Issues in Economics Today

Ninth Edition

The McGraw-Hill Series Economics

ESSENTIALS OF ECONOMICS

Brue, McConnell, and Flynn
Essentials of Economics
Fourth Edition

Mandel
M: Economics—The Basics
Fourth Edition

Schiller
Essentials of Economics
Eleventh Edition

PRINCIPLES OF ECONOMICS

Asarta and Butters
Connect Master: Economics
Second Edition

Colander
Economics, Microeconomics, and Macroeconomics
Eleventh Edition

Frank, Bernanke, Antonovics, and Heffetz
Principles of Economics, Principles of Microeconomics, Principles of Macroeconomics
Seventh Edition

Frank, Bernanke, Antonovics, and Heffetz
Streamlined Editions: Principles of Economics, Principles of Microeconomics, Principles of Macroeconomics
Fourth Edition

Karlan and Morduch
Economics, Microeconomics, and Macroeconomics
Third Edition

McConnell, Brue, and Flynn
Economics, Microeconomics, Macroeconomics
Twenty-Second Edition

McConnell, Brue, and Flynn
Brief Editions: Microeconomics and Macroeconomics
Third Edition

Samuelson and Nordhaus
Economics, Microeconomics, and Macroeconomics
Nineteenth Edition

Schiller
The Economy Today, The Micro Economy Today, and The Macro Economy Today
Fifteenth Edition

Slavin
Economics, Microeconomics, and Macroeconomics
Twelfth Edition

ECONOMICS OF SOCIAL ISSUES

Guell
Issues in Economics Today
Ninth Edition

Register and Grimes
Economics of Social Issues
Twenty-First Edition

ECONOMETRICS AND DATA ANALYTICS

Hilmer and Hilmer
Practical Econometrics
First Edition

Prince
Predictive Analytics for Business Strategy
First Edition

MANAGERIAL ECONOMICS

Baye and Prince
Managerial Economics and Business Strategy
Ninth Edition

Brickley, Smith, and Zimmerman
Managerial Economics and Organizational Architecture
Seventh Edition

Thomas and Maurice
Managerial Economics
Thirteenth Edition

INTERMEDIATE ECONOMICS

Bernheim and Whinston
Microeconomics
Second Edition

Dornbusch, Fischer, and Startz
Macroeconomics
Thirteenth Edition

Frank
Microeconomics and Behavior
Ninth Edition

ADVANCED ECONOMICS

Romer
Advanced Macroeconomics
Fifth Edition

MONEY AND BANKING

Cecchetti and Schoenholtz
Money, Banking, and Financial Markets
Sixth Edition

URBAN ECONOMICS

O'Sullivan
Urban Economics
Ninth Edition

LABOR ECONOMICS

Borjas
Labor Economics
Eighth Edition

McConnell, Brue, and Macpherson
Contemporary Labor Economics
Twelfth Edition

PUBLIC FINANCE

Rosen and Gayer
Public Finance
Tenth Edition

ENVIRONMENTAL ECONOMICS

Field and Field
Environmental Economics: An Introduction
Eighth Edition

INTERNATIONAL ECONOMICS

Appleyard and Field
International Economics
Ninth Edition

Pugel
International Economics
Seventeenth Edition

Issues in Economics Today

Ninth Edition

ROBERT C. GUELL
Indiana State University

ISSUES IN ECONOMICS TODAY, NINTH EDITION

Published by McGraw-Hill Education, 2 Penn Plaza, New York, NY 10121.

Some ancillaries, including electronic and print components, may not be available to customers outside the United States.

This book is printed on acid-free paper.

1 2 3 4 5 6 7 8 9 LWI 24 23 22 21 20

ISBN 978-1-260-22532-7 (bound edition)
MHID 1-260-22532-1 (bound edition)
ISBN 978-1-264-04927-1 (loose-leaf edition)
MHID 1-264-04927-7 (loose-leaf edition)

Director: *Anke Weekes*
Associate Portfolio Manager: *Kevin White*
Product Developer: *Sarah Wood*
Marketing Manager: *Bobby Pearson*
Content Project Managers: *Lisa Bruflodt, Emily Windelborn*
Buyer: *Sandy Ludovissy*
Designer: *Matt Diamond*
Content Licensing Specialist: *Brianna Kirschbaum*
Cover Image: ©*4 PM production/Shutterstock*
Compositor: *Aptara®, Inc.*

All credits appearing on page or at the end of the book are considered to be an extension of the copyright page.

Library of Congress Cataloging-in-Publication Data

Names: Guell, Robert C., author.
Title: Issues in economics today / Robert C. Guell, Indiana State University.
Description: Ninth edition. | New York, NY : McGraw-Hill Education, [2021] | Series: The McGraw-Hill economics series | Includes index.
Identifiers: LCCN 2019030840 (print) | LCCN 2019030841 (ebook) | ISBN 9781260225327 (hardcover) | ISBN 1260225321 (MHID) | ISBN 9781264049271 (spiral bound) | ISBN 9781264049301 (ebook) | ISBN 9781264049325 (ebook other)
Subjects: LCSH: Economics.
Classification: LCC HB87 .G83 2021 (print) | LCC HB87 (ebook) | DDC 330–dc23
LC record available at https://lccn.loc.gov/2019030840
LC ebook record available at https://lccn.loc.gov/2019030841

mheducation.com/highered

To Lilly, Blake, and Henry

About the **Author**

Dr. Robert C. Guell (pronounced "Gill") is a professor of economics at Indiana State University in Terre Haute, Indiana. He earned a B.A. in statistics and economics in 1986 and an M.S. in economics one year later from the University of Missouri–Columbia. In 1991, he earned a Ph.D. from Syracuse University, where he discovered the thrill of teaching. He has taught courses for freshmen, upper-division undergraduates, and graduate students from the principles level, through public finance, all the way to mathematical economics and econometrics.

Dr. Guell has published numerous peer-reviewed articles in scholarly journals. He has worked extensively in the area of pharmaceutical economics, suggesting that the private market's patent system, while necessary for drug innovation, is unnecessary and inefficient for production.

In 1998, Dr. Guell was the youngest faculty member ever to have been given Indiana State University's Caleb Mills Distinguished Teaching Award. His talent as a champion of quality teaching was recognized again in 2000 when he was named project manager for the Lilly Project to Transform the First-Year Experience, a Lilly Endowment–funded project to raise first-year persistence rates at Indiana State University. He was ISU's Coordinator of First-Year Programs until January 2008, when he happily stepped aside to rejoin his department full time.

Dr. Guell's passion for teaching economics led him to request an assignment with the largest impact. The one-semester general education basic economics course became the vehicle to express that passion. Unsatisfied with the books available for the course, he made it his calling to produce what you have before you today—an all-in-one readable issues-based text.

Brief Contents

Table of Contents

Preface

This book is designed for a one-semester issues-based general education economics course, and its purpose is to interest the nonbusiness, noneconomics major in what the discipline of economics can do. Students of the "issues approach" will master the basic economic theory necessary to explore a variety of real-world issues. If this is the only economics course they ever take, they will at least gain enough insight to be able to intelligently discuss the way economic theory applies to important issues in the world today.

Until the first edition of this book was published, instructors who chose the issues approach to teaching a one-semester general economics course had to compromise in one of the following ways: they could (1) pick a book that presents the issues but that is devoid of economic theory, (2) pick a book that intertwines the issues with the theory, (3) ask students to buy two books, or (4) place a large number of readings on library reserve.

Each of these alternatives presents problems. If the course is based entirely on an issues text, students will leave with the incorrect impression that economics is a nonrigorous discipline that assumes that all of the issues are relevant to all students in the course. In fact, some issues are not relevant to some students and others are relevant only when the issue makes news. For example, at Syracuse my students never understood why farm price supports were interesting, whereas at Indiana State no student that I have met has ever lived in a rent-controlled apartment. The problem associated with using multiple books is the obvious one of expense. Having multiple reserve readings, still a legitimate option, requires a great deal of time on the part of students, teachers, and librarians and is usually not convenient to students.

The ninth edition of this book meets both student and instructor needs simultaneously. By making the entire portfolio of chapters available for instructors to select and include in a print book as they see fit within McGraw-Hill's CREATE platform, we allow instructors maximum flexibility to design a product that keeps students interested.

HOW TO USE THIS BOOK

Issues in Economics Today includes 8 intensive core theory chapters and 40 shorter issues chapters. The book is designed to allow faculty flexibility in approach. Some colleagues like to intertwine theory and issues while others like to lay the theoretical foundation first before heading into the issues. Some faculty will choose to set a theme for their course and pick issues consistent with that theme while others will let their students decide what issues interest them. There is no right way to use the book except that **under no circumstances is it imagined that the entire book be covered.**

Mc Graw Hill create®

McGraw-Hill CREATE

To address the recommendation that no instructor should assign the entire book to be covered in their course, the ninth edition takes advantage of the capabilities in McGraw-Hill's CREATE platform (www.mcgrawhillcreate.com) to give instructors the flexibility to easily design a print product customized to their issues course: Instructors can easily add chapters to their product in the same way someone might add purchases to their cart when online shopping. Once the table of contents is set, the instructor can easily view the net price of their course text (often much lower once extraneous chapters have been removed). When the product is approved by the instructor, the system will generate an ISBN for the customized product, which can be provided to the bookstore. Once an order is placed, the copies will be printed on demand for each institution. The process is very straightforward; however, a McGraw-Hill representative can assist instructors or build products based on syllabi if required. This workflow makes it feasible for an instructor to revisit their product and make tweaks every time they teach the course. It also makes it a possibility for me to author and make available chapters that address current economic issues in a timely manner as events arise.

Organization of the Issues Chapters

There are 40 issues chapters that I have divided into the following categories: Macroeconomic Issues (Chapters 9–16), International Issues (Chapters 17–20), Externalities and Market Failure (Chapters 22–23), Health Issues (Chapters 24–26), Government Solutions to Societal Problems (Chapters 27–31), Price Control Issues (Chapters 32–34), and Miscellaneous Markets (Chapters 36–48). These groupings will be helpful as you navigate through the Contents looking for a particular topic. To help you decide which issues chapters to cover, see the table on pages xxx–xxxi, entitled "Required Theory Table." It shows at a glance which theory chapters need to be covered before pursuing each of the issues chapters. On pages xxviii–xxix, the table entitled "Issues for Different Course Themes" includes my recommendations for courses that focus on social policy, international issues, election year issues, or business. Within the CREATE platform these different course structures are already assembled into ready-made Express Books to make it easy for you to customize your text according to these themes.

CHANGES TO THE NINTH EDITION

The main focus of this revision was to ensure readability, accessibility, and relevance. Every chapter saw extensive revisions to enhance these attributes. In addition, as with previous editions, all data references and data intensive graphs were updated to reflect the most recent release of the information. Finally, in every chapter, end-of-chapter questions were revised to align with learning objectives and to ensure completeness.

Individual Chapter Updates

Chapter 1 Extensively revised the Economic Growth section.
Chapter 2 Augmented the determinants of supply and demand discussion to ensure clarity.
Chapter 3 Added to the determinants of elasticity.
Chapter 4 Greater connections drawn between the verbal, graphical, and numerical explanations of production and cost.
Chapter 7 Retitled the chapter to "Money, Interest Rates, and Present Value." Moved/added the material on the roles and attributes of money to this chapter and described cryptocurrency.
Chapter 8 Added a discussion of the Tax Cuts and Jobs Act.
Chapter 9 Added a discussion of the Tax Cuts and Jobs Act.
Chapter 10 Noted President Trump's challenge to Federal Reserve independence.
Chapter 11 Used the 2019 government shutdown over the funding for a border wall as the primary example of what happens when Congress and the president fail to agree on spending bills.
Chapter 12 Removed the section on CBO projections.

Chapter 13 Noted the degree to which housing prices have recovered most of their losses.
Chapter 15 Added a discussion of the Tax Cuts and Jobs Act.
Chapter 17 Added a discussion of Trump's use of tariffs (and their consequences) as a weapon in trade negotiations.
Chapter 18 Extensively revised the section on foreign exchange markets.
Chapter 19 Added a discussion of Brexit.
Chapter 21 Added a discussion of Trump-era changes to trade agreements.
Chapter 22 Added a discussion of state laws regarding marijuana.
Chapter 23 Added a discussion of a carbon tax.
Chapter 24 Described the impact of the removal of the individual mandate. Added to the discussion of international cancer survival rates.
Chapter 25 Changed the language regarding Medicare's financial health to one of solvency. Noted the increase in the number of states expanding Medicaid.
Chapter 28 Added an extensive discussion of violent, nonviolent, and white-collar crime. Also added a discussion of the First Step Act. Revised significantly to ensure inclusivity of language.
Chapter 29 Made extensive reference to issues of intellectual property and anti-trust allegations in the technology sector.
Chapter 30 Revised significantly to ensure inclusivity of language.
Chapter 31 Added an extensive discussion of the various proposals to shrink income and wealth inequality.
Chapter 32 Removed the farm land price discussion.
Chapter 33 Added a map of state minimum wage laws.
Chapter 36 Noted the removal of high-stakes testing.
Chapter 37 Revised the discussion on textbooks.
Chapter 38 Described the idea of a Universal Basic Income.
Chapter 39 Extensively revised the characteristics of Head Start beneficiaries.
Chapter 40 Removed the section on who Social Security helps/hurts.
Chapter 41 Extensively revised the structure discussion based on the Tax Cuts and Jobs Act.
Chapter 42 Noted OPEC's decreased ability to control prices in light of modern drilling techniques that expanded production in the United States.
Chapter 43 Removed most of discussion regarding the monopoly of motor sports.
Chapter 44 Recast the Accounting Scandals of 2001 and 2002 section in terms of all corporate bankruptcies. Distinguished between Chapter 11 and Chapter 13 bankruptcies.
Chapter 45 Referenced the *Janus* ruling regarding public unions.
Chapter 46 Noted the degree to which Walmart's advantages have been decreasing.
Chapter 47 Revised the discussion of sports gambling in light of a recent Supreme Court ruling.

FEATURES

- *A conversational writing style* makes it easier for students not majoring in economics to connect with the material. The book puts students at ease and allows them to feel more confident and open to learning.
- *Chapter Outline and Learning Objectives* set the stage at the beginning of each chapter to let the student see how the chapter is organized and anticipate the concepts that will be covered.
- *Key Terms* are defined in the margins and recapped at the end of the chapters.
- *Summaries* at the end of each chapter reinforce the material that has been covered.

- *Issues Chapters You Are Ready for Now* are found at the end of each theory chapter, so students can go straight to the issues chapters that interest them once they've mastered the necessary theoretical principles.
- *Quiz Yourself* presents questions for self-quizzing at the end of each chapter.
- *Think about This* asks provocative questions that encourage students to think about how economic theories apply to the real world by putting themselves in the economic driver's seat. This feature facilitates active learning so that the students will learn the concepts more thoroughly.
- *Talk about This* includes questions designed to trigger discussion.
- *For More Insight See* sends the students to websites and publications to find additional material on a given topic. Since economic issues are particularly time-sensitive, this feature not only helps students learn to do research on the web but also keeps the course as fresh and current as today's newspaper.
- *Short Answer Questions* are included so that faculty may ask students questions that will help faculty assess student understanding of complex economic phenomena.

RESOURCES TO SUPPORT LEARNING

The content and reliability of supplements are of primary importance to the users of the book. Because of this, I am personally involved in crafting and checking all of the following ancillaries, which are available for quick download and convenient access via the instructor resource material available through Connect.

Connect Problems

The multiple choice questions from the end-of-chapter materials are assignable in Connect, providing students with instant feedback on their answers. Additionally, over 200 Connect-only questions are also available.

Instructor's Manual

In addition to a traditional outline of each chapter's content and updated references to data sources for each chapter, the Instructor's Manual offers key-point icons to emphasize the importance of particular concepts. Another distinctive feature is that each figure is broken into subfigures with explanations that can be offered at each stage. Solutions to the end of chapter questions are also provided.

Test Bank

The test bank includes 80–200 multiple-choice questions for the core theory chapters and 60–100 multiple-choice questions for the issues chapters. These questions test students' knowledge of key terms, key concepts, theory and graph recognition, theory and graph application, and numeracy, as well as questions about different explanations given by economists regarding particular economic phenomena.

Test Builder in Connect

Available within Connect, Test Builder is a cloud-based tool that enables instructors to format tests that can be printed or administered within a LMS. Test Builder offers a modern, streamlined interface for easy content configuration that matches course needs, without requiring a download.

Test Builder allows you to:

- access all test bank content from a particular title.
- easily pinpoint the most relevant content through robust filtering options.
- manipulate the order of questions or scramble questions and/or answers.
- pin questions to a specific location within a test.
- determine your preferred treatment of algorithmic questions.
- choose the layout and spacing.
- add instructions and configure default settings.

Test Builder provides a secure interface for better protection of content and allows for just-in-time updates to flow directly into assessments.

PowerPoint Presentations

Revised with accessibility in mind, the PowerPoint slides include a brief, detailed review of the important ideas covered in each chapter, accompanied by relevant tables and figures featured within the text and accessible descriptions for all figures compatible with most screen reader technology. You can edit, print, or rearrange the slides to fit the needs of your course.

Assurance of Learning Ready

Many education institutions today are focused on the notion of *assurance of learning*, an important element of some accreditation standards. *Issues in Economics Today* supports assurance of learning objectives with a simple, yet powerful solution.

Instructors can use Connect to easily query for learning outcomes/objectives that directly relate to the learning objectives of the course. You can then use the reporting features of Connect to aggregate student results in similar fashion, making the collection and presentation of assurance of learning data simple and easy.

AACSB Statement

McGraw-Hill Global Education is a product corporate member of AACSB International. Understanding the importance and value of AACSB accreditation, *Issues in Economics Today* has sought to recognize the curricula guidelines detailed in the AACSB standards for business accreditation by connecting questions in the test bank and end-of-chapter material to the general knowledge and skill guidelines found in the AACSB standards.

It is important to note that the statements contained in *Issues in Economics Today* are provided only as a guide for the users of this text. The AACSB leaves content coverage and assessment within the purview of individual schools, the mission of the school, and the faculty. While *Issues in Economics Today* and the teaching package make no claim of any specific AACSB qualification or evaluation, we have labeled questions according to the general knowledge and skill areas.

ACKNOWLEDGMENTS

This text would not have been possible but for the efforts of a number of people. I thank Indiana State University and its Department of Economics for their continued support of this project. In particular, I thank my chair, John Conant, for his unflagging support, both moral and material. I am indebted to the personnel of McGraw-Hill Education for their work in gathering and compiling peer reviews. I want to thank Kelsey Darin. Kelsey was an undergraduate student at Indiana State who (for the prior edition) spent countless hours updating each data reference, table, and graph. After the text was complete, she helped me ensure that every PowerPoint slide, Instructor's Manual entry, and test bank and Connect question aligned with the material. When she graduated in 2017, she did so with a love for publishing and relentlessly pursued a career in it. That October she landed a job with McGraw-Hill's Chicago (then Burr Ridge) office. When the time came for me to produce a ninth edition, Anke Weekes (Director, Economics, Business and Management) was kind enough to facilitate her working with me again. Thanks to countless WebEx-fueled weekends and evenings, we were able to collaborate on this ninth edition. We tackled every sentence, concept, and explanation to ensure the text would resonate with a modern student. She pressed me time and again to be sure that examples were as up to date as possible and reminded me that examples from the Reagan, Bush, Clinton, and Bush (W) eras were not good enough. I maintain that there are three people who can tell me I am wrong and I immediately assume I am wrong: one gave birth to me, I have been married to another for 32 years, and then along came Kelsey. We did this together. We kept the tone conversational and made sure the examples were relatable. Thank you.

I thank the many participants in McGraw-Hill Symposia who happily offered great insight on the best way to teach interesting issues. Finally, I thank the following peer reviewers whose insight substantially enhanced this book:

Alex Aichinger
Northwestern State University

Thomas Andrews
West Chester University

Michael Araujo
Quinsigamond Community College

Lee Ash
Skagit Valley College

Robert J. Bartelli
Labette Community College

Daria J. Bernard
University of Delaware

Roberta Biby
Grand Valley State University

Ann Marie Callahan
Caldwell College

R. Edward Chatterton
Lock Haven University

Russ Cheatham
Cumberland University

Joab Corey
Florida State University

Ann M. Eike
University of Kentucky

Herb Elliott
All Hancock College

John A. Flanders
Central Methodist University

Holly Fretwell
Montana State University

Neil Garston
CSULA

E. B. Gendel
Woodbury College

Glenn Graham
SUNY-Oswego

Abbas P. Grammy
California State University, Bakersfield

Sheryl Hadley
Johnson Community College

Suzanne Hayes
University of Nebraska, Kearney

Rolf Hemmerling
Greenville Technical College

John S. Heywood
University of Wisconsin-Milwaukee

Richard Hoogerwerf
Marian College

Scott Hunt
Columbus State Community College

Hans Isakson
University of Northern Iowa

Debra Israel
Indiana State University

Allan Jenkins
University of Nebraska, Kearney

Dick Johnson
Skagit Valley Community College

Gary Langer
Roosevelt University

Tom Larson
California State University–Los Angeles

Raymond Lee
Benedict College

Gary D. Lemon
DePauw University

Alston Lippert
University of South Carolina

Patrick McMurry
Missouri Western State University

Tom Means
San Jose State University

Kimberly Merritt
Oklahoma Christian University

Daniel Morvey
Piedmont Technical College

Richard Newton
Augusta Technical College

Inge O'Connor
Syracuse University

Nathan Perry
University of Utah

Chris Phillips
Somerset Community College

Patrick Price
University of Louisiana at Lafayette

Taghi Ramin
William Patterson University

Michael Ryan
Western Michigan University

John Sabelhaus
University of Maryland

Sue Lynn Sasser
University of Central Oklahoma

Brenda M. Saunders
Somerset Community College

Robert D. Schuttler
Marian University

Millicent M. Sites
Carson-Newman College

Rebecca Smith
Mississippi State University

Arun K. Srinivasan
Indiana University Southeast

Frank Tenkorang
University of Nebraska, Kearney

Tara Thornberry
Maysville Community and Technical College

Michelle Villinski
DePauw University

Darlene Voeltz
Rochester Community and Technical College

William Walsh
University of St. Thomas

Wendel Weaver
Oklahoma Wesleyan University

Janet L. Wolcutt
Wichita State University

Derek K. Yonai
Campbell University

Ben Young
University of Missouri, Kansas City
Johnson County Community College

FOR INSTRUCTORS

You're in the driver's seat.

Want to build your own course? No problem. Prefer to use our turnkey, prebuilt course? Easy. Want to make changes throughout the semester? Sure. And you'll save time with Connect's auto-grading too.

65%
Less Time Grading

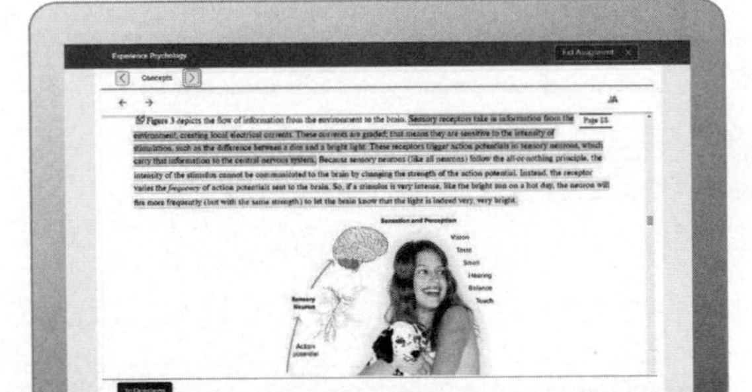

Laptop: McGraw-Hill; Woman/dog: George Doyle/Getty Images

They'll thank you for it.

Adaptive study resources like SmartBook® 2.0 help your students be better prepared in less time. You can transform your class time from dull definitions to dynamic debates. Find out more about the powerful personalized learning experience available in SmartBook 2.0 at **www.mheducation.com/highered/connect/smartbook**

Make it simple, make it affordable.

Connect makes it easy with seamless integration using any of the major Learning Management Systems—Blackboard®, Canvas, and D2L, among others—to let you organize your course in one convenient location. Give your students access to digital materials at a discount with our inclusive access program. Ask your McGraw-Hill representative for more information.

Padlock: Jobalou/Getty Images

Solutions for your challenges.

A product isn't a solution. Real solutions are affordable, reliable, and come with training and ongoing support when you need it and how you want it. Our Customer Experience Group can also help you troubleshoot tech problems—although Connect's 99% uptime means you might not need to call them. See for yourself at **status.mheducation.com**

Checkmark: Jobalou/Getty Images

FOR STUDENTS

Effective, efficient studying.

Connect helps you be more productive with your study time and get better grades using tools like SmartBook 2.0, which highlights key concepts and creates a personalized study plan. Connect sets you up for success, so you walk into class with confidence and walk out with better grades.

Study anytime, anywhere.

Download the free ReadAnywhere app and access your online eBook or SmartBook 2.0 assignments when it's convenient, even if you're offline. And since the app automatically syncs with your eBook and SmartBook 2.0 assignments in Connect, all of your work is available every time you open it. Find out more at **www.mheducation.com/readanywhere**

"I really liked this app—it made it easy to study when you don't have your text-book in front of you."

- Jordan Cunningham,
Eastern Washington University

Calendar: owattaphotos/Getty Images

No surprises.

The Connect Calendar and Reports tools keep you on track with the work you need to get done and your assignment scores. Life gets busy; Connect tools help you keep learning through it all.

Learning for everyone.

McGraw-Hill works directly with Accessibility Services Departments and faculty to meet the learning needs of all students. Please contact your Accessibility Services office and ask them to email accessibility@mheducation.com, or visit **www.mheducation.com/about/accessibility** for more information.

Top: Jenner Images/Getty Images, Left: Hero Images/Getty Images, Right: Hero Images/Getty Images

Issues for **Different Course Themes**

Social Policy

22. The Line between Legal and Illegal Goods
24. Health Care
25. Government-Provided Health Insurance: Medicaid, Medicare, and the Children's Health Insurance Program
26. The Economics of Prescription Drugs
30. The Economics of Race and Sex Discrimination
31. Income and Wealth Inequality: What's Fair?
33. Minimum Wage
36. The Economics of K–12 Education
37. College and University Education: Why Is It So Expensive?
38. Poverty and Welfare
47. The Economic Impact of Casino and Sports Gambling

Election Year

9. Fiscal Policy
11. Federal Spending
14. The Recession of 2007–2009: Causes and Policy Responses
15. Is Economic Stagnation the New Normal?
16. Is the (Fiscal) Sky Falling? An Examination of Unfunded Social Security, Medicare, and State and Local Pension Liabilities
17. International Trade: Does It Jeopardize American Jobs?
23. Natural Resources, the Environment, and Climate Change
24. Health Care
27. So You Want to Be a Lawyer: Economics and the Law
28. The Economics of Crime
30. The Economics of Race and Sex Discrimination
33. Minimum Wage
37. College and University Education: Why Is It So Expensive?
40. Social Security

International Issues

12. Federal Deficits, Surpluses, and the National Debt
15. Is Economic Stagnation the New Normal?
17. International Trade: Does It Jeopardize American Jobs?
18. International Finance and Exchange Rates
19. The European Union, Debt Crisis, and Brexit
20. Economic Growth and Development
21. Are Trade Agreements Good for Us?
22. The Line between Legal and Illegal Goods
23. Natural Resources, the Environment, and Climate Change
32. Farm Policy
42. Energy Prices
48. Terrorism

Business Issues

10. Monetary Policy
11. Federal Spending
13. The Housing Bubble
14. The Recession of 2007–2009: Causes and Policy Responses
17. International Trade: Does It Jeopardize American Jobs?
24. Health Care
26. The Economics of Prescription Drugs
29. Antitrust
34. Ticket Brokers and Ticket Scalping
41. Personal Income Taxes
42. Energy Prices
44. The Stock Market and Crashes

45. Unions
46. Walmart: Always Low Prices (and Low Wages)—Always

Social Justice

14. The Recession of 2007–2009: Causes and Policy Responses
15. Is Economic Stagnation the New Normal?
23. Natural Resources, the Environment, and Climate Change
24. Health Care
25. Government-Provided Health Insurance: Medicaid, Medicare, and the Children's Health Insurance Program
26. The Economics of Prescription Drugs
30. The Economics of Race and Sex Discrimination
31. Income and Wealth Inequality: What's Fair?
33. Minimum Wage
35. Rent Control
36. The Economics of K–12 Education
37. College and University Education: Why Is It So Expensive?
38. Poverty and Welfare
39. Head Start
40. Social Security

Health and Education Policies

11. Federal Spending
16. Is the (Fiscal) Sky Falling?: An Examination of Unfunded Social Security, Medicare, and State and Local Pension Liabilities
23. Natural Resources, the Environment, and Climate Change
24. Health Care
25. Government-Provided Health Insurance: Medicaid, Medicare, and the Children's Health Insurance Program
26. The Economics of Prescription Drugs
30. The Economics of Race and Sex Discrimination
31. Income and Wealth Inequality: What's Fair?
36. The Economics of K–12 Education
37. College and University Education: Why Is It So Expensive?
38. Poverty and Welfare
39. Head Start
40. Social Security

The Most Popular Issues Chosen by Students

14. The Recession of 2007–2009: Causes and Policy Responses
17. International Trade: Does It Jeopardize American Jobs?
22. The Line between Legal and Illegal Goods
23. Natural Resources, the Environment, and Climate Change
24. Health Care
28. The Economics of Crime
30. The Economics of Race and Sex Discrimination
33. Minimum Wage
42. Energy Prices
43. If We Build It, Will They Come? and Other Sports Questions
44. The Stock Market and Crashes
47. The Economic Impact of Casino and Sports Gambling

Required **Theory Table**

Core Theory Required								
1	**2**	**3**	**4**	**5**	**6**	**7**	**8**	
					X	X	X	9. Fiscal Policy
					X	X	X	10. Monetary Policy
X								11. Federal Spending
					X		X	12. Federal Deficits, Surpluses, and the National Debt
					X	X	X	13. The Housing Bubble
					X	X	X	14. The Recession of 2007–2009: Causes and Policy Responses
					X	X	X	15. Is Economic Stagnation the New Normal?
					X	X	X	16. Is the (Fiscal) Sky Falling?: An Examination of Unfunded Social Security, Medicare, and State and Local Pension Liabilities
X	X	X						17. International Trade: Does It Jeopardize American Jobs?
	X							18. International Finance and Exchange Rates
X	X				X	X	X	19. The European Union, Debt Crisis, and Brexit
	X				X		X	20. Economic Growth and Development
X	X	X						21. Are Trade Agreements Good for Us?
X	X	X						22. The Line between Legal and Illegal Goods
X	X	X	X	X		X		23. Natural Resources, the Environment, and Climate Change
X	X	X						24. Health Care
X	X	X						25. Government-Provided Health Insurance: Medicaid, Medicare, and the Children's Health Insurance Program
X	X	X	X	X				26. The Economics of Prescription Drugs
X	X	X					X	27. So You Want to Be a Lawyer: Economics and the Law
X	X	X						28. The Economics of Crime
	X	X	X	X				29. Antitrust
	X							30. The Economics of Race and Sex Discrimination
X	X					X		31. Income and Wealth Inequality: What's Fair?
X	X	X						32. Farm Policy
X	X	X						33. Minimum Wage
	X	X		X				34. Ticket Brokers and Ticket Scalping
	X	X						35. Rent Control
X						X		36. The Economics of K–12 Education
X	X	X	X	X		X		37. College and University Education: Why Is It So Expensive?
X								38. Poverty and Welfare
X						X		39. Head Start
						X		40. Social Security

Core Theory Required								
1	2	3	4	5	6	7	8	
						X		41. Personal Income Taxes
	X	X	X					42. Energy Prices
X						X		43. If We Build It, Will They Come? And Other Sports Questions
						X		44. The Stock Market and Crashes
	X	X	X	X				45. Unions
X	X	X	X	X				46. Walmart: Always Low Prices (and Low Wages)—Always
X					X	X	X	47. The Economic Impact of Casino and Sports Gambling
X								48. The Economics of Terrorism

CHAPTER ONE

Economics: The Study of Opportunity Cost

Learning Objectives

After reading this chapter you should be able to:

LO1 Define the key terms of economics and opportunity cost and understand how a production possibilities frontier exemplifies the trade-offs that exist in life.

LO2 Distinguish between increasing and constant opportunity cost and understand why each might happen in the real world.

LO3 Define *economic growth* and distinguish between specialized and generalized economic growth in the context of a production possibilities frontier.

LO4 Analyze an argument by thinking economically, while recognizing and avoiding logical traps.

Chapter Outline

This book exists to give you a glimpse into how economists think. This chapter starts that process by defining the discipline of economics and its most basic concept: opportunity cost. You get your first look at how economists work by modeling opportunity cost through the use of a diagram called a production possibilities frontier. You then get a road map to the economy and to the remainder of the book in the form of a circular flow diagram. The heart of this chapter is dedicated to explaining what makes the economics profession distinctive. You will see that economists tackle problems using marginal analysis, and in doing so, you will see why. You will explore the difference between positive and normative analyses and examine economic incentives. As the chapter concludes, you will be forewarned regarding the logical traps that frequently get in the way of economists and noneconomists alike.

Economics and Opportunity Cost

Economics Defined

economics
The study of the allocation and use of scarce resources to satisfy unlimited human wants.

Some define **economics** as a hard requirement for general education or a major; others, a "dismal science"; and still others, the study of the allocation and use of scarce resources to satisfy unlimited human wants. The reality is that economics is all three. It deserves its reputation as a difficult course, its practitioners are always disappointing the public by insisting that there is a cost to everything, and it really is a social science dealing with the fact that humans want more than resources are capable of satisfying.

On another level, the study of economics is the application of complicated jargon and graphs to common sense. You already know a lot of economics. You know, for instance, that choices have consequences; that having more money is more fun than having less; and that even though you are rich relative to a starving refugee, you are less rich than you would like to be. Of course, there are many other economic lessons that you learn simply by being alive.

However, there is a systematic way of thinking about those economic ideas, and that is what this course and this book provide. All jargon with special meaning to economists will be in **bold,** with its definition, sometimes also in jargon, close by in the text as well as in the margin. If the definition is in "econ-speak" rather than commonsense English, you will also find an English translation nearby.

scarce
Not freely available and lacking an infinite source.

resource
Anything that is consumed directly or used to make things that will ultimately be consumed.

Two terms in this definition of economics, *scarce* and *resources*, need clarification. Each has a particular meaning to economists. Something is **scarce** when there is not a freely available and infinite source of it. A **resource** is anything we either consume directly or use to make things that we will ultimately consume.

There are four basic resources that society can allocate: land, labor, capital, and the entrepreneurship of its people. Any other resource, like oil, steel, or corn, is made available to a society when it allocates one or more of the basic resources to uncover, create, or harvest it.

Choices Have Consequences

opportunity cost
The forgone alternative of the choice made.

In this course and with this book you will be faced with a choice: Do you read and study, or do you sleep and party? This choice illustrates the first and most basic concept of economics: opportunity cost. **Opportunity cost** is the forgone alternative of the choice made.

If that sounds like a tortured definition, try this: Opportunity cost is "what you would have done had you not done what you did." It is important to keep in mind that the "forgone alternative" is the next best choice. It is not all the things "you could have done had you not done what you did," but it is the best of these alternatives because presumably that is "what you would have done."

If, for example, you decide at some point before finishing your assigned reading to put down this book, you will be implicitly saying that you would rather do something else. In terms of the course you are taking, the "opportunity cost" of such a poor decision could well be the lower grade that results from lost understanding.

Unfortunately, no matter what you do, you cannot escape opportunity cost. If you remain responsible and continue to read, the opportunity cost would be what you would do with the time saved. You are giving up the opportunity to watch something on *Netflix*, play the latest multiplayer game, sleep, or study something else. To you, the preferred alternative would be the opportunity cost of reading.

As an aside, professors see many students trying to avoid opportunity cost by multi-tasking. Scanning your Facebook account, reading your English, texting your significant other, or studying your biology during your economics class may seem like you are simply using time that has no opportunity cost. It is not. Students who attempt to multitask frequently miss details, instructions, or concepts when attention is divided. The opportunity cost of the attempt is the lost understanding that could have been gained had you focused your attention in class.

Modeling Opportunity Cost Using the Production Possibilities Frontier

The Intuition behind Our First Graph

production possibilities frontier
A graph that relates the amounts of different goods that can be produced in a fully employed society.

model
A simplification of the real world that can be manipulated to explain the real world.

simplifying assumption
An assumption that may, on its face, be silly but allows for a clearer explanation.

The concept of opportunity cost can be further illustrated by looking at something called a **production possibilities frontier.** This graph, Figure 1.1, is the first of more than 100 that you will see in this book. It is an example of a **model,** a simplification of the real world that we can manipulate to explain the real world. This particular model relates the amounts of different goods that can be produced in a fully employed society.

In order to be useful, models need to capture the essence of a problem in an accessible and understandable form. For a book (paper or electronic), we are still limited to two dimensions. This gives us the first opportunity to introduce something called a **simplifying assumption.** A simplifying assumption is one that may, on its face, be silly but allows for a clearer explanation. A good one also has the characteristic that the conclusions that spring from it are valid in its more complicated scenario.

For our production possibilities frontier, we will make several simplifying assumptions. We will assume that there are only two goods in the world, that these goods are pizza and soft drinks, and that they will be produced with limited resources and an unaltered method of turning those resources into pizza and soda.

For another simplification, suppose that there are five types of people in the world: (1) those really good at producing pizza but lousy at producing soda, (2) those pretty good at producing pizza and not so good at producing soda, (3) those modestly talented at both, (4) those good at producing soda and not so good at producing pizza, and (5) those really good at producing soda but lousy at producing pizza.

The Starting Point for a Production Possibilities Frontier

If we imagine that our resource is the time of our workers, it can be consumed directly in the form of their leisure or it can be combined with other resources to produce goods and services. This resource is also scarce because there is not an infinite number of people to work, those people can do only so much work, they will not work without being paid, and there is only so much soda that can be produced—even if all the people on the planet devote their lives to the production of soda. Of course, this point also holds if we apply the scarce resource to the production of pizza. There is only so much pizza that can be produced even if everyone on the planet is producing pizza.

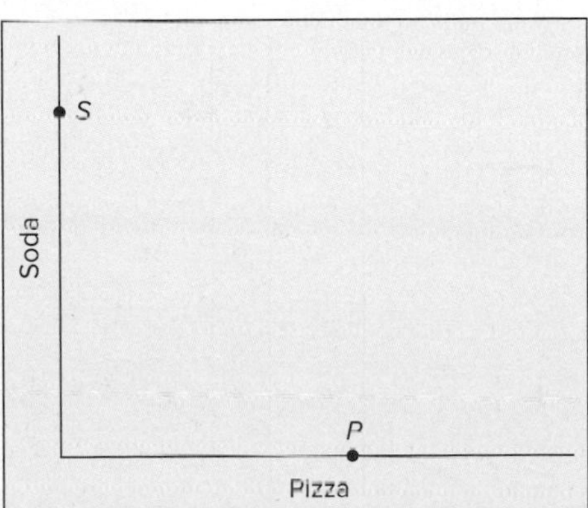

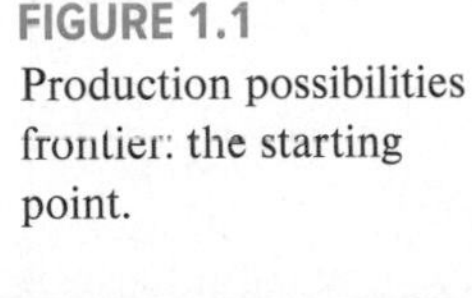

FIGURE 1.1
Production possibilities frontier: the starting point.

This notion of scarcity gives us the two extreme points, *S* and *P*, in Figure 1.1. Point *S* represents the situation where all resources are devoted to the production of soda; point *P* represents the situation where all resources are devoted to the production of pizza. In both cases, all the resources in the world are devoted to the production of a specific good, yet production is still limited. It is limited by the ability of people and by the number of people and machines we have to help those people do their jobs. So that it is clear, remember that the production possibilities frontier is about choices. So far, we have only examined the extreme points. One point, *P*, represents only pizza and no soda, while the other one, *S*, represents only soda and no pizza. Remember also that we can pick only one of them. We cannot have both *S* sodas and *P* pizzas. In reality, we can have some soda and some pizza. We can devote a portion of our resources to pizza and others to soda. As a result, there are many points between *S* and *P* that are possible.

Points between the Extremes of a Production Possibilities Frontier

To proceed, assume you want something to eat with your soda, and ask yourself what kind of people you would remove from soda production to foster pizza production. Clearly, you would remove those who are not contributing much to the soda production but would contribute greatly to pizza production. That is, those with the attributes of people in group 1 (the "pizza chefs") above: really good at pizza, lousy at soda.

Figure 1.2 shows us what happens if we go ahead and move that group. As you see, this increases pizza production to a respectable level while not costing society much soda. Point *X* in Figure 1.2 represents that new soda-pizza combination. There everyone except those "pizza chefs" are still making soda, and the pizza chefs are efficiently cranking out as many pizzas as they can on their own. The thing is, though we gained a great deal of pizza production, we lost some soda production. That's why point *X*, while to the right of point *S*, is also lower than point *S*.

If we continue this process further, we are not blessed with a similar effect. The reason is that if we move toward greater pizza production, we do not have those pizza chefs to call on; instead we have our group 2, who are pretty good at pizza and not so good at soda. What that means is even though pizza production rises, it does not rise as much as it did before. On top of that, our soda production falls more than it had before because when we moved the pizza chefs, they were "lousy" at soda. Now we are moving workers who are simply not so good at soda. Our soda losses are growing at an increasing rate. Thus we have point *Y* in Figure 1.3.

Going further, point *M* in Figure 1.4 results from moving the workers from group 3 (those with "modest" talent at both) from soda to pizza, point *Z* results from moving group 4 workers to pizza, and point *P* results from moving group 5 workers to pizza.

Connecting points like this creates Figure 1.5: a production possibilities frontier. This curve represents the most pizza that can be produced for any given amount of soda or, interpreted differently, the most soda that can be produced for any given amount of pizza.

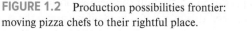

FIGURE 1.2 Production possibilities frontier: moving pizza chefs to their rightful place.

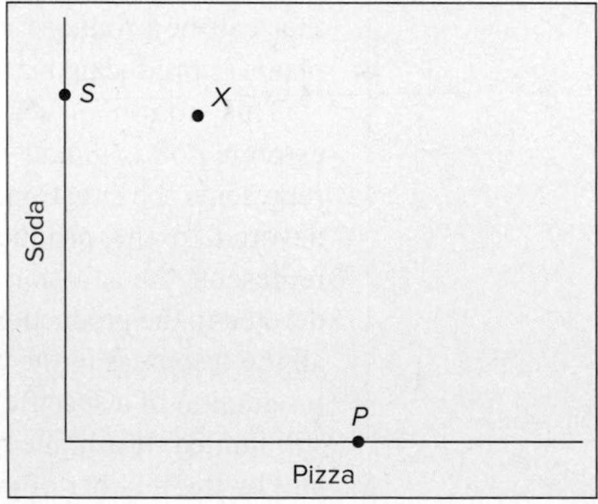

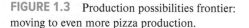

FIGURE 1.3 Production possibilities frontier: moving to even more pizza production.

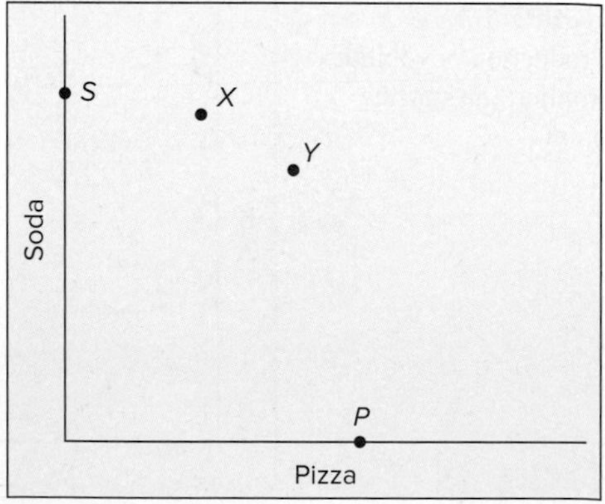

FIGURE 1.4 All points on a production possibilities frontier.

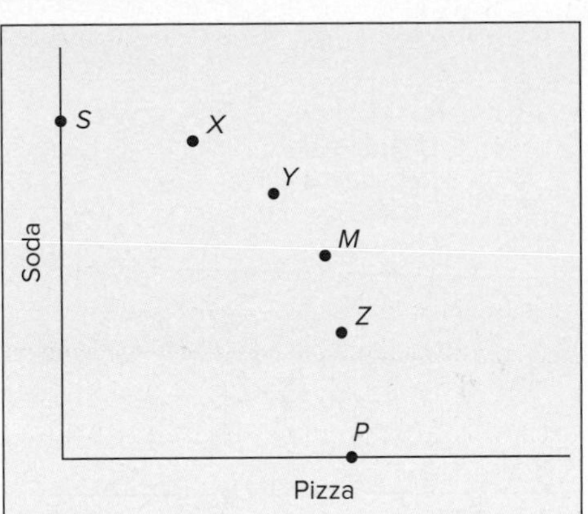

FIGURE 1.5 A fully labeled production possibilities frontier: the case when people are different.

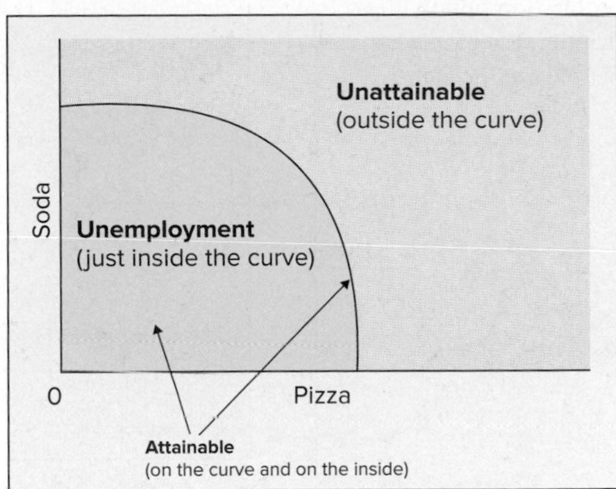

Attributes of the Production Possibilities Frontier

unemployment
A situation that occurs when resources are not being fully utilized.

attainable
Levels of production that are possible with the given resources.

unattainable
Levels of production that are not possible with the given resources.

Of course, if you can produce any combination on the production possibilities frontier, you can produce less than that as well. If you do produce at points inside a production possibilities frontier, there are unemployed resources, or **unemployment** for short. Therefore, all points on or inside the production possibilities frontier are **attainable.**

Conversely, since the production possibilities frontier represents the maximum amount of one good that you can produce for a given level of production of another, those points outside the production possibilities frontier are **unattainable.** This means that currently available resources and technology are insufficient to produce amounts greater than those illustrated on the frontier. On the graph, everything beyond the frontier is unattainable.

The preceding discussion illustrates something you need to be wary of in this book. Words you think you know may mean something entirely different to economists. Thus far we have at least three such words: *unemployment, frontier,* and *good.* You may think of unemployment as the condition of someone wanting a job but not having one. Economists do not disagree but expand that definition to resources other than labor. For example, on the interior of the production possibilities frontier there is unemployment, but that unemployment may be of capital. The word *frontier* is used to describe the boundary of production, not a wooded area with bears to avoid. The word *good,* to an economist, is a generic term for anything we consume. In the example, soda and pizza are goods.

In the soda and pizza example, there were people of different talents for soda and pizza production. The pizza chef had far different skills from the soda master. If, on the other hand, everyone were identical in their soda and pizza production capabilities, then points would fall on the line, as seen in Figure 1.6.

Increasing and Constant Opportunity Cost

Figures 1.5 and 1.6 have important similarities and differences. In both, the points on the production possibilities frontier are the most of one good that can be produced for a given amount of the other good. In both, the points on the curve and inside it are attainable and those on the outside of it are unattainable. In both, the opportunity cost of moving from one point to another is the amount of one good you have to give up to get another. They differ in one important way, however: whether opportunity cost is increasing or constant.

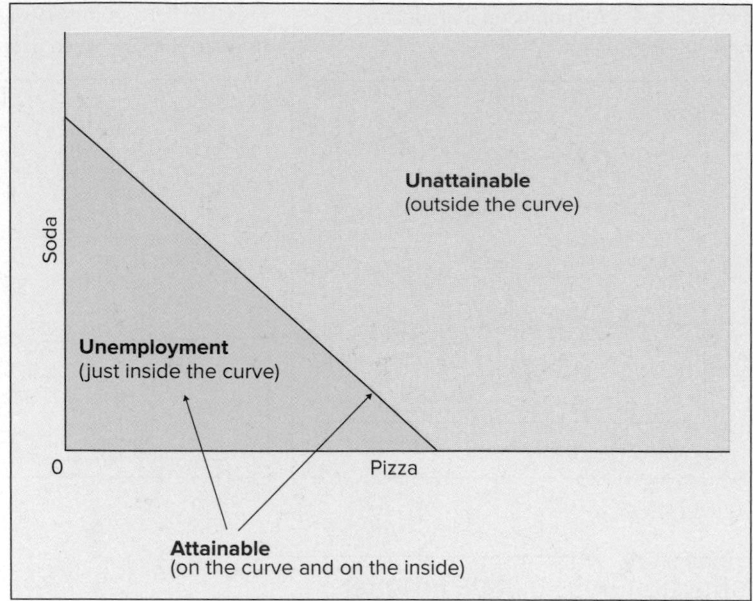

FIGURE 1.6
A fully labeled production possibilities frontier: the case when people are the same.

If the production possibilities frontier is not a line but is bowed out away from the origin, then opportunity cost is increasing. The reason for this is that as we add more resources to the production of pizza, we are using fewer resources to produce soda. Compounding that problem, at each stage as we take the resources away from soda and put them into pizza, we are moving workers who are worse at pizza production and better at soda production than those moved in the previous stage. This means that the increase in pizza production is diminishing and the loss in soda production is increasing. An economist would call this an example of increasing opportunity cost.

If the production possibilities frontier is a straight line that is not bowed out away from the origin, then opportunity cost is constant. If every worker possesses identical skill, though you still have to give up some soda to get pizza, this is not compounded by anything. The resources you put into producing more pizza are just as good as the resources used to get you to that point, and the resources taken away from the soda are similarly just as good as the resources used up to that point. An economist would call this an example of constant opportunity cost.

Economic Growth

How Is Growth Modeled?

economic growth
The circumstance where greater production opportunities exist.

Economic growth can be modeled using the production possibilities frontier. Economic growth is the circumstance where greater production opportunities exist. This can happen either because there are more resources available or because an innovation allows for those resources to produce more output. Economic growth can also happen in the context of increasing opportunity cost or constant opportunity cost. In the top three graphs of Figure 1.7, there is increasing opportunity cost between pizza and soda, whereas in the bottom three graphs of that figure, there is constant opportunity cost.

FIGURE 1.7
Modeling economic growth.

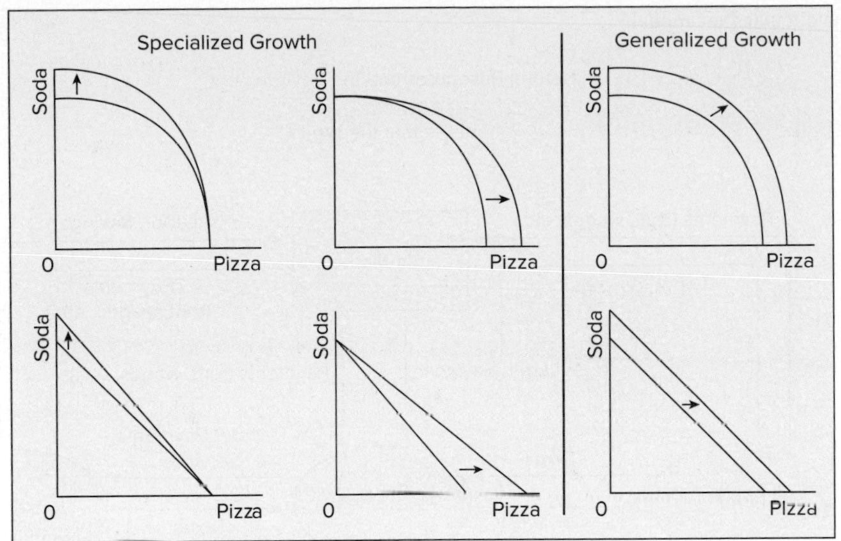

generalized growth The circumstance where innovation directly allows for greater production of all goods.

Generalized growth, the circumstance where innovation directly allows for greater production of all goods, is depicted on the right side of Figure 1.7. The most obvious example of generalized growth is when there is an overall increase in available labor or an increase in labor productivity. Having women enter the labor force in large numbers during the 1960s through the 1990s increased the availability of labor. The increase in the portion of the population with a college education that occurred at the same time would constitute an increase in the ability of that labor resource. In both cases, the production possibilities frontier moves outward from the origin.

specialized growth The circumstance where innovation directly allows for greater production of a particular good yet production of other goods is indirectly enabled.

Generalized growth is distinct from **specialized growth**. Specialized growth is the circumstance where innovation directly allows for greater production of a particular good yet production of other goods is indirectly enabled. Specialized growth is depicted on the left side of Figure 1.7.

The indirect, or enabled, growth exists because fewer resources are required to produce the good where the production innovation is occurring, thereby making more resources available to produce the other good where the innovation is not occurring. For instance, suppose you have a machine that allows more pizza to be produced with fewer workers. Some of the freed-up workers could be tasked with producing more soda, and you would have more of both goods. The impact on pizza would be direct while the impact on sodas would be indirect.

The Big Picture

circular flow model A model that depicts the interactions of all economic actors.

Now that we have looked at our first "simplified" model of the economy, it's time to get an idea of the "Big Picture." Think of Figure 1.8 as your road map to the book. This **circular flow model** is designed to put all of the pieces that follow in perspective. It shows firms, workers, investors, savers, buyers, and sellers interacting in markets and dealing with government. It has humanity taking natural resources from the environment and combining them with domestic and foreign financial and human resources to produce goods and services. Finally, it has humanity interacting in markets.

FIGURE 1.8 The circular flow model.

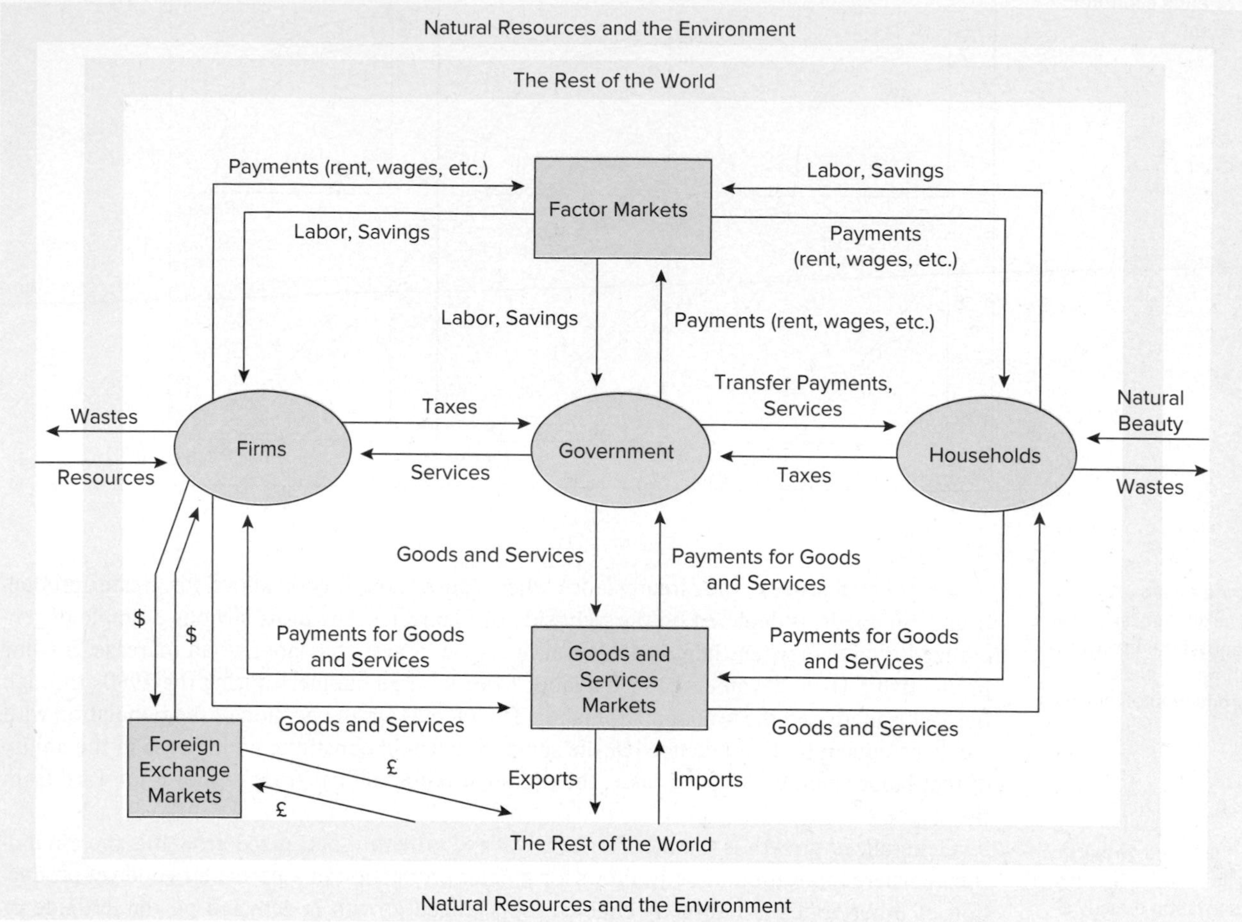

market
Any mechanism by which buyers and sellers negotiate an exchange.

factor market
A mechanism by which buyers and sellers of labor and financial capital negotiate an exchange.

foreign exchange market
A mechanism by which buyers and sellers of the currencies of various countries negotiate an exchange.

goods and services market
A mechanism by which buyers and sellers of goods and services negotiate an exchange.

Circular Flow Model: A Model That Shows the Interactions of All Economic Actors

The ovals in the diagram represent entities of specific kinds: There are households, firms, and governments. Households provide labor for wages. They use those wages to buy goods and services and pay their taxes. They receive services from government. Some save, some borrow, and many do both. Firms provide wages to households and pay taxes to government while getting labor from their workers and services from the government.

The rectangles in the diagram represent **markets** of various kinds: There are factor markets, foreign exchange markets, and goods and services markets. **Factor markets** are where workers and firms, and borrowers and savers interact to set wages and interest rates. **Foreign exchange markets** are where holders of various currencies interact to facilitate international trade. **Goods and services markets** are where consumers and producers interact to negotiate exchange of goods like cars, and services like dry cleaning. While some of these interactions occur in physical places, others do not. For instance, most financial interactions occur within computer networks.

On the exterior of this model are "The Rest of the World" and "Natural Resources and the Environment." The former allows us to explicitly think about foreign trade and foreign exchange, while the latter lets us think about the use of natural resources and the implications of economic activity on the environment.

Thinking Economically

Marginal Analysis

marginal analysis A form of analysis whereby incremental changes are examined to determine the net impact of those changes.

One of the central tools of economics is **marginal analysis**. Economists typically look at problems by analyzing incremental changes to determine the net impact of those changes. When people buy something, they compare the value of what they purchase to the value of what they give up. When companies produce goods for sale, they compare the money they generate from sales to the costs they will incur from the production process. When you were a teen, you engaged in marginal analysis when it came to the state of your room. You weighed the cleanliness gained against the opportunity cost of the time required. You decided it was "clean enough" when the next minute of cleaning would be better spent doing something else.

optimization assumption An assumption that suggests that the person in question is trying to maximize some objective.

Economists generally make an **optimization assumption.** This is an assumption that suggests that the person in question is trying to maximize some objective. For example, consumers are assumed to be making decisions that maximize their happiness subject to a scarce amount of money. Companies are assumed to maximize profits.

marginal benefit The increase in the benefit that results from an action.

marginal cost The increase in the cost that results from an action.

net benefit The difference between all benefits and all costs.

Economists see that these problems can be tackled using marginal analysis. Economists compare the **marginal benefit** of an action with its **marginal cost.** Something is worth doing only if the increase in benefits equals or exceeds the increase in costs. If the marginal benefit of an action steadily decreases and the marginal cost of an action steadily increases, then a person maximizes **net benefit** by doing that action until the marginal benefit equals the marginal cost. This is the essence of marginal analysis, and we will see it in action throughout this book.

Positive and Normative Analysis

positive analysis A form of analysis that seeks to understand the way things are and why they are that way.

normative analysis A form of analysis that seeks to understand the way things should be.

When people look at the world, they often see things as they are and compare the way things are to the way they think things should be. They see a major league shortstop sign a contract for a quarter of a billion dollars over 10 years while their high school teachers make less than $40,000 a year. Economists, and social scientists in general, distinguish views of "the way things are" from "the way things should be," calling the former **positive analysis** and the latter **normative analysis.** Although there are economists who utilize both forms of analysis, more economists are comfortable explaining why things are the way they are than are comfortable suggesting the way things should be. Some critics look at this as self-delusion on the part of economists, using the argument that we choose which information to weigh more heavily based on normative beliefs. For instance, economists long ago decided what would count as production. They decided to include only goods and services that were sold in markets because it was too hard to count things we do for ourselves (like laundry, cooking, and lawn care). Feminist economists maintain that this distinction diminished the production of women because women engage much more in home production than men.

Economic Incentives

incentives Something that influences a decision we make.

What kinds of choices we make as individuals and as a society depend on our preferences. Returning to the soda and pizza example, whether we like soda or pizza, or in what combinations we most like them, will have an important impact on what we choose to produce and consume. But also high on the list of things that determine which combinations of things we will produce and consume are **incentives.** Something is an incentive if it influences a decision we make. Some incentives are part of a market, like prices. Others are imposed by an outside force like a government, and they can positively reinforce behaviors that are desired or deter behaviors that are not. This means that you are still able to produce and consume what you want, but something—perhaps a tax or a government regulation—is encouraging a particular choice. For example, by taxing beer and not soda, the government encourages you to steer toward soda and away from beer.

On a deeper level, an incentive may motivate you to do something you would not ordinarily do. For instance, many incentives are offered in the tax system. Tax credits and deductions for college tuition are considered incentives that will persuade people to get an education. For many people who would go to college anyway, these are not incentives. However, to some people who were perhaps considering college but had not made a decision, any influence these tax benefits would have on the decision would constitute an incentive.

An important and sometimes unfortunate aspect of incentives is that they create unintended consequences. Taxes are an area where some argue that the unintended consequences can be predicted from the incentives that arise out of programs. If welfare payments were reduced when the recipient found part-time employment, some predict that the recipient would not look for part-time employment.

Impediments to Thinking Economically

Fallacy of Composition

One of the key traps to thinking economically is assuming that the total economic impact of something is always and simply equal to the sum of the individual parts. The **fallacy of composition** is an important logical trap to avoid because invalid economic conclusions will inevitably be drawn.

fallacy of composition
The mistake in logic that suggests that the total economic impact of something is always and simply equal to the sum of the individual parts.

Outside of economics, cake constitutes a famous illustration of why the fallacy of composition is just that—a fallacy. Imagine a cake. Now imagine the ingredients that go into making the cake. Imagine eating the cake and the satisfaction you get from that. Now compare that level of satisfaction to what you would have if you separately poured flour, sugar, and baking powder down your throat, washed it down with a couple of raw eggs and some cooking oil, and then stuck your head in an oven. The baked combination is obviously better than its individual parts.

As an example within economics, we will learn in Chapter 5 that when many farmers are making high profits, others will want to join in. If they do join in, will all of the old and new farmers be making high profits? We will see that the new farmers' extra production will ultimately drive prices down so far that neither the older nor the newer farmers make money.

When we are making economic judgments, we must do so with care. The sums of the individual parts must not be confused with the whole. The two can be, and often are, different.

Correlation ≠ Causation

When people are attempting to think economically, another trap they may fall into is assuming that because two variables changed simultaneously, one caused the other to happen.

For instance, if you weighed all people under age 30 and also asked them how many dates they had had in their lifetime, you would find a **direct correlation,** meaning that it appears that the more people weigh, the more dates they have had. This does not imply **causation.** Heavier people do not necessarily get more dates and dating does not make us gain weight. In this case, the two variables happen to be correlated with age. People in their twenties weigh more and have had a longer opportunity to have dates than have teens, preteens, and young children.

direct correlation
A higher level of one variable is associated with a higher level of the other variable.

causation
A change in one variable makes another variable change.

When politicians attempt to take credit for good economic times with the claim that their policies caused the good economic times to happen, we must be suspicious. Of course, we must be equally suspicious if they attempt to pin the blame on their incumbent opponent if bad economic times existed during their opponent's time in office. While their claims may be true, it is perfectly plausible that the policies and the economy were unrelated, or that the economy did well or did poorly despite the policies.

When economists look at cause and effect, they frequently attempt to generate a **counterfactual.** A counterfactual is an educated guess about what would have happened had a policy or an event not occurred. A well-constructed and convincing counterfactual can help determine

counterfactual
An educated guess as to what would have happened had a policy or an event not occurred.

whether a policy (like the 2008 Troubled Asset Relief Program or TARP) made things better than they otherwise would have been. It is not enough to say that the economy lost millions of jobs after a policy was passed and therefore the policy was bad. You must be able to construct a scenario of what would have happened had the policy not been enacted. This is often the reason why economists will disagree and seem absolutely convinced that those with whom they are disagreeing are wrong. Whether the Bush administration's TARP program, the Federal Reserve's lowering of interest rates through unprecedented purchases of long-term debt, or the Obama stimulus package made the economic downturn of the time better than it would have been depends entirely on your counterfactual.

inverse correlation A higher level of one variable is associated with a lower level of the other variable.

Sometimes two variables move in opposite directions. This **inverse correlation** can also be misinterpreted as being causal. If you were to get season tickets to your college's football games and observe the amount of skin (bare arms, legs, and midriffs) showing on the fans and compare that to the amount of hot chocolate sold during the game, you would find that when people show more skin they also consume less hot chocolate. If you came to the conclusion that one caused the other to happen you would, of course, be wrong. Obviously, the weather caused each to occur.

Kick It Up a Notch

DEMONSTRATING CONSTANT AND INCREASING OPPORTUNITY COST ON A PRODUCTION POSSIBILITIES FRONTIER

Economists use the production possibilities frontier to show the concepts of increasing and constant opportunity cost. If we start with no pizza and only soda but then move in increments to change our mix, there is opportunity cost. Just how much depends on whether it is increasing or constant.

Demonstrating Increasing Opportunity Cost

For example, in Figure 1.9, if we go from the point on the graph where we are producing no pizza to the point where we are producing a single unit, a unit whose numbers could be in the billions, our opportunity cost would be characterized by lost units of soda. On Figure 1.9, the opportunity cost of going from 0 units of pizza to 1 unit of pizza is 1 unit of soda. Choosing to increase pizza production from 1 unit to 2 units has an opportunity cost that is 3 units of soda. Similarly, increasing pizza production from 2 to 3 units has an opportunity cost of 6 units of soda. As is visually obvious, the opportunity cost of going from 0 to 1 is smaller than going from 2 to 3. Economists refer to this by saying that the opportunity cost is increasing.

Demonstrating Constant Opportunity Cost

Similarly, we can use Figure 1.10 to show constant opportunity cost. The opportunity cost of moving from producing no pizza to 1 unit of pizza is 3 units of soda. Shifting production from 1 unit to 2 units of pizza and from 2 to 3 units also has an opportunity cost of 3 units of soda. In this case, the opportunity cost of going from 0 units to 1 unit is the same as going from 2 to 3 units. Here, we say that the opportunity cost is constant.

What this all means is simple: Choices have consequences. Sometimes those consequences are great and sometimes they are small. If studying for five hours moves you from an F to a B on a test, then the higher grade has a low opportunity cost in terms of lost television watching. Viewed from the other side, the opportunity cost of another five hours of television watching (instead of studying to get a good grade) could be substantial. Opportunity cost is everywhere and is a consequence of every decision you make.

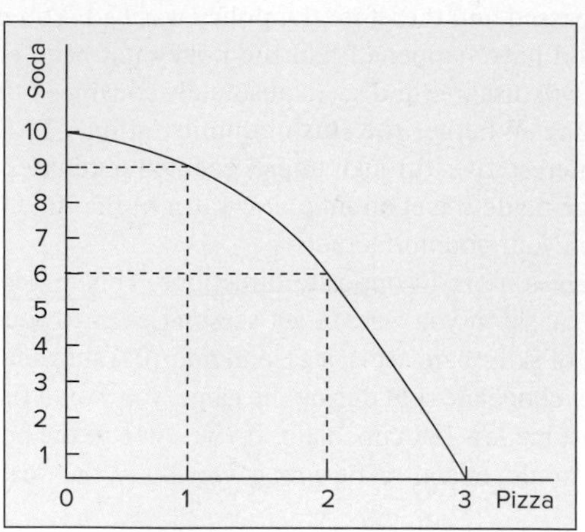

FIGURE 1.9 Illustrating increasing opportunity costs.

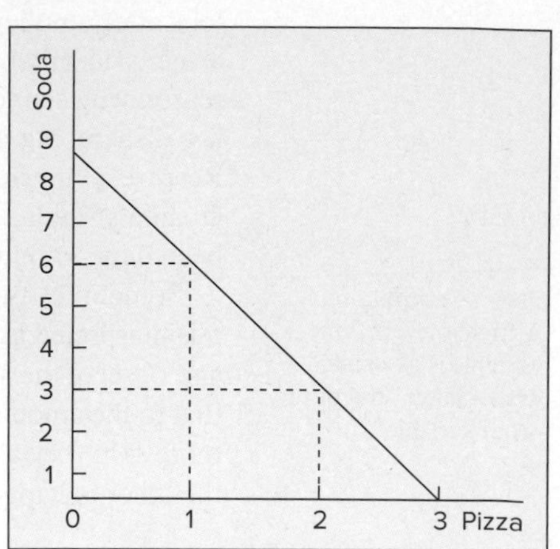

FIGURE 1.10 Illustrating constant opportunity costs.

Summary

In this chapter we learned the definition of economics, that choices have consequences, and that those consequences are called opportunity cost. We modeled choices using a production possibilities frontier. We also learned that, depending on our assumptions, opportunity cost can be increasing or constant. We created a road map to the entire economy and to the rest of this book by developing a circular flow diagram to show the various markets, individuals, firms, and governments interacting in society. Last, we explored the meaning of thinking economically by examining marginal analysis, positive and normative analysis, incentives, and the flaws of logic that may get in the way of economically accurate thinking.

Key Terms

attainable
causation
circular flow model
counterfactual
direct correlation
economic growth
economics
factor market
fallacy of composition
foreign exchange market
generalized growth
goods and services market
incentives
inverse correlation
marginal analysis
marginal benefit
marginal cost
market
model
net benefit
normative analysis
opportunity cost
optimization assumption
positive analysis
production possibilities frontier
resource
scarce
simplifying assumption
specialized growth
unattainable
unemployment

Issues Chapters You Are Ready for Now

Federal Spending
Poverty and Welfare
If We Build It, Will They Come? And Other Sports Questions

Quiz Yourself

1. Scarcity implies that the allocation decision chosen by society can
   a. not make more of any one good.
   b. always make more of any good.
   c. typically make more of one good but at the expense of making less of another.
   d. always make more of all goods simultaneously.
2. A production possibilities frontier is a simple model of
   a. allocating scarce inputs to the production of alternative outputs.
   b. price and production/consumption in a market.
   c. the cost of producing goods.
   d. the number of inputs required to produce varying levels of output.
3. The underlying reason that there are unattainable points on a production possibilities frontier is that there
   a. is government.
   b. are always choices that must be made.
   c. are scarce resources within a fixed level of technology.
   d. is unemployment of resources.
4. The underlying reason production possibilities frontiers are likely to be bowed out (rather than linear) is
   a. choices have consequences.
   b. there are always opportunity costs.
   c. some resources and people can be better used producing one good rather than another.
   d. there is always some level of unemployment.
5. If you were modeling the impact of the introduction of computer automation into manufacturing on a production possibilities frontier (PPF) with two manufactured goods on their respective axes, it would be more likely that the result would be
   a. generalized growth with the PPF moving both up and right.
   b. specialized growth with the PPF moving both up and right.
   c. generalized growth with the PPF just moving up and not to the right.
   d. specialized growth with the PPF just moving up and not to the right.
6. The optimization assumption suggests that people make
   a. irrational decisions.
   b. unpredictable decisions.
   c. decisions to make themselves as well off as possible.
   d. decisions without thinking very hard.
7. Imagine an economist ordering donuts one-by-one. When deciding how many donuts to order, she would pick that number where the enjoyment of the ________ equals the enjoyment she could get from using the money on another good.
   a. first donut
   b. last/marginal donut
   c. average/typical donut
   d. total number of donuts
8. Of course, all individual students are better off if they get better grades. If you were to conclude that all students would be better off if everyone received an A, you would
   a. have fallen victim to the fallacy of scarcity.
   b. be right.
   c. have fallen victim to the fallacy of composition.
   d. be mistaking correlation with causation.

9. If you were to conclude, after carefully examining data and using proper evaluation techniques, that a tax credit for attending college benefits the poor more than a tax deduction (of equal total cost to the government) would, you would have engaged in ____________ analysis to reach that conclusion.
   a. negative
   b. positive
   c. normative
   d. creative

Short Answer Questions

1. Suppose you buy a new car. What is the opportunity cost of doing so?
2. Suppose you decided to study all last week for this exam instead of doing anything fun. What was the opportunity cost of doing so? Why might the opportunity cost (defined in terms of fun lost) be expected to increase?
3. Suppose you hear a political candidate claim credit or lay blame for an economic outcome. How can you tell whether the candidate is correct? What would you need to know?
4. If you get a 25 percent pay increase, you are better off. Explain why some people would *not* be better off if their employer gave them a 25 percent pay increase.
5. Suppose you were to analyze the state and the economy at the moment. You say to your friends, "The economy has been growing more slowly in the last 10 years than it did in the previous 20 years. The government should cut taxes to stimulate the economy." What portion of that statement is "positive" and what portion of that statement is "normative"?

Think about This

What was your opportunity cost of attending college?

Think about the most expensive thing you have ever purchased. What could you have done with the money? Which outcome would have made you better off–what you did or what you could have done?

Think about the last time you took a series of tests during a short period of time (high school or college finals work here). How did you decide how much time to spend on each subject? How might the study of economics help you make that allocation decision in the future?

Talk about This

Discuss whether you believe people make rational decisions based on the optimization assumption.

Discuss what kinds of noneconomic (something you would normally not think of as an economic decision) trade-offs could be modeled with a production possibilities frontier?

Graphing: Yes, You Can.

Whether you like it or not, graphing is an important part of "getting" economics. If you have ventured to this appendix, it is likely that your instructor agrees and wants you to have a firm foundation for what you are about to do. This appendix is geared to the student who never understood what a graph was trying to tell them–to those who look at a complex diagram and see a bunch of stray lines that have no meaning. Those of us who teach economics have often lost our students at the moment we went to the board, overhead projector, or computer display to draw a graph. Let's get off on the right foot with learning what a graph is and what it can tell us.

CARTESIAN COORDINATES

As the subheading suggests, Cartesian coordinates are named for their inventor, Frenchman René Descartes. As the legend goes, he was staring at the ceiling and began following the path of a fly. He discovered that he could use just two numbers to pinpoint the placement of the fly on the ceiling every time it landed. So lie back for a moment and look at the ceiling.

origin The point on the graph where both the variables are zero (0,0).

***y*-axis** The vertical axis.

***x*-axis** The horizontal axis.

Now pick a corner of the room where the ceiling meets two walls; that will be your reference point, called the **origin**. Assuming the walls are square to one another, call the wall that runs on your left the ***y*-axis** and the wall on your right the ***x*-axis**. Now find a spot on the ceiling that stands out–a spider, a small stain, a vent, anything. Draw the shortest possible imaginary line from your spot to the ceiling to the wall on the right. Call that point *A*. Do the same thing for the wall on the left and call that point *B*. You can identify that point on the ceiling using just two numbers. The first number is the distance along the *x*-axis from the corner to *A* and the second is the distance along the *y*-axis from the corner to *B*. In Figure 1A.1, the point that is marked is 9 units along the *x*-axis and 11 units along the *y*-axis, so it is shown as (9,11).

FIGURE 1A.1
Graphing a point.

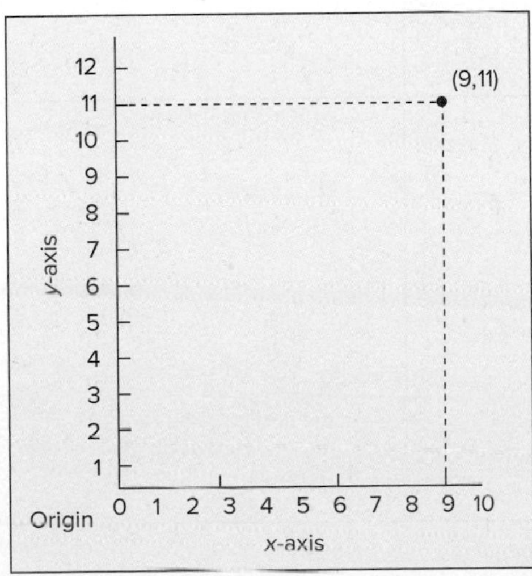

PLEASE! NOT $Y = MX + B$ . . . SORRY.

slope
The increase in the value of the y-axis variable for a 1-unit increase in the value of the x-axis variable.

x-intercept
The value of the x-axis variable when the y-axis variable is zero.

y-intercept
The value of the y-axis variable when the x-axis variable is zero.

Whether you want to recall the experience or not, you were first exposed to the **slope**, **x-intercept**, and **y-intercept** of a line and the dreaded $y = mx + b$ form of the line in your first algebra class. Whether that was in 7th, 8th, 9th, or 10th grade, enough time has passed that a refresh is in order. The equation $y = mx + b$ is a line because if you get all of the x, y combinations that come about from plugging in random values of x and computing what you get for y and then graph them, they comprise a line. That line will cross the y-axis at b, because if you plug in 0 for x in the $y = mx + b$ equation, mx is 0 (because anything multiplied by zero is zero), so all you are left with is b. Therefore, b is the y-intercept. It will cross the x-axis at $-b/m$. Therefore, the x-intercept is $-b/m$.

As you will (perhaps not so vividly) recall, the slope is the "rise over the run." That means it is the amount by which y rises divided by the amount by which x rises. Suppose we let x start at 3 and rise to 4. If that happens, then y goes from $m3 + b$ to $m4 + b$. Therefore, y rises by m. The rise is m, the run is 1, so the slope is $m/1$, or just m. There is nothing magic about the choice of 3; we could have used any number and we would have gotten the same result. The slope is m.

If m and b are positive, you get a graph like Figure 1A.2. If m is positive and b is negative, you get something like Figure 1A.3. If m is negative and b is positive, you get a graph like Figure 1A.4, and finally, if they are both negative, you get something like Figure 1A.5. If m is large and positive, the line is upward sloping and steep; small and positive means that it is upward sloping and relatively flat. If m is really negative, then the line is downward sloping and steep, and if it is slightly negative, then the line is downward sloping and flat.

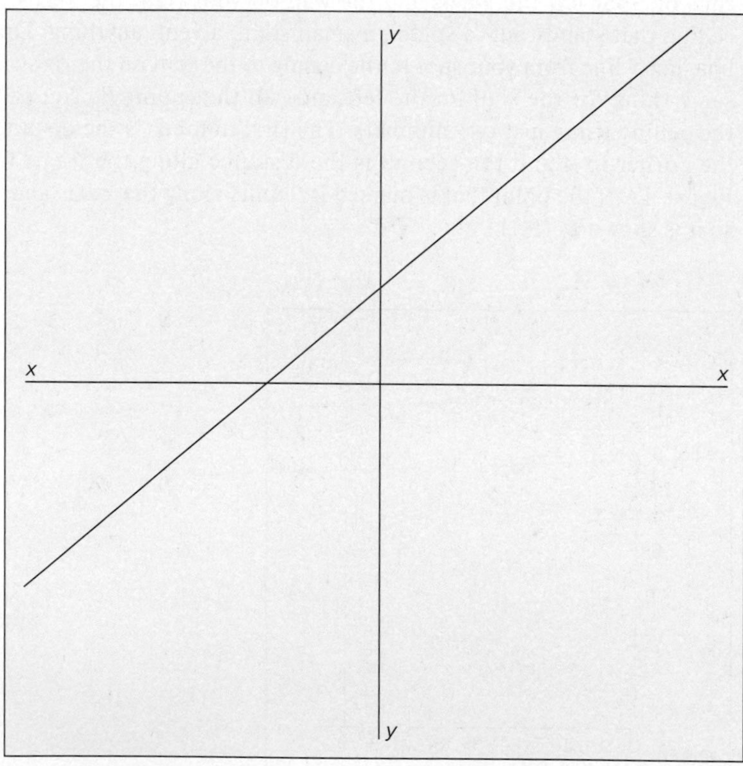

FIGURE 1A.2
Graphing a line
$y = mx + b$
$m > 0, b > 0.$

FIGURE 1A.3
Graphing a line
$y = mx + b$
$m > 0, b < 0.$

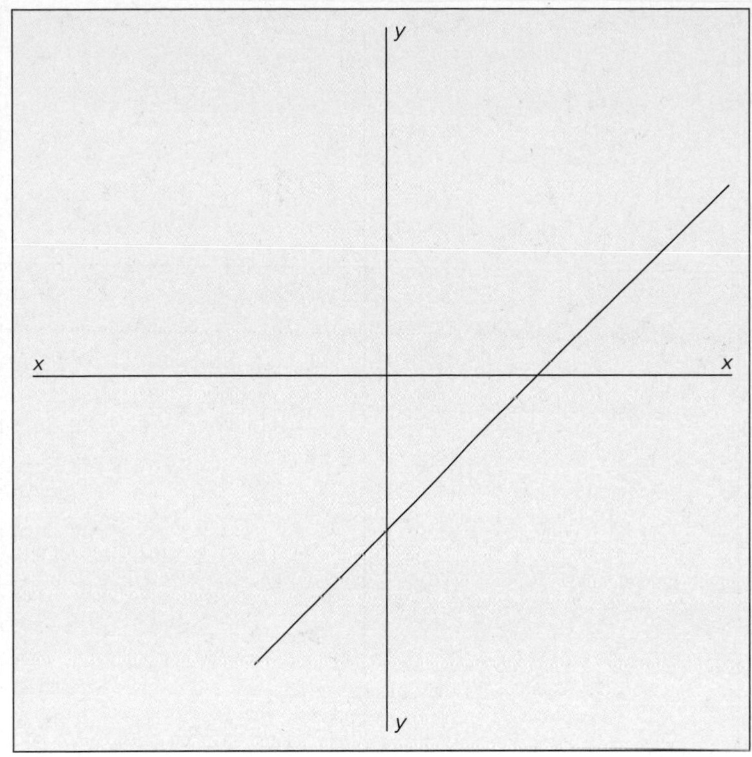

FIGURE 1A.4
Graphing a line
$y = mx + b$
$m < 0, b > 0.$

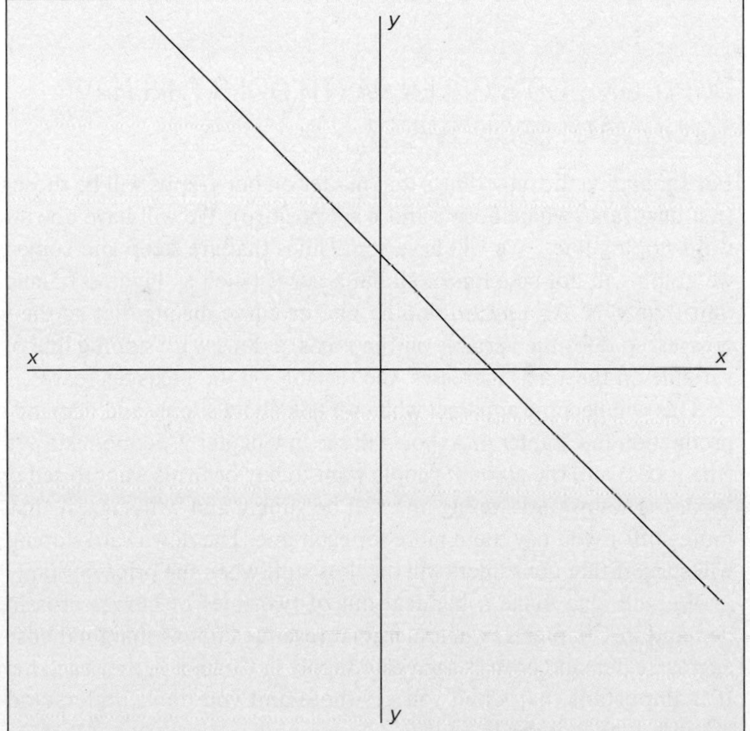

FIGURE 1A.5
Graphing a line
$y = mx + b$
$m < 0, b < 0.$

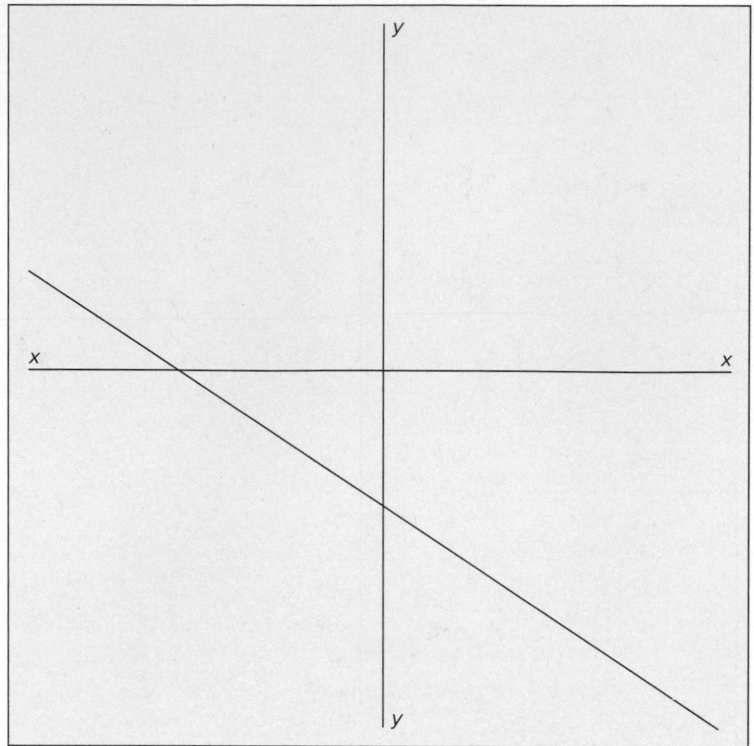

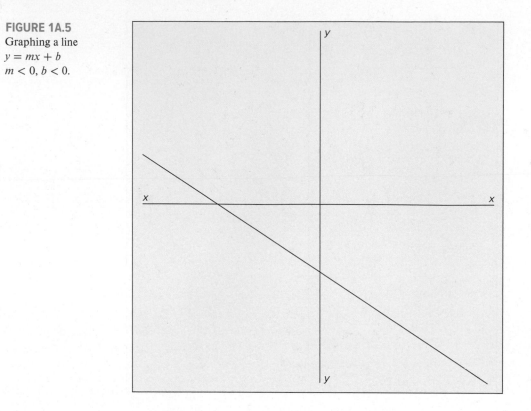

WHAT ON GOD'S GREEN EARTH DOES THIS HAVE TO DO WITH ECONOMICS?

For simplicity, the only things that matter on our graphs will be those things that happen in the first quadrant (where both x and y are positive). We will have downward-sloping lines and upward-sloping lines. We will have some lines that are steep and some that are flat. Often, what we graph will not be a line at all but a curve (such as Figures 1.5 and 1.8). That is less important than this: An upward-sloping line or curve means that as the variable on the x-axis increases, so does the variable on the y-axis; a downward-sloping line or curve means that as the variable on the x-axis increases, the variable on the y-axis decreases.

This will become apparent when we talk about supply and demand in Chapter 2 and costs of production in Chapter 4. As you will see in Chapter 2, economists put price on the vertical axis (the y-axis) and the amount people want to buy or firms want to sell on the horizontal axis (the x-axis). The upward-sloping line will be supply and will suggest that companies will produce more stuff if you pay them more for each one. The downward-sloping line will be demand and will suggest that consumers will buy less stuff when the price per unit rises.

We will also make a big deal out of two lines or curves crossing. When supply crosses demand in Chapter 2, when marginal revenue crosses marginal cost in Chapter 5, and when aggregate demand crosses aggregate supply in Chapter 8, they each have particular significance. It is important that when you get there and you don't understand why two lines crossing matters at all . . . **ASK!**

CHAPTER TWO

Supply and Demand

Learning Objectives

After reading this chapter you should be able to:

LO1 Construct a supply and demand model.

LO2 Define and explain the terms associated with the supply and demand model.

LO3 Explain the assumptions of individual and firm behavior that support the supply and demand model.

LO4 List the determinants of supply and those of demand and demonstrate the impact of changes in those determinants on a supply and demand diagram.

Chapter Outline

Supply and Demand Defined

The Supply and Demand Model

All about Demand

All about Supply

Determinants of Demand

Determinants of Supply

The Effect of Changes in Price Expectations on the Supply and Demand Model

Kick It Up a Notch: Why the New Equilibrium?

Summary

This is the make-or-break chapter of the book: You cannot understand economics without understanding supply and demand nor can you effectively apply the lessons of economics to most of the issues laid out in Chapters 9–48. This isn't one of those topics that you will never use. Once you understand it, it will inform things you do and answer questions you have almost every day.

You probably are familiar with the words *supply and demand* through television, newspapers, or conversation. The phrase is frequently used by people in a way an economist would not use it. This chapter is intended to show you what economists mean when they discuss supply and demand and use its associated model. This will enable you to use the model and jargon correctly as we apply it to a variety of economic issues.

Arriving at that level of understanding will take some time. We begin by introducing some of the language we will be using. It may be tempting for you to read too fast, to skim through, figuring that you are familiar with all the words. Don't. As we discussed in Chapter 1, the language has precise meaning to economists, and it is not necessarily the same as the meaning you associate with it.

Our next step is laying out the supply and demand model itself, starting with brief explanations of the term *demand* and then the term *supply*. We then put them together on one graph to form our first look at the model and our first look at what economists call *equilibrium*. With the model in place, we pause a moment to examine, in considerable detail, its individual elements. We use commonsense stories to explain why, for demand, price and quantity are negatively related and why, for supply, they are positively related.

With a rudimentary understanding of the supply and demand model, we explore what happens in it when demand changes and then explore what happens in it when supply changes. We conclude the chapter by showing why a new equilibrium results when there are changes to demand or supply. We do this by imagining the consequences of laws that might forbid such changes to price.

Supply and Demand Defined

Markets

supply and demand The name of the most important model in all of economics.

price The amount of money that must be paid for a unit of output.

output The good or service produced for sale.

market Any mechanism by which buyers and sellers negotiate an exchange.

consumers People in a market who want to exchange money for goods or services.

producers People in a market who want to exchange goods or services for money.

equilibrium price The price at which no consumers wish they could have purchased more goods at the price; no producers wish that they could have sold more.

equilibrium quantity The amount of output exchanged at the equilibrium price.

Supply and demand is the name of the most important model in all of economics. Economists use it to provide insight into the movements in **price** and **output.** Remember from Chapter 1 that a model is a simplification of a complicated real-life phenomenon. This model assumes that there is a **market** where buyers and sellers get together to trade. **Consumers** are assumed to bring money to the market, whereas **producers** are assumed to bring goods or services to the market. Consumers want to exchange their money for goods or services while producers want to exchange the goods or services they have for money.

It is important that you understand that the word *market* has a very specific meaning to economists. A market exists anywhere that buyers and sellers negotiate price and perform an exchange. Therefore, they have to be able to communicate and they have to be able to exchange. Take, as an example, the market for used midsized sedans. There are people who are looking to buy them and people who are looking to sell them. Prior to the Internet, most of the communication was geographically constrained. Buyers went to used-car lots or read ads in the newspaper. People who wanted to unload a car advertised by word of mouth, by newspaper, or sold to a dealer. With the Internet, the market is greatly expanded because communication (autotrader.com; craigslist.com, etc.) is easier, but you still are unlikely to buy a car in Seattle if you live in Miami because the cost of getting the car from Seattle is prohibitive.

The supply and demand model assumes that there are many consumers and producers, so that no one of them can dictate price. There is a price at which neither consumers nor producers leave with less value than they came with; no consumers wish they could have purchased more goods at the price; no producers wish they could have sold more at that price—in short, everyone is better off for participating. Economists call such a price an **equilibrium price** and the amount that consumers buy from producers an **equilibrium quantity.** The nuts and bolts of this model are the supply and demand curves. The demand curve shows the relationship between the price consumers have to pay and how much they "want to buy," whereas the supply curve shows the relationship between the price firms receive and how much producers "want to sell." Economists refer to the amount that consumers want to buy at any particular price as *quantity demanded* and the amount that firms want to sell at any particular price as *quantity supplied.*

People participate in markets because markets make their participants better off. Markets evolved because our ancestors recognized that self-sufficiency, though possible, did not allow people to take advantage of their particular skills. A social creation of humans, markets have been shaped by humankind to bring people together to exchange goods and services and, because these exchanges have always been voluntary, participants have always left exchanges content that they have gained from the market's existence. Thus markets have endured as a useful social institution because they continue to advance our individual and societal standard of living.

Quantity Demanded and Quantity Supplied

quantity demanded The amount consumers are willing and able to buy at a particular price during a particular period of time.

This is one place where everything you have read, heard, or seen in the media will confuse you because economists use these terms very differently from the way they are used outside of economics. Economists insist on highlighting the difference between *demand* and **quantity demanded.** If you look carefully, there is an important distinction buried in the detail regarding

ECONOMIC SYSTEMS AND ECONOMIC FREEDOM

capitalist economy
An economic system where markets, in particular markets for financial resources, are free.

socialist economy
An economic system where a significant part (but not all) of the decisions regarding the allocation of financial resources is made by a governmental authority.

communist economy
An economic system where governmental authorities determine the allocation, use, and distribution of financial resources.

Markets exist whether the underlying economic system is **capitalist**, **socialist**, or **communist**. A capitalist economy is so named because, in addition to there being free markets that determine prices and quantities for most goods and services, there are free markets in financial capital. Whether people have money to lend because they have saved it or inherited it, in a capitalist system they control it. The profit that the capital generates goes to the owner of the capital.

In a communist system, capital and the profit that it generates are controlled by a government authority. The government authority decides how the money is used. In a socialist system, a significant part of the profit generated by financial capital goes to the government in the form of taxes. The government then uses the tax money to counter the wealth impacts of the distribution of profit.

No country is completely capitalist and few (possibly North Korea) are completely communist. Each country exists along a spectrum. The politically conservative Heritage Foundation, in conjunction with the *Wall Street Journal*, developed an Index of Economic Freedom that measures the degree to which countries have free capital flows, minimal government regulation of business and labor, minimal limits on trade, and a legal system conducive to business. Selected countries are listed in the table below.

It is also worth noting that this is the first, but certainly not the last, time that this text will use a source with a political agenda. That usage, however, will be balanced.

Index of Economic Freedom Table

Top 20	Bottom 20	Other Countries and Their Rank	
Hong Kong	Central African Republic	Germany	24
Singapore	Burundi	Norway	26
New Zealand	Mozambique	Israel	27
Switzerland	Turkmenistan	South Korea	29
Australia	Suriname	Japan	30
Ireland	Sudan	Austria	31
United Kingdom	Sierra Leone	Uruguay	40
Canada	Kiribati	Peru	45
United Arab Emirates	Djibouti	Belgium	48
Taiwan	Ecuador	Spain	57
Iceland	Algeria	Mexico	66
United States	Timor-Leste	France	71
Netherlands	Bolivia	Italy	80
Denmark	Equatorial Guinea	Saudi Arabia	91
Estonia	Zimbabwe	Russia	98
Georgia	Republic of Congo	China	100
Luxembourg	Eritrea	India	129
Chile	Cuba	Greece	138
Sweden	Venezuela	Brazil	150
Finland	North Korea		

Source: The Heritage Foundation. "Country Rankings, 2019 Index of Economic Freedom." Accessed June 17, 2019. www.heritage.org/index/Ranking

quantity demanded. In particular, it is how much consumers are willing and able to buy at a *particular price* during a *particular period of time*. Demand, on the other hand, shows how much consumers want to buy at all prices. Demand is a relationship, whereas quantity demanded is a particular point on that relationship. An identical distinction exists with supply. **Quantity supplied** is how much firms are willing and able to sell at a particular price during a particular period of time, whereas supply shows how much firms want to sell at all prices.

quantity supplied Amount firms are willing and able to sell at a particular price during a particular period of time.

Ceteris Paribus

Social scientists in general, and economists in particular, believe in something called the scientific method, one aspect of which suggests that to isolate the effect of one variable on another you have to separate out the impacts of everything else. Unlike chemistry or biology, though, economists are rarely able to put their subjects (people) into a lab and experiment on them. For instance, economists cannot create a capitalist system in one area of town, a socialist system in another, and a communist system in a third so as to test which economic system serves society best. Economists must observe in the context of their models. So, even though life does not progress one change at a time, our model allows us to focus on one change at a time. This brings us to a Latin phrase commonly used by economists, **ceteris paribus,** which means "other things equal." This phrase, when added to a definition or a conclusion, means that though there are many other factors that could affect a phenomenon in real life, the statement is focusing on the impact of one variable while holding other factors constant.

ceteris paribus Latin for "other things equal."

Demand and Supply

For our demand curve, we want to know what the relationship is between price and quantity demanded. Determining this relationship is difficult because the relationship depends on such things as whether people are rich or poor, whether the good is in or out of fashion, or how much rival goods cost. To get around this, we assume we are looking at the relationship between price and quantity demanded in such a way that none of the other variables are changing. Thus, **demand** is the relationship between price and quantity demanded, ceteris paribus.

Precisely, the same logic applies to supply. There are many things upon which the relationship between price and quantity supplied depends: how much workers must be paid, the cost of materials, or the availability of technology. Again we assume these things do not change, so **supply** is the relationship between price and quantity supplied, ceteris paribus.

demand The relationship between price and quantity demanded, ceteris paribus.

supply The relationship between price and quantity supplied, ceteris paribus.

The Supply and Demand Model

Demand

We have put it off long enough—let's look at the supply and demand model. To plot a demand curve, let's first tell ourselves a reasonable story and put the relevant information in a table. In many downtown areas, there are vendors selling food and drink from stands. To simplify the issue, let's suppose we are looking at the market for bottled orange juice sold by these street vendors and that the customers buy the bottles of orange juice from those vendors and consume the juice throughout the day in their downtown offices. There are obviously lots of things that will affect the supply and demand for these bottles of orange juice, but for the moment, we are going to assume they are held constant.

We start this inquiry with the price of a bottle of orange juice at zero and ask how many will be wanted. Probably a lot, but not as many as you might think. People get tired of drinking the same thing over and over again, and even if they were going to get a bunch to save for later, they still have to carry it to their offices. Suppose, for mathematical simplicity, that there are only

Table 2.1
Demand schedule for bottles of orange juice.

Price ($)	Individual Quantity Demanded	Market Quantity Demanded (10,000 people)*
0	5	50,000
0.50	4	40,000
1.00	3	30,000
1.50	2	20,000
2.00	1	10,000
2.50	0	0

*This is ceteris paribus at work, holding the number and type of people constant.

10,000 people in this area and that at a price of zero each person wants only five bottles per day. That would mean that, at a price of zero, there would be a quantity demanded of 50,000 drinks.

Suppose the price were raised to 50 cents per bottle. Each individual would have to consider whether they wanted a bottle of orange juice or 50 cents. Let's say the average person decides to buy only four per day at that price. As a result of the price increase, the quantity demanded for the market would be 40,000. Suppose another 50-cent increase would decrease the amount wanted by the average person to three. The quantity demanded in the market would fall to 30,000. Without belaboring the point further, price increases would decrease the amount the average person would buy until at $2 per bottle the average person wanted only one, and at $2.50 the average person would buy none. Table 2.1 depicts the options we have just suggested in the form of what is called a **demand schedule.** A demand schedule presents the price and quantity demanded for a good in tabular form.

demand schedule
Presentation, in tabular form, of the price and quantity demanded for a good.

This information can also be displayed on a graph. As a matter of fact, that is how you will nearly always see it. Figure 2.1 is a graph of a demand curve. Note that the vertical axis is labeled *P* for price per unit and the horizontal axis is labeled *Q/t* for quantity per unit time. You probably anticipated the first label, but the second may require a short explanation. Quantity per unit time is the number of orange juice bottles that the 10,000 people will want per day. There must be a time reference for quantities demanded and for quantities supplied. The dark dots represent the points from our demand schedule, and when we connect the dots we create a demand curve.

Supply

Now, using the same example, let's think about the sellers of orange juice bottles. Suppose, for the sake of this example, that there are 10 completely independent street vendors selling orange juice bottles, and that there aren't any brand names of the vendors or for the orange juice. Now ask yourself how many orange juice bottles a business would attempt to sell at various prices. Obviously they would not want to give any away, so at a price of zero, quantity supplied would be zero. Even at a very low price, such as 50 cents per bottle, they might not want to sell any because the cost to the vendor of either buying or filling the bottle might be more than the 50 cents per bottle they would get from customers. As prices rise, vendors would be willing to put forth more and more effort to make more and more money. For the sake of this example, we will assume that at $1.00 per bottle each business will sell a bottle to anyone who would come up to them, but the vendors won't go out of their way to sell more than that. They will station themselves where there are a lot of people and simply sell to them.

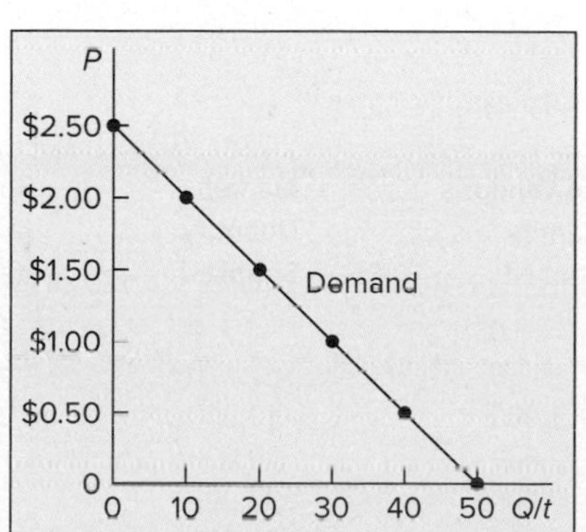

FIGURE 2.1
The demand curve.

Table 2.2 Supply schedule for bottles of orange juice.

Price ($)	One Vendor's Quantity Supplied	The Market's Quantity Supplied (all 10 concession vendors)
0	0	0
0.50	0	0
1.00	1,000	10,000
1.50	2,000	20,000
2.00	3,000	30,000
2.50	4,000	40,000

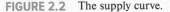

FIGURE 2.2 The supply curve.

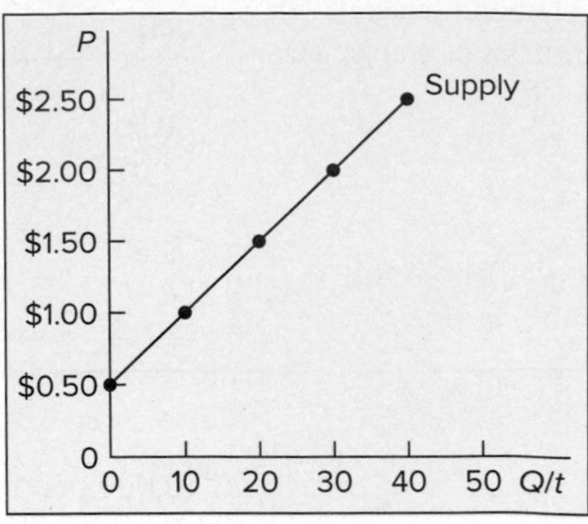

supply schedule Presentation, in tabular form, of the price and quantity supplied for a good.

Suppose that as the price people are willing to pay rises, the vendors hire people to hawk the orange juice bottles to drum up sales. Let's say that at $1.50, they will each want to hire enough hawkers to sell 2,000 bottles per day and that at $2.00, they will hire enough to sell 3,000 per day. Finally, suppose that at $2.50 per bottle, they will hire enough hawkers to sell 4,000 per day. Table 2.2 displays this information in a **supply schedule,** which presents in tabular form the price and quantity supplied for a good.

This information can also be displayed on a graph. Figure 2.2 shows the supply curve with the axes labeled the same as Figure 2.1: price and quantity per unit of time. Here the dark dots represent the points from our supply schedule. When we connect the dots, we create a supply curve.

equilibrium The point where the amount that consumers want to buy and the amount firms want to sell are the same. This occurs where the supply curve and the demand curve cross.

Equilibrium

Table 2.3 combines the supply schedule and the demand schedule into a single schedule, and Figure 2.3 combines the supply curve and demand curve on one diagram. They both show us that at prices below $1.50, consumers want more orange juice bottles than vendors are willing to provide and that at prices above $1.50, they want fewer bottles than vendors are willing to sell. Where the supply and demand curves cross, the amount that consumers want to buy and the amount firms want to sell are the same. This is called an **equilibrium.**

shortage The condition where firms do not want to sell as many goods as consumers want to buy.

surplus The condition where firms want to sell more goods than consumers want to buy.

Shortages and Surpluses

When the price is too low we have a **shortage.** Firms do not want to sell as many goods as consumers want to buy. Likewise, when the price is too high we have a **surplus.** Firms want to sell more goods than consumers want to buy.

Table 2.3 Supply and demand schedules with shortage and surplus.

Price ($)	Individual Quantity Demanded	Market Quantity Demanded	One Vendor's Quantity Supplied	Market Quantity Supplied	Shortage (excess demand)	Surplus (excess supply)
0	5	50,000	0	0	50,000	
0.50	4	40,000	0	0	40,000	
1.00	3	30,000	1,000	10,000	20,000	
1.50	2	20,000	2,000	20,000		
2.00	1	10,000	3,000	30,000		20,000
2.50	0	0	4,000	40,000		40,000

Imagine that the vendors start to run out of bottled orange juice. There is an obvious shortage. According to the model of supply and demand, this will have occurred because the price was too low. With long lines of people wanting to buy bottles in front of them, the vendors will see that in the face of a shortage, or **excess demand,** they can raise the price and still sell their product.

excess demand
Another term for shortage.

excess supply
Another term for surplus.

The opposite will occur if there is a surplus, or **excess supply.** If the price is too high, the vendors will want to sell more bottles than consumers will want to buy. Instead of long lines, there will be excess inventory and firms will see that in the face of a surplus, they should lower prices to sell more product.

FIGURE 2.3 The supply and demand model and equilibrium price and quantity.

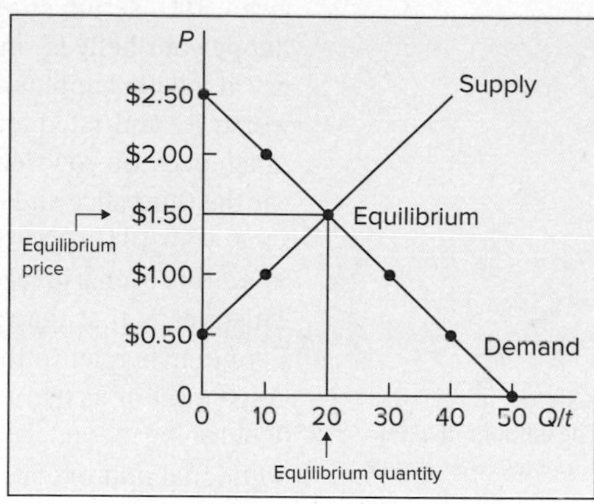

With self-interested sellers, shortages and surpluses are short-lived. Firms react to changes in inventories by changing the price they charge. They react to shortages with price increases and surpluses with price cuts, and as a result either situation is temporary.

All about Demand

The Law of Demand

We know from this chapter's section on definitions that demand is the relationship between price and quantity demanded, ceteris paribus, and we followed a reasonably believable story about orange juice vendors. That story implied that there was a negative relationship between price and quantity demanded. Because of the relationship, the demand curve we drew was downward sloping. The negative relationship between price and quantity demanded is called the **law of demand.** This "law" is not really a law but is common sense applied to the following rather constant observation: When prices are higher, we tend to buy less.

law of demand
The statement that the relationship between price and quantity demanded is a negative or inverse one.

Why Does the Law of Demand Make Sense?

Why do we see this negative relationship so often? There are three distinct reasons. First, when you go to the store and find that the good you want is highly priced, you search for an acceptable substitute that costs less. If you buy something else, you are substituting another good for the one that you originally wanted because the original good's price is too high. Economists say that this is a **substitution effect.** You buy less of what you originally wanted when its price is high because you use something else instead.

substitution effect
Purchasing less of a product than originally wanted when its price is high because a lower priced product is available.

real-balances effect
When a price increases, your buying power is decreased, causing you to buy less.

Second, suppose you cannot find an acceptable substitute. In this case, you buy less of the good because you cannot afford as much. What has happened is that your real buying power has fallen (even though the money you have in your wallet is the same) because prices have risen. This does not necessarily work for all goods (especially basic necessities like water), but generally economists call this a **real-balances effect** because when a price increases, it decreases your buying power, causing you to buy less.

The third reason we see a negative relationship between price and quantity demanded can be explained with either great detail, or a useful, though not always completely accurate, shortcut. You are in this course and your professor has chosen this book because you do not need the great detail, so you will get the shortcut. It starts from the premise that what you are willing to pay for something depends on how many you have recently had. With this in mind, consider the following silly but illustrative example. Suppose I give you $10 and I ask how much you would pay for pizza slices at lunch. Suppose further that as part of this experiment you are given truth serum so you have to honestly tell me two things: (1) on a scale from 1 to 10, how happy your belly is; and (2) how much you valued each slice in terms of money. Starting hungry at a belly happiness index (BHI) of 1, suppose that you eat one slice and tell me that it was worth $3 and rated a 5 on the BHI. Now you eat another slice and tell me it wasn't worth as much because you were not as hungry, so you say it was worth $2 and your BHI rose to 8. You eat the third slice and tell me that, because you were somewhat full at the time you ate the third slice, your BHI only rose to 9 and the slice was only worth $1.

In this scenario, each time you consume a slice, the value you place on the next slice falls. This means that the value you place on a good depends on how many you have already had. Economists refer to the amount of extra happiness[1] that people get from an additional unit of consumption as **marginal utility** and say that it decreases as you consume more. This **law of diminishing marginal utility** suggests that the amount of additional happiness that you get from an additional unit of consumption falls with each additional unit. Stated more simply, because each additional slice increases your happiness less than the previous slice, the most you would be willing to pay for each additional slice is less than the previous one. The third reason why a demand curve is downward sloping, then, is that for most goods there is diminishing marginal utility.

marginal utility The amount of extra happiness that people get from an additional unit of consumption.

law of diminishing marginal utility The amount of additional happiness that you get from an additional unit of consumption falls with each additional unit.

It is often helpful to view the demand curve as more than a way of finding how much of a good a person wants at a particular price. In addition, you can use it to find out how much a person is "willing to pay" for a particular amount of the good. Whenever you come across this phrase, think "the most they would be willing to pay." Of course you would always want to pay less, but looked at this way the demand curve also represents the most you would be willing to pay for different amounts of a good, ceteris paribus.

All about Supply

The Law of Supply

We also know from our section on definitions that supply is the relationship between price and quantity supplied, ceteris paribus, and we followed a story about how many orange juice bottles a vendor would want to sell in a city. That story implied that there was a positive relationship between price and quantity supplied. Because of that, the supply curve we drew was upward sloping. The positive relationship between price and quantity supplied is called the **law of supply.** Like all other laws in economics, this one isn't a law either but is more like a hypothesis that is supported by nearly all the evidence nearly all the time. Stated more simply: When prices are higher, firms tend to want to sell more.

law of supply The statement that there is a positive relationship between price and quantity supplied.

Why Does the Law of Supply Make Sense?

Although believable intuitively, the technical reason that a supply curve is upward sloping takes up much of Chapters 4 and 5. What follows is a simplified (though probably not simple) explanation that will be repeated and expanded in Chapters 4 and 5.

[1] This is why this discussion has been an intellectual shortcut. Most economists do not believe that you can measure happiness in the same way that you measure distance or temperature. This means that though you can say you are happier in one circumstance than in another, you cannot say how much happier you are. All is not lost, though, because we can get the same idea through the concept of indifference. The reason no one-semester course textbooks explain the downward-sloping nature of demand using the concept of indifference is that it takes too long and gets you no further in your understanding than the last two paragraphs have. Thus, the shortcut of marginal utility nets the same result in a lot less time and is judged by most teachers of one-semester economics courses as useful.

Suppose the downtown area where the vendors are selling orange juice bottles has varying areas of population density. It is relatively easy to sell where there are more people, like at a subway exit, and progressively more difficult to sell as you get away from those population centers. As a result, even if vendors hire hawkers to go out and sell orange juice bottles, it is going to get harder and harder to sell a lot when they go out into portions of the downtown area with fewer pedestrians. Even though it is harder to sell, as the price rises, it is still possible and even likely that it would be worth it for vendors to hire hawkers. So even when the last hawkers hired sell far fewer bottles than the first ones, the vendors hire them because they make money doing so. When the price is low, high-cost sales methods aren't worth it, and when the price is high, they are worth it. There might even be a price high enough that the vendors would be willing to deliver individual bottles to individual offices. While this would be very inefficient relative to simply standing at a subway exit, if the vendors have sold all they can this way and the price is high enough, it could still be profitable to the vendors to do so.

What this means, and what Chapters 4 and 5 demonstrate in detail, is that the reason the supply curve is upward sloping is that it costs more per unit to sell more units. In this example, the orange juice bottles were not more expensive to produce, but the cost of hawking them made them increasingly expensive to sell in increasingly remote areas.

In addition, when firms decide which good to produce, they will want to produce the one that makes them the most money. Suppose our orange juice vendors have only so much space in the coolers in their carts. In this case, the vendors do not care whether they sell orange juice or water; they simply want to make a profit. If consumers are willing to pay more for bottled water, the vendors will stock their carts with bottled water. Relative to water, when orange juice prices are higher, the vendor is willing to take water out of the cart and replace it with orange juice. When orange juice prices are lower, the vendor does the opposite.

Determinants of Demand

In the previous section we talked about holding other things constant. Now is the time to consider what happens when things change. As we alluded to in the section on definitions, there are many things that affect the demand relationship for a good. These include how much the good is liked, how much income people have, how much other goods cost, the population of

DETERMINANTS OF DEMAND

Taste

Determinant of whether the good is in fashion or whether conditions are right for many people to want the good.

Income

Inferior goods: Goods for which higher incomes result in decreased purchases.

Normal goods: Goods for which higher incomes result in increased purchases.

Price of other goods

Substitute: Goods used instead of one another.

Complement: Goods that are used together.

Population of potential buyers

The number of people potentially interested in a product.

Expected future price

The price that you expect will exist in the future.

Excise taxes

A per unit or percentage tax on a good or service that must be paid by consumers.

Subsidies

A per unit or percentage subsidy for a good or service that is granted to consumers.

potential buyers, the expectations of the price in the future, and any taxes or subsidies there are on the good. These variables will change how much of the good is wanted as well as how much someone is willing to pay for it. Again "willing to pay" is shorthand for the most someone is willing to pay. If people want more of the good, this also translates into willingness to pay prices that they would not have paid before the determinant change occurred.

Taste

Taste is the word that economists use to describe whether the good is in fashion or whether conditions are right for many people to want the good. A high level of taste means that the good is in fashion or highly desired; a low level of taste means that few people want it. It works on demand in an obvious way: As the general desirability of the good increases, people's willingness to pay increases. They will pay higher prices and they will want more of it. Going back to the orange juice example, the taste for orange juice would rise during cold and flu season as people were trying to boost their immune systems believing that orange juice aids in keeping viruses at bay.

Income

For most goods, an increase in income will lead to an increase in the amount that consumers want. In cases where you buy more of a good when you have more income, economists call the good *normal*. If the good is normal and your income rises, you are able to buy more and you want to buy more of the good and you are willing to pay more for it.

For some goods, income works in an opposite way. Consider a couple of staples in the college diet, instant ramen noodles and macaroni and cheese. No matter which of these you eat, you can fill your belly for under a dollar. Now ask yourself how many pouches, boxes, or bags of this stuff you would buy if your grandmother died and left you $25,000. Answer: not many, particularly if you have been eating them because you could not afford other things to eat. This example shows you that it is not always the case that the more you make, the more you buy. In cases where you buy less of a good when you have more income, economists call the good *inferior*. If the good is inferior and your income rises, you are able to buy more, but you want to buy less of the good, and you will need lower prices to induce you to buy any particular quantity.

Returning to our orange juice example, if people consume more bottles of orange juice as their incomes rise, then orange juice is a normal good. If they consume fewer bottles of orange juice when their incomes rise, it is an inferior good.

Price of Other Goods

Similarly, there is no straightforward answer to the question of how you will change your willingness to purchase a good if the price of another good rises. It is possible that if the price of beef rises, you will switch to chicken. In that case, you would be willing to pay more for chicken and want to buy more of it. Likewise, if the price of hot dogs increases, you will decide to buy fewer of them. Since hot dog buns have little good use other than to surround hot dogs, you will need fewer of these too. Economists say that goods used instead of one another (e.g., chicken and beef) are *substitutes* and that goods that are used together (e.g., hot dogs and hot dog buns) are *complements*.

Examples of substitutes and complements abound. Peanut butter and jelly are often considered complements because they are typically used together to produce sandwiches. Pepperoni and sausage might be considered substitutes because they are alternative meats for a pizza. To confuse matters, though, goods can be substitutes to some people and complements to others. My father-in-law considered peanut butter and jelly to be equally good bagel spreads, so to him they were substitutes. The Meat Lover's Pizza by Pizza Hut includes both sausage and pepperoni, so to people who like this pizza the two may be complements.

Once again, returning to orange juice bottles: Orange juice and grapefruit juice are likely substitutes for one another while orange juice and vodka are likely to be complements because people (of legal drinking age) may mix them together to form a "screwdriver."

Population of Potential Buyers

The number of people potentially interested in a product will clearly have an impact on its demand. So, as the downtown population rises, more people are potentially interested in buying bottles of orange juice. Clearly the larger the city, the more people come downtown to work and shop, meaning more people will buy orange juice. Or, for instance, in the dark ages of the 1970s, when there were only a few computer-literate people, only a few people were interested in buying computers. Then schoolchildren, and especially college students, began to rely on computers for their schoolwork, creating a group of potentially interested customers when they graduated. Economists shorten this concept of the number of people potentially interested in a product to call it the *population*.

Expected Future Price

When the expected future price (usually shortened to just *expected price*) of a good rises, this induces a stock-up effect. Let's suppose that a winter freeze destroys a large number of the orange groves. Forward-thinking consumers will see the impending increase in orange juice prices and be motivated to stock up now before the price increase takes hold. Similarly, smokers stock up on cigarettes when a tax increase is expected. Frugal drivers buy gas on Wednesdays, before the nearly universal weekend price increase. If there is an expectation that an increase in price is imminent, consumers will be willing to pay more and they will want to buy now rather than later. Of course, if there is a widely held belief that prices are about to fall, consumers will do the opposite and wait for that price decrease.

Excise Taxes

Sometimes governments want to discourage the consumption of a good and will place a *tax* on it. Such a tax causes consumers to pay more per unit than they otherwise would and, as a result, decreases the amount that they wish to purchase. Suppose that a city wanted to encourage the recycling of plastic bottles and that consumers had to pay $1 extra per orange juice bottle that they purchased. That would mean that the new demand curve would be $1 lower at every quantity than the original one.

Subsidies

Sometimes governments want to encourage the consumption of a good and will create a *subsidy* for it. Such a subsidy would mean that consumers pay less per unit than they otherwise would and, as a result, increases the amount that they wish to purchase. Suppose that a city in Florida wanted its citizens to be seen by tourists drinking Florida orange juice. To encourage consumers to do so, it would allow them to pay $1 less per orange juice bottle that they purchased. That would mean that the new demand curve would be $1 higher at every quantity than the original one.

The Effect of Changes in the Determinants of Demand on the Supply and Demand Model

Tables 2.4 and 2.5 summarize how the determinants of demand work on the supply and demand diagram. Table 2.4 indicates the impact of increases in the variables listed above, whereas Table 2.5 indicates the impact of decreases in those variables. The final column of each table refers to the figure that illustrates the appropriate demand shift. Figure 2.4 shows the impact of an increase in demand, while Figure 2.5 shows the impact of a decrease in demand. In each figure,

Table 2.4 Movements in the demand curve: increases in the values of the determinants.

An Increase in	Causes Demand to	Causes the Demand Curve to Move to the	Is Shown in Figure
Taste	Increase	Right	2.4
Income, normal good	Increase	Right	2.4
Income, inferior good	Decrease	Left	2.5
Price of other goods, complement	Decrease	Left	2.5
Price of other goods, substitute	Increase	Right	2.4
Population	Increase	Right	2.4
Expected future price	Increase	Right	2.4
Excise tax	Decrease	Left	2.5
Subsidy	Increase	Right	2.4

Table 2.5 Movements in the demand curve: decreases in the values of the determinants.

A Decrease in	Causes Demand to	Causes the Demand Curve to Move to the	Is Shown in Figure
Taste	Decrease	Left	2.5
Income, normal good	Decrease	Left	2.5
Income, inferior good	Increase	Right	2.4
Price of other goods, complement	Increase	Right	2.4
Price of other goods, substitute	Decrease	Left	2.5
Population	Decrease	Left	2.5
Expected future price	Decrease	Left	2.5
Excise tax	Increase	Right	2.4
Subsidy	Decrease	Left	2.5

FIGURE 2.4 The effect of an increase in demand on the supply and demand model.

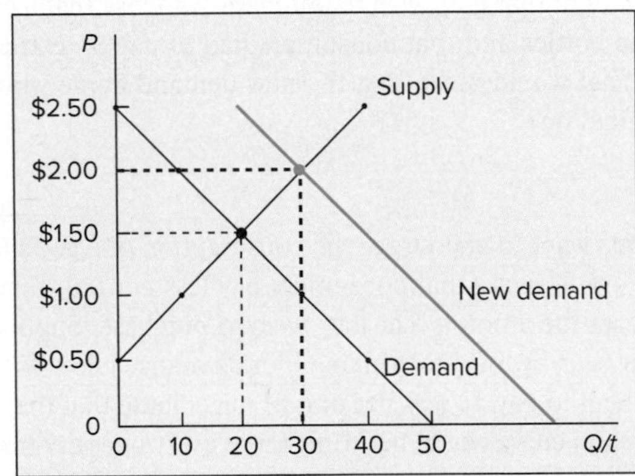

FIGURE 2.5 The effect of a decrease in demand on the supply and demand model.

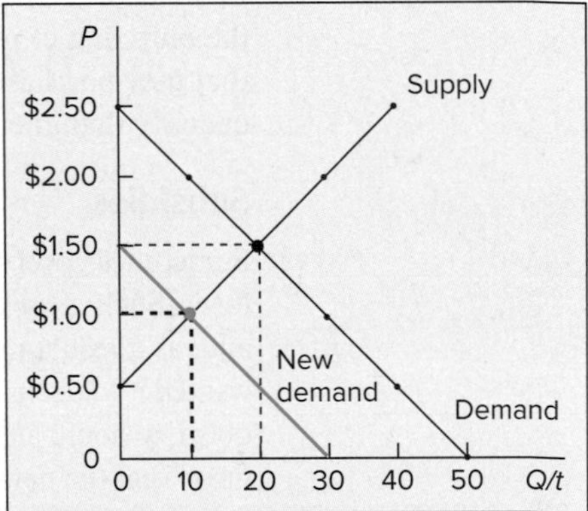

the original supply and demand curves are shown in black and the new demand curve is shown in the gold color. The original equilibrium is shown with the big black dot, and the new equilibrium is shown with the big gold-colored dot.

Tables 2.4 and 2.5 as they apply to Figures 2.4 and 2.5 may seduce you into thinking the best way of using this information is to memorize it. As the verb *seduce* suggests, that is a very bad learning strategy. The best use of these tables and figures is to use them to check your economic intuition.

As an example, suppose you are tasked with drawing a supply and demand diagram for hot dog buns showing the impact of an increase in the price of hot dogs. First, you would recognize hot dogs and hot dog buns as complements and that when the price of a complement rises, you will consume fewer hot dogs (because the demand for hot dogs is downward sloping), meaning you would need fewer hot dog buns. Second, you would recognize that behavior as a decrease in the demand for hot dog buns. Third, you would draw a supply and demand diagram for hot dog buns showing a leftward movement in demand for hot dog buns because a decrease in demand is depicted by shifting demand to the left. You would then check your analysis against the information in Table 2.4 (because it is an increase in the price of hot dogs impacting hot dog buns); look down to the "Price of other goods, complement" row then across to see that your intuition that demand should move left was correct and that the drawing of a figure like Figure 2.5 is accurate.

Determinants of Supply

Again, the definitions section alluded to the types of things that can change the supply relationship. They include changes in the price of inputs, technology, price of other potential outputs, the number of sellers, expected future price, and any taxes or subsidies there are on the good. Again we are assuming that other things are held constant.

Price of Inputs

The *price of inputs* refers to the costs to firms of all the things necessary to produce output. If an input is used to make a product, then the input costs money and therefore has a price even though its name may change. Obvious examples of inputs are raw material, labor, and equipment. The price of a raw material is simply its price. (Though this sounds like a circular definition, think about our orange juice bottles example. The bottles, the orange juice itself, and coolers to keep the bottles in each have a price.) The price of labor is the wage + benefit cost to employers associated with hiring a person. (Everything that employers pay for that is not paid directly to workers–health insurance, unemployment insurance, worker's compensation, and so on–is defined as benefits.) The price of equipment can affect supply, but just as often, what matters is the rental cost of leased equipment or the interest + depreciation rates that must be paid on the equipment bought with borrowed money. (Interest is the price of borrowed money, and depreciation is the rate at which machines lose value owing to wear and tear.)

DETERMINANTS OF SUPPLY

Price of inputs
Costs to firms of all the things necessary to produce output.

Technology
The method by which inputs are turned into output.

Price of other potential output
When firms have to decide which good to produce, they will want to produce the one that makes them the most money.

Number of sellers
The number of firms competing in the same market.

Expected future price
Firms want to hold back sales to wait for higher prices and unload inventory before prices fall.

Excise taxes
A per unit or percentage tax on a good or service that must be paid by producers.

Subsidies
A per unit or percentage subsidy for a good or service that is granted to producers.

Technology

Within economics, the word *technology* refers to the ability to turn input into output. In our previous example of selling bottles of orange juice in a city, a technological advance that would allow vendors to keep the bottles fresh without ice or refrigeration would reduce costs. This technology would increase output and lower costs. As we are using it here, technology can change because of increases in the ability of employees to work harder and smarter, or it can change because new devices make employees more efficient.

Another example of how increases in technology change markets can be seen in the *very illegal* term-paper business. If you wanted to buy term papers in the 1960s, you would have had to pay people to go to the library to look stuff up in card catalogs of alphabetized index cards and indices of periodicals to find source material. Because access to copy machines was limited, they would have then had to read the material in the library. Finally, they would have had to type the paper on a typewriter, and they would have been able to fix mistakes only with Wite-Out®. Paying people to do this would have been expensive.

In the 1970s, all the steps were the same except copy machines would have allowed the people you hired to read source material in their homes. In the 1980s, primitive computers would have allowed them to gather limited quantities of source material on a computer and to write the paper using a hard-to-use, not very flexible word processor. By the 1990s, writers of term papers could look up material on the Internet, print it, read it, and write the paper, all from the comfort of their own bedrooms. In each of these periods, producers of such contraband had to find a way to sell their papers. Often informal networks had to be created and payment had to be in cash.

In the early 2000s, you could go to any number of term-paper sites on the Internet and download a paper by simply entering a credit card number. Because it was easier to produce papers in less time than used to be the case, sellers of term papers could charge lower prices and produce more papers. Today, TurnitIn® and other companies have made it exceptionally easy for faculty to detect previously produced work. The result is that purchased papers have to be, more-or-less, original. That raises costs tremendously.

Price of Other Potential Outputs

The *price of other potential outputs* refers to the same idea that we referenced when indicating why the supply curve is upward sloping, except now we focus on what happens to the existing supply curve when the price of the other good changes. As we said, vendors have only so much space in the coolers in their carts. During a hot summer's day, they may discover that they sell out of bottles of water and have plenty of leftover bottles of orange juice. If consumers are willing to pay more for bottled water, the vendors will stock their carts with bottled water. They will stock those carts with the combination of water and orange juice that makes them the most money. As the price of water rises, the supply of orange juice will fall because vendors want to stock water.

Number of Sellers

The *number of sellers*, that is, the number of firms competing in the same market, is important because as the number of firms increases, so does total market production. Using the orange juice example, we assumed that there were 10 different vendors. If these vendors are all making a significant profit, it is likely that other entrepreneurs will want to set up their competing stands. This raises total market supply. Similarly, if there were losses, some of those vendors may quit the business, reducing total market supply.

Expected Future Price

The *expected future price* should sound familiar because it is also something that will change demand. In the context of supply, it refers to a firm's desire to hold back sales to wait for higher prices and its desire to sell its goods and thus lower its inventory before prices fall. Firms want to sell their goods when they can make the most money regardless of when that time is. A warning that a hurricane is coming will bid up the current price of gas-powered generators because firms will want to retain those they have in stock to sell at high prices after the hurricane hits. Conversely, if firms figure that their goods will be out of fashion soon, they will want to sell them now.

Let's return to the example of the freeze that decimated the orange groves. Not only will buyers of orange juice be motivated to stock up to avoid the increase in price, sellers will know that a price increase is coming and will want to hold on to what they have. As a result, the expected future price not only changes demand for a good, it changes supply as well. Of course, it also works in the other direction. If a bumper orange crop is expected, orange juice prices will be expected to fall and those currently holding orange juice will be motivated to sell their current inventories before the price falls too much.

Excise Taxes

As we indicated in the context of demand, sometimes a government wants to discourage the consumption of a good. In so doing it can *tax* producers or consumers. If it wants the tax to be collected on the production side, it will place a tax on that good and compel firms to pay it. Note that the impact of the tax (and who it hurts) doesn't depend on whether the tax is on the demand side or the supply side; it depends on the Chapter 3 concept of elasticity. In any event, a tax is modeled by moving the supply curve vertically higher by the amount of the tax. So a city can encourage recycling of plastic bottles by charging firms $1 extra per orange juice bottle that they sell. That would mean that the new supply curve would be $1 higher at every quantity than the old one.

Subsidies

Similarly, *subsidies* can be applied to the firm producing the good rather than to the consumer. A $1 subsidy would be modeled with the new supply curve $1 lower at every quantity than the old one. If the government wanted to encourage orange juice consumption, it could create a subsidy and pay that subsidy to firms rather than to consumers. The result would be precisely the same either way as firms would lower their prices to attract the sales that would result in those subsidies being paid to the firms.

The Effect of Changes in the Determinants of Supply on the Supply and Demand Model

Tables 2.6 and 2.7 summarize how determinants of supply affect a supply and demand model. Table 2.6 indicates the impact of increases in the variables listed above, whereas Table 2.7

Table 2.6 Movements in the supply curve: increases in the values of the determinants.

An Increase in	Causes Supply to	Causes the Supply Curve to Move to the	Is Shown in Figure
Price of inputs	Decrease	Left	2.7
Technology	Increase	Right	2.6
Price of other potential outputs	Decrease	Left	2.7
Number of sellers	Increase	Right	2.6
Expected future price	Decrease	Left	2.7
Excise tax	Decrease	Left	2.7
Subsidy	Increase	Right	2.6

Table 2.7 Movements in the supply curve: decreases in the values of the determinants.

An Decrease in	Causes Supply to	Causes the Supply Curve to Move to the	Is Shown in Figure
Price of inputs	Increase	Right	2.6
Technology	Decrease	Left	2.7
Price of other potential outputs	Increase	Right	2.6
Number of sellers	Decrease	Left	2.7
Expected price	Increase	Right	2.6
Excise tax	Increase	Right	2.6
Subsidy	Decrease	Left	2.7

FIGURE 2.6 The effect of an increase in supply on the supply and demand model.

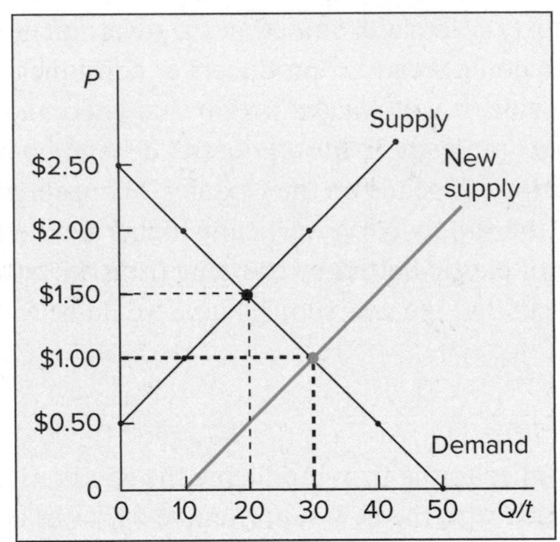

FIGURE 2.7 The effect of a decrease in supply on the supply and demand model.

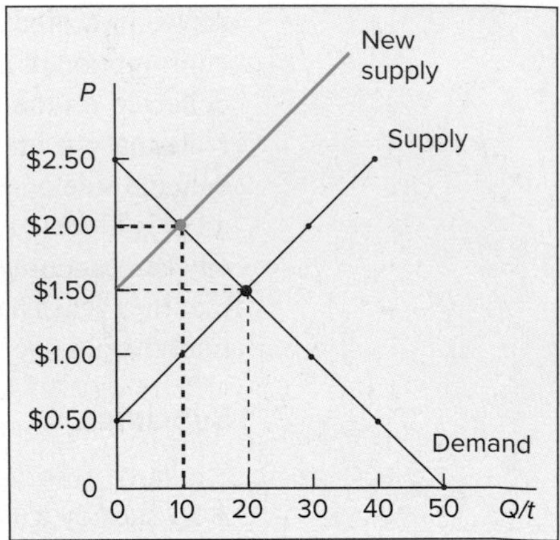

indicates the impact of decreases in those variables. It is important to understand that on the supply side, an increase in supply is shown by a movement to the right in the supply curve and a decrease in supply is shown by a movement to the left in the supply curve. As with Tables 2.4 and 2.5, the final columns of Tables 2.6 and 2.7 refer to the figure that illustrates the appropriate supply shift. Figure 2.6 shows the impact of an increase in supply, while Figure 2.7 shows the impact of a decrease in supply. Just as it was for Tables 2.4 and 2.5 and Figures 2.4 and 2.5, the original supply and demand curves are shown in black and the original equilibrium is shown with the big black dot. This time the new supply curve is shown in the gold color with the new equilibrium shown with the big gold-colored dot.

After having read the admonition against memorizing regarding the demand shifts, you can guess what's next: Don't try to memorize Tables 2.6 and 2.7 as they apply to Figures 2.6 and 2.7. The best use of these tables and figures is to use them to check your economic intuition. As an example, suppose you are tasked with drawing a supply and demand diagram for gasoline showing the impact of an increase in the price of crude oil. First, you would recognize that crude oil is the primary input to gasoline so that, when crude oil prices rise, refineries would have to increase their gasoline prices to compensate for those higher production costs. Second, you would recognize that as a decrease in the supply of gasoline. Third, you would draw a supply and demand diagram for gasoline showing a leftward movement in supply for gasoline because a decrease in supply is depicted by shifting supply to the left. You would then check your analysis against the information in Table 2.6 (because it is an increase in the price of crude impacting gasoline); look down to the "Price of inputs" row then across to see that your intuition that supply should move left was correct and that the drawing of a figure like Figure 2.7 is correct accurate.

The Effect of Changes in Price Expectations on the Supply and Demand Model

If you have not already noticed, expected future price is both a determinant of demand and a determinant of supply. This means that if the expected future price changes, both the supply and demand curves change as well. If the expected future price rises, consumers will want to stock up, thereby increasing demand. Firms, on the other hand, will want to hold back their inventory to wait for the price increase, thereby decreasing supply. In this case, we do not know what will happen to equilibrium quantity because the demand shift will, by itself, increase quantity, whereas the supply shift will, by itself, decrease quantity. Whether there is a net increase or decrease in equilibrium quantity depends on which shift is greater. On the other hand, the effect on price is known, and it amounts to a self-fulfilling prophecy because a credible prediction of a future price increase will hasten an actual current price increase.

When expected prices rise, we know that the current price will rise, but we do not know what will happen to the quantity. This is because we do not know whether firms' desire to wait for price increases will be stronger than consumers' desire to stock up. When the price is expected to fall, firms will want to sell their inventory and consumers will want to wait for the new lower prices.

When expected prices fall we know that the current price will fall, but we again do not know what will happen to the quantity. This is because we do not know whether firms' desire to unload inventory will be stronger than consumers' desire to wait for lower prices.

Kick It Up a Notch

WHY THE NEW EQUILIBRIUM?

When either the supply curve or the demand curve shifts, the equilibrium has to change. If it does not, one of two things will happen: There will be a shortage where consumers want to buy more than firms want to sell, or there will be a surplus where firms want to sell more than consumers want to buy.

To show that this is the case, imagine that there is an increase in the demand for a good and firms do not increase the price. As shown in Figure 2.8, keeping the price at the old equilibrium would yield a situation where consumers would want more (40 units) than firms would be willing to sell (20 units). The resulting shortage would not be eliminated unless there was an increase in the price.

A somewhat different problem would happen if firms did not lower their price in the face of decreased demand. Figure 2.9 shows that keeping the price at the old equilibrium after a decrease in demand would yield a situation where consumers would want fewer (0 units) than firms would be willing to sell (20 units). The resulting surplus would not be eliminated unless there was a decrease in the price.

Just as we needed a new equilibrium when there was a change in demand, we need one when there is a change in supply. Figure 2.10 shows that keeping the price at the old equilibrium when supply increases yields a situation where consumers want fewer (20 units) than firms are willing to sell (40 units). The resulting surplus will not be eliminated unless there is a decrease in the price.

FIGURE 2.8 The shortage that is created when demand increases if price and quantity do not.

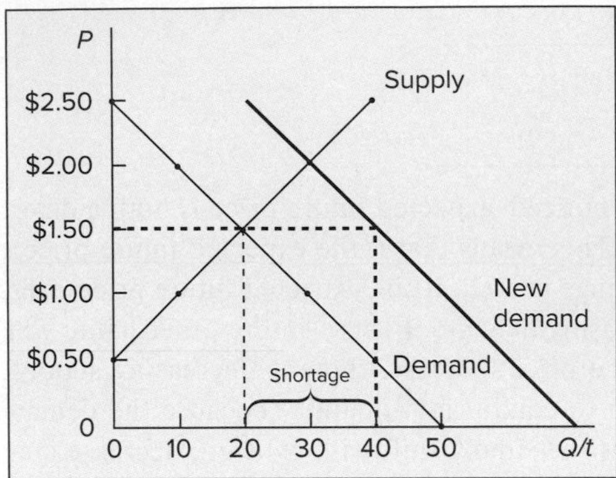

FIGURE 2.9 The surplus that is created when demand decreases if price and quantity do not.

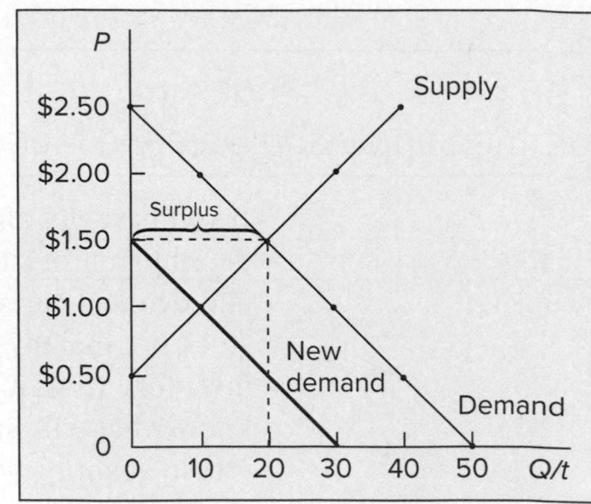

FIGURE 2.10 The surplus that is created when supply increases if price and quantity do not.

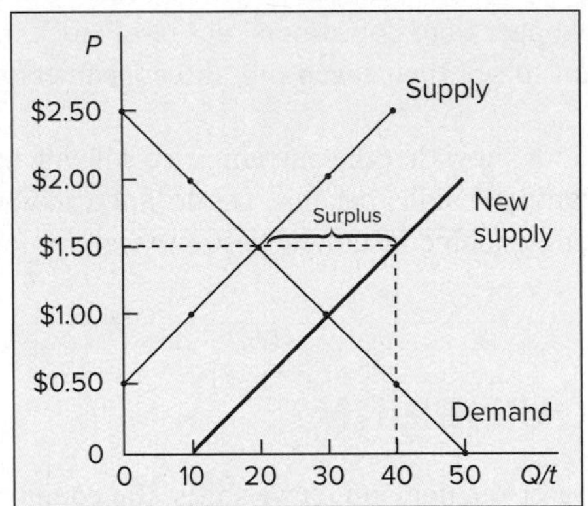

FIGURE 2.11 The shortage that is created when supply decreases if price and quantity do not.

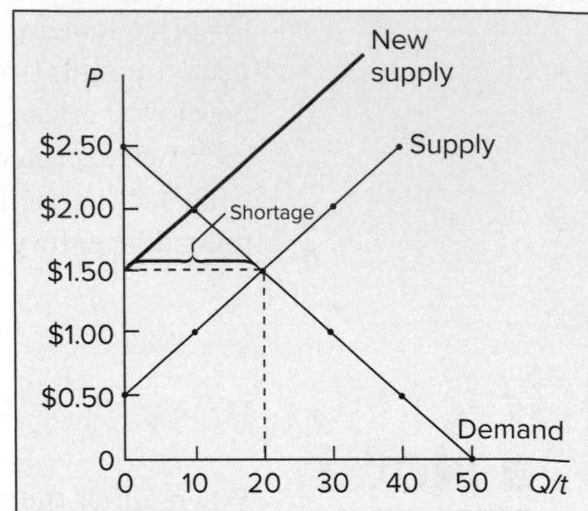

Finally, if firms do not raise their prices in the face of decreased supply, there will be a shortage. Figure 2.11 shows that keeping the price at the old equilibrium in the face of decreased supply yields a situation where consumers want more (20 units) than firms are willing to sell (0 units). The resulting shortage will be eliminated unless there is an increase in the price.

What can you conclude? A change in either the supply or demand curve will change the price at which the quantity consumers want to buy equals the quantity that firms want to sell. If the price does not change, either a surplus or a shortage will ensue.

price gouging
The negative term applied to the circumstance when firms raise prices substantially when demand increases unexpectedly.

price ceiling
Price above which a commodity may not sell.

There are circumstances when a new equilibrium will not be achieved. For instance, **price gouging** is the name given to the situation in which a rapid increase in demand is followed by a rapid increase in price. When demand increases, firms do not have to raise prices to cover costs; they raise prices because they can. Laws preventing price gouging are relatively common.

If you sell ice and have a volume to sell, in many states you are not allowed to raise the price of it more than a specified percentage if your community loses electrical power. Economists call the maximum price allowed by law a **price ceiling.** Once the price hits that level, it cannot rise further, which often results in a shortage for that good. Other examples of price ceilings include rent control and laws that prevent ticket scalping.

price floor
Price below which a commodity may not sell.

Similarly, equilibrium will not be achieved if there is a **price floor.** This exists when a price may not fall below a certain legally prescribed level. In that circumstance, there is a surplus of the good. Examples of this include farm price supports and the existence of the minimum wage.

Detailed descriptions of the effects of price ceilings and floors are left to their applications in the chapters on rent control, ticket scalping, farm price supports, and the minimum wage.

Summary

The supply and demand model is the single most important model in economics. More than half the issues that you deal with in the latter part of this book will rely on your ability to put an economics problem into the context of this model. In the course of this chapter, we explained the supply and demand model by providing all of the language. We explained both supply and demand in isolation and then put them together in the form of a coherent model. We then talked about the variables that might change demand and then which ones might change supply. We showed that prices and quantities sold must change to maintain an equilibrium once one of these shifts occurs.

Key Terms

capitalist economy
ceteris paribus
communist economy
consumers
demand
demand schedule
equilibrium
equilibrium price
equilibrium quantity
excess demand
excess supply
law of demand
law of diminishing marginal utility
law of supply
marginal utility
market
output
price
price ceiling
price floor
price gouging
producers
quantity demanded
quantity supplied
real-balances effect
shortage
socialist economy
substitution effect
supply
supply and demand
supply schedule
surplus

Issues Chapters You Are Ready for Now

International Finance and Exchange Rates
The Economics of Race and Sex Discrimination

Quiz Yourself

1. The supply and demand model examines how prices and quantities are determined
   a. in markets.
   b. by governments.
   c. by consumers only.
   d. by producers only.
2. A change in the price of lumber will impact
   a. the demand for lumber.
   b. the supply of lumber.
   c. the quantity demanded and quantity supplied of lumber but neither the supply nor the demand for lumber.
   d. both the supply and demand for lumber.

3. Choose the appropriate Latin phrase. When an economics student draws a supply and demand diagram to model an increase in income, she is assuming this change happens
   a. semper fidelis.
   b. ceteris paribus.
   c. ipso facto.
   d. de facto.

4. The point where supply and demand cross is called equilibrium because
   a. nothing will cause it to move (even if demand changes).
   b. nothing will cause it to move (even if supply changes).
   c. once the price settles there, unless supply or demand changes, it will not move.
   d. price will move away from it quickly.

5. If the supply and demand curves cross at a price of $5, at any price above that, there will be
   a. an equilibrium.
   b. a surplus.
   c. a shortage.
   d. a crisis.

6. If the supply and demand curves cross at a quantity of 10, then the price necessary to get firms to sell more than that will have to be __________ equilibrium.
   a. above
   b. at
   c. below
   d. within 10 percent either way of

7. Which of the following will impact both supply and demand?
   a. A change in price
   b. A change in quantity
   c. A change in expected future price
   d. A change in income

8. An increase in the income of consumers will cause the
   a. supply of all goods to rise.
   b. demand for all goods to rise.
   c. supply of all goods to fall.
   d. the demand for some goods to rise and for others to fall.

9. Without an increase in price, an increase in demand will lead to
   a. a shortage.
   b. a surplus.
   c. socialism.
   d. equilibrium.

10. An important reason for the downward-sloping nature of the demand curve is that
    a. consumers rarely make substitutions between goods when the price of one changes.
    b. consumers frequently make substitutions between goods when the price of one changes.
    c. consumers have unlimited resources.
    d. the consumption of most goods comes with increasing marginal utility.

11. The underlying reason for the upward-sloping nature of the supply curve is that
    a. the production of most goods comes with increasing marginal benefits.
    b. the production of most goods comes with increasing marginal costs.
    c. the consumption of most goods comes with decreasing marginal utility.
    d. the consumption of most goods comes with increasing marginal utility.

12. If Florida vegetable farmers can plant either green peppers or tomatoes on their land with equal profitability and there is an increase in the price of green peppers, which of the following will result?
    a. A movement to the right in the demand for tomatoes
    b. A movement to the left in the demand for tomatoes
    c. A movement to the right in the supply of tomatoes
    d. A movement to the left in the supply of tomatoes

13. Part of the Patient Protection and Affordable Care Act involved a tax on indoor tanning that tanning salons are required to collect from tanners and send to the federal government. Which of the following would be the predicted result?
    a. A movement to the right in the demand for tanning
    b. A movement to the left in the demand for tanning
    c. A movement to the right in the supply of tanning
    d. A movement to the left in the supply of tanning

14. As the baby boom generation (born between 1946 and 1964) ages, which of the following is a likely outcome?
    a. A movement to the left in the demand for nursing home beds
    b. A movement to the left in the supply of nursing home beds
    c. A movement to the right in the supply of nursing home beds
    d. A movement to the right in the demand for nursing home beds

Short Answer Questions

1. Use your own demand for pizza to illustrate the notion of diminishing marginal utility. Explain why that concept means your demand for pizza-by-the-slice is downward sloping.
2. Suppose you have been given money by your friends and sent to get beverages for a party. Use your demand for those beverages to illustrate why the concept of the "real-balances effect" will mean your demand is downward sloping.
3. If there is an alteration to the price of a complement to a good, why is that a change in *demand* when an alteration in the price of the good itself is a change in the *quantity demanded*?
4. If there is an alteration in the price of an input used to produce a good, why is that a change in *supply* when an alteration in the price of the good itself is a change in the *quantity supplied*?

Think about This

Using simple supply and demand analysis, think about the system of allocating human kidneys. The law that forbids the sale of human organs, but allows their voluntary donation, means that there is a bigger shortage of kidneys than there otherwise would be. Does this fact alter your view of the law forbidding the sale of human organs? How about blood?

Talk about This

Are markets always right? List some markets that you think get the production or price of a good wrong. What do these goods have in common?

CHAPTER THREE

The Concept of Elasticity and Consumer and Producer Surplus

Learning Objectives

After reading this chapter you should be able to:

LO1 Define *elasticity,* recognize its importance in economics, and apply the concept to various real-world goods and services.

LO2 Connect the relationship between the concept of elasticity and the appearance of the demand curve.

LO3 Demonstrate that a market equilibrium provides both buyers and sellers with benefits.

LO4 Define *deadweight loss* and apply it to various policies.

Chapter Outline

Now that we have a supply and demand model, we can change our focus to the ability of consumers and producers to react to price changes. That ability to react, called *elasticity,* will be very important to us as we apply the supply and demand model to different economic issues. We will see how differently sloped demand and supply curves will reflect the degree to which shifts in one curve or the other will affect equilibrium quantity.

The last third of the chapter is central in our analysis of several issues. We will see how the supply and demand model can be used to explain why markets are effective in pleasing both consumers and producers. Though we know that consumers long for low prices and producers for high prices, we will realize that when a consumer buys something from a producer, both can be pleased with the outcome. We will also see why the *net benefit to society* is lower when prices are not at equilibrium.

Elasticity of Demand

Intuition

In the previous chapter, we learned that a change in either supply or demand will result in a change to the equilibrium price-quantity combination. We did not discuss whether price was impacted more than quantity or vice versa. For instance, if costs to a firm go up, it is reasonable to ask whether the firm will pass that price increase on to consumers or be willing to accept lower profits. Exploring this question motivates our examination of the concept of elasticity.

If the good is one that you need to survive with no good substitutes, or if it is one on which very little money is spent, the firm may be able to pass on its increased costs to consumers in the form of higher prices. On the other hand, if a good is a luxury, a good you can do without, has many substitutes, or already consumes a lot of income, you may buy fewer. In this case, the firm must absorb the costs associated with the price increase.

elasticity The responsiveness of quantity to a change in another variable.

price elasticity of demand The responsiveness of quantity demanded to a change in price.

price elasticity of supply The responsiveness of quantity supplied to a change in price.

income elasticity of demand The responsiveness of quantity demanded to a change in income.

cross-price elasticity of demand The responsiveness of quantity demanded of one good to a change in the price of another good.

elastic The circumstance when the percentage change in quantity is larger than the percentage change in price.

inelastic The circumstance when the percentage change in quantity is smaller than the percentage change in price.

unitary elastic The circumstance when the percentage change in quantity is equal to the percentage change in price.

Definition of Elasticity and Its Formula

In general, **elasticity** is the responsiveness of quantity to a change in another variable. The two most commonly referred to elasticities are the **price elasticity of demand** and the **price elasticity of supply.** Respectively, these are the responsiveness of quantity demanded to a change in price and the responsiveness of quantity supplied to a change in price.

Other elasticities include the **income elasticity of demand** and the **cross-price elasticity of demand.** The former measures the responsiveness of quantity demanded to changes in income, and the latter measures the responsiveness of quantity demanded to changes in the price of another good. All of these elasticities (and others) are central to determining who is right in many economic debates on subjects as varied as the minimum wage and tax policy. Fortunately, they are all very similar in their formulation. So we will start with the most basic one: price elasticity of demand.

The price elasticity of demand is measured by looking at how a percentage change in price affects the percentage change in quantity demanded. The formula for elasticity is:

$$\text{Elasticity} = \frac{\%\Delta Q}{\%\Delta \text{P}} = \frac{\Delta Q/Q^*}{\Delta P/P^*}$$

where

$$\begin{aligned} \% &= \text{percent} \\ \Delta &= \text{change} \\ P^* &= \text{price } (P \text{ star}) \\ Q^* &= \text{quantity } (Q \text{ star}) \end{aligned}$$

The other elasticities (including ones not discussed here) are similar in that the percentage change in either quantity demanded or quantity supplied is in the numerator and the percentage change in the price, income, or other price is in the denominator.

Because the demand curve is downward sloping, an increase in price will therefore cause a decrease in quantity. For example, if a 5 percent increase in price leads to a 10 percent decrease in quantity, the elasticity is $-0.10/.05$. Because the important thing about elasticity is the value itself, it is acceptable and less complicated for us to ignore the minus sign.

Elasticity Labels

This brings us to an important distinction that will be vital when we look at issues that hinge on whether demand is elastic or inelastic—for example, whether increasing the tax on cigarettes leads to decreases in teen smoking or just leads to vaping. Economists say that demand is **elastic** when the percentage change in quantity is larger than the percentage change in price and **inelastic** when the percentage change in quantity is smaller than the percentage change in price. Looking at the formula, if the computed elasticity is greater than 1, then demand is elastic; when it is less than 1, then demand is inelastic. When the percentage change in quantity is the same as the percentage change in price (the computed elasticity is exactly 1), demand is **unitary elastic.**

Alternative Ways to Understand Elasticity

To see this more clearly, let's examine it using three different thought processes. Our first explanation will focus on the slope of the demand curve. Then we will look at the topic but confine ourselves to only words. Lastly, we will focus on how much money is spent on the good.

The Graphical Explanation

We first examine the elasticity phenomenon using graphical skills. To see that slope matters, look at Figures 3.1 and 3.2. Obviously, Figure 3.1 depicts a relatively flat demand curve, while Figure 3.2 depicts a relatively steep one. You can see that both go through the point $P = \$8$, $Q = 4$. Suppose you were to ask how much price would have to rise in order to induce a reduction in quantity demanded to 3. In Figure 3.1, you can see that it would take an increase from \$8 to \$9, whereas in Figure 3.2 it would require an increase from \$8 to \$12. This implies that on the steeper curve (Figure 3.2) demand is less elastic, and on the flatter one (Figure 3.1) it is more elastic. In Figure 3.1, a 12.5 percent increase in prices results in a 25 percent reduction in quantity.[1] In Figure 3.2, price must increase 50 percent to generate a 25 percent decrease in quantity.

FIGURE 3.1 At a given price, a flatter demand curve is more elastic than a steeper one.

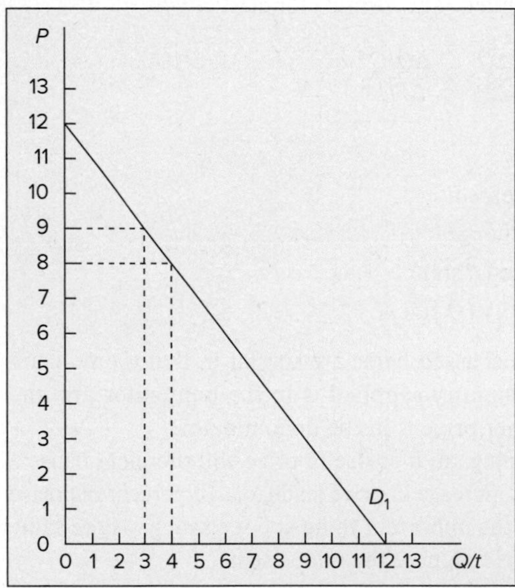

FIGURE 3.2 At a given price, a steeper demand curve is more inelastic than a flatter one.

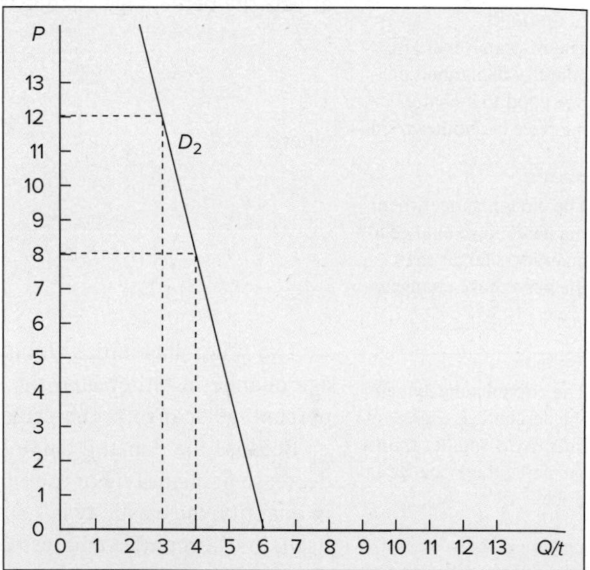

[1] A price increase from \$8 to \$9 is a 12.5 percent increase because it is the fraction 1/8. It is a 25 percent decrease in quantity because it went from 4 to 3 (1/4).

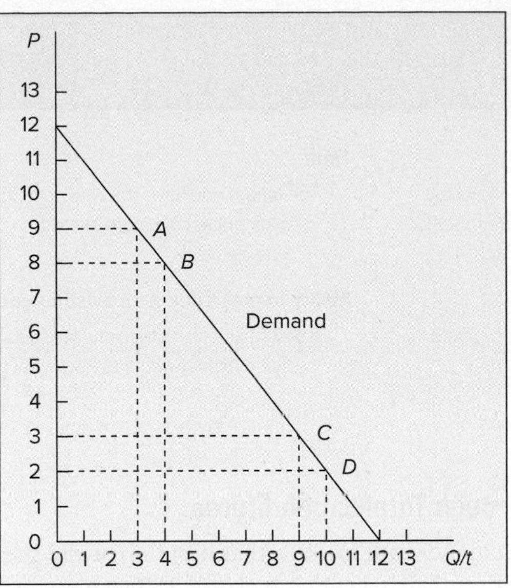

FIGURE 3.3
The higher the price, the greater the elasticity.

This is not to say that slope and elasticity are the same thing; it just means that slope matters. The flatter demand curve (Figure 3.1) depicts a situation where quantity demanded is more responsive to changes in price. The steeper one (Figure 3.2) depicts a situation where quantity demanded is less responsive to price. It is critically important, however, that the implied conclusion—that a flatter demand curve is more elastic than a steeper one—requires that you examine elasticity at the same price-quantity point.

Figure 3.3 examines a different question but shows why the last paragraph was so important. It illustrates that elasticity changes depending on where on the demand curve you are. Specifically, it shows that the higher the price, the greater the elasticity. The price increase from \$2 to \$3 causes a decrease in quantity from 10 to 9. The same size increase in price from \$8 to \$9 causes the same size decrease in quantity from 4 to 3. This is because the slope of this demand curve is the same at all those points. Looking at the formula again, we see it is the percentage changes that matter and not just the size of those changes. Even though the price increases and quantity decreases are the same, the percentage changes are very different.

From point *D* to *C*, the percentage change in price from \$2 to \$3 is a sizable 50 percent, while the percentage change in quantity from 10 to 9 is negligible, only 10 percent. Since the percentage change in the price is greater than the percentage change in the quantity, demand is inelastic between points *D* and *C* (elasticity is low).

On the other hand, from point *B* to *A*, the percentage change from \$8 to \$9 is only 12.5 percent, whereas the percentage change in quantity from 4 to 3 is large (25 percent). As a result, demand between points *B* and *A* is elastic (elasticity is high).

The Verbal Explanation

Although the graphical explanation of elasticity is highly accurate, if it does not make sense to you, it is useless. Recall the original definition of elasticity (the reaction of quantity to a change in price). If you really need a product because there are no good substitutes (like insulin for a diabetic), you will hardly change the amount you buy when the price changes. Thus there is little, if any, reaction of quantity to changes in price. The demand curve for a good you "need" is going to be rather steep. If the good is a luxury item, you are more likely to eliminate it from your budget if it becomes overly expensive. In this case, there is a substantial reaction of quantity to a change in price. The demand curve for a luxury is likely to be flatter.

In addition, price changes for goods that consume little of your income (like drinking water) are not likely to lead to big quantity changes. This is because even if their price increases greatly, you can still easily afford them. Goods that consume a significant portion of your income are more likely to have elastic demand because you are less able to afford large price increases. In this case, goods with low prices are likely to have inelastic demand and goods with high prices are likely to have elastic demand.

DETERMINANTS OF ELASTICITY OF DEMAND

Number and closeness of substitutes

The more alternatives you have, the less likely you are to pay high prices for a good and the more likely you are to settle for an adequate alternative.

Portion of the budget

When a good consumes a significant portion of a consumer's budget, it is more likely to be elastic.

Time

The longer you have to come up with alternatives to paying high prices, the more likely it is you will shift to those alternatives.

Ability to make due with existing goods

If you can stretch the useful life from a good you already have, the elasticity of the replacement will be higher.

Seeing Elasticity through Total Expenditures

total expenditure rule If the price and the amount you spend both move in the same direction, then demand is inelastic, whereas if they move in opposite directions, demand is elastic.

If we wanted to, we could use math to show that if the price and the amount you spend both move in the same direction, then demand is inelastic. If they move in opposite directions, however, demand is elastic. This **total expenditure rule** of elasticity also allows us to quickly judge whether demand is elastic or inelastic. For instance, when the price of cigarettes goes up, smokers usually have to spend more on them. When the prices of luxuries go up, many of us spend less on them (because we do without them). In this way, we can find out whether our demand for a good is elastic or inelastic. All we need to do is to ask whether a price increase will cause us to spend more or less on that good.

More on Elasticity

Determinants of Elasticity of Demand

Key factors of the three elasticity explanations are important in determining whether a good is elastic or inelastic. The first is the number and closeness of substitutes. When there are many substitutes that all serve nearly as well as the good in question, demand is likely to be more elastic, because price increases induce consumers to purchase other goods. Whether price increases can be easily absorbed into a person's budget also matters. If price increases cannot be absorbed—which is likely to be the case if the good takes up a significant portion of the budget of consumers—when they occur, significant quantity reductions will follow. And although timing was not mentioned above, given time, close substitutes can be found or invented. One way or another, consumers will frequently find ways around paying higher prices.

One of those substitutes could be the continued use of something the consumer already has. Cars, for instance, have greater elasticity than razor blades because owners can easily continue to drive the cars they have until a sale price induces them to buy a replacement, whereas shavers can stretch the use of a razor for only a limited number of days.

Elasticity and the Demand Curve

Supply changes will have very different results depending on the elasticity of demand. As you can see from the figures on the next page, an identical supply change can affect only price (Figure 3.4), only quantity (Figure 3.5), price much more than quantity (Figure 3.6), or quantity much more than price (Figure 3.7).

FIGURE 3.4 Perfectly inelastic demand.

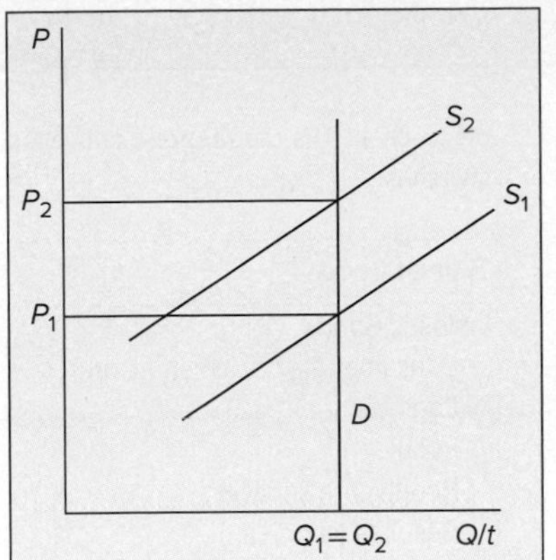

FIGURE 3.5 Perfectly elastic demand.

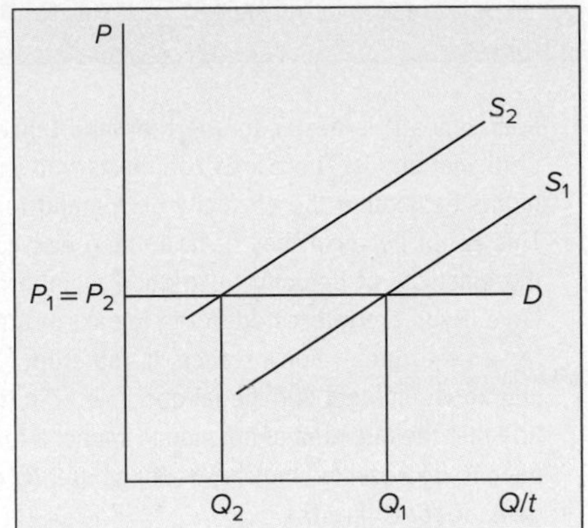

FIGURE 3.6 Inelastic demand.

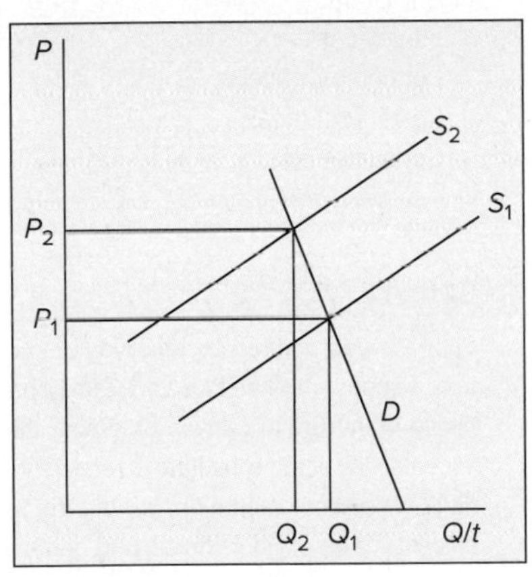

FIGURE 3.7 Elastic demand.

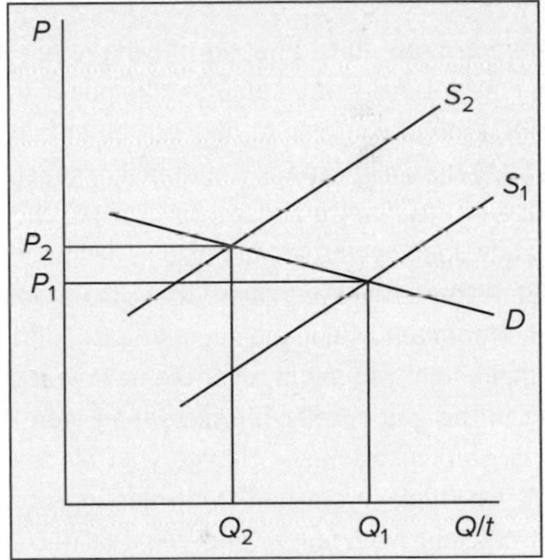

perfectly inelastic The condition of demand when price changes have no effect on quantity.

perfectly elastic The condition of demand when price cannot change.

In Figure 3.4, the demand curve is **perfectly inelastic** because price changes have no effect on quantity. In Figure 3.5, the demand curve is **perfectly elastic** because price cannot change. As we saw in Figures 3.2 and 3.3, a linear demand curve is elastic at high prices and inelastic at low prices. In Figure 3.6, demand is inelastic over the entire range shown because at every point the percentage change in price is larger than the percentage change in quantity. This will be true when the demand curve is nearly vertical. In Figure 3.7, demand is elastic over the entire range, because at every point, the percentage change in price is smaller than the percentage change in quantity. This will be true when the demand curve is nearly horizontal.

If we recall the elasticity formula, we can use this explanation to compute the appropriate elasticity numbers for each of these elasticity labels. For perfectly elastic demand the computed elasticity is ∞ (infinity), while for perfectly inelastic demand the computed elasticity is 0 (zero). Remembering that unitary elastic demand computes to 1 (one), it makes sense that elastic demand will compute to greater than 1 but less than ∞, and inelastic demand will compute to less than 1 but greater than 0.

ELASTICITY: SOME ILLUSTRATIVE EXAMPLES

Sometimes it is easier to see the importance of elasticity with particular goods. There are economists who spend their days and nights estimating the elasticity of demand for particular goods. This is not because they have nothing else to do. It is because the elasticity of demand for a good is important information to have if you are interested in the impact of a price increase or a tax on that good. For instance, if you study the chapter on the line between legal and illegal goods later in the course, you will find that the question of how much impact a tax on cigarettes will have in decreasing smoking depends greatly on the elasticity of demand for cigarettes.

Consider the goods listed in the following table and their elasticities. You should be able to tell yourself stories (like the ones included here). The key to the question of whether a good is elastic or not is whether there is an acceptable substitute.

SAMPLE STORY 1

There are few substitutes for driving to and from work. Though you may or may not be able to take public transportation or carpool, though you may or may not be able to trade in your SUV for a fuel-efficient car, it would take a substantial change in the price of gasoline to cause you to make the substitution immediately upon seeing an increase in gas prices. This is especially true if you did not anticipate that prices would remain high. On the other hand, if you did see that gasoline prices were going to remain high, you might, over the next year or so, consider trading in the gas guzzler for something more fuel efficient. Similarly, you cannot easily change your electric bill, but over time you can replace an inefficient electric forced-air furnace with an efficient heat pump, and you can decide to put electronic devices that draw electricity even when they look like they are off (such as TVs, coffeepots, and even cell phone chargers) on switches.

Type of Good	Price Elasticity
Inelastic Goods	
Consumer electricity (short-run)	0.13
Eggs	0.06
Food	0.21
Health care services	0.18
Gasoline (short-run)	0.08
Gasoline (long-run)	0.24
Highway and bridge tolls	0.10
Unitary Elastic Good (or close to it)	
Shellfish	0.89
Cars	1.14
Elastic Goods	
Luxury car	3.70
Foreign air travel	1.77
Restaurant meals	2.27
Consumer electricity (long-run)	1.89

Sources: Variety of sources combined by author

SAMPLE STORY 2

Suppose you wanted to take your family on an interesting vacation. Suppose further that your family had narrowed its choices to hiking in the Grand Canyon or seeing the sights in Paris. Given the acceptability of the substitute, a relatively small change in the price of flights and accommodations for the trip to France would have a significant impact on your choice. A 10 percent change in the price would result in a nearly 18 percent change in the chance of going to Paris.

Elasticity of Supply

Before moving on, we need to stop and say that nearly everything we have just learned about the price elasticity of demand can be applied to the price elasticity of supply. Firms selling goods may be in a situation where they have already brought goods to market that are quite perishable and, therefore, must be sold regardless of their price. We may have other situations where producing more of the goods can be accomplished but only at a sharply increased price. We can imagine a third circumstance where prices do not have to rise much in order to motivate further sales and, finally, it is possible that firms may be willing to produce as many goods as buyers want at the current market price. In the first scenario, the supply curve would be vertical. In the second and third scenarios, the supply curve would be upward sloping, with the second being a steeply sloped supply curve, and the third being a relatively flat one. The final scenario would likely result in a horizontal supply curve. Some examples of goods with varying elasticities might be helpful here. In the very short run, the elasticity of supply of fresh fruit at a farmers' market is perfectly inelastic as long as the fruit will spoil if it goes unsold. In

FIGURE 3.8 Perfectly inelastic supply.

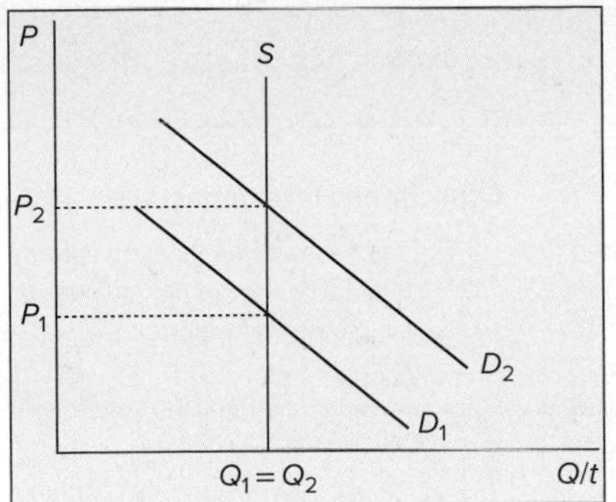

FIGURE 3.9 Inelastic supply.

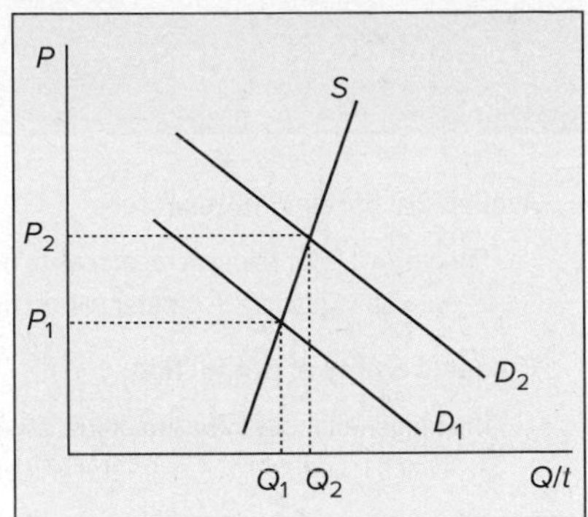

FIGURE 3.10 Elastic supply.

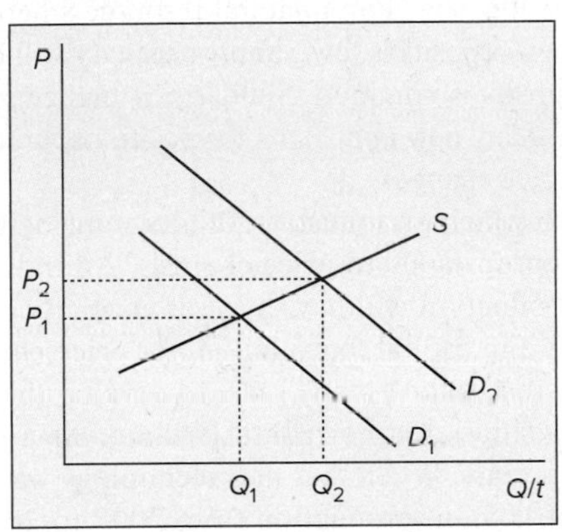

FIGURE 3.11 Perfectly elastic supply.

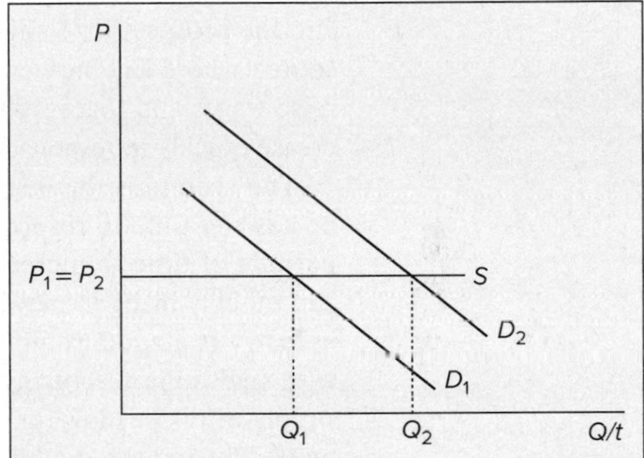

the relatively short run and in the United States, the supply of gasoline is inelastic because most refineries are not easily capable of expanding or contracting output. They run 24 hours per day, seven days a week, and are brought offline only for maintenance. In the longer run, there are myriad goods where firms can bring new production online. A relatively small increase in the profit margin on a good can motivate significantly greater production. There are very few real-world examples of perfectly elastic supply.

Replicating the idea of Figures 3.4 through 3.7 where we had a constant shift in supply and saw what happened with varying elasticities of demand, Figures 3.8 through 3.11 show what happens when demand shifts with varying elasticities of supply. In Figure 3.8, the supply curve is perfectly inelastic and vertical. As a result of an increase in demand, price rises greatly, but quantity does not change at all. In Figure 3.9, the supply curve is inelastic and steeply sloped so the change in demand causes prices to rise quite a bit and quantity to rise, albeit not very much. If supply is elastic, such as it is in Figure 3.10, the demand increase causes prices to rise only a little and quantity to rise substantially. Finally, in the case where supply is perfectly elastic, as it is in Figure 3.11, the increase in demand causes only an increase in quantity and no effect is seen on price.

Determinants of the Elasticity of Supply

There are also key factors that are important in determining whether supply is likely to be elastic or inelastic. The first is the degree to which the relevant resources used for production

DETERMINANTS OF ELASTICITY OF SUPPLY

Availability of relevant resources

The easier it is for relevant resources to be developed or attracted into an industry, the greater will be the supply elasticity.

Time and agility of production

The longer an industry has to adjust production, or the ease with which it can do so, the greater will be the supply elasticity.

Capacity and inventories

The farther away an industry is to its production capacity combined with the degree to which it can easily and cheaply use inventories as a buffer, the greater will be the elasticity of supply.

are available. That availability can be achieved either by their development or by the ability to attract those resources into the industry. For a natural resource where the location is known and the prospect for finding new deposits is low, supply elasticity will be smaller than for a resource where finding new deposits is common. Similarly, if higher prices motivate firms to raise wages and that results in many new applicants for positions, productive capacity can increase quickly in response to price changes.

The second is the degree to which an industry exhibits some agility in their production or has the time to respond appropriately to price changes. An industry that requires long periods of time to increase production will have a lower elasticity of supply than one that can quickly bring in new labor and capital to exploit minor price changes. Here, the energy industry is a good example in that it took many years to develop the technology associated with hydraulic fracturing (fracking) and horizontal drilling. As a result, the elasticity of supply of oil was low for many years. When that new technology was on full display, in particular during the doubling of U.S. oil production from 2008 to 2019, elasticity of supply increased markedly.

The final determinant of elasticity of supply is the degree to which a firm is close to its production capacity combined with the degree to which it can easily and cheaply use inventories as a buffer. An industry that is always running at full capacity and can't cheaply store its output will have very low elasticity of supply. The clearest and most frequently observed example of this is in the gasoline-refining business. Refineries are always running at full capacity—24/7/365. The only exception to that is when they shut down for maintenance, which occurs when they switch from winter blends to summer blends (in March) and back again (in October). You see the price at the pump rise in those months because there is no spare capacity and the cost of storage is quite high.

Consumer and Producer Surplus

Consumer Surplus

Most people think that when consumers buy goods, only the firm is better off as a result of the exchange. They do not often acknowledge that consumers are also better off. It turns out that consumers often get much more value than they part with. Recall from "All about Demand" in Chapter 2 that the demand curve represents the marginal utility of the good. This means that the amount each additional unit of the good is worth to the consumer can be read from the demand curve.

COMPARING THE GAIN TO THE GAINERS WITH THE LOSS TO THE LOSERS

When there are win–win scenarios such as the case outlined, economists generally favor uninhibited exchange. When there are losers, economists look to consumer surplus–producer surplus analysis to weigh the gain to the gainers against the loss to the losers. To you, whether free trade is a good thing or not depends on whether you are a Kia owner who saved several thousand dollars on your car or an unemployed United Auto Workers union member. Whether a new Walmart Supercenter is good for your town depends on whether you are a consumer paying lower prices for steak or a meat cutter unemployed because the Kroger that you worked for closed. Generally, but by no means universally, economists favor market outcomes because they make the calculation that the gain to the gainers outweighs the loss to the losers. Whether it is trade between the United States and Korea or Walmart outcompeting Kroger, free-trade economists insist that lower prices generate a gain in consumer surplus that is greater than the net loss in producer surplus.

Figure 3.12 demonstrates consumers win in an exchange and provides a measure of the degree to which they win. The value the consumers place on each unit of the good is their marginal benefit for that unit. That is how much they would have paid for that unit. As a result, the total value to consumers is simply the sum of those marginal benefits for each unit and is the area under the demand curve from O to Q^*. It looks like ⏢ (trapezoid) and is bounded by the letters $OACQ^*$. The total amount of money they pay for these goods is the price, P^*, times the amount they buy, Q^*, so it looks like □ (rectangle) and is bounded by the letters OP^*CQ^*. The difference between the areas is the triangle that represents the value to the consumers minus the amount they pay the producer. Economists call that **consumer surplus;** it looks like ◺ (triangle) and is bounded by the letters P^*AC.

consumer surplus
The value you get that is in excess of what you pay to get it.

Producer Surplus

Firms also benefit from an exchange. In the Chapter 2 section "All about Supply," we learned that the supply curve is upward sloping because it is the marginal cost curve and marginal cost is increasing. Just as we added together marginal benefits to get the value to the consumers in Figure 3.12, we now add together marginal costs for each unit in Figure 3.13 to get the total variable cost to the producer (which is the difference between all its costs and those it

FIGURE 3.12 Consumer surplus.

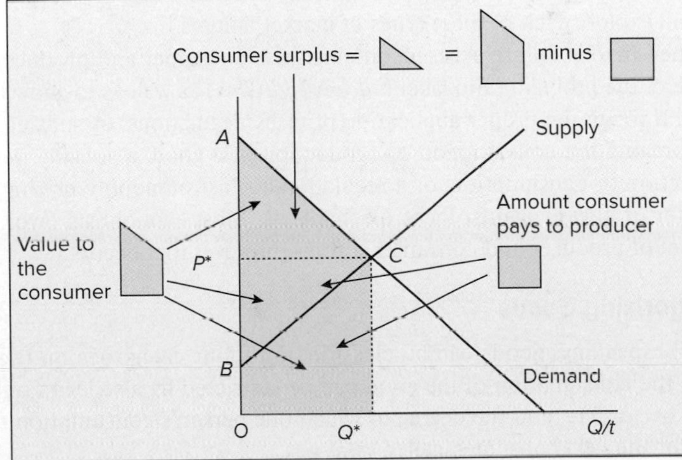

FIGURE 3.13 Producer surplus.

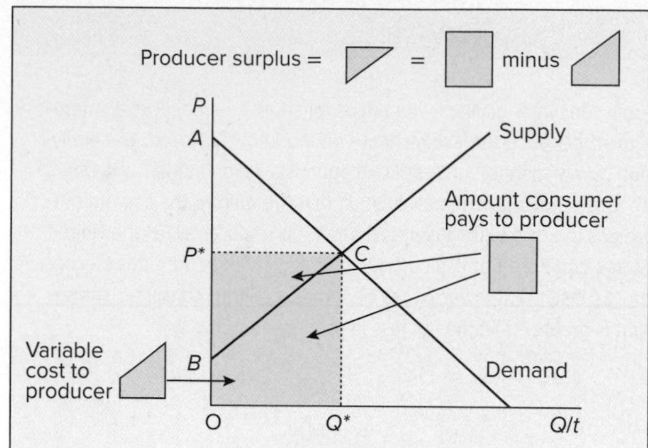

FIGURE 3.14 Net benefit to society.

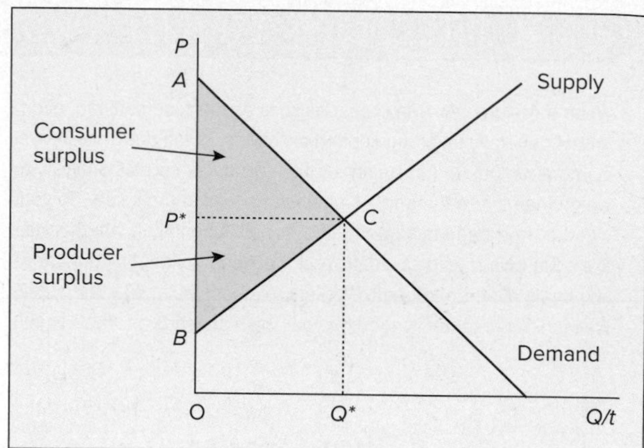

needs to start up its business). As a result, we can measure the total variable cost as the area under the supply curve from O to Q^*, which looks like ◺ (trapezoid) and is bounded by the letters $OBCQ^*$. The amount consumers pay producers is the same OP^*CQ^* rectangle it was in Figure 3.12, □ (rectangle). The difference is what economists call **producer surplus;** it looks like ◸ (triangle) and is bounded by the letters BP^*C.

producer surplus
The money the firm gets that is in excess of its marginal costs.

The *net benefit to society,* shown in Figure 3.14, is the consumer surplus plus the producer surplus. That is, if the market did not exist, consumers would lose their consumer surplus and the producers would lose their producer surplus. Because the market exists, both are better off.

Market Failure

Reread the last sentence of the preceding paragraph. It seems to suggest that the market works perfectly and that there is never cause for government to intervene. Intuitively you know that is not true. A market can fail for a number of reasons: The actions of a consumer or producer can harm an innocent third party, a good may not be one for which a company can profit from selling even though society profits from its existence, the buyer may not be able to make a well-informed choice given the complexity of the decision, a buyer or a seller may have radically different information about a good or service, or a buyer or seller may have too much power over the price. Each of these problems leads to **market failure**—the circumstance where the market outcome is not the economically efficient outcome. In the issue chapters to come, you will explore each of these types of market failures.

market failure
The circumstance where the market outcome is not the economically efficient outcome.

When market failure exists, economists use consumer and producer surplus to analyze the degree of the problem (and label it *deadweight loss*) as well as to show how the problem can be solved through the proper application of taxes, regulations, or subsidies. Whether this is a tax discouraging the consumption or production of a good, a subsidy designed to encourage its production or consumption, or a regulation against monopoly pricing, economists are not always for or always against these mechanisms. Most economists favor policies that maximize the sum of producer and consumer surplus, however that occurs.

exclusivity
The degree to which the consumption of the good can be restricted by a seller to only those who pay for it.

rivalry
The degree to which one person's consumption reduces the value of the good for the next consumer.

Categorizing Goods

Broadly speaking, goods can be classified into four categories on the basis of the degree to which the consumption of the good can be restricted by a seller to only those who pay for it, called **exclusivity,** and the degree to which one person's consumption reduces the value of the good for the next consumer, called **rivalry.**

purely private good
A good with the characteristics of both exclusivity and rivalry.

purely public good
A good with neither of the characteristics of exclusivity or rivalry.

excludable public good
A good with the characteristic of exclusivity but not of rivalry.

congestible public good
A good with the characteristic of rivalry but not of exclusivity.

network good
a type of good for which you need other people consuming it for it to have any use to you.

A slice of pizza has a high degree of both qualities; the seller can easily prevent you from consuming their pizza if you do not pay for it, and once you have eaten a slice of pizza, that particular piece is not available to others. As a result, economists would label pizza as a **purely private good** because both exclusivity and rivalry exist. On the other hand, the army protects all citizens from foreign invasion regardless of how much they pay in taxes, and their success at doing so is not diminished at all by how many people they have to defend. Economists label national defense as a **purely public good** because it is one for which there is neither rivalry nor exclusivity.

In addition to those extremes, there are goods that have a high degree of one characteristic and a low degree of the other. Cable companies can easily exclude their consumers from getting HBO, but one consumer's viewing of HBO does not affect another's viewing. HBO is excludable, but there is no rivalry. Economists call such goods **excludable public goods.** Similarly, a city street is an example of a good for which it would be nearly impossible to prevent usage by citizens and one for which rivalry is common (think traffic jams).[2] Such goods are what economists call **congestible public goods.**

There is another type of good for which you actually need other people consuming it for it to have any use to you. Economists call this type of good a **network good.** The first landline telephones were an early example of this type of good. Social media apps such as Facebook, Instagram, and Twitter, as well as the more nefarious ones like Yik-Yak, Tinder, and Kik, all require other users to be active in order for the apps to have any value.

[2]While you may think license plates allow for exclusivity, they do not serve the entire function in that once you have a licensed car, it is very difficult to charge you based on usage. As technology increases, GPS receivers and transmitters may make it possible to charge drivers based on where and when they drive.

Kick It Up a Notch

DEADWEIGHT LOSS

deadweight loss
The loss in societal welfare associated with production being too little or too great.

In Figures 3.15 and 3.16, the market is not at equilibrium. The net benefit to society (consumer surplus plus the producer surplus) is not as large as it is at equilibrium. At equilibrium, it is *ABC* and is as big as it can be. If consumption is more than Q^*, then consumers are paying more than they think a product is worth, or producers are not meeting their marginal costs, or both. If consumption is less than Q^*, consumers wish they could buy more (and they would get more consumer surplus), or firms wish they could sell more (and they would get more producer surplus), or both. If the triangle is smaller than *ABC,* then there is **deadweight loss.** Deadweight

FIGURE 3.15 Deadweight loss with a price higher than P^*.

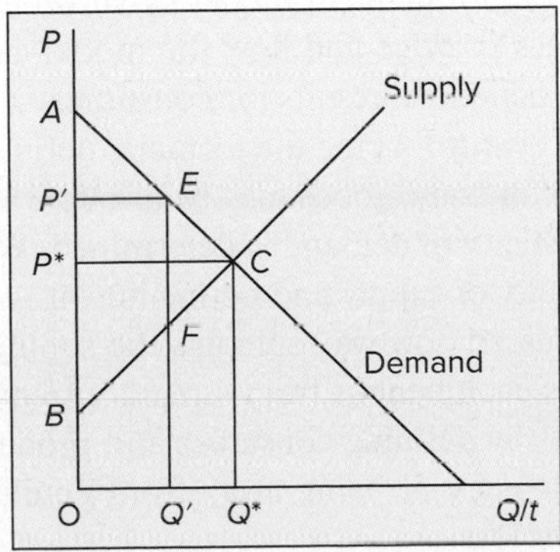

FIGURE 3.16 Deadweight loss with a price lower than P^*.

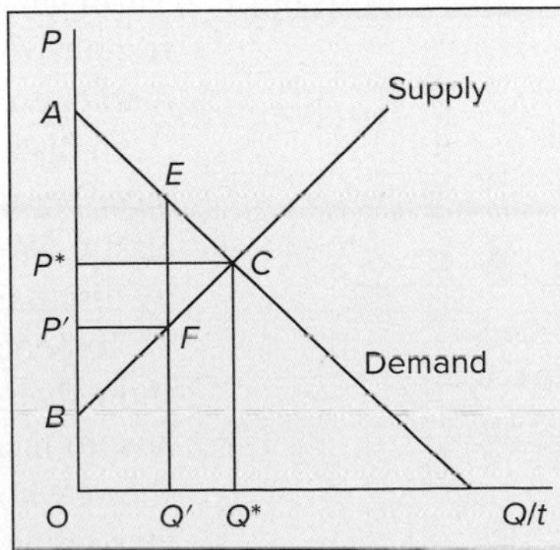

loss is the measure economists use to discuss the inefficiency of markets when a problem like air pollution exists or when government establishes an impediment to a free floating price, such as the minimum wage.

To see how deadweight loss fits our supply and demand diagram, suppose that for some reason the price cannot be at P^* but is instead at P' (P prime). Figure 3.15 shows the impact of this when P' is greater than P^*, and Figure 3.16 shows the impact when P' is less than P^*. In either circumstance, the new quantity will be less than equilibrium because consumers will not be willing to buy more than Q' at P' in Figure 3.15, and producers will not be willing to sell more than Q' in Figure 3.16 at P'.

In Figure 3.15, the price is higher than P^*. At that higher price, though producers will want to sell many more than the previous equilibrium quantity, consumers will want to buy fewer. Unless the consumers are compelled to buy things they do not want, they will buy only Q'.

Given that, we can find the consumer and producer surplus in this market and compare it to what it was in Figure 3.14. The area under the demand curve represents the value to the consumers of Q' goods, which is OAEQ'. The price P' times the quantity Q' is the amount of money consumers will pay to get Q', represented by the area O$P'EQ'$. The difference between these, $P'AE$, is the consumer surplus. It costs the producer OBFQ' in terms of variable costs to make these goods. The difference between the money consumers pay them and their costs, $BP'EF$, is the producer surplus. The sum of consumer and producer surplus in this case is $BAEF$, but this is less than ABC, which is what this sum was in Figure 3.14. This means that the area FEC is lost as a result of being at P' instead of P^*, and this is the deadweight loss of being at P' instead of P^*.

In Figure 3.16, the price is lower than P^*. At that lower price, though, producers will not want to sell as much as they did at the previous equilibrium and consumers will want to buy more. Unless producers are compelled to sell things they do not want to sell, they will produce only Q'. Again we can find the consumer and producer surplus in this market and compare it to what it was in Figure 3.14. The area under the demand curve still represents the value to the consumer of Q' goods and is still OAEQ'. The price P' times the quantity Q' is still the amount of money consumers will pay to get Q', but this is now represented by the area O$P'FQ'$. The difference between these, the consumer surplus, is now $P'AEF$. Whereas the costs of the producer, OBFQ', remain the same, the revenue has fallen, so the producer surplus falls to $BP'F$. The sum of consumer and producer surplus is also $BAEF$, which is still less than it was in Figure 3.14. The deadweight loss is again represented by the area FEC.

Summary

This chapter expanded on the supply and demand model by showing the importance of the responsiveness of quantity to changes in price and how the model can be used to show that market exchange results in mutually beneficial results for consumers and producers.

In discussing elasticity we began by introducing the formula, defining the terms *elastic* and *inelastic,* and exploring why demand for some goods may be elastic while for others may be inelastic. We then considered how elasticity of demand is determined. We continued our elasticity discussions by defining the elasticity of supply and noting how it is determined.

To conclude the chapter, we discussed how we could use the supply and demand model to show that consumers and producers each benefit from a market transaction, and we showed how to measure the benefit each gets by defining consumer and producer surplus. Finally, we showed how we measure the inefficiency of being away from equilibrium by defining and illustrating the concept of deadweight loss.

Key Terms

congestible public good
consumer surplus
cross-price elasticity of demand
deadweight loss
elastic
elasticity
excludable public good
exclusivity
income elasticity of demand
inelastic
market failure
network good
perfectly elastic
perfectly inelastic
price elasticity of demand
price elasticity of supply
producer surplus
purely private good
purely public good
rivalry
total expenditure rule
unitary elastic

Issues Chapters You Are Ready for Now

International Trade: Does It Jeopardize American Jobs?
The Line between Legal and Illegal Goods
Health Care
Government-Provided Health Insurance
Farm Policy
Minimum Wage

Quiz Yourself

1. The elasticity of demand is related to the slope of the demand curve
   a. and only the slope of the demand curve.
   b. but also the (price, quantity) position on the demand curve.
   c. but also the slope of the supply curve.
   d. and whether the good is normal or inferior.
2. If a firm cannot determine whether the demand for the good it sells is elastic or inelastic but discovers that every time it raises its price, its total revenue declines, it can conclude its
   a. demand is unitary elastic.
   b. demand is elastic.
   c. demand is inelastic.
   d. demand is perfectly inelastic.
3. Suppose you observe that minor changes in supply seem to cause dramatic changes in price. You would conclude that
   a. demand is unitary elastic.
   b. demand is elastic.
   c. demand is inelastic.
   d. demand is perfectly inelastic.
4. The fact that the demand for pasta is inelastic should not surprise you because
   a. it is a very cheap food.
   b. the demand for nearly all food products is inelastic.
   c. the supply of pasta is inelastic.
   d. it is so expensive.
5. In the last five years, the elasticity of supply for gasoline has increased dramatically. All other things equal, this would be expected to contribute to
   a. greater price stability.
   b. greater price volatility.
   c. greater demand.
   d. uncertain demand.
6. Combined, the consumer surplus and producer surplus at equilibrium is
   a. lower than it would be at prices below equilibrium.
   b. lower than it would be at prices above equilibrium.
   c. typically negative.
   d. as big as it can be.

7. When looking at the impact of a change in trade policy, economists use consumer and producer surplus to look at the winners and losers. Free-trade economists insist that
   a. no one loses.
   b. everyone loses.
   c. there are winners and losers but that the gain to the winners is greater than the loss to the losers.
   d. there are winners and losers but that the loss to the losers is greater than the gain to the winners.
8. When a satellite television company gains a subscriber, there is no impact on existing subscribers. That is, there is no rivalry in the consumption for their service. This is an example of a
   a. purely private good.
   b. purely public good.
   c. congestible public good.
   d. excludable public good.
9. Policy makers have considered putting computer chips in cars that would allow tax collectors to charge people on the basis of how often they drive during rush hours. These policy makers are dealing with the fact that public roads are
   a. purely private goods.
   b. purely public goods.
   c. congestible public goods.
   d. excludable public goods.

Short Answer Questions

1. Give an example of a good that you believe has perfectly inelastic demand for most people. Then explain why you believe that is the case.
2. Give an example of a good that you believe has inelastic demand (not perfectly inelastic) for most people. Then explain why you believe that is the case.
3. Give an example of something you hate to do, and imagine that you could pay someone else to do that thing for you. Explain why both you and the person you pay could end up better off.
4. Give an example of a situation where the government compels you to do something you do not want to do. Why might that be a reasonable requirement? When might it be unreasonable?
5. Suppose you hear the following: "They just increased taxes on cigarettes and on high-priced cigars." Use the concept of elasticity to describe who will be hurt by those taxes. Is a change in the price of the good itself a change in the quantity supplied?

Think about This

Suppose both gasoline supply and demand are highly inelastic. Knowing that a change in the expected price of gasoline will shift both supply and demand, explain how these combined facts can lead you to an understanding of wildly changing gasoline prices.

Talk about This

Talk about your alternative choices for colleges. What schools did you consider? Was tuition a consideration? Does your college's proximity to other schools imply anything about your school's ability to raise revenue by raising tuition?

Behind the Numbers

Hirschman, Ira, Claire McKnight, and John Pucher, "Highway and Bridge Toll Elasticities," *Transportation* 22 (May 1995).

Food Demand and Nutrient Elasticities, www.ers.usda.gov/publications/tb1887/tb1887.pdf

Schaller, Bruce, "Transportation Elasticities," *Transportation* 26 (1999), pp. 283–297.

Gasoline Elasticities: Hughes, Jonathan E., Christopher R. Knittel, and Daniel Sperling. Evidence of a Shift in the Short-Run Price Elasticity of Gasoline Demand (September 5, 2006). Available at SSRN: http://www.nber.org/papers/w12530

CHAPTER FOUR

Firm Production, Cost, and Revenue

Learning Objectives

After reading this chapter you should be able to:

LO1 Demonstrate the relationship between production and costs and the relationship between sales and revenues.

LO2 Explain that models of production are based on the assumption that firms seek to maximize profit.

LO3 Demonstrate how profit maximization dictates that firms set production so that marginal cost equals marginal revenue.

Chapter Outline

---

profit
The money that a firm makes: revenue - cost.

cost
The expense that must be incurred to produce goods and services for sale.

revenue
The money that comes into the firm from the sale of goods and services.

economic cost
All costs of a business: those that must be paid as well as those incurred in the form of forgone opportunities.

accounting cost
Only those costs that must be explicitly paid by the owner of a business.

The business of business is making money, and the money business makes is called **profit.** How it makes that profit is by selling its goods for more than it costs to make them. For this chapter (and for most of this book) we'll make the simplifying assumption that nothing influences business other than maximizing profit. Although this is an exaggeration, it is reasonably close to the truth, and accepting it as the truth simplifies our task considerably.

With the profit maximization assumption in place, we can break things down into cost and revenue. **Cost** is the expense that businesses must incur to produce goods for sale. **Revenue** is the money that comes into the firm from the sale of its goods.

It is important to understand why economists focus on costs that are incurred rather than simply those costs that must be paid, called *expenses*. Accountants focus only on expenses, but economists also consider the *opportunity cost* of choices. To fully understand the concepts of **economic cost** and **accounting cost,** consider a new startup business whose owner quits a $50,000 per year job and cashes savings of $100,000 (earning 1 percent) to get started. An accountant would not consider the $50,000 of forgone job-related income or the $1,000 per year in forgone interest as costs of the business, but an economist would. For the remainder of this chapter and all of the next, all costs refer to economic costs.

That said, because profit is the difference between revenues and costs, we will be able to use what we have learned regarding these concepts to find how much production our profit-maximizing firm will choose. We then explore the production process and the costs that it generates, move on to discuss the revenue side, and then put the two together to show how, under different circumstances, firms choose their production levels.

We'll carry one example from the beginning of this explanation to the end. Let's assume that the industry we are examining is the computer memory industry, the industry that makes the chips that enable computers to use and quickly access information. Let's suppose that the production of computer memory requires three things: expensive machines, highly trained people, and very inexpensive plastic and metal from which the chips are made. To make things even easier, let's assume that the plastic and metal used to make the chips are free.

So far we have had a section entitled "Kick It Up a Notch" in every chapter. The problem with this chapter is that material presented is already "kicked up" plenty. Complicating matters further, some students need a verbal explanation, some need to "see" it in the form of a graph, while still others can only get their arms around a concrete numerical example. To deal with that, we'll explain each of them using just words, a graphical explanation, and a numerical example.

Production

Just Words

To understand costs, we need to know how much money it takes to produce goods. First we need to know what resources are necessary for production. Then we can construct an input–output relationship called a **production function**, shown in the form of a graph and accompanying table. Our graph will show how many resources we need to produce various amounts of output. From the production function, we can derive how much various amounts of production cost. From the resulting **cost function**, we will be able to determine how much each unit costs on average to produce and how much each additional unit costs.

production function
A graph that shows how many resources are needed to produce various amounts of output.

cost function
A graph that shows how much various amounts of production cost.

Of course, this is putting the cart before the horse. Before the firm decides how many to produce, it has to decide what to produce. In our example, the memory chip firm did not decide to make chips for the fun of it. Early computer designers decided that their computers would work better if they had a short-term place to store and quickly retrieve information. Chip-making companies were founded to provide the computer industry with the parts to make short-term storage of data possible. For the remainder of this section and this chapter, we assume that the firm is up and running and is simply trying to figure out how many chips to make at any given time.

To make any product, you typically have **fixed** and **variable inputs.** That is, you have resources that you cannot change and resources that you can. In our example, the plant and the equipment in the plant are considered fixed inputs because they are not easily changed, added to, or subtracted from. On the other hand, the labor to operate those machines is easily changed. You can hire and fire more easily and quickly than you can replace a machine. People and other resources that can be easily changed are called variable inputs.

fixed inputs
Resources that cannot be easily changed.

variable inputs
Resources that can be easily changed.

The first step in our process of figuring out how many memory chips to make is to map out how many resources are needed to produce various amounts of these chips. Another simplifying assumption: Though the manufacture of most things, including computer memory, requires both labor and materials, we will simplify the problem and assume it only takes labor.

Without any personnel there is no production. If there are only a few workers, production is both low and inefficient because workers are not able to specialize in particular parts of the production process. They waste time moving from one part of the process to another, and they take time to build momentum, working at each stage only to find that when they get good at it, it is time to move on to another stage in order to create one unit of a finished good.

The addition of a few more workers solves that problem and production levels increase greatly. Workers divide the tasks in such a way that each can build momentum and does not have to switch jobs. This specialization is called the **division of labor,** and its impact is such that for a small increase in labor a dramatic increase in output is gained.

division of labor
Workers divide the tasks in such a way that each can build momentum and not have to switch jobs.

At some point, though, there are enough workers to get the job done and more workers produce little additional output. Some jobs, too, just cannot be easily divided. Although it is usually the case that having more workers increases output, eventually workers find that the existing plant and equipment are too limiting for them to get the most out of new employees. As a result, output increases but not as fast as it had before. This phenomenon, referred to by economists as **diminishing returns,** is a central assumption of this chapter as well as the next.

diminishing returns
The notion that there exists a point where, because there are some fixed inputs like plant and equipment, the addition of resources increases production, but does so at a decreasing rate.

Graphical Explanation

Using the same ideas just presented, let's analyze Figure 4.1. The axes correspond to our simple assumption. Labor is hired to produce output. The horizontal axis shows labor, while the vertical axis shows the output of memory. Point *A* begins at the origin because, as was pointed out in the preceding section, if you have no workers, you have no output. Where there are too few workers to staff the plant, they have to waste time moving from one stage of production to the next, so the increase in production associated with the first group of workers is relatively low. This idea is represented by point *B*. The curve is bowed to the right between points *A* and *C* because of the division of labor. That is, as you add the same number of workers, you get the benefits from those workers specializing and *production increases at an increasing rate*.

Once you get to point *C*, though, there is not enough plant and equipment to accommodate more workers efficiently. Mathematicians call point *C* an *inflection point* because the curve goes from increasing at an increasing rate to increasing at a decreasing rate. In more simple terms, it stops steepening and starts flattening. At point *D*, the curve clearly bows to the left because of diminishing returns to the existing plant and equipment.

Numerical Example

Now, let's consider the same concept using the numbers that comprise Table 4.1. Continuing with the memory chips example, suppose the first column represents the groups of workers, the second column represents the total output produced, and the third column represents the extra output added with the inclusion of the group. Because memory chips cannot make themselves, zero labor corresponds to zero output. Suppose that the first group of workers hired produces 100 units, but when a second group is added a total of 317 units is produced. That is, the second group adds 217 units to production. Suppose the third group adds somewhat less, 183 units, so the total becomes 500 units. If it takes 5 groups of workers to produce 700, 9 to produce 900, and 13 to produce 1,000, then we have a story similar to what we saw in the

FIGURE 4.1 The production function in graphical form.

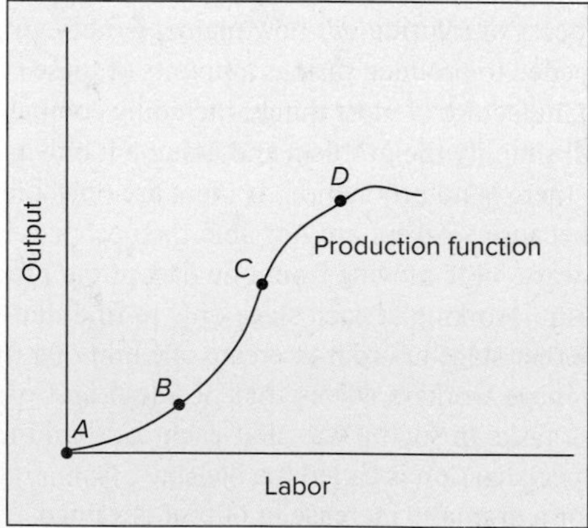

Table 4.1 The production function in tabular form.

Labor	Total Output	Extra Output of the Group
0	0	
1	100	100
2	317	217
3	500	183
4	610	110
5	700	90
6	770	70
7	830	60
8	870	40
9	900	30
13	1,000	

graphical explanation. That is, as we added workers we got more production. The first group of workers was not very efficient because they could not specialize, whereas the second group was efficient because they could. Efficiency continued to grow until it peaked when the fourth group was added. Once the fifth group of workers was hired, and beyond, efficiency waned because the workers were limited by the existing plant and equipment.

We have now explained production in terms of how a varying number of workers can be combined with a fixed amount of plant and equipment to make computer memory chips. We work next on how much it costs to hire those workers and pay for that machinery.

Costs

Just Words

Once we know how many workers it takes to produce our memory chips, we can find out how much it costs to make those chips. The first thing to consider is that there are costs of production that we cannot change. In our example, these **fixed costs** are the costs of the plant and equipment that we own. Costs that we can change, like the number of workers we hire for our plant, are called **variable costs.** The task now is to compare the number of memory chips we make against the costs of making those chips. To accomplish this we need to explore four cost concepts: marginal cost, average total cost, average variable cost, and average fixed cost.

fixed costs
Costs of production that cannot be changed.

variable costs
Costs of production that can be changed.

As we mentioned in Chapter 1, economists frequently use marginal analysis as a method of examination to determine the net impact of incremental changes. For the cost function, **marginal cost (MC)** is the increase in cost associated with a one-unit increase in production. Conceptually, **total cost** is the sum of fixed and variable costs. In order to produce more units, total cost will always continue to rise, so marginal cost will always be positive as each additional unit is produced.

marginal cost (MC)
The addition to cost associated with one additional unit of output.

total cost
The sum of fixed and variable costs.

Total cost rises quickly at low levels of output because of fixed costs, so marginal cost is going to be high at low levels of output. Once equipment is in place and the plant is running, fixed costs pay off because more units of output are being created. Of course, variable costs continue to rise, but not nearly as much as the initial amount of the fixed cost. This means that total cost is not increasing at the same rate as it was when production began. Therefore, marginal cost is lower at moderate levels of output.

Eventually, the efficiencies of the division of labor and specialization have been maximized, and it requires more and more labor to achieve additional one-unit increases in output. It is for this reason that marginal cost begins to increase rapidly as quantity continues to increase more slowly. Thus, marginal cost starts high, decreases for a while, and then increases again.

Average total cost (ATC) is the per unit cost of production. Because this includes fixed cost, which can be very high, average total cost will be high at low levels of production. It will shrink as production gets more efficient and the fixed costs become spread over greater levels of output. As production rises to higher levels where marginal costs are increasing, these two effects will begin to counteract each other and the drop in average total costs will slow. Eventually, the increases in marginal cost will overwhelm the effect of spreading fixed costs over higher levels of output and average total cost will rise again.

average total cost (ATC)
Total cost divided by output, the cost per unit of production.

Average variable cost (AVC) is dictated by the same changes in efficiency that gave us the marginal cost curve. Because it is an average, however, the movements are dampened; the highs are not as high and the lows are not as low. Like average total cost and marginal cost, average variable cost starts high, decreases for a while, and then increases again.

average variable cost (AVC)
Total variable cost divided by output, the average variable cost per unit of production.

Average fixed cost (AFC) falls continuously because the fixed costs of production are being spread over greater and greater levels of production. It is also the difference between ATC and AVC (which will be important when it comes to graphing it).

average fixed cost (AFC)
Total fixed cost divided by output, the average fixed cost per unit of production.

FIGURE 4.2 Total cost function.

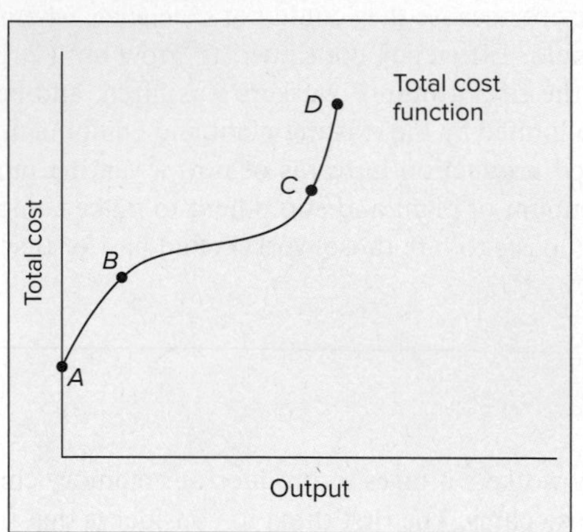

FIGURE 4.3 Marginal cost, average total cost, and average variable cost.

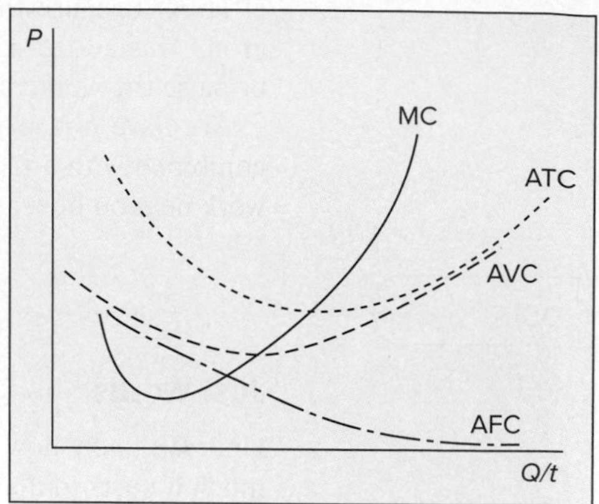

These cost concepts serve as the basis for much of what follows in this chapter, the next one, and our subsequent study of issues.

Graphical Explanation

Looking back at Figure 4.1, you can see that at point *A* we will not have to pay anything to our workers (because we have no workers to pay), but we still have to pay fixed costs. As a result, point *A* in Figure 4.1 corresponds to point *A* in Figure 4.2. We have workers at point *B* whom we have to pay, yet they are not all that productive. Remember that this is not their fault, because there are too few of them to allow specialization. Point *B* in Figure 4.2 is therefore higher than point *A* (because we have to pay them) but not much farther to the right (because they are not making that many chips).

Point *C* in Figure 4.1 indicates that the workers were quite productive. Another way of thinking about this is that for one extra dollar in cost, the increased production is greater at *C* than it was at *B*. Thus, point *C* in Figure 4.2 is also higher than point *B* but is significantly farther to the right. Point *D* in Figure 4.1 shows us where extra workers did not add much to production because of diminishing returns. Again the workers cost money, so point *D* in Figure 4.2 is higher than point *C* but is not that much farther to the right. Connecting these points, we have a total cost function. *Our graph shows how the function helps* us understand and make decisions about the cost of production and the amount produced.

Thus far we have focused on finding the total cost of producing various amounts of output. When we get total revenue, we will be able to find the profit. Before we go there, though, we are going to need graphical representations of the four other cost functions: marginal cost, the average variable cost, the average fixed cost, and the average total cost. This is done in Figure 4.3 with a step-by-step explanation in the accompanying box.

Numerical Example

Again we are dealing with concepts that may be easier to comprehend when there are numbers attached. Following the numerical example used in Table 4.1, consider Table 4.2 (on the next page). The first column is *Output*. The second, *Total Variable Cost,* is based on the $2,500 per unit of labor from Table 4.1 that is required to produce that output. The third, *Total Fixed Cost,* is the cost of plant and equipment and is unchanging. The fourth, *Total Cost,* is the sum of total variable cost and total fixed cost. The fifth, *Marginal Cost,* is the increase in total cost from each level of production. The sixth, *Average Total Cost,* is the per unit cost; the seventh,

DRAWING THE ATC-AVC-MC DIAGRAM

If you are inclined to replicate Figure 4.3 yourself (or are required to in your course) try the following:

1. Draw a sweeping check-shaped MC curve.
2. Draw a symmetrical U-shaped AVC curve that bottoms out on MC.
3. Draw an asymmetrical U-shaped ATC curve that also bottoms out on MC (a bit higher than the AVC curve bottoms out) where the vertical distance between ATC and AVC is longer on the left than it is on the right side of the diagram. (For the mathematically inclined, this is what you get if you have a cubic total cost function.)

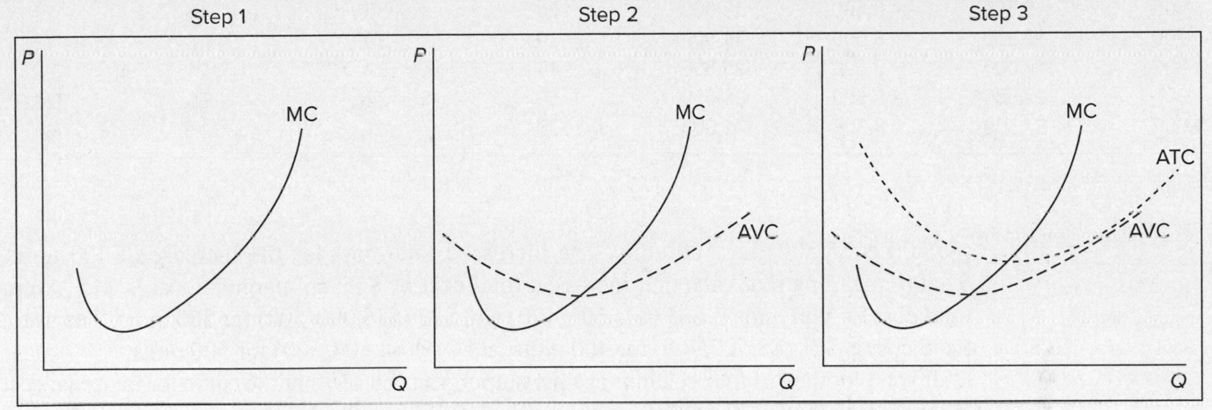

Average Variable Cost, is per unit variable cost; and the eighth, *Average Fixed Cost,* is per unit fixed cost.

These derivations take economics majors several class periods to understand. We'll skip that but outline why Figure 4.3 looks the way it does. Starting with the easiest one, average fixed cost, it is constantly decreasing because the same costs are being spread over more and more units of output. Marginal cost, average total cost, and average variable cost all start high, decrease, and then increase. The manner in which they do that, though, is somewhat complicated.

Marginal cost is the increase in costs associated with a one-unit increase in production. That means it is the "rise over the run" in the total cost curve, which means it is the slope of the total cost curve. You can see in Table 4.2 that total cost rises rapidly at the beginning (rising $25 per unit), flattens out (rising at only $10 per unit at 300 units), and then rises rapidly again (rising at $100 per unit at the end).

Average total cost and average variable cost are both U-shaped because they start high and decrease. Average total cost starts at $110, declines to $30, then rises from there. Average variable cost starts at $25 and drops to $15 before rising. The difference between the two curves is average fixed costs. Because average fixed cost diminishes as production increases, the gap between the average total cost and average variable cost diminishes from $85 to $8.50. Both average total cost and average variable cost are cut from below by the marginal cost curve at their respective minimums. This happens when, because of diminishing returns, marginal costs increase to the point where, first, average variable cost, then average total cost, starts to rise as well.

To see how each column in Table 4.2 is computed, let's look at a production increase from 400 to 500 units. The variable costs associated with producing 400 units are $6,000. Variable costs rise to $7,500 when output rises to 500 units. Fixed costs are $8,500 in both cases. That means that total cost is $14,500 ($6,000 + $8,500) for 400 units and rises to $16,000

Table 4.2 Numerical example: cost functions.

Output	Total Variable Cost	Total Fixed Cost	Total Cost	Marginal Cost*	Average Total Cost	Average Variable Cost	Average Fixed Cost
0	0	8,500	8,500				
100	2,500	8,500	11,000	25	110	25	85
200	3,800	8,500	12,300	13	62	19	43
300	4,800	8,500	13,300	10	44	16	28
400	6,000	8,500	14,500	12	36	15	21
500	7,500	8,500	16,000	15	32	15	17
600	9,500	8,500	18,000	20	30	16	14
700	12,500	8,500	21,000	30	30	18	12
800	17,000	8,500	25,500	45	32	21	10.6
900	22,500	8,500	31,000	55	34	25	9.4
1,000	32,500	8,500	41,000	100	41	32.5	8.5

*Change in total cost/change in output.

($7,500 + $8,500) for 500 units. The increased total cost for the increase of 100 units is $1,500, meaning that each unit increased total cost by $15, so marginal cost is $15. Average total cost for 400 units is $36 ($14,500/400) and $32 ($16,000/500) for 500 units. The average fixed cost is $21 ($8,500/400) for 400 units and $17 ($8,500/500) for 500 units.

If you plot the last four columns against output, you will see that the curve for marginal cost is indeed check-shaped, those for average total cost and average variable cost are both U-shaped, and the average fixed cost curve decreases steadily. You can also see that at 300 units of output marginal cost is at its minimum. Further, you can see that the marginal cost curve cuts the average variable cost curve at its minimum (500 units of output). The marginal cost curve also cuts the average total cost curve at its minimum (700 units of output).

Revenue

Just Words

The other side of any production decision is the amount of money that will be generated from the sale of the goods. To get a handle on revenue, we will need to know whether the business has competition and, if so, how much. For instance, if a business faces many other competitors that produce goods like the ones it produces, its behavior will be different from what it would be if it had the market to itself.

In some industries, like agriculture, the price that the firm receives remains unchanged regardless of how much it has to sell. In other industries, like those that supply electric power, the amount sold affects the price. To explore this difference, let's first assume our memory chip maker is one of many chip makers. Then we will see what happens when we assume that it is the only one.

If our chip-making firm has many competitors, the price is set in a market that it cannot control. The supply of and the demand for chips determine how much the firm can charge. To see the futility of trying to set its own price, imagine that it tried to have a price higher than the market price. If it did, computer makers could and would buy all their chips from our firm's competitors. The firm could, of course, set a price lower than the market price. If it did, it would get to sell all it produced. On the other hand, it could do that at the market price. Because our firm wants to maximize profit and because it can always sell as much as it wants at or below the market price, it will always want to charge the market price.

marginal revenue (MR) Additional revenue the firm receives from the sale of each unit.

This price also happens to be the additional revenue the firm receives from the sale of each unit. To see why this **marginal revenue (MR)** is the same as the price, consider a thought experiment. If the market price is $5, how much will revenue be if our firm sells one unit? Answer: $5. How much will revenue be if it sells two units? Answer: $10. The increase in revenue associated with any sale is therefore $5. This is true whether you let the price be $5, $10, or $600; the price is the marginal revenue.

If, on the other hand, we are the only ones selling computer chips, computer makers have to buy their memory chips from our firm. This situation is quite different from the case where there were many competitors. Instead of just taking a price given to it by the market, our firm is setting the price. Instead of being a small, insignificant part of the market, it is the market. Unfortunately, to sell more, the firm has no recourse other than lowering the price it charges. For instance, if it is currently selling 1 million chips a week and it wants to increase its sales to 2 million a week, it must lower the price to everyone, even those who would have bought 1 million at the higher price.

Graphical Explanation

Figures 4.4 and 4.5 show how marginal revenue is created graphically. In Figure 4.4, the firm has many competitors. Its price is determined for it by the market. As a result, the market price is its marginal revenue. It can sell as many as it wishes at that market price. For each additional one it sells, its revenue increases by the price, so its marginal revenue is a horizontal line equal to the price.

In Figure 4.5, the situation is more complicated. The marginal revenue curve starts on the vertical axis where the demand curve starts. That is because when it sells its first unit, revenue increases from zero to whatever the price was for that first unit. From there, prices must fall in order to increase sales. For a linear demand curve, the marginal revenue curve is exactly twice as steep. (You can see that in the table or ask your teacher for the calculus-based demonstration.)

Numerical Example

Using the same numerical example, suppose that our firm is one of many and has no control over price. Suppose further that the price in the market for memory is $45 per unit. This means that the total revenue (TR) increases by $45 for each unit sold and the marginal revenue is thus $45 for each unit sold. This is illustrated in Table 4.3.

If there are no competitors, then the market demand for memory is simply the demand for our firm's memory. This means that our firm must lower its price to induce consumers to buy more memory. Another way of looking at precisely the same thing is to notice that a firm without competition can force the price higher by restricting its output. As before, total

FIGURE 4.4 Setting the price when there are many competitors.

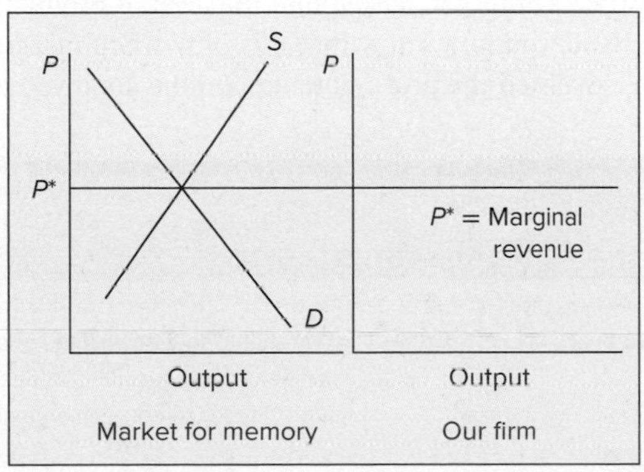

FIGURE 4.5 Marginal revenue when we have no competitors.

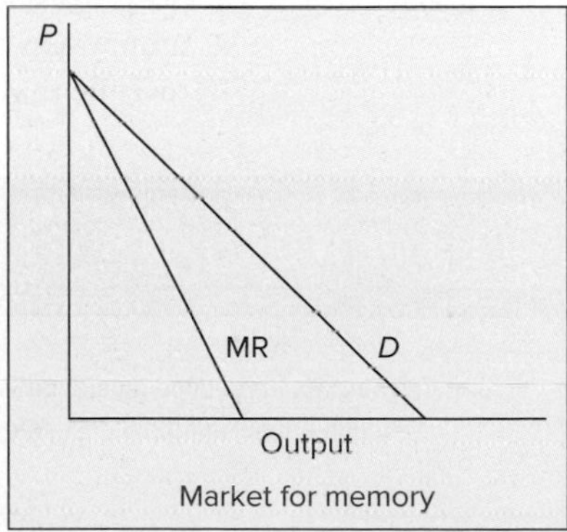

Table 4.3 Numerical example: revenue when there are many competitors.

Q	Price	TR	MR*
0	45	0	
100	45	4,500	45
200	45	9,000	45
300	45	13,500	45
400	45	18,000	45
500	45	22,500	45
600	45	27,000	45
700	45	31,500	45
800	45	36,000	45
900	45	40,500	45
1,000	45	45,000	45

*Change in total revenue/change in output.

Table 4.4 Numerical example: revenue when there are no competitors.

Q	Price	TR	MR*
0	75	0	
100	70	7,000	70
200	65	13,000	60
300	60	18,000	50
400	55	22,000	40
500	50	25,000	30
600	45	27,000	20
700	40	28,000	10
800	35	28,000	0
900	30	27,000	−10
1,000	25	25,000	−20

*Change in total revenue/change in output.

revenue is price times quantity, but because price changes to drive output, the marginal revenue falls. This is illustrated in Table 4.4.

Maximizing Profit

Just Words

perfect competition
A situation in a market where there are many firms producing the same good.

monopoly
A situation in a market where there is only one firm producing the good.

As mentioned, the level of output for the business that will maximize profit very much depends on whether the business is in **perfect competition** (i.e., one of many producing the same thing) or is a **monopoly** (i.e., it has no competitors). Regardless of whether it has many competitors or it has the market to itself, we assume firms produce and sell the amount that will maximize profit. In economic terms, this ends up meaning that every firm should produce an amount such that marginal revenue equals marginal cost (MR = MC). Recall the Chapter 1 concept of marginal analysis; this is our first opportunity to see it at work.

This is not as difficult as it seems. Remember that marginal revenue is the amount the firm brings in from selling one more unit, and the marginal cost is the amount of money that it costs to produce one more unit. To illustrate, suppose you start by selling a fixed number, say, 10 units. If you sell an eleventh and you make money on that sale (MR > MC), you should do it again and sell at least one more. If you sell an eleventh and you lose money on that sale (MR < MC), you should reduce sales by at least one. If marginal revenue is less than marginal cost for the eleventh chip, you should not have produced it. To maximize profit, you could repeat this one-by-one process until you have found the level of production that makes the most money. On the other hand, you now know that it is only when marginal cost equals marginal revenue that you have exhausted the profit potential on the good you are trying to sell.

THE RULES OF PRODUCTION

- A firm should produce an amount such that marginal revenue equals marginal cost (MR = MC).
- A firm should shut down if the price is less than the average variable cost (P < AVC) at the quantity where marginal revenue equals marginal cost.

Of course, it is possible that our entire business is a loser. In the age of word processors and cheap personal computers, the manual typewriter business would be a loser even if it was the only firm in this industry. The exception to the rule that a firm should produce where marginal cost equals marginal revenue occurs when the best alternative is to do nothing; that is, sometimes the best decision is to shut down the business. This occurs when the amount that you sell a good for is not enough to cover the variable costs that went into the production of the good. The firm should shut down if the price is less than the average variable cost (P < AVC).

Numerical Example

To illustrate profit maximization when there are many competitors, we need to combine the information in Tables 4.1 and 4.3; when there are no competitors, we need to combine the information in Tables 4.3 and 4.4. In either case, we need to pick a quantity to maximize profit. This is done where marginal cost equals marginal revenue. Table 4.5 illustrates this for the case where there are many competitors, and Table 4.6 does it for the case where there are no competitors. In Table 4.5, we see that the firm that has many competitors maximizes profit at $10,500, and this happens when the firm produces 800.[1] In Table 4.6, we see that the firm that has no competitors has its profit maximized at $9,000, and this happens when it produces 600. The graphical demonstration that profit is maximized where marginal cost equals marginal revenue is where we pick up in the next chapter.

Table 4.5
Numerical example: profit maximization when there are many competitors.

Q	Price	TR	TC	MR	MC	Profit
0	45	0	8,500	0	0	−8,500
100	45	4,500	11,000	45	25	−6,500
200	45	9,000	12,300	45	13	−3,300
300	45	13,500	13,300	45	10	200
400	45	18,000	14,500	45	12	3,500
500	45	22,500	16,000	45	15	6,500
600	45	27,000	18,000	45	20	9,000
700	45	31,500	21,000	45	30	10,500
800	**45**	**36,000**	**25,500**	**45**	**45**	**10,500**
900	45	40,500	31,000	45	55	9,500
1,000	45	45,000	41,000	45	100	4,000

Table 4.6
Numerical example: profit maximization when there are no competitors.

Q	Price	TR	TC	MR	MC	Profit
0	75	0	8,500	0	0	−8,500
100	70	7,000	11,000	70	25	−4,000
200	65	13,000	12,300	60	13	700
300	60	18,000	13,300	50	10	4,700
400	55	22,000	14,500	40	12	7,500
500	50	25,000	16,000	30	15	9,000
600	**45**	**27,000**	**18,000**	**20**	**20**	**9,000**
700	40	28,000	21,000	10	30	7,000
800	35	28,000	25,500	0	45	2,500
900	30	27,000	31,000	−10	55	−4,000
1,000	25	25,000	41,000	−20	100	−16,000

[1]In the next chapter, we will see that firms with many competitors see their profits disappear because new firms enter, thereby increasing market supply and lowering the price.

Summary

This chapter has illustrated production, costs, revenues, and profit maximization. For each concept and relationship, we considered verbal, graphical, and numerical explanations. We assumed that businesses choose their production levels to maximize profit and that, as a result, they set it where marginal cost equals marginal revenue.

Key Terms

accounting cost
average fixed cost (AFC)
average total cost (ATC)
average variable cost (AVC)
cost
cost function
diminishing returns
division of labor
economic cost
fixed costs
fixed inputs
marginal cost (MC)
marginal revenue (MR)
monopoly
perfect competition
production function
profit
revenue
total cost
variable costs
variable inputs

Quiz Yourself

1. When firms add workers and become more efficient, they are benefiting from
   a. the division of labor.
   b. diminishing returns.
   c. increasing marginal costs.
   d. diminishing marginal utility.
2. When firms add workers and find that the additional workers add less to output than their predecessors did, they are experiencing
   a. the division of labor.
   b. diminishing returns.
   c. increasing marginal costs.
   d. diminishing marginal utility.
3. Suppose a firm has $1,000,000 in fixed costs and variable costs equal to $100; for every unit it produces,
   a. its marginal costs are decreasing.
   b. its fixed costs are decreasing.
   c. its average costs are decreasing.
   d. marginal costs are increasing.
4. The marginal cost curve will intersect the average total cost curve at the latter's minimum as long as
   a. fixed costs are rising.
   b. average costs are decreasing.
   c. marginal costs eventually increase.
   d. marginal costs continually decrease.
5. Whether marginal revenue is constant or decreasing depends on
   a. whether the firm is benefiting from the division of labor.
   b. whether the firm is dealing with diminishing returns.
   c. the number of firms the competitor faces; if there are no other competing firms, it will be constant.
   d. the number of firms the competitor faces; if there are many competing firms, it will be constant.

6. When a firm chooses to shut down, it is
   a. making a poor decision because it should always produce where marginal cost equals marginal revenue.
   b. making a poor decision because it should always produce where average total cost exceeds average revenue.
   c. making a good decision as long as the price it is getting is less than its average total cost.
   d. making a good decision as long as the price it is getting is less than its average variable cost.
7. The result that a firm should produce where MC = MR (except when the shutdown condition is met) is based on the assumption that it is attempting to
   a. maximize profit.
   b. maximize market share.
   c. minimize marginal cost.
   d. minimize average total cost.
8. If a firm's marginal revenue exceeds its marginal cost,
   a. there is potential profit if it produces one less unit.
   b. there is potential profit if it produces one more unit.
   c. the firm is maximizing profit.
   d. the firm should shut down.

Short Answer Questions

1. What key assumption for perfect competition would lead you to believe that fast food is not a perfectly competitive industry? Explain why.
2. Suppose your favorite sports team is losing by an insurmountable score. What does the shutdown condition suggest the team should do? Explain why.
3. Does raising the price always increase revenue for the firm raising the price?
4. If your college leadership sought your advice on setting tuition, why would it matter if your college was the only college for miles?

Think about This

Why is it that when a firm has no competition it typically must lower the price to all consumers in order to sell more? What would have to happen for it to be able to lower the price only to new consumers?

Talk about This

We assume that the price to all consumers is the same. List the cases where the price to one person is different from the price to another. Why might a firm do this?

CHAPTER FIVE

Perfect Competition, Monopoly, and Economic versus Normal Profit

Learning Objectives

After reading this chapter you should be able to:

LO1 Illustrate maximized economic profit for perfectly competitive firms and monopolistic firms.

LO2 Distinguish between normal and economic profit.

LO3 Demonstrate and explain why economic profit disappears under perfect competition and monopolistic competition but not under oligopoly and monopoly.

LO4 Describe why, under perfect competition, the supply curve is the marginal cost curve above average variable cost.

Chapter Outline

In this chapter, we build on Chapter 4 to describe firms in different competitive situations. We show how firms at opposite ends of the competitive spectrum maximize profits. We show why, when there are many firms competing against one another, substantial profits are unsustainable. We conclude by demonstrating why the supply curve from Chapter 2 was upward sloping.

To start, we show that some firms, such as family farms, are among millions of firms in an industry, whereas other firms completely dominate their industry. We move on to show that there is a competitive continuum between these extremes. We categorize firms along this range and provide lists of distinguishing characteristics of firms in each category. We then establish a measure of the degree of competition in an industry and show that most familiar industries fall between the extremes.

In Chapter 4, we operated under the assumption that firms seek to maximize profits. What we want to do now is determine how well firms in various competitive situations succeed in sustaining profits. This allows us to show why it is that family farmers cannot seem to make consistently high profits, whereas Apple, Google, and Microsoft can. We'll approach these questions by separating profit into two categories: the profit that is necessary for firms to stay in business and the profit that is in excess of that level.

Last, we see that the supply curve laid out in Chapter 2 was indeed upward sloping for a reason. We will show that under perfect competition, an upward-sloping supply curve stems from the check-shaped marginal cost curve we studied in Chapter 4.

From Perfect Competition to Monopoly

As discussed in Chapter 4, the shape of the marginal revenue curve depends on whether there are many or no competitors. Figure 5.1 lays out these extreme cases by combining the cost curves from the previous chapter with the marginal revenue curve appropriate to the competitive situation. On the left, the cost curves are overlaid onto the marginal revenue curve from the many competitors case. On the right, the cost curves are overlaid onto the demand and marginal revenue curves from the no competitors case. The amount that both firms choose to produce in each case is labeled Q^*. The price they charge is labeled P^*.

Perfect Competition

The key difference between the cases outlined is the number of competitors. When the number of competitors is large, the firm (e.g., a dairy farm) simply must accept the market price as given but can sell as many goods as it can profitably produce at that price. When there are no competitors, the firm (e.g., Microsoft) can set any price it wants but can sell only the number that consumers want to buy at that price. Of course, not every firm is faced with the stark either–or difference. Some firms (e.g., Exxon) have only a few competitors in markets of similar or identical products, and other firms (e.g., McDonald's) have many competitors in markets where each has its own signature brand.

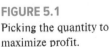

perfect competition A market type characterized by many small firms that have no control over price, are selling identical products, each have sufficient information to make good decisions, and face the threat of entry of new firms.

Perfect competition is a market type defined by a set of characteristics. It arises when firms face a large number of competitors that individually have no influence on the price they can charge, sell goods indistinguishable from one another, have good information about market conditions, and also face the threat of entry of new competitors. This may seem like an odd name given that the best examples of perfect competition are of sellers that do not really "compete" in the way noneconomists normally think of "competition." Whether it is Midwestern grain farmers; Western ranchers; Florida or California vegetable growers; Wisconsin, New York, or California dairy operations; or Georgia peach growers, the common conception of competition does not seem to apply. As individuals, they do not advertise. A conversation with any of these farmers would reveal that their best friends are their neighbor farmers. When one farm's equipment breaks down or a farmer has a significant health crisis at a critical planting or harvesting time, the neighborhood farmers come to help. That sounds more like cooperation than competition. So why do economists call this "perfect competition" when there does not seem to

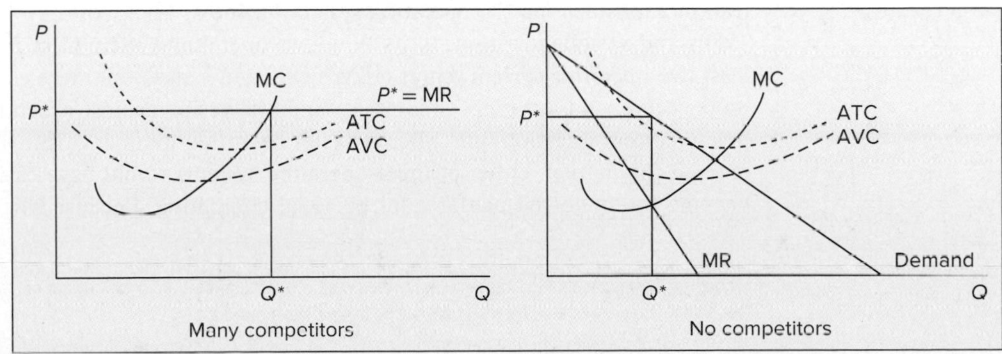

FIGURE 5.1 Picking the quantity to maximize profit.

CHARACTERISTICS OF PERFECT COMPETITION

- A large number of competitors, so that no one firm can influence the price.
- The good a firm sells is indistinguishable from those its competitors sell.
- Firms have good sales and cost forecasts.
- There is no legal or economic barrier to entry into or exit from the market.

be any true competition? The reason this is "perfect" goes back to the first characteristic of perfect competition: No one firm has any control over price. No farmers, of any farm product, have any control over the price of their produce when they sell it on the wholesale market.[1]

Monopoly

monopoly
The market form in which there is only one seller.

Monopolies exist at the other end of the spectrum, when we have markets in which there is only one firm. The important thing to know about the concept of **monopoly** is that the existence of many firms does not necessarily mean the firms are in competition. For instance, Consolidated Edison was the exclusive provider of residential electrical power to New York City, and Commonwealth Edison still is the exclusive service provider of residential electrical power to Chicago. There are hundreds of companies that provide residential electricity service in the United States, but very few of them compete with one another. While the generation of electricity is a competitive industry, the residential service providers are not competitors because they cannot sell in another's area. Just as a cement contractor in Little Rock, Arkansas, is not competing with a cement contractor in Miami for roadwork in south Florida because of transportation costs, electric companies do not compete with one another because they cannot access the same buyers. For monopoly, all that is necessary is that one firm and only one firm sells to the customers in a given market.

Some firms get their monopoly power because the law prevents others from entering the market. An example of a legal barrier to entry is a patent. For example, until recently, Gilead Sciences was the only firm with a medicinal cure to Hepatitis C. It was, therefore, the only firm that could produce and sell the drug.[2] On the other hand, some firms get their monopoly power by becoming such a large firm that competing against them is impossible. The frustration that consumers have with monopolies is the lack of choice that results from there being only one seller. While many may understand and accept the lack of choice when the good being sold is a utility with very high fixed costs, and others may understand and accept the need for patents and copyrights to motivate innovation, monopolies where the barriers to entry are simply associated with the size of the one monopolizing company often create anger and frustration. Consider the PC operating system business. Microsoft developed DOS in the early 1980s and various iterations of its Windows operating system after that. There have been at least two operating system genres (IBM's OS2 and Linux) that were considerably more stable, more secure, and less glitchy than the Windows version against which they attempted to compete. Without question, had Microsoft not been the dominant firm when these competitors entered the market, either of these operating systems would have easily beaten Windows to become the preferred platform for personal computing. Because Microsoft had the leading

[1] Though they may be able to charge any price they want at a local farmers' market, they are not perfect competitors there. In that setting, they are one of a few farmers selling that particular produce.

[2] Competing drugs (with different formulations by different manufacturers) entered the market in 2017.

position, it has been able to maintain it. Whether or not all of Microsoft's tactics were legal has certainly been questioned, but its ability to keep people buying its products has not. It maintains a dominant position because it has a dominant position.

Monopolistic Competition

monopolistic competition A situation in a market where there are many firms producing similar but not identical goods.

Now that we have established the extremes of the continuum of competition, it is time to explore what lies in between those extremes. While perfect competition is the most competitive market form, it is closely followed by **monopolistic competition.** This is the situation where there are many firms that sell slightly different products. In the fast-food market, there are quite a few firms (McDonald's, Wendy's, Burger King, etc., in burgers; KFC, Taco Bell, etc., in various niches), but they do not sell exactly the same good. McDonald's has a monopoly on the Big Mac and Happy Meal, but its competitors offer many close substitutes. This means that each firm has a monopoly on its particular menu, but the demand curve for the product is quite elastic. (Remember from Chapter 3 that the number of close substitutes determines elasticity.)

Oligopoly

oligopoly A situation in a market where there are very few discernible competitors.

Moving further along the continuum toward monopoly, we find **oligopoly.** That is the situation where there are very few discernible competitors. In the cell phone business, for example, there are major companies like AT&T, Sprint, and Verizon Wireless. In the soft drink business, there are Coke and Pepsi. In some markets, firms sell exactly the same thing, whereas in other markets, firms sell close substitutes. In either case, firms are acting in oligopolistic ways and referred to as oligopolies.

Which Model Fits Reality

Tables 5.1 and 5.2 summarize these market forms by providing examples and distinguishing characteristics of each type. That does not mean we will spend a great deal of time in the issues chapters worrying about market forms. Recall that in Chapter 2 we implicitly assumed that all markets were perfectly competitive. It turns out that very few markets meet the extreme criteria necessary to be categorized as perfect competition.

Table 5.1 Examples of different market forms.

Perfect Competition	Monopolistic Competition	Oligopoly	Monopoly
Agricultural products Lumber	Fast food Clothing	Smartphones Soft drinks	Operating systems Local residential electric power

Table 5.2 Distinguishing characteristics between market forms.

Characteristic	Perfect Competition	Monopolistic Competition	Oligopoly	Monopoly
Number of firms	Many (often thousands or even millions)	Several*	Few* (usually two to five)	One
Barriers to entry	None	Few	Substantial	Insurmountable, at least in the short run
Product similarity	Identical	Similar but not identical	Similar or identical	NA

*There is dispute about the line that separates monopolistic competition and oligopoly.

Most of the products that meet the criteria of perfect competition are agricultural; few products outside this area can make that claim. It may strike you, then, as somewhat curious that we will assume that most markets are perfectly competitive when we move into the issues. We do this because the supply and demand model is simple enough so that it can be used to explain and describe most markets where there are several competitors and the products are similar. You should understand that your instructor and I (the author) make this simplifying assumption reluctantly but knowingly.

Finally, you should be prepared for a high level of ambiguity in how particular markets fit into these forms. For instance, in the 1960s, for most Americans shopping for cars, there were "the big three" (GM, Ford, and Chrysler). Now there are more than 20 recognizable car companies, and the industry fits best under monopolistic competition. The personal computer business is similar in that there was only one firm, IBM, for many years, but today there are a dozen or more selling laptops and desktops. They all sell essentially the same thing but have a monopoly over their brand. The smartphone operating system industry is dominated by Apple and Google, with the device industry being dominated by Huawei, Apple, and Samsung.

Similarly, if you want to fly from New York to Los Angeles, you have a number of alternatives, perhaps not so many that it would be perfect competition but certainly enough to classify this service as monopolistic competition. On the other hand, if you want to fly directly from Indianapolis to Atlanta, you have two choices for nonstop flights (Southwest and Delta). If you want to fly directly from Syracuse to Detroit, you have only one choice (Delta). Where airline travel fits depends greatly on to where, and from where, you are traveling. In particular, it depends on who has a hub in the respective airports.

concentration ratio
A measure of the market power held by the top firms in an industry. For a specific number of firms (n), it is the percentage of total sales in the industry accounted for by top n firms.

Further, there is no magic line that separates oligopoly from monopolistic competition. Economists who study these things will often look to something called a **concentration ratio** that measures the percentage of total market sales for the top firms (from 4 firms to 100 firms). So even though there are several tobacco companies selling cigarettes, one company, Philip Morris, holds nearly half the U.S. market, and the top four hold all but 1 percent of the market. If there were several equally competitive firms, it would suggest monopolistic competition. Instead, there are several firms, but a few dominate, so oligopoly is a better fit. Table 5.3 presents 4-, 8-, and 50-firm concentration ratios for specific industries.

Table 5.3 Concentration ratios and Herfindahl-Hirschman indices for various industries, 2012.

	Concentration Ratios			
Industry Group	**4 Largest Firms**	**8 Largest Firms**	**50 Largest Firms**	**Herfindahl-Hirschman Index**
Breakfast cereals	79.2	93.7	100.0	2,332.5
Ice cream	45.9	64.6	94.0	665.8
Beer	87.8	90.8	95.9	3,560.7
Wine	45.3	58.0	75.2	785.3
Clothing	10.3	15.0	38.3	54.0
Computers and peripherals	31.5	46.0	80.6	421.9
Furniture	23.7	30.9	52.8	233.7
Automobile manufacturing	60.2	88.7	99.7	1,177.90
Cellular service	89.1	95.2	98.8	*

*This industry is so concentrated that the Census Bureau cannot report exactly how concentrated it is because doing so would provide competing firms with sales information of their individual competitors.

Not published for service providers.

Source: U.S. Census Bureau. "2012 Economic Census of the United States."

Herfindahl-Hirschman Index
A measure of market concentration developed by adding the sum of squared market shares.

Another index that economists, particularly those in the antitrust division of the Department of Justice, use is the **Herfindahl-Hirschman Index** (HHI). Instead of just adding together market shares of the largest firms, this adds the square of the market shares. This distinguishes a market where five firms have equal market shares from one in which the big firm has a large proportion of sales and the others simply split the rest. If the market share is between 0 and 100 percent and there are *N* firms, the HHI ranges between 10,000/*N* and 10,000. A number between 1,000 and 1,800 is considered moderately concentrated, while an index value greater than 1,800 is considered highly concentrated. The index value for breakfast cereals is above 2,500 and the one for cellular service is so high that the Census Bureau (that regularly published the statistics) must suppress the actual number to "protect the identity of any business. . . ." Essentially the industry is so concentrated that reporting the actual value provides the largest businesses information on others.

Supply under Perfect Competition

Normal versus Economic Profit

Let's return to the example we used in Chapter 4: the business of selling memory chips. If we are one of many firms competing in this industry, making a sustained profit will be deceptively difficult. Though we can sell all that we produce (because we are only a small part of the market), we can't count on the price remaining high enough for us to make a profit. That is because of our assumption of free entry into and exit from this market. Any time there are abnormally large profits, other firms will want to start making memory chips. Remember that Chapter 2 presented evidence that an increase in the number of sellers will move the supply curve to the right, thus lowering market price. If price falls, our marginal revenue curve will fall as well. As a matter of fact, it will fall all the way to where profit is normal. **Normal profit** is the level of profit that business owners could get in their next best alternative investment. The next best alternative would be whatever investment an owner would choose if he or she decided to go out of business. Any profit above normal profit is called **economic profit.**

normal profit
The level of profit that business owners could get in their next best alternative investment.

economic profit
Any profit above normal profit.

Return to Figure 5.1. In both examples, the firms are making an economic profit. We know that because the price they are charging is greater than their average total cost (P > ATC). If they were only making normal profit, the price would exactly equal average total cost (P = ATC).

If business owners do not make their normal profit, they will quit the business and move into another. This means that we might think of normal profit as the salary the business owners pay themselves and, as such, part of the "cost of doing business." If they make less than normal profit, then the salary they can pay themselves is too low to keep them in the industry. In that sense, normal profit is built in to ATC. On the other hand, if profits are routinely more than that, others will want to enter the industry. This means that in the long run profit will shrink to normal levels.

When and Why Economic Profits Go to Zero

Fortunately for our chip maker, although the firm cannot make long-run economic profits, it is not going to lose money (make less than normal profit) for long either. When firms lose more money than their fixed costs, they shut down. In the short run, firms will continue to produce when they lose less than their fixed costs, but as time passes these firms will also want to shut down. So, though our chip maker can make economic profit in the short run and lose money in the short run, the effect of free entry and exit in this market will cause the marginal revenue

A NEARLY PERFECT EXAMPLE OF THE IMPORTANCE OF ENTRY AND EXIT

A nearly perfect example of the importance of entry and exit in explaining why and when economic profits go to zero is the crude oil industry and the experience since 2014. Prior to mid-2014, hydraulic fracturing and horizontal drilling, though invented, hadn't had a dramatic impact on world oil supplies. Because of that, OPEC countries had tight control over supplies and the market was largely oligopolistic (with OPEC operating like one enormously powerful firm in a market with other, smaller producers). OPEC made the decisions and everyone else just went along.

In 2014, that began to change when those new technologies transformed the industry. North Dakota's production took off and once-idled oil fields in Texas and Oklahoma resumed production. The result was a dramatic decline in crude prices. From $107 per barrel in mid-2014, to below $30 per barrel in early 2016, the economic profit was completely wrung out of the industry due to entry. Economic losses replaced economic profits. Though producers usually pump from a well until it's dry, when the price drops, they don't drill new wells. That is because most of the costs associated with oil production are drilling costs, not pumping costs.

Since that time, oil prices have remained stable (by historic standards) as entry (drilling) occurs when prices rise and exit (pumping a well until it's dry and then not drilling a new one) occurs when prices fall. When entry and exit are relatively easy, as they are now in the oil industry, economic profits dwindle. When entry was impossible, OPEC could charge what it wanted. For OPEC members, those "good old days" are not likely to reappear.

curve to settle at the minimum of the U-shaped average total cost. Any short-run profit or loss will evaporate in the long run because new competitors will enter or old ones will exit. Both of these behaviors drive the price toward the minimum of average total cost where profit is normal.

Though profit also shrinks to its normal level under monopolistic competition, there is no mechanism for profits to shrink to normal levels under oligopoly or monopoly. This is because the mechanism that shrinks profit is entry. Because entry is almost insurmountable under monopoly and substantially difficult under oligopoly, new firms do not come in to put the pressure on the price to fall. For the same reason, it is uncommon for firms to exit.

At this point, we need to pause for a moment to define more explicitly what economists mean by short run and long run. To an economist, the distinction between the two is whether the firm has the ability to change its fixed inputs. So far, we have assumed that we cannot change things like plant and equipment (our fixed inputs), and this is true in what we call the **short run.** In the **long run,** there is enough time (or sufficient flexibility) to change these inputs and their costs are no longer fixed. We can either buy more plant and more equipment, or we can sell what we have. The distinction is thus not only one of time but of flexibility; in the long run, we are more flexible and in the short run less flexible.

short run
The period of time where a firm cannot change things like plant and equipment.

long run
The period of time where a firm can change things like plant and equipment.

Why Supply Is Marginal Cost under Perfect Competition

Showing that, under perfect competition, supply and marginal cost are interchangeable is important for several of the issues that follow, but it is also notoriously difficult. That is why we will go back to the three approaches used in Chapter 4. We'll start with the "Just Words" and "Numerical Example" approaches and end with the "Graphical Explanation."

Just Words

In order to see that, under perfect competition, supply and marginal cost are interchangeable, you need to recall two key facts from Chapter 4: (1) All profit-maximizing firms will choose to produce where marginal cost equals marginal revenue (as long as price is greater than average variable cost) and (2) under perfect competition, price and marginal revenue are the same.

With that in mind, imagine that a perfectly competitive firm is trying to decide how much to produce. It will take the price that is given to it by the market (which is also the firm's marginal revenue) and set production where that price equals its marginal cost. If the price rises or falls, it will do the calculation again. In every case, the quantity at which marginal revenue equals marginal cost is the same as the quantity at which price equals marginal cost. In every case, the relationship between quantity produced and the marginal cost of producing it (the marginal cost curve) is the same as the relationship between the quantity produced and the price at which it is sold (the supply curve). So, under perfect competition, supply and marginal cost are interchangeable.

Numerical Example

Using the memory chips example again, you can see from Table 4.2 that the average variable cost reaches a minimum at $15 per unit at the quantity of 500 units. This is important because at any price below $15, the firm will choose not to produce any units. To see that, suppose the price were $12 per unit. Marginal cost equals marginal revenue ($12) at 400 units, but at 400 units the firm's total revenue will be $4,800 ($12 × 400), while its total cost will be $14,500, and it will lose more money by continuing production ($9,700 = $14,500 − $4,800) than it would if it simply shut down ($8,500).

At every price above $15, the firm either makes money or at least loses less than $8,500, and therefore it makes sense for the firm to produce where marginal cost equals marginal revenue. If the price were exactly $15, the firm would produce 500 units, have $7,500 ($15 × 500) in total revenue, $16,000 in total cost, and lose exactly its fixed costs, meaning the firm will continue to produce. If the price were $20, the firm would produce 600 units, bringing $12,000 in revenue while costing $18,000, and the loss is $6,000. The firm would rather lose $6,000 than $8,500 (what it would lose if it shut down), so it produces 600 units.

As the price rises to $30, it produces 700 units, has both revenue and cost of $21,000, and breaks even. At a price of $45 it produces 800 units, has revenue of $36,000, costs of $25,500, and makes a profit. At a price of $55 it produces 900 units, has revenue of $49,500, costs of $31,000, and its profit increases. Finally, at a price of $100, it produces 1,000, has revenue of $100,000, costs of $41,000, and its profit increases further. Putting it all together, the firm's supply curve is its marginal cost curve (out of the minimum of average variable cost) because optimal firm production is where marginal revenue (which is price) equals marginal cost. Therefore, the relationship between its marginal cost and its production (its marginal cost curve) is the same as the relationship between the price it will receive and its production (its supply curve).

Graphical Explanation

Figure 5.2 shows the chip maker's ATC-AVC-MC cost curve diagram with four potential marginal revenue curves. For each, if there is pressure on the price to change in the short run, this is indicated with a short arrow in the direction of the pressure. If there is long-run pressure, this is indicated with a long arrow. At the first price/marginal revenue, MR_1, the loss is so big that firms want to exit in both the short and the long run. This will reduce the number of sellers, and the market price will rise in both the short run and the long run. At MR_2, the chip maker is losing money but not enough for it to shut down. So, though the firm does not want to shut down in the short run, it will want to shut down rather than invest money in new equipment as the old equipment wears out. Therefore, the long-run pressure is for the price to rise. At MR_4 our chip maker is making an economic profit. If this happens, others will want to join the chip-making industry and there will be short- and long run pressure for the price to fall. It is

FIGURE 5.2 In perfect competition, the market price is under pressure to move to where economic profit is zero.

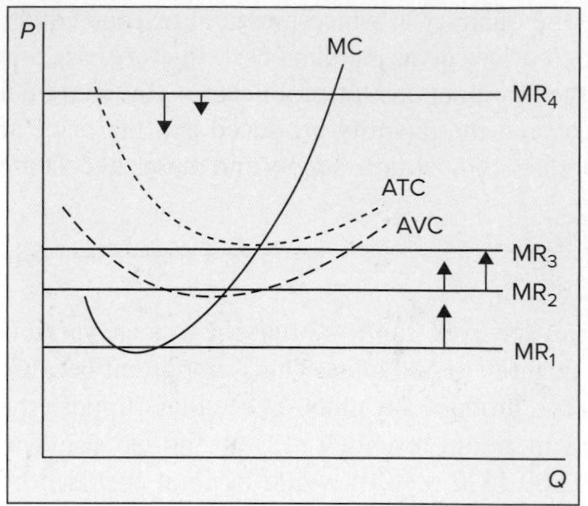

FIGURE 5.3 Points where MC = MR in perfect competition.

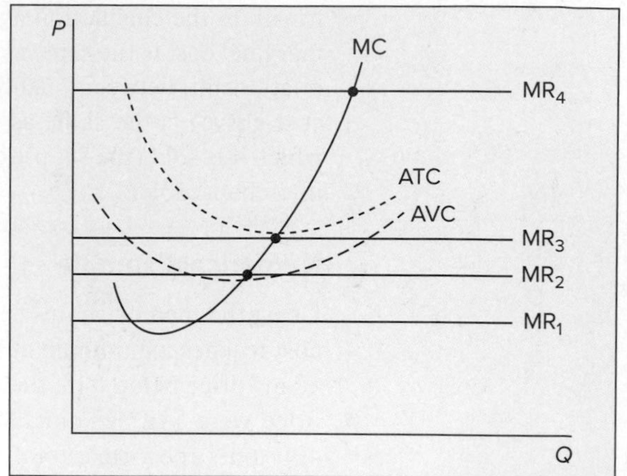

only when the price is at MR_3 that there is no pressure on the price. That is because the firm is making normal profit at that price.

Now to why under perfect competition a firm's supply curve is its marginal cost curve out of the minimum of its average variable cost. In Figure 5.3, the arrows from Figure 5.2 have been taken away and the points where the firm will produce are indicated by a dot. These points appear where marginal cost crosses marginal revenue, a circumstance that will occur only if firms do not shut down.

In our final manipulation of the figure, we arrive at one of the most important implications of perfect competition. Connecting the dots of Figure 5.3 makes clear the relationship between the price of the chips our firm is selling and the number of chips our firm is willing to produce. If that sounds familiar, it is because that is exactly the definition of supply. As a result, we now know that supply, under perfect competition, is marginal cost out of the minimum of average variable cost. This, of course, also demonstrates why the supply curve is upward sloping: Marginal cost is increasing.

FIGURE 5.4 Derivation of supply: marginal cost out of the minimum of average variable cost.

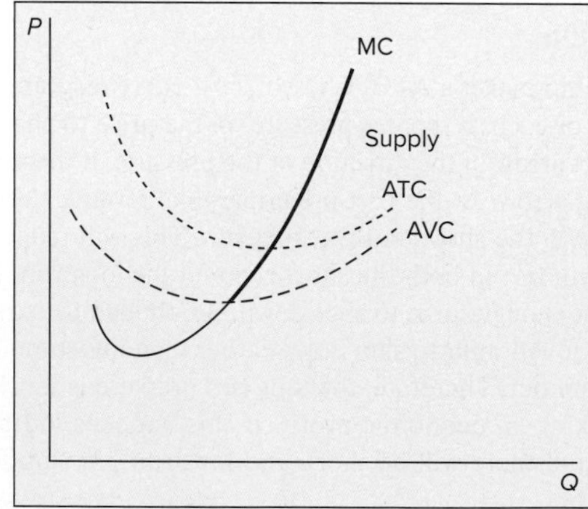

Although more difficult to show than it is worth, it is important to state that there is no supply curve under monopolistic competition, oligopoly, or monopoly. To understand the reason, note that Figure 5.4 generates the supply curve by finding the production levels with a variety of different prices. Recall from Figure 3.5 that these horizontal price lines also represent perfectly elastic demand curves for a particular firm's output. This same derivation does not work for the other market forms because the elasticity of demand for a firm's output is not perfectly elastic and demand curves of different elasticities result in different profit-maximizing firm output.

Summary

This chapter built on the previous one in which costs and revenues were defined and illustrated. We saw the distinction between perfect competition and monopoly and that they are the endpoints of the market form continuum. We said that most markets operate somewhere in the middle of this continuum. Further, we distinguished between normal and economic profit, and showed why economic profit disappears under perfect competition but not under monopoly. Last, we saw that under perfect competition, the supply curve from Chapter 2 is the part of the check-shaped marginal cost curve from Chapter 4 that is above average variable cost and is therefore upward sloping.

Key Terms

- concentration ratio
- economic profit
- Herfindahl-Hirschman Index
- long run
- monopolistic competition
- monopoly
- normal profit
- oligopoly
- perfect competition
- short run

Issues Chapters You Are Ready for Now

- The Economics of Prescription Drugs
- Ticket Brokers and Ticket Scalping
- The Economics of K-12 Education
- Energy Prices
- Unions
- Walmart: Always Low Prices (and Low Wages)—Always
- The Economic Impact of Casino and Sports Gambling

Quiz Yourself

1. An industry in which there are two competitors is likely to be characterized by
   a. monopoly.
   b. oligopoly.
   c. monopolistic competition.
   d. perfect competition.
2. An industry in which there are a very large number of firms is likely to be characterized by
   a. monopoly.
   b. oligopoly.
   c. monopolistic competition.
   d. perfect competition.
3. Owing to its usefulness and relative simplicity, the supply and demand model is often used
   a. because nearly every major industry in the United States is governed by perfect competition.
   b. because nearly every major industry in the United States is governed by monopoly.
   c. even though, strictly speaking, few industries in the United States are governed by perfect competition.
   d. even though it has no connection to economic reality.
4. Whether a firm stays in business or shuts down depends heavily on the concept of
   a. economic profit.
   b. actual profit.
   c. market share.
   d. concentration ratios.

5. Economic theory would suggest that the profitability of an industry would be
   a. directly related to the number of firms competing in the industry.
   b. inversely related to the number of firms competing in the industry.
   c. unrelated to the number of firms competing in the industry.
   d. zero in the long run, regardless of market structure.
6. If there were three firms in an industry with identical sales, the concentration ratio would be ____ and the HHI would be ____.
   a. 100 percent; 33.33
   b. 33.33 percent; 3,333
   c. 100 percent; 3,333
   d. 100 percent; 10,000
7. An indicator of the degree of competition in an industry is the concentration ratio. It measures
   a. the percentage of sales in the industry by the largest firms.
   b. the percentage of profit in the industry by the smallest firms.
   c. the sales in the industry as a percentage of all consumption in the United States.
   d. the profitability of the industry.
8. Suppose you overheard two of your fellow economics students arguing about where Internet service fits into the spectrum of market forms.
   a. The one arguing that it is a monopoly would clearly be correct.
   b. The one arguing that it is an oligopoly would clearly be correct.
   c. Neither would be correct.
   d. Both could be correct because if the one arguing for monopoly lived in a small town with one option and the other lived in a city with three options, both would be correct given their experience.
9. In a diagram of perfect competition, the marginal revenue line moves up and down when there is exit and entry, respectively, because
   a. the market demand for the good rises and falls when there is exit and entry, respectively.
   b. the market demand for the good rises and falls when there is entry and exit, respectively.
   c. the market supply for the good rises and falls when there is exit and entry, respectively.
   d. the market supply for the good rises and falls when there is entry and exit, respectively.
10. Under perfect competition, the supply curve is
    a. the marginal cost curve for all price-quantity combinations.
    b. the marginal cost curve, but only that portion that is downward sloping.
    c. the marginal cost curve, but only that portion that is upward sloping.
    d. the marginal cost curve, but only that portion that is above the minimum of average variable cost.

Short Answer Questions

1. Imagine an owner of a firm is thinking about raising prices. Describe the consequences of doing so as a monopolist, oligopolist, monopolistic competitor, and perfect competitor.
2. What are the key differences between monopolistic competition and perfect competition?

3. Describe why there is pressure on the price to fall when P > ATC. Is there a long- and short-run distinction in the answer?
4. Describe why there is pressure on the price to fall when P < ATC. Is there a long- and short-run distinction in the answer?

Think about This

One of the concerns about Walmart's entry into the grocery business in the latter part of the 1990s was that it would set low prices, drive little stores out of business, and then raise prices to monopoly levels when it had no competition. That hasn't happened, but that doesn't mean it couldn't happen. Under what conditions, and in what industries, might such a strategy work?

Talk about This

List the monopolies that used to exist when you were growing up that are now facing increased competition. Compare that list to a list provided by your instructor (who is presumably older than you). What current monopolies are likely to be threatened with entry in the future?

Behind the Numbers

U.S. Census Bureau: www.census.gov/econ/concentration.html

- Concentration ratios for largest 4, 8, and 50 firms in various industries
- Herfindahl-Hirchman Index

CHAPTER SIX

Every Macroeconomic Word You Ever Heard: Gross Domestic Product, Inflation, Unemployment, Recession, and Depression

Learning Objectives

After reading this chapter you should be able to:

LO1 Describe how the economy is measured.

LO2 Describe how gross domestic product is calculated.

LO3 Calculate inflation using a price index.

LO4 Describe real gross domestic product and judge its use as the measure of the economy's health.

LO5 Describe how unemployment is measured and enumerate the types of unemployment that economists recognize.

LO6 Describe the alternative measures of productivity.

LO7 Describe the necessity for seasonal adjustment in most economic data.

LO8 Define and apply the vocabulary of the business cycle.

Chapter Outline

We shift gears now to talk about the economy as a whole rather than the consumption or production of specific goods. What we covered in Chapters 2 through 5 is called **microeconomics**, because it deals with individual markets and firms. The prefix *micro*, meaning small, applies here because of the narrow scope of microeconomics. The opposite prefix, *macro*, means large, so **macroeconomics** deals with the economy as a whole. When you read or hear "economic news" you more often than not get macroeconomic news. With this type of news, you often encounter the same words over and over again. In this chapter, we'll define and explain the vocabulary of macroeconomics.

microeconomics
The part of the discipline of economics that deals with individual markets and firms.

macroeconomics
The part of the discipline of economics that deals with the economy as a whole.

We begin the chapter by examining the methods by which we measure the macroeconomy. In that process, we define and explain gross domestic product, inflation, and how and why the gross domestic product is adjusted for inflation. From there, we explain how unemployment is measured, and we proceed to a discussion of the business cycle. You will see that all of these economic measures have flaws that economists recognize and study and that, though real gross domestic product is an accepted measure of the economy's health, it is not a perfect measure of our nation's overall health.

This is by far the most easily understood chapter of all the theory chapters, but you should make sure that you understand the terms and the concepts behind them thoroughly. Chapter 8 and other macro-oriented issues chapters rely on them heavily.

Measuring the Economy

Measuring Nominal Output

To determine how well or how poorly the economy is doing, we measure economic activity by adding up the dollar value of all of the goods and services produced for final sale in the United States in a year. The **gross domestic product (GDP)** is the primary measure of the health of the economy, and some important concepts within this definition need to be highlighted:

gross domestic product (GDP)
The dollar value of all of the goods and services produced for final sale in the United States in a year.

1. This is a dollar-denominated measure that is subject to price variability.
2. Only "final" sales are counted.
3. The goods that are counted must be goods produced within the United States.

The first issue listed above requires a complete explanation of *inflation*. However, we can easily explore the second and third items here.

To avoid the double-counting of certain economic activity, only final sales are counted. Let's consider the production and sale of two hypothetical loaves of bread. The first loaf is produced by a woman who grows and grinds the wheat, mixes the dough, bakes the loaf, and sells it to a customer all by herself. The other loaf begins with a farmer who grows the wheat and sells it to a miller, who grinds it into flour and sells the flour to a baker, who mixes the dough, bakes the loaf, and sells the loaf to a retailer, who sells the loaf to a customer. If both loaves are of equal quality, then both should be sold for the same price: say, one dollar. Clearly both loaves contribute the same to the amount of bread available to society, so both should count the same when we measure economic activity. If you summed all of the intermediate sales along the way, however, the second loaf would count more than the first. By only counting final sales, you treat equal loaves equally. Both result in the same impact on GDP.

The other aspect of this measure is that it counts production only if it takes place within the borders of the United States. This means the Fords produced in Mexico are not counted in the U.S. GDP, but the Hondas produced in Ohio are.

The actual computation of the GDP is done in two distinct ways. One way is to count all those things for which people pay money. This is called the *expenditures approach.* The expenditures approach adds up all of the following: consumption (C), investment (I), government spending on goods and services (G), and exports (X); then it subtracts imports (M). Using the expenditures approach, GDP is therefore computed as C+ I + G + X − M.

The other approach, which counts all those ways in which people earn money, is called the *income approach.* This approach adds up employee compensation, interest, rents, profits, and depreciation and then subtracts income earned in other countries and indirect business taxes (such as sales taxes). Both approaches yield the same result because the money that the buyer "spends" is, by definition, the seller's "income." Therefore, adding up everyone's income and everyone's spending yields the same sum.

The sources that the government uses to compute this information are wide and varied. They are known as the National Income and Product Accounts, and compiling them is complicated and time-consuming. For instance, while the government knows quickly and reliably how much it spends on goods and services, nearly every other piece of information included in the GDP has to come from forms that businesses send to the government: tax forms, unemployment insurance forms, reports of sales and sales taxes, and other documentation. It is therefore obvious, but it warrants noting, that trying to produce the final GDP quickly is difficult. What actually happens is that government economists use sampling techniques to produce preliminary estimates that are repeatedly updated as more information is submitted. When all information is in, sometimes more than a year after the first preliminary estimate is made, a final GDP value is published.[1]

HOW DOES IT COUNT IN GDP?

Issue	How It Counts in GDP (C + I + G + X − M)
A product made in one year but sold in a later year	GDP counts the value of the product made but not yet sold as an increase to business INVESTMENT (I), of which inventories are a part. So if it is made in December, investment increases at that time. When it is sold, investment drops but either CONSUMPTION (C) or EXPORTS (X) increases. Typically a good goes into inventories at its wholesale value so when it is sold at the retail level, the increase in consumption or exports is greater than the decrease in inventories.
A used car is sold	The only part of a used car sale that counts is the markup from its purchase price from the previous owner to the sale to the next owner. That is the value the used car dealer created in cleaning and preparing the car for sale.
Stock sold in a stock market	Personal investment and business investment are two different things. It is only when a business uses the sale of (initial public offering) stock to raise money to buy equipment and inventory that there is any intersection between the two concepts.
How illegal drug sales are counted	The simple fact is they aren't, and it isn't because they shouldn't be. Only recorded sales (typically sales tax reports) that are part of the system of business reporting to state and federal governments count.

[1] Even then, some components are estimates.

Measuring Prices and Inflation

As we said in the previous section, measuring price changes is important. Whether price changes account for changes in the GDP or whether actual production changes account for those changes is vital to the question of whether we are better off in one period than we were in a previous period. A GDP number that increases because prices rise is less desirable than a GDP value that increases because people are actually buying products in greater quantities. For instance, let's make the simplifying assumption that there is only one good in society, cheese, we produce 10 trillion tons of cheese in one year, and cheese is sold at a price of $1/ton. That is vastly better than if we produce only one ton of cheese that is sold at a price of $10 trillion. Clearly, to discuss the value of production, we must discuss how we measure prices.

The way that government economists measure prices is intricate. Each month, employees of the Bureau of Labor Statistics (BLS) survey the prices of a **market basket** of goods and services in an effort to see if the total cost of that market basket has changed in the current year from what it was in the previous year. To do this, they have to establish what should go into that market basket through a process of figuring out what average people buy and in what quantities they buy it. This market basket then makes up a kind of "grocery list" of sorts. With the rapid expansion of available products, the BLS has recently chosen to update the market basket every two years. Their old practice of updating the market basket only every 10 years led to significant problems.[2]

market basket Goods that average people buy and the quantities they buy them in.

The "list" of items for which government employees go out every month to find prices is very specific, not only indicating what model number or UPC code to look for but also specifying stores in which the goods need to be located. Frequently, especially with electronic equipment, the item that the employee is supposed to find no longer exists or no longer exists at the specified store. In that case, employees must use their best judgment to find a suitable substitute and record key attributes of the good.[3]

For each month for which the list is in effect, BLS employees find the prices of everything on the list. These numbers are put into the form of an index number. For indexes of this type, a **base year** is chosen. This is the year to which all other prices are compared. When they finish, a national average is computed. The result constitutes the first key piece of information necessary to compute future inflation: It is the national average of the total cost of the market basket. It is called the **price of the market basket in the base year.** In succeeding months, a new national average is generated on the basis of new information on prices.

base year Year to which all other prices are compared

price of the market basket in the base year National average of the total cost of the market basket.

To use this information to measure inflation in any given year, we have to go through three distinct steps:

1. We find the price of the market basket in the relevant years.
2. We compute a price index for the relevant years.
3. We compute the percentage of change in the relevant price indices.

After arriving at the price of the market basket in the base year, we must also find the price of the market basket in the other years of interest. For instance, if you ultimately wanted to know the inflation rate for 2018, you would need the price of the market basket in the base year, 1998, the price of the market basket at the beginning of 2018, and finally the price of the market basket at the beginning of 2019.

[2] In 1996, the Boskin Commission established that measuring inflation the original way overstated the true inflation rate by 1.1 percentage points. In response to this criticism and in recognition of these problems, the BLS corrected some of these flaws by going to a two-year cycle on market basket updates.

[3] The BLS then constructs a "hedonic price" for these goods. A hedonic price is an educated guess at what the price of the original good would have been given its characteristics. The BLS constructs hedonic prices for clothes dryers, microwave ovens, refrigerators, camcorders, consumer audio products, DVD players, and college textbooks.

price index
A device that centers the price of the market basket around 100.

consumer price index (CPI)
The price index based on what average consumers buy.

inflation
The percentage change in the consumer price index.

Next, a **price index,** which centers the price of the market basket around 100, is computed for the beginning of 2018 and 2019. For instance, the **consumer price index (CPI)** for 2018 is

$$\text{CPI in 2018} = \frac{\text{Price of the market basket in 2018}}{\text{Price of the market basket in the base year of 1998}} \times 100\%$$

This formula can be interpreted to mean that in the base year the CPI is 100. At other times, as prices rise, the CPI will rise above 100. If prices eventually become twice what they were in the base year, the CPI will be 200.

Inflation is the percentage change in the price index. To compute, you take the CPI at the beginning of the year and the CPI at the beginning of the next year and plug them into the following formula

$$\text{Inflation during 2018} = \frac{\text{CPI on January 1, 2019} - \text{CPI on January 1, 2018}}{\text{CPI on January 1, 2018}} \times 100\%$$

cost-of-living adjustment (COLA)
A device that compensates people for the fact that changes in inflation change the spending power of their income.

As a practical matter, the CPI is important for another reason. For economists, it is important because it is used to generate not only an inflation rate, the percentage increase in the CPI, but also the **cost-of-living adjustment,** or **COLA.** This adjustment compensates people for the fact that changes in inflation also change the spending power of their income. For social security recipients and others on pensions that pay a COLA, as well as union members with contracts that are tied to a COLA, this represents the extra income they get each year to compensate them for inflation.[4] Table 6.1 presents a historical picture of the CPI.

Problems Measuring Inflation

We now have a measure of inflation that gives us helpful information on how the total price of a given market basket changes. For several reasons, however, it does not do a very good job measuring the true impact of inflation. The first way in which the CPI can estimate inflation inaccurately is the result of the two-year period between changes in the market basket. Specifically, large price decreases that occur in the first two years after the introduction of a product are ignored.

Table 6.1
CPI and inflation in selected years, 1920–2018; base years 1982–1984.

Year	CPI	Inflation Rate (%)	Year	CPI	Inflation Rate (%)	Year	CPI	Inflation Rate (%)
1920	19.4		2001	177.4	1.6	2010	220.5	1.4
1930	16.1		2002	181.8	2.5	2011	227.1	3.0
1940	14.1		2003	185.5	2.0	2012	231.1	1.8
1950	25.0		2004	191.7	3.3	2013	234.7	1.5
1960	29.8		2005	198.1	3.3	2014	236.3	0.7
1970	39.8		2006	203.1	2.5	2015	237.8	0.7
1980	86.4	12.4	2007	211.4	4.1	2016	242.8	2.1
1990	134.2	6.3	2008	211.4	0.0	2017	247.9	2.1
2000	174.6	3.4	2009	217.4	2.8	2018	252.7	1.9

Note: CPI is year-end figure.

Source: Bureau of Labor Statistics. https://data.bls.gov/pdq/SurveyOutputServlet

[4] Social Security uses the end of June CPI to compute the COLA. By law, Social Security checks to individuals cannot fall, which means that if prices fall, the Social Security Administration simply does not increase benefits until the CPI rises to above its previous higher level. Because the June 2008 to June 2009 CPI fell and because the June 2010 level did not rise to the June 2008 level, Social Security recipients received no COLA for two years. The same thing happened in 2015 when plummeting gasoline prices held the CPI down so much that overall inflation was zero.

INFLATION'S WINNERS AND LOSERS

An interesting aspect of inflation is that it creates its own set of winners and losers. People living on fixed incomes will be highly sensitive to inflation, and because people who borrow money are paying it back with dollars that are less valuable than the money they borrowed, both they and the lending institutions from whom they borrow will have a stake in the rate of inflation.

Anyone receiving a fixed amount of money per month or per year through an investment or having a fixed amount of cash that they must stretch over a long period of time will be unambiguously hurt by inflation. They will see their buying power drop incrementally over time. To see how important that is, suppose a 65-year-old new retiree sets up an annuity so that she gets $20,000 a year until she dies. If she lives 20 additional years and inflation is running at 5 percent per year, the buying power of that money will be 62 percent lower. Even if inflation is running at a modest 2 percent per year, her buying power will be 33 percent lower. While good financial planners will account for this when setting up such annuities for their clients, retirees who forgo investment advice can get caught in this trap.

In the arena of borrowing and lending, there are also winners and losers. Here the important question is not necessarily whether there is inflation but whether inflation is greater than was expected by the respective parties. If inflation is greater than was expected when the interest rate on the loan was established, then borrowers are winners because they are paying the loan back using less valuable dollars than they anticipated. If borrowers are the winners, then lenders are clearly the losers in that they are receiving less valuable dollars in return. Of course, each "dollar" is still worth a dollar, but with inflation running above expectations, each dollar buys less than it was expected to be able to buy when the loan was established.

On the other hand, if inflation runs less than was expected, the lender is the winner and the borrower is the loser. The borrower is paying the loan back with dollars that have more spending power than they were anticipated to have and the lender is receiving those more valuable dollars.

The history of consumer electronics provides many examples of this. The very first mass-marketed calculator, the HP-35, sold for nearly $400. It was less than a quarter of that price in two years. The first VHS and DVD players were more than $1,000 and soon were under $400 (and under $50 today). Apple's first iPhone was $600 and fell to a third of that within a few years.[5] When the market basket updates were on a 10-year cycle, most consumer electronics did not come into the market basket until several years after their introduction. In all of these cases, large price decreases and significant quality improvements occurred long before their inclusion. Though the CPI methodology will eventually pick up the final fall in prices once the products are included, it will fail to pick up the initial price drops.

The second way in which the CPI may assess inflation inaccurately relates to quality improvements in electronics, which may occur so quickly that by the end of the final year of the market basket, the good that was originally included no longer exists. The best example of this is the personal computer. Recognizing this, in 2006, the BLS began to adjust for quality improvements in certain goods.

Third, people have significantly changed the places in which they buy goods. For instance, in the 1950s, television sets were, by and large, purchased in department stores or small appliance stores. Although the personal service customers received during this period undoubtedly exceeded the level of service we now get at large discount stores or warehouse clubs, the price we pay when we make our purchases at discount stores is also much lower. One of the impacts of e-retailers such as Amazon is that some consumers are shifting their purchases in favor of greater convenience. Consumers who shop this way are showing their preference for convenience over low prices.

If you remember, the government employees who go looking at prices do so at the specific stores designated at the beginning of the life of the market basket. Because they change the store to match consumer behavior only when they change the market basket, they may fail to capture

[5] In more recent years, Apple changed its marketing strategy to upgrade speed, size, and features rather than to lower price.

OTHER PRICE INDICES

core CPI
The consumer price index that has had the impact of food and energy costs removed.

core PCE
The Personal Consumption Expenditures deflator that has had the impact of food and energy costs removed.

Personal Consumption Expenditures deflator
A chain-based price index that adjusts for the substitution problem.

Producer Price Index
A price index based on what firms buy.

Because inflation is damaging to an economy and extreme inflation can be very dangerous, the Federal Reserve Board keeps close tabs on it. As we will see in Chapters 8 and 12, the Fed, for short, adjusts short-term interest rates to keep inflation in check. If you look behind the numbers of the CPI you find that it is highly variable. That is why the Fed looks at two more stable price indices. Both are called the core rates because they eliminate the impact of highly volatile food and energy prices. The **core CPI** is based on the traditional CPI, while the **core PCE** strips out the costs of food and energy from a different price index, called the **Personal Consumption Expenditures deflator.** You can see from Figure 6.1 that the core CPI and the core PCE are much more stable than the CPI itself. Because the Fed does not want to overreact to rapid changes in volatile sectors, it focuses its attention on these core measures.

Finally, there is also an index of input items for firms, called the **Producer Price Index.** It is often useful as a look ahead at what inflation will be in a few months as firms turn those inputs into goods that they sell.

FIGURE 6.1 CPI, core CPI, and core PCE.

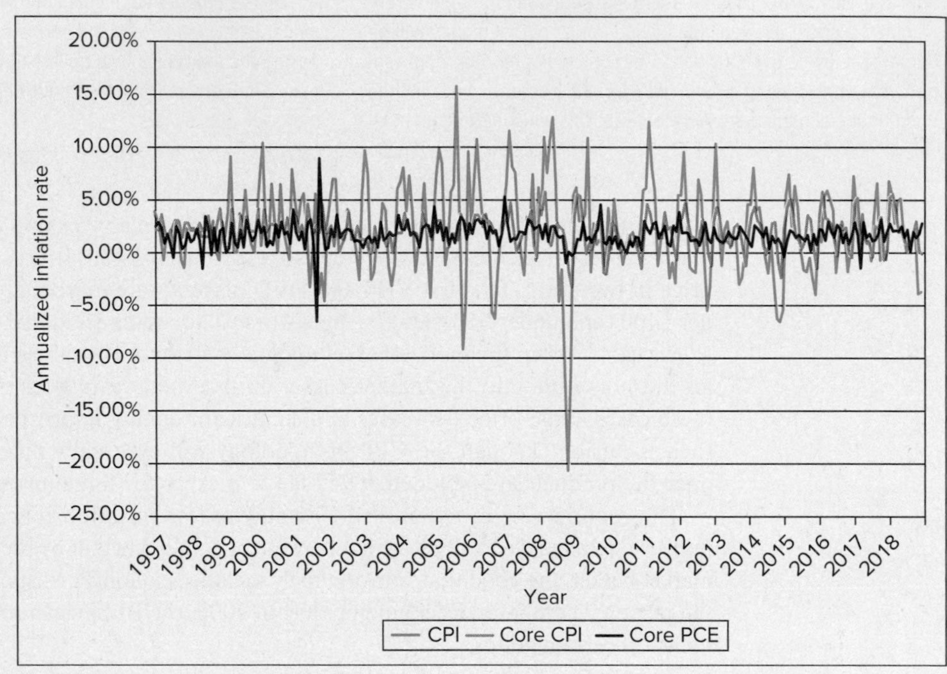

a significant source of price decreases. In this way, the BLS continues to lag behind actual behavior regarding Internet shopping.

Fourth, when prices change dramatically, people look for substitutes. Because the market basket is fixed for a two-year period, it is implicitly assumed that people mindlessly buy exactly the same amount of everything, every period, regardless of prices. This is surely a silly assumption for economists to make, given that much of Chapter 2 was devoted to how people react to price changes. For an example of how failing to account for substitution can overstate the effects of an increase in the price of one good, consider energy prices. In 2008, gasoline prices climbed from $2 per gallon to more than $4.20 per gallon. Many people sold their SUVs and bought more fuel-efficient cars, or simply drove less. When prices fell between 2014 and 2019 to $2.00, automakers began eliminating cars from their lineups in favor of those same gas-hogging SUVs.

In response to this criticism and in recognition of these problems, the BLS began an effort to correct some of these flaws. First, as mentioned above, they make an explicit effort to account for the consumer electronics quality problem. Second, they now reestablish the market basket every 2 years rather than every 10 years. This allows for new goods to enter the market basket much more quickly and have at least a portion of the initial drops in price count. It also allows the BLS to account for substitution between goods when there are long-term changes in prices. This **chain-based index** represents progress as far as economists are concerned.

chain-based index
A price index based on an annually adjusted market basket.

Still, these efforts have not solved the problem entirely. In a summary of the issues, David Lebow and Jeremy Rudd reported that the degree of error in the CPI has been cut to less than a percentage point. Though better than before, their 0.8 percentage point estimate for the overstatement is significant. Over the course of 30 years, tax brackets and CPI-adjusted benefits will be overadjusted by 27 percent.

Real Gross Domestic Product and Why It Is Not Synonymous with Social Welfare

Real Gross Domestic Product

Having examined inflation and how it is measured, we can return to gross domestic product. As we said, one of the concerns with GDP measurement is that changes in prices can affect the GDP just as easily as changes in output. To cleanse our GDP measure of the price changes, we use a price index called a **GDP deflator (GDPDEF)**. This inflation-adjusted measure of GDP is called the **real gross domestic product (RGDP)**.

GDP deflator (GDPDEF)
The price index used to adjust GDP for inflation, including all goods rather than a market basket.

real gross domestic product (RGDP)
An inflation-adjusted measure of GDP.

RGDP is computed by taking current production of goods and services and multiplying those by their previous year prices and then adding these up across different goods and services. The current production of new goods and services is then added to this figure. This process is different from that which creates the CPI in that the market basket changes from year to year, so the choice of a base year is somewhat arbitrary. Past practice had been to align the base year choice with changes in the composition of the market basket. That is no longer the case. To change the base year, all it takes is a little algebra to convert the data from one base year to another. Still, it allows for a comparison of total production from one year to the next while eliminating the effects of inflation. Further, many economists feel more comfortable computing inflation using the GDP deflator approach (which is the annual percentage increase in the GDP deflator) than the CPI approach. That is because the GDP deflator more accurately measures inflation's impact. Figure 6.2 shows the trajectory of RGDP since World War II using 2012 as the base year.

Problems with RGDP

Even with its adjustments, RGDP is not a flawless measure. Besides having the GDP deflator suffer from many of the problems that the CPI suffers from, RGDP has several other problems.

First, it does not give your mother or father much credit. When either one does things around the house—laundry, cooking, yard work, and the like—the value created in the process is not counted in GDP. It is not counted because it is not sold. Much work gets done and much value is created without sales. I, for instance, installed a large wooden fence around my backyard. Had I gotten a contractor to do it, it would have cost $8,000. Instead, I drafted my son and son-in-law. It cost only $3,000 for supplies, and the GDP missed as much as $5,000 of the value that was created.

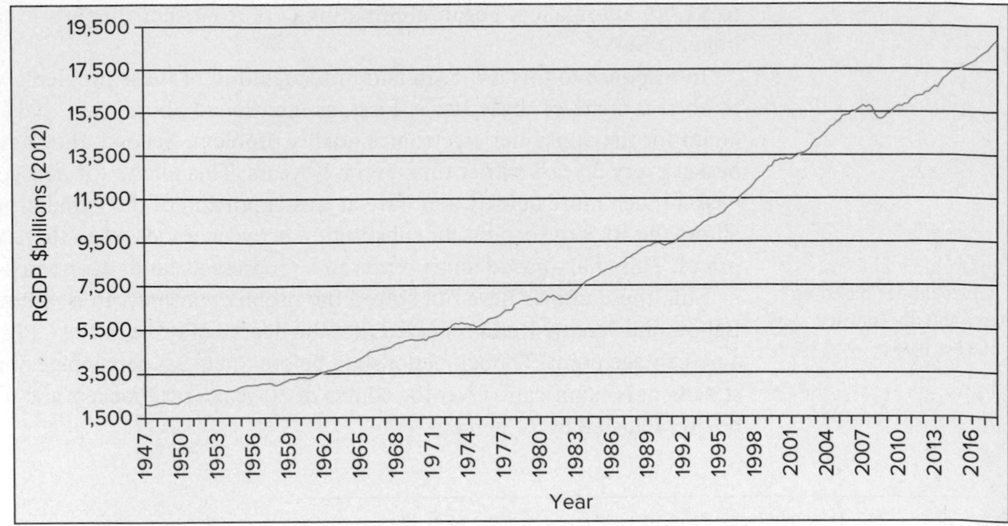

FIGURE 6.2
Post–World War II real gross domestic product by quarter, billions of 2012 dollars.

Source: U.S. Bureau of Economic Analysis. Gross Domestic Product, www.bea.gov

Second, RGDP does not see that leisure is valuable. If we all worked ourselves to the bone and never took days off, GDP would rise, but we would be worse off for it. Clearly, in a fully employed society, people who retire voluntarily reduce GDP by the amount of work they would have done. Just as clearly, people retire voluntarily because they are happier fishing, golfing, lollygagging, or volunteering than working.

Third, what people buy is not considered important in the computation of GDP. The substantial increase in government spending on homeland security that resulted from the terrorist attacks of 2001 and beyond was quite likely necessary given the threat, but we are not better off as a society for having to spend this money. We spend it in an attempt to re-create the old sense of security. Spending more money on something that used to require less does not make us better off.

Fourth, the population of the United States is always growing. If RGDP does not grow at the rate that the population does, then the per capita RGDP (the inflation-adjusted goods and services going to the average person) will fall.

Fifth, we can sacrifice environmental quality of life for economic gain, but again we would not necessarily be better off. There is untapped crude oil under the coral reefs off the coast of Florida and under the vast tundra of northern Alaska. The 2010 Deepwater Horizon disaster (where 5 million barrels of crude oil spilled into the Gulf of Mexico) clearly demonstrated that drilling for oil in environmentally sensitive areas comes at a cost. When the process of "fracking" opened up vast quantities of natural gas for use throughout western Pennsylvania in 2008–2011, GDP was clearly and positively affected. In 2012, President Obama rejected the path of the Keystone pipeline and was criticized by Republicans for doing so. Their argument was that he was constraining GDP. In both cases, both sides are essentially correct. More drilling does increase GDP and reducing that new drilling does decrease GDP, but in both cases those concerned for the environment have a serious point. Any increase in GDP should be offset by the impact on the environment. No one in the government makes this adjustment. We would increase RGDP if we pumped this oil and gas, but the price of doing so would have to include its impact on the environment.

Sixth, just as the laundry and yard work your parents do does not count because the service does not get sold in a market, goods or services sold under the table do not get counted either. The illegal drugs that people buy do not get recorded anywhere. Similarly, if you mowed lawns or babysat as a teenager, it is unlikely you reported any of that income to the government. If you do not report the income on your taxes and your employer does not either, this economic activity does not appear as part of the

GDP. This omission is especially important when it comes to the effect of higher tax rates. Studies reflect the obvious: When taxes are higher, people do more of their work under the table.

For all of these reasons, RGDP cannot be considered a perfect measure of social welfare. Still it remains the primary measure of the economic health of the country. Any attempt to account for the problems outlined above would subject the measure to value judgments about the intrinsic worth of certain goods for which there is little agreement. Therefore, economists generally accept RGDP for what it can tell us while remaining aware of its limitations.

Measuring and Describing Unemployment

Measuring Unemployment

Losing one's job is the most traumatic thing that a person can go through short of the loss of a loved one. Economists therefore consider the unemployment rate to be one of the most important indicators both of the economy and of well-being in general. When people who want and need to work cannot find suitable employment, they lose not only income but also self-esteem. The problem for economists is distinguishing in a meaningful way between stay-at-home parents who might work outside the home if they were paid $50,000 a year and unemployed autoworkers who refuse to go from $20 an hour assembling cars to the minimum wage flipping burgers. At what point does the lack of a job go from being the economy's fault for not generating good jobs to being the person's fault for not having realistic expectations? This is an important question, but it is nearly impossible to answer.

The government measures unemployment by conducting phone surveys. The first thing the people making the surveys do is verify that they are speaking to a person age 16 or over. (This is because people under 16 are not counted, whether they are working or not.) Second, they ensure that the person they are talking to is not in the military. (Those in prison, mental health facilities, or active duty military do not count.) Third, they ask if the person has done work for pay or worked more than 15 hours a week in a family business during the previous week. If the answer to that question is yes, then the person is considered employed. If the answer to that question is no, then the person is asked if he or she looked for work during the week, that is, whether he or she filled out an application or made a job inquiry. If the answer to that question is yes, then the person is considered unemployed.

As mentioned previously, not everyone counts. For instance, the total U.S. population in 2018 was 327 million. Of those, 65 million were under the age of 16, 1.4 million were in the military, 2.2 million were incarcerated, and 1.8 million were institutionalized in mental health facilities (with about half of those being over 85 years old and in homes for the aged). As a result the civilian, noninstitutionalized population of working age was 259 million.

labor force participation rate The percentage of the civilian, noninstitutionalized population that is either employed or searching for a job.

labor force All nonmilitary personnel who are over 16 and are employed or are unemployed and actively seeking employment.

The percentage of the civilian, noninstitutionalized population that is either employed or searching for a job—called the **labor force participation rate**—increased substantially between the end of World War II and the turn of the century. Figure 6.3 shows that the rate increased from 59 percent after the war to 67.3 percent in 2000. While there were multiple causes, the biggest cause dwarfed all others: women. In 1948, the labor force participation rate for men in their prime working ages (25–54) was 98 percent, while it was only 34 percent for women. The combined labor force participation rate for men and women peaked in April of 2000. That same month, the rate had fallen to 91 percent for men but had risen to 77 percent for women. At the end of 2018, the aggregate labor force participation rate was 63.1 percent, the rate for men ages 25–54 had fallen further to 89 percent and the rate for women in that age group had fallen to 75.9 percent.

From those surveys, the government creates two numbers: the labor force and the unemployment rate. The **labor force** is generated by adding the employed to the unemployed. The

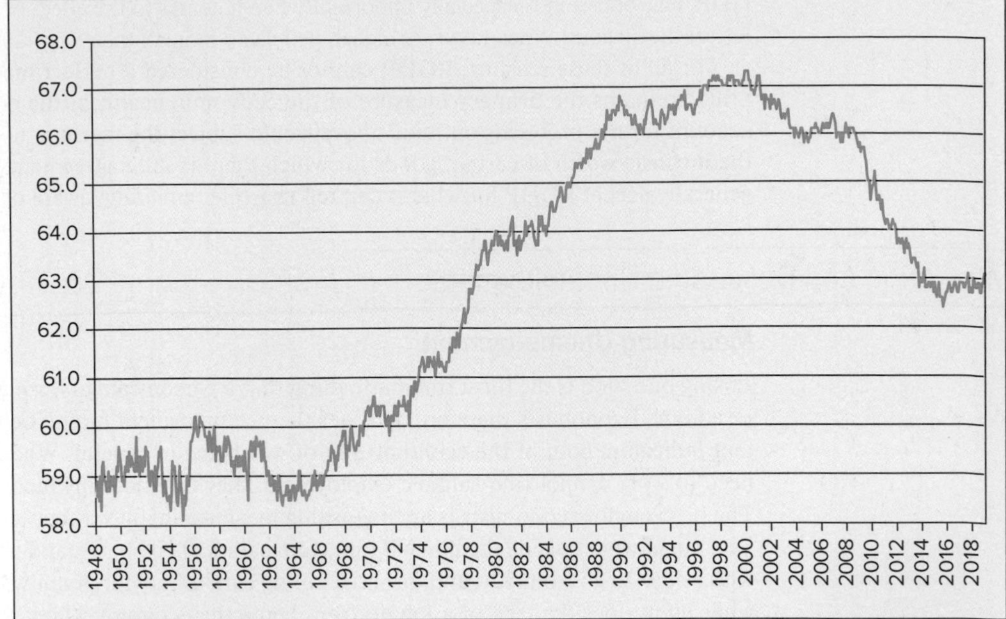

FIGURE 6.3
Labor force participation rate.

Source: Bureau of Labor Statistics. https://data.bls.gov/timeseries/LNS11300000

unemployment rate The percentage of people in the workforce who do not have jobs and are actively seeking them.

unemployment rate is the unemployed divided by the labor force and should be interpreted as the percentage of people in the workforce who do not have jobs and are actively seeking them. Both of these numbers are announced on the first Friday of every month.

Problems Measuring Unemployment

The lower line in Figure 6.4 shows the unemployment rate. However, this measure of the unemployment rate has some flaws. First, it does not count any people who are so discouraged that they stop looking for work as being unemployed. Second, it counts those people who are (correctly or incorrectly) encouraged by positive economic news to look for work before there really is any work as being unemployed. Third, it fails to recognize the plight of workers who are working significantly below their skill level or those who would like to work full time but are stuck in part-time jobs. Those suffering from either of these last two problems are referred to as **underemployed.**

underemployment The state of working significantly below skill level or working fewer hours than desired.

discouraged-worker effect Bad news induces people to stop looking for work, causing the unemployment rate to fall.

encouraged-worker effect Good news induces people to start looking for work, causing the unemployment rate to rise (until they succeed in finding work).

The first two flaws are important because they subject the unemployment rate to incorrect interpretation. For example, if there are 10 people, 8 who work and 2 who are looking for work, then the unemployment rate is 20 percent. If things turn bad, so that one of the two decides to stop looking, the unemployment rate falls to 11 percent (1/9). Thus, bad news in this case causes the unemployment rate to fall. This is called the **discouraged-worker effect,** a process that can be reversed. That is, good news causes people to look for work before there is any, and the unemployment rate rises back to 20 percent. This is called the **encouraged-worker effect.** The upper two lines of Figure 6.4 show how the unemployment rate would be impacted if the discouraged workers and those underemployed were included.

These two effects were prominent during the 2007–2009 recession and beyond. The clearest examples of the discouraged-worker effect were in the January and February 2011 reports (for December and January unemployment, respectively). During that two-month period, three-quarters of 1 million people left the labor force, due in large part to the fact that their unemployment compensation had expired. The unemployed are required to look for work while they collect unemployment compensation. Once the benefits ran out, with no opportunities out there, many unemployed simply gave up their search. When they did, the unemployment rate fell dramatically (from 9.6 percent to 9.0 percent). Even though there were hundreds of

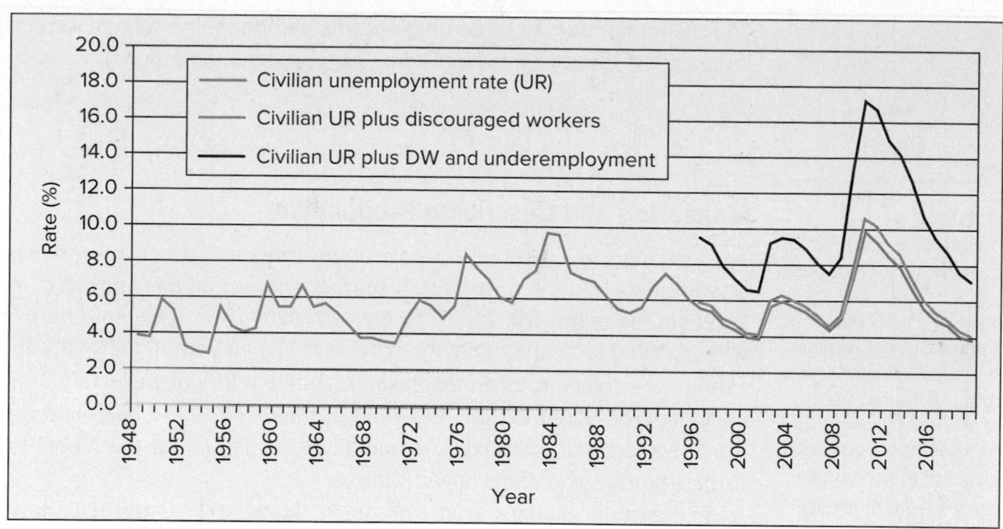

FIGURE 6.4
Post-World War II unemployment rates: the civilian unemployment rate (UR) and the rates as they would be if we include discouraged workers (DW) and the underemployed.

Source: Bureau of Labor Statistics, United States Department of Labor. http://data.bls.gov/cgi-bin/srgate

Series: LNS12000000; LNS 14000000; LNS12032194; LNU05026645.

thousands of people without jobs, the discouraged-worker effect had the impact of decreasing the unemployment rate.

Toward the end of a long employment dry spell, there is a predictable phenomenon where good news causes a significant increase in job seekers. Between October and November of 2010, 470,000 people joined the labor force, but only 397,000 got jobs. The result was, although this was a better-than-average period for new job creation, the unemployment rate rose from 9.5 percent to 9.8 percent. Here, the encouraged-worker effect had the impact of increasing the unemployment rate because more people were looking for jobs.

cyclical unemployment State that exists when people lose their jobs because of a temporary downturn in the economy.

Types of Unemployment

Economists further divide the unemployed by reasons for unemployment. If people lose their jobs because of a temporary downturn in the economy, economists call them **cyclically unemployed.** The **seasonally unemployed** are those people who lose their jobs predictably every year at the same time, like lifeguards in Michigan.

seasonal unemployment State that exists when people lose their jobs predictably every year at the same time.

A third type of unemployment is more problematic and permanent. If people lose their jobs because of a change in the economy that makes their particular skill obsolete (either because the industry ceases to exist or because it moves to another country), they are referred to as **structurally unemployed.** These are typically the most difficult people to reemploy because their wage expectations are higher than the positions that remain in the economy that they can fill.

structural unemployment State that exists when people lose their jobs because of a change in the economy that makes their particular skill obsolete.

Conversely, a fourth type of unemployment often results from good things in the economy. If things are going well and people get better jobs or at least are encouraged to go out and look for better jobs, they sometimes add to the unemployment rate. For instance, if people hear there are better jobs out there and quit their jobs to devote time to looking for them, they might be surveyed when they are unemployed. Still others may be part of a two-earner family where one gets a promotion that requires that the family move to another city and the spouse who does not get promoted quits to find work in that new city. During the time that such people are looking for work, they are categorized as **frictionally unemployed.** These people are unemployed for a short time, but they have skills that employers will want. It just takes time to find the appropriate job. Thus, this type of unemployment exists in any smoothly functioning economy as long as it takes time to find similar or better work.

frictional unemployment Short-term unemployment during a transition to an equal or better job.

Typically, between a quarter and a third of unemployed people are laid off subject to recall (cyclically unemployed), an equal number voluntarily leave their jobs (frictionally unemployed), and the remainder are let go involuntarily without being subject to recall (though not all of this latter group should be referred to as structurally unemployed).

Productivity

productivity
The increase in output for the same levels of inputs.

labor force productivity
The measure of productivity that is expressed as output per labor hour.

Multifactor productivity/ Total factor productivity
The measure of productivity that is expressed as the output that cannot be explained by an increase in labor, capital, or materials.

Measuring and Describing Productivity

As described in Chapter 1, an economy can grow because more resources are available or because the ability to turn those resources into output has improved. **Productivity** speaks to the latter source of growth. **Labor force productivity** is the total amount of output per worker hour, whereas **total factor productivity,** otherwise known as **multifactor productivity,** is the output that cannot be explained by an increase in labor, capital, or materials. It is measured as the difference between actual output and what output would have been had inputs remained constant. For this reason, it is called a "residual" and is named for the Nobel Prize-winning economist Robert Solow, who came up with the measure.

The annual changes are displayed in Figure 6.5 as dashed lines. Because those annual changes are so clearly volatile, the five-year moving average of those changes is displayed in solid lines, and it is those that are more valuable to inspect. What is clear is that the rapid increase in productivity (measured either way) that occurred during the post-World War II

FIGURE 6.5 Annual changes (AC) and five-year moving averages (5 yr MA) of labor productivity and multifactor productivity.

Sources: Bureau of Labor Statistics, United States Department of Labor. http://www.bls.gov/bls/productivity.htm; http://www.bls.gov/mfp/trends_in_multifactor_productivity.pdf

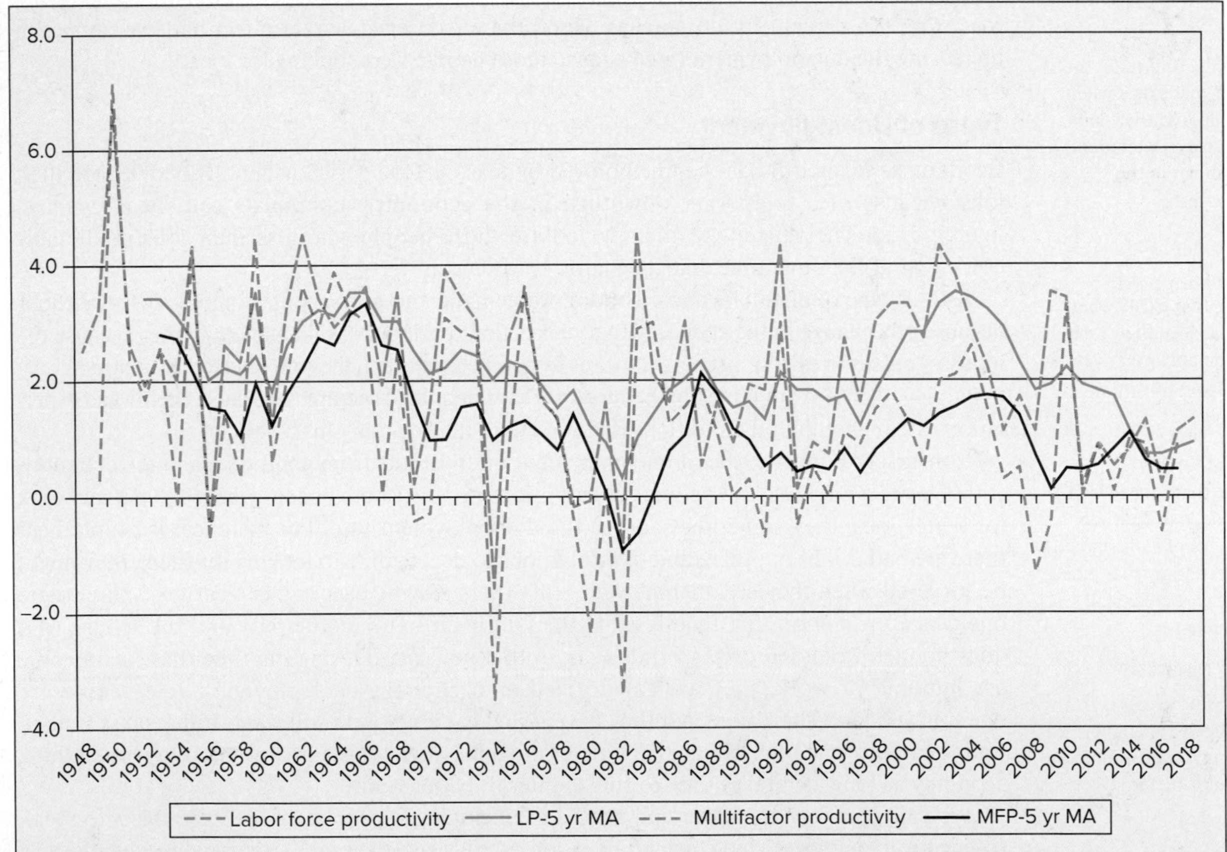

period up to the late 1960s was dramatically higher than that which occurred during the 1980s and early 1990s. A brief spike in productivity occurred during the late 1990s and early 2000s when manufacturing firms began to utilize robotic production and many service-based firms began to substitute automation for human interactions (e.g., ATMs and phone-trees). During and after the Great Recession, those productivity gains evaporated.

Seasonal Adjustment

Almost all economic data published by the U.S. government come in two forms, seasonally adjusted and nonseasonally adjusted. Seasonal adjustment takes into account predictable, calendar-based changes. For instance, in the run-up to the Christmas shopping season, employment increases. First it increases at those manufacturing facilities that produce goods and then through the wholesale and retail trade sector as those goods are transported for sale and ultimately sold. When the season ends, there is typically a one-percentage point increase in the nonseasonally adjusted unemployment rate from December to January. Seasonal adjustment takes that into account. The good thing about seasonal adjustment is that it allows you to better understand what the change in the unemployment rate is telling you about the state of the economy. Without it, you may hear that the unemployment rate increased by one-half of one percentage point from December to January and mistakenly view that as a troubling sign regarding the economy. If the typical increase is a full percentage point and the actual increase is less than that, it is a good sign.

The same thing is true regarding prices. Fresh fruits and vegetables are cheaper when they are in season and more expensive when they are out of season. When they are out of season, they must be imported from another country where they are in season or, at the very least, brought in from a warm-climate area like California or Florida. Gasoline prices are typically higher in March and October because that is when refineries are required to switch from producing winter formulations to summer ones or vice versa. The dip in refining capacity during that time creates temporary price spikes. Seasonal adjustment takes that into account by smoothing out the changes attributable to this effect.

business cycle
Regular pattern of ups and downs in the economy.

trough
The lowest point in the business cycle.

Business Cycles

recovery
The part of the growth period of the business cycle from the trough to the previous peak.

expansion
The part of the growth period of the business cycle from the previous peak to the new peak.

peak
The highest point in the business cycle.

recession
The declining period of at least two consecutive quarters in the business cycle.

Over the years, there has been such a regular pattern of ups and downs in the economy that economists have put a name to it: the **business cycle**. Figure 6.6 shows the general pattern of the economy over time. Though the general trend is up, you can see that the path is rarely a straight line. With real gross domestic product on one axis and time on the other, you can see that a business cycle has five main components.

FIGURE 6.6 The business cycle.

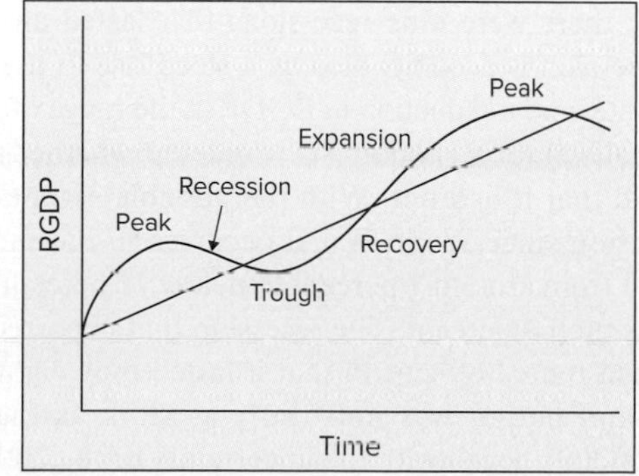

The **trough** is the lowest point in the business cycle. The **recovery** is the period of growth in RGDP from the trough to the previous peak, that is, the period where RGDP gets back to where it was before the recession began. The **expansion** is the period of growth in RGDP from the previous peak to the new peak. The **peak** is the period where the growth in RGDP slows and eventually stops. Traditionally, a **recession** has been defined as a period of at least two consecutive quarters when the RGDP falls. This definition has, at times, been ignored as the National Bureau for Economic Research's

IF INFLATION IS BAD, HOW CAN DEFLATION BE WORSE?

deflation
A general reduction in prices.

From 1970 through the late 1990s, the predominant concern over prices was their propensity to rise too rapidly. Inflation concerns reached their peak in the late 1970s and early 1980s as prices were rising at or near 10 percent per year. Given that, why would it be a problem for prices to decline? The answer is actually somewhat simple. People delay buying big-ticket items when they are certain it will be cheaper if they are patient.

When inflation is running between 1 and 2 percent per year, it is not in anyone's interest to not buy things in hopes that prices will decline, because they won't. On the other hand, if prices are falling, then there is such a motivation. If consumers do not buy goods in anticipation of price declines, then the people who make those goods will see demand fall. They cut costs by cutting wages and benefits, or worse, by laying people off. When profits decline, the value of stocks declines. With less wealth, stockholders spend less on consumer goods. The final straw is when housing prices start to fall. When that happens, people can easily owe more on their house than their house is worth. That results in a dramatic contraction in their willingness to maintain it and the elimination of their ability to borrow money against its equity (since they now have none).

From the late 1980s until 2003, Japan experienced a significant **deflation** in asset prices with the Japanese stock market, as measured by its principal index, the Nikkei 225, falling from nearly 40,000 points to less than 8,000. Beginning in 2003, it recovered so that by early 2007 it was above 18,000 points. During that 13-year period, Japanese real estate values also plummeted. So, though Japan's economy was once the envy of the Western world, its deflation-led economic slump lasted much longer than a typical recession. More recently, the bursting of the housing bubble in the United States in 2007, the demise of the commercial real estate market, and the dramatic drop in world oil prices from mid-2008 through 2009 caused many economists to worry that this same fate would strike the United States.

It was precisely this concern that kept the Federal Reserve focused on ensuring that the fragile recovery of 2010 and 2011 continued. The Fed's overriding fear was that a deflationary spiral would be nearly impossible to stop. This led the Fed to policies, like the much discussed second round of quantitative easing (dubbed QE2), that under normal circumstances would have been viewed as disastrously inflationary. The goal of these policies was to prevent deflation.

Business Cycle Dating Committee has attempted a more commonsense approach to establishing the beginning and ending dates for recessions.

The 2007–2009 recession, for instance, was determined to have begun in late 2007 despite there being a slightly positive first quarter and significantly positive second quarter of 2008. This was because the downturn clearly started in late 2007 and the first half of 2008 was aided by a stimulus package that provided rebate checks to millions of Americans. By the time those rebates worked their way through the system and the financial crisis of Fall 2008 took hold, it was apparent to these economists that the recession began in late 2007.

Between 1950 and 2018, there were nine recessions that lasted an average of nine and a half months. Typically, a recession is accompanied by a steep rise in the unemployment rate, a moderation in the inflation rate, and a reduction in RGDP in the range of 2 percent to 3 percent.

Many times in the last half-century, economists wondered whether the business cycle had been "repealed" only to find that it had not. With the possible exception of the recession of 2007–2009, the worst recession since World War II occurred in the early 1980s. At that time the unemployment rate went from around 7 percent to nearly 11 percent, and the inflation rate went from 13 percent to less than 4 percent. The recession that occurred in 1990 as a result of Iraq's invasion of Kuwait had muted effects, in that it lasted only eight months. Its effect on unemployment, inflation, and output was not nearly as stark as that of the recession of 1981–1982. The recession of 2001 began with the uncertainty of the 2000 presidential election

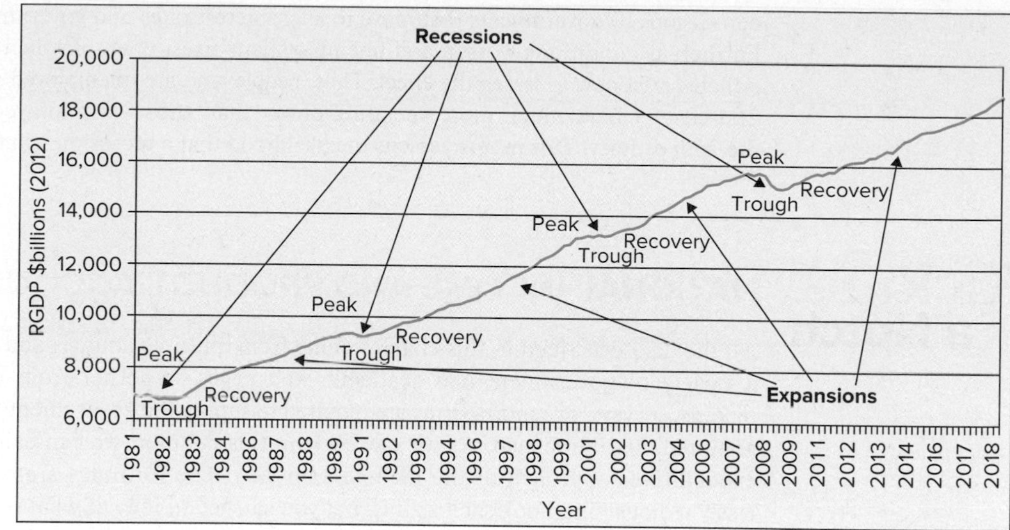

FIGURE 6.7
An example of four business cycles: 1981 to 2018.
Source: Bureau of Economic Analysis, www.bea.gov

and ended in November of 2001. The Great Recession clearly ended the string of short and shallow recessions. While it was not particularly long by historic standards, it was very deep. Figure 6.7 shows the four business cycles from 1981 to 2018.

The potential for a recession has been lessened in some economists' eyes by the globalization of the U.S. economy. Those who argue from this point of view suggest that with greater international trade, countries moving into recessions are bolstered by international demand for their products. Conversely, countries that are in strong recoveries have that impact dampened because purchases that were once domestic often are made from foreign sources.

On the other hand, some economists warned that the Asian–Russian–Latin American financial crisis of the late 1990s shows how one region's economy can begin a domino effect that is destabilizing. Just as a string of dominoes is more stable when barriers are strategically placed between dominoes, economies may be more stable if the troubles in one country are insulated from the troubles in another. The health of the U.S. economy during the period did, in the end, stabilize the world economy.

Unfortunately, there were few corners of the globe that stood in the way of the 2007–2009 recession. Begun by declining demand in the United States and rapidly increasing world energy prices, it got an unwelcome boost with the collapse of real estate markets around the world and the subsequent foreclosure-induced financial crisis of late 2008. Whether globalization dampened or amplified the recession will be a matter for future macroeconomic historians to determine.

depression
Severe recession typically resulting in a financial panic and bank closures, unemployment rates exceeding 20 percent, prolonged retrenchment in RGDP on the magnitude of 10 percent or more, and significant deflation.

A phenomenon that has not visited the United States in nearly 60 years is **depression.** Although there is no formal economic distinction between a recession and a depression, there certainly is little doubt that we have not experienced a depression since the 1930s. Depressions are severe recessions usually characterized by any one of the following problems: financial panic and bank closures, unemployment rates exceeding 20 percent, prolonged retrenchment in RGDP on the magnitude of 10 percent or more, and significant deflation. The closest the United States or Europe has come was the Great Recession of 2008–2009. The Asian financial crisis of the late 1990s was also close in terms of its short-term impact, but it was of relatively short duration.

Lessening the likelihood of depression are the economic and social safety nets (e.g., unemployment insurance, welfare) that exist in most modern economies. The recessions that occur when people lack the confidence to buy things can be prevented from becoming depressions by governments that move to alter interest rates and government spending policies. Further, as conditions worsen and unemployment rises, unemployment insurance and other policies exist now to lessen the effect. Thus, people who are unemployed at the beginning of the 21st century have much more spending power than those unemployed at the beginning of the 20th century. This in turn lessens the likelihood that a recession will turn into a depression.

Kick It Up a Notch

NATIONAL INCOME AND PRODUCT ACCOUNTING

All the data described in this chapter come from multiple sources and can be accessed from a variety of government and academic web pages. Whether from tax reports, sales tax records, surveys, or reports firms are required to supply the government, the data are collected, analyzed, and published. As we saw early in this chapter, we can calculate GDP using the expenditures approach or the income approach. The formulas are complicated and needlessly tedious for a book such as this, but you can get an idea of what is needed for GDP from the table below. You should also note that for a variety of statistical and methodological reasons the numbers don't add up to be precisely equal, so a "statistical discrepancy" is always present.

Alternative calculations for gross domestic product in billions, 2018.

Expenditures Approach	Amount	Income Approach	Amount
Personal consumption	14,188.4	Employee compensation	11,036.6
Gross private investment	3,766.3	All profits	5,137.0
Government consumption and investment expenditures	3,569.4	Indirect business taxes	1,383.7
Net exports	−658.9		
		Depreciation	3,340.6
		Statistical discrepancy	−32.8
Gross domestic product	20,865.1*	Gross domestic product	20,865.1*

Expenditures Approach: Table 1.1.5; Income Approach: Table 1.10.

* Rounding error

Source: Bureau of Economic Analysis, www.bea.gov

Summary

This chapter presented the basic vocabulary of the macroeconomy and explored many of the measures of it–measures that are not without flaw. We saw that the measure of output is gross domestic product, that prices and inflation are measured using a price index, and that the most frequently referred to price index is the CPI. Moreover, we discussed why GDP is adjusted for inflation to create RGDP and that this, though also flawed, is a key measure of economic health. Further, the chapter explained how unemployment is measured, that this measure is subject to some concern, and that economists divide the unemployed into types depending on how they got that way. We proceeded to explain the influence of productivity on growth in real GDP as well as explain the need for seasonal adjustment in economic measures. We concluded by discussing the language of the business cycle.

Key Terms

base year
business cycle
chain-based index
consumer price index (CPI)
core CPI
core PCE
cost-of-living adjustment (COLA)
cyclical unemployment
deflation
depression
discouraged-worker effect
encouraged-worker effect
expansion
frictional unemployment
GDP deflator (GDPDEF)
gross domestic product (GDP)
inflation
labor force
labor force participation rate
labor force productivity
macroeconomics
market basket
microeconomics
multifactor productivity
peak
Personal Consumption Expenditures deflator
price index
price of the market basket in the base year
Producer Price Index
productivity
real gross domestic product (RGDP)
recession
recovery
seasonal unemployment
structural unemployment
total factor productivity
trough
underemployment
unemployment rate

Quiz Yourself

1. In measuring gross domestic product (GDP), goods produced by foreign firms in the United States are
   a. counted, and so are goods produced by American firms in foreign countries.
   b. counted, but goods produced by American firms in foreign countries are not counted.
   c. not counted, but goods produced by American firms in foreign countries are counted.
   d. not counted, and goods produced by American firms in foreign countries are also not counted.
2. Gross domestic product (GDP) is counted using two methods: one that counts all the ways people ________________ money and another that counts all the ways people ________________ money.
   a. earn; spend
   b. spend; save
   c. earn; save
   d. loan; borrow
3. Inflation is measured using ________________ in a price index.
   a. the absolute increase
   b. a multiyear weighted average increase
   c. the percentage year-to-year increase
   d. logarithm-adjusted absolute increase
4. If inflation increases unexpectedly because of an increase in oil prices, this helps
   a. borrowers.
   b. lenders.
   c. people on fixed incomes.
   d. workers.
5. The consumer price index (CPI) is a heavily criticized measure of inflation because
   a. the government does nothing to fix its known deficiencies.
   b. it consistently understates the increase in the cost of living.
   c. it consistently overstates the increase in the cost of living.
   d. the government constantly makes adjustments to it without a good reason.

6. One problem with using real gross domestic product (RGDP) as a measure of social welfare is that
   a. it fails to count home production.
   b. it fails to count services, a growing part of the economy.
   c. it double, triple, and sometimes quadruple counts goods that are produced in stages.
   d. it fails to account for imports, a growing part of the economy.
7. In 2019, General Motors announced the closure of its Lordstown, Ohio, assembly plant. Those laid off as a result would likely be classified as
   a. seasonally unemployed.
   b. cyclically unemployed.
   c. frictionally unemployed.
   d. structurally unemployed.
8. If there are 325 million Americans, 162 million with jobs (with 2 million of those in the active duty military), 8 million who are out of work and looking for jobs, and 155 million who do not have jobs and are not looking for work, what is the unemployment rate?
   a. 8/170 or 4.7 percent
   b. 163/325 or 50.2 percent
   c. 8/168 or 4.8 percent
   d. 8/155 or 5.2 percent
9. Which measure of productivity describes the increase in production that occurs after accounting for the changes in all inputs?
   a. Labor force productivity
   b. Multifactor productivity
   c. Tangential productivity
   d. Marginal productivity
10. Seasonal adjustment is used in economic data to _____ the changes in those variables that are the result of regular patterns associated with the calendar.
    a. eliminate
    b. accentuate
    c. overcome
    d. prepare for
11. On a graph of real gross domestic product (RGDP) over time, recessions appear as
    a. relatively short and shallow drops on an otherwise increasing path.
    b. long, sharp declines on an otherwise increasing path.
    c. the dips on a path that increases and decreases equally.
    d. the periods where the rate of growth, while still positive, slows.
12. Of these, economists consider this the worst:
    a. inflation of 5 percent.
    b. recession.
    c. deflation of 1 percent.
    d. depression.

Short Answer Questions

1. Explain why an economist would focus on real GDP rather than nominal GDP.
2. Suppose you walked into an unemployment office and found the following people: a laid-off mall Santa Claus, an unemployed auto-industry worker (who is subject to callback by their company), a woman who lost her job at a manufacturer because the company relocated to Mexico, and a nurse who just moved to town because his wife recently started a

new job. Assign the following labels to the people above: cyclically unemployed, frictionally unemployed, structurally unemployed, and seasonally unemployed. Then, explain your assignment of the terms to each person.

Think about This

Economists have argued for many years that the CPI overstates the cost of living. The degree of that overstatement has been the subject for significant economic research. Part of the problem in resolving the agreed-upon problems is that any correction has the effect of reducing Social Security checks and increasing taxes. Should economic measures be subject to political debate?

Talk about This

Economist Joseph Schumpeter once argued that people are too often lulled into an unproductively comfortable state when they have continuous employment. His conclusion was that recessions (more accurately, depressions, in his era) were good because they forced people to be creative and entrepreneurial. He labeled this "creative destruction." Do you agree with the premise of his argument? Do you agree with his conclusion?

For More Insight See

Hausman, Jerry. "Sources of Bias and Solutions to Bias in the Consumer Price Index." *Journal of Economic Perspectives* 17, no. 1, pp. 23–44.

Lebow, David E., and Jeremy B. Rudd. "Measurement Error in the Consumer Price Index: Where Do We Stand?" *Journal of Economic Literature* XLI, pp. 159–201.

"Measuring the Economy"—www.bea.gov/national/pdf/nipa_primer.pdf

Behind the Numbers

Bureau of Labor Statistics (BLS): www.bls.gov/cps

- Labor force participation rate
- Unemployment rate

Bureau of Labor Statistics (BLS): www.bls.gov/cpi

- CPI, PPI, Core CPI
- Inflation rates

Bureau of Labor Statistics (BLS): www.bls.gov/bls/productivity.htm

- Labor productivity
- Multifactor productivity

Federal Reserve Economic Data (FRED): fred.stlouisfed.org

- PCE, core PCE

Bureau of Economic Analysis (BEA): www.bea.gov

- GDP, RGDP

CHAPTER SEVEN

Money, Interest Rates, and Present Value

Learning Objectives

After reading this chapter you should be able to:

LO1 Describe the attributes of money and explain its value in an economy.

LO2 Describe what interest rates are and differentiate nominal from real interest rates.

LO3 Describe the use of present value calculations in determining the value of a payment stream.

LO4 Apply the tool of present value when thinking about economic decisions where the costs and benefits of decisions happen at different times.

Chapter Outline

The single-most important economic invention in the history of humanity is money. Money allows people to exploit their strengths and diminish their weaknesses. Instead of having to be self-sufficient in everything, money lets you do one thing: buy and sell goods and services with efficiency. You collect money when you sell something or perform a service and then use that money to buy everything else.

One of the great things about money is that you can borrow and lend it. That is useful because many economic decisions take place over time. That is, the time at which the benefits of a given decision are gained is different from the time the costs are incurred. For instance, when you save money, you put off the ability to buy something now so that you have even more money to spend in the future. When you borrow, you get to consume a good before you have sufficient means to pay for it. Thus, we agree to give up a single sum now for a larger amount that we will receive later, or we agree to pay a certain amount per month over a series of months rather than pay a single sum now. In this market, as in any market, there is a price and a quantity, and there is a buyer and a seller. In this chapter, we explore borrowing, lending, investing, and saving decisions.

We begin by exploring the qualities and attributes of money. We move to discussing interest rates, the price of money, and how they are determined. We look at the importance of anticipated inflation in this decision so as to draw a distinction between nominal and real interest rates.

We conclude by looking at financial decisions. We will see that any particular decision to borrow, save, lend, or invest depends on what economists call *present value.* We will examine scenarios in which we save or borrow a sum of money now in order to get a larger sum of money later. We will also provide more complicated examples in which the payments we make or receive are spread over time.

Money

money
Anything that is generally accepted as a representation of value.

currency
Money that takes on a physical form (cash or coin).

barter
Direct exchange of a good or service for another good or service.

Money serves several purposes in an economy. **Money** is anything that is generally accepted as a representation of value. **Currency** is the type of money that has a physical form (cash and coin). It might surprise you to know that a very small portion of money exists in a physical form. When you swipe your debit card at a Starbucks, the store is willing to take that electronic authorization to a take portion of your checking account. That means what is in your checking account is money just like the piece of paper in your wallet. That does not mean that a debit card is currency; it is simply access to money. At the end of 2018, there was $1.6 trillion in U.S. currency in existence and another $2.1 trillion in checking accounts (and other accounts where checks are permitted).

The greatness of the invention of money replaced **barter.** Barter is the direct exchange of a good or service for another good or service. For instance, if you washed your roommate's car in exchange for the right to use that car for a date, that would be a barter. Money makes these exchanges much more efficient. You don't have to find someone willing to make that deal. You could simply rent a car and pay the rental agency money that you earned at a job.

Functions of Money

store of value
The fact that money preserves value over time.

medium of exchange
The attribute of money that it facilitates trades.

unit of exchange
The attribute of money that allows you to compare relative values of goods and services.

Money provides a way to capture the value of what you produce in an easily stored fashion. If you are chicken farmer, you don't have to carry chickens around to pay for things you want. You can sell your chickens for money and use the money that you received to make a purchase once you find something you want. In that sense, it is a **store of value.** That means it preserves the value over time.

It is also generally accepted for the purpose of exchanging goods. As a **medium of exchange,** it facilitates trades better than the barter of goods. Everyone readily accepts money in exchange for work because they know someone else will readily accept it for goods and services. The chicken farmer is much more likely to find someone to accept money in exchange for feed as opposed to someone willing to accept a hen.

Finally, money allows people to make relative judgments of value because it operates as a **unit of exchange.** You can say that a large whole chicken is worth four gallons of milk because the former costs $10.00, and the latter costs $2.50.

Attributes of Money

acceptability
The attribute of money that causes people to have a willingness to receive it.

scarcity
The limited characteristic of money.

To fulfill these functions of money, that money must have particular attributes, many of which build on one another. The most important attribute is also the one most easily lost: **acceptability.** This means that people will take it. They take it because others will take it. If doubts creep in about whether others will take it, then you are less likely to take it.

Scarcity fosters acceptability because scarcity means that the money will serve its function as a store of value. Scarcity results from the knowledge that there is only a limited amount of it or a confidence and that those in charge of creating it will not produce excessive amounts. That is one reason people, particularly in times of crisis, tend to hold gold or gold-backed currency. If you know you can exchange gold-backed currency for a specified amount of gold, and gold remains scarce, that currency will maintain its value in a way that an unbacked currency will not. Throughout history, desperate governments have resorted to printing so much money that scarcity is lost. When scarcity is lost, acceptability is lost.

divisibility
The ability to divide money into progressively smaller units.

portability
The ability to carry money.

privacy
The attribute of money where transactions are not easily traced.

The next two attributes, **divisibility** and **portability,** are technical in nature. The first is the ability to divide the money into units that can be divided into ever-smaller amounts. Currency units can be divided into ever-smaller denominations (a quarter, dime, nickel, penny) in ways that chickens cannot. The second is the ability to carry it. Simply put, a chicken is more difficult to carry than a coin.

The final attribute, **privacy,** is very important to some and is the main reason for the development and popularity of cryptocurrencies (such as Bitcoin). If you want to engage in a transaction using your checking account (with either a check or debit card), that transaction is easily traced. Money that allows you to keep your transactions from being traced makes it more widely accepted, particularly when you are dealing with someone who is on the wrong side of the law (or the country whose currency is usually used).

That is not a big deal if you are buying a gallon of milk. That is a problem if you are selling or buying something more nefarious. A drug cartel needs to move money from where the goods are sold to where the leaders want it stored without record. Likewise, an adversary of the United States doesn't want a dollar-denominated transfer because the U.S. government could freeze those accounts.

Good Money

Good money has all the attributes of money. Table 7.1 compares a variety of forms of money and their attributes. Chickens can be privately exchanged and are scarce, but they are not widely accepted, divisible, or portable. Therefore, chickens make terrible money.

Gold (or any precious metal) makes pretty good money because it can be characterized by some attributes but not others. It is accepted, but its purity is not always clear from its appearance. Twenty-four carat gold is 99.9 percent gold, whereas 12 carat gold is only 50 percent gold. It is hard to see the difference just by looking at a gold coin. It is difficult to carry (because of its weight) and hard to divide into very small amounts without carrying around a hyper-accurate scale.

That is why the original paper currencies were backed by gold. The paper, usually produced by a bank, allowed the holder of that paper to exchange it for goods because the seller knew they could always turn that paper in for the described amount of gold at the bank. As long as the bank was able to detect counterfeits, the system worked. People were essentially making exchanges using "lightweight" gold.

The problem with bank-produced paper currency was that banks could easily produce more pieces of paper than they had gold to back it. The other problem with gold-backed currency is that the total amount of known gold in the world grows much more slowly than economic activity. As a result, if there is fixed amount of gold, prices (including wages) must continuously drop until more gold is discovered.

That, and a host of very important macroeconomic problems (described in the chapter entitled "Monetary Policy") associated with gold-backed currency, led to unbacked currency.

Table 7.1
Attributes of money for various types of currency.

	Chickens	Gold	Gold-Backed Currency	Unbacked Currency	Cryptocurrency
Acceptability	No	Yes/ Somewhat	Yes	Yes	Somewhat
Scarcity	Yes	Yes	Yes	Yes	Yes
Divisibility	No	Somewhat	Yes	Yes	Yes
Portability	No	No	Yes	Yes	Yes
Privacy (of transactions)	Yes	Yes	Somewhat	Somewhat	Yes

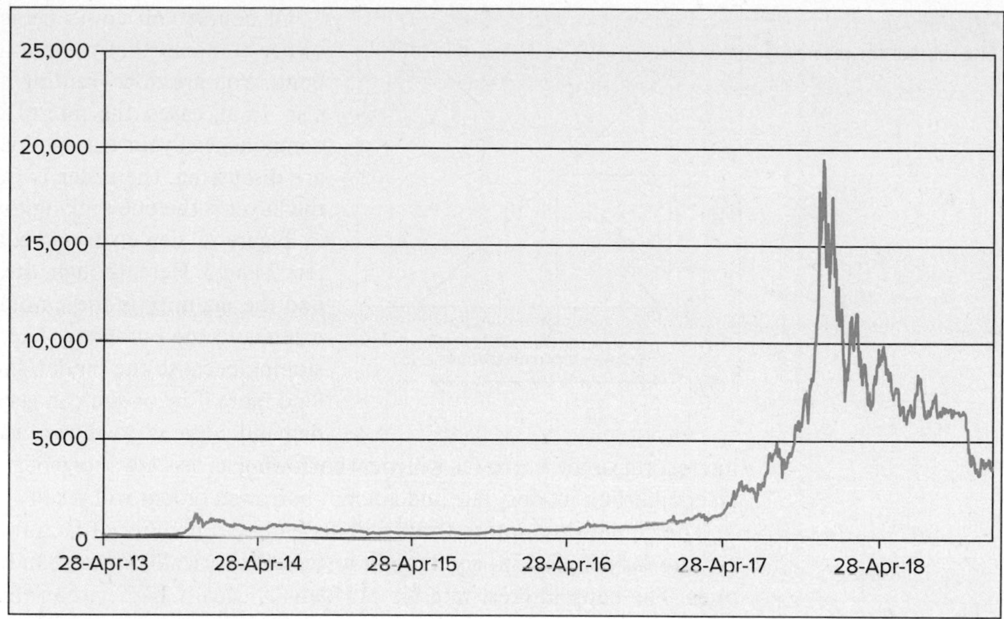

FIGURE 7.1
Bitcoin prices: 2013–2018.

Source: CoinMarketCap. coinmarketcap.com

There is literally nothing that guarantees the value of the dollar, pound, yen, or euro. It is only the trust people have in those charged with regulating scarcity (in the United States, that is the Federal Reserve) that keeps acceptability going.

Because unbacked paper currencies replaced gold-backed currencies, things remained relatively stable. The birth of cryptocurrencies began in reaction to the use of banking regulation by the United States, Europe, and other countries to stop particular uses of money. Terrorist organizations, for instance, need to be able to provide their members with resources. If they do it in a national currency using the banking system, those transactions are easily traced. That allows nations to order the banks that operate in their countries to disclose account information. It also allows those nations to freeze accounts. Bitcoin and other forms of cryptocurrency are untraceable. Research suggests that something like 20 percent of the volume is facilitating illegal activity.[1] The Bitcoin–dollar exchange rate from its creation to early 2019 is shown in Figure 7.1. Its volatility is, in large part, due to its tenuous acceptability.

Interest Rates

The Market for Money

interest rate
The percentage, usually expressed in annual terms, of a balance that is paid by a borrower to a lender that is in addition to the original amount borrowed or lent.

When people lend or borrow money, we call the price at which they do this the **interest rate.** A useful way to think of this market for money is to imagine yourself renting a moving van. When you rent such a vehicle, the owner is letting you use it for a predetermined period of time at a predetermined price. Now, instead of renting a van, think about renting money. The owner of the money is letting you use the money for a period of time at a predetermined price. The period of time is typically denoted per year, and the price is an annual interest rate. This means that when you are borrowing money to buy a car or home or seeking money from investors, you must pay interest.

[1]https://papers.ssrn.com/sol3/papers.cfm?abstract_id=3102645

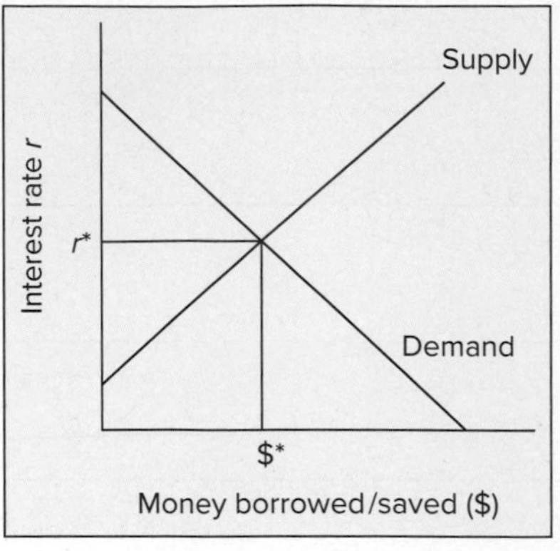

FIGURE 7.2
The market for money.

Of course you could be on the other side as the owner of money that you put in a bank or use to buy a bond. You are now "renting" the money to someone else. In all cases, the rate of interest is an important component in your transaction. In this market that we are discussing, the seller is the one with money, and the buyer is the one seeking the money.

Figure 7.2 depicts a market like one we saw in Chapters 2 and 3. Here, though, the price is the interest rate and the quantity is the amount that the lender/saver extends to the borrower. The supply curve is upward sloping because the lender/saver will be motivated to lend more if he or she can get a higher return, and the demand curve is downward sloping because at higher interest rates, the borrower will view borrowing as less advantageous. As in any other market, an equilibrium interest rate and amount borrowed or lent will result.

The equilibrium interest rate will depend on a number of factors. For instance, the interest rate for people with good credit histories is typically lower than it is for people with poor ones. The bank interest rate for car loans is usually higher than the interest rate for home loans. Credit card interest rates are very high. The reason for these differential rates is the degree of risk. A lender cannot assume that a borrower will pay every loan back in full. Lenders are taking a risk and part of what dictates their decisions is the likelihood that the borrowers will pay back the loans and the consequences if they do not. Credit cards are typically not secured by anything, and, as a result, credit card interest rates are higher than home loans. If a buyer defaults on a home loan, the lender can take possession and ultimately sell the house.

Nominal Interest Rates versus Real Interest Rates

nominal interest rate
The advertised rate of interest.

real interest rate
The rate of interest after inflation expectations are accounted for; the compensation for waiting to consume.

When the interest rate for a certificate of deposit (CD) or car loan is advertised publicly, that is referred to by economists as the **nominal interest rate.** Though this is the rate of interest referred to in Figure 7.2, it is not as interesting to economists as what they refer to as the **real interest rate.** The real interest rate is the rate of interest after inflation expectations have been taken into account. Inflation, which was explained in Chapter 6, is the increase in prices in percentage terms. Inflation is critical for our discussion of interest rates because both borrowers and lenders consider the benefits and costs of their decisions in terms of the consumption gained and lost. Since the borrower is presumably going to take the money to buy something now and pay the money back later to a lender who will then buy something with the repaid money and interest, the change in prices is important. Let's consider a concrete example.

Suppose you agree to lend a friend $500 if he agrees to pay you back next year with 10 percent interest. This means that next year you will get $550. Suppose that both of you will end up buying iPads with the money and that today it costs exactly $500. If the price of these devices goes up to $600 by the time he repays you the money, then you have lost due to inflation. He got his iPad and you did not have enough for one even after waiting a year to get it. On the other hand, if iPads increased only to $525, then you could afford one when you got your money and would have $25 extra for waiting the year to get it. As you can see, inflation heavily impacted this borrowing/lending decision and may have influenced your behavior as the lender if you knew what the rate of inflation would be.

Although no one knows for sure what inflation will be in the coming year, people are able to use recent experience as a guide. As a result, borrowers and lenders form inflation expectations. If you require $25 compensation for waiting a year to buy your iPad and you expect the price to increase by $25, then you will require $550 be paid to you. The first $25 compensates you for the higher prices that will exist when you go to buy yours, and the second $25 compensates you for waiting the year to buy it.

What this means for economists is that the nominal interest rate is equal to the sum of inflation expectations and the real interest rate.[2]

Present Value

present value
The interest-adjusted value of future payment streams.

It is easy to see that $100 is more than $50. It is much more difficult to compare $50 today against $100 six years from now. To put dollar values on an even playing field, we compare monies using a concept called **present value.** Using an appropriate interest rate, though, you can compare money paid at two different times. We say that two amounts paid apart from one another in time are equal in present value if the money paid now could be invested at an appropriate interest rate and generate an amount that turns out to be equal to a higher amount that is paid later.

Simple Calculations

The math required to fully understand present value is somewhat complicated and is displayed below:

$$\text{Present value} = \frac{\text{payment}}{(1 + r)^n}$$

where

payment = payment to be received in the future
r = interest rate
n = number of years before payment is received

Fortunately, the concept and its conclusions are not as complicated as the math. The idea is that the payment in the future needs to be deflated by a factor equal to 1 plus the interest rate for every year that is to pass before the payment is made. If the interest rate is 10 percent and 10 years are to pass, then the payment is deflated 10 times by 1.10.

To use a particular example, consider what $200 paid 10 years from now is worth in present value if the interest rate is 10 percent. To compute this, we need to multiply 1.10 by itself 10 times. The result is 2.5937, so the present value is $200/2.5937, or approximately $77.11. This means that if you had $77.11 today, and you invested it at 10 percent interest for 10 years, you would have $200. Stated differently, if 10 years from now you were going to receive $200 and wanted to borrow against it and the going rate was 10 percent, you could borrow only $77.31.

As mentioned, the factor 2.5937 was computed by multiplying 1.1 by itself 10 times (a process called compounding). Table 7.2 provides factors for several different interest rates for several different periods. The interest rate appears at the top, and the left column indicates the number of years between the time when the borrower gets the money and the time he or she pays it back. The body of the table displays how much money the borrower will have to pay back for every dollar borrowed. For instance, every dollar you borrow on a credit card with a 20 percent interest rate that you fail to pay back within five years costs you $2.49, the original dollar plus $1.49 of interest.

[2] There is a mathematical cross-product term as well, but it is very small when the inflation and real interest rates are low.

Table 7.2 The amount payable for every dollar borrowed for several interest rates and loan durations.

	Interest Rate (%)				
Year	20	10	5	2	1
30	$237.38	$17.45	$4.32	$1.81	$1.35
10	6.19	2.59	1.63	1.22	1.10
5	2.49	1.61	1.28	1.10	1.05
1	1.20	1.10	1.05	1.02	1.01

Mortgages, Car Payments, and Other Multipayment Examples

Using present value, we can calculate what kind of house or car we can afford. Here, instead of borrowing a single sum and paying it off with a single payment, we are borrowing a single sum and paying it off in small increments. Of course, we could think of situations where we save in small increments to generate a single sum, like saving for a vacation, or situations where we save in small increments to generate other increments, like saving for retirement and in turn receiving a monthly check several years later. These are simply extensions of present value.

For each of these examples, there is a wonderfully elegant formula that would allow us to plug in various numbers and draw useful conclusions. These formulas, while interesting to those who study financial management issues, are not necessary for us to understand how we might use the present value idea in these other contexts.

For that, let's turn to Table 7.3, where we will try to evaluate whether a particular business deal is a good idea. Suppose that an investment of $100 each year for five years will, starting in the sixth year, return a payout of $100 a year that will continue for the next seven years.

Though the total of benefits is greater than the total of costs, whether this is a good business deal depends on the interest rate. In Table 7.3, if the interest rate is 5 percent, the present value of benefits is larger than the present value of costs. At 8 percent and 10 percent the present value of benefits is less than the present value of costs. That means that a business whose goal was to maximize profit would go ahead with the investment if interest rates were 5 percent and not if the interest rate was 8 or 10 percent. The interest rate where the present value of costs and benefits are equal is called the **internal rate of return.** In this case, it is about 5.8 percent. Generally, when the interest rate that must be paid is less than the internal rate of return, then

internal rate of return The interest rate where the present value of costs and benefits is equal.

Table 7.3 Present value of costs and benefits at alternative interest rates.

Year	Cost	Benefit	PV Cost @5%	PV Benefit @5%	PV Cost @8%	PV Benefit @8%	PV Cost @10%	PV Benefit @10%
1	100		100.00		100.00		100.00	
2	100		95.24		92.59		90.91	
3	100		90.70		85.73		82.64	
4	100		86.38		79.38		75.13	
5	100		82.27		73.50		68.30	
6		100		78.35		68.06		62.09
7		100		74.62		63.02		56.45
8		100		71.07		58.35		51.32
9		100		67.68		54.03		46.65
10		100		64.46		50.02		42.41
11		100		61.39		46.32		38.55
12		100		58.47		42.89		35.05
	500	700	454.59	476.04	431.20	382.69	416.98	332.52

Table 7.4
Monthly payments required on a $1,000 loan for various interest rates and various loan durations.

	Interest Rate (%)				
Year	**20**	**10**	**5**	**2**	**1**
30	16.71	8.78	5.37	3.70	3.22
10	19.33	13.22	10.61	9.20	8.76
5	26.49	21.25	18.87	17.53	17.09
1	92.63	87.92	85.61	84.24	83.79

the present value of benefits exceeds the present value of costs which is precisely the definition of a good business deal.

All mortgages and car payments are similarly calculated, though these are somewhat more simple because there is only one time when there is a benefit (when the money goes to the borrower for the house/car), and multiple times where there are payments required. To give you some perspective on how much you would have to make in monthly payments on a variety of loans, consider Table 7.4, a very abbreviated set of present value factors. Again, at the top are the various yearly interest rates, and in the left column are the various loan durations. Thus, a $1,000 computer purchased on a 20 percent interest credit card will cost the buyer $26.49 every month for five years. This translates into $1,589.63 in total payments over the five-year loan.

We can use Table 7.4 to determine the typical monthly payments on purchases that you might make in the coming years. We just saw that if you purchase a $1,000 computer using a typical credit card, you will have to pay $26.49 per month for five years to pay off the loan. If you buy a $30,000 car with a five-year payoff period and get a 10 percent interest bank loan, you will have monthly payments of $637.50 (30 × $21.25). If you buy the same car during a financing promotion when the car company loans you the cost of the car at only 2 percent interest, your payments will be only $525.90 (30 × $17.53) per month. Last, if you purchase a $100,000 home with a 30-year mortgage at 5 percent interest, it will cost you $537 (100 × 5.37) per month.

Future Value

future value
The interest-adjusted value of past payments.

The present value formula can be algebraically rearranged to become a **future value** formula. Future value is the interest-adjusted value of past payments. Using the same variables from the present value formula,

$$\text{Future value} = \text{payment} \times (1 + r)^n$$

This calculation is useful when you are looking to save an amount now for an expense that will occur at a later time. If, for instance, you had $10,000 and wanted to save it to give to your newborn daughter upon her high school graduation, you might put it in an 18-year certificate of deposit earning 4 percent. If you plug in those numbers ($n = 18$, $r = .04$), you will find that she could cash it in for $20,258.17.

Rule of 72
A shortcut that allows you to estimate the time it would take for an investment to double by dividing 72 by the annual interest rate.

Both present value and future value calculations are central to problems in business, especially in the discipline of finance. Both require a calculator with a y^x key or a spreadsheet program to make the exponential calculations. Before calculators and computers were common, car dealers and real estate agents used a shortcut, called the **Rule of 72,** which allowed them to estimate these calculations in their head relatively quickly. Note from the preceding calculation that the $10,000 CD roughly doubled when saved at 4 percent for 18 years. The Rule of 72 allows you to estimate the time it would take for an investment to double by dividing 72 by the annual interest rate (72/4 = 18).

SPREADSHEETS MAKE COMPLICATED CALCULATIONS QUICK AND EASY

Spreadsheet programs, such as Microsoft's Excel®, allow for quick and easy processing of complicated financial calculations. For instance, the PMT function allows users to calculate the payment that, when made over several periods, will pay off a loan. The PV function allows users to calculate how much they can borrow to buy a home or car when they can afford a particular payment. The FV function helps users determine how much money they will have when they retire or when they are ready to put a child through school if they were to save a particular amount per pay period. The IRR function allows users to calculate the internal rate of return on an investment that takes the form of a flow of uneven payments. The RATE function allows users to calculate the rate of return they are earning on an investment that promises to pay a particular amount in the future should the user save either a fixed amount now or follow a regular savings plan.

Function	Form of the Function	Example Problem	Example Solution
Payment (PMT)	@PMT(rate,nper,pv,fv)	How much would you have to pay per month on a four-year $30,000 car loan when the bank charges you 5%?	@PMT (.05/12,4*12,30000)
		How much would you have to save per month if you wanted to have $20,000 for a car five years from now if you could earn 3% interest?	@PMT (.03/12,5*12,0,20000)
Present Value (PV)	@PV(rate,nper,pmt,fv)	How much could you borrow if you could afford $500 per month payments on a house on a 30-year 4% mortgage?	@PV (.04/12,30*12,500)
		How much could you borrow at 7% if you were going to receive $10,000 in two years and use that money to pay all of your loan at that time?	@PV (.07,2,0,10000)
Future Value (FV)	@FV(rate,nper,pmt,pv)	How much would you have in an account in 20 years if you saved $1,000 per month and earned 1% on those savings?	@FV (.01/12,20*12,1000)
		How much would you have in an account in 15 years if you put $15,000 into an account that earned 9%?	@FV (.09,15,0,15000)
Internal Rate of Return (IRR)	@IRR (range on the sheet)	What is the internal rate of return for an investment that costs $100 the first year, $50 the second, but earns $200 in the third year and $40 in the fourth?	C –100 –50 200 40 @IRR(C1:C4)
	@RATE(nper,pmt,pv,fv)	What is the internal rate of return for an investment that costs $10,000 but returns $4,000 for three years?	@Rate (4,4000, −10000)
		What is the internal rate of return for an investment that costs $1,000 per year but returns $15,000 after 10 years?	@Rate (10, −1000,0,15000)

Kick It Up a Notch

RISK AND REWARD

Investing is risky business. Some investments do not pay off as expected. Economists look at **risk** as the possibility that the investor will not get those anticipated payoffs. There are two basic types of risk, **default risk,** where the borrower doesn't pay the debts, and **market risk,** where the market value of a stock or bond changes in an unanticipated manner. To compensate the investor, a greater reward is offered. Economists call that greater reward the **risk premium.** Because longer-term predictions are often less accurate than shorter-term ones, there is also a relationship between the reward an investor receives and the length of time the investor must wait to get that reward. Economists call that relationship between reward and the time you have to wait to get it the **yield curve.** A sample yield curve for loaning money to the federal government is shown in Figure 7.3.

risk
The possibility that the investor will not get anticipated payoffs.

default risk
The risk to the investor that the borrower will not pay.

market risk
The risk that the market value of an asset will change in an unanticipated manner.

risk premium
The reward investors receive for taking greater risk.

yield curve
The relationship between reward and the time until the reward is received.

FIGURE 7.3 Yield curve for U.S. treasuries, January 2016, with maturities to 2046.

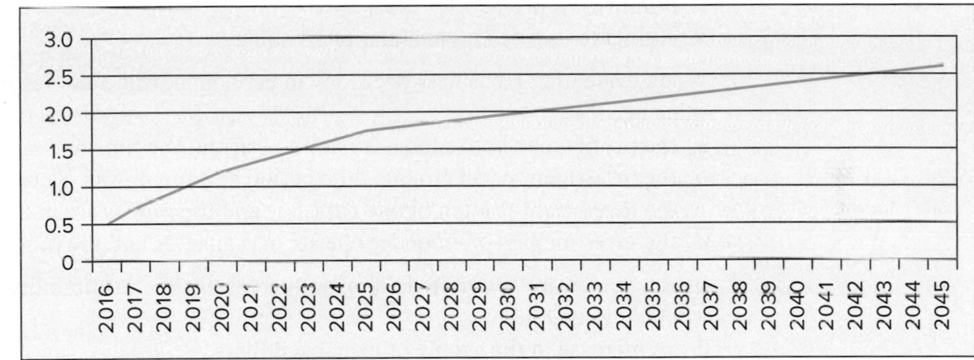

Summary

This chapter introduced money and described why it is such a valuable societal invention. It went on to describe the concept of interest rates and showed that the market for money is no different conceptually from the market for any other good. The interest rate was explained as the price of borrowing money. The difference between real and nominal interest rates was explained, highlighting the notion that real interest rates account for anticipated inflation. These concepts were expanded to explain present value and future value and how those concepts can be used to evaluate economic decisions where payments are made or received over a span of time.

Key Terms

acceptability
barter
currency
default risk
divisibility
future value
interest rate
internal rate of return
market risk
medium of exchange
money
nominal interest rate
portability
present value
privacy
real interest rate
risk
risk premium
Rule of 72
scarcity
store of value
unit of exchange
yield curve

Issues Chapters You Are Ready for Now

The Economics of Crime
The Economics of K–12 Education
College and University Education: Why Is It So Expensive?
Social Security
Personal Income Taxes
The Stock Market and Crashes

Quiz Yourself

1. Which of the following is not necessary for something to be considered "good" money?
   a. Scarcity
   b. A written declaration that it is money somewhere on it
   c. Acceptability
   d. Portability
2. If a government printed money and distributed it to people, this would ____ and thus diminish its acceptability.
   a. diminish its divisibility
   b. diminish its scarcity
   c. diminish its privacy
   d. eliminate its role as a medium of exchange
3. When evaluating a business decision, an economist will often resort to the use of present value because
   a. the profits may not be large enough to warrant the time and attention of the investor.
   b. the investment occurs in one time period and the profits occur in another.
   c. the investment is often in one currency and the profits are in another.
   d. the investment is often under one set of managers and the profits are under another.
4. In the market for loanable dollars, an increase in the profitability of investments overall will be revealed in
   a. an increase in the supply of loanable dollars.
   b. an increase in the demand for loanable dollars.
   c. a decrease in the supply of loanable dollars.
   d. a decrease in the demand for loanable dollars.
5. When evaluating whether or not to make an investment, one should focus on the ________ because doing so takes into account anticipated inflation.
   a. nominal interest rate
   b. real interest rate
   c. exchange rate
   d. junk bond rate
6. Suppose your grandmother told you (today) that she had set aside an amount of money in a savings account bearing 3 percent interest that was sufficient to give you a $5,000 graduation present in exactly four years. How much would she have had to set aside?
   a. $5,000
   b. $\$5{,}000 \times (1.03)^4$
   c. $\$5{,}000/(1.03)^4$
   d. $\$5{,}000/(1 + 0.034)$
7. Using an interest rate of 5 percent, which figure has the largest present value?
   a. $5,000
   b. $5,050 to be received two years from now
   c. $5,075 to be received three years from now
   d. $5,500 to be received 10 years from now

8. Using an interest rate of 5 percent, which figure has the smallest present value?
   a. \$5,000
   b. \$5,050 to be received two years from now
   c. \$5,075 to be received three years from now
   d. \$5,500 to be received 10 years from now

9. The present value of a \$1,000 payment received two years from now at 5 percent annual interest will be less than \$900 because of
   a. taxes.
   b. compounding.
   c. withholding.
   d. inflation.

10. A 60-month car loan (where no down payment was made) with a 6 percent interest rate and a monthly payment of \$500 would allow the borrower to buy a car that costs
   a. \$35,500.
   b. \$30,000.
   c. \$25,863.
   d. \$28,200.

Short Answer Questions

1. Why is the present value of money to be paid in the future less than the amount to be paid, but the future value of money invested now and withdrawn later is greater than the original investment?
2. Why is it that \$400 per month paid over five years will not be enough to buy a \$24,000 car?
3. Why is there usually a positive relationship between the time a bond will mature (how long the investor has to wait to get her money) and the interest rate on that bond?

Think about This

The amount of principal paid in the early stages of a mortgage is relatively modest. On a \$100,000 loan, at 6 percent for 360 months, the first payment is almost exactly \$600 with \$500 going for interest and \$100 going toward principal. Before 2008's financial meltdown, many new homebuyers were getting "interest-only" mortgages. (They paid \$500 per month for the first five years and then \$644 per month thereafter.) Do you think this was a good idea?

Talk about This

College students and young people generally get themselves into credit problems because they do not fully understand the consequences of borrowing and overestimate their ability to pay loans back. Should your college censor campus bulletin boards and remove credit card offers from mail you receive in residence halls?

Bankruptcy laws prevent people from defaulting on student loans, which means even if you do declare bankruptcy on your credit card debt, you cannot get out from money you owe in student loans. Were you aware of this when you took out a student loan, and would that impact your decision to take out a student loan?

CHAPTER EIGHT

Aggregate Demand and Aggregate Supply

Learning Objectives

After reading this chapter you should be able to:

LO1 Apply and manipulate the aggregate supply and aggregate demand model of macroeconomics.

LO2 Explain why the aggregate demand curve is downward sloping and why there is controversy over the shape of the aggregate supply curve.

LO3 List the determinants of aggregate supply and aggregate demand and illustrate impacts of changes in those determinants on price and output levels.

LO4 Discriminate between demand-pull and cost-push inflation.

LO5 Distinguish between supply-side economic policies and demand-side economic policies.

Chapter Outline

Now that we have explored the language of macroeconomics and some of the measurement issues, it is time that we turn our attention to modeling the macroeconomy. In this chapter, we follow the familiar path of Chapter 2. The supply and demand model explained there is used to describe one market. This model, the aggregate supply and aggregate demand model, is used to illustrate the economy as a whole.

Remember that models are not perfect. They rest on simplifying assumptions that allow us to focus on the essentials of what we are looking at in a way that clarifies the big picture. In microeconomics, supply and demand is a well-understood and relatively well-accepted framework with which to look at particular industries. Regrettably, in macroeconomics no such comparable model exists.

The closest we come to finding a workable model that is relatively easy to use and that is flexible enough to encompass a variety of differing viewpoints is the aggregate supply and aggregate demand model. It also has the virtue of mirroring the supply and demand model that we studied in Chapter 2, so the concepts are less foreign than they would be with a completely new model.

The reason for caution with regard to macroeconomic models is that, unlike microeconomic models, where there is only one market for one good or service, many interrelated goods and services are combined in order to analyze the entire economy. Whereas we can readily list five important things that influence the price of apples, we would need more than five pages to list the important things that affect the economy as a whole. The macroeconomy is just much bigger and much more complex than any particular market. With this caution in mind, we proceed in this chapter with the aggregate supply–aggregate demand model knowing that, although not perfect, it is reasonably suited to the purpose at hand.

Following the method of presentation in Chapter 2, we explain this model by first examining aggregate demand and aggregate supply individually. Then we look at them together, as part of one model. Just as in Chapter 2, where we then looked at why supply and demand might change, we examine why aggregate supply and aggregate demand might change and what happens when they do. Last, we use the aggregate supply–aggregate demand model to explain, albeit very briefly, supply-side economics.

Aggregate Demand

Definition

aggregate demand (AD) The amounts of real domestic output that domestic consumers, businesses, governments, and foreign buyers collectively will desire to purchase at each possible price level.

Aggregate demand (AD) is a measure of the amount of goods and services that will be purchased at various prices. It shows the quantities of real domestic output that domestic consumers, businesses, governments, and foreign buyers collectively will desire to purchase at each possible price level. We use real gross domestic product (RGDP) as the measure of output and the price index associated with the RGDP calculation as our measure of the price level. Throughout this chapter, RGDP, output, and spending are largely synonymous. The result is Figure 8.1, with RGDP on the horizontal axis and the price index (PI) on the vertical axis.

real-balances effect Because higher prices reduce real spending power, prices and output are negatively related.

foreign purchases effect When domestic prices are high relative to their imported alternatives, a country will export less to foreign buyers and a country will import more from foreign producers. Therefore, higher prices lead to less domestic output.

interest rate effect Higher prices lead to inflation, which leads to less borrowing and a lowering of RGDP.

Why Aggregate Demand Is Downward Sloping

Just as in Chapter 2, when we asserted that the demand curve was downward sloping and then discussed why this makes sense, we do the same now. As shown in Figure 8.1, the aggregate demand curve does, in fact, relate all prices to real output in a negative or inverse manner. This can be explained by the **real-balances effect**, the **foreign purchases effect**, and the **interest rate effect**.

FIGURE 8.1 Aggregate demand curve.

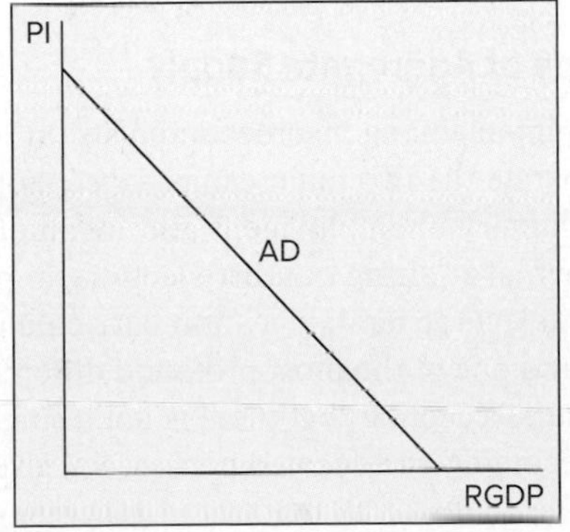

The real-balances effect is the idea that any wealth that people have in cash or non-interest-bearing accounts becomes less valuable as prices rise. If people have less ability to buy real goods and services when prices are higher, then output and prices are negatively related. This is easily confused with the identically named explanation for a downward-sloping demand curve in Chapter 2. The logic is similar. The Chapter 2 explanation regarded how much money there is in an individual's wallet, whereas this regards how much money society has in forms of money that bear no interest (cash and checking accounts).

The second reason why the aggregate demand curve is downward sloping is the foreign purchases effect. As prices rise in the United States, Americans will be more willing to buy imports and less willing to buy American-made goods. Foreigners will also be less willing to buy U.S. goods, thus reducing our exports to them. If you remember the expenditures approach from Chapter 6, you will recall that any increase in imports reduces U.S. GDP.

The interest rate effect simply means that higher prices lead to inflation. This in turn leads to less borrowing and a lowering of RGDP. The definition of aggregate demand will help explain the significance of interest rates as they relate to the downward-sloping nature of the aggregate demand curve. Recall from Chapter 6 that, using the expenditure approach, GDP is calculated by adding total consumption, business investment, government spending on goods and services, and exports and then subtracting imports from that sum. Two of those items, consumption and business investment, are interest-sensitive. When people buy homes, cars, home furnishings, or any good expected to last longer than three years (what economists call *durable goods*), they make the purchase by borrowing the money. When interest rates are high, the payments people can expect to make on the consumption of these goods will be higher than they are when interest rates are lower. When businesses borrow money to build a new plant or buy new equipment, the payments they must make to their creditors are also determined by the interest rate. Any time the interest rate rises, the volume of both large-dollar-item consumption and business investment will fall because the interest rates have caused costs to be greater. Recall from Chapter 7 that inflation increases interest rates, so if prices rise, inflation rises; if inflation rises, interest rates rise; if interest rates rise, consumption and investment fall; if consumption and investment fall, then RGDP falls.

Aggregate Supply

Definition

aggregate supply (AS) The level of real domestic output available at each possible price level.

full employment The level of unemployment that would exist if cyclical unemployment were zero.

Aggregate supply (AS) is a measure of the level of real domestic output available at each possible price level. If you want to know why macroeconomists disagree regarding the wisdom of particular policies, you can usually isolate the source of that disagreement to different opinions regarding the shape of the aggregate supply curve. The differing viewpoints hinge on what is called **full employment**. Most economists say that full employment exists when cyclical unemployment is zero, but that means that there are still unemployed people at "full employment." Specifically, the so-called structurally unemployed, the people whose industry has moved or no longer exists, are without work. In addition, the frictionally unemployed, those who quit because they are looking for better jobs or because their spouse found a better job in a new location, are out of work during what is referred to as "full employment."

Competing Views of the Shape of Aggregate Supply

We have a serious divergence of opinion among macroeconomists on several important definitions. The following questions separate the two main camps of economists: What constitutes full employment, and how are voluntary unemployment and involuntary unemployment defined? While what follows may seem like "airing out dirty laundry in public," it also serves as an excellent "teachable moment" in your general education curriculum. Profound differences of opinion exist in all disciplines, and one of the most profound differences of opinion in macroeconomics focuses on these issues. Accepting that there is not a single right answer to every question is an important step in becoming an educated person. So, given that caution. . . .

Classical economists believe in the ability of all markets to generate good outcomes without government involvement. They believe that if minimum-wage jobs are available and unemployed

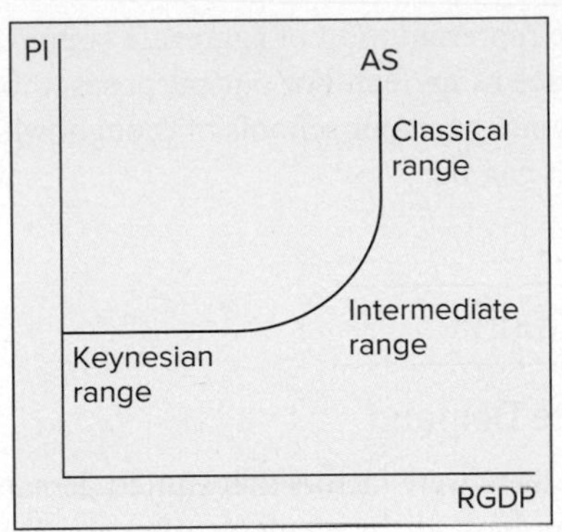

FIGURE 8.2
The aggregate supply curve.

steel workers choose not to take them, they are not involuntarily unemployed, just deluded about their prospects. As a result, they believe that cyclical unemployment is zero and therefore we will, by definition, always be at full employment because changes in the labor market will ensure that each person who wants a job will have one. If people are not willing to work for the market equilibrium wage, then they do not count anyway—at least within the definition of full employment held by classical economists.

Keynesian economists take the opposite view. These economists, followers of the early 20th-century economist John Maynard Keynes, argue that there are always more people willing to work than there are jobs available and that, as a practical matter, we have never actually reached full employment. To Keynesians, the concept of full employment is irrelevant. Thus, however many people are employed, Keynesians argue there could always be more and increases in aggregate demand are needed to employ them.

Figure 8.2 illustrates these differing views. Classical economists believe that the aggregate supply curve is vertical all the time. They believe that prices and wages will constantly equilibrate all markets, so increases in aggregate demand will only increase prices, and the underlying RGDP will remain unchanged.

As an example, recall the memory chip-making firm we studied in Chapters 4 and 5. Suppose it has many competitors that are identical to it. If aggregate demand increases, leading to an increase in demand for computers and therefore memory chips, our firm will want to expand output. Classical economists argue that since all markets are at full employment, our firm will have to raise the wage it pays to attract more employees to produce those extra chips. Whether or not the firm succeeds in hiring workers from the competition, total industry output will remain the same, since the total number of workers will not have changed. The only thing that will change if the classical economists are right is that prices will rise.

On the other hand, Keynesian economists believe that prices and wages are rigid and that unemployment results from that fact. The only way to employ these people, so the Keynesians' argument goes, is to increase aggregate demand. Moreover, since prices do not change, the aggregate supply curve should be thought of as horizontal. Again, using our chip maker as an example, if there are many unemployed workers available for hire into the chip-making business, then increasing output to meet increased demand does not require that wages rise.

The *intermediate range* between these two schools of thought is that some industries are at full employment, while other industries are not. If this is the case, an increase in aggregate demand may simply increase prices in some industries and simply increase output in others. Thus, in aggregate, RGDP rises a little and prices rise a little. If some industries, like computer chip makers, are at full employment and others, like steel, are not, then an increase in aggregate demand that increases demand for these two products will cause only inflation in the chip industry and only an increase in output in the steel industry.

We can now return to how these differences of opinion are reflected in the aggregate supply curve depicted in Figure 8.2. As you can see, the vertical portion corresponds to what classical economists believe and is so indicated because any increase in aggregate demand will simply increase prices and not output. Similarly, the horizontal region corresponds to what Keynesian economists believe and is labeled as such because any increase in aggregate demand will simply increase output but not prices. The intermediate range connects the two ideological extremes and does so on the assumption that the classical economists may be right for some industries and the Keynesians for others. The intermediate range between the "vertical" and "horizontal" extremes is an upward-sloping curve.

You should understand that the representation of aggregate supply in Figure 8.2 is not one that most economists would embrace as perfect. For our purposes, though, it allows us to deal with the differences of opinion among the major schools of thought within macroeconomics in a way that is as uncomplicated as it can be.

Shifts in Aggregate Demand and Aggregate Supply

Variables That Shift Aggregate Demand

Just as we saw in Chapter 2, where there were factors that shifted demand, there are also factors that shift aggregate demand. If you look at the elements of aggregate demand, you will find clues to what these might be. Anything that affects people's willingness to consume, government's desire or need to spend money on goods and services, a business's desire to invest in new plant and equipment, or net exports (exports minus imports) will affect aggregate demand.

For instance, taxes on personal or business income will affect consumption and investment, respectively. With higher tax rates, consumers have less take-home income to spend. With higher business or corporate tax rates, prospective business ventures are not as attractive as they might otherwise be. Thus any increase in personal or business taxes will lower aggregate demand, shifting it to the left on the graph, and any decrease will raise it, shifting it to the right on the graph.

An increase in interest rates will have a similar effect. As we saw in Figure 7.2 and as we described in the previous discussion on the interest rate effect, increases in interest costs diminish individuals' and businesses' willingness to borrow money. The result is that aggregate demand decreases and moves to the left on the graph.

Any increase in business and consumer confidence will be followed by an increase in, and a movement to the right of, aggregate demand. This result occurs because as consumers become more confident in their own financial situation, they are more willing to assume debt to buy durable goods. As businesses have more confidence in their ability to sell products, they will invest more in productive capacity. Actions of both consumers and producers will shift aggregate demand to the right. Any reduction in that confidence will, of course, have the opposite effect. It will lessen aggregate demand and move the curve to the left on the graph.

For reasons explained in the nearby box, "Why a Strong Dollar Isn't Necessarily Good," if the dollar becomes stronger, exports will fall and imports will rise. Thus, a strong dollar reduces aggregate demand, moving it to the left on the graph. Of course, a weaker dollar has the opposite impact. Aggregate demand increases and moves the curve to the right on the graph.

DETERMINANTS OF AGGREGATE DEMAND

Taxes

The amount people are required to pay for government services.

Interest rates

The rate borrowers must pay lenders.

Consumer and business confidence

The degree to which consumers and business have positive expectations of the future.

Strength of the dollar

The exchange rate between the dollar and another country's currency.

Government spending

The dollar value of government purchases of goods and services.

WHY A STRONG DOLLAR ISN'T NECESSARILY GOOD

There is something vaguely unpatriotic about saying there are problems with a "strong dollar." Nevertheless, it is true. As an example, take the euro (€)–dollar ($) relationship and apply it to the hypothetical case where a German and an American are car shopping. Suppose each person is looking to buy a midsized sedan and each is comparing a German-made car with an American-made alternative. Each, after extensive research, has decided they are of equal quality and overall appeal and that each will simply buy whichever one is cheaper.

Keeping in mind that the euro was created in the 1990s to replace various European currencies and its value was originally pegged to equal one U.S. dollar, then if they are of equal value, the exchange rate is 1–1 (one euro equals one U.S. dollar). That would mean that if each of the cars was equally priced in both the United States and Germany, both cars would cost $30,000 in the United States and both cars would cost 30,000€ in Germany.

Now suppose that American dealers of German cars must buy those cars from Germany for 25,000€ and that German dealers of American cars must buy those cars from the United States for $25,000. That means that American dealers pay $25,000 to a bank to get 25,000€ and German dealers pay 25,000€ to a bank to get $25,000.

If the dollar gets substantially stronger so that the exchange rate moves to 1.00–0.75 (one euro equals 75 cents), then German dealers of American cars would have to pay 33,333€ to a bank to get $25,000 to buy the car from America. To maintain the 5,000€ margin the dealers had been making at the old exchange rate, they would have to raise the price of American cars in Germany to 38,333€. The American dealer of German cars would now need only $18,750 to get the 25,000€ and could therefore maintain the $5,000 margin by charging a price of $23,750 for German cars. Thus, the American is now more likely to buy the imported (German) car and the German is more likely to buy the domestic (German) car. Thus, a stronger dollar increases imports and decreases exports in the United States.

Recall from Chapter 6 that GDP is the sum of consumer spending, business spending, government spending, and net exports. Because government spending is in this list, and because aggregate demand is synonymous with GDP here, a change in government spending directly changes aggregate demand. An increase in government spending causes an increase in aggregate demand, and a decrease in government spending causes a decrease in aggregate demand. Therefore, an increase in government spending will move the aggregate demand curve to the right and a decrease in government spending will move the curve to the left.

These impacts are summarized in Table 8.1. The effect of an increase in aggregate demand is shown in Figure 8.3, and the effect of a decrease in aggregate demand is shown in Figure 8.4.

Table 8.1
The impact of changes in the determinants of aggregate demand.

Variable	**Part of GDP Calculation Affected**	**Effect of an Increase in Variable on the Movement of Aggregate Demand**	**Effect of a Decrease in the Variable on the Movement of Aggregate Demand**
Taxes	Consumption and Investment	Decreases AD so curve moves left	Increases AD so curve moves right
Interest rates	Consumption and Investment	Decreases AD so curve moves left	Increases AD so curve moves right
Consumer and business confidence	Consumption and Investment	Increases AD so curve moves right	Decreases AD so curve moves left
Strength of the dollar	Exports and Imports	Decreases AD so curve moves left	Increases AD so curve moves right
Government spending	Government spending	Increases AD so curve moves right	Decreases AD so curve moves left

FIGURE 8.3 Aggregate demand increases, causing it to move to the right on the graph.

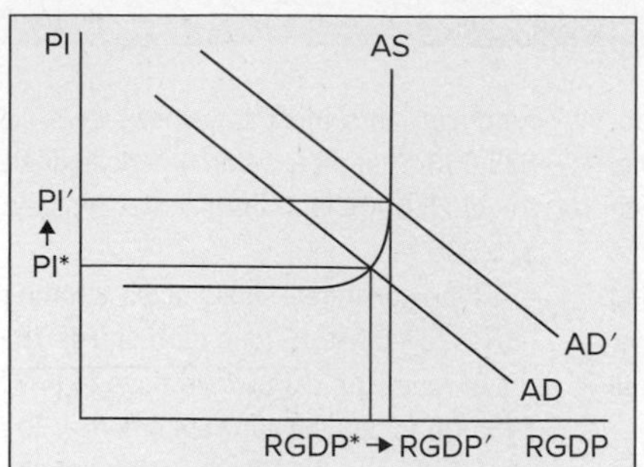

FIGURE 8.4 Aggregate demand decreases, causing it to move to the left on the graph.

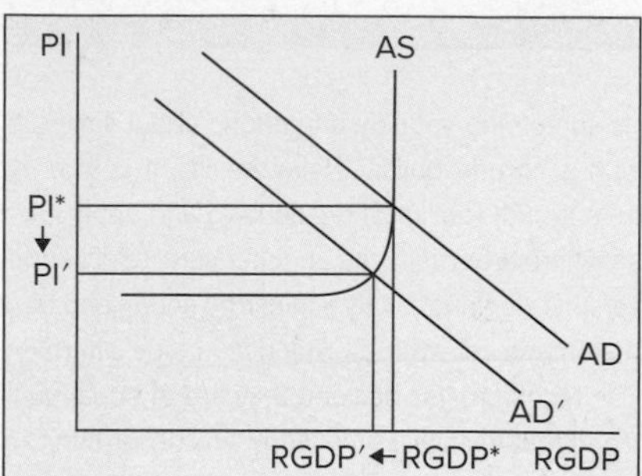

Recall, if you will, the Chapter 2 admonition against trying to memorize Table 8.1 as it applies to Figures 8.3 and 8.4. Here, as it was in the Chapter 2 discussion of supply and demand determinants and curve shifts, the advice is to use these tables and figures to confirm against your own intuition and understanding.

For example, if you were analyzing a tax increase, you would understand that taxes take money out of the hands of consumers and business and thereby reduce the ability of these groups to buy goods and services. That impact decreases aggregate demand. An aggregate demand decrease is depicted as leftward movement of the aggregate demand curve. Were you to follow that intuition and understanding, you could check your conclusion against Table 8.1 and Figure 8.4.

Variables That Shift Aggregate Supply

Just as there are factors that will change aggregate demand, there are important factors that will change aggregate supply. These are factors that are important to business. Any change that increases business costs will be important in terms of aggregate supply. Other variables that impact aggregate supply are factors affecting productivity and government regulations.

Any factor that will increase costs of production will hurt aggregate supply. That is, an increase in labor costs or other input costs will decrease aggregate supply and shift the curve to the left, whereas a decrease in those costs will increase aggregate supply and move the curve to the right. Along with other costs of doing business, interest rates also impact the aggregate supply curve in that they affect borrowing costs on lines of credit used to minimize cash-flow problems.

Similarly, if government regulations increase costs of production in some way, then aggregate supply will decrease, which causes the aggregate supply curve to shift to the left. Deregulation will have the opposite impact because firms can eliminate costs of complying with regulations. Last, if firms become more productive, perhaps through the use of better technology, then aggregate supply will increase, and the curve will shift to the right.

DETERMINANTS OF AGGREGATE SUPPLY

Input prices

The costs to business associated with producing goods and services.

Productivity

The efficiency with which inputs can be turned into output.

Government regulation

The rules that prevent businesses from engaging in certain practices.

Table 8.2
The impact of changes in the determinants of aggregate supply.

Variable	Effect of an Increase in the Variable on the Movement of Aggregate Supply	Effect of a Decrease in the Variable on the Movement of Aggregate Supply
Input prices	Decreases AS so curve moves up and left	Increases AS so curve moves down and right
Productivity	Increases AS so curve moves down and right	Decreases AS so curve moves up and left
Government regulation	Decreases AS so curve moves up and left	Increases AS so curve moves down and right

Table 8.2 summarizes these impacts; Figures 8.5 and 8.6 illustrate the impacts of these shifts on an aggregate supply–aggregate demand diagram. Figure 8.5 shows the impact of an increase in aggregate supply, and Figure 8.6 shows a decrease in aggregate supply.

Now apply the admonition against memorization to Table 8.2 as it applies to Figures 8.5 and 8.6. For example, if you were analyzing a productivity increase, you would determine that productivity increases enhance the ability of firms to produce goods and services. That increases aggregate supply. An aggregate supply increase is depicted as a movement down and to the right. Were you to follow that intuition and understanding, you could check your conclusion against Table 8.2 and Figure 8.5.

Causes of Inflation

demand-pull inflation Inflation caused by an increase in aggregate demand.

cost-push inflation Inflation caused by a decrease in aggregate supply.

As can be seen in Figures 8.3 and 8.6, increases in prices can result from demand-side or supply-side impacts. Anything that causes the aggregate demand curve to move to the right increases prices. Economists refer to the inflation caused by this phenomenon as **demand-pull inflation.** Anything that causes the aggregate supply curve to move to the left also increases prices. Economists refer to this type of inflation as **cost-push inflation.**

Many of the things that move the aggregate demand curve to the right are things that government manipulates. If government spending is increased or taxes are decreased, aggregate demand is increased and demand-pull inflation occurs. There have been periods of U.S. history where government policy was responsible for the inflation of the time.

FIGURE 8.5 Aggregate supply increases causing it to move to the right on the graph.

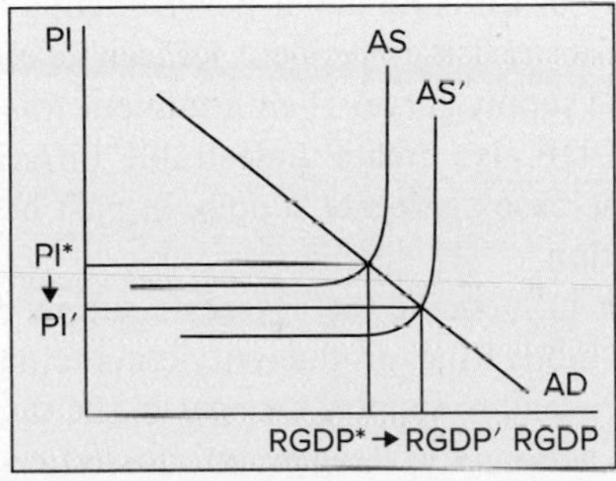

FIGURE 8.6 Aggregate supply decreases causing it to move to the left on the graph.

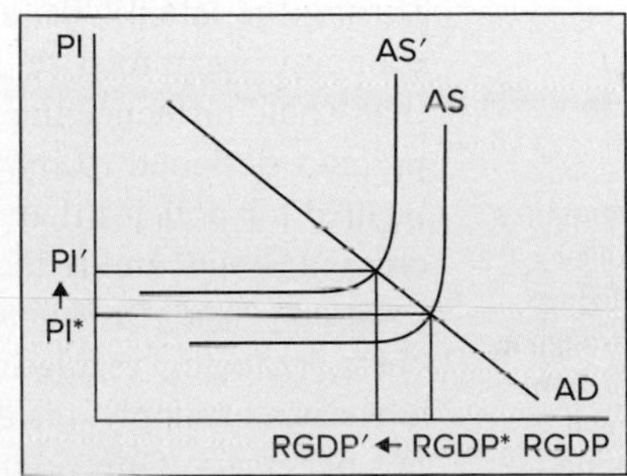

During the 1960s, when President Lyndon Johnson was simultaneously carrying on the Vietnam War and attempting to wage a war on poverty, there was a substantial concern of demand-pull inflation. Government spending was increasing rapidly, and though taxes during this period also increased, inflation increased from 1 percent in 1965 to 6 percent in 1970.

At other times, inflation can be the result of aggregate supply factors. For example, an increase in wages due to either market actions or legislation will move the aggregate supply curve to the left, thereby increasing prices. Increases in such things as oil prices will have a similar effect on the aggregate supply curve.

Looking back, the inflation of the late 1970s was largely attributable to increases in oil prices. Oil, a significant input to production throughout the economy, increased from $5.21 per barrel in 1973 to $35.15 per barrel in 1981. This, in turn, contributed to inflation rising from 3 percent in 1972 to 18 percent in the first quarter of 1980. Similarly, the short spike in inflation during 2007 through early 2008 was due, in large part, to the tripling of world oil prices during the same period.

How the Government Can Influence (but Probably Not Control) the Economy

By looking at the determinants of aggregate demand and aggregate supply, it is clear that government can influence the economy in a number of ways. Taxes, interest rates, the strength of the dollar, and government spending make up four of the five determinants of aggregate demand outlined in Table 8.1, and these are quite clearly areas where the government can exert influence. Input prices and government regulation are determinants of aggregate supply described in Table 8.2.

Demand-Side Economics

While Chapters 9 and 10 offer more detail on how government policy makers can influence the economy via the demand side, it is worth mentioning here as well. By raising or lowering taxes or by raising or lowering spending, Congress and the president can influence aggregate demand and thereby influence prices and RGDP. Similarly, by raising or lowering target interest rates, the Federal Reserve can influence aggregate demand. To a lesser extent, governments—through their ability to buy or sell world currencies—can influence the value of their own currency. These are the means by which government can steer an economy out of a recession.

Recent history is filled with examples of attempts to manipulate the economy through factors that impact aggregate demand. In 2001, short-term interest rates were cut; in late 2008, rates were cut to nearly zero; in 2003, 2008, and 2017, tax cuts were enacted to boost the economy; and in 2009, the Obama administration pushed through a nearly $1 trillion package of spending increases and tax cuts.

Supply-Side Economics

During the late 1970s, a new way of thinking about government's ability to influence the economy began to arise. Economists advising President Reagan advocated for policy actions that would influence the aggregate supply curve. Their argument was that aggregate demand policies designed to increase RGDP also create undesirable inflationary pressures. They pushed for policies that would increase aggregate supply, in part because they result in increased RGDP and reduced inflation.

supply-side economics Government policy intended to influence the economy through aggregate supply by lowering input costs and reducing regulation.

Supply-side economics involves influencing the aggregate supply curve by lowering input costs, reducing regulation, and motivating productivity-enhancing investments. Though advocates of supply-side economics tend to support changes in the tax code, such changes are not necessary. Only some of the actions the Reagan administration (1981–1989) took are properly understood as supply-side actions: Tax cuts aimed at businesses (the investment tax credit and accelerated depreciation schedules), tax code changes that significantly reduced marginal tax rates, attempts at deregulation and lax enforcement of existing regulations, and vetoing of increases in the minimum wage are clearly supply-side policies. These policies, advocates suggest, increased the incentive to innovate, take risks, and work hard by increasing after-tax rewards or by removing impediments.

President Reagan's policies had many detractors as well. The tax rate reductions to individuals and significant increase to defense spending created historically high deficits. Moreover, those policies are more accurately described as demand side.

The biggest supply-side impact in the 1980s was that the price of a barrel of oil fell from $40 to less than $10. Very few of the shifts in tax policy through the 1990s to the election of President Trump can be argued to have had significant supply-side impacts. The Trump-era policies that are highly favorable to business (significant deregulation regarding banking and energy and the reduction in business taxes) are examples of such policies. Like similar policies of President Reagan, they have many detractors.

Summary

This chapter introduced the aggregate demand and aggregate supply model that we will use when discussing the macroeconomy and macroeconomic issues. We first examined aggregate demand and aggregate supply in isolation, explaining why aggregate demand is downward sloping. We also looked at the shape of the aggregate supply curve in the context of the differences between classical and Keynesian views of both aggregate supply and full employment. Combined, we were able to show what happens to the curves as well as overall prices and RGDP when certain macroeconomic variables change. In that way, we used the model to explain the concepts of cost-push and demand-pull inflation and of supply-side economics.

Key Terms

aggregate demand (AD)
aggregate supply (AS)
cost-push inflation
demand-pull inflation
foreign purchases effect
full employment
interest rate effect
real-balances effect
supply-side economics

Issues Chapters You Are Ready for Now

Fiscal Policy
Monetary Policy
Federal Deficits, Surpluses, and the National Debt
The Housing Bubble
Is Economic Stagnation the New Normal?

Quiz Yourself

1. Any event that creates a "crisis in confidence" is likely to lead to
   a. higher aggregate prices.
   b. higher aggregate output.
   c. lower aggregate prices.
   d. inflation.
2. Use the aggregate supply–aggregate demand model to determine which of the following will lead to higher prices.
   a. A tax increase
   b. A fall in world oil prices
   c. An increase in interest rates
   d. An increase in government spending

3. Use the aggregate supply–aggregate demand model to determine which of the following will lead to higher aggregate output.
   a. A tax increase
   b. A spike in world oil prices
   c. A cut in interest rates
   d. A cut in government spending
4. Congress and the president have control of the tax system and government spending. As a result, their policies will directly impact
   a. aggregate supply.
   b. aggregate demand.
   c. residual demand.
   d. the demand for loanable dollars.
5. The Federal Reserve has indirect control over short-term interest rates, and, as a result, their ability to control economic activity is through
   a. aggregate supply.
   b. aggregate demand.
   c. residual demand.
   d. the exchange rate.
6. An economist worrying about the economic impact of environmental regulations would model that impact with a
   a. decrease in aggregate supply.
   b. increase in aggregate supply.
   c. decrease in aggregate demand.
   d. increase in aggregate demand.
7. Disagreements about the shape of the aggregate supply curve focus on the degree of ___________ in the economy.
   a. unemployment
   b. inflation
   c. fraud
   d. confidence
8. The use of a backward L-shaped aggregate supply curve allows us to ________________ in a way that other shapes would not.
   a. consider various levels of prices
   b. consider different macroeconomic points of view
   c. deal with shifting curves
   d. create an equilibrium
9. Which of the following could create demand-pull inflation?
   a. A recession
   b. An increase in taxes
   c. An increase in interest rates
   d. A decrease in taxes

Short Answer Questions

1. Of the reasons that the aggregate demand curve and the demand curve are downward sloping, each has one labeled the "real balance effect." How are they different?
2. If we want our president to "do something" about the economy, what do we usually have in mind? How can we use the aggregate demand–aggregate supply model to show that what we have in mind will work?

3. Suppose a president says: "We are in a crisis and on the verge of another Great Depression. We need to increase government spending to give the economy a boost." What determinant of aggregate demand is the president counting on to keep us out of that depression? What determinant of aggregate demand is the president hoping you do not respond to?
4. Explain the chain of events that connect an overall price increase to a decrease in aggregate demand using the interest rate effect.
5. Define aggregate demand. Then, list and explain the intuitive reasons why aggregate demand is downward sloping.
6. Discuss the shape of the aggregate supply curve by listing and explaining the reasons behind the various ranges.
7. List and explain the three ways that the Federal Reserve controls the money supply (i.e., tools of the monetary authority).

Think about This

President Harry Truman once lamented that he wanted a "one-handed economist" because we economists have a tendency to say "on the one hand . . . but on the other hand. . . ." Economists have never made very good presidential aides because we respect the uncertainty of things; we rarely give straight answers because there are rarely simple, straight answers to give. Macroeconomics generally, and the aggregate supply–aggregate demand model specifically, embrace that uncertainty. If you were a political leader, would you want a "one-handed" economist?

Talk about This

The aggregate supply–aggregate demand model can be useful in predicting macroeconomic consequences of policy actions (like tax cuts, government spending increases, regulatory actions, interest rate adjustments). It does not tell you about the distributional aspects of policy actions. For instance, a regulatory requirement that all employers offer health insurance would shift the aggregate supply curve to the left, increasing prices and decreasing real GDP. Does that make it a bad idea? Would the impact of such a regulation on health care availability counteract these macroeconomic consequences in your mind?

CHAPTER NINE

Fiscal Policy

Learning Objectives

After reading this chapter you should be able to:

LO1 Describe and model discretionary and nondiscretionary fiscal policy using an aggregate supply and aggregate demand diagram.

LO2 Distinguish between aggregate demand and aggregate supply shocks.

LO3 Summarize the problems associated with discretionary fiscal policy.

LO4 Explain why nondiscretionary fiscal policy is the primary means by which the economy is stabilized today.

Chapter Outline

When you want government to "do something" about the economy, you are typically referring to **fiscal policy,** which was considered a vital tool in macroeconomics at one time. Fiscal policy is the purposeful movements in government spending or tax policy designed to influence the path of an economy. In the United States, fiscal policy is determined by the Congress and the president.

fiscal policy
The purposeful movements in government spending or tax policy designed to influence the path of an economy.

discretionary fiscal policy
Government spending and tax changes enacted at the time of the problem to alter the economy.

nondiscretionary fiscal policy
A set of policies that are built into the system to stabilize the economy.

Fiscal policy is not simply one idea; it is really two. **Discretionary fiscal policy** consists of actions taken at the time of a problem to alter the economy of the moment. **Nondiscretionary fiscal policy** is the set of policies that are built into the system to stabilize the economy when growth is either too fast or too slow.

We start this chapter by describing nondiscretionary and discretionary fiscal policy. Then we consider the benefits of nondiscretionary fiscal policy and explain why some argue that discretionary fiscal policy cannot claim similar benefits. We use that discussion to examine why policy makers had abandoned discretionary fiscal policy for many years. We finish by discussing the largest recent example of discretionary fiscal policy: the 2009 Obama stimulus package.

Nondiscretionary and Discretionary Fiscal Policy

How They Work

The difference between nondiscretionary and discretionary fiscal policy is that one is automatic and the other is not. Nondiscretionary fiscal policy, for example, includes government policies that automatically stimulate the economy when it needs stimulus and dampen it when it needs to be dampened. Under discretionary fiscal policy, Congress and the president must agree on a course of action to stimulate or dampen the economy at a specific time.

Nondiscretionary fiscal policy is at work every day as a result of policies enacted years ago. Every time you get a raise, move to a better job, or earn money in the stock market, the government takes a portion of your improved income via taxes. The effect on your assets becomes more pronounced as you advance in the tax brackets, because when you make more money, you pay a higher percentage of that income in taxes. If you happened to have been a welfare recipient and you have found a job, the effect is even greater. Not only is the government now not providing you with benefits, but it is also withholding taxes from your pay. In both cases, the effect of nondiscretionary fiscal policy is dampening the increase in your income.

Of course, nondiscretionary fiscal policy can have the opposite effect as well. If you lose your job, get demoted, or lose a lot of money in the stock market, your tax burden falls. Likewise, if you lose your job and are granted welfare, the effect is again magnified. The government is not taking money from you but is giving money to you. This stimulates the economy somewhat, and it thus has the effect of helping to counteract the loss you incurred.

Because our progressive income tax system increases the percentage that you pay in taxes as you make more money and because federal and state programs are in place that offer economic assistance when you need it, nondiscretionary fiscal policy is constantly working to stabilize the economy. No one uses any discretion—that is, makes any decisions—to make it work. Therefore, it is called nondiscretionary fiscal policy. Because the actions are built into the system, nondiscretionary fiscal policy is often referred to as a *built-in stabilizer.*

With discretionary fiscal policy, on the other hand, action is required by Congress and the president. When each decides that the economy is in need of a specific action that will properly stimulate or dampen it, the usual actions that they consider involve changes in taxes or spending policies. Historically, fiscal policy has been used to stimulate an economy in recession but rarely to dampen an economy that is growing rapidly.[1]

The specific policy actions used in the past were tax cuts and funding of public works projects to give jobs to people who were unemployed. In the mid-1970s, for example, President Gerald Ford sought to provide each taxpayer with a tax rebate of $50. During the Great Depression, many unemployed workers found jobs in government programs that were enacted to build roads, dams, and bridges.

During his 2008 campaign, President Barack Obama promised a middle-class tax cut while promising to repeal tax cuts passed during the prior administration that primarily benefited wealthy Americans earning more than $250,000 per year. President Obama's election in the midst of the financial crisis of Fall 2008 was quickly followed by the worst holiday shopping period in 40 years. In this context, the Obama administration spent considerable time during the transition contemplating a fiscal stimulus package. What emerged included tax cuts for individuals, an extension of and an increase in unemployment benefits, aid to state and local governments both to account for the expected increases in Medicaid enrollment and to forestall the need for significant state and local budget cuts, spending on a series of projects that were priorities for Democrats, and spending on what were called "shovel-ready" infrastructure projects.

The individual tax cuts in the Obama stimulus package were structured differently from the Bush era cuts. The Bush rebates came first with paper checks, then with a combination of paper checks and direct deposits to banks. With each rebate, there was a period of time from its passage to the time when the money was in the hands of consumers.

The economists advising President Obama were convinced that there were two significant problems with the Bush-era rebates that made them less effective. They took too long to get into taxpayers' hands and too much of the money was saved by them rather than spent. These economists believed that by changing withholding tables they could speed up the process as well as induce more spending by giving nearly every worker smaller amounts per week rather than a large amount at once in the form of a rebate or when the worker filed for their refund.[2]

Using Aggregate Supply and Aggregate Demand to Model Fiscal Policy

Our aggregate supply and aggregate demand model is a useful tool for examining the effect of both forms of fiscal policy. Both discretionary and nondiscretionary fiscal policy work to move the aggregate demand curve. Figure 9.1 shows the effect of expansionary fiscal policy, and Figure 9.2 shows the effect of contractionary fiscal policy. **Expansionary fiscal policy** options, such as increased government spending and decreases in taxes, are reflected in an aggregate demand curve that moves to the right.

Expansionary fiscal policy
Changes to tax and government spending intended to increase RGDP.

[1]A one-year 10 percent surtax was added to income taxes in the Lyndon Johnson administration. Some justified this action as an effort to combat inflation.

[2]The IRS provides tables to employers that direct them to withhold taxes from employees' paychecks. These are usually adjusted at the first of the year. These tax cuts altered the tables mid-year.

FIGURE 9.1 Expansionary fiscal policy.

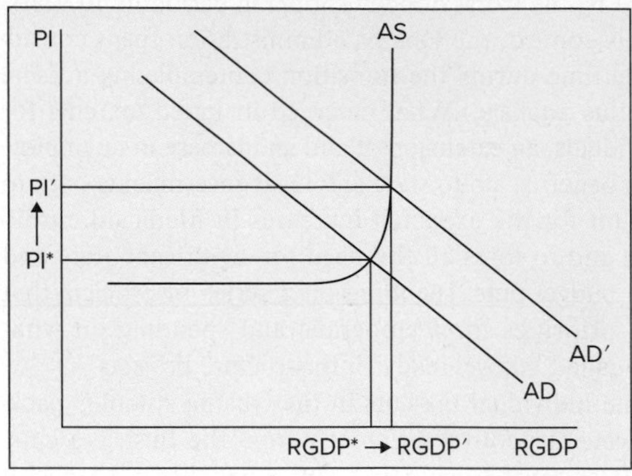

FIGURE 9.2 Contractionary fiscal policy.

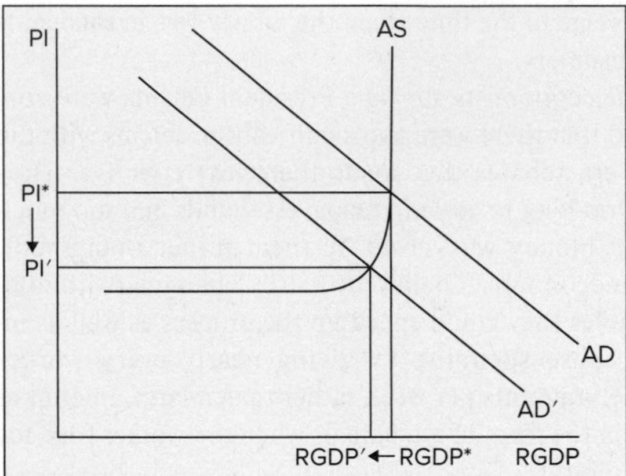

Contractionary fiscal policy
Changes to tax and government spending intended to decrease RGDP.

Contractionary fiscal policy options, including decreased government spending and increases in taxes, are seen in an aggregate demand curve that moves to the left.

It should be noted that there is considerable debate over whether any fiscal policy will have a real impact on the economy. A useful but relatively simplistic way of thinking about this argument is to frame it in terms of where on the aggregate supply curve the economy lies. Those who believe that we are on the vertical portion of the curve (classical economists) argue that any expansionary fiscal policy will be completely ineffective. It will merely create inflation without bolstering output.

It is worth mentioning that the money necessary to engage in expansionary fiscal policy does not come out of thin air. The increased government spending and the reduced tax revenue generate a shortfall that must be compensated by either borrowing or printing the requisite money. Economists do not consider the latter option a good one because inflation is nearly always the result. Thus, deficits financed through borrowing money tend to be the result of expansionary fiscal policy.

Using Fiscal Policy to Counteract "Shocks"

Aggregate Demand Shocks

Neither expansionary nor contractionary actions happen in a vacuum. Both are enacted as a result of the economy moving unexpectedly to make RGDP much higher or much lower than policy makers think is healthy. Figures 9.3 and 9.4 show the impact of these **shocks**, or unexpected moves. In each we suppose that aggregate demand is what moves unexpectedly, and in each we start with it at AD_1.

shock
Any unanticipated economic event.

FIGURE 9.3 A negative aggregate demand shock.

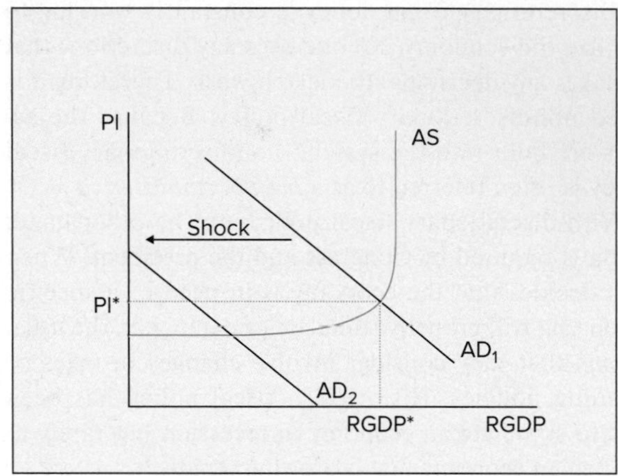

FIGURE 9.4 A positive aggregate demand shock.

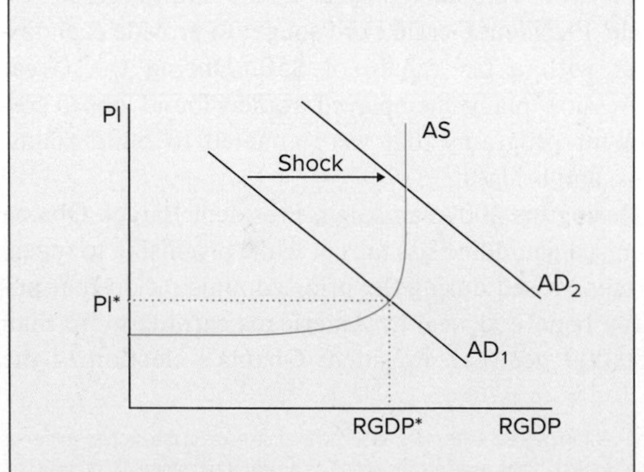

FIGURE 9.5 Nondiscretionary and discretionary fiscal policy as it combats a recession.

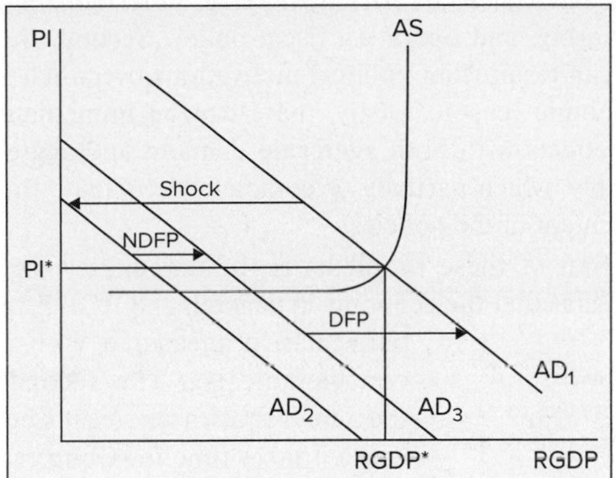

FIGURE 9.6 Nondiscretionary and discretionary fiscal policy as it combats an overheated economy.

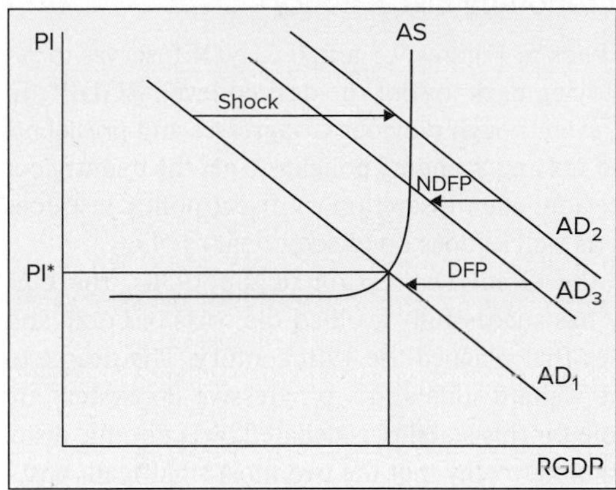

aggregate demand shock An unexpected event that causes aggregate demand to increase or decrease.

Because of a shock, it unexpectedly moves to AD_2. If a negative **aggregate demand shock** causes a recession, like Figure 9.3, then the aggregate demand curve moves from AD_1 to AD_2. People will lose their jobs, and as a result, welfare spending will rise and tax payments will fall. As Figure 9.5 shows, expansionary nondiscretionary fiscal policy (NDFP) shifts the aggregate demand curve partially back to the original aggregate demand curve (to AD_3). Expansionary discretionary fiscal policy (DFP) (either increases in government spending or decreases in taxes) can potentially shift aggregate demand all the way back to AD_1.

If a positive aggregate demand shock causes an overheated economy, like Figure 9.4, then the aggregate demand curve moves from AD_1 to AD_2. When people get better jobs or raises, welfare spending will fall and tax revenue will rise. As Figure 9.6 shows, contractionary NDFP shifts the aggregate demand curve partially back to the original aggregate demand curve (to AD_3). Contractionary DFP (either decreases in government spending or increases in taxes) can potentially shift aggregate demand all the way back to AD_1.

In both cases, nondiscretionary fiscal policy moves aggregate demand back toward AD_1 to AD_3, and discretionary fiscal policy can shift aggregate demand all the way back to AD_1 again. In theory, regardless of whether the economy experiences a positive or negative aggregate demand shock, the government can use both discretionary and nondiscretionary fiscal policy to reinstate a healthy economy.

At this point, we need to consider what could happen that would unexpectedly shift aggregate demand. There are a number of reasons and each involves the reaction of people to their predictions of the future. If people's positive view of the health of the economy spurs them to buy new cars or furnishings, the aggregate demand curve will move to the right. If the opposite happens and people decide to delay buying these expensive items because of negative feelings about the economy, the aggregate demand curve will move to the left. Tracking the "feeling" that people have about the economy is not easy and therefore large, unexpected swings can upset the economy.

Aggregate Supply Shocks

Along with aggregate demand shocks, we must also deal with the problem of aggregate supply shocks. Usually, an **aggregate supply shock** involves an important natural resource. It should come as no surprise that recent aggregate supply shocks have all involved the price of oil. During the 1973 Arab-Israeli war, for example, the price of oil climbed dramatically. During the Iran–Iraq war, the price of oil fell dramatically as both sides increased production to pay for war material. The tripling of world oil prices from 2007 to mid-2008 and the dramatic plummeting of those prices from the summer of 2008 through early 2009 each had dramatic aggregate supply impacts.

aggregate supply shock An unexpected event that causes aggregate supply to increase or decrease.

Whether drastic changes are positive or negative, policy makers are frequently called upon to do something to counter that aggregate supply shock, and, because they very frequently have little control over the events that cause those shocks, they may wish to use discretionary fiscal policy to mitigate the economic impact.

Evaluating Fiscal Policy

Nondiscretionary Fiscal Policy

Looking back at Figures 9.5 and 9.6, NDFP serves to get output moving back toward the desired level, RGDP*. In addition, even though previous Congresses and presidents developed tax and spending policies to get the country out of a recession, such discretionary fiscal policy just does not work as well as does nondiscretionary policy.

Since the Great Depression of the 1930s, the U.S. economy has successfully avoided the sorts of boom and bust cycles that plagued the 19th century. The degree to which the welfare state and a progressive tax system are responsible for this stability is debated by economic historians. It is noteworthy that the two most significant post-World War II recessions, the one in 1982 and the one that extended from late 2007 to mid-2009, were far less onerous than any of the financial panics of the 1800s.

Discretionary Fiscal Policy

Given that discussion, and the near universal appreciation of the positive impact of nondiscretionary policy, you might think that discretionary fiscal policy would work as well. In fact, among macroeconomists, it's net impact is highly controversial. It wasn't always that way. In the aftermath of the Great Depression and the belief that Roosevelt's New Deal policies contributed to economic stability, most economists were confident that discretionary fiscal policy would essentially eliminate the instability of recessions. However, by 1980, most economists had given up on discretionary fiscal policy. Coincidentally or not, during the 20 years that followed, the United States experienced half the usual number of recessions.

What transformed economists from overconfident discretionary fiscal policy champions in the 1960s to profound skeptics in the 1980s was the very poor performance of these policies during the 1970s. The preceding aggregate demand and aggregate supply analysis is nice to examine, and the nondiscretionary fiscal policy part does work as advertised, but discretionary fiscal policy was more of a fantasy of economists. In the 1950s and 1960s, economists were confident that Congress could know exactly how much stimulus or dampening would be necessary to get the economy back to a desired level of RGDP. Congress would then pass a bill that the president would sign to implement that policy. As a practical matter, it just did not work in the ways economists predicted it would.

The reasons discretionary fiscal policy does not work as well as advertised (or perhaps at all) are threefold. First, the failures can be attributed to lags in recognizing, administering, and operating fiscal policy. Second, the failures can result from political motivations overwhelming economic reason. Lastly, there can be immediate counter-effects with both aggregate demand and aggregate supply, which partially or completely eliminate the positive intent of the policies.

The first of these problems is the **recognition lag**, which means that the economy in general, and RGDP, in particular, is measured with a considerable lag. The second, the **administrative lag**, results because it takes time for Congress and the president to agree on a course of action. The third, the **operational lag**, results because it takes quite awhile for the full impact of a government program or tax change to have its effect on the economy.

recognition lag
The time it takes to measure the state of the economy.

administrative lag
The time it takes for Congress and the president to agree on a course of action.

operational lag
The time it takes for the full impact of a government program or tax change to have its effect on the economy.

The recognition lag results from the fact that GDP is not easily and immediately measured. Quarterly GDP is first estimated using reasonably good predictors that are available soon after the end of the quarter. Later, more data are brought to bear and GDP is reestimated. Only after many months is a final GDP figure given. Thus we do not know for sure whether we are in a recession until months after it begins. Similarly, we do not know when we are out of a recession until months after it ends. There are many historic examples of this issue. The most recent of which is the 2007–2009 recession. It was late in the fall of 2008 before the National Bureau of Economic Research Business Cycle Dating Committee identified Fall 2007 as the beginning of the recession. While it was clear by late in the summer of 2008 that the economy was slowing dramatically, it was a full year after the recession began before it was universally acknowledged. The recession of 2007–2009 was not declared to have ended in June 2009 until September 2010.

The administrative lag results from the inherent inefficiency of American democracy. We have two legislative bodies that must first agree with each other and then must agree with the president. The president, the House, or the Senate can delay or derail fiscal policy. Even if they choose to work on a given problem, Congress never solves a problem without disagreements. They may agree, for example, that we are in a recession but will not be able to decide whether to engage in discretionary fiscal policy through tax cuts or through spending programs. Even when they agree on that, they may argue over the kinds of tax cuts to make, who should get them, what kinds of spending programs would be appropriate, and the congressional districts that should be benefited. By the time they finally agree, of course, more time has passed.

This is quite well illustrated by the political wrangling over the 2008 financial system rescue plan and the 2009 stimulus package. Both presidential candidates were in agreement that the Troubled Asset Relief Program (TARP) was necessary, but it took nearly a month for the plan to pass. Even with significant majorities in both houses and two and a half months from his election to his swearing in, it took President Obama five additional weeks to get a stimulus plan through Congress. Much of the disagreement surrounded the size and composition of the package. Conservative economists and members of Congress were concerned about the budget deficit implications of the package. Liberal economists and members of Congress were concerned that the package would be of insufficient size to have the desired impact. These are perfectly legitimate differences of opinion, but the debate took time. That delayed the intended impact.

The operational lag offers the final roadblock to effective discretionary fiscal policy. Even supposing that Congress and the president agree on time that a policy is needed and they agree on the type of policy, it takes months, if not years, for discretionary fiscal policy to have its desired effects.

If the discretionary fiscal policy takes the form of increases in highway construction, a program that increases the numbers of jobs available, federal contracts usually do not pay the entire amount up front. Contractors are paid in the stages of building, and it takes quite awhile to go from the beginning of a large construction project to its end. To avoid this delay, the Obama stimulus package hoped to include mostly "shovel-ready" infrastructure plans. The idea was to take plans that had already gone through the design phase. In so doing, the hope was to get these projects started the moment funds became available. When the recession of 2007–2009 ended in June 2009, less than 10 percent of the stimulus funds from the bill that had passed that February had been spent.

As for the tax aspects of fiscal policy, the vast majority of the money going to taxpayers went to them well after it was needed. The 2001, 2003, 2008, and 2009 tax cuts provide evidence that properly structured ones can make their way into the economy somewhat quickly. The downside to these relatively quick tax cuts is that their impacts are often muted by those who use the extra money to save or to pay down existing debt. This is why many economists, particularly liberal ones, argue for spending increases as the primary tool of discretionary fiscal policy.

The Political Problems with Fiscal Policy

Another argument against discretionary fiscal policy is that even if it worked, vote-obsessed politicians would not use it properly. Aside from the bias toward expansionary fiscal policy alluded to in the introduction, there is the question of who will be affected by any changes in taxation or spending policies. In addition, there is the complication caused by politicians too concerned with reelection. They seek to expand the economy in presidential election years only to act responsibly after the election.

The first of these issues raises questions of political motivation. Whether large-scale, federally funded building projects are needed is one question; where they will go is quite another. History is filled with examples of powerful members of Congress, for purely political reasons, manipulating the process of project selection. Noted economist James Buchanan and others have suggested that all federal spending, but in particular that spending that is done in the name of fiscal policy, is susceptible to this kind of problem.

There is also the problem of the **political business cycle.** It is suggested that politicians, particularly presidents, will add new spending and tax policies to their pre-election-year budgets to boost the economy in time for their own or their party's reelection. Table 9.1 suggests that this might be the case, given that the average of growth rates in the fourth year of presidential terms of office is slightly higher than that of first-year growth rates.

political business cycle Politically motivated fiscal policy used for short-term gain just prior to elections.

Criticism from the Right and Left

There were many economists, mainly on the conservative end of the spectrum, who advised against a fiscal stimulus of any kind and then were only too happy to say "I told you so" when, by their calculations, the impact of the 2009 stimulus package was less than the Obama administration had predicted. John Cogan, John Taylor, and others argued that the impact was, if anything, small and temporary, and quite possibly negative. They argued that

Table 9.1 Real growth rates by presidential terms.

Source: Bureau of Economic Analysis, www.bea.gov

President	First Year	Second Year	Third Year	Fourth Year
Truman	−0.5	8.7	8.1	4.1
Eisenhower I	4.7	−0.6	7.1	2.1
Eisenhower II	2.1	−0.7	6.9	2.6
Kennedy/Johnson	2.6	6.1	4.4	5.8
Johnson	6.5	6.6	2.7	4.9
Nixon I	3.1	0.2	3.3	5.2
Nixon II/Ford	5.6	−0.5	−0.2	5.4
Carter	4.6	5.6	3.2	−0.2
Reagan I	2.6	−1.9	4.6	7.3
Reagan II	4.2	3.5	3.5	4.2
Bush GHW	3.7	1.9	−0.1	3.6
Clinton I	2.7	4.0	2.7	3.8
Clinton II	4.5	4.5	4.7	4.1
Bush GW I	1.0	1.8	2.8	3.8
Bush GW II	3.3	2.7	1.8	−0.3
Obama I	−2.8	2.5	1.6	2.2
Obama II	1.8	2.5	2.9	1.6
Trump	2.2	2.9		
Average	2.9	2.8	3.5	3.5

the only way to truly stimulate consumption and investment is to make long-term structural changes to tax rates in ways that consumers and businesses can confidently predict that their future after-tax income will be higher.

Liberal (and Nobel Prize–winning) economist Paul Krugman was just as critical of the stimulus package as these conservative economists, yet his point of attack was that it was predictably too small to have any of its desired impacts. While dismissing the conservative economists' estimation of the importance of, as he called it, "the confidence fairy," he and others argued as early as December 2008 that policy makers were understating what was necessary by a factor of at least two. Since that time, Krugman repeatedly pointed to the fact that total government spending declined in 2010 and 2011 because state and local governments were cutting back on spending by more than the federal government was increasing spending.

The Rise, Fall, and Rebirth of Discretionary Fiscal Policy

In the 1970s, it became apparent to policy makers that discretionary fiscal policy was not an adequate way to stabilize the economy. The lags were too important to ignore because the recessions of the 1970s had been too short for them to be recognized, laws to be passed, and money spent in time to have any effect.

An odd coincidence happened on the way to the grave for discretionary fiscal policy. When the 2001 Bush tax cut passed in May of that year, it was not known that we were already in a recession. In addition, instead of implementing the tax cut prospectively, it was made retroactive to the beginning of the year, and instead of having taxpayers wait until they filed their tax forms in 2002 to claim their money, rebate checks were sent out in anticipation of those cuts. These checks started arriving in August and September of that year and were nearly fully dispersed when the terrorist attacks of September 11 occurred. Together with a series of interest rate cuts, these tax cuts had the fortunate coincidence of stimulating the economy at precisely the time the stimulus was needed.

The Obama Stimulus Plan

The clearest sign that discretionary fiscal policy was back as a policy tool under active consideration came with the election of Barack Obama as president of the United States. Prior to that, it had been more than 30 years since policy makers actively sought to increase aggregate demand through increases in government spending rather than through tax rebates.

As shown in Table 9.2, the plan itself had four basic elements. The first was to shore up the state-run unemployment, welfare, and Medicaid systems. Though the money had to be appropriated through an act of Congress, this is best labeled as nondiscretionary fiscal policy as it is a regular part of the federal government's response to economic difficulty. The second element in the plan is not as readily categorized because though it was "discretionary" in that the federal government could have chosen to let states ride out the recession on their own, it was intended to allow states to make it through the 2009 and 2010 fiscal years without having to cut budgets and raise taxes. In essence, this portion was designed to allow states—that often are constitutionally prevented from borrowing—to engage in their own form of nondiscretionary fiscal policy. The remainder was clearly discretionary as it was motivated by a desire to speed a recovery rather than to simply mitigate the impact of it. Whether any of it worked at all is the subject of the nearby box.

Table 9.2 The Obama stimulus plan as originally enacted.

Source: http://webarchive.loc.gov/all/20090930210842/, http://www.recovery.gov/Pages/home.aspx.

Stimulus Plan Element	Amount in $ Millions
Nondiscretionary fiscal policy: Unemployment, welfare, Medicaid	$135,832
Aid to states	53,600
Discretionary fiscal policy: Tax cuts	301,135
Discretionary fiscal policy: Spending increases	300,047

The recovery.gov site was removed. The Library of Congress archives previous versions of government websites. That site's archive can be found at http://webarchive.loc.gov/all/20090930210842/http://www.recovery.gov/Pages/home.aspx

DID THE OBAMA STIMULUS WORK?

The question of whether the Obama stimulus package worked or not depends entirely on what you assume the counterfactual to be. Recall that a "counterfactual" to a policy is a story associated with what the result would have most likely been had there been no change in policy. Had there been no stimulus package of any kind, had there been no assistance to states to cover higher unemployment and Medicaid claims, had there been no extension of Bush-era tax rates, had there been no "Making Work Pay" credit, had there been no money for shovel-ready projects, Cash-for-Clunkers, or for alternative energy development, what would have been the result? The judged effectiveness of the stimulus package as a whole, therefore, depends on how you create the counterfactual.

There are, generally speaking, two branches of counterfactuals: Keynesian ones and Ricardian equivalence ones. Keynesian counterfactuals assume that the $787 billion stimulus was all new money being spent and was not displacing any money that would have been spent elsewhere, by someone, even perhaps by another level of government. Ricardian equivalence counterfactuals assume that people foresee that current and temporary increases in the deficit will ultimately necessitate future tax increases or spending cuts to pay for it, or that federal grants received by states are offset by reductions in what states would have otherwise borrowed. In this way, currently higher deficits and the private and other level government reactions to those deficits completely wipe out any effect of the policy.

For instance, if you assume that people only bought the cars they did because of the Cash-for-Clunkers program so that all spending on those cars, including the subsidy, was induced by the program, you would, by the evidence, be wrong. In fact, most of the cars purchased during that period were by people who happened to be in the market for a new car anyway and had a "clunker" to trade in. Similarly, if you assume that states would have chosen not to borrow money to provide for Medicaid coverage for those people who were forced on to the program because they lost their jobs, you would count the extra money provided to the states for that purpose by the federal government as extra money that was spent that wouldn't have been. That is probably wrong in some states and correct in others.

However, sometimes the money spent as part of the stimulus was clearly new money that resulted from the stimulus. Even the most strident anti-stimulus economists acknowledge that unemployment benefits were extended and made more generous using federal money and that money was available only through the stimulus. The fact that almost all that money was spent by relatively poor recipients has a stimulatory impact. Some economists would still quibble with this as stimulus because they would argue that those who were unemployed and receiving long-term benefits were less likely to accept the reality of lesser jobs at lower wages and that the benefits merely extended their ability to convince or even delude themselves that their old jobs would reappear at their old wage levels.

The stimulus plan's supporters point to the relatively short period of economic distress in the United States relative to ongoing challenges in Europe where there was relatively little appetite for stimulus. They argue that the United States emerged from the Great Recession to rates of growth that were, while slow, generally more brisk than were European nations'. Detractors simply point to the very slow recovery in real GDP and very slow drop in unemployment in the United States. They point to investments in companies that ultimately went bankrupt or to shovel-ready projects that had little infrastructure-enhancing purpose. They point to large decreases in the percentage of the population working or seeking work, the primary driver for reduced rates of unemployment.

There is no consensus on this topic. Noble Prize winners are on both sides of the debate. If the measure to be used to judge its overall effectiveness is the median estimate of its ultimate impact, then the impact was modestly effective. Several economists have prepared estimates of the impact of the stimulus. A simple summary of the studies done on the topic is included below. Given that the term *stimulus* became a political "dirty word" shortly after the package's passage, it appears that academic economists have a greater appetite for discretionary fiscal policy than does the public.

Study	Authors	Conclusions
"Did the Stimulus Stimulate? Real Time Estimates of the Effects of the American Recovery and Reinvestment Act"	James Feyrer, Bruce Sacerdote	Significantly positive
"Does State Fiscal Relief during Recessions Increase Employment? Evidence from the American Recovery and Reinvestment Act"	Gabriel Chodorow-Reich, Laura Feiveson, Zachary Liscow, and William Gui Woolston	Significantly positive
"Estimated Impact of the American Recovery and Reinvestment Act on Employment and Economic Output from January 2011 through March 2011"	Benjamin Page and Felix Reichling	Mostly positive
"Targeted Transfers and the Fiscal Response to the Great Recession"	Hyunseung Oh and Ricardo Reis	Mildly positive
"Estimated Impact of the American Recovery and Reinvestment Act on Employment and Economic Output in 2014"	Congressional Budget Office	Mildly positive
"The American Recovery and Reinvestment Act: Public Sector Jobs Saved, Private Sector Jobs Forestalled"	Timothy Conley and Bill Dupor	No impact
"An Empirical Analysis of the Revival of Fiscal Activism in the 2000s"	John B. Taylor	No impact

A more detailed summary of these and other papers can be found at www.washingtonpost.com under the title "Did the Stimulus Work? A Review of the Nine Best Studies on the Subject." It was authored by Dylan Matthews.

Kick It Up a Notch AGGREGATE SUPPLY SHOCKS

In both Figures 9.7 and 9.8 we start out with AS_1 crossing AD_1 so that prices are at PI* and output is at RGDP*. A hypothetical shock moves aggregate supply to AS_2. If the aggregate supply shock is negative and it raises input prices substantially, as in Figure 9.7, people will lose their jobs as RGDP falls. Nondiscretionary fiscal policy will kick in at this point, though, because the loss of jobs will mean an increase in welfare spending and a decrease in taxes. This will cause aggregate demand to shift to the right to AD_2. If the president and Congress then decide to go further with discretionary fiscal policy in an effort to get output back to RGDP*, they will have to cut taxes or raise spending to do so. The problem is that the shock itself and the nondiscretionary fiscal policy that was implemented have already created high inflation. Discretionary fiscal policy can only serve to worsen the problem.

On the other hand, if the aggregate supply shock is that input prices have fallen, as depicted in Figure 9.8, output increases. Nondiscretionary fiscal policy is such that taxes increase and welfare spending decreases. When this happens, aggregate demand falls to AD_2. In this case, there is no need for discretionary fiscal policy because, even though there is a shock, it is only for the good. Both the shock and the nondiscretionary fiscal policy also serve to calm inflation.

FIGURE 9.7 Nondiscretionary and discretionary fiscal policy in the wake of a negative aggregate supply shock.

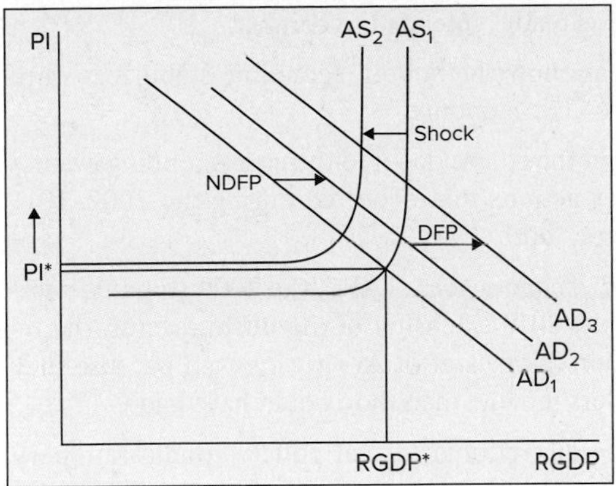

FIGURE 9.8 Nondiscretionary fiscal policy in the wake of a positive aggregate supply shock.

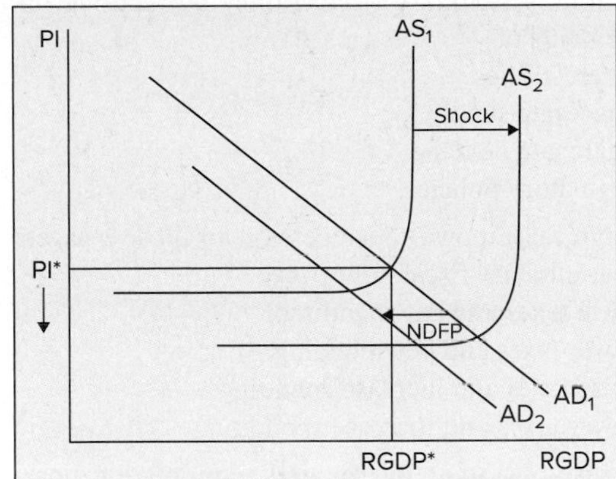

Summary

You now can distinguish between discretionary and nondiscretionary fiscal policy and know how to model them using an aggregate supply and aggregate demand diagram. You understand that different policies are used to counteract aggregate demand and aggregate supply shocks. You also now understand that though there are considerable problems associated with discretionary fiscal policy, it has seen a recent revival. Still, nondiscretionary fiscal policy remains the primary means by which we stabilize our economy.

Key Terms

administrative lag
aggregate demand shock
aggregate supply shock
contractionary fiscal policy
discretionary fiscal policy
expansionary fiscal policy
fiscal policy
nondiscretionary fiscal policy
operational lag
political business cycle
recognition lag
shock

Quiz Yourself

1. The existence of the federal income tax and the welfare system serve as the primary elements of
   a. discretionary fiscal policy.
   b. nondiscretionary fiscal policy.
   c. monetary policy.
   d. exchange rate policy.
2. Adjustments to tax and spending policies serve as primary elements of
   a. discretionary fiscal policy.
   b. nondiscretionary fiscal policy.
   c. monetary policy.
   d. exchange rate policy.
3. Discretionary fiscal policy is the purview of
   a. Congress only.
   b. the president only.
   c. Congress and the president collectively through law.
   d. the Federal Reserve.
4. Nondiscretionary fiscal policy has its impact by
   a. magnifying the economic ups and downs already occurring.
   b. purposefully adjusting interest rates.
   c. focusing Congress's attention on economic policy.
   d. dampening the economic ups and downs already occurring.

5. The aggregate demand–aggregate supply model examines the impact of discretionary fiscal policy and nondiscretionary fiscal policy by focusing on movements of
   a. interest rates.
   b. aggregate supply.
   c. aggregate demand.
   d. regulatory policies.
6. One typical response to a recession for those engaged in discretionary fiscal policy is to
   a. raise taxes and cut spending.
   b. lower taxes and cut spending.
   c. raise taxes and increase spending.
   d. lower taxes and increase spending.
7. One response to an overheated economy for those engaged in discretionary fiscal policy is to
   a. raise taxes and cut spending.
   b. lower taxes and cut spending.
   c. raise taxes and increase spending.
   d. lower taxes and increase spending.
8. In 2001, it was not clear that the recession had started until well after it had begun. In retrospect, this was an example of the
   a. administrative lag.
   b. operational lag.
   c. recognition lag.
   d. implementation lag.
9. Nondiscretionary fiscal policy has the advantage over discretionary fiscal policy in that
   a. the latter requires action by the Congress and president (who often cannot agree).
   b. the former only makes use of taxes.
   c. the latter can only make use of changes to interest rates.
   d. the former only makes use of the welfare state.
10. Discretionary fiscal policy as a tool for managing an economy is
   a. universally applauded as being helpful.
   b. universally criticized as never being effective.
   c. considered by many to be effective but subject to several concerns over timing and motive.
   d. inconsistent with the aggregate demand-aggregate supply model.
11. The oil price decreases from 2014 to 2016 are an example of a
   a. positive aggregate demand shock.
   b. negative aggregate demand shock.
   c. positive aggregate supply shock.
   d. negative aggregate supply shock.

Short Answer Questions

1. Which lag described in this chapter is the concept of "shovel-ready" intended to combat.
2. Explain how the built-in economic stabilizers work in the U.S. economy.
3. Assign the correct label to the corresponding events/policy actions that occurred during the 2007–2011 time period.

   Events/policy actions: TARP, the 2009 stimulus package, the 2010 extension of the Bush tax cuts, the reduction in taxes most Americans paid because they had less income than they would have had.

   Label: discretionary fiscal policy, nondiscretionary fiscal policy.

Think about This

Concerns over the recognition, administrative, and operational lags as well as the concern that discretionary fiscal policy is subject to political biases have caused some economists to believe Congress and the president should do nothing in the face of a recession. Even if they are correct, is it realistic to expect the public to embrace elected officials who do nothing?

Talk about This

The third and fourth years of presidential terms have higher average rates of real growth than the first and second years. Do you think this is a coincidence or is it a reflection of political reality that politicians are more concerned about reelection than about creating long-run economic growth?

For More Insight See

Journal of Economic Perspectives 14, no. 3 (Summer 2000). See articles written by Alberto Alesina, John B. Taylor, Alan Auerbach, and Daniel Feenberg, and Douglas Elmendorf and Louise Sheiner.

Any textbook entitled *Intermediate Macroeconomics* will have a chapter on fiscal policy.

Behind the Numbers

Bureau of Economic Analysis (BEA): www.bea.gov

- GDP
- RGDP

Bureau of Economic Analysis (BEA): www.bea.gov/newsreleases/rels.htm

- Early estimates of GDP

CHAPTER TEN

Monetary Policy

Learning Objectives

After reading this chapter you should be able to:

LO1 Describe the role of the Federal Reserve of the United States.

LO2 Describe the goals of monetary policy.

LO3 Describe the tools of monetary policy and utilize the aggregate supply and aggregate demand model to illustrate how monetary policy works.

LO4 Describe the recent history of monetary policy and the Federal Reserve's role in the 2007–2009 recession.

Chapter Outline

Throughout the 2007-2009 recession and beyond, the role of the Federal Reserve—usually called the Fed—in shaping the economy of the United States has grown from mysterious yet important to absolutely central, with politicians, the media, and, on some days, ordinary Americans attentive to its actions. No more important aspect of our daily lives is run by people with as little accountability as those who are its executive officers.

The Federal Reserve began in 1913 as a response to the boom and bust nature of the financial world of the late 19th and early 20th centuries. It has become a government institution every bit as important in the lives of people as the three branches of government. In a matter of a couple of hours, one person, the chair of the Federal Reserve Board, can influence stock prices by 5 percent, cause mortgage interest rates to rise or fall by a full percentage point, and set in place a course of action that will raise or lower the unemployment rate by one percentage point or more. The chair can do this, moreover, without the approval of or even consultation with any elected person. Fortunately, the chairs appointed by presidents and confirmed by the Senate have all been people of impeccable character. Even if their wisdom has been clouded at some points, a hint of corruption in this area of government would be devastating to world financial markets in particular and, by extension, to the whole world economy.

We will use the context of the 2007-2009 recession, and the very slow recovery from it, to explore the goals of monetary policy and then discuss the tools the Federal Reserve has to meet those goals. We will begin the discussion of those tools by first focusing on the traditional and ordinary tools of monetary policy and then examine the extraordinary ones that were first employed in 2008 as the Federal Reserve attempted to stabilize first the financial markets and later the overall economy. As we move through the chapter, we will consider why the Fed exists and why its political independence is important. Next we review some of the history of the pre-2008 use of monetary policy and consider the extraordinary actions of the Federal Reserve during and after the 2007-2009 recession. We conclude by describing the process by which the Fed is likely to unwind those policies and return to its traditional function.

It is worth noting, particularly for those who may have completed Chapter 9, monetary policy differs from fiscal policy in important respects. Where fiscal policy is the purview of Congress and the president, monetary policy is governed by the Federal Reserve. Fiscal policy utilizes changes to tax and spending policies, whereas monetary policy utilizes changes to interest rates.

Goals, Tools, and a Model of Monetary Policy

The Federal Reserve has never had a "tool" that would directly impact the economy. Its goals must be met using an intermediate target with the hope and expectation that the end result of hitting the intermediate target will satisfy the ultimate goal. Though the *monetary transmission mechanism*, the means by which the intermediate target allows you to hit the ultimate goal, will be explained later, consider this metaphor: Most modern cars have electronic throttle controls (gas pedals). Pushing the gas pedals doesn't directly increase gas flow to the engine, it causes the electronics of the car to do that. If your goal is a steady speed and your speedometer is broken, you can achieve your goal through the use of an intermediate target: steady pressure on the pedal.

Goals of Monetary Policy

The most important historical role for monetary policy and its implementing institution, the Federal Reserve, has been to prevent boom and bust cycles by regulating banks and other financial institutions. While the role of dampening the boom and bust cycle remains an important part of the job, the mechanism by which this is achieved has changed dramatically. At first, the Fed simply ensured the financial soundness of institutions. Now it also directly manipulates interest rates to change the borrowing habits of banks, businesses, and consumers. In this way, the Fed seeks to maintain low levels of inflation and sustainable levels of RGDP growth.

Traditional and Ordinary Tools of Monetary Policy

For the better part of the last 50 years, the Federal Reserve and other similar central banks around the world have been conducting monetary policy in a similar fashion. They pick an intermediate target variable that works the best to achieve their goals and use the basic tools at their disposal to hit that target. If they see that the target is outside of a desired range, they use those tools to nudge the variable back within the range. There have been times when the Fed has found that it can hit the intermediate target but that fails to result in its goal.

Returning to the example of the gas pedal and the broken speedometer, if you are on a hilly section of road, steady pressure on the gas pedal doesn't keep your speed steady. You have to use your position relative to other cars as the intermediate target. There have been times when the Fed has had to abandon one intermediate target in favor of another.

In the 1970s, the target was the **federal funds rate**—the market-determined rate at which banks borrow from one another to meet obligations imposed on it by the Federal Reserve. As inflation increased rapidly in the late 1970s, targeting the federal funds rate proved to be impossible. That was because keeping the federal funds rate low required that the Fed continuously increase the supply of money. As more money was available to purchase limited goods, those increases created even greater inflation. This caused interest rates to rise rather than fall. In October 1979, as the rate of inflation continued to rise, the Fed formally stopped using the federal funds rate as its target and shifted to targeting **M2.** M2 is what is known as a **monetary aggregate.** M2 is a broad measure of money because it includes cash, checking accounts, savings accounts, and small certificates of deposit (CDs). **M1,** a narrower monetary aggregate, includes only cash and checking accounts.[1] By the summer of 1982, the economy was in the midst of a deep recession. The result was that inflation subsided. A statistical side effect of recessions is that monetary aggregates become unstable. The result of that instability in M2 was that the Fed returned to targeting the federal funds rate. In general, when inflation is high, a monetary aggregate is a good target, but when the economy is in recession or in a period of typical growth, the federal funds rate serves as a better target.

federal funds rate
The market-determined rate at which banks borrow from one another to meet obligations imposed on it by the Federal Reserve.

M2
M1 + saving accounts + small CDs.

monetary aggregate
A measure of the quantity of money in the economy.

M1
Cash + coin + checking accounts.

inflation targeting
A policy whereby a central bank publishes a desired range of a specified inflationary measure and then uses the tools of monetary policy to bring that measure of inflation into that desired range.

The European Central Bank currently targets inflation rather than a monetary aggregate or interest rate. **Inflation targeting** is relatively new as a concept and involves publishing a desired range of a specified inflationary measure and then using the tools of monetary policy to bring inflation into that desired range. Many argue that from the time Benjamin Bernanke took over as Fed chair

[1]In 2006, the Fed abandoned its use of M3 as a useful measure as it was becoming unstable and therefore an unreliable measure.

MONEY CREATION

One of the lessons that economists routinely teach students in courses designed for economics and business majors is the notion of "money creation." The banking system can create more "money" than physically exists in the form of coin and cash. This was implied in our definitions of the monetary aggregates (M1, M2, etc.) because if money were only currency, then there would be no need to add checkable accounts and CDs.

The banking system creates money by issuing a series of loans. To see how, let's assume that there are several people (John, Paul, George, Ringo, Simon, Randy, and Paula) and several banks (1st National, 2nd National, 3rd National, and 4th National. Suppose John makes a $1,000 deposit at 1st National, and that bank loans Paul $900 (10 percent, or $100, must be held as part of that bank's reserves). Suppose Paul buys something from George, who deposits that $900 at 2nd National. Then suppose that Ringo borrows $810 (again 10 percent, or $90, must be held at the Fed) from 2nd National to buy something from Simon, who deposits that money in 3rd National. If Randy borrows $729 (10 percent, or $81, must be held at the Fed) from 3rd National to buy something from Paula and Paula deposits that money in 4th National and . . . You get the point—this could go on forever. In the end there are deposits totaling $10,000 ($1,000 + $900 + $810 + $729 + . . .) that resulted from that initial $1,000. The bottom line is this: the banking system can create more money than physically exists.

in 2006 to the beginning of the financial crisis in the fall of 2007, the Fed engaged in what amounted to inflation targeting. The Fed made clear through its regular announcements that it was closely monitoring the core PCE deflator described in Chapter 6.

Whatever is targeted, the mechanism by which the Fed regularly analyzes the target is **open-market operations.** Open-market operations result when the Fed buys and sells government debt. The Fed owns approximately half a trillion dollars of the short-term government bonds that make up a portion of the national debt, and it sells (to banks) a portion of that reserve of bonds when it wants to get money out of the banking system. It buys bonds (from those same banks) when it wants to add to the supply of money that is in circulation.

open-market operations
The buying and selling of bonds, which, respectively, increases or decreases the money supply, thereby influencing interest rates.

One of the important functions of the Federal Reserve is to serve as a direct lender to banks. That means the interest rate that the Fed charges those banks serves as one of the tools of monetary policy. Banks with sufficient creditworthiness can borrow unlimited amounts from the Fed at the primary credit rate. The **primary credit rate or discount rate** is typically one percentage point higher than the federal funds rate. Banks with lesser credit ratings face higher rates.[2]

primary credit rate or discount rate
The rate at which banks with excellent credit can borrow from the Federal Reserve.

The last way that the Federal Reserve can impact interest rates is by altering the proportion that the bank can lend from the deposits it receives. The **reserve ratio** requires that a specific percentage of every dollar deposited be placed in a Federal Reserve bank. If the ratio is lowered, the bank has more money to lend, whereas if the ratio is raised, the bank has less money to lend. For the vast majority of banks in 2019, the reserve ratio was 10 percent.

reserve ratio
The percentage of every dollar deposited in a checking account that a bank must maintain at a Federal Reserve branch.

Modeling Monetary Policy

The way monetary policy is supposed to work is through what is called the *monetary transmission* mechanism. The Federal Reserve can use any of its tools (open-market operations, the adjustments to the discount rate, and adjustments to the reserve ratio) to increase or decrease the supply of loanable funds, which in turn impacts short-term interest rates. The expansionary and contractionary impacts of such policies are shown in Figures 10.1 and 10.2, respectively. The only real question is whether the causation arrow (the arrow between the loanable funds diagram and the AS-AD diagram) is operating.

Let's begin by showing that each of the Fed's tools can impact interest rates. If the Federal Reserve uses open market operations to buy bonds, it increases the amount of money that banks and other financial institutions can loan. This increases the supply of loanable

[2]Prior to 2003, the Federal Reserve utilized another key interest rate to signal its intentions, the discount rate. This was the interest rate at which the Fed itself loaned money to banks, usually buying a portion of a bank's loan portfolio. The discount rate (as the primary credit rate was called then) was below the federal funds rate, but banks were hesitant to use this service too often because it brought with it the potential for extra scrutiny from auditors.

FIGURE 10.1 Expansionary monetary policy: buying bonds, lowering the discount rate, or lowering the reserve ratio.

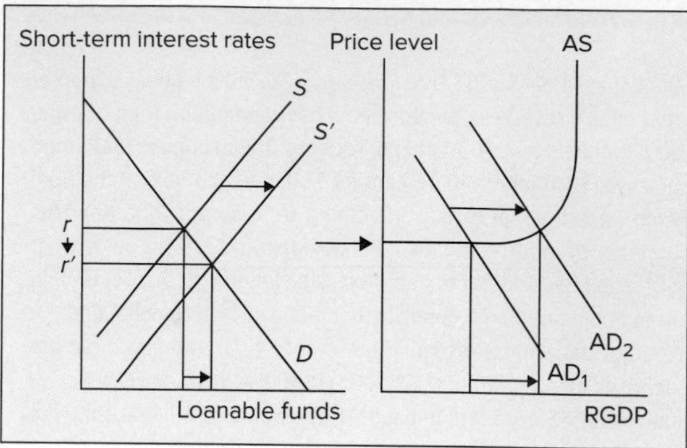

FIGURE 10.2 Contractionary monetary policy: selling bonds, raising the discount rate, or raising the reserve ratio.

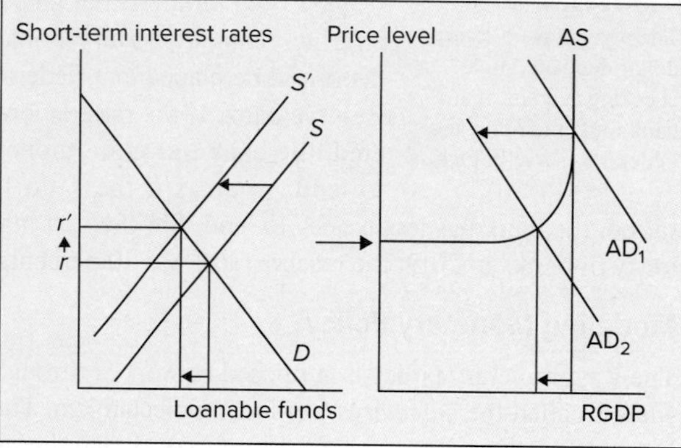

funds in Figure 10.1 and decreases the interest rate in this market. The Fed can just as easily have an opposite desire to increase interest rates. The left panel of Figure 10.2 shows what happens when the Fed sells bonds in an effort to increase interest rates. The increase in interest rates is accomplished when the Fed reduces the supply of loanable funds.

Because the federal funds rate is determined by market forces between banks and is not determined directly by the Fed, the way the Fed can influence that rate is by increasing or decreasing the supply of generally available funds for loans. Its rationale is that this action will indirectly influence the federal funds rate. There is enough linkage between the quantity of money that is generally available for loans and the interest rate that banks charge each other that this seems to work fairly well.

As we noted, the Federal Reserve can impact interest rates by changing the reserve ratio. If the ratio is lowered, the bank has more money to lend and the supply of loanable funds moves to the right, as it does in the left panel of Figure 10.1. If the ratio is raised, the bank has less money to lend and the supply of loanable funds moves to the left, as is indicated in the left panel of Figure 10.2.

As you saw in Chapter 8, one of the determinants of aggregate demand is interest rates. The influence of interest rates stems from the fact that investors want to borrow more to buy plant and equipment when interest rates are lower. In addition, consumers are more willing to buy expensive durable goods like cars and home furnishings when interest rates are lower. For the person who pays cash, the lower interest rate effect is indirect in that buyers sacrifice less interest income when they take money out of savings to buy something. The person who borrows money to buy a car is more likely to buy that car and more likely to buy a nicer, more expensive car because of the lower interest rate.

An increase in the money supply or a lowering of the federal funds or discount rate allows banks to make more loans. These are loans that they can make only if they lower interest rates to ordinary borrowers. The lowering of interest rates causes the aggregate demand curve to rise as a result of increases in investment and interest-sensitive consumption. This is shown in the right panel of Figure 10.1. An identical but opposite story can be told concerning a decrease in the money supply. Less is available for banks to lend, a circumstance that allows them to raise the interest rates they charge to ordinary borrowers. Raising such rates causes a reduction in investment and interest-sensitive consumption. This in turn causes aggregate demand to fall, as is shown in the right panel of Figure 10.2.

The Monetary Transmission Mechanism

Now we get to the question of whether changing short-term interest rates (using any of the tools) impacts the overall economy in the desired fashion. That is, does the change in the left panel of Figure 10.1 cause the change in the right panel of Figure 10.1, and does the same work for Figure 10.2? The process by which the use of a monetary policy tool impacts the overall economy is called **monetary transmission.**

monetary transmission The process by which the use of a monetary policy tool impacts the overall economy.

Economists disagree about the effectiveness of monetary policy, especially in the long run and in circumstances of extreme economic uncertainty. Let's take the first of these two concerns. Whereas there is some doubt among economists about whether the Fed has the ability to alter short-term economic outcomes in normal economic circumstances, the doubt is much more widely held concerning its long-term ability to increase output through sustained increases in the money supply.

The underlying reason for this skepticism is that sustained increases in the money supply will be factored in by investors, who will anticipate that substantial inflation will result from such a policy. Thus, though it may look as if the Fed could use the logic from Figure 10.1 to continuously foster long-run rapid growth, not many economists believe the Fed has this power. As a result, Figures 10.1 and 10.2 should be taken as relevant only in the short term.

Conventional monetary policy is less effective in times of extreme economic uncertainty than Figures 10.1 and 10.2 suggest. This is because borrowers' confidence is so shaken (by actual unemployment, the threat of unemployment, or reduced demand for what their business produces) that any small modifications to borrowing costs are trivial compared to these underlying problems. This was certainly the case during the Great Depression, but you don't have to go back that far for a clear example of what economists call a **liquidity trap.** A liquidity trap exists when even zero or near zero interest rates do not stimulate borrowing.

liquidity trap
A situation where zero or near zero interest rates do not stimulate borrowing.

With a global economic slowdown under way in 2008 and 2009, firms had more than adequate capital to produce the significantly reduced volume of goods and services consumers were ready to purchase. As a result, the reduction in interest rates that normally may have motivated firms to borrow money to buy new capital did not influence them in the slightest. Furthermore, consumers who might have been persuaded to borrow money to buy cars, homes, or home furnishings were more concerned about the likelihood that they would keep their jobs, so they continued to save their money. Moreover, the bursting of the housing bubble, which reduced home prices by an average of more than 20 percent, made many potential borrowers think twice about taking on more debt.

The supply side of the liquidity trap can be demonstrated with the help of the data on required and excess reserves of banks displayed in Figure 10.3. As previously

FIGURE 10.3 Proportion of bank reserves held by banks that are required and excess.

Source: Board of Governors of the Federal Reserve System, www.federalreserve.gov/econresdata/statisticsdata.htm

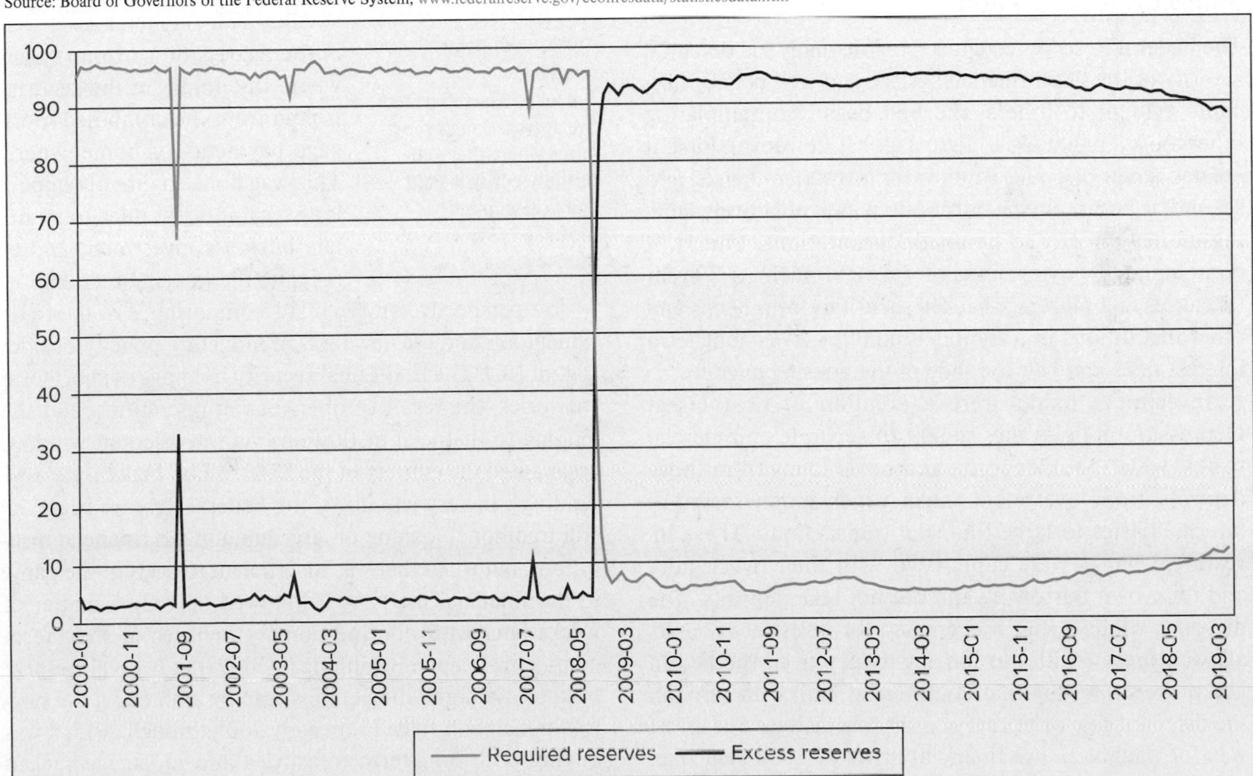

described, large banks are compelled to hold 10 percent of their deposits in the form of required reserves at the Federal Reserve. They can loan the other 90 percent as they see fit. During normal economic times, that is exactly what they do. With the quite obvious and notable exception of September of 2001, bank reserves were basically equal to required reserves. Upward of 95 percent of their reserves were required while the remainder were simply viewed as a cushion against unusual daily activity. The excess reserves were loaned overnight in the federal funds market. In late 2008, as the financial crisis hit in full force, the proportion of reserves that were considered "excess" went from 5 percent of the total to 90 percent of the total, and this occurred over a short three-month window. That these proportions did not revert to normal through mid-2019 suggests that, at least from the banks' perspective, the liquidity trap was in full effect. Because the Federal Reserve paid a modest interest rate on these deposits, the risk-adjusted profits the banks could earn by depositing their excess reserves with the Federal Reserve were sufficient to have them do that rather than loaning it to businesses and consumers.

The Additional Tools of Monetary Policy Created in 2008

The Federal Reserve recognized before many the potential severity of the 2008 financial crisis, and well before it became evident to others, the Fed began contemplating other tools it might use to fight a global slowdown. First, it created a new discount window for investment banks, and second, it began buying corporate paper, effectively lending money directly to nonbank corporations. Finally, it contemplated buying longer-term debt such as 30-year treasuries and mortgage-backed securities from banks and other institutions in a frantic attempt to lower long-term interest rates and halt the slide of the housing market.

Investment banks were a creation of post–Great Depression policies that sought to separate commercial banks, which took deposits and made loans from those deposits, from investment banks, which simply served as intermediaries to large financial transactions. These investment banks were capitalized with their own equity and their own borrowing and did not take deposits. The discount window that was created for investment banks allowed these entities to borrow money from the Fed in much the same way that commercial banks do through the discount rate or primary credit rate facility. The effort was for naught as the financial crisis of 2008 sent one, Lehman Brothers, into liquidation and threatened the health of the remaining two, Morgan Stanley and Goldman Sachs.

Additionally, the Fed began buying corporate paper when even well-capitalized and well-run corporations were having difficulty finding buyers for their short-term debt. **Corporate paper** is the name given to short-term debt offered by large corporations. These corporations routinely borrow billions of dollars for inventory-building purposes or to deal with uneven sales knowing that they will easily be able to pay off the debt with the proceeds of future sales. Without this market, many corporations could not operate. Because the financial system was not working properly in the fall of 2008, the Fed stepped in to support these loans.

corporate paper
Short-term debt offered by large corporations.

At times during 2008–2013, the Federal Reserve began buying long-term debt in a process called **quantitative easing.** This process referred to making much more money available to the economy through the purchase of 20- and 30-year U.S. treasuries and mortgage-backed securities. A **mortgage-backed security** is a financial asset that is the aggregation of mortgages where the holder of the security is paid from the combined mortgage payments of homeowners. This was done to directly impact long-term interest rates to stimulate business investment and to re-ignite the housing market.

quantitative easing
The process by which the Federal Reserve buys long-term securities in order to decrease long-term interest rates to directly stimulate business investment and housing markets.

mortgage-backed security
Financial asset that is the aggregation of mortgages where the holder of the security is paid from the combined mortgage payments of homeowners.

For perspective on the relative importance of the traditional tools and the new tools of monetary policy, consider Figure 10.4. The traditional security holdings of short-term treasuries, the result of open-market operations, and the lending to financial institutions via the discount window, constituted the entirety of the $860 billion Federal Reserve holdings. In very late 2008, the Federal Reserve began its still traditional loaning of large amounts to financial institutions, but when that was insufficient to prevent the panic in the financial markets, it followed up only a matter of weeks later with nontraditional purchases of short-term commercial paper. Beginning in 2009, the Federal Reserve tried to overcome the liquidity trap by embracing the nontraditional tools fully. From early 2009 through 2015, it was buying both long-term treasuries and mortgage-backed securities in such volume that by early 2015, the total

FIGURE 10.4 Federal Reserve holdings 2007–2019.

Source: Board of Governors of the Federal Reserve System, www.federalreserve.gov/econresdata/statisticsdata.htm

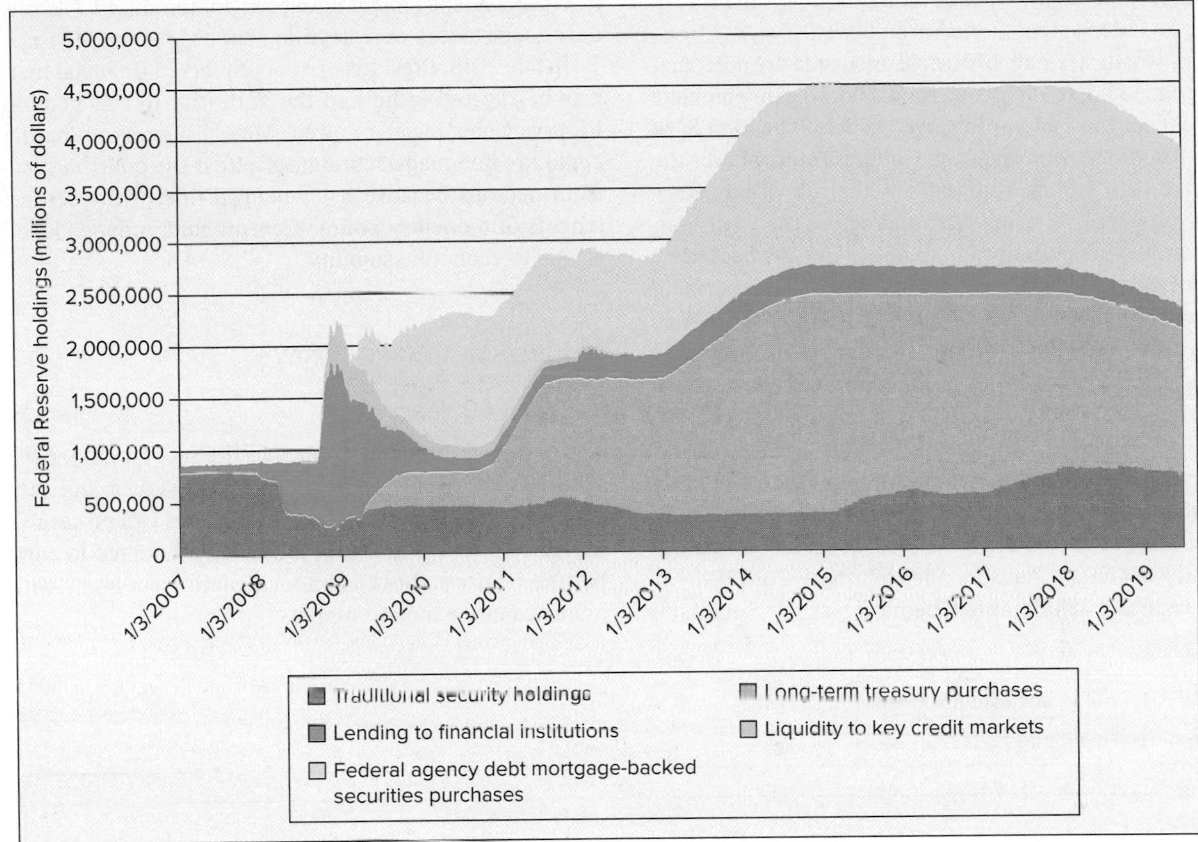

Federal Reserve holdings had quintupled. From 2015 to 2017, the Fed held its portfolio relatively constant. As the RGDP started growing more rapidly in 2017 and 2018, the Fed began to raise interest rates and begin the long, slow process of reducing its portfolio.

Central Bank Independence

The Fed's power over the economy is substantial because it can do what it thinks is best without fear of being contradicted. Its independence from political control gives it awesome power and awesome responsibility to use that power judiciously. The Fed is so independent that it can slow growth or even put the nation into a recession in an effort to stamp out inflation. Economists generally agree that the Fed must be free from political control in order to take the necessary action to fight inflation. Experience across nations in the latter half of the 20th century provides rather powerful evidence that this is true.

Long-run economic growth requires that the financial markets have faith that money invested in a country will not lose value as a result of excessive inflation. When people are concerned about inflation, interest rates increase. Higher interest rates make investments more expensive. Since growth occurs only when investments in the future take place, long-term growth depends on the existence of a believable **monetary authority**—the general name given to the entity that controls monetary policy in a country. While a politically controlled monetary authority could generate that faith if it never wavered from potentially unpopular policies, experience tells us this does not happen. We know this because those countries with a history of independent monetary authorities have experienced lower inflation rates, lower interest rates, and higher real growth rates than countries without that history of independence. The United States, Germany, Switzerland, Japan, Canada, and the Netherlands are

monetary authority
The general name given to the entity that controls monetary policy in a country.

examples of countries with such independence, whereas Spain and Italy are examples of countries without it. For the stability we enjoy, we are willing to accept the risk of having an independent monetary authority.

It is worth a small historical interlude to note that Congress could, by simply passing a law, regain complete control over the Federal Reserve. Article I, Section 8, of the U.S. Constitution gives the Congress control over the power to coin money. It never took the role of monetary policy very seriously, however; and before the Civil War, paper money was usually a banknote, typically backed by gold, of an individual private bank. With its authorizing of the printing of money during and after the Civil War, prices fluctuated so fast that three significant financial panics in the span of 60 years convinced Congress to create the Federal Reserve in 1913. If Congress became sufficiently motivated, it could return to the business of controlling the supply of money and, indirectly, interest rates. Under ordinary circumstances, the continuous consultations between Federal Reserve Chair Bernanke, Treasury Secretary Paulson, and then New York Federal Reserve Bank Chair and Obama Treasury Secretary designate Geithner that occurred in the fall of 2008 would have raised concerns about the degree to which this independence might have been compromised. Clearly, the circumstances were anything but ordinary at the time.

In late 2018, President Trump unnerved financial markets by suggesting he had the authority to fire Federal Reserve Chair Jerome Powell. Merely suggesting that he could fire him made economists across the political spectrum nervous because it challenged one of the central tenants of monetary policy: Central bank independence is vital to economic stability.

Modern Monetary Policy

The Last 40 Years

The history of monetary policy in the second half of the 20th century is one of increasing importance and self-confidence, and its effect on interest rates can be seen in Figure 10.5. In the late 1970s, the Fed attempted to combat the oil-price shocks and a stagnating economy with increases in the money supply.

FIGURE 10.5 Key interest rates from 1955 to 2015.

Source: Board of Governors of the Federal Reserve System, www.federalreserve.gov/econresdata/statisticsdata.htm

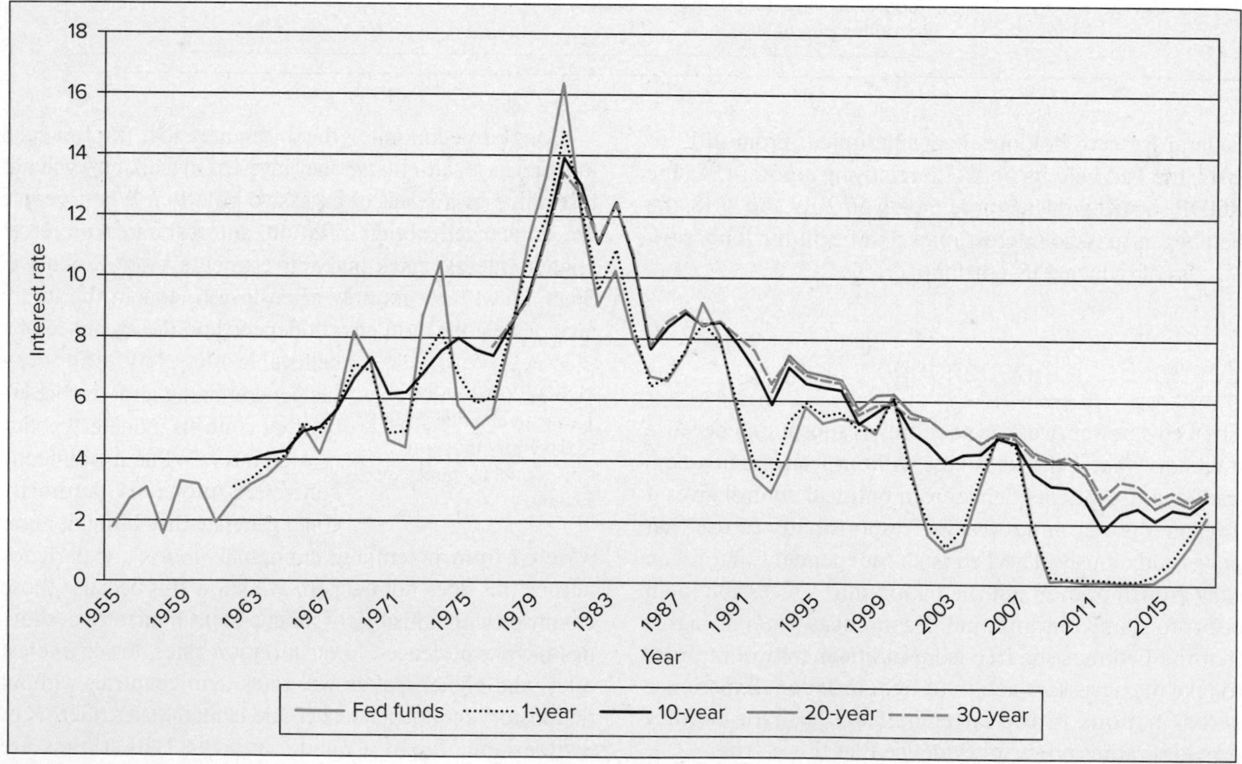

Unfortunately, these efforts served only to add to inflation. In 1981, the Fed changed course with a high-stakes war on inflation. It sent interest rates soaring. Its grip on M2 was such that the federal funds rate increased to nearly 20 percent, while the discount rate increased to 13 percent. By most measures, the resulting recession of 1981–1982 was the worst in post–World War II history. The unemployment rate peaked higher, RGDP fell more, and the reduction in inflation was greater than in any of the other post-1946 recessions. It also had the distinction of being the only recession caused intentionally by the Fed.

Since that time, the Fed has learned from its mistakes. For one thing, since the recession of 1982, it has not had to fight a significant inflation battle. In part this has been because it has been vigilant about not contributing to inflation.

After 1984, the highest inflation rate has been 5 percent. Not having to battle double-digit inflation but only having to keep it under control has made the Fed's job a little easier. In 1988, 1995, and again in 1999 and 2000, the Fed preemptively kept inflation in check by quickly increasing interest rates to slow an economy on the verge of creating inflation. It also worked to prevent a recession in 1994 by quickly lowering interest rates.

Its response to the 1990 recession was slow, but it was probably forgivably slow. In the months leading up to Iraq's invasion of Kuwait, RGDP growth was slow, inflation was picking up, and consumer indebtedness was starting to peak. On top of that, the Fed was determined to wait for the outcome of a budget deal. At the time, the federal deficit was more than $250 billion, it was headed toward $400 billion, and the Fed wanted to hold President Bush's (George Herbert Walker) and the Democratic leadership in Congress's collective feet to the fire and force them to act.

Unfortunately, Saddam Hussein's Iraq did not wait for the completion of the budget deal. After the invasion of Kuwait, gasoline prices increased sharply, and these circumstances precipitated an equally sharp decline in consumer confidence. Had the Fed acted immediately, it might have had better success keeping the United States out of the 1990–1991 recession, but its focus was on the deficit. It was also wary of duplicating the mistakes of the late 1970s by trying to battle cost-push inflation (inflation caused by movements in aggregate supply to the left) with increases in the money supply.

Whether explicitly or by chance, the Fed simply let the recession happen. It appeared to decide that there was little it could or should do to prevent it. Fortunately, however, the 1990–1991 recession was one of the shortest and the least disruptive recessions on record. Inflation never became a significant problem in part because consumer credit card debt was so high. Thus, except for a short spike in gas prices, inflation was negligible during this period. Unemployment rose but it came nowhere near 1982's modern record of 11 percent. During the first 18 months of the recovery, from June 1992 through the end of 1993, the economy was so weak, however, that it was unclear at the time whether it was a recovery or just an extension of the recession. In 1992 and 1993, the Fed stepped in with a significant reduction in interest rates, and by the last quarter of 1994, the economy was humming along nicely.

From 1994 on, the Fed kept a vigilant eye on inflation. Where necessary, as in 1995, the Fed let its guard down enough to prevent a slowdown from becoming a recession. By 1998, Fed governors were feeling rather proud of themselves. Unemployment was at a 30-year low, inflation was nowhere in sight, and longtime Fed Chair Alan Greenspan had successfully kept the stock market in check by offering advice against "irrational exuberance." In 1998, the economy was doing fine. It was in no need of increases or decreases in interest rates. Then the Asian financial crisis hit.

The Asian financial crisis resulted from a series of bad loans made in the Pacific Rim nations of Thailand, Malaysia, South Korea, and Indonesia, and from failed attempts by these countries to hold their foreign exchange rates constant.

The Fed's response to the crisis was guarded at first. It wanted to prevent the crisis from spreading but did not want its action to have the effect of importing the crisis to the United States. Stock prices in the United States did fall 20 percent in three months, and many economists began to predict that a recession would occur in the United States within a year. The Fed lowered interest rates a full percentage point, enough of an action to increase U.S. demand for imported goods. This helped stabilize Asia. In turn, the dollar became so strong relative to Asian currencies that the relative price of imports purchased by Americans fell enough to offset any domestic price increases.

The recession of 2001 served as another example of monetary policy, its uses, and its limitations. Beginning with the ambiguous nature of the 2000 presidential election, the recession of 2001 was met with 12 separate cuts in interest rates by the Federal Reserve. By 2003, the federal funds rate was at its lowest level in more than 40 years. For a time, in the spring of 2003, 30-year fixed mortgage interest rates were below 5 percent for the first time ever.

PUBLIC ENEMY #1: INFLATION OR DEFLATION?

In the late 1980s and through the decade of the 1990s, criticism started to be heard from the left and right that the Fed was overly concerned about the reappearance of inflation and not sufficiently concerned about the average person. Whether it has admitted it in public or not, since the late 1970s and early 1980s, the Fed had considered inflation public enemy number one. This had been true whether inflation was really a problem, as it was in 1979 and 1980; had the possibility of being a problem, as in 1988, 1995, and 1999–2000; or was a theoretical threat on the distant horizon.

Only when the country or the world was in trouble and inflation was less than 3 percent, as was the United States in 1993 and 2001 and the world in 1994, has the Federal Reserve relaxed its vigilance against inflation. In being focused on inflation, it has cut recoveries short or starved them of sufficient cash to really get going.

In late 2002–early 2003, and again in late 2008 and 2009, a new public enemy number one had begun to come into view: deflation. Recall from Chapter 6 that deflation is the opposite of inflation but is no less of a concern. Deflation has the effect of encouraging people not to buy now. This is because they know that if they wait, they will save money. This can be self-perpetuating in that by not buying, consumers force businesses to cut prices. This causes profits to fall and layoffs to occur, and buying diminishes even further. Even moderate deflation is worse than inflation in this regard. The Japanese experience with deflation in the late 1980s and 1990s offered very slow growth and stagnant employment. The Fed understood this potential quite well in 2003 when it again began to consider further interest rate cuts. It also understood this well when it drove short-term interest rates to zero in the fall of 2008. The deflation of 2008 was confined mostly to housing (20 percent), energy (60 percent), and to some producer commodities such as corn (40 percent), soybeans (40 percent), and raw metal prices (20 percent to 50 percent). The core PCE did not decrease during the period.

As can be seen from Figure 10.6, the crowning period of this aggressive monetary policy was between 1999 and 2006. The Federal Reserve Board's Open-Market Committee aggressively increased their federal funds rate target to combat economic circumstances. In mid-1999, the Fed aggressively raised interest rates six separate times.

The Fed was in the process of easing credit conditions in 2001 when the attacks of September 11, 2001, occurred. When stock markets opened the following Monday, it was with a Federal Reserve announcement that it was aggressively moving interest rates lower. With 13 rate cuts in a period of two-and-one-half years, the

FIGURE 10.6 Aggressive monetary policy between 1999 and 2019.

Source: Board of Governors of the Federal Reserve System. https://www.federalreserve.gov/monetarypolicy/openmarket.htm

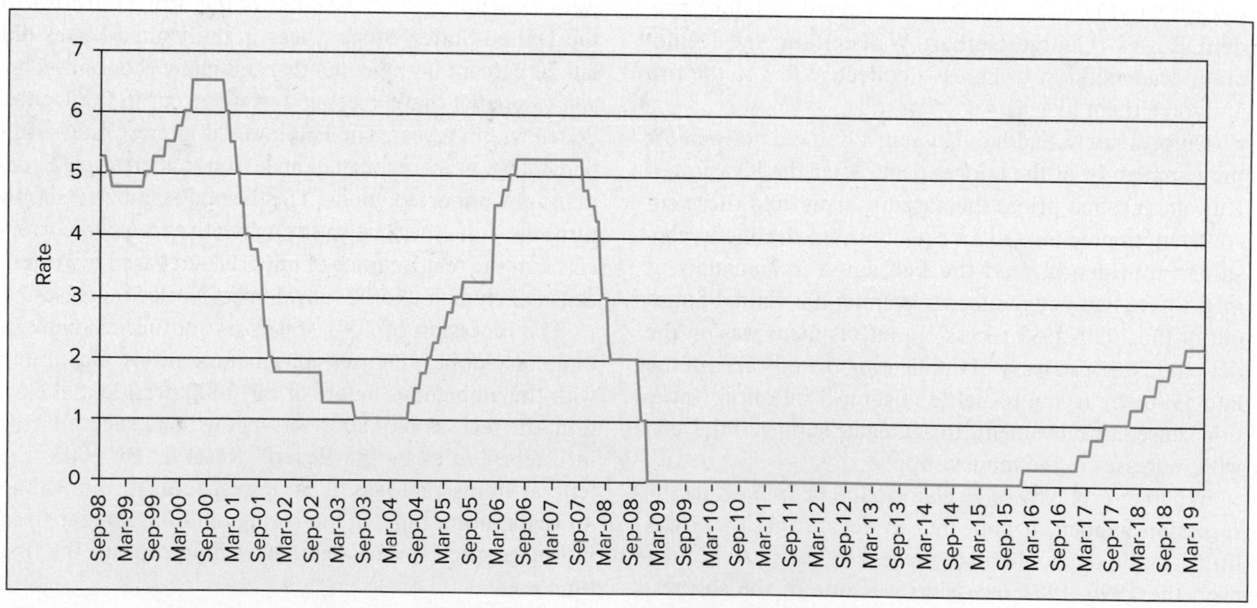

sluggish economy slowly rebounded through 2002 and grew much more rapidly through 2003 and 2004. In response, the Fed raised interest rates to more normal historical levels in 10 steps through mid-2005. As mentioned repeatedly through this chapter, the Federal Reserve's response to the financial crisis of 2008 was swift, if not entirely effective. It lowered short-term interest rates to nearly zero in an attempt to forestall, or at least dampen, the impact of the recession.

Economists will debate whether these interest rate changes had the desired impact, but consider this: Between June 2003 and June 2004, and again in 2008 and 2009, the Fed was pretty much out of tools. The Fed can't force businesses borrow money to invest in new plant and equipment and can't make consumers borrow to buy expensive consumer durables. Once the interest rate has been driven to nearly zero, decisions to borrow money are determined by the confidence that the borrower has in his or her ability to repay the money.

The Great Recession (2008–2009) and the decade that followed represent a unique moment in the history of monetary policy. Central banks across the globe engaged in sustained efforts to keep interest rates low for an extended period of time. As can be seen in Figure 10.7, the U.S. Federal Reserve was hardly alone in its massive purchases of financial assets. Both the Federal Reserve and the Bank of England quintupled the size of their respective portfolios. The European Central Bank started along the path the Fed was on and abandoned the effort at the same time the Fed doubled-down. The Bank of Japan, late to the show, tripled its holdings in the span of three years.

In the case of the U.S. Federal Reserve, it purchased nearly \$2 trillion in mortgage-backed securities and nearly \$2 trillion in long-term treasuries in three separate stages. The result was that \$3.7 trillion was in the economy, with most of it in bank reserves (typically held at the Fed as excess reserves). In late 2014, the Fed stopped pushing new money into the system, and in late 2015, it began the long process of pulling it out.

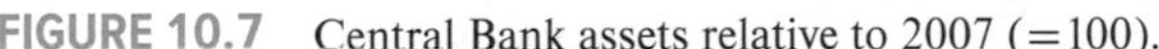
FIGURE 10.7 Central Bank assets relative to 2007 (=100).

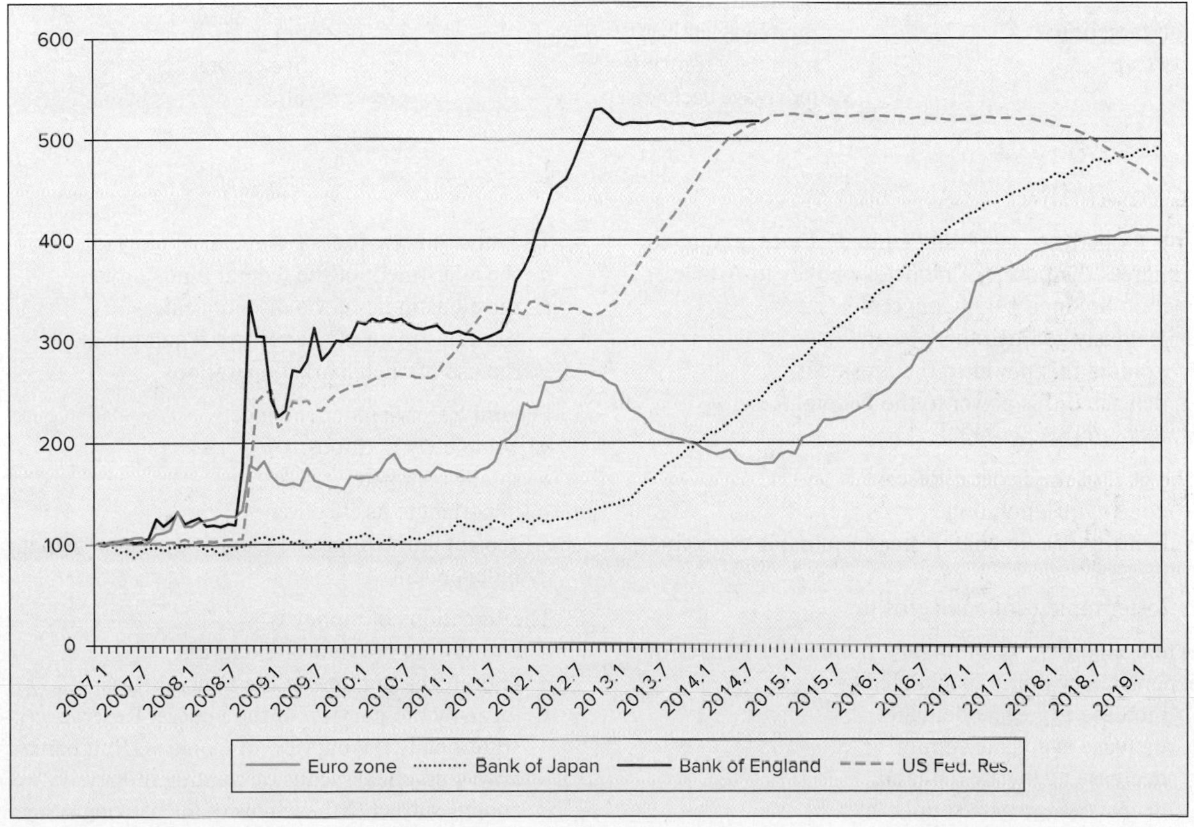

Through 2016 and into 2017, the efforts to remove that money involved simply letting the instruments that were purchased mature. It was, and remains, a balancing act. The removal of the money at too rapid a pace could set off a recession. Indeed, the slow growth of 2016 created precisely that concern. As growth picked up in 2017 and 2018, the effort to raise interest rates sped up, with interest rates rising one-quarter of a point every quarter. By the end of 2018 and into early 2019, when global slow-growth concerns mounted, the Fed slowed its efforts by pausing the rate increases.

Summary

With your newfound wealth of knowledge, you now understand the role of the Federal Reserve of the United States and its primary goal to maintain macroeconomic stability. You see that the Fed's own apparent measure of success in meeting this goal has been the ability to control inflation. You know the tools of monetary policy, understand how they work, and are able to apply that knowledge to an aggregate supply–aggregate demand model to illustrate the impacts of both expansionary and contractionary efforts. You explored the recent history of monetary policy and know how it has shaped the Federal Reserve's current fixation with inflation. Finally, you understand that economists, though worried about the consequences of inflation, are more concerned when deflation takes hold.

Key Terms

corporate paper
federal funds rate
inflation targeting
liquidity trap
M1
M2
monetary aggregate
monetary authority
monetary transmission
mortgage-backed security
open-market operations
primary credit rate or discount rate
quantitative easing
reserve ratio

Quiz Yourself

1. The Constitution of the United States grants to Congress the power of monetary policy in Article 1, Section 8. Since 1913, Congress has
   a. jealously guarded this power.
   b. granted this power to the president.
   c. delegated this power to the Federal Reserve.
   d. ignored this power.
2. The goal of the Federal Reserve is to
   a. control inflation only.
   b. control inflation and foster sustainable economic growth.
   c. foster rapid economic growth.
3. When engaging in monetary policy, the impact of expansionary policy is modeled by a(n)
   a. increase aggregate demand.
   b. increase aggregate supply.
   c. decrease aggregate demand.
   d. decrease aggregate supply.
4. The most precise tool of monetary policy is
   a. the adjustment of the federal funds target.
   b. the adjustment of the discount rate.
   c. the adjustment of the reserve requirement.
   d. the use of open-market operations.
5. Federal Reserve independence is
   a. completely fictitious.
   b. totally complete.
   c. important to its effectiveness.
   d. subject to the Supreme Court's desire to keep it independent.
6. The "creation" of money is
   a. entirely the purview of Congress.
   b. entirely the purview of the Federal Reserve.
   c. formally the purview of the Federal Reserve, constitutionally the purview of Congress, but banks have a practical means of creating money.
   d. entirely subject to the whims of the banking system.

7. During the Great Recession, the Federal Reserve
   a. used only its traditional tools.
   b. used tools it had never used before.
   c. was entirely passive.
   d. ignored the recession's existence.
8. The ability of the Federal Reserve to control interest rates using its traditional tools is
   a. limited almost entirely to short-term rates.
   b. limited almost entirely to long-term rates.
   c. limited almost entirely to intermediate-term rates.
   d. unlimited.
9. Which of the following tools would have likely had the impact of raising short-term interest rates the most?
   a. Cutting the federal funds target by 0.25 percent
   b. Buying $1 million in bonds
   c. Raising the reserve requirement from 8 percent to 15 percent
   d. Raising personal income tax rates by 1 percentage point

Short Answer Questions

1. Explain how open-market operations work.
2. Explain the difference between the discount rate and the federal funds rate.
3. Explain how lowering the reserve ratio affects the economy.
4. Explain how the 2010–2013 quantitative easing through the Federal Reserve purchase of mortgage-backed securities is different in style from what it usually does.

Think about This

Because the chairs of the Federal Reserve Board can have an enormous impact on policy decisions of the Fed and thereby the economy, their selection has been the subject of great political interest. Politically motivated monetary policy could be ruinous economic policy. Previous Fed chairs have understood that their functional independence from congressional interference depends on the apolitical nature of their decisions. What would the economic consequences be if this balance was upset by a president who nominated a Fed chair dedicated to protecting the president's political party?

Talk about This

Presidents tend to nominate Fed chairs on the basis of advice from those working daily in the financial markets. Who should have an impact on the choice of the Fed chair? Specifically, Fed policy can favor financial interests or the interests of workers. Should unions or others with a claim to represent workers have an impact on the selection of the Fed chair?

For More Insight See

Colander, David, "The Stories We Tell: A Reconsideration of AS/AD Analysis," *Journal of Economic Perspectives* 9, no. 3 (Summer 1995), pp. 169–188.

Ramo, Joshua Cooper, "The Three Marketeers," *Time*, February 15, 1999, pp. 34–42.

Steiger, Douglas, James H. Stock, and Mark W. Watson, "The NAIRU, Unemployment and Monetary Policy," *Journal of Economic Perspectives* 11, no. 1 (Winter 1997), pp. 33–50.

Behind the Numbers

Bureau of Labor Statistics (BLS): www.bls.gov/cpi

- CPI
- Inflation rates

Federal Reserve Board: www.federalreserve.gov/data.htm

- Interest rates
- Federal Reserve balance sheet

CHAPTER ELEVEN

Federal Spending

Learning Objectives

After reading this chapter you should be able to:

LO1 Describe the process of creating the federal budget of the United States.

LO2 Show that mandatory spending has steadily increased because of various entitlement programs and interest on the national debt.

LO3 Summarize the elements of discretionary spending.

LO4 Explain how marginal analysis is used to examine federal spending.

LO5 Distinguish between current-services and baseline budgeting.

LO6 Use the concept of opportunity cost to examine the elements of federal spending.

Chapter Outline

The federal government of the United States spends nearly $5 trillion each year on everything from welfare to national defense. This chapter focuses attention on how the government spends that money, a perfect example of how, in public policy, we use the concept of opportunity cost that was introduced in Chapter 1.

We start with a brief primer on what the Constitution requires before money can be spent. We then discuss the difference between mandatory and discretionary spending and how the balance between the two has shifted over the years. Next we describe where the money was budgeted in the 2020 fiscal year, how that budget reflects on our priorities, and how the shift in distribution over the years reflects a shift in priorities. We focus our attention, in particular, on health, Social Security, and defense spending, which make up the bulk of the federal budget. We use the Chapter 1 notion of marginal analysis to discuss both the size of federal spending and the distribution of it among various programs. Finally, we describe baseline and current-services budgeting and use Medicare and defense to discuss the differences.

As can be seen in Figure 11.1, federal spending as a percentage of GDP stayed between 18 percent and 22 percent for 22 years. After peaking in 1952 as a result of the Korean War, this measure trended up from 16 percent in 1955 to a peak at 23.5 percent in 1982 as spending on social programs increased. The Reagan years saw a slow decline only to rebound in the George Herbert Walker Bush years as billions were spent in a bailout of failed savings and loan associations. Since that time, the size of the federal government, measured as a percentage of GDP, fell to its lowest point in 25 years only to rise again in the wake of the September 11, 2001, attacks and the subsequent wars in Afghanistan and Iraq. The $750 billion Troubled Asset Relief Program (TARP) passed in October 2008, and the $787 billion Obama stimulus package passed in February 2009 greatly altered this figure. After the Great Recession peak of 24.4 percent, federal spending as a percentage of GDP is projected to stabilize at around 21 percent.

FIGURE 11.1 Federal spending as a percentage of GDP.

Source: The Office of Management and Budget. https://www.whitehouse.gov/omb/historical-tables/

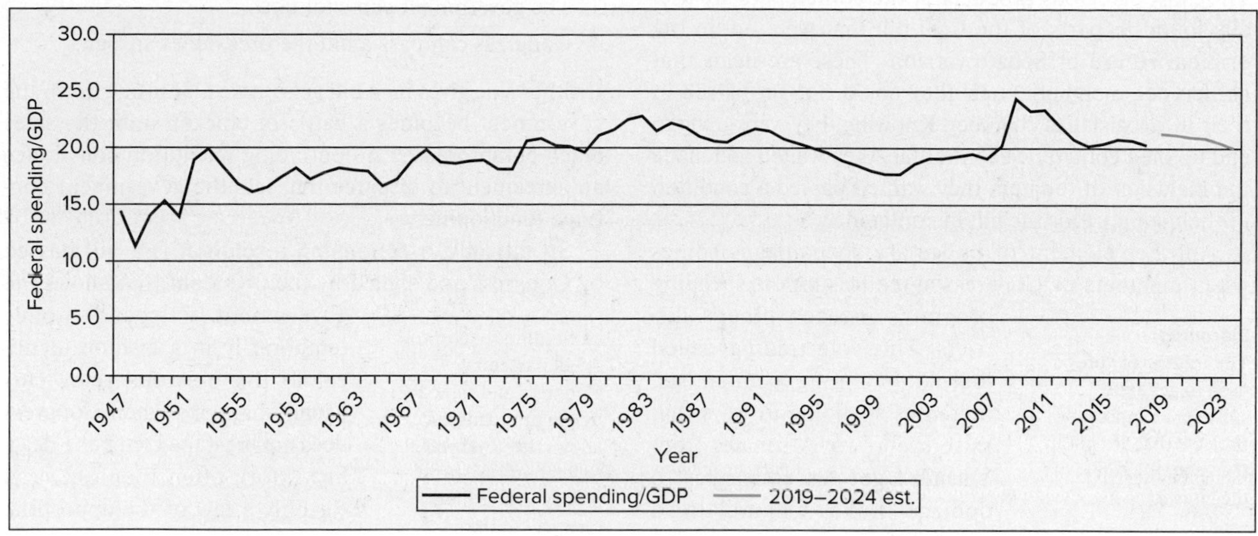

A Primer on the Constitution and Spending Money

What the Constitution Says

According to the Constitution of the United States of America, "No money shall be drawn from the treasury, but in consequence of appropriations made by law." This means that unless Congress passes an appropriations bill and the president either signs it or has a veto overturned, no money can be spent. The president and Congress thus must reach either an agreement or a compromise on spending priorities so that Congress will pass an appropriation bill that the president will sign.

Under normal procedures, the president sends a proposed budget to Congress in late winter or early spring. The Congress often uses that budget as a blueprint upon which it bases a budget plan of its own. It uses its version as it debates and negotiates with the executive branch of government. When both sides reach agreement on a final budget, Congress passes appropriations bills to actually spend the money that has been budgeted.

All of this work must be completed by October 1 because the government's fiscal year starts then and goes to September 30 of the following year. (So the 2020 fiscal year began October 1, 2019, and ended September 30, 2020.) When these bills are passed and signed by the president, they become law and money can be spent. Otherwise, money cannot be spent.

Shenanigans

This process has a myriad of places for shenanigans. Chief among these are actions taken by the various subcommittee and committee chairs and in the House-Senate conferences. The chairs of the appropriations subcommittees and the chairs of the full committees can and do influence how much gets allocated in the federal budget and where it gets spent. Whereas spending on social insurance programs like Medicaid, Medicare, and Social Security cannot be easily altered, highway spending and defense spending are prime targets for spending on items of local rather than national interest. The chair of a subcommittee like the one on highway spending can fund the building of bridges and highways in his or her district much more easily than anyone else can. As with roads and bridges, defense is also an area where the powerful chairs of the subcommittees and the full committees work to ensure that federal money is spent in their districts. Recent history is filled with examples of weapons systems that are not wanted by the military but are being built because the production facilities are in districts or states of powerful members of Congress.

Even worse, members of the conference committees, who are charged with putting together good compromise bills, have been known to spend significant time making sure money is included for their states or districts and less time making sure the bill is good for the country. Members of Congress who have seniority over other members are the ones who are assigned to such committees. Such appointments are considered rewards for years of service. The most egregious products of the conferences are usually found in parts of the final bill that were not in the original House or Senate version. These are items that conference members knew they could not get passed in their own legislative chamber. Knowing they were going to end up on a conference committee, they waited and made the inclusion of the item they wanted passed a condition of their support for the bill in conference.

Another element of budgetary shenanigans comes when members of Congress agree to support spending programs in each other's districts. This vote trading, called **logrolling** among economists, increases spending in ways that raise eyebrows. A senator from Vermont got his colleagues to declare Lake Champlain a Great Lake so that it would qualify for an environmental program. Promises to quell this type of spending are rarely kept.

logrolling
The trading of votes used to generate sufficient support for projects that are not in the general interest of the country.

Dealing with Disagreements

The appropriations process seldom moves smoothly, and the process is particularly rough when the political party in control of the White House is not in control of Congress. Nothing illustrates this better than the Trump administration's insistence on building a border wall. Disagreements abound when this is the case, and rarely can one party "have its way" with the budget. In 2008, President Obama was elected to office with large majorities in both the House of Representatives and Senate. Yet, Senate budget rules required that he garner 60 votes for his stimulus package. He could do that only with Republican votes. Even then, he was in a considerably more advantageous position than Presidents Clinton and Bush. Neither could count on their respective political parties to support their budget priorities, and both dealt with periods when Congress was controlled by the other party. It has been a truly rare circumstance in recent American history where a president had sufficient political party and ideological majorities in Congress to get his way. Thus, the usual case for much of the late 20th century featured long and protracted budget debates.

When Congress either does not pass appropriations bills that are acceptable to the president or passes bills the president does not want, there are only four choices:

1. Congress can pass what the president wants.
2. The President can sign what Congress passes.
3. The government can shut down.
4. Congress can pass a bill the president can sign.

If either side gives in, a bill gets passed. Shutting down the government becomes a battle of chicken until the sides reach compromises. A continuing resolution constitutes an agreement to disagree that lets the government continue functioning.

Specifically, a **continuing resolution** is a bill passed by Congress and signed by the president that allows the government to spend money temporarily in a fashion identical to the previous year. This usually happens when Congress does not meet the October 1 deadline. More often than not, it is for only a few of the appropriations bills and for only a few weeks, but in 2013, almost the entire budget was passed as a continuing resolution. The 2019 battle between President Trump and congressional Democrats only reinforces the point. Unless they agree to a solution, there is no solution.

continuing resolution
A bill passed by Congress and signed by the president that allows the government to temporarily spend money in a fashion identical to the previous year.

Using Our Understanding of Opportunity Cost

The federal budget of the United States is an illustrative example of opportunity cost. Whenever money is spent in one area, it cannot be spent in another. Although more money can be spent in all areas, this also has an opportunity cost. When money is taken from taxpayers, their ability to enjoy private consumption is reduced. Deficit spending is also not without opportunity cost. Interest payments add up into the future, and money for private investment is reduced.

Some economists argue that the opportunity cost of government deficit spending is such that for every dollar the federal government borrows and spends, a dollar is removed from private investment. If these economists are correct, this phenomenon, called **crowding out,** is an example of opportunity cost at work: Government cannot spend money and benefit everyone. In the process, someone is harmed. Other economists suggest that crowding out is less than complete,

crowding out
The opportunity cost of government deficit spending such that private investment is reduced.

which means that for every dollar of government spending something less than a dollar of private spending is lost. In either case, there is an opportunity cost to the money spent.

The remainder of this section describes the choices that must be made by Congress and the president when establishing a spending plan.

Mandatory versus Discretionary Spending

Although the actual budget proposal of the president runs to more than 1,000 pages and is incredibly detailed and precise, Figure 11.2 offers its basic distribution of spending. You can see that the broadest of its distinctions is the difference between mandatory and discretionary spending. **Mandatory spending** delineates those items for which a previously passed law requires that money be spent, while **discretionary spending** is subject to annual appropriations decisions. For instance, current law states that people are entitled to certain benefits that must be paid regardless of other budget details. Future laws could overturn those now in existence, but the benefits that are currently provided through Social Security, Medicare, Medicaid, and welfare are so firmly entrenched in our society that in reality the money spent on them is untouchable. These four areas of the budget are often referred to as **entitlement** spending because the people for whom they are intended are, quite literally, entitled to the money they receive based on their situation. Entitlement spending is a subset of mandatory spending, which also includes interest on the national debt.

mandatory spending
Budget items for which a previously passed law requires that money be spent.

discretionary spending
Budget items for which an annual appropriations bill must be passed so that money can be spent.

entitlement
A program where if people meet certain income or demographic criteria they are automatically eligible to receive benefits.

The appropriations for defense, student loans, the courts, and so on, occur annually and, as a result, are considered discretionary. While these budgets rarely change drastically from the previous year, a failure to pass an appropriations bill can significantly affect the operations in these areas.

On this discretionary side of the budget, there are three main components: defense, international policy and foreign aid, and everything else (broken out in Table 11.1). The most misunderstood and controversial of these is international policy. Of the $54 billion spent in this area, $14 billion is spent to maintain the State Department and its embassies in other countries and to pay our dues to the United Nations and other international organizations. The remaining $40 billion goes to other countries in the form of foreign aid.

As you can see from Figure 11.3, the proportion of the budget devoted to discretionary spending has decreased from over 65 percent to just over 30 percent, while the proportion devoted to mandatory spending has skyrocketed. Current projections suggest that by 2024, less than one-quarter of all federal spending will be discretionary. The biggest reason for this split is that so much of the budget is now paying for a social welfare state that runs, more or less, on autopilot. The rules for each program establish who is eligible to receive benefits from them, and as the programs have been created and as the population has aged, more and more people are eligible for more and more benefits.

This brings us back to the inescapable notion of opportunity cost. Every time a new entitlement program is created, such as the prescription drug coverage for

FIGURE 11.2 Fiscal Year 2019 spending (in billions) and percentage of federal budget.

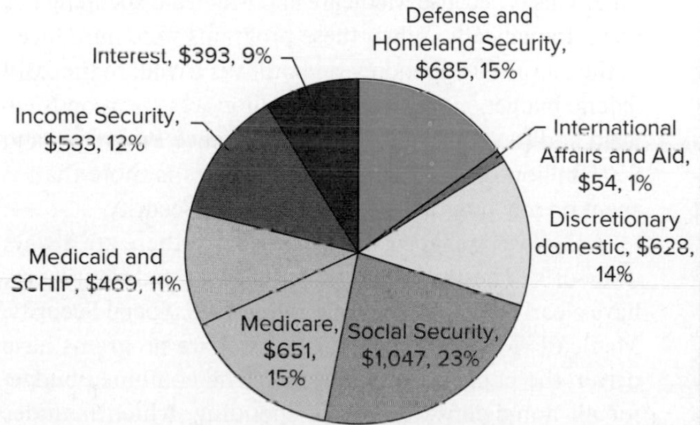

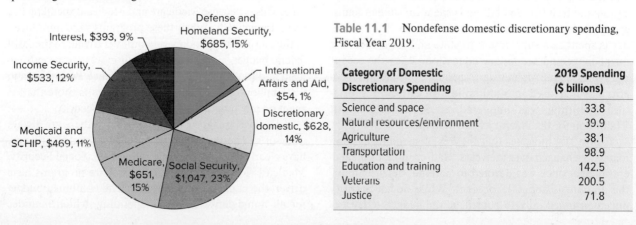

Table 11.1 Nondefense domestic discretionary spending, Fiscal Year 2019.

Category of Domestic Discretionary Spending	2019 Spending ($ billions)
Science and space	33.8
Natural resources/environment	39.9
Agriculture	38.1
Transportation	98.9
Education and training	142.5
Veterans	200.5
Justice	71.8

FIGURE 11.3 Mandatory and discretionary spending as a percentage of total federal spending, 1962–2024.

Source: The Office of Management and Budget. https://www.whitehouse.gov/omb/historical-tables/

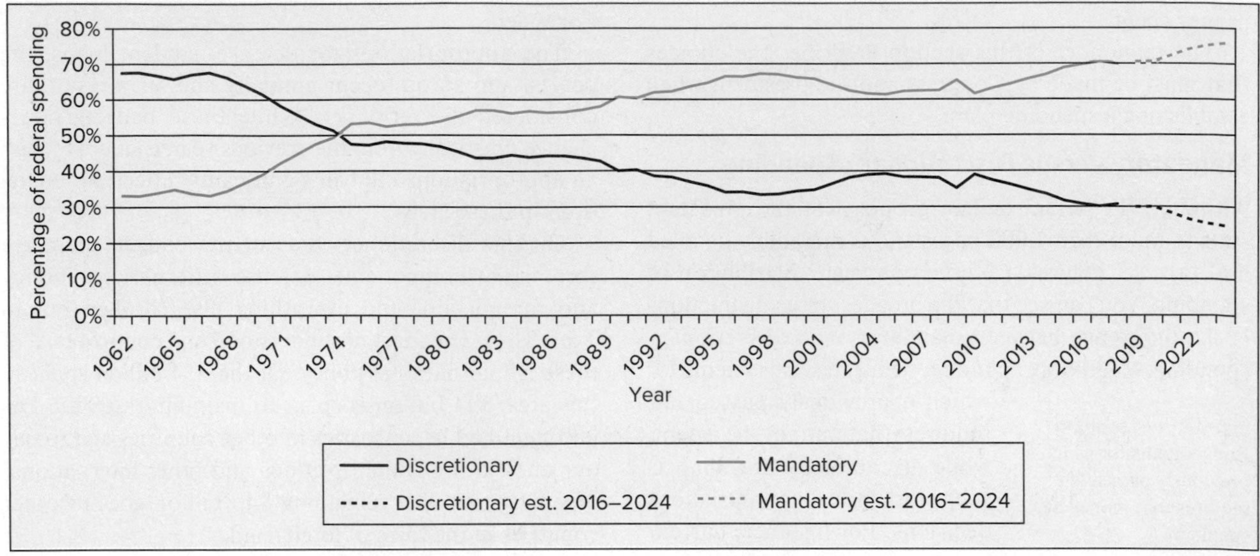

Medicare recipients, it not only costs money now and in the future but also reduces the amount of flexibility of future Congresses and presidents as less and less of the budget can be devoted to other priorities.

Where the Money Goes

As you can see from Figure 11.2, defense, Social Security, Medicare, Medicaid, and net interest take up $3.2 trillion of the $4.7 trillion spent each year. The rest is allocated to other welfare programs such as Temporary Assistance for Needy Families (TANF) or food stamps, or it is spent in the relatively smaller discretionary spending amounts listed in Table 11.1. The biggest of these areas of spending are under the Department of Education and its education and training programs. Of the $143 billion spent on education and training, $64 billion is spent on student loans, grants, and the federal work-study program. The remainder is spent as a supplement to state and local spending on primary and secondary education. With the recent wars in Iraq and Afghanistan, spending on veterans' benefits has increased to $200 billion. In 2019, transportation spending was budgeted at $99 billion, with $72 billion for the federal justice system.

Figure 11.4 indicates that the mix of spending has dramatically changed over the years. Half or more of the federal budget once was devoted to national defense; today the amount is about 15 percent. While Social Security once consumed only 15 percent of the budget, today it is approximately 24 percent. Net interest paid increased from less than 10 percent to more than 15 percent only to fall to 9 percent as a result of the surpluses of the late 1990s and early 2000s and the historically low interest rates of 2001 through 2004. As deficits grew during 2005–2007 and then exploded during and in the decade following the 2007–2009 recession, the portion of the budget devoted to paying interest on the debt will certainly rise to more than 10 percent. The only reason it has not already exceeded that amount is that the Federal Reserve has used its power to buy this debt to temporarily reduce the interest rate.

An area of spending that has increased remarkably since 1970 is federal spending in support of health care. As seen in Figure 11.5, adjusted for inflation, federal spending on health care has risen more than 1,000 percent over that time. This is because Medicare and Medicaid spending has risen dramatically. When these programs were introduced in the late 1960s, spending on both was trivial. In the 2019 federal budget, more than $469 billion was spent on Medicaid and the Children's Health Insurance Programs, and $771 billion on Medicare. Together, this is more than is spent on any program other than Social Security.

Again, we are faced with the fact that there are always trade-offs. The trade-offs that we have made until now have clearly been in favor of entitlements. Social Security, Medicare, Medicaid, and various welfare programs have driven the budget for many years. The combined budget for all non-defense domestic spending, which includes

FIGURE 11.4 Composition of federal spending.

Source: The Office of Management and Budget. https://www.whitehouse.gov/omb/historical-tables/

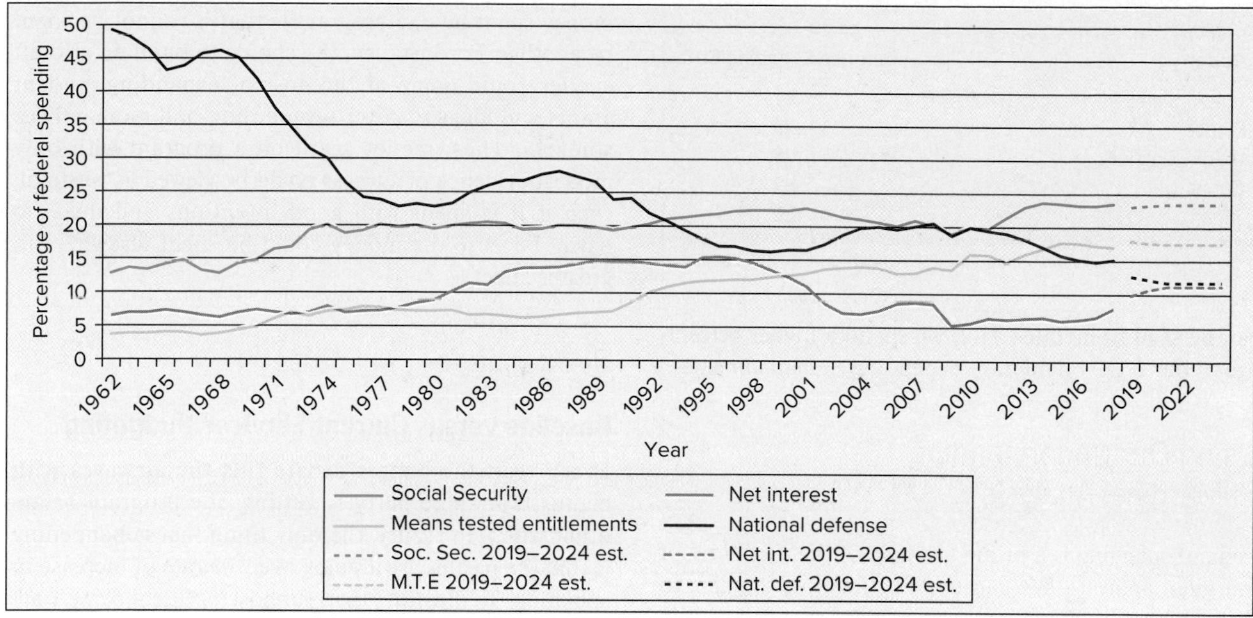

FIGURE 11.5 Real health spending by the federal government, 1962–2024 billions of 2000 dollars.

Source: The Office of Management and Budget. https://www.whitehouse.gov/omb/historical-tables/

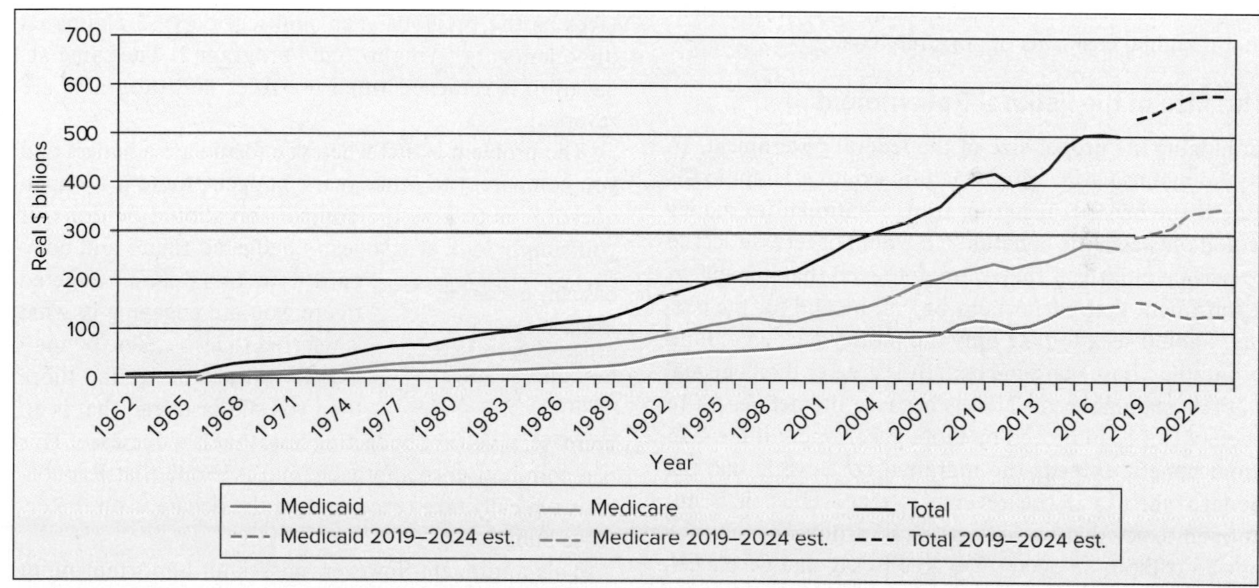

everything from the federal judiciary to student loans, is exceeded by only one program, Social Security. The choice that we have made to ensure that elderly people and persons who are disabled have steady and reliable incomes comes at a cost.

Another choice that we have made is to exercise our military power in other parts of the world. Though some would argue that we had no real choice being the world's only superpower, the military spending necessary to carry out that responsibility has an opportunity cost. As

Table 11.2 International comparisons of defense spending as a percentage of GDP, 2017.

Source: The World Bank. https://data.worldbank.org/indicator/MS.MIL.XPND.GD.ZS

Country	Defense Spending/GDP
United States	3.1
France	2.3
United Kingdom	1.8
Germany	1.2
Japan	0.9

can be seen from Table 11.2, we spend a higher percentage of our GDP on military expenditures than our allies.

Using Our Understanding of Marginal Analysis

Federal spending is a prime example of the usefulness of marginal analysis. We can use this form of thinking to discuss whether the federal government spends too little or too much and whether the distribution of spending on various spending priorities is appropriate. Recall from Chapter 1 that marginal analysis compares the marginal benefit of an action with its marginal cost. In particular, that marginal cost is its opportunity cost.

The Size of the Federal Government

In judging the proper size of the federal government, an economist using marginal analysis would attempt to decide if the benefits resulting from additional tax money would outweigh the benefits that would otherwise accrue to private citizens if they were not taxed that amount. A government that purports to be "of, by and for the people" should seek to take only the money needed to fund programs whose marginal benefit is greater than or equal to their marginal cost. That is because the net benefit to society can be improved by more government if the marginal benefit exceeds the marginal cost, while that net benefit shrinks if the reverse is true. Thus, it is not enough to say that we are getting $5 trillion in value for our $5 trillion; we need to be able to say that we are getting a dollar's worth of value for the last dollar of those $5 trillion.

The Distribution of Federal Spending

Just as government should seek to maximize the net benefit to society by picking the optimal size of government, it should ensure that the distribution of spending between various priorities is optimal as well. Once the optimal size is established, the opportunity cost of money spent by one program is that it cannot be spent by another. For instance, the choice to build an aircraft carrier could come at the cost of expanding student grants and loans to cover several thousand more college students. Thus, money spent on a program with only modest evidence of success could be viewed as wasteful, even if it is spent with good intentions and does no harm, because the money could be spent elsewhere to greater effect.

Budgeting for the Future

Baseline versus Current-Services Budgeting

Every year, the budget debate fills the airwaves with claims that some party is gutting one program or another when, in reality, the only thing that is happening is that the parties are arguing over the rate of increase in spending. To illustrate that, suppose political party 1 advocates for spending on program 1, and political party 2 advocates for spending on program 2. Almost invariably, when political party 1 suggests increasing program 2 by less than would be necessary to offer the same services as the previous year, political party 2 claims its opponents are trying to "cut" program 2. The same accusation is returned when the roles and programs are reversed.

The problem is that when you formulate a budget and you compare it to other years' budgets, there is an open question as to how the comparison should be done. If you simply look at last year's budgeted figure and compare it to this year's budgeted figure, you are engaging in what is referred to as **baseline budgeting.** If you are budgeting more than you did last year, that is an increase; if you are budgeting less, that is a decrease. This is a commonsense approach, and it is one that Republicans typically take (except when the debate is on the defense budget).

baseline budgeting Using last year's budgeted figure to set this year's budgeted figure.

This approach, however, misses an important point that is vital to interests Democrats support. They wish to ensure that government services are available to everyone who is eligible to receive them. There is no guarantee that baseline budgeting will provide enough money to provide those services. A reasonable question to ask in budgeting is one that Democrats tend to ask:

current-services budgeting
Using an estimate of the costs of providing the same level of services next year as last.

"How much will it cost to perform services this year in a manner identical to last year?" This is referred to as **current-services budgeting.** Current-services budgeting takes into account such things as overall inflation, inflation in the specific sector, and an increase in the number of people being served. If you want to guarantee enough money to provide identical services in the future, then merely starting with the previous year's baselines may not work. This has been particularly true in the health care field because new, more effective treatments become available. Thus, the question is whether the new spending required to meet the old standard of care will be sufficient to meet the new standard.

Summary

You now understand the process that goes into creating the federal budget of the United States. You know that in percentage terms, a large and increasing part of the budget is devoted to spending on items for which no annual vote is taken. You now see that this mandatory spending funds Social Security, Medicare, Medicaid, various welfare programs, and the costs of interest on the national debt. You understand that the rest is spent almost equally on domestic concerns and spending on defense. You see that a relatively small amount is spent on foreign aid and other obligations to international organizations such as the United Nations. You understand the difference between current-services and baseline budgeting and why this difference is at the heart of many political debates. Most important, you now understand that the idea of opportunity cost–choices have consequences, and money spent in one area cannot be spent in another–is central to a proper analysis of budgeting.

Key Terms

baseline budgeting
continuing resolution
crowding out
current-services budgeting
discretionary spending
entitlement
logrolling
mandatory spending

Quiz Yourself

1. Federal spending is typically ______________ percent of GDP.
   a. less than 10
   b. between 18 and 22
   c. between 25 and 30
   d. more than 30
2. The FY 2020 federal budget was around
   a. $5 million.
   b. $5 billion.
   c. $5 trillion.
   d. $5 quadrillion.
3. Disagreements between the Congress and the president about the federal budget occur frequently. When they cannot agree on a budget but want to keep the government running, they
   a. use the president's budget.
   b. use Congress's budget.
   c. use a budget created by an independent budget commission.
   d. pass a continuing resolution.
4. Mandatory spending implies spending that is
   a. required by a previously passed set of laws.
   b. required by the U.S. Constitution.
   c. needed more than discretionary spending.
   d. off-limits for any cuts at any time.
5. Defense spending is part of
   a. mandatory spending.
   b. discretionary spending.
   c. off-budget spending.
   d. unauthorized spending.
6. The largest single item in federal spending is
   a. international aid.
   b. welfare.
   c. interest on the debt.
   d. Social Security.
7. Total federal spending on health care, after adjusting for inflation, has been
   a. growing.
   b. relatively constant.
   c. declining slowly.
   d. declining rapidly.

8. In determining whether the federal government is the right size, an economist would determine whether
   a. the first dollar spent produced \$1 worth of social good.
   b. the average dollar spent produced \$1 worth of social good.
   c. the last/marginal dollar spent produced \$1 worth of social good.
   d. an amount of social good was created equal to the amount spent.
9. In determining whether the distribution of federal spending among various agencies was correct, an economist would want to make sure
   a. that each agency manager got what (s)he thought was needed in that area.
   b. that the last/marginal dollar spent in each area produced the same amount of social good.
   c. that the average dollar spent in each area produced the same amount of social good.
   d. that the total amount of money spent in each agency produced the same level of social good.
10. Suppose budget analysts are projecting that a particular program's costs will increase faster than overall inflation (primarily) because there will be an increase in the number of people eligible for it (e.g., Social Security and an aging population). If there is an increase in the budget by only the amount necessary to cover inflationary increases, this would be considered
    a. an increase if you were using either baseline or current-services budgeting.
    b. an increase if you were using baseline budgeting but a cut if you were using current-services budgeting.
    c. an increase if you were using current-services budgeting but a cut if you were using baseline budgeting.
    d. a cut if you were using either baseline or current-services budgeting.
11. Which of the following could be considered the opportunity cost of spending more money on defense through the purchase of a weapons system?
    a. The cost of the weapons system purchased
    b. The extra security associated with the system
    c. The money that could have been used on education
    d. The difference between the cost of the system and its benefits

Short Answer Questions

1. Explain how mandatory spending comes about relative to discretionary spending. Then assign the following programs to each: interest payments on the debt, national defense, Social Security, food stamps.
2. In order of magnitude, rank the following spending from greatest to smallest: Social Security, national defense, Medicare, federal support for education, space exploration, and foreign aid.
3. Explain what would transpire for new government expenditures to crowd out other economic activity.
4. One political party believes government spending is too high; another party thinks it is too low. Which party will argue for current-services budgeting as a practice for setting government budgets? Explain why.

Think about This

The Medicare prescription drug benefit passed during 2003 comes at a significant long-term cost (at least \$720 billion over 10 years). Consider the opportunity cost of this spending in terms of tax cuts, deficit reduction, or spending on other priorities. Would you have committed the federal government to this spending?

Talk about This

When Congress and the president do not agree on a spending package and cannot agree on a continuing resolution, the government shuts down all but emergency services. What, in your mind, should be considered under the umbrella of "emergency"?

For More Insight See

Lee, Ronald, and Jonathan Skinner, "Will Aging Baby Boomers Bust the Federal Budget?" *Journal of Economic Perspectives* 13, no. 1 (Winter 1999).

Lynch, Thomas, *Public Budgeting in the United States* (Englewood Cliffs, NJ: Prentice Hall, 1979).

Behind the Numbers

White House Office of Management and Budget (OMB): www.whitehouse.gov/omb/historical-tables

- Federal spending
- Mandatory and discretionary spending
- Composition of federal spending
- Federal government health spending

World Bank: data.worldbank.org

- International comparisons of government spending

CHAPTER TWELVE

Federal Deficits, Surpluses, and the National Debt

Learning Objectives

After reading this chapter you should be able to:

LO1 Distinguish between the federal budget deficits/surpluses and the national debt.

LO2 Associate significant deficits as resulting from wars and severe recessions/depressions.

LO3 Recognize that economists evaluate the importance of a deficit or debt relative to GDP.

LO4 Compare the U.S. national debt-to-GDP ratio relative to U.S. history and to other countries.

LO5 Explain that the federal government owns much of the debt and list what agencies own that debt.

LO6 Summarize the different positions taken by economists on the issue of a balanced-budget amendment to the U.S. Constitution.

Chapter Outline

The purpose of this chapter is to discuss the history of the deficits, those few surpluses, and the national debt of the U.S. federal government. After a brief history, we discuss the main causes of deficits and debt. We examine how economists view the federal debt and how they compare the current situation with other countries and U.S. history. When we discover who actually owns the federal debt, you may be surprised to learn that a significant portion of it is owned by the federal government itself. We conclude by discussing whether a balanced-budget amendment to the U.S. Constitution makes sense as economic policy.

Surpluses, Deficits, and the Debt: Definitions and History

Definitions

Defining **budget deficit, budget surplus,** or **national debt** ought to be simple, but because of the way the federal government does its accounting, the definitions are not as simple as they could be. For instance, you may think that if you did the math, a surplus would result when the total amount of tax revenue generated was greater than the total amount spent. Likewise, if spending exceeded revenue, the result would be a deficit, and the debt would be the sum of the annual deficits minus the sum of the annual surpluses.

budget deficit
The amount by which expenditures exceed revenues.

budget surplus
The amount by which revenues exceed expenditures.

national debt
The total amount owed by the federal government.

The problem is that those definitions are not quite right because the deficit or surplus for a year is the combination of what are referred to as the off- and on-budget deficits and surpluses. Social Security, Medicare, and other parts of the budget that have trust funds attached to them

off-budget
Parts of the budget designated by Congress as separate from the normal budget. Programs that operate with their own revenue sources and have trust funds; Social Security, Medicare, and the Postal Service are examples.

on-budget
Parts of the budget that rely entirely or mostly on general revenue.

are considered **off-budget.** The part of the federal budget that operates from year to year without a trust fund is **on-budget.**

History

The annual budget of the United States is never actually balanced because no one has ever attempted to make the revenue projections exactly match the expenditure projections. The closest we ever came to a strictly balanced budget was a $3,800 deficit in 1835 (which, even accounting for inflation, would be less than $100,000 today). Why is the budget never balanced? Congress passes the budget *before* it knows exactly how much revenue will be generated. When the United States operated under the Articles of Confederation, before the Constitution was ratified, it had a considerable debt (more than $75 million) from the American Revolutionary War and no money to pay it. In fact, the Continental Congress had no power to tax during the war. Almost all of the money necessary to fight and win it was borrowed. In the first 58 years of constitutional government in the United States, from 1791 to 1849, there were more years of surplus (36) than deficit (23), and over that time, the country ran a net surplus of $60 million. As a matter of fact, in 1836 the debt had all been repaid and President Andrew Jackson got Congress to give states money. Congress missed the mark and gave away $37,000 too much.

The American Civil War ended notions that the country would ever again go without a national debt. Two billion dollars was borrowed to fight that war, and even though in the 35 years after the war there were more years with a surplus (21) than a deficit (14), the debt remained at $2 billion by 1900. As a matter of fact, in the first 30 years of the 20th century, there were almost as many years of surplus (13) as deficit (17). The debt during that period grew because the deficits during the two-year U.S. involvement in World War I were twice the size of the combined surplus in the other years. The longest uninterrupted period of debt reduction began just after World War I and lasted until 1930, the first full year of the Great Depression. Surpluses ruled for 11 consecutive years. In general, U.S. economic history prior to the Great Depression can be summarized as one in which the expenses of wars created the debt, and steady efforts were made to eliminate the debt when the wars ended.

Since 1930, however, deficits have been more the rule than the exception. During the 89 years from 1930 to 2018, there were only 12 years with surpluses (three years in the 1940s, three in the 1950s, two in the 1960s, two in the 1990s, and two in the 2000s), whereas there were 77 with deficits. Also during that time, the national debt grew from $50 billion to $21.5 trillion. Adjusting the deficits and surpluses for inflation, we can compare the relative size of the various years, and this is shown in Figure 12.1.

Figure 12.1 also portrays an important division between the total budget and the off-budget surpluses and deficits. Recall that the total budget is the combination of the on- and off-budget numbers. In recent times, especially after changes in Social Security in 1982 that resulted in a hefty increase in taxes in anticipation of the large number of retirements among baby boomers, the off-budget surplus has been substantial. In all but 12 of the 82 years depicted in Figure 12.1, the off-budget part of the system was in surplus. For the 27 years between 1983 and 2020, the Social Security and Medicare taxes were much greater than expenditures. These off-budget surpluses masked the severity of budget deficits in the late 1980s and created the illusion of surpluses in the late 1990s. It was only in fiscal years 1999 and 2000 that the on-budget side (which is the difference between the total deficit/surplus and off-budget deficit/surplus) was showing a surplus. Deficits surged after the Bush-era tax cuts and spending increases resulting from the terrorist attacks of September 11, 2001, and the subsequent wars in Iraq and Afghanistan. The deficits were projected to hover in the $400 billion per year range when, in 2008, the recession and financial collapse took place.

It is worth noting that in the decade since the Great Recession, deficits, which had swelled to $1.5 trillion annually, were brought down to less than a third of that level by 2017. The Trump-era tax cuts and the continued surge in baby boom retirements (resulting in Social Security and Medicare spending increases enough to eliminate the off-budget surpluses) have and will likely mean that trillion dollar deficits will continue into the 2020s.

Figure 12.2 displays the trend in deficits as a percentage of GDP. On the left side of the graph, the large annual deficits were for the expenses of war, just as 19th-century deficits were. In addition to the other upheaval caused by the Great Depression and World War II, budget deficits, measured in 2012 dollars in Figure 12.1 and measured as

FIGURE 12.1 The total and off-budget deficits and surpluses since 1940, in billions of 2012 dollars.

Source: The Office of Management and Budget. https://www.whitehouse.gov/omb/historical-tables/

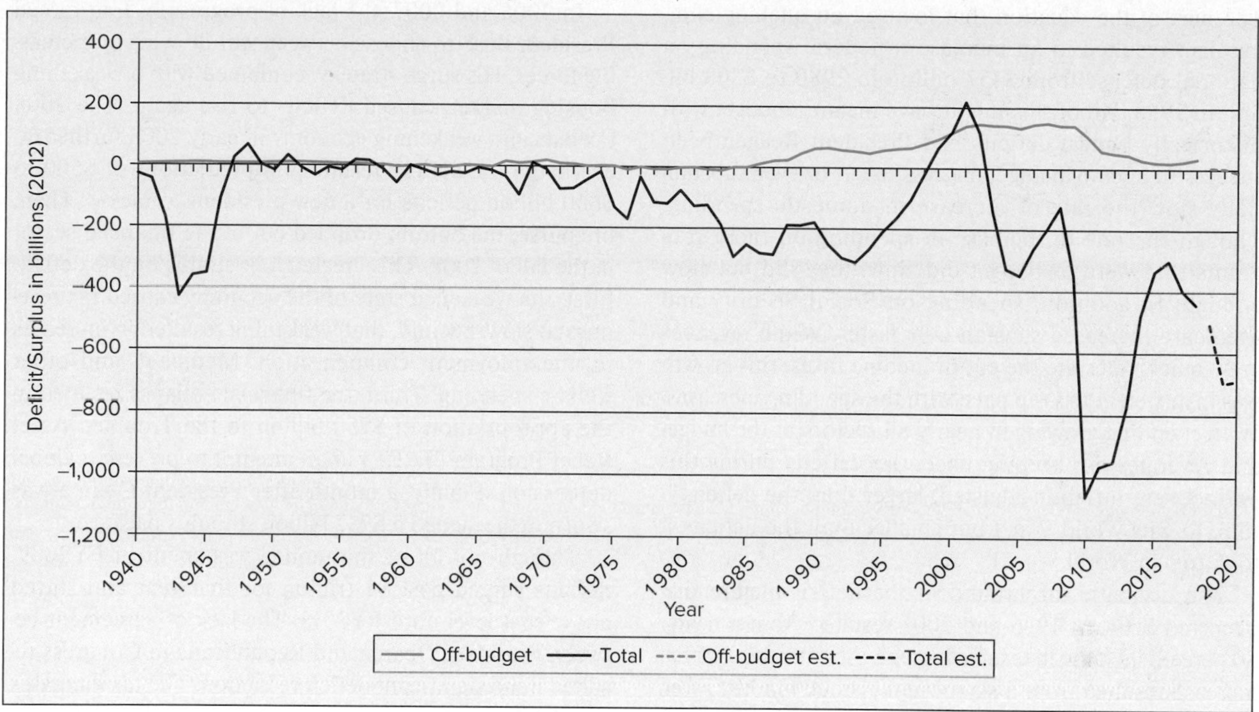

a percentage of GDP in Figure 12.2, peaked at more than $400 billion a year, or nearly a third of GDP.

The deficits of the 1980s and 1990s were caused by a confluence of events. In 1981, President Reagan took office on a platform dedicated to decreasing the size of the federal government and lessening the threat of communism. Part of this meant that he worked to reduce federal income taxes. Tax rates were slashed and important

FIGURE 12.2 Deficits as a percentage of GDP: 1940–2024.

Source: The Office of Management and Budget. https://www.whitehouse.gov/omb/historical-tables/

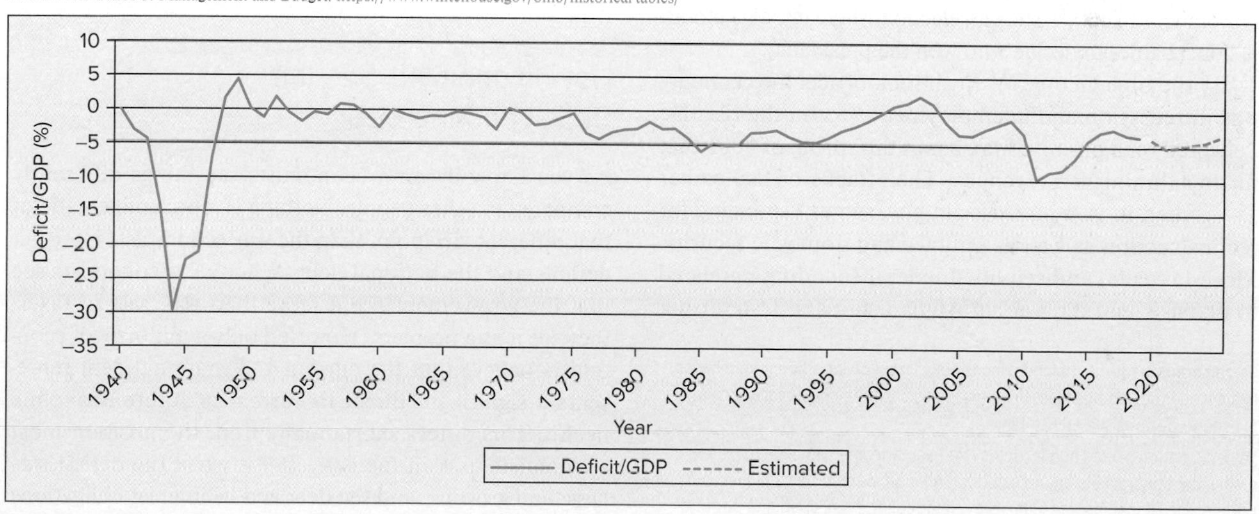

deductions and exemptions were indexed[1] for inflation to prevent *bracket creep*[2] from raising taxes in later years. The part of the equation that focused on quelling communism resulted in an increase in federal spending on national defense from $157 billion in 1980 to $303 billion in 1988. All of this might have meant a budget with historically typical deficits had President Reagan been successful in convincing Congress to cut or even substantially slow the rate of increase in domestic spending. Though the rate of increase in spending on those programs that were on-budget did slow, they did not slow enough. In addition, spending on Social Security and Medicare increased substantially faster. While revenues grew quickly despite the cut in income taxes, this growth was insufficient to keep pace with the spending increases. With spending growing in nearly all sectors of the budget and revenues not keeping pace, the deficits during this period were inflation-adjusted, larger than the deficits it took to win World War I but smaller than the deficits it took to win World War II.

The dramatic turnaround in the deficit picture that occurred between 1996 and 2001 resulted from a nearly 50 percent increase in taxable income. About a third of that increase resulted from a skyrocketing stock market. From 1991 to 2000, taxable capital gains income increased from just over $100 billion to more than $630 billion. As a result, a deficit that had been approaching $300 billion in 1992 turned into a $236 billion surplus in 2000.

Beginning in 2000, things began to unravel. In March, the stock market reached its peak and began a rapid decline with the Dow Industrial average losing 40 percent of its value and the NASDAQ losing 75 percent of its value. Taxable capital gains income was cut by more than half in that time. In November of 2000, we had an election where it took a month of court battles to decide who won the presidency.

By the time George W. Bush took office, the economy was in recession and unemployment was on the rise. He delivered on a promised tax cut in the spring of 2001 that further diminished revenues. The attacks of September 11 resulted in vast increases in government spending for reconstruction as well as military and domestic security. More tax cuts, undisciplined federal spending unrelated to defense, and the wars in Afghanistan and Iraq further swelled the deficit such that by 2005, the total budget deficit was more than $239 billion.

In 2006 and 2007, the lack of progress in Iraq forced President Bush to choose between withdrawing or increasing forces. His surge strategy, combined with a weakening housing market, caused deficits to rise again. The 2008 tax cuts and weakening economy in early 2008 further exacerbated the deficit, resulting in predictions of $500 to $600 billion deficits for a new president to tackle. Then, of course, the bottom dropped out of the financial sector in the fall of 2008. This created four strains on the deficit. First, the weakened state of the economy caused tax revenues to slow. Second, that weakening resulted in increases in unemployment compensation, Medicaid, and other welfare spending. Third, the financial collapse resulted in the appropriation of $750 billion to the Troubled Asset Relief Program (TARP) in an attempt to prevent a global depression. Finally, a month after President Obama was sworn in, he signed a $787 billion stimulus package.

Though not all of the money was spent in FY2009, deficits surged past $1 trillion for that year and stayed above that level until FY2013. The lack of agreement between President Obama and Republicans in Congress resulted in no significant deficit reduction. The tax increases on high-income taxpayers and the sequester (automatic budget cuts) of 2013 combined with a modestly growing economy had the effect of reducing trillion dollar per year deficits by 30 to 50 percent between 2013 and 2016.

Trillion dollar deficits are projected to return in FY2020 and beyond. For this, Democrats blame the Trump-era tax cuts, while Republicans blame the rapid increases in entitlement spending (which reached an all-time high of 12 percent of GDP in 2019).

How Economists See the Deficit and the Debt

As you know by now, economists see things differently compared to other people. Nothing is more emblematic of that different viewpoint than the way economists interpret deficits and the national debt. When noneconomists see that the government spent more than was paid in taxes, they see it as a problem. However, only a minority of economists believe that the current U.S. national debt represents a significant threat to current or future economic health. This differs substantially from the position most economists took in the early 1990s when the deficit was large and growing, and the debt and its interest obligations were becoming rapidly burdensome.

[1]Recall from Chapter 6 that indexing is adjusting a dollar amount for inflation. It is called indexing because an index, in this case the consumer price index, is used to perform the adjustment.

[2]When inflation occurs and incomes rise exactly in line with inflation, then, unless the tax brackets are adjusted for inflation, people pay a higher percentage of that income in taxes even though the real spending power of their income has remained unchanged.

Operating and Capital Budgets

To see things from an economist's perspective, consider first that the debt is made up of a series of budget deficits over time. The next thing to realize about the budget is that, again from an economist's viewpoint, it is calculated improperly. It should be divided between **operating** and **capital budgets.** Things that are big, expensive, and will last several years ought not be accounted for in the same way as federal purchases of toilet paper. Highways, dams, and buildings are certainly going to be around for a while, and it makes little economic sense to account for them as though they are going to disappear at the end of the year.

operating budget
That part of the federal budget devoted to spending on goods and services that will be used in the current year.

capital budget
That part of the federal budget devoted to spending on goods that will last several years.

Away from government, what businesses normally do with such large investments is create a *capital budget*. An investment in an asset with a long life simply must generate profits over the years that are more than sufficient to make payments on the asset. The expenses of the business that are used to pay for items that are used soon after they are paid for, like labor, paper, and phone calls, go into an *operating budget*. As long as the revenue of the firm is sufficient to cover the operating budget and make the appropriate payments on the capital previously purchased, the business is fine, even if it is carrying a large debt. If big corporations did their accounting the way the federal government does, they would rarely show a profit.

One problem with separating a capital budget from an operating budget is trying to determine what spending is an investment that should go into the capital budget and what spending is not. Liberal politicians tend to argue that nearly all social spending should be included in the capital budget. Conservatives, on the other hand, usually say that nearly all military spending should be included in the capital budget. Each would label its spending recommendations as investments in the future and the other's as consumption. This distinction is important because balancing the budget is harder as more goes into the operating side. Moreover, it is more a political shell game than an exercise grounded in fundamental economic principles.

Cyclical and Structural Deficits

Another way in which economists look at the deficit differently from other people is that they divide it between its structural and cyclical components. In Chapter 6 we broke unemployment into four parts—seasonal, frictional, cyclical, and structural. We can do a similar thing here. The part of the deficit that is attributable to the economy not being at full employment is called the **cyclical deficit**, and the part of the deficit that would remain even if we were at full employment is called a **structural deficit.** If the deficit is large because the economy is not doing well, then the economy is the issue, not the deficit. If the deficit is large even when the economy is doing relatively well, then the deficit is a problem. Economists who think deficits can be used to stimulate a lackluster economy label that part of the deficit attributable to that purpose as **functional finance.**

cyclical deficit
That part of the deficit attributable to the economy's not being at full employment.

structural deficit
That part of the deficit that would remain even if the economy were at full employment.

functional finance
That part of the budget attributable to programs designed to get an economy out of a recession.

The Debt as a Percentage of GDP

There are other reasons why most economists did not view the national debt (as it stood during the pre-2008 periods) as all that troubling. Among these was that, as a percentage of national income, the national debt was not anywhere near as high as it had been in the immediate aftermath of World War II. If you look at Figure 12.3, you will see that the ratio of national debt to the GDP was greater than 100 percent after World War II and, while it increased to near 70 percent in the 1990s, it fell sharply in the late 1990s when deficits turned into surpluses. Of course, that lasted only a short time as large deficits resumed bringing the debt-to-GDP ratio back near the 70 percent level. With the global economic downturn and the subsequent TARP and stimulus plans all occurring in relatively short order, the debt shot up to near 100 percent of GDP by 2011. Current projections suggest a debt level above 100 percent of GDP will exist through 2024.

International Comparisons

Though the relevant measure of debt differs among countries,[3] what is clear is that government debts have increased throughout the developed world. As can be seen

[3]The Organization for Economic Cooperation and Development (OECD) and World Bank definitions of public sector (PS) debt differ. The OECD discontinued its published series. World Bank Gross PS includes all public sector debt (including state/provincial/local). World Bank-Central includes only the central government debt. These numbers differ greatly in more federal systems (e.g., the United States and Canada) and less in centralized systems (e.g., the United Kingdom).

FIGURE 12.3 Debt as a percentage of GDP: 1940–2024.

Source: The Office of Management and Budget. https://www.whitehouse.gov/omb/historical-tables/

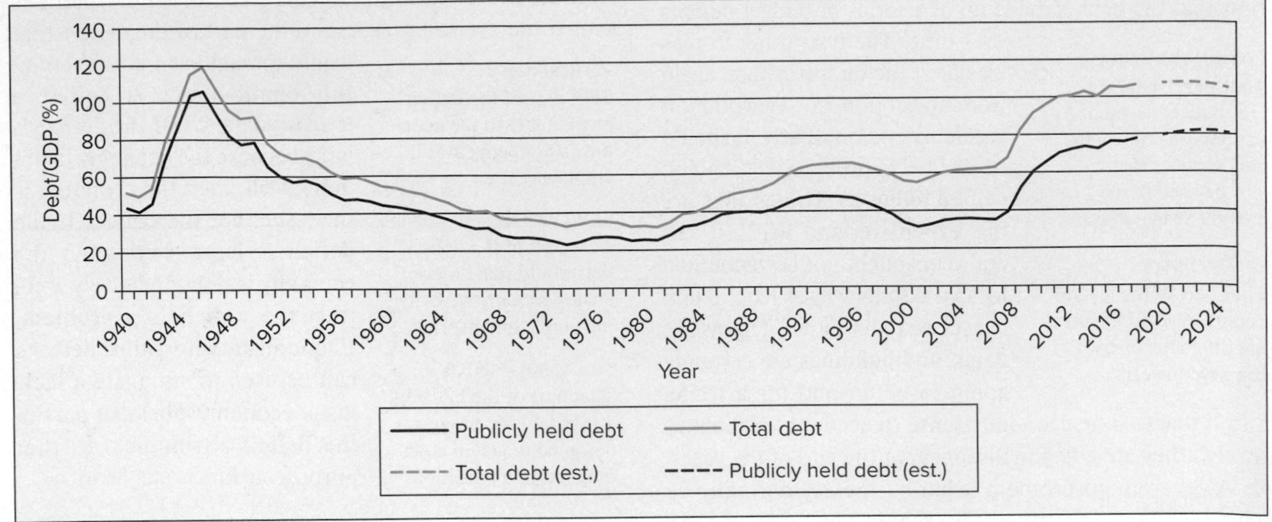

in Table 12.1, the U.S. debt-to-GDP ratio was well within the norms of the rest of the world for the period between 1970 and 2005. Though still nowhere near the levels of Italy and Japan, this debt-to-GDP ratio that had been significantly better than Canada's and Germany's, and only somewhat worse than that of the United Kingdom, is now noticeably worse than any of those countries. The country that has really begun to tread close to its ability to manage its debt is Japan. Once regarded as an example of fiscal responsibility, Japan has seen its national debt balloon from 10.6 percent of GDP in 1970 to more than 230 percent in 2015.

Generational Accounting

Some economists look at the deficit and surplus in a completely different fashion. These economists, led by Alan Auerbach and Laurence Kotlikoff, argue that, instead

Table 12.1 International comparisons of gross public sector (PS) and gross central debt-to-GDP ratios.

Sources: www.oecd.org; databank.worldbank.org.

Year	Canada			United States			United Kingdom			Germany			Italy			Japan		
	OECD Gross PS	World Bank Gross PS	World Bank Gross Central	OECD Gross PS	World Bank Gross PS	World Bank Gross Central	OECD Gross PS	World Bank Gross PS	World Bank Gross Central	OECD Gross PS	World Bank Gross PS	World Bank Gross Central	OECD Gross PS	World Bank Gross PS	World Bank Gross Central	OECD Gross PS	World Bank Gross PS	World Bank Gross Central
1970	54.1			44.5			78.0			17.5			38.1			10.6		
1975	44.9			42.8			62.1			23.1			57.4			20.2		
1980	45.6			39.8			54.5			30.2			58.0			47.9		
1985	66.3			53.5			59.4			41.6			82.1			64.2		
1990	74.5			66.6			33.0			41.5			103.7			68.6		
1995	100.3	131.2	74.9	74.2	83.1	70.0	52.7	49.0	46.8	57.2			125.5			87.1		
2000	82.1	108.1	56.1	55.2	61.5	53.0	45.6	42.3	41.3	60.4	58.9	37.7	121.6	105.1	101.9	136.7	136.5	101.0
2005	70.3	94.5	42.9	62.4	78.5	56.3	46.5	43.7	42.4	71.1	66.9	40.8	120.5	101.9	96.8	177.3	182.1	143.6
2010	84.4	105.3	49.5	92.8	116.0	85.6	81.3	79.7	77.9	79.9	81.0	51.6	131.3	115.3	108.5	198.4	212.5	174.6
2015	114.9	113.4	47.2	136.6	136.6	96.5	109.4	94.0	90.7	79.0	70.8	45.0	157.0	131.6	126.5	236.8	230.5	192.3
2018		109.1	43.5		135.5	98.4		91.6	89.0		61.0	39.5		133.0	127.8		231.4	195.0

of looking at the deficit as a meaningful number, we should look at the "net tax rate" that the current policies imply for future generations. To understand their argument, recall the discussion of present value from Chapter 7. These economists and others argue that if you look at the difference between the present value of what people of different generations pay in taxes and the transfers that they get in government benefits, you can compute a net tax rate. They claim that this number has been getting steadily worse for younger generations. Specifically, future generations will face a terrible tax burden because of the deficits of the last 40 years and the entitlement crises of Social Security and Medicare.

Who Owns the Debt?

The question of who owns the bonds that a nation sells to finance its debt is an important aspect of any nation's debt. Although this may seem like an irrelevant issue, you may be surprised to learn that the U.S. government owes itself more than a quarter of the debt. That is what separates the total and publicly held debts in Figure 12.3 and is the point of Figure 12.4. There are two ways in which the federal government lends itself money:

1. The Federal Reserve uses federal debt for the purposes of open-market operations.
2. The federal trust funds invest money by lending it to other parts of the federal government.

As you may recall from Chapter 10, the Federal Reserve of the United States (the Fed) has three options for moving the economy: open-market operations, changing key interest rates, and changing the reserve ratio. Open-market operations are activities that result in the Fed buying or selling bonds. To get money into the economy, it buys bonds, and to remove money from the system, it sells bonds. Since the role of the Federal Reserve is to keep inflation on an even keel, it must steadily increase the money supply to keep pace with the growth in the economy. Doing so requires that the Fed constantly buy bonds. In this way, the federal government owes itself a growing amount of money. If you think that is silly, consider that when the federal government borrows money from itself it also pays itself interest, and, as a matter of fact, in the early 1990s, it was borrowing money from itself to pay interest to itself.

The government also owes itself money through the various trust funds it maintains for Social Security, Medicare, highways, airports, and other smaller parts of the government entities. By law, these trust funds are allowed to invest their money in federal bonds only. Given that these bonds are the safest investment on the planet, this makes sense, but the bonds also return among the lowest interest rates available. In any event, when these programs have more revenue than they spend, the excess is lent to other parts of the government and is money that the government will not have to borrow on the open market.

From Figure 12.4, we see that the amount of federal debt that is held by the public tends to fall unless the deficit and debt are rising quickly. When these are rising quickly, the Federal Reserve is reluctant to buy a great amount of debt in a short period of time because injecting

FIGURE 12.4 Who owns our debt? Percentage of the debt held by the public, trust funds, and the Federal Reserve.

Source: The Office of Management and Budget. https://www.whitehouse.gov/omb/historical-tables/

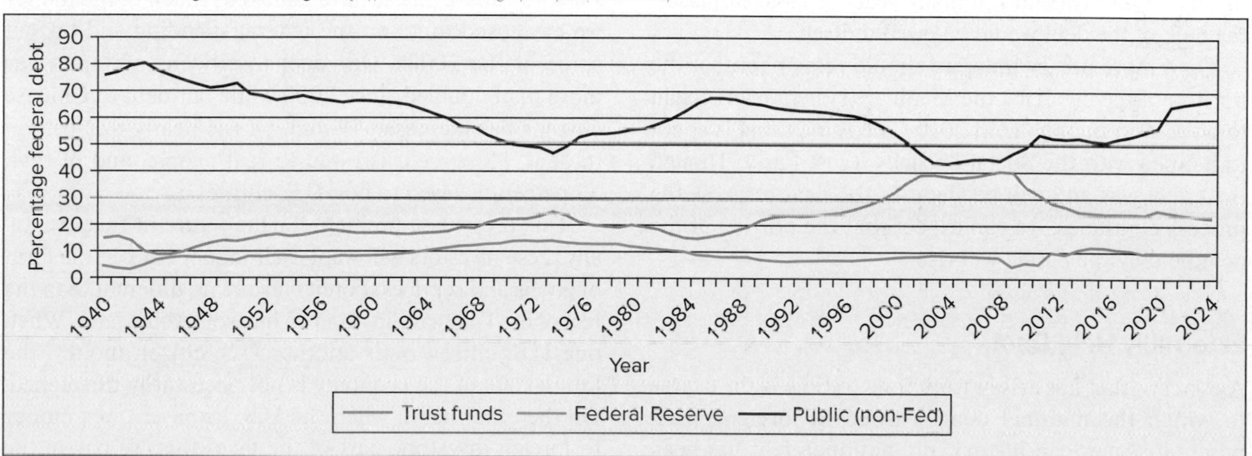

FIGURE 12.5 U.S. debt owed to foreign entitites.

Source: U.S. Department of the Treasury. https://www.treasury.gov/resource-center/data-chart-center/tic/pages/ticsec2.aspx

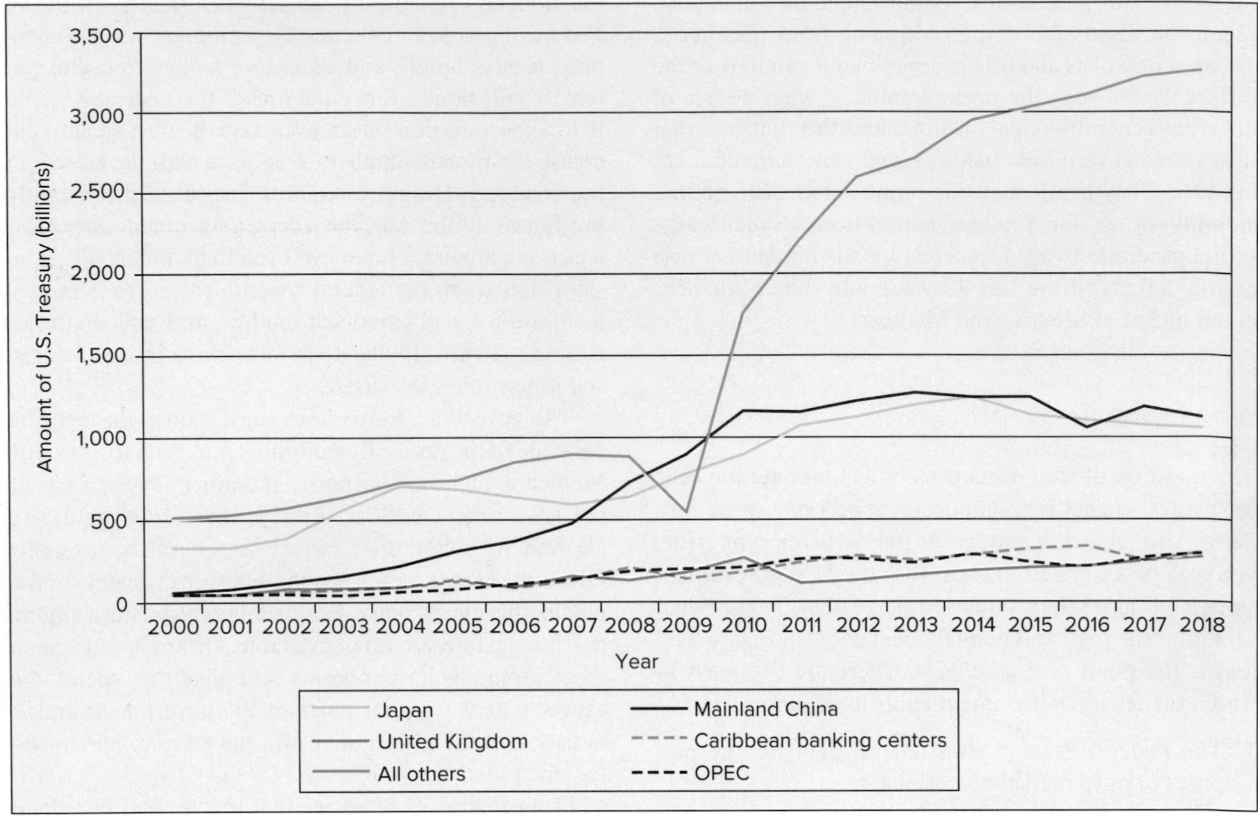

large quantities of new money in the system can create inflation. Any time large deficits exist, bonds must be sold to the public, and the overall proportion held by the public rises. When the deficit is not large or there is a surplus, the percentage held by the public will fall. It is conceivable that if the government ran many years of large surpluses, the bulk of the debt would be owed to itself.

On a more dreary note, we should remember that the portion of the debt that the Medicare system owns began to be sold to the public in 2010. The same thing is about to happen with the Social Security Trust Fund. Though the effect was and will be slight in the near term, as the process continues, we can expect that the portion of the debt held by the public will rise.

Externally Held Debt

A concern that has arisen from time to time is the degree to which the national debt is owed to foreigners. At points in American history, the national debt has been owed to citizens of other nations. While we could consider this flattering, in that these non-Americans view the United States as a safe place for their savings, it can also be a problem if too much debt is owed to foreigners.

Figure 12.5 demonstrates that, in large measure, the Japanese and Chinese have loaned us much of the money we have used to go on the federal spending and tax cut spree of the 2000s. Our debt to citizens of Japan has more than doubled since 2000 while our debt to Chinese citizens has increased 19-fold. Of the nearly $22 trillion in debt, 55 percent is owed to real people, and of that, 53 percent is owed to non-U.S. entities.

This presents a problem for the future in that eventually these investors will want their money back in the form of goods and services. Foreigners are no different than the rest of us: They save in order to buy something later. When one U.S. citizen owes another U.S. citizen money, the future state of the economy is not necessarily threatened. On the other hand, when the U.S. taxpayer owes money to foreign investors, part of the taxes that we pay in the future will go to pay them interest rather than to pay for schools, defense, or our criminal justice system.

A Balanced-Budget Amendment

One of the important debates of the final quarter of the 20th century was whether we need an amendment to the U.S. Constitution requiring a balanced federal budget. Economists argue both sides of this issue, but the majority believe it is not a good idea. Those who are opposed reason that an inflexible amendment could cause recessions to turn into depressions because the provisions of the amendment would mandate tax increases and spending cuts at precisely the time when the opposite would be needed. Those in favor of the amendment argue that the politicians' performance in the latter half of the 20th century is evidence of Congress's inability to show the discipline necessary to bring budgets into balance. Balancing the federal budget, it is argued, is necessary to generate low interest rates, which bring about long-term, investment-led growth.

Opponents of balanced budgets and of a constitutional amendment that makes them mandatory offer their best argument against a balanced-budget amendment by appealing to the aggregate supply–aggregate demand model that was explained in Chapter 8. The left panel of Figure 12.6 depicts this model and what would happen if we entered a recession. If aggregate demand were to shrink from AD_1 to AD_2 and a balanced-budget amendment were not required, two things would happen: (1) People would make less money and therefore pay less in taxes, and (2) people would require more assistance from government and spending would have to rise. This would happen without any new laws having to be passed. This nondiscretionary fiscal policy is built into the system and is called a *built-in stabilizer.* This stabilizer would result in aggregate demand returning in the direction from which it came, perhaps to AD_3. If a balanced-budget amendment were in place, we would be without the built-in stabilizer and the movement back to AD_3 would not happen. A recession would thus be worse than it would be otherwise have to be.

Of course the opposite could happen, and the right side of Figure 12.6 depicts that eventuality. Because spending on welfare programs and unemployment benefits would fall and tax revenues would rise, an increase in aggregate demand would result in surpluses. Without a balanced-budget requirement (that might force the money to be spent or taxes cut), aggregate demand would fall back to AD_3. With such a requirement, aggregate demand would not bounce back and the economic boom would be more extensive than otherwise. Therefore, a balanced-budget amendment would be **procyclical** because good times would be even better and bad times even worse than they would be without such a requirement. This "boom or bust" phenomenon was part of the economic landscape of the 19th century. Avoiding that outcome has been one of the successes of the economics profession in the post–World War II era.

procyclical
Situation that renders good times better and bad times worse.

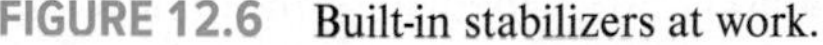

FIGURE 12.6 Built-in stabilizers at work.

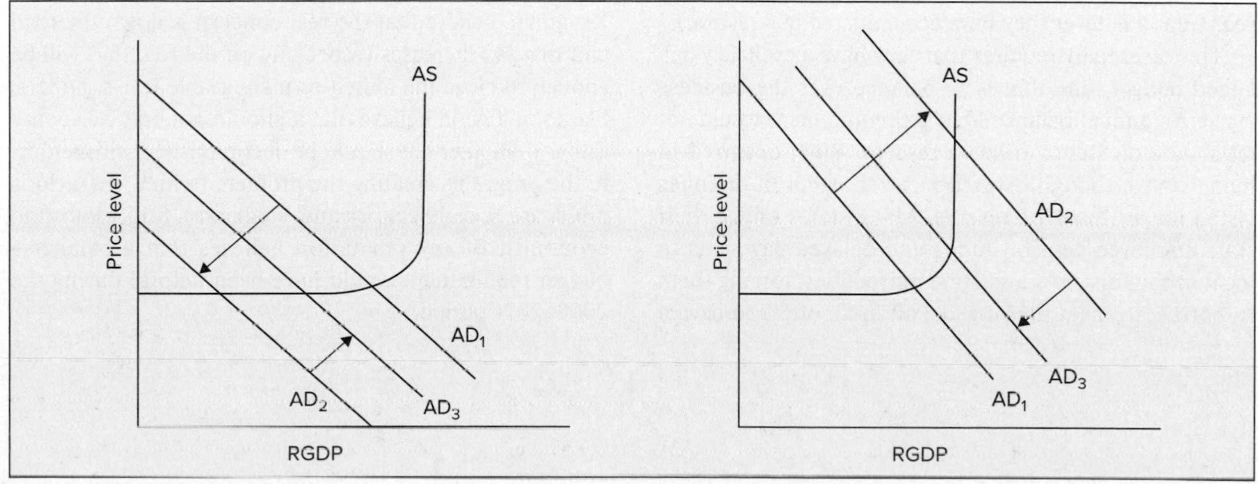

The best argument for mandating a balanced budget in some way, however, is that an elimination of federal borrowing would go a long way to reducing interest rates. The results of the 1990s support the idea that reducing the deficit can create a virtuous cycle in which lower deficits create lower interest rates. With lower interest rates, the economy grows, tax revenues increase, the deficit decreases even more, and so on. While this occurred without a balanced-budget amendment in the late 1990s, the 1960s through the early 1990s was a period of extensive borrowing with little fiscal discipline by either political party.

In the 1990s, both the Republican and Democratic parties claimed that reducing the federal deficit was important. Both parties, under President Bush (George Herbert Walker) with a Democratic Congress and President Clinton with a mostly Republican Congress, attempted to reduce the deficit. Each did it with means consistent with their party's philosophy. They were successful because a reduction in the demand for loanable funds by the federal government translated into lower interest rates. In particular, mortgage interest rates were lower during this period than they had been in 30 years. Lower interest rates meant more business investment as well. What ensued was the most dramatic drop in the deficit and the longest peacetime expansion since the end of World War II.

Both proponents and opponents of such an amendment point to the behavior of the states during the 1990s and early 2000s. Opponents note that the fiscal crises the states experienced between 2002 and 2006, and again in 2009, were a direct result of the constitutional requirements to have balanced budgets. Though the constitutions of the states are varied in this regard, they generally suggest that they can spend no more than the revenue for that year (plus whatever they have accumulated in a reserve).

This essentially requires that they have a cyclically balanced budget, one that is in balance over the business cycle. An annual balanced-budget requirement would not let a state create or utilize a reserve. What occurred in many states, though, was that the shortfall in revenues lasted longer than the reserve. Many states raided their state employee pension funds and delayed payments to local school districts and state universities, forcing them to borrow to meet their needs, all in an effort to have a "balanced budget." Opponents argue that governments will resort to these and other "smoke and mirror" tactics when forced to render any balanced-budget amendment meaningless.

The arguments relating to a balanced-budget amendment were rendered moot when, in 2008, the federal government borrowed hundreds of billions of dollars for the spring 2008 stimulus and especially after the fall 2008 TARP plan required the federal government to borrow nearly a trillion dollars to save the financial system from meltdown.

The initial Obama budget, curiously if not ironically named "A New Era of Responsibility," called for annual deficits of more than $1 trillion for 2009 and 2010 and deficits above $700 billion for many years after that. It has turned out that the deficit picture was somewhat worse than that with trillion dollar deficits extending into 2013. It is important to understand, though, that the majority of economists would acknowledge that imposing a balanced budget in this period would have seriously diminished the government's ability to stabilize the economy.

Economists, even those among a group that might be called deficit "hawks," were not upset by the record deficits of 2009 and 2010. The fear of these economists is that without a serious reduction in the deficit over the course of the next few years, when the large Medicare and Social Security bills due to retiring baby boomers come due, there will be little ability of the federal government to make good on those promises, even with borrowed money. We are only at the very beginning of that process. Those fears will only grow in the coming decade.

Economists' opinions vary widely in terms of how and when these deficits should be closed. Some, like Paul Krugman, believe that the real concern is down the road and that tax increases (especially on the wealthy) will be enough to close the deficit to manageable levels. Others, like John Taylor, believe that it should not only be sooner rather than later but should be accomplished with reform to the programs creating the problem (which, in Taylor's mind, are Social Security and Medicare). Still, almost no economist of any reputation believes that a balanced-budget requirement would have been helpful during the 2008–2011 period.

Summary

You now understand how economists look at federal budget deficits and surpluses and the national debt. You know that deficits have been more often than not caused by wars and that economists are less interested in the raw numbers of the debt and deficits than in more sophisticated measures. You are aware of U.S. economic history and that comparisons with other countries indicate that the United States had a relatively moderate national debt-to-GDP ratio, but that the deficits of the period from 2008 to 2012 have raised debt concerns dramatically. You know that the federal government actually owns much of the debt, and you should understand why most economists oppose an amendment to the U.S. Constitution that would mandate that it maintain a balanced budget.

Key Terms

budget deficit
budget surplus
capital budget
cyclical deficit
functional finance
national debt
off-budget
on-budget
operating budget
procyclical
structural deficit

Quiz Yourself

1. When considering the importance of the national debt, economists generally focus on
   a. the debt as a percentage of GDP.
   b. the increase in the debt.
   c. the level of the debt.
   d. the percentage of the debt held by the Federal Reserve.
2. The Obama-era (2009–2016) deficits were, to that time,
   a. the largest deficits ever when measured as a percentage of GDP.
   b. the largest deficits in nominal dollar terms, but not the largest deficits as a percentage of GDP.
   c. much smaller (in nominal dollars and as a percentage of GDP) than those run by previous administrations.
   d. quite typical (as a percentage of GDP) of those run by previous administrations.
3. The off-budget–on-budget distinction
   a. is important because two large programs, Social Security and Medicare, largely run off-budget.
   b. is a historical fiction.
   c. deals with long-lasting products of government (like roads and bridges).
   d. is important because defense is run off-budget.
4. The U.S. budget
   a. is required to be balanced.
   b. is never truly balanced, but historically surpluses are more common than deficits.
   c. is never truly balanced, but historically surpluses are less common than deficits.
   d. is typically balanced except in time of war.
5. The portion of the national debt owed to citizens of other countries is
   a. economically irrelevant however big it is.
   b. economically important, but it has been falling in recent years.
   c. economically important, and it has been rising in recent years.
   d. practically inconsequential because it is so small.
6. When looking at a balanced-budget amendment to the U.S. Constitution, economists are
   a. universally opposed to it.
   b. universally in favor of it.
   c. of two minds with opponents concerned about its procyclical nature.
   d. of two minds with proponents excited about its procyclical nature.
7. By way of international comparison, recent U.S. deficits have increased the ratio of debt to GDP
   a. such that the United States has the highest ratio in the industrialized world.
   b. but every other industrialized nation's ratio is much worse.
   c. but the United States' ratio is still lower than that of Germany, Canada, and Japan.
   d. such that only Japan's ratio is worse.

Short Answer Questions

1. If you ranked eras in terms of times in which the national debt was the biggest, what measures could you use and why? How would the measures differ when ranking the deficits of the 1940s, 1980s, and 2010s?
2. Why might you distinguish between borrowing to rebuild roads and bridges and borrowing to increase food stamp allocations?
3. Suppose the deficit were to be $500 billion during normal times, but increases to $1 trillion because we are in a recession, then increases again to $1.5 trillion because the government attempts to stimulate the economy. Which of these amounts are the structural deficit and the cyclical deficit and which amount represents functional finance?
4. Explain why to whom a country owes its money matters in terms of the true burden a national debt will have on future generations.
5. Explain why what deficit spending buys matters in terms of the true burden a national debt will have on future generations.

Think about This

The United States and China have had foreign policy disputes in the past. The most problematic situation could arise over the status of Taiwan. Does owing Chinese investors nearly $1 trillion make this problem more or less likely to come to a head? Does economic interdependence promote peace?

Talk about This

What is the opportunity cost of running a high deficit? How might this opportunity cost depend on the shape of the supply curve for loanable funds? What does it tell you about the supply curve for loanable funds when interest rates remained low even while the United States went from a $200 billion surplus to a $1.5 trillion deficit over 15 years?

For More Insight See

Journal of Economic Perspectives 10, no. 1 (Winter 1996). See articles by Alan J. Auerbach, Ronald Lee, Jonathan Skinner, and Douglas Bernheim.

Ronald, Lee, and Jonathan Skinner, "Will Aging Baby Boomers Bust the Federal Budget?" *Journal of Economic Perspectives* 13, no. 1 (Winter 1999).

Behind the Numbers

U.S. Bureau of Economic Analysis (BEA): www.bea.gov

- GDP
- RGDP

White House Office of Management and Budget (OMB): www.whitehouse.gov/omb/historical-tables

- Off-budget vs. on-budget
- Total deficit and surplus
- Debt and debt sources

Organisation for Economic Cooperation and Development (OECD): www.oecd.org

- International comparisons of gross debt-to-GDP ratios

CHAPTER THIRTEEN

The Housing Bubble

Learning Objectives

After reading this chapter you should be able to:

- LO1 List the fundamental determinants of housing prices.
- LO2 Compare and contrast the components of a traditional mortgage, an interest-only mortgage, and a negative-amortization mortgage.
- LO3 Discuss how a bubble can be created in a market based on unrealistic expectations.
- LO4 Summarize the consequences of a burst housing bubble on the U.S. economy.

Chapter Outline

In this chapter, you will learn about the U.S. housing market, mortgages, and lending practices. Specifically, you will discover how housing prices are determined, and how housing prices are determined in a hot, bubble market. Finally, you will examine the bursting of such a bubble in 2006 and 2007 and see that it was only the first wave of housing foreclosures that ultimately started the Great Recession.

How Much Is a House Really Worth?

As you can see from Figure 13.1, between 1997 and mid-2006, housing prices in many major urban areas rose much faster than overall inflation (as measured by the core PCE) and much faster than housing prices in other areas. This housing price index, created by economists Karl Case and Robert Shiller, has a base year of 2000 and measures the increase in prices in major metropolitan areas. While the price of all goods consumers buy (excluding food and energy) increased about 13 percent between 2000 and 2006, and while home prices in Dallas and Cleveland increased a mere 25 percent, home prices in Miami and Los Angeles almost tripled. Starting in mid-2006, the housing market in many metropolitan areas collapsed. Home prices in Phoenix dropped 41 percent, while those in Las Vegas and Miami dropped 39 percent and 38 percent, respectively. To understand why this happened, we need to remember some fundamental concepts, including opportunity cost, supply and demand, and interest rates and present value.

The key ingredients in what a house is fundamentally worth pertain to the opportunity cost of the land upon which the home sits, the cost of home construction in the community, the characteristics of the home itself, and the income of prospective buyers.

Referring back to Figure 13.1, the reason Dallas's home prices never increased at the rate of those in other areas is that buildable land is abundant in north-central Texas. The area is flat, with relatively few alternative uses. Unlike Los Angeles, San Francisco, or Miami, Dallas has almost no physical barriers to expansion. This means that the supply of buildable land is quite elastic. That doesn't mean land is created, but rather land use is changed from ranching to residential use, and this can be done very easily. So even if there is a significant increase in the demand for homes, the price of an existing house can, therefore, not increase beyond that of the alternative of building a new one. While building farther away from the city center (and there are actually two city centers because Ft. Worth is practically

FIGURE 13.1 Case-Shiller indices.

Source: Federal Reserve Bank of St. Louis. https://fred.stlouisfed.org/

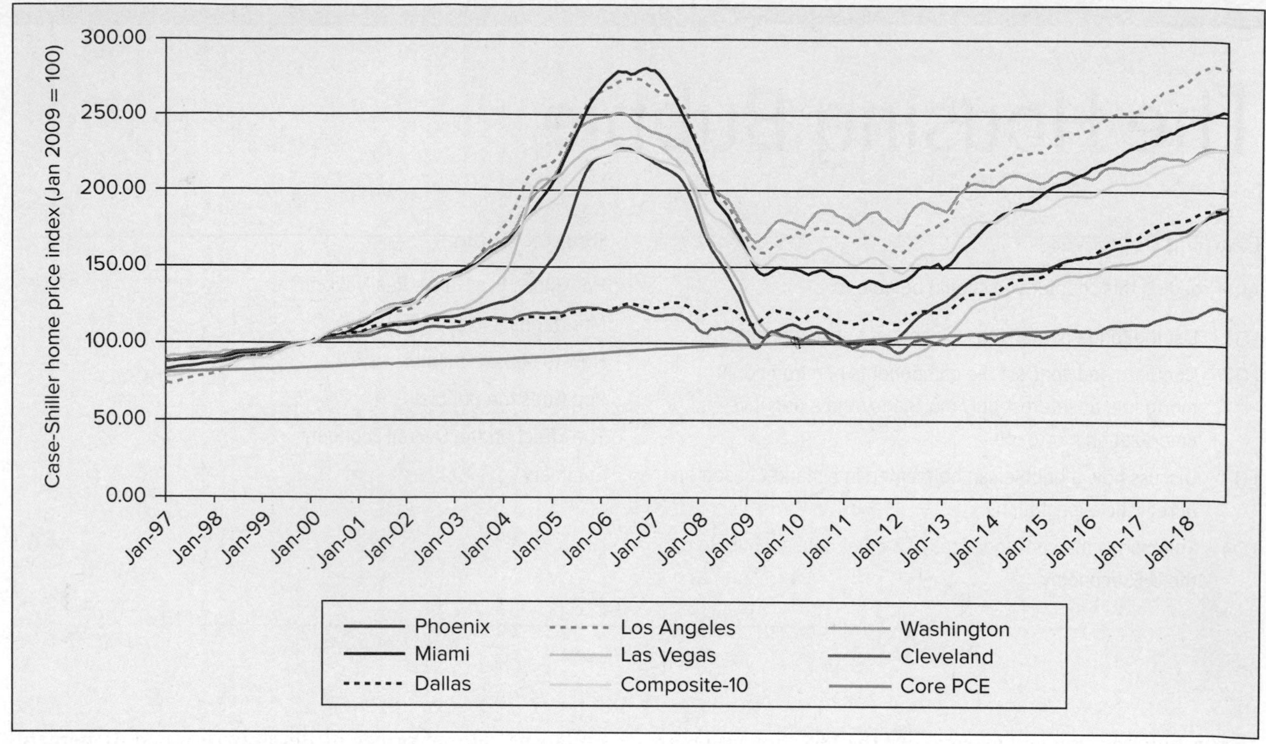

next door) can be inconvenient, resulting from the longer commute, most home buyers would gladly drive 10 to 20 minutes longer per day if they can save tens of thousands of dollars on the price of the home.

The supply of buildable land in Los Angeles, San Francisco, and Miami is quite inelastic because there are oceans, beaches, environmental regulations, and either swamps or mountains that render some land unsuitable for residential building. An increase in demand for homes in these cities will inevitably result in higher prices.

The next biggest factors in explaining home prices are demand-side factors such as the characteristics of the home and the income of the buyers. It is obvious that a home with all modern amenities will sell for more than an older one in need of repair. The income of a community's potential buyers is important as well. The Department of Housing and Urban Development estimated that median family income in San Francisco and Washington D.C. is substantially higher (nearly $100,000) than median family income in Dallas and Cleveland (about $60,000). Table 13.1 ranks cities on housing affordability using the ratio of median housing prices to median income. Clearly, the cities are not randomly distributed geographically. California has 18 of the top 20 least affordable cities and the Midwest is home to 15 of the top 20 most affordable cities.

Population growth/decline figures into housing prices. The city of Detroit is the only city in the world to have gone from a population exceeding 2 million to a population of less than 1 million. This means that for every new home is built, more than one home will go vacant. In growing areas, new neighborhoods are constantly created. The Atlanta metropolitan area has seen an increase in home prices based almost entirely on its increase in population.

Though the housing bubble of the early 2000s burst later in the decade, in the decade of the 2010s, housing prices recovered those losses.

Mortgages

As we learned in Chapter 7's review of present value and interest rates, the mathematics of amortization are relatively straightforward. In determining a car payment or a

Table 13.1 Most affordable and least affordable places to live.

Source: National Association of Home Builders. https://www.nahb.org

Least Affordable		Most Affordable	
1	San Francisco–Redwood City–South San Francisco, CA	1	Cumberland, MD–WV
2	Los Angeles–Long Beach–Glendale, CA	2	Kokomo, IN
3	Santa Cruz–Watsonville, CA	3	Wheeling, WV-OH
4	Salinas, CA	4	Davenport–Moline–Rock Island, IA–IL
5	Anaheim–Santa Ana–Irvine, CA	5	Elmira, NY
6	San Jose–Sunnyvale–Santa Clara, CA	6	Youngstown–Warren–Boardman, OH–PA
7	San Luis Obispo–Paso Robles–Arroyo Grande, CA	7	Fairbanks, AK
8	San Diego–Carlsbad, CA	8	Binghamton, NY
9	San Rafael, CA	9	Springfield, OH
10	Napa, CA	10	Springfield, IL
11	Oakland–Hayward-Berkeley, CA	11	Mansfield, OH
12	Santa Rosa, CA	12	Monroe, MI
13	Oxnard–Thousand Oaks–Ventura, CA	13	Scranton–Wilkes-Barre–Hazleton, PA
14	Merced, CA	14	Canton–Massillon, OH
15	Santa Maria–Santa Barbara, CA	15	Carbondale–Marion, IL
16	Vallejo–Fairfield, CA	16	Lansing–East Lansing, MI
17	Stockton–Lodi, CA	17	Rockford, IL
18	Kahului–Wailuku–Lahaina, HI	18	Syracuse, NY
19	Miami–Miami Beach–Kendall, FL	19	Bay City, MI
20	Modesto, CA	20	Utica–Rome, NY

mortgage payment, you find the monthly payment that will pay off the debt, at a particular interest rate, over a particular period of time. A mortgage, besides being a formal piece of paper, is a payment scheme designed to bring the original debt to zero over a period of time.

In the good old days, when your great grandparents bought a home, mortgages were all structured the same. The home buyer would be required to pay 20 percent of the value of the home, and the bank would loan the remaining 80 percent. On top of that, your great grandparents were compelled to provide verifiable documentation of their income, assets, and debts. Even if they had the 20 percent to put down on the home, if their mortgage payment, their estimated annual property taxes, and home owners insurance were more than 30 percent of the verifiable income, your great grandparents' banker would have been reluctant to lend them the money. They would have counseled your great grandparents to buy a smaller home. A final aspect of "old-fashioned" mortgages was that your great grandparents' banker would have held the mortgage. This meant that if your great grandparents defaulted on their mortgage, their hometown bank would take the loss.

To understand how your great grandparents' mortgage would work, look at Table 13.2. Doing an apples-to apples comparison, in a traditional mortgage, the payment lasts for 30 years. Setting aside the fact that home prices and interest rates have changed, let's assume a loan of $250,000, for 30 years, at 5 percent interest. A financial calculator or a spreadsheet program can help you compute the payment to be $1,342 per month. That is $1,342 the first month, the last month, and every month in between.

Now let's turn to the evolutionary and revolutionary changes that have occurred in the mortgage market. The first significant change came in 1968 when Congress spun off the Federal National Mortgage Association (more commonly known as Fannie Mae) and authorized it as a government-sponsored enterprise to buy home mortgages from banks and other financial institutions that wrote them. Fannie Mae would **securitize** them; that is, it bundled those mortgages together and then sold shares of itself to investors. In so doing, it spread the geographic risk of mortgages that resulted from banks holding a significant portion of the portfolios in local markets. This reduced the risk to any one bank of going bankrupt as a result of a local economic downturn. This reduced the risk to

securitize
The process of bundling nonfinancial assets (typically mortgages) together and then reselling them as either shares or as financial instruments to investors.

Table 13.2 Traditional, zero-interest, and negative-amortization mortgages, 30 years, 5 percent.

	Traditional Mortgage			Interest-Only, 5 Years			Interest-Only, 10 Years			Negative-Amortization, 5 Years		
Payment Number	Payment	Interest	Balance	Payment	Interest	Balance	Payment	Interest	Balance	Payment	Interest	Balance
0			$250,000			$250,000			$250,000			$250,000
1	$1,342	$1,042	249,700	$1,042	$1,042	250,000	$1,042	$1,042	250,000	$ 521	$1,042	250,521
2	1,342	1,040	249,398	1,042	1,042	250,000	1,042	1,042	250,000	522	1,044	251,043
3	1,342	1,039	249,095	1,042	1,042	250,000	1,042	1,042	250,000	523	1,046	251,566
4	1,342	1,038	248,791	1,042	1,042	250,000	1,042	1,042	250,000	524	1,048	252,090
.	.	.	.	.	.	.	.	.	.	.	.	.
.	.	.	.	.	.	.	.	.	.	.	.	.
.	.	.	.	.	.	.	.	.	.	.	.	.
57	1,342	963	230,719	1,042	1,042	250,000	1,042	1,042	250,000	585	1,170	281,487
58	1,342	961	230,338	1,042	1,042	250,000	1,042	1,042	250,000	586	1,173	282,074
59	1,342	960	229,956	1,042	1,042	250,000	1,042	1,042	250,000	588	1,175	282,661
60	1,342	958	229,572	1,042	1,042	250,000	1,042	1,042	250,000	589	1,178	283,250
61	1,342	957	229,186	1,461	1,042	249,580	1,042	1,042	250,000	1,656	1,180	282,775
62	1,342	955	228,799	1,461	1,040	249,159	1,042	1,042	250,000	1,656	1,178	282,297
63	1,342	953	228,410	1,461	1,038	248,735	1,042	1,042	250,000	1,656	1,176	281,817
64	1,342	952	228,020	1,461	1,036	248,310	1,042	1,042	250,000	1,656	1,174	281,336
.	.	.	.	.	.	.	.	.	.	.	.	.
.	.	.	.	.	.	.	.	.	.	.	.	.
.	.	.	.	.	.	.	.	.	.	.	.	.
117	1,342	855	204,827	1,461	932	223,053	1,042	1,042	250,000	1,656	1,056	252,720
118	1,342	853	204,338	1,461	929	222,521	1,042	1,042	250,000	1,656	1,053	252,117
119	1,342	851	203,848	1,461	927	221,987	1,042	1,042	250,000	1,656	1,050	251,512
120	1,342	849	203,355	1,461	925	221,450	1,042	1,042	250,000	1,656	1,048	250,904
121	1,342	847	202,860	1,461	923	220,912	1,650	1,042	249,392	1,656	1,045	250,293
122	1,342	845	202,364	1,461	920	220,371	1,650	1,039	248,781	1,656	1,043	249,680
123	1,342	843	201,865	1,461	918	219,827	1,650	1,037	248,168	1,656	1,040	249,065
.	.	.	.	.	.	.	.	.	.	.	.	.
.	.	.	.	.	.	.	.	.	.	.	.	.
.	.	.	.	.	.	.	.	.	.	.	.	.
358	1,342	17	2,667	1,461	18	2,905	1,650	20	3,279	1,656	21	3,291
359	1,342	11	1,336	1,461	12	1,455	1,650	14	1,643	1,656	14	1,649
360	1,342	6	0	1,461	6	0	1,650	7	0	1,656	7	0

investors and thereby reduced home mortgage interest rates. Its sister organization, the Federal Home Loan Mortgage Corporation (commonly known as Freddie Mac), was founded in 1970 and did much the same thing except that it focused on selling these bundled mortgage-backed securities to other investors. Neither the principal nor the profits of either entity was explicitly guaranteed by the federal government, but investors believed there to be an implicit understanding that should these entities have difficulty, the federal government would provide a bailout.

Beginning in the late 1980s, mortgages were offered where the buyer would have to put down only 5 percent or 10 percent rather than the traditional 20 percent. Though they would have to pay for an insurance policy (that would pay the bank in case of default), this made home buying an option for millions of Americans who previously could not afford the down payment. In the early part of the 2000s, zero-down mortgages became common. Only paperwork costs would be charged when the house was sold.

Beginning in 2002, **interest-only mortgages** and even **negative-amortization mortgages** became available. An interest-only mortgage, as the name suggests, has the buyer paying only interest for the first few (typically 5 or 10) years of a mortgage and then paying off the balance over the remainder of the mortgage. A negative-amortization mortgage does much the same thing, except buyers get to choose how much they want their payment to be in the first few years of the mortgage. These **pick-a-pay mortgages** (also known as pay option adjustable rate mortgages) would typically have the buyer paying about half the interest accrued each month on the mortgage so the outstanding balance on the mortgage would rise over time. After a few years, the mortgage would convert to a standard type and the balance would be paid off over the remaining years. Though borrowers "chose" these risky options, many were sold on them by mortgage brokers who, themselves, faced no risk.

interest-only mortgage
A mortgage that allows the buyer to pay only the interest portion of the typical payment for the first few years of a mortgage. The mortgage resets to a traditional mortgage after that period, typically at a higher payment.

negative-amortization mortgage
A mortgage that allows the buyer to pay less than the interest portion of the typical payment for the first few years of a mortgage. The mortgage resets to a traditional mortgage after that period, typically at a higher payment.

pick-a-pay mortgage
A variety of negative-amortization mortgage that allows the buyer to choose a payment for the first few years of a mortgage.

Now let's compare the traditional mortgages to the interest-only mortgages and negative-amortization mortgages. Again, comparing apples-to-apples suppose the home owner is borrowing $250,000, for 30 years, at 5 percent interest. Looking at Table 13.2, you see that an interest-only mortgage saves the buyer $300 per month for the interest-only period, but the payment increases substantially once the mortgage converts to a traditional version. Because with most negative-amortization mortgages, the borrower gets to choose how much to pay during the initial payment period, let's assume they take an option of paying half the interest they owe each month. As a result, the outstanding balance rises, so the payment rises, albeit very slowly until the point where it converts to a traditional mortgage, and then the payment nearly triples.

These interest-only and negative-amortization mortgages were popular with home buyers because they allowed someone of modest means to get into a home they might otherwise not be able to afford. What is unclear is the degree to which borrowers adequately understood the terms of these mortgages. They may have simply not read their documentation, or they may have been convinced that regardless of how high their mortgage payments rose, the ever-increasing value of their home would allow them to take out a second mortgage with a home equity line of credit. Of the interest-only and negative-amortization mortgages issued during 2006 and 2007, approximately half came with built-in home equity lines of credit. This provided borrowers with the false assurance that if they had trouble making their payment, they could borrow that payment.

How to Make a Bubble

As NASDAQ investors of the late 1990s discovered, bubbles are created by the expectation of higher prices causing people to buy assets based on that expectation rather than the aforementioned fundamentals. When you are told to "buy now before the price goes up" and you do, you only add to the volume of the bubble. People buy on the expectation that prices will rise faster than their ability to afford those same assets later so they become convinced to buy now. What really stimulates a bubble is borrowed money. If you had to put 20 percent down on a home, the increased price would affect your ability to react to that expectation. With the ability to put nothing down, and pay only half the interest, the buyer's ability to continue fueling the bubble is sustained, not diminished.

As NASDAQ bubble-riders remember, bubbles are fun when they are inflating. Why? Suppose you bought that $250,000 home in Miami in January 2002. Suppose you put nothing down and took out a negative-amortization mortgage. In Miami, from January 2002 to January 2007, the average home more than doubled in value. So you may owe $283,250 on the house you bought for $250,000, but who cares? It's now worth $500,000. Having trouble making the payments that have now increased from $589 per month to $1,656? No problem. You now have $216,750 in equity in that home and since you signed up for a home equity line of credit when you signed up for the mortgage, you can use your home like an ATM. You can even buy an SUV and take a vacation!

While that explains the demand side of the housing bubble, bubbles require ruinous mistakes on both the demand side and the supply side. So you may be asking why banks would lend money to these borrowers. This takes us back to the first of the evolutionary changes in the mortgage market: securitization. While your grandparents' mortgage was owned by their local bank, these mortgages were immediately sold. It was no longer part of the local banker's job to counsel home buyers against borrowing more than they could afford. Remember that old 30 percent rule? The banker no longer cared that you could not afford the payment because the banker was going to sell the mortgage within days of writing it, which eliminated any burden or risk on the banker. If you defaulted on the mortgage, it was someone else's problem. In addition, about half of negative-amortization mortgages were "liar loans" in that the bankers who wrote the mortgages purposefully did not verify the income or assets of the borrower. They merely consulted the credit agencies. If your credit was good enough that they could sell your mortgage to Fannie Mae or Freddie Mac, they wrote the mortgage and sold it within days.[1]

There is one other aspect of the modern mortgage market that may have contributed to the mess, and that is the noticeable absence of the intimidation involved in the closing process. Your grandparents sat across the table from a banker who went through each piece of paper associated with the mortgage. Your grandparents paid very close attention, in part because they were afraid that if they didn't, somehow the mortgage would not go through. Today, a click here or a phone call there, and you can be approved by a mortgage company with no local interest whatsoever. That means that you get a package of papers that you simply have to take down to a notary public (a designation of a person who certifies that the person signing is indeed the named party) and sign where the "sign here" tabs are located. This eliminates one of the places where a borrower might better understand the features of a mortgage (such as the tripling of the required payment after the fifth year).

Foreign investors whose money was at risk began to openly worry about the impact of a collapse of the mortgage market. This fear created an instrument that, perversely, only added to the bubble. By the middle of the 2000s, it became more difficult to sell the securitized mortgages because of the growing fear of foreclosures. The same entities that bought the mortgages, securitized them, and then sold them to investors, now offered to sell the investors **credit default swaps.** In this case, the credit default swap acted like an insurance policy that promised to pay the holder of the securitized mortgage should the borrowers fail to pay their debts. This satisfied the investors' concern for security, and the bubble continued to grow. The problem was that these insurance policies were not regulated like typical insurance policies. A typical home owners or auto insurance company is compelled to have sufficient capital to pay claims and is often required to carry reinsurance. Though credit default swaps are, most certainly, insurance policies, those that sold them were not regulated as if they were. Though some in Congress and others in regulatory bodies began to question these practices, the underlying feel-good story of record rates of home ownership and increasing home owner wealth (at least paper wealth) overwhelmed these voices of concern. This was the now infamous AIG's most profitable line of business for several years prior to its needed bailout by the Federal Reserve.

credit default swap Insurance on a mortgage-backed security.

Pop Goes the Bubble!

What the feel-good story relies upon heavily is the fiction that home prices only increase. Home prices can fall. Imagine this story somewhat differently. Suppose the price of the home falls from $250,000 to $200,000 because the home was only 1,500 square feet, had few amenities, and was in a relatively unattractive neighborhood. That is, suppose the fundamentals start to take over and the speculative demand to buy a house at any price goes away, meaning that the only reason its price exceeded what was rational for its location was a bubble mentality (like NASDAQ in 1999

[1]The bank may still take your payment every month, but they are only servicing it. They send that payment to the true owner.

and 2000). Now the poor home owner, who paid $250,000 for a home that is worth only $200,000, must pay $1,656 per month because he or she owes $283,250.

What are the options? Not many. First, if the home owners sell their home, they will owe $83,250 plus real estate fees of approximately $12,000, and they will have nowhere to live. If they do not have sufficient funds in savings, they will have to negotiate some other noncollateralized loan to pay off that amount before they can buy another home. Their only option to escape the massive debt is bankruptcy. This is a very bad option because they not only lose the home in which they live but they become unable to buy another home for years to come. Of course, they also eliminate their ability to buy cars, furniture, or anything else on credit as well. Their ability to go on vacation is quashed by their inability to qualify for credit cards, and their ability to pay off their existing credit card debt is eliminated because they no longer have equity in their home.

People who used this form of negative-amortization loan to purchase a home did so either because they believed their income in a few years would be sufficient to cover the increased mortgage payment, or they believed that housing prices would continue to rise, or they believed that a combination of the two would cause everything to turn out in the end. Unfortunately, it didn't "turn out in the end" for many borrowers. Beginning in 2006, foreclosures and near foreclosures (homes more than 30 days in arrears) began to skyrocket. In 2007, foreclosures were up 51 percent from 2006, and in 2008, they were up 82 percent on top of that. In Nevada in early 2009, 1 in 14 homes was in some sort of foreclosure process. In one month alone, November 2008, 1 in 76 homes in Nevada received foreclosure paperwork. The hardest hit states were California, Nevada, and Florida. It is not hard to see why. Consider Table 13.3 and the ability of the median family, with median income, to buy the median house in those locations we examined in Figure 13.1. Even if they chose a conventional mortgage, their 2006 mortgage payments, insurance, and property taxes would be well above 30 percent of their income in the "bubble" cities. One estimate in 2008 suggested that 1 in 6 households in the United States was above this 30 percent guideline, and 1 in 20 was paying more than half of its income in housing costs. Given that, it is no wonder that home prices stopped rising in 2006.

The shakeout after the collapse in housing has had a notable impact on the ability of the median-income family to afford the median home in these markets. At the peak of housing prices in 2006, with a 6 percent mortgage a median family would have to spend 43 percent of their income on housing. In 2018, in all of the communities sampled in Table 13.3, the percentage of household income a median family would have to spend on housing was significantly lower than it was in 2006. So, despite the fact that housing prices had fully recovered, housing was more affordable.

The Effect on the Overall Economy

At the beginning, the bursting of the housing bubble had a modest impact slowing the rate of growth of the overall economy in 2006 and 2007 by about 1 percent. By late

Table 13.3 Measuring housing affordability in major cities, 2006 and 2018.

Sources: HUD estimated from Home Mortgage Disclosure Act Reports; National Association of Realtors.

	Median Family Income		Median Sale Price of an Existing Single-Family Home		Approximate Annual Mortgage Payments (30 years)		Approximate Home Owners Insurance*		Approximate Property Tax*		Total Annual Housing Costs		Home Costs as a Percentage of Income	
	2006	2018	2006	2018	2006 (6)%	2018 (4.25)%	2006	2018	2006	2018	2006	2018	2006	2018
Phoenix	$64.0	$69.1	$218.8	$269.8	$12.5	$15.9	$2.0	$2.0	$4.0	$4.0	$18.5	$21.9	38.2%	31.7%
Los Angeles	63.0	69.3	506.8	590.8	29.0	34.9	2.0	2.0	4.0	4.0	35.0	40.9	80.9	59.0
Washington	109.2	117.2	388.6	424.0	22.3	25.0	2.0	2.0	4.0	4.0	28.3	31.0	38.1	26.5
Miami	49.9	52.3	290.0	350.0	16.6	20.7	2.0	2.0	4.0	4.0	22.6	26.7	65.8	51.0
Las Vegas	59.2	64.8	221.5	288.8	12.7	17.0	2.0	2.0	4.0	4.0	18.7	23.0	42.9	35.6
Cleveland	66.1	70.7	132.0	153.3	7.6	9.0	2.0	2.0	4.0	4.0	13.6	15.0	24.7	21.3
Dallas	70.4	77.2	210.0	260.0	12.0	15.3	2.0	2.0	4.0	4.0	18.0	21.3	25.9	27.7

*Author estimate.

2007 and into 2008, as foreclosures ballooned, the impact snowballed. It was not until the fall of 2008 that the true impact of the crisis came to light. In order to avoid a massive financial meltdown, the Treasury Department took ownership of both Fannie Mae and Freddie Mac, the Federal Reserve took a significant ownership stake in the insurance giant AIG, and Congress passed the Troubled Assets Relief Program (TARP) to save the nation's largest banks from the consequences of their ill-advised practices.

From September 2008 through the end of that year, credit markets were almost entirely frozen. This meant that institutions that were otherwise healthy could not access credit markets in a normal and necessary fashion. As the news that fall was almost entirely bad, consumers simply stopped buying anything that was not absolutely necessary. Depending on the automaker, car purchases fell between 40 percent and 67 percent, and by December, GM and Chrysler required TARP funds to survive. The year culminated with the worst Christmas shopping season in more than 40 years.

The final post-mortem has not been written on what the ultimate impact of the housing bubble was. It certainly caused the steepest decline in economic activity since the Great Depression. It certainly led to relatively modest government deficits obliterating all post-World War II deficit records (whether in real or nominal terms) and states having to cut billions from their own budgets. Judging by the Composite-10 of the Case-Shiller Index, the housing market ultimately bottomed out in 2012. By 2018, most housing prices had rebounded to their 2006 highs. A look back at Figure 13.1 shows an issue that slowed the process of the housing market finding its "bottom" was the difficulty in selling homes for which more was owed than the home was worth. Part of that problem is that with securitization it is a difficult, time-consuming, and lawyer-filled process to engage in what is called a **short sale.** A short sale involves a buyer and a seller agreeing to a price and the mortgage company agreeing to write off the difference between the price of the home and what is owed on the mortgage. It took many years for the stock of "underwater" houses to be sold.

short sale
A sale of a home where the amount owed is more than the sale price and in which the seller seeks to have the remaining balance forgiven.

It will be left to Chapter 14 to review the effectiveness of TARP and the 2009 stimulus package as well as the Federal Reserve's attempt to stabilize markets by buying long-term treasuries and mortgage-backed securities.

Summary

You now understand the fundamental elements that determine housing prices, how homes are typically financed, and that modern types of mortgages offer an alternative to traditional 20 percent down, constant-payment mortgages. You also learned that unrealistic expectations in housing prices can create spiraling price increases and that such bubbles inevitably burst and can have a significant economic impact such as the one that popped in 2007 that influenced the Great Recession of 2008–2009.

Key Terms

credit default swap
interest-only mortgage
negative-amortization mortgage
pick-a-pay mortgage
securitize
short sale

Quiz Yourself

1. The type of mortgage that allows you to make the lowest possible payment is called a(n)
   a. zero-down mortgage.
   b. traditional constant-payment, 20 percent down mortgage.
   c. interest-only mortgage.
   d. negative-amortization mortgage.
2. In which type of mortgage do you build equity the fastest?
   a. A zero-down mortgage
   b. A traditional constant-payment, 20 percent down mortgage
   c. An interest-only mortgage
   d. A negative-amortization mortgage

3. In which type of mortgage do you neither build nor lose equity?
   a. A zero-down mortgage
   b. A traditional constant-payment, 20 percent down mortgage
   c. An interest-only mortgage
   d. A negative-amortization mortgage
4. Fundamentally, housing prices are a function of the home's
   a. location and amenities.
   b. amenities only.
   c. location only.
   d. interest rates only.
5. A housing bubble occurs when ______________ drive(s) prices more than fundamental factors.
   a. the price of gasoline
   b. a home's expected future price
   c. interest rate changes
   d. property tax increases
6. A bursting of a housing bubble could create more problems than the NASDAQ crash in 2000 because the housing bubble involves
   a. assets, and NASDAQ was about debts.
   b. risky forms of debt.
   c. more people.
   d. fewer people.
7. The bursting of the housing bubble triggered
   a. the Great Depression.
   b. the Great Recession.
   c. the Great Moderation.

Short Answer Questions

1. Explain how mortgage securitization makes it easier to borrow money to buy a house but harder to deal with when a house is sold for a loss.
2. Explain why securitization contributed to the problem of people buying homes using mortgages for which they did not know all the details (such as the negative-amortization mortgages referred to in the text).
3. Explain why the Federal Reserve felt it necessary to bail out AIG and what result it was attempting to avoid.
4. Explain the role of the credit default swap and why the attempt to make things safer for investors made things worse for everyone.

Think about This

Bubbles are a great deal easier to identify after they burst. Believe it or not there were many who did not believe that the housing market was in a bubble until well into 2008 when it was obvious to everyone. (If you can get your hands on the fourth edition's web chapter on this subject, you can see that I thought it was one, but because prices were stabilizing when I wrote it, I wasn't sure.) The same thing was true with the stock market in 1929 and 2000. Fast-forward 30 years and imagine yourself in a position of trying to manage your retirement savings. How are you going to tell if your portfolio is really worth what your 401(k) statements say or whether it is a bubble all over again?

Talk about This

We are in a post–housing bubble world in which millions of families owe substantially more money on their homes than they can sell them for. Recent changes to bankruptcy laws make it more difficult to declare bankruptcy, which leaves many fully employed, hardworking people trapped in their homes with no means of financial escape. As we reconsider financial regulation, should we treat negative-amortization mortgages and interest-only mortgages like cocaine: banned to prevent you from making a lifetime mistake?

Behind the Numbers

Federal Reserve Economic Data (FRED): fred.stlouisfed.org

- Case-Shiller Index

National Association of Realtors: www.nar.realtors

- Home prices

National Association of Home Builders: www.nahb.com

- Affordability

CHAPTER FOURTEEN

The Recession of 2007–2009: Causes and Policy Responses

Learning Objectives

After reading this chapter you should be able to:

LO1 Describe the cause of the 2007–2009 recession.

LO2 Enumerate the consequences of the recession.

LO3 Describe and model the discretionary and nondiscretionary fiscal policy, monetary policy, and TARP program to combat the recession.

LO4 Enumerate and describe the components of the fiscal stimulus package passed in the early days of the Obama administration.

Chapter Outline

The recession of 2007-2009 was one of the most, if not the most, severe recessions in post-World War II history. In terms of peak unemployment, it was the second worst since the Great Depression. In terms of the drop in real GDP and in terms of how long it took for real GDP to recover to its prerecession peak, it was the worst. It began in the fall of 2007 looking very much like the short and shallow recessions of 1991 and 2001. Then, in the fall of 2008, the bursting of the housing bubble and the decimation of the financial sector set off a series of economic shocks.

This chapter will begin with a look at economic activity in 2005 and 2007, discuss the most significant cause of the recession—the bursting housing bubble—the attempts in early 2008 to make it another short and shallow one, the financial sector meltdown of the fall of 2008, and the policy responses from the Federal Reserve, the Congress, and Presidents Bush and Obama. The chapter will conclude with a summary of the debate surrounding whether these policies were effective in either shortening or mitigating the impact of the recession.

Before It Began

As can be seen in Figure 14.1, RGDP growth was progressing at about the 20-year average (2.7 percent annually) until the final quarter of 2007. As you can see in Figure 14.2, this was despite gasoline prices that had nearly doubled from their early 2005 levels. What was providing the steam behind this growth? Housing.

While a full discussion of how the housing bubble was created (and subsequently how it burst) can be found in Chapter 13, we'll provide a much briefer version here. As can be seen from Figure 14.3, the price of homes (as measured by the Case-Shiller Home Price Index Composite-10) was increasing at an astonishing rate. While this may have made buying a home difficult

FIGURE 14.1 RGDP (billions, 2000) 2005.1–2007.3.

Source: Bureau of Economic Analysis. https://www.bea.gov/national/xls/gdplev.xls

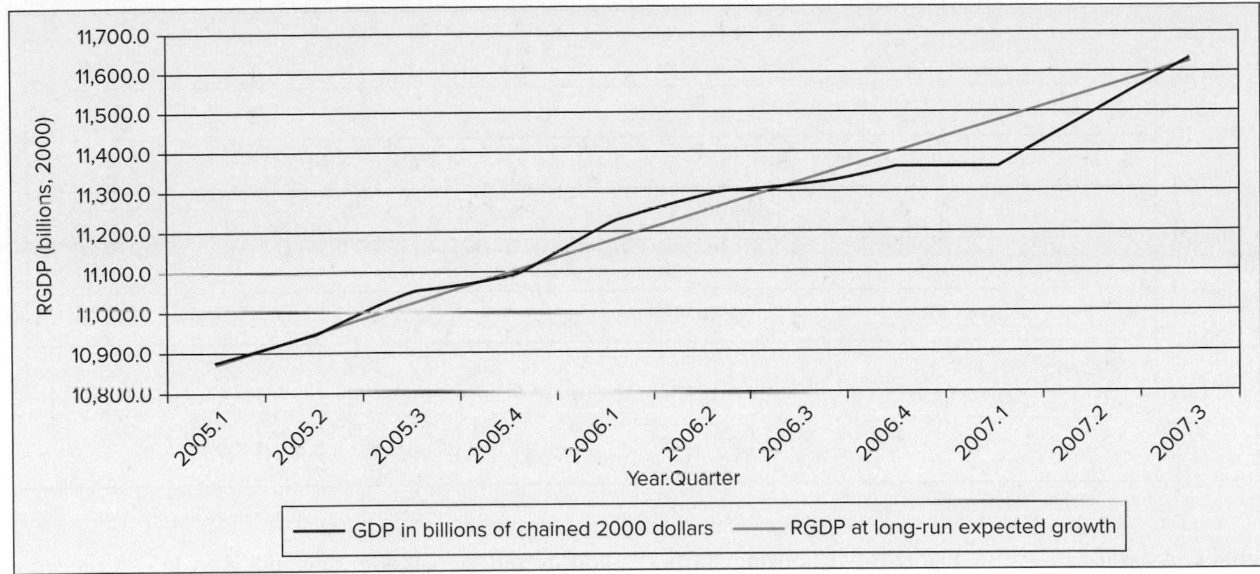

under normal circumstances, these were anything but normal circumstances. Lenders were eager to make loans of almost any amount to people wanting to buy a home. This was because between early 2000 and late 2005, the annual rate of appreciation in homes averaged 14.2 percent. At that annual increase in prices, it was erroneously thought, even if the borrower defaulted on the loan, the bank would lose no money because they could unload the house for more than the value of the borrower's loan.

This housing price escalation fueled two distinct housing booms: home building and home equity lines of

FIGURE 14.2 Average price of gasoline in cents.

Source: U.S. Energy Information Administration. https://www.eia.gov/petroleum/gasdiesel/

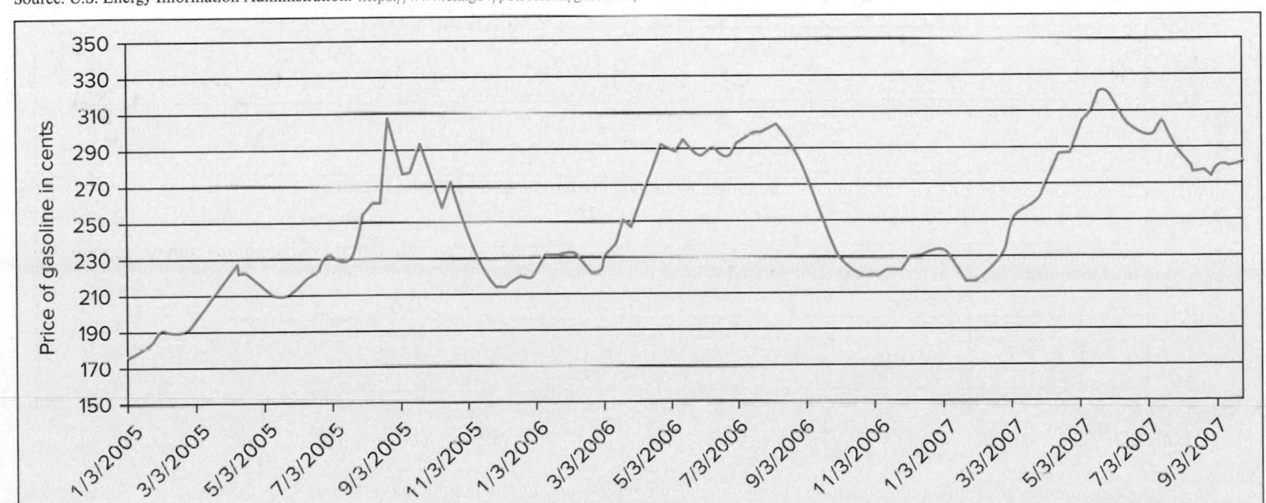

FIGURE 14.3 Case-Shiller Price Index (Composite-10).

Source: Federal Reserve Bank of St. Louis. https://fred.stlouisfed.org

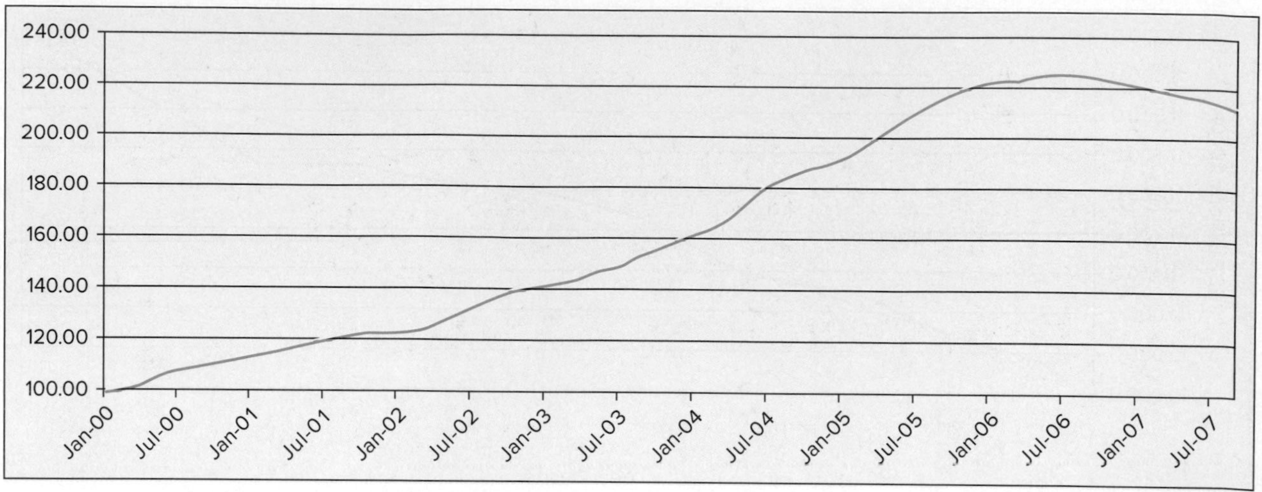

credit. As you can see in Figure 14.4, housing starts, though fluctuating with the weather, steadily increased between 2001 and 2007, and as you can see in Figure 14.5, nonrevolving credit, which includes home mortgages, home equity lines of credit, and car loans, increased at a 7.1 percent annual rate. Revolving debt, mostly credit card debt, increased at a 5.2 percent rate.

During this period, the most significant policy concern of the Federal Reserve was the increase in inflation that was resulting from rapidly increasing energy prices and overall increases in demand. As you can see from Figure 14.6, the Federal Reserve increased its targeted federal funds rate 14 times between June 2004 and June 2006 from 1 percent to 5.25 percent. At one point in January 2006, the concern over inflation was so great the Fed increased the federal funds rate 1.25 percentage points in one step. Given that the vast majority of increases and decreases in the federal funds rate have been limited to one-quarter of a point changes, this was considered a very aggressive action to combat inflation.

FIGURE 14.4 Single family housing starts.

Source: U. S. Census Bureau. https://www.census.gov/construction/nrc/index.html

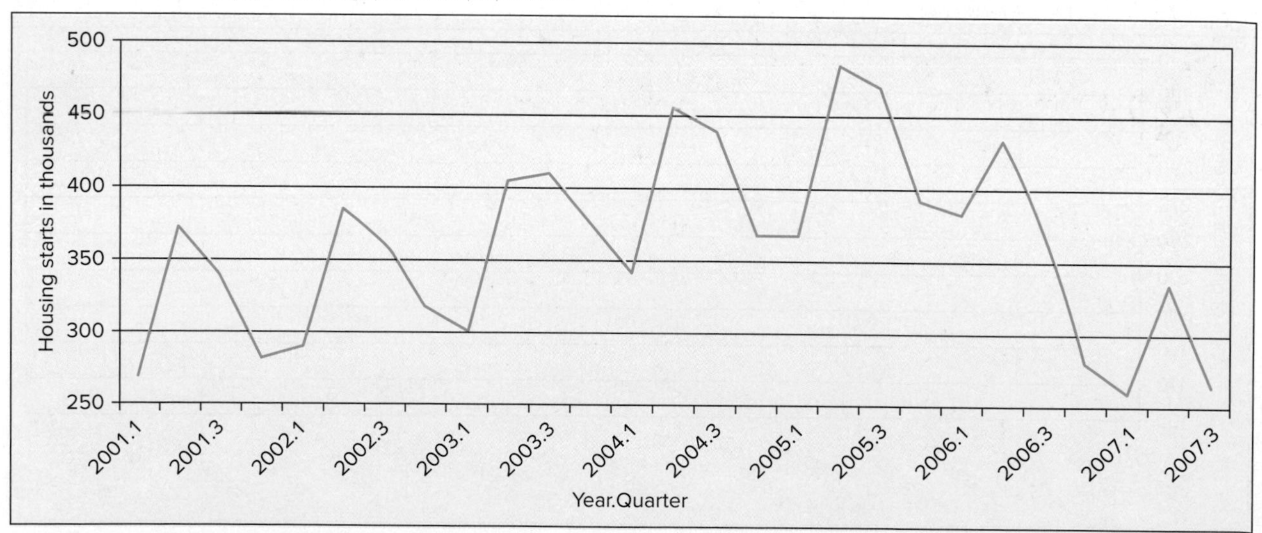

FIGURE 14.5 Revolving and nonrevolving household debt.

Source: Board of Governors of the Federal Reserve System. https://www.federalreserve.gov/Releases/G19/hist/

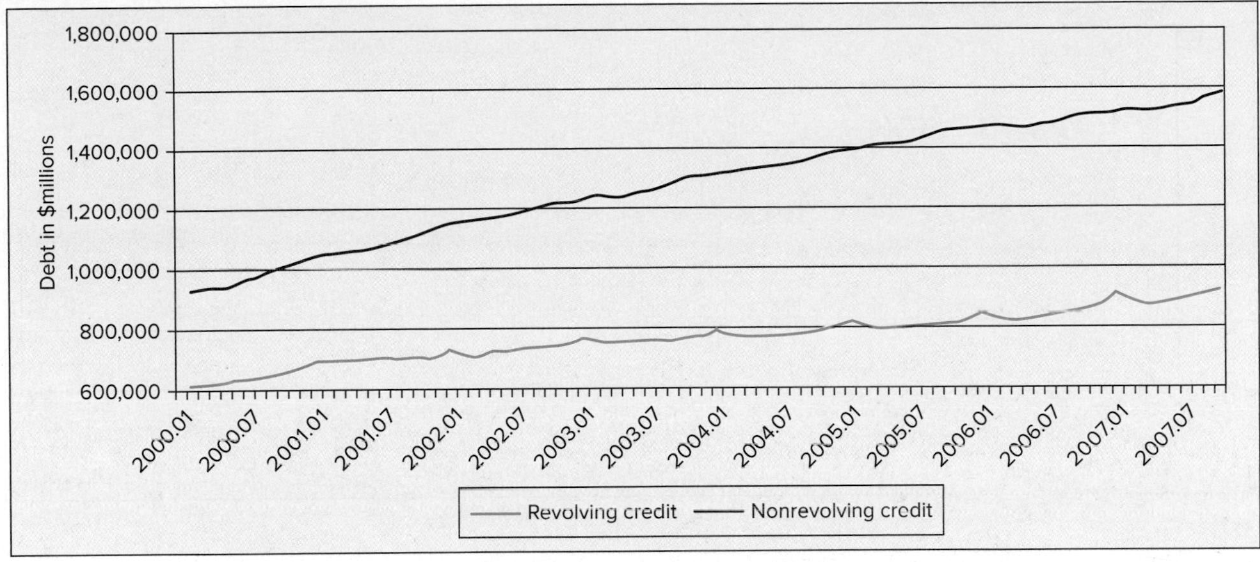

Late 2007: The Recession Begins as Do the Initial Policy Reactions

We know now that the National Bureau of Economic Research Business Cycle Dating Committee has pinned the beginning of the recession as late Fall 2007. It was evident to policy makers that a slowdown was about to occur in late 2007. As can be seen in Figure 14.7, the Federal Reserve began cutting its federal funds rate in September 2007 and didn't stop cutting the rate until it was at zero in December 2008.

The Bush administration began lobbying in early 2008 for a stimulus package. Its preferred mechanism was to make its tax cuts of 2003 permanent, as well as to provide tax rebates to taxpayers. It failed in securing the former but succeeded in garnering the latter. By early in the

FIGURE 14.6 The federal funds rate.

Source: Board of Governors of the Federal Reserve System. https://fred.stlouisfed.org

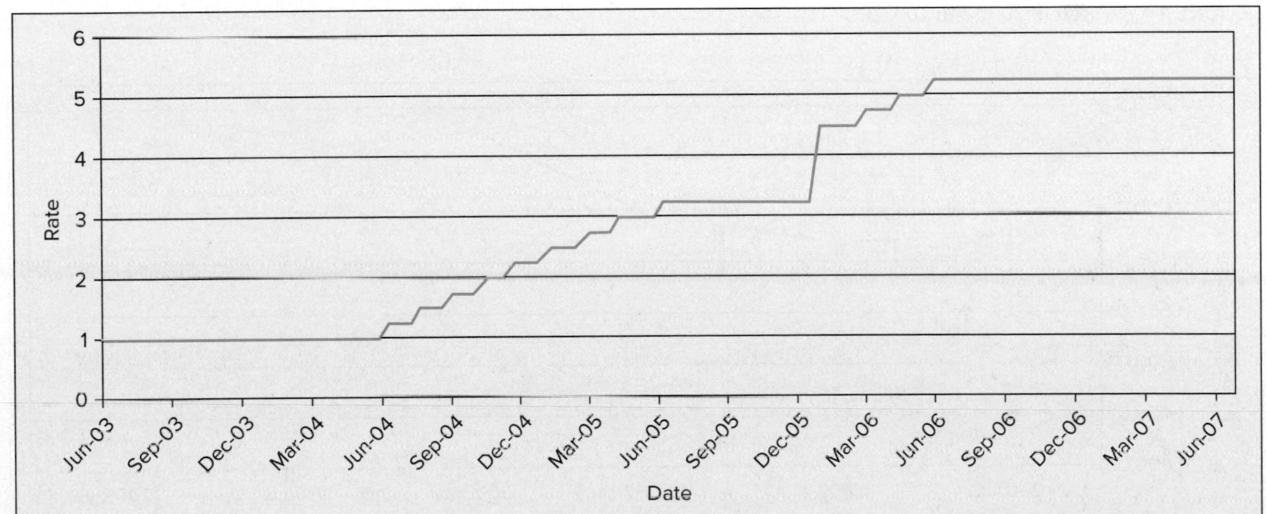

FIGURE 14.7 Federal funds rate September 2007–December 2008.

Source: Board of Governors of the Federal Reserve System. https://fred.stlouisfed.org

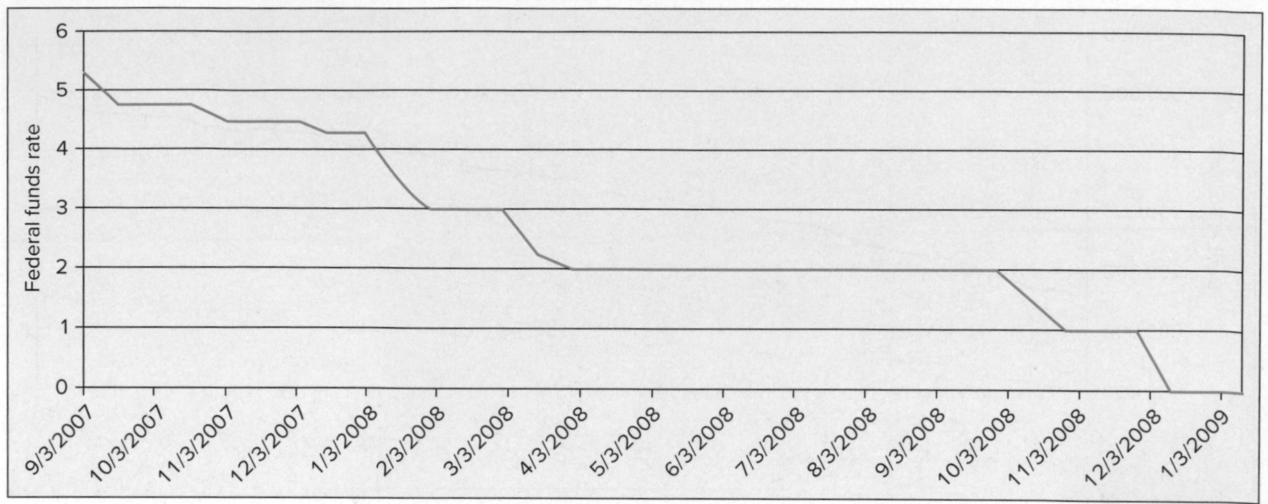

spring of 2008, the rebate plan was enacted, and by early summer, millions of Americans received $600 per individual, $1,200 per married couple. For most, this money was deposited directly into checking accounts by early summer. For the rest, rebate checks were mailed before the end of the summer. If you look at Figure 14.8, you can see that this $158 billion package had a significant short-run impact. Economic growth in the third quarter of 2008 was consistent with a healthy economy, but the economy was not at all healthy. Oil prices were rising to $145 per barrel and home foreclosures were increasing rapidly.

The Bottom Falls Out in Fall 2008

In the late summer and early fall of 2008, a crisis of confidence in the financial sector threatened to freeze capital markets in a way not seen since the Great Depression of the 1930s. During the summer, the rating agencies, Moody's and Standard and Poor's, were downgrading mortgage backed securities and the companies that held them as significant elements of their portfolios. The Federal Reserve created several loan programs to assist various bank and non-bank entities to cope with the difficult credit markets.

FIGURE 14.8 RGDP 2007.2 to 2008.3.

Source: Bureau of Economic Analysis. https://www.bea.gov/national/xls/gdplev.xls

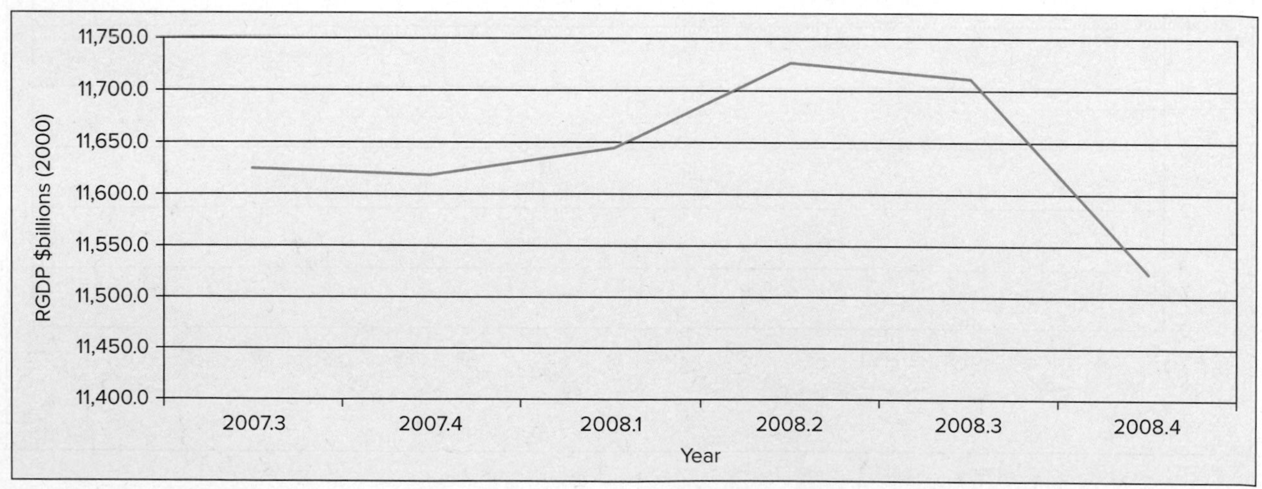

MARK-TO-MARKET

mark-to-market
An accounting rule that requires banks to revise their balance sheets to reflect the drop in the value of any financial assets they hold.

There are many economists, mostly conservatives, who believe that the real cause of the Great Recession was an obscure accounting rule forced on banks as a result of accounting scandals. The law, Sarbanes–Oxley (2002), required banks to revise their balance sheets to reflect the drop in the value of the mortgage-backed securities they held. The rule, called **mark-to-market**, when implemented at the height of the economic uncertainty of mid-2008, prevented banks from making perfectly normal loans because the banks were technically insolvent (had fewer assets than liabilities).

The economists who blame this accounting rule maintain that if the rule wasn't in place to begin with, the Great Recession would not have been that "great." They note that lending almost completely froze in the third quarter of 2008, and when the rule was suspended in October of that year, the healing of the banking sector began. These economists do not credit TARP, the Obama stimulus package, or any of the extraordinary monetary policy actions taken between 2008 and 2015. They pin it all on this obscure rule.

On September 7, 2008, the Treasury Department placed Fannie Mae and Freddie Mac in conservatorship[1], because it realized that these government-supported entities were essentially bankrupt. Within a week, Lehman Brothers filed for bankruptcy, and two days later, the Fed lent the insurance giant AIG $85 billion (which ultimately became $182.5 billion). Two weeks later, then Treasury Secretary Paulson and Federal Reserve Chair Bernanke went to Congress seeking $700 billion for their planned Troubled Asset Relief Program (TARP). Two weeks after that, Wachovia teetered on the edge of bankruptcy and was purchased by Wells Fargo.

Within the span of two months, from Labor Day weekend to Election Day 2008, the financial system was on the verge of collapse. The terrible news, repeated on a daily basis, produced such a crisis of confidence that Christmas 2008 was the worst holiday shopping season in 40 years. As can be seen in Figure 14.9, unemployment

FIGURE 14.9 Unemployment rates 2006–2009.

Source: Bureau of Labor Statistics, United States Department of Labor.

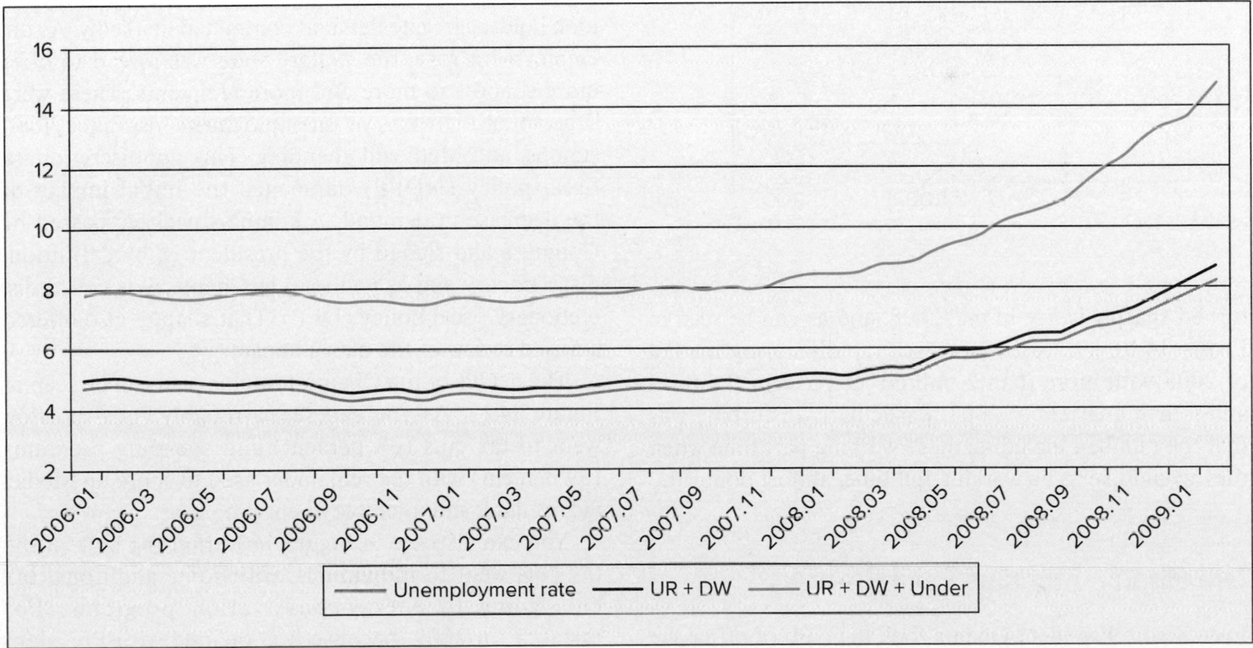

[1]Conservatorship involves temporarily placing an entity under the control of another entity.

FIGURE 14.10 Net change in employment (2009).

Source: Bureau of Labor Statistics, http://data.bls.gov/cgi-bin/srgate (LNS12000000)

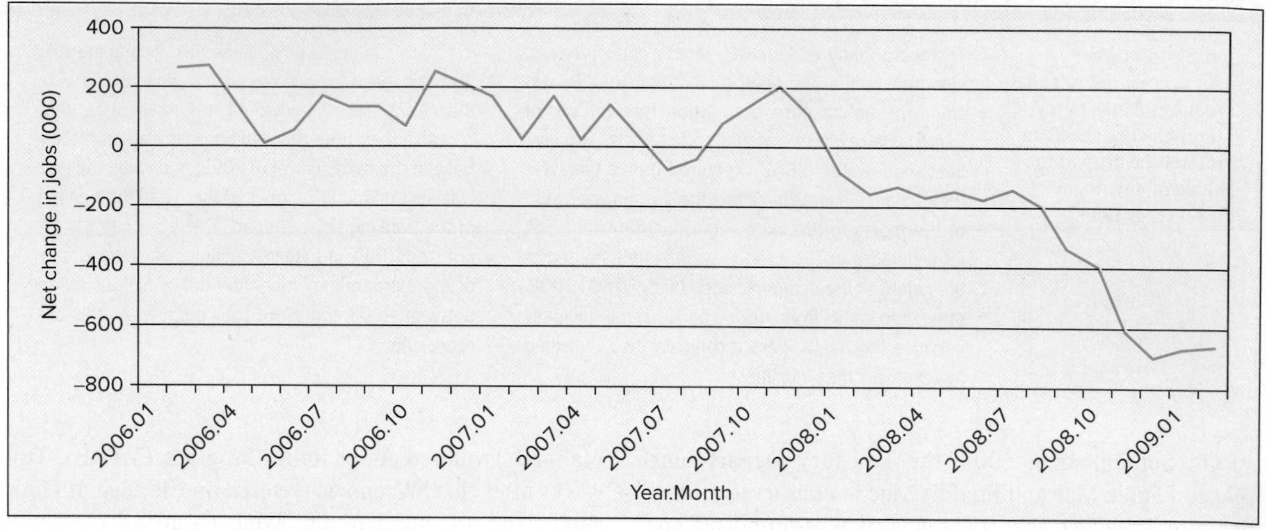

FIGURE 14.11 Modeling the impact of nondiscretionary fiscal policy and the Obama stimulus package (discretionary fiscal policy).

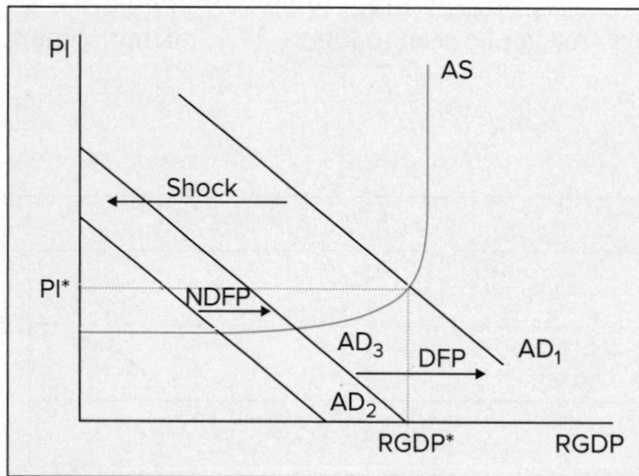

turned sharply worse in mid-2008, and as can be seen in Figure 14.10, job losses increased rapidly during the fall of 2008 with more than 2 million jobs lost in the third and fourth quarters of 2008. Particularly disturbing was that the number, including those working part time when they would like to be working full time, almost doubled.

The Obama Stimulus Package

Even before President Obama took the oath of office, he was deeply involved in negotiations with the incoming Congress to produce a stimulus package. While President Bush had engaged fiscal policy in the form of tax rebates, as the Obama plan emerged, it was not confined to tax changes but included significant spending.

As you can see in Figure 14.11, the aggregate demand–aggregate supply model can be used to model both the recession as well as the built-in and discretionary policy reactions. As the initial crisis of consumer confidence took hold, aggregate demand contracted markedly. As unemployment rose, the welfare state was forced to offer more support to more and more recipients. There were substantial increases in unemployment insurance, food stamps, and Medicaid spending. This nondiscretionary fiscal policy (NDFP) dampened the initial impact of the decrease in demand. A stimulus package passed by Congress and signed by the president is, by definition, discretionary and as you read in Chapter 9 is called discretionary fiscal policy (DFP). That chapter also offered a mixed review of the plan's impact.

The details of the Obama stimulus plan can be seen in Figure 14.12. As you can see, a roughly equal portion went to tax cuts (38 percent) and spending programs (39 percent) with the remainder used to shore up Medicaid, welfare, and unemployment programs.

You can also see in Figure 14.12 that the bulk of the tax cuts went to individuals, with some additional tax cuts going to energy-conservation programs. For instance, in 2009, because it coincided with President Obama's environmental policies, the purchase of

FIGURE 14.12 The Obama stimulus plan in detail.

Source: www.cbo.gov.

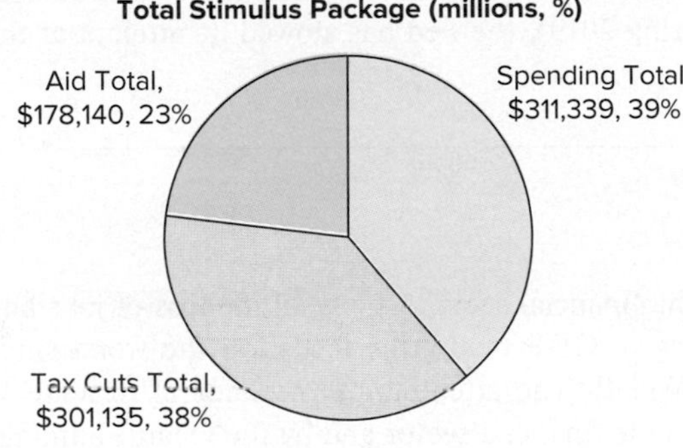

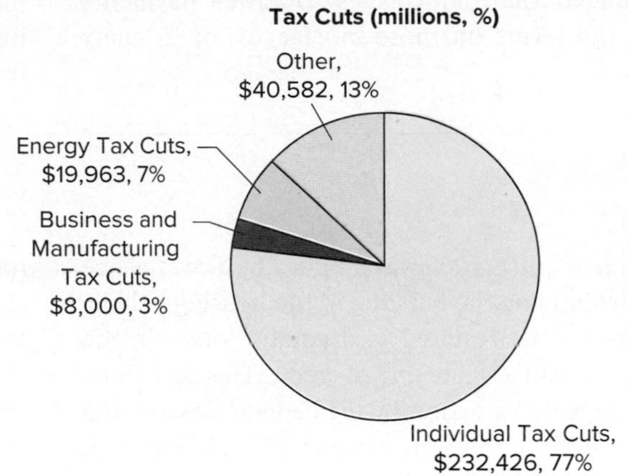

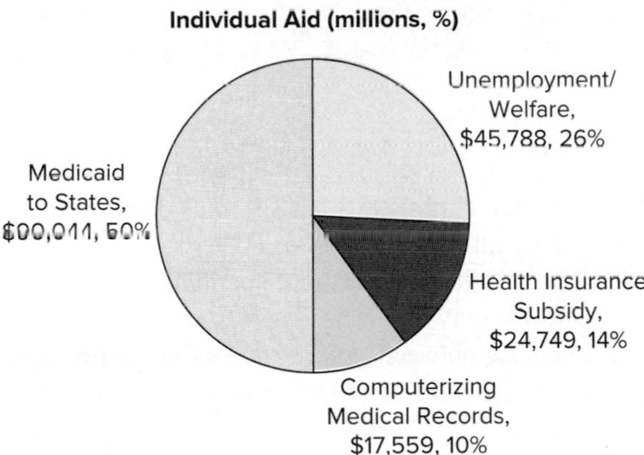

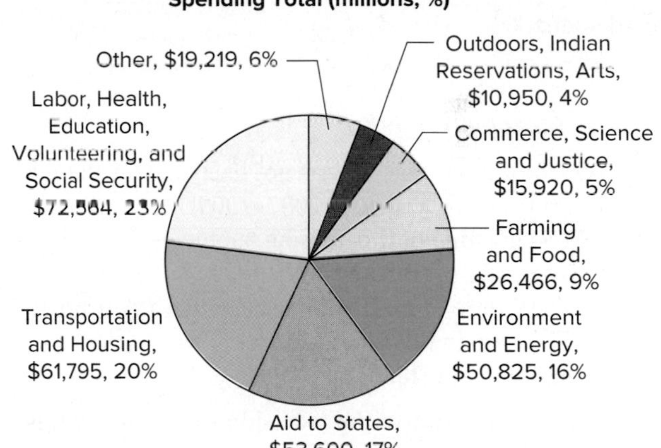

energy-efficient appliances was given preferential treatment. About half of the aid to individuals came in the form of money to states to help them provide Medicaid, given the anticipated increase in enrollment caused by the recession. About a quarter of the individual aid went to increase unemployment benefits by $25 per week and to extend benefits beyond the already approved 26 weeks.

Extraordinary Monetary Stimulus

At the same time the Obama administration was engaging in expansionary discretionary fiscal policy, called a fiscal stimulus, the Federal Reserve was engaging in the most expansive monetary stimulus in its history. Long after the tax cuts and spending increases expired, the monetary stimulus continued. For a detailed look at the monetary policy of this period, it would be worthwhile to read (or reread) Chapter 10's discussion of the "The Additional Tools of Monetary Policy Created during 2008" and to examine Figure 10.4. The short version is this: The Federal Reserve's portfolio of assets quadrupled between 2008 and 2015, and that tripling meant that there was available to the banking system three times more money in 2015 than there was in 2008. Moreover, the stimulus continued through 2015 as the Federal Reserve was purchasing $40 billion in mortgage-backed securities and another $40 billion in long-term treasuries each and every month.

This dramatic increase in loanable money kept interest rates extraordinarily low for the entire period. In

2012 and 2013, home mortgage interest rates were below 3 percent for those with good credit. That allowed those who refinanced their mortgages to lower payments or shorten the terms on those mortgages, or in many cases, both.

Whether this monetary stimulus was effective is also open for debate and will likely not be settled among economists until the stimulus has been reversed. At this writing (Spring 2019), the Fed has slowed its attempt at the reversal.

Summary

The recession of 2007–2009 was initiated by a confluence of events surrounding the bursting of the housing bubble. The housing bubble resulted in dramatic losses in the financial sector and a tightening of credit. This tightening was despite repeated attempts by the Federal Reserve, the Bush administration, and the Obama administration to revive the financial sector. The resulting loss of jobs and shrinking of GDP made this recession the worst since World War II. The attempts by the Federal Reserve to shore up the financial sector and by the Obama administration to stimulate the economy were breathtaking in their magnitude, though much debated in their impact.

Key Term

mark-to-market

Quiz Yourself

1. Which of the following was not likely a contributing factor to the recession of 2007–2009?
   a. The bursting of the housing bubble
   b. The 2008 tax rebates
   c. The failure of major financial service companies
   d. The drop in oil prices from $150 to $40 per barrel in late 2008
2. In the years prior to the recession the economy was growing
   a. at about its typical rate.
   b. at a rate much slower than typical.
   c. at a rate much faster than typical.
3. Gasoline prices ________ in late 2007 through mid-2008.
   a. spiked
   b. increased relatively slowly
   c. remained constant
   d. plunged
4. The Federal Reserve's response to the recession of 2007–2008 was
   a. clearly effective in shortening the recession.
   b. quick but not obviously effective in shortening the recession.
   c. slow and subject to criticism for being rather timid.
   d. procyclical in that it had precisely the opposite impact as intended.
5. The Obama administration's stimulus package was
   a. almost entirely made up of tax cuts.
   b. almost entirely made up of spending on "shovel-ready" projects.
   c. a balance between tax cuts, spending on projects, and shoring up the unemployment and welfare systems.
   d. almost entirely spent on welfare programs.
6. The job losses during this recession were
   a. typical of a short recession.
   b. nonexistent.
   c. significant and rapid.

Short Answer Questions

1. Explain each of the following in terms of whether they were discretionary fiscal policy, nondiscretionary fiscal policy, or monetary policy: TARP, the AIG bailout, the 2009 stimulus package, the rapid increase in unemployment compensation spending, the rapid reductions in state sales, and income tax revenues resulting from people having lower incomes.
2. How was "quantitative easing" different from what the Federal Reserve normally does?
3. Which lag described in Chapter 9 did the concept of "shovel-ready" intend to combat?

Think about This

Nobel Prize-winning economist Paul Krugman repeatedly warned through 2008 and 2009 that it was far worse for Congress to be too timid than too aggressive. In retrospect, was he correct? What would have been the result of a $1.5 trillion stimulus package?

Talk about This

What lessons would you draw from the recession of 2007–2009? What could have realistically been attempted in the middle of the housing boom to forestall the bust that came after?

Behind the Numbers

Bureau of Labor Statistics (BLS): www.bls.gov/cps

- Job losses
- Unemployment rates

Bureau of Economic Analysis (BEA): www.bea.gov

- GDP, RGDP

Federal Reserve Board: www.federalreserve.gov/data.htm

- Interest rates
- Federal Reserve balance sheet

Federal Reserve Economic Data (FRED): fred.stlouisfed.org

- Case-Shiller Index

CHAPTER FIFTEEN

Is Economic Stagnation the New Normal?

Learning Objectives

After reading this chapter you should be able to:

LO1 Describe the historical rates of per capita real GDP growth from 1950 to 2018.

LO2 Enumerate the sources of economic growth and explain why some of those sources cannot be repeated, while others may be repeated.

LO3 Describe the causes and consequences of slowing economic growth and describe the debate as to whether a shrinking middle class is best labeled a cause or a consequence.

LO4 Describe and model the alternative suggestions for jump-starting economic growth.

Chapter Outline

As the economies of the West recovered from the Great Recession at historically anemic rates, economists began to worry that the era of sustained, standard-of-living-enhancing economic growth was at an end. For decades the U.S. economy grew at a healthy and steady pace. While interrupted by recessions, that pace was considered sustainable. Whether measured in terms of real GDP growth, or per capita real GDP growth, Table 15.1 shows that during the period from 1950 to 2000, economic growth was fairly constant. The annualized rate of growth in per capita real GDP was between 2 and 3 percent.

Between 2000 and 2016, the "new normal" was a phrase that crept into the economic lexicon to both describe and accustom people to the unpleasant realization that growth could no longer be expected to increase standards of living across the board. The outlook for economic growth produced by the Organization for Economic Cooperation and Development (OECD) across the world's richer countries shows just how slow growth is projected to be. This chapter puts this in historical context, offers an explanation for why growth was so slow during this time, and concludes by considering whether the more robust growth of 2017 and 2018 is sustainable.

Table 15.1 Real growth in the United States.

Decade/ Period	Annualized Growth in RGDP	Annualized Growth in Population (%)	Annualized Growth in Per Capita RGDP
1950s	3.33	1.72	1.74
1960s	4.24	1.2	3.06
1970s	3.19	1.00	3.23
1980s	3.14	0.98	2.23
1990s	3.03	1.01	1.90
2000s	1.40	0.90	0.71
2010–2016	2.10	0.74	1.30
2017–2018	2.77	0.70	2.25

Periods of Robust Economic Growth

Estimates of real GDP growth for the pre–Civil War era vary, but they clearly show that the United States grew at rather modest rates (on a per capita basis). A startling statistic generated by economic historians suggests that between 1300 and 1750 per capita real economic growth was essentially zero. Another suggests that growth between the Revolutionary War and the Civil War was not much better at 1 percent. Pre–Industrial Revolution growth was limited by modest improvements in tools and animal-based energy (i.e., mules, horses, and oxen pulling plows). Though the cotton gin created a 50-fold increase in the amount of lint that could be separated from seed on a cotton plant, it was still operated by a hand crank with the energy of a slave.

What ignited the years of growth after the Civil War was the use of carbon-based energy (i.e., oil, natural gas, and coal), which fueled the Industrial Revolution's assembly-line manufacture of goods. Electric lighting added to this productivity by opening up the entire day for production. This torrential rate of growth created not only cars, airplanes, and useful home appliances; it created middle-class jobs for the people who produced those goods. Those jobs created incomes that were then used to purchase those goods. The virtuous cycle of growth enabling more growth made it such that from the end of the U.S. Civil War to the beginning of the Great Depression, annual growth in real per capita GDP averaged 1.75 percent.

Toward the end of the pre–World War II portion of the Industrial Revolution, political change and economic growth also resulted in unionization of employees, the substantial raising of wages, the dramatic improvement in working conditions, the ending of child-labor practices, a minimum wage, and the standardization of the 40-hour workweek. Laws protecting workers' rights to organize, collectively bargain, and strike were passed. That growth and those laws created a broad U.S. middle class. Though conservative, pro-business economists would give more of the credit to growth and liberal, pro-labor economists would give more credit to labor-friendly laws, it is clear that the combination created a large, healthy, and stable middle class.

Sources of Growth

From 1950 to 2007, per capita real GDP growth averaged 2.16 percent. That growth had several "mothers." During the 1950s through the 1990s, the labor force participation rate for women of prime working age (25–54) increased from 36 percent to 77 percent. All those extra workers clearly boosted overall economic output.

Technological growth also played an important role in increasing economic output. The use of carbon-based energy to power manufacturing and electric lighting to elongate the production day produced incredible gains. As a result of these technological innovations, labor productivity increased at a rapid pace for much of this period. Looking back at Chapter 6's statistics on productivity, the five-year moving average of labor productivity exceeded 2 percent (for all but a select few years) during the period from 1950 to 1975. Though it slowed dramatically, to below 2 percent for most of the period from 1975 to 2000, it once again rose rapidly in the pre–Great Recession 2000s as robotic- and computer-assisted manufacturing once again boosted production.[1]

Workers also became more productive, in part, because of increases in worker educational attainment. Though explored more deeply in Chapters 36 and 37, it is worth noting here that the percentage of Americans ages 25 to 64 with at least a high school diploma increased from 45 percent just after World War II to around 85 percent by 1980. That figure stabilized until 2000 when it increased further to in excess of 90 percent. The college completion rate for that same population increased from under 5 percent prior to World War II to more than 34 percent in 2018.

Another source of growth during the period was globalization. International trade created new markets for U.S. goods while also creating new goods for American markets. Of course, globalization also contributed to job losses, particularly for manufacturing workers, but economists are consistent that the impact on output was positive.

Causes and Consequences of Slowing Growth

Causes

Slowing economic growth, on both a RGDP basis and a per capita RGDP basis, has several causes and consequences. In terms of causes, the two most significant have been the slowing of production-related technological improvements and the general reversal of the increases to the labor force participation rate. Demographic changes

[1] Multifactor productivity, though notably slower overall, showed essentially the same pattern and timing.

have also occurred that resulted in slower growth. The population is not only growing at a slower rate; it is aging. The lingering consequences of the Great Recession are also not to be discounted. Tighter credit standards and greater financial regulations have made it more challenging for small businesses to operate and grow. We will take each of these, in turn.

Though technological improvements have been dramatic since 2000, few inventions have been particularly important to production. The cell phone and its offspring, the smartphone, have enabled us to do things as we walk from one place to another or as we wait in line somewhere, but we don't do much of anything that is productive with those devices. While some of us may write or respond to work-related e-mail, most of us are reading for entertainment (e.g., a book in our Kindle app), participating in social media (e.g., Instagram), or watching a show or video (e.g., Netflix or YouTube). The smartphone, tablet, and applications to which we are addicted do not increase the productivity of the workforce in the way that the electric light did. The DVR, smart TV, and proliferation of streaming media outlets that feed them may increase the joy associated with our leisure time, but they do not add to production.

The increase in labor productivity of the 1990s and early 2000s was due to the application of computer technology to manufacturing, agriculture, retail, wholesale, and service providers. Auto companies now use robotic spot welders, thereby increasing the consistency of those welds. Sawmills use laser imaging and computerized cutting programs to increase the amount of lumber that can be produced from each log. Hyper-accurate GPS-driven planters have increased yields in farm fields. Self-scanning checkouts are now common, which allow one cashier to monitor several lanes at once. Interconnected supply-chain management software has allowed Walmart and others to order goods, load trucks, and restock shelves with greater efficiency. Banking and payment processing efficiency has increased dramatically because of computerized processes and electronic transfers.

On the other hand, Netflix, Twitter, and the myriad gaming apps do absolutely nothing positive for production.

Another significant cause related to slowing growth is the significant decline in the labor force participation rate. Whereas men in their prime working ages used to participate at rates nearing 98 percent, that rate fell to 88 percent in 2013. Though still high, consider this: The percentage of men NOT working or looking for work while in their prime working years is six times higher than it was in the 1950s. Women in this age group, who constituted one of the "mothers" of earlier growth, have also departed the labor force albeit at a much slower rate. At 36 percent in 1950, the rate for women ages 25 to 54 peaked at 77.3 percent in 2000. By 2015, the rate had fallen to 73.3 percent. Young people have also left the labor force. In the early 1950s, approximately 60 percent of people between the ages of 16 and 24 were in the labor force. That number increased to a peak of 69 percent in the middle 1980s but dropped to 54 percent in 2014.

Another major cause of declining RGDP growth is the slowing increase in the population. This is one reason to focus on the per capita statistic. From 1950 to 1964, the U.S. population grew at between 1.4 percent and 2.2 percent per year, largely due to the postwar baby boom. The birth control pill slowed that rate such that it ranged between 0.8 percent and 1 percent from 1966 to 2009. The Census Bureau predicts that growth in the U.S. population is likely to slow to less than 0.4 percent.

A related cause is the changing demographic mix of the population. The percentage of the U.S. population under the age of 25 and over the age of 65 has changed dramatically over time. In 1970, 46 percent of the population was under the age of 25 and 9.8 percent was over the age of 65. By 2010, 33 percent of the population was under 25 while 13 percent was over 65. That is, the population in 2010 in their peak earning years was 54 percent. That number is now falling. By 2018, it had fallen to 53 percent and is projected to continue falling to under 50 percent by 2040.

The Great Recession was not just an economic problem for those who suffered it; it created several problems that lingered far longer than the recession. Chapter 13 described the extraordinary measures undertaken by the Federal Reserve. Those artificially low interest rates should have caused an increase in business investment. The reality is that business investment did not revive, and that is likely because of the higher standards that banks applied to commercial and industrial loans. Those higher standards are at least somewhat attributable to new financial regulations imposed on banks shortly after the Great Recession.

Consequences

One of the elements that is a cause to some, a consequence to others, and to still others both a cause and a consequence, is the declining middle class (a subject explored in some depth in Chapter 31, "Income and

Table 15.2
Pew Charitable Trust percentage of income held by income quintiles.

	Quintiles				
Year	**Lowest**	**Lower Middle**	**Middle**	**Upper Middle**	**Highest**
1971	16	9	61	10	4
1981	17	9	59	12	3
1991	18	9	56	12	5
2001	18	9	54	11	7
2011	20	9	51	12	8
2015	20	9	50	12	9

Source: The American Middle Class Is Losing Ground. Pew Research Center, December 9, 2015.

Wealth Inequality: What's Fair?"). The longer-term consequences relate to the overall social and economic health and welfare of the American population. In particular, with incomes growing more slowly than that projected by the Medicare and Social Security Trustees, the financial viability of those programs could be called into question.

The percentage of Americans in the middle class has seen a recent and troubling decline. The Pew Charitable Trust defines the middle class as those households with incomes between 67 percent and 200 percent of the median household income by household size. For 2015, a three-person household with income between $42,000 and $126,000 would qualify as being in the middle class. As Table 15.2 shows, the middle class has been shrinking since the 1970s, but much of that shrinkage was because those near the top boundary of the definition had their incomes rise pushing them into the "upper-middle" category. Now it is shrinking because households nearest the bottom boundary of the definition are having their incomes fall into the "lower-middle" category and those at the bottom of the "lower-middle" category are falling into the "lowest" category.

Though a shrinking middle class can be viewed as merely a consequence of a slowly growing economy, it can also be viewed as a cause of that slowly growing economy. That perspective, that the distribution of income is contributing to the lack of income, is typically held by economists on the left. They hold this perspective because people in the lower and middle classes tend to use most of their income for the purpose of bolstering their consumption. Further, those at the top of the income distribution tend to use their income for the purpose of making more income for themselves. The conclusion of those inclined to support income redistribution is that there is a positive macroeconomic impact to the change in distribution. When they buy, their spending is someone else's income and their income is generated by someone else's purchases of the goods and services they produce. At the very least, the money in the hands of the highest-income individuals tends to be spent or invested much more slowly than money in the hands of those not in the highest strata. In this way, the consequence can also be a cause.

Where economists generally agree, because it is simply math, is that when growth runs at 1 percent per capita rather than 2 percent per capita, the average newborn child today can count on having about half as much income when they retire. That is because growth is mathematically exponential. It isn't just 65 years of 1 percent lost for a 65 percent difference, it is 1.01^{65}, or a 91 percent difference. The result of slower growth is that the typical person has substantially lower income. There are fewer opportunities, fewer jobs, lower pay, and lower tax revenue. This means that commitments that were made years ago, such as Social Security and Medicare, will become increasingly difficult to maintain. It also means that new promises, perhaps government-subsidized child care or universal paid family leave, not only can't be kept; they can't even be responsibly considered. A society with twice as much income can do many more things for its citizenry. Growth not only helps those who earn the money; it also helps those who depend on government because government depends on revenue growth to support social programs.

One startling statistic that jolts and depresses at the same time is one that relates to suicide. According to the Centers for Disease Control and Prevention, between 2000 and 2016, the suicide rate for those between the ages of 45 and 64 increased from 13.5 to 19.2 per 100,000. This increase has been more pronounced among whites than among other ethnicities. Already twice the rate for whites as for African Americans, the suicide rate for whites increased from 11.3 per 100,000 to 14.7. When growth is slow and good-paying jobs are hard to find, depression can lead to suicide.

What Can Be Done to Jump-Start Growth, or Is This the New Normal?

Just as the cause of the slow-growth predicament is subject to debate, the conclusions economists draw are also subject to debate. There are essentially two camps: "get used to it, this is the new normal" and "we can do better." Within the "we can do better" camp there are also two camps with two vastly different solution sets. Liberals suggest a massive increase in stimulus to stimulate aggregate demand. Conservatives suggest an equally massive change to the regulatory system and tax structure.

Chief among the "new normal" group of economists is Robert Gordon. In his book, *The Rise and Fall of American Growth*, Gordon argues that the sources of economic growth of the post–Civil War period through 2000 have all but evaporated. Specifically, there isn't a large new workforce waiting to be tapped. Women entering the workforce in great numbers can only happen once. There is no significant portion of the day to be turned to productive use like there was when electric lighting allowed for round-the-clock manufacturing. The conversion to carbon-based energy from human or animal energy happened, and its benefits can't be repeated. Even if we can convert completely to non-carbon–based energy sources, that will not increase output. Such a conversion may save the planet from climate change, but it will not increase production because electrically powered equipment does not run any better just because the source of that electricity has changed.

A group Gordon labels "techno-optimists" disagrees with his assertions that the days of robust growth are behind us. They point to driverless cars and trucks as an example of productivity enhancements that are only a few years away from having a dramatic impact. If all the labor devoted to over-the-road trucking were to be replaced with driverless vehicles, that labor could be used to produce other goods and services. Further into the future, it is not hard to imagine that artificially intelligent robots could engage in home production in much the same way that current robots have increased productivity in factories. People might be able to engage in GDP-recognized productive activities rather than cooking, cleaning, shopping, or doing laundry. These techno-optimists imagine a world in which technology increases growth at once-again robust rates.

Back in the real world where we do our own cooking and cleaning, conservative and liberal economists debate what can be done to get the United States back on track.

FIGURE 15.1 Growth through increases in aggregate demand.

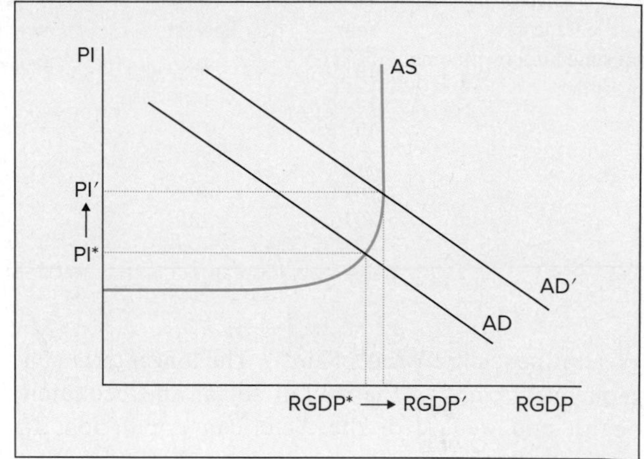

FIGURE 15.2 Growth through increases in aggregate supply.

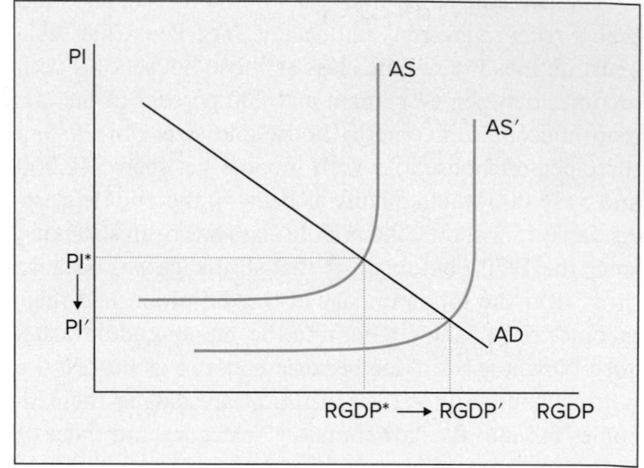

Liberals typically advocate for policies that increase aggregate demand, while conservatives look to aggregate supply increasing actions. Figures 15.1 and 15.2 show these alternatives.

Liberals/Democrats would use the Chapter 8 levers of middle-class tax cuts and increases to government spending to shift aggregate demand rightward, as shown in Figure 15.1. It is argued that that would stimulate the virtuous cycle. Greater demand would foster more business investment and more jobs (both to produce the greater number of goods and services and to increase the jobs associated with building new businesses). That would create more income and even greater middle-class demand. An abrupt rightward shift in aggregate demand would generate faster future rightward shifts in aggregate demand. This assertion is based on the notion that there is a level of growth that must be achieved to be self-sustaining. That is because consumer confidence is bolstered by increasing growth, and increased consumer confidence is itself a cause of economic growth.

Conservatives/Republicans argued (and, as a result of the Trump election in 2016, got an opportunity to test the proposition) that a reduction in the U.S. corporate income tax rate and a reform and simplification of the U.S. personal income tax system would generate aggregate supply increases, as shown in Figure 15.2. The U.S. corporate income tax (considering both state and federal tax systems) placed one of the highest business tax burdens, on U.S. companies. It also motivated companies with large international divisions to locate and hide those profits in foreign countries. Profits are only taxed in the United States when they reach U.S. shores, so companies simply leave those profits overseas because stockholders are better off when they do. The Tax Cuts and Jobs Act of 2017 was passed by a Republican Congress and signed by President Trump. It was their attempt to prove the "new normal" narrative wrong. Returning to Table 15.1, growth in per capita RGDP returned to its 1950–2010 average for 2017 and 2018. Whether that was, as Democratic critics claimed, as a result of a "sugar high" (of tax cuts) that would soon dissipate or, as Republicans claimed, as a result of new investments and increased consumer and business confidence will only be known given time.

Summary

The rapid slowing of U.S. real economic growth from 2 percent per capita to less than 1 percent per capita is a significant problem not only for the near term but also for the long term. Caused by both demographic shifts and a decline in productivity-enhancing technological improvements, the decline in growth has led to a decline in the U.S. middle class and to reduced expectations for the future. If it ends up that slow growth is the "new normal," economic opportunities for today's generation of young people will likely lead to many more of them living below their parent's economic status for the first time in more than 150 years. Perhaps even more depressing is that there is no consensus regarding a solution to this quandary. The 2016 elections gave Republicans the opportunity to test their side of the argument, and time will tell whether they were right.

Quiz Yourself

1. Per capita real economic growth during the pre-Revolutionary War era was
   a. negative.
   b. zero.
   c. 1 percent.
   d. 2 percent.
2. Per capita real economic growth during the Industrial Revolution through the mid-1970s was
   a. negative.
   b. zero.
   c. 1 percent.
   d. 2 percent.
3. The impact of slowing economic growth over a long period of time is
   a. negligible.
   b. the lost growth times the number of years.
   c. substantial because of the exponential aspect of growth.
4. The large increase in the labor force participation rate that occurred between 1950 and 2000 was because
   a. women's participation in the labor force doubled.
   b. men's participation in the labor force increased.
   c. the proportion of the population over 65 increased.
   d. young people's participation in the labor force doubled.
5. The large increase in the labor force participation rate is ________ source of growth.
   a. a duplicatable
   b. an unduplicatable
6. What source of rapid (1950–1975) growth is not duplicatable?
   a. Electrification of lighting
   b. Increases in education
   c. Increases in productivity

7. One issue that some call a consequence and others call a cause of slowing growth is a(n)
   a. slowing rate of increase in the population.
   b. change in the demographic mix of people to nonworking populations.
   c. declining middle class.
   d. increase in the labor force participation rate among women.

8. To counter the slowing rate of economic growth, liberal economists would recommend
   a. taxation and spending policies that decrease aggregate demand.
   b. taxation and spending policies that increase aggregate demand.
   c. corporate and personal income tax policies that decrease aggregate supply.
   d. corporate and personal income tax policies that increase aggregate supply.

9. To counter the slowing rate of economic growth, conservative economists would recommend
   a. taxation and spending policies that decrease aggregate demand.
   b. taxation and spending policies that increase aggregate demand.
   c. corporate and personal income tax policies that decrease aggregate supply.
   d. corporate and personal income tax policies that increase aggregate supply.

10. The rate of economic growth in 2017 through the first quarter of 2019 was ____ the rate of economic growth from 2010 through 2016.
   a. slower than
   b. the same as
   c. faster than

Short Answer Questions

1. Why is it that some believe that slowing growth is a cause of a declining middle class and others believe the causality is reversed? Could it be both?
2. Why would a cut in the rate of growth from 2 percent to 1 percent have more than a 10 percent impact if it lasted 10 years?

Think about This

Part of the reason that the economy is slowing is that both men and women in their prime working years are decreasing their labor force participation rate. This could be because more couples are choosing to sacrifice income for the benefits associated with having one stay at home during the period when their children are young. If this is the case, is it a problem? Is it merely a consequence of a choice that individuals are making?

Talk about This

Bernie Sanders and Donald Trump both tapped into a 2016 electorate troubled by the same thing: a slowing economy pinching the middle class (or a pinching middle class slowing the economy). Both targeted trade deals, but neither noted any of the causes cited by economists (left and right). What is your explanation for why?

For More Insight See

Gordon, Robert, *The Rise and Fall of American Growth* (Princeton University Press).

Behind the Numbers

Pew Charitable Trust: www.pewsocialtrends.org/2015/12/09/the-american-middle-class-is-losing-ground/

Bureau of Economic Analysis (BEA): www.bea.gov

- GDP, RGDP

U.S. Census Bureau: www.census.gov

- Population

CHAPTER SIXTEEN

Is the (Fiscal) Sky Falling?: An Examination of Unfunded Social Security, Medicare, and State and Local Pension Liabilities

Learning Objectives

After reading this chapter you should be able to:

LO1 Describe the source of the problem of the largest fiscal challenges facing the federal and state and local governments.

LO2 Compare and contrast defined benefit and defined contribution pension plans.

LO3 Describe the scope and degree of underfunding of each of the sources of fiscal problems.

LO4 Evaluate the likelihood of each of the scenarios in which the underfunding of Social Security, Medicare, and pensions for state and local government employees presents smaller problems than expected.

Chapter Outline

The story of "Chicken Little" is one in which the lead character claims that "the sky is falling" though the only thing that fell was an acorn. This chapter examines whether the fiscal sky is falling and uses the concept of present value to consider the question of whether the promises made by politicians of the past with regard to Social Security, Medicare, and defined benefit pensions to employees of state and local governments can be kept.

What Is the Source of the Problem?

As you may go on to read in Chapters 25 and 40, Medicare Part A and Social Security are funded through a system of payroll taxes. Working 40 quarters and paying taxes entitle people to subsidized hospital care as well as a pension based on the highest 35 years of earnings. For many employees of state and local governments, pension benefits are typically based on only the last three to five years of salary.

All three systems are either **entitlements** or **defined benefit programs** in that if you participate

entitlement
A program where if people meet certain income or demographic criteria, they are automatically eligible to receive benefits.

defined benefit program
A pension plan that defines eligibility for retirement and benefits according to a set of rules and a formula.

for the required period of time, you get a benefit according to their respective rules and formulas. For instance, defined benefit plans frequently have a rule defining retirement eligibility that is structured around the variable years-of-service + age. When this number exceeds a particular level (often 85), the person is eligible to retire. This is why a teacher who began teaching in a school district at age 25 can retire at full benefits at 55.

defined contribution program
A pension plan in which those enrolled, as well as their employer, contribute to an account according to a formula, and the investment of that account is under the control of the employee.

This plan differs from a **defined contribution program.** In a defined contribution program, those enrolled, as well as their employer, contribute to an account according to a formula (which can be 100 percent employee, 100 percent employer, or a mix), and the investment of that account is under the control of the employee. Under defined contribution systems, retirees only get what their account accumulates.

Under a defined benefit program, because you pay according to a formula and you receive benefits according to a formula, there is the possibility that the formula will be wrong (on either side), resulting in a surplus (more than enough has been collected to pay the promised benefits) or a deficit (not enough has been collected and invested to pay the benefits). As is probably obvious, politicians would love the former because they can increase benefit payouts, but the latter is more likely. It is the latter that has occurred and now plagues the public pension system. Because you only get out of an investment what you put in plus what it earns, in a defined contribution plan there are no surpluses or deficits.

Defined benefit programs used to dominate the world of employee retirement systems, but they quickly fell out of favor as fewer and fewer workers spent their entire careers working for the same employer. This is important because under most defined contribution plans, there is a minimum years-of-service requirement, and people who work 15 years with three different employers would usually get nothing or at least substantially less in aggregate pensions than they would if they worked 45 years with one employer. Because significantly fewer employees spend their careers with one private employer and because a large number of public employees stay with their original employer, it is now the norm for employees in the private sector to have defined contribution plans and for public employees to have defined benefit plans.

Defined benefit plans, because they involve employers investing money on the behalf of employees, require either a degree of trust or a degree of regulation. The **Employee Retirement Income Security Act of 1974 (ERISA)** provides regulation for defined benefit plans offered by private employers. The rules require that the funds in the accounts meet the actuarial requirements to keep them fully funded. This simply means that, accounting for expected returns on investments, life expectancy of pensioners, and so forth, the assets of the investments must be able to meet the liabilities, which to the fund are the pension payments to retirees. They must also make payments to the Pension Guaranty Trust Corporation, which operates as a government insurance company in cases where the pension fund cannot meet its obligations and the company that is supposed to pay in goes bankrupt. This guarantees pensioners that their defined benefit plans will pay pensions if the company that sponsored them is unable to pay its pension obligations (usually because of bankruptcy).

Employee Retirement Income Security Act of 1974 (ERISA)
A regulatory system for defined benefit plans.

Another thing that ERISA requires private companies to do is have sufficient funds to pay for any benefit it offers. It must also invest those funds with a third party.

How Big Is the Social Security and Medicare Problem?

It is important to understand that ERISA applies most stringently to private pensions, whereas public pensions, namely Social Security and state and local pensions, do not have to be fully funded. The absence of a requirement for a fully funded system is the crux of the problem. Social Security is, in present value terms under a range of assumptions, underfunded by between $11 and $14 trillion dollars, state pension funds are underfunded by $3 trillion, and local government pension funds are underfunded by more than one-half trillion. On top of that, though it is not a pension fund, Medicare is underfunded by another $4.7 trillion.

Let's begin at the federal level. The Social Security and Medicare system had one gigantic, and perhaps even fatal, operational assumption: Current employees could pay for current retirees. This assumption was necessary so that people could begin collecting benefits when the programs passed (in 1935 and 1966, respectively). Otherwise, the programs would have been collecting taxes and providing nearly no benefits for several years. Unfortunately for both systems, that mechanism requires that the number of babies born in a year remain roughly stable or grow at a steady rate so that eventually the ratio of workers per retiree can remain roughly constant. With the dearth of babies born between 1931 and 1945, due first to the scarcity of food during the Great Depression, which made many women at least temporarily infertile, and, second, World War II, which made young men temporarily scarce, and the subsequent baby boom of the postwar era, that assumption did not hold.

The result was that in 1982 analysts anticipated that beginning in 2008, as the first baby boomers became eligible for early-retirement Social Security benefits, and extending until around 2040, both Social Security and Medicare would have insufficient funds to pay for the anticipated benefits. In that year, a compromise was enacted that significantly raised payroll taxes in order to create the Social Security and Medicare trust funds and raised the full-benefit retirement age from 65 to 67.

As of 2018, those accounts remain seriously underfunded. As can be seen in Figure 16.1, the annual deficits in these programs alone will, very soon, reach very high levels. Because these deficits will occur mostly in the future, there are two reasonable ways of looking at them. The first, presented in Figure 16.1, displays them by discounting using the present value methodology of Chapter 7. Using an interest rate associated with long-term U.S. treasuries, 2.42 percent,[1] the annual deficits are discounted and plotted below. The area between the 0-line and the Social Security line is the degree of the problem with regard to that program going out 75 years.[2] It is $49 trillion. Similarly, between the 0-line and the Medicare line is the degree of the deficit in that program, which is $14 trillion. For perspective, at this writing the sum of those two numbers is nearly three times GDP. That means that as of 2019, the total liabilities of the United States are more than $85 trillion (the sum of the national debt and the unfunded liabilities of Social Security and Medicare).

To compound the problem, there will be a decreasing percentage of the population working to pay that enormous bill. As can be seen in Figure 16.2, the dependency ratio, the ratio of the population dependent on others to support them to the population supporting them, will rise from around 28 percent to more than 38 percent in the next 20 years and to nearly 44 percent within the next 75 years.

There are many factors to consider when evaluating the size of these problems. For instance, the earning capacity of the next generations will be greater than the earning capacity of today's generation. Moreover,

[1] The zero-coupon bond yield at this chapter's writing (April 2019).

[2] This is the length of time the Social Security and Medicare trustees are required to consider and report upon.

FIGURE 16.1 The present value of the annual Social Security and Medicare deficits: 2018–2095.

Source: Social Security Administration. "2018 OASDI Trustees Report." https://www.ssa.gov/OACT/TR/2018/

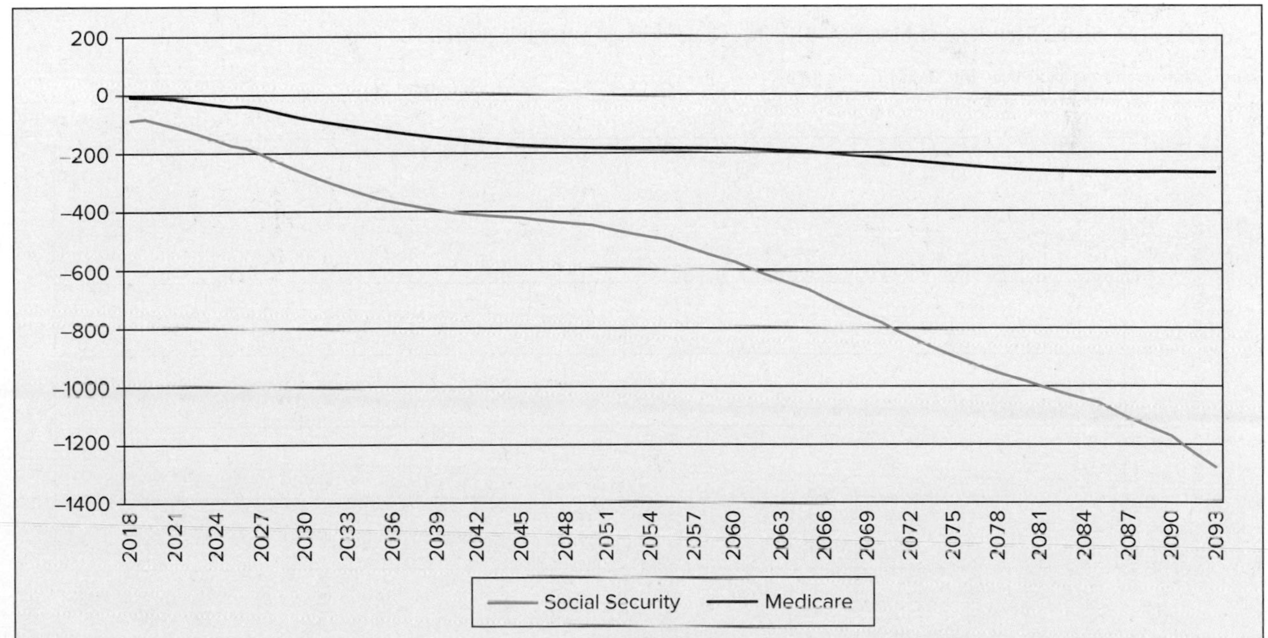

FIGURE 16.2 The dependency ratio: 2010–2095.

Source: Social Security Administration. "2018 OASDI Trustees Report." https://www.ssa.gov/OACT/TR/2018/

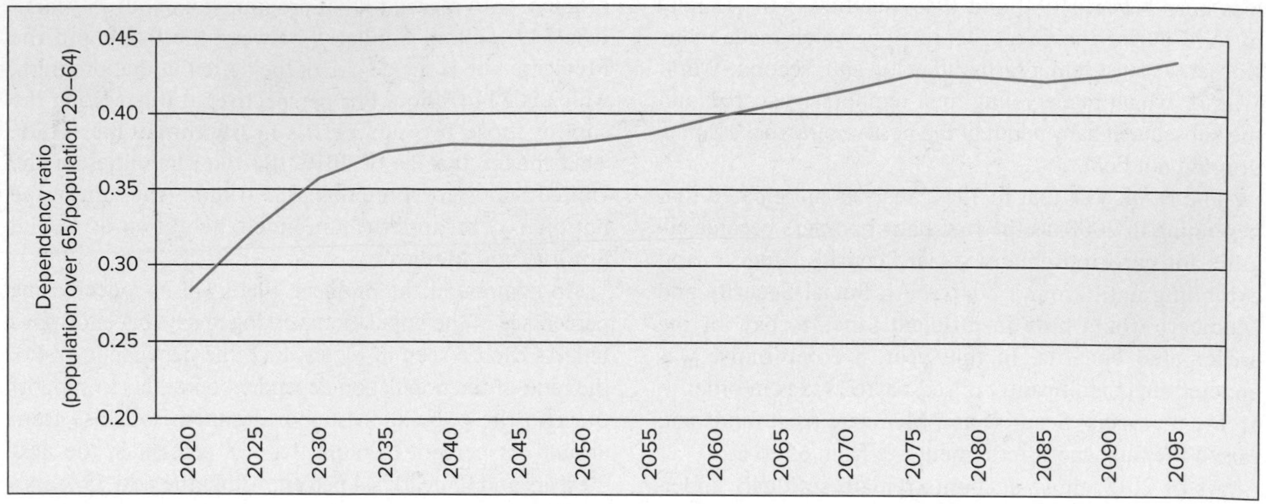

through immigration and birth, the U.S. population will grow, making it somewhat likely that the problem could present less of a burden than these figures imply. In Figure 16.3, we see that U.S. taxpayers could pay for these deficits with an amount of money equal to around 1 percent of payroll over the next decade. Though, by this measure, these deficits as a percentage of payroll rise to 5 percent in rapid order between 2020 and 2035, they only grow by another 1.5 percentage points in the ensuing 40 years.

How Big Is the State and Local Pension Problem?

State and local governments provide their own pensions in addition to Social Security. They do so, by and large, using defined benefit plans. The budget standoff in Illinois in 2015 and 2016 was a direct result of the unfunded pension liability problem there. The Republican governor and the Democratic state legislature could not

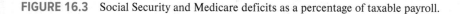

FIGURE 16.3 Social Security and Medicare deficits as a percentage of taxable payroll.

Source: Social Security Administration. "2018 OASDI Trustees Report." https://www.ssa.gov/OACT/TR/2018/

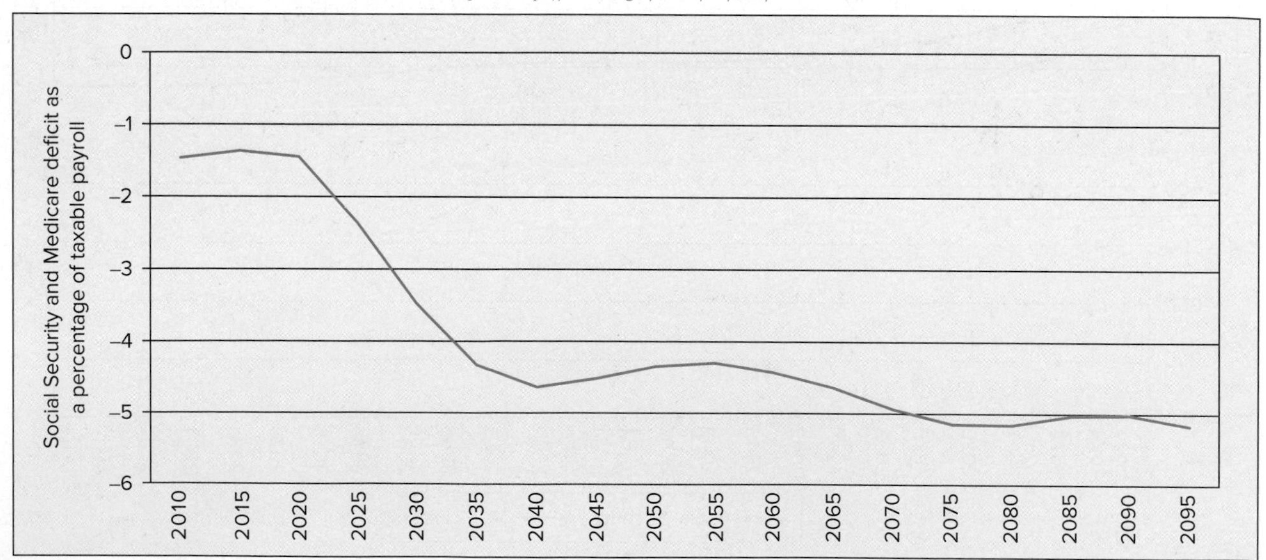

Table 16.1 State pension liabilities, 2010.

Source: Novy-Marx, Robert, and Joshua Rauh. "Public Pension Promises: How Big Are They and What Are They Worth?" *The Journal of Finance* 66, no. 4 (2011): 1–53.

State Name	Liabilities, Stated	Liabilities, Treasury Rate	Pension Assets	State Name	Liabilities, Stated	Liabilities, Treasury Rate	Pension Assets
Alabama	42.0	61.8	21.4	Montana	9.1	12.4	5.3
Alaska	15.3	21.7	12.4	Nebraska	8.4	11.6	5.5
Arizona	43.6	73.5	24.8	Nevada	25.4	36.3	18.8
Arkansas	21.5	30.4	14.6	New Hampshire	8.5	12.5	4.3
California	518.1	699.7	329.6	New Jersey	132.8	191.2	67.2
Colorado	57.3	86.2	28.8	New Mexico	28.8	39.8	15.9
Connecticut	45.3	69.1	20.1	New York	239.8	325.7	192.8
Delaware	7.6	10.9	5.8	North Carolina	74.9	101.8	64.0
Florida	136.4	186.3	96.5	North Dakota	4.4	6.3	2.7
Georgia	75.8	110.1	53.1	Ohio	197.5	281.4	114.7
Hawaii	17.5	24.2	8.1	Oklahoma	33.6	45.9	15.8
Idaho	11.7	16.6	8.7	Oregon	57.5	80.7	42.9
Illinois	151.0	233.0	65.7	Pennsylvania	110.6	164.5	64.3
Indiana	37.3	49.8	19.6	Rhode Island	13.9	20.5	6.6
Iowa	26.0	35.0	18.0	South Carolina	42.4	63.5	20.3
Kansas	21.3	30.3	10.2	South Dakota	7.4	10.3	5.6
Kentucky	45.2	63.4	21.1	Tennessee	36.7	49.6	26.4
Louisiana	36.8	54.8	18.4	Texas	191.2	268.4	126.1
Maine	14.4	20.1	8.3	Utah	22.6	31.2	14.7
Maryland	52.7	72.1	28.6	Vermont	4.0	5.7	2.4
Massachusetts	59.7	86.9	32.7	Virginia	69.1	89.6	41.3
Michigan	73.2	103.1	39.5	Washington	62.3	86.4	43.5
Minnesota	60.6	91.0	35.9	West Virginia	13.7	18.3	7.2
Mississippi	31.4	44.2	15.5	Wisconsin	79.7	114.6	58.4
Missouri	53.5	75.2	33.1	Wyoming	7.0	9.8	4.4

agree on a budget because of, among other things, the pension issue. That standoff was made substantially worse when the Illinois Supreme Court ruled that Illinois public pensions were "inviolate"—meaning they could not be lower than promised—and that this extended to everyone currently or previously working for state or local government in Illinois. The consequences of that standoff included little things, like closing interstate rest areas for unpaid sewer bills; and really big things, like failing to honor state scholarships at public universities across the state and furloughs to several employees of those institutions.

How big is the problem of state pensions? You can see the degree to which these unfunded liabilities will affect each state by looking at 2010 pension liability data in Table 16.1. Produced by economists Robert Novy-Marx and Joshua Rauh, their methodology began by examining the liabilities that these states acknowledge and the assets they claimed, but then made adjustments to the discount rate that these states use to establish those liabilities. Finding those discount rates unreasonably high, they instead chose to use what they determined to be a more reasonable rate—the rate that you would get on U.S. Treasury bonds.[3] What they found was that in 2010 states had roughly $3 trillion in unfunded liabilities in their state-funded pension plans. When they updated the aggregate number using 2013 data, they found that the problem was growing and that the gap was as much as $3.3 trillion.

These same scholars duplicated this analysis for county and municipal pensions. Using a comprehensive

[3] The technical reasons for this consideration are beyond the scope of this text; however, from Chapter 7 you understand that higher rates of discount mean that liabilities far off into the future will have a smaller present value. The authors argue that the discount rates on the liabilities are overstated for political purposes to mask the actual size of the problem.

Table 16.2 County and municipal pension liabilities, 2010.

Source: Novy-Marx, Robert (University of Rochester and NBER) and Joshua Rauth (Kellogg School of Management and NBER). www.kellogg.northwestern.edu/faculty/rauh/research/nmrlocal20101011.pdf.

Name (Number of Plans)	Liabilities, Stated Basis, June 2009 ($B)	Liabilities, Treasury Rate	Net Pension Assets ($B)	Unfunded Liability ($B)	Unfunded Liability/ Revenue	Unfunded Liability per Household ($)
Chicago	46.3	66.6	21.8	44.8	763%	41,966
New York City	155.8	214.8	92.6	122.2	276	38,886
San Francisco	16.3	22.6	11.9	8.7	306	34,940
Boston	7.4	11.0	3.6	7.5	430	30,901
Detroit	8.1	11.0	4.6	6.4	402	18,643
Los Angeles	34.6	49.3	23.2	26.1	378	18,193
Philadelphia	9.0	13.0	3.4	9.7	290	16,690
Cincinnati	2.2	3.2	1.2	2.0	321	15,681
Baltimore	4.4	6.4	2.7	3.7	260	15,420
Milwaukee	4.4	6.7	3.3	3.4	687	14,853
Fairfax County	8.3	11.1	5.5	5.6	169	14,415
Hartford	1.2	1.6	0.9	0.7	249	14,333
St. Paul	1.5	2.2	0.8	1.4	464	13,686
Jacksonville	4.1	6.0	2.0	4.0	278	12,994
Dallas	7.4	10.8	4.6	6.3	298	12,856
Contra Costa County	6.3	8.7	3.7	5.0	425	12,771
Santa Barbara County	2.3	3.3	1.4	1.8	329	11,995
Kern County	4.2	5.6	2.0	3.6	612	11,919
San Jose	5.4	7.5	3.4	4.1	321	11,391
Houston	11.1	16.4	7.2	9.1	356	10,804
Nashville Davidson	2.9	4.1	1.8	2.3	151	10,048
Arlington County	1.5	2.0	1.2	0.8	103	10,000

(but not universal) list of cities and counties and their pension plans, they performed similar calculations for those local governments. What they found, as shown in Table 16.2, was that for those counties and cities they could include in their database, there was $383 billion in unfunded liabilities on pensions, and if that was extrapolated to the remaining population of local governments, they have a total of $574 billion in unfunded pension liabilities. Some of those cities had laughably large unfunded liabilities. For instance, the city of Chicago had so many outstanding liabilities that if every household in the city contributed $40,000 to the city, it would still be insufficient to entirely eliminate the gap. Even worse, because the state of Illinois had not contributed anywhere near enough money to its pension funds for state employees (such as teachers, college professors, state highway patrol, prison guards), it would take almost an additional $30,000 to cover those liabilities. Even the substantial increase in the stock market that occurred since the publication of these estimates has not been sufficient to close the gap between liabilities and assets. That is because, according to the Boston Center for Retirement Research, liabilities actually grew as fast as the value of assets.

To put a bow on this, imagine a household in Chicago wanted to pay off its share of all unfunded Social Security, Medicare, and pension liabilities (completely ignoring the other portions of the national debt); they would have to come up with more than $215,000, of which one-third would be their state and local liabilities. If this fiscal "sky is falling" prediction is accurate, the fiscal sky will fall in the next 20 years. That is the period in which the Medicare problem will hit its present-value peak, the state and local pension problem will peak, and the Social Security problem will still be increasing.

Is It Possible That the Fiscal Sky Isn't about to Fall?

It is at least plausible that the preceding analysis overstates the actual problem that Americans will face. Optimists point to a number of factors that could make these problems substantially smaller in scope. First, the analysis is predicated on the ability of the authors of the Social Security and Medicare trustees' reports to predict wages, life expectancy, GDP, interest rates, and other economic variables 20, 30, 50, 75 years in advance. Additionally, there are any number of changes that could make the next 20 years only slightly uncomfortable with regard to these underfunded programs. Incomes could grow at a more rapid, but still historically reasonable, rate, or the programs' benefits could be curtailed.

Aside from the possibility that the forecasts are simply wrong, consider the most likely and most important source for potential optimism. Taxable incomes could grow at the relatively rapid rate they did in the 1980s and 1990s and do so for a sustained period. Similarly, productivity and/or technological increases could be sufficient to raise RGDP growth expectations from the 2 percent to 3 percent they have been to 3.5 percent to 4.5 percent. A one percentage point increase in growth would make the U.S. RGDP 28 percent higher in 25 years than it is now projected to be at that time, which would be more than enough to make the funding of those particular programs substantially less onerous.

Second, programmatic changes could be made, especially to Social Security, that could eliminate the largest part of the long-term problem. For instance, some combination of tax increases (either eliminating the maximum taxable earnings for Social Security, increasing tax rates 1 percent across the board on both employers and employees, or extending Social Security taxes to unearned income) or benefits changes (eliminating the option for taking benefits at 62, raising the retirement age to 70, using price inflation rather than wage inflation to adjust benefits for the cost of living) could be enacted. If these were enacted immediately, most of the problem in Social Security could be eliminated.

Whether state and local governments can break the promises they have already made to their teachers, firefighters, police, and other workers is another story. There would certainly be political and even legal challenges to such changes. As governors around the country were seeing between 2011 and 2016, it is politically difficult to require public workers to contribute (more) to their pensions; so, though there could be a political solution that would require higher contribution levels by the workers themselves, if that does not occur soon, it will not be enough to solve the state and local pension problem. That would leave state and local governments with no option but to cut benefits to current retirees (which would ignite an even more furious political and legal challenge) or to seek a bailout from higher levels of government.

The biggest challenge to optimists is Medicare. Its problems were almost completely ignored within the Affordable Care Act. That plan's focus was on expanding eligibility and not on realistic cost control. Second, Medicare's fiscal challenges will be upon us in the 2020s, while the others will strike in the 2030s.

Summary

Whether or not you believe the "sky is falling" on fiscal issues relating to Social Security, Medicare, and the pensions systems for state and local government workers, you now understand the source of the problem. Combined, various levels of government have underfunded programs for retirees by trillions of dollars. You know that the Medicare challenge will occur first, followed shortly thereafter by the state and local pension challenge. The Social Security shortfall will not become acute until the 2030s but remains the largest fiscal challenge. You understand that because these liabilities will occur so far in the future that the rate at which you discount them and the rate at which the economy will grow can significantly alter the estimated scope of the problem.

Key Terms

defined benefit program
defined contribution program
ERISA
entitlement

Quiz Yourself

1. In terms of magnitude, which of the following has the greatest fiscal shortfall?
   a. State pension funds
   b. Local pension funds
   c. Medicare
   d. Social Security
2. In terms of when fiscal shortfalls are likely to require significant changes to budgets or program rules, which of the following is likely to occur first?
   a. State pension funds
   b. Local pension funds
   c. Medicare
   d. Social Security
3. Using a higher rate of discount (or interest rate)
   a. makes no difference when calculating the present value of future liabilities.
   b. raises the present value of future liabilities.
   c. lowers the present value of future liabilities.
4. The dependency ratio in the United States is
   a. growing.
   b. steady.
   c. falling rapidly.
   d. falling slowly.
5. State and local pensions for government employees are usually structured as
   a. defined benefit plans.
   b. defined contribution plans.
   c. entitlements.
   d. determined year to year.
6. Deficits cannot occur in
   a. defined benefit plans.
   b. defined contribution plans.
   c. entitlement budgets.
   d. state and local budgets.

Short Answer Questions

1. Why does the discount rate matter when evaluating the future liabilities of defined benefit pension plans?
2. Why does it matter whether you have a defined contribution plan or a defined benefit plan in terms of whether there is a degree of underfunding that your boss might not be telling you about?
3. Why would a schoolteacher be a better candidate for a defined benefit pension than a computer programmer?
4. Why would the Pension Guaranty Trust or something like it be necessary in defined benefit plans?
5. Is Social Security closer to a defined benefit plan or a defined contribution plan?

Think about This

When you go into the voting booth, which type of politician appeals to you: the optimistic sort that seeks to assure you that brighter days are ahead or the pessimistic sort that seeks to warn you of impending disaster? Are voters the source of the problem?

Talk about This

Suppose nothing is done about state and local pension issues and state and local governments face a choice of either paying their retired teachers what they were promised in terms of pensions or paying current teachers enough to ensure an adequate education for children. (Suppose for the purpose of this discussion, you are convinced at the state level if you impose a tax increase, too many citizens will leave to go to another state, rendering the tax rate increase ineffective.)

Behind the Numbers

Social Security Administration, Trustees' Report: www.ssa.gov/OACT/TR/2018/tr2018.pdf

- Social Security Trust Fund balances
- Medicare Trust Fund balances

Pew Charitable Trusts: www.pewtrusts.org/en/projects/public-sector-retirement-systems

Novy-Marx, Robert, and Joshua Rauh, "Public Pension Promises: How Big Are They and What Are They Worth?" *Journal of Finance,* 62, pp. 2123–2167.

Novy-Marx, Robert (University of Rochester and NBER), and Joshua Rauth (Kellogg School of Management and NBER)–www.kellogg.northwestern.edu/faculty/rauh/research/nmrlocal20101011.pdf

CHAPTER SEVENTEEN

International Trade: Does It Jeopardize American Jobs?

Learning Objectives

After reading this chapter you should be able to:

LO1 Name the principal trading partners of the United States and the goods that are most often traded.

LO2 Illustrate how international trade benefits both trade partners.

LO3 Define the principles of absolute and comparative advantage and apply these definitions to prove the benefits from trade.

LO4 Compare and evaluate the reasons for limiting trade and illustrate the mechanisms for doing so.

LO5 Conclude that limiting trade protects some industries and jobs, but at a very high cost.

LO6 Enumerate attempts to use trade as a diplomatic weapon and evaluate the success of those attempts.

Chapter Outline

One of the more important economic developments of the last 40 years is the increased globalization of our economy. Whereas the world used to be composed of more than 150 countries whose economies were mostly independent of one another, nearly all economies of the world now depend heavily on one another.

As you can see from Figure 17.1, exports make up 12.5 percent of the U.S. economy while imports make up more than 15.4 percent. The Great Recession significantly, but only temporarily, impacted this trend. The increasing importance of the international sector has led political leaders to worry about whether this trend is a good one. Are American jobs being unfairly taken by workers from other countries? If so, is this trend toward globalization avoidable?

We address these questions first by explaining why economists generally believe that international trade is good for both parties. Then we discuss the reasons for limiting international trade, distinguishing between reasons that economists embrace and those that they do not. Next we discuss the methods by which trade is limited. To conclude, we consider whether trade can be used as a tool in political or diplomatic disagreements.

What We Trade and with Whom

Trade in the United States is not only growing; it is also encompassing a diverse set of goods and services, as seen in Table 17.1. We trade in obvious goods and some not so obvious goods. We import TVs, computers, and other electronics, as well as steel and oil. We export financial services and airplanes. We simultaneously export and import large quantities of automobiles, chemicals, and services. While that may sound somewhat odd, it is not as

FIGURE 17.1 Increasing importance of international trade.

Source: United States Census Bureau. www.census.gov/foreign-trade/statistics/index.html.

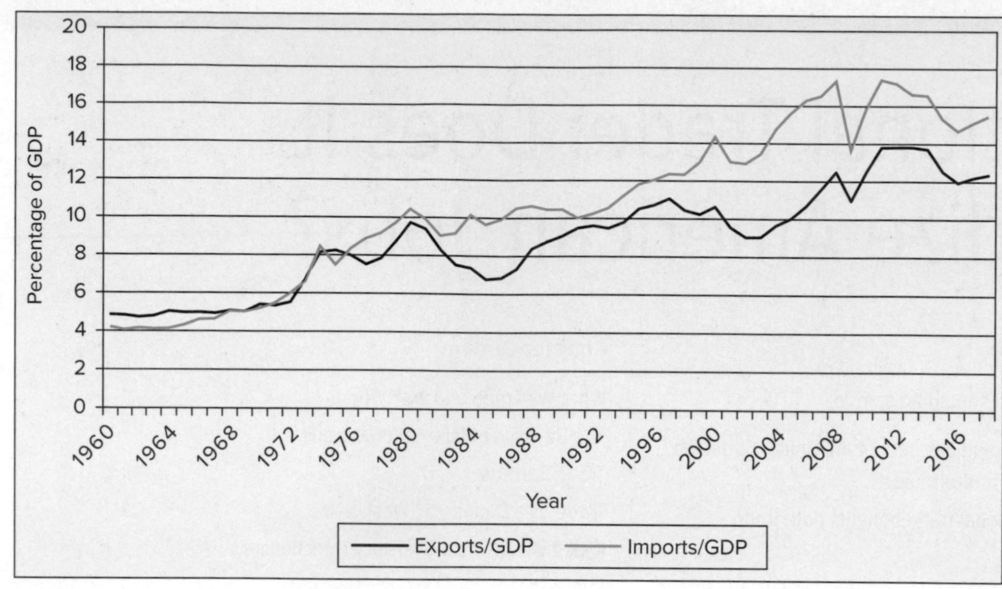

Table 17.1 U.S. exports and imports of goods and services.

Sources: International Trade Administration. www.trade.gov; TradeStats Express ™. http://tse.export.gov.

Exports		Imports	
Transportation equipment	285.9	Computer and electronic products	414.0
Computer and electronic products	213.2	Transportation equipment	402.7
Chemicals	207.5	Chemicals	253.6
Machinery, except electrical	142.6	Machinery, except electrical	188.6
Petroleum and coal products	102.6	Oil and gas	166.7
Miscellaneous manufactured commodities	83.8	Miscellaneous manufactured commodities	129.0
Oil and gas	75.5	Electrical equipment; appliances and components	125.9
Agricultural products	67.2	Primary metal manufacturing	96.2
Food manufactures	66.4	Apparel manufacturing products	87.8
Electrical equipment; appliances and components	62.5	Goods returned to Canada (Exp); US goods returned and reimports (Imp)	80.5
Primary metal manufacturing	59.3	Fabricated metal products; Nesoi	78.1
Services	828.4	Services	559.2
Total	2500.8	Total	3122.9

strange as it may sound. There are a wide variety of cars, and we are importing some and exporting others. Similarly, though we export and import computers, this also shows the degree to which many products are made all over the globe.

If you open up any computer, you will find components that were made in a variety of places. The memory comes from one country, the hard drive from another, and the CPU from still another. Your computer may have been assembled in the United States, but it was made from components that could have been produced in 10 other countries. You can see that it is difficult to decide where it was really made. In part, this is one reason why the trade deficit we have with China is so high. China is the final assembly point for significant consumer electronics, and it is the final assembly point that gets credit (in our trade data) for their export to us.

There is one good on the list of exports that also may intrigue you—"Oil and gas." It includes refined products, so any oil imported to the United States as crude oil into the refineries around Houston, Texas, and is then sold in Mexico, would appear as an export of a petroleum product of the United States. Recent legislation has also allowed for the exportation of crude oil.

The final item in Table 17.1 that also might seem out of place is the trade in services. It is hard to imagine that we would import babysitting and lawn-mowing services, but it is much more plausible in areas of financial services and, specifically, in insurance. An American insurance company can easily sell life insurance to Canadians, and vice versa. Services make up a large and rapidly growing area of trade, and it is one area where the United States has a substantial trade surplus.

A concern to many Americans, evident in their election of President Trump, is the growth in trade deficits. Table 17.2 shows those deficits of several countries/regions, while Figure 17.2 shows those deficits over time.

Table 17.2 U.S. exports, imports, and trade balances of goods with selected countries and regions of the world, 2018.

Source: United States Census Bureau. https://www.census.gov/foreign-trade/statistics/country/index.html

Country	Exports ($ billions)	Imports ($ billions)	Balance ($ billions)
Canada	298.7	318.5	−19.8
Mexico	265.0	346.5	−81.5
Japan	75.0	142.6	−67.6
China	120.3	539.5	−419.2
OPEC	58.9	80.0	−21.1
Europe	370.3	572.7	202.4
Africa	26.0	35.8	−9.9
World	2500.8	3122.9	−622.1

The Benefits of International Trade

Comparative and Absolute Advantage

To illustrate the benefits of trade, it is useful to distinguish between two kinds of "advantages" that people can have. Consider a brain surgeon and her secretary. Suppose that the surgeon worked her way through school by typing

FIGURE 17.2 Trade balances with selected partners.

Source: United States Census Bureau. https://www.census.gov/foreign-trade/balance/index.html

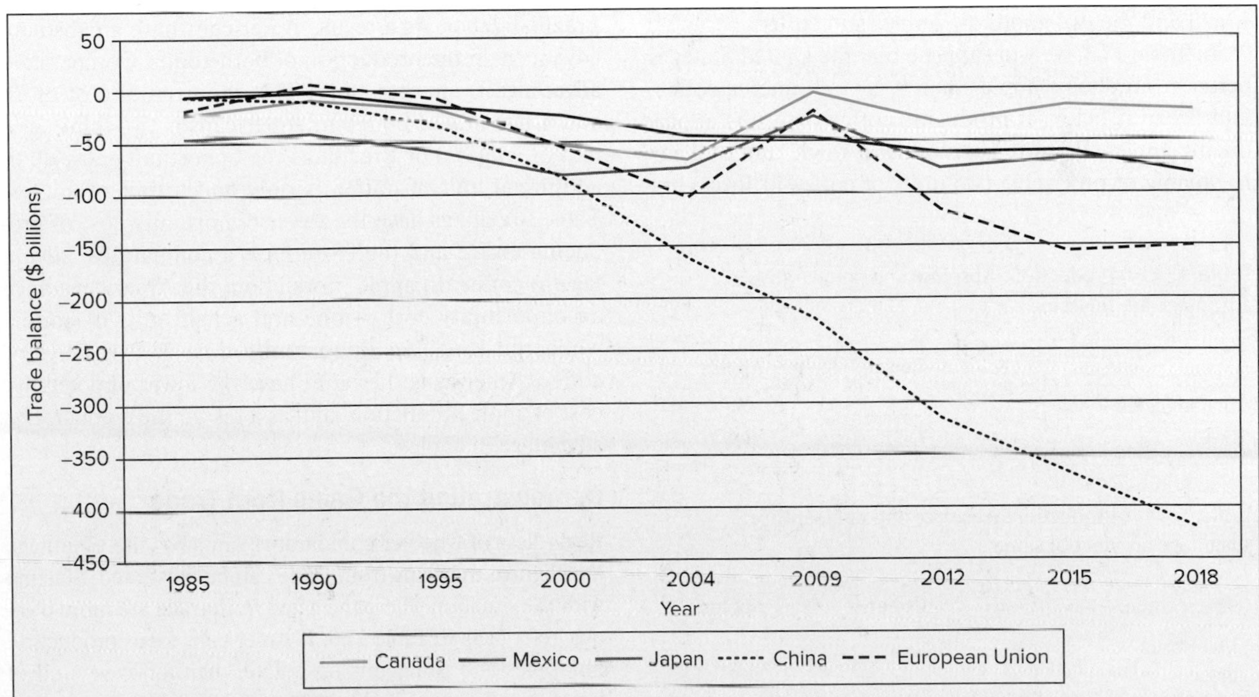

papers and that she types faster than her current secretary. If she is better at both typing and surgery, would it be better for her to do both and fire her secretary? The answer is no; she will be better off having her slow-typing secretary do the typing. Making the decision relies on the notion of opportunity cost that we discussed in Chapter 1.

To review, opportunity cost is what you give up by making the choices that you do. In the case of the secretary and the surgeon, if the surgeon does her own typing, she must give up at least some of her lucrative surgeries. On the other hand, if she delegates the typing, she will pay the secretary only a small fraction of the money she would earn performing extra surgeries. In this case, she has an **absolute advantage** in both surgery and typing, because she is better at both things than the competition. Her secretary has a **comparative advantage** at typing because the secretary has a lower opportunity cost of doing the typing than does the surgeon.

absolute advantage The ability to produce a good better, faster, or more quickly than a competitor.

comparative advantage The ability to produce a good at a lower opportunity cost of the resources used.

As a simple example of how this applies to international trade, consider Tables 17.3 and 17.4. We can illustrate comparative and absolute advantage and the benefits from trade for each of two countries by relating their individual production of two goods. We will suppose that the two countries are the United States and Brazil and the two goods are apples and coffee.

In Table 17.3, we will suppose that the United States is better at producing apples than it is at producing coffee, and Brazil is better at producing coffee than it is at producing apples. We will assume that a single unit of labor is capable of producing two units of coffee in Brazil but only one unit of apples. In the United States that situation is reversed. One unit of labor produces two units of apples but only one unit of coffee. Because one unit of labor in the United States can produce more apples than one unit of labor in Brazil, the United States has the absolute advantage in apples. Similarly, it is clear that Brazil has an absolute advantage in coffee.

To analyze comparative advantage, we need to measure what is sacrificed when the two countries allocate one unit of labor. For instance, when Americans produce an additional unit of coffee, they are giving up two apples. When Brazilians produce an additional unit of coffee, they are giving up only one-half of a unit of apples. Brazilians therefore have the lower opportunity cost of producing coffee. Similarly, when Americans produce an additional unit of apples they give up one-half a unit of coffee, and when Brazilians do so they give up two units of coffee. As a result, Americans have a lower opportunity cost for apples. This means that in addition to having an absolute advantage in coffee, Brazilians also have a comparative advantage in coffee. Similarly, Americans have a comparative advantage as well as an absolute advantage in apples.

These advantages do not need to be aligned. Consider Table 17.4, which shows where the Americans are assumed to have an absolute advantage in the production of both goods. A single unit of American labor can produce more apples and more coffee than a single unit of Brazilian labor. As a result, Americans have an absolute advantage in the production of both goods. Comparative advantage is another story. The opportunity cost of an additional unit of coffee to Americans is two-thirds of a unit of apples. For Brazilians the opportunity cost of an additional unit of coffee is only half a unit of apples. Thus, Brazilians have the lower opportunity cost of producing coffee and therefore have a comparative advantage in coffee. In apple production, the Americans have an opportunity cost of one and a half units of coffee, while the Brazilian opportunity cost is two units of coffee. Americans therefore have the lower opportunity cost of apple production and, as a result, the comparative advantage in apples.

Table 17.3 Production: Absolute and comparative advantage are the same.

	Coffee	Apples
United States	1	2
Brazil	2	1

Table 17.4 Production: Absolute and comparative advantage are not the same.

	Coffee	Apples
United States	3	2
Brazil	2	1

Demonstrating the Gains from Trade

Regardless of whether comparative and absolute advantage are aligned, the gains from trade can be illustrated. Starting with the situation where the gains from trade are more obvious, refer back to Table 17.3. If Americans focus production on apples and Brazilians on coffee, then for every unit of labor that Americans move to apples and Brazilians move to coffee, there is a worldwide increase in total production of one unit of apples and one unit of coffee.

To see that each is better off with trade than without it, suppose there is a total of 30 units of labor in each country and each prefers apples and coffee in equal amounts. Before trade, there will be 10 Americans producing 20 units of apples and 20 Americans producing 20 units of coffee. Similarly, there will be 10 Brazilians producing 20 units of coffee and 20 Brazilians producing 20 units of apples.

To see that trade makes both better off, we need to know the **terms of trade**, the amount of one good required to get the other. If we suppose that it comes to one unit of apples for one unit of coffee, then we have our answer. The Brazilians will produce only coffee and make a total of 60 units, and the Americans will produce only apples and produce 60 units. The Brazilians will ship 30 units of coffee to the United States in exchange for 30 units of apples, and in the end, each will be able to consume 30 units of each and be better off with trade than without it because each country has 10 more units of each good.

terms of trade
The amount of a good one country must give up to obtain another good from the other country, usually expressed as a ratio.

Trade is also beneficial when one country has the absolute advantage in both goods. Turning back to Table 17.4 we can show that there are gains from trade here as well. Prior to trade, the Brazilian situation is unchanged from the preceding example, but the American situation is such that 12 Americans are producing 36 units of coffee and 18 Americans are producing 36 units of apples. Again, if both focus more on the good for which they have a comparative advantage, coffee for Brazilians and apples for Americans, and the terms of trade adjust appropriately, then the Americans will again ship apples to Brazil for coffee, and both will be better off. Economists conclude that, at least theoretically, trade can improve the lives of the people it involves.

Production Possibilities Frontier Analysis

We can show the gains using our Chapter 1 production possibilities frontier as well. Recall that a production possibilities frontier shows the output combinations that a country can accomplish on its own. If we assume either of the scenarios presented above, then the production possibilities frontiers for the two countries, shown in Figure 17.3, would have different slopes. The Brazilian production possibilities frontier would be flatter and the United States' steeper.

FIGURE 17.3 Increased consumption possibilities with trade.

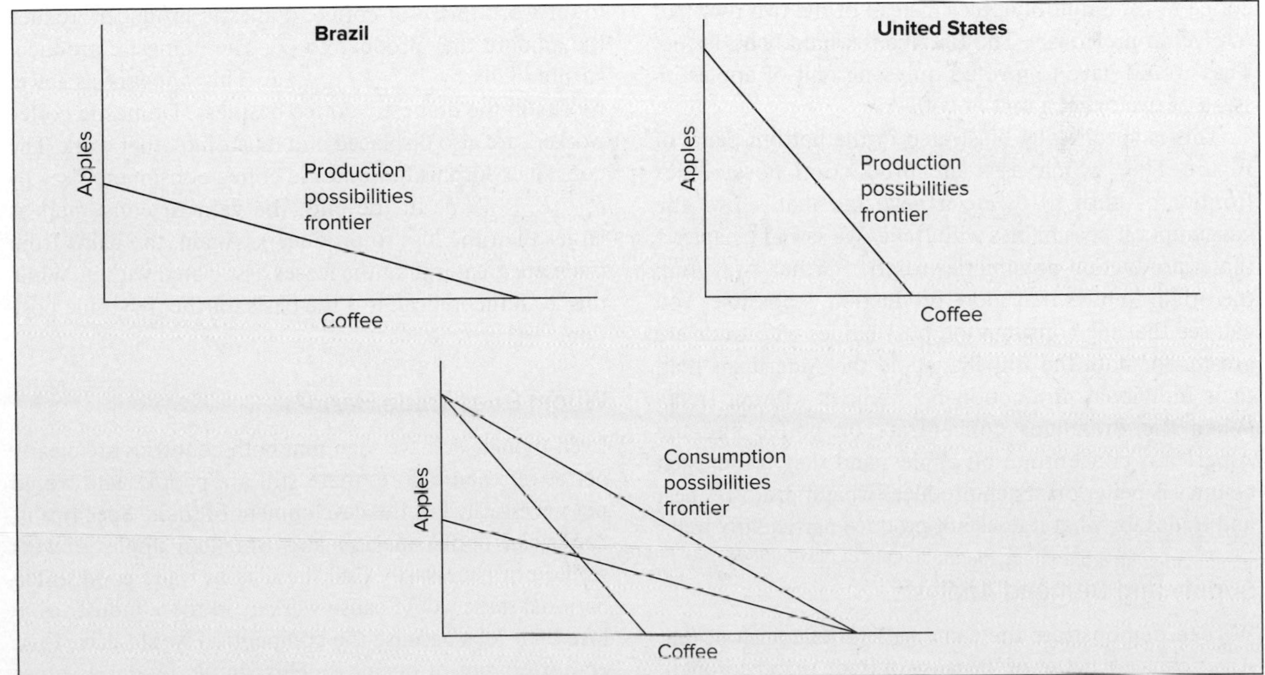

FIGURE 17.4 Gains from trade.

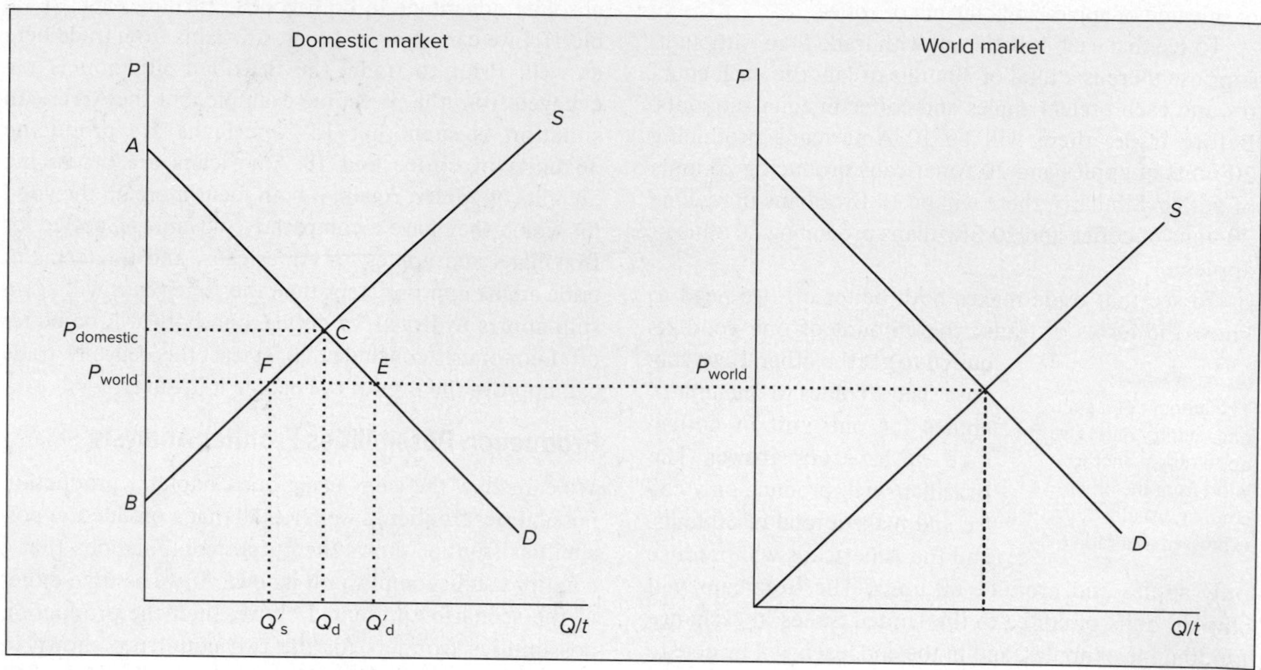

If we again assume the one-for-one terms of trade and perfect specialization in the goods for which each country has a comparative advantage, it would improve the situation for both the Americans and the Brazilians. The Americans would now have to give up only one unit of coffee to get a unit of apples instead of the two they had to give up previously. The Brazilians would benefit, too. They would have to give up only one unit of apples instead of two to get a unit of coffee.

This is specifically illustrated in the bottom panel of Figure 17.3, which uses the production possibilities frontier of both to create a new line that shows the consumption possibilities with trade. We saw in Chapter 1 that a production possibilities frontier farther away from the origin implies that more production is possible. You can see that the consumption possibilities with trade are greater for both the Brazilians and the Americans than their individual production possibilities without trade. When the Brazilians concentrate on coffee and the Americans concentrate on apples, and they trade, each country is better off. Each produces what it produces best and trades for what it does not produce particularly well.

Supply and Demand Analysis

We can demonstrate the same general conclusion, that Americans are better off because of trade than without it, using supply and demand. Using Figure 17.4, suppose there is a market for domestically produced coffee (from Hawaii perhaps). In a world without trade, the market price of coffee is $P_{domestic}$ and the amount that the domestic industry produces is Q'_d. If there is trade and there is a lower world price of coffee, domestic producers reduce the amount they produce to Q'_s. The domestic producer surplus falls by $P_{world}P_{domestic}CF$. This appears as lower profits in the domestic coffee business. Domestic coffee workers are also displaced and must find other work. The consumer surplus to domestic coffee consumers rises by $P_{world}P_{domestic}CE$. In the end, the gain to consumers is larger than the loss to producers. Again, the gains from trade are greater than the losses associated with it. While this is all theoretical, it is the basis for the free-trade position.

Whom Does Trade Harm?

Even though we have seen that both countries are clearly better off than before, there still are people who would not necessarily like the development of trade. Specifically, American coffee makers and Brazilian apple growers would not necessarily find the idea of trade good. International trade would cause workers in these industries to lose their jobs because the competition would drive their employers out of business. This simple model assumes that the unemployed could find new work in the expanding industries in their respective countries or in other industries generally. This assumption, however, while not bad in the long run, ignores the pain of people losing their jobs and needing to attain new skills. In addition, these displaced workers are likely to get jobs at wages below those they were previously earning.

A relatively recent phenomenon is the development of **outsourcing.** The term is generally understood by economists to narrowly apply to a firm's use of contractors to perform services that were previously performed within the firm. So, if a computer peripheral company that used to have a technical support line in the United States now contracts to have this service provided by a foreign company, this would be considered outsourcing. The press often refers to anything that used to be done domestically that is now done off-shore as outsourcing. Economists refer to this as **off-shoring.** An example here would be a manufacturer, like Ford, that used to assemble all of its F-150 pickup truck line in the United States, moving a portion of that operation to Mexico. In either case, the same issue arises. Domestic workers are required to find new jobs.

outsourcing
A firm's use of contractors to perform services that were previously performed within the firm.

off-shoring
A form of outsourcing where the services are performed in another country.

It is important to note, though, that in a typical non-recession year 30 million of approximately 140 million jobs are eliminated and about 31 million new jobs are created. While some of the 30 million jobs that are eliminated are eliminated because companies engage in outsourcing or off-shoring, more jobs are created than are lost.

Trade Barriers

Reasons for Limiting Trade

Because it is possible that with free trade some businesses shut down and some workers lose their jobs, it is useful to summarize some of the questionable and some of the good reasons to limit trade. The questionable reasons begin with protecting jobs within the industries that are being affected by better or cheaper imports. The good reasons are as numerous as they are narrow. We may choose not to trade with other countries in certain goods because those goods may be important to our national security or national identity. Producing such goods at home is therefore important in and of itself. We may choose not to trade with countries that gain their comparative advantage through lax worker safety rules, lax environmental laws, or because they allow businesses to employ child labor.

Though there are clearly short-run costs to free trade, when people lose their jobs to foreign competition and need retraining to get new ones, the long-term benefits usually outweigh these. When labor unions argue against free trade, it is often because the industry that they represent has lost its comparative advantage to other countries. Though this comparative advantage is sometimes lost because of labor or environmental protections, it is usually because the other country has developed a better or more cost-effective method of producing the good. Protecting an industry in such circumstances is not beneficial for two reasons:

1. For capitalism to work, not only must success be rewarded, but failure must be punished. If companies see that the government will prevent international competition, they will become lax, and they will not produce the best goods for the lowest prices.
2. If other countries see that we protect our firms from competition, they will certainly feel free to do the same. Instead of everyone benefiting from trade, we will return to the days before trade and lose consumption possibilities. We will lose our ability to export our goods to countries where our products are better and cheaper than domestic goods.

The preceding points notwithstanding, there are still good and legitimate reasons for limiting trade even when other countries produce better or cheaper goods. If, for instance, a country other than the United States produced the best and cheapest combat aircraft and it also happened to be a potential wartime enemy of the United States, the United States would be seriously misguided to shut down its own combat aircraft industry and buy planes from the other country. For national security reasons, guaranteed access to war material is important for countries.

Countries also limit trade for reasons that are similar to national defense. If a nation's identity is tied to a particular commodity the way the Japanese identity is tied to rice, for example, it makes sense for the government to limit imports of the commodity so that its domestic producers can survive. Though there is enough productive capacity in the south-central United States to supply the entire rice consumption needs of Japan, and though the Japanese continue to pay more than five times the world market price for rice to maintain a domestic industry, this economically inefficient trade restriction can be justified on two grounds. First, Japan without a rice industry is not Japan; and second, in case of a naval war in the Pacific, it is hard to imagine the United States or any other country devoting significant naval resources to protect rice shipments to Japan.

A final reason for limiting trade is that other countries may get their comparative advantage by using production processes that indirectly harm other countries or that other countries find offensive. If a country lowers its production costs, for example, by polluting in a way that would not be allowed in the United States, the United States might reasonably decide not to let that country sell its products here. This is especially true if the pollution ultimately causes health problems. The United States might not want to allow the importation of chemicals and other environmentally onerous products from Mexico if, as a byproduct of their manufacture, they pollute the Rio Grande.

In addition to environmental objections, countries may find certain labor practices so immoral that they do not allow importation of goods from countries that engage in them. For instance, it is against U.S. law to import any good made with slave labor or prison labor. In addition, the United States will not knowingly allow the importation of goods made with forced or indentured child labor, and the U.S. government requires that its contractors certify that no child labor was used in the production of its goods.[1] Several countries allow children as young as eight to work in factories several hours a day. For example, if you own a soccer ball, it was probably made outside the United States, and the production likely involved at least one child who would not be allowed to work in the United States. The garment industry joins sporting goods in utilizing child labor and engaging in other labor practices that are not legal in the United States. Child labor has existed in nearly every country at some point, and its use is attributable almost entirely to high rates of poverty. In addition, some economists argue that outlawing child labor is not necessarily good for the children involved if their only alternative is severe poverty. Despite this, many see the issue less in economic terms and more in moral ones.

Other reasons for limiting trade appeal to only a limited number of economists. The first of these, the infant-industry argument, says that trade protection is required to give an industry in a country time to get on its feet. In theory, there may be an argument for temporary shelter from competition, but in practice, it often happens that trade is permanently limited.

The second of these limited-appeal arguments is the antidumping argument. **Dumping** occurs when international competitors charge less than their cost in order to drive out competition. The argument is that competitors do this to gain a monopoly in the long run. The problem with this argument is ascertaining the true marginal cost of the international competitor. Inefficient domestic producers' assertions of dumping often hinge on the notion that since they cannot produce at such low costs, it must be impossible. The crux of the dumping argument is the attempt at generating a monopoly, and there are few, if any, industries in which such a strategy has prevailed.

dumping
The exporting of goods below cost to drive competitors out of business.

Methods of Limiting Trade

Once a nation has decided to limit trade, it must choose a method. There are three main methods for limiting trade: A country can put a tax on imported goods, limit the quantity of a good that can be imported, or put regulations on goods that are imported to make it more difficult for the goods to be imported.

The most widely used method for limiting trade is the use of a tax on imports, called a **tariff.** Figure 17.5 shows that if a country wants to limit the amount of a good imported to Q_{limit}, a tax can be put on the good that is sufficient to move the supply curve to where it intersects the demand curve at that output. With such a tariff the price increases to P_{limit}, where domestic producers have a better chance of competing. In addition, the

tariff
A tax on imports.

FIGURE 17.5 The effect of tariffs and quotas.

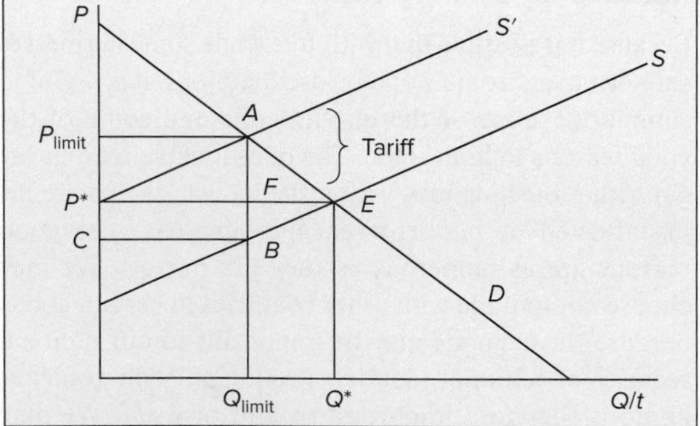

[1]See Executive Order 13126, Executive Order on Child Labor, https://www.federalregister.gov/documents/1999/06/16/99-15491/prohibition-of-acquisition-of-products-produced-by-forced-or-indentured-child-labor

government gets $CP_{limit}AB$ in tax revenue that it can use to retrain workers or to provide other sorts of compensation.

The second method of limiting trade, a **quota,** places a legal restriction on the quantity of a good coming into the country. Also shown in Figure 17.5, this method is popular in that it has the effect of raising the price that domestic producers can charge to P_{limit}. Instead of shifting the supply curve to S' with the tariff, the new supply curve is just truncated at Q_{limit}. The main difference between a quota and a tariff is that with a quota the government of the importing country receives no tax revenue. Importers get to raise their prices and they get to keep the extra money as profit. Even though it appears this method would seem to be much worse than a tariff for the importing country, quotas sometimes provide political advantages. Often it is less of a diplomatic problem for a country to impose a quota on the imports of another country. Also, as has happened before in the automobile business, it is sometimes possible to get an exporting country to agree to limit its exports voluntarily. While this operates exactly like a quota, the exporting country retains the power to end the action rather than giving that power to the importing country. In the early 1980s, Japan willingly limited exports of cars to the United States when congressional action was threatened.

quota
A legal restriction on the amount of a good coming into the country.

The final method by which a country can limit the imports of another country utilizes a recognized right of a country to inspect goods imported. If a country does not want a particular good coming into the country, it can establish rules for its import that effectively make importation too costly. This method is effective, nearly impossible to evade, and becomes apparent only when the rules become silly. The method is seen mostly with the importation of agricultural products. Although it is perfectly legitimate for a country to want to inspect a shipment to look for certain diseases, bugs, or parasites, countries will sometimes use such inspection as an excuse to limit imports. Because the goods themselves are usually perishable, this can raise the cost to prohibitive levels and effectively prevent any attempts to break into a new market.

Many examples of these **nontariff barriers** exist. Some are perfectly logical; others are dubious. An outbreak of mad cow disease began to affect English herds in 1999, resulting in a ban on English beef sold in Europe. A concern over the potential of allergic reactions in genetically altered corn resulted in a similar European ban on Starlink corn. The European ban on milk from cows that had been given bovine growth hormone (BGH) and the Japanese ban on American apples in the 1980s appear to be examples of the use of nontariff barriers for strictly protectionist reasons.

nontariff barriers
Barriers to trade resulting from regulatory actions.

Trade as a Diplomatic Weapon

There are countless examples in the last 70 years of international trade being used to make a diplomatic point or to solve a diplomatic problem. Since the late 1950s, the United States has imposed trade sanctions against Cuba to destabilize Fidel Castro. In 1979, in response to Iran's refusal to free American diplomats being held hostage in its embassy, the United States made it illegal to trade with Iran. In 1980, in response to the Soviet invasion of Afghanistan, the United States imposed a grain embargo, making it illegal to sell wheat to Russia. In the middle 1980s, in response to a series of terrorist acts by the Libyan government and its surrogates, the United States declared it illegal to buy Libyan oil. In the early 1990s, after Iraq invaded Kuwait, the United Nations imposed economic sanctions against Iraq in hopes that Iraq would retreat. Iraq did not retreat, the Gulf War was fought, and afterward, further economic sanctions were used in attempts to pressure Iraq into giving up its weapons of mass destruction. This too failed.[2] In 2012 and 2013, both Iran and North Korea were sanctioned by the United States and other allies for refusal to give up nuclear weapons. Neither budged.

Manipulating trade simply has not been particularly effective as a method of influencing diplomacy. Castro has outlasted nine U.S. presidents; the Iranians did not buckle to such pressure; the Soviets, the Libyans, and the Iraqis followed their lead. The main reason that cutting off trade has not worked as a diplomatic tool is that it has been impossible to implement adequately. There have always been other avenues that the countries in question could use for trade. The Iranians had never sold much oil to the United States, and they found few problems selling their output to other countries. Argentinean and Australian farmers were only too happy to sell their grain to the Soviets, and the Libyans and the Iraqis had few problems breaking the sanctions imposed on them because many other countries felt free to break them. In theory, limiting trade appears to be a powerful diplomatic tool. In reality, it has not been very effective.

[2]Recently released interrogations of Saddam Hussein show that he failed to comply with these UN directives because Iraq had no such weapons after 1995, but that he wanted the Iranians to believe Iraq was stronger militarily than it was.

Kick It Up a Notch COSTS OF PROTECTIONISM

Reasons and mechanisms for limiting trade are available, but their use incurs substantial economic costs. We can examine those costs using Figure 17.5 and our consumer and producer surplus analysis from Chapter 3. Whatever the mechanism is for limiting trade, if the price of the imported good increases to P_{limit} and the quantity is reduced to Q_{limit}, then there are winners and losers from the protectionist measures. The losers are consumers because their consumer surplus falls by $P^*P_{limit}AE$. Domestic producers are winners because they get a higher price, and foreign producers are losers because their sales are limited. The net gain to producers from a quota, or alternatively the net gain to producers plus the tariff revenue to the government, is $CP_{limit}AB - BFE$. In any event, there is a net loss to society from the protectionist measures of *ABE*.

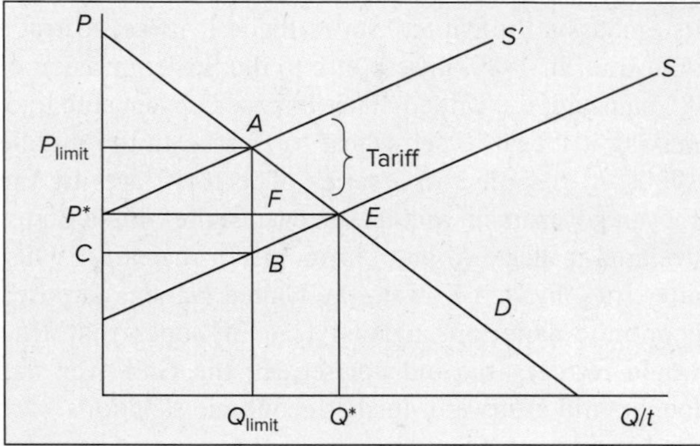

In practice this loss can be very substantial. Table 17.5 illustrates the net loss to the United States from trade protection in certain industries. It also demonstrates the net loss per job that the protectionist measures save. This table clearly shows the efficiency costs to American consumers from tariffs and quotas. We pay a few dollars more for many goods, but these figures add up to more than \$32 billion to save 191,664 jobs. At \$169,000 per job saved, trade protectionism is one of the worst jobs programs in place.

Table 17.5 Total cost of trade protectionism.

Source: Hufbauer, Gary Clyde, and Kimberly Ann Elliott. *Measuring the Costs of Protection in the United States*. Washington: Institute for International Economics, 1994.

Industry	Total Cost to Consumers ($ millions)	Jobs Saved	Cost per Job Saved ($)
Food and beverage	$ 2,947	6,035	$ 488,000
Textiles and light industry	26,443	179,102	148,000
Chemical products	484	514	942,000
Machinery	542	1,556	348,000
Miscellaneous	1,895	4,457	425,000
Total	32,311	191,664	169,000

Summary

You now understand that the United States trades many goods with many partners and that we have a massive trade deficit, but that both we and our trading partners benefit from international trade. You are now able to use the principles of absolute and comparative advantage as well as a production possibilities frontier to demonstrate why that is the case. You know the reasons for limiting trade and alternative mechanisms for doing so and that limiting trade comes at a very high cost. Last, you now see that the use of trade as a diplomatic weapon has been largely a failure.

Key Terms

absolute advantage
comparative advantage
dumping
nontariff barriers
outsourcing
off-shoring
quota
tariff
terms of trade

Quiz Yourself

1. If you add exports and imports, America's most significant trading partner is
   a. Saudi Arabia.
   b. Europe.
   c. China.
   d. Japan.
2. Suppose Germany can (with one unit of labor) produce six units of good A and four units of good B. Suppose (also with one unit of labor) Vietnam can produce only four units of good A and two units of good B. Which of the following statements is true?
   a. There is no point in the two countries engaging in trade because Germany has an absolute advantage in both goods.
   b. There is no point in the two countries engaging in trade because Vietnam has an absolute advantage in both goods.
   c. There is no point in the two countries engaging in trade because Germany has a comparative advantage in both goods.
   d. There is value to both countries from specializing and trading because Germany has a comparative advantage in good A and Vietnam has a comparative advantage in good B.
3. Theoretically speaking, all trade is based on
   a. comparative advantage.
   b. absolute advantage.
   c. numerical advantage.
   d. political advantage.
4. Since 1950, the trends in U.S. international trade are such that
   a. imports are increasing and exports are decreasing.
   b. imports are decreasing and exports are increasing.
   c. both imports and exports are decreasing.
   d. both imports and exports are increasing.
5. Using linear production possibilities frontiers in a simple two-good, two-country model, comparative advantage is evident when
   a. one country can make more of both goods than the other.
   b. the slopes of the two production possibilities frontiers are identical.
   c. the slopes of the two production possibilities frontiers are different.
   d. one country is incapable of producing one good.
6. Using linear production possibilities frontiers in a simple two-good, two-country model, absolute advantage is evident when
   a. one country can make more of a good than the other country can.
   b. the slopes of the two production possibilities frontiers are identical.
   c. the slopes of the two production possibilities frontiers are different.
   d. one country is incapable of producing one good.
7. Of the following justifications for limiting trade, which one would economists be least likely to endorse? Some goods should not be imported because
   a. they are important for national defense (e.g., tanks, fighter airplanes).
   b. they are important for national identity (e.g., television programs).
   c. their production employs many people (e.g., cars).
   d. other countries use child labor to gain a comparative advantage (e.g., clothing).
8. When choosing to limit trade, a country can impose a tax on imported goods. This is called
   a. an estate tax.
   b. a tariff.
   c. a quota.
   d. a capital gains tax.
9. Economists are concerned when nontariff (regulatory) barriers are used to prevent imports for a good that
   a. is produced via questionable means (e.g., banning milk produced from cows injected with bovine growth hormone).
   b. is produced via more efficient use of labor.
   c. may spread disease (e.g., banning beef from countries that have experienced mad cow disease).
   d. violates local standards for decency.

Short Answer Questions

1. Use the concept of comparative and absolute advantage to illustrate why a fast-typing business executive might dictate letters on a digital audio recorder for her secretary to type rather than type them herself.
2. List some reasons why the United States might import and export cars, airplanes, chemicals, and petroleum products.
3. Construct an argument against "energy independence" as a policy goal for the United States using the notion of comparative advantage.
4. Explain why a tariff on imported oil would be better than an import quota as a means by which to achieve energy independence.

Think about This

Today's transportation infrastructure makes international trade more efficient than intra-U.S. trade was 100 years ago. What this means is that it is easier today for a shirt made in China to get to California than it was for a shirt made in Georgia to make it to Missouri in 1900. The U.S. Constitution has always banned states from regulating trade between states. This amounted to a within United States free-trade agreement. Can we use the experience of the United States between 1900 and 2000 to predict what would happen in world trade if there was free trade across the globe?

Talk about This

Simple trade theory suggests that a country should not import and export the same good. It should either import the good or export the good, but not both. Reality is that intraindustry trade is common. What might explain this?

For More Insight See

Journal of Economic Perspectives 12, no. 4 (Fall 1998). See articles by Dani Rodrik; Maurice Obstfeld; and Robert C. Feenstra and Jeffrey G. Williamson, pp. 3–72.

Journal of Economic Perspectives 9, no. 3 (Summer 1995). See articles by J. David Richardson and Adrian Wood, pp. 57–80.

Krugman, Paul R. "Is Free Trade Passe?" *Journal of Economic Perspectives* 1, no. 2 (Fall 1987), pp. 131–144.

Any text with a title like *International Economics*.

Behind the Numbers

Bureau of Economic Analysis (BEA): www.bea.gov/data/economic-accounts/international

- Exports
- Imports

U.S. Bureau of Economic Analysis (BEA): www.bea.gov

- GDP

U.S. Census Bureau: www.census.gov/foreign-trade/balance/index.html

- Trade balances with countries

CHAPTER EIGHTEEN

International Finance and Exchange Rates

Learning Objectives

After reading this chapter you should be able to:

LO1 Describe the importance of international financial transactions in the global economy.

LO2 Discuss how foreign exchange markets facilitate trade.

LO3 Analyze how alternative foreign exchange systems operate.

LO4 List the determinants of foreign exchange rates.

Chapter Outline

If you have studied the chapter "International Trade: Does It Jeopardize American Jobs?," you know that globalization is one of the central historical facts of the late 20th and early 21st centuries. In the United States alone, as a percentage of GDP, exports have more than doubled and imports have more than tripled. Since 1970, U.S. investment abroad as a percentage of GDP has increased 10-fold and foreign investment in the United States as a percentage of GDP has increased 15-fold. What the previous two sentences imply is that a massive accumulation of trade deficits has resulted in the transition of the United States from the world's largest creditor nation to the world's largest debtor nation. In addition to discussing the financial implications of increasing trade, increasing American trade deficits, and increasing globalization, this chapter discusses the exchange of the world's currencies.

International Financial Transactions

In order for international trade to occur, international currencies must be transacted to allow for that trade. There is almost no barter left in the world. Because of that, there is no guarantee that the value of what is imported will equal the value of what is exported. There is also no guarantee that the amount of money Americans invest abroad will equal the amount of money others invest in America. To understand international finance, you have to begin with three basic accounting concepts: balance of trade, current account balances, and capital account balances.

To illustrate this, consider an example of a good manufactured in one country and purchased in another. When Americans buy iPhones, though the iPhone is made by an American-owned company, Apple, it is assembled in China, with components manufactured in several countries. We will wait to talk about currency exchanges until the next section, but we know that the Chinese company needs yuan, the currency of China, in order to pay its employees. Ignoring that detail for the moment, suppose that there is American currency, say $100,000,000, that has left the United States. Whoever ends up with that $100,000,000 can buy things that are made in the United States: Unless they exchange it into yuan, they can buy financial assets, like U.S. government debt; they can buy physical assets that remain in the United States, like land, buildings, or manufacturing facilities; or they can simply hold on to dollars. This latter option is rarely chosen unless the holder lives in a country where the dollar is a better form of money than the home currency, or the holder

Table 18.1 Balance of payments, United States, 2018 ($ millions).

Source: Bureau of Economic Analysis. https://www.bea.gov/data/intl-trade-investment/international-transactions

Major Accounting Item	Sub Accounting Item	Sub Accounting Component	Component Amount	Sub Accounting Balance	Balance
Current Account	Balance of trade	Exports	2,500,756	−622,106	−488,472
		Imports	3,122,862		
	Balance of short-term investment income	Income to the United States	1,060,362	244,296	
		Payments from the United States	816,066		
	Net Transfers (taxes, private payments)			110,661	
Financial Account	Change in the ownership of assets	U.S.-owned assets abroad	301,618	499,295	−488,472
		Foreign-owned assets in the United States	800,913		
	Financial derivatives net + capital transfers net			−10,852	
	Statistical discrepancy and net derivatives			−40,492	

is engaged in an internationally illegal activity where holding cash makes them less traceable. In short, that $100,000,000 has to return to the United States somehow. The "how" is the key question.

Measures of International Transactions

Table 18.1 displays the elements of the **balance of payments,** the accounting system for how money moves between countries to facilitate the purchase of goods, services, financial instruments, and physical investments. What "balances" with the balance of payments is the current account and the capital account. The **current account** represents the impacts of trade, short-term investment payments, and American payments of foreign taxes, foreign payments of American taxes, and the net transfer of private money. This net transfer is most often seen when migrant workers send money home to their families who live outside the United States. As you can see, mostly because of the enormous trade deficit, there is a massive current account deficit of $488 billion.

balance of payments The accounting system for how money moves between countries to facilitate the purchase of goods, services, financial instruments, and physical investments.

current account The portion of the balance of payments accounting that represents the impacts of trade, short-term investment payments, and American payments of foreign taxes, foreign payments of American taxes, and the net transfer of private money.

Over time, the current account and the balance of trade mirror one another quite closely. Figure 18.1 maps both as a percentage of GDP from 1960 to 2018. For all but one of the last 37 years, the balance of each has been negative. The exploding trade deficits of the 1990s and the 2000s can be seen as trade and current account deficits that had reached previous records in the middle 1980s and grew to in excess of 5 percent of GDP from 2003 to 2008. Both of these deficits fell rapidly during the recession as Americans cut import demand significantly. In 2018, the current account deficit was a typical 3 percent of GDP.

FIGURE 18.1 Current account and balance of trade as a percentage of GDP (1960–2018).

Source: Bureau of Economic Analysis. https://www.bea.gov/data/intl-trade-investment/international-transactions

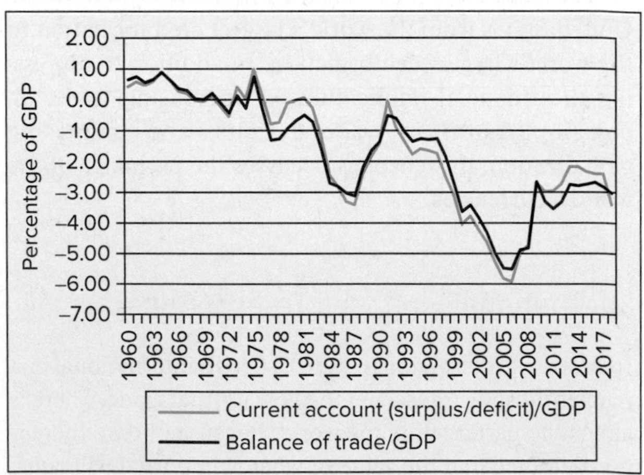

FIGURE 18.2 Foreign purchases of U.S. assets and U.S. purchases of foreign assets as a percentage of GDP (1960–2018).

Source: Bureau of Economic Analysis, https://www.bea.gov/data/intl-trade-investment/international-transactions

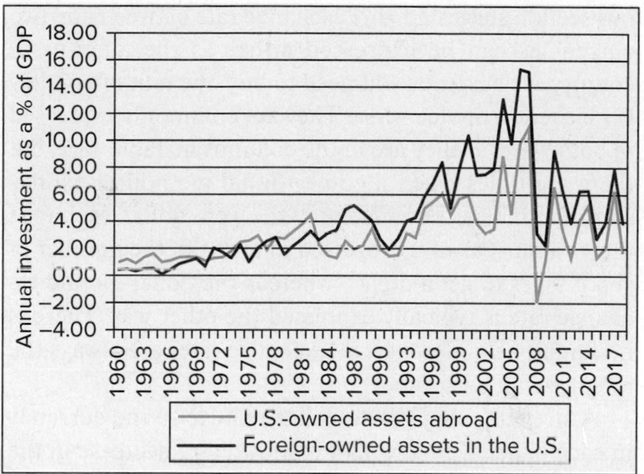

financial account Represents the changes in holding of longer-term financial and physical assets by citizens of one country in another country.

The **financial account** represents the changes in holding of longer-term financial and physical assets by citizens of one country in another country. The most significant elements of the financial account are the amount of foreign investment in the United States and the amount of investment by Americans in other countries. Recall that when iPhones are sold, the holders of dollars have to do something with the money. For the most part, they buy U.S. financial and physical assets. The balance of the financial account, plus or minus a statistical discrepancy, is (other than a small set of other transactions) the opposite of the balance of the current account.

As can be seen in Figure 18.2, the globalization of asset holding has grown markedly. From less than 1 percent of GDP for much of the 1960s to 10 to 15 times those levels today, the international ownership of financial and physical assets is quite clearly a sign of the times. Figures 18.1 and 18.2 are directly related in that the level of the current account deficit line in Figure 18.1 is the difference between the two lines in Figure 18.2.

The other feature of Figure 18.2 that is worth noting is that after the Great Recession, the pattern of the 1990s resumed.

Foreign Exchange Markets

To understand the importance and the complexity of dealing with exchanging currencies, consider the simple act of buying an iPhone. When you pay $500, $1,000, or more for that phone, that money goes several places. It starts with the store owner, who uses some of it to pay employees and other business expenses and uses some to pay Apple for the phone. The rest is profit. For many years, Apple Inc. has contracted with a company in China (Foxconn) to assemble its products from parts made all over the world. This is where the complication of exchanging currencies arises. People want to be paid in their own currency. In China, it's the yuan (u-wan. It is also known by its other name, the "renminbi").

Let's look at this U.S. dollar-for-yuan exchange. At first glance, Figure 18.3 looks like any ordinary supply and demand diagram. Upon further examination, though, the labels are different. That difference stems from the fact that a form of currency is being exchanged for another form of currency. A typical supply and demand diagram of market exchange involves a trade of a currency for a good or a service.

Moreover, keeping supply and demand straight isn't quite as easy either. The demand for yuan is also the supply of U.S. dollars, and the demand for U.S. dollars is also the supply of yuan. The place on the diagram for a "price" is replaced with an exchange rate. An **exchange rate** is the amount of one currency that must be given up to gain a unit of another currency. In Figure 18.3, it is expressed as U.S. dollars per unit of yuan. It could just as easily have been expressed as yuan per unit of U.S. dollars.

exchange rate The amount of one currency that must be given up to gain a unit of another currency.

For this reason, the curves and axes labels use somewhat roundabout language. The vertical axis of Figure 18.3 is labeled "Price of yuan in U.S. dollars" because it is the number of U.S. dollars that must be given up to get a quantity of yuan. The horizontal axis is the

FIGURE 18.3 Yuan to U.S. dollar.

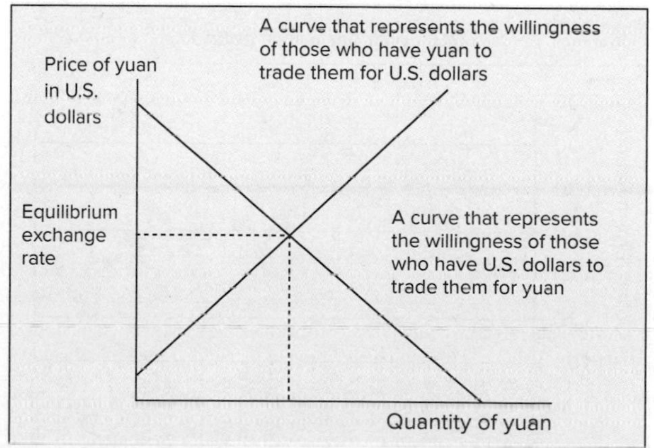

quantity of yuan exchanged. What would normally be called a demand curve is the "curve that represents the willingness of those who have U.S. dollars to trade them for yuan." What would normally be called a supply curve is the "curve that represents the willingness of those who have yuan to trade them for U.S. dollars."

Going back to our iPhone example, this simple purchase involves a number of different currencies that must be exchanged because the components are produced throughout Asia. If currency exchange is as easy as going to the bank with a $20 bill and asking for 20 $1 bills, then **foreign exchange** is not an obstacle to trade. In most of the Western world, it is a relatively simple proposition for a corporation to get the currencies it needs.

foreign exchange The conversion of the currency of one country for the currency of another.

There are foreign exchange markets in all large cities that have stock markets. In most countries, exchange rates are like any freely traded asset. The price, or in this case the exchange rate, changes over time. A look at Figure 18.4 shows the exchange rate between the dollar and other key currencies around the world. As the previous section suggested, any exchange rate between any two currencies can be expressed either as the amount of country A's currency you need to buy one unit of country B's currency, or vice versa. They are commonly expressed in both ways, as they are in the columns in Table 18.2, but there are times when a conventional method of expression dominates. For instance, the yen-dollar exchange rate is almost always expressed in terms of the number of yen it takes to get a dollar, whereas the dollar-pound exchange rate is typically expressed the other way. There is no functional difference, as exchange rates are always the reciprocal of each other.

A strengthening of the dollar relative to the currency in each panel of Figure 18.4 is shown as a decrease in the

FIGURE 18.4 Exchange rates between the dollar and four major currencies.

Source: Board of Governors of the Federal Reserve System. https://www.federalreserve.gov/releases/h10/current/

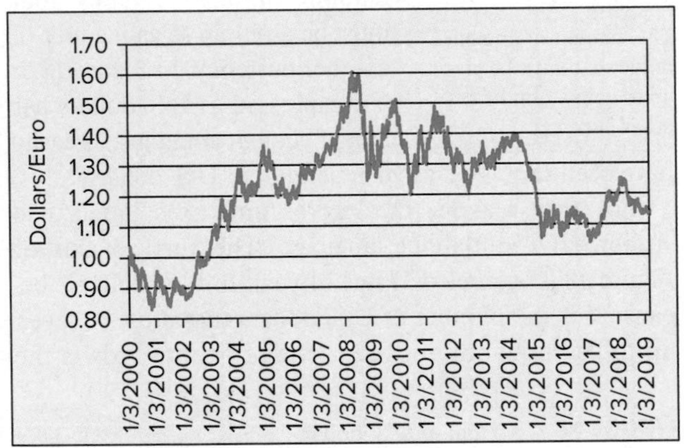

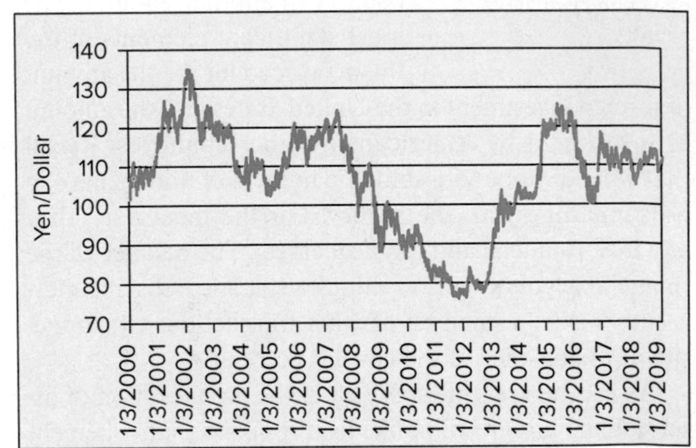

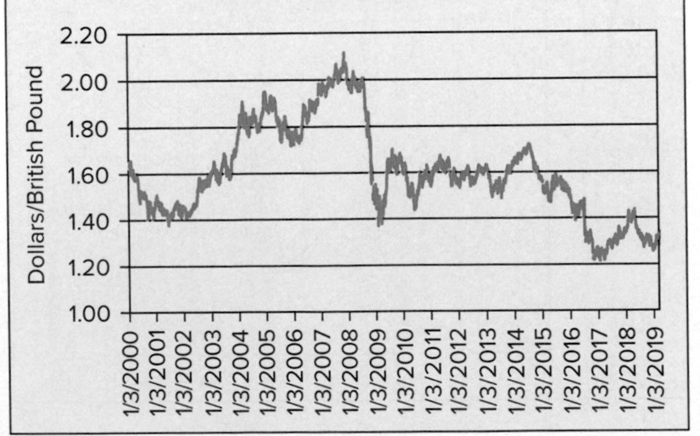

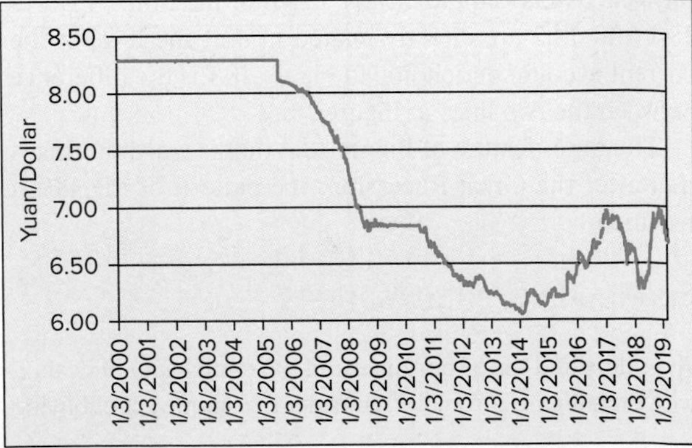

Table 18.2 Exchange rates between several currencies and the U.S. dollar, March 7, 2019.

Source: X-RATES. http://www.x-rates.com

Foreign Currency	Amount of Currency Needed to Get $1	Amount of U.S. Dollars Needed to Get One Unit of the Currency
Brazilian Real	3.882702	0.257553
British Pound	0.763608	1.309572
Canadian Dollar	1.344757	0.743629
Chinese Yuan Renminbi	6.715131	0.148917
Euro	0.891146	1.122150
Japanese Yen	111.639568	0.008957
Mexican Peso	19.558847	0.051128
South Korean Won	1133.871246	0.000882

dollar per other currency line and an increase in the other currency per dollar line. So between July 2008 and November 2008, the dollar strengthened relative to the euro and pound and weakened relative to the yen.

Not every country allows its people to freely trade their currency for other world currencies. Moreover, the Chinese government does not let its currency move at the whim of market forces. It was not until 2005 that the Chinese government let its currency move, and even then it was only slowly, and not nearly as fast as free market forces would have moved it.

In 2010, China began a slow process of letting the yuan float with other currencies in a managed way. Between 2014 and 2019, the yuan exchange rate with the dollar began to move in a way that resembled the movements of a market-determined currency.

Alternative Foreign Exchange Systems

Throughout modern history, currencies have been exchanged to facilitate trade. During that time, there have been three models for setting those exchange rates. As suggested by Figure 18.4, most exchange rates are determined by market forces. An increase in the demand for a currency will strengthen it relative to another currency. While this is the system that dominates today, it has not always been that way and as intimated above with reference to the Chinese yuan, market forces can be controlled by governments.

Floating Exchange Rate System

Though we have already discussed the market, let's quickly review the role of the market in determining exchange rates. In a **floating exchange rate system,** there is no government control over exchange rates. The market for various currencies is determined solely by the forces of supply and demand. Shifts in the curves from Figure 18.3 are determined by the factors outlined in the next section.

floating exchange rate system
Foreign exchange rate system where there is no government control over exchange rates.

Fixed Exchange Rate System

We now turn our attention to the system that was common between World War II and the early 1970s. One of the perceived ills of the exchange rate system of the 1920s and 1930s was that, because it was determined by markets, it created uncertainty for traders. In the days before options markets (where traders could lock in exchange rates for the future), the concern was that uncertain exchange rates dampened trade, which was bad for the world economy. As a result, after World War II a **fixed exchange rate system** was enacted.

fixed exchange rate system
Foreign exchange rate system whereby the country (or group of countries) must stand ready to purchase or sell its currency in exchange for foreign currencies or gold so that any excess demand or excess supply is immediately eliminated.

Under a fixed exchange rate system, the country (or group of countries) that wishes exchange rates to be fixed relative to other countries' currencies must stand ready to purchase or sell its currency in exchange for foreign currencies or gold so that any excess demand or excess supply is immediately eliminated. (The gold standard is simply one way in which a country can achieve a fixed exchange rate.)

For instance, if you look at the yuan–dollar exchange rate from Figure 18.4, the exchange rate remained constant for an extended period of time. In that system, depicted in panel A of Figure 18.5, an increase in the demand for yuan must be met immediately with an increase in the supply of yuan by the Chinese government. That is not difficult for a country to maintain. It can always print more of its own currency. Panel B shows the opposite problem. Were the demand for yuan to decrease, the Chinese government would have to reduce the supply of its own currency. This can be done by it supplying the necessary dollars to buy the yuan, or as panel B shows, removing yuan from the system, typically through exchanging other currencies or gold. If, once again, you focus on Figure 18.4 from early 2006 to early 2009, the Chinese government let the yuan strengthen in value from 8 yuan to the dollar to a new set level of 6.8 yuan to the dollar.

FIGURE 18.5 Alternative exchange rate systems.

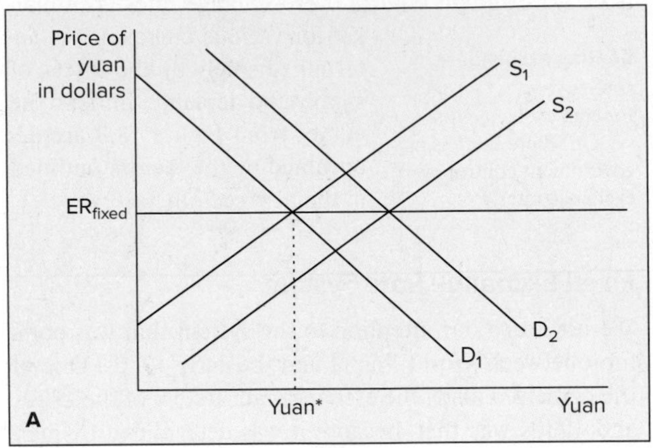

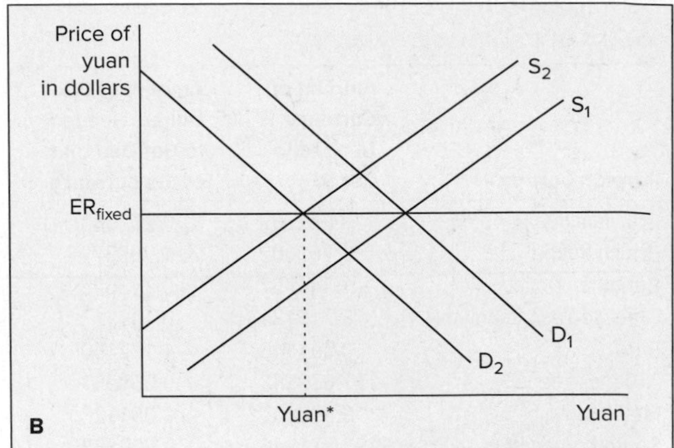

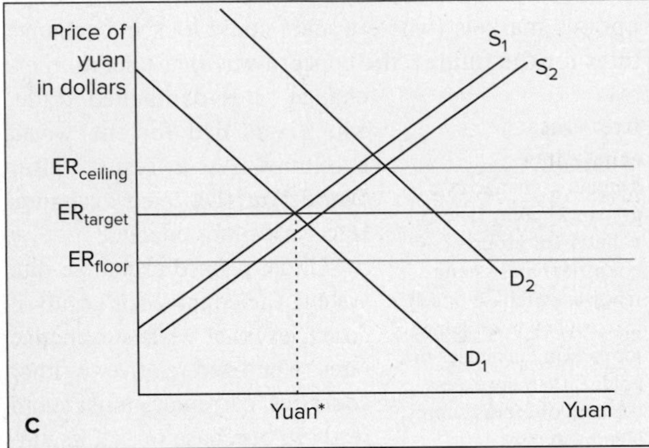

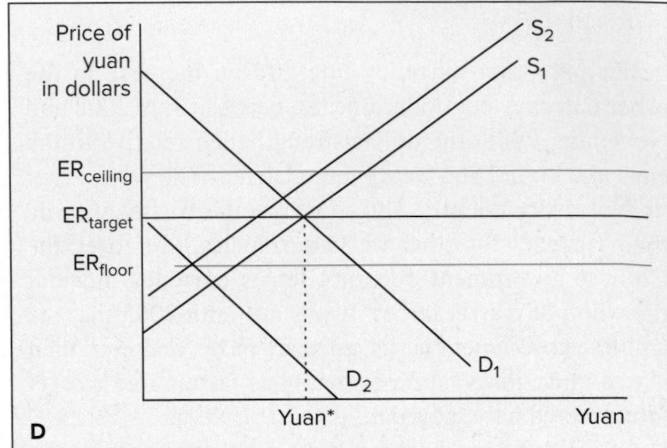

Managed Flat Exchange Rate System

Starting in 2010, the Chinese government began to let the yuan float but ensured that it stayed within an acceptable range. During that time, it was never less valuable than 7 yuan to the dollar and never more valuable than 6 yuan to the dollar. This highlights the third system: a **managed float exchange rate system.** In this system, governments decide the range of exchange rates they will allow the market to create, and act only when either the top end (noted as the "ceiling" in panels C and D of Figure 18.4) or the bottom end (noted as the "floor" in panels C and D of Figure 18.4) of that range is breached. In this circumstance, the government need not change the supply of its currency by the amount necessary to bring about the target exchange rate. It must only bring it back into the desired range. Graphs C and D work exactly like panels A and B except that the government(s) managing the exchange rate must increase or decrease the supply of the currency by a smaller amount so as to maintain the desired range.

managed float exchange rate system Foreign exchange rate system whereby governments decide the range of exchange rates they will allow the market to create, and act only when either the top end or the bottom end of that range is breached.

In post–World War II history the world has seen major currencies exchanged in all three fashions. As indicated above, immediately after World War II the fixed exchange rate system dominated. The system became unsustainable in the early 1970s, and from that point to today, the system has been (for nearly every country) a floating exchange rate system with periods of managed float when exchange rates changed too markedly for politicians to stomach.

Determinants of Exchange Rates

Recall from our discussion of supply and demand in Chapter 2 and from our discussion of aggregate supply and aggregate demand in Chapter 8, we presented the models and then presented the reasons why each of the curves might shift. We need to replicate that here except that we need to remember that there really is no distinction between supply and demand, so we will look at the factors that will strengthen or weaken an exchange rate. Since each exchange rate applies only to the two countries involved, the factors are expressed relative to one another.

So returning to our discussion of the U.S. dollar and Chinese yuan, the dollar can get stronger or weaker relative to the yuan if either the desire of yuan holders to acquire U.S. dollars changes or the desire of U.S. dollar holders to acquire yuan changes. An increase in the desire of either to have U.S. dollars rather than yuan would strengthen the U.S. dollar, causing the price of yuan–the U.S. dollar-to-yuan exchange rate–to fall. A decrease in the desire of either Americans or Chinese to have U.S. dollars will weaken the U.S. dollar, causing the price of yuan–the U.S. dollar-to-yuan exchange rate–to rise. So, what specific factors determine the desirability of various currencies?

The first and typically most important factor for exchange rates is the trade imbalance between the two countries. The United States has a significant trade deficit relative to China. If the yuan and dollar are determined in markets (and we know from the above discussion of exchange rate systems they are not), the yuan will strengthen relative to the dollar. This is because there will be more dollars in the foreign exchange markets than there are yuan to sustain the current exchange rate.

The second factor influencing exchange rates is the relative real interest rate being offered on investments in the two countries. This combines two ideas, because the real interest rate is the difference between nominal interest and expected inflation. If inflation is expected to be the same in the two countries, because investors will seek the maximum return on their investment regardless of where that happens, they will seek the currency of the country with the highest interest rate. As a result, the currency of the country with the higher interest rate will strengthen relative to the one with the lower interest rate. If the interest rates of the two countries are the same, the country with the lower anticipated rate of inflation will see its currency strengthen relative to the country with the higher anticipated inflation rate.

The third factor is the relative safety of assets held in a particular country. This is why the dollar nearly always strengthens in times of international strife. The U.S. government, though in significant debt, holds the distinction of being the one government that has paid every debt it has ever incurred. Being a haven for international investors seeking safety means that the dollar strengthens even when strife is triggered in the United States. The dollar strengthened slightly in the wake of 9/11 and strengthened mightily relative to the euro and pound during the 2008 financial crisis (which started in, but was not confined to, the United States).

Summary

For foreign trade to exist, currencies must be traded. Whenever trade between two countries is not balanced, the money that is not returned to the country maintaining a trade deficit will have to return eventually and will be used to buy assets in that country. As a result, trade balances, which are augmented by short-term investment flows, will be balanced by longer-term asset ownership exchanges. In this way, the current account and capital account balance. The United States runs a large trade deficit and as a result runs a large current account deficit. This is balanced by a substantial capital account surplus. The markets in which these currencies are exchanged can be allowed to function freely and without government intervention, or they can be managed by governments to maintain either fixed exchange rates or exchange rates within an acceptable range. Whether a currency is strong or weak typically depends on the trade balance between the two countries, the relative inflation rates, the relative interest rates, and the relative safety of investments in the countries.

Key Terms

balance of payments
current account
exchange rate
financial account
fixed exchange rate system
floating exchange rate system
foreign exchange
managed float exchange rate system

Quiz Yourself

1. Which two numbers "balance"?
   a. The current account and exports
   b. The financial account and the current account
   c. Exports and imports
   d. Short-term investment income and short-term investment payments
2. From the perspective of people in a particular country, a strong currency is
   a. good for both its importers and exporters.
   b. bad for both its importers and exporters.
   c. good for its importers and bad for its exporters.
   d. good for its exporters and bad for its importers.
3. The dollar to yuan exchange rate will equal
   a. the yuan to dollar exchange rate.
   b. the reciprocal of the yuan to dollar exchange rate.
   c. the yuan to euro exchange rate.
   d. the square of the yuan to dollar exchange rate.
4. If one country determines it wants a fixed exchange rate with another
   a. it can do nothing on its own but must have the cooperation of the other country.
   b. it only needs to announce its desired exchange rate, and that will result.
   c. it must be prepared to purchase or sell its own currency in the market to maintain the exchange rate.
5. An increase in the expected inflation rate in one country will
   a. strengthen its currency.
   b. weaken its currency.
   c. have no impact on the exchange rate between its currency and other currencies.

Short Answer Questions

1. Explain why the current account and the trade balance are so closely aligned.
2. Explain or illustrate why it is that if $1 will buy you 0.8€ that 1€ must equal $1.25.
3. If you had $1,000 and wanted to get the most for it and you believed that the dollar would get weaker relative to the yen by 10 percent and that you could earn 5 percent in the United States and only 1 percent in Japan, show that you would still want to invest in a yen-denominated asset.
4. If you were a U.S. politician seeking to strengthen the dollar, how might you accomplish that, and what would the consequence be of the attempt?

Talk about This

Until the presidency of Donald Trump, the United States accepted that countries utilize tariffs and currency manipulation to advantage themselves with fear of retaliation by the United States. This was viewed (by the establishment of both political parties) as one of the consequences of America being the world leader. President Trump changed that policy by threatening and executing retaliatory tariffs to punish countries that put tariffs on the United States. Was he right to abandon past policies?

Think about This

Suppose there are two countries (A and B). Suppose Country A has a currency exchange rate with Country B of 0.89, and Country B has a currency exchange rate with Country A of 1.12. Currency exchange rates between two countries are always the reciprocal of each other. Why is that the case? What would happen if currency exchange rates between countries deviated from the reciprocal?

Behind the Numbers

U.S. Bureau of Economic Analysis (BEA): www.bea.gov/data/economic-accounts/international

- Balance of trade
- Current account
- Financial account

Federal Reserve Board: www.federalreserve.gov/releases/h10/hist

- Historical exchange rates

Currency exchange website such as: www.x-rates.com

- Various currency exchange rates

CHAPTER NINETEEN

The European Union, Debt Crisis, and Brexit

Learning Objectives

After reading this chapter you should be able to:

LO1 Describe the creation of the European Union and the euro.

LO2 Explain the consequences of the European Union.

LO3 Distinguish between the causes of the Irish and Spanish debt crises and the Italian and Greek debt crises.

LO4 Describe why the policies that the United States used to mitigate the Great Recession were largely unavailable to those European nations faced with crises.

LO5 Explain the reasons why some countries considered, but decided against, exiting the euro while the United Kingdom decided to exit the European Union.

Chapter Outline

From late 2008 through 2019, Europe has been in a state of economic turmoil, moving from recession, to stagnation, to debt crises, to Brexit. In the process, there was a constant threat that Europe's troubles would/could drag the world into another, perhaps even deeper, global recession. In this chapter, we explore the causes of Europe's problems during this period by going back to the scene of the crime—the creation of the euro. We proceed with an analysis of the impact of the euro's creation on housing markets in Ireland and Spain and on the borrowing habits of Italy and Greece. We then describe why the existence of the euro made it very difficult for governments in the most hard-hit countries to recover and why there is so much disagreement over the austerity policies many countries were compelled to employ to secure the help of healthier European economies. We conclude by recognizing that some countries may be better off (or at least perceive they will be better off) if they leave either the European Union, the euro, or both.

In the Beginning There Were 17 Currencies in 17 Countries

After World War II when country borders were redrawn by the allied powers, each European country reestablished its individual currencies. Germany had the mark, France had the franc, Italy had the lira, Greece had the drachma, and so on. Very quickly it became clear to the governments of Germany, France, and the United Kingdom that the European economies would recover more quickly with a free-trade union allowing freight to travel between the countries without having to stop at each border. In 1958, the European Union's predecessor, the European Economic Community, was created to establish travel and trade rules throughout the member nations.[1] Through the years, the movement toward European integration intensified, culminating in a series of referendum votes in the 1990s approving the Maastricht Treaty that created a common currency for 16 countries.[2] The currency (the euro) was first used exclusively in financial markets from 1999 to 2001 and has circulated as the currency of the member states since.

By joining the euro, countries gave up a major symbol of their sovereignty, their currency. They also gave up the ability to use monetary policy (described in Chapter 10) as individual countries because they had to cede that authority to the European Central Bank (the counterpart to the U.S.' Federal Reserve). It was for these reasons that some European Union nations, most notably the United Kingdom, refused to join. The transition process was remarkably smooth. Bank balances were converted from home currencies to euro-denominated balances at specified rates, and actual paper and coin currency was recalled and exchanged. This typically occurred when businesses would deposit their local currency at local banks. At that time, they would receive credit for those deposits in euros.

Several other provisions of the Treaty on the Functioning of the European Union were implemented to avoid the kind of economic catastrophe that we have seen in Greece and Spain. One such provision, Article 126, was that countries were required to maintain a deficit-to-GDP ratio of less than 3 percent and work to a debt-to-GDP ratio of less than 60 percent. Another, Article 123, stated that the European Central Bank could not purchase member nation debt. A third, Article 125, prohibited bailouts of one country by the union or by any member state unless it was viewed as necessary to avoid a systemic financial collapse of the entire union.

The Effect of the Euro

The effect of the creation of the euro and these provisions was that the poorer members, some southern European countries, in particular, saw relatively rapid growth. As can be seen in Figure 19.1, growth in Ireland, Spain, and Greece exceeded that of the euro area and the United States from 2001 through 2007.

As can be seen in Figure 19.2, there was a considerable discrepancy between the per capita GDP of these countries. With the European Union-27 member nations indexed as 100, the interpretation of the data below is that in 2001 Greece had a per capita GDP 50 percent

FIGURE 19.1 GDP growth in euro countries and the United States.

Source: European Central Bank, www.ecb.int/stats/html/index.en.html.

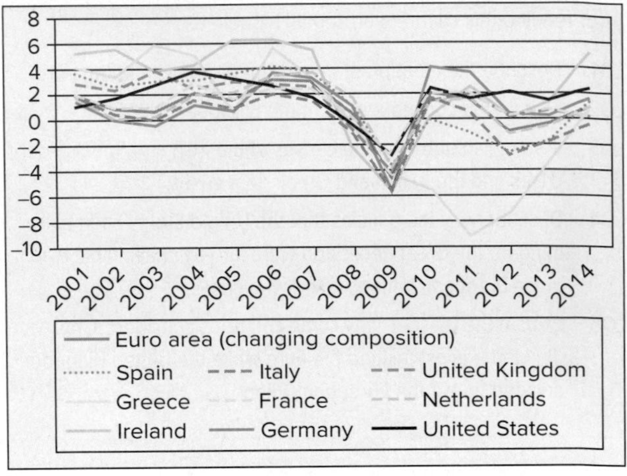

FIGURE 19.2 Per capita GDP across Europe and the United States relative to EU-27.

Source: Eurostat. European Union, ec.europa.eu/eurostat/data/database.

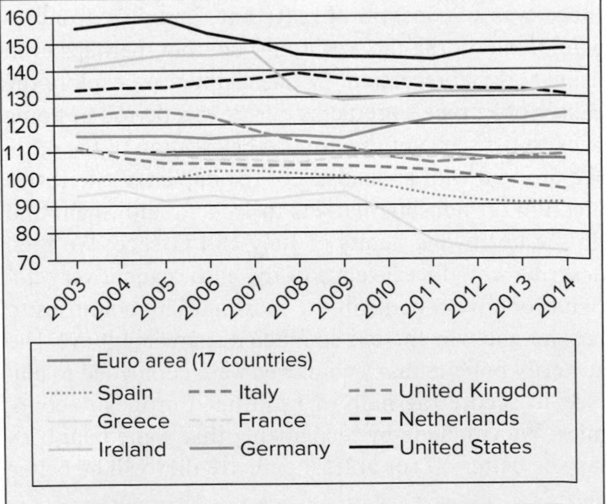

[1] Current members: Austria, **Belgium,** Bulgaria, Croatia, Cyprus, Czechia, Denmark, Estonia, Finland, **France, Germany**, Greece, Hungary, Ireland, **Italy,** Latvia, Lithuania, **Luxembourg,** Malta, the **Netherlands,** Poland, Portugal, Romania, Slovakia, Slovenia, Spain, Sweden, and the United Kingdom. **Bold = original members**

[2] There are now 19 countries that are part of the currency union. They are Austria, Belgium, Cyprus, Estonia, Finland, France, Germany, Greece, Ireland, Italy, Luxembourg, Malta, the Netherlands, Portugal, Slovakia, Slovenia, and Spain. Estonia, Latvia, and Lithuania were not part of the original 16. Further, millions more live in countries with currencies whose value is pegged to the euro.

FIGURE 19.3 Long-term interest rates.

Source: European Central Bank, www.ecb.europa.eu/stats/html/index.en.html.

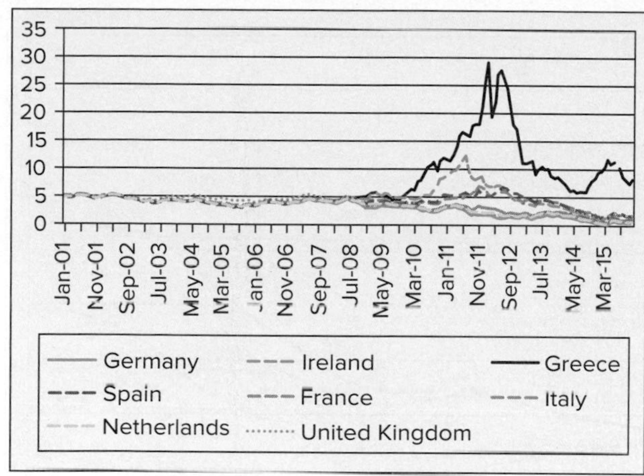

FIGURE 19.4 Housing prices in Spain, Ireland, and the United States.

Sources: www.statcentral.ie; www.standardandpoors.com.

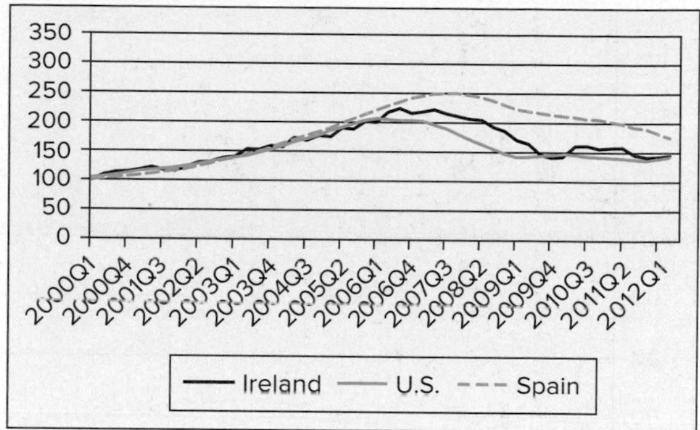

lower than the Netherlands and Germany. Spain was 15 percent poorer than Germany.

Because these countries were growing faster than the richer countries, it promoted considerable lending to poorer member countries largely because interest rates to poorer member countries converged to the already low rates of the richer member countries. This was because investors believed that a loan to a euro-member country or a financial institution in a euro-member country was largely the same regardless of whether that nation was relatively rich or poor. As can be seen in Figure 19.3, the interest rates on 10-year government debt were, during the period from 2001 to 2007, largely identical across Europe's largest governments.

These low interest rates and the relatively attractive weather of Ireland and Spain generated housing bubbles in those two countries that were even more inflated than those in the United States. Figure 19.4 shows that, between 2000 and 2009 and relative to the first quarter in 2000, housing prices doubled in the United States, but increased by 125 percent in Spain and by 150 percent in Ireland. The sources of those mortgage loans, however, differed. In the United States, Fannie Mae and Freddie Mac bought and securitized mortgages as mortgage-backed securities (MBS). In Europe, the instrument was the "covered bond." Using that method, mortgage loans remained with the originating bank (unlike in the United States where the originating bank sold the mortgages within days) and then sold bonds that were backed by those mortgages.

As a result, a bank in the United States that did not purchase MBS for its own portfolio could have largely escaped the housing crisis. In Europe, however, any bank that made the loans and any financial institution that purchased the covered bonds were vulnerable to this crisis. In both Ireland and Spain, the bursting of the housing bubble severely damaged banks in those countries but also threatened larger German and French banks because this is where the money originated. Had there been no covering of the Irish and Spanish bonds by German and French banks, there would have been insufficient funds for Irish and Spanish banks to lend to people buying homes there, which would have stopped the housing bubble altogether.

In Italy, the recession and fiscal crisis had a very different origin. Italy's economy was simply and steadily on the decline for some time. In 2000, its per capita GDP was 18 percent higher than the EU-27 average. By 2010, it was at the EU-27 average. That is, on a relative basis, Italians spent the decade getting poorer. This has structural and political origins. The structural origin was twofold. First, Italy is aging more rapidly than any other major European economy because the birthrate has plummeted for 40 years. Fewer births mean fewer workers supporting its pension system. Second, it already had a relatively high debt. As can be seen in Figure 19.5, the Italian national debt was relatively high for the period prior to the crisis, and its deficits, as shown in Figure 19.6, were also high. Politically, Italy's prime minister was an egotistical, womanizing media mogul with no desire to tackle difficult structural issues such as reforming a pension system for a declining population.

In Greece, the origins were far worse. Its debt was always high and its deficits were worse. If it is possible, they were actually worse than the data show them to be

FIGURE 19.5 Debt to GDP.

Source: Eurostat. https://ec.europa.eu/eurostat/web/government-finance-statistics/data/main-tables

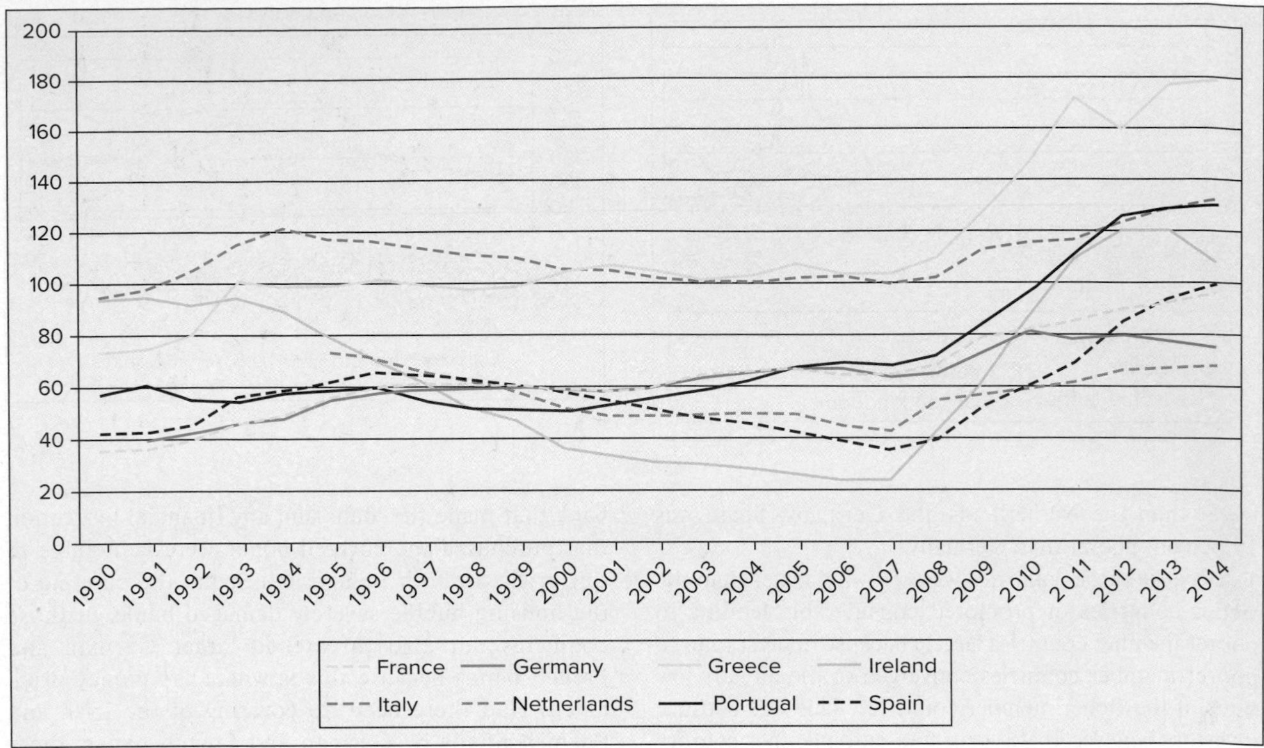

because it was widely believed that the true deficit in Greece was worse than they reported to the European Union. Tax evasion by individuals and businesses in Greece was so pervasive as to be unsolvable. People claimed that they would begin to pay their share when others did.

Why Couldn't They Pull Themselves Out? The United States Did

Though the start of the decline in economic activity began in the United Kingdom, it got its first major push in the United States with the collapse of the American housing bubble in late 2008. The United States did three big things to counter the impact of the Great Recession: (1) TARP (the bank bailout), (2) acts of monetary policy on an unprecedented scale, and (3) fiscal policy–induced explosions in deficits in the form of Bush and Obama stimulus packages. The United Kingdom and France did the latter; Germany did not. The deficits in Germany in 2009 and 2010 were on the scale of their 2001–2005 deficits, whereas the deficits in the United States and France were two to three times those levels.

As for monetary policy, as Chapters 10, 13, and 14 noted, the Federal Reserve of the United States created and exercised authority in the area of monetary policy well beyond what any previous Federal Reserve chairperson would recognize. As a result of those actions, interest rates throughout the United States were at or near all-time lows. The Treasury was borrowing money on the short-term market for nearly zero interest. In the long-term market, interest rates were so low that 15-year mortgages were being offered for less than half of previous 1960s-era records. These record-low interest rates were the direct result of the Federal Reserve's policy of buying large volumes of mortgage-backed securities and long-term treasuries.

Why did European nations not do the same thing? Simply put, they couldn't. They couldn't do so individually because interest rates were too high, and they couldn't do so collectively because of the Article 123 provision that prohibited the purchase of member-nation debt by the European Central Bank. Italy, Ireland, Greece, and Spain did not have any tools of monetary

FIGURE 19.6 Deficits to GDP.

Source: Eurostat. https://ec.europa.eu/eurostat/web/government-finance-statistics/data/main-tables

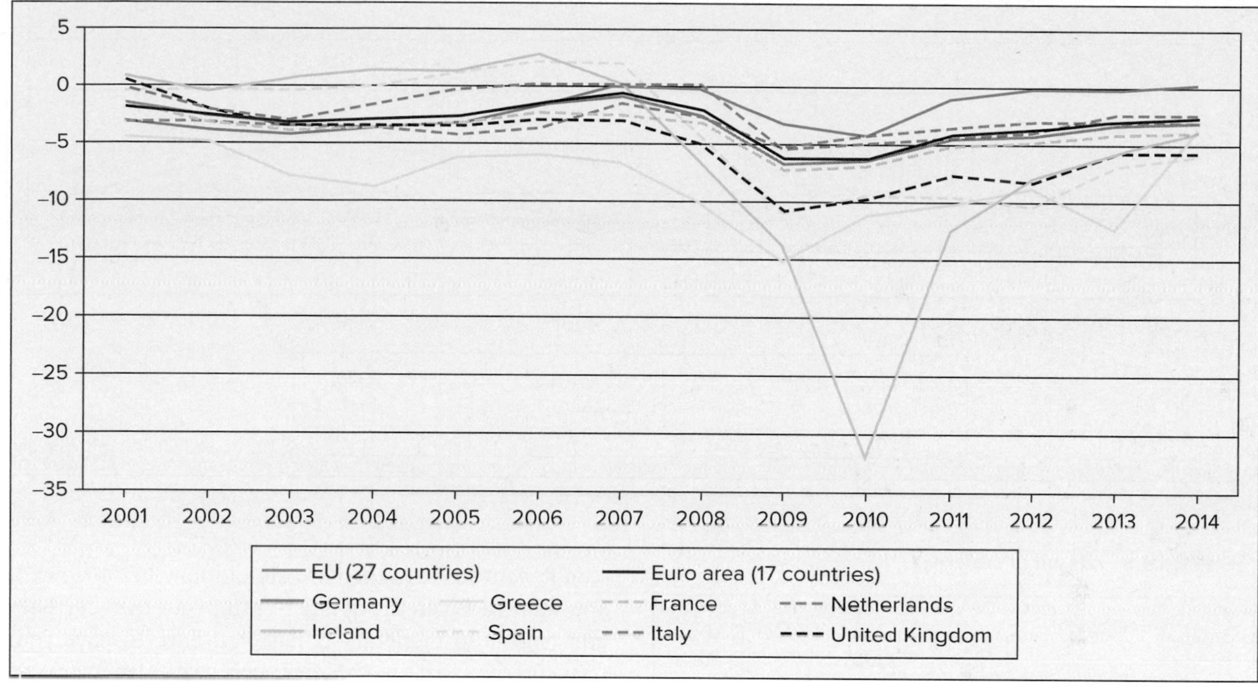

policy, let alone the expanded ones, because just like the state of Maryland doesn't have its own central bank, neither do individual EU countries.

Further, at its creation, the European Central Bank had one and only one mission–inflation control–and it is governed by the Germans, Dutch, French, and Belgians, who have little interest in generating a threat of inflation for themselves by engaging in monetary policy that would help the Greeks, Spanish, Italians, and Irish. To make things worse, the individual country's governments had limited ability at best to engage in their own version of TARP, though the Irish tried. They would have had to borrow money to do so and, as can be seen by Figure 19.3, the interest rates they faced were prohibitive. Further, and for the same reason, they could not engage in fiscal policy to stimulate their economies on their own because, again, they would have to borrow the money to do it. The bottom line is that everything the United States did to minimize the impact of the Great Recession was unavailable to the weaker economies of Europe, largely because they had no control over the value of their currency and had no ability to borrow at reasonable interest rates.

Because there was a growing recognition among the Germans and French that their economies were threatened by the instability of weaker ones, there was a willingness among them to help the Greeks, Spanish, Irish, and Italians. This formal recognition of the threat to the EU, generally, allowed for the cross-national bailouts because the systemic risk clauses of Articles 123 and 125 were invoked. For political and economic purposes, though, the Germans and French insisted that the weaker economies reform their budgets before they received the assistance. In each case, the demand was for spending cuts and tax increases. These policies had consequences. Figure 19.7 shows that unemployment rose everywhere but rose more dramatically in these weaker economies. Governments laid off employees, cut pensions, and increased taxes in an attempt to reduce their deficits.

From a Keynesian economist's point of view, this is a predictable result of austerity. As can be seen from Figure 19.8, a decrease in government spending and an increase in taxes will result in a decrease in aggregate demand. That will result in a decrease in economic activity, and that will result in an increase in unemployment. Austerity could even be self-defeating. The loss of jobs would increase demands on the social safety net and decrease tax revenues. Austerity can ultimately lead to a larger deficit if the actions of budget cuts and tax increases

FIGURE 19.7 Unemployment rates in Europe.

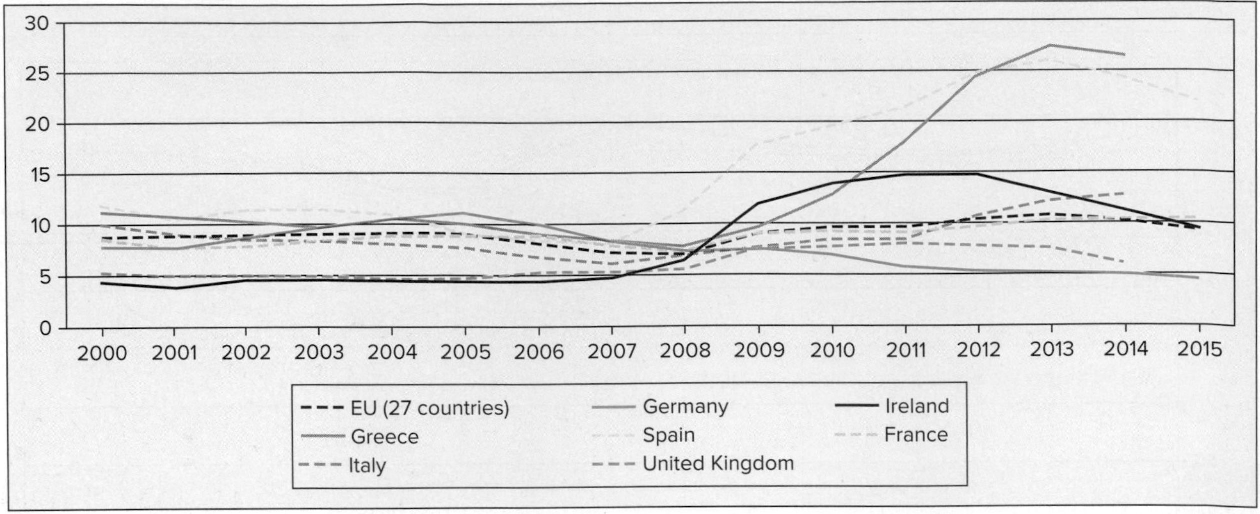

FIGURE 19.8 Result of austerity.

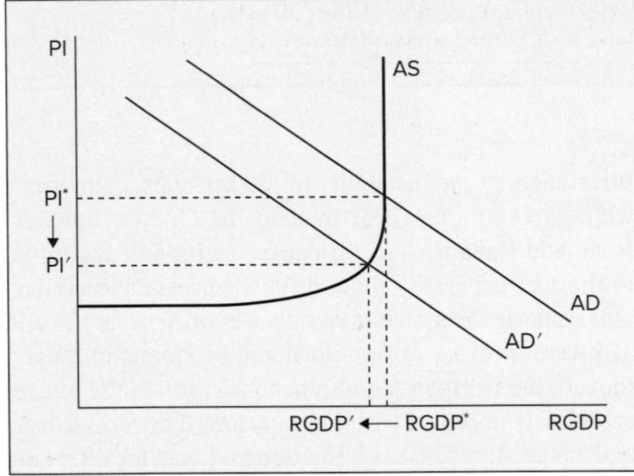

plunge the economy into such a poor state that the impacts on the economy generate larger revenue losses than the deficit reductions resulting from the budget cuts and tax increases. Greece's economy contracted in eight of the nine years from 2008 to 2016. Italy's contracted from 2008 to 2013 and has grown anemically (exceeding 1 percent only once) since. On the other hand, Spain and Ireland have rebounded nicely.

Was It Too Late to Leave the Euro?

For much of 2011 and 2012, there was speculation that Greece would leave the euro. The reasons why Greece would want to leave the euro should now be obvious. If you want to regain the ability to print your own currency and engage in monetary policy, you have to have your own currency to do it. Creating their own currency would not be difficult. Getting people to accept it, however, would be challenging. Yet, if the Greek government were to order all Greek banks to convert euro-denominated accounts into drachma-denominated accounts, the effect would be quick. Though the Greek government could easily issue this order, they would have little power to maintain the value of the drachma, and its value would almost certainly plummet.

The inflation in Greece would be dramatic. From some perspectives, that would be a good thing. That's because inflation would operate as an across-the-board tax on everyone. Your 1,000 euro account would have 1,000 drachmas in it, and then the drachma would lose half its value. You would be able to buy about half as much from the rest of Europe as you had been able to buy, and you would look to Greek providers of the goods or services because their drachma-denominated prices would look relatively more attractive. The attractive aspect of the idea of the "Grexit" (Greek exit from the euro) is that it would quickly stabilize Greece by taxing each Greek by half their wealth as inflation of 100 percent cuts the buying power of wealth in half.

But, alas, it isn't that easy. Smart Greeks had already anticipated the change. They became convinced that it would eventually happen that way, so they closed their euro-denominated banks accounts in Greece and opened new ones in other countries. They converted their euros into assets that were inaccessible by the Greek government. Though the threatened action never materialized, it still had an impact. The only people with any euro-denominated accounts in Greece were those who were either poor (and therefore couldn't afford to do their banking with a foreign bank) or unaware (and therefore vulnerable).

This bankrupted Greek banks because they did not have the euros to pay off their depositors. Understand that no American bank could withstand a demand by a large number of its depositors for a cash withdrawal ei ther. Thus, the threat of a Greek exit both increased its likelihood and diminished its viability and desirability. It also made it harder for France and Germany to keep them in the currency union. The problem was made worse because if Greece left, it would be difficult to contain Spanish concerns that their country would be next. That would jeopardize Spanish banks. Spain would topple Italy and, if Italy was toppled, the euro would be a memory. As a result, as difficult as it was to achieve, the Germans and French felt compelled to keep Greece in the euro. It was a mess that only got better very slowly. No country left the euro, but the 2010s were a miserable time to live and work in southern Europe.

The irony is that Greece needed to leave the euro at a time that it could not, and Germany and France needed Greece to leave the euro but could not allow it to happen out of fear of what the consequences might be.

Brexit and Beyond

At this writing (Spring 2019), Brexit (the exit of the United Kingdom from the European Union) remains uncertain. In March 2019, the British Parliament voted multiple times on multiple resolutions and resolved nothing. On one day in March 2019, the parliament voted on eight separate resolutions ranging from a "no-deal" crash out of the EU to authorizing a new referendum. No resolution garnered a majority. As a result, they succeeded only in delaying their decision.

The issues that led to the June 2016 referendum were largely based on a dissatisfaction with the reaction of the European Union to the Great Recession and a fear by many that their country was losing its national identity. The economic unhappiness stemmed from the fact that Europe didn't recover well from the recession. Its growth rates were very low, lower than those which existed in the United States, and there was a second recession in 2012–2013. The euro area did not get back to its 2008 level of RDGP until late 2015. (By contrast, the United States recovered fully by early 2011.) Those arguing for Brexit were quick to label EU policy makers as incompetent.

Immigration laws were set by the European Union and meant that anyone living in it could live and work anywhere else within the Union. This meant that many eastern and southern Europeans were living and working in the United Kingdom, and (at least the perception was that) they were keeping wages in the United Kingdom stagnant.

Finally, the issue of sovereignty was concerning. Business practices were effectively determined by regulators of the European Union stationed in Brussels. Some of the loss of sovereignty was considered necessary while the Cold War (1948–1990) was going on but was an unnecessary intrusion on British life in the post-Cost War era.

Anger reached a peak in 2016 and culminated in a surprising vote by the British people to leave. The reaction was varied. England and Wales had voted in favor of Brexit by healthy margins, but Scotland and Northern Ireland voted against it by even wider margins. The Irish and Northern Irish had only come to terms with their own issues 20 years prior. Their history, involving 30 years of Catholic–Protestant violence (euphemistically referred to in the United Kingdom as "the troubles"), made them keenly sensitive to having an enforced national border cutting across the island.

One immediate result of the Brexit vote was that the prime minister at the time, Dave Cameron, resigned and Teresa May was left with the unenviable task of negotiating an exit. Those negotiations managed to produce an almost unanimous dislike of the elements of her negotiated exit agreement with the EU leadership. Those who wanted completely out of the EU were dismayed that the price of remaining in the free-trade zone of the Union. Specifically, it required them to adhere to regulations produced in Brussels without being able to vote for representatives in Brussels. Those who didn't want to leave the Union in the first place were opposed because they continued to maintain that leaving the EU was a mistake.

If Brexit goes well for the United Kingdom (which is somewhat difficult to imagine), it could spark other countries to pursue an exit as well. If it goes as poorly, as it appears it will, remaining countries may realize that they can't escape the Union.

Summary

From late 2008 through 2012, the United States experienced and made its way through the Great Recession, while Europe stumbled from one economic crisis to the next. At the center of recent European difficulties is the fact that they created a currency, the euro, thereby unifying their monetary systems without unifying their fiscal systems. As a result, whether it was Ireland and Spain with housing-bubble-related crises or Italy and Greece with fiscal crises, the challenge for stronger EU countries was how to save the euro without the tools the United States used to weather the Great Recession. Having managed to keep Greece from exiting the euro zone, the EU was faced with the United Kingdom attempting a Brexit. The 2010s have been a period of great difficulty in Europe.

Quiz Yourself

1. The cause of the European financial crisis had its origins in
   a. the creation of the euro.
   b. vast overspending in Germany.
   c. uncompetitive tax collections in Greece.
   d. speculative home buying in Belgium.
2. One clear benefit to all members of the European Union was that
   a. mutually beneficial trade was made much easier.
   b. it allowed countries to engage in currency manipulation to their own benefit.
   c. it allowed poorer countries to borrow money at lower interest rates.
   d. it made immigration between countries more difficult.
3. The proximate cause of the Spanish problem was
   a. vast overspending during the previous decade.
   b. lax tax collections during the previous decade.
   c. a burst housing bubble.
   d. both *a* and *b*.
4. The proximate cause of the Greek problem was
   a. vast overspending during the previous decade.
   b. lax tax collections during the previous decade.
   c. a burst housing bubble.
   d. both *a* and *b*.
5. The reason the Greeks didn't use a plan similar to TARP to save their banks was that
   a. the Greek Central Bank had no funds.
   b. the interest rates Greece would have had to pay on the loans would have been unaffordable.
   c. banks weren't a problem in Greece.
   d. there was no political will in Greece to borrow that kind of money.
6. The reason the European Central Bank (ECB) didn't initially engage in the kind of expansionary monetary policy that the Federal Reserve did for the United States was that
   a. the ECB didn't view the problem as serious.
   b. the ECB could not raise the capital.
   c. the provisions of the treaty that created the ECB did not allow for it to buy the debt of member nations unless there was systemic risk.
   d. there was no debt for the ECB to buy.
7. The reason the ECB did not want the Greeks to exit the euro was that
   a. Greece was viewed as a valuable member in temporary distress.
   b. Greece was viewed as so unimportant that it did not want the perception that countries were leaving for any reason.
   c. Greece was a founding member, and political friendships were important to the ECB leaders.
   d. Greece was viewed as the first domino in a series of dominos that, if Greece left, it would jeopardize the whole euro system.

Short Answer Questions

1. What should the Maastricht Treaty have included to allow for an adequate response to the various European economic crises?
2. When would be the right time and what would be the correct mechanism for getting a country out of the euro?
3. What would be the problems associated with the ECB being allowed to purchase the debt of member nations?

Think about This

For full integration of the European Union, some argue that the nations should be like states of the United States with the central government having limited and enumerated powers. What would those powers be?

If Greece is analogous to Mississippi (relatively poor) and Germany is analogous to New York (relatively rich), what is present in the United States that makes it relatively easy for Mississippi to be in the same country as New York that is absent that makes it relatively hard for Greece and Germany to imagine themselves in the same country?

Talk about This

The bursting of the housing bubble hit Phoenix and Miami much harder than Dallas/Ft. Worth. Why should the taxpayers of Texas have consented to programs that helped only citizens of Phoenix and Miami? Why, then, should Germans care if the Irish housing bubble caused problems in Ireland?

Behind the Numbers

European Central Bank: www.ecb.europa.eu/stats/html/index.en.html

- GDP growth in EU countries
- Interest rates for EU government debt

Eurostat: ec.europa.eu/eurostat/data/database

- U.S. vs EU per capita GDP
- EU country government debt

Standard & Poors: www.standardandpoors

- Housing prices

CHAPTER TWENTY

Economic Growth and Development

Learning Objectives

After reading this chapter you should be able to:

LO1 Summarize why developed countries tend to grow faster than less developed ones.

LO2 Explain why creating an environment for economic growth in a developing country is a very different and much harder challenge than fostering growth in an already developed country.

LO3 List the legal, political, and institutional factors that have historically limited growth in many developing countries.

Chapter Outline

Economists have been trying to explain economic growth and development for as long as there have been economists. Why, for instance, does a country such as the United States command nearly one-quarter of the world's yearly economic output while having less than 5 percent of the world's population? Why did the United States grow faster than France during the last two decades? Why can't sub-Saharan Africa catch an economic break? Why has politically repressed China grown so rapidly for more than two decades, while India, a democracy for decades, grew much more slowly? Why has South Korea blossomed from a developing country to a developed one? This chapter combines a little bit of macroeconomics, a little bit of international trade, a little of government policy, and frankly, a little bit of guesswork. Economic development is one of the least well-settled areas of economics in part because even the Nobel Prize-winning models perform poorly in explaining why some countries grew and others did not.

Let's start by dividing the question of economic growth and development into two very different questions: Why do already developed countries grow at different rates? Why do underdeveloped countries rarely reach a point where they can emerge from their meager circumstances?

Growth in Developed Countries

If we revisit the aggregate demand–aggregate supply model from Chapter 8, we can begin to consider how developed countries grow. An economy can grow because of sustained increases in aggregate demand but only when there is a simultaneous sustained increase in aggregate supply. To see why, remember the shape of the aggregate supply curve. It starts out flat, begins to slope upward, and finally becomes vertical. If aggregate supply does not grow, then eventually increases in aggregate demand have no impact on real economic growth because sooner or later we will hit the vertical portion of the aggregate supply curve and RGDP growth will stop.

We also learned in Chapter 8 that deflation can be a very dangerous economic circumstance, so without increases in aggregate demand, increases in aggregate supply can conceivably bring a developed economy to a standstill as deflationary pressures diminish people's willingness to buy big-ticket items. This implies that long-term economic growth results from increases in aggregate demand and sustained increases in aggregate supply.

What fosters increases in aggregate demand? Again Chapter 8 gives us a clue, but a deceptive one. If we just look at the determinants of aggregate demand and what might be done to increase it, we note we can increase government spending, increase business and consumer confidence, decrease interest rates, decrease taxes, or weaken the dollar. As Figure 20.1 indicates, each will have the desired impact. The problem is you cannot do these in a sustained fashion.

First, we cannot continually decrease interest rates or taxes. Zero is an absolute minimum for each. We cannot continually increase government spending or eventually deficits will increase interest rates. Consumer confidence is unlikely to grow continually as it is almost always influenced by factors beyond anyone's control. This leads us to the conclusion that the ultimate determinant of economic growth in developed countries is likely to come from the aggregate supply side. Increases in aggregate demand simply help sustain such growth.

What fosters increases in aggregate supply? Government regulation can't continuously decrease and neither can wages or other input prices. However, worker productivity can continue to increase. Workers, aligned with the right machines and technology, can always produce more than they produced the previous year if they work smarter, better, and more efficiently. When they do, we see the results shown in Figure 20.2: more output and lower prices.

Note that the word "harder" was not on the previous list of ways to increase productivity over the long run. People can work harder, but at some point, human endurance reaches a maximum. Getting more output from workers usually requires providing them with the education, tools, and technology.

Therefore, the economy can grow or contract in the short run for a variety of reasons mostly due to changes in aggregate demand, but the ultimate source of long-term growth in developed countries is increases in worker productivity. Remember, that this does not mean that workers must work longer hours, that they must work at a faster pace, or that we need bosses intolerant of anything but the bottom line. Long-run, sustainable increases in worker productivity usually come about because of an increase in the education of workers and an improvement in the tools with which they work.

What feeds the worker productivity engine? Worker productivity is driven by policies that contribute to long-term capital formation and worker education and training. If saving is discouraged and consumption is encouraged beyond that which is sustainable, there is not a plentiful supply of loanable funds. If the benefits from saving money are exorbitantly taxed, then the motivation to save money is diminished. Growth requires a healthy capital market on the demand side as well. This means that rates of taxation on the gains from that capital must be at levels so that after-tax returns to businesses are sufficiently motivating for investment. A developed and motivated workforce is also a prerequisite to economic growth. Workers must be motivated to get the right amount of education and to then productively apply that

FIGURE 20.1 Increases in aggregate demand.

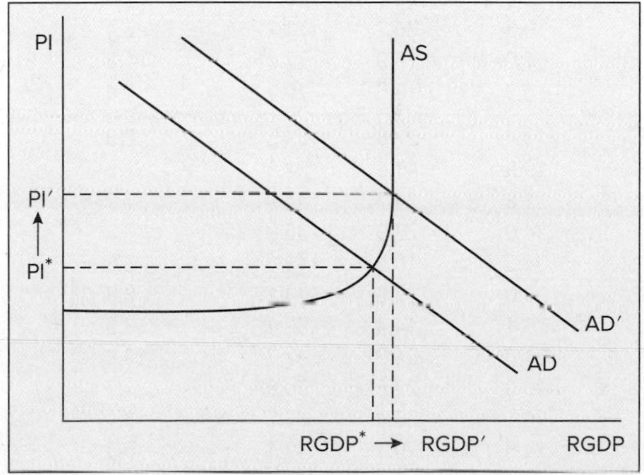

FIGURE 20.2 Increases in aggregate supply.

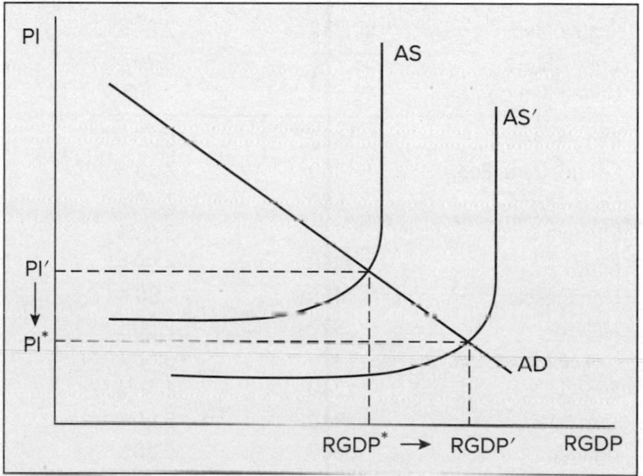

education in the workforce. With moderate marginal tax rates, rates of interest and inflation, reasonable regulatory policies, a sound education system, and a sound welfare system that does not overly compensate the unemployed, developed economies will continue to grow.

Comparing Developed and Developing Countries

Besides the obvious, income, what is different about rich and poor countries? Table 20.1 brings this all into stark relief. The countries listed on the top of the table have per capita gross national income (GNI)[1] of more than $20,000, while the countries at the bottom of the table have per capita GNI of less than $2,000. There are other stark differences that appear on this table. While those at the top of the table generally have a large "middle class," those at the bottom do not. The **Gini index,** a measure of overall income disparity, is generally higher in poorer countries than in richer ones. Those at the top of the table have very little of their GNI coming from agriculture and a significant portion coming from services, while those at the bottom experience the reverse. If you go all the way back to Chapter 2's reference to the Heritage Foundation's Index of Economic Freedom, you will also note that those at the top also tend to be the most economically free, while those at the bottom tend to be classified as the most unfree.

Gini index
A measure of overall income disparity.

[1]Gross national income modifies gross domestic product by adding in income earned abroad and makes other relatively small adjustments. For the most part, GNI is a better measure for comparing incomes across development categories.

Table 20.1 International comparisons.

Source: The World Bank DataBank, http://databank.worldbank.org.

Country Name	2017 Gross National Income per Capita (PPP)	1990–2017 Annualized Rate of per Capita GNI Growth	Distribution of Family Income—Gini Index	GDP—Composition by Sector			Inflation Rate (consumer prices) 2017
				Agriculture	Industry	Services	
Australia	51,360	3.90%	34.7	2.8	23.0	67.0	3.7
Belgium	41,790	2.80%	27.7	0.6	19.8	68.8	1.7
Canada	42,870	2.70%	34.0				2.3
France	37,970	2.20%	32.7	1.5	17.4	70.2	1.0
Germany	43,490	2.50%	27.0	0.6	27.6	61.9	1.5
Greece	18,090	0.59%	31.7	3.5	14.8	68.9	0.7
Japan	38,550	1.10%	32.1	1.2	29.3	68.8	−0.2
Korea, Rep.	28,380	5.50%	30.2	2.0	35.9	52.8	2.3
Netherlands	46,180	3.00%	28.2	1.9	17.5	70.4	1.1
Singapore	54,530	3.53%	*	0.0	23.2	70.4	0.9
Spain	27,180	2.90%	36.2	2.6	21.6	66.4	1.0
Switzerland	80,560	2.80%	32.3	0.6	25.2	71.2	0.4
United States	58,270	3.20%	41.5	1.0	18.9	77.0	1.8
United Kingdom	40,530	2.90%	33.2	0.5	18.6	70.1	2.0
Bangladesh	1470	5.70%	32.4	13.4	27.8	53.5	6.3
Congo, Dem. Rep.	460	−2.38%		19.9	41.6	34.1	-2.5
Cote d'Ivoire	1580	2.70%	41.5	21.6	24.7	44.9	-1.7
Ethiopia	740	3.80%	39.1	34.0	22.9	36.9	6.3
Kenya	1460	4.90%	40.8	34.6	16.5	43.6	8.6
Madagascar	400	1.80%	47.5	20.0	22.6	44.1	8.3
Malawi	320	2.00%	39.0	26.1	14.4	52.4	13.5
Mozambique	420	3.00%	45.6	21.3	24.9	47.7	12.9
Senegal	1240	1.10%	40.3	16.0	22.6	50.9	1.7
Tanzania	910	5.50%	37.6	30.1	26.4	37.5	5.1
Uganda	600	2.20%	39.5	24.6	20.3	47.1	6.3

There is also an accounting issue that we need to discuss. In Chapter 6, we noted that RGDP and social welfare are not synonymous. One of the reasons that is true is the existence of the underground economy. Though the primary example in that discussion was the United States, consider the notion of the underground economy in a developing country like Ethiopia. While many people in the United States engage in a little "cash-on-the-side" business (lawn mowing, babysitting, illegal drug dealing) where the efforts are not counted, many people in Ethiopia make their own clothing, grow or raise their own food, and trade one good or service for another. As a result, whereas the underground economy is 10 percent of the U.S. production, as much as half a developing country's economy can be in nonmarket transactions. This is why the comparable figures for each country shown in Table 20.1 are adjusted using the notion of **purchasing power parity.** Economists have estimated what it costs to purchase a similar market basket of goods and services in each country and used that to estimate GNI.

purchasing power parity
Using the cost of a similar market basket of goods across countries to compare an economic variable like gross national income.

Fostering (and Inhibiting) Development

Modern models of economic development, like the Solow Growth Model, named after its Nobel Prize-winning author, provided the basis for much discussion on the subject of how economies would grow. The central prediction of that model, and of many others that it spawned, was that economies would converge in their levels of economic development. That is, poor countries would grow faster than rich ones to the point where levels of per capita GDP would not differ substantially. Even a brief look at Table 20.1 shows that this has not been the case.[2]

The remainder of this chapter will focus on how a country might move from below the line in Table 20.1 to above it and what might prevent it from doing so. First, we need to appreciate that the challenges for policy makers in developing countries are substantially different and often substantially more difficult than the challenges of developed countries. Those at the top of the table attempt to use sound fiscal, monetary, and regulatory policies within an overarching democratic political structure to foster long-term increases in labor productivity; low levels of inflation; moderate levels of taxation; and reasonable labor, safety, and environmental regulations. That is difficult enough, but all too often, policy makers in countries at the bottom of the table don't typically have a political, governmental, or banking structure to do any of these things. Furthermore, they are faced with choices that go beyond simply future consumption versus present consumption, but of future consumption versus present survival.

[2]That is not to say that these models are without value. They provided the basis for much of what we know about economic development, but in all honesty, this is an area of economics for which little consensus exists.

The Challenges Facing Developing Countries

To see why developing countries face such challenges, put yourself in the position of an open-minded company manager with a decision to make. Do you locate a manufacturing facility in a developed or a developing country? Your goal, of course, would be to bring as much profit to your stockholders as possible. You would probably be enticed by the low cost of labor and land in the developing country. Hourly wages in developed countries are almost always 5 to 10 times higher and, at times, 20 to 100 times higher than those in a developing one. On the other hand, you would also have to recognize the potential pitfalls detailed in subsequent sections.

Low Rates of Basic Literacy

It's hard to find a quality labor force in a developing country because, though wages are low, the typical resident has little formal education. They may not be able to read or do rudimentary mathematics. Without the basic ability to follow written instructions, the workers in the developing country may need to be managed much more closely than workers who can read and follow instructions.

Lack of Infrastructure

Second, even if you can adapt your production processes to take advantage of the low-skill, low-wage workers, you still do not have the basic financial, physical, or legal infrastructure in place to maintain it. Local banks are necessary for access to credit, and to transmit profits out of the country. They may not exist or may be constrained in their ability to provide the financial services necessary for your business. Roads, bridges, rail lines, and ports are all necessary to transmit goods around the country and around the world. Without the ability to quickly move your finished products to the rest of the world, any cost advantage you had in wages might evaporate because of your inability to move your products. Finally, legal protections are necessary for the owners of invested property. Whether those protections are based on social conventions, law enforcement, or trustworthy governments, a social infrastructure protecting investments is necessary for those investments to occur.

Political Instability

Trustworthy governments are hard to find in the developing world. This can be because these governments are all too often corrupt, unstable, or both. Take Nigeria, for example. Sitting on one of the largest deposits of oil in the world, its long-standing civil war has prevented it from taking ultimate advantage of its resource. You may be able to get low-wage labor to get the oil out of the ground, but you have to pay bribes to the various warring factions to avoid having your equipment stolen, damaged, or destroyed, and you have to worry about your skilled engineers being kidnapped. Do you locate there or do you attempt to make your money elsewhere?

Corruption

Even when a government is stable, the concern that the political leadership will simply take invested property is paramount. Take Uzbekistan, for example. It is also sitting on significant oil and natural gas reserves, but its political leadership is so corrupt that you never know from one year to the next whether the leadership will nationalize those assets. Countries such as these have a culture that expects and accepts this type of corruption. Managers coming from the cultures of developed economies are not, for the most part, comfortable investing in countries where bribery is common or expected.

Lack of Independent Central Banking

If you look at the list of countries on the top of Table 20.1 and compare them with those at the bottom, you will note that the United States, Europe, and the economically successful countries of East Asia all have systems in place to control inflation. As described in Chapter 10, each has a central bank that sets interest rate policies, and in each case, there is a degree of central bank independence from political control. In developing countries, these banks are not only not independent, in some cases they do not exist. That means that when there is a central bank, it is often under the control of the ruling party, king, general, or junta. When no central bank exists, banking crises are common. In fact, the United States was without a functional central bank for much of the 1800s and experienced several banking crises.

Without an independent central bank in a developing country, when its ruler wants to print money to build a new palace or to pay soldiers for protection, he or she can and will. There are many examples of independent central bankers fighting inflation at the expense of an elected leader's popularity. Leaders in countries with democratic traditions and independent central banks understand that the long-term effect of fighting inflation is far more important than the short-term benefit that is gained from being able to spend newly printed money.

Inability to Repatriate Profits

Your ability to move money out of a country can also be limited by government policies. In many developing countries, you can bring as much **hard currency** (a term used to describe currencies like the dollar, euro, yen, and pound whose value remains predictable) into the country as you wish, but you cannot reverse the transaction as easily. So, if you were making a profit in the currency of the host country, you may not be able to convert that into hard currency. This is less of a problem if you are manufacturing in a developing country for sale in a developed country, but it is a problem if you are selling goods in the developing country and wishing to turn those profits into hard currency. Knowing that, you may be less likely to invest in the developing country.

hard currency
A term used to describe currencies like the dollar, euro, yen, and pound whose value remains predictable.

A Need to Focus on the Basics

Developing countries, especially the ones listed in the bottom half of Table 20.1, must focus on the very basic necessities of life. Even a well-meaning government would have a difficult time choosing between expending resources on education, health care, or food. The opportunity cost of extra spending on making education more widely available could well be a lack of adequate food or health care for others. With so many people engaged in subsistence agriculture, with so little capital with which to work, and with live births per adult woman above five, these countries are not in a position to invest in their future because their present is so bleak.

In addition, health concerns in these countries can be overwhelming. The countries on the bottom of Table 20.1 are predominantly in sub-Saharan Africa. These countries have been ravaged by HIV/AIDS to such a degree that notions of long-term economic development have become secondary to survival.

What Works

The best examples of countries rising above their 1960s economic status to become newly developed countries are the countries of East Asia. China and South Korea, in particular, have grown at a rather brisk pace for very long. Both got to their present position in different ways. South Korea's success economically coincided with its liberalization politically, while China's success occurred while it was relatively unfree politically. It is not just about natural resources either. Though Saudi Arabia and Kuwait have grown almost entirely as a result of enormous oil wealth, Japan's growth through the 1970s and 1980s was despite the fact that it has no natural resources upon which to capitalize.

The basic building blocks for what fosters economic growth tend to begin with education, a low or manageable level of government corruption, and a level of political and financial stability that create confidence among foreign investors. Countries that have grown have created political and financial stability, physical and social infrastructures that generate confidence, and predictable, if not democratic, governments. South Korea's economy continues to grow because its government and central bank reaction to the late 1990s Asian financial crisis created confidence among investors that their banking system could adapt to challenges. The Chinese economy started slowing substantially when investors began to doubt that the government would ultimately respect their intellectual property and let them repatriate profits.

Summary

You now understand that economic growth in developed countries is mostly a function of their ability to increase worker productivity and that economic growth in developing countries is often hampered by the lack of social, political, financial, legal, and economic institutions that are prerequisite to economic growth. You recognize the magnitude of the gap between developed and developing countries and that the countries that have moved from developing to developed did so in different ways.

Key Terms

Gini index

Hard currency

Purchasing power parity

Quiz Yourself

1. For developed economies, sustained increases in aggregate demand, absent increases in aggregate supply, will result in
   a. growth for a while, but ultimately, they will result in only inflation.
   b. continuous economic growth.
   c. deflationary risks.
   d. a boom and bust cycle.
2. For developing economies, sustained increases in aggregate demand, absent increases in aggregate supply, will result in
   a. growth for a while, but ultimately, they will result in only inflation.
   b. continuous economic growth.
   c. deflationary risks.
   d. a boom and bust cycle.
3. In order to sustain economic growth in a developed economy, it is important for
   a. taxes to continuously decrease.
   b. government spending to continually increase.
   c. worker productivity to increase.
   d. worker productivity to decrease.
4. One of the biggest problems for developing countries is that they all too often
   a. are ruled by representative democracies.
   b. are populated by people unwilling to work hard.
   c. lack the financial, physical, and social infrastructure to grow.
   d. indulge in wasteful consumption.

5. For the ruler of a developing country, the opportunity cost of a choice to invest in universal education
   a. is the reduction in health care spending.
   b. does not exist because food is a necessity.
   c. is much lower than a similar choice for the ruler of a developed country.
   d. cannot be measured.
6. Which advantage does a typical developing country have in attempting to draw foreign investment?
   a. Very low wages
   b. Poor education
   c. Easy profit repatriation
   d. Independent central banks

Short Answer Questions

1. What does Mexico have to do in order to grow economically? What does Germany need to do to grow economically? Why are those likely to be different answers?
2. What is the long-term consequence to U.S. economic growth of having an education system that lags behind that of other countries?
3. What issues will China face if it wants to continue to grow?

Think about This

Go to the CIA Factbook web pages cited below and explore the economic statistics of the following countries: Brazil, Egypt, India, Malaysia, and South Africa. Each has a per capita GDP between $3,000 and $15,000 per year. What country in that list do you believe is most likely to move into the class of "developed" countries? That is, which is likely to have its per capita GDP rise the fastest and why?

Talk about This

Suppose you had to decide whether or not to invest in formal education for the masses, but the opportunity cost of doing so was reducing health expenditures for the sick and aged. What choice would you make?

CHAPTER TWENTY-ONE

Are Trade Agreements Good for Us?

Learning Objectives

After reading this chapter you should be able to:

- LO1 Conclude that economists generally believe free trade is better than restricted trade.
- LO2 Show how trade agreements facilitate the opening of trade and why such agreements are sometimes necessary.
- LO3 Describe the function of trade agreements and institutions.
- LO4 Evaluate whether trade agreements are working as advertised.
- LO5 Enumerate the economic and political concerns that free-trade agreements generate.
- LO6 Conclude that, for most economists, trade agreements are good policy.

Chapter Outline

One of the few things Republican and Democratic administrations from the 1980s to 2016 agreed upon was that free trade was good for the United States. The 2016 election of President Trump marked a change in that philosophy. This chapter describes the institutions of free trade created during the previous administrations and summarizes the Trump administration's policies toward them.

NAFTA
North American Free Trade Agreement involving the United States, Mexico, and Canada.

CAFTA
The Central America Free Trade Agreement involving the United States and five Central American countries: Costa Rica, El Salvador, Guatemala, Honduras, and Nicaragua.

Previous administrations based their free-trade reasoning on the grounds that Americans would routinely outcompete their international trade partners. The logic was that jobs that were gained and the increases in living standards from such trade would outweigh any losses. The foundation for this argument relies heavily on the theory of international trade that we addressed in Chapter 17.

GATT
General Agreement on Tariffs and Trade, a world trade agreement.

WTO
The World Trade Organization, an institution that arbitrates trade disputes.

NAFTA, the North American Free Trade Agreement; **CAFTA,** the Central America Free Trade Agreement; **GATT,** the General Agreement on Tariffs and Trade; and the **WTO,** the World Trade Organization, are the spearheads of pre-Trump trade policy. The TPP, Trans-Pacific Partnership, was an agreement among 12 countries (including the United States). President Trump, fulfilling a campaign promise, ended U.S. participation. The other 11 countries remain in the agreement. This chapter explains the purposes of each agreement and reviews the arguments for and against them. As a first step, we summarize the theoretical argument for free trade. We then explicate some of the details of the agreements. Finally, we examine the effect of these agreements on trade, income inequality, workers' wages, and environmental health.

The Benefits of Free Trade

The economic benefits from trade are so often assumed to be obvious that economists do not feel the need to explain them. Most noneconomists, however, assume that trade is a zero-sum game that can be characterized by the phrase "your win is my loss." Nothing could misrepresent trade more thoroughly. Nowhere in the field of economics is there such a discrepancy between what economists know and what noneconomists consider to be the conventional wisdom. If the explanation that follows does not present the economists' argument on the benefits of international trade in sufficient detail, you will find additional information in Chapter 17, which covers international trade.

Suppose that the United States and Mexico are the only countries in the world and that they produce only two goods: low-tech (LT) and high-tech (HT). Further, suppose that U.S. workers can make both LT and HT more quickly and in greater numbers than Mexican workers. Why would the United States want to trade with Mexico when it can produce both goods itself? To see the possibilities, assume that workers in the United States and Mexico are divided between high skill and low skill and that everyone is fully employed in both countries. To see how effective they are, assume that Table 21.1 represents the number of workers needed to produce specific amounts of each good in each country.

Table 21.1 shows that it takes one high-skill U.S. worker to make one HT good, that one high-skill Mexican worker can produce three LT goods, and so on. The suggestion here is that high-skill workers in the United States are more proficient than anyone else at all forms of production and that Mexican low-skill workers are less proficient across the board. The low-skill American worker is assumed to be better at HT production than the high-skill Mexican worker (perhaps because the American is working with better machines), but the two are equal in LT production.

If 100 American low-skill workers were to shift from the production of LT to the production of HT and 120 Mexican workers were to shift from HT to LT, then there would be 50 more HT goods and 300 fewer LT goods produced in the United States. In Mexico, there would be 40 fewer HT goods and 360 more LT goods produced. The world (limited in this case to the United States and Mexico) would have a net addition of 10 HT goods and 60 LT goods. Given a fair distribution of these gains from trade, each side would be better off.

As a result of the increased competition from Mexican LT firms, the workers in LT firms in the United States would lose their jobs. They would quickly get new jobs in the HT firms, however, as increased demand for American HT goods increases demand for laborers capable of such production. While there are more than a few places where the argument that trade is good for all can be criticized, it remains the basic position of economists. Most economists are convinced that trade provides increased standards of living and regardless of how many workers are displaced, they will always be absorbed into the growing industries.

Why Do We Need Trade Agreements?

You may instinctively distrust this economists' view of trade. You may be asking, "If free trade is so good, why do we need agreements to keep it in place?" The answer is twofold: one economic, the other political.

Strategic Trade

Strategic trade policies are policies designed to get more of the benefits from trade in a country than would exist under free trade. On the economic front, there are circumstances under which a country can increase its share of free-trade

strategic trade policies Policies designed to get more of the benefits from trade in a country than would exist under free trade.

Table 21.1 Production of workers: number of workers needed to produce a number of goods.

Source: U.S. Census Bureau, www.census.gov/foreign-trade/statistics/index.html.

	High Tech		Low Tech	
	High Skill	Low Skill	High Skill	Low Skill
United States	1 produces 1	2 produce 1	1 produces 4	1 produces 3
Mexico	3 produce 1	4 produce 1	1 produces 3	1 produces 1

benefits. That is, a country can increase its benefits from trade by implementing tariffs, quotas, and the like; if it does, however, the sum of the benefits from trade to the two trading partners deteriorates.

Although the circumstances under which strategic trade is better for a country than free trade are somewhat complicated, one example might shed some light. Suppose a large country is the dominant world player in the production of a particular good and another large country is a much smaller player. The monopoly power of the large company can overwhelm the other country's small company. Economists have shown that, at least theoretically, the country with the small company can subsidize its exports and increase its profits by more than the subsidy. The typical example of this has been the Boeing–Airbus competition in the manufacture of large aircraft. In practical terms, Airbus's subsidy from France and Britain has been greater than its profits.

The Chapter 1 idea of the fallacy of composition can be employed here. If an action makes the person who takes it better off, it is not necessarily true that everyone would be better off taking the action.

Special Interests

Whenever there is trade, there are individuals who see themselves as the losers. Typically, these are the folks who are the most visible. When a plant closes in an American town to move production to a facility in another country, the job losses from trade are obvious for all to see. The jobs created by trade are more difficult for the average worker to see. As a result, workers left with pink slips become vocal opponents of trade, and those who benefit from it do not attribute that benefit to trade. This is because workers do not always know where the goods they are producing are sold.

An even greater political problem occurs if the loser from trade has sufficient political strength to convince elected officials that restricting trade is in the officeholders' electoral interest. Again, because many of the beneficiaries of free trade—consumers paying lower prices and workers having better jobs—do not see these gains as attributable to trade, they are far less vocal in favor of trade. There are two groups whose voices are typically raised in favor of trade, business interests and farmers. As a result, it appears to the political world as though free trade is a battle between workers on one side and big business and farmers on the other. In such a circumstance, though free trade is rather obviously the better outcome to economists, it is not so obvious to elected officials.

What Trade Agreements Prevent

To see how misplaced self-interest can lead to a deterioration of trade benefits, let's return to our hypothetical example of trade between Mexico and the United States. If the low-skill, LT workers in the United States fear that trade will cost their jobs, they can seek a **tariff** (a tax on imports) or a **quota** (a limit on imports) from the U.S. government. Each would raise the price of imported goods, and the former would bring tax revenue to the U.S. government. If Mexico does not retaliate by levying its own tariffs or quotas, our exports of HT goods will remain unchanged. This will be good for the United States. However, it will be less good for the United States than it is bad for Mexico. Importantly, though, it will be worse for the world as a whole. If Mexico does retaliate, it can make itself better off than if it does not retaliate. It will do so with tariffs or quotas of its own. Again, the degree to which Mexico will make itself better off is outweighed by the damage done to the United States, which will retaliate further. Soon there will be no gains from trade because there will be no trade.

tariff
A tax on imports.

quota
A limit on imports.

Trade agreements prevent countries from starting on the slippery slope of trade retaliation. Because a country is better off with free trade than with no trade, free trade wins. The problem is that countries will always be tempted to raise some barriers in hopes that no one will retaliate. When countries get into a tariff war and retaliation is met with more retaliation, not only are any small advantages lost, but all other advantages from trade are lost. Countries thus need trade agreements to keep themselves from the temptation of creating trade barriers.

The history and politics of trade are somewhat strange. The first Republican president, Abraham Lincoln, ran for his first U.S. House seat on a platform that called for high tariffs. Such protectionist trade policy was a staple of Republican political philosophy, and it was exemplified by the disastrous Smoot–Hawley tariff law of the 1930s. Not until the 1950s did Republicans begin to change and to embrace free trade, and they did so because their constituents in business argued that they could be more profitable with trade. During the same time, Democrats, the party most identified with labor unions, switched from being the free-trade party to the protectionist party, and they did so because the unions saw trade hurting their members. In 1993, Democratic president Bill Clinton started to move his party back to a free-trade position just as some Republicans were moving back to their traditional protectionist position. In 2005, most Democrats in Congress remained sympathetic to the protectionist concerns of labor and most Republicans remained free traders. It was in this context that President George W. Bush brought the CAFTA to Congress with a goal of spreading the idea of free trade throughout the Americas. It passed by only one vote. The election of President Trump created a significant split within the Republican party on trade. Whether this disruption is permanent or fleeting remains to be seen.

Trade Agreements and Institutions

Alphabet Soup

The North American Free Trade Agreement, NAFTA, was first proposed by President Ronald Reagan, negotiated by President George Bush (George Herbert Walker), and, after being amended, pushed through Congress and signed by President Bill Clinton. It created a geographical area of free trade in which the United States, Canada, and Mexico agreed to (1) very low tariffs and (2) procedures whereby some tariffs could remain in place. An important element in the agreement was a formalized grievance process whereby disputes could be discussed.

The General Agreement on Tariffs and Trade, GATT, is another agreement negotiated across the terms of many presidents. GATT established the conditions under which signatory nations could set tariffs and quotas. GATT came into existence just after World War II, but its most recent version, the Uruguay Round, has had the greatest free-trade focus. Even under stretched definitions, GATT cannot be called a free-trade agreement, but it has moved nations in that direction. In reality, it simply makes the rules for tariffs and retaliation more explicit.

The rules of GATT require that retaliation be proportional. When in 1999, for example, much of western Europe gave favorable treatment in banana sales to its former colonies, the United States, at the behest of major fruit companies like Dole, retaliated by threatening a tariff on European leather goods. Although the connection between bananas and purses is tenuous, it was deemed acceptable retaliation under GATT. It makes sense under GATT because the trade in question is roughly the same. In operational terms, GATT is an agreement that says "there are ways you can impose tariffs and other ways you cannot impose them."

The Uruguay Round also took up the issue of intellectual property rights and restrictions. Prior to the 1990s, the laws of China, South Korea, and other Asian nations had not recognized the right of people to own ideas the way that copyright and patent laws allowed them to in Western countries. They engaged in copying and selling copyrighted materials like CDs, books, and computer software with impunity. In addition, much to the dismay of the U.S. government and the industries whose markets were affected, many nations whose television and movie industries were unable to compete with Hollywood limited the importing of American shows and movies.

On the issue of copyright infringement, Asian governments promised a crackdown on entrepreneurs' openly making and selling copies of widely distributed music and software CDs. At one time, there were more illegal than legal copies of Windows in China. It was the position of the United States that this represented a theft from American artists, producers, record companies, and software producers and, as such, it should be banned. On this issue, GATT recognized copyright infringement as an area worthy of tariff retaliation.

Another priority for the United States was the distribution of American-made movies and television shows. The American entertainment industry sells its output throughout the world. Many countries, however, have "domestic content" rules that require at least a certain percentage of all movies shown in a theater and programs shown on television be produced (1) in the home country and (2) with domestic actors. The United States objects to these rules because they have the effect of limiting U.S. exports. Even though movies and television programs represent an important area of American export, the final negotiations leading up to the conclusion of the Uruguay Round of GATT in 1997 did not ultimately resolve this issue in favor of the United States.

One aspect of GATT that was resolved in a manner favorable to the United States was the power given to the WTO. Until 1997, trade disputes involving countries reverted to no more than "yes, it is fair" versus "no, it is not fair" conflicts. There were no institutions charged with the task of finding the truth in such disputes. The WTO's job is now to resolve those disputes. Although the WTO has no greater power than to suggest who is in the right and who is not, it is hoped that complaints with and without merit will be separated and that disputes will be resolved more easily.

Are They Working?

From the outcomes of NAFTA, GATT, and the WTO, it is hard to tell which side of the argument over trade agreements was more wrong in its predictions. While trade has grown rapidly among the United States, Canada, and Mexico after NAFTA, it had grown rapidly before NAFTA. While some jobs were lost as firms left to go to Mexico, the overall economy created more jobs in a shorter period than at any time in U.S. history. So, what was the impact of these agreements?

Take a look at Figure 21.1. In inflation-adjusted terms, exports to, and imports from, both Canada and Mexico are at or near all-time highs. Whether NAFTA had anything to do with these increases is the question. To investigate that, let's compare annualized inflation-adjusted rates of growth in trade among the United States, Canada, and Mexico and compare those to similar rates for trade in general. From Table 21.2, we see that inflation-adjusted exports to Mexico were rising at 10.2 percent per year prior to NAFTA and rose at 12.9 percent immediately after NAFTA. Subsequently, exports to Mexico and imports from Mexico have been rising at a somewhat faster rate than they have been for the United States with the entire world. The experience with Canadian trade is different. Both exports and imports grew at slower rates after NAFTA than prior to it. All trade, and in particular trade within NAFTA, was significantly altered by the 2007–2009 recession.

It is also worth noting that it was not until 2011 that NAFTA was fully implemented. The last piece hinged on whether Mexican truckers, driving Mexican-licensed trucks would be allowed on U.S. highways. Though Canadian trucks were allowed to drive on American roads, it had not been the case that Mexican trucks were afforded the same right. The concern among the trucking industry and its main union, the Teamsters, was that they would be forced to compete with companies paying their drivers much less than union wages. While that concern was not dealt with, President Obama established regulations to hold the Mexican trucks themselves to the same safety and inspection standards as U.S. trucks.

The impact that NAFTA has had on jobs is also in dispute. The NAFTA Transitional Adjustment Assistance Program was enacted to provide for retraining benefits as a result of NAFTA-induced job losses. The degree to which this was needed was hotly debated at the time. Two

FIGURE 21.1 NAFTA trade.

Source: U.S. Census Bureau. https://www.census.gov/foreign-trade/balance/index.html

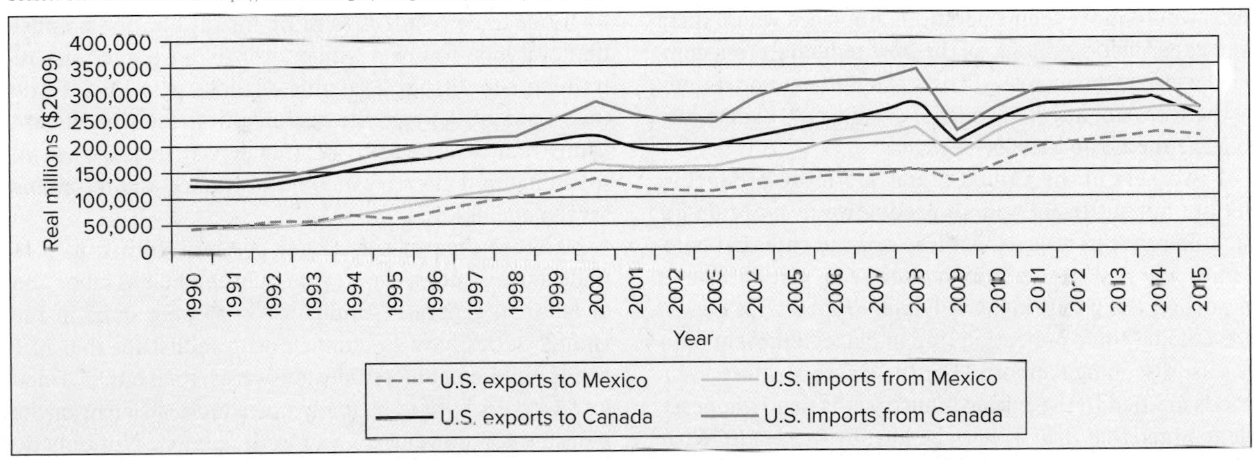

Table 21.2 Percentage of annual real growth rates of U.S. exports and imports, Canada, Mexico, and world.

Source: U.S. Census Bureau. https://www.census.gov/foreign-trade/balance/index.html

	1990 to 1994	1995 to 1998	1999 to 2007	2008 to 2015
U.S. exports to Mexico	10.2%	12.9%	2.7%	3.7%
U.S. imports from Mexico	8.2	9.8	5.0	6.8
U.S. exports to Canada	4.3	4.1	2.1	3.0
U.S. imports from Canada	4.9	3.5	3.2	3.8
U.S. total exports	3.5	2.9	3.6	4.9
U.S. total imports	3.3	4.1	4.9	6.7

economists, Gary Hufbauer and Jeffery Schott, estimated the impact in 2005 to be slightly positive. The Economic Policy Institute (EPI) estimated that though 1 million jobs were created as a result of the rising exports, 2 million were lost due to more rapidly rising imports. The EPI estimated that this caused a $7.6 billion net drag on employee wages with the hardest hit states being in the industrial Midwest.

Economic and Political Impacts of Trade

Of much greater concern to those objecting to free-trade agreements than its effects on trade in general is its impact on workers' wages, wage inequality, labor treatment in general, and the environment. Before we discuss whether worries about these variables have been borne out as a result of the trade pacts we have been discussing, it will be useful to look at them individually to explain the specific concerns.

Average manufacturing wages in the United States are substantially higher than those in Mexico, Canada, and nearly every other nation. If the productivity of workers were the same worldwide, you would expect that corporations would move their operations to places where there is cheaper labor. As long as the cost reduction to a company exceeds the increased costs of shipment and as long as there are not any trade barriers, you would expect jobs to leave the United States.

If workers in the United States are more productive but are not sufficiently more productive to make up for the difference in wages, then it is still the case that companies will make more money producing elsewhere and importing the goods into the United States. This can be prevented if trade protections are in place to prevent or to at least discourage imports. For the workers whose livelihoods are tied to the exiting industry, it is nearly impossible to argue that they will not be hurt by free trade. What advocates of free trade suggest is that there are enough gains from trade to finance a retraining program for workers who are displaced.

We need only to look at the number of workers and the quantity of imports in certain industries to get an idea of the magnitude of worker displacement that is involved. Since 1960, millions of jobs associated with the production of cars, car parts, steel, electronics, apparel, and textiles have lost to imports. Unfortunately, these industries (with the exception of textiles) provided the best paying low- to semi-skilled jobs during the 1960s through the 1970s, and their loss contributed to one of the main problems of the second half of the 20th century, the lack of employment prospects for people without a college education.[1] Using the CPI, real wages for production workers in the United States have fallen since 1970,[2] while wages for high-skill workers increased. This increasing gap between the haves and the have-nots has increased the tension concerning trade tremendously.

Free trade benefits workers only if they keep their jobs. By and large, the educated have kept their jobs and even gotten better ones. For such people, the prices of goods they purchase are cheaper than they would be if they were produced in the United States, and, with jobs that pay well, they have enjoyed a sharp increase in their standard of living. Many people who have lost their jobs, in comparison, have found new ones, but the new ones do not allow them to maintain their previous standard of living. The collective loss of steel production in Pennsylvania, auto production in the Midwest, and electronics production throughout the United States has seriously lessened the number of high-paying jobs. It is therefore not surprising that professionals and some highly educated people are in favor of free trade and that people who have been hurt by it, frequently those without a college education, are against it.

If our trade policy is to move forward on the premise that everyone can be a winner, we will have to ensure retraining benefits are available to those who lose. To do this, some of the benefits accruing to those who benefit from trade will need to be transferred in the form of spending on temporary income assistance and retraining for the unemployed.

Another area of significant concern with regard to trade agreements is the treatment both of child labor and of labor in general. If industries that were once in the United States have to compete with industries that hire young children at incredibly low wages, then either American workers have to be many times more efficient or the industry will move to a lower-wage country. Not only do many Americans consider child labor immoral, but they think anything that promotes its existence is immoral as well. If they perceive free trade as responsible for promoting child labor, they may very well consider free trade itself to be immoral.

It is not just the treatment of children that is of concern. Labor costs are kept down in impoverished

[1] The extent to which trade exacerbates this is debated because this trend may have been inevitable.

[2] This is accurate unless you modify the CPI as suggested in Chapter 6, in which case the real wages for production workers have risen slightly.

countries in large part because workers fear losing even a bad job. The concentration of wealth is so great among the few people who control the industries that employers can get away with threatening workers with an inability to work anywhere. The employers collude to keep wages low. Workers have few rights and, even if they have legal rights, they are unwilling to invoke them against an employer for fear that they will lose the job they have. Such fundamental rights as freedom from physical torture, breaks for regular meals or bathroom visits, a 40-hour workweek, and collective bargaining are but dreams to many of the world's workforce.

Free trade gives countries with such a lack of workers' rights a competitive advantage against American and European firms. That is because they must pay higher wages and accord workers better rights. To compete, these Western firms must have efficiencies that their competitors cannot achieve with a poorly trained workforce. This is not difficult for high-skill areas such as software development, but it is nearly impossible for textile and apparel production. When a job takes very little skill or is not intellectually challenging, then a poorly treated, poorly trained, or poorly paid worker can compete. It is only when the job requires complex thinking that workers who are well treated, highly trained, and well paid are going to outproduce the poorly treated, poorly trained, and poorly paid by enough to justify those who hire them keeping production in the United States.

A last area where free-trade agreements are criticized is the environment. The maquiladoras, concentrations of industries on the Mexican side of the border with the United States, produce some of the most toxic substances in the world. Those toxic substances are produced wherever the manufacturing takes place, but their handling, an important factor, differs. For instance, in the United States, the wastewater from these manufacturing plants would have to be cleaned to a near-drinkable standard. In Mexico, however, less than 10 percent of industrial wastewater is treated with that degree of stringency. This is an obvious example of how the comparative advantage gained and exploited through free trade is not wanted or good. Since much of the waste travels along the Rio Grande and affects Texans directly, it would be better for them if production were in the States, even though it would cost more.

Free-trade agreements can deal with these issues. Whereas it is impossible to impose U.S. labor and environmental standards on other countries, it is possible to set forth principles in the accords that require that the less-developed countries continually increase standards in designated areas. Although neither NAFTA nor CAFTA does all of this, they do work toward that end. And GATT, while less strict than either NAFTA or CAFTA, also requires that signatories adhere to the international treaties on labor rights that they have already signed.

The election of President Trump in 2016 upended an established consensus among economists that free-trade agreements were a goal worth pursuing. He threatened to impose and actually imposed tariffs on imports from allies and adversaries alike. He demanded renegotiations of NAFTA and concessions from the Chinese. At this writing, very little is clear about the ultimate outcome.

The renegotiated elements that resulted from discussions with Canada and Mexico produced a renamed agreement (the U.S., Mexico, Canada Agreement) and a few concessions on dairy exports to Canada, but little else. The domestic content requirements for cars make it somewhat more likely that those cars will be produced in North America, but that doesn't mean they will be produced in the United States. The steel tariffs imposed on allies may have protected the domestic steel industry—but at the cost of higher steel and car prices. Perhaps the most important data point undercutting the strategy of the Trump agenda is that the U.S. trade deficit increased in 2017 ($552 billion) and 2018 ($622 billion) from its 2016 level ($498 billion).

The Bottom Line

The bottom line on international trade pacts is this: Most economists favor them for two basic reasons:

1. Economists generally favor allowing people to buy what they want from whom they want and to sell what they want to whomever they want, without restriction, as long as doing so does not harm an innocent third party.
2. More to the point of this chapter, they favor trade pacts because, if they are negotiated with care, such pacts enhance global economic well-being.

While free trade eliminates some jobs in some areas, it creates more jobs in other areas. Some countries with high poverty rates and low wages will gain jobs in areas where training and education are relatively unimportant. Other countries, including the United States, will benefit by being able to sell goods that highly skilled workers must produce.

With regard to free trade, economists insist that with income support and retraining, the gains from trade are nearly always sufficient to offset the losses of the people harmed by trade. What we need to understand is that if the people who gain from trade get all of the benefits and the people who get laid off are forgotten, then free trade is going to be seen and will in fact become just another way the rich get richer and the poor get poorer.

One interesting spin on those who lose their jobs is the notion of **creative destruction** introduced by Joseph Schumpeter. Schumpeter's thesis is that workers' desire for job security and their complacency when they have it is such that they do not seek better opportunities unless they are forced. If this logic is to be believed, then free trade does such people a favor by sending them into unemployment. Because most economists firmly believe that people do what they think is in their best interests, it may be that they know that there are better opportunities out there but are simply more comfortable where they are. This would suggest that unemployment is not really a favor. However, it is just not as bad as many fear because the massive and burgeoning service sector in the United States has absorbed many of those whose jobs were lost due to trade.

creative destruction The notion that people need to lose their jobs involuntarily in order to seize better opportunities.

Whether or not we have NAFTA, CAFTA, GATT, or any other trade agreement, what labor unions, workers, and young people in general have to understand is that the days are over when a high school diploma guaranteed that the employee would earn middle-class wages. The trends toward more computerized and mechanized manufacturing are not going to be reversed. The jobs that are available now are in operating, repairing, or designing the new machines. These jobs, moreover, require training and higher education.

Summary

You now understand that economists generally see that free trade is better than restricted trade and that trade agreements that facilitate the opening of trade are seen by most economists as a good thing. You understand why economists insist that free trade is good and why it is that agreements to maintain it are sometimes necessary. You are familiar with NAFTA, CAFTA, GATT, and the WTO as trade agreements and institutions, and you understand some of the positions regarding whether they are working as advertised. You understand the economic and political concerns that free-trade agreements generate, and you know that the bottom line for most economists is that such agreements are good policy. You also know that the Trump administration attempted to disrupt this consensus.

Key Terms

CAFTA
creative destruction
GATT
NAFTA
quota
strategic trade policies
tariff
WTO

Quiz Yourself

1. Trade agreements are often necessary because
   a. free trade is in no one's best interest.
   b. limiting trade is in no one's best interest.
   c. limiting trade helps those doing the limiting but typically by less than it hurts those who are limited.
   d. limiting trade helps those doing the limiting and typically by more than it hurts those who are limited.

2. Trade agreements are enforced
   a. militarily by the United States.
   b. militarily by the United Nations.
   c. by the consent of the parties to abide by the judgment of the arbitrators.
   d. only by the willingness of the parties to respond favorably to each other.

3. Which concept from Chapter 1 can be used to explain how it is possible for it to be in the individual interest of each nation to engage in protectionist policies but for everyone to be worse off if they all engage in protectionist policies?
   a. The fallacy of composition
   b. That correlation does not necessarily equate to causation
   c. That all resources are scarce
   d. That the right policy option is one chosen at the "margin"

4. Free-trade agreements
   a. are just that, about tariff and quota-free trade.
   b. have very little to do with the trade of goods and services and more to do with currency exchange.
   c. are about making trade freer than it was before and rarely about making it completely free.
   d. only impact the trade of goods and rarely impact the trade of services.

5. When one country objects to the trade restrictions of another, the provisions of trade treaties typically
   a. allow it to militarily exact retribution against the offending party.
   b. require that it submit its objections to a recognized, decision-making body to determine whether the practice is allowed.
   c. require that the offending country immediately stop the action pending a review of the case by a recognized, decision-making body.
   d. provide no form of relief.

6. The World Trade Organization governs the provisions of
   a. NAFTA.
   b. GATT.
   c. CAFTA.
   d. TPP.

7. From the perspective of the United States, a major accomplishment of the 1999 round of GATT was
   a. the complete banning of "domestic content" provisions in movie and television production.
   b. the creation of major restrictions on child labor.
   c. the worldwide adoption of U.S. environmental practices.
   d. the recognition of copyright protection for software, music, and movies.

8. The consensus among economists is that NAFTA's impact on the U.S. economy was/is
   a. enormously positive.
   b. enormously negative.
   c. marginal in net though it has increased both imports and exports.
   d. marginal in net because it has affected neither imports nor exports.

9. Joseph Schumpeter coined the phrase "creative destruction." The idea of creative destruction is that
   a. people need to be forced from their comfort zone in order to make crucial decisions that enhance their economic prospects.
   b. unemployment affects society more negatively than thought because it breeds social discontent.
   c. unemployment is good because it keeps prices down.
   d. competition for resources is inherently destructive.

Short Answer Questions

1. Why might it be easier to see a job lost because of NAFTA than to see a job created by it?
2. Why might an agreement like NAFTA increase GDP but not be favored by union members?
3. Why would free-trade agreements be easier to negotiate between similar countries than with ones that had very different methods of production, safety standards, and wages.

Think about This

Look at the ingredients list on the next nondiet soda you buy. The second ingredient behind water is high-fructose corn syrup. If you do the same thing in Canada or Mexico, the second ingredient is sugar. The reason for the difference is that the United States imposes a quota on cane sugar imports (to protect sugar beet growers in Minnesota and California). Is this good policy?

Talk about This

Protesters insist that the economic benefits of trade have social costs that go unrecognized. Whether or not you agree with them, make a list of those social costs. Open your closet and look at the labels on your clothing. Look for the labels on your consumer electronics to see where they were made. Are you, individually, better off with cheap clothing and electronics? In that context, do we owe something to those who bear those social costs?

For More Insight See

"China and the WTO," *Economist,* April 3, 1999, pp. 14–15.

Hufbauer, Gary, and Jeffery Schott, *NAFTA Revisited: Achievements and Challenges*. Institute for International Economics, 2005.

Husted, Steven, and Michael Melvin, *International Economics* (Reading, MA: Addison-Wesley, 1997), esp. Chapter 8.

Krugman, Paul R., and Maurice Obstfeld, *International Economics: Theory and Policy* (Reading, MA: Addison-Wesley, 1997), esp. Chapter 11.

Scott, Robert, Carlos Salas, and Bruce Campbell, *Revising NAFTA: Still Not Working for North America's Workers,* Economic Policy Institute Briefing Paper #173, September 2006.

The Seattle Times, December 4, 1999, and the *Seattle Times* WTO web page, http://old.seattletimes.com/special/wto/

Whitelaw, Kevin, "Banana-Trade Split," *U.S. News & World Report,* January 11, 1999, p. 49.

Behind the Numbers

U.S. Census Bureau: www.census.gov/foreign-trade/balance/index.html

- Trade balances with countries

CHAPTER TWENTY-TWO

The Line between Legal and Illegal Goods

Learning Objectives

After reading this chapter you should be able to:

LO1 Apply the supply and demand model and the concepts of consumer and producer surplus to the markets for tobacco, alcohol, and illegal goods and services.

LO2 Summarize why economists endorse interference in a market for reasons related to the information and costs to innocent third parties.

LO3 Utilize the concept of elasticity of demand to analyze who gets hurt by taxes on tobacco and alcohol.

LO4 Analyze the impact of drug legalization.

Chapter Outline

Let's face it. No mother wants her child to start smoking or drinking, or to engage in illegal activity. These are not healthy activities. Nevertheless, economists don't usually suggest that a good or service should be banned outright just because it is not good for you. This chapter uses the tools of supply and demand, elasticity, and consumer and producer surplus to look at these particular goods and services and the reason some are regulated, some are taxed, and still others are illegal.

Fourteen percent of the American population smokes, and the average American consumes nearly 25 gallons of beer a year. With that much smoking and drinking, tobacco and alcohol are obviously important parts of the American economy. The tobacco industry employs 13,020 people a year, and it has annual shipments of $41.4 billion. The alcohol industry employs 91,692 people, and its annual sales amount to $69.7 billion. Because certain goods and services are illegal, it is impossible to know exactly how much money is spent on them or how many people are employed in their production. What is known is that nearly half of all adults under 35 have used some form of illicit drug at least once their lifetime.

Before looking closely at the economics of these goods and services, we will review the fundamentals of supply and demand to remind ourselves of how equilibrium within a market serves the interests of both the consumer and the producer. Then we will turn to reasons why selling and using these goods are regulated, taxed, or banned and why economists might support such restrictions. Along the way, we'll focus not only on secondhand smoke, drunk driving, the spread of disease, and increases in crime but also on the issues of age restrictions, warning labels, and prohibition. After a brief discussion of the importance of elasticity, we'll use the concept within our supply and demand model to indicate who gets hurt by the considerable taxes that are levied on both tobacco and alcohol. Finally, we'll discuss why tobacco and alcohol are legal, why other goods and services are not, and what decriminalization of these goods and services would likely bring.

An Economic Model of Tobacco, Alcohol, and Illegal Goods and Services

We'll use the market that was presented in Chapter 2 as the basis for our analysis of these goods. To be general, we'll just call the good or service in question "the offending good." You can substitute whatever example you wish because the analysis is exactly the same. As we did with the market in that chapter, we will assume that there are many buyers and sellers, that the demand curve for each is downward sloping, and that the supply curve for each is upward sloping. For the time being, we will pretend that there are no negative consequences to innocent third parties. We will also pretend that all the people who engage in these activities know exactly what the consequences of their choices are. While these are fanciful assumptions, the approach gives us a starting point that we can use to analyze these markets. To prove that the markets benefit both the consumers and the producers, we have to refer to the consumer and producer surplus analysis that was presented in Chapter 3.

We start with a few facts that are presented in Figure 22.1. Consumers buy Q^* goods and pay P^* for each. This means that consumers pay producers an amount of money that is simultaneously less than the value the consumers place on the good and more than it cost the producers to provide it. That is, consumers are happier with the good or service than they were with the money they gave up, and producers make a profit. The gain to the consumers is P^*AB and is called their consumer surplus. The profit to the producer is CP^*B and is called their producer surplus.

As a result of this analysis, we can state that the sale of this offending good makes both consumers and producers better off than they would have been without the sale. The sum of the consumer surplus and the producer surplus is CAB. If it were illegal to buy and sell these goods and services, and if everyone obeyed the law, consumers and producers would both be worse off. Before you have a fit at this conclusion, though, remember that it was arrived at only after we made some fanciful assumptions.

FIGURE 22.1 Market for an offending good.

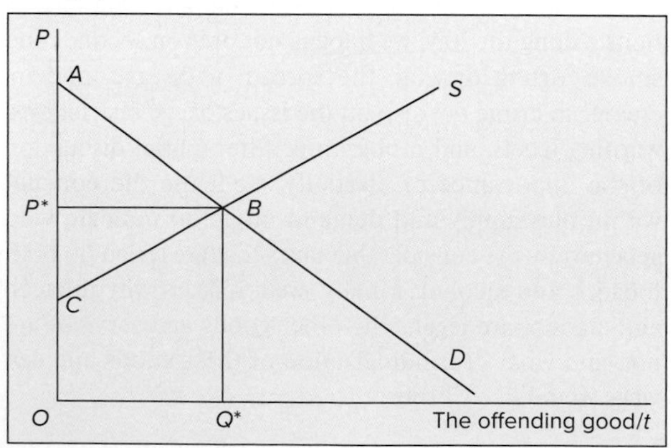

Why Is Regulation Warranted?

It is now time to recognize reality and to deal with the very real problems of tobacco, alcohol, and illegal goods and services. The goods themselves are very addictive. There are harmful effects to innocent third parties from secondhand smoke, drunk driving, and the spread of disease. In addition, the use of any one of these goods or services negatively affects spouses and children. Their presence has caused experts in public health to persuade legislators to implement restrictions, regulations, taxes, or outright bans.

When people argue for government intervention in a market, they do so from many points of view. Economists, who tend to decry unwarranted intervention, generally categorize reasons into three broad areas. First, they deem it possible for people to suffer from a lack of knowledge or an inability to think clearly. When that is the case, it may be appropriate for the government to step in with information or with warnings of danger. It may even be appropriate for government to make decisions for people. Second, they accept that the good or service may have adverse impacts on people other than the consumer or producer. Those costs, which are ignored in a market, must be taken into account by the government. Last, and least appealing among economists, is that consumption or production of the good may be immoral. That is, even though buying or selling the good may not hurt anybody in a physical sense, its production or consumption hurts society in general.

The Information Problem

For legal goods, advertising is intended to draw people to a product, and advertisers want their ads to be memorable. When the advertising is for products like tobacco and alcohol, we sometimes bemoan the effectiveness of the ads. For children of the 1950s and 1960s, the Marlboro Man™ was the image of health and rugged individualism. For children of the 1980s and 1990s, the R. J. Reynolds' Joe Camel™ was as recognizable as Mickey Mouse. In 1998, tobacco advertising was ended as part of a legal settlement. Still, Anheuser-Busch's series of Budweiser and Bud Light ads have been quite effective with Super Bowl audiences for decades. Though economists recognize the role of advertising in markets for goods that are legal, they debate the usefulness of advertising bans when the goods are legal for only a specified group (i.e., those old enough to drink or smoke).

For illegal goods, advertising is not an issue; the real "information" problem is the degree to which people do not adequately weigh the likelihood or impact of addiction. Government's reaction to this can be one of education, restriction, or prohibition. In the United States, we use education to dissuade young people from using drugs and reinforce that with prohibition. In all but certain counties in Nevada, the government's response to prostitution is simply one of prohibition.

The addiction argument clearly applies to cocaine, ecstasy, and methamphetamine. The reasoning is that potential users may not know or fully comprehend that these drugs can be addictive and what the impact of that addiction will be on users. The argument as it applies to prostitution is somewhat different. When prostitutes get started in the sex business, they may not fully realize the consequences of their actions. Some advocacy groups that seek to maintain and strengthen the ban on prostitution, for instance, claim that prostitutes generally begin their trade as children.

Estimates place the number of U.S. prostitutes under the age of 18 at between 300,000 and 600,000, with 100,000 new victims per year. People engaged in prostitution, especially at an early age, might not realize that sex workers are sexually assaulted on a regular basis or that the illegal drugs provided to them when they get started are used as a means to keep them under control and dependent. Further, there is widespread concern of a growing market for sexual slaves. The girls caught up in this horrific practice are not convinced to participate but are either abducted or told that they have been chosen to live in the West because of their academic potential or because there is a market for live-in child-care workers. Only after their arrival in the West do they learn their fate. Finally, these groups also make the point that more than 80 percent of prostitutes are the victims of childhood incest and that the sex industry capitalizes on this sense of degradation.

In general, then, economists suggest that the information problem can be dealt with using education, age restrictions, or prohibition. The appropriate tool depends on the degree of the problem. For example, the government requires that packages of cigarettes and bottles of alcohol display warning labels that describe the consequences of smoking and drinking. Thus, requiring warning labels and banning advertising on the grounds that these promotions serve only to cloud the judgment of consumers is acceptable to economists. We take "providing knowledge" a step further when we ensure that every new generation knows the addictive nature of smoking and drinking through programs in schools.

Of course, there are times when we simply do not trust young people to make good decisions, even when they have all the information. In these cases, we either make it illegal to buy the goods or services or we require that people reach a certain age before they can buy them. Economists are not at all uncomfortable forbidding children from consuming tobacco products for two reasons. First, the vast majority of smokers began their nicotine addictions well before becoming adults. Second, there is evidence that the tobacco companies aided addictions through their marketing efforts. Because only a tiny fraction of smokers began smoking as adults, preventing children from having ready access to cigarettes is in society's interest and in the child's long-term interest.

Ultimately, the reason many economists embrace the prohibition of cocaine, ecstasy, and methamphetamine is that for these the addiction problem is often immediate and permanent.

External Costs

Few economists object when government interferes in a market in which someone other than the consumer or producer is hurt by the consumption or production of a good. These externalities are important considerations for market regulation because the point of market efficiency is that everyone either benefits from, or is left unaffected by, a transaction. If that does not happen, then standing by and allowing the market to take care of itself is not always acceptable.

The externalities that result from the use of tobacco are the illnesses and deaths associated with secondhand smoke and the increased health care expenditures incurred by people who do not smoke but must pay increased premiums for health insurance to cover the expenses of smokers. It is not the concern of most economists that (knowledgeable) smokers hurt themselves by smoking. It is the concern of economists that those smokers tend to pass on costs to others.

The sale of drugs often affects someone other than the buyer or seller of the drug. As a result, at least some of the costs of that market are not being accounted for by

EXAMINING THE EXTERNALITIES

There are a few facts on crime that we ought to consider when dealing with illegal drugs in particular. First, 24 percent of all violent crimes (13 percent for rapes) are committed while the perpetrator is on drugs. Second, 55 percent of inmates in jail, detention, or prison used drugs during the month leading up to their arrest. Last, we spend $6 billion on drug interdiction at the federal level, another $28.5 billion in other drug control expenses, and $87 billion on incarceration in this country every year. One-sixth of those incarcerated now are there for drug-related offenses. What effect would legalization have on these statistics? We would save a lot of money—one-sixth of the incarceration costs and all of the interdiction costs. If overall use increased, as it probably would, violent crime would increase as those who were not addicts before legalization became addicts after legalization and, once addicted, became more prone to violent tendencies.

BATTLING NEGATIVE EXTERNALITIES WHILE CREATING OTHER PROBLEMS

Solving the externalities associated with a good by enforcing a prohibition strategy creates a problem. Sometimes the solution can be worse than the problem it was intended to solve. Much drug violence exists only because of laws criminalizing drug use. If cocaine and methamphetamine were legal and inexpensive, there would be less of a need for addicts to rob in order to get money to buy them. There would likely be fewer drive-by shootings to protect turf. There would be no need for the hundreds of thousands of prison beds devoted to drug offenders. It is for this reason that you find a significant number of economists, even very conservative economists, favoring drug legalization. They appreciate that drugs carry with them externalities but see the solution as worse than the problem.

the buyer or seller. If addicts are more likely to commit crime than nonaddicts, then neither the addict nor the dealer is accounting for the rising number of innocent victims when they sell their goods. Similarly, if a person gets a venereal disease from a visit to a prostitute and passes that disease on to an unsuspecting third party, then there is an external cost. Someone who is not part of the original transaction is being affected because of the transaction.

Establishing who should be counted as an innocent victim, though, is not as easy as it might sound. Children clearly are innocent victims, but are nonsmoking spouses? Some economists suggest that as part of the give and take of a marriage, smokers and their nonsmoking partners negotiate the rules for smoking in a household. If they decide it is alright for one to smoke and the other to be negatively affected, then smoking and its implications do not constitute an externality; it is simply one of the costs of the marriage. Other economists disagree. They suggest that regulations are needed to protect any people who are not consumers themselves.[1]

However you determine who is an innocent victim, people subjected to secondhand smoke have higher rates of lung-related illness than exist in the general population. Children in the presence of smokers are much more likely to die from sudden infant death syndrome (SIDS), asthma, and other lung illnesses. Before smoking in restaurants, bars, and airplanes was banned, nonsmoking servers, bartenders, and flight attendants reported higher than typical rates of lung illnesses. The costs of treating these innocent victims are ignored by both smokers and tobacco companies. Economists detest ignored costs. Whether economists support corrective actions when there are such costs depends on the degree of those costs and whether eliminating them is worth the loss of private benefits. In addition, there are twice as many smokers on Medicaid than their proportion within the general population warrants. They, of course, produce some rather substantial costs to the program. If they were not smoking, Medicaid would cost taxpayers less. Here, the innocent victim is the taxpayer.

Externalities also exist in less likely places. Since smokers typically die 10 years earlier than comparable nonsmokers, if they have group life insurance policies whose rates are the same for both smokers and nonsmokers, the expected net payout for smokers' beneficiaries is more than for nonsmokers' beneficiaries. Life insurance rates are therefore higher for nonsmokers than they should be and the rates for smokers are lower than they should be.[2]

[1]This is the same argument that some economists use to suggest that government need not regulate workplace safety. Risk takers must be compensated adequately or they would not take the risk.

[2]This externality is avoided when life insurance companies differentiate their premiums for smokers and nonsmokers. The degree of the employer subsidy would have to depend on this as well.

These facts combine to suggest that when smokers buy cigarettes, the full cost of smoking not only is not paid at the cash register but is not even fully incurred by the smoker.

This is not to say that economists hold unanimous opinions of these matters. Some suggest that there is a benefit to nonsmokers when other people smoke. These benefits come from two separate but related aspects of smoking. First, as mentioned previously, people who smoke for long periods of time die several years earlier than comparable people who never smoked. Smokers and nonsmokers pay into Social Security and other pension plans, but nonsmokers have some of their retirement essentially subsidized by smokers, because the smokers die before they have collected the benefits to which they were entitled.

A second form of subsidy that smokers grant nonsmokers is that not only do they die early, but they die more suddenly than nonsmokers. When smokers over the age of 60 become ill, their lifetime of smoking has so depressed their immune systems that they die of illnesses that nonsmokers are more likely to survive. They also succumb to those illnesses much faster and less is spent attempting to save them. Even though the money is spent sooner, it is much less. It is grimly ironic then that by dying more quickly than nonsmokers, smokers sometimes cost the health system less than do nonsmokers. By dying early and quickly, smokers avoid expenses that nonsmokers eventually need to pay. Because more than one-quarter of Medicare expenses are incurred during the last year of elderly people's lives, hastening their deaths saves money. If this gruesome fact is taken into account, the net external costs of smoking become negligible in the eyes of some economists.

Though there is a morbid economic upside to smoking, there is no such benefit to drunk driving. There are more than 1 million arrests a year for driving under the influence of alcohol. While that number has come down substantially over the last decade, it is still more than high enough to represent a significant problem. Of the roughly 34,247 accidents that result in 37,133 traffic fatalities each year, 28 percent involve at least one person whose blood alcohol level is over the legal limit. Another 5 percent involve someone who has a legal, but still measurable, blood alcohol content. Even when someone does not die, alcohol is a contributing factor in nearly a third of a million automobile accidents a year.

Despite these troubling statistics, it is time to try to look at the issue from a dispassionate viewpoint. To model the problem of the externalities that are associated with people who drive under the influence of alcohol, we need to alter our supply and demand diagram to account for the extra costs for which their behavior is responsible. To understand Figure 22.2, you need to recall that under perfect competition the supply curve is the marginal cost curve to the firms in the business. Any costs that are borne by neither the seller nor the buyer must be added to these costs to create the social cost of the good. On the assumption that the only people who benefit from the consumption of the good are the consumers themselves, the demand curve is the private and social marginal benefit curve. So instead of coming to the market solution of a price-quantity combination P^*-Q^*, the socially optimal combination is P'-Q'. That is, if there is a market for a good where some of the costs spill over to others, then the market will produce too much of the good and charge too little for it.

FIGURE 22.2 Modeling externalities.

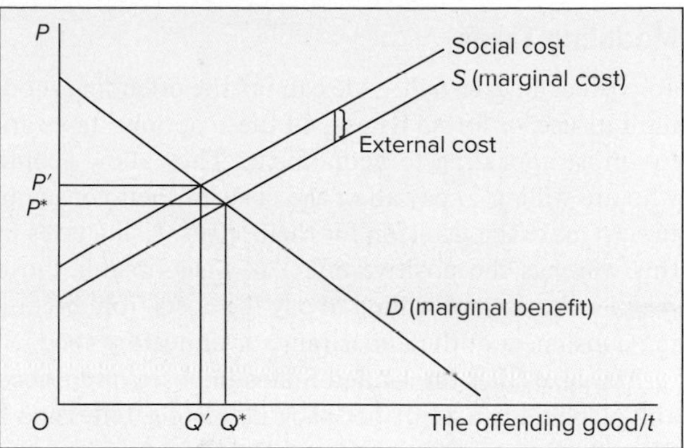

Morality Issues

We have looked now at the first two circumstances under which economists consider it acceptable for government to intervene in the market. Besides lack of information and externalities that may harm innocent people, a final reason why government might regulate a free market is that the market may be for a good or service that is considered to be immoral. For believers in certain major world religions, alcohol, tobacco, drugs, and prostitution are accorded this status. While appeals to righteousness are not particularly meaningful to economists on an academic level, they are certainly important to many other people. Many religions consider drinking a sin, and a few feel the same way about smoking.

Taxes on Tobacco and Alcohol

Modeling Taxes

To correct an externality, we can tax the offending good, limit its use, or forbid its use. Of these options, taxes are the most appealing to economists. They allow people who are willing to pay all of the costs of their consumption to make the decision for themselves. Using taxes in this way has the positive effect of discouraging those people who are not willing to pay the costs from becoming consumers of the undesirable or unhealthy good.

The taxes that the United States imposes on tobacco and alcohol are a $1.01 per pack tax on cigarettes and a 33-cent per six-pack tax on beer. The federal taxes on tobacco raise approximately $14 billion a year, while the taxes on alcohol raise $10 billion. States also tax these goods, collecting $18 billion in tobacco taxes and nearly $10 billion in alcohol taxes.

Figure 22.3 shows that the effect of the federal taxation on cigarettes and alcohol is to raise the price from P^* to P' and to lower consumption from Q^* to Q'. An important thing to notice about this effect is that smoking and drinking do not stop. This means that the deleterious effects of secondhand smoke and drunk driving do not stop either. They are simply reduced. If the tax is set equal to the dollar value of such externalities, then in theory the tax revenue raised is sufficient to cover the costs of the externalities. One problem, though, is that the tax impacts the considerate and rude alike. Smokers who light up alone do not cause secondhand smoke, whereas smokers who blow it in your face do. A per-pack tax affects both equally.

In any event, a policy short of prohibition implies that there are an economically acceptable number of expected drunk driving deaths and childhood secondhand-smoke-induced illnesses. The idea is that as long as we have an adequate sum of money available to compensate the people who are affected, it is acceptable for smokers to smoke, drinkers to drink, and people to be influenced in negative ways by their behavior.

People who are not economists have a very difficult time with the "acceptability" of deaths and illnesses. The basic idea is that people drink and smoke because they enjoy doing so. Looking back to Figure 22.3, that means Q' is the right level of production and consumption of the offending good. If we take taxing and regulating too far, the reduction in enjoyment by users would outweigh the effect of the reduction on innocent victims.

The notion of acceptable deaths is a difficult one for many to accept. Consider this though: The Brain Injury Association reports that approximately 5 children die each year on playgrounds as a result of falls and other injuries. We continue to send our children out on recess because we weigh what is to be gained with what is to be lost and judge the risk of injury or even death to be tolerable. We drive to work because we see that what is gained–income–is greater than what is lost–a small risk of injury or death.

FIGURE 22.3 Modeling taxes.

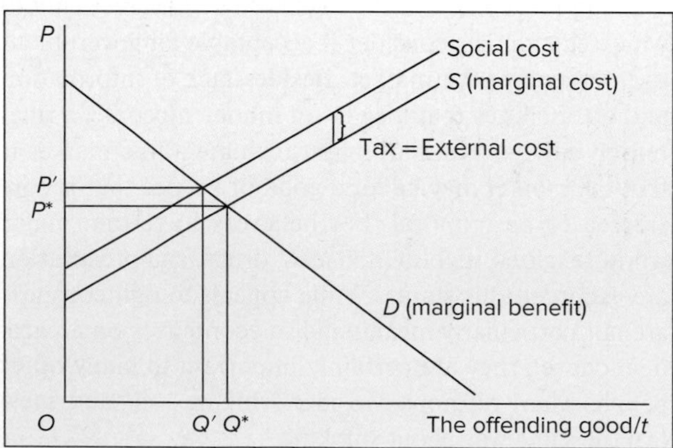

The Tobacco Settlement and Why Elasticity Matters

For quite some time, legislators have given particular consideration to raising the taxes on tobacco. The settlement between several states and the big tobacco companies that was reached in 1998 requires that the companies pay the states more than $250 billion over 25 years to compensate them for Medicaid expenses the states paid that were created by smoking. The companies will then pass on those taxes to the smokers who buy their products. To see how a sequence like this works, we need to look at the supply and demand curve for tobacco.

First, it should be remembered that when someone is addicted to a product, as smokers are to cigarettes, the demand curve for the good is highly inelastic. If you look at Figure 22.4, you see that a tax will again raise the price from P^* to P'. If you compare the size of the tax (P'' to P') to the amount of the price increase, you see that smokers will be paying for most of this tax increase and that tobacco companies will pay comparatively less (P^* to P' versus P^* to P''). Because smokers are, on average, far poorer than the average of the general population, this tax is as regressive as any tax we can imagine. Because consumption falls only from Q^* to Q', it is also disturbing that the tax will not have a significant influence on how much people smoke.

FIGURE 22.4 Tax on tobacco with inelastic demand.

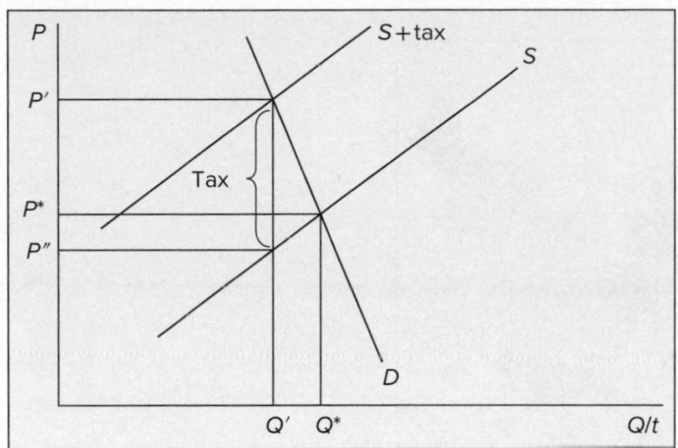

When you look at teen smoking, the picture is not quite as bleak. Because the habit of smoking consumes a much larger portion of teenagers' incomes compared to adults, the elasticity of demand for cigarettes by young people is much greater. That is, demand is more elastic and the demand curve is flatter. If you were to draw such a demand curve, you would see that the burden of the tax would still fall mainly on consumers. You would also see that tobacco companies would be paying a greater proportion of the tax. Further smoking, at least teen smoking, would be reduced by more. Until quite recently, economists' estimates were that elasticities for cigarettes were as low as 0.2 for adults and as high as 0.5 for children. Under these circumstances, an increase of one dollar in cigarette prices would diminish adult smoking by 10 percent, but it would diminish smoking by children by 25 percent. More recent studies of cigarette elasticity put adult elasticity at 0.8 for adults. This is quite likely the result of electronic cigarettes and the degree to which they provide an alternative to users.

A study of the elasticity of demand for beer put it at 0.53, which suggests a tax that adds 10 percent to the price of a six-pack would reduce consumption by 5.3 percent.

Why Are Certain Goods and Services Illegal?

The debate over whether drugs and prostitution should be legal usually comes down to a comparison of the negative consequences of what is currently legal, tobacco and alcohol, with what is currently illegal. Clearly a case can be made that the aggregate impact of tobacco and alcohol is much greater than the aggregate impact of illegal drugs and prostitution. As you can tell by now, economists are less interested in "aggregate" impacts than "marginal" ones.

Here, the case can be made that the negative externalities associated with one person purchasing one more unit of the illegal goods are greater than the negative externalities associated with one person purchasing one unit of a legal good. The other argument that could be made to justify the current state of the law is that the unknown or underestimated consequences to the consumer of using drugs or engaging in prostitution are substantially greater than those with regard to alcohol. Of course, the opposite case could be made as well.

The Impact of Decriminalization on the Market for the Goods

Figure 22.5 displays the legality of marijuana as of February 2019. Ten states and the District of Columbia have made marijuana fully legal, while 15 continue to treat it as fully illegal. For the other 25 states, they either decriminalize it, make it legal for medical purposes, or both. The varying state laws and the impacts of those changes have allowed economists to examine the impact of legalization.

Theoretical Perspective

Given the previous discussion, suppose a good or service is currently illegal. What would result from making it legal? The first thing that would likely happen as a result of making a good legal is that the concerns of both consumers and producers about getting caught would evaporate. Because getting caught would not be a problem any longer, any shift to the left of supply that resulted from illicit operation would cease to exist. Similarly, any shift to the left in the demand curve by those who might have wanted to partake of the illicit good but did not because it was illegal would cease to exist. The net result of legalizing a previously illegal activity would be a movement in the demand curve to the right and a movement in the supply curve to the right.

Another impact of decriminalization would occur on the elasticity of demand and, to a lesser degree, supply. When a good is illegal, it is often the case that the consumers of the good are addicted to it in some sense. Therefore, the demand curve for such a good is likely to be very inelastic.

When legal, a good's demand is likely to be more elastic than when it is illegal. That is because, when it is legal, a higher proportion of consumers are just trying the good

FIGURE 22.5 State marijuana laws, February 2019.

Source: https://disa.com/map-of-marijuana-legality-by-state

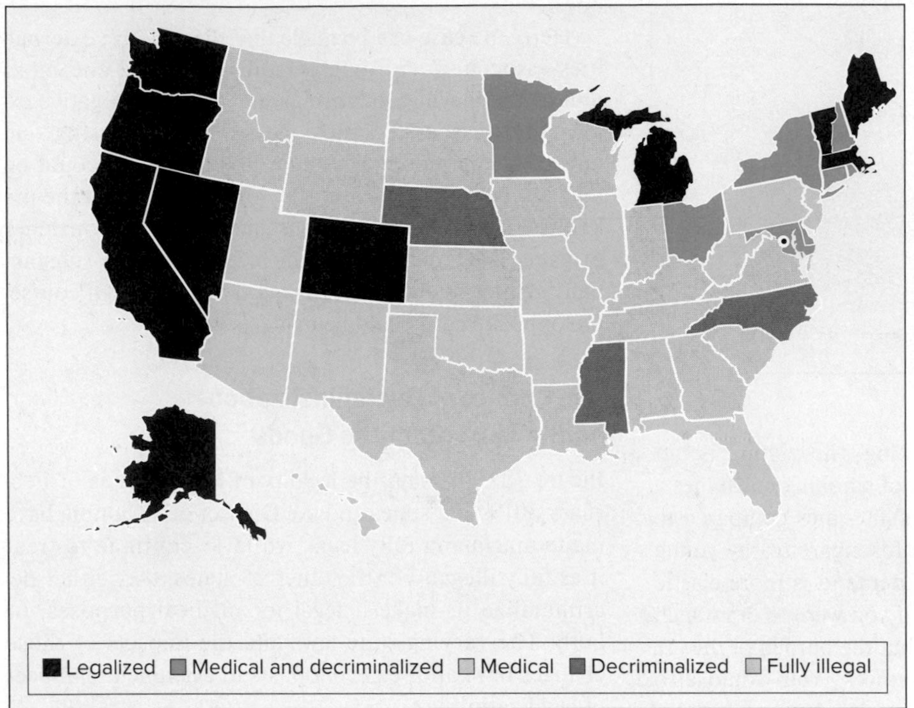

or use it recreationally. Similarly, once people have made the decision to become a seller of an illicit good, the price they sell it for is not usually a stimulus to sell it in great quantities. This is because the risks of getting caught may prevent sellers from expanding their operation quickly as prices rise.

Therefore, from either side, the supply and demand curves are less elastic when the good or service is illegal than when it is legal. The net result here is that both curves flatten out when the good is made legal. Figure 22.6 depicts the effect of legalizing a previously illegal good. The demand curve flattens and moves right, and the supply curve flattens and moves right. If the supply curve movement is more than the demand curve movement, as it is in Figure 22.6, the net result is a lowering of price. Not shown, but equally plausible, is the case where the demand curve movement is greater than the supply curve movement and the price rises.

Thus, the direction of a price change as a result of decriminalization depends on whether the reduction in risk to dealers or prostitutes is greater than the increase in interest by consumers. Because the conventional wisdom is that legalization would lower the price, conventional

FIGURE 22.6 Making an illegal good legal or vice versa.

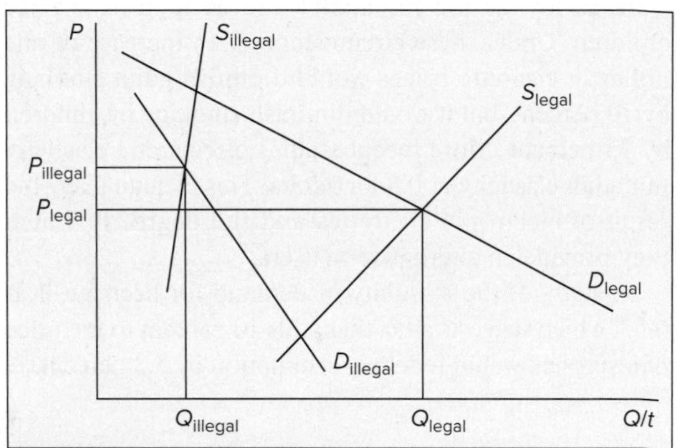

wisdom is just that: The supply curve shift will be greater than the demand curve shift.

Empirical Perspective

As a result of the theoretical ambiguity, there is place for economists to examine how changes in laws and prices will change behavior. Economists Rosalie Pacula and

Russell Lundberg have summarized the studies on a variety of potential impacts of legalizing marijuana, in particular. They note that there are two "prices" that consumers face when making decisions: the price of the drug itself and the potential "price" they might face if caught engaging in an illegal act. On the first question, they estimate that the elasticity (of using within a year, among high school age youth) is between 0.3 and 0.5. Among adult users, they estimate the elasticity at 0.25. On the second question, decriminalization increases use by 7 to 10 percent.

The External Costs of Decriminalization

Ultimately, whether legalization makes sense to you depends on whether you believe the external costs of these activities are significant enough to pay the significant costs of punishing users and dealers. One potential solution that many pro-legalizers suggest is that we tax and regulate drug sales and prostitution in order to take into account and pay for the externalities.

Looking back to Figure 22.3, you see that we simply added a tax equal to the external cost that was examined in Figure 22.2 to get the P', Q' result. That is, a proper taxation scheme can compensate for the problems of an externality. There is money to educate against the use of the illicit good or to compensate victims of users of the questionable good.

The problem is that if the external costs are very great, the tax will have to be very high. If the tax is very high, there will be a motivation to have a black market in untaxed goods. As evidence of this, consider that in Canada a prohibitively high tax created a black market for cigarettes. In this case, people drove to the United States, bought cigarettes, took them back to Canada, and sold them. In another similar case, while prostitution is legal in Nevada, it is highly regulated. That regulation leads to prostitutes avoiding regulation by working on their own outside the regulated brothels. Whenever a tax is too high or regulation too severe, a black market will exist beside a legal market.

Summary

You now understand how we can apply a supply and demand model and the concepts of consumer and producer surplus to tobacco, alcohol, drugs, and prostitution. You understand that there are reasons that economists endorse interference in a market, reasons that relate to information and costs to innocent third parties. You have seen how the question of who gets hurt by taxes on tobacco and alcohol is dependent on the elasticity of demand for these goods. Finally, you have seen the argument for the current state of the law with regard to the treatment of these goods and the economic consequences of decriminalization.

Quiz Yourself

1. When justifying the wisdom of tobacco taxes, economists focus almost entirely on
   a. the cost to cigarette companies of production.
   b. the cost to cigarette smokers for the cigarettes themselves.
   c. the cost to cigarette smokers for their extra health care expenses.
   d. the costs to nonsmokers (like secondhand smoke).
2. When discussing an addictive drug, an economist is likely to focus on
   a. both the external costs and the "information problem" associated with addiction.
   b. the moral costs exclusively.
   c. the cost of the drug to the user.
   d. the costs of production.
3. If you became convinced that marijuana was neither addictive nor contributed to externalities, then banning it creates
   a. a social benefit without social cost.
   b. deadweight loss.
   c. a vacuum.
   d. a social benefit with an exact countering social cost.
4. Decriminalizing a drug is likely to lead to a price decrease if
   a. the anticipated supply effect is greater than the anticipated demand effect.
   b. the anticipated demand effect is greater than the anticipated supply effect.
   c. the anticipated demand effect is exactly equal to the anticipated supply effect.
   d. both demand and supply decrease.

5. Compared to a recreational user of a drug, an addicted user's elasticity of demand is
   a. much more elastic.
   b. much less elastic.
   c. much less.
   d. flatter.
6. If policy makers were to attempt to set a tax equal to the external costs of alcohol, one would have to evaluate
   a. the cost of production.
   b. the price paid by consumers.
   c. the value of innocent lives lost to drunk driving.
   d. the value of the shortened lives of alcoholics.
7. When examining the "right tax" on a good that produces an externality, the tax should be such that
   a. it is greater than the externality.
   b. it is less than the externality.
   c. it is exactly equal to the externality.
   d. it makes consumption prohibitively expensive for anyone.
8. One unsettling consequence of setting a tax on tobacco sufficiently high to reduce consumption would be that it would
   a. likely reduce Medicare costs.
   b. likely increase tobacco revenues to farmers.
   c. likely increase tobacco company profits.
   d. make Social Security's financial outlook worse.
9. The introduction of e-cigarettes provides a substitute for regular cigarettes. The result is likely that the elasticity of
   a. supply increases.
   b. supply decreases.
   c. demand increases.
   d. demand decreases.

Short Answer Questions

1. If the United States is able to continue reducing the incidence of children smoking, how might that end up costing more in the long run in terms of health-related expenses?
2. If the United States were to legalize marijuana production, what might the negative externalities be and what current negative externalities might be lessened?
3. If the United States were to eliminate the drinking age, what might you predict the outcome to be in terms of externalities?
4. What does the "legalize and tax" method of dealing with currently illegal drugs imply about how proponents of this approach view the ability to put a dollar value on human life?

Think about This

There are considerate smokers and inconsiderate smokers. Secondhand smoke is not an issue when smokers are considerate (in that they smoke where no one is around to breathe it). Should these smokers be taxed when they are producing no harm to society?

Talk about This

As unsavory as it sounds, there are travel agents who book "sex tours" in parts of Asia. Travelers visit prostitutes in various locations. While some of the brothel operators mandate "safe" practices, others allow the patrons to pay extra if they wish to participate in "unsafe" practices. Should you be able to pay someone to risk their lives in this manner?

For More Insight See

Grossman, Michael, Jody Sindelar, John Mullahy, and Richard Anderson, "Alcohol and Cigarette Taxes," *Journal of Economic Perspectives* 7, no. 4 (1993), pp. 211–222.

Thorton, Mark, *The Economics of Prohibition* (Salt Lake City: University of Utah Press, 1991).

Behind the Numbers

Department of the Treasury, Alcohol and Tobacco Tax and Trade Bureau: www.ttb.gov/statistics/
- Alcohol and tobacco tax collections

Tax Policy Center of the Urban Institute and Brookings Institution: www.taxpolicycenter.org
- Alcohol and tobacco tax rates

U.S. Census Bureau, Annual Survey of Manufacturers: www.census.gov/programs-surveys/asm.html
- Employment
- Value of shipments

White House Office of National Drug Control Policy: www.whitehouse.gov/ondcp/
- Drug control funding

National Highway Traffic and Safety Administration: www.nhtsa.dot.gov
- Traffic fatalities
- Blood alcohol

Department of Justice, Bureau of Justice Statistics: bjs.gov/content/pub/pdf/p11.pdf
- Incarcerations
- Incarceration costs

Department of Justice, Bureau of Justice Statistics: bjs.gov/content/pub/pdf/cvus08.pdf
- Victimization information

CHAPTER TWENTY-THREE

Natural Resources, the Environment, and Climate Change

Learning Objectives

After reading this chapter you should be able to:

LO1 Apply the principles of present value to natural resource development.

LO2 Apply marginal analysis to answer the question of how clean is clean enough.

LO3 Apply the concept of externalities to explain why pollution warrants government intervention in the market.

LO4 Describe why pollution is much more likely to occur on publicly owned property than on private property.

LO5 Summarize the variety of environmental problems that exist in the world as well as the economic solutions that exist to address these problems.

Chapter Outline

Responsible management of the natural resources of the country and protecting the environment are increasingly popular positions for politicians to take. On the surface, the solution to the first of these is to create a system of usage that leaves resources for the next generation, while the solution to the second problem seems rather simple: Stop polluting. For an economist, though, not only is the problem more complicated, but the solution is as well. The environmental problems of modern society are substantial and varied: unsustainable usage of natural resources, pollution of the water and air, the potential extinction of 1,865 species of plants and animals, acid rain that puts forests and fish in jeopardy, and greenhouse effects that are probably responsible for rapidly rising global temperatures.

To most environmentalists, solving these problems involves strict questions of right and wrong. Economists, on the other hand, want to look also at costs and benefits. Recall that economics is about the "allocation of scarce resources to satisfy unlimited human wants." With both the environment and natural resources, there are competing interests: economic growth for the present and sustainability for the future. Where economics can be particularly helpful is in the area of efficiency. Developing a plan that reduces pollution is not difficult, but it is hard to create one that reduces pollution in a way that will minimize the economic costs. That is what economists bring to the discussion.

Using Natural Resources

The earth is a bounty of **limited natural resources** such as land, oil, natural gas, coal, mineral ores (iron, copper, etc.), and **renewable natural resources** such as fresh water, wood, and wildlife. The question for a society is how to deploy those resources in such a way that maximizes their long-run usefulness. For a society to do that, it must weigh the value of those resources to those who are living now against the value of those natural resources to generations to come. The issue can be summarized as one of **stewardship,** which is the management of resources in a fashion that weighs their value through time.

limited natural resources
Resources that cannot be replaced.

renewable natural resources
Resources that can be replaced.

stewardship
The management of resources in a fashion that weighs their value through time.

In the simplest sense, suppose you have a resource that you can use now or you can leave unused and preserve it for later. Suppose you also know what people will pay for it now, and you have a good estimate of what they will pay for it in the future. In order to determine whether you should use it now or leave it until another time, you must use the Chapter 7 concept of present value. To keep things simple, suppose the resource is costless to find, extract, and process and produces a constant value per unit in each time when it is used. Finally, assume that there are a fixed number of units to be extracted and consumed. Any positive interest rate will yield a conclusion that you should use it all now—the exact opposite of **sustainability.** Sustainability is the idea that you should only use renewable resources at the rate at which they can be replaced, and it means that you use limited natural resources at the lowest possible rate in order to preserve them for future generations.

sustainability
The idea that you should only use renewable resources at the rate at which they can be replaced.

However, the simple introduction of a downward-sloping demand curve for that resource results in a trade-off between present use and future use that will result in a motivation among resource owners to conserve even with a positive discount rate. The downward-sloping demand curve accomplishes this because increasing the present use decreases its marginal benefit.

Suppose, for the purpose of illustration, the resource is oil and that oil is used to produce gasoline. Recall from Chapters 2 and 3 that the demand for gasoline represents its marginal benefit to its user. If an additional unit of oil is going to be utilized now, it has a decreasing marginal benefit to the refiner because there is a decreasing marginal utility for gasoline among consumers. The refiner must reduce the price to sell the extra gasoline. The question for the oil company is whether it is worthwhile to drill for oil now and refine more gasoline now when doing so requires reducing the price of gasoline now. In doing so, the oil company is foregoing the opportunity to wait and sell that gasoline later at a price that is likely higher. Though those later profits will have to be discounted, they can well outweigh the profits from producing and selling now.

An upward-sloping supply curve can also aid in motivating conservation. Continuing with the example of oil, the shale oil of the North Dakota area has been known to exist for half a century and yet went largely untapped even when oil prices peaked in 1980 and again in 2008. That is because it is very expensive to access. The marginal cost of producing more oil, if that oil is from a location such as that, is very high, so few companies tried to extract it until recently. As a result, there is conservation of difficult-to-extract resources because the marginal costs are greater than the marginal revenues.

This means that market forces, on both the demand and the supply side, will lead to some degree of conservation. The greater the discount rate, the lesser the degree of conservation, and the lower the discount rate, the greater the degree of conservation. This leads some environmentalists to conclude the morally correct discount rate is zero. Economists typically would not go so far as to say that. Economists would more frequently assert that the rate of utilization should be socially optimal for everyone involved, those present and those in the future. These economists would suggest, in the case of oil, that the rate of utilization should also factor in the likelihood that with greater scarcity of oil, alternatives to oil will become more profitable to develop. History tells us that when society requires an alternative, prices adjust so that an alternative becomes profitable.

How Clean Is Clean Enough?

For many of you, when you were 10, your bedroom was a wreck. When asked whether a room is clean, a 10-year-old will respond with a reply that is pure economics: "Clean enough." With that reply, 10-year-olds are asserting that to them, further cleaning is simply not worth the effort. In the language of economics, children are asserting that the

FIGURE 23.1 Clean enough.

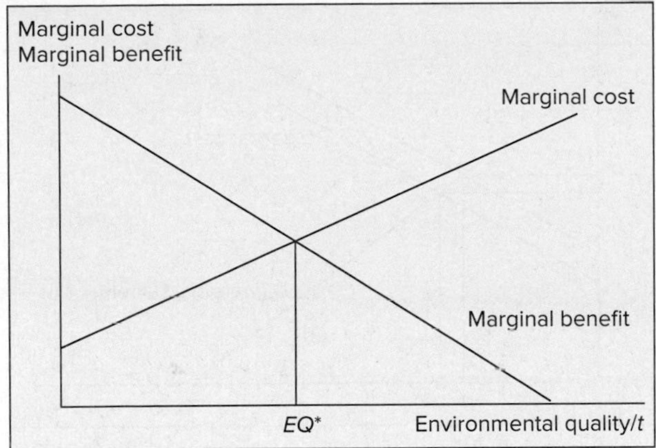

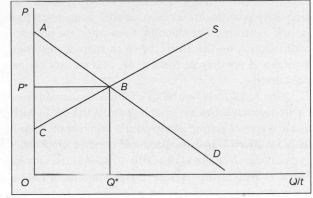

marginal benefit of cleaning more (the value they place on additional cleanliness) is less than the marginal cost of cleaning more (the value they place on play time).

Economists apply the same standard to environmental issues–merely on a larger scale than a child's bedroom. The opportunity cost of a cleaner environment is lost economic satisfaction. We can use marginal cost–marginal benefit analysis to analyze this problem, but only if we make some simplifying assumptions.

Let's assume for the moment that we have a generally accepted measure of environmental quality. Let's further assume that the really dirty stuff is relatively easy to clean but that achieving higher levels of cleanliness is harder and harder. Using the dirty room analogy, you know that the quickest way to make your room look cleaner is to pick up the dirty clothes, which can be done in seconds. Once you get down to straightening and dusting the knick-knack shelves, the benefits are slight and the time required is great. This implies that the marginal cost of achieving greater cleanliness is increasing, while, at the same time, its marginal benefit is decreasing. As shown in Figure 23.1, this means that the maximum net benefit of environmental cleanup is *EQ**, where the marginal benefit equals the marginal cost.

The Externalities Approach

We created many of the original environmental problems (such as polluting the air and water) when we produced and consumed goods considering only the costs and benefits that directly affected us. As we saw in Chapters 2 and 3, doing this is usually fine, but problems often arise when the actions we take impose costs on or present benefits to

FIGURE 23.2 When the market works.

others. Economists call costs or benefits that are incurred by someone other than the producer or consumer **externalities.** We begin this chapter by reviewing why a market without externalities serves everyone. We then explore why there is a problem with markets when externalities are present. After that, we examine the specific environmental problems discussed previously. We conclude with a look at what economics can offer in the way of solutions.

externalities
Effects of a transaction that hurt or help people who are not a part of that transaction.

When the Market Works for Everyone

As we learned in Chapter 3, a market works very well in a world where all the costs and benefits of production are confined to producers and consumers. Figure 23.2 depicts that the market price–quantity combination, *P*–Q**, provides benefits to consumers, *OABQ**, at a cost to them of *OP*BQ**. The difference, *P*AB*, is called *consumer surplus,* that is, what consumers get in net benefits. Similarly, for the producer, the variable costs of production, *OCBQ**, are lower than revenue generated from sales, *OP*BQ**. The difference, *CP*B*, is called the *producer surplus.* Thus when the market does not generate costs or benefits to anyone other than consumers and producers, both benefit and no one loses.

When the Market Does Not Work for Everyone

The main problem with the model just described is that it does not take into account that there are nearly always indirect costs to others in either the production or consumption of a good. There are, for example, very few goods that do not require some form of energy for their production. Whether that energy is generated from the direct combustion of a steel mill's smelting facility or electricity generated from burning coal, some fossil fuel is used in nearly all production. Even when the power is hydroelectric, nuclear, wind, or solar, there are environmental and possibly aesthetic costs that are not always considered.

Using fossil fuels like oil or coal creates a number of environmental problems from beginning to end. In each of the stages of getting energy to the user, people or animals are affected. In extraction, land is either temporarily or permanently altered. The 2010 oil spill in the Gulf of Mexico clearly points out that extraction creates a negative externality.

Transporting oil, natural gas, and coal consumes energy. Transporting the first two carries with it the potential for an environmental catastrophe like the rupturing of the *Exxon Valdez* disaster and the resulting massive oil spill in Alaska's Prince William Sound. By far the greatest problem, though, is created when fossil fuels are burned. Particulate matter creates breathing problems that are unpleasant for some and life-threatening for others. Burning coal releases sulfur into the air and it produces acid rain. If current scientific predictions of the United Nations Intergovernmental Panel on Climate Change are found to be true, greenhouse gases will cause significant changes in the world's climate.

You may believe that alternatives like hydroelectric, wind, or solar power offer externality-free energy, but, like fossil fuels, each has its own problems. As the Japanese experience of 2011 points out, though nuclear power is potentially clean, it is also potentially disastrous, and even accounting for disasters ignores the problem of how to store nuclear waste. Hydroelectric power requires the destruction of river valleys, eliminating habitat as rivers flood the area behind the dams. While wind and solar power are clean in that they do not pollute the air or water, the sheer number of collectors needed to produce an amount of electricity that is equal to the amount produced by coal at the present time is vast. Therefore, this option has the potential of destroying thousands upon thousands of acres of land that we now consider to have great scenic beauty.

Figure 23.3 depicts the problem as an economist would see it. Whereas firms pay attention to the costs of production of their goods, unless forced to, they tend to ignore the environmental costs of their production. Similarly, consumers pay attention to how much a good costs them, but it often serves their purposes to ignore the costs to those around them. Costs to people other than

FIGURE 23.3 When a market does not work.

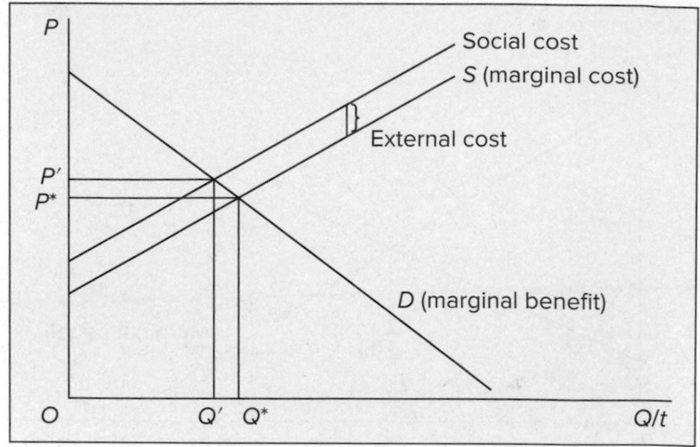

the producers and consumers are considered to be unaccounted for in the market. The existence of such costs is unacceptable to an economist. The fundamental flaw with the market is that unless all costs are accounted for, it will produce too much and charge too little. To find the true cost of production and consumption of a good that includes the effects on innocent bystanders, called the **social cost**, you need to add the external cost to the private costs (measured on the supply curve). When these costs are accounted for, the price is to be P' rather than P^*, and the amount produced is Q' rather than Q^*.

social cost
The true cost of production and consumption of a good that includes the effects on innocent bystanders.

Unless you believe that a pristine environment is a matter of right and wrong, allowing no compromises to your position, you will have to accept the existence of some environmental problems even when you account for all the costs. For example, Figure 23.2 does not display a thoroughly clean environment, but it does show how the costs of pollution are weighed against the benefits of consumption.

We may decide, for instance, that even though some pesticides threaten certain species, they enhance food production enough that using them is worth the cost. The species are still threatened, but at least the cost is recognized. Similarly, we may decide that reformulating gasoline to reduce emissions by 80 percent is worth 20 cents per gallon but that reducing it another 10 percent is not worth the dollar a gallon it would take to accomplish that level of reduction. Here, the costs of pollution are weighed, but so are the benefits of consumption. There are substances for which the optimal level is zero. This occurs when the marginal benefit of the production or use of even one drop of the good is less than its social cost.

The Property Rights Approach to the Environment and Natural Resources

A Nobel Prize-winning economist by the name of Ronald Coase came up with a completely different method of dealing with pollution. His widely cited theorem states that markets with externalities can be made to be efficient. This can be done by simply assigning rights to the polluted property, but it requires that bargaining costs not be prohibitive. To see why this is so, we need to first look at why ownership matters.

Why You Do Not Mess Up Your Own Property

Consider a relatively simple problem. Why is it that you are much more willing to litter in a park than you are to litter in your own residence hall, apartment, or house? The reason is that you have property rights in the place you live and you make your own place less valuable when you litter in it. You do not own the park. Though your littering diminishes the value of the park, it does not diminish your own wealth.

This explains why people treat many forms of common property worse than they treat their own. If you have ever lived on a cul-de-sac, you will have noted that the circle of grass in the center of the turnaround was in demonstrably worse shape (or at least less well landscaped) than the surrounding lawns. People tend to treat their own property better than they do public property.

Why You Do Mess Up Common Property

Common property is property that is without a discernible individual owner. This property is usually owned by the government, a neighborhood association, or some other collective group. The problem with common property is that even though it may be worth a great deal to the group, the benefits of treating the property well are not worth the costs to any one individual. Economists refer to this as the "tragedy of the commons."

common property
Property that is not owned by any individual but is owned by government or has some other collective ownership.

Consider again the problem of a neighborhood park. Suppose that a city agrees to pay the up-front costs of a park for a neighborhood of 100 homes. It buys the playground equipment, plants trees and grass, but then turns the park over to the neighborhood. What happens when the grass needs to be cut, a tree falls, or the surface under the playground equipment needs to be rejuvenated? While each neighbor may consider the individual benefit to be worth one-hundredth of the cost of this regular maintenance, often no one will view maintenance for the entire neighborhood as worth the time or money. The ultimate problem is that no one owns the property. As a result, while the social benefit of the maintenance is greater than its cost, the benefit to an individual is much lower than its cost to that individual.

Natural Resources and the Importance of Property Rights

Economists use many of the same tools to explore the use of natural resources as we use when dealing with pollution. Whether the resource in question is mineral, timber, energy, or the oceans' bounty, economists note that the extraction, cutting, removal, or harvesting imposes costs on someone other than the producer or consumer. It doesn't matter whether this results from the fact that the land is owned by the government or not owned by anyone at all, or because the process of garnering the resource is itself polluting. What matters is that all of the costs must be acknowledged.

Economists also bring another element to the table: the notion of present value. The value of an untapped resource to its owner is the present value of the profit associated with exploiting it over a period of time. In this way, there is an optimal rate of exploitation, which is the rate that maximizes the present value. Suppose you owned a resource such as a forest of timber. You could clear-cut it and sell all of it at once. Then you would have to plant new trees, wait for the trees to grow tall enough to harvest, and repeat the cycle. On the other hand, you could cut only those trees that had achieved an optimal height and leave the rest for another year. You would have a few trees to cut every year. An economist would look at this and say that whichever rate of exploitation maximizes the present value of the profit emanating from that timber would be the optimal exploitation rate. Assuming that no timber company can influence prices, then there is no value to waiting to harvest trees unless some are relatively immature. The motivation to wait comes from the fact that trees grow, and thereby grow more valuable. If the interest rate is high (and exceeds the rate of tree growth), then that favors the cut-it-now rate, while if the interest rate is low, that favors the let-it-grow rate.

The problem comes when no one owns the resources that are being harvested. For instance, the oceans are notoriously overfished because there is no value to leaving the fish to grow bigger. Similarly, when logging companies buy the right to harvest trees on federal land, those contracts need to be well specified and well enforced or the company will have no motivation to leave the smaller trees for a later date, especially if the contract expires before the trees grow to maturity. This is much less of a problem on private property because the owner must weigh the present value of the profit from taking an immature tree against the present value of the profit from taking it a few years later. It is often the case that the logging company that owns the property it is working on will leave the smaller trees because it is in its interest to do so.

Environmental Problems and Their Economic Solutions

Environmental Problems

We face many environmental problems, some obvious and others not so obvious. Specific problems include water and air pollution, plant and animal species that face extinction, the effects of acid rain, landfills that are overflowing, limited natural resources that are being depleted, and global warming. In this section, we look briefly at each.

When humans are affected by the economic activity of other humans, the problem is relatively easy to solve. People complain when they are being hurt. When producers pollute the air or water, there are concerned people who have to breathe the affected air or want to drink or swim in the affected water. They will lobby their representatives for pollution regulations. In fact, the Environmental Protection Agency (EPA) was created in 1969 in response to pleas that environmental regulations be enforced. The Clean Air Act of 1970 and the Clean Water Act of 1972 were additional responses to people's perceptions that problems existed and their desire to have them addressed.

By most measures, these laws have been effective. The nation's air and water are much cleaner than they were 50 years ago. Air pollution has been addressed with regulations that range from requirements that smokestack emissions be "scrubbed" before being released to requirements that cars have catalytic converters and burn unleaded gasoline. Since the Clean Air Act's inception, the amount of sulfur dioxide (SO_2) in the air has been reduced by 91 percent, carbon monoxide by 71 percent, particulate matter by 30 percent, and lead by 99 percent. As can be seen in Figure 23.4, even since 1980, the Clean Air Act has resulted in significant reductions in all measured forms of air pollution.

Regarding water pollution, municipal wastewater facilities now have to return untreated water to rivers and streams in nearly drinkable form. Companies can no longer discharge waste materials into rivers or lakes,

FIGURE 23.4 Pollutant concentrations.

Source: Environmental Protection Agency, www.epa.gov.

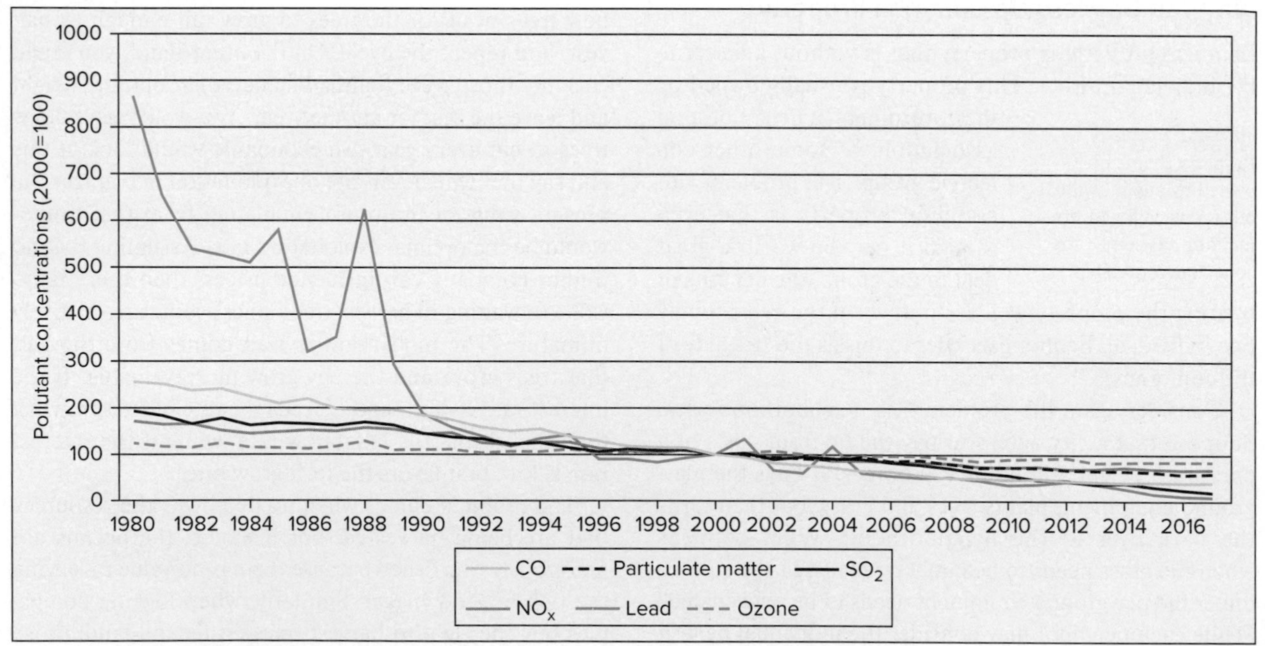

either. Though some of the damage to these bodies of water is permanent, most are improving. Classic examples of this include the Cuyahoga River near Cleveland, Ohio, which was so polluted that it once actually caught fire. Now it is clean enough that people can eat its fish. On the bottom of Onondaga Lake in Syracuse, New York, several feet of toxic sludge was removed, and the "Allied Waste Beds" designation on the map of the city was deleted.

When air and water are unacceptably dirty, the problem is fairly obvious. However, it is more difficult to see damage to wildlife, making it harder to address the problem. Plants and animals do not object as they become extinct. Fortunately for them there are scientists who monitor their health. To illustrate the difficulty of convincing people of problems with wildlife, though, it took threatening of our national symbol, the bald eagle, to bring about legislative action. The Endangered Species Act of 1973 has resulted in lists of plants and animals that are either threatened or, more serious, endangered. Currently there are in the United States alone 303 threatened and 503 endangered animal species, as well as 172 threatened and 772 endangered plant species. Since the inception of the act, 56 species have been removed from the lists, and a number, including the bald eagle, which in 2007 was deemed fully recovered, have been delisted entirely.

Although 34 North American species of birds and mammals have become extinct since the 1500s, none that has been listed since 1973 has succumbed. Some species would have become extinct without the help of humans, but the rate of extinction is estimated to have increased at least 10-fold since the time of the first known human.

The key to keeping plant and animal life from extinction is to prevent the loss of habitat. This is why the Endangered Species Act is a problem for economic growth. The lost logging associated with preserving a single mating pair of spotted owls in the American Northwest amounts to $650 million. While strict environmentalists advocate for the preservation of species, regardless of the economic costs of doing so, the costs are foremost in the minds of the people whose livelihoods are threatened by this law's requirements.

A piece of environmental legislation that combines protections for both wildlife and habitat is the Clean Air Act of 1990. In this legislation, the targeted problem is acid rain. Acid rain is created when power plants burn high-sulfur coal and the SO_2 emissions from that burning combine in the atmosphere with various nitrogen oxides (NO_2, NO_3, etc.) to create a dilute form of sulfuric acid. In particular, the coal that is burned in the Midwest creates an acid that travels to the northeastern states in clouds, and the rain that subsequently forms has caused trees to die and lakes to become deadly for fish.

The legislation limits the quantity of sulfur that industry can put into the air. To comply with the law's provisions, firms can buy more expensive low-sulfur coal, equipment to clean up the emissions, or another firm's pollution permits. Offering options like the trading of pollution permits is considered to be very innovative. It allows companies to clean the environment in the cheapest way possible, and, as we will discuss later, this innovative way of dealing with pollution has earned economists a place at the table in discussing environmental problems.

An additional environmental problem is that landfill space is being used faster than new space is created. The problem here is less an environmental problem than a location problem. Modern landfills are required to prove that no contamination leaks into groundwater. No homeowners want garbage in their neighborhoods, and Congress has steadfastly refused to allow states to keep others from exporting their garbage. A consequence of this stance is that more New York City garbage is put in out-of-state landfills than in those in New York. Because the interstate commerce clause of the U.S. Constitution prevents states from refusing to accept out-of-state garbage, and because of the way the U.S. population is distributed, the burden of siting new landfills has shifted from the East to the Midwest.

The economic implications of changes in Earth's climate are what we will discuss last in this chapter. It is a fairly well-settled scientific fact that the globe is warming. The warmest years on record are concentrated in the 2010s. The problem is that unless they were told by a scientist that this is bad, most people would neither have noticed nor objected to the change in temperature. Though summers have been somewhat warmer, winters—especially at night—have been still warmer. Who is likely to object if winter weather is milder than usual?

Meteorologists tell us that the earth's temperature has risen about 1.5° Fahrenheit in the entire 20th century. The average, though, is 3.0° higher in 2016 than it was in 1970. It is a change that is simply too small for the typical person to detect. Over time, however, the problems with global warming will become more obvious. With temperatures that are anywhere from 5° to 10° higher by the end of the 21st century, several things may happen. The bad things include a thawing of the polar ice caps, which scientists say will be accompanied by a flooding of coastal cities and islands. Soils may become dry, making it more difficult to grow grains. People will use more refrigerants for air conditioning. Warm-weather diseases like malaria and yellow fever may proliferate, and certain areas of the world will become deserts, in a process labeled with the frightening word *desertification*.

On the other hand, some good things will happen if global temperatures rise. Growing seasons will lengthen in northern climates, less energy will be needed to heat homes and businesses in those areas, and the impact of cold-weather diseases like colds and the flu will diminish. A good way of imagining the positive impact is to realize that though there will be places where the climate will get "too hot," some places that were once "too cold" will now be "just right."

This is not to suggest that there will necessarily be an even trade by any means. While temperature zones will change relatively quickly, forests can move only extremely slowly. Thus some forests whose trees require a specific temperature band to be healthy will die long before new ones appear. There is also new research suggesting that only about half of the increased carbon dioxide, which may be good for some species of plant life, can be absorbed.

A statistic of vital importance to environmental economists is the responsiveness of climate to CO_2 concentrations. One estimate suggests a doubling of CO_2 leads to an increase in global temperatures anywhere from 1° Celsius to 4.5° Celsius (relative to preindustrial levels).

Economic Solutions: Using Taxes to Solve Environmental Problems

To solve the environmental problems that we face, we have to encourage or require clean behaviors, or we must discourage unclean behaviors or render them illegal. To varying degrees, all these methods work. America's history of environmental regulations clearly indicates that we have been moving successfully from forms of regulation that concentrate on punishing people to forms where we provide incentives that make clean behavior profitable.

Most environmental regulation still prohibits certain actions that damage the air, water, or wildlife. For instance, the Clean Water Act prohibits dumping of untreated industrial waste into a river. Mandating that the environment be protected, however, is not necessarily the best way to deal with all environmental issues. For instance, it is hypothetically possible that production of a cure for a terrible disease may turn out to be very dirty. In such a case, it might be in society's best interest to sacrifice the environment.

FIGURE 23.5 Solving the problem with a pollution tax.

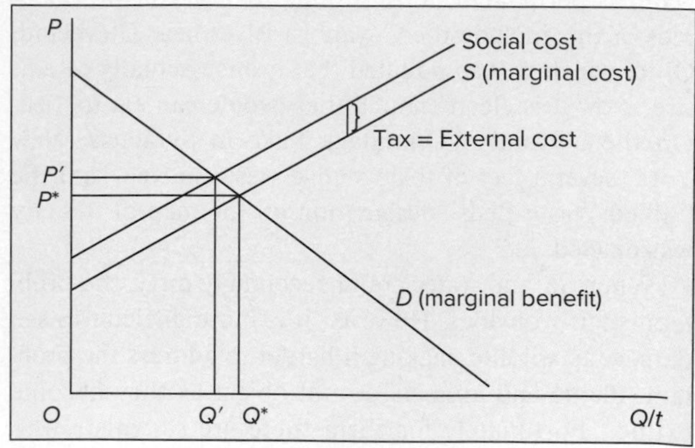

Instead of an outright ban, a polluting activity could be heavily taxed. Activities that were sufficiently profitable to cover whatever tax was levied could continue.

A tax could conceivably be used to discourage any polluting activity, including the creation of garbage or the use of fossil fuels. As Figure 23.5 indicates, a tax would be set that was equal to the external cost, that is, the dollar-denominated value of the pollution. Production of the good would fall to Q', its socially optimal level, and the price would increase to P'. There would be enough tax revenue to compensate those affected by the pollution resulting from a garbage dump or, perhaps, to fund research on nonpolluting technologies. Assuming a connection between energy use and global warming and between global warming and hurricane flooding, such a fund might also be used to deal with flood relief from hurricanes.

Economic Solutions: Using Property Rights to Solve Environmental Problems

Coase's theorem holds that it does not matter if you grant the property right to the polluter or the victim of the pollution. If you say that people have a right to clean air, then Coase suggests that the polluter would buy the right to pollute from the people; if you say that polluters have the right to do what they want, then Coase suggests that the people will pay polluters to be cleaner. Either way, the right amount of production and pollution will result.

An interesting adaptation of Coase's ideas was the Clean Air Act of 1990 and its use of effluent[1] permits.

[1] Effluent is the general term for the stuff that comes out of a smokestack.

The law provides that each emitter of certain restricted pollutants can be granted a fixed number of permits ceding the right to pollute a specific amount. In 1990, the quota of polluted emissions was slightly less than the historical levels of pollution. Any firm that polluted less than that amount could sell its remaining rights to pollute to those that polluted more than their permits allowed. In 2000, in the second phase of the Clean Air Act of 1990, emission rights were reduced further, and each time the act is reauthorized, further reductions are required. In this way pollution is reduced over time, while polluters have options that allow them flexibility in meeting the reductions.

In 2008, the Supreme Court compelled the EPA to regulate greenhouse gases (GHG) as pollutants, and though the outgoing Bush administration chose not to rush into this area, the Obama administration was quite willing to get involved. Its preferred method was to use this same **cap-and-trade** method. Cap-and-trade gets its name from the process by which the government sets a "cap" on the level of pollution that is allowable and then allows polluters to "trade" the right to pollute. By giving the rights away each year, and in diminishing amounts, the reductions are achieved in the most economically efficient manner possible. Specifically, we get the most output (usually electrical power) subject to our societal goal of pollution reductions. This happens because power companies have different opportunity costs associated with reducing pollution. Those that have a high opportunity cost will buy permits from those that have a low opportunity cost. Consider the following uncomplicated example. Suppose there are only two electrical companies and both have older coal-powered generators that generate a great deal of pollution. Each one will have to reduce pollution slightly unless it wishes to buy permits from the other. Suppose one is close to a natural gas pipeline, but the costs of switching to cleaner-burning natural gas have been heretofore just beyond what would have made economic sense for the firm. Suppose the options to the other firm are much more prohibitive. Suppose, finally, that electrical power demand is increasing, so each will be expected to produce more electricity and will therefore generate more pollution in the future. Because they cannot both increase pollution, the firm that has the lower cost option of reducing pollution will do so and be compensated for doing so by selling its permits to the firm with the higher costs. Society's goal of both meeting the increase in electrical demand and reducing pollution is furthered.

cap-and-trade
The method of reducing a pollutant whereby the government gives to polluters, or auctions, a capped amount of pollution permits and then allows those permits to be sold in a market.

For the purposes of acid rain reduction under the 1990 Clean Air Act, each permit grants its holder approximately one ton of SO_2 emissions. Total emissions of SO_2 over the life of this provision of the 1990 act have been cut 91 percent to 2.5 million tons per year. Surprising as it may seem, the price of those emission permits was falling through the 1990s and mid-2000s from $200 to $100. Though those prices spiked in 2006 at more than $1,500, today they are less than $6. At first this was because power companies have found it a profitable part of their business to find ways to reduce pollution. And though the reduction in the number of available permits and the increase in electrical power demand put pressure on the permit prices to rise, electric utilities are using new, cleaner technologies either to reduce the number of permits they have to buy or to make money selling their rights. More recently, though, the biggest driver in clearing the air of SO_2 and nitric oxides has been the reduction in natural gas prices. Natural gas, being a much cleaner burning fuel, allowed utilities to reduce their purchases of permits substantially. Thus the pressure on the price of these permits to decrease that has resulted from this innovation has greatly outweighed the pressure to rise.

Though the cap-and-trade idea was originally one created by economic conservatives in the 1980s as a way to use market forces to deal with environmental challenges, it became a useful political target in 2010. Dubbed "cap and tax," the policy option, instead became something conservatives could pin on political opponents in 2010. It worked so well that even with a 60 to 40 majority in the U.S. Senate, Democrats were unable to muster the votes to pass cap-and-trade as part of their energy bill, which subsequently stalled as a result.

The reasons conservatives opposed cap-and-trade were not all purely political. The acid-rain–producing pollutants were clearly identifiable as to their source—specifically, power plants and other large combustion units with obvious smokestacks. The problem with using cap-and-trade for CO_2 and other greenhouse gases is that there are many more polluters to monitor and regulate. It is relatively simple to monitor the two gases that overwhelmingly come from a few sources. It would be impossible to accurately monitor GHGs emanating from every car, home, business, and farm.

In early 2019, a new idea for dealing with CO_2 emissions was offered by a cross-section of U.S. economists:

a **carbon tax.** A carbon tax would, proportionally to the carbon emissions associated with the use, tax energy consumption. Gasoline would get one rating; coal another; natural gas, a third; and hydroelectric, solar, and wind would have a rating of zero. In order to generate support from conservative economists who might scrutinize an increase in taxes, the entirety of the revenue would be used to fund a per-person rebate that would be deposited regularly into people's bank accounts. A letter advocating for this approach was signed by nearly 4,000 U.S. economists (including myself).

carbon tax A tax levied on the amount of carbon emitted from a particular energy source.

No Solution: When There Is No Government to Tax or Regulate

If the problem of climate change were just an American problem, the federal government could use cap-and-trade or a carbon tax to solve it. It is more challenging because climate change is a global problem. When an environmental problem is confined to one jurisdiction, the government, whether it be local, state, or national, can enact legislation to tackle the problem. When the problem is international, such as with global warming, there is no government to impose a regulatory or tax-based solution.

The Kyoto Protocol is a treaty to which the United States was an original signatory. Such treaties require U.S. Senate approval, so President Clinton's signature was pointless from the start because there were not 20 votes for ratification and he knew that when he signed it. Shortly after his election, President Bush formally pulled the United States out of the agreement noting the significant economic impact compliance would have. He also noted that the agreement did not limit China or India, two rapidly growing energy consumers, in any meaningful way. China now produces two and one-half times the amount of greenhouse gases as it did when the protocols were created, and India produces nearly twice as much. In terms of GHGs per dollar of GDP, these countries now rival the United States.

With the election of President Obama, the position of the U.S. government toward GHG regulation changed. He signed the Paris Agreement in 2015 that required that each country commit itself to reduced carbon emissions. The problem for agreement critics was that it left both the choice of a target and the enforcement to each individual country. Critics suggested that, for these reasons, China was not doing its part. President Trump pulled the United States out of the agreement, giving this and other reasons for doing so.

Assume, for a moment, that at some point there will be an agreement to affirmatively tackle the issue forthrightly. To understand the economic consequences of doing so, consider what would have to happen to gasoline prices to garner a 25 percent reduction in GHGs. Recall that the short-run price elasticity of demand for gasoline is 0.08, while it is 0.24 in the long run. Extrapolation would imply that the price of carbon-based energy would have to quadruple in order to get that 25 percent reduction in the short run though a doubling would be sufficient to accomplish the same thing in the long run. That is likely the upper bound of what is necessary because a doubling of carbon-emitting energy prices would induce energy consumers to look to nonemitting sources. Accounting for the substitution to these other sources, some economists have estimated that the tax on emissions necessary to reduce GHG by 13 percent could be as little as $36 per ton of GHG to as much as $70 per ton. For perspective, a typical car produces a little less than 1 pound of GHG per mile driven, and if you do a bunch of algebra, that translates to an appropriate tax of as little as 20 cents per gallon to as much as $1.75 per gallon.

An alternative solution (favored by liberal politicians and environmentalists) is raising mileage standards for passenger vehicles. This forces an automobile manufacturer to meet a particular standard for the average vehicle it sells. To meet the standard, car companies end up selling their electric and fuel-efficient gasoline cars at a steep discount. This forces the price of larger, less efficient vehicles higher. It essentially puts consumers in the position of deciding whether they want an environmentally friendly car at below cost or pay a premium for the less environmentally friendly SUV.

There is one other concern regarding any of these solutions. They could, theoretically, put American producers of goods at a disadvantage because of the higher costs of energy. The carbon tax proposal suggests appropriate taxes on imported goods when those goods come from countries without similar carbon emission controls in place. It would also repay the tax to the producer when the companies sell their goods to countries without limits.

Regardless of whether environmentalists or their critics are right, the issue illustrates the difficulty in dealing with international environmental problems. There is little economic motivation for a single country to impose high costs on itself, and there is no world government to impose those high costs on everyone. So while the politics in the United States have swung back and forth with regard to American participation in international agreements on climate change, two things should be clear: We have to deal with it, and dealing with it will be made more difficult because of the global nature of the problem.

Summary

You now understand how to use the concept of externalities to explain why pollution warrants government intervention in the market. You understand why pollution is much more likely to occur on publicly owned property than on private property, and you have a cursory understanding of the variety of environmental problems that exist in the world. You now also have an understanding of some economic solutions to these problems.

Key Terms

cap-and-trade
carbon tax
common property
externalities
limited natural resource
renewable natural resource
social cost
stewardship
sustainability

Quiz Yourself

1. When finding the optimal usage rate for a nonrenewable resource, an economist is likely to rely on the idea of
   a. externalities.
   b. present value.
   c. average cost and benefit.
   d. consumer surplus.
2. The notion of "clean enough" is
   a. appealing to an economist thinking about average benefit and average cost.
   b. appealing to an economist thinking about marginal benefit and marginal cost.
   c. appealing to an economist thinking about total benefit and total cost.
   d. completely rejected as a concept by an economist.
3. If a chemical does environmental damage but is used in the production of a good that provides satisfaction to the consumer and profit to the producer, an economist will
   a. insist that the market be left alone.
   b. insist that the chemical be completely banned.
   c. seek to impose a tax on either the chemical or the good.
   d. suggest that consumers voluntarily cut back their consumption.
4. An example of an externality that we see every day is
   a. people paying high prices for gasoline.
   b. people enjoying their ability to drive to work.
   c. oil companies making record profits.
   d. the emissions from a car's tailpipe.
5. When tackling local environmental problems, taxes and regulations can be useful. The reason that global problems (like global warming) are more difficult to control is that
   a. it is in the global interest to ignore the problem.
   b. it is not in any individual country's interest that the problem be solved.
   c. there is no ability to enforce those taxes or regulations.
   d. the "marginal" country is unknown.
6. Overfishing certain parts of the ocean and certain species of fish has been a problem for centuries with countries actually going to war over fishing disputes. Ronald Coase would suggest that there would be no problem if
   a. someone owned (and could control) the ocean.
   b. people stopped eating fish.
   c. people reacted according to the golden rule.
   d. countries agreed to voluntary restrictions on fishing.

7. The evidence on many environmental pollutants (lead in the air and water, sulfur in the air, etc.) is that they
   a. are not nearly as harmful as once thought.
   b. are increasing at an alarming rate.
   c. have decreased substantially in the last 40 years.
   d. have stabilized in the air at their all-time high.
8. An environmental economist would likely recommend which of the following policies?
   a. The elimination of fossil fuel consumption
   b. A tax on gasoline equal to the environmental damage caused by one gallon of gasoline
   c. A tax on gasoline greater than the environmental damage caused by one gallon of gasoline
   d. Voluntary limits on driving

Short Answer Questions

1. Why would an increasing marginal cost of producing oil lead to a more spread-out utilization plan?
2. Why would saving some species be worth the cost of saving them while another species might not be?
3. Why would "cap-and-trade" be more aligned with those who wish to use private market innovations to solve environmental problems than a regulatory-based environmental system?

Think about This

Fossil fuels were the "clean" alternative to wood burning and overcame wood as a source of fuel only when it became cheaper to use. If left unchecked, this will happen to fossil fuels as well because this limited resource will eventually become more scarce than its alternatives (solar-, wind-, hydroelectric-, or biomass-generated power). Should we just wait it out?

Talk about This

Every power source entails some environmental consequence. Nuclear power leaves behind waste that is dangerous for thousands of years. Hydroelectric power destroys the habitat of valley-dwelling animals. Wind and solar power require vast spaces for collection devices. Combustible fuels typically leave a heat-trapping gas. Currently, the dominant U.S. fuel sources are fossil based (coal, oil, natural gas). While other countries have turned toward nuclear power, we have not. Given that our power needs are continuously growing, what are your solutions?

For More Insight See

Joskow, Paul L., A. Denny Ellerman, Richard Schmalensee, Juan Pablo Montero, and Elizabeth M. Bailey, *Markets for Clean Air: The U.S. Acid Rain Program* (Cambridge, U.K.: Cambridge University Press, 2000).

Journal of Economic Perspectives 12, no. 3 (Summer 1998). See articles by Gardner M. Brown Jr., and Jason F. Shogren; Andrew Metrick and Martin Weitzman; Robert Innes, Stephen Polasky, and John Tschirhart; and Richard Schmalensee, pp. 1–88.

Journal of Economic Perspectives 9, no. 4 (Fall 1995). See articles by Michael E. Porter and Claas van der Linde; Karen Palmer, Wallace E. Oates, and Paul R. Portney, pp. 97–132.

Journal of Economic Perspectives 7, no. 4 (Fall 1993). See articles by Richard Schmalensee; William D. Nordhaus; John P. Weyant; James M. Poteba and Gacielka Chichilinsky; and Geoffrey Heal, pp. 3–86.

Any environmental economics textbook, for instance, *Economics and the Environment* by Eban Goodstein.

Behind the Numbers

Environmental Protection Agency: www.epa.gov/air-emissions-inventories/air-pollutant-emissions-trends-data

- Air quality and emissions data
- Outdoor air pollution

Environmental Protection Agency: www.epa.gov/airmarkets

- Emission permit prices

National Oceanic and Atmospheric Administration: www.noaa.gov

- Climate data

U.S. Fish and Wildlife Service: www.fws.gov/endangered

- Threatened, endangered, and delisted species

CHAPTER TWENTY-FOUR

Health Care

Learning Objectives

After reading this chapter you should be able to:

LO1 Summarize how the system of health care finance seriously alters the market for health care services.

LO2 Summarize the sources and uses of health care spending.

LO3 Analyze the health care industry using the supply and demand model and discuss the limitations of the model when applied to this industry.

LO4 Demonstrate that both private insurance and taxpayer-financed health care systems increase the overall price of health care.

LO5 Compare and contrast privately financed and single-payer, taxpayer-financed health care systems by noting their respective advantages and disadvantages.

Chapter Outline

Health care in the United States has two characteristics that seem to be fundamentally inconsistent. No other country can match the United States in terms of the quality of care that is available, but no developed country experiences a similarly high infant mortality rate. In addition, in no other country are doctors as skilled, and in no other country are doctors as highly paid. In no other country is the quality of care as high, but in no other developed country is care denied so often because patients are unable to pay for it. At its root, the problem of having high-quality care that is not available to everyone who needs it is attributed only to the way we finance health care.

In this chapter, we explain health care in the United States by first detailing the money spent and by whom it is spent. We discuss how private and public insurance work in the United States and discuss the problems associated with each. We then turn to why the economics of health care differs so much from the economics of any other good. Along the way, we compare our health care financing system with the model used in most other developed countries and hit the high points of the Patient Protection and Affordable Care Act (PPACA).

Where the Money Goes and Where It Comes From

Health care is one of the most important sectors of our economy. In 2017, a little more than one-sixth of GDP ($3.49 trillion of $19.49 trillion) was spent on health-related goods and services. Of that, the government's portion was nearly half (45 percent, or $1.58 trillion). In political terms, when Republicans accuse Democrats of wanting the government to take over health care, the reality is, government already has almost half of it.

Medicare
Public health insurance in the United States that covers those over age 65.

Of the $1.58 trillion that government spent on health care in the United States in 2017, some $706 billion was spent on **Medicare** (the government health insurance program

Medicaid
Public health insurance in the United States that covers the poor.

for the elderly) and $582 billion was spent on **Medicaid** (the government health insurance program for the poor). The remainder was spent by all levels of government on local, state, and veterans' hospitals and in support of medical research.

Of the $1.91 trillion that was spent on health care in the private sector in 2017, some $1.18 trillion came from premiums paid to insurance companies by businesses, households, or governments (or to employers' self-insured systems). People paid an additional $366 billion in out-of-pocket expenditures, and the remainder was spent by private medical research companies.

In general, of the $3.49 trillion spent on health care in the United States in 2017, $1.14 trillion went to hospitals and $694 billion went to doctors. Drugs accounted for $333 billion and medical research spending accounted for $51 billion.

Insurance in the United States

Most people in the United States are covered by some form of health insurance for at least part of the year. In 2017, for example, 91 percent of the 323 million people in the United States had coverage for at least a portion of the year, and 9 percent had no coverage at all. The coverage during that year came from a variety of sources. The largest group, 181 million people, was covered by group insurance policies, 52 million had individual policies, 56 million were on Medicare, 62 million were on Medicaid,[1] and of those, 12 million were on both.

How Insurance Works

Whether we are discussing health insurance, life insurance, or auto insurance, private insurance of any kind operates similarly. There is a small chance that something bad will happen to you, and there is a large chance that nothing bad will happen to you. You spend a little money on insurance that will cushion the effects of the bad prospect, should it occur. In other words, you pay a premium so that if the bad thing happens, the insurance provider (whether it be the government or an insurance company) will pay to make things better. In the case of health insurance, people pay premiums so that when they get sick, their provider pays most of the expense related to their illnesses.

[1]Because Medicaid's enrollment is fluid, many more people have Medicaid at some point during the year.

risk averse
A characteristic of a person who would pay extra to guarantee the expected outcome.

risk neutral
A characteristic of a person who would not pay extra to guarantee the expected outcome.

It is perfectly rational to buy insurance even when the average expense you would face is less than the cost of the insurance. The reason is that most people are **risk averse:** They prefer to be guaranteed a particular outcome, even when the odds are that for the average person, over an average lifetime, insurance is more expensive than the problem they are insuring themselves against. As an example, suppose there is a 1 percent chance that you will have a major health-related expense of $100,000 and a 99 percent chance that you will have only $1,000 of typical health expenses. A **risk-neutral** person would look at the expected expense, $1,990,[2] and not be willing to pay any more than that for full insurance coverage. People who are risk averse, on the other hand, would be willing to pay more than that to guarantee themselves that they would not have to pay very large health bills out of pocket.

Nearly all private health insurance plans have a number of characteristics in common. You owe a premium that, for most Americans, is paid partly by you and partly by your employer.[3] Insurance companies use premiums for three things: (1) to pay doctor and hospital bills of their patients, (2) to cover administrative expenses, and (3) to provide profits for the owners (usually shareholders) of the insurance company.

If you get sick and have a health expense, it is usually the case that both you and your insurance company will pay part of the bill. There are four key pieces of vocabulary that determine who pays how much. The **deductible** is the amount of health spending a year that you have to pay before the insurance company pays anything. This very much depends on the type of plan you have but can be as low as nothing and as high as several thousand dollars. Annually, the typical deductible for a plan is between $1,400 and $2,700 per person and between $2,800 and $6,300 per family. For instance, if you have an insurance plan with a $2,000 deductible and you have a covered medical expense that totals $5,000,

deductible
The amount of health spending a year that you have to pay before the insurance company pays anything.

[2]$0.99 \times \$1,000 + 0.01 \times \$100,000 = \$1,990$.

[3]This aspect is actually an artifact of World War II. Because of inflation fears during that time, it was against the law to raise wages to attract workers. Instead, companies increased benefits in the form of group insurance subsidies, and the practice survived the war.

you will have to pay $2,000 before your insurance company pays anything. Average deductibles have increased dramatically as many people with the ability to cover large medical expenses have opted for high-deductible health plans. Though the deductibles are often $5,000 to $10,000, the premiums are lower.

The **co-payment** is either a set amount or the percentage of the bill, after the deductible has been taken out, that you have to pay. Typical office visit co-payments are around $25 per visit. Co-insurance rates, the percentage version of co-payments, range between 20 percent and 25 percent. The national average is 20 percent. The **maximum out of pocket** is the most that a person or family will have to pay over a year for all covered health expenses. This means that a $500,000 health expense will not bankrupt the typical person because the maximum out of pocket is usually between $3,000 and $5,200 a year.

co-payment
Either a set amount or the percentage of the bill, after the deductible has been taken out, that you have to pay.

maximum out of pocket
The most that a person or family will have to pay over a year for all covered health expenses.

Varieties of Private Insurance

There are several types of private insurance plans, but they can be classified into three large groups: (1) fee for service, (2) health maintenance, and (3) preferred provider. A fee-for-service provider allows sick people to go to any doctor they want, wherever they want, for whatever ails them. The doctor then bills the insurance company, the insurance company pays its share, and the doctor bills the patient for the remainder. Because there are few controls on spending in a system like this, it is very costly. Patients and doctors, however, have few complaints.

A health maintenance organization (HMO) requires that people see specific doctors at the beginning of any problem. A doctor in this role is referred to as a **primary care physician (PCP)** or, familiarly, as a *gatekeeper*. Patients can see specialists only after their PCP, or gatekeeper, makes a referral, and the PCP has the responsibility of making sure that patients get the appropriate care as inexpensively as possible. Usually HMO PCPs receive a fixed fee for every patient assigned, and specialists are either salaried or also have fixed fees for every referral. Patients and doctors complain about the controls on spending in HMOs, but these serve to keep costs manageable.

primary care physician (PCP)
Physician in managed care operations charged with making the initial diagnosis and making referrals. Also called a *gatekeeper*.

preferred provider organization (PPO)
A type of insurance where certain doctors, hospitals, and other providers have negotiated fee reductions in exchange for a preferred designation.

A **preferred provider organization (PPO)** is somewhat of a hybrid. People can choose the doctor they want from a list of doctors. The doctors agree to charge a specific amount per procedure or disease, and they take a lower fee than usual in order to be guaranteed a large number of potential patients.

Table 24.1 outlines the advantages and disadvantages of each of these private insurance options from the patient's standpoint.

Table 24.1 Advantages and disadvantages to patients of different forms of private insurance.

Insurance Type	Advantages	Disadvantages
Fee for service	Maximum physician choice Little insurance company meddling in doctors' decisions	Highest premiums, deductibles, and co-payment rates because of little control over expensive and unnecessary procedures
HMO	Maximum control over expensive and unnecessary procedures so premiums, deductibles, and co-payment rates are low	Minimal physician choice Significant meddling in physician decisions, especially when differing procedures have significant cost differences
PPO	Some physician choice Moderate premiums, deductibles, and co-payment rates Some control over expensive procedures Minor meddling in physician decisions	

Public Insurance

Public insurance, provided by the government, is divided into three main programs: Medicare, Medicaid, and the Children's Health Insurance Program (CHIP). Medicare is available to eligible citizens who are 65 and older. It works very much like a generous fee-for-service health insurance plan, except that the burden for high premiums is placed on the taxpayer rather than on the patient or the patient's employer. The tax that funds Medicare appears on your paycheck in the same place your Social Security tax does; they are both under FICA (Federal Insurance Contributions Act). The portion that is used for Medicare is 1.45 percent of your salary, wages, and tips; you and your employer each pay that rate. For part of Medicare, money is also taken from the general tax revenues of the government.

Medicare is generous in the following sense: By private health care standards, its premiums are very low, and the co-payments and the deductibles are also low. In truth, Medicare is really two programs, a compulsory program that covers hospital-related expenses and a voluntary program that covers doctors' charges. In 2019, those who were eligible for the compulsory version, Medicare Part A, and worked at least 30 quarters or were married to someone who worked at least 30 quarters paid a $240 monthly premium. Those who worked less than 30 quarters and certain individuals with disabilities who have exhausted other entitlement paid $437 per month, and for those who worked more than 40 quarters, it was free. The voluntary version, Medicare Part B, cost beneficiaries between $135.50 and $460.50 per month in 2019 depending on their 2017 income, which covered doctor-related expenses. Elderly people who are eligible for the primary welfare program for the old and poor, Supplemental Security Income, have Medicaid pick up the Part A premium and often the Part B premium as well.

In contrast with Medicare, Medicaid is a no-premium, no-deductible, very low or no co-payment health plan for the poor.[4] Under Medicaid, doctors are reimbursed at rates that are low relative to what Medicare pays and extremely low relative to what private insurance pays. Hospitals and doctors can and do refuse to treat Medicaid patients when they judge the reimbursement rates to be too low.

Prior to the passage of the Affordable Care Act, there were 49 million Americans who survived, at least part of the year, without any health insurance at all. Many of these are people who move from one job to another and whose insurance runs out while they are unemployed.[5]

Among the uninsured are the nearly 4 million who are under 18. In the 1990s, that figure was more than 16 million. It was in response to that statistic that CHIP was created. Its function is like that of Medicaid, but it is focused, as the name suggests, on children who live in families where the primary earners do not have insurance through their employer and do not make enough to purchase it themselves.

Economic Models of Health Care

We can use our supply and demand model to examine what happens when the good in question is not something tangible, like an apple, but intangible, like health care. In addition, in the context of this model, we can explore how the health care finance system alters people's behavior.

Why Health Care Is Not Just Another Good

Health care is not like any other good. You can look at an apple grown today and say that it is comparable to an apple grown in 2005 or 1885. An apple is pretty much the same through time. On the other hand, medical advances have made it such that medical care is substantially more effective than it used to be. Though the medical CPI has risen at or above the overall rate of inflation for several years, we cannot be sure how much of this increase is an increase in prices and how much is an increase in quality.

To illustrate, let's discuss the treatment of acquired immunodeficiency syndrome (AIDS). In 1985, there was no standard treatment for AIDS. Morphine was sometimes given to ease pain—a terribly ineffective but "cheap" treatment compared to today. In 2001, the treatment became a "drug cocktail" of zidovudine (AZT) and a group of protease inhibitors. Newer drug cocktails cost more than $30,000 per patient per year, but they can sustain a good quality of life for several years. Which "treatment" costs more? You do not have to answer the question because you know that you are not pricing the same thing. The quality of the treatment has improved so greatly that to say that the price of the treatment has increased is simply wrong. The quality of the treatment has improved, and because there was no effective treatment to compare the current one to, the "price" has fallen from infinity.

[4]States may impose small co-payments to discourage abusive overuse.

[5]Workers have the right to continue their employer-sponsored health insurance even after they quit or are fired. The problem is that most employers do not continue subsidizing the premiums, which means people are not likely to be able to afford to exercise this right.

HOW THE PPACA EXPANDED COVERAGE

There are three significant provisions of the PPACA that serve to expand coverage to those who have been without it. First, employers of more than 50 full-time employees are required to provide their employees with at least a minimal insurance plan or else pay a fine. Second, Medicaid was expanded in states where the state agreed to pay a small portion of the extra cost. That expansion, where it occurred, allowed health insurance coverage for everyone (rather than just the children) in families earning under 133 percent (which because of an income exemption amounted to 138 percent) of the poverty line. Third, subsidies are paid to those earning under 400 percent of the poverty line when they purchase health insurance through an approved exchange.

These provisions are not without controversy. The first provision forces employers that do not provide at least minimal health insurance to pay a fine if even one of their employees is given a subsidy to buy insurance. This provision has some economists worried that the PPACA lessens the incentive that firms have to employ new workers by raising the cost of that worker. The Medicaid expansion worried governors and legislatures regarding its impact on state budgets so much that 37 states (including Washington D.C.) have agreed to the expansion or a similar alternative using a waiver process. Finally, because the PPACA was such a charged political issue for so long, only 24 states have agreed to create the exchanges.

Many of the complaints about the increase in the cost of health care over the past few years are misdirected. The cost of things that do not change in quality (syringes, bandages, etc.) has surely increased. But, just as surely, we cannot measure the price of things whose quality is constantly changing. A night in a hospital, for instance, is not the same today as it was in 1985. Though some definitions are the same (e.g., semiprivate has meant and still means two beds in a room), other aspects of the night's stay are different. Today sophisticated medical equipment, including beds that monitor vital signs, are standard. These didn't exist when you were born.

Another key problem with using a supply and demand model for health care services is that one of the assumptions that we made for such a model to work was perfect knowledge. One of the reasons we go to the doctor in the first place is that we do not know what is wrong with us. We go not only to stop the pain but also to find out why the pain exists. This is distinctly different from buying an apple. We know what an apple is, we know why we want it, and we know what it costs to get one. In health care, we have to trust the seller (the doctor) to tell us what we need and how much it will cost.

Implications of Public Insurance

Though considerations such as these are important, we can still examine the effect of our financing system on the supply and demand model for health care services. As you can see in Figure 24.1, if there were no program to provide health care services to the poor, the nonpoor would get many services and the poor few. If D_{poor} is the demand for health care by the poor and D_{nonpoor} is the demand for health care by the nonpoor, then $D_{\text{poor + nonpoor}}$ is the market demand for health care services. This is found by adding the two demand curves together horizontally. Specifically, at each price, the quantity demanded of the poor is added to the quantity demanded of the nonpoor. If the supply curve is as shown, then the price is P^* and the poor consume Q_{poor}, much less than the nonpoor, Q_{nonpoor}.

On the other hand, if the poor were to get the services at no cost, then the situation might be quite different. Figure 24.2 shows that in this case, the market demand is the amount that the poor would consume if it were free to them, Q_{poor}, plus the demand by the nonpoor. As you can see, the poor would consume much more, Q_{poor}, while the nonpoor would consume less. Prices would also be higher for both the poor and nonpoor.

FIGURE 24.1 Health care: who gets it without subsidies.

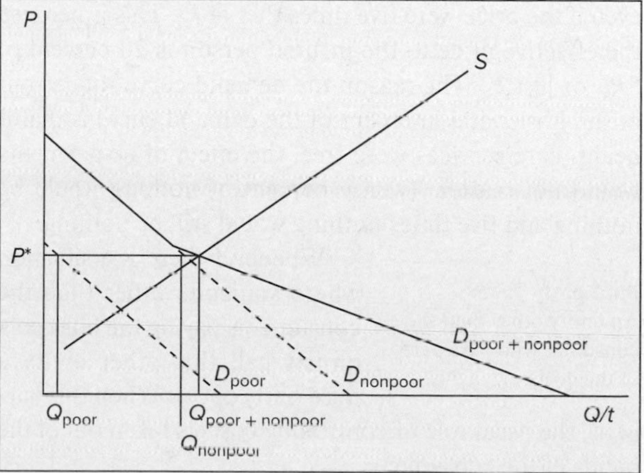

FIGURE 24.2 Health care: who gets it with subsidies.

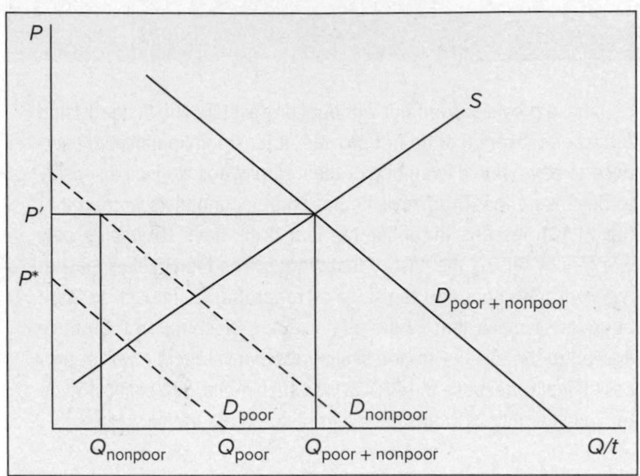

FIGURE 24.3 The effect of co-payments on the market for health care.

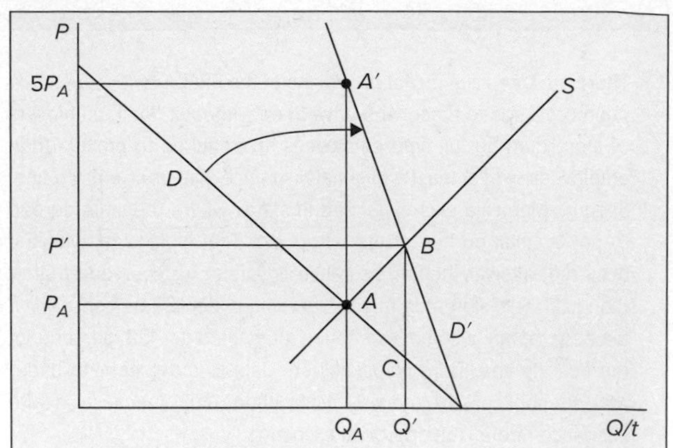

Efficiency Problems with Private Insurance

What private insurance does to the market for health care is as disruptive as public insurance. Recall the idea of co-payments: After the deductible is met, for every dollar of covered medical expense, a low percentage (usually 20 percent) is paid by the patient and the remainder is paid by the insurance company. How does that affect the demand for health care? For simplicity's sake, assume the deductible has either been met or is zero.

Figure 24.3 shows that the demand curve will rotate out to the right (from *D* to *D*′) and that this will cause a greater consumption of health care services and higher prices. Let's look at why the curve rotates this way. Take the equilibrium point prior to any insurance; call that point *A*. A person is willing to pay P_A and consumes Q_A medical services prior to insurance. Suppose that person now has insurance with a 20 percent co-payment rate. If that is the case, that person would be willing to consume Q_A medical services even if the price were five times that of P_A. This is because the effective price to the insured person is 20 percent of $5P_A$, or just P_A. The reason the demand curve rotates out of the horizontal intercept of the demand curve is that if health care services were free, the effect of co-payments would not matter. Twenty percent of nothing would be nothing and five times nothing would still be nothing.

third-party payer
An entity other than the consumer who pays part of the costs.

Whenever there is a situation where someone other than the consumer is paying the bill, economists call this other entity a **third-party payer.** When this happens, the usual role of controlling costs is taken out of the hands of the consumer.

Since our demand curve rotates out, we buy more health care services and pay more for them. The good news is that this effect is lessened if the underlying demand curve, *D*, is itself inelastic. It can certainly be argued that the demand for health care services is relatively inelastic, and the evidence from an extensive study started in the late 1970s and published in 1987 suggests just that. This is because we would not have an unnecessary operation even if it got less expensive, and most people will have a necessary operation even if the price is high. This study suggests that patient sensitivity to price is greater for visits to doctors than for hospitalizations. Overall health elasticity estimates from this study indicate that a 10 percent increase in the out-of-pocket expenses of the patient is associated with a 1 percent to 3 percent reduction in health care utilization. More recent studies have identified elasticities by type of health care service. The conclusions of these studies follow reasonable intuition. Trips to the emergency room are highly inelastic, whereas prescription drugs are (while still inelastic) much more elastic.

The increase in health care utilization also has an efficiency implication. Recall from the Chapter 3 discussion of consumer and producer surplus that the deadweight loss is the means by which economists measure inefficiency. Here, the triangle *ABC* is the amount of the inefficiency.

moral hazard
Having insurance increases the demand for the insured good.

Another area of inefficiency with health care insurance in particular comes in the form of **moral hazard.** People who have insurance consume more health care. This is a problem with all forms of insurance, and the clearest example is in automobile insurance. If you drive more recklessly when you have insurance than when you do not, having insurance makes you more likely to need insurance. In the field of health care, if having insurance makes you more likely to get tested for certain diseases, or even worse, fail to exercise or eat right, then moral hazard is a problem.

A final area of inefficiency in the health insurance market is the greatest threat to its existence, **adverse selection.** Adverse selection arises when, instead of a true cross-section of the population buying insurance, those in most need of insurance are the most willing to pay for insurance and drive up the price of insurance with their illnesses to such a degree that those people who are not as sick leave the market altogether.

adverse selection
Those in most need of insurance are the most willing to pay for insurance and drive up the price of insurance with their illnesses to such a degree that those people who are not as sick leave the market altogether.

To understand the problem, suppose there are three types of people who initially do not know their own health status and their own need for health insurance. Unbeknownst to them, they are the "healthy," "somewhat healthy," or "unhealthy." Suppose the healthiest category of people have no serious illnesses in their foreseeable future and face few risks other than accidents that are equally likely to occur throughout the population. Suppose the unhealthiest category of people face many risks associated with expensive treatments as well as those same injury risks. Now suppose there are two periods: now and later. If no one knows his or her health status "now" and everyone is risk averse, everyone will likely buy insurance "now." They will pay the costs of that insurance (through premiums), which will equal the average cost of care plus the administrative costs plus the profit for the insurance company. In that sense, when no one knows anything, insurance works fine. Once people know their health status, they will be able to compare the premiums to their expected costs by going it alone. If the difference is dramatic, the healthiest group may drop their insurance coverage. Doing so will raise the average costs to everyone else left in the insurance pool. It may raise costs so much that the somewhat healthy people drop their insurance. This has been labeled by some as the "insurance death spiral."

You can solve this particular problem of adverse selection in one of three ways: charging unhealthy people more than healthy people (which is what we do with car insurance in that bad drivers pay more), having a system in which everyone gets insurance through some means other than individual choice (which could be through their employer or through the government), or we can mandate that people buy health insurance. The first method is considered, by many, unethical because lack of coverage is frequently translated as lack of care and lack of care for the sick is considered immoral.

The second method, which is what most of those in group insurance experience, is the system that existed in the United States prior to health care reform in 2010. Prior to that time, most Americans had insurance either through the government or through their employer, while some purchased it as individuals; and some of those in the individual market who were sick were denied coverage by insurers. The PPACA changed that. Insurance companies were required to cover them without considering their health status. Ending that option for insurance companies, though, left the companies vulnerable to adverse selection.

The resolution to this problem and the final method of dealing with adverse selection is **mandation.** Mandation is the requirement that everyone buy insurance. By requiring the healthy to buy insurance (forcing them to pay a tax or fine if they do not), the problem of adverse selection disappears. The fine that was included in the PPACA was repealed in 2017 as part of the Trump tax cuts.

mandation
The requirement to purchase insurance.

Major Changes to Insurance Resulting from PPACA

Several provisions of the bill change how the health insurance industry operates. Under laws existing prior to the enactment of PPACA, health insurers could cut off dependent children from coverage under their parents' health insurance the first year after their children reached 23 and were free to consider, charge more for, and deny coverage for any medical condition a prospective client had prior to purchasing insurance through the company.

Insurance companies could set annual and lifetime limits on how much they would cover. They were free to set prior conditions by which they could rescind coverage, and they could raise the rates of those who became ill (and therefore expensive to the company). They were free to charge rates that were different for men and women. They were not subject to government intervention regarding premiums, profit, and the proportion of premiums associated with administrative costs. Much of this ended as a result of the passage of PPACA.

The law as it stands requires that health insurers allow dependent children to stay on their parents' health insurance through age 26, that the insurers accept everyone without regard to health status, charge the same to healthy and the unhealthy alike, and charge the same for men and women. They can no longer set annual or lifetime limits. Lastly, they cannot rescind coverage or raise rates on the sick.

To the untrained eye and ear, each of these provisions might be considered unambiguously good, but consider that each one of them will come with a cost that will, in all likelihood, be passed on to the people who pay the premiums for health insurance, the people who work for companies who provide them with health insurance, and the people who buy goods and services from those companies. Take the simplest of these provisions, the extension of dependent coverage to children through age 26. This provision means that young adults will be able to go to graduate school and/or have some time to find that first good job. However, their parents' employer will face extra costs associated with having them on their health insurance plan.

How will employers and employees react? That depends on the elasticity of demand and supply for labor, the elasticity of demand for the good or service the employer produces, and some other factors. For some workers, paychecks will be smaller than they would otherwise be. For some firms, they may employ fewer workers than they might have. Still others may take a hit to profits. Finally, firms that can raise prices to pay for these costs may do so, and these extra costs will be dispersed to consumers. The cost of this provision will go somewhere. While that is good for 24- to 26-year-olds, it is not necessarily good for society.

All of the other provisions have a similar problem associated with them. Again, the benefits to those not cut off, or not charged more, or not denied coverage will be greater. However, those costs and burdens will go somewhere. Take another example. Women, on average, are more costly than men throughout the health care life cycle because they face cancer risks—specifically, ovarian, breast, and uterine cancer—that men either do not face or, in the case of breast cancer, do with much less frequency. Just as in the auto insurance industry teenage boys pay more for car insurance than teenage girls because boys get in more serious accidents than do girls, women used to have to pay more for individual health insurance, and groups that were disproportionately comprised of women paid more than groups of the same size that were disproportionately comprised of men. What does that mean with regard to this provision? Unlike the situation that existed prior to the passage of the PPACA (where men were paying less than women, all other things equal), men and women pay the same amount. Premiums for men had to increase to allow for premiums for women to fall.

The aforementioned provisions affecting insurance that present the greatest challenge to the health insurance industry itself are the provisions that prevent insurance companies from denying coverage to people based on preexisting conditions. This, by itself, could (were it not accompanied with another provision requiring that everyone buy health insurance or have it provided to them) lead to the end of all private individualized health insurance, through the aforementioned death spiral.

The resolution to the death spiral imagined by the PPACA is through a combination of provisions that expand coverage. Through a large expansion of Medicaid via state-run insurance exchanges, and through an employer requirement (all explained later in this chapter), coverage could be extended to three-quarters of those who are currently uninsured. Still, those provisions alone would likely not be enough to forestall the death spiral. This is why the PPACA included the requirement that everyone buy insurance if insurance is not provided to them. Requiring the healthy to buy insurance (forcing them to pay a tax or fine if they do not) makes the problem of adverse selection disappear. That is why the removal of the fine associated with lacking health insurance is such an issue.

In the individual health insurance market, insurance companies have significantly less freedom to charge differential prices to buyers. They are allowed to charge older customers no more than three times what they charge younger ones (though younger ones typically cost one-fifth or less than what older ones cost), and only are able to charge 50 percent more to tobacco users. They may set up broad geographic price differences and may charge more for larger families than smaller ones. This all is opposed to few, if any, federal limits that had been in place with regard to market segmentation. Remember that, under normal circumstances, insurers maximize profits by charging premiums based on actual experience.

There is another, in the grand scheme of things, relatively minor provision change that is potentially important to young people; that is the provision that requires that administrative costs and profits make up not more than 20 percent of premiums. It is this provision that affects those in the relatively low-wage restaurant and retail industries.

The Blood and Organ Problem

One problem associated with our current health care system is the scarcity of blood and organs. To an economist, the shortage of blood and organs is directly and unambiguously determined by the fact that it is illegal for people to sell these items for medical use. The ban on the sale of blood and organs for medical use is almost entirely justified on moral grounds. For instance, it is not illegal to sell your blood for use in cosmetics.

If a price can be forced to be zero, the quantity supplied will be reduced and the quantity demanded enhanced. This offers another moral dilemma. If a market were allowed, there would be people who would not be able to pay the price for a needed organ, and, as a result, they would die while someone else who could afford that organ would live. On the other side of that moral debate, though, is the fact that if there were a legal market, more organs would become available and more people would live.

Note that although both the supply and demand for organs are inelastic, neither is perfectly inelastic.[6] There are people who would choose not to pay an exorbitant price to live, and there are people who would be more likely to sign their donor cards if there were a high reward that they could bestow on their heirs by doing so.

The downside of such a market is similar to the downside of the market for tobacco. Poor information can cause people to make life-altering mistakes. For instance, you can live on one kidney, and therefore you could sell the other if the price were right. However, you might underestimate the likelihood that you will ultimately need that other kidney. The sale of organs may be a poor idea, but selling blood may not. There is little economic reason to ban the sale of blood for medical purposes because, unlike organs, blood is self-replenishing.

[6]If both were perfectly inelastic at different quantities, there would be no market-clearing price.

Comparing the United States with the Rest of the World

Every industrialized nation has a distinct health care system. The one thing that is common throughout the rest of the developed world, though, is that government is the health care provider, insurer, or insurer of last resort. There are distinct advantages to the way the rest of the world does this, but there are disadvantages as well. Having a **single-payer system,** where the government collects significantly high taxes to pay for everyone's health care, benefits those who could not afford health care any other way. It creates serious shortages as well.

single-payer system The government collects (usually very high) taxes to pay for everyone's health care.

In Canada, the United Kingdom, and much of Europe, being a citizen of the country grants you unlimited rights to necessary health care that is either free or close to it. While the financial arrangements (shown in Table 24.2) in these countries differ, the citizenry need not worry about access to basic health care regardless of their ability to pay. This helps explain the very low

Table 24.2 International health care finance schemes.

Sources: OECD Health Data, www.oecd.org; Kaiser Family Foundation, www.healthsystemtracker.org.

Country	Government Health Expenditures as a Percentage of Total, 2017	Government/ Compulsory Insurance as a Percentage of Total, 2015	Hospitals	Physicians	Function of Private Insurance
Australia	67.7	68.2	Mostly public	A	a
Canada	70.5	70.5	Mostly private	A, B	a
France	79.1	76.6	Mostly public	A	b
Germany	84.8	84.3	Mix of public and private	A	a
Japan	NA	84.1	Mostly private	A, B	None
United Kingdom	79.4	79.6	Mostly public trusts	C	a
United States	49.1*	81.9*	Mostly private	A	c

A–mostly private fee for service.
B–government-imposed fee schedule.
C–public employees.
a–option to purchase private insurance for all expenses.
b–option to purchase private insurance for noncovered expenses.
c–all non-Medicare, non-Medicaid.
* The significant differences between these figures (not present for other countries) reflect the ACA requirements that large employers provide insurance to their employees.

Table 24.3 International comparisons of health expenditures, infant mortality, and life expectancy.

Sources: databank.worldbank.org; stats.oecd.org; www.thelancet.com.

		Australia	Canada	France	Germany	Japan	United Kingdom	United States
	Health expenditures/GDP, 2015	9.3	10.4	11.5	11.1	10.9	9.8	16.8
	Infant mortality rate per 1,000 births, 2015	3.2	4.7	3.5	3.3	2.1	3.8	5.8
	Life expectancy, 2015	84.5	83.9	82.4	80.7	83.9	81.0	78.7
Five-Year Survival Rates	Prostate cancer	94.5	93.6	93.1	91.6	93.0	88.7	97.4
	Breast cancer	89.5	88.2	86.7	86.0	89.4	85.6	90.2
	Ovarian cancer	42.0	40.9	43.5	41.2	46.3	36.2	43.4
	Cervical cancer	66.4	66.6	65.0	65.2	71.4	63.8	62.6
	Colon cancer	70.7	67.0	63.7	64.8	67.8	60.0	64.9
	Leukemia (adult)*	51.1	55.2	59.2	53.6	18.9	47.4	51.8
	Melanoma	92.9	89.1	90.8	93.1	69.0	90.9	90.8
	Lung cancer	19.4	20.6	17.3	18.3	32.9	13.3	21.2
	Pancreatic cancer	12.0	10.8	8.6	10.7	8.4	6.8	11.5
	Childhood leukemia	92.3	92.6	88.6	91.1	87.6	92.2	89.5
	Childhood brain cancer	67.1	72.7	70.8	69.5	69.6	71.9	78.2

*2005–2009

occurrences of infant mortality and relatively long life spans in these countries, as seen in Table 24.3. The unemployed and the employed, the working and the retired, the young and the old, the rich and the poor are treated with a degree of equality that cannot be claimed in the United States. In addition, because the doctors are paid salaries by the government instead of fees for seeing patients, they do not have an incentive to order expensive tests and perform costly surgeries. Further, as government employees, they are usually protected from lawsuits. Thus universal access is accomplished at lower overall costs than in the United States.

This, however, comes at a cost. These countries have severe doctor shortages because, in an effort to control costs, physicians are paid much less than they are paid in the United States. One principal reason many foreign-born physicians practice in the United States is that they can make a great deal more money here than in their own countries. In addition, there is no monetary incentive to become a doctor when you cannot get rich by being one. The effect of having salaried doctors is also seen when these doctors are reluctant to put in long hours. Physicians are among the hardest-working people in the United States. You can also see the effect of this public health provision in the five-year survival rates of various cancers. Of the countries listed in Table 24.3, the United States enjoys survival rates that are at or above the median (of those countries) in all but 1 of the 11 cancers listed. It also ranks first or second (in terms of survival rates) in 5 of the 11 cancers. If you rank the countries for these survival rates and average those ranks, only Australia performs better than the United States.

Another favorable factor of the U.S. system is immediate access to procedures that require long waiting periods elsewhere. In the United States a 50-year-old man with blocked arteries is hospitalized and operated on within hours of being admitted, whereas the waiting period for bypass surgery in Canada has been as high as six months. Though some waiting periods have shortened, this is in part due to the recognition by physicians that expensive procedures must be rationed. In the United States the elderly with kidney disease will be given dialysis as long as they are physically able to stand it (lengthening life by a year or more). A similar English patient cannot schedule routine dialysis treatments under the British government-run system. Finally, an American with an arthritic joint can count on the fact that (after a process of testing less costly treatments) he or she will be outfitted with an artificial joint. Such is not the case in Canada or the United Kingdom.

Another important area that would be lost if the United States were to go to a single-payer system would be innovation. Prescription drug, medical device, and medical procedure innovation has been highly concentrated in the United States, largely because the innovator makes money that cannot be made in the single-payer countries. Furthermore, the innovation that takes place abroad is likely motivated by profits that can be made in the United States. As a result, very few health care economists believe that turning the United States into a single-payer environment would be good for health care innovation.

Last, because doctors are typically immune from lawsuits in countries with single-payer systems, accountability for mistakes is left to professional standards boards. While these mechanisms can work, very often they end up being a system for physicians to protect their own.

Summary

You should now understand how the system of health care finance seriously alters the market for health care services. You also understand that in the United States about half of the health care tab is picked up by the taxpayer, with the remainder being picked up either by patients directly or through their insurance companies. You understand why health care is not like most other goods that economists study but that we can look at it using the tools of supply and demand. You understand that both taxpayer-financed health care and private insurance-financed health care increase the overall price of health care. Last, you understand why a single-payer, taxpayer-financed health care system would have both advantages and disadvantages.

Key Terms

adverse selection
co-payment
deductible
mandation
maximum out of pocket
Medicaid
Medicare
moral hazard
primary care physician (PCP)
preferred provider organization (PPO)
risk averse
risk neutral
single-payer system
third-party payer

Quiz Yourself

1. The existence of health insurance as a means of paying for health care tends to _____ health care.
   a. increase the supply of
   b. decrease the supply of
   c. increase the demand for
   d. decrease the demand for
2. The primary motivation for the purchase of any insurance is grounded in the fact that most people are
   a. risk lovers.
   b. risk averse.
   c. risk neutral.
3. The risk-averse person will buy health insurance
   a. only if the expected health costs equal the insurance premium.
   b. only if the expected health costs are greater than the insurance premium.
   c. even if the expected health costs are less than the insurance premium.
   d. under no circumstances.
4. The government, in the form of Medicare, Medicaid, and the Children's Health Insurance Program, pays for __________ of health care costs.
   a. less than 10 percent
   b. slightly less than half
   c. about 75 percent
   d. all
5. If you have a \$2,000 covered health expense, a deductible of \$500, and a 20 percent co-pay, then you pay __________ and the insurance company pays __________.
   a. \$1,500; \$500
   b. \$1,000; \$1,000
   c. \$800; \$1,200
   d. \$700; \$800

6. Which of the following forms of private insurance is likely to have the lowest premiums and least doctor choice flexibility?
   a. Medicare
   b. An HMO
   c. A PPO
   d. A fee-for-service plan
7. Medical care inflation is likely to be easily overstated (if you look simply at the increase in the cost of a hospital stay) because that calculation ignores
   a. the original costs.
   b. the new costs.
   c. quality increases.
   d. quality decreases.
8. The problem of the "third-party payer" arises in health care in the form of
   a. doctors having to pay part of their own expenses.
   b. government and/or private insurance paying a significant part of the costs.
   c. patients having to pay a significant part of the costs.
   d. hospitals not being able to collect from many patients.
9. One significant feature of a "single-payer" system lacking in the U.S. system is
   a. government involvement in health care.
   b. coverage for the elderly.
   c. coverage for the poor.
   d. universal coverage.
10. Compared to other countries, the United States spends _____ (as a percentage of GDP). Compared to other countries, U.S. survival rates for a variety of cancers are _____.
    a. more; worse
    b. less; worse
    c. more; better
    d. less; better

Short Answer Questions

1. Why would eliminating the ability to deny coverage to those with preexisting conditions require mandation to accompany it?
2. Why would risk-averse people be more likely to buy insurance?
3. For whom would a mini-med health insurance policy be a good policy to have relative to the alternative and why?
4. Why is it more likely that health expenses will rise faster in the United States than in Canada or the United Kingdom?
5. How might you apply the notion of "moral hazard" to decisions you make about exercise?

Think about This

List the pros and cons associated with the U.S. system of financing health care relative to the U.K. system. Do the same relative to the Canadian system. Use your understanding of opportunity cost to think about why we can't have "the best of both worlds."

Talk about This

In the United States a terminally ill patient can decide to decline extraordinary medical treatment, but in all cases the patient, or the spouse, is the one who makes that decision (either with prior instructions or by making his or her wishes known to the health care provider). In the United Kingdom, the government can, and does, limit the availability of extraordinary medical treatment. Thus, though care is free (or nearly free) to the patient, it can be limited against their will. The U.K. government's contention is that health care resources are scarce and they would be wasted extending the life of a terminally ill patient by a few days. Which is worse, the aspect of the U.S. system where people are denied care when they are unable to pay, or the U.K. system where they are denied care because their treatment would not lead to a significant increase in the quality of life?

For More Insight See

Health Care Finance Association statistical tables–www.hcfa.gov

Phelps, Charles E., *Health Economics* (Reading, MA: Addison-Wesley, 2009).

www.census.gov/prod/2004pubs/04statab/health.pdf
International Comparisons of Types of Health Care Finance Systems–www.nao.org.uk/publications

Behind the Numbers

Statistical Abstract of the United States; comparative international statistics–www.census.gov/compendia/statab

Health care expenditures.
Centers for Medicare and Medicaid Services; historical tables–www.cms.gov/NationalHealthExpendData

Health insurance coverage.

Coverage type–

www.census.gov/hhes/www/hlthins/hlthins.html

Lack of coverage.

Centers for Disease Control and Prevention–

www.cdc.gov/nchs/nhis.htm

Centers for Medicare and Medicaid Services: www.cms.gov

- Medicare and Medicaid spending
- Medicare and Medicaid enrollment
- Medicare premiums

U.S. Census Bureau: www.census.gov

- Health insurance coverage

Organisation for Economic Cooperation and Development (OECD): www.oecd.org

- International comparisons of health spending.

World Bank: databank.worldbank.org

- International comparisons of health outcomes

"Global surveillance of trends in cancer survival 2000–14 (CONCORD-3): Analysis of individual records for 37 513 025 patients diagnosed with one of 18 cancers from 322 population-based registries in 71 countries," www.thelancet.com, Vol 391

- International comparisons of cancer survival rates

CHAPTER TWENTY-FIVE

Government-Provided Health Insurance: Medicaid, Medicare, and the Children's Health Insurance Program

Learning Objectives

After reading this chapter you should be able to:

LO1 Describe the Medicaid program.

LO2 Describe the Medicare program.

LO3 Distinguish Medicaid from Medicare and understand their relationship.

LO4 Describe the Children's Health Insurance Program.

Chapter Outline

Since the early 1900s, the United States has been subsidizing medical care for citizens whose incomes are extremely low. The number of people who were covered by some form of federal medical care increased until 1967, when the Medicaid program was established. From that point on, millions of Americans have benefited from free medical care. In 2017, 46 million children and another 28 million adults had nearly all of their medical expenses paid for by Medicaid and its companion program, the Children's Health Insurance Program (CHIP).

In this chapter, we describe the Medicaid program in full, and we provide information about the people who are eligible for its benefits and what coverage they receive. We also discuss the groups that draw most heavily on Medicaid benefits. We describe the relationship between the federal government and individual states as it relates to funding and administering the Medicaid program. We outline how doctors and hospitals are reimbursed when they work with patients whose costs are paid through Medicaid. We use our supply and demand model to explain why Medicaid costs so much, and we focus attention on Medicaid's treatment of two very different populations: the very old and the very young. Then, we consider provisions in Medicaid that are intended to control costs.

Medicare and Social Security are the centerpieces of the United States' policy for the elderly. Social Security ensures an income for the retired, and Medicare guarantees heavily subsidized health insurance for everyone over 65, retired or not. Social Security began in the New Deal 1930s; Medicare in the second great wave of social programs during the Johnson administration's Great Society of the 1960s. In its first full year in operation, 1967, the cost of its benefits totaled \$2.7 billion; by 2018 it cost \$700 billion.

Medicare comprises two programs: Medicare Part A, a mandatory program that covers expenses derived from hospital stays; and Medicare Part B, a voluntary program that covers doctor visits. The Medicare section begins by laying out why a government health insurance program for the elderly makes economic sense and reviews the problems that such health insurance programs inevitably face. After discussing how each part of Medicare works, we focus on ways that each part has attempted to control costs. We then look at the Medicare Trust Fund and its projected problems in staying solvent, and we suggest ways Medicare can delay or prevent the shortfall. As part of that discussion, we talk about the relationship between Medicaid and Medicare, the program for Americans 65 or older.

Finally, we explore CHIP and its function of providing health insurance to the children of working families that do not have employer-provided health insurance.

Medicaid: What, Who, and How Much

Medicaid was established in 1964 to consolidate and expand existing programs that had been charged with providing health care to those who could not otherwise afford it. In 2017, the program cost the federal and state governments $582 billion. We begin our discussion of the Medicaid system by describing who is eligible, what is covered, who is enrolled, which groups cost the most, the relationship the federal government has with the states, and how doctors and hospitals are reimbursed.

People who are eligible for Medicaid must meet one of many criteria. In general, anyone who is in a family that is eligible for cash assistance under Temporary Assistance to Needy Families (TANF) or Supplemental Security Income (SSI) is automatically eligible for Medicaid. Eligibility standards were altered by the Patient Protection and Affordable Care Act (PPACA) such that many more adults are covered by Medicaid. Prior to that act's passage, any children under 19 whose parents' income was less than 133 percent of the appropriate poverty line for their family size or pregnant women and children under a year old whose family income was less than 185 percent of that poverty line were also eligible, as were relatively few others who were affected by a variety of other rules. Under the rules prior to 2014, adults who did not have children under the age of 19 could have very little income and not be covered by Medicaid because their wealth made them ineligible for TANF or SSI.

The PPACA, as originally passed, required states to expand Medicaid eligibility to include anyone in the household if the household income was less than 133 percent[1] of the poverty line unless the states were willing to forgo all federal money for Medicaid. The Supreme Court decision that validated many parts of the act invalidated this provision. This meant that states could decide whether or not to participate. This also meant that although Medicaid enrolled more than 61 million, and CHIP enrolled another 7.9 million, only half of those whose incomes were below 150 percent of the poverty line received its benefits. By 2019, 37 states had chosen to expand their Medicaid programs.

Medicaid pays for nearly everything that is considered necessary from a medical standpoint, but it also leaves other procedures optional for states to cover if they wish. Doctor visits, emergency room visits, surgery, outpatient procedures, medicines, birth control pills, permanent and semipermanent birth control procedures and devices, eye care, long-term care—you name it, Medicaid probably pays for it. Literally, the only things that are not covered are most abortions, cosmetic surgeries, and drugs for weight loss and hair growth. Abortions are paid for by Medicaid in only a few states, and in those states the state must pay the whole fee. Whenever a pregnancy is the result of rape or incest, or threatens the life of the mother, Medicaid pays as it would for any other procedure.

Far more women and young people are served by Medicaid than their respective proportions in the general population. Whereas 51 percent of the population is female, nearly 54 percent of the Medicaid population is. Only 22 percent of the population is under 18, yet 39 percent of the Medicaid population is under 18. If you look simply at the adults on Medicaid, 59 percent are female.

In racial makeup, Medicaid recipients mirror the population of those who live in poverty nearly perfectly: 40 percent white, 21 percent black, and 25 percent Hispanic.

Medicaid is a cooperative effort of federal and state governments. The federal government mandates that the states enroll all people who are eligible, and it gives them guidelines to use if they wish to enroll others. States have the option of covering or denying certain specified expenses (like the previously mentioned abortions), as they wish.

The federal mandates are partially covered by federal matching money, and states are reimbursed according to their relative GDPs. Poorer states are given greater reimbursement rates, and richer states are given smaller ones.

[1]Though technically the cutoff is 133 percent of the poverty line, there is an income exemption in the calculation, which makes the effective percentage 138 percent.

Twelve states get the minimum 50 percent matching percentage from the federal government, while nine other states and the District of Columbia get at least a 70 percent match. To motivate state participation in Medicaid's eligibility standards, the PPACA temporarily raised these rates 7.6 to 15 percentage points to assist states' transition. The differential rates made Medicaid less of a burden for poorer states to fund.

Regardless of whether states participate in the expanded Medicaid provisions, some states make it easier to enroll in Medicaid than others. States have different income and wealth standards for TANF, and people who are eligible for Medicaid in New York and Wisconsin, for example, would not be eligible in states like Texas and Arkansas. This difference is effective only for adults, since children under one year of age are eligible, regardless of the state they live in, under a federal standard evaluating whether the family's income is less than 185 percent of the poverty line. All other children are similarly eligible as long as their family's income is less than 133 percent of the poverty line.

When doctors and hospitals treat patients whose bills are paid by Medicaid, they are reimbursed by the state at widely varying rates. States pay different amounts for the same procedures. These variations arise because Medicaid payments start at the state level with the federal government matching the state's payments. States must set reimbursement rates high enough that there are enough physicians and hospitals in all areas willing to treat Medicaid patients. When many physicians are in competition with one another, rates can be lower; when there are few, rates must be higher.

For doctors and hospitals, Medicaid is an all-or-nothing proposition. When doctors and hospitals agree to take Medicaid patients, they agree to accept the state reimbursement rate as payment in full. This means that they cannot bill patients for any portion of the cost. They also agree to take any and all Medicaid patients who need treatment. They cannot limit their practice to a certain percentage, and they cannot accept patients with one disease and not another. Finding these restrictions to be unreasonable and reimbursement rates too low, many private hospitals and prestigious doctors do not accept Medicaid patients.

Combined, these provisions make it so that states make many of the implementing decisions about what they will cover and at what rates they will reimburse providers. They do this knowing that the federal government will pick up between one-third and two-thirds of the total bill.

Why Medicaid Costs So Much

Medicaid is an expensive program. To examine why it costs as much as it does, it will be helpful to put it into our supply and demand context. In 2017, the federal and state governments spent $582 billion to provide health care for 74 million Americans of Medicaid and Medicaid's companion program, CHIP. Netting out the CHIP enrollment and costs, that amount translates to just under $8,000 per recipient. People who are not on Medicaid spend about the same as that. As a matter of fact, until quite recently those on Medicaid accounted for substantially greater per capita expenditures than those not on Medicaid. Why is it that the expenses of people who pay for their own health care are almost identical to the expenses of people whose health care is paid through Medicaid?

Let's turn to our supply and demand model for an explanation. As it is with any other good, the demand for health care is downward sloping. This is because when the price is high, people forgo care for ailments that are not all that troubling. Although price is always a concern, there are ailments that people will treat regardless of cost. Likewise, a standard upward-sloping supply curve makes sense because it takes more money to get doctors and hospitals to provide the greater quantities of care and the higher quality of care that we desire.

Figure 25.1 differs from every other supply and demand diagram you have seen, though, in that we have separated the demand by people in poverty from the demand by the people whose incomes are above the poverty line. The demand curve $D_{nonpoor}$ for the nonpoor is farther

FIGURE 25.1 The supply and demand for health care without Medicaid.

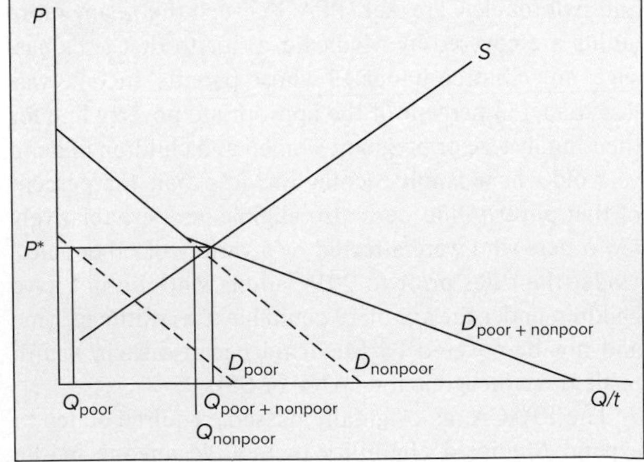

to the right than the demand curve D_{poor} for the poor. To get the market demand curve $D_{poor + nonpoor}$, we must add the quantities of care that both the nonpoor and poor want at each price. At some prices, the poor cannot afford any health care, and they therefore do not demand any health care. As prices fall, the poor begin to demand health care, and the nonpoor begin to demand more health care. To find where the market demand curve cuts the horizontal axis, you must add the quantity of health care that each population would want if it were provided free of charge. This horizontal adding of demand curves gives us the market demand curve.

Where the market demand curve $D_{poor + nonpoor}$ crosses the market supply curve *S*, we get the equilibrium price P^* and quantity $Q_{poor + nonpoor}$. When we take that price over to the nonpoor person's demand curve, we can read off the quantity of health care the nonpoor person will get as $Q_{nonpoor}$. Taking it further, to the poor person's demand curve, we can read off what the poor person wants as Q_{poor}. If the health care system is such that the poor cannot get access to care at affordable prices, there will be a disparity between the health care received by the nonpoor and the poor that some people will consider unacceptable.

If the poor are provided health care free of charge, as they are with Medicaid, a different problem arises. The market demand curve does not stay as it was in Figure 25.1 but moves to its position in Figure 25.2. This new demand curve is made by adding the quantity Q_{poor} of care poor people will want if it is free to the demand curve $D_{nonpoor}$ for the nonpoor. This results in the market demand curve in Figure 25.2 being parallel to the demand curve for the nonpoor. At the intersection of market supply and market demand, the price rises to P', which is substantially above its old price at P^*. It also results in greater access for the poor and less access for the nonpoor because the price the nonpoor pay has risen so substantially. Figure 25.2 exaggerates this effect, but in the real world, Medicaid recipients consume slightly less health care than those who have private insurance.

FIGURE 25.2 The supply and demand for health care with Medicaid.

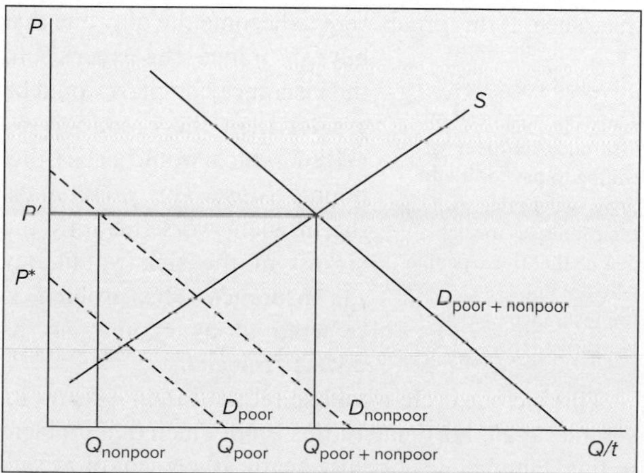

Why Spending Is Greater on the Elderly

In terms of expenses, Medicaid dollars are spent disproportionately on the elderly. This is because older people need care that tends to be more expensive, and they need it more often than those who are younger. The average Medicaid recipient utilized about $8,000 in medical care in 2017. In the last year for which there are age-specific expenditure data, 2014, the average child who was covered by Medicaid cost the government one-sixth the amount the average person over 65 cost. Thus, though children make up slightly less than half of Medicaid's population, they account for only 20 percent of the bills, and although those over 65 (and not disabled) make up less than 10 percent of its population, they account for 20 percent of the bills. This is in addition to the $700 billion that they account for in Medicare bills.

As mentioned previously, the central reason that Medicaid spending per person is so much greater for the elderly than for children is the elderly suffer from much more expensive maladies. However, there is another reason that comes in a close second: nursing home care. Nursing home care is not part of either Medicare Part A or Part B. People who are elderly must therefore pay for this care themselves, unless, of course, they cannot. When elderly people's incomes are low enough that they qualify for assistance, Medicaid will cover nursing home care. This can cost anywhere between $43,000 and $92,000 per year, constituting a substantial outlay for Medicaid. In the final analysis, Medicaid spends 25 percent of its total budget on long-term care, of which about three-quarters is on care for the aged.

The problem that this generates for elderly Americans is that they have to qualify for Medicaid before Medicaid will start paying. For widows and widowers, this is not that difficult; they simply pay all their medical and nursing home expenses until their money is gone. Then, Medicaid starts paying. Oftentimes, adult children with power of attorney try to hasten the point at which Medicaid pays their parents' medical expenses by draining the wealth of their parents by making gifts of it to themselves and their children. It is legal to do this but only up to a point. Any money that is given to children and grandchildren in the name of the elderly relatives in the two-year period leading up to their enrollment in Medicaid is treated as a semifraudulent way of avoiding paying for nursing home care. The government monitors this and takes back any money that was given away within that period.

Giving away an elderly person's assets does not solve the nursing home problem entirely because many times an elderly married couple has one partner who needs care and another who does not. This is especially true when an otherwise healthy person gets Alzheimer's disease. Medicaid used to require that the entire household's wealth be spent down before it would pay anything to a nursing home. This left many healthy spouses destitute because of the need to finance health care for their partner. At the time, the only alternative for the couple was to file for divorce the minute one of them was placed in a nursing home. That way, the assets were divided in half so that only half would be spent down, and the other half would be available for the healthy spouse. The needless emotional trauma of divorcing a longtime spouse is now avoided because the law now allows the assets of the couple's household to be divided equally between what will be spent down and what will be left untouched when one member of the married couple is admitted to a nursing home.

Cost-Saving Measures in Medicaid

During the early 1990s, Medicaid costs were rising by more than 10 percent per year. This trend, coupled with other welfare concerns, motivated many of the welfare reform measures of the middle part of that decade. During that time states began to shift their Medicaid systems from individual doctors reimbursed for expenses to health maintenance organizations (HMOs). From 1990 to 2018, doctors in HMOs went from treating fewer than 5 percent of Medicaid patients to treating more than half of them.

When HMOs are in place, people are denied coverage unless it is authorized by the doctors who have been designated as their primary care physicians. Under HMOs, primary care physicians are charged with providing basic care, and they are the only people who can refer patients to specialists. The use of HMOs has stemmed the unfortunate practice of Medicaid patients' use of emergency room treatments for basic care. Nonemergency Medicaid patients are now counseled that if they show up at an emergency room for treatment of nonserious matters, they may be refused service. They are also counseled about the benefits of having a physician who follows their particular health needs. In this way, HMOs are saving the state and federal governments money and, at the same time, they are helping to improve the health of the people they serve.

Medicare: Public Insurance and the Elderly

Why Private Insurance May Not Work

There are two main arguments for government provision of health insurance for the elderly: equity and efficiency. While it was appropriate in earlier times to argue that it was only fair to provide for the elderly in that the elderly were poorer than younger people, such arguments are less appropriate today. Today's elderly are among the least likely of our citizens to be in poverty, due in some measure to Medicare and Medicaid. What remains are arguments that the market cannot provide health insurance efficiently to people who are not in groups.

The problem with health insurance, in general, is that people who really need it, those who are sick, are more than willing to pay very high prices for it; and those who are healthy are only willing to pay low prices. Most people think of two kinds of health expenses when they are thinking about buying insurance, the expenses they are rather sure they will incur and expenses of which they are not as certain. They will buy insurance readily if the expenses they expect are greater than the premiums they have to pay. People will pay for insurance that covers them in areas they are not certain they will need, but if premiums are too high, only the sickest will want to buy insurance. If this group were to become the only one that buys insurance, the expenses to the insurance company would be greater than the premiums received, which would cause premiums to rise. This would make the problem worse, as only the sickest of the sick would buy the insurance. This problem is referred to by economists as **adverse selection.**

adverse selection
Those in most need of insurance are the most willing to pay for it and drive up its price with their illnesses to such a degree that those people who are not as sick leave the insurance market altogether.

This vicious cycle would spiral until there was no insurance at all. Fortunately, this is not much of a problem in the United States because nearly 90 percent of private health insurance is group insurance that employers buy for their employees. In each group, there are undoubtedly some people who are sick, some who are healthy, and many who are somewhere in between. The healthy subsidize the sick. Because being part of a group affords such important benefits both to the insurance companies and to members of the group, people who buy health insurance as individuals always run into problems (such as adverse selection) not encountered by people who buy into group health insurance.

This would not be a problem if the elderly were still with their employers. They are not; they are retired, and many employers do not offer membership in company health groups to retirees. With the efficacy of offering health plans to people in groups, and with millions of individual retirees needing health insurance, it makes sense for the government to offer such insurance, and it does so through Medicare.

What remains debatable about Medicare is who pays for it—its beneficiaries (as with normal health insurance), or all taxpayers, or a combination of these groups. At the outset, it was intended that the cost split would be about 50–50, proportions that offered the elderly a substantial subsidy. Today the subsidy is such that about three-quarters of the total expenses are paid out of tax dollars and only about a quarter by its beneficiaries.

Why Medicare's Costs Are High

All government health insurance programs suffer from problems of cost control. Those problems that are compounded in an era of rapid advances in medical technology that vastly improve health care but increase costs as well. Anytime the consumption of a good is subsidized via insurance, several basic problems ensue. The first problem is the risk of artificially increasing consumption. The second problem, referred to by economists as the **third-party payer** problem, is that by insuring consumers and thereby insulating them from costs, neither consumers nor producers have incentives for holding down costs. These and other insurance problems were explained in detail in Chapter 24 on health care.

third-party payer
An entity other than the consumer who pays part of the costs.

As with all other government health insurance programs, then, the costs of Medicare have escalated dramatically. Figure 25.3 shows the increase in the costs of Medicare since its inception in 1967.

For most programs, spending can rise only because prices rise or beneficiaries become more numerous.

FIGURE 25.3 Medicare spending in billions of 2009 dollars.

Source: Office of Management and Budget. https://www.whitehouse.gov/omb/historical-tables/

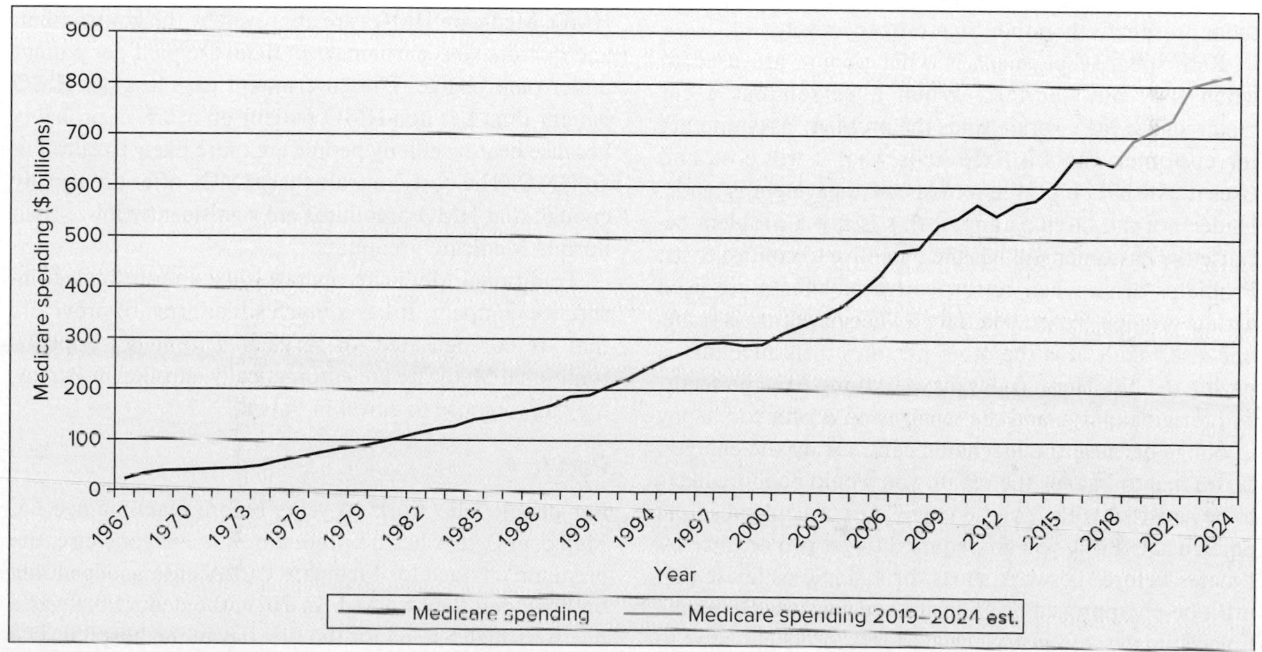

Medicare spending has risen for these reasons and one other: increases in numbers of available medical services. Medicare beneficiaries are not limited to the medical procedures that existed in 1967. They can avail themselves of the best that medical science has to offer. This means that some patients who would have died previously, and who therefore would no longer be drawing on Medicare's resources, are now given medicines and procedures that are allowing them to live much longer.

It would be unconscionable to deny medical treatment to Medicare patients, even if it would be expensive to improve their life or life span. Moreover, it would be unrealistic to assume that they would deny themselves expensive treatments in the name of cost savings. Thus, as treatments for health problems continue to become more effective and life expectancies increase, we will see a continued escalation of Medicare spending. As you will see in our section on the Medicare Trust Fund, it is this quickly increasing expense that has put Medicare on a path such that the current sources of funding will soon be insufficient.

One of the ways to deal with this kind of problem is to transfer the incentive to save money from the consumer to the producer. While it is usually consumers who want to limit the amount of money they pay, with insurance, this incentive is either drastically reduced or even eliminated. As discussed above, if no one has an incentive to control expenses, no one will. It is possible, though, to make producers the cost-conscious parties by paying them prospectively rather than retrospectively.

Retrospective payment is what people are used to when they buy services. When a person has a car repaired, a garage worker finds the problem, asks whether the customer wants it fixed, tells what it will cost, and fixes it. At that point, the retrospective payment is made. Under normal circumstances, this is not a problem because the customer still has the incentive to control costs. Problems arise when retrospective payments are used with insurance. When you have an accident that is someone else's fault, it is the other person's insurance that is paying the bill. Here, you want everything fixed perfectly, with original parts, and the repair shop is only too happy to oblige because the mechanic can rack up the charges. If you had to pay for the repair, you would be more likely to be satisfied with "good enough" and accept substitute parts. That is why you are required to get two or three estimates before the work starts, or a single estimate that must be preapproved by an insurance adjuster. Both multiple estimates and insurance adjusters' oversight serve to keep repair shops competing with one another and prevent or lessen overbilling.

In health care, it is unusual for an insurance company to have you go to several doctors to get estimates, though some may require second opinions. This is why some insurance companies and Medicare have gone to a system of prospective payments. Prospective payments are made prior to the service being performed. The hospital gets paid up front to treat its patients, and it then has an incentive to keep costs below what it has been paid. In the private arena, HMOs are designed to take advantage of such payments. Gatekeeper doctors, who are usually family practice physicians, pediatricians, or obstetrician/gynecologists, are paid specified sums per patient under their care, and they are paid the sums whether the patients require a great deal of care or no care at all.

Medicare's Nuts and Bolts

As we discussed before, Medicare is divided into two categories. Medicare Part A is mandatory for people over age 65, and it covers hospital care. Medicare Part B is voluntary, and it covers doctor visits. Medicare Part D covers prescription drugs. No part of Medicare covers long-term nursing home care.

Provider Types

The first choice a Medicare recipient has to make is whether to choose traditional Medicare or a Medicare HMO. Medicare HMOs are approved by the government, and doctors who participate in them are paid per patient under their charge. The government pays less per HMO patient than per non-HMO patient on average, probably because healthy elderly people are more likely to enroll in an HMO. The cost controls that HMOs offer are usually enough that HMO premiums are significantly lower than normal Medicare premiums.

Traditional Medicare operates like a more typical insurance company. It has a much wider array of providers that are compensated for services. People who opt for traditional Medicare are automatically enrolled in Part A; they may choose to enroll in Part B.

Part A

For people who work 10 years before reaching age 65, Medicare Part A has no premium. For everyone else, the premium charged for Medicare Part A differs, depending on how long they worked. In 2019, the deductible was a relatively high $1,364 for the first day in the hospital. The costs for the next 60 days were paid by Medicare. After 60 days in the hospital, patients paid $341 per day, Medicare paid the rest, and after 90 days patients paid $682 per day. From day 91 on, patients have a 60-day reserve of days upon which to draw. When that reserve is gone, patients must pay the rest themselves.

From the hospital's position, Medicare is paying amounts that it has determined for specific diagnoses. These prospective payments are determined by where the patients' ailments put them on a list of more than 500 diagnosis-related groups (DRGs). All Medicare patients who enter the hospital are placed in a DRG, and rather than paying for specific expenses that are incurred, Medicare pays the hospital a predetermined amount that is considered appropriate for that DRG. This motivates the hospital to keep costs under control. Medicare had paid for every bandage, meal, and service until the mid-1980s, when it found that hospitals were racking up costs of questionable medical value just to increase their profit margins. Under fixed payments for DRGs, Medicare has kept much better control of cost increases. This policy has also led to a significant shortening of average hospital stays for specific problems. The current system also provides an incentive for hospitals to discharge patients as soon as possible.

This system for reimbursement is not without its critics. Specifically, President Obama noted this prospective payment system paid hospitals based on what the patients had rather than what the hospitals did. This criticism is not new, but the balance was struck when the DRG-based prospective reimbursement was instituted. Specifically, paying hospitals on performance (how much patients improve from when they were admitted) will cause hospitals to specialize in low-mortality, low-risk treatments. Paying hospitals based on the services they provide will motivate hospitals to overtreat patients, thereby running up the costs. Though not without its critics, the current system is favored by most health economists as being one that keeps costs down, and with Medicare costs rising rapidly in the near future due to the aging of the baby boom generation, this is of primary concern.

Part B

Medicare Part B, the voluntary insurance program that pays for visits to doctors, has a monthly premium and an annual deductible. In 2019, the premium depended on a person's income. For those with incomes under $85,000 ($170,000 for married couples filing joint tax returns), the premium was $135.50 and the deductible was $185. Because neither the premium nor the deductible has increased at the rate of medical inflation, this part of the program is now being subsidized at a rate approaching 75 percent. This means that for every dollar a patient pays, Medicare Part B pays $3 out of tax revenues. Accordingly, there is virtually no reason for an elderly person not to enroll in Part B. For those who cannot afford the premium, Medicaid typically intervenes. For everyone else, that $135.50 premium is a small enough amount that nearly 100 percent of the non-Medicaid eligible elderly are enrolled.

From a doctor's perspective, Medicare Part B pays a regional standard for each treatment. Unlike Part A, Part B is billed expense by expense with retrospective payment. Medicaid pays a fixed amount for each service, but each service is billed individually rather than being grouped in a DRG.

The reason that prospective payments do not work for Medicare Part B is that, with a huge range of possible ailments, there are many potential doctors a patient may want to see. It would be impossible to predict such choices in advance, and since no single doctor or hospital is in total charge of their care under Part B, prospective payments cannot be made to work.

Prescription Drug Coverage (Part D)

As part of the 2003 reauthorization of Medicare, the costs of prescription drugs are now covered. Prior to this change, health care economists were of two minds. First, they saw a distortion of the market when surgery was covered but medicines were not. Second, they noted Medicare's precarious financial state and worried that the additional benefit would make it that much worse.

As expensive as most drugs are, drug-based treatments are less expensive than their surgical alternatives. Because Medicare did not cover prescription drugs and it did cover surgery, patients may have elected surgery even though it may have been more expensive.

On the other side of the debate were the concerns over the cost of any prescription drug program. Initial estimates in the 2003 Medicare reauthorization placed the cost of such a program at $400 billion over 10 years. Those estimates were quickly revised. In 2018, it cost nearly $100 billion.

What must be understood about any such estimates is that they are highly sensitive to assumptions about price elasticity for drugs. If the estimator uses data on the number of prescriptions filled and multiplies that number by the cost per prescription covered by the government (assuming perfectly inelastic demand), this would seriously underestimate costs. This is because if there is any elasticity of demand, there will be an increase in purchases because of the insurance. Moreover, there are often people who will benefit from prescriptions who did not go to the doctor because they know they will get a prescription slip they cannot afford to fill. In addition, there were elderly who used to get multiple prescriptions and fill only a fraction of them because they could not afford to fill them all. Together, these issues explain why original cost estimates understated the true costs of the program.

The 2003 reauthorization also introduced means testing to Medicare. The Republican-authored bill made premiums and coverage dependent on income and required most seniors to pay as much as $3,600 out of pocket. Medicare Part D is not really a national plan but was intended to foster many private alternatives with substantial government subsidies. Premiums, deductibles, and co-pays are features of each plan and are highly localized, and as a result much more confusing to beneficiaries than Medicare Part A or B. Democrats, who had sought a government-run program akin to the other parts of Medicare, generally opposed the plan. Republican defenders sought to introduce private market incentives to keep costs under control.

Neither seems to have the upper hand on this issue as the system was initially very confusing, but the most recent estimates suggest that it will cost the government 50 percent less than it was originally projected to cost. A particularly troubling part of the original law was the existence of a "donut hole," where coverage began at one level of individual spending, then stopped until another higher level of spending was arrived at, and then began again. The donut hole was reduced under the PPACA.

Cost Control Provisions in Medicare

Medicare has been attempting to keep costs under control since its inception, but, unfortunately, it has enjoyed little success. Ultimately, the reasons for this lack of success boil down to two:

1. Medical care is increasingly sophisticated, with continually improving success rates, and it is therefore more costly.
2. There is no economic incentive for either patient or doctor to control costs.

While the aforementioned DRGs have helped control costs in Part A, and Medicare HMOs have helped control costs in Part B, neither has been foolproof. The DRGs, however, have succeeded in doing a couple of important things with regard to costs. First, basing the payments on DRGs has given hospitals the incentive to take many procedures that used to require one night in the hospital and turn them into outpatient procedures. Second, hospitals have put pressure on doctors and patients to shorten the average length of stay of many multiday procedures.

Given that DRGs pay a fixed amount for a procedure, hospitals have the incentive to cut costs. Since one of a hospital's greatest costs is keeping someone in a bed overnight, converting a procedure that formerly involved a hospital stay to one that is done on an outpatient basis helps to raise profits. Heart bypass surgery is not likely to be an outpatient procedure anytime soon, but many other procedures are candidates. While many people are concerned about the health consequences of turning out patients who would have stayed a night, there has been little medical evidence that sending people home right away has had adverse effects.

A second area where costs have come down is the shortening of the length of stay for many multiday procedures. Surgeries that used to require a three- or four-day stay in the hospital to recuperate now require only two or three. In part this is because surgeons are better at limiting the trauma to the body from surgery, and in part it is because postsurgical rehabilitation has improved.[2]

The Medicare Trust Fund

One of the greatest concerns today is the fiscal health of the Medicare program that provides for our elderly's physical health. The Medicare Trust Fund enjoyed assets of $290 billion in 2018. This trust fund was set up to handle the anticipated medical expenses of the baby boom generation. Like the Social Security Trust Fund, it deliberately collected more in taxes than was necessary in order to build savings for the period when it was anticipated that the high numbers of the baby boom generation were likely to strain the system. Like the Social Security Trust

[2]While the data on length of stay have not shown a decline, this is misleading because of the aforementioned outpatient substitution. Since the length-of-stay data are based on the number of days a patient stays in a hospital, the procedures that are now outpatient do not count at all. If length of stay for the other procedures had remained the same as it was before the outpatient substitution, then the overall average would have risen substantially since whenever you remove short stays and leave only the longer stays, the average rises. Since the overall average has remained constant, we know the length of stay for longer-stay procedures has fallen.

Fund, the Medicare Trust Fund is invested only in U.S. government debt. In 1997, however, the trustees of the Medicare Trust Fund issued an alarming report. They estimated that long before the serious crisis hit, the trust fund would be insolvent. While later trustees' reports have been somewhat more optimistic about the fiscal health of the program, eventual insolvency remains its conclusion. In fact, in 2008, the balance of the trust fund began to shrink for the first time in its history.

The annual reports have been based on three different projections of the future: one very optimistic, the second very pessimistic, and the third on what the trustees judged to be the most realistic assumptions. Assumptions have been made about two economic variables and two demographic variables. The economic considerations have been the growth in inflation-adjusted wages and the real interest rate. The demographic variables have been the fertility rate and life expectancy. The higher the projected growth rate in wages, the more projected tax revenues would be; the higher the projected real interest rate, the better return on the trust fund would be; and because it is held that greater numbers of children will produce more tax revenue, the higher the projected fertility rate, the greater the projected tax revenues. Last, longer projected life expectancy would be anticipated to create greater Medicare expenses.

Figure 25.4 shows the actual balance of the Medicare Trust Fund from 1970 to 2017 and the projected balance of the trust fund until 2027 under the alternative assumptions just outlined. The estimates of low costs are based on the following assumptions: Real wages will grow quickly, at a rate of 1.8 percent; real interest rates will be a high rate of 3.2 percent; and fertility will be high, at 2.2 children per woman. The figures that reflect the estimate of high costs are just the opposite: Real wages will grow at 0.6 percent; real interest rates will be 2.2 percent; and fertility will be 1.8 children per woman. The intermediate cost projections are that real wages will rise at 1.2 percent; real interest rates will be at 2.7 percent; and the average woman will have 2.0 children.

If the assumptions leading to high costs are correct, Medicare is genuinely on the verge of insolvency. If the costs turn out to be low, the year of insolvency is beyond the immediate projections of the report, but it still happens in 2026.

To forestall the projected insolvency, it seems reasonable to consider simply raising taxes along the way in a pay-as-you-go format. This would presuppose that nothing is done to alter the current program. If we go to a pay-as-you-go system where taxes have to increase each year to meet the health care needs of the elderly, tax rates may rise substantially.

Under current law, the payroll tax that funds Part A of Medicare is 2.9 percent. That is, you and your employer each contribute 1.45 percent of everything you make on the job. (The self-employed contribute the full 2.9 percent.) Under the most likely scenario, the rate would more than double to 3.3 percent each.

If raising taxes to the necessary levels is unacceptable, other solutions may be explored. The age at which people

FIGURE 25.4 The Medicare Trust Fund under alternative assumptions.

Source: Medicare Trustees Report. https://www.cms.gov/Research-Statistics-Data-and-Systems/Statistics-Trends-and-Reports/ReportsTrustFunds/Downloads/TR2019.pdf

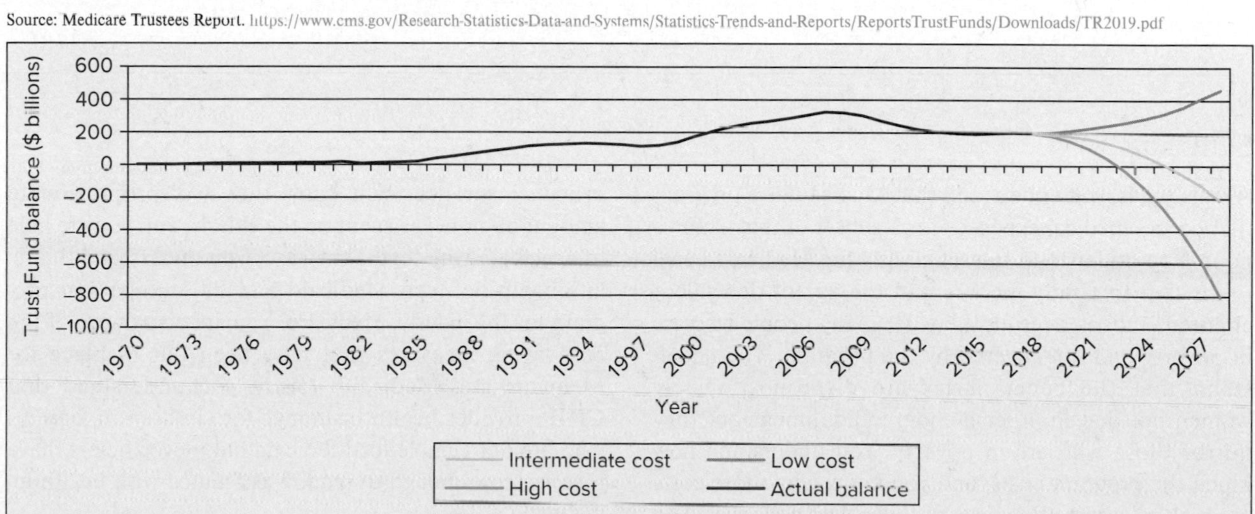

become eligible could be raised, premiums and deductibles could be raised to their inflation-adjusted 1970 level or beyond, all beneficiaries could be required to have gatekeeper physicians (as in HMOs), and it could be mandated that at certain income or wealth levels the elderly would get reduced subsidies. Many people are dissatisfied with these alternatives, and none meet with the approval of the main lobbying organization for the elderly, the American Association of Retired Persons.

The Relationship between Medicaid and Medicare

Besides beginning with the same act of Congress and besides sharing the first six letters of their eight-letter titles, Medicare and Medicaid share other features. The most significant is a commingling of tasks when people are both old and poor. Medicare was set up to deal with only the aged and Medicaid was set up to deal with only the poor. When someone is both old and poor, both programs come into play.

When a person is of an age to be eligible for Medicare and is also poor and qualifies on that ground for Medicaid, the first to pay is Medicare. Medicaid is the payer of last resort. Since Medicare has two parts and since Medicaid's costs are shared by both the federal and state governments, the story gets even more complicated.

All elderly are required to participate in Medicare Part A, which covers hospital expenses, and they can elect to participate in Medicare Part B, coverage for doctors' visits. When people are poor as well and qualify for Medicaid, the Medicare premiums and deductibles for Part A are paid by Medicaid and the remainder are paid by Medicare. For Part B, the state can then elect to pay the Medicare Part B premiums and deductibles and have Medicare Part B pick up the bulk of the expenses. In any event, when elderly people are eligible for Medicaid, there is significant overlap between Medicare and Medicaid.

The Children's Health Insurance Program

In 1997, CHIP was created to help the children of the working poor. It allowed states either to expand Medicaid coverage to those making less than 200 percent of the poverty line or to create a separate program to serve that population. The states have chosen a variety of strategies to implement their programs. In general, though, when a child's low-income parents have no insurance through their employer, they can purchase highly subsidized health insurance. Though the premiums vary from state to state, they are a tiny fraction of what they would be for private insurance. Similarly, the deductibles and copayments are low as well. An interesting feature is that well-baby visits and immunizations are required to be free for children in the program.

The program is structured very much like Medicaid in that there is a matching rate for states depending on their per capita income and minimum coverage expectations to ensure that all covered children are given adequate care regardless of where they live. The matching rates are closely tied to the regular Medicaid matching rates but are, on average, 23 percentage points higher. The program now serves more than 9.4 million children at a cost of more than $17 billion per year.

Summary

At this point, you understand that Medicaid is a program that covers medical expenses for a subset of this nation's poor. You understand that eligibility for Medicaid benefits is tied to family income and the age of dependent children, and, as a result, there are many people who are in poverty and not covered by the program. You understand that the beneficiaries are disproportionately women but that in other demographic dimensions they mirror those who are in poverty. You understand how much the program costs, and you know why those costs are high relative to the costs of those who are covered by private insurance. You know that a disproportionate amount of money is spent on the elderly, and you are able to articulate why that is the case. You understand the relationship between Medicaid and the companion program for the elderly, Medicare. You are also aware of the cost-saving measures that have been put in place for Medicare and Medicaid. Lastly, you understand that CHIP provides health insurance for children in families who are not eligible for Medicaid but, nevertheless, have incomes low enough to require assistance with health insurance.

Key Terms

adverse selection

third-party payer

Quiz Yourself

1. In 2019, in a Medicaid expansion state, a member of a family earning less than 133 percent of the poverty line is
   a. ineligible for any health care assistance.
   b. eligible for Medicare's prescription drug plan only.
   c. eligible for all of Medicare.
   d. eligible for Medicaid.
2. When a 65-year-old goes to the hospital, the part of Medicare that pays for the hospital bill is
   a. Part A.
   b. Part B.
   c. Part C.
   d. Part D.
3. Medicare Part A funding is mainly through
   a. premiums.
   b. payroll taxes (attached to Social Security).
   c. states.
   d. general federal revenues.
4. When a program like Medicaid is introduced, the market demand curve for health care will
   a. increase and flatten.
   b. increase and become more steep.
   c. decrease and flatten.
   d. decrease and become more steep.
5. Medicaid spending per recipient is
   a. twice that of the average citizen's use of health care.
   b. somewhat less than the average citizen's use of health care.
   c. somewhat greater than the average citizen's use of health care.
   d. half that of the average citizen's use of health care.
6. The DRG system controls Medicare expenses by
   a. preventing doctors from using particular procedures.
   b. paying hospitals after they submit bills.
   c. paying hospitals on the basis of a disease or injury rather than expenses.
   d. paying the patient who then pays the hospital.
7. The Medicare Trust Fund is necessary because
   a. current expenses are greater than current revenues.
   b. current expenses are less than current revenues.
   c. future expenses will be greater than future revenues.
   d. future expenses will be less than future revenues.
8. CHIP
   a. was eliminated as part of the PPACA.
   b. covers the elderly.
   c. covers the children of those not poor enough to qualify for Medicaid.
   d. covers those not old enough for Medicare.

Short Answer Questions

1. How might the elasticity of demand for a health care service be used to estimate the demand created for a health care service when there is a new program for government coverage?
2. Why is the Medicare Trust Fund estimated date of fund exhaustion so dependent on the assumption made with regard to economic growth, interest rates, and political changes?
3. What are the benefits and costs associated with reimbursing hospitals based on their actual services performed rather than based on the problems the patients have when they come to the hospital?

Think about This

One of the suggestions for providing the working poor with health insurance has been to require employers to provide health insurance benefits for all workers by having employers "buy them into Medicaid." Requiring this would raise the cost to employers of hiring new workers. Under what circumstances would this be good for workers? Under what circumstances would it not be good?

Talk about This

When public provision of health care is discussed in most political arenas, providing more coverage (e.g., prescriptions and long-term care) for the elderly typically garners more attention than expanding coverage to the working poor. Why is that? Is this the right priority in your mind?

For More Insight See

Garrett, Major, "Medicare: Healthier for Now," *U.S. News & World Report,* April 12, 1999, p. 29.

Lee, Ronald, and Jonathan Skinner, "Will Aging Baby Boomers Bust the Federal Budget?" *Journal of Economic Perspectives* 13 (Winter 1999), pp. 117–140.

Miller, Matthew, "Premium Idea," *The New Republic,* April 12, 1999, pp. 24–27.

Newhouse, Joseph, "Policy Watch: Medicare," *Journal of Economic Perspectives* 10 (Summer 1996), pp. 159–168.

Phelps, Charles, *Health Economics* (Reading, MA: Addison-Wesley, 1997), esp. Chapter 13.

"Survey: Health Care," *The Economist,* July 6, 1991.

Behind the Numbers

Centers for Medicare and Medicaid Services: www.cms.gov

- Medicare, Medicaid, and CHIP spending
- Medicare, Medicaid, and CHIP enrollment
- Medicare premiums and deductible
- Trust Fund balance and projection

Kaiser Family Foundation: www.kff.org

- Gender and ethnicity statistics

CHAPTER TWENTY-SIX

The Economics of Prescription Drugs

Learning Objectives

After reading this chapter you should be able to:

LO1 Apply the concepts of monopoly as well as consumer and producer surplus to the economics of prescription drugs.

LO2 Summarize why most health economists view prescription drugs as relatively inexpensive, even though most noneconomists view them as very expensive.

LO3 Explain why most health economists do not favor price controls on prescription drugs.

LO4 Identify the consequences of an approval process that is too stringent or too lax.

Chapter Outline

When people go to the doctor because they are sick or injured, they want the doctor to make them better. For certain injuries, they may expect active treatments, like surgery. It is just part of the human psychological makeup to want to know that "everything is being done" to restore the patient's health. The same holds for the treatment of illnesses. Nothing is more frustrating to patients than to be told they have a "virus," because they accurately translate that to mean "go home and go to bed because there is nothing we can do for you."

On the other hand, if patients go home having filled a prescription for a drug, they feel better simply because they think that taking medicine will make them well. In part they think this because the prescription drug industry has been so successful in treating everything from infections to impotence. When we have a virus and there is no prescription forthcoming, we lose hope for a quick end to our illness. In this sense, we go to the doctor hoping for prescriptions because it is usually a drug the doctor prescribes, rather than something the doctor actually does, that makes us better.

It seems all the more strange to economists, then, that prescription drugs get as much criticism as they do when it comes to expense. The amount of money spent on prescription drugs is actually trivial relative to all health spending. In 2017, for example, all U.S. health spending amounted to more than $3.5 trillion dollars, and 10 percent of that was spent on prescription drugs.

This chapter has several purposes. We look at the degree to which prescription drug manufacturers are profiteers or Good Samaritans. We use our monopoly model to discern why drugs are so costly, and we examine some new drugs and discuss whether they are expensive necessities or relatively inexpensive godsends. In doing this, we will see the fundamental reasons why prescription drug companies are likely to remain unpopular even as they continue to provide important medicines. Last, we look at how other countries control prescription drug prices, and we offer a perspective on whether the United States should follow suit.

Profiteers or Benevolent Scientists?

Among the more interesting advertisements of the 1990s were the pharmaceutical industry's feel-good television spots that focused on a variety of hardworking scientists endeavoring to conquer a disease. These ads differed somewhat from the ads that commonly try to get us to go to the doctor to ask about problems like hair loss, seasonal allergies, or other afflictions. Just as McDonald's wants to sell burgers, pharmaceutical companies are trying to sell us particular drugs. The feel-good ads are there, not to have us buy any particular product, but to persuade us to feel better about the industry in general.

Usually, the earlier ads discussed an emotional attachment the scientists had with curing the disease on which they were working. A friend, spouse, relative, or parent had the disease, and this, we were supposed to believe, motivated the scientist to spend long nights crouched over a microscope in search of a cure. With no attempt to criticize the scientists' sincerity, however, we know deep down that whether or not something altruistic motivates the scientist, what motivates the drug company is profit.

As with any invention, the fundamental economic problem is how to reward the inventor. Unless the inventor is given exclusive rights to his or her idea once the item has been invented, copycats can steal it. Knowing this, inventors have little economic incentive to innovate. This is why we have laws that govern copyrights and **patents.** Within existing laws, a patent-holding inventor is the only person who can sell the invention for as long as the patent exists.

patent
A right granted by government to an inventor to be the exclusive seller of that invention for a limited period of time.

orphan drug
A drug that treats someone with a disease that afflicts few people.

Monopoly power is particularly important in the so-called **orphan drug** industry, an industry that deals with diseases that afflict few people. Therapies that benefit small numbers of patients cannot hope to generate sufficient profits during normal patent lives for companies to justify research. For this reason, drugs that are labeled orphan drugs are granted very long patent lives so that profits, though small, can be expected to last long into the future. Without this aspect of the patent law, research on such diseases would never be instituted by scientists working in the private sector.

In economic terms, monopoly power gives the inventor total control. As you recall from Chapter 5, monopoly means that there is one seller. It means, in turn, that there are no other companies producing the particular drug. When the drug is one-of-a-kind, as AZT (an early AIDS treatment) was in the early 1990s, and it is the only hope a patient has, its monopoly power is dramatic. It is all the more dramatic when the disease it treats is fatal. Since most drugs cost very little to produce but may, as in the case of AIDS drugs, cost billions to discover and test, consumers (and voters) are conflicted about high prices. We know that companies need to be rewarded for their investments, but we also find it troublesome that money has the power to determine whether a person gets a drug and lives or does not get a drug and dies.

On the other hand, when the drug is one of many, and it treats a non-life-threatening condition, as do the anti-heartburn medications Nexium and Zantac, we are not at all conflicted. The problem is not life and death, and the power the companies have to charge high prices is limited only by competition and consumers' willingness to suffer through ailments that are merely annoying.

Whether we view drug companies as profiteers or benevolent scientists rests on whether they, in the end, do good and whether they charge what are perceived to be fair prices. Drug companies make a great deal of money, but they incur a great deal of risk. Much economic research has gone into studying whether their profits are out of line in comparison with those of similar industries. Although that research has not settled on a definitive answer, it does suggest that the rate of return to stockholders in the pharmaceutical industry is either at or slightly above that of similar industries. What is clear is that prescription drugs have both improved the quality of life for millions and made companies billions in profit.

Monopoly Power Applied to Drugs

As stated previously, the key economic attribute of the prescription drug industry is monopoly. While patents do expire and competition takes place in the form of generic drugs, monopoly reigns for the life of the patient. Figure 26.1 is the same graph that we saw in Chapter 5 illustrating a monopolist's price and production decisions. As you know, a monopolist is the only seller of a good. This means that the demand curve that a monopolistic firm faces for its goods is the entire market demand curve. For such a firm, this has good and bad aspects. In contrast to perfect competition, the seller does not have to worry about other firms. However, if the firm wants to sell more goods, it not only has to lower the

FIGURE 26.1 The prescription drug monopolist.

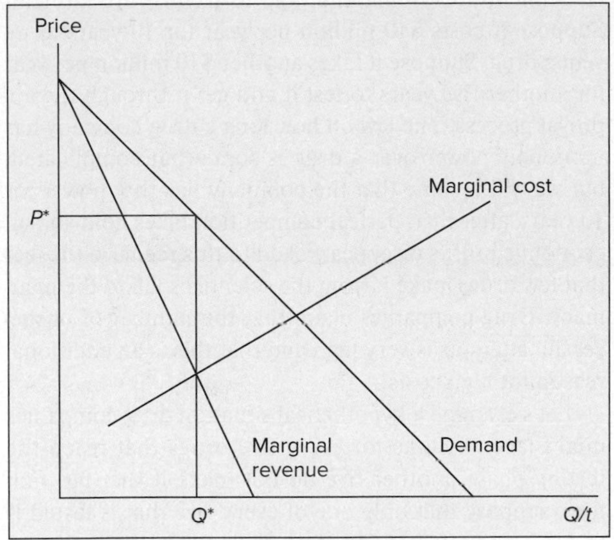

FIGURE 26.2 Comparing monopoly and perfect competition in prescription drugs.

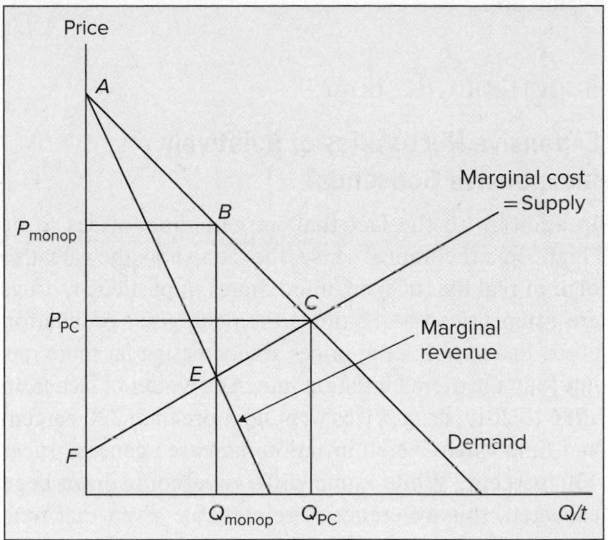

price to the people who will buy the extra goods; it has to lower the price to everyone in the market. This includes the people who would have purchased their goods at high prices, so the money gained from increasing sales is partially offset by the money that is lost from having to lower prices. The good news for the firm is that raising the price does not cause all customers to leave, as it does under perfect competition because they cannot buy the drug from another seller. Furthermore, we know that (because marginal revenue is positive) the firm increases its revenue.

Figure 26.1 depicts a drug company that is the sole provider of a certain drug. It indicates that the marginal revenue curve, the curve that represents the additional revenue to the firm associated with the sale of one more unit of the good, is downward sloping rather than flat, as it would be under perfect competition.

Using the tools of consumer and producer surplus, we can show that with the price equal to P^* and the quantity equal to Q^*, relative to the societal optimum, the price is too high and the quantity too low. This can be seen by looking at Figure 26.2 and the assumptions that go along with it. For a moment, suppose that the proper comparison to make with regard to the monopolistic production of prescription drugs is perfect competition.[1] As you saw in Chapter 5, the marginal cost curve for a perfect competitor—out of the minimum of average variable cost—was the supply curve. If you adapt that notion here, the marginal cost curve for this monopolist in Figure 26.1 is also what the supply curve would be if the market were under perfect competition.

The perfectly competitive market would produce Q_{PC} at a price of P_{PC}, because this is where supply crosses demand. The monopolistic producer charges much more, P_{monop}, and produces less, Q_{monop}, because this is where marginal cost equals marginal revenue. Our consumer and producer surplus analysis, then, allows us to show that companies profit not only at the expense of sick people, but also at the expense of society as a whole.

Under perfect competition, the consumer surplus (the area under the demand curve but above the price line) at the perfectly competitive price-quantity combination is $P_{PC}AC$, and the producer surplus (the area above the supply curve but under the price line) is $FP_{PC}C$. Under monopoly, the consumer surplus shrinks to $P_{monop}AB$, and the producer surplus rises to $FP_{monop}BE$.

Why is this important? Because it gives you a net result—you can compare the winners to the losers. Specifically, producers are better off but not by as much as consumers are worse off. Stated differently, the **deadweight loss,** or loss to society of producing at the wrong price-quantity combination, can be shown as the difference between the sum of consumer and

deadweight loss The loss in social welfare associated with production being too little or too great.

[1]Because of the large innovation costs, this is a poor assumption for the industry at all stages of production but a reasonable one after the drug has been invented and approved.

producer surplus between the perfect competition and monopoly situations. That area is depicted as *EBC* in Figure 26.2.

Important Questions

Expensive Necessities or Relatively Inexpensive Godsends?

In addition to the fact that we can show prices to be "high" in a theoretical sense, the data show they are also high in real life. In the United States in particular, drugs are often priced at 10 times their marginal production costs. In addition, drug prices are increasing far more rapidly than the overall inflation rate. As a matter of fact, from 1986 to 2019, drug prices went up more than 320 percent at a time when overall inflation increased general prices 130 percent. While some difference could have been expected, this difference is remarkable given that nonprescription drugs declined from 2009 to 2019.

The reasons for increased prescription drug prices are many and varied, but they boil down to a few important issues: development costs, regulation, and litigation. There is also a problem with the mismeasurement of inflation in drug prices.

Development of new drugs costs a great deal of money, and drug companies need to recoup costs before they can make a profit. Since the "easy" diseases already have cures or treatments, firms and their scientists are left with some very difficult diseases to research. The training required to even understand how to start researching drug therapies takes several years after a researcher has earned a doctorate or a medical degree. People who get that kind of education for that long a period of time are going to command very high salaries once they start working. In addition to high labor costs, the equipment needed for this kind of work is specialized and expensive.

The capital and labor costs of drug research are extended even further by the years required to take a drug from successful trials to government approval. Typically, new drugs are first tested on small animals. They are then tested on primates. These tests are followed by small-scale human trials, designed primarily to gauge safety. Finally, a large-scale human trial requires that the drug be shown to work effectively while not causing unacceptable side effects. This lengthy process is expensive, and it significantly extends the time before the company's revenue stream starts.

The concept of present value can shed light on how this contributes to the high costs of drugs. Let's use a numerical example to illustrate these issues. Assume a drug company sees that 1 million patients with a particular ailment are willing and able to pay for a treatment. Suppose it costs \$10 million per year for 10 years to invent a drug. Suppose it takes another \$10 million per year for another five years to test it and get it through the approval process. The law on how long a drug company has monopoly power over a drug is somewhat complicated, but we will assume that the company has that power for 10 years; after that, perfect competition takes hold and all economic profits disappear.[2] Add to this scenario the fact that few drugs make it from the scientist's lab to the pharmacy. Drug companies claim that the number of unsuccessful attempts is very high and that this is an additional reason for high costs.

Let's examine a hypothetical situation drug companies might face. Assume for every five drugs that reach the testing phase another five do not make it that far. Further, suppose that only one of every five that is tested is shown to be safe and effective. Thus for every 11 that incur invention costs, there are five that also incur testing costs. Only one produces revenue. Suppose at the very beginning of this process the manufacturer does not know which of these 11 plausible ideas will pay off, but it does know that one of them will. Also suppose that the manufacturer has a good idea that marginal production costs will amount to \$10 per patient per year.

Given all that, if you applied the present value analysis from Chapter 7, you could determine the profit that the firm would have to generate annually to cover its costs (including the opportunity cost of its invested money). Specifically, at a 10 percent real rate of return, the anticipated profit to the manufacturer from this one drug would have to be \$520 million per year for the drug company to make back its initial investment. Thus, even if you ignore all of the markups that wholesalers and retailers charge from the manufacturer to the patient, the price per patient per year for our hypothetical example will have to be \$530 (\$520 million in profit/1 million patients + \$10 in production costs).

In addition to all the preceding considerations, drug prices are made higher because of society's propensity for suing pharmaceutical companies. Pharmaceutical firms have deep pockets. They produce products that do not work all the time and that sometimes do more harm

[2]Manufacturers typically will make some economic profits on drugs after the expiration of the patent because of brand loyalty among physicians and patients. Drug company representatives encourage that loyalty with gifts. Sometimes these gifts are as innocuous as drug company pens while at other times they are expensive company-sponsored vacations.

than good. In the last 20 years, Vioxx and other Cox-2 inhibitors were approved to treat arthritis and inflammatory issues for people with pain beyond the scope of over-the-counter medications. They had their safety questioned because they were shown to cause heart problems. Merck, the manufacturer of Vioxx, paid nearly $9 billion in settlements and legal fees on this issue alone. With the fear of such judgments in mind, pharmaceutical firms will increase their prices so they have enough money on hand to account for such judgments and to have profit left over. In countries where lawsuits and judgments are limited, the prices of drugs tend to be lower because the impact of legal judgments will be less significant.

Another phenomenon we must account for in analyzing the prices of drugs is that drug price indexes suffer from all of the problems that affect other major price indexes. The consumer price index's lapses, discussed briefly in Chapter 6, are especially problematic with drugs. For an illustration of this, you need look no further than birth control pills. The pills available in the early 1960s are nothing like those that are available now. The side effects of the early pills were much more severe than they are today. Part of the increase in the current price of birth control pills can be attributed to the improvement of quality rather than to the effects of inflation. Thus, a portion of that reported 320 percent increase in prescription drug prices is better understood as an increase in quality.

Taking all of the preceding into account, we are left with the fact that either drug prices are high or they seem to be high. The lifetime cost of treating AIDS is more than $400,000. The cost of treating hepatitis C has just recently come down from its original $100,000 price. A new drug was just recently approved to treat postpartum depression. At introduction, it carried a $34,000 price tag.

These drugs are obviously very expensive and if they treated diseases for which the patient was blameless or treated people who have health insurance, we might not consider these costs a problem. The patients who need these are usually complicit in their fate and frequently do not have insurance. That either leaves them untreated or puts enormous cost pressure on Medicaid.

To counter some of the preceding negative characteristics, it must be said that the prescription drug industry can also lay claim to lowering health costs in some areas and to improving lives in nearly all areas. Drugs treat some diseases that either used to require surgery or, worse, that simply went untreated. There are also drugs that improve the quality of life and do so in a number of important areas. Some nonemergency heart conditions can now be treated with drug therapies rather than $30,000–$50,000 bypass or $10,000–$20,000 catheterization surgeries. Although the drugs are expensive and cannot be used when a patient is suffering from near-complete arterial blockages, they can slowly open up the arteries, and they have been shown to have a success rate that is comparable to more invasive alternatives.

In other areas, new drugs have simply improved life. From ailments as irritating as seasonal allergies to those as trivial as heartburn, to those as debilitating as asthma, new drugs have made the lives of people of all ages much better. While seasonal allergies and heartburn are never life-threatening, people's lives are changed when they are successfully treated.

Before the invention of nonsedating antihistamines such as Seldane[3] and Claritin, allergy sufferers struggled to accomplish anything outdoors in the spring and fall. These medications let allergy sufferers play golf, mow the lawn, and do many other enjoyable and productive things that used to induce fits of sneezing. Claritin was also shown to be safe enough that the Food and Drug Administration (FDA) allowed the drug to go "over the counter" (meaning no prescription is required) in 2003. Before anti-heartburn medications such as Nexium,[4] spicy, high-acid, or rich dishes were simply off-limits for many middle-aged people. While it may seem trivial to the young, being unable to eat favorite foods affects people's quality of life. Being able to eat pizza, Cajun wings, or a piquant sauce does not rank high in the sphere of important medical issues, but being able to indulge once in a while does make life a little more enjoyable.

These latter cases are also not life-threatening, but they do represent serious quality-of-life issues. The drugs that treat these ailments may not be critical to life, but they represent significant advances for people. As a result, people may want them. They may resent that the drugs are somewhat costly. However, when compared to the alternative scenario where these life-improving drugs aren't available at all, their existence (even at a high price) is properly viewed as a blessing of modern science.

Why then do prescription drugs get such a bad reputation? It is the reality that drug prices have increased significantly faster than inflation along with perceptions that economists claim are not well founded. Our perceptions tell us that the costs of prescription drugs are much

[3]This drug was pulled from the market because it was shown to interact in potentially fatal ways with heart medications.

[4]In extreme cases, this drug has reduced the risk of esophageal cancer.

higher than the actual 10 percent of medical spending for which they are responsible. For every dollar of expense incurred in hospital or doctor visits, there is a corresponding patient out-of-pocket cost (7.5 percent and 20 percent, respectively). For prescription drugs, out-of-pocket costs are much higher, at 33 percent. This leaves the patient more aware of and sensitive to increases in drug costs than increases in the costs of hospitals and doctors.

Price Controls: Are They the Answer?

Another of the facts that must be faced with regard to drug prices is that they are higher in the United States than anywhere else in the world. That is because in most other countries drug prices are regulated. Whether the drug prices themselves are controlled or the profits from their sales are controlled, people in other countries pay much less for drugs than we do. Go to El Paso, Texas, and price a drug, and you will find it at half price or less across the border in Mexico. You find the same thing in Detroit relative to Windsor, Canada. The drug is not safer in El Paso or Detroit; it is only more expensive. As a matter of fact, it is often in exactly the same package. Prices are lower in other parts of the world, and one of the reasons is certainly price controls.

Would we be better off if the government controlled the price of drugs? Probably not. The world's drug inventors eye the profit that they get in the United States when they pour billions into their scientists and laboratories. If they could not make a profit in the United States, there would be no place to make one and they would not put the money into innovation. To mix metaphors, the United States is the drug industry's cash cow; by controlling prices, we would be killing the golden goose just as she is producing some very important life-improving and life-saving eggs.

The law with respect to prescription drugs is in flux, with both political parties considering changes to patent laws in advance of the 2020 election. It has been against the law for companies to buy prescription drugs in a foreign country and resell them in the United States. Otherwise, a drug company could sell its products to a Canadian company at a low price determined by Canadian law. That Canadian company would then resell them to a U.S. retailer, thereby avoiding the high price in the United States. This would have the same effect as allowing Canada to control U.S. prices. Though it has been considered for more than 20 years, reimportation is still illegal.

FDA Approval: Too Stringent or Too Lax?

The approval for, and the regulation of, prescription drugs is performed by the FDA. In the early 1990s, the FDA was under scrutiny for not allowing drugs to come to market quickly enough. The issue then was magnified by the excruciatingly slow process of approving AIDS drugs. As described earlier, the FDA's process is a multistage one where a drug is tested first for its safety and then for its effectiveness. A drug can be marketed only if both meet a high scientific standard.

While this sounds very good, the problem is that people will die of afflictions for which there are already existing drug therapies. For example, in the early 1990s, the AIDS-combating protease inhibitors had been shown to be safe, but scientists had not yet had the time to show their effectiveness. Reasoning that unforeseen drug interactions were the least of their worries, dying AIDS patients wanted the drugs immediately. The problem of overly stringent FDA regulation is that people die when they could be saved with a less-stringent process.

During the mid-1990s, the FDA began to experiment with a fast-track approval process. Here, drugs that are shown to be safe get an expedited review for effectiveness. The problem is that the initial safety review is conducted using a relatively small sample of people, while the effectiveness review is conducted using a much larger one. Adverse drug interactions and relatively rare and unforeseen safety issues come to light during this effectiveness testing. Expediting the effectiveness testing causes some safety issues to be missed, and as a result the FDA sometimes has to subsequently pull drugs off the shelves. This was Fen-Phen's fate, and it may end up being the fate of all Cox-2 inhibitors.

This is a prime example of how marginal analysis can be used to aid in decision-making. The marginal benefit of increasing FDA stringency is the decrease in the health problems accruing to those who take approved drugs that later are found to be unsafe. The marginal cost of increasing FDA stringency is the forgone increase in the health of people who could have been treated but were not. The optimal degree of FDA stringency is where the marginal cost equals the marginal benefit.

Whether a particular drug is approved to be sold over the counter is also a matter for FDA approval. When a new drug shows that it is sufficiently safe that it can be used by consumers with little or no consultation with a doctor, the FDA will approve it for use over the counter. When that occurs, the price of the drug falls precipitously because it can be more easily mass-marketed.

Summary

You are now able to apply the concept of monopoly as well as consumer and producer surplus to the analysis of the costs of prescription drugs. You are able to apply those concepts to see the reasons most health economists view prescription drugs as relatively inexpensive even though most noneconomists view them as very expensive. You also understand why it is that most health economists do not favor price controls on prescription drugs. Last, you understand how economists see the issue of FDA approval and the appropriate degree of stringency.

Key Terms

deadweight loss | orphan drug | patent

Quiz Yourself

1. The prescription drug industry is characterized by products that have
   a. low fixed costs and low marginal costs.
   b. low fixed costs and high marginal costs.
   c. high fixed costs and low marginal costs.
   d. high fixed costs and high marginal costs.
2. A patent is necessary to motivate innovation in areas where the innovation is
   a. costly to figure out and easily copied.
   b. cheap to figure out and difficult to copy.
   c. costly to figure out and difficult to copy.
   d. cheap to figure out and easily copied.
3. The reason orphan drug laws were created was that the motivation to invent drugs for these diseases was
   a. much greater than normal because prices could be high.
   b. much less than normal because prices would be too low.
   c. much less than normal because firms anticipated few sales.
   d. much greater than normal because firms anticipated high sales.
4. The market form for a new drug in an area where there are no competitors is
   a. perfect competition.
   b. monopolistic competition.
   c. oligopoly.
   d. monopoly.
5. The market form for a new drug in an area that has one other drug is
   a. perfect competition.
   b. monopolistic competition.
   c. oligopoly.
   d. monopoly.
6. Which of the following explains why drug prices are lower in other countries than they are in the United States?
   a. U.S. prices are controlled.
   b. Drugs are allowed to be reimported into the United States.
   c. Other countries use price and profit controls.
   d. The United States is the only country investing in new drugs.
7. The approval process for new drugs, if governed by economic thinking, should set stringency standards so that the ____________________ equals the ________________.
   a. total cost; total benefit
   b. average cost; average benefit
   c. marginal cost; marginal benefit
   d. cost of production; revenue from sales
8. When an existing prescription drug goes over the counter
   a. everyone wins.
   b. drug companies win but consumers lose.
   c. drug companies lose but consumers win.
   d. drug companies likely win because of the increase in sales, and consumers may win depending on whether prescriptions are covered by insurance.

Short Answer Questions

1. What reasons are there for not limiting the price, or at least the increase in the price, of prescription drugs that have already been invented?
2. What are the reasons why, even if it is in the best interests of every other country to limit prescription

drug prices, it might not be in the best interests of the United States to limit those prices?

3. Why might legalizing drug re-importation be equivalent to limiting drug prices?
4. What is lost in terms of societal welfare if, in the cause of safety, a drug or medical device has its approval delayed by a year or two?

Think about This

Vioxx and other Cox-2 inhibitors were invented because the existing pain medications (when taken for persistent pain) did damage to the lining of the stomach. After years of clinical trials, they were determined to be safe. It was only after use by millions of people that we became aware of the fact that they affected the heart. Under what conditions should their makers be legally liable for these side effects?

Talk about This

When a disease has no cure, people with the disease have no options. Suppose a prescription drug is invented but is so expensive that some patients cannot afford it. Are we better off with a drug being available but only to those with insurance? What are the social consequences of this?

For More Insight See

Scherer, F. M., "Pricing, Profits, and Technological Progress in the Pharmaceutical Industry," *Journal of Economic Perspectives* 7, no. 3 (Summer 1993), pp. 97–115.

Behind the Numbers

Bureau of Labor Statistics: www.bls.gov/cpi

- Prescription drug prices
- Overall prices

CHAPTER TWENTY-SEVEN

So You Want to Be a Lawyer: Economics and the Law

Learning Objectives

After reading this chapter you should be able to:

LO1 Describe private property, intellectual property, and contracts and relate their importance in enabling economic growth.

LO2 Explain how a carefully crafted system of bankruptcy aids economic activity.

LO3 Describe the role of civil litigation in a society and discuss how economists participate in that arena.

Chapter Outline

In this chapter, we outline the importance of government institutions and make the case that a sound legal environment is helpful in promoting economic activity. We start by describing why a system of laws is a prerequisite to a healthy economy. We explain the foundational elements of private property, intellectual property, contracts, and bankruptcy. We conclude by describing why a system of legal challenges can either aid or detract from economic efficiency depending on how it is applied.

As Chapter 3 illustrated, there are times when markets fail and governments are needed to correct those failures. One of the potential failures of markets identified in that chapter was for public goods. Those are goods where you need a government to provide the service because there is no ability of the private market to do so. Clearly, government is necessary to protect us from physical harm. We need armies and police forces to keep others from hurting us. Those services are provided by government in response to a clear market failure. This chapter focuses on the legal framework under which our economy operates.

Private Property

Suppose you have a quiz on this chapter in the next hour and you are reading this book so you can study. Now also suppose that you are smart and could get a decent grade on that quiz without reading carefully. The friend sitting next to you does not have a book and is not as smart as you are. He could claim to "need" it more than you and that the gain to him of reading it is greater than the loss to you of not reading it. All that may be true, but the book is your **private property** to do with what you wish. You sacrificed money to buy it. It is yours. If your friend took it from you, you could have him charged with theft. Here, government plays the role of protecting and respecting the importance of private property.

private property
Land and other physical items that are owned by individuals or a group of individuals.

Why does protecting private property foster economic growth? First, it motivates you to work hard. If you work hard and produce goods and services for others, people will pay you for them. In exchange, if you make a lot of money, you can buy stuff. You cannot count on getting to enjoy the benefits of your hard work if your earnings, or the stuff you buy with those earnings, can be taken by others without consequence. Second, government's protection of private property motivates you to save. If you save your earnings rather than immediately consuming them, you are (perhaps indirectly) providing the financial capital for others to buy productive machinery that they would otherwise not be able to buy. You get the reward of interest and the borrowers have the opportunity to increase their business's profit. If fear of theft caused you to consume everything you earned right away, you would not save. You would be worse off because of the forgone interest, and the borrower would be worse off because of the forgone profit.

Intellectual Property

Usually, owning private property is the product of your hard work. Once in a while that hard work is a result of your brain power, imagination, creativity, or insight. This **intellectual property** is also protected from those tempted to steal it. This book is protected by a **copyright.** Similarly the recipe to the vaccine protecting you from HPV and its cancerous consequences is patented. For the life of the **patent,** only the inventing company can produce it. Finally, if you created a brand name for a product, that name could not be used without your consent. The instrument that protects your intellectual property in this case is called a **trademark.**

intellectual property
Written and recorded works, ideas, formulas, and other creative intangible property that are owned by individuals or a group of individuals.

copyright
A right granted by government to a creator of a written or recorded work to be the exclusive seller of that work for a limited period of time.

patent
A right granted by government to an inventor to be the exclusive seller of that invention for a limited period of time.

trademark
A right granted by government to a business to be the exclusive user of a phrase, logo, or name of such a business.

Contracts

As economies develop, contracts are required because transactions get more complicated. This typically occurs because the exchange between parties is not at the same time. When I buy a Snickers bar with cash at a gas station, I do not need to sign a contract because I have paid for the Snickers bar when I received it. However, I need a **contract** with my publisher because I wrote this book several months before you bought it. I was paid my portion of the amount you paid for it about six to nine months after you bought it. Without a contract, the publisher could simply keep the money, or perhaps hold on to it for years rather than months. My contract protects me from my publisher should it decide to be dishonest. That contract also protects my publisher from my laziness. When I wrote the first edition, they paid me money in advance on the condition that I would deliver on my promise of a book they could sell.

contract
Written agreement by which each party is bound to provide other parties with goods, services, or financial consideration in exchange for other goods, services, or financial considerations.

Contracts protect both parties and make promises binding by something other than good word. If I thought there was a chance that I would not be paid, I would not have taken many months to write it and the publisher would not have made money on it. If the publisher could not hold me to our agreement that I would deliver a book, they would not have paid me in advance. From our Chapter 3 concepts of producer and consumer surplus, society is better off when the book is produced. I make royalties, my publisher makes a profit, and you learn about why contracts are necessary. Everyone is better off because of the existence of contracts.

Enforcing Various Property Rights and Contracts

Just because we have a law that says you cannot do something does not mean that it is not done. Someone must enforce a law in order for it to be recognized and widely respected. If someone steals your money, car, or other property, you call the police. Assuming that person is caught and convicted, the punishment is typically jail time. If someone copies your song, book, drug, or marketing trademark, or violates his or her part in a contract, you must appeal to a different part of government: the civil court system. That means you have to hire a lawyer and get a court date for a judge and jury to determine whether a theft of intellectual property has occurred. If they agree with your claim, the intellectual property thief or contract violator is punished by being ordered to stop the violation and pay you the money you are owed. The theft of intellectual property rarely results in jail time because it is usually one corporation stealing from another. The punishment is that the guilty corporation has to pay the victimized corporation.

So, even when markets are perfectly competitive, contracts and property rights are imperative to an economy's success, and government, whether it be the police or the courts, is needed to enforce those rights. Countries without stable and effective governments are typically not successful in fostering healthy economies. Lawlessness is a major impediment to economic growth. In 2016, the World Justice Project named Venezuela, Cambodia, Afghanistan, and Egypt as the most lawless countries. It is not a coincidence that their economies were in shambles.

Negative Consequences of Private Property Rights

Though a system of private property rights clearly motivates people to work hard and be creative, it also creates other ethical and economic issues. If you have discussed Chapters 26 and 37 (Prescription Drugs, and College Education, respectively), you have become acquainted with some of these issues. Ethically, how do we accept a level of global wealth inequality that arises from our system of private property? Is it ethical to possess the means by which to manage the AIDs problem and not allow the poor countries in Africa to produce the medications to do so? Is it ethical to charge $125 for a textbook that costs $15 to produce? Is it economically efficient to have monopoly production, with the resulting deadweight loss, in these markets? Economists generally agree that the system of private property motivates these goods to be produced in the first place and that removing the property rights protections would seriously reduce the incentive to produce them. The ethical conundrum and the monopoly-induced inefficiency are the price we pay for creating those incentives.

Bankruptcy

Sometimes people and firms are unable to meet their financial obligations. Either because they have been confronted with hard economic times, have had health issues that turned into financial troubles, or simply spent more than they could afford, sometimes people cannot repay the money they owe. The entities (such as banks, hospitals, or credit card companies) that are owed are called **creditors.** **Bankruptcy** allows people to start fresh with their debts. The bankruptcy laws have options that allow a person entering bankruptcy to restructure their debts in a way that will allow them to stay in their homes or keep their cars. If a bankruptcy judge allows them to, this option is usually the least disruptive. On the other hand, some people want to get out of debt altogether.

creditors
Entities (such as banks, hospitals, or credit card companies) that are owed money.

bankruptcy
The legal state that allows debtors to be protected from the actions of their creditors.

A perfectly reasonable question to ask at this point is why, if we need government to enforce contracts, would it make sense to allow people to not repay their debts? For the answer, recall the Chapter 1 notion of incentives. Suppose you are in great debt and whatever you earn would go to paying on that debt. You would have no incentive to work if you knew there was no way to repay your debts. Providing a system of bankruptcy that allows people a way out of debt has the benefit of energizing their incentives to work hard. Of course, when abused, a system of bankruptcy allows people to consume without ever intending to pay for it. In 2005, Congress recognized this concern when it reformed the bankruptcy laws to put tighter controls on who could declare bankruptcy and for what purposes.

Since this is a college textbook and you likely are a college student, it is also important for you to know that part of the way society pays for the subsidized interest rates on student loans is to make it so that you cannot escape them if you declare bankruptcy. They will follow you forever.

Civil Liability

Sometimes the harm one person does to another is not from taking something from them but from accidentally, negligently, or purposefully injuring them. Suppose you are driving along and crash into me in your car, and I die. My wife and children are clearly harmed. How much they have been harmed depends on what their lives are like without me compared to the way life was with me. Using this fairly straightforward principle and the notion of liability, we can determine how much my family should get from you and your insurance company.

Before we address how much harm you have done, let's think about how the accident occurred. If you were driving the speed limit, had adequately maintained your car, were not impaired by alcohol, and were not talking on your cell phone, but instead were blinded by the sun when you came around a corner, we can argue that this was an accident. In most states, your liability is limited because, though you were at fault, it was an accident. Most states protect the perpetrator of true accidents by limiting their liability. If you were drinking, neglected your brakes, or were chatting on your cell phone, your liability may be unlimited. Similarly, if you killed me on purpose because this book had bored you to tears one too many times, you would not only face civil liability, but criminal liability as well.

How much my wife has been harmed, though, is independent of the degree of your liability. So now let's assume that you were drunk and your employer knew it when he sent you out on a delivery. There is no limit on your liability or your employer's. We can now look at your legal exposure by dividing it into monetary losses and nonmonetary losses. This division is similar to the distinction we made between accounting cost and economic cost in Chapter 4.

Let's start with the monetary losses that are relatively easy to quantify. Suppose I make $75,000 per year as a professor at my university and I get pension, health, and other benefits totaling another $25,000 per year. You could find the present value of $100,000 per year for the rest of my working life and, depending on the interest rate chosen and the length of time I am likely to work, get a pretty good starting point for how much monetary damage you have done to my family. The present value of $100,000 per year for 25 years discounting at 5 percent is a little more than $1.4 million.

The problem is that you have not taken into account any pay increases I might earn. You have not figured in how much this book will earn in royalties that will now be paid to a substitute author. You have not taken into account the fact that I might have died from something else. You have assumed that I will not be fired or will not quit well before retirement age. You have assumed I will retire at the "average" time. You have assumed an interest rate that is based on an assumed inflation rate. Economists make assumptions about these types of variables when testifying in trials. Using those assumptions, they present the court with an expected present value of losses. Let's pretend for a moment that your estimates of these variables are accurate and you can modify your simple present value calculation appropriately. Having done so, you are still missing the nonmonetary losses.

If you review the reasons RGDP is not synonymous with social welfare from Chapter 6, you will remember that RGDP only accounts for transactions that occur in markets. My choice to sell my labor to my university is a market decision, and both my salary and my benefits count. What does not count there, and has not counted so far, is my work around the house. I am a good husband in that I do my share of the cooking, cleaning, and shopping. What's the loss associated with that? What about the loss to my family's psychological well-being? These implicit losses are real, but difficult to quantify.

Let's suppose, for now, that the jury takes all of this into account and generates a solid, defensible verdict and jury award. Is it good for the economy? Many would argue that it is because this type of jury award forces people to understand and account for the actions they take that risk harming other people. If you recall from Chapter 3, markets fail when a person makes an economic decision without thinking about the harm done to an innocent third party. Having people think about the economic consequences of their actions helps ensure that those actions are the correct ones. So, if juries get their awards right, this serves to cause individuals and businesses to consider all the costs they impose on a society.

The problem is that juries sometimes wildly inflate the less easy-to-quantify losses. Though I am a good guy, I am not worth $100 million even if the jury wants to make a statement against drunk driving or driving while cell-phone talking. When firms are concerned that even when they make good-faith mistakes, they will jeopardize their very existence (because of an appropriate jury award), they will be overly cautious. A good example of this concern is the arena of prescription drugs.

When drugs go through the FDA approval process, they are tested for both their effectiveness in treating the specific ailment for which they are prescribed and their safety. Assuming they are approved, they are marketed. The advertisements are often humorous without intending to be. The pitch person talks very calmly about the drug and its uses, and then someone else talks very fast about possible side effects. Part of the rationale behind the fast-talking discussion of side effects is to limit the liability of the drug maker.

Consider Vioxx. It was the first in a line of painkillers designed for arthritic patients who cannot take aspirin or Tylenol because these cheap over-the-counter medications damage the lining of the stomach. After Vioxx and several other similar Cox-2 inhibitors passed the approval process, a link between heart problems and these drugs was discovered. The companies that invented and marketed them did not immediately pull the drugs when the first questions were raised, but rather waited until the links were confirmed. When those ill effects were confirmed, it was off to the races with civil liability lawsuits because they waited.

Why would individuals hire attorneys when they might lose a lawsuit? The answer is because they don't have to worry about losing. **Contingency attorneys** are lawyers who agree to take a case on the stipulation that if their client loses, the client owes nothing. If they win, the lawyer typically gets one-third of the judgment or settlement. Contingency attorneys take cases knowing that they may only win a few of them, but as long as the settlements in the cases that they win are very high, they can still make a very nice living.

contingency attorney
A lawyer who agrees to take a percentage of any judgment or settlement. The attorney is paid only if the client wins the case.

class action lawsuits
Suits where similarly harmed people are joined together into one party so as to sue one or more defendants.

In other cases, where the losses to individuals are very low but where there are many similarly situated victims, attorneys create class actions. **Class actions lawsuits** are suits where the concerns of many wronged parties are grouped into one "class." A good example is my former 2002 Honda Odyssey. For whatever reason, it was proven that the odometer on that model overestimated the true distance traveled by 5 percent. The losses to individuals were very small, but the losses to the estimated 6 million Honda owners were not small in total. Because Honda settled the suit, they agreed to pay for any repairs that they would have paid for had the odometer reading been accurate. So if I had a 36,000-mile warranty and my engine blew at 37,000 miles, they would agree to fix it for free. Under the settlement, if I had already had the repair done, I could submit receipts for a refund. Those who leased minivans could recover a portion of their mileage overage charges. What also happened in this case, and what happens in many class action lawsuits, is that the lawyers get paid, usually rather well. In the Honda case, the lawyers netted close to $10 million.

Another example of a class action suit is the Takata airbag issue. Takata is a Japanese manufacturer of airbag components for a variety of automakers (BMW, Chrysler, Daimler, Ford, General Motors, Honda, Mazda, Mitsubishi, Nissan, Subaru, and Toyota). At issue was the tendency (under certain conditions) of Takata airbags to deploy with sufficient explosive force to turn the airbag housing into lethal shrapnel. By mid-2019, there were 17 U.S. deaths and more than 200 injuries attributed to this issue. While there was, and remains, a national recall of those airbags, people who own those cars had to wait, in many cases years, before enough became available to replace the impacted ones. The loss to those families directly impacted by a death or injury would be settled individually. The losses to the owners who experienced lower-than-otherwise resale values for their vehicles would be dealt with by class action.

Whether this is good for the economy generally depends on whether the losses recovered by the wronged parties are significant. It also depends on whether firms are more careful to account for these types of errors, and whether the firms overcompensate for the fear of losses by not producing useful goods that might generate such suits. The question of whether class action suits are, in net, useful devices to protect people is an open question. On one hand, they motivate businesses to ensure their products are working properly. On the other hand, the lawsuits and the threat of lawsuits can dampen innovation. Contingency attorneys overwhelmingly favor Democrats while business interests seeking a limit on their liability overwhelmingly favor Republicans.

Summary

In this chapter, we explored the role of government and the law with respect to property, intellectual property, contracts, bankruptcy, and civil liability. We learned that these legal provisions add to economic efficiency but come at a cost. We also discovered that bankruptcy and civil litigation can be used as tools to enhance economic efficiency but also have the potential to dampen innovation.

Key Terms

bankruptcy
class action lawsuit
contingency attorney
contract
copyright
creditors
intellectual property
patent
private property
trademark

Quiz Yourself

1. For a market economy to function, economists insist that government must protect
   a. private property.
   b. rights to free speech.
   c. freedom of assembly.
   d. free access to health care.
2. The type of private property that is protected by a copyright or patent is
   a. land.
   b. financial capital.
   c. intellectual property.
   d. personal property.
3. A monopolistic competitor's brand identity is protected by a
   a. trademark.
   b. patent.
   c. copyright.
   d. bond.
4. Economists insist that bankruptcy laws are always harmful to a well-functioning economy.
   a. True
   b. False
5. Bankruptcy laws
   a. always require total liquidation of all assets to pay debts.
   b. allow for those filing to restructure their debts.
   c. typically require those filing to pay a fine or serve a term in jail/prison.
   d. always allows for the forgiveness of all debts.
6. When one party harms another and the harmed party hires a lawyer who will collect only if the harmed party wins the suit, that party has hired a
   a. personal injury attorney.
   b. contingency attorney.
   c. corporate lawyer.
   d. disbarred attorney.
7. If an attorney wishes to combine the small claims of many people into one lawsuit against a defendant, he or she is engaging in a
   a. summary judgment.
   b. frivolous tort.
   c. pointed claim.
   d. class action lawsuit.

Short Answer Questions

1. Mortgages are a form of contract. Why might it not be in the best interests of the borrower, the lender, or the house buyer that such a contract be enforced if the value of the house is much less than the outstanding balance on the mortgage?
2. What are the potential costs and benefits associated with allowing for intellectual property rights? Do they always motivate innovation? Could they inhibit innovation? How?
3. What are the benefits of having a system that allows for bankruptcy? What are the costs?
4. In 2011, the Supreme Court heard a case in which lawyers were attempting to certify that all women who worked for Walmart were a single class. What would make you skeptical of such a large "class," and why would having a large class such as this make it more likely that the plaintiffs would get some settlement in their favor?

Think about This

When an economy creates intellectual property rights, it must enforce those rights. This is somewhat easy to do within a country but very difficult to do when the violator is outside the country. In China copyright infringement runs rampant, and DVDs and CDs are copied and sold by street vendors for much less than these movies and albums sell for in the United States. The United States made this an important part of trade negotiations and emphasized it more than it emphasized adherence to international labor standards. Which issue is more important to you and why?

Talk about This

The Republican and Democratic parties differ greatly on their view of personal injury and class action lawsuits. Republicans argue that these suits place a significant drain on the economy and reduce the motivation for innovation, especially in the medical arena. Democrats counter that consumers must have recourse when they are hurt or their interests are damaged by corporations. Suppose, at some level, they are both right. Where would you balance the interests of everyone in a growing but safe economy?

CHAPTER TWENTY-EIGHT

The Economics of Crime

Learning Objectives

After reading this chapter you should be able to:

- LO1 Differentiate between violent and nonviolent crime.
- LO2 Describe who generally commits crime.
- LO3 Conclude that economists who study crime often assume that criminals are rational.
- LO4 Analyze the cost of crime to society.
- LO5 Apply the principles of incentives, marginal cost, and marginal benefit to crime control.

Chapter Outline

Crime is a problem that does not naturally spring to mind as one for which economists would have much of value to contribute. Other than early work on crime by Nobel Prize–winning economist Gary Becker, we have not used much of our research time and money on this subject. Still, there are areas where economic analysis is uniquely suited to deal with the problems of crime. For instance, a potential criminal makes a decision to commit a crime based on the income potential of legal work, the profit (monetary or otherwise) to be gained from the crime, and the chance and consequence of getting caught. This is not all that different from an investment decision in which small gains in safe assets are compared to large gains in risky assets. When viewed this way, economics and criminology have some important links.

The first thing we do in exploring the economics of crime is to differentiate between violent and nonviolent crime. The next task is to look at who commits crime. We then see what a theoretical "investment-like" decision would tell us about who we should expect will commit crimes. Next, we use cost–benefit analysis to discuss how the noncriminal public should devote resources in the areas of crime prevention, detection, apprehension, and punishment. Last, we use economics to study whether the goals of life imprisonment and the death penalty have the desired effects of deterring or preventing future crime.

Types of Crime

There are two basic types of crime, violent and nonviolent crime. **Violent crime** occurs when harm is done to the victim (e.g., murder, assault, rape, robbery, etc.), aggressive action is taken by the criminal (e.g., breaking and entering, burglary, etc.), or threats are made by the criminal against a victim. **Nonviolent crimes** occur when someone simply takes what is not his/hers (theft/larceny), uses or sells illegal substances, and schemes to defraud someone of money (e.g., embezzlement, fraud, writing bad checks, etc.). Fraud crimes are often referred to as *white-collar crimes* because they are committed by people who work in office, or white-collar, jobs.

violent crime
Crime that occurs where harm is done to a victim, aggressive action is taken by the criminal, or threats are made against a victim.

nonviolent crime
Crime that occurs where someone takes what is not theirs, uses or sells an illegal substance, or engages in fraud.

Who Commits Crimes

White-Collar Crime

Table 28.1 shows the sex and racial and ethnic statistics for arrests associated with nonviolent crimes. Aside from the

Table 28.1 Nonviolent crime arrests by race and ethnicity (percentage).

Sources: Federal Bureau of Investigation. "Table 21, Arrests by Race and Ethnicity, 2016. 2016 Crime in the United States." https://ucr.fbi.gov/crime-in-the-u.s/2016/crime-in-the-u.s.-2016/topic-pages/tables/table-21; U.S. Department of Justice. "Table 42, Arrests by Sex, 2015. 2015 Crime in the United States." https://ucr.fbi.gov/crime-in-the-u.s/2015/crime-in-the-u.s.-2015/tables/table-42

	Male	Female	White*	Black*	Hispanic	Non-Hispanic
U.S. population	49.2	50.8	76.6	13.4	18.1	81.9
Forgery and counterfeiting	64.7	35.3	65.5	31.9	15.9	84.1
Fraud	61.3	38.7	67.0	30.5	11.5	88.5
Embezzlement	49.8	50.2	61.4	35.8	12.0	88.0
Stolen property; buying, receiving, possessing	78.6	21.5	64.2	33.4	19.7	80.3

*Includes those who also identify as Hispanic. Though the Census statistics divide the population into White, not-Hispanic; Black, Not-Hispanic; and Hispanic, crime statistics do not.

white-collar crime of embezzlement, men are significantly more likely to commit nonviolent crime compared to women. Relative to their percentage of the overall U.S. population, whites are somewhat less likely to be arrested for nonviolent crimes, Hispanics are somewhat less likely (except for stolen property receiving), while blacks are much more likely.

White-collar crimes tend to be committed by older people who work in offices. The average embezzler, for instance, is 48 years old. Just over half of embezzlers are women, and most work for a company with fewer than 100 employees. One-quarter of these embezzlers were engaged in their crime for more than five years, and one-quarter garnered more than $1 million. More than one-third are perpetrated within the accounting or finance department of their company. Outside of financial services, the most affected industry is government (typically, local government).

The way in which these crimes are executed frequently involves the creation of fake employees or vendors. The accounting, payroll, and accounts payable divisions of small businesses are particularly susceptible. A prototypical embezzlement scheme involves an employee who pays people or vendors setting up a modest, ongoing, and (most importantly) nonsuspicious stream of payments to a former employee, fake employee, or vendor—with the direct deposit going into an account under the control of the perpetrating employee. Cash businesses (e.g., concessions, restaurants) are often the target of embezzlement because of the ease with which a small amount can be taken from deposits.

Tax fraud cases overwhelmingly tend to be committed by men, ages 50 and older, who either fail to pay owed taxes or fail to report earned income. The racial and ethnic mix of these perpetrators differs from their representation in the overall U.S. population. Slightly less than half of these offenders are white, 30 percent are black, 13 percent are Hispanic, and 8 percent fall outside those three descriptions. Most people guilty of tax fraud serve less than two years and do so in minimum security facilities.

Violent Crime and Nonfraud, Nonviolent Crime

Table 28.2 summarizes the arrest statistics for several violent crimes. The data show that men and minorities

Table 28.2 Violent crime arrests by race and ethnicity (percentage).

Sources: Federal Bureau of Investigation. "Table 21, Arrests by Race and Ethnicity, 2016. 2016 Crime in the United States." https://ucr.fbi.gov/crime-in-the-u.s/2016/crime-in-the-u.s.-2016/topic-pages/tables/table-21; U.S. Department of Justice. "Table 42, Arrests by Sex, 2015. 2015 Crime in the United States." https://ucr.fbi.gov/crime-in-the-u.s/2015/crime-in-the-u.s.-2015/tables/table-42

	Male	Female	White*	Black*	Hispanic	Non-Hispanic
U.S. population	49.2	50.8	76.6	13.4	18.1	81.9
Murder and nonnegligent manslaughter	88.5	11.5	44.7	52.6	20.0	80.0
Rape	97.1	2.9	67.6	29.1	27.0	73.0
Robbery	85.6	14.4	43.4	54.5	21.1	78.9
Aggravated assault	76.9	23.1	62.8	33.3	24.4	75.6

*Includes those who also identify as Hispanic. Though the Census statistics divide the population into White, not-Hispanic; Black, Not-Hispanic; and Hispanic, crime statistics do not.

Table 28.3 Murder victims and perpetrators by sex, race, and ethnicity.

Source: Federal Bureau of Investigation. "Expanded Homicide Data Table 3, Murder Race, Ethnicity, and Sex of Victim by Race, Ethnicity, and Sex of Offender, 2016. 2016 Crime in the United States." https://ucr.fbi.gov/crime-in-the-u.s/2016/crime-in-the-u.s.-2016/tables/expanded-homicide-data-table-3.xls

		Perpetrator			Perpetrator			Perpetrator	
		Male	Female		White*	Black*		Hispanic	Non-Hispanic
Victim	Male	64.1	7.1	White	46.0	8.6	Hispanic	16.5	5.1
	Female	26.1	2.6	Black	3.9	41.5	Non-Hispanic	5.7	72.7

*Includes those who also identify as Hispanic. Though the Census statistics divide the population into White, not-Hispanic; Black, Not-Hispanic; and Hispanic, crime statistics do not.

are much more likely to be arrested for these violent crimes (particularly murder and robbery).

Table 28.3 shows (in cases where both the victim and the perpetrator are known) who tends to murder whom. It clearly indicates that murder is not random. Whites are far more likely to kill other whites, blacks are far more likely to kill other blacks, and Hispanics are far more likely to kill other Hispanics. Men are much more likely to kill . . . period.

Tables 28.1, 28,2 and 28.3 show the age distribution of various crimes. In particular, it is clear that violent crime is an occupation of the young. The less violent the crime, the more likely it is to be engaged in by people who are somewhat older. Fraud-based crimes, in particular, tend to be committed by older people.

These statistics come to us from two sources: police reports and surveys of crime victims. Those who view the police as racially biased may argue that statistics that come from police reports are racially biased, but it is hard to believe that crime victims would have an interest in biasing their reports. Falsely reporting the physical characteristics of an attacker to the police would diminish the likelihood that the perpetrator would be caught, and doing so in a survey would not serve any useful purpose. Regardless of whether you measure crime by looking at arrest reports sent to the FBI or by looking at victimization surveys, the data indicate conclusively that minorities commit far more crimes than their 38 percent proportion of the populace.

The Rational Criminal Model

In the late 1960s, Gary Becker developed the rational criminal model to explain crime in terms of a simple decision of risk versus return. The low-return investment, which in this case is work at a legal (but low-paying) job, has a low return, but the worker carries no risk of being arrested. On the other hand, the high-return investment, stealing or selling illegal goods, has a high return, but it puts the thief or drug dealer at risk of being caught and punished. In this context, a criminal is no different from an investment banker who is deciding whether to invest in tried-and-true U.S. Treasury bonds or a risky initial public offering of an Internet stock. Just as investors have a portfolio that contains a mix of risky and safe assets, you would expect to see that most criminals have legitimate jobs as well. This is, in fact, the case.

To properly contextualize what is suggested by the rational criminal model, we should take some time to explain what economists mean when they use the word *rational*. To an economist, if people know what it is they want, the constraints they face, the costs of getting what they want, and choose to proceed with getting it, then they are rational. This does not mean that these rational people will do what society thinks is best for them. It means only that their actions are consistent with their goals, constraints, and costs. By this standard, all but the insane are rational.

Crime Falls When Legal Income Rises

If a person has the potential for earning a higher income through legal means than illegal ones, then the person would be just plain stupid to pick the risky and lower-earning alternative of a life of crime. If you have the skills to be a doctor or lawyer and have a six-figure salary, the alternative of making $50,000 while selling cocaine is not all that attractive. Thus, the rational criminal theory correctly predicts that people with high legal incomes are not likely to be prevalent in the criminal and prison population.

This conclusion may seem trivially easy to come to, but what is not trivial is how a person with a set of intermediate skills, earning $10 an hour, or about $20,000 a year, would treat the issue. To be at that level of income in today's society, most people have only completed high school. It is therefore significant that less than half of those in the prison population graduated from high school, and 33 percent were not working at a legal job just prior to being arrested. Weighing a $20,000 a year job against a high-risk, high-income criminal life is hard, and the decision could go either way.

A full-time minimum-wage worker, earning approximately $14,500 (in 2019), would see the opportunity of earning a high criminal income as a significantly greater temptation than would a person making much more. We would expect that greater economic alternatives in the legal realm would translate into less crime, and fewer opportunities would lead to more crime. Why, then, did crime escalate during the sustained economic growth in the middle to late 1980s and fall during the sustained growth of the middle to late 1990s? The answer lies in the placing of economic opportunities.

If our rational criminal theory is accurate, raising a middle-, upper-middle-, or high-income person's economic prospects should have little to no effect on crime. Even without a growth in income, such a person would have virtually no incentive to commit crime. An increase in income would simply lessen a trivially small temptation and would have no appreciable impact on crime. On the other hand, if the economic prospects changed at the low end of the economic scale, the effect on crime would likely be substantial. This all assumes that the gain to the criminal is monetary. If the gain to the criminal is the "high" a person might get from taking the risk, or even the distasteful satisfaction one might get from inflicting suffering on another person, then the analysis is more difficult. In the case of the 2019 college admissions scandal (where rich people paid direct and indirect brides to get their kids into elite colleges), the gain to the criminal isn't necessarily monetary, but rather the satisfaction of helping their child.

All that said, let's focus on crimes of monetary gain. In the decade and a half from the mid-1970s to the early 1990s, income inequality rose. Average income rose because the upper half of the income scale did very well, while people with little education and few job skills saw their real spending power remain stagnant or fall.[1] What you would expect to see from our rational criminal model did, in fact, happen. Crime increased substantially through the period, and it did so more in the lower-income groups than in the higher-income groups.

[1]Chapter 6 shows that because the CPI overstates the effects of inflation, real incomes for the poor did not fall but rose slightly.

Crime Falls When the Likelihood and Consequences of Getting Caught Rise

The other variable that can impact the rational criminal model is the probability and consequences of getting caught. We know that crime pays (either monetarily or with satisfaction) when you do not get caught. We also know that choosing to become a criminal becomes less attractive when the chances of getting away with crime diminish and when the potential punishment becomes more severe. It is usually true that if you knew you would get caught, you would choose a legal occupation. Sometimes, however, this is not true. For some women who possess low levels of education and few marketable skills, for example, the occupation of prostitute (assuming it is a choice) may be appealing even though it typically entails getting caught regularly and going to jail for a few days as a part of the cost of doing business. The important thing here is that even given the lost time in jail, for such women, prostitution pays better than legal work.

To deter potential criminals from committing crimes, there are two things that society can do. It can make the chances of punishment greater, and it can make the punishment more severe. In its simplest terms, the first implies that by having more police, judges, and jails we can increase the likelihood that criminals will be caught, be convicted quickly, and go to jail. The second suggests that the solution is to make the sentences longer or the fines greater.

Though these may seem like two aspects of the same approach, in part because we are talking about increasing spending on the same kinds of people, they are really distinct in their intent. The first is intended to make criminals less confident that they will get away with their activities. This is where the allocation of funding comes into play. Depending on where in the judicial system the money is spent, this can provide additional funding for cops on the street, making detection and apprehension more likely, or it can provide funds for greater numbers of effective prosecutors, who may garner greater numbers of postarrest guilty verdicts. This differs from spending more money on prisons and allowing judges to sentence convicted criminals to longer terms.

Assuming that criminals are rational, their own estimation of the likelihood of getting caught is almost certainly based upon their experiences. A criminal with a long history of getting away with crime is going to place a low estimate on that probability. That is likely the reason behind the observation that embezzlers do what they do. Typical embezzlers were engaged in ongoing crimes for five years before getting caught. This may also be why embezzlers jeopardized their relatively comfortable lifestyle to engage in this crime–they assumed that they would not get caught.

Problems with the Rationality Assumption

Criminologists and sociologists have a difficult time granting the assumption that the decision to become a criminal is a rational economic decision made by people capable of evaluating complex choices. In support of their view, you only have to look at the percentage of crime that is seemingly senseless. For example, 22 percent of murders involved a family member killing another family member. School shootings are not explainable using models of rationality. One of the main criticisms of economic models is that they assume too much intellectual capacity on the part of humans. For instance, it might be argued that if criminals could evaluate the options as rationally as economists claim they can, they probably would be smart enough not to turn to crime. Despite its limitations, economists use the idea of the "rational criminal" when looking at criminality; and, as was seen above, the rational criminal model is often consistent with what we know about crime.

The Costs of Crime

In the latest year for which there are comprehensive national data, 2015, we spent a total of $284 billion on the police, the judiciary, and prisons. In 2017, 9 million persons were arrested and some 606,571 of that number were sentenced to jail. There were more than 2.2 million Americans in state or federal jails and prisons. This was all done in response to the 1.2 million violent and 7.7 million property crimes that were reported that year. When we see these numbers, we wonder whether the money we spend is worth it, and whether the distribution of spending on police, justice, and prisons is optimal.

If we put any faith in the rational criminal model, we are convinced that by spending money in this way, we can change the probability of criminals being punished and the extent of their punishments. Of course, we could also talk about spending money to raise the legal income potential of people. Some people argue, for example, that we should take money that originally allocated for building new prisons and put it into education and social programs like Head Start and employment training programs that might help people to get out of poverty. Others point to data that indicate that these programs do not work and suggest that building prisons is the best of a set of bad alternatives.

To answer the central questions of whether we, as a society, are spending the right amount of money on crime control and whether we are spending it on the right mix of control mechanisms, we need to examine how much crime there is and how much it costs us. Using a variety of criminological surveys, we know that, of the crimes reported annually, more than twice that number are actually committed. Though most murders get reported, robberies, rapes, and other crimes tend not to be universally reported. Some of this may be attributed to the rationality of crime victims. If the chances of catching the perpetrator are low and the psychological and monetary costs of testifying are high, then some victims may not report crimes committed against them.

How Much Does an Average Crime Cost?

When a crime is committed, there are several different kinds of costs to consider. If we could put a dollar value on the average crime, we could, at least theoretically, generate an estimate of the cost of crime in general. The first and most obvious cost of crime is the value of items taken or stolen. This is fairly easily measured, but it is not always very important, especially if the crime is a form of assault rather than a form of theft. Even when the crime is a simple theft, if the stolen item is replaced with insurance, the cost of the crime to the victim doesn't account for the loss to society of the theft. Insurance rates, for instance, will rise when thefts are prevalent as will extraneous theft-prevention activities that add little to actual economic well-being.

As difficult as it is to estimate tangible costs of crime, it is much harder to estimate the costs of crimes like murder, rape, and assault, because so much of those costs are intangible. There are some aspects of these that are easier to estimate than others. For example, an assault victim who cannot work for a few days has a loss that is at least quantifiable. On the other hand, a sexual assault victim's loss in terms of quality of life is not so easily quantified. Moreover, there is no way of knowing whether being a victim of a crime causes people to be less ambitious or productive than they would have been otherwise. The monetary value of psychological trauma that comes with victimization is also difficult to estimate.

There are two general methods that are used to estimate these intangible losses. The first looks at how much money individuals pay to avoid crimes by looking at the relative price of homes in high- and low-crime neighborhoods. This allows economists to create a

THINGS THAT MATTER IN CRIME

A 2015 study by the Brennan Center for Justice conducted by economists and criminologists separated out the impact of various policies on the decline in crime that occurred during the 1990s and 2000s. Their study examined the impact of increased incarcerations, increased numbers of police, the use of CompStat policies that used sophisticated statistics to deploy resources, the increased prevalence of the death penalty, and the increased prevalence of right-to-carry laws. They looked at economic factors such as consumer confidence, income growth, and unemployment. They also considered social and demographic trends, ranging from the decreased use of crack cocaine and alcohol, to a decrease in the percentage of the population in their prime crime years (ages 16–24).

They began by noting the nearly 50 percent drop in the crime rate since 1991. With violent crime dropping by 51 percent and property crime dropping by 43 percent, something caused it to happen, and these scholars wanted to figure out what that was. They wanted to know whether it was any of the various policies that were tried or whether the drop was caused by something unrelated to crime policy.

One key conclusion was a wonderful example of diminishing returns. At first, during the 1990s, increased rates of incarceration had a significant impact, explaining as much as 10 percent of the drop in crime. Later, in the period from 2000 to 2013, rates of incarceration had no additional impact on crime. They found much the same thing with the impact of increasing the numbers of police. At first there was a large impact, but later there was no impact. Those with good economic intuition should not be surprised that diminishing returns would show itself in crime reduction.

The state of the local economy was a consistent factor in explaining crime rates as was the drop in the use of alcohol. CompStat also showed itself to have a positive effect in reducing crime but only as the methodology was honed in the 2000s.

Two interesting theories appeared during the 2000s (and in this textbox in previous editions of this book) to explain the drop in crime in the 1990s; both had their origins in changes that occurred during the 1970s. The first of these theories was that the legalization of abortion increased the average degree of "wantedness" of the children who were born in the 1970s and thereby resulted in fewer poorly parented children in the 1980s and 1990s. With fewer poorly parented children in the 1970s and 1980s, that, it was hypothesized, would have resulted in fewer crimes in the 1990s. The second of these theories tied atmospheric lead concentrations to criminal conduct. This theory offered as proof that the increase in atmospheric lead that occurred because of increased driving in the 1950s and 1960s was, 20 years later, associated with an increase in crime in the 1970s and 1990s. It further argued that the subsequent decrease in atmospheric lead because of 1970s-era laws that eliminated it from gasoline led to decreased crime in the 1990s. The explanation, that lead in young children inhibits the judgment centers of the brain, seemed plausible. However, once all factors were taken into account, both of these theories were held to be without empirical support.

Policy favorites of the political right, increased use of the death penalty and increased prevalence of right-to-carry laws, were also shown to be without merit.

"willingness-to-pay" measure. If people are willing to pay \$100,000 extra to reduce their likelihood of victimization by half, then crime "costs" \$200,000. This method can be used to estimate the value of a human life. If someone is willing to pay \$100 to reduce their likelihood of death from one in 5,000 to one in 10,000, then they are implicitly saying their life is worth \$100/0.0002 = \$500,000.

Another method uses jury awards in wrongful death and personal injury cases to establish loss estimates. In this method, the average jury award to the widow of a drunken driving victim is used as a proxy for the value of the life lost. The average jury award to a nonfatal accident might stand in for the intangible loss from a nonfatal assault.

If we simply ignore all of the estimated costs of pain and suffering and lives lost, then the cost of the average crime is estimated at approximately \$1,000. For each crime, the estimates of the value of pain and suffering depend on methodology. For murder, the estimates cluster around \$4 million. For rape, estimates cluster around \$100,000. For other assaults, they cluster around \$25,000. Other crimes have much lower estimated costs, such as \$6,000 for car theft and \$2,500 for household burglary. On average, the cost estimates per crime including pain and suffering are around \$15,000.

How Much Crime Does an Average Criminal Commit?

We can use these figures to estimate the cost of letting criminals go free and compare that to the cost of keeping them in jail. If we know how many crimes the average criminal commits, we can multiply the average cost per crime by the average number of crimes committed in a year to determine the costs imposed on society by the early release of a still violent criminal. Viewed differently, we can examine the cost of choosing not to catch and jail a criminal. That is, we might realize that some crime is not worth preventing.

Even when we interpret sophisticated criminological surveys, we find that the average number of crimes committed by the average criminal ranges all the way from 180 down to 10. Most economists are comfortable with estimates in the range of 10 to 20 crimes. If we assume for a moment that crime would stay the same if we eliminated all expenditures on law enforcement, the average savings from keeping average criminals off the street would range from 10 crimes per criminal times $1,000 per crime, or $10,000, to 20 crimes per criminal times $15,000 per crime, or $300,000.

Optimal Spending on Crime Control

What Is the Optimal Amount to Spend?

The average cost of incarceration is $39,545 per year, and the total cost of incarcerations, $87 billion. Assuming that crime rates would rise if we eliminated all expenditures on law enforcement—either by the average criminal committing more crimes or because otherwise law-abiding citizens turn to crime—it is quite clear that the money we spend on prisons is worth it. Even though more than 1.6 million people are in state or federal prisons at a cost of approximately $56 billion per year, this may be a good expenditure.

The question of whether we spend the optimal amount on keeping people in prisons, however, remains to be answered. At this time, there are far more than double the number of felons on the street than in prison. These are people who have served their sentences, been released on parole, or were never imprisoned in the first place. If they are committing crimes at a rate similar to the 10 to 20 crimes a year that incarcerated criminals were committing, then we have too few people in prison.

Of key concern to economists is not necessarily whether the total amount spent on crime control exceeds the total amount saved from preventing crime, but whether we are spending the correct amount. At its heart, the problem is exactly the same as the profit-maximizing problem for a business firm. The mere fact that a firm's revenues exceed its costs does not mean that profit is as high as it could be. That means we are less interested in the costs and benefits of capturing, trying, and incarcerating the "average" criminal than we are in incarcerating the "marginal" criminal.

Think of it this way. Suppose we catch a prolific thief who costs society $100,000 a year, and it costs $39,545 per year to incarcerate him. Now suppose we catch a part-time thief who costs society only $10,000 per year, and it still costs $39,545 per year. The intermediate or average thief costs society $55,000 each year, and we spend $39,545 per year keeping him incarcerated. This does not mean we should not have incarcerated the part-time thief. The marginal benefit to society of incarcerating him was less than the marginal cost.

Applying this information to the problem of optimal crime control means that we would need to look at who the people are who get arrested and put away when we increase spending on criminal justice. The practical problem is much harder to figure out than it is for a firm. In business, we can see how much extra material and labor costs go into producing another unit of output and judge whether that is greater than the price, but we cannot easily determine which extra criminals are caught as a result of our spending more on police. Are these criminals more or less prolific than the average criminal caught before the spending increase? Much of the research on crime assumes that the "marginal" criminal is just like the "average" criminal, but it is merely an assumption.

Is the Money Spent in the Right Way?

Whether we spend the right amount of money is interesting, but equally interesting is whether we spend the money in the right way. Again, marginal analysis is of use. If we spend $284 billion on the system, the allocation between police, justice, and incarceration should depend on how effective the marginal dollar is in combating crime in each category. If the optimal distribution is accomplished, the marginal benefit of a dollar should be equal in the three areas.

Are the Right People in Jail?

Of course, there is the related issue of whether the right people are in jail. Of the 1.6 million people who are in prisons and 727,000 in local jails, just under half are there for violent crimes. The remainder are there for nonviolent crimes such as burglary, drug possession, and drug distribution. In the 1980s, society faced a problem. If these prison spaces were being used for drug offenders rather than violent criminals or thieves, perhaps the wrong people were in jail. We could release violent criminals in order to make room in prisons for drug users, or build more prisons, or let the drug users go.

In recognition of this choice, state and local governments decided to go on a prison-building spree during the 1980s and 1990s. In Texas, for example, prison capacity was nearly doubling every four years. This phenomenon was certainly not confined to any one state, as state after state went to "truth in sentencing" laws that required criminals to serve at least 85 percent of their sentence. In Florida and Texas, felons had been serving less than one-third of their sentences, a disparity these states and others found unacceptable.

In recent years critics have called into question the practice of incarcerating so many people, for so long. These critics have noted that the increase in incarceration frequency and duration has impacted the African American population disproportionately. Those who counter this argument turn to the data on crime that show (again, without regard to whether you use victimization surveys or police reports) that minorities commit a disproportionate amount of violent crime and that the drop in the crime rate that resulted from these incarcerations is worth the cost. If you accept their conclusion that the increase in incarcerations in the 1990s decreased crime (which evidence shows occurred) and in the 2000s (which new evidence suggests did not occur), that need not require you to accept that the increase in the cost (both monetary and social) is worth it.

Partly in response to this movement, President Trump worked with an interesting coalition of interested parties (Kanye West, Van Jones, and Rep. John Lewis on the left and Senators Lee and Grassley on the right) to pass the First Step Act. The purpose of the bill was to reduce the number of people incarcerated in federal prisons for long sentences for drug offenses where no violence occurred.

What Laws Should We Rigorously Enforce?

In a formal way, economists look at crime control measures from a cost–benefit point of view. In Figure 28.1 the vertical axis represents the amount of marginal benefit and marginal cost associated with catching, adjudicating, and imprisoning an additional criminal. We will make three assumptions:

1. The marginal benefits are decreasing for each additional criminal.
2. We will deal with serious crimes first and petty crimes last.
3. The dollar benefits of preventing these crimes will fall.

Furthermore, we will assume that the marginal cost of dealing with criminals increases because the petty criminals violating trivial laws are assumed to be more expensive to catch and convict than are criminals whose crimes are more serious. This assumption is predicated on the idea that we would have to have very many and, most important, less competent police[2] to catch such violators.

FIGURE 28.1 Marginal cost and marginal benefit analysis and crime.

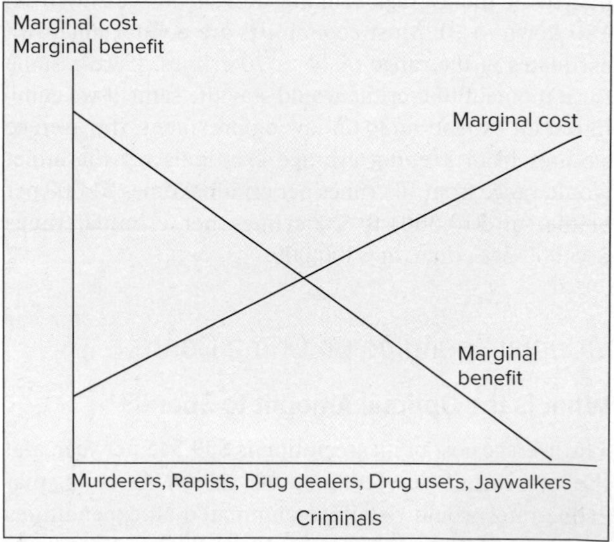

Figure 28.1 indicates that it makes sense to spend the money to catch, prosecute, and imprison all murderers, rapists, and high-end drug dealers. It also indicates that it makes no sense to do the same for jaywalkers, drug users, and low-end drug dealers. Though this picture is simplistic in its assumptions, you can see, roughly, how an economist reasons on the issue of crime control. Spend the money on the really bad guys rather than spending it on the not-so-bad guys.

That leaves one last issue to deal with in determining how we spend our law enforcement dollars: How do we divide the money among the various sectors? States, for example, have spent a growing part of their budgets to deal with crime and in doing so have changed the percentage that they allocate to the different sectors. The increase in resources has gone to prisons and police, with a smaller percentage of money allocated to adjudication. Competent police are more effective in deterring criminals and apprehending criminals who have not yet been deterred. It also means that people sentenced stay in jail longer. The downside of this is that more cases are plea-bargained than ever before. That is because, with more prison cells, those arrested run the risk of actually serving very long sentences if they go to trial. Those cells give prosecutors more leverage.

[2]We assume they are likely to be less competent because cities hire the more competent of their applicant pool first, and these are all gone when it comes time to hire more.

Since the increases in spending have not funded all sectors of the system evenly, criminals are more likely to be caught, plea to a crime that is less severe than the one they actually committed, and go to jail. The length of term they face has probably increased because 85 percent of a short sentence is often longer than 33 percent of a long one. Part of the reduction in crime since the early 1990s is also attributable to this policy of sending greater numbers of criminals to prison. A small minority of criminals commit a majority of the crime, and they now must stay in prison longer. Though estimates vary, an increase of 10 percent in the prison population has been shown to result in a 4 percent to 6 percent decrease in crime. Whereas some of this may be deterrence, it is likely that simply holding criminals prevents them from committing the crimes they would have committed had they been left on the streets.

What Is the Optimal Sentence?

One of the major debates of our time is whether criminals convicted of murder and other heinous crimes should be put to death or incarcerated with no opportunity for parole. While many religious leaders and laypersons alike approach this as a moral issue, economists again tend to look at it from the standpoint of the costs and benefits. If you sentence men and women to death, the sentences are carried out only after a long and drawn-out appeal process. At least one-quarter of those on death row die of natural causes. In economic terms, we must decide whether spending a lot of money over a 10-year period is worth the savings in imprisonment expenses. Life sentences, which are routinely given in murder cases, also have cost issues to face. If a 75-year-old is released from prison, is he or she likely to again become a menace to society?

To examine whether the death penalty saves money or costs money, we need to recall the Chapter 7 concept of present value. Suppose it would take $1 million invested now to make the payments to house, adjudicate appeals, and put to death a condemned inmate. Suppose it would cost less than $1 million invested now to simply house the inmate from the time he or she is sentenced to the time that inmate would have died if given a life sentence. In such a circumstance, the death penalty costs money. Otherwise, it saves money. This of course assumes that the death penalty is not a deterrent. It may also be that society wants to ensure justice without regard to the price.

The cost–benefit trade-off is important also in establishing sentence length. Since nearly no crime is committed by 80-year-olds, does it make sense to sentence people to life in prison? Why not let them out when the chances of committing a crime have largely disappeared? It is not hard to figure that, as time goes on, a person violent enough to kill at age 18 is not as likely to commit murder at 50 and is even less likely to at 70. This point may not be worth considering since the life expectancy in prison is such that few inmates sentenced to life live long enough to outlive their own violent tendencies. Prison life is hard, and the food and medical care are not designed to keeping people healthy in their "golden years." Ironically, this makes the death penalty even less economically sensible since the "lifer's" life is not going to be that long.

Summary

You should now understand how economics, and in particular the use of marginal benefit–marginal cost analysis, can contribute to the debate over crime and crime control. Besides knowing who it is that generally commits crime and why, you have seen that economists often model criminals as rational people who are influenced by the risks and rewards of their decisions. You have seen how much crime costs society and how much we spend to control it. You have seen how an economist analyzes crime control to answer questions about whether society is spending the right amount on the right criminals, on the right crimes, while imposing the right sentences.

Key Terms

nonvoilent crimes

violent crimes

Quiz Yourself

1. When accountants take money from their employers (by directing money to personal accounts), this is classified as
   a. a violent crime.
   b. the nonviolent crime of embezzlement.
   c. the violent crime of fraud.
   d. the nonviolent crime of burglary.

2. If judges had to be trained as economists before taking their position, they might use ________ analysis when deciding on the right sentence.
   a. marginal
   b. punitive
   c. religious
   d. average

3. The optimal level of police protection would compare the ________________ with the ________________.
   a. marginal cost of hiring an additional officer; marginal benefit of crime reduction
   b. average cost of all officers; average benefit per officer of crime reduction
   c. total cost of all officers; average benefit of crime reduction
   d. length of the average sentence; history of sentences, per crime

4. If a crime prevention mechanism works initially, but increasing it further has no additional impact that is an example of
   a. diminishing returns.
   b. downward-sloping demand.
   c. the division of labor.
   d. economic loss.

5. To an economist, the correct distribution of money among police, the justice system, and prisons is one that
   a. sets an equal amount to each.
   b. sets the amount each gets equal to its average benefit.
   c. sets the amount each gets so that none is wasted.
   d. sets the amount each gets so that no other element could get better use (in terms of crime reduction) of the marginal dollar.

6. The rational criminal model explains crimes of
   a. passion.
   b. stupidity.
   c. profit.
   d. love.

7. The rational criminal model draws a parallel to the thought processes of
   a. investors.
   b. educators.
   c. law enforcement officers.
   d. politicians.

Short Answer Questions

1. How would you use marginal benefit and marginal cost analysis to determine the correct sentence length for a particular crime?
2. How could you use marginal benefit and marginal cost analysis to determine whether money would be better spent keeping prisoners incarcerated or on employing more police?
3. Why is it important to use marginal analysis in examining crime policies rather than "average" (cost and benefit) analysis?
4. What other policy changes could you make now that would have a similarly delayed impact on crime several years from now?

Think about This

The rational criminal model is often invoked to explain the behavior of drug dealers and their pushers. Economist Steven Levitt disputes this by suggesting that drug dealers engage in behaviors that are just as irrational as those who play the lottery. Is drug dealing rational?

Talk about This

Under what circumstances would you engage in a criminal activity? Would your actions be rational?

For More Insight See

Journal of Economic Perspectives 10, no. 1 (Winter 1996). See articles by John J. DiIulio; and Richard B. Freeman and Isaac Ehrlich, pp. 3–8.

Cohen, Mark, *The Costs of Crime and Justice* (New York: Routledge, 2005).

Levitt, Steven D., "Understanding Why Crime Fell in the 1990s: Four Factors That Explain the Decline and Six That Do Not," *Journal of Economic Perspectives* 18, no. 1 (Winter 2004).

Reyes, Jessica Wolpaw, "Environmental Policy as Social Policy? The Impact of Childhood Lead Exposure on Crime," *The B.E. Journal of Economic Analysis & Policy* 7, no. 1 (2007), Contributions, Article 51.

"What Caused the Crime Decline?" Roeder, Eisen, and Bowling. Brennan Center for Justice. www.brennancenter.org/publication/what-caused-crime-decline, 2015.

Behind the Numbers

Department of Justice; Bureau of Justice Statistics: www.bjs.gov

- Crime (violent and nonviolent) statistics
- Arrest statistics
- Victimization statistics
- Crime control spending

CHAPTER TWENTY-NINE

Antitrust

Learning Objectives

After reading this chapter you should be able to:

LO1 Identify the economic inefficiencies associated with monopolies and explain why some monopolies are inevitable and even good for society.

LO2 Summarize the laws that regulate the existence and pricing behavior of monopolies.

LO3 Provide examples of how antitrust law has been applied to specific industries within the United States.

Chapter Outline

When a business treats us badly, most of us get a high degree of satisfaction by announcing that we will never return. When the business is the phone, gas, electric, or water company, though, it is frustrating because in most cases we cannot get those goods or services somewhere else because those businesses are monopolists. It is likely that you have only one source of cable television, electricity, water, or natural gas. When a representative of a monopolistic company makes you mad, you and the representative know that you have no alternatives; you are stuck. You can scream and complain, but in the end, you must continue using the same company for service. For capitalism to function, these situations work best when there are both the incentive generated by potentially high profits and the downside of potential bankruptcy to keep firms working in the consumer's best interest. Without such incentives, a company's profit motive tends to work against consumers rather than in their best interests.

It is for this reason that we have laws that inhibit firms from becoming monopolies through mergers, and we have laws that prevent the monopolies that do exist from using their power to the detriment of consumers. That said, we will review the characteristics of monopoly that concern economists and discuss situations where monopolies may be necessary evils. We then turn to laws that are in place to protect consumers from the problems that monopolists cause. We attempt to determine how many competitors are needed for competition to work, and we provide a few examples of firms that have been accused of using their monopoly power to the detriment of their customers.

What's Wrong with Monopoly?

High Prices, Low Output, and Deadweight Loss

Figure 29.1 illustrates the core of the problem with monopolies. Recall that a monopolist controls an entire market. That is, when we diagram the monopolistic situation, the market demand curve will be the demand curve for the firm's output. What follows from this is that to sell more of its good, the firm has to progressively lower the price it charges. When the firm lowers prices, the resulting graph shows that the marginal revenue curve is not flat, as it is under perfect competition, but is downward sloping (with a slope twice that of the demand curve).

Assuming that its goal is to maximize profits, a monopolistic organization will sell its output at a price that is determined by the point on the graph at which marginal cost and marginal revenue are equal. In Figure 29.1

FIGURE 29.1 Perfect competition versus monopoly.

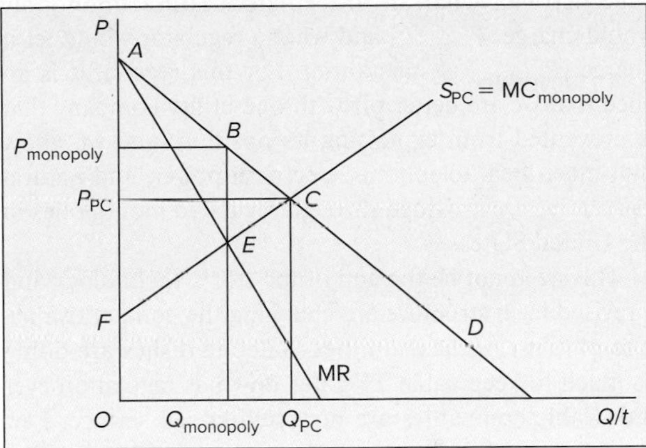

that output level is $Q_{monopoly}$. The price a monopolistic firm would charge for that output can be found by going up from $Q_{monopoly}$ to the demand curve and over to the price axis to get $P_{monopoly}$.

To compare this monopoly outcome to what would exist in an industry composed of many firms in perfect competition, we need to recall that the supply curve for each individual perfect competitor is its marginal cost curve. To find the industry supply curve, we would horizontally add the individual supply curves together. When we do that we find that we have also created the marginal cost curve for an industry ruled by one firm. That is why, in Figure 29.1, the supply curve for the industry of perfect competitors is also labeled as the marginal cost curve for the monopolist. It is simply a different interpretation of the same information. It is not, however, the monopolist's supply curve. There is no such thing because monopolists do not take the price as given; they search for the price that makes them the most money.

Given that, we can say that if an industry is characterized by many perfectly competitive firms rather than a monopolistic firm, then the price-quantity combination will be where supply equals demand: P_{PC}, Q_{PC}.

Under perfect competition, we know that the consumer surplus, depicted as the area under the demand curve but above the price line, would be $P_{PC}AC$, and the producer surplus, depicted as the area under the price curve but above the supply or marginal cost curve, would be $FP_{PC}C$ for a combined social benefit of *FAC*. (See Chapter 3 if you need to review consumer and producer surplus.) In an industry that is ruled by just one firm rather than many, the consumer surplus is much smaller and the producer surplus somewhat larger. To be precise, the consumer surplus shrinks to $P_{monopoly}AB$, and the producer surplus grows to $FP_{monopoly}BE$. The combined area is *FABE*. This is smaller than the combined area under perfect competition by the triangle *EBC*. Economists call this area deadweight loss because it represents the loss in economic benefits to society that results from an inefficiency–that is, a monopolist.

The desire to eliminate deadweight loss is at the center of why economists, usually reluctant to let government control markets, generally accept the need for government to intervene in monopoly cases.

Reduced Innovation

Another problem with monopolies–both those subject to price control by government and those that are government-owned, like the post office–is the reduction in the motivation to innovate. When there are no competitors to keep a business innovating, it can easily get lazy. Monopolies like your local water company are much less likely to engage in cost-saving or service-enhancing innovation when they are not threatened with competition. Even worse, since they use their costs to justify their prices to regulators, they have an incentive to pad costs that make their own jobs easier. Layers of middle management can easily grow. They can be justified as improving customer service when they are really about making life easier for upper management.

This problem is not limited to privately held monopolies. The U.S. Postal Service (USPS) is a government-held monopoly for mail. It did not consider overnight delivery important until Federal Express and United Parcel Service developed the business. Cost-saving or service-enhancing technology is less likely to come from the USPS than it is from the private package delivery companies.

Natural Monopolies and Necessary Monopolies

Natural Monopoly

Many of the monopolies that we deal with every day are inevitable. The utilities–electricity, natural gas, local telephone service, sewers, and cable television–are monopolies where there are very high fixed costs and diminishing marginal costs. On an intuitive level, you understand that you would not want several hundred wires or pipes coming in and out of your house. It would be ugly and expensive for there to be many different electric companies vying for your business. Changes in technology and

FIGURE 29.2 Natural monopoly.

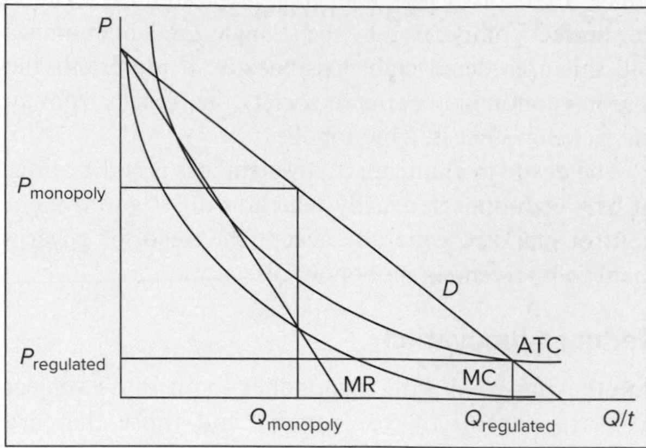

reforms of the regulatory structure are rapidly changing the way these utilities do business. Still, each locale typically has only one provider of these services.

If you look at Figure 29.2, you can see the problem in the context of Chapter 4's cost curves. Instead of the marginal cost (MC) curve sloping up and the average total cost (ATC) curve being U-shaped, both are downward sloping and steadily flattening. In a typical monopoly, the fixed costs of stringing wires or burying pipes are so great that output levels never get to where MC is rising. The ATC and MC curves might take on their familiar shapes if quantities were very much larger. If it is easier to imagine, just think of this graph as showing the left side of those two curves.

It is the large fixed costs that represent a potentially insurmountable economic **barrier to entry.** Recall from Chapter 5 that one of the four requirements for perfect competition is freedom of entry and exit. When fixed costs are high, it is nearly impossible for a new firm to get started in the market. If the fixed costs are significant, then having more than one firm bearing them is not cost-efficient. In this case, a carefully regulated monopoly may save consumers money. The quality of regulation is definitely the key, because the company will want to charge $P_{monopoly}$ and produce only $Q_{monopoly}$. The monopolist wants to exploit the power it has, and it is part of the government's job to provide the regulation that prevents that from happening.

barrier to entry
A legal or economic mechanism that prevents firms from competing in an industry.

Government regulators will allow monopolies to earn a *normal profit,* the profit consistent with what a similar investment would get them in another industry. This is depicted in Figure 29.2 as the point at which ATC crosses the demand curve, *D.* It should be clear that the difference between what an unregulated natural monopoly would charge, $P_{monopoly}$, and what a regulator would let it charge, $P_{regulated}$, is substantial. For this reason, it is argued that we are better off with one utility company that is prevented from exploiting its position, and we know that most local telephone, electrical power, and natural gas service are provided through regulated monopolies in the United States.

This need not be the end of the story. Technology and a revised legal structure are changing the competitive nature of many of these utilities. Satellite dishes are doing as much to keep cable TV rates down as regulation ever did. Cable companies are now selling cell service. Few young people have a home phone; they simply use cellular phones.

Though the poorly thought-out 1990s-era California electricity deregulation experiment was a disaster, some communities are deregulating the electric power industry successfully. Some forms of deregulation have the existing provider charge a fee to access the delivery system. It may be that in the near future these once-inevitable natural monopolies will face competition.

Patents, Copyrights, and Other Necessary Monopolies

Copyrights and patents are examples of other legalized monopolies that society has decided are needed for the economy to work well. The only way singers, authors, or moviemakers make money on their creative work is through their exclusive right to sell it. Monopoly power is given to record companies, publishers, and movie producers so they can make enough money to motivate their efforts.

For example, services like Napster and LimeWire allowed anyone with access to the Internet to download music that other people had uploaded through peer-to-peer sharing networks for free. Many in the music industry believed that the mass online distribution of such material violated copyright laws. They were correct and a federal court terminated the original Napster.[1] The economic issue at the time was how this type of service affected the motivation to produce new music. What's interesting now is that downloaded music has become another interesting antitrust example with Apple and Spotify arguing in court over whether Apple was inappropriately exploiting its App Store.

[1]Napster is now owned by Rhapsody and operates under a subscription-based model similar to Spotify Premium.

Patents are given to inventors of new things for the same reason that copyrights are given to writers and performers. Patents expire after a number of years, depending on the type of invention. While the patent is in force, however, the inventor is the only one who has the right to sell his or her invention. Whether the invention is a new drug, or a vast improvement on a familiar product or service, the invention belongs to the inventor. In the modern era, scientists usually work for a big company that retains the right to buy their ideas for $1 each. Although this may seem unfair, scientists are often part of a team that jointly creates ideas. In addition, because inventing is a risky business with inventions only rarely becoming successful in the marketplace, the companies guarantee the scientist an income. For that, they get to keep the high returns.

In any event, the exclusive right to sell something creates the incentive to be creative or innovative, as the case may be. The author of the book you are reading right now would like to think he would have written this book for the good of his own students' understanding, but the truth is he is working for money, too. Lest you think I am the only one, ask yourself whether you too are not motivated to work by money. Writers, singers, moviemakers, and inventors need protection. Without that protection, the inventor would know that the costs they incurred perfecting their invention would not be covered because competitors could exploit the invention without having paid for its development.

The rationale for other monopolies is that they provide a social good. The USPS performs the social service of providing equal mail service at an equal price to everyone anywhere in the United States. Though its detractors suggest that a privatized system would be more efficient and cost less, its defenders believe that the "social good" is sufficient to justify any monopoly inefficiencies.

Monopolies and the Law

The Sherman Anti-Trust Act

Under the law, it is not illegal to be a monopoly. It is not even against the law for a company to establish itself as a monopoly. The Sherman Anti-Trust Act of 1890, however, makes it illegal for a company to use its monopoly power in one market to enhance its position in another.[2] According to the Sherman Act, it is also illegal to attempt to control a market in all of its stages of production.

As we saw above, there are cases where monopoly power is a good thing. As a matter of fact, it is the ultimate incentive for a business. If a manufacturer is so good that it makes a product so much better than that of its competition, then it will, of course, benefit by having no competition. As long as the company is that good and as long as it continues to price its product low enough that other firms see no point in entering the market, there is no demonstrable harm from having a monopoly. The result is that there is no violation of antitrust law. Later in the chapter, we will see that Microsoft claims to be a company that has performed so well that it became a monopoly in the operating system business.

As we said previously, it is against the law to use monopoly power in a given area to generate business in another area. This is what Spotify accused Apple of doing. That is, Spotify argued that Apple's App Store monopoly enabled it to derive revenue because of its market power in the app and device business.

Antitrust law also forbids a company from controlling the entire production-to-sales process for a particular good. This is what got Standard Oil in trouble with the government in the early 1900s. At one time, Standard Oil dominated the oil and gasoline industry through its ownership and control of drilling equipment, oil wells, refineries, pipelines, distribution networks, and gas stations. This was found at the time to be illegal, and it is still illegal.

Other parts of the law work toward preventing companies from becoming monopolistic by merging. It is very much against the law for two separate companies, in an industry of only a few, to share information or to collude on setting prices. This is called "price fixing," and local gasoline stations are accused of it all the time. Just as someone realized that companies could fix prices if they merged, Congress gave power to the Federal Trade Commission (FTC) to allow or to deny proposed mergers. When two airlines merge and it is a merger that would lead to a monopoly at an important airport, the FTC intervenes. It can simply prohibit the merger, or it can require that the airline sell its gate access to another airline.

The interesting exception to this general rule is the case of Sirius/XM radio. Both companies were on the verge of bankruptcy before their 2008 merger and only narrowly avoided it in 2009 afterward. The question before the antitrust division of the Justice Department was not whether having two satellite radio providers was better than one; it was whether one was better than zero. It decided that one was better than zero.

[2]While a number of important laws amending and clarifying the Sherman Act have been enacted since 1890, for simplicity and brevity we will consider this one body of antitrust law.

What Constitutes a Monopoly?

One of the new areas of economic research asks an interesting question: How many firms does it take to ensure competition? We have assumed that we needed many, but we have not produced a number. Some economists have begun to argue that one is actually enough. They argue that if the one entity that comprises the monopoly is afraid of potential competition, and prices its goods low enough that no one decides to enter the market, we have what ordinarily comes only with perfect competition. In this hypothetical example, however, it has come with only a single firm.

To see this at work, imagine an airport that is served by only one major airline. Speculate on how it will price its tickets as a monopolist or as if it had many competitors. It turns out that under certain conditions, it will be sufficiently frightened at the prospect of another carrier coming in that it will price its tickets very close to a competitive level and significantly below the potential monopoly level.

As a concrete example, Southwest Airlines has a reputation of causing other airlines to lower their fares when they are in competition with Southwest and in some places where they are not. It faces few work-rule inefficiencies that plague other airlines. Southwest can get at least one additional flight more than its competitors, out of a plane and crew each day. This means it can outcompete everyone else on the price of tickets.

Suppose you are in charge of pricing tickets for another airline and you have a monopoly in a particular city. You know that Southwest chooses its next target city on the basis of its ability to charge much less than the price that is currently being charged. What will you do? You keep your price low in hopes that Southwest will ignore you.

contestable markets hypothesis
One firm is all that is necessary for competitive prices to exist as long as that firm is threatened by hit-and-run entry.

To its firm believers, this **contestable markets hypothesis** means that the answer to the question of how many firms it takes to have competitive prices is *one,* as long as it is one that is scared.

Examples of Antitrust Action

Standard Oil

When John D. Rockefeller established Standard Oil, no one knew how petroleum would change the world. By the time the huge monopoly that was Standard Oil was disbanded, Rockefeller had become the richest man the world had ever known. If you measure personal wealth as the percentage of all U.S. wealth, Jeff Bezos would have to triple his to come close to Rockefeller's. Rockefeller got as rich as he did by controlling the entire petroleum production process. He owned the oil fields, all the drilling equipment, all the pipelines and trucks that distributed it, and he licensed all the retail outlets that sold his gas, oil, and kerosene.

This kind of monopoly, called a **trust,** involves the single ownership of all stages of production, and it has been accomplished to this degree only a few times. A comparable situation would occur if Bill Gates owned not only Microsoft but also Intel, Dell, Apple, Hewlett-Packard, and all other computer hardware manufacturers, and he licensed franchises to all of the retail outlets that sold computers.

trust
A single company having ownership of all stages of production in a particular industry.

In Rockefeller's case, he used the total control he had over the oil production business to gain control over the pipelines and the retail outlets. He did this by simply refusing to use pipelines that refused to sell to him, and he refused to sell his products to stations that he did not license. He then used this power to make even more money by buying the pipelines at low prices and by selling his products to filling stations at high prices. Our debt to Rockefeller is that much of the law making trusts illegal simply makes illegal what he did so well.

The dissolution of Standard Oil made several companies out of one. Each competed with the others for pipeline services and to sign up gas stations. Among others, we know these companies today as Exxon, Amoco, and Standard Oil. The lessons that Rockefeller taught the world were learned very well, and most developed countries now have laws that make it illegal to use monopoly pressure to limit competition.

IBM

International Business Machines, better known as IBM, began as a producer of typewriters and adding machines. By the 1960s, however, IBM was well into the business of computers. Back then, a state-of-the-art mainframe computer with the computational capacity of a current smartphone would fill several rooms. Moreover, if you needed that kind of computing, you had one choice, IBM.

As the monopolist in mainframe computers, IBM could use this power as an advantage over the companies that produced mainframe software as well as other hardware. In 1969, the Justice Department sued, arguing that IBM was using its monopoly in one area, the central processing units for mainframes, to develop a monopoly in other mainframe areas.

This lawsuit dragged on in court for years. By 1977, a startup at the time, Apple, developed the first personal computer, and somewhat later, IBM decided to join this market and began to make computers for the home and office. These computers were novel, and they possessed far more power than the computers that flew to the moon. By the early 1980s, it became apparent that the mainframe market was dying as the PC's popularity grew. In 1982, the case was dropped because even if IBM had a monopoly in mainframe processors, which it no longer had, it was no longer an important area of business.

One of the reasons that IBM lost any chance of generating a monopoly in PCs was that it had licensed the operating system of that original PC, called DOS (disk operating system), to a little-known company in Washington called Microsoft. Further, it was buying its microprocessors, so named because they were physically much smaller than the processors developed for the mainframes, from another little-known company called Intel. When others found that they too could put parts together to make a computer and use Microsoft's DOS to run it, all chances of an IBM monopoly were gone.

Microsoft

In the mid-1980s, Apple introduced a new personal computer, called a Macintosh. It was the first PC to use icons on a monitor and a mouse, instead of using typed-in commands to tell the computer what to do. Microsoft followed suit shortly thereafter. It called its new operating system Windows. While the first two versions of Windows were terrible and could have lost Microsoft its advantage in operating systems in 1992, Windows 3.1 was introduced and soon took over the industry.

Since that time, Windows has dominated the operating system market. The only serious threat that Windows faced during this time was IBM's introduction of OS/2 and its follow-on Warp. Unlike Windows, IBM's version could work on more than one task at a time.

If the Justice Department and many of Microsoft's critics are to be believed, this made Microsoft very nervous. Critics charged that it was at this point that Microsoft began using its preeminence in the industry to pressure software companies to write exclusively for the soon-to-be released version of Windows. The Justice Department also charged that Microsoft pressured the vendors of hardware components not to provide software that would work with the IBM operating system. If Microsoft did those things, it was in flagrant violation of the law.

Later, Microsoft ran into other problems. The Internet grew to a degree that Microsoft had seriously underestimated, and Netscape grabbed well over three-quarters of the market for Internet browsers. On top of that, Sun Microsystems created Java, a programming language that is compatible with Windows, Apple, or any other computer. This threatened not only the Windows monopoly position, but the domination of the Windows Office Suite as well. In reaction to these events, Microsoft created Internet Explorer as its alternative to Netscape Navigator and integrated it into the operating system.

Even more troubling to the Justice Department was its contention that Microsoft was insisting that PC makers not put any product on their PCs that competed with a Microsoft product. Specifically, it was alleged that Microsoft would not sell Windows to PC makers if they also bundled their PC with Netscape or Corel's WordPerfect Suite.

Last, it was believed by many in the industry that there were secret parts of Windows 98 that made computers using non-Microsoft products crash. If this was true, users of these non-Microsoft products would conveniently blame the makers of those products and want the "more reliable" Microsoft software.

What the Justice Department charged in the trial of 1998 and 1999 was that Microsoft had used and was using the tactics of Rockefeller to drive out other competitors. On April 3, 2000, the judge for the case, Thomas Penfield Jackson, ruled first that the evidence showed that Microsoft wanted to monopolize a variety of areas of software, that it used its monopoly in Windows to further a monopoly in Office Suite, to build one for the Internet Explorer, and to prevent competition from, among others, Sun's Java. He further ruled that Microsoft had harmed consumers in the process. In his June 7, 2000, ruling ordering a breakup of the company into an operating system business and an applications business, he also showed that he believed that Microsoft had indeed used secret parts of Windows to cause other software to crash. By ordering that it "shall not take any action it knows will interfere with or degrade the performance of any non-Microsoft" software and by ordering that it disclose the "interfaces," the software that allows applications to talk to the operating system, he was clearly implying that at some point in time Microsoft had done both. On appeal to a U.S. Court of Appeals, the important finding of facts with regard to the illegal activities of Microsoft was upheld, but the breakup remedy was not. Prior to September 11, 2001, the Department of Justice was intently focused on settling the case and had taken the breakup off the table.

In November of that year, the Department of Justice ended the fight with Microsoft on terms quite friendly to the software giant. While some of the states that had sued alongside the federal government stuck to their guns, by 2003, when California settled for $1.1 billion in vouchers to the state's citizens and AOL Time-Warner (the parent of Netscape) settled for $750 million, the battle was pretty much over.

Apple, Google, and the European Union

Apple and Google have each found themselves in the European Union's crosshairs. Both were essentially charged with the same crime: using market dominance in one area to gain market dominance in another. While the U.S. government has yet to claim that either has run afoul of antitrust laws, the European Union has made such claims. In Apple's case, their concern was that by making it such that iTunes songs only play on iPods (and later, iPhones) and computers with the iTunes software, they were and are using these products to simultaneously reinforce market power in both players and the music itself. With the introduction of the iPhone in 2007, there was a reasonable fear that Apple could continue to leverage their dominance in music to dominate cell phones as well. In Google's case, it was the allegation that Google was using its search engine functionality to privilege its own shopping service.

Summary

You now understand why economists worry about monopolies, and why some monopolies have been seen as inevitable and even good for society. You know that laws were enacted to regulate the existence and pricing behavior of monopolies. Last, you saw how that body of law was applied to Standard Oil, IBM, Microsoft, Apple, and Google.

Key Terms

barrier to entry

contestable markets hypothesis

trust

Quiz Yourself

1. Antitrust law is designed to limit the impact of
   a. monopoly.
   b. oligopoly.
   c. monopolistic competition.
   d. perfect competition.
2. One of the concerns about monopolies is that they
   a. reduce the motivation to innovate.
   b. reduce the motivation to earn a profit.
   c. hire people at an excessive level.
   d. waste resources in pursuit of the next invention.
3. Monopoly creates prices that are ________ which would exist under perfect competition.
   a. lower than that
   b. equal to that
   c. greater than that
   d. more volatile than that
4. Using the monopoly power in one area to compel customers to buy goods in another area
   a. is a violation of the Sherman Anti-Trust Act.
   b. is legal but bad business practice.
   c. is illegal but would be bad business practice anyway.
   d. is legal and a recommended strategy.
5. Standard Oil's trust involved monopolizing
   a. gas stations only.
   b. oil exploration only.
   c. refining.
   d. all aspects of the petroleum industry.
6. The suit against Microsoft accused it of
   a. using its own innovation to thwart competition.
   b. using its Windows monopoly to foster other monopolies.
   c. incorporating more innovations into the Office Suite.
   d. charging more than Windows was worth.

Short Answer Questions

1. Music, television, and movie streaming services are examples of a situation where there are good and bad attributes associated with the fact that there are very few participants. List the positives and negatives.
2. Facebook, Google, and Amazon came under increasing scrutiny during 2019. All three claimed they were not monopolies. List the attributes that suggest they are monopolies. List those that suggest they are not.

Think about This

Those who opposed the Department of Justice suit against Microsoft argue that the company was responsible for great innovation. They argue that the "next Microsoft" would be reluctant to be as successful. Does this criticism make sense to you? Would a multibillion-dollar corporation be limited in innovation for any reason?

Talk about This

If Apple used the high market share in iPhones to generate a monopoly in music streaming via Apple Music, would that be a concern to you?

For More Insight See

Journal of Economic Perspectives 1, no. 2 (Fall 1987). See articles by Steven C. Salop, Lawrence J. White, Franklin M. Fisher, and Richard Schmalensee, pp. 3–54.

Online Newshour, "The Microsoft Antitrust Case," http://www.pbs.org/newshour/bb/cyberspace/july-dec99/microsoft_index.html.

CHAPTER THIRTY

The Economics of Race and Sex Discrimination

Learning Objectives

After reading this chapter you should be able to:

LO1 Describe how economists measure income disparity between races and sexes.

LO2 Define discrimination and explain how it is measured.

LO3 Model discrimination in the labor market and summarize the evidence for its existence in other markets.

LO4 Describe the forms of affirmative action.

Chapter Outline

Discrimination has been a part of the American experience since before there was a United States. That discrimination exists is not a surprise, but its precise detection and measurement are not as simple as they may seem. Some of the differences in income and wealth have diminished, but nontrivial gaps remain. In this chapter, we explore the economic status of women and minorities, discuss the varieties of discrimination economists recognize, and explain them. In so doing, we discuss the means of detecting discrimination and seek to model its impact on wages. We explain why, absent legally sanctioned discrimination, some economists thought wage gaps would close quickly, yet others correctly predicted that those gaps would remain, even in the presence of laws forbidding discriminatory practices. Finally, we conclude with a discussion of affirmative action, its economic justification, and forms.

Before analyzing the data, it is important to preface this conversation with a discussion of language and labels. The Census Bureau (at this writing) categorizes people as either men or women. With regard to race and ethnicity, they use the word "black" rather than "African American." When referencing data, we will use the word "black" to match the source, but when describing a person, we will use "African American."

The Economic Status of Women and Minorities

Women

Women are becoming an ever-growing part of the U.S. economy. The **labor force participation rate** for women rose for decades, from 38 percent in the early 1960s to 60.3 percent in 2000. Today, it is 57.3 percent. While the rate for men is higher than that for women, 69 percent, it has been, until quite recently, decreasing. Demographers, the people who study population trends, adjust the labor force participation rate to reflect the fact that as the U.S. population ages, more people are in age groups that are retired. For this reason, they suggest that the real importance of women in the workplace is even greater than the raw participation rate suggests.

labor force participation rate
The percentage of the population of a group that is employed or seeking employment.

Though men and women are approaching equality in income and wealth, men still have 59 percent more income than women, earn 23 percent more in wages for full-time employment, and are less likely to be in poverty.

Finally, single men, ages 35–54, have 40 percent more wealth than single women. These differences are summarized in Table 30.1.

This is not to suggest that the economic status of women is not improving. Figure 30.1 shows that the ratio of women's to men's weekly wages for full-time employment and the similar ratio for income from all sources continue to increase. Still, as Table 30.2 suggests, even when you look at identical professions, women currently earn less than men.

Minorities

There are two clear trends in the data on economic and social conditions affecting different races. Inequality within races is clearly documented, and the degree of inequality is lessening. The clearest sign of this phenomenon of shrinking-but-not-yet-zero inequality can be seen in the data on median family income for white and black families. Figure 30.2 shows us that since 1967 median family income has risen from $8,234 to $79,749 for white families and from $4,875 to $50,870 for black families.

Figure 30.3 indicates that while the income gap between black and white people is widening in absolute terms, the ratio of white median family income to black median family income is narrowing. This means that while white families still enjoy the benefits of more income, the income of black families is increasing at a faster rate than that of white families.

Table 30.1 Economic differences between men and women.

Sources: United States Census Bureau. www.census.gov/topics/income-poverty/income.html; www.bls.gov/cps/cpsaat39.pdf; www.census.gov/topics/income-poverty/wealth.html; www.census.gov/topics/income-poverty/poverty.html.

	Men	Women
Income from all sources	$40,396	$25,486
Median weekly wages for full-time employment	$973	$789
Mean net worth (singles, 35–54)*	$96,790	$69,140
Poverty rate	10.9%	13.6%

*Data exclude the wealthiest 1 percent.

Table 30.2 Median full-time wage earnings: selected occupations.

Source: U.S. Bureau of Labor Statistics. www.bls.gov/cps/cpsaat39.pdf.

Occupation	Women's Earnings as a Percentage of Men's
Physicians	67%
Lawyers	80%
Managers/executives	73%
Teachers (elementary)	94%

FIGURE 30.1 Ratio of women's income to men's.

Source: United States Census Bureau, www.census.gov.

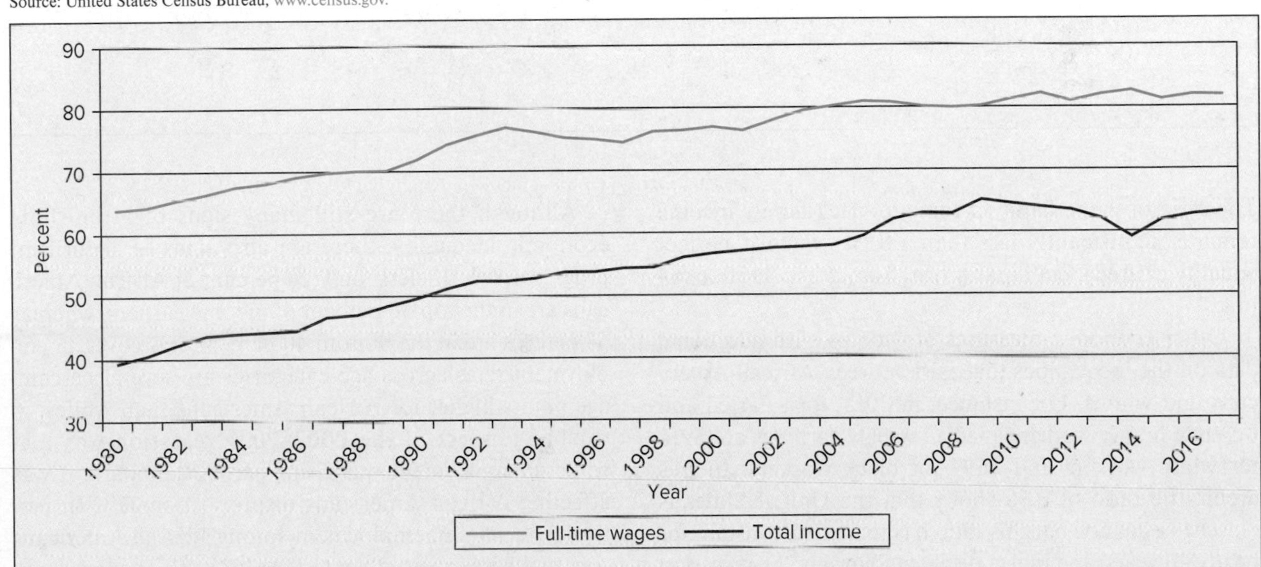

FIGURE 30.2 Median family income.

Source: United States Census Bureau, www.census.gov.

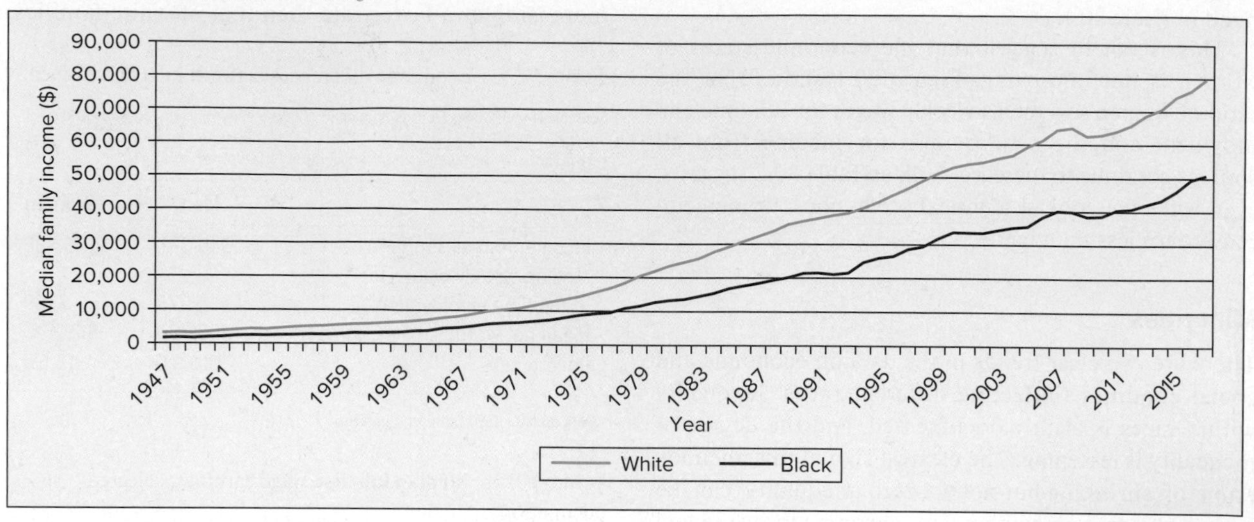

FIGURE 30.3 Ratio of black to white family income.

Source: United States Census Bureau, www.census.gov/topics/income-poverty/income.html.

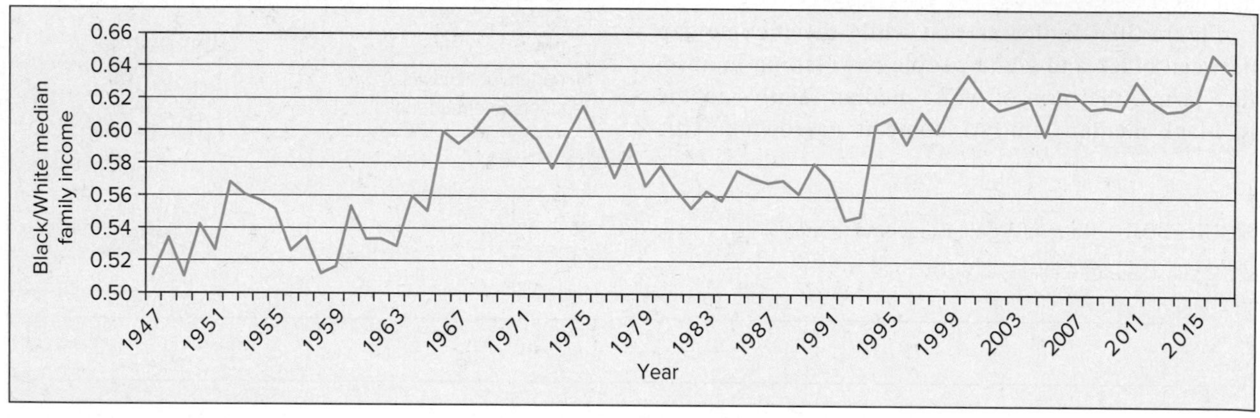

The ratio of white family income to black family income remains significantly less than 1.0 (its value if perfect equality existed), but it has grown from .52 in 1950 to .64 in 2017.

Other economic measures provide us with additional data on the inequalities that exist between African Americans and whites. For instance, in 2018, for salaried and full-time hourly workers, median weekly earnings are $916 for white workers and $694 for black workers. In this arena, the ratio of 0.76 shows that the United States is closer to equality, but this ratio has remained constant for nearly 40 years, and in fact declined following the recession of 2007–2009.

Although there are still many signs of astonishing economic inequality, there are also signs of significant progress. Nevertheless, only 24 percent of African Americans are in the top 40 percent of income earners, whereas 57 percent are in the bottom 40 percent; moreover, unemployment rates across age categories are several percentage points higher for African Americans than whites. A troubling aspect of the 2007–2009 recession was that while unemployment was rising across the board, it was affecting African Americans disproportionately. In particular, teenage unemployment among African Americans rose to 49.2 percent in September of 2010. That level was more than twice white teenage unemployment.

We cannot escape the fact that African American children are more than twice as likely as white children to be in a female-headed household. Because family structure is a key determinant of economic well-being, this social problem of single-parent (overwhelmingly female) households is a major cause of the economic disparity that African Americans face.

It must be noted, too, that African Americans are disproportionately the victims of crime. In any given year, 2.18 out of 100 African Americans are victims of violent crime, whereas only 2.08 out of 100 whites are so victimized. African Americans are 14 percent more likely than whites to be victims of serious violent crime (such as rape, robbery, and aggravated assault).

With regard to educational achievement, African Americans are graduating from high school at a much faster rate than they were in 1960. African Americans also saw a more significant increase in post-secondary degrees conferred than whites. The number of associate's, bachelor's, master's, and doctoral degrees conferred on African Americans increased (from 2005 to 2015) at much higher rates.

Definitions and Detection of Discrimination

Discrimination, Definitions, and the Law

On the surface, it would seem that defining discrimination would not be that difficult. If you treat people in a certain way because they are female, African American, or Hispanic, you are discriminating. To make matters more complicated, however, there are two types of discrimination rather than just one. If you treat two otherwise equal people differently and do so on the basis of their sex or race, then this is called **disparate treatment discrimination.** If, on the other hand, you do something that is not necessarily discriminatory on its face but that impacts some groups more negatively than others, you are engaging in what is called **adverse impact discrimination.**

disparate treatment discrimination
Treating two otherwise equal people differently on the basis of race.

adverse impact discrimination
Doing something that is not necessarily discriminatory on its face but that impacts some groups more negatively than others.

While both forms of discrimination are usually illegal, adverse impact discrimination can be both legal and justified. While that may sound odd, consider the following: it is legal as long as the persons or companies doing the discriminating can show that what they are doing makes sense for their needs. If whites sued the National Football League (NFL) on the basis that defensive backs were disproportionately black, there would be two legal hurdles. The first hurdle would be for whites, the group at whom the discrimination had supposedly been aimed, to show the "adverse impact." They could do this easily, by showing that the United States is majority white and that from 2003 to 2018 there were no white cornerbacks. With adverse impact proved, the burden of proof would be transferred to the accused, in this case the NFL. The NFL would have to show a "business necessity" that led the teams to make the choices they made. The NFL would win in court if the teams could point to the NFL Combine and its tests of speed, strength, and conditioning to show that (1) these tests did predict the ability to cover receivers and (2) they chose defensive backs on the basis of these tests. Thus, while disparate treatment discrimination is always illegal, adverse impact discrimination is illegal only when it cannot be defended on business necessity grounds.

The more common example of disparate treatment discrimination arises when an employer uses a rule-of-thumb approach to hiring. Rules of thumb are useful in that they can be simple guidelines for people making complex decisions. Some economists who study disparate treatment discrimination assert that rules of thumb for hiring are generally perpetuated long past the time when they are relevant. Furthermore, they suggest that many of those rules of thumb were never very good predictors of performance. One that was propagated in the world of broadcasting was that men, being generally more interested in sports, would make better sports broadcasters. Although it may be true that men watch more sports, that does not mean that a certain man or woman would be a better broadcaster. Furthermore, many rules of thumb, like the sexist notion that men are better drivers, never were good predictors of performance on the job.

Even when there is a concretely accurate rule of thumb, discrimination is illegal. This form of discrimination is the economic equivalent of racial profiling, which we hear about with regard to police tactics. In economics, such discrimination is labeled by some as **rational or statistical discrimination** because it is based on sound statistical evidence. It is referred to as "rational" only because it is consistent with the recognized goal of firms of maximizing profit. For instance, it is a fact of life in the United States that when a bank consults with

rational or statistical discrimination
Unequal treatment of classes of people that is based on sound statistical evidence and is consistent with profit maximization.

SOCIOLOGY OR ECONOMICS: WHY WOMEN EARN LESS THAN MEN

A multitude of studies compare women's pay to men's. Many economists do the comparison by controlling for education, full- or part-time status, experience, job requirements, and a host of other factors to determine whether men and women earn the same income for the same work. Sociologists and nearly all feminists view this as fallacious because they see these as symptoms of continued mistreatment of women, rather than economic phenomena that should be statistically controlled. The issues are:

- **All income versus earned income:** As shown in Table 30.1, if you focus on the broad issue of relative incomes, women earn only 63 percent of what men do, but if you focus more narrowly on the differences between what women and men earn when they both work full time, the ratio is narrower: Women earn 81 percent of what men do.
- **Experience with the same employer:** Men have been with their current employer for a median 4.3 years; the comparable figure for females is 4.0 years. It is notable that this gap has nearly been eliminated in recent years.
- **Different professions:** Only 40 percent of lawyers, 43 percent of doctors, and 15 percent of engineers are women. On the other hand, women account for 94 percent of secretaries, 88 percent of nurses, 80 percent of elementary school teachers, 93 percent of day-care workers, and 81 percent of social workers.
- **Pregnancy and child rearing:** While it is illegal to discriminate based on pregnancy, any opportunity that a woman loses and a man gains can result in young professional fathers being promoted more quickly than young professional mothers. Since only women can give birth and 96 percent of stay-at-home parents are women, women lose opportunities.
- **Flexible employment:** For reasons that are primarily sociological, women rather than men pick flexible employment so that they can deal with their family's needs. Flexible jobs also tend to be lower paying.

Are these legitimate economic consequences of choices that people make freely and knowingly, or are they manifestations of discrimination itself? That is a debate for you to have with fellow students and professors of economics and sociology.

the best statisticians and economists, it finds that African Americans were, from 2007 to 2010, 6 percent more likely to default on a home loan. This is true even when the study holds income, occupation, and a host of other important variables constant. If lenders use this information to charge African Americans a higher interest rate for mortgages, or if they use this information to set a higher standard for African Americans to qualify for a loan, they are guilty of "statistical" discrimination.[1] Regardless of whether it makes economic sense, it is illegal to use race in any part of the lending decision.

One reason that statistical discrimination is illegal is that sometimes the statistics themselves are biased. There is evidence that banks are more likely to proceed to foreclosure and move to complete that foreclosure on a loan that is in arrears when the borrower is African American.

Detecting and Measuring Discrimination

Detecting and measuring the extent of discrimination in an authoritative way are not always easy. If a Hispanic female high school dropout and an affluent white male college professor each went into a bank to ask for a loan, and the high school dropout was denied the loan and the professor got one, we would not automatically assume we were looking at a case of gender or race discrimination. We would have to analyze the reasons one person got the loan and the other did not.

There are two ways that economists try to do this. First, they use the statistical technique called "regression" to look for systematic patterns in the data. Once they figure the appropriate values using a statistical computer program, regression analysis tells them the impact of one variable on another, holding the effects of other variables constant. It allows them to say, with degrees of certainty, that a variable like race or sex has a specific impact on another variable, like whether or not a loan was approved, even when they hold other variables like income constant. When many different people, from many different backgrounds, with different incomes and debt histories seek loans from many different banks, the regression technique can, when correctly applied, determine whether being a certain race or gender makes an applicant less likely to get a loan.

The second technique involves creating fake identities for people who are identical except for race or sex. These "auditors" approach a situation one after the other to see if they are treated differently. Since everything other than

[1]Another interpretation of this finding is that it is actually whites who are being discriminated against since, all else being equal, they are defaulting less frequently than African Americans. This implies that they are being turned down too often.

race is held constant, any differences in the way the auditors are treated must be related to race. A fascinating example of this work was conducted by economists Bertrand and Mullainathan. They showed that on purely fictitious and functionally identical résumés, applicants with names like "Emily" and "Greg" were statistically, substantially, and depressingly more likely to be called for an interview than applicants with names like "Lakisha" and "Jamal."

These two techniques have their critics. This may, at least in part, be because of the somewhat different conclusions the techniques have led economists to make. Generally, regression techniques expose a smaller race bias problem across the board than is exposed by audit techniques. Typically, those who advocate regression measurement rather than using auditors say that the fictitious auditors themselves may create part of the disparity by the way they act. They also say that the exactness of the match is less than reliable. On the other hand, the advocates of auditing suggest that variables included in regressions, like intelligence scores, are themselves biased or indicative of other past discriminatory practices and therefore tend to understate the true problem.

Discrimination in Labor, Consumption, and Lending

We turn now to three areas of the economy in which professional economists have studied discrimination in some depth. These areas are the labor market, where people sell their labor to firms; the goods market, where people buy things; and the lending market, where people borrow money.

Labor Market Discrimination

We can start exploring the effect of discrimination in the labor market by assuming a world, like the 1960s, where it is legal and openly practiced. In Figure 30.4, suppose there are two kinds of jobs: jobs that only whites are allowed to do and jobs that whites are allowed to do but African Americans must do if they want jobs.[2] In a world where there is no discrimination (that will be denoted with a subscript "ND"), the nondiscriminatory supply curve, S_{ND}, crosses the demand curve at a wage, W_{ND}, that is equal for African Americans and whites. In the world where such discrimination is legal and binding, the supply of workers available to perform tasks limited to whites only (left panel) is less, S_D, and therefore the wage that must be paid to whites is greater. Because African Americans must perform the other tasks, the supply of workers available in that market (S_D in the right panel) is greater, and therefore, the wage is lower.

Thus when discrimination is legal, whites make more than African Americans (i.e., $W_{white} > W_{AA}$). The question is: If discrimination is illegal, is that sufficient to eliminate the wage differential? Beginning with the work of economist Gary Becker, the profession showed theoretically that without a legal basis, discrimination and wage differentials would disappear. In the 1960s, economists were confident that profit-oriented but open-minded business owners would want to make as much money as possible and would therefore ignore a person's race. If employers hired people to do what used to be considered "a white man's job" and were right in assuming that the only reason African Americans had been previously prevented from doing the job before was racism, then the African Americans would be able to do the job just as well as whites. That, in and of itself, however, would not motivate profit-oriented business owners to hire African Americans. It is that they could offer African Americans a little bit more than they were making but less than what the owners were currently paying whites. In Figure 30.4, this would be between W_{AA} and W_{white}.

If profit-oriented managers were to hire African Americans at just above the W_{AA} wage that is depicted in the right panel of Figure 30.4, they could get all the labor they need at much lower cost than they would have had to pay white workers, W_{white}. Thus, the business manager's desire to make money could serve to narrow the wage gap, at least a little.

The hopeful prediction is that as other managers see the advantage of hiring lower-paid, equally skilled African

FIGURE 30.4 The effect of racism on wages.

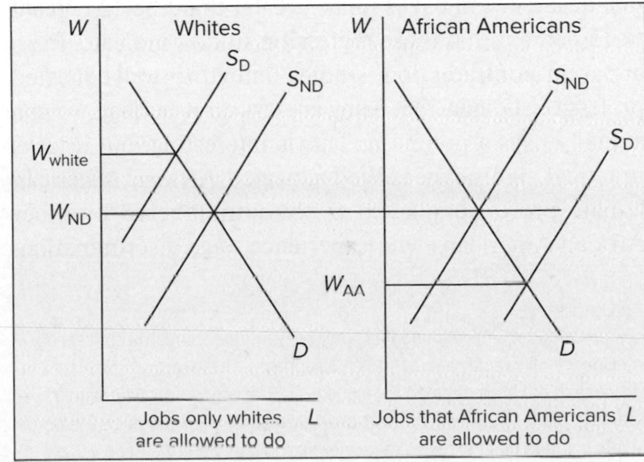

[2]This analysis works the same for modeling sex discrimination.

American labor, the wages among African Americans would continue to rise as firms seeking cheaper labor attempt to outbid each other. A traditional economist argues that, in time, nothing more than removing legal impediments is required to achieve equality. Their conclusion is that bigotry is inconsistent with profit maximization.

The Equal Pay Act and the Civil Rights Act were passed in 1963 and 1964, respectively. Considering that wages are not equal after all that time, there must be obstacles that simple economic incentives have not been able to overcome in equalizing wages. The first thing to consider is that the model presumes greed (the desire for money) trumps bigotry. When the bigot has market power (and as a result has economic profit to spend) they may be willing to pay to support their bigotry.

Another potentially faulty assumption in the model is that some people will patronize only businesses where not any of "them" are around. Even if you are an open-minded, profit-oriented manager, if you see that your business decreases whenever you hire more of a particular group, you may decide to hire only members of the preferred group, and you will pay more to attract them. You may do this even though you know it is illegal and morally wrong. As a result, the conclusion that profit maximization is inconsistent with bigotry doesn't hold.

It is for these reasons that, even though the wage gap between whites and African Americans has shrunk, it has not disappeared. Regression analysis shows that it remains between 12 percent and 15 percent.[3] Remember that the regression results hold constant things that are supposed to determine pay such as education and occupation. Because some African Americans have attained a lower average level of education and because they are less prevalent in high-income occupations, you would expect that they would be paid less. This also means that the actual difference in pay is much greater than the 12 percent to 15 percent that these regression studies indicate. In an apparent contradiction, studies limited to well-educated professionals show that being an African American woman actually pays a premium. This is interesting, but it lacks practical significance. Well-educated African American female professionals are vastly outnumbered by other African Americans who experience wage discrimination.

[3]Some economists have found that when they include standardized tests of intelligence, this remaining difference disappears. These tests and their use in this context are hotly debated by economists. The economists who employ the results of the tests believe the tests are truly tests of intelligence, whereas others contend that the tests are racially biased and therefore of no value.

Consumption Market and Lending Market Discrimination

While it is easy to imagine discrimination in the labor market, where people either are denied positions or are hired for lower pay, it is harder to imagine in the market for goods. You never see a Walmart charge a white man $65 for a car battery and then charge a Hispanic woman $75. There are areas in the goods market, however, and especially in the services market, where the races can and are treated differently.

At first it would seem rather silly for a business to discriminate and decline profitable sales. What you have to consider, though, is that audits performed by various economists and government investigators have shown that discrimination is in fact quite prevalent in real estate, apartment rentals, and car sales.

In real estate, audits show that real estate agents of both races tend to show white clients more houses. Moreover, they tend to show white families houses in all-white neighborhoods while diverting African American families to houses in African American or integrated neighborhoods. The same results were evident when auditors looked for rentals. Why would real estate agents do this? Why, in particular, would African American real estate agents do this? There appear to be a couple of explanations.

The first possibility is that agents are simply trying to make the clients happy, and they think they are doing this—and may in fact be doing this—by showing housing in areas where they think the clients want to live. Salespeople make judgments all the time about what will make their clients happy, and they do so with very little basis. The economists who uncovered this attribute it to racism and call it discrimination. If a significant segment of African Americans really do want to live in integrated neighborhoods rather than move into another neighborhood to become the only minority family in the area, the economists are incorrect when they label this behavior as discrimination.

The second possibility is that real estate agents have regular clients in the neighborhoods that contain the apartments or houses that are available, and they do not want to anger their regular clients. The audits do not include interviews of the agents, so the data do not show whether either of these scenarios account for the discriminatory practices that exist when realtors are showing properties to their clients.

Another area where economists have found race and sex discrimination in the market for goods is in automobile sales. According to John Yinger's research, auditors found that even when they used the same bargaining strategy, made it clear they would be paying cash, and were talking about the same car, dealers charged African Americans and women more. The usual method of the audit had matched pairs (African Americans and whites, men and women) going into the same dealership within a short period of time and asking a salesperson to tell them the asking price for a specific car. In each case, the auditors would then offer a price they had previously decided to offer and then they would use a "split the difference" bargaining technique until they arrived at a final price. What happened was that the initial offer made by both African American and white car dealers was lower for whites than it was for African Americans. The dealers also agreed to sell cars to whites for lower prices than those for African Americans. The economists who performed these audits concluded that, on the average, African American women pay $1,000 more, African American men pay $800 more, and white women pay $400 more for a car than do white men.

Why would dealers do this? Though the bias was less evident when the dealers themselves were women or minorities, they still discriminated against African Americans and women. It seems as if either the dealers did not want the sales or dealers have preconceived notions of sales resistance and bargaining strategies. It may be they believe they can outmaneuver African American and female customers.

Another area where economists have investigated and found serious race discrimination is the area of mortgage lending. Because it is rare that banks offer anything but a single interest rate, the question is whether African Americans are more likely to be denied for loans than are whites. Again, audits, constructed and reported upon by Helen Ladd, found that given nearly identical economic characteristics, African Americans were somewhat more likely than whites to be turned down for a loan. It seems likely here that, short of bigotry, banks, which use both objective and subjective standards to make their decisions, have discriminatory prejudice in their subjective standards.

Some economists claim to have noted sex discrimination in retirement annuities. Whether it is actually discrimination, men have better choices than women because women live longer than men by more than half a decade. Insurance companies that offer annuities must charge women more than men, offer fewer benefits to women than men, or split the difference in some other way so that women pay somewhat more and are paid somewhat less. Making it illegal to charge women more than men for such annuities would not change these facts. It would merely force companies to indulge in what would amount to a redistribution of wealth from men to women.

Affirmative Action

The Economics of Affirmative Action

As you saw in the preceding discussion, there are conditions under which discriminatory behavior sadly continues long after it is declared illegal. Either because employers may be bigoted or because employers may have customers who are bigoted, discrimination in employment exists even in a perfectly competitive market. This means that the perfectly competitive market may fail to arrive at the socially optimal level of employment for minorities. Minorities will be underemployed and underpaid, and whites and men will be overpaid for the work they are doing and get jobs for which they are not as qualified.

Anytime a market fails to achieve the price and quantity combination where consumer and producer surplus combined are maximized, economists are interested in actions that can correct that market's failure. Though corrective policies for failed markets have costs, they are seen by economists as necessary investments that will ultimately pay dividends. In this context, the corrective policies are called **affirmative action.** Affirmative action is any policy that is taken to speed up the process of achieving equality.

affirmative action
Any policy that is taken to speed up the process of achieving equality.

The costs of affirmative action policies range from the costs of more thorough searches for employees to the cost of monitoring fair hiring practices with a fully staffed human resources office. These costs can be seen in the same context as any costs associated with correcting a failed market. For example, though it costs industry money to clean up pollution, associated expenditures, which are mandated by the government, make us better off in the aggregate than we would be without them. When affirmative action is utilized to correct an inequality that is seen as permanent, its supporters view it very much like pollution control expenses: It is money spent to fix a market failure. If affirmative action exists to speed up a transition from inequality to equality that would have happened eventually anyway, these are seen as costs that diminish the market failure by shortening the time it exists.

On the other hand, if the market differences between minorities and whites and between men and women only reflect the differences in the skills of the groups, then the market is not failing. If this is the case, then any attempt at affirmative action imposes a cost on, rather than a benefit to, the economy. In such a case, the costs of affirmative action should be viewed as buying "fairness" rather than fixing a market failure.

MYTHS OF AFFIRMATIVE ACTION

Economists Roland Fryer and Glenn Loury studied affirmative action policies and concluded that the mythology of the practice sometimes overwhelms the reality.

Myth 1: Affirmative Action Can Involve Goals and Timetables while Avoiding Quotas
They argue that because those looking for discrimination cannot see into the heart of the potential accused, the hiring, loaning, or admitting entity will likely create an "implicit quota" to achieve its goal.

Myth 2: Color-Blind Policies Offer an Efficient Substitute for Color-Sighted Affirmative Action
They point to reactions in California, Florida, and Texas when affirmative action policies were banned in college admissions. They argue that the attempt to use income or high school location as a proxy was ineffective and that getting the best, most diverse class of students is hampered by using proxies for race rather than race itself.

Myth 3: Affirmative Action Undercuts the Incentive to Invest in Yourself
They argue that though whites may not see as much payoff to educational investments, African Americans will see a greater payoff to education. Which effect is greater, they argue, is an unsettled empirical question.

Myth 4: Equal Opportunity Is Enough to Ensure Racial Equality
They argue that social networks ("who you know") matter a great deal in hiring practices. Specifically, previous advantages (such as a parent's admission to a prestigious university) are likely to maintain themselves for a very long time (because of practices such as legacy admissions).

Myth 5: The Earlier in, the Better
They argue that this is an empirical question where the data have not yet shown that earlier investments in more equal education will assist later outcomes in graduation rates.

Myth 6: Many Nonminority Citizens Are Directly Affected by Affirmative Action
They argue that far more whites and men believe they are passed over because of affirmative action policies than actually are.

Myth 7: Affirmative Action Always Helps Its Beneficiaries
They argue that affirmative action has reduced the graduation and bar passage rates of African American law school students because they are admitted to schools where they are less likely to flourish.

Even if traditional economic models correctly predicted that pay gaps between men and women and between whites and minorities would eventually be eliminated without needing such influences as affirmative action, there is the problem of time. Affirmative action resulted because proponents wanted to achieve equality more quickly. To the degree that equality is not arriving fast enough through economic incentives, advocates have asserted that further affirmative action be taken to speed up the process.

Gradations of Affirmative Action

Affirmative action takes many forms. It constitutes a range of policies that mildly adjust existing personnel processes to ones that impose significant restrictions on those systems. As a result, they range from the inconsequential to the highly consequential. For years, many critics equated affirmative action with a system of quotas that mandated the number of people who must be hired, promoted, or admitted. As a matter of fact, explicit quotas are rare and, unless they have been ordered through a court decision, they are illegal. On the other hand, many other policies can be employed without resorting to quotas.

One form of affirmative action is simply to ensure that all potentially qualified employees know about a particular job. So, for instance, if you were hiring production workers in a southwestern city, affirmative action could consist of your advertising in both the English and Spanish newspapers. If you were hiring in a city that had a radio station whose audience was primarily African American, under this form of affirmative action you would advertise there alongside radio stations where audiences were predominantly white. This form of affirmative action requires that employers cast the net wide when looking for new hires. It places very little burden on employers and it gives no one any sort of unfair advantage. The only people who might be perceived as disadvantaged would be those who previously had an unfair advantage. These might be those who were less qualified but got jobs because minorities were not aware particular jobs were available.

Another form of affirmative action has held that if two applicants are judged to have equal qualifications for a position, then the one who is a member of a minority should automatically be hired. Just as in baseball where "tie goes to the runner," this form of affirmative action suggests that "tie goes to the minority."

A third, higher level of affirmative action is one in which an employer sets a level of qualification that is appropriate for a job, hires all minorities who meet the standard, and then fills the remaining slots with nonminorities. When universities make decisions about whom to admit, and they use criteria to further affirmative action, they often conduct them in the following way: A school will decide that an SAT of 1,000 is sufficient to make graduation likely and admit all minorities who meet that standard. The remainder of the student body is then generated from the best of the rest, a pool of students whose SATs may well be above 1,000.

A fourth version of affirmative action, just short of a quota, is establishing a guideline that employers should try to meet. The idea behind this is to ensure that employers can be somewhat flexible while also ensuring that the proportion of minorities not be allowed to drop too low. In military promotions, for example, if the racial, ethnic, and gender proportions of those promoted are not roughly equal to the racial, ethnic, and gender proportions of those eligible for promotion, the promotions board must file a report justifying the discrepancy. That means that though there is no specific number that must be promoted, any deviation from the guideline is suspect.

The final version of strictness associated with affirmative action is quotas. Surprisingly, the quotas that most people think of when they think of affirmative action are actually against the law as a general practice. Quotas are legal only when court-mandated, through either a verdict or a consent decree (an agreement that is backed by the court). Sufficient grounds must exist to show that a particular employer or university has been guilty of discrimination in the past to make quotas legal. What troubles some economists is the degree to which businesses engage in quota-like hiring practices designed to protect themselves from legal troubles.

Summary

You now understand the economic implications of discrimination. You can describe how economists measure the impact of discrimination, detect its existence, and explain its importance. You know how labor market discrimination can be modeled, which implies that discriminatory pay gaps should close over time, but the reality is that the rate of closure is slow. You understand that economists have detected discrimination in real estate and auto markets. You know what affirmative action is in its various forms.

Key Terms

adverse impact discrimination
affirmative action
disparate treatment discrimination
labor force participation rate
rational or statistical discrimination

Quiz Yourself

1. How academics look at the evidence on how much women make relative to men is an issue that very much depends on
   a. which year you examine.
   b. which state you examine.
   c. whether you consider some variables as "choices" or as "further evidence of discrimination."
   d. which court is examining the evidence.
2. The family income of African Americans relative to whites has
   a. increased from 40 percent in the 1920s to 90 percent today.
   b. increased from 50 percent in the 1950s to around 60 percent in the 1970s, rising only slightly since.
   c. remained constant since the 1950s.
   d. decreased steadily since the 1960s.
3. The method of detecting sex discrimination most likely to minimize it would be to use
   a. simple differences in income between men and women.
   b. simple differences in full-time wages for men and women.
   c. regression techniques.
   d. auditing techniques.

4. The method of detecting sex discrimination most likely to maximize it would be to use
   a. simple differences in income between men and women.
   b. simple differences in full-time wages for men and women.
   c. regression techniques.
   d. auditing techniques.
5. The way in which discrimination in hiring translates into differential wages is
   a. only related to the restriction on the supply of labor in the area where the favored group works.
   b. only related to the excessive expansion of the supply of labor in the area where the discriminated-against group must work.
   c. related to labor demand differences for the favored and unfavored groups.
   d. related to both the restriction on supply for the favored group and the excessive supply for the discriminated-against group.
6. If a woman does not get an interview for a job requiring heavy lifting because the manager has noted that the average woman can lift less than the average man, this is
   a. a legal example of statistical discrimination.
   b. an illegal example of statistical discrimination.
   c. a legal example of adverse impact discrimination.
   d. an illegal example of adverse impact discrimination.
7. Those who believe that wages paid to minorities will rise without government intervention believe that bosses are primarily motivated by
   a. profit.
   b. religion.
   c. doing right.
   d. helping minorities.
8. Affirmative action
   a. can take many forms.
   b. is almost always a racial quota.
   c. applies only to women.
   d. has typically been declared unconstitutional.

Short Answer Questions

1. Describe the process by which greed, absent sexism or bigotry on the part of business owners, can lead to the reduction in wage gaps between men and women and between whites and minorities.
2. What are the reasons that income gaps between men and women and whites and minorities may persist even in the absence of sexism or racism by business owners?
3. Suppose an establishment has absolutely no overt history of employment discrimination but has a goal of reducing race or gender gaps in its employment. What are the legal means by which it may reduce that gap?

Think about This

Think about your chosen major, your favorite restaurant, or the place you live. Are they predominantly male, female, African American, or white? Would you feel comfortable going outside the social norms in your choices? Are those social norms limiting?

Talk about This

Who is going to raise your children? Who is going to sacrifice a career for their care, an illness, their after-school activities, etc.?

For More Insight See

Bertrand, Marianne, and Sendhil Mullainathan, "Are Emily and Greg More Employable Than Lakisha and Jamal? A Field Experiment on Labor Market Discrimination," *America Economic Review* 94, no. 4 (September 2004).

Blau, Francine, Marianne Ferber, and Anne Winkler, *The Economics of Women, Men and Work,* 3rd ed. (Upper Saddle River, NJ: Prentice Hall, 1998).

Curry, George E., ed., *The Affirmative Action Debate* (Reading, MA: Addison-Wesley, 1996).

Feiner, Susan F., *Race and Gender in the American Economy* (Englewood Cliffs, NJ: Prentice Hall, 1994).

Fryer, Roland, and Glenn Loury, "Affirmative Action and Its Mythology," *Journal of Economic Perspectives* 19, no. 3 (2005).

Journal of Economic Perspectives 12, no. 2 (Spring 1998). See articles by John Yinger; William A. Darity, Jr., and Patrick L. Mason; Helen F. Ladd; and Kenneth J. Arrow, James J. Heckman, and Glenn C. Loury, pp. 23–126.

Sowell, Thomas, *Race and Economics* (New York: David McKay, 1975).

Waldfogel, Jane, "Understanding the 'Family Gap' in Pay for Women with Children," *Journal of Economic Perspectives* 12, no. 1 (Winter 1998), pp. 137–156.

Behind the Numbers

U.S. Census Bureau; historical income tables: www.census.gov/hhes/www/income

- Income and wealth
- Median family income
- Income by race and gender

U.S. Census Bureau; historical income tables: www.census.gov/hhes/wealth

- Wealth

Bureau of Labor Statistics: www.bls.gov/cps/cpsaat39.pdf

- Median earnings and ratio of men's to women's income

CHAPTER THIRTY-ONE

Income and Wealth Inequality: What's Fair?

Learning Objectives

After reading this chapter you should be able to:

LO1 Describe how income inequality is measured.

LO2 Describe how wealth inequality is measured.

LO3 Explain why income and wealth inequality exists in the United States.

LO4 Describe the costs and benefits of income inequality.

LO5 Describe the concepts of income mobility and intergenerational income mobility as well as what data indicate about them in the United States.

LO6 Summarize the proposed solutions to income and wealth inequality.

Chapter Outline

Since the mid-2000s, the American political left has been particularly concerned about rising income and wealth inequality. It is not hard to see why. In 2007, the proportion of income going to the top 1 percent peaked at 23 percent (three times its 1970 level). In 2011, the Occupy Wall Street movement made headlines and, in 2016, presidential candidate Bernie Sanders made the issue the centerpiece of his unsuccessful campaign for the Democratic nomination. Four years later, half of the field of candidates for the Democratic nomination advocated for policies (such as a tax on wealth) that had been unheard of in previous generations. Income inequality has many measures, causes, and consequences. We will begin by showing narrow and broad measures of income and wealth inequality and how those measures have changed through the years. The focus will shift from measures of the top and bottom ends of the income and wealth scales to the issues associated with the shrinking middle class. We will continue by analyzing the causes and effects of both income and wealth inequality and conclude by discussing why some inequality is necessary to reward productivity and success, while excessive inequality has potentially troublesome social and economic consequences.

Measurement of Inequality

Income Inequality

The popular press measure of inequality looks at the percentage of total income going to the top 1 percent of earners. The data available for this type of analysis are garnered from an IRS publication (*Statistics of Income: Individual Income Tax*). The data only become available three years after the fact. As can be seen in Figure 31.1, the same year (2010) the inequality issue gained widespread attention in the United States coincided with the worst of the financial-crisis-precipitated recession. This happened for two reasons: First, conventional wisdom

FIGURE 31.1 Conventionally measured income inequality.

Source: The Internal Revenue Service, www.irs.gov.

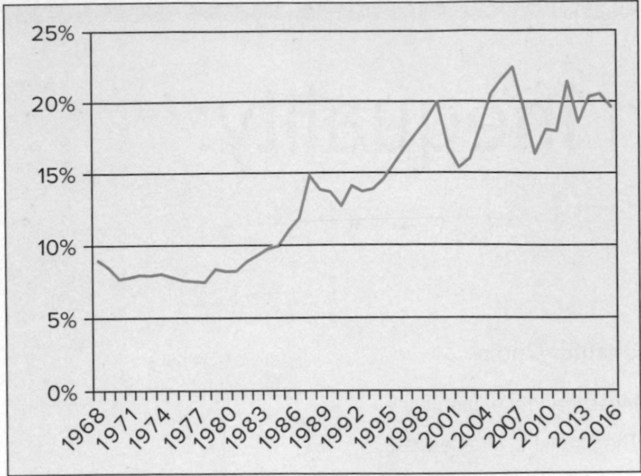

FIGURE 31.2 Conventionally measured income inequality.

Source: The Internal Revenue Service, www.irs.gov.

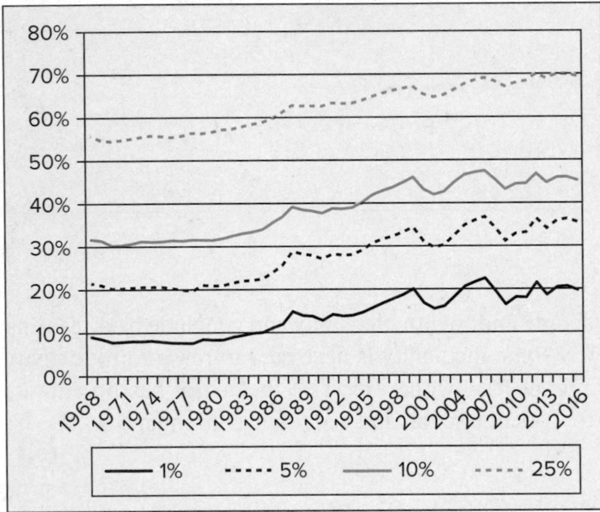

placed the blame for the recession on wealthy financial interests; and second, the IRS report for 2007 showed that the "top 1 percent" share of income had risen to 22.49 percent. Those most troubled with this level of income inequality noted that in 1978 that same measure showed the "top 1 percent" share stood at only 7.55 percent. For that period and using that measure, the share of the top 1 percent of income earners had tripled.

Clearly, as can be seen in both Figures 31.1 and 31.2, and using the share of income from more broadly defined groups, as more data became available, they showed that the increase from 2001 to 2007 was largely

FIGURE 31.3 Ratio of returns to population.

Source: The Internal Revenue Service, www.irs.gov.

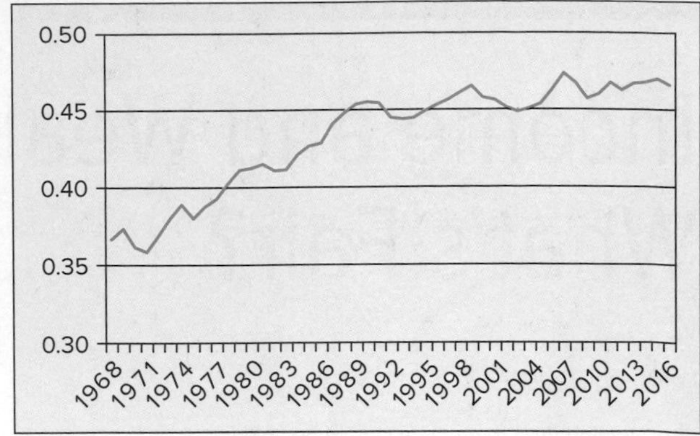

transitory. It peaked at the time of the tech boom in the 1990s and peaked again just prior to the financial crisis. The biggest increase in systemic inequality had actually occurred during the 1980s and 1990s. The period of the 2000s was marked by highly variable income inequality measures.

As compelling as this may appear, there are problems using only this measure of income inequality. The first of these relates to the rapid increase in the proportion of Americans filing tax returns, while the second relates to the special tax treatment of capital gains.

Regarding tax filings, Figure 31.3 shows that from 1971 to 1998, there was such a rapid increase in the number of income tax returns filed that the proportion of the population completing income tax returns rose from 36 to 47 percent. There are three basic reasons this occurred: (1) More people were filing as "head of household" because more people who were not married or were divorced had children; (2) more young people (under 24) were working at part-time jobs during this period than had been in previous generations; and (3) the new Child Tax Credit combined with the refundable[1] and greatly expanded Earned Income Tax Credit (EITC) was creating a motivation for low-earning households to file tax returns when they were not legally required to (because they could garner a tax refund in an amount vastly

[1]A refundable tax credit is one whereby a household can receive more from the federal government in the form of a return than is owed in tax or withheld. The Earned Income Tax Credit (which was greatly expanded in both the Reagan and Clinton administrations) and the Child Tax Credit (which was created in the Clinton administration and doubled in size during the G. W. Bush administration) are both (mostly) refundable. A portion of the American Opportunity Credit (a tax credit to support a college education) is also refundable.

FIGURE 31.4 Top 1 percent adjusted for the increase in all returns.

Source: The Internal Revenue Service, www.irs.gov and author calculations.

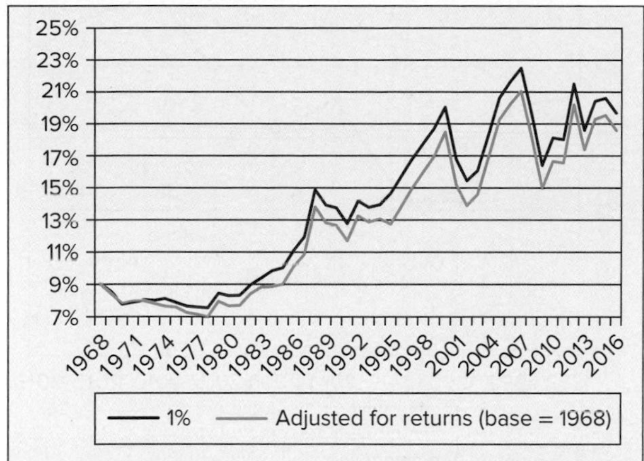

FIGURE 31.5 Maximum capital gain tax rate.

Source: The Internal Revenue Service, www.irs.gov.

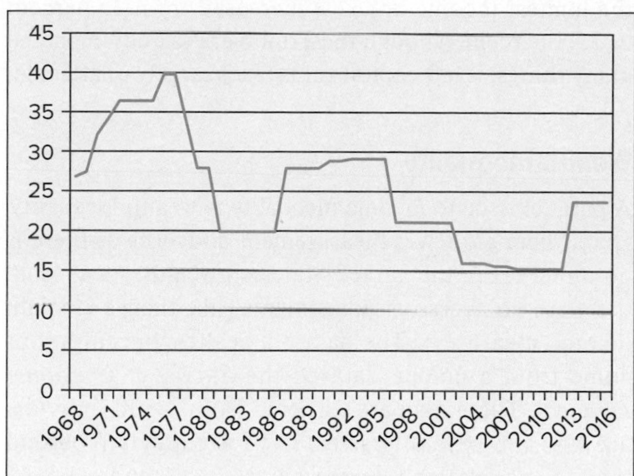

exceeding their tax withholding). When filings increase faster than the population increases, and when nearly all extra filings are in the lower 99 percent, that expands the 1 percent group to cover more people than it otherwise would. For instance, in 2007, 32 million more filings were received than there would have been had only 36 percent of the population filed. With 32 million more filings, there were 322,000 filings more in the top 1 percent. Essentially, the conventional measure scooped some of the 2 percent into the 1 percent. Correcting for that effect results in a 1.4 percent decrease in the top 1 percent's systemic share. This is displayed in Figure 31.4.

Regarding the impact that changes to the tax treatment of capital gains have had on the measure of inequality, there is potentially a much larger effect. For the benefit of those not steeped in finance or tax issues, *capital gains* are those gains garnered from selling an asset for more than was paid for it. In the United States, capital gains are only taxed on "realization" rather than "accrual." This means that taxes are only owed on the gain if the gain is "realized" in the form of a sale. Further, capital gains are forgiven at death, which means that if there is an accrued gain and a person sells, he or she realizes the gain and owes the tax. If the person dies prior to the realization, the gain is tax free (except for inheritance taxes) and the heirs can immediately sell that asset (with its gains) tax free. It is only if the heirs hold the asset that any gains are taxed, but even then, the "stepped-up basis" means that its value on the day the person died becomes its effective purchase price. There are good economic reasons for this treatment that are beyond the scope of this chapter, but this point needs to be raised: Capital gains realizations, and therefore payments of capital gains taxes, are almost entirely voluntary and easily avoided. Higher tax rates encourage tax avoidance through nonrealization, and lower tax rates encourage realization. Figure 31.5 shows that the rate that high-income earners pay on those capital gains has changed over the years. That rate reached a peak in the late 1970s at nearly 40 percent and from 2003 to 2012 was at its all-time low level of 15 percent. This impacts the measure of income inequality markedly in that, were capital gains tax rates as high in 2007 as they were in the late 1970s, far fewer gains would have been realized, and therefore far fewer gains reported to the IRS. The accrued income would have existed, but the measured income would not. If tax rates on capital gains had remained the same, presumably the rate of realization would have remained the same. Because a higher percentage of capital gains probably went unrealized during the 1970s, incomes of the top 1 percent were likely understated. Looked at differently, if tax rates had remained at their mid-1970s peak, fewer realizations would have occurred and less income would have been reported by the top 1 percent. Either way, a decrease in the capital gains tax rate would be reflected in an increase in the observed measure of the share of income of the top 1 percent though inequality may not have changed at all. Accounting for the tax-returns effect and the capital gains effect, the top 1 percent's share would have increased from 7.55 percent to 13.09 percent rather than to 22.49 percent.

One consequence of the reelection of President Obama in 2012 was that he negotiated an increase in the top capital gains tax rate for 2013 and beyond. For those holding assets beyond a year, the tax rate (for those in the highest income bracket) increased from 15 percent to 23.8 percent. Though the Trump-era tax cut impacted many things, it left capital gains taxes largely unaffected.

Wealth Inequality

A parallel issue to income inequality is wealth inequality. Here, there are fewer measurement concerns as there is no direct tax in the United States on wealth. As a result, there are no necessary adjustments (like there were with income measures). The data on wealth concentrations come from a unique dataset: the *Survey of Consumer Finances*. These data are garnered from 4,500 individuals who are carefully selected to accurately represent the U.S. population's demographics (age, gender, household type, etc.) but also to achieve an appropriate representation of households according to economic characteristics (homeowners vs. renters, high-income vs. low-income individuals, as well as those with defined benefit pensions vs. those with defined contribution pensions). Part of the survey's usefulness is that there is what is known in statistics as "oversampling" of high-income and high-wealth households to get a more accurate representation of households in those categories. Those "oversampled" households are then weighted downward to make sure they do not bias the results of the survey. Conducted on behalf of the Federal Reserve by the University of Chicago, it is widely considered the gold standard of economic surveys.

Its results show that wealth inequality is similarly high and is higher than it once was. The share of the top 10 percent, which was 67 percent in 1989, grew to 77.1 percent by 2016. Figure 31.6 shows that the share of the top 1 percent grew markedly (from 30 percent to 36 percent) with the rise in the stock market during the 1990s and has been relatively stable. The relatively (but not extraordinarily) rich (i.e., the 9 percent in the top 10 percent but not in the top 1 percent) fared very well during the period after 1995. Figure 31.7 shows that the upper-middle class and the bottom half have seen their relative wealth shares fall. While the decrease in the bottom half's share from 2007 to 2016 (from 2.5 percent to 1 percent) is likely the result of the bursting of the housing bubble in 2008 through 2010, both household types have seen systematic declines in their wealth shares since 1989.

Another measure of wealth inequality is the ratio of mean wealth to median wealth. Mean (the simple average of) wealth differs from the median (the midpoint of) wealth because rich people are very rich, and modest percentage changes in their wealth are still very large and as such will change the mean significantly even if they have no effect on the median person's wealth. Figure 31.8 shows that during the 1989 to 2007 period, wealth (in inflation-adjusted dollars) rose 60 percent for the median household, but the mean rose 86 percent; that is, the rich got richer faster than did others. Again, most of that effect was

FIGURE 31.6 Share of wealth: top 10 percent.

Source: Survey of Consumer Finances

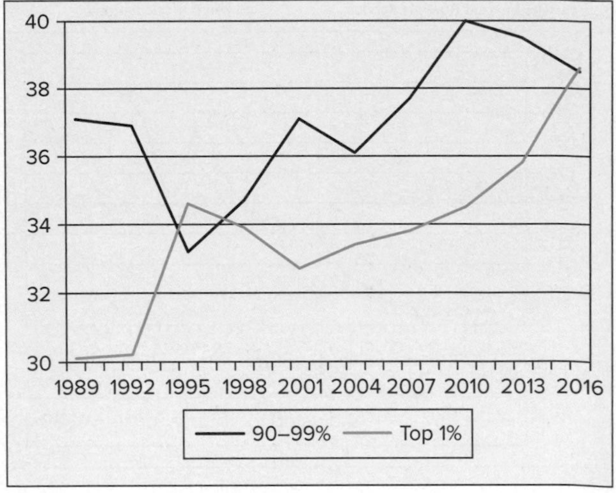

FIGURE 31.7 Share of wealth: bottom 90 percent.

Source: Survey of Consumer Finances

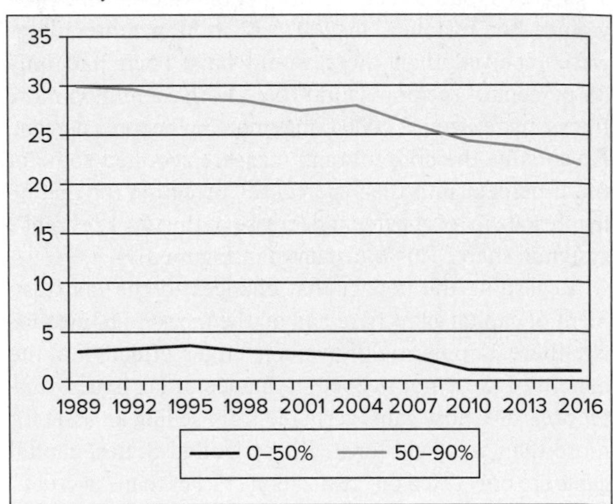

FIGURE 31.8 Median and mean wealth and their ratio (2010 dollars).

Source: Survey of Consumer Finances

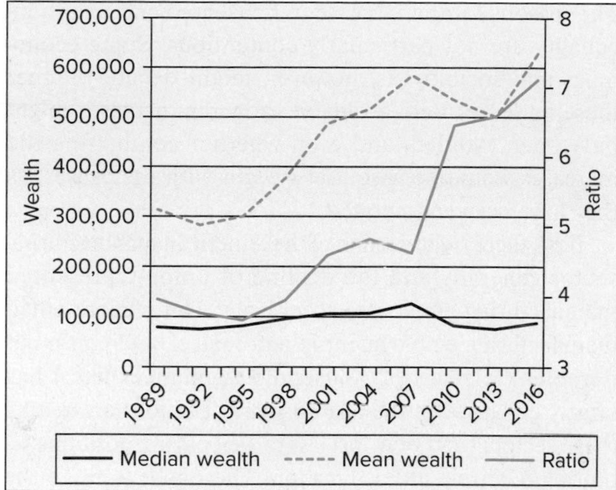

a result of the increase in the stock market from 1989 to 2000. The gains from 2001 to 2007 were more the result of the housing bubble, and because the average household benefited more (in net wealth terms) from the increase in housing-related wealth than did the rich (who have far less of the wealth tied up in their homes), the relative increase in median and mean wealth for that period was approximately equal. When the housing bubble collapsed, however, the median household's wealth fell 40 percent, all the way back to its 1989 inflation-adjusted level, while the mean value dropped only 15 percent. This caused the mean to median ratio, which had been rising steadily from 1995 to 2004, to spike. In 2016, it stood at 7.11. This means that the high end is so high that mean wealth is 7.11 times higher than the median household's wealth.

The Shrinking Middle Class

While income inequality has been increasing, the middle class in the United States is shrinking. These two issues are similar but not necessarily identical. The inequality issue is about incomes of those at the very top increasing faster than everyone else's (or increasing while everyone else's has remained stagnant or fallen). The issue of the shrinking middle class is associated, mostly, with the loss of income by those in the middle. For this study, the Pew Charitable Trust defined the middle class as those households with incomes between 67 percent and 200 percent of the median household income by household size. In 2014, a three-person household with income between $42,000 and $126,000 would qualify as being in the middle class. Table 31.1 shows the percentage of households by Pew's income classes.

Table 31.1 Percentages of people within Pew Charitable Trust income classes.

Source: Pew Research Center. "The American Middle Class Is Losing Ground." Last updated December 9, 2015. https://www.pewsocialtrends.org/2015/12/09/the-american-middle-class-is-losing-ground/.

Year	Lowest	Lower Middle	Middle	Upper Middle	Highest
1971	16	9	61	10	4
1981	17	9	59	12	3
1991	18	9	56	12	5
2001	18	9	54	11	7
2011	20	9	51	12	8
2015	20	9	50	12	9

Without regard to definitions, the middle class can shrink or expand because the income of people near the definitional thresholds changes. For instance, a surge in earnings of people just under the 200 percent definitional threshold would shrink the middle class by moving them into the "upper middle." That would be an unambiguously good thing. To some degree, that is what happened in the 1970s through the 1990s. Another unambiguously good thing would be if people moved into the middle class because they were below the lower threshold and moved above it. This did not occur in the 45 years of this Pew study.

On the other hand, if people are falling below the 67 percent definitional threshold into the "lower middle" group, or worse, moving from the lower middle to the lowest group, that is unambiguously bad. Not just because the middle class is shrinking but because of the way in which it is shrinking.

A graphical display of the income distribution is not a standard bell curve. It actually looks a great deal more like the two distributions shown in Figure 31.9. There are many people at the lower end of the distribution with an ever-decreasing percentage in each income category thereafter. The middle class is represented by the shaded portion. If the middle class shrinks, more of the distribution is outside the shaded area. In particular, a movement from the black distribution to the brown one would constitute a shrinking of the middle class.

The economic and political consequences of the shrinking middle class are enormous. When people's

FIGURE 31.9 Income distribution.

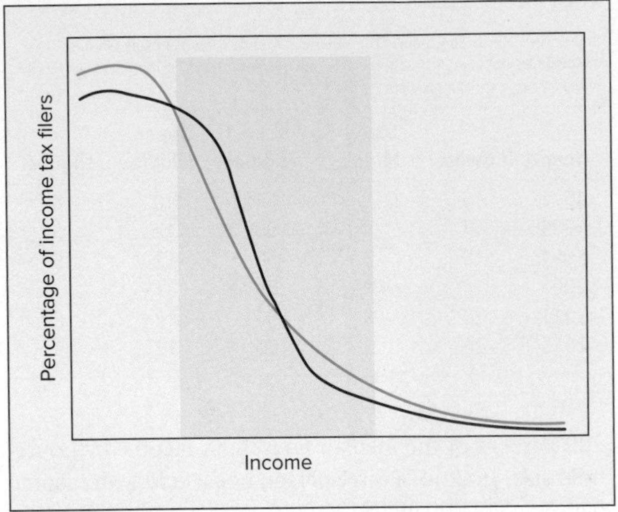

incomes become less equal and fewer people can describe themselves as being in the middle class, fewer people are likely to embrace a market-based economic system. On the other hand, as long as people view the system as fundamentally fair, even those who find themselves at the bottom of the income distribution will see the economic results of their life as a consequence of their own choices. Increases in income inequality, therefore, cause more people to question the fairness of a market-based economy.

When people question the fairness of a market-based economy, they will seek policies that insulate them from the harshness of that system. The British vote to leave the European Union, for instance, could be viewed as such a reaction by that population. The popularity of 2016 presidential candidates Donald Trump and Bernie Sanders and their anti-trade prescriptions is another. Those insulating policies (reducing immigration or erecting trade barriers) inhibit the free flow of people, labor, investments, goods, and services. Those who argue for such policies do not necessarily care because they assert that the benefits from free trade and the free movement of those goods, services, financial resources, and people only favor the rich. Those who argue against such policies typically argue that the policies shrink the size of the economic pie and therefore reduce what is available to everyone. That system is threatened when market-based systems produce outcomes that are viewed by the majority as unfair or "rigged." Polls throughout 2018 and 2019 found an increasingly favorable view (particularly among the young) of socialism and an increasingly negative view of capitalism.

Causes of Household Income and Wealth Inequality

The reasons for the increase in household and wealth inequality are not particularly contentious. Some economists and sociologists, however, might debate whether these increases were avoidable, how the increases might have been avoided, and even whether combatting the increases would be wise. Let's begin with the causes, as they have been enumerated.

First, there is the decline of the American manufacturing sector generally and the decline of union-represented manufacturing employees specifically. Union-represented manufacturing employment in autos, steel, and consumer durables (televisions, household appliances, etc.) has largely collapsed in the last 40 years. The jobs created by these sectors (and now lost) were well-paying positions requiring relatively little education. These jobs were, to the hardworking, a ticket to a middle-class lifestyle.

Robotic production and international competition for the goods produced by these industries are largely to blame for the elimination of manufacturing jobs. Specifically, fewer and fewer jobs are being performed by physically challenging labor, and more and more jobs are being performed by intellectually challenging labor. As a result, the premium paid to the brightest and most well educated continues to grow, and the relative wage of those performing manual labor has diminished. A worker today can be responsible for the output, while supervising the actions of computer- and robotically driven manufacturing that once required several workers to perform physically demanding tasks.

International competition for goods-producing industries has made it extraordinarily difficult for domestic manufacturers to compete if and when they have high wages and generous benefit packages. Domestic steel and auto production declined in the 1970s and 1980s, and while their decline continued through today (particularly by American companies), the 1990s and 2000s saw a significant decline in the production of consumer electronics, appliances, and household products. Many economists considered this trend inevitable. Immediately following World War II, there was no major economy, other than the American one, with its economy and infrastructure more or less intact. For that reason, American manufacturing had significant market power relative to the rest of the world. If a buyer wanted steel, for the better part of the 1950s and into the 1960s, he or she had to buy it from the United States. The same was largely true of automobiles through the 1970s and for consumer electronics and durables through the 1980s. With that market power, companies in the United States could pass on their higher wage costs to the world's consumers.

American unions could therefore bargain for higher wages, and because there was no international competition in these areas, the manufacturers were motivated to pay those wages and offer better benefits. Again, because they could pass on the increased costs to consumers, they were not only not compelled to keep costs under control, but it was also in their interests to avoid sales-reducing strikes. As time progressed the economies of first, Germany and Japan, then Korea and China, and perhaps soon, India and Africa were able to undercut high American prices with the one advantage they had: lower wages. Short of isolating the U.S. economy, there was nothing the United States could have done to stop this pressure. As a result, downward pressure on American wages, under the story accepted by many, was an inevitable outcome of the late 20th century.

All of this speaks to why incomes (and wealth) of those at the bottom would remain stagnant or decline, but what would explain why those at the top did so well? For this we have to turn to the aspects of global changes that benefited those at the top. The first of these changes involves the movement of global capital, while the second involves changes in the consumption-saving patterns of those not at the top.

After World War II and through the 1980s, the vast majority of financial capital used to grow businesses was locally generated. That is, Americans lent their money to other Americans to build businesses, finance homes, and so forth. Today, a bond used to finance a company or a mortgage taken out to buy a home could very easily have its origins in Saudi Arabia or China. The foreign entity saves the money from profits earned in their global enterprises, converts that money to dollars, and invests it in U.S. markets. Capital markets have become much more profitable to those engaged in them and those engaged in them are, almost always, very wealthy people.

Furthermore, American saving rates have fallen precipitously since the 1960s. A home that used to require a 20 percent down payment can now be acquired for 10 percent (or less) down. A car that used to be purchased for cash is now far more likely to be financed with a loan or leased with terms so generous as to allow the consumer to simply sign his or her name and drive away with a new car. The savers, who used to come from all walks of life, are now far more likely to come from the higher end of the income scale.

To some degree, public policy since the 1980s has been more favorable to those at the high end of the income and wealth distribution than it was in years prior. Inheritance tax rates have fallen throughout the United States relative to where they were in the 1970s. Nationally, in inflation-adjusted terms, inheritance taxes are collected on fewer households than used to be subject to them and at lower rates. This is true at the federal and state levels. If there are two ways of being rich—inheriting your wealth or earning your wealth—policy changes are making the former easier.

The other significant tax policy change prior to the 1980s is the treatment of investment-based income. Capital gains tax rates as well as tax rates on carried interest (a form of income associated with an investment or hedge fund manager's exceeding a specified return goal), which were treated as ordinary income in the late 1980s and early 1990s, are now taxed at a lower rate than other earned income.

Finally, with all of this happening to increase income inequality, there had existed a counterweight to it in the 1960s through the 1980s. Specifically, the increasing labor force participation of women had turned millions of one-earner households into two-earner households. That meant the wage-and-salary earning class experienced rapidly increasing family incomes (especially during the early part of this period) from the increase in the number of income earners in those families. As the trend finished running its course, this counterweight was no longer holding back the movement toward inequality resulting from the other forces.

Costs and Benefits of Income Inequality

Market economies rely on the principle that individuals earn an income that is positively related to the value of what they provide to that society where that value is measured by what others are willing to pay. If it is not positively related, some (perhaps many) individuals will stop doing what they are doing and do something else more lucrative or less demanding. If physicians and other professionals who require higher levels of education do not earn more than ordinary laborers, then only those who wish to stay in school for long periods of time to engage in their desired profession will do so. If that happens, there will be too few trained physicians, engineers, scientists, and managers. Income inequality provides a motivation for both those who wish to be at the high end of the income distribution to work to achieve it and those

Table 31.2 Income mobility from 1987 to 1996 and from 1996 to 2005.

Source: United States Department of the Treasury. "Income Mobility in the U.S. from 1996 to 2005, Report of the Department of the Treasury." Last updated November 13, 2007. https://www.treasury.gov/resource-center/tax-policy/Documents/Report-Income-Mobility-2008.pdf.

		Lowest	Second	Middle	Fourth	Highest	Total	Top 1%
Lowest	1987–1996	38.9	28.3	14.9	10.6	7.3	100	0.3
	1996–2005	37.8	27.1	16.1	11.8	7.2	100	0.3
Second	1987–1996	14.2	33.8	26.4	16.4	9.3	100	0.2
	1996–2005	15.8	30.1	28	17.2	9	100	0.2
Middle	1987–1996	6.1	17.4	33.9	28.4	14.2	100	0.3
	1996–2005	5.9	14	32.6	31.1	16.3	100	0.3
Fourth	1987–1996	3	7.5	19.4	40.1	30	100	0.5
	1996–2005	3.1	5.7	15.5	41.9	33.8	100	0.3
Highest	1987–1996	1.8	2.5	7.3	20.6	67.8	100	5.4
	1996–2005	2	2	5.7	17.2	73.2	100	4.8
Top 1%	1987–1996	2.1	0.9	2.5	4.7	89.9	100	46
	1996–2005	2.7	1	1.5	4.5	90.3	100	44.7
All Income	1987–1996	11.3	16.5	20.1	24.1	28	100	1.5
	1996–2005	11.7	14.7	19.1	24.4	30	100	1.3

who wish to avoid being at the low end of the income distribution to work to avoid that result as well.

To see this in your own life, imagine that the profession you wish to embark upon paid only the minimum wage. Would you continue pursuing a degree in order to engage in that profession? Some of you might, but most of you would change your degree program to do something more lucrative–if for no other reason than to pay off your student loans or make the time in college worth the expense.

Significant income inequality has a social downside as well, especially when the level of inequality is viewed by those in the middle and at the bottom of the distribution as unjustified by the aforementioned social benefits associated with meeting market needs. When the poor believe that their poverty is a result of choices they made or a result of things they did or failed to do, income inequality does not present a challenge to capitalism. On the other hand, when those in the middle or at the bottom of the distribution believe that the system is rigged in favor of the rich remaining rich, social disorder (demonstrations, riots, etc.) can be the result. Social disorder can threaten the system that allows for income inequality in the first place, and as a result, it is frequently in the interests of those at the top of the distribution to ensure that those in the middle and at the bottom believe that the inequality is justified.

A positive view of income inequality by those in the middle and at the bottom can be achieved as long as there is the widespread belief that there exists upward income and wealth mobility in society. It is therefore important for those at the top of the income distribution to create the reality of opportunity or at least maintain a widespread belief in a myth of opportunity.

Table 31.2 shows the degree of income mobility from 1987 to 1998 and from 1996 to 2005. What it shows is that 38.9 percent of those in the lowest quintile in 1987 were also in the lowest quintile in 1996. What it also shows is that 17.9 percent of those in the lowest quintile in 1987 were in one of the two highest quintiles in 1996. From 1996 to 2005, these figures were largely the same, given that 37.8 percent of the poor in 1996 were also poor in 2005 and that 19 percent of the poor in 1996 were in one of the top two quintiles in 2005. At the other end, it shows that 55.3 percent (100 percent − 44.7 percent) of those in the 1 percent in 1996 weren't in the top 1 percent in 2005.

Another way of looking at income mobility is the degree to which the income quintile of parents and the income quintile of their children are related; that is, whether or not you inherit your parents' wealth, you often inherit your parents' values, work ethic, and social standing and that translates into higher income.[2] This

[2]For instance, my fraternal grandfather earned a law degree; my father, brother, sister, and daughter (as well as I) earned PhDs. That is highly unlikely to be random.

Table 31.3 Cross-country intergenerational income elasticities.

Source: Corak, Miles. "Do Poor Children Become Poor Adults? Lessons from a Cross-Country Comparison of Generational Earnings Mobility." Last modified March 2006. http://ftp.iza.org/dp1993.pdf.

Country	Elasticity
Denmark	0.15
Norway	0.17
Finland	0.18
Canada	0.19
Sweden	0.27
Germany	0.32
France	0.41
United States	0.47
United Kingdom	0.50

intergenerational income relationship has been estimated by economists for a variety of countries using a variety of methodologies. Canadian economist Miles Corak summarized the results that are displayed in Table 31.3. Higher numbers suggest a stronger relationship between parental and child income. This analysis shows that the U.S. claim to be "the land of opportunity" isn't backed up by the data, at least not recently.

Solutions to Income and Wealth Inequality

In 2019, the Democratic nominees for president competed with one another over how to address income inequality. All were determined to overturn the 2017 Jobs and Tax Cut Act that was passed by the Republicans in Congress and President Trump. That act lowered business tax rates (corporate and noncorporate alike) as well as lowering rates for individuals. The Tax Policy Center, a nonpartisan think tank, estimated that between 20 and 25 percent of the benefits of these provisions would accrue to the top 1 percent of income earners.

One candidate in particular, Senator Elizabeth Warren of Massachusetts, advocated for a 2 percent wealth tax on wealth over $50 billion and 3 percent on wealth over $1 billion. The constitutionality of such a tax at the federal level is dubious[3] but, nevertheless, provides an interesting talking point. Senator Warren, backed by many left-leaning economists, believes that there is no way to address wealth inequality indirectly. As a result, she and her supporters propose that we tax the result: very high wealth by a narrow group.

Another 2020 presidential candidate, former Governor of Colorado John Hickenlooper, suggested a different (and obviously constitutional) way of getting at the wealth of the rich. He suggested eliminating a provision of the tax code referred to earlier that allows for the *stepped-up basis at death* for capital gains. He suggested taxing those gains on the last tax return of the person who dies instead of allowing them to be untaxed. In that way, the tax can be collected within one year of the death of the investor.

Economic conservatives do not tend to offer solutions to wealth inequality issues because many believe that it stems from free people engaging in free exchange. However, there is a segment of conservative economists who believes that some of the gains stem from a rigging of the rules. For example, there are provisions of the tax code that continue to allow the shielding of income from any taxes. Through their political donations, the rich are frequently able to steer these provisions in their favor.

On the corporate side, Apple and Amazon made a combined $11 billion in 2018 and paid no federal corporate income taxes. A large part of the explanation is that the companies can treat capital and equipment investments in the same way that they treat buying paper—as an expense.

[3]The U.S. Constitution only allowed direct taxes (taxes on income and wealth are direct taxes; sales and inheritance taxes are indirect because they are taxes on sales or transfers) when the total paid by citizens of the states was proportional to their population. The 16th Amendment allowed for an income tax only.

Summary

The United States has significant income and wealth inequality. Part of the increase in income inequality is explained by measurement issues. The systemic increase in income inequality is explainable by demographic factors and factors relating to tax policy. Inequality has benefits in that a higher income is a market reward for higher productivity, while it has costs related to social discord. Social discord is a more likely outcome when income mobility is low or decreasing, and in the present-day United States, both are the case. The solutions to this inequality are as contentious as today's politics.

Quiz Yourself

1. Income inequality, when measured as the percentage of total income going to the top 1 percent, increased most rapidly during the
   a. 1950s.
   b. 1960s.
   c. 1980s and 1990s.
   d. 2000s.
2. Income inequality, as conventionally measured, is ____ when you ignore the fact that a higher percentage of the population is filing tax forms.
   a. overstated
   b. understated
   c. properly stated
3. Income inequality, as conventionally measured, is ____ when you ignore the decreases in the capital gains tax rate.
   a. overstated
   b. understated
   c. properly stated
4. Wealth inequality is _____ related to the ratio of mean to median wealth.
   a. positively
   b. negatively
   c. not
5. Which of the following had the effect of decreasing income inequality?
   a. The increase in the female labor force participation rate
   b. The increase in globalization of capital
   c. The increase in globalization of trade in steel, autos, and consumer durables
   d. The increase in robotic production
6. Which of the following had the effect of increasing income inequality?
   a. The increase in the female labor force participation rate
   b. The decrease in globalization of capital
   c. The increase in globalization of trade in steel, autos, and consumer durables
   d. The decrease in robotic production
7. The benefits of income inequality are
   a. always greater than the costs.
   b. always less than the costs.
   c. associated with rewarding hard work and work that society values.
   d. associated with the social discord that it creates.
8. Social discord resulting from income inequality can be lessened if there is (are)
   a. high levels of intergenerational income mobility.
   b. high levels of income mobility of individuals.
   c. belief that the economic system is rigged in favor of the rich.
   d. *a* and *b*
9. The notion that the United States is the "land of opportunity" where who your parents are and how much they earn is unrelated to your income is (relative to other industrial powers)
   a. clearly shown in the data to be accurate.
   b. clearly shown in the data to be inaccurate.
   c. not supported, but there aren't data to support the conclusion that it isn't true either.

Short Answer Questions

1. Illustrate how adding a tax benefit to people at the low end of the income scale (causing many new people to file taxes to get those benefits) alters the percentage of income reported to be held by the top portion.
2. Illustrate how, when the rich get richer (and everyone else maintains the same level of wealth), the ratio of the mean to the median wealth rises.

Think about This

Are the poor adults with whom you are familiar poor because of things they did (got pregnant at an early age, committed a crime that prevented them from a getting a good job), things they failed to do (finish their education, work hard), things that happened to them (they were the victim of an accident, or were left with children to attend to), or is the system rigged against poor people?

What policy would you suggest to a national leader to increase income mobility?

Talk about This

Many politicians (mostly Democrats) speak about income inequality and propose solutions that revolve around directly taking from the 1 percent (e.g., higher income or wealth taxes) to provide to programs (e.g., free college) for the 99 percent. Set those policies aside for a moment. Brainstorm policies that would focus on increasing income mobility (i.e., making it easier to rise or fall between income classes).

Behind the Numbers

U.S. Census Bureau: www.census.gov/topics/income-poverty/wealth/data/tables.html

- Wealth distribution

Federal Reserve: www.federalreserve.gov/pubs/feds/2009/200913/200913pap.pdf

- Income mobility

Internal Revenue Service: www.irs.gov/statistics/soi-tax-stats-individual-income-tax-return-form-1040-statistics

- Income distribution

Corak, Miles, "Do Poor Children Become Poor Adults? Lessons from a Cross Country Comparison of Generational Earnings Mobility," ftp.iza.org/dp1993.pdf.

- Intergenerational income mobility

CHAPTER THIRTY-TWO

Farm Policy

Learning Objectives

After reading this chapter you should be able to:

LO1 Conclude that economists generally are against price supports in agriculture.

LO2 Conclude that price variation is the best of a set of poor economic justifications for farm price supports.

LO3 Demonstrate economists' reasoning in opposing farm price supports by using concepts of supply and demand and consumer and producer surplus.

LO4 Compare the mechanisms that are typically used to enforce price supports and describe their historic use.

Chapter Outline

Farm policy in the United States has been contradictory. Sometimes farmers are depicted as strong, independent men and women who simply need the government to stay out of their way. At other times, they are depicted as desperate victims in need of help. In political speeches, family farms are spoken of with the same sentiment as motherhood and apple pie.

It is ironic, then, that without almost continuous government grants and low-interest loans, many farmers would have declared bankruptcy long ago. Help for farmers has come from government in many forms. The government has bought and stored excess production, bought and given away excess production, bought livestock to prevent oversupply, and paid farmers not to farm.

We look at the history of farm prices since 1950, and we draw on that history to discuss why government has intervened and will probably continue to feel motivated to intervene in agriculture. We use the basic supply and demand model and the concepts of consumer and producer surplus to discuss the impact of farm price supports. In that discussion, as we said, we review the history of farm price supports and the various ways that farmers have received assistance.

Farm Prices since 1950

A look at Figure 32.1 quickly tells you that farm prices are anything but stable. While beef, hogs, milk, corn, and soybeans are sold in different units, by displaying prices relative to where they were in 1982, we can show all of them on one graph. Recall from Chapter 6's use of a price index and a base year, a number higher than 100 indicates a price in a selected year for that commodity that exceeds its 1982 level. A number below 100 indicates the opposite.

Whereas the prices of all the products shown in Figure 32.1 were higher in 2018 than they were in 1950, as recently as 2005, several were lower than they were in 1982. Since, according to the CPI, overall inflation was 151 percent from 1982 to 2018, farmers who produced the same crops in the same amounts and with the same costs would have experienced a 40 percent (100/251) loss in real income if they were only able to get the same price they received in 1982. Hog prices in particular took a beating between 1998 and 2000, yielding at times less than 45 percent of their 1982 levels. Any farmers who had not gotten more productive by this time would have seen a standard of living only 33 percent of their 1982 level.

FIGURE 32.1 Farm prices relative to their 1982 levels.

Source: Bureau of Labor Statistics.

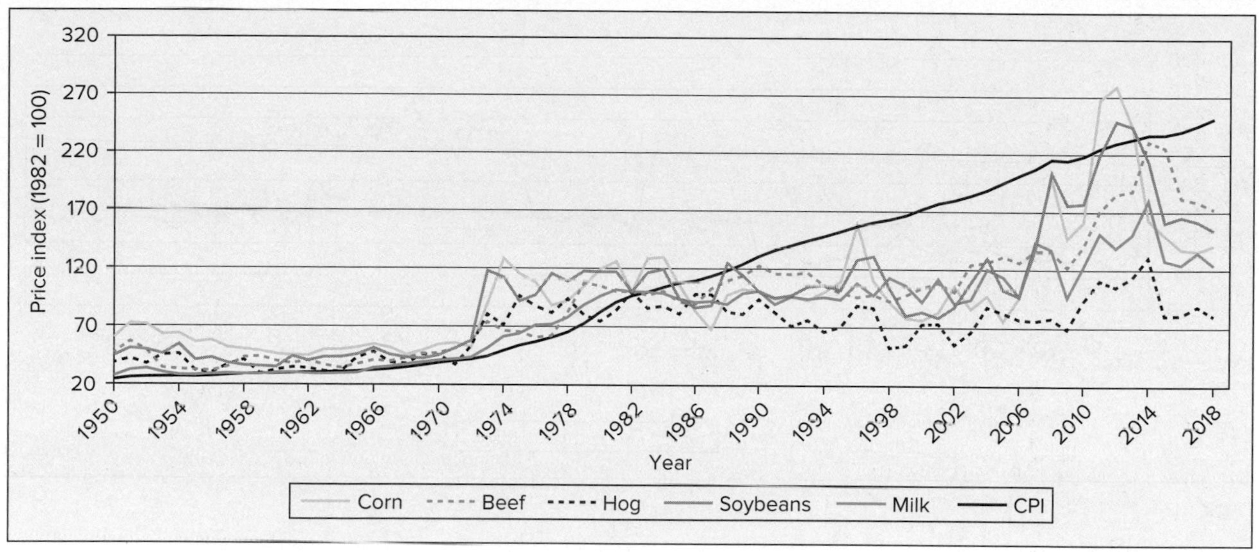

Until quite recently, prices for most farm commodities have risen far more slowly than overall consumer prices. Beginning in 2006, there was a dramatic increase in nearly all farm prices that carried through until 2013. Since that time, however, there has been a dramatic retreat. From their respective peaks to 2018, farm prices fell between 25 and 50 percent.

If you look carefully at Figure 32.1, you will see that there was a sharp jump in all of these commodity prices in the early 1970s and again in 2008, and then again between 2010 and 2013. Corn, soybean, and hog prices doubled in the four years from 1972 to 1975. Before 1975, corn, soybean, and milk prices had been the most stable, but since 1976, corn has joined beef as a commodity with great price instability.[1] In 2007 and 2008, most farm commodities doubled or even tripled in price. By far the greatest increase was seen in corn and soybeans. Going back to Chapter 2, you will remember that when one good is an input into another, an increase in that input price will drive the price of the output to rise. Corn and soybean meal are frequently used as animal feed. For our purposes, that means that they are inputs to beef and pork. Recall from the Chapter 2 notion of "alternative outputs," that when two different goods can be easily produced from the same inputs, the two prices will almost always mirror one another. If you have ever traveled from Ohio through Indiana, Illinois, Iowa, or Missouri, the farms along the highway are almost always planted in corn and soybeans. An increase in the demand for one will cause a decrease in the supply of the other. Farmers will plant whatever makes them the most profit, and as a result, the prices will move in tandem. What occurred in 2007 and 2008 was a spike in the demand for corn resulting from its potential use in corn-based ethanol.

Corn and Gasoline

Let's examine that corn–gasoline relationship in greater detail. What had once been a nonexistent relationship began to emerge in 2004 as subsidies and mandates for alternative fuels for cars and trucks became part of the U.S. energy landscape. Corn-based ethanol was a major part of President Bush's energy strategy and played a role in President Obama's energy strategy. Flex-fuel vehicles are an increasing portion of the rolling stock on American roads, and as a result the overall demand for corn has risen.

In addition, ethanol is now an increasing portion of the total fuel demand, so much so that 38 percent of the corn grown is now used for that purpose. As can be seen

[1]We are defining stability here as the ratio of the standard deviation of real prices to their mean.

FIGURE 32.2 Relative prices of gas and corn.

Source: Bureau of Labor Statistics.

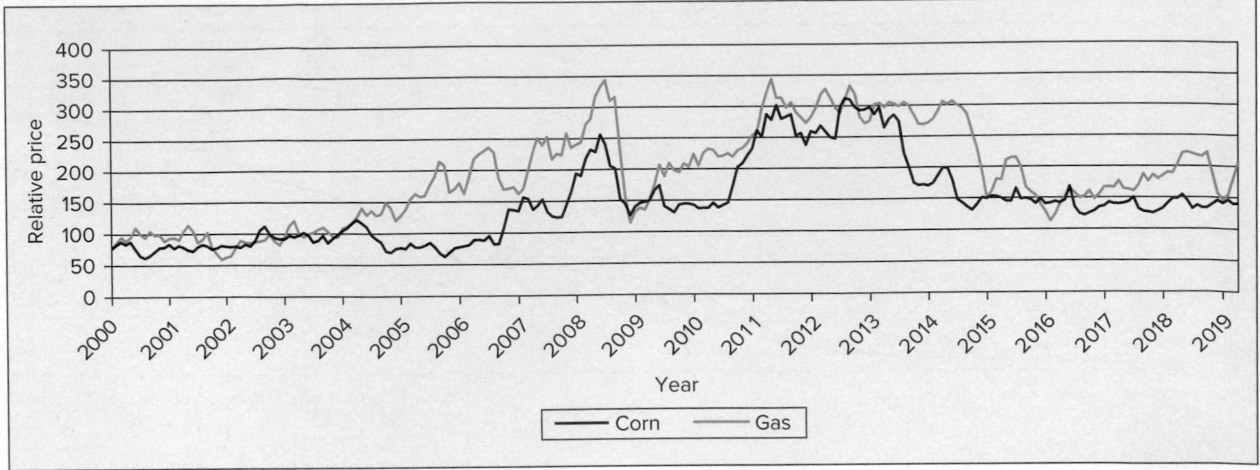

in Figure 32.2, prior to 2004 there was almost no relationship between the two prices, but between late 2004 and early 2009 the price per bushel of corn more than tripled in reaction to the tripling of gasoline prices. Going back to our Chapter 2 discussion of demand and supply determinants, ethanol is a substitute for gasoline and corn is an input to ethanol. A steadily high gasoline price would be expected to, and in fact did, lead to an increase in corn demand and corn prices.

Had gasoline prices remained at their summer 2008 highs, corn probably would have as well. When the demand for gasoline fell dramatically with the declining economy, the price of corn plummeted as well. By the end of 2008, the price of corn was about half of its mid-2008 high. The prices once again mirrored each other in the rise through late 2010 and into 2014.

Because ethanol is only a viable substitute for gasoline when gasoline prices are high, with the dramatic drop in gasoline prices that occurred from 2015 to 2016, the link between corn and gasoline prices was largely severed.

Price Variation as a Justification for Government Intervention

Economists agree on few things, but one area where there is wide agreement is on the inadvisability of government intervention in agriculture. As a result, appeals for intervention tend to be based on sentiment rather than analysis. Although such sentimental appeals have not persuaded many economists, they have swayed politicians. The family farm is so revered in America, even by people who have never lived on or even near one, that economists have had little success forestalling farm bailouts. That said, there are reasons for government intervention in agriculture that a few academic economists, particularly agricultural economists, accept.

The Case for Price Supports

The most compelling of the reasons for government intervention in agricultural markets is that price variability makes farming an economically risky occupation. Supporters think that small farmers need some government action to survive the aforementioned variability. The government's assistance in this might take the form of buying and storing excess crops when prices are too low and selling them out of inventory when prices rebound. This would do nothing to change the long-term price of crops, but it would stabilize prices.

There are two sources of price instability for any good: supply uncertainty and demand uncertainty. Sources of supply uncertainty are obvious: the weather and other natural phenomena like diseases and insect damage. The source of demand variability is mostly the unpredictability of international markets and whether there is demand for American crops by other countries.

The weather and other aspects of nature determine whether crops will do well, and there is not a great deal farmers can control once planting is complete. They can plant different varieties of corn and soybeans based on the lateness of the planting season, but once the seeds are sown, most of the economic decisions are made. Grain farmers, for example, are powerless to do anything if market conditions change after planting. At harvest they will reap what they sowed–no more, no less.

On the demand side, variability comes from the quantities of goods other countries buy. In part, this is supply-side variability in other nations. For instance, if the weather is bad in the other major exporting countries of grain like Argentina, Australia, Canada, and Russia, then demand will be high in importing countries for American grain. The United States is the largest source of grain exports to the world, but prices are usually somewhat high compared to other countries. For this reason, food importers buy all they can from these other countries; then they buy the rest of what they need from the United States. If the weather in the exporting countries is bad, then importing countries will need larger quantities of U.S. grain. Likewise, if their weather is good, importing countries will not need much U.S. grain. With the weather and other variable forces, there are few goods whose prices fluctuate as much as basic farm prices.

The Case against Price Supports

Though price variability is the most compelling reason for government interference in agriculture, it is not a persuasive reason for many economists. *Option markets* for agricultural goods exist and offer many opportunities to ensure that prices at harvest are known in advance. Such markets serve as insurance to farmers on prices.

To see how using an option market might work, suppose you planted your crop in May and expected it to yield 10,000 bushels. When you plant your crop, you can buy an option to sell 10,000 bushels at harvest for a specific price. If the price at harvest is lower than the price specified in the option, you can exercise the option and sell your harvest at the higher contract price. If the price is higher, you do not need the option. This is comparable to buying automobile insurance. You will use it if you have an accident; you will not if you avoid a wreck.

In addition, if you fear your crop might fail, you can protect yourself by purchasing crop insurance. Crop insurance pays farmers a portion of what they would have likely harvested had their crops not been subject to a drought, storm, flood, or freeze. With these two forms of insurance (options and crop insurance), farmers can deal with the aspects of farming over which they have no control without government help. If farmers do not buy options or crop insurance, it is typically because, like all financial instruments and insurance, they cost money. Even when things go well, profit margins on farms are low enough that some farmers believe they cannot afford insurance.

Consumer and Producer Surplus Analysis of Price Floors

One Floor in One Market

All of the many forms of support that government can give to farmers can be modeled with our supply and demand model, and we can discuss their implications using the consumer and producer surplus language that was introduced in Chapter 3. This section quickly reviews that language and uses Figure 32.3 to look at the impact of farm price supports on the economy.

In Chapter 3, we learned that consumer surplus is the difference between how much consumers value a good and the price they have to pay for it. Producer surplus is the difference between the amount producers get from consumers and the variable cost of production. The demand curve represents what consumers are willing to pay for a good, and we interpret that as how much they value the good. In Chapter 5, we saw that the supply curve in a perfectly competitive market is made up of the marginal cost curves of the many entities that comprise the market. The area under the supply curve thus represents the variable costs of production.

At the equilibrium point (P^*, Q^*), consumers have a consumer surplus of P^*AC. Similarly, the producer benefits as well. The firms net a producer surplus of HP^*C. The combined surpluses make up the value to society of the exchange, a value represented as HAC.

FIGURE 32.3 Price floors in a supply and demand model.

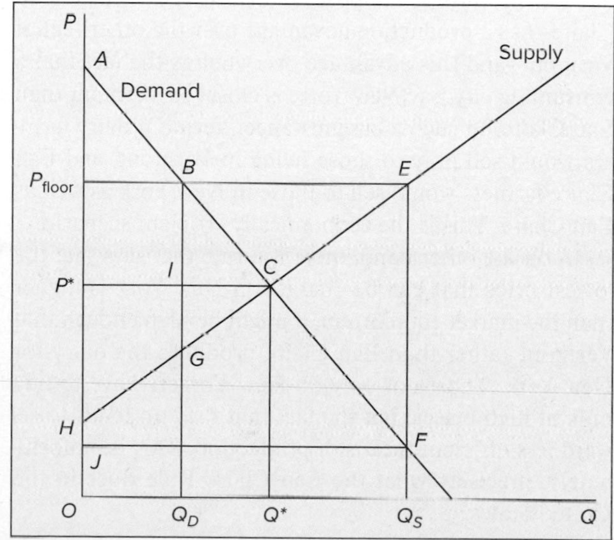

If the government sets a **price floor** of P_{floor}, it must enforce it. While we will not talk until the next section about how government might enforce the price floor, assume for the moment that it is possible. Because consumers will want only Q_D, this is all that will be sold. The consumer surplus will shrink (to $P_{floor}AB$), while the producer surplus will grow (to $HP_{floor}BG$). However, in this case, the net benefit to society is only *HABG*, which is smaller than the net benefit before the price floor was established (*HAC*). Economists label the difference between the net benefit to society in both circumstances, *GBC*, deadweight loss. To see why this is the case, turn to "Kick It Up a Notch" at the end of the chapter.

price floor
Price below which a commodity may not sell.

Variable Floors in Multiple Markets

Support for farmers and their price supports dates back to the Great Depression, when dairy farmers could not sell their products, and they convinced the government to set minimum prices. The so-called Eau Claire Rule came about at this time. Put in place so that farmers outside Wisconsin could survive and remain in business, the Eau Claire Rule sets the minimum price for milk as a function of a farm's proximity to this small Wisconsin city. To this day, a dairy farmer in central Wisconsin gets a substantially lower subsidy than a similar farmer in the other dairy capitals of central New York or northern California.

To see the effect of this, consider three geographically distinct areas. Suppose two of these are rural areas, where dairy products are both produced and consumed, and the third area is a city where these products are consumed but not produced. Suppose one rural area–call it Eau Claire–has a production advantage over the other–call it Vermont–and this advantage overwhelms the fact that a consuming city, say New York, is closer to Vermont than Eau Claire. In such a circumstance, Vermont dairy farmers would sell only to those living in Vermont, and Eau Claire farmers would sell to those in New York as well as Eau Claire. This is the economically efficient scenario.

If, on the other hand, there is a rule that says that the lowest price that can be charged in New York is higher than the market equilibrium, it might be high enough that Vermont rather than Eau Claire produces the dairy for New York. Thus, not only do New Yorkers have to buy milk at high prices, but the fact that they do tends to reward less efficient means of production. This is, unfortunately, precisely what the Eau Claire Rule does in the United States.

What Would Happen without Price Supports?

If there were no price supports, how low could prices go? The first thing to understand is that like everyone else, farmers have options other than farming. If prices become too low, they will sell the farm and work somewhere else. In this sense, farmers are like any other small businessperson who must decide when they have had enough. While being your own boss has clear advantages, the advantages must also be weighed against risks and the anxiety associated with farming.

For most farmers, the upside outweighs the downside. Even with lower income, they would rather continue farming than work for someone else. On the other hand, there is a price for which the rate of return to farming is just too low. When that point is reached, farmers auction their assets, pay their debts, and move on with their lives. As a result, prices cannot fall below the level where farmers are better off not farming. If they did, the farmers would leave the market, thereby reducing the number of sellers, and that would put upward pressure on the price.

Price Support Mechanisms and Their History

Price Support Mechanisms

As we noted in the previous section, there are many ways of enforcing a price support. The reason an enforcement mechanism is required in agriculture and not in other price floor situations is that production happens and most costs are incurred well before sales are made or even arranged. For instance, the minimum wage is a form of price floor. The buyer of labor, the boss, cannot pay the seller of labor, the worker, any less than the minimum wage, just as the buyer of the agricultural product cannot pay the farmer any less than the price floor. The supply and demand analysis of the minimum wage shows that more people want to work than there are jobs available. This is not as much of a problem in normal work as it is in farming because, unlike farming, the workers are not working and then looking to see if the boss will pay them. They are hired and then they do the work. Farmers, on the other hand, grow and harvest their crops before they have a known buyer. Raising the price that farmers get to P_{floor} will not do farmers any good if many of them end up having truckloads of grain to sell and no one willing to buy them. They will have incurred all of the costs of working, but they will not derive any revenue from their work.

For this reason, the government must enforce the price floor in a manner that ensures either that only Q_D is produced or that Q_S is wanted. There are several ways that this can be done. The government can limit what farmers produce by allocating rights to sell among farmers. With rights to sell, farmers can sell only what their rights allow. The government can pay farmers to participate by allowing anyone to sell at P^*, while allowing only those who agreed to limit production to sell at P_{floor}. The government can then buy all that farmers want to produce. At its discretion it can then give the good away to foreign or domestic recipients that could not afford to buy it at P_{floor}, or the government can buy and store all that farmers want to produce at P_{floor}.

The government's least expensive option to keep prices high, however, is to limit the amount that a farmer can produce. It can do this by allowing only licensed farmers to produce specific quantities. At times in U.S. history, you had to have a license to grow peanuts and chewing-grade tobacco. If you examine Figure 32.3 again, you will see that by limiting the number of farmers and the amount of acreage that can be devoted to this production, the P_{floor} price can be maintained and farmers will produce only Q_D.

The government's next least expensive option is to pay farmers not to produce as much as they might otherwise choose. In the past, the government paid farmers not to plant in certain fields, and it even paid them not to farm altogether. Moreover, to affect the price of milk, the government bought dairy herds and sent them off to slaughter. The government, of course, is able to decrease production when it pays farmers not to produce. The effectiveness of this method is lessened, however, by increases in productivity and by new people becoming farmers. In the case of milk, farmers who had their herds bought were not allowed to get back into dairy farming for several years, even if they wanted to, but that did not prevent others from becoming farmers. It did not prevent remaining farmers from increasing their herds, and it did not prevent others from increasing the productivity of their cows, using artificial hormones. Grain farmers also experienced this form of price support. Many were paid to have idle fields, fields that could be used for hay but not for cash grains like wheat, soybeans, or corn. In general, government subsidies have persuaded a significant numbers of farmers either to do something else or limit production.

An expensive option for the government has been to let farmers grow all they want and either pay them the difference between the market price and the price floor or simply buy whatever was not purchased by consumers. Figure 32.3 shows that it is very expensive for the government to choose either of these options. If it chooses the former, it will have to pay farmers the difference between P_{floor} and the price that Q_S will sell for on the open market, shown in Figure 32.3 as J, for all Q_S. This totals $JP_{floor}EF$. If the government chooses the latter option, it will have to buy the difference between Q_S and Q_D for the P_{floor}, price. That totals Q_D-BEQ_S.

If it buys what is left by consumers, the government still has to figure out what to do with the excess. There are three options: let it spoil, give it away, or store it. The first does not cost anything more than trucking the surplus to a place where it can be dumped. Giving the excess away sounds more appealing, but if you give people something that they would have ordinarily purchased, you still are not solving the agriculture price problem. You are reducing demand even further by the amount you are giving to consumers. You can only give the good to people who are so poor that they would have gone without, and you are most likely to find such people in the developing world. It may sound somewhat cynical, but the government of the United States is a leading contributor of foodstuffs to victims of starvation and natural disaster in the developing world in part because the United States has an excess that it needs to unload.

Even though the most expensive option for the government is to store the excess, it has, at various times, stored milk and grains. Milk has been stored either as a powder or in the form of block American cheese. While both can be stored at near room temperature, a cool, dry environment is more conducive to long-term storage. Abandoned salt mines have served that purpose well.

Storing grain is somewhat easier. It does not require any processing, the way milk does, but it is still subject to rotting if it gets wet. However it is stored, this alternative is very expensive.

History of Price Supports

At various times, the United States has employed every imaginable way of supporting agriculture prices. At one point, it could have idled all grain farms in the United States for a year and still had enough in storage to process into food and feed livestock. In the middle of the 1982 recession, there was enough excess dairy that the government gave every poor person who showed up for it several pounds of cheese and several boxes of powdered milk. In the middle 1980s, thousands of dairy farmers around the country went into early retirement when the government paid top dollar for their herds.

As we said before, the support for agricultural price supports grew out of the depression of the 1930s. Agricultural prices fell so far so fast that farm bankruptcies skyrocketed. Politicians reacted by putting price floors on a number of agricultural products, most notably dairy. The Reagan administration tried to lessen the cost of agriculture subsidies by limiting supply, rather than serving as a buyer of last resort. First, it sold and gave away much of its excess stocks of grain and dairy products. Then, it offered farmers payments not to farm. The ultimate act in this regard was the policy to thin dairy herds. This policy led to nearly a 10 percent reduction in farmland under active cultivation. While we proceed down a path of restricting output rather than buying up excess, many thousands of farmers are still paid many billions of dollars not to farm many millions of acres.

The 1996 Freedom to Farm Act began yet another long phase of practices leading away from agricultural price supports. By 2002, the United States was supposed to exist without supports for milk or grain, but alas, support continued with the federal government spending $19 billion in 2009. Supports totaled $16.7 billion in 2018 and are projected to fall to $13.1 billion in 2024.

Kick It Up a Notch

Referring back to Figure 32.3, at equilibrium, (P^*,Q^*), consumers pay the producers OP^*CQ^*, but they value what they get at $OACQ^*$. This means they have a consumer surplus of P^*AC. Similarly, the producer benefits as well. The producer receives the OP^*CQ^* in revenue and variable costs are only $OHCQ^*$. This means that the producer surplus is HP^*C. The combined surpluses comprise the value to society of the exchange, *HAC*.

If the government sets a price floor of P_{floor}, consumers will want only Q_D. They will pay the $OP_{floor}BQ_D$ to producers. Consumers will value this at $OABQ_D$, and there will be consumer surplus of $P_{floor}AB$. It will cost producers $OHGQ_D$, so producer surplus will be $HP_{floor}BG$. The net benefit to society will be *HABG*. Therefore, the deadweight loss will be the difference between the net benefit to society with and without the price floor, *GBC*.

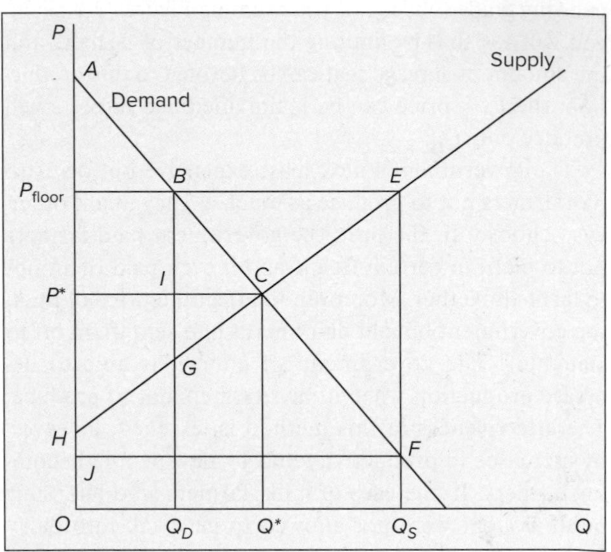

Summary

Now that you have plowed your way through this chapter, you understand why economists generally are not in favor of agricultural price supports. You know that though price variation is real, there are mechanisms that farmers can use to compensate for that without government intervention. You are now able to employ the supply and demand model and consumer and producer surplus analysis to demonstrate the inefficiency caused by price floors. Last, you understand how price floors have worked in practice.

Key Term

price floor

Quiz Yourself

1. Economists ____ farm price supports.
   a. support
   b. oppose
   c. are indifferent toward
2. The economic rationale for farm price supports is generally
   a. weak, but relies on price variability.
   b. weak, but relies on the unavailability of crop insurance.
   c. strong, and relies on the fact that prices are too high.
   d. strong, and relies on the importance of Iowa in presidential elections.
3. Price supports in the United States have
   a. always relied on the government paying farmers to set aside land.
   b. always relied on the government buying excess crops.
   c. always relied on forbidding production above certain levels.
   d. utilized a wide variety of means to raise prices and reduce output.
4. Farm price supports are typically for
   a. basic commodities like raw milk and grain.
   b. fruits and vegetables.
   c. refined products like flour.
   d. manufactured products like breakfast cereals.
5. A price support mechanism
   a. can only regulate supply.
   b. can only regulate demand.
   c. must involve government purchases.
   d. can involve government manipulation of the supply or demand of the good.
6. In Figure 32.3, maintaining P_{floor} as the target minimum price (rather than equilibrium) would
   a. raise consumer surplus more than it would decrease producer surplus.
   b. raise producer surplus more than it would decrease consumer surplus.
   c. involve creating deadweight loss.
   d. enhance the welfare of consumers and producers.
7. Looking at Figure 32.3, maintaining P_{floor} as the target minimum price (rather than equilibrium) by having the government purchase the amount farmers wished to produce would cost the government ____________ dollars.
   a. OP^*CQ^*
   b. Q_DBEQ_S
   c. $OP_{\text{floor}}BQ_D$
   d. BCG

Short Answer Questions

1. Given what you know about the relationship between corn and beef and corn and soybeans and corn and gasoline, an increase in the price of corn (due to a new insect that eats the roots out of corn) would have what impact on soybeans, beef, and gasoline?
2. If the price floor for corn is $3 per bushel and it is raised to $4 per bushel, what is the impact of that policy if the market price of corn is $6.50 per bushel?
3. During the 1980s many considered urban sprawl to be a serious problem for farmland. What would the mechanism be for "farm sprawl" reversing that?

Think about This

How much does it matter from the perspective of market form (monopoly, oligopoly, perfect competition) if there are 100, 1,000, or 1,000,000 farms producing raw grain?

Talk about This

Farm price supports are intended to help "the family farmer" but in reality often help multimillion-dollar farms. When Congress limited the size of the check that any particular farm could receive, farmers divided their farms into separate entities with different family members owning different farms so that they could continue to collect money. The "family farmer," defined as a simple farm with one house and the occupants of that house working the land, no longer produces a significant portion of the raw grain, cattle, or milk in the United States. Is the family farm more of a social myth than an actual entity?

For More Insight See

Gardner, Bruce L., "Changing Economic Perspectives on the Farm Problem," *Journal of Economic Literature* 30, no. 1 (March 1992), pp. 62–101.

Behind the Numbers

Bureau of Labor Statistics (BLS): www.bls.gov/ppi

- Farm product prices

CHAPTER THIRTY-THREE

Minimum Wage

Learning Objectives

After reading this chapter you should be able to:

LO1 Apply supply and demand to a labor market.

LO2 Describe the purpose of a minimum wage.

LO3 Conclude that the minimum wage must be higher than the equilibrium wage in order to be relevant.

LO4 Apply consumer and producer surplus to identify real-world winners and losers of a minimum-wage increase.

LO5 Apply the concept of elasticity to the question of whether a minimum-wage increase would increase unemployment.

LO6 Explain why some economists view the Earned Income Tax Credit as an alternative to a minimum wage.

Chapter Outline

The **minimum wage** is the lowest wage that may legally be paid for an hour's work, subject to government restrictions. In 1938, the first minimum wage was set at 25 cents per hour, and the amount has been increased periodically over the years. As of May 2019, the federal minimum wage was $7.25 per hour.

minimum wage
The lowest wage that may legally be paid for an hour's work.

living wage
A wage sufficient to keep a family out of poverty.

The minimum wage has traditionally been justified as a mechanism to ensure a **living wage,** that is, a wage sufficient to keep a family out of poverty. As you can see in Figure 33.1, the minimum wage was always sufficient to keep an individual above the poverty line. However, it has been (typically) insufficient to keep families above relevant poverty thresholds. Since 1985, the minimum wage has been insufficient to maintain a one-earner, minimum-wage family (constituting more than an individual) above the poverty line. For instance, to accomplish the feat of keeping a family of four above the poverty line, the minimum wage for a single full-time earner would have to be above $12 per hour.

Figure 33.2 indicates that although the minimum wage itself has been increased several times since 1938, its real value, that is, the value adjusted for inflation in 1999 dollars, rose for the first 30 years of its existence and has steadily fallen since. The inflation-adjusted minimum wage was at its lowest level just before an increase in 2007. Without some increase in the near future, it will fall below even that level. It reached its highest inflation-adjusted level in 1968 at $11.54 per hour (2018 dollars).[1] There has been no increase since the last step increase in 2009.

Over time, economists have tended to argue against the minimum wage. In this chapter, we explain those arguments along with the reasons why, until recently, most economists thought raising the minimum wage was wrongheaded. We also look at the arguments that suggest it may have been economists who were misguided.

[1]The poverty line used here is the official poverty line, with which there are many problems. Review the chapter "Poverty and Welfare" to understand this issue.

FIGURE 33.1 The ratio of the earnings of a full-time minimum-wage worker to the poverty line for various family sizes.

Sources: U.S. Census Bureau. www.census.gov/data/tables/time-series/demo/income-poverty/historical-poverty-thresholds.html; United States Department of Labor. www.dol.gov/dol/topic/wages/minimumwage.htm.

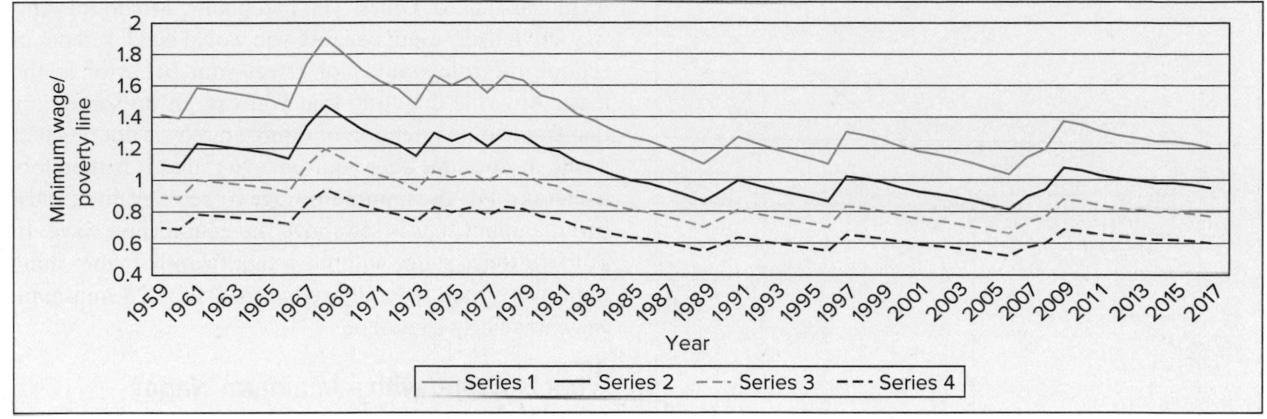

FIGURE 33.2 The nominal and real minimum wage, 1938–2018, in 2018 dollars.

Source: United States Department of Labor. https://www.dol.gov/whd/minwage/chart.htm.

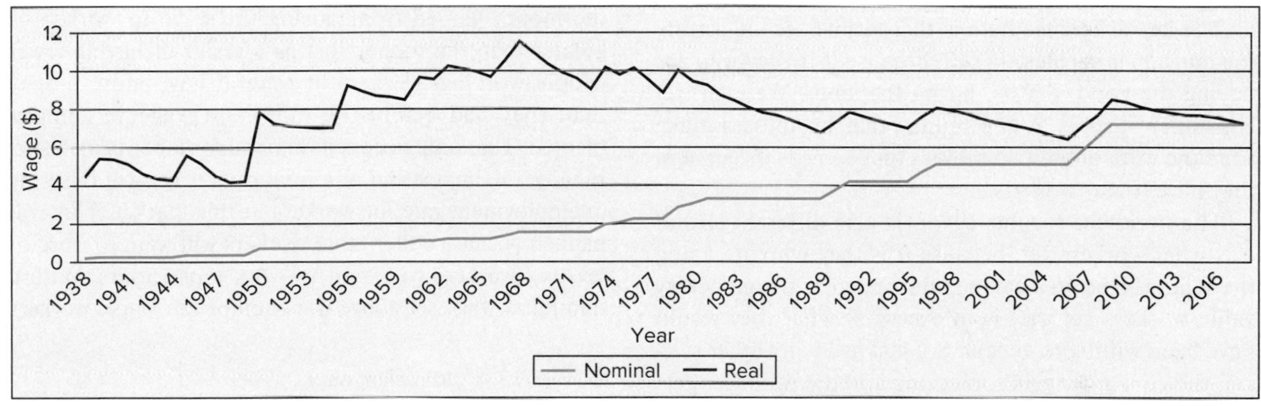

Traditional Economic Analysis of a Minimum Wage

Labor Markets and Consumer and Producer Surplus

Most economists have had few good things to say about the idea of establishing a minimum wage, and they have based that opinion on a traditional supply and demand analysis of the issue. Figure 33.3 represents a market for low-skill, minimum-wage labor. The good being sold in this market is labor, and the price at which it is sold is the wage. The supply is composed of workers who will want to work more at higher pay, implying an upward-sloping supply curve; demand is composed of bosses seeking to hire that labor. The employers are assumed to want fewer laborers at higher wages, implying a downward-sloping demand curve. Without a law that sets its actual dollar amount, the wage would be set in this market at the point where the supply and demand curves meet. At this equilibrium, there would be no shortage and no surplus. The wage would be W^* and there would be L^* labor. The market clearing equilibrium is a wage at which no one who wants a job at that wage is without one, and no employers who want workers at that wage are unable to get them.

In this situation, workers would be paid a total of OW^*CL^* dollars. When we addressed the notion of consumer and producer surplus in Chapter 3, we stated that the consumer surplus is the area under the demand curve but above the price line, while the producer surplus is the area under the price line and above the supply curve. Of course, in this case, the price is the wage.

FIGURE 33.3 Labor market.

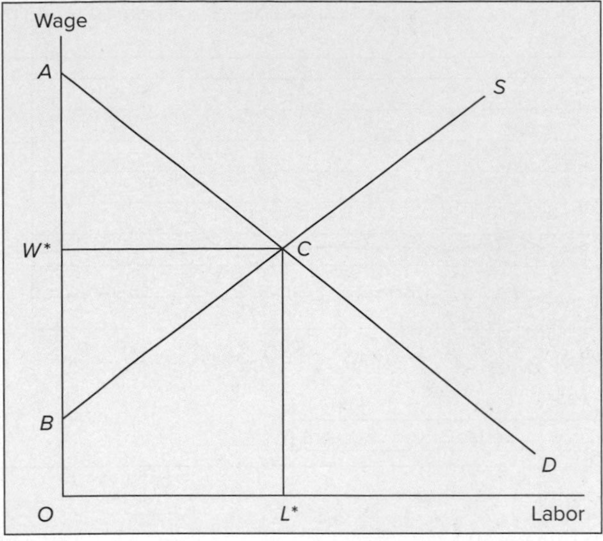

The key difference here is that businesses are getting the consumer surplus, W^*AC, because it is they who are buying the good, that is, hiring the labor. We interpret consumer surplus as the money that businesses make from the work of their employees that exceeds the amount they have to pay workers.

The producer surplus BW^*C is also different in that it is what workers get, because it is they who are doing the selling. This area can be interpreted as the monetary value workers get that is in excess of what they would have been willing to accept. So, just as in any other market, the consumer gets something and the producer gets something.

A Relevant versus an Irrelevant Minimum Wage

If a minimum wage is set below W^*, would businesses pay the minimum wage rather than the higher W^*? Surprisingly, the answer is no, they would not: To get workers in the numbers that are most profitable to the business, employers have to pay the higher W^*. They would rather pay more than the minimum because, even though their labor costs then rise at a higher rate, the output of the extra workers will generate enough additional revenue to pay the workers and produce an increased profit. In addition, it is in their best interests to pay W^*, because otherwise their competitors will outbid them for labor. Thus, any minimum wage set below W^* is irrelevant, because firms make more profit offering W^* rather than a lesser amount.

If you are not yet convinced that setting a minimum wage may be irrelevant, consider what would happen if your professors told you that you would fail if you showed up in class naked. Unless you had planned to do this anyway, an unlikely event because you would be kicked out of school, the rule would not affect your behavior in the least. Any rule dictating that you cannot do something that you had no intention of doing anyway is not much of a rule. It does not alter your behavior, and it is therefore irrelevant. For the minimum wage to be relevant, it must be an amount that is set above the equilibrium wage. In 2019, in those states without a significantly higher minimum wage than federally required, the $7.25 minimum wage was likely irrelevant.

What Is Wrong with a Minimum Wage?

As seen in Figure 33.4, a minimum wage that has been set above the equilibrium wage has several effects. First, it raises the wage from W^* to W_{min}. Second, it reduces the amount of labor sold from L^* to L_{min}. Third, as long as the money gained from raising the wage to workers is greater than the money lost as a result of having fewer people working, workers in general have more money than they had before the minimum wage was implemented. That only occurs if demand for labor is inelastic. Finally, the imposition of a minimum wage will raise the unemployment rate for workers in this market. This will happen because either more workers will want to work or existing workers will want to work more hours. With a minimum wage set above the equilibrium wage, workers

FIGURE 33.4 Minimum wage.

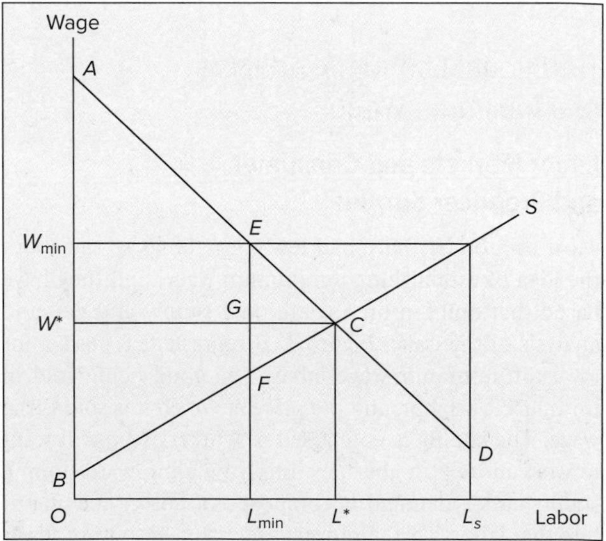

CITIES, STATES, AND $15 PER HOUR

Because the federal minimum wage remained constant for nearly a decade, states and cities began to take the initiative to impose a higher minimum wage within their jurisdictions. As of May 2019, the 29 states and several cities have minimum-wage laws that are higher than the federally mandated minimum wage. Moreover, in an effort to prevent the inflationary erosion of their state minimum wage, 16 states and the District of Columbia index their minimum wage to some measure of inflation.

Throughout 2016–2018, several cities and five states adopted $15 minimum-wage laws. Most of those laws will phase in that higher rate over a few years. Many economists, even those for whom increases in the minimum wage are considered wise, are concerned. That concern is centered on the observation that an increase to $15 per hour is not, what they call, "modest." When increases in the minimum wage are modest compared to the existing wage, there is far less motivation for business owners to make expensive adjustments to their production processes. However, when the increases are very large and when those increases come with built-in adjustments for future inflation, the motivation is not only high but sustained.

The owner of a prototypical fast-food outlet facing an immodest increase in the minimum wage must respond. That is because, as the National Restaurant Association reports, the profit margin at a typical restaurant is frequently smaller than the projected increased wage bill. It is not a matter of reduced profits to business owners going instead to their workers; it is a matter of those businesses closing. As a result, owners must increase prices or reduce labor. To reduce labor, they must find labor-reducing capital substitutions. An example of this type of substitution from the past is the moving of soft drink dispensing to the consumer side of the counter. Presently, McDonald's, Taco Bell, Panera, and others are moving to automated ordering kiosks. Mobile ordering apps significantly decrease order-taking expenses as well as providing convenience to consumers. It is not entirely out of the realm of possibilities that Domino's and Papa John's will be among the first large-scale buyers of driverless cars. Very high minimum wages will surely produce job-saving innovations that will just as surely undercut the purpose of those increased wages.

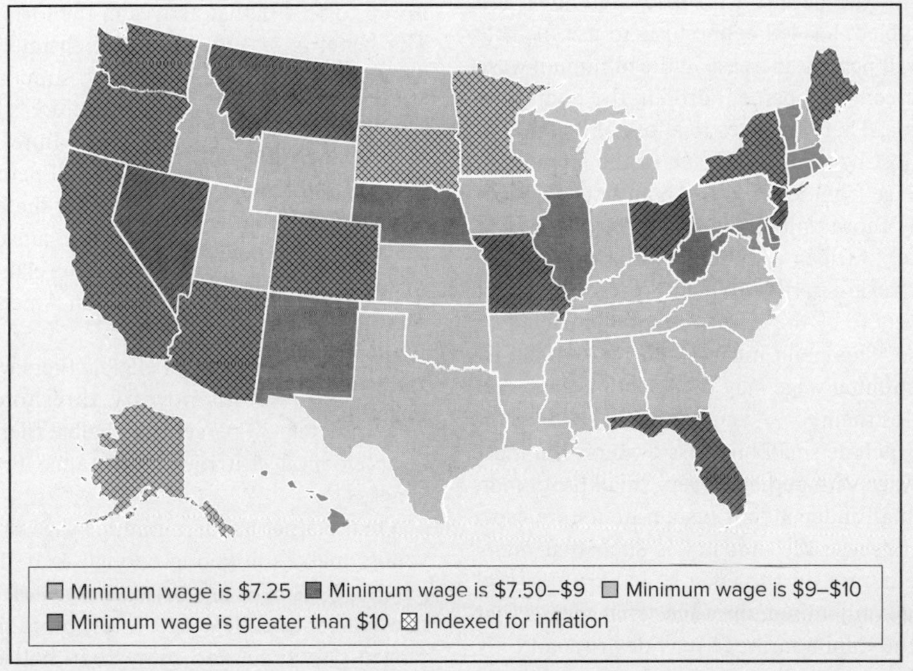

want to provide L_s labor, whereas they used to want to work only L^*. Further complicating this is that employers now want to hire labor only up to L_{min} rather than the L^* they had wanted previously.

In the end, the consumer surplus shrinks to $W_{min}AE$ and producer surplus grows. The sum of the consumer and producer surpluses is less than it was without the minimum wage, by the triangle *FEC*.

Under the minimum wage, there are winners and losers. The winners are those workers who get a wage increase and are still able to continue working as much as they want. The losers are men and women who used to be working and are now unemployed ($L^* - L_{min}$). The important part of this analysis is that what is gained by workers is less than what employers lose. We are thus confronted with what economists label deadweight loss, the net loss to society by the area *FEC*. To see this graphically, go to "Kick It Up a Notch" located at the end of the chapter.

Real-World Implications of the Minimum Wage

Though rather elegant as a mechanism to analyze the impacts of a minimum wage, consumer and producer surplus analysis does not put it in terms easy for the average person to understand. The winners are the more than 4 million people who work for the minimum wage and get a pay increase because they keep their jobs.

The losers are the people who lose their jobs. Research on the subject has led economists to use the rule of thumb that a 10 percent increase in the minimum wage results in a 1 percent to 3 percent drop in the number of jobs held by teens. That translates to a loss of 360,000 to 1,050,000 jobs lost by teens as a result of the increase in the minimum wage from $5.15 to $7.25 an hour.[2] Economists who study those unlucky teens find that they are disproportionately African American, Hispanic, or uneducated. Without regard to race, those who are the poorest are the most likely to be the ones adversely impacted by such an increase. This point must not be missed. An increase in the minimum wage may very well hurt the poor more than it helps them.

Other losers include small business owners who must pay the higher wage with perhaps a very small profit margin to do so. Small independent restaurateurs are especially hard hit because the industry is such that many new entrepreneurs are on the edge of bankruptcy and can afford to pay only minimum wage. That means that an increase in the minimum wage may destroy not only the jobs these entrepreneurs are creating but also the entrepreneurs themselves.

[2]This assumes that at $5.15, the minimum wage was above equilibrium. The evidence is that the equilibrium wage was higher than $5.15 for much of 2004 and beyond, making $5.15 an irrelevant minimum wage.

Finally, the losers include anyone who buys goods or services produced by minimum-wage workers, because part of the increase is passed on to them in the form of higher prices.

Alternatives to the Minimum Wage

It is for all of these reasons and more that until recently most economists could not endorse increases in the minimum wage. Those who took the position that the minimum wage was an inappropriate cure for the problems of poorly paid workers highlighted the fact that most workers who earned minimum wage were under 24. Nearly one-third of these people were under 19 and therefore very unlikely to be supporting a family. Combine this with the fact that many of those who earn the minimum wage and are over age 24 are spouses who work only to supplement the income of the family's primary income producer and are nowhere near poverty.

In the eyes of many economists, a better alternative is the Earned Income Tax Credit (EITC). Low-income, working families with three or more children are eligible for up to $6,431 that arrives in the form of a tax refund. The benefits of EITC are concentrated on the people who actually need the money to support their families. According to the Brookings Institution's MetroTax model (developed using the U.S. Census Bureau's 2015 American Community Survey), nearly 20 percent of tax filers in the United States were eligible for the EITC. Of course, to receive the credit, the family unit must file a tax return claiming it. If all eligible family units claimed the credit, it would affect more than 72 million Americans (including 31 million children).

The median income of eligible filers was $14,479—well below any relevant poverty threshold. In addition, approximately 33 percent of eligible filers were receiving Supplemental Nutrition Assistance Program (SNAP) benefits.

On the other hand, minimum-wage workers tend to be young, many still young enough to be living with their parents (one-fifth are between ages of 16 and 19) and one-quarter of college age. Many more than half are employed part time, and more than half of those people work less than 24 hours per week.

The Tax Policy Center estimates that the EITC alone lifts 8 million Americans above their poverty threshold. This contrasts dramatically with the minimum wage, where upward of 80 percent of the benefits accrue to households not in poverty.

The EITC, while born in the 1970s, saw great increases starting during the administration of President Ronald Reagan. It was during this administration that the minimum wage saw a long period of real decline in its value. It was President Reagan's view that the minimum wage was a poor mechanism to help the poor and that the EITC could help working poor families without hurting businesses. While President Clinton's first budget increased taxes for many, it also greatly increased the EITC. Moreover, though he pushed through an increase in the minimum wage as well, the increased level of the EITC has had a greater effect on the working poor.

Rebuttals to the Traditional Analysis

In contrast to the preceding section, important points of rebuttal to the traditional analysis have gained respectability in recent years among economists. They focus on three main arguments. Macroeconomic argument suggests, first, that the effect of a decrease in income by business owners is somewhat offset by the effect of an increase in income by the lower-income people. Low-income people tend to have much lower rates of saving than high-income people. That means that low-income people spend more of their income than do high-income people. The work effort argument is that the good in question, labor, is not as definable as most other goods and that with better pay, workers can be induced to work harder. If they do, the increase in the wage becomes less of a burden on employers. The elasticity argument is that the demand for labor may be so inelastic that the traditional analysis needs to reflect this fact. If it does, the negative aspects of the minimum wage will be small.

The Macroeconomics Argument

The first argument in rebuttal to the traditional analysis relies on an aspect of macroeconomics that suggests that if you track all of the times a particular amount of money is spent, you can figure the total impact of new spending. Or, as is appropriate in this case, you can examine the net effect of monies being spent by different people. If, for instance, business owners save most of their profit rather than spend or invest it, then something less than the entire profit of the business works its way through the economy in the form of additional spending. On the other hand, if business owners relinquish more of that profit to workers because of the imposition of a higher minimum wage, then almost all of that money will be spent. Men and women who are paid the minimum wage tend to save very little, and they often spend nearly all of their additional income. Because money is spent rather than saved, total consumption in the economy rises. From a macroeconomic standpoint, any negative effects of a minimum-wage increase range from being offset, to being nonexistent, to being positive.

Suppose, for example, that the result of an increase in the minimum wage is to increase the incomes for workers by $75, while creating a $100 loss in profit to businesses. Remember that it is not simply a direct transfer; workers' gains are offset by losses to business that are greater. The $25 difference, the deadweight loss, is the amount of damage to GDP. This gap can be overcome if the effect of low-skill workers' spending is greater than the effect of bosses spending it. If low-skill workers spend all of their increased income, and bosses spend or invest only 80 percent of theirs, the net effect of raising the minimum wage is that GDP shrinks by $5 rather than by $25. This is because 80 percent of $100 is only $5 more than 100 percent of $75. This is, of course, predicated on the assumption that a higher minimum wage has the net effect of increasing the income of minimum-wage workers.

The Work Effort Argument

The second argument is probably correct in assuming that people adjust the effort they put in at work depending on how happy they are with their employer. This means that the graphs in Figures 33.3 and 33.4 are not as stable as we previously thought them to be. The good "labor" is not as fixed as most other goods for which we use this supply and demand model. People can work hard or slack off, and there is not a great deal that an employer can do to force slackers to work harder. If higher pay translates into workers who are happier and perform more work per hour, it may be the case that some if not all of the impact of forcing wages to rise will be mitigated. In this way, the minimum-wage increase may pay for itself. On the other hand, if it did pay for itself, the implication would be that employers were either ignorant of this fact or are not maximizing profit. Neither of these assumptions sits well with most economists. It is more plausible that such an increase merely lessens the negative impact.

FIGURE 33.5 The minimum wage in the short run.

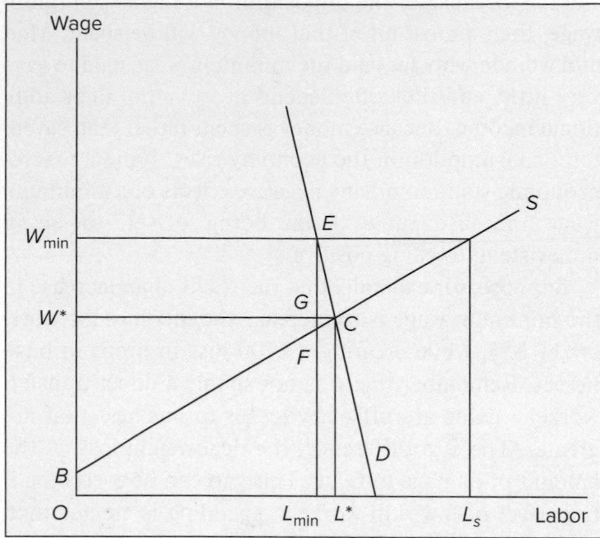

The Elasticity Argument

The last argument used to rebut traditional analysis simply tweaks the traditional analysis to suggest that the negative impact of an increase in the minimum wage is very small. Any increase can thus be interpreted as simply a transfer of money from business owners to workers. Comparing Figure 33.5 to Figure 33.4, you will find that the only real difference is that the demand curve is steeper, that is, more inelastic, in Figure 33.5. The net amount that workers gain is very great, and the resulting unemployment of those who had jobs before, $L^* - L_{min}$, is very low. As we said when we discussed elasticity in Chapter 3, there are four things that will influence elasticity. Two of them are the number of close substitutes and time to invent them.

Given that in the short run there are very few substitutes for having workers on the job, this rebuttal seems, of the three mentioned, the most persuasive to traditional economists. Most economists still believe that the existence of a minimum wage will reduce employment in the long run. They maintain that the only reason the gain to workers is great and the net loss to society is small is that this is an analysis that works only in the short run.

They argue that in the long run, business owners will search until they find substitutes for labor such as easier-to-use machines and self-serve devices. If you look at the fast-food industry and the equipment that it uses, you will find that the companies involved are always looking for new ways to reduce the need for employees, and they have had great success in their endeavors. Putting the drink machines and self-ordering kiosks in the lobby and using chain ovens or broilers that cook food for exactly the correct amount of time without needing employee monitoring are just a couple of examples of how employers of minimum-wage workers have substituted capital for labor.

Where Are Economists Now?

If the more recent nontraditional analysis is correct, it is probably because in the short run there is not much deadweight loss to be overcome. The combined impact of the macroeconomic effect and the work effort effect is therefore enough to completely eliminate the problem. The data on whether recent minimum-wage increases have had a net negative impact on unemployment for the 1990 and 1996 increases are mixed. Two influential economists, David Card and Andrew Krueger, published a study of the minimum wage utilizing data on fast-food employment. They surveyed establishments in two neighboring states in a period where one increased its minimum wage and another did not. They found that the increase did not negatively impact, and perhaps positively impacted, employment in the state that raised its minimum wage.

Since this study ran against the conventional wisdom of labor economists, many were quick to try to duplicate their results. The attempts to replicate the work of Card and Krueger turned up serious data and methodology problems. As a result of the newer work casting doubt on the Card and Krueger conclusion, most labor economists have not moved much from their earlier assessment. In particular, many still use the teen employment rule of thumb mentioned earlier but concede that a 10 percent increase in the minimum wage translates to a 1 percent or 3 percent decrease in teen employment. In particular, according to Jeffrey Clemens, it is young workers without a high school degree, those most likely to be working for a minimum wage, who seem to have been hit by the greatest reduction in employment opportunities. In any event, economists have expended considerable time rethinking an issue that they thought they had settled a long time ago.

Kick It Up a Notch

Referring back to Figure 33.4, we can firmly establish the winners and losers and more rigorously defend the claim that the gain to workers from a minimum wage is less than the loss to firms and unemployed workers. Remember that the benefit to workers from an increase in the minimum wage is the increase in their producer surplus. Without a minimum wage, the producer surplus is BW^*C, while with the minimum wage it is $BW_{min}EF$. The consumer surplus is the benefit to firms hiring the labor. They go from having a consumer surplus of W^*AC without the minimum wage to a consumer surplus of $W_{min}AE$ with it. The gain to workers is $W^*W_{min}EG - GFC$, while the loss to firms is $W^*W_{min}EG + GEC$. The net effect is the gain to workers minus the loss to firms, which is $-FEC$. Because the net effect is negative, economists refer to this as the deadweight loss.

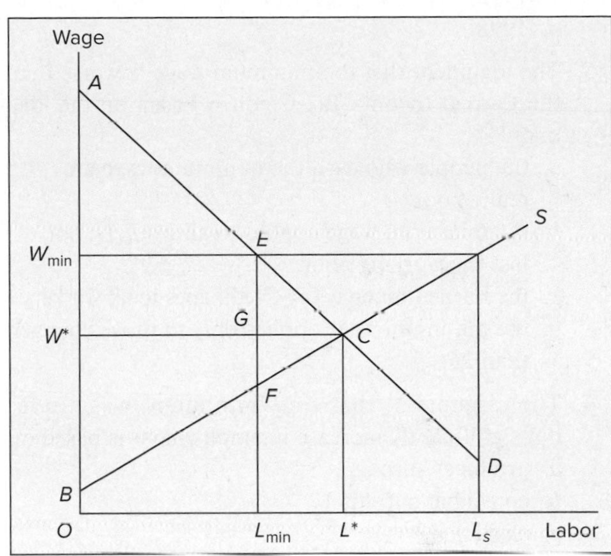

Summary

After this exploration of the minimum wage, you understand why it exists and what its implications are for our supply and demand model for labor. You know how to use consumer and producer surplus techniques to identify the winners and losers of any minimum-wage increase and then apply real-world observations. You understand that the Earned Income Tax Credit is an alternative to it. Finally, you understand that some economists favor increasing the minimum wage and base their arguments in the observations that labor demand is inelastic, low-income people are more likely to spend their income, and workers may be inclined to work harder when paid more.

Key Terms

living wage

minimum wage

Quiz Yourself

1. Between 1998 and 2007, the real minimum wage
   a. rose rapidly.
   b. rose slowly.
   c. remained constant.
   d. fell rapidly.
2. In order for the minimum wage to reach its 1968 high in real terms (1999 dollars), it would have to rise to slightly more than _________ per hour.
   a. $8
   b. $9
   c. $10
   d. $12
3. In order for a minimum wage to be relevant, it must be ______ the equilibrium wage.
   a. above
   b. below
   c. equal to

4. The last time the minimum wage alone was sufficient to keep a family of three above the poverty line was
   a. 1979.
   b. 1985.
   c. 1990.
   d. 1998.

5. The argument that the minimum wage is worse than the Earned Income Tax Credit is based on the idea that
   a. the people who earn the minimum wage are really poor.
   b. the minimum wage applies to all workers, not just the working poor.
   c. the Earned Income Tax Credit goes to all workers.
   d. the minimum wage applies only to those younger than 25.

6. The argument that the minimum wage does not significantly increase unemployment is based on
   a. producer surplus.
   b. consumer surplus.
   c. elasticity.
   d. aggregate demand.

7. The argument that the minimum wage hurts society more than it helps is based on __________________ analysis.
   a. consumer and producer surplus
   b. production possibilities
   c. aggregate supply–aggregate demand
   d. marginal

8. The argument that employers would actually not lose money if the minimum wage were raised is based on
   a. the idea that workers would spend the extra money buying goods from their employer.
   b. the idea that workers would work overtime without having to be paid.
   c. the idea that workers would be more productive if they felt they were adequately compensated.
   d. the elasticity of demand for labor.

Short Answer Questions

1. Who is most likely to benefit from an increase in the minimum wage?

2. Who is most likely to lose from an increase in the minimum wage? Who of those might have thought an increase was in their best interests?

3. Suppose you knew that there was going to be 20 percent inflation between now and five years from now, and suppose you knew that the minimum wage was only enough to get a family of three to 80 percent of the poverty line. How much would you have to raise the minimum wage over that period in order to make the minimum wage earn enough to be at that poverty line?

Think about This

Several states have set the minimum wage in their states higher than the federal minimum wage. If doing so places them at a competitive disadvantage for new business this might be counterproductive. On the other hand, the minimum wage is typically relevant only in low-paid service jobs. Who makes the minimum wage in your community? Would your community be better off with a higher minimum wage?

Talk about This

One of the principal opponents to minimum-wage increases is the umbrella organization for small business. Many states with higher minimum wages than the federal level exempt businesses with few employees. Should small businesses be exempt from minimum-wage laws?

For More Insight See

Brown, Charles, "Minimum Wages Laws: Are They Overrated?" *Journal of Economic Perspectives* 2, no. 3 (Summer 1988), pp. 133–146.

Brown, Charles, Curtis Gilroy, and Andrew Kohen, "The Effect of the Minimum Wage on Employment and Unemployment," *Journal of Economic Literature* 20, no. 2 (June 1982), pp. 487–528.

Card, David, and Alan Krueger, *Myth and Measurement: The New Economics of the Minimum Wage* (Princeton, NJ: Princeton University Press, 1995).

Behind the Numbers

Department of Labor: www.dol.gov/dol/topic/wages/minimumwage.htm

- Historic minimum wage levels

Department of Labor: www.dol.gov/whd/minwage/mw-consolidated.htm

- State and local minimum wage laws

U.S. Census Bureau: www.census.gov/data/tables/time-series/demo/income-poverty/historical-poverty-thresholds.html

- Poverty thresholds

Internal Revenue Service: www.irs.gov

- EITC eligibility standards and amounts

Adams, Scott, and David Neumark, "A Decade of Living Wages: What Have We Learned?" Public Policy Institute of California: www.ppic.org/main/publication.asp?i=620.

CHAPTER THIRTY-FOUR

Ticket Brokers and Ticket Scalping

Learning Objectives

After reading this chapter you should be able to:

- LO1 Define ticket scalping and describe why it exists.
- LO2 Identify the appropriate market form to analyze ticket sales to an event.
- LO3 Contrast the typical marginal cost curve with the one appropriate for ticket sales.
- LO4 Enumerate the reasons why promoters may rationally charge less for an event than they could, and conclude that the result of this is a shortage of tickets.
- LO5 Describe why the conditions of a shortage typically create a scalping market.
- LO6 Summarize why economists generally value the scalping market, see very little reason to make laws regulating it, and see very little functional distinction between the legal and illegal forms of scalping that exist across the country.

Chapter Outline

If you want to see a concert, game, race, or any other event that is sold out, you probably know that you can always get a ticket–for a price. Some tickets command prices that are many times their face value. History is filled with examples. In the 1990s, scalpers were getting more than $1,000 for a ticket to see Michael Jordan's last game as a Chicago Bull. In 2017, Adele tickets were selling for several times that. Hamilton tickets have sold for more than their face value in many cities for many years. Some events are once in a lifetime, whereas other reoccurring events like the Super Bowl and the World Series are events that are important enough to some people that they are willing to pay more than face value for a ticket.

While in many cities it is illegal to sell a ticket for more than face value, in every major city there is a way of getting such tickets when they are the only ones available. Economists are almost always against laws that prevent people from selling things they possess. They reason that if one person would rather have $500 than a ticket to a game and another person would rather have a ticket to a game than $500, then both parties benefit from the exchange.

In this chapter, we will define ticket scalping and offer an economic explanation for it. We begin that explanation by using our monopoly pricing model from Chapter 5 to understand the promoter's ticket-pricing scheme. We show that for scalping to exist, promoters must underprice their tickets, and we consider why they do this. We use our supply and demand model and the notions of consumer and producer surplus to see how scalping helps consumers and scalpers alike. We talk about the mechanism by which scalpers become "legit" by calling themselves "brokers" or by offering packages that combine the tickets with other amenities.

Defining Brokering and Scalping

Brokering tickets is the act of buying tickets and selling them at a price higher than face value when such a transaction is legal. **Scalping** tickets is the act of buying tickets and selling them at a price higher than face value when such a transaction is illegal. Thus, the practice is considered scalping only when it is done illegally. Regardless of semantic differences, for many fans and performers, scalpers and brokers are the worst form of predator; they obtain large blocks of tickets before other people get them and then they sell the tickets at prices that earn them a profit. They do not produce anything. Those who engage in scalping view themselves as simply providing a service from which they make a living. To others, they are simply parasites.

brokering
The act of buying a ticket and legally selling it at a price higher than its face value.

scalping
The act of buying a ticket and illegally selling it at a price higher than its face value.

For economists, scalpers perform a function that "fixes" pricing that promoters set improperly. As we will see, scalping can exist profitably only when enough fans are willing to pay more for tickets than the face value of the ticket and there are more buyers willing to pay face value than there are seats.

This does not necessarily mean the event sells out. If some seats are really good and others are really terrible, then the good ones, at courtside, might be scalped, while those in "nosebleed territory" might remain unsold. However, there cannot be unsold seats right next to seats for which scalpers wish to charge more than face value. When traditional ticket outlets sell decent seats at face value, these will be sold out before scalpers can sell any. Modern scalping operations use computer programs to buy as many tickets as possible instead of relying on people to stand in line. Ticketmaster has attempted to use technology to end this practice. It has been largely unsuccessful.

An Economic Model of Ticket Sales

The question we can pose at this point is, "Why would a promoter charge less for a ticket than it is worth?" To answer the question, we need to consider what determines the price a promoter should charge. To model that, we need to return to Chapter 5 to see which market model is more appropriate for ticket sales, perfect competition or monopoly. Because there is ultimately only one seller of the tickets, the promoter, the monopoly model is clearly more appropriate than the perfect competition model, in which there are many sellers.

FIGURE 34.1 Marginal cost.

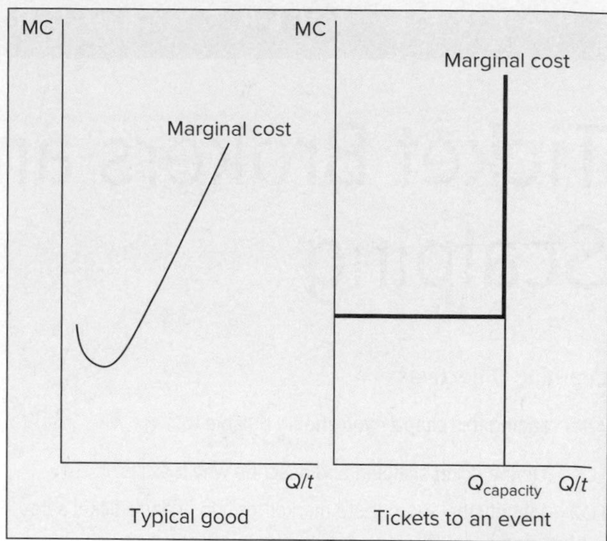

Marginal Cost

To complicate things, remember the shape of the marginal cost curve that was introduced in Chapter 4. It is a check-shaped curve, as seen in the left panel of Figure 34.1. For ticket sales to a sporting event or a concert, marginal cost looks a little different. The right-hand side of Figure 34.1 shows that up to the capacity of the stadium, the marginal cost is more likely to be constant. The costs of printing and selling tickets and cleaning up after each additional fan remain relatively constant. These extra costs are likely to be the same for the thousandth fan as the hundred-thousandth fan. At capacity, however, the extra cost of selling to another person grows astronomically, as new construction would have to occur to add more seats.

The Promoter as Monopolist

When promoters are attempting to maximize profits and trying to determine what price to charge for events, they must gauge what the demand will be for the event. Once they have done that, they can look at this problem as any other monopolist would. Recall that we have always assumed that firms seek to maximize profit. Though revenue would be maximized where marginal revenue cuts the horizontal axis, this is not where the

FIGURE 34.2 The profit-maximizing promoter's choice of price and ticket sales.

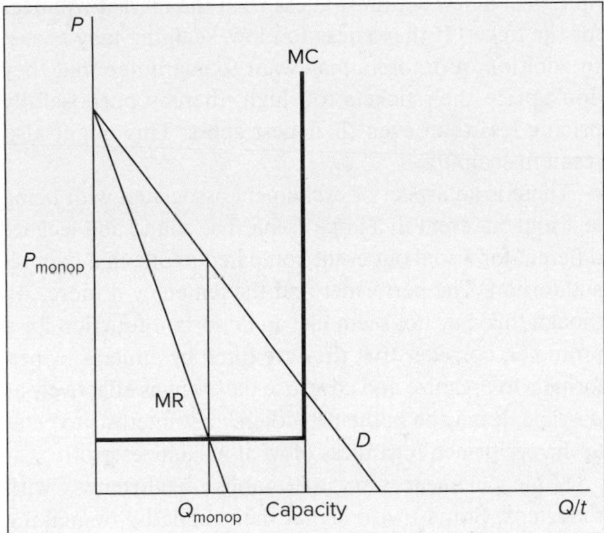

FIGURE 34.3 The perfect arena.

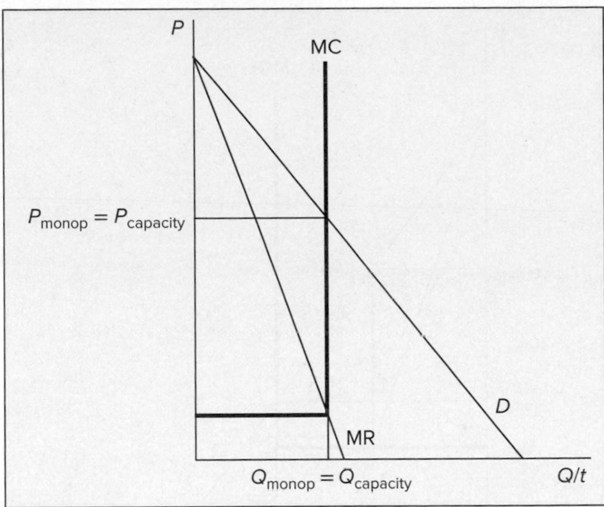

profit-maximizing promoters operate. As is depicted in Figure 34.2, they project the number of sales and set the price so that MR = MC. This means that they would sell Q_{monop} tickets for P_{monop} each.

An interesting aspect of this approach is that it may make sense for promoters to see that the arena is only partially filled. Promoters refrain from selling additional tickets when they would have to lower the price too far in order to sell out the facility. You should not be surprised by this conclusion, especially if you are at a school that does not have a popular athletic program. Consider a school whose men's basketball team draws between 4,000 and 6,000 fans per game, while the women's team draws fewer than 1,000 per game. If the athletic department were to price tickets to sell out the arena, tickets would be nearly free for the men's games and the department would have to pay people to attend the women's games. That is not a comment on the quality of women's basketball, but rather on the sociology of spectator sports. Clearly, it makes sense for universities like this to charge more for the men's games and to charge something (usually less) for the women's games. The university is still maximizing profit, even if there is only one sellout per decade.

The Perfect Arena

To a promoter, the size of the facility is significant. In a promoter's eyes, the perfect facility would be represented by the one depicted in Figure 34.3, where the capacity is equal to the number of seats that the promoter wants to sell. That is, the facility with perfect capacity is the one where marginal cost intersects marginal revenue at the quantity that is exactly equal to the capacity of the facility. Of course, promoters cannot always find the perfect facility. Most medium and small cities have only one or two places to hold an event like a concert, and even in other places, the perfect arena or concert hall may not be available.

In a big city with many venues of many different sizes, a promoter should seek the facility whose size ensures that the marginal cost will cross marginal revenue at the capacity. On the assumption that facilities that are unnecessarily large cost the promoter more to rent, booking this "perfect" facility maximizes profit.

In each case mentioned so far, there is no market for scalpers because the face value of the ticket is the price at which it is sold. Scalping makes sense only if the market price of the ticket is greater than the face value. The only way for that to happen is if the promoter charges less than the profit-maximizing amount (i.e., sell more than where marginal revenue = marginal cost). This is seen in Figure 34.4, where the ticket is priced at or below the price that would sell out the facility rather than the price that would maximize profits for the promoter. In a city like Chicago, Los Angeles, or New York, there are multiple venues. A wise promoter can pick the site where $Q_{monop} = Q_{capacity}$. In a small city, such as Dubuque, Terre Haute, or Traverse City, there may be only one or two venues for an event. In that case, the promoter has to pick among the imperfect choices.

FIGURE 34.4 Capacity versus profit-maximizing prices.

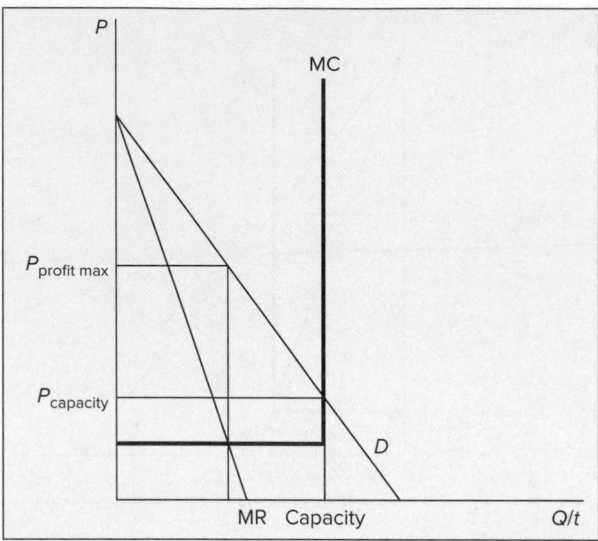

Why Promoters Charge Less Than They Could

We should acknowledge that promoters and performers might have different motivations. Promoters want to maximize profits. Performers want what they want. However, promoters usually do what the performers want them to do. So, why might promoters sell out a facility rather than maximize profits? First, they may not have good information on the price they ought to charge. This uncertainty might motivate them to err on the safe side and charge a lower price. Second, there may be some "excitement" factor to a full stadium that appeals to the performers that is worth the loss of profit. Third, the performers may want a reputation of charging a "fair price" for their events and are willing to forgo maximum profit to further that reputation. Fourth, the performers may want some mechanism other than price to separate the "real fans" from those who go to events simply because they have money. Fifth, ancillary sales of shirts and other memorabilia are important sources of revenue for performers and promoters alike. It may be that the revenue gained by these sales exceeds the lost revenue associated with low ticket prices. Viewed that way, low ticket prices may lead to increasing audience size and may therefore maximize profit after all. Last, it may be in the long-run best interest of the performers to charge a low price for tickets so that the largest possible audience can provide word-of-mouth advertising for them and generate interest for their talent.

Sometimes promoters do not know precisely what price to charge for an event. More often than not, promoters of a new act must guess what the market will bear for the ticket. If they guess too low, scalping may ensue. In addition, promoters may want to guarantee that they don't price their tickets too high, thereby purposefully pricing less than even their best guess. This might also result in scalping.

There is an aspect of excitement associated with being at a sold-out event in a large arena. The sound and feel are different for a sold-out event compared to one in a half-full auditorium. The performer and the fan enjoy it more. Although this may not seem like an important function for a promoter, consider that they are hired by athletes or performers to organize and advertise the event as effectively as possible. It may be in the promoters' best interests to cater to the performer, regardless of what maximizes profit.

Some performers try to establish a closeness with their fans. Some try to signal their empathy by making sure ticket prices are low enough that "ordinary" fans can afford to go. This means that performers and promoters are willing to accept less money for the good feeling that charging "fair" prices gives them.

In your parent's day (prior to Ticketmaster), fans would camp out for tickets. Performers loved the image of fans camping out to hear them perform. In that circumstance, performers may have preferred fans who were willing to camp out for tickets more than those simply willing to pay a lot of money. The people who were willing to camp out to get front-row seats were far more likely to convey enthusiasm for performers than those with deep pockets.

When you go to a concert, you often spend as much on parking, concessions, shirts, and other promotional items as you do on the ticket. If promoters charge too much, they forgo that important other revenue as well. In the big picture, low ticket prices may be profit maximizing after all.

Promoters of new bands may decide that it is in their long-run interest to keep ticket prices low so that the band is seen by as many people as possible. By setting low ticket prices early in a performer's career, they may be more likely to turn a one-hit wonder into a star.

For any one of the reasons in this section, promoters may choose to sell their tickets at prices below their monopoly market value and perhaps even below the price that would guarantee a sellout. In any event, a price below what they see as the free market value will cause scalpers to buy tickets at the lower price in order to sell them at a higher price.

An Economic Model of Scalping

A market characterized by ticket scalping will have a typical demand curve. It will reflect the demand by those who do not get tickets through the box office. For many events, such as any home game played by the Green Bay Packers, tickets only go to those who subscribe or have had tickets for many, many years. This "right of first refusal" on tickets is so valuable that married couples' divorce agreements have been held up over this right. If you want to go to a single Packers game, you likely have to resort to the scalpers' market.

The demand curve for these tickets is downward sloping just as it is for any other good. If the event is a "must see," then you expect a demand curve farther to the right or perhaps more inelastic, or steeper, because tickets for a "once-in-a-lifetime event" have fewer substitutes than tickets for events that will be repeated. The elasticity of demand will be expected to be less.

The supply curve for this market is upward sloping (and not vertical), not because the number of tickets is not limited but because in order to get tickets away from those who have them, you have to give up more and more to persuade more and more rabid fans to give up their tickets. Figure 34.5 reflects the market for scalped tickets.

If the price is required to stay at the face value of the ticket, then there will be fewer tickets than potential buyers. To an economist, this is the very definition of a shortage. Note that the supply curve may start below $P_{\text{face value}}$ or above it. In Figure 34.5, the supply curve starts below the face value. To understand why, consider that there are people who have tickets for an event who are willing to sell them for less than they paid because they do not want to go. Why would you buy a ticket for an event you did not want to attend? Suppose you had season tickets to the Los Angeles Lakers and a ticket to the California 500 NASCAR race. Suppose the L.A. Clippers were playing the Lakers on the day of the race. You paid face value for the ticket, and you are willing to take almost anything for that game's ticket because you have decided to go to the race.

FIGURE 34.5 A scalpers' market.

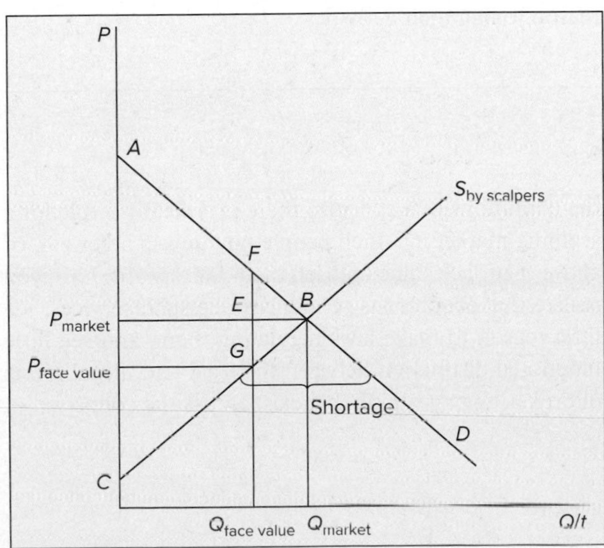

If scalping is illegal, only $Q_{\text{face value}}$, the tickets that people are willing to sell for the face value will be sold. If those are the only tickets that are sold, then the people who are willing to pay more than face value will not find any to buy. Some people will go to the game when they would rather have received P_{market} and stayed home. Others will stay home, when they would rather have paid P_{market} and gone to the game.

Without scalping, there is a shortage and a loss of societal benefit. That loss, measured by the loss in consumer and producer surplus, can also be seen in Figure 34.5. The loss of welfare to people who want to see the game at the scalper's price is *EFB*, while the loss to people who would like to have sold their tickets is *GEB*. The total loss to society when scalping is forbidden is *GFB*.

In this circumstance, is the permission to scalp tickets creating a problem or solving one? Economists figure that scalpers are solving the shortage by taking tickets from those who have them and value them least and transferring them to those who do not have them and value them most. For this the scalper makes a profit. Many musicians dislike this practice intensely. They take great offense at the fact they are the ones performing and someone else is profiting at the expense of their fans.

Legitimate Scalpers

In some states, all forms of scalping are legal; in others, none are. In a growing number of states, scalping remains illegal, but "brokers" are allowed to sell tickets for more than they pay for them. The only difference between a scalper and a broker is that the scalper walks around an event's perimeter trying to sell tickets, while the broker does it from a desk and a phone. The scalper demands cash; the broker takes credit cards.

Another way that scalpers have become legitimate is by pairing their services with those of a travel agent. It is legal in nearly every state for travel agents to create

STUBHUB, TICKETMASTER, AND THE NFL TICKET EXCHANGE

After-market ticket exchanges used to be solely in the province of a perfectly competitive market of individuals who would buy tickets at ticket counters or on the street and then resell them outside of events. No longer. StubHub changed that with its web-enabled methods of connecting buyers and sellers of tickets. Street scalpers still exist today, but businesses such as StubHub have allowed buyers to have some assurance of the authenticity of the tickets being sold and knowledge of the location of those tickets within the event space. When the sports leagues saw how much money could be made in the after-market ticket business, they wanted a piece of the profits.

Today, the after-market ticket exchange business has become intertwined with the primary ticket market. StubHub is the official ticket exchange for Major League Baseball. The official exchange outlet for the National Football League, NFL Ticket Exchange, is a cooperative arrangement between the league and Ticketmaster. Ticketmaster also has the National Hockey League and National Basketball Association business through league-branded websites. These arrangements pay off well for both the leagues and the business facilitating the exchange. The leagues can keep their ticket prices lower than market price levels, yet simultaneously benefit from higher market prices because they receive a sizable cut from the exchanges.

How do they enforce the "official" status of their preferred ticket exchange partner? When there are competing claims to a seat, the person who bought it from the "official" website gets it. I witnessed how this plays out in during a 2015 NFL game in Indianapolis. A couple sitting one row in front of my wife and I were confronted by another couple who had purchased the same seats on the NFL Ticket Exchange. The usher escorted the couple who purchased the seats on StubHub aside and told them (in a voice loud enough that everyone around could hear) that only official tickets would be honored when there was a dispute. The usher told the couple they could buy standing-room seats or be escorted out of the building.

What does this do? It converts the perfectly competitive market for tickets back to a near-monopoly. There are still street scalpers, but the official websites have gained significant market power based on these agreements. This clearly benefits the leagues to the detriment of fans. The leagues can effectively sell individual game tickets at market prices, while claiming to sell them at low prices. It may fool those who aren't familiar with economics but not those who are.

packages with hotel rooms, cab rides, and the like, and then offer these along with the tickets. Suppose you want a ticket to the latest "fight of the century." If it is in a no-scalping state and you cannot get tickets the normal way, you can still get the ticket because travel agents can combine a \$100 ticket with a \$100 hotel room and a \$10 cab ride and call it a \$500 "excursion." This is legal nearly everywhere, even when "scalping" is not.

It must be reinforced, therefore, that economists generally disapprove of anti-scalping regulations. Whether as legal brokers or illegal scalpers, the sellers are providing services. They are not only fixing the market shortage left by the promoter; they are also providing convenience. Because scalpers and brokers provide us with a convenience and harm no one in the process, there is little economic reason to ban their activities.

Summary

You now know what ticket scalping is and why it exists. You acknowledge that the market for tickets falls within the monopoly model and that the typical marginal cost curve presented in Chapter 4 is not appropriate for ticket sales. You understand why promoters may rationally charge less for an event than they could and that the result of this is a shortage of tickets. You recognize that under the conditions of a shortage there is typically a role for a scalping market in which people buy tickets below, at, or above their face value and sell them for a profit. Last, you realize that economists generally value such services, see little reason to make laws regulating them, and see little functional distinction between the legal and illegal forms of brokering or scalping that exist across the country.

Key Terms

brokering

scalping

Quiz Yourself

1. Ticket scalping is a symptom of
   a. ill-informed promoters.
   b. market prices being greater than the face value of the ticket.
   c. market prices being less than the face value of the ticket.
   d. ill-informed consumers.

2. Economists ____________________ the activities of ticket brokers and scalpers.
   a. draw no distinction between
   b. separately model
   c. draw a stark contrast between
   d. ignore

3. The optimal venue for an event is one where
   a. the number of seats exceeds the number where marginal cost equals marginal revenue.
   b. the number of seats is less than the number where marginal cost equals marginal revenue.
   c. the number of seats is exactly the number where marginal cost equals marginal revenue.
   d. marginal revenue exceeds marginal cost for all seats.

4. The distinct feature of the marginal cost curve in the analysis of venues is that it is a
   a. vertical line.
   b. horizontal line.
   c. check-shaped curve.
   d. backward L.

5. The model for a promoter is ________________ whereas the model for scalpers is that of ________ __________.
   a. monopoly; monopolistic competition
   b. monopolistic competition; perfect competition
   c. monopoly; oligopoly
   d. monopoly; perfect competition

6. Ticket scalping flourishes when there is ________ in the market for tickets at the price charged by the promoter.
   a. a surplus
   b. a shortage
   c. an equilibrium
   d. an externality

7. If anti-scalping laws are perfectly enforced, it will result in
   a. deadweight loss.
   b. a significant increase in consumer surplus.
   c. a significant increase in producer surplus.
   d. a significant loss to people who are going to the event.

Short Answer Questions

1. What is the difference between StubHub and a ticket scalper walking in front of a stadium?
2. Explain why it is not a contradiction for a ticket scalper to carry a sign that says "Need Tickets" on one side when it says "Have Tickets" on the other side (indicating he is both buying and selling tickets)?
3. Suppose you have a ticket to an event that is on a very important day to your spouse and you know it will cost you if you go to the event. How is the scalper good for you?
4. Suppose you need a ticket to a sold-out event for which your spouse had asked you to buy tickets a long time ago (and you forgot). Would you be made better off with or without anti-scalping laws when those laws are closely enforced?

Think about This

There are laws in many states and communities against scalping. Many promoters will let people buy only a limited number of tickets for fear that the buyer will simply resell them later. Why would a promoter care who buys the tickets? If you became a performer, would you care?

Talk about This

Some scalpers will pay college students who have camped out for a concert to buy extra tickets for them so that they can later resell them. Because this is against the law in some places, there is some risk for the scalper in that the students could simply resell the tickets themselves. If you were standing in line for tickets, what would you do?

For More Insight See

Happel, Stephen, and Marianne Jennings, "The Folly of Anti-Scalping Laws," *The Cato Journal* 15, no. 1 (Spring/Summer 1995), pp. 65–76.

CHAPTER THIRTY-FIVE

Rent Control

Learning Objectives

After reading this chapter you should be able to:

LO1 Use the principles of supply and demand to model the effect of rent control.

LO2 Identify the reasons for controlling rents.

LO3 Summarize why economists generally oppose rent controls.

LO4 Demonstrate that the consequences of controlling rent increases over time.

LO5 Use the supply and demand model to explain why eliminating rent control can be in a city's general interests but not in the interests of the voters of that city.

Chapter Outline

Several cities in the United States have enacted laws that control the amount of rent that a landlord can charge. Some, like New York City, have laws that date from World War II. Many of these laws were coincident to laws that controlled prices of all goods and services. When the general price controls expired, New York City chose to extend them for rents in the city. Others, like the more than 100 New Jersey cities with such laws, began their excursion into rent control by simply extending the price controls imposed by President Nixon in 1971. San Francisco, Los Angeles, and San Jose adopted controls when skyrocketing land prices drove rents up in California in the late 1970s and early 1980s. In 2019, in addition to New York, New Jersey, and California, there are state rent control statutes in Oregon, Maryland, and the District of Columbia. In five others, local rent control laws are permitted.

Rent control laws typically specify how often rents can be increased and by how much. Some rent control laws prevent rents from being increased as long as a tenant continues to rent the same apartment. As we analyze the issue of rent control, the first thing we examine is how rents are established in a free market. Then, we discuss what might motivate governments to control rents, and we examine the long- and short-term consequences of preventing rent increases.

Rents in a Free Market

In a free market, rents are determined in the same manner as the price of any other good or service. The supply of apartments is determined by how much it costs landlords to build them and how their profitability compares with other investments. The demand for apartments is based on the number of people seeking apartments, how much it costs to rent in the city as opposed to buying or renting in a neighboring community, and the income of the potential tenants.

When landlords choose to invest their money in apartment buildings, they are motivated by exactly the same things that motivate other investors. They look for the highest possible rate of return on their investments subject to a limited amount of risk. The costs associated with being a landlord are more varied and variable than they are with most other investments. The most prominent cost is the building itself. If the investor borrows money to build or buy the building, the cost is the interest portion of the monthly mortgage payment. If the investor buys the building without borrowing, the cost of the building is the interest rate that the investor could have received in his or her next best investment. In this sense, the costs involved in investing in rental properties are not all that different from other investments.

Some costs of owning rental property, though, are considerably more variable. Landlords must fix all of the problems in a building. They have to deal with tenants who do not pay their rent on time and those who leave before their lease expires. Landlords are also confronted with tenants who cause more damage to their apartments than their security deposits cover. It is for this reason that people who are highly organized and handy find investing in apartment buildings highly profitable. They use their skills to save money on maintenance.

People looking for a place to live have a similar set of concerns. They must decide whether to buy or rent. If they buy, they not only have to find a house, they must be ready to pay a down payment, and they must consider how they will pay for their own repairs. If they rent, they must decide where to rent. In a large city, the cost of renting close to work is greater, but the time and expenses involved in commuting are avoided. If rents in the city are low, people are more likely to live in the city. If they are high, people are more likely to live farther away.

Figure 35.1 shows that a market for rental apartments generates an equilibrium number of apartments rented, Q^*, and an equilibrium rent, R^*. Such a market can be affected by a number of factors. If interest rates rise, for example, the cost to landlords rises and more people want to become renters. This is because the home mortgage payments that represent the cost of alternatives to renters increase. Increased costs to landlords and greater numbers of potential tenants both lead to higher rents.

It is important to mention that there are several rental markets for different types of rental housing. For instance, landlords who rent to young college-age people anticipate having repair costs at the end of the lease that landlords who rent to older people do not anticipate. Landlords who rent apartments to people with a low and uncertain income must deal with the probability that some of their tenants will always be late paying their rent. Landlords who rent apartments that command higher rents will not.

With such an array of apartment types and rents, it is often the case that renters are self-segregating. Apartments close to colleges and universities have higher rents than similar apartment buildings elsewhere, because college students value lower transportation costs and are willing to pay higher rents so they can take advantage of them. People who are not college students do not value being close to the school. Because they have a homogeneous population, a landlord will require security deposits that are higher than typical for such apartments. This is important because it would be illegal to have a differential security deposit for different types of people. (They may require more for legitimate distinctions such as those that might exist for pet owners or smokers.)

FIGURE 35.1 The market for rental apartments without rent control.

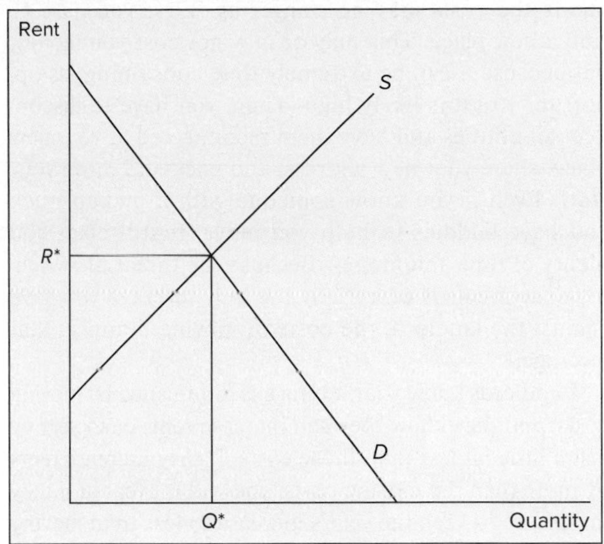

Landlords cannot charge men more than women despite experience that tells them that they may have to pay more in repair costs after a college-age male tenant leaves as compared to a college-age female. The Fair Housing Act says that they cannot set rents based on gender, race, religion, or age.

Reasons for Controlling Rents

When landlords face increased costs, they need to raise rents to make the rate of return on their investments of rental apartments equal to that of other, comparable investments. Few people begrudge landlords rent increases when they are necessary to make the owners a reasonable profit. On the other hand, like all business owners, landlords want to increase prices to increase profits. What prevents landlords from raising rents is exactly what prevents any business from raising prices: Their competition will take their customers. In this area, though, landlords have an advantage over businesspeople who sell other goods.

When you switch brands of toothpaste, beer, or anything else, no cost is involved. When you change apartments the costs may be staggering. First you have to find a new place. This may or may not cost you money, but because it can be extremely time consuming, its opportunity cost is likely high. Then, you have to disconnect all utilities and have them reconnected at your new place, share your new address, and pack and move your stuff. Even if you know someone with a pickup truck and have buddies to help you move, it still costs you plenty of time and money. Because the threat of switching apartments is essentially the only leverage you have against the landlord, the costs of moving diminish that leverage.

Landlords know your leverage is diminished by moving costs, and they know they can increase rents each year by just a little bit less than those costs. If they increase rents by more than the moving costs, you will move; but if they make sure to keep the year's increase to less than moving costs, you will decide it is in your economic interest to renew your lease and pay the extra rent. In the last two decades, overall prices have risen 52 percent. Rents have increased 85 percent.

This process cannot continue forever, because that would imply that rents always increase faster than other prices. If they did, investors would build new apartments in hopes of getting the higher-than-average return on investment. With new apartments, there would be a rent war, and renters would be its winners. On the other hand, it is possible for a rent war not to start for a few years. This in turn may be all that is required for politicians to mistake a temporary situation for one that's permanent and that can be solved only through the imposing of rent controls. As we will see later, once rent control is imposed in a city, it is nearly impossible to discontinue it.

Consequences of Rent Control

Rent control is a form of **price ceiling** where the price is not allowed to rise above a specified level. Once rent control is in place, the market for rental apartments is no longer governed by supply and demand alone, but also by the often obscure rules that politicians have written into the legislation. The consequences of any price ceiling in general, and of rent control laws in particular, depend on the elasticity of the supply and demand curves. Those elasticities are dependent on the number of close substitutes and on time. Because close substitutes can be better developed over time, the two are closely related. We will put them together under the idea of time and discuss the consequences in the short run as being different from the consequences in the long run.

price ceiling
The level above which a price may not rise.

Note that for a price ceiling to be relevant it must be lower than the equilibrium price. Imagine what would happen if the ceiling were, in fact, above the equilibrium price. If landlords charged more than the equilibrium rent, their renters would move to other landlords' buildings. Since landlords do not find it in their best interest to do this, setting rents by law at a rate lower than equilibrium has the effect of telling landlords that they cannot do something that is not in their best interests anyway. It is exactly as if a professor were to tell you that you cannot attend her class naked. You were not going to partake of class in the buff anyway, so having her tell you not to do so is irrelevant.

We can analyze the consequences of rent control more systematically by examining Figure 35.2. First note that in Figure 35.2 there are two panels. The panel on the left indicates the consequences of rent control in the short run, while the panel on the right indicates the consequences in the long run. There are important

FIGURE 35.2 The short- and long-run consequences of rent control.

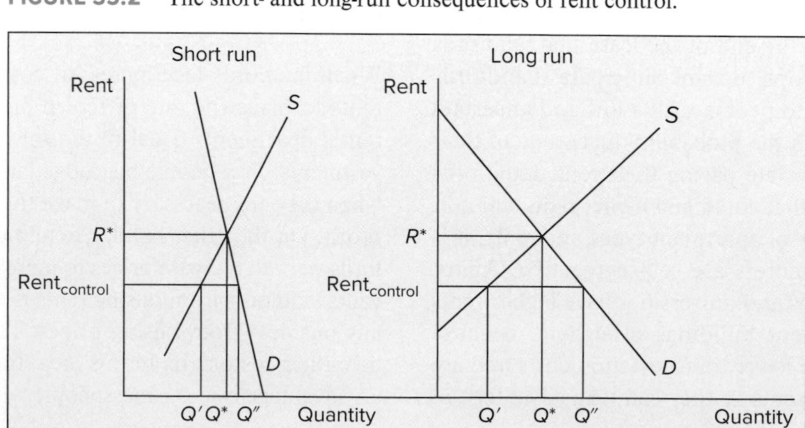

long-run and short-run differences because, if you recall from Chapter 3, an important determinant of the elasticity of supply and demand is time.

The inelasticity of the supply and demand curves in the short run makes sense because renters and landlords have little time or ability to change their respective behaviors. Apartment owners are going to lease most of their units regardless of what the market rent is. It is only with apartments that require significant maintenance that landlords will base the decision on getting them ready to rent on the amount of money they can get for them. Again, in the short run, this is likely to be a very small percentage of the units under their control.

Focusing on what they have in common for a moment, we see that the equilibrium rent, R^*, is being superseded by a legal limit, $R_{control}$. The first consequence of this is the one legislators intended: Rents are lowered, landlords make less than they would without rent control, and renters either pay less in rent or get more for their money.

Reducing the rent also results in the quantity demanded, Q'', exceeding the quantity supplied, Q'. The quantity of apartments rented decreased because a certain number of apartments ($Q^* - Q'$) that would have been rented before rent control are not being offered for rent after rent control. To see why this is the case, imagine yourself as a landlord with a building of apartments of varying difficulty to maintain. The more difficult ones, say, basement apartments, which require more frequent painting because humid conditions cause early deterioration, will not be rented unless at least R^* rent is paid. Thus, the second consequence of rent control is that the number of apartments that would ordinarily be rented is decreased.

The final consequence of rent control, which happens in both the short run and the long run, is that people will seek apartments in the rent-controlled community who had not sought to rent there in the past. Specifically, there will be $Q'' - Q^*$ apartments demanded at $R_{control}$ that had not been demanded at R^*.

The magnitude of these consequences and the reactions of people to the consequences determine the severity of the shortage. In the short run, for instance, the rent reduction comes at a fairly small cost. The shortage of apartments caused by rent control is small in the short run because both the supply curve and demand curve are likely to be inelastic.

Likewise, renters who live in the community are not likely to want to move to a better apartment immediately following the introduction of rent control. Renters who live outside a community, on the other hand, are not likely to want to move into the community until there is a substantial difference between their current rents and those in the rent-controlled city.

It is important to note that most rent control laws do not lower rents but simply prevent them from increasing. If overall inflation is 2 percent per year and rents are not allowed to rise, it takes several years for a significant difference between equilibrium rents and controlled rents to develop. It is only when that difference becomes large enough that landlords do not fix apartments and tenants start moving that the full effect of rent control will begin to be felt.

Once this long-run scenario develops, the serious flaws in rent control begin to overwhelm the benefits. The difference between Q' and Q^* in Figure 35.2 begins to widen significantly as landlords who would have built or refurbished apartment complexes in the community decide not to make that investment. The gap between Q'' and Q^* also grows as commuters who live outside the community seek to rent in town, attracted by the lower rents.

Where the system goes from here depends on its rules. For instance, one set of problems is generated if rents can increase by only a fixed percentage each year regardless of who lives there. If, on the other hand, rents cannot increase at all for the duration of a tenant's stay, another set of problems is created. Rules with regard to subletting and eviction tend to exacerbate the problems.

Some rent control laws allow modest yearly increases in rents. Usually, though, these increases do not keep up with either inflation or what equilibrium would have been. In New York City, the difference has had more than 60 years to build up, so rent-controlled apartments are very inexpensive places to live. They can be rented for a third or less of their free-market rent. This makes for a perverse scenario in which those looking for an apartment turn not to the newspaper's real estate section but to the obituaries.[1]

When markets are controlled, they will sometimes go underground. These *shadow markets*, as they are called by some economists, are generated because there are people who have legal rights to something of value—an apartment, say, whose rent is below equilibrium—and there are people who want them. It is illustrative that in New York City more transactions for rent-controlled apartments happen in the shadow market than through typical real estate practices. The evidence for this is the scarce number of rent-controlled apartments advertised in the newspapers.

To illustrate how the shadow market works, suppose you know someone who has a loved one die and no local relatives are looking for a cheap apartment. You can go to the funeral, pretend to be sad, and see if you can get the dead person's apartment. Of course everyone knows this, so, on

[1]When the difference between equilibrium rents and market rents is wide enough, the only apartments that become available are those whose occupants have died.

the sly, the dead tenant's executers attempt to sell the right to the apartment to the highest bidder. It is a common occurrence, in cities with laws such as this, for people to pay what amounts to a bribe to rent a rent-regulated apartment.

The law in other communities is even more strict: Rents cannot increase until the lease expires, and since the renter can perpetually renew the lease, this happens only when the owner dies unexpectedly. If the heirs of a deceased renter can swing it, they sublet with the original renter's name still on a lease that is decades old. Again, the right to sublet an apartment is sold to the highest bidder, sometimes through multiple generations.

Typically, the only recourse that owners of buildings whose rents never increase have is to make the buildings miserable places to live. Because rents are so low, there is little money for repairs, so repairs simply are not made. Additionally, if owners can get every tenant in a building to leave, they can gut the building and start over again. Refurbished buildings are treated as new ones, and the owners can set charges that are subject only to the market.

The other alternative that the owner has once the building is empty is to refurbish and sell the apartments as individual condominiums. Renters know this and will fight moving out as long as they can. They do not do this to spite the owner. They do it because they know that finding a rent-controlled apartment is difficult. Without one, they would be one of many (Q'') wanting to rent one of the few (Q') available apartments. This is why, in rent control communities, tenants often do their own repairs or pay for them out of pocket. The only recourse that tenants have against landlords who do not pay for necessary repairs is to report them to the city health department. Sometimes the health department can get a court order for the landlord to make repairs, sometimes they cannot. This sort of pressure rarely works. Owners simply abandon the buildings, leaving tenants worse off than if they had not reported the problem.

Thus, one reaction of landlords is to reduce the quality of the apartment they are renting. Charging the same rent for a lesser apartment is the same as raising the rent. As a result, economists suggest that, in the long run, rent controls are ineffective because landlords raise rent on the sly, not by explicitly raising rent, but by lowering quality.

Why Does Rent Control Survive?

With all of these strange long-run consequences, it makes sense to ask why cities continue controlling rents. The answer is simple, and it can be traced to the ballot box. Let's start with the obvious: You do not get to vote in a community unless you live there. People who live in a suburb cannot vote in a city's election, even though the result of the election directly affects them. The only people who can vote on a referendum to eliminate rent control are the people who live in the city (many of whom live in rent-controlled apartments). So, the people who benefit from rent control get to vote, and those who lose as a result of rent control do not get to vote. It isn't hard to predict the result of that vote.

Figure 35.2 helps to make this clear. The people hurt by rent control are (1) landlords and (2) people who can no longer find an apartment in the city ($Q^* - Q'$). The first group is a minuscule number whose plight is not treated that seriously by candidates.[2] The second group had to move out of town to find a place to live. Either way, the majority of the people left in the community (Q') are simply better off than they would be were rent control to be discontinued.

In Boston, though, the 1995 repeal of rent controls led to none of the problems that rent control supporters had predicted. Rents in previously controlled apartments did rise, but new construction ensued. This had the effect of holding down increases in rents.

[2]This is not to say that these landlords have no influence. Through campaign contributions, landlords, particularly the high-profile ones, are able to make their case and have received consideration on a number of development issues of concern to them. Nevertheless, this influence has not led to the undoing of rent control in New York.

Summary

You are now able to use the model of supply and demand to show the effects of rent control. You understand that though there are reasons for controlling rents, these are typically short term in nature and that economists generally are against rent controls. You know that the consequences of controlling rents differ given the time horizon, and the short-term benefits to the renter are usually offset by long-term losses to landlords and renters who cannot get housing in a community. Last, you are now able to use the supply and demand model to explain why eliminating rent control can be in a city's general interest but not in the interests of the voters of that city.

Key Term

price ceiling

Quiz Yourself

1. The principal argument in favor of rent control is that
   a. landlords and all tenants are helped.
   b. landlords have the ability to raise rents because they know it is costly for tenants to move.
   c. landlords are harmed.
   d. all tenants are helped equally.
2. The principal argument against rent control is that
   a. landlords and all tenants are made worse off.
   b. landlords and a few tenants are made worse off by less than the majority of tenants that are made better off.
   c. landlords and a few tenants are made worse off by more than the majority of tenants that are made better off.
   d. all tenants are made better off.
3. In the long run, rent control has ________________ impact because, over time, supply and demand become ____________ elastic.
   a. an increasing; more
   b. a decreasing; more
   c. an increasing; less
   d. a decreasing; less
4. Rent control is an example of a ________________.
   a. price ceiling
   b. price floor
   c. price irrelevancy
   d. price equalization
5. If the equilibrium rent is ___________ the controlled level, then rent control laws are ________________.
   a. above; necessary
   b. above; irrelevant
   c. below; necessary
   d. below; irrelevant
6. Which of the following is likely to occur after several years of relevant rent control?
   a. Rents exceeding equilibrium
   b. An increase in available housing
   c. A decrease in available housing
   d. Rents equaling equilibrium
7. History suggests that rent control laws
   a. tend to be declared unconstitutional.
   b. tend to be overturned soon after they are adopted.
   c. tend to become a permanent fixture of a community.
   d. are incredibly unpopular.

Short Answer Questions

1. Illustrate the impact of rent control laws when demand is quite elastic, quite inelastic, and modestly elastic. Show how the deadweight loss changes with elasticity.
2. Apartment buildings fall into disrepair when they cannot be profitably operated. Show how this might impact a rent-controlled market for apartments in the short run versus the long run.

Think about This

Rent control laws, like minimum-wage laws apply to everyone, not simply the poor. Should there be provisions to apply rent control only to those who need the lower rent?

Talk about This

In smaller cities, being a landlord is a way for handy men and women to invest in property, fix it up, and rent it out. It allows them to save and invest some of their own sweat. Should rent control laws exempt these types of landlords?

For More Insight See

Keating, W. Dennis, Michael Teitz, and Andrejs Skaburskis, *Rent Control: Regulation and the Rental Housing Market* (New Brunswick, NJ: Center for Urban Policy Research, 1998).

CHAPTER THIRTY-SIX

The Economics of K–12 Education

Learning Objectives

After reading this chapter you should be able to:

LO1 Analyze education as an investment that not only pays dividends to the person getting the education, but also positively affects society at large.

LO2 Summarize the debate over whether spending more on education will yield more significant returns.

LO3 Summarize the controversies associated with school reform.

LO4 Explain why many economists argue that the current structure of education limits the ability of policy makers to improve outcomes with greater spending.

Chapter Outline

From a strictly economic perspective, the amount of time and money we spend on educating ourselves and our fellow citizens is amazing. Required to stay in school until we are at least 16, and in some cases until we are 18, we are strongly encouraged to graduate from high school, and when we do, we are offered substantial subsidies to get some form of higher education. Some of us even continue on to earn graduate degrees. In the end, it is easily possible that we have spent the first third of our lives acquiring an education. Our parents and our government have encouraged us to invest in ourselves even while contributing nothing of substance to society during that time. Since most people retire before they die, the typical postgraduate educated person has fewer than 40 years to earn enough to pay back, figuratively, what he or she invested in formal education.

In general, parents and grandparents are enthusiastic supporters of schools, at least financially. People without children in school have other reasons for supporting them. In this chapter, we explore some of the reasons people give for supporting education. We try to determine whether society is getting its money's worth for elementary and secondary education.

In considering the elementary and secondary level, we look at how much money is spent on education and attempt to determine whether taxpayers are getting value for their money. To that end, we plot measures of cost, and we look at the ratio of the numbers of students to teachers. Lastly, we examine measures of success such as students' performances on standardized tests and the numbers of degrees that are granted.

Investments in Human Capital

In Chapters 4 and 5, we spoke of capital as though the concept were confined to machines. Here, we turn to another form of capital, **human capital.** This refers to the ability of a person to create goods and services. Education and training play an important role in developing human capital.

human capital
The ability of a person to create goods and services.

Present Value Analysis

In Chapter 7's discussion of present value and investments, we learned it is possible to invest too little or too much in anything, including human capital. Determining the right amount depends on the **net present value,** the difference between the present value of benefits and the present value of costs.

net present value
The difference between the present value of benefits and the present value of costs.

The investment we make in the education of our own children we do out of love for them, but it also makes sense from an economic point of view. If there were no "free"[1] public schools, we would look first at the present value of the cost of educating a child from kindergarten through high school. We would then subtract that from the present value of the child's increased earning potential because of that education. If at that point we found that the net was positive, then we would conclude that, for the parent, the investment would be a wise one.

Again, from the view of the parent, an even more refined look at this analysis would subtract out those costs that would occur anyway. Consider the modern family with two working parents or a single parent. If there were no public school, they would have day-care expenses whether or not the child were educated. That means, at the margin, the cost of educating a child is the difference between the tuition to the school and the day-care costs. This reduces the relevant costs, and it makes education an even better investment.

External Benefits

Of course, K-12 education is public and has been for so long that we may not even think of asking why. There are societal as well as economic reasons for having free public education. Societally, benefits accrue to us all from having children become educated, whether or not they are our own children. Economically, benefits accrue to us because people who are educated are less likely to be on welfare or commit crimes. They are more likely to be productive citizens who pay more in taxes than they cost in government benefits. An additional benefit that we derive from public school education is that having children of all races, ethnic groups, religions, and income classes in the same schools may foster social stability. Thus, the **external benefits** of K-12 education justify having a considerable subsidy to that education.

FIGURE 36.1 External benefits of K-12 education.

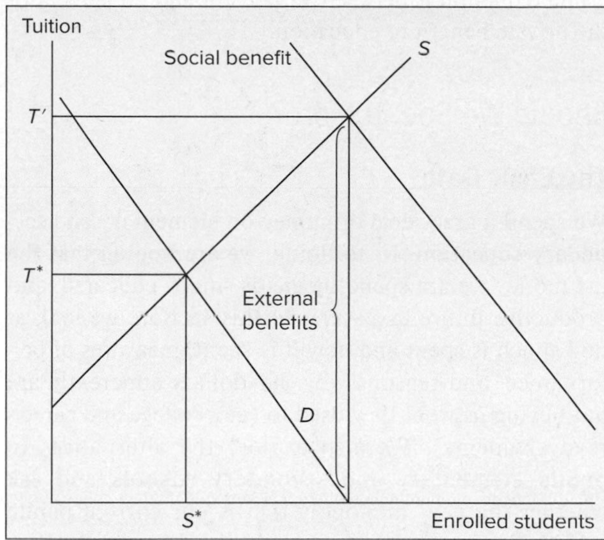

external benefits
Benefits that accrue to someone other than the consumer or producer of the good or service.

We can use our supply and demand diagram to illustrate the inefficiency of just having unsubsidized private education. Consider Figure 36.1 and what it suggests the price of education should be to the parents of the children to be educated. The price is the annual tuition, and the quantity is the number of kids educated in a year. At low tuition rates, more will be invested in education, and when it is free, everyone will take advantage of it by going to school. The resulting demand curve is downward sloping, but if tuition is low, schools will be willing to educate fewer students.

The equilibrium tuition, T^*, and the equilibrium number of enrolled students, S^*, are what the unsubsidized market would yield. If there is an external benefit of the size shown, then the optimal number of students is much greater than the market amount. In this case, the optimal number of students is everyone and the optimal price is zero. This means that taxpayers pay T per student. From a theoretical point of view, this does not necessarily mean that the school must be government-owned and -operated. In the United States, except for some experiments in a variety of places, this is precisely what it means.

Specific estimates of the magnitude of this external impact have started to emerge. Economists Lance

[1] "Free" is in quotes for two reasons. First, eight states require a textbook rental fee that, in Indiana at least, is between $100 and $200 per student per year. This fee is waived for students qualifying for the Federal School Lunch program. Second, the taxpayer pays for this public education. Thus, "free" should be read as "free to the parents except for any fees that might be involved."

Lochner and Enrico Moretti estimate that the impact of crime reduction is between 12 percent and 26 percent of the private benefit to education.

Should We Spend More?

The Basic Data

We spend a great deal of money on elementary and secondary education. In so doing, we are hoping that the tax money we are spending yields smart, educated, and productive future taxpayers. In this section, we look at how much is spent and how it is spent, measures of performance, and reasons why our dollars apparently are not buying us what they used to (i.e., college and career-ready students). We also explore the alternatives to public elementary and secondary schools and ask whether the near monopoly that is our current public school system is serving our interests adequately.

As of 2016, the United States was spending nearly $700 billion to educate 56.4 million elementary and secondary students. In exploring whether this amount of money is justified, we can look at how inflation-adjusted spending per pupil has been tracked over time and compare the amounts that have been spent with outcomes such as test scores and graduation rates. It is important that we look at things in this way because as the number of students rises, the number of classrooms needed rises too. This not only raises construction and maintenance costs; it also increases the number of teachers that are needed. Thus, whether or not spending increases, it is spending per pupil that matters. In addition, because inflation makes a 1960 dollar more valuable than a 2018 dollar, we need to adjust the spending figures for inflation.

From Figure 36.2, you can see that even when it is adjusted for inflation, spending per student increased dramatically over the years. While there was a leveling off in the period of economic turmoil in the late 1970s and early 1980s and another during the early 1990s, there was, nonetheless, a marked increase from $3,716 (2018 dollars) per student in 1960 to its peak of $14,128 in 2009. The trauma to state budgets caused by the Great Recession led to a nearly 9 percent decline in inflation-adjusted per-pupil spending. This constituted the first substantial period of decreased real spending for K-12 education since the Great Depression. Most of those cuts were restored by 2016.

One consequence of the longer term increase in spending since 1960 is that it served to decrease average class size dramatically. As can be seen in Figure 36.3, in 1960 there were more than 26 students per class; there are currently 15.6. The resource constraints caused by the Great Recession are also reflected by a 4 percent increase in average class sizes from their all-time low achieved in 2009. If the demands on what needs to be taught have remained constant, such a significant long-term reduction in the number of students in a class

FIGURE 36.2 Spending per pupil in 2018 dollars.

Source: *Digest of Education Statistics,* http://nces.ed.gov/programs/digest.

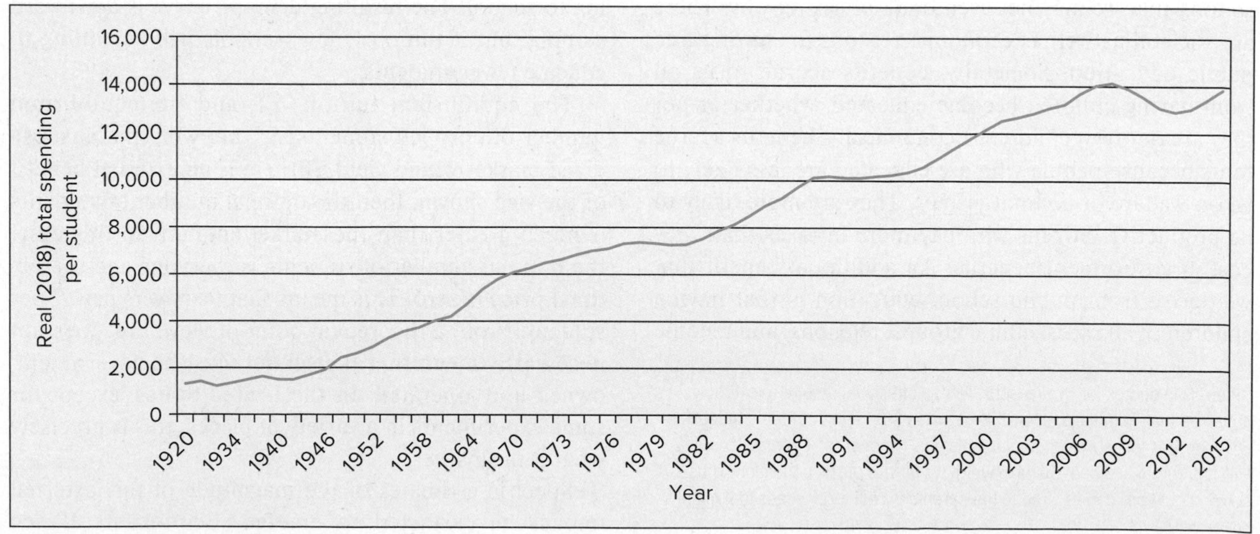

FIGURE 36.3 Student-to-teacher ratios.

Source: *Digest of Education Statistics*, http://nces.ed.gov/programs/digest.

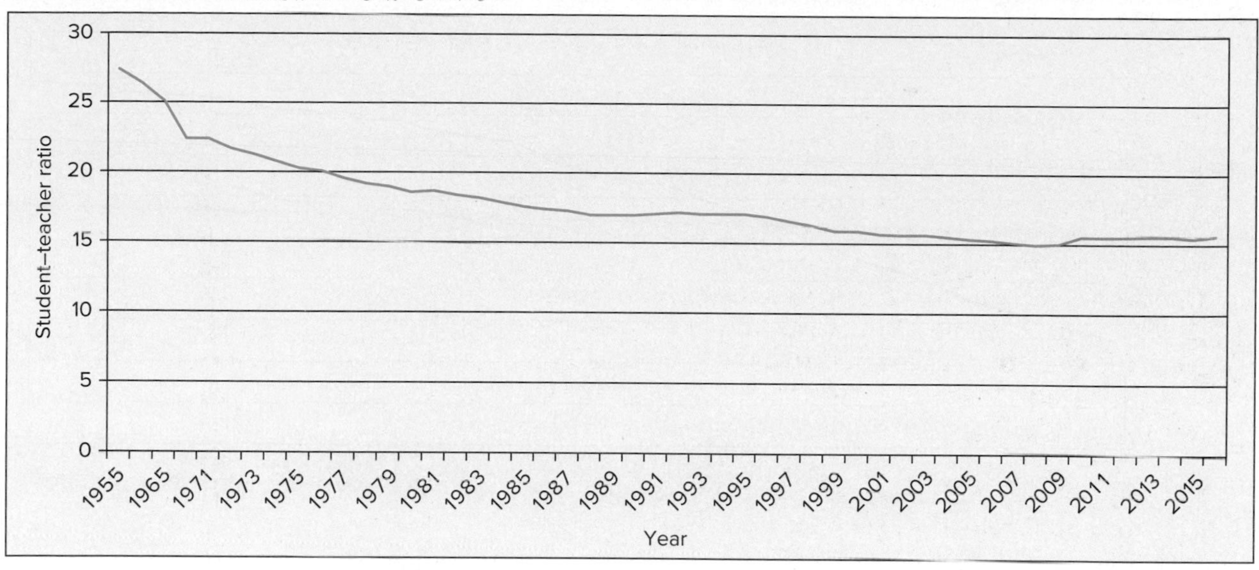

FIGURE 36.4 SATs for college-bound students.

Source: *Digest of Education Statistics*, http://nces.ed.gov/programs/digest.

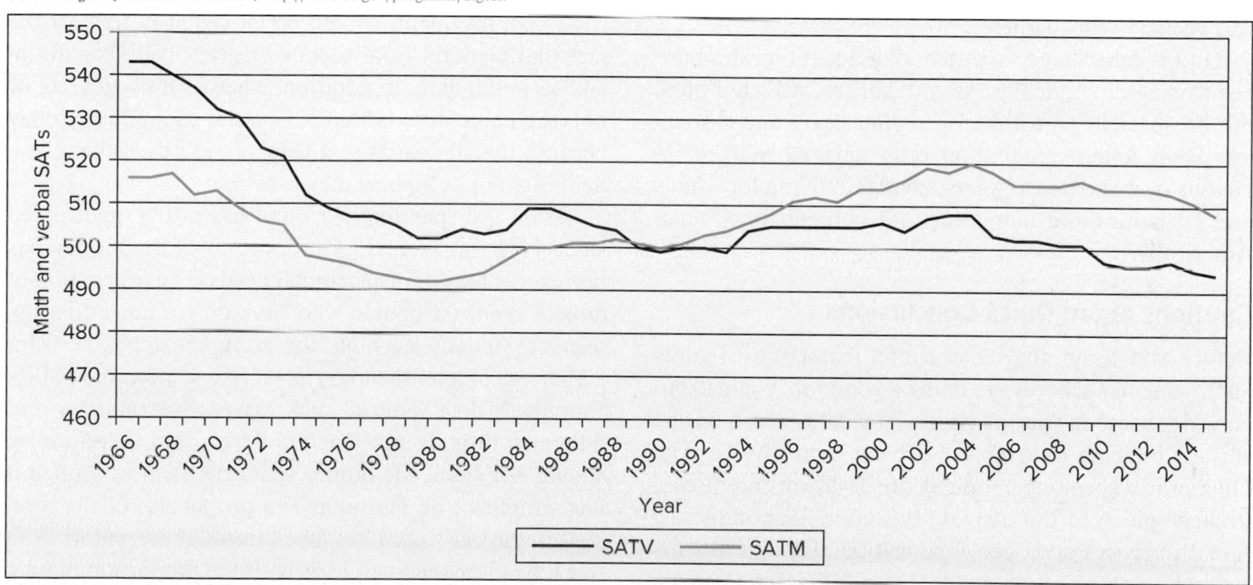

would be expected to have a similarly significant impact on the success of students. By some measures it has, and by others, it has not.

Figure 36.4 indicates that students' scores on the SATs over the same period did not respond in proportion to the reductions in class sizes, and there is no clear evidence that reducing class size led to an improvement in SAT scores for college-bound students. If anything, the opposite happened. Average math SATs plummeted while class sizes were falling and rebounded during the time when class sizes leveled off. The decline in verbal SATs bottomed out later and the rebound was less

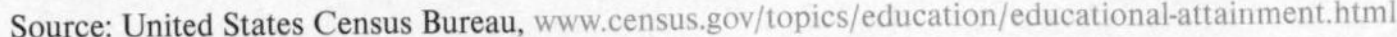

FIGURE 36.5 High school graduation rates.

Source: United States Census Bureau, www.census.gov/topics/education/educational-attainment.html.

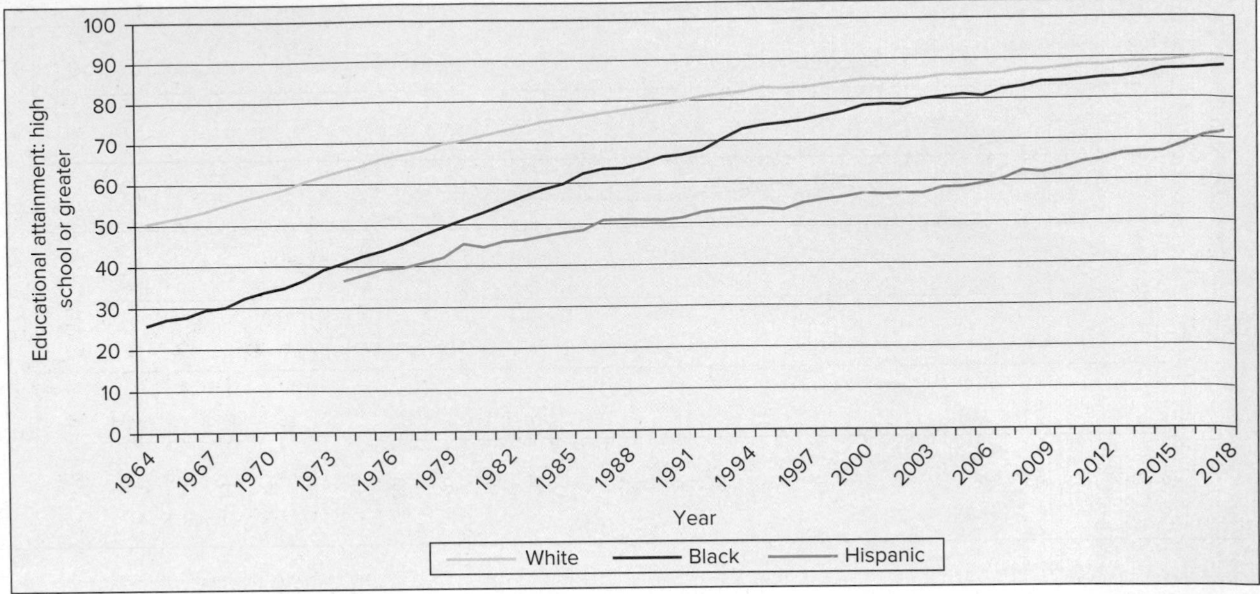

dramatic. These scores are 57 points below where they had been 55 years earlier.[2]

On the other hand, high school graduation rates have been rising dramatically. As you can see in Figure 36.5, this is especially true for African Americans and Hispanics. High school graduation rates showed marked increases over the last 59 years, nearly doubling for whites and Hispanics and increasing 242 percent for African Americans.

Cautions about Quick Conclusions

Before you draw any conclusions from these figures about whether schools are doing a good job, you need to consider some mitigating issues. The data, which on the surface indicate that there has been more than a doubling of real spending per pupil, are easily misinterpreted because much of the increase has gone for noninstructional purposes and special education. Though it is depressing on the surface, the low SAT scores can be accounted for in part by the increasing proportion of students from low socioeconomic groups taking the SAT.

The high school graduation rate, which on the surface shows improvement, should be looked at in light of the fact that General Equivalency Degrees (GEDs) are included in the data. In addition, whether it is accurate or not, the perception is that it is easier to graduate today because the standards that teachers use to evaluate students are not as high as they used to be.

While real spending per pupil has nearly quadrupled since 1960, an increasing proportion of the money has been going for noninstructional needs. The proportion of dollars spent on people who have only a tangential impact on student learning, for example, has gone from 32 percent of total spending in 1960 to 47 percent in 2016. Employees like janitors, bus drivers, secretaries, and administrators do not teach children, and therefore we should not count the money spent on them as though it has an impact on learning. The proportion of the total staff in the classroom has fallen from 70 percent in 1950 to a little more than half in 2016. If the proportion of total spending on noninstructional employees had remained constant, then the overall rate of increase could be telling us something about whether we have been getting the same value for our tax dollars. It has not remained constant, so we cannot. It is still the case, however, that real instructional spending per pupil has doubled.

Some of the real instructional spending per pupil that has doubled since 1960 has been devoted to legally

[2]The 3-test version of the SAT may have had an impact as the scores dropped markedly for the year in which it was adopted. The three distinct recentering exercises have also been accounted for in these data. In those exercises, the College Board provided conversion tables to equate one year's SAT with another. Each time, past SATs were adjusted higher.

mandated special education instruction. In 2018, 13.7 percent of the student population was labeled with disabilities and thus eligible for subsidized assistance through various state and federal programs. Most students who have been labeled as having physical disabilities do not require many extra resources, but some require quite expensive services. Although the Americans with Disabilities Act (ADA) requires that the school provide all necessary assistance to such children while they are in school, the money that it costs to do so should not be called a spending increase for purposes of deciding whether annual costs per pupil are too high. Such spending does not directly benefit students without disabilities, so it should be netted out of the analysis.

If we include the spending that funds ADA-required programs in our analysis, the figures on class sizes are understated. Because the figures are derived by simply dividing the number of students by the number of teachers, and because many of the additional teachers focus on only a few children, the correct number for analysis should be the number of students not requiring extra services divided by the number of their teachers.

In the past 59 years, real total spending per pupil has increased, real total instructional spending per pupil has increased, and real total instructional spending has increased for students without ADA-defined conditions. The SAT and other test scores are lower today than they were 59 years ago. While we would not expect increased spending on bus drivers or students with severe academic problems to increase SAT scores, we have every reason to expect a real increase in spending on instruction of students without disabilities to increase test scores. Because spending has increased and test scores have decreased, it seems logical to conclude that we are not getting the same value for our taxpayer dollars. That conclusion may not be warranted, though, because the number of students taking the tests has increased and the number going to college has increased. If we look at the entire range of students, moreover, we will see that greater numbers of those who earn lower scores are represented than used to be the case. For instance, if a high school senior class of 10 students has 5 going to college and they averaged a combined score of 1,000 (on the two-score SAT), is that better than a class of 10 students where the first 5 average a 1,000 and the 6th, a less-qualified student, gets an 800? Because more people are taking the SAT now than in 1960, and because the quality of the students who would not have taken it then but take it now is lower than the quality of students who would have taken it anyway, logic would suggest that we should expect average SAT scores to decrease. Even an unchanged SAT average would indicate that today's schools are doing a better job.

Test scores have fallen as spending has increased, and we have speculated about why increased spending has not resulted in higher test scores. Let's look now at graduation rates. Though graduation rates have risen substantially over the decades, there is an open question as to whether this can necessarily be viewed as an improvement. For one thing, prior to 2014 when the exam changed (becoming substantially more difficult), more people had earned a GED diploma than at any other time in history. Some of them had dropped out of school for various reasons. Others were prisoners who had learned that completing a GED shaved time off their sentence. It was admirable that they would do this, regardless of who they were, but even though the "E" used to stand for equivalence, few employers consider it to be the equal of a high school diploma. The best evidence for this assertion is that the income of GED holders is still far closer to the income of high school dropouts than it is to high school graduates who have not gone to college. We need to consider this when we make positive statements about the marked increase in graduation rates for Hispanics and African Americans. Because they hold a vastly disproportionate number of the GEDs, we have to be careful to interpret the increases in graduation rates.

Additionally, there is a common perception that high schools engage in what is referred to as "social promotion," that is, the granting of diplomas for survival rather than for achievement, a trend that critics say has increased in recent years. In response to laws such as No Child Left Behind, states began implementing exit exams for students to combat this perception. The result was a concerning increase in the number of students who had passed all other requirements for graduation but could not pass the tests. The subsequent Every Student Succeeds Act (ESSA) eliminated the absolute requirement for high-stakes testing.

Literature on Whether More Money Will Improve Educational Outcomes

There is vast literature written by economists on whether increases in spending can guarantee an increase in educational outcomes. The premise that "you get what you pay for" and that more money will make things better can be traced to the production function that we outlined in Chapter 4. Recall that this function maps the relationship between inputs and the resulting outputs. We used workers as the example of inputs and showed that more workers translated into more outputs (or finished goods) until the point where the limited capital stock or the structure of the business prevented additional workers from having a positive impact on output.

Applying that idea to education, let's assume that the input is teachers and the output is some agreed-on measure of education outcomes. Each of these assumptions requires some clarification. First, whether it is best to hire more teachers (a higher quantity) to reduce class size, pay teachers more money to get better ones, or a combination of these two alternatives is certainly an open question. For the purposes of our graph, we will simply assume quality and quantity are interchangeable concepts. Second, while standardized test scores do not necessarily qualify as an agreed-on measure of outcomes, for simplicity of explanation we will assume that they do. Given all that, Figure 36.6 shows the relationship between teachers and test scores.

Eric Hanushek, a leading economist on the issue of education, summarized 377 studies where one or more measures of input like student-to-teacher ratio (the quantity of teachers), teacher education, and teacher experience (the quality of teachers) were used to explain test scores. He reported that most of these studies found no relationship between test scores and these inputs and nearly as many found a negative one as a positive one. This stunning conclusion, however—that money does not matter and that spending more is a waste of taxpayer resources—is in some dispute by other economists. These economists contend that test scores are less important than the earnings of graduates. They state that over the last century, graduates of schools in states that spent more had more earning power than those who graduated in states that spent less. All economists who study the issue have found, moreover, that educational outcomes are determined mostly by factors that are largely beyond the control of schools, such as family income and family structure.

These results are not as contradictory as they might seem. Figure 36.6 indicates that it might very well be that the structure of public schools has been such that more money had a significant impact in the 1940s through the 1960s because we were spending so little in real terms and were on the steep, upward-sloping part of the curve. The argument that Hanushek and others make is that it appears that we are now "on the flat of the curve," meaning that we have done all we can do with more teachers. The implication is that we need to look at something else to improve outcomes.

FIGURE 36.6 Educational production function.

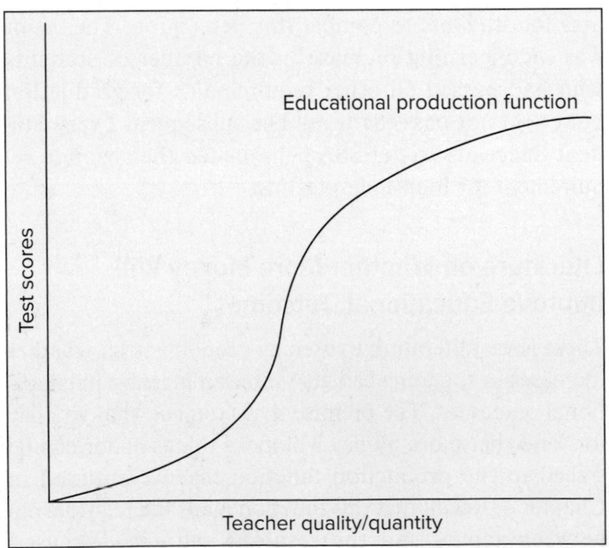

School Reform Issues

If we are in fact on the flat part of the educational production function and more money will not improve outcomes until the structure is changed, it is reasonable to ask what the structure is and why it is limiting. There are two separate issues with regard to the structure that we explore in this section. The first is that the public education system operates as a monopoly and as such tends not to be responsive to the desires of individual students and parents. The second is that teachers' salaries are usually not dependent on their performance. We'll also explore whether private schools and government-provided vouchers to pay for them might help to improve formal education.

The Public School Monopoly

In Chapter 5 we saw that in industries dominated by monopolies, prices are higher and output is less than it would be under perfect competition. Public schools operate in most communities as a monopoly. Though there are private schools and homeschooling, these are not real options to most parents. Even more interesting is that this monopoly charges you, in the form of state and local taxes, whether or not you use the schools. It would be as if your electric company could continue sending you a bill even after you decided to buy your own electric generator.

There are reasons for this. If you believe that the external benefits of K-12 education are so great that they justify being subsidized, then parents who choose to send their children to private schools should not be exempt from school-related taxes because they are getting those external benefits.

Ultimately, the problem with a monopoly is that it becomes unresponsive to the needs and desires of its customers. In the case of public schools, there is no compelling monetary incentive for the school to help a child with a particular need or to foster excellence in another child. Consider the following problem that exists at the beginning of every school year in nearly every school in the country. Schools have teachers of varying quality, and many parents know which ones are better. Parents want their kids to have the best teachers, and the principal must disappoint some of these parents. Under competition, a disappointed parent could threaten to move to another school. Under competition, the principal would have at least a budgetary incentive to make teachers better. Under the current system in most school districts, the parents are simply told, "That's the way it is."

Merit Pay and Tenure

One of the areas that distinguish teachers from other professionals is the lack of economic performance incentives and the presence of lifetime job security. One study found that individual teacher quality does matter. Economist Jonah Rockoff, in particular, discovered that he could isolate the impact of individual teachers and identify the better ones statistically by carefully matching student achievement to their past teachers. One might imagine a system could exist where good teachers were paid for good results and poor teachers would be encouraged (by their lack of pay) to leave the profession. It would take more than a good imagination to enact such a system. The reason is that most teachers in the United States are represented by a union that is an independent union, an affiliate of the National Education Association, or the American Federation of Teachers. Unions in general, and teachers' unions in particular, prefer that pay be based solely on education and seniority.

This means that a poor teacher with more experience earns more than a good teacher with fewer years in the classroom. This is a problem because energetic teachers can become discouraged by the lack of monetary recognition for their efforts. Any time pay is based strictly on who you are rather than what you do, there is an incentive to do as little as possible.

The other serious obstacle to rewarding good teachers and getting rid of bad ones is teacher tenure. Much like tenure in colleges and universities, K–12 educators are often granted tenure after they have successfully met certain criteria and taught for a set number of years. This means that, short of some abusive behavior, they cannot be fired. This further adds to the lack of performance incentives among teachers.

Many teachers and their union representatives argue several points in defense of this system. First, they argue that as professionals they are above economic considerations and teach to the best of their ability all the time. Second, they argue that granting a principal the power to fire senior teachers and offer merit pay would foster unproductive favoritism. Only those who supported the principal would keep their jobs or get large pay increases. Last, they argue that pay in general is low relative to other professionals and that any additional money should raise all teachers' pay to a higher level.

An additional obstacle facing the current educational system is the degree to which talented women have fled teaching jobs. Economists Caroline Hoxby and Andrew Leigh have identified a frightening degree of movement of high-capability women away from teaching and an even more frightening shift of less capable women toward teaching. This, combined with the fact that very few men, capable or otherwise, choose teaching as a profession, means that salaries will have to rise in order to reattract bright men and women to the profession of teaching. Teachers' salaries, although they have risen with inflation, have fallen relative to the salaries of equally credentialed occupations. These economists argue that economics has overcome the sociological tendency of women to be attracted to teaching as a profession and only more pay will reverse this trend.

Private versus Public Education

In the presence of failed or failing public schools, many people have begun to ask whether private schools should be allowed to receive public funds. In general, students from private schools perform dramatically better and have far fewer discipline problems than students in public schools. This happens even though most private schools exist with funding that is far less than that of public schools.

When private schools outperform public schools, it can be attributed to a variety of factors. Because parents pay tuition to private schools out of their own pockets, we can surmise that most students come from homes where education matters and tend to be wealthier than their counterparts in public schools, and it is unlikely they possess ADA-specified conditions.

The question is whether, after separating out these factors, private schools do outperform. The answer is an equivocal "yes." If you look at public school students who fit a profile similar to private school students, private schools do a little more with somewhat fewer resources. The difference is not as dramatic as it is without this filter, but it still exists. The primary reason is that parents' involvement is higher and administrative costs are lower in private schools.

There is a concern, however, as it relates to private schools that they would be motivated to admit the easiest to educate. By and large, students with higher test scores, students from two-parent households, and students without significant physical or psychological challenges are easier to teach than other students. **Cherry-picking,** the act of choosing students easy to educate, would leave the hardest and most expensive students in the public schools.

cherry-picking
The act of admitting only students who are easy to educate, leaving the harder and more expensive ones for public schools.

School Vouchers

The question raised by the preceding analysis is whether parents should be allowed to take their children out of a public school and have them placed in another public school or a private school that is then given the taxpayer money that would have gone to educate the child in the public school. With cost savings and a general dislike of teachers' unions in mind, this option is popular among Republicans. Democrats, strict believers in the "public" part of public education, generally oppose attempts at privatization.

There are, however, ongoing experiments with school vouchers. The school system in Milwaukee, Wisconsin, for example, has been operating a school choice program since 1990. In this system, low-income parents can obtain vouchers to send their children to secular (i.e., nonreligious) private schools. The degree of parental disgust with public schools can be seen in the fact that there was space for only a third of those who applied for the vouchers.[3]

The results of this experiment and others like it are mixed. Until recently, only a research team at the University of Wisconsin had access to the data and they concluded that, compared to all other Milwaukee public school students, children did no better. Research that ensued after the data were released to the general academic community suggests that those in the program for three or more years did better (3 to 5 percentile points on reading and 5 to 12 on math) than those who applied but were denied due to space limitations.

The debate continues on the wisdom of school vouchers from a variety of perspectives, political, ethical, and economic. Research conducted separately by Helen Ladd and Derek Neal suggests that vouchers and charter schools have not performed so well, or so badly as to settle the issue from the perspective of effectiveness. Part of the problem in such analysis is that parents who show an interest in getting their children out of failing public schools are likely to nurture their children in either setting. If those who succeed in getting their children out of the failing schools and into charter schools are highly motivated parents, then any success in the charter schools is likely to be overstated with simple analysis. These researchers found that controlling for that bias, the impact of charter schools is modest at best. A 2019 study of Boston area charter schools reported evidence that suggested otherwise. Cohodes, Setren, and Walters reported that when highly successful charter schools were offered funding to replicate their results in other locations using the same education practices, they were indeed successful. The Boston system eliminated the cherry-picking problem by engaging in a lottery for limited spots in those charter schools. The comparisons were, therefore, to students who "lost" that lottery. The conclusion of these authors was that when the educational practices were highly standardized, their successes were able to be replicated.

Collective Bargaining

An issue that developed in the aftermath of the 2010 midterm elections was the degree to which the collective bargaining rights of teachers had led to, or even contributed to, a perceived decline in education outcomes in public elementary and secondary schools. Indiana and Wisconsin limited the collective bargaining rights of their teachers (as well as other public employees). The changes were, at least in part, motivated by the desire to control non-salary-related costs.

If you read Chapter 16 and its discussion of the public employee pension crisis that is about to hit many states, you understand that it is not current teachers' salaries that are considered the problem, but instead it is their pensions. These pensions are frequently defined benefit pensions with a "rule of 85" clause that allows any teacher in a state to retire with full benefits (typically 75 percent of their salary) when their age plus their years of service equals 85.

The perception in Wisconsin was that collective bargaining led to these types of pension arrangements,

[3]State law mandated that in such a circumstance the awarding of vouchers would be determined at random.

which allowed teachers to retire at full benefits at age 55. That was considered more generous than the state could afford.

Associated with that same collective bargaining issue was the realization that state education budgets across the country were going to be cut, and it was through collective bargaining that teachers' unions had negotiated "last in, first out" clauses for layoffs. Those in favor of significant educational reform felt that these provisions would inappropriately require that excellent young teachers be let go, while poor (yet experienced) teachers remained. Those opposed to the stripping of collective bargaining rights for teachers objected to what they described as the vilification of experienced teachers.

Summary

You now understand that education is an investment in human capital and that this investment not only increases the earnings of the person being educated but has positive externalities as well. You also understand that spending more money will not necessarily yield even more returns. Moreover, you are aware of the debate centering on whether, with the current education structure, we are on the "flat" of the education production function. You now understand the controversies behind the school reform issues of tenure, merit pay, vouchers, and collective bargaining.

Key Terms

cherry-picking
external benefits
human capital
net present value

Quiz Yourself

1. The evidence on the impact of spending on K-12 education outcomes suggests that, ceteris paribus, the
   a. more a school district spends, the better it does.
   b. more a school district spends, the worse it does.
   c. more a school district spends on expensive buildings, the better it does.
   d. amount of money a school district spends has no consistent positive or negative impact on outcomes.
2. The fact that education benefits not just the person being educated but society as a whole, suggests that there is a
   a. positive externality.
   b. negative externality.
   c. high level of fixed costs.
   d. monopoly.
3. The argument that spending more money on teachers has little impact on educational outcomes in K-12 is
   a. inconsistent with any economic model.
   b. consistent with the upward-sloping nature of a production function.
   c. consistent with the downward-sloping nature of a demand curve.
   d. consistent with the flat part of the production function.
4. The institution of teacher tenure is meant to
   a. ensure job security for teachers with 10 years of experience.
   b. ensure that teachers do not get fired for political reasons.
   c. allow teachers to engage in any behavior they wish.
   d. allow for the easy firing of incompetent teachers.
5. The evidence on charter schools is that they have had
   a. no impact in any locations they have been tried.
   b. an enormously positive impact on education generally.
   c. a negative impact on students.
   d. some impact in some locations, but there is no generally obvious positive impact.
6. If all K-12 schools were privately owned with a constant subsidy paid by the government to the school for each student enrolled, what would be one potential and likely negative consequence?
   a. Cherry-picking
   b. Collective bargaining
   c. Tenure
   d. Vouchers

7. In most school districts, all other characteristics held constant, an excellent teacher earns _______ a poor teacher.
   a. the same as
   b. more than
   c. less than

Short Answer Questions

1. Explain how the data in Figures 36.2 through 36.5 (increasing real spending per pupil, decreasing class sizes, decreasing SATs, and increasing graduation rates) can be occurring at the same time.
2. Use the production function "flat of the curve" explanation to describe why more money spent on education may not have a significant impact.
3. Provide an explanation for why it is possible that average SATs that are declining might be consistent with the assertion that more people are prepared for college than ever before.
4. Suppose you were to find yourself between an advocate for education who claimed that you have to pay teachers more in order to get more qualified teachers and an advocate for education reform who claimed that paying the same teachers more money won't help. Explain why they both might be correct.

Think about This

As bad as the gender discrimination of the 1950s and 1960s was to the career aspirations of smart women, there was a silver lining to the dark cloud: School systems could hire very smart, very capable, and very motivated women to be elementary teachers and do so for relatively modest salaries. Suppose you were a school board member in the 1980s and noticed the decline in abilities of the new graduates. What would you have done to reattract great women to the teaching profession?

Talk about This

Should teachers' salaries be tied to their performance? How would you measure their performance? Should the performance-evaluation mechanisms be strictly based on quantitative factors (e.g., test scores) or should they reflect the subjective judgments of administrators?

For More Insight See

Greene, Jay P., Paul E. Peterson, Jiangtao Du, Leesa Boeger, and Curtis L. Frazier, *The Effectiveness of School Choice in Milwaukee: A Secondary Analysis of Data from the Program's Evaluation.* Education and Urban Society, 1999; http://journals.sagepub.com/doi/10.1177/0013124599031002005

Hoxby, Caroline M., and Andrew Leigh, "Pulled Away or Pushed Out? Explaining the Decline in Teacher Aptitude in the United States," *American Economic Review* 94, no. 2 (May 2004).

Journal of Economic Perspectives 10, no. 4 (Fall 1996). See articles by Francine D. Blau; Eric Hanushek; David Card and Alan B. Krueger; and Caroline Minter Hoxby, pp. 3–72.

Journal of Economic Perspectives 16, no. 4 (Fall 2002). See articles by Helen Ladd and Derek Neal, pp. 3–44.

Lochner, Lance, and E. Moretti, "The Effect of Education on Crime: Evidence from Prison Inmates, Arrests, and Self-Reports," *American Economic Review* 94, no. 2 (May 2004).

Rockoff, Jonah E., "The Impact of Individual Teachers on Student Achievement: Evidence from Panel Data," *American Economic Review* 94, no. 2 (May 2004).

Behind the Numbers

Department of Education, National Center for Education Statistics: nces.ed.gov/programs/digest

- Enrollment
- Spending
- Student–teacher ratios
- SATs

U.S. Census Bureau: www.census.gov/topics/education/educational-attainment.html

- Educational attainment by race/ethnicity

CHAPTER THIRTY-SEVEN

College and University Education: Why Is It So Expensive?

Learning Objectives

After reading this chapter you should be able to:

LO1 Explain why a college education is so expensive and why those costs have been rising faster than inflation.

LO2 Demonstrate why some level of subsidies to a college education make sense.

LO3 Explain the role of textbooks in rising higher education costs

LO4 Apply the principle of present value to determine whether college education is a wise investment.

LO5 Recall that the United States has a greater percentage of citizens with a college degree than most other developed countries.

Chapter Outline

In Chapter 36, we raised questions about the costs and effectiveness of education through grade 12. Here, we explore whether students in colleges and universities are receiving good value for their money. In 2017, a little more than $569 billion was spent educating 20 million college students, which works out to $28,781 per student, per year. Obviously, it costs substantially more for higher education than it does for students in elementary or secondary schools. Moreover, tuition, room, and board have increased 767 percent over the last 37 years—a period when overall prices increased only 154 percent. Figure 37.1 shows that both college tuition and college textbook prices have increased much more rapidly than inflation.

To find out why this is the case, we examine some of the economic issues involving higher education. We include a discussion of why it costs more (including the role of textbook prices) and whether those costs are worth it to the college student consumer. We proceed to describe how higher education is financed in the United States.

Why Are the Costs So High?

The reasons why college costs more than high school per student are both obvious and hidden. First, the obvious: On the average, college professors earn salaries that are twice those of elementary and secondary teachers. Colleges have libraries that dwarf what we might see in a high school, and librarians have no choice but to subscribe to wildly expensive journals, including many in the sciences that have five-figure subscription prices.

FIGURE 37.1 College costs relative to CPI.

Source: Bureau of Labor Statistics. https://www.bls.gov/cpi/home.htm

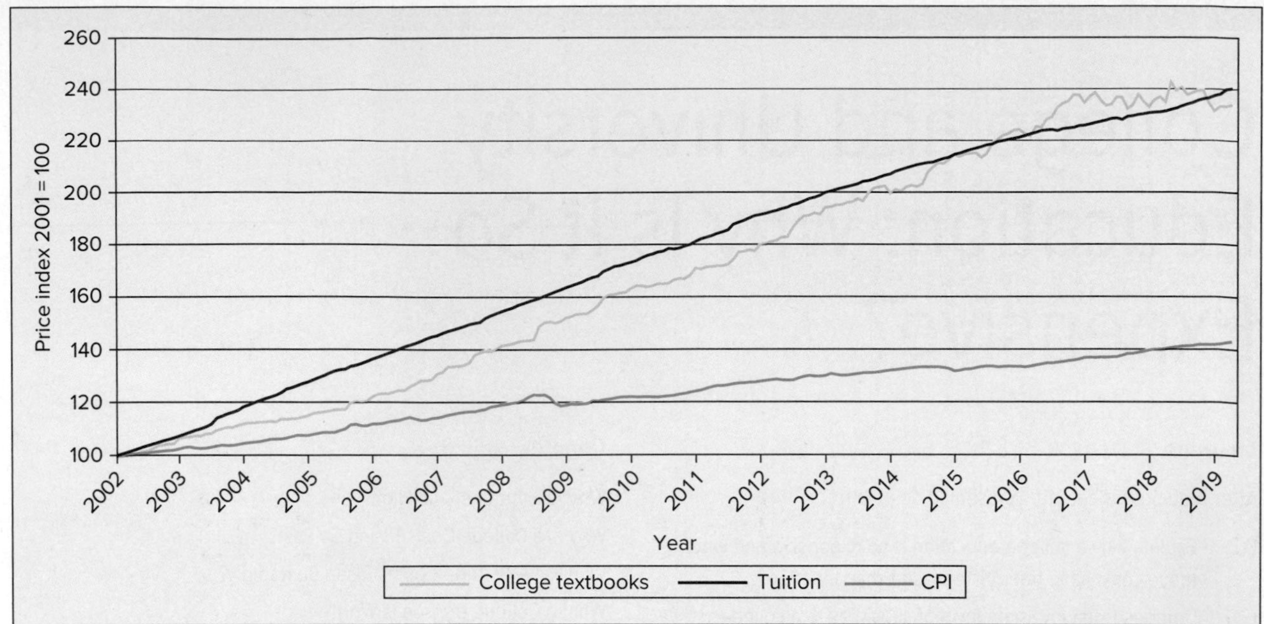

Additionally, college professors teach far less than high school teachers. A professor at a research-oriented university may teach only 3 to 6 hours a week, while a professor in a teaching-oriented community college may average 12 to 15 hours a week. High school teachers are in the classroom from around 8 a.m. to around 3 p.m., with some time off for lunch and preparation. They may teach five- or six-hour-long classes, five days a week. In net, a high school teacher is in class more in a single day than some professors are in a week.

Exploring reasons for the disparities between K-12 and college teachers surfaces less obvious reasons why per-pupil college costs are so high. Educators at all levels must maintain a high level of expertise in their field. At the college level, it is accepted that professors need time for reading and studying. Professors who teach at the higher end of a discipline need particularly great amounts of time for scholarly study. Many professors are also judged by the degree to which they advance knowledge in their academic discipline. This research commands most of a professor's time at most universities, whether or not they are regarded as prestigious. A sad fact of the higher education landscape is that for a professor to advance within an institution, or to advance from a less prestigious school to a more prestigious one, research and other scholarly activity are more important than teaching.

That research is expensive. Research for an English professor requires a well-stocked library and a state-of-the-art computer. This is cheap compared to what it costs to set up a biologist to do advanced research. Not only do biologists require the well-stocked library; they require a laboratory with equipment that can separate DNA and magnify samples so that individual cells can be seen. The cost of some of this equipment is so high that if you used that money to equip high schools, you could equip all the high school labs of a medium-sized city for what it costs to fund the laboratory of a single professor at Harvard, MIT, or Stanford. On the other hand, research generates a considerable amount of money to universities. At nearly $50 billion (for public institutions) in 2017, the revenue associated with grants and contracts is the next biggest source of higher education revenue next to tuition at $79 billion.

A final reason why college is so expensive relates to subsidies. As shown in the previous chapter about K-12 education, a college education provides private benefits to its students as well as external benefits to the public at large. The private benefits include the higher incomes college graduates earn as well as the fun college students have in and especially out of the classroom. The external benefits include the fact that the college educated pay far more in taxes over a lifetime than do those without such an

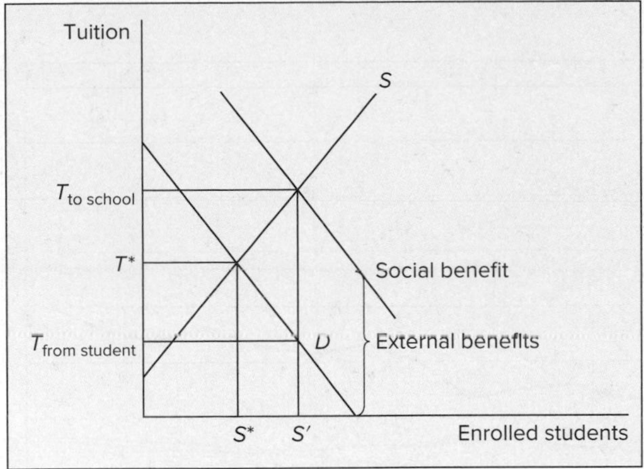

FIGURE 37.2 External benefits of a college education.

education as well as the increased knowledge they bring to their voting and leadership activities. Thus, though perhaps not as significant as the external benefits of K–12 education, they are still high enough to justify having a considerable subsidy to that education.

Just as we used our supply and demand diagram in Chapter 36 to illustrate the inefficiency of just having unsubsidized private K–12 education, we can apply the same models and principles here. Consider Figure 37.2 and what it suggests about the price of a college education. The price is the annual tuition and the quantity is the number of college students educated in a year. At low tuition rates, more students will invest in a college education, so the resulting demand curve is downward sloping. However, if tuition is low, colleges and universities will be willing to educate fewer students.

The equilibrium tuition, T^*, and the equilibrium number of enrolled students, S^*, are what the unsubsidized market would yield. If there is an external benefit of the size shown, then the optimal number of students is much greater than the market amount. Unlike the K–12 case, the optimal number of students is likely not everyone and the optimal price is likely not zero. It does mean that students should not have to pay all of the costs. Students should pay $T_{from\ student}$, and taxpayers should (in the form of a subsidy) pay the rest so that the school gets the amount they need, $T_{to\ school}$, to teach S' students. Notice, though, what happens to the cost per student (not just to the student). It rises from the T^* to $T_{to\ school}$. Subsidizing something contributes to its higher costs because schools can charge more than they otherwise could.

Why Are College Costs Rising So Fast?

As can be seen from Figure 37.3, though tuition has been rising fast, the rise in the revenues to universities has more to do with their other enterprises than it does with tuition. Total revenues to public universities increased by $268 billion over the period 1995 to 2017. Tuition increases only accounted for $55 billion of that increase. The staples of a public university's budget—especially a public university that is not the flagship of the state—are its tuition, its state (and to a lesser degree federal and local) appropriation, and its housing-based auxiliaries (shown in the figure as "Aux-Non-Hospital").

There is little doubt, however, that the mix in revenues has changed dramatically throughout the years, even ignoring the largest part of the increase: that is, the increase in gift, investment, grant and contract, and affiliated hospital-derived income.[1] Figure 37.4 shows how the sources of revenue to universities changed from 1995 to 2017 when you ignore those elements. Clearly, the relative sizes of the wedges of the pie have changed markedly. The worst of it was during and immediately after the Great Recession. From 2007 to 2013, total federal, state, and local appropriations to public universities fell from nearly $80 billion to less than $71 billion. At that same time, tuition revenue increased by 42 percent. Figure 37.4 shows that the share of revenues attributable to appropriations fell from 57 percent in 1995 to 44 percent in 2017, with almost the entirety of that difference being absorbed within tuition. Essentially, public universities are justifying rapid increases in tuition on the relative decline in state appropriations.

Another reason for the increase in the cost of higher education is the degree to which student expectations of their environment have changed. The contrast between post-World War II student housing and modern student housing is remarkable. The floor of 40 two-to-a-room 10 × 15-foot prison cells with a common shower and bathroom facility has been replaced by suite-style housing with private or semiprivate showers and bathrooms. According to the National Center for Education Statistics IPEDS data, between 2002 and 2017 all of that construction led to a 337 percent increase in long-term debt at four-year public institutions. Those costs have been passed on to students. Further, while not always directly demanding modern exercise facilities, students have

[1]Some larger state universities operate hospitals as part of their medical schools, and the revenue from those hospitals significantly distorts the relative size of the revenue sources.

FIGURE 37.3 Revenue to public degree-granting universities.

Source: National Center for Education Statistics. https://nces.ed.gov/programs/digest/d13/tables/dt13_333.10.asp.
*2001–2002 and 2002–2003 interpolated from available data

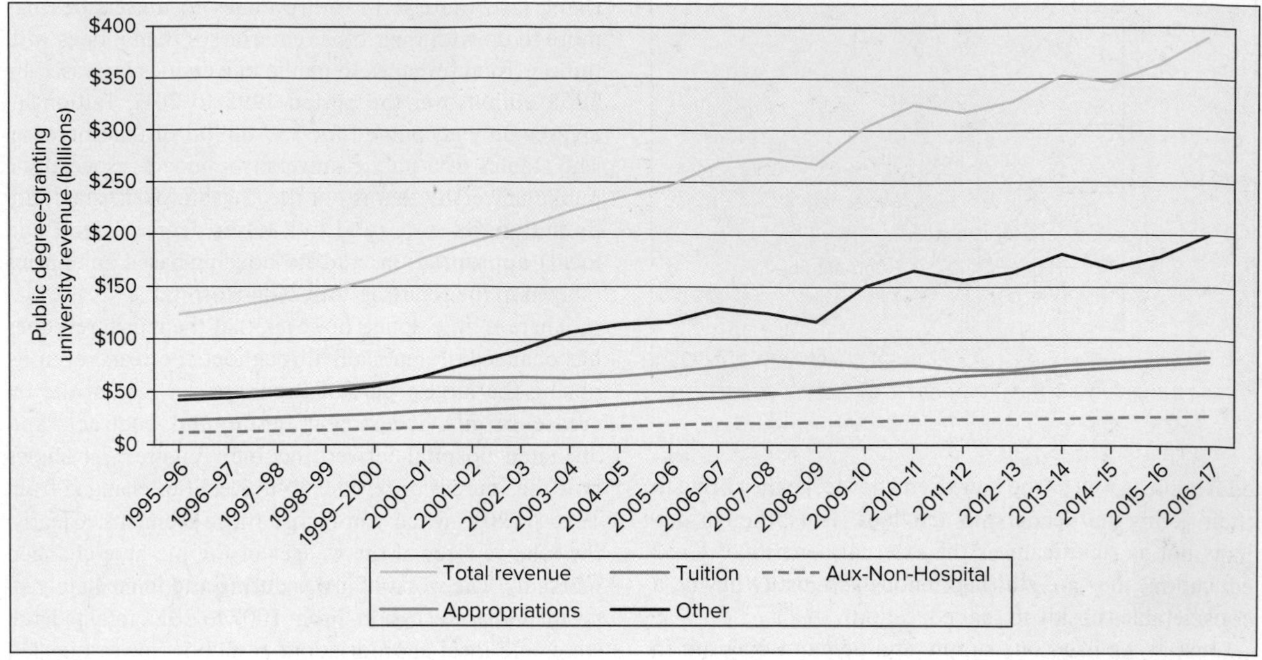

FIGURE 37.4 Share of university revenue: Appropriations, tuition, and non-hospital auxiliaries.

Source: National Center for Education Statistics, http://nces.ed.gov/programs/digest.

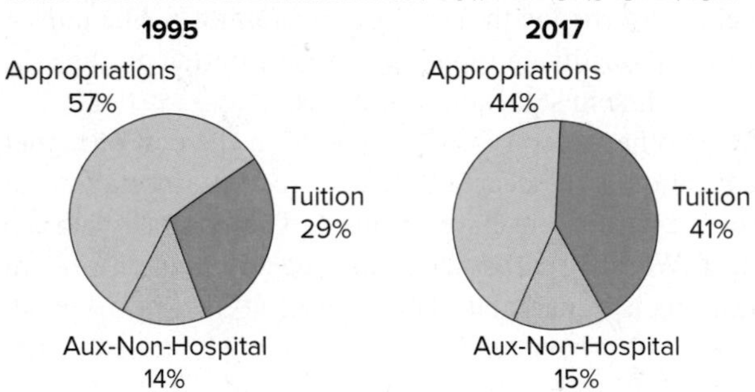

chosen to enroll on campuses that have built them. The costs of constructing and equipping these recreation centers have been passed on to students in the form of either dedicated fees or higher tuition. Universities have built them largely for enrollment reasons. As public universities have become increasingly dependent on tuition revenue, they have become increasingly sensitive to student desires. In particular, out-of-state and international students are particularly prized by public institutions. While state legislatures have placed limits on tuition increases to in-state students, they have largely let institutions charge out-of-state students whatever they wish.

Why Have Textbook Costs Risen So Rapidly?

The market for college textbooks is a good example of many economic concepts: fixed and variable costs, the impact of patents and copyrights on the market for a good, the fuzziness of the line between oligopoly and monopolistic competition, and the degree to which increased technology increases supply. Before we get too deep into the analysis, you should understand how a textbook is developed.

Either solicited or unsolicited, a faculty member will write a chapter or two to show a publisher why this new book would be better than those that exist. Very few of these prospective books make it past this step. Those sample chapters that meet the publisher's expectations are sent to faculty who, when the book is published, might consider using the book for their course. They are compensated for their feedback and, if the publisher senses from that feedback that the book will be successful, a contract is established that specifies how the author is to be paid. Typically, the author earns a **royalty,** which is a percentage of the sales (in the neighborhood of 15 percent) to bookstores (based on the wholesale price, net of returns). An **advance** is usually offered to the author (of a first edition) against future royalties. The book takes at least one year to write, revise, edit, and publish. Often, a first edition takes much longer than subsequent editions because it is typically reviewed by a collection of faculty around the country.

royalty
The amount of money paid to authors. Typically paid on a percentage basis.

advance
The amount of money paid to authors prior to a book's publication. This is typically counted against future royalties.

Once available for sale, the book is offered (in the form of a sample) to faculty that teach a course in which the book might be used. Faculty place their orders with their respective bookstores and the bookstores order them prior to the beginning of the semester.

To see where the money goes on the sale of a new book, consider the one you are reading. As shown in Figure 37.5, suppose this book sold for $200 as a new book in a university's bookstore. The book was sold to the bookstore for $160, so its expenses and profit come out of the store's $40 markup. I get 15 percent of the amount that the publisher gets, or $24. The publisher keeps between $126 and $131. The publisher's costs include very high fixed costs for such things as student assessments and digital supplements for instructors as well as costs associated with editorial staff and marketing. Looking at the physical book market, the variable costs also include the cost of the paper, ink, and printing of the book itself. In all, the marginal production cost of a textbook is less than $10, sometimes as little as $5. If it is an electronic book, the variable costs can be essentially zero. The $126–$131 margin that the publisher makes must cover all the fixed costs of production.

Here it gets tricky because the publisher, and by extension the author, makes money (when the book is physical) only when a new book is sold. You do not have to be in college very long to know that you can buy used textbooks for much less than new ones and that you can sell your books back to the bookstore at the end of the semester. Typically a physical book that sells new for $200 will sell used for $160. The bookstore will have purchased that used book from a previous student at the

FIGURE 37.5 Where your textbook dollar goes.

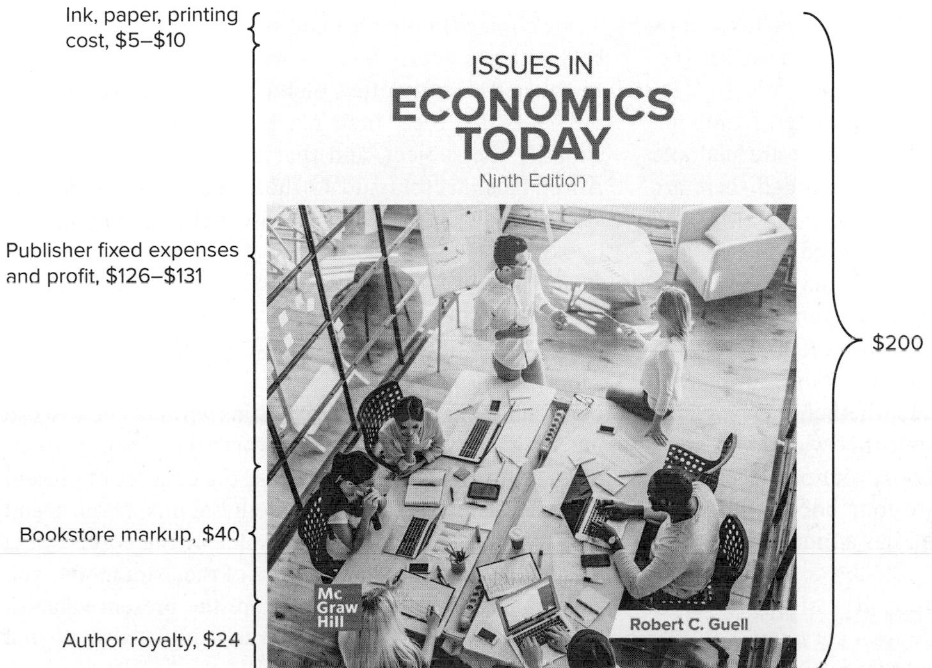

same university for around $100.[2] The bookstore then stocks both new books and used books and makes a profit on either. There is some risk for the bookstore in overstocking a new book, since they have to pay a restocking fee to return new books to the publisher, but there is enormous risk in overstocking used books.

The bottom line for publishers is that they are in business to make money, and new sales increase profits and used book sales eat into profits. That is why several publishers are engaging in interesting tactics to minimize the impact of the used book market. The favored strategy among several publishers is to offer the book primarily in electronic (or loose-leaf) form. If they can limit the number of bound physical books in circulation, they can effectively limit students to electronically delivered books. They can do this by offering a much lower price. Doing so makes sense for the publisher if it can gain more revenue than if it sold a physical, bound book once at full price. The only way that works, though, is if there aren't physical, bound books in circulation.

A second significant cause behind the expense of textbooks is the market form. The book you are reading is the intellectual property of its owner. I gave that intellectual property to the publisher in exchange for the royalties they pay me for sales on the book. The copyright gives McGraw-Hill the exclusive right to sell this material. It also prohibits you from going to FedEx Office and making copies for your friends. Copyrights are necessary to bring intellectual property to market because without them producers of the books, songs, and inventions would have no financial motivation to produce them (because of the threat of duplication).

In some disciplines there is one standard textbook that everyone uses, while in others there are multiple texts that look very much the same. Though there are hundreds of textbooks on the market, most are not good substitutes for another. It does little good to bring your economics text to your poetry class. In the end, your professor probably had a relatively small number of books from which to choose. If you are using this book while taking a general education economics course for nonmajors, your professor had to decide whether to spend most of the semester covering economic theory or do an issues approach. Having chosen this book, your professor chose the issues approach. There are four books that really work in this niche. McGraw-Hill has a monopoly on this book, but it is a competitor in this niche. The market form best suited to this area is monopolistic competition.

The market for principles of economics texts is much greater and there are many more choices. There are four really big sellers and several scattered players. This is also an example of monopolistic competition. The differences between books is quite slight (mostly in presentation and emphasis and digital components), but the publishers still retain their monopoly rights. For an example of an area in which there are fewer sellers, consider the market for graduate-level textbooks in mathematical economics. For all intents and purposes, there are two. One is so old, I used it, and the other one is a few years old. This is an example of oligopoly. Some areas of study are so narrow, with such a small market, that there is only one book.

A third reason why textbooks have increased rapidly in price is that, like prescription drugs, in most cases the consumer doesn't get to pick a cheaper alternative. Textbooks are chosen for you by faculty members who can be completely oblivious to the price that will be charged for the book. If that is the case, when students go to the bookstore and get their books, they cannot choose which book to buy (beyond their choice of used versus new, buy versus rent, or print versus e-book). They must decide to obtain the book or not. Thus the price of the book is, frequently, irrelevant in the adoption decision. Under good circumstances, the adoption decision is typically made after a professor has looked at the choices in the area and selected the one that goes best with the course and the way the professor teaches. In the end, faculty often pick books that have the supplements that meet their needs, have illustrations that simplify the subject, and that are pleasing to the eye. All of these factors add to the price of the book. The student is then made to choose between buying the book or not.

What a College Degree Is Worth

Now that we have seen a few reasons why college costs so much, we can ask whether it is worth the expense. To explore this question, we need to use the concept of present value. If the interest-adjusted amount of money you spend on your education, the present value of the costs, is less than the interest-adjusted amount of the extra money you earn as a result of your education, the present value of the benefits, then your college education is worth the money you pay for it.

[2] There are several reasons why a student might get less than the full buy-back price. Some include the existence of key codes for online content or custom content. Bookstores almost never repurchase loose-leaf books.

AVOIDING HIGH TEXTBOOK PRICES

In recent years, there have been three significant changes to the textbook market that have jolted publishers. The first of these is the advent of a relatively old niche market for textbook rentals. Chegg and other Internet companies have revived this relatively small market in a significant way. These companies typically charge approximately half the retail price of the book but compel you to return the book to avoid being charged for the other half. To accomplish this, they will typically take a customer's credit card information for the sale and, if the book is not returned, charge it again. This amounts to the same issue as buying new books and selling them back, but the student doesn't take the risk that the book will be out of edition (and therefore worth much less).

Additionally, companies are beginning to see their e-book alternatives grow in popularity. Again this is like renting a book but the book does not have to be returned. Typically, it becomes inaccessible after a defined period.

An increasing number of faculty who have seen their students struggle with being able to afford their textbooks have chosen a path that is both interesting as an economist and troublesome as an author. It had been the case that when a new edition of a textbook came out, nearly every faculty member would adopt that new edition and the old editions would be of almost no value in the market. For instance, when the fifth edition of this book became available in the spring of 2010, it sold in bookstores for $125 and rented on Chegg for half that. At the same time, the fourth edition, which had sold in bookstores for $120 the semester before, was selling for less than $10 on the Internet's many used-book outlets.

What seems to be occurring now is that some faculty direct the bookstore to order the old edition for everyone in their class so students are in the same position. The faculty member has stayed with the author's book, but there are no profits for the publisher or royalties for the author. The long-run impact of this strategy will, however, result in decreasing its viability as a strategy. As more faculty fail to "roll" to the new edition, the price of old editions will rise on the Internet as their easy availability shrinks. In addition, traditional bookstores will have an increasing difficulty finding and stocking the old editions in sufficient quantity to meet the demand.

Finally, there are open educational resources (OERs). These are frequently books that failed to thrive in the market and the author was released to find another publisher. These books are usually made available for Internet reading only and are free. The open-resource publisher makes money if a student wants a printed version. The author makes very little. Faculty who adopt OERs are left without the ancillaries (such as online homework, test banks, etc.).

Assume for a moment that four years of college cost you $10,000 a year in out-of-pocket expenses and you give up another $12,000 a year in what you would have earned had you worked full time. The total cost of your education is then $22,000 a year, or a total of about $88,000. Since the expenses incurred in the second, third, and fourth years are in the future, you must discount them by the appropriate interest rate. Now assume that instead of making an extra $12,000 a year without a degree, you will earn the degree and then make an extra $36,000 a year. The benefit from going to college is the extra $24,000 you earn a year. We use $24,000 because this is roughly the difference in median income of households headed by people who have college degrees over that same figure for households headed by people with only a high school education. We must again discount these benefits, as they will happen in the future. If we assume that all of these dollar figures are inflation-adjusted and the real interest rate is 3 percent, then the present value of the costs is roughly $82,000 and the present value of 40 years of $24,000 extra a year is $553,333. The net present value of a college degree is $473,333, making it so that dropping out of college is likely the most expensive noncriminal mistake you could ever make. Conversely, doing well in college may be the most lucrative thing you ever do.

How Do People Pay for College?

Many college students recognize the benefits of education but cannot see themselves paying for them. While we have just shown that it makes sense to complete college even if you have to borrow all of the money to do it, you know that taking out student loans does not mean you get a degree. There is some risk involved. You must weigh the risk of having the only thing you take away from college be debt against the benefit that you get the $473,333 in net present value. In addition, according to CollegeBoard, though it seems as if a college degree costs you a lot of money, consider the fact that at a regional bachelors-only public university you are getting a subsidy of nearly $0.85 for every $1 you spend. At flagship doctoral granting state institutions, the subsidy is $0.65. The subsidy at a private university is less, but it is still substantial and usually comes in the form of institutional financial aid and subsidized student loans. Subsidies to universities are computed from the value of interest-reduced loans and gifts to the universities. Whether you are a student at a public or private university, you are paying great sums of money, sums that would be even greater were it not for subsidies from national, state, and private sources.

One of the interesting changes over the decades has been the change in the way students pay for their portion of the costs of a higher education. In the 1940s, World War II veterans received the GI Bill, which allowed many former soldiers to go to college. Not only was their tuition paid, but they were also granted a stipend upon which to live. In the 1960s and 1970s, the federal government instituted programs such as the Pell Grant, which provided a similar benefit to children of poor families. In the 1980s, President Reagan shifted the focus to making student loans available at subsidized rates. In the 1990s, President Clinton reformulated the loan process by increasing federal government involvement and sponsored educational income tax deductions and credits. As a rarely discussed part of the Patient Protection and Affordable Care Act, President Obama's legislation reformed the student loan program to bypass banks. The loans, instead, are administered out of the U.S. Department of Education. Taken together, these transformations have allowed more students to access some form of aid, but the aid is now more likely to come in the form of a subsidized loan.

Nationally, between 1992 and 2016, the percentage of students on some form of aid increased from 58 percent to 86.4 percent, and the percentage borrowing to pay for college increased from 34 percent to 55 percent, while the percentage receiving federally funded education grants has slowly increased to 45 percent.

Figure 37.6 shows that if we measure the success of higher education by looking at degrees granted, there is success across races/ethnicities. On the other hand, the United States is rapidly being caught (and surpassed) by other developed countries in the percentage of adults with a college education. Until recently, the United States led OCED countries with one-third of the adult population ages 25 to 64 having at least a four-year college education. Counting those with some college, including two-year degrees, Canada, Japan, and South Korea have surpassed the United States. Most disturbing is that the rate for young adults (24–35) places the United States behind 10 other countries. The United States is not becoming less educated. It is that others are surpassing us. The college attainment rate for Americans has remained steady through the years, while the rate for other countries has increased rapidly. This could ultimately threaten the comparative advantage the United States had held in this particular area.

FIGURE 37.6 College graduates as a percentage of the 24 and older population.

Source: United States Census Bureau. https://www.census.gov/data/tables/time-series/demo/educational-attainment/cps-historical-time-series.html.

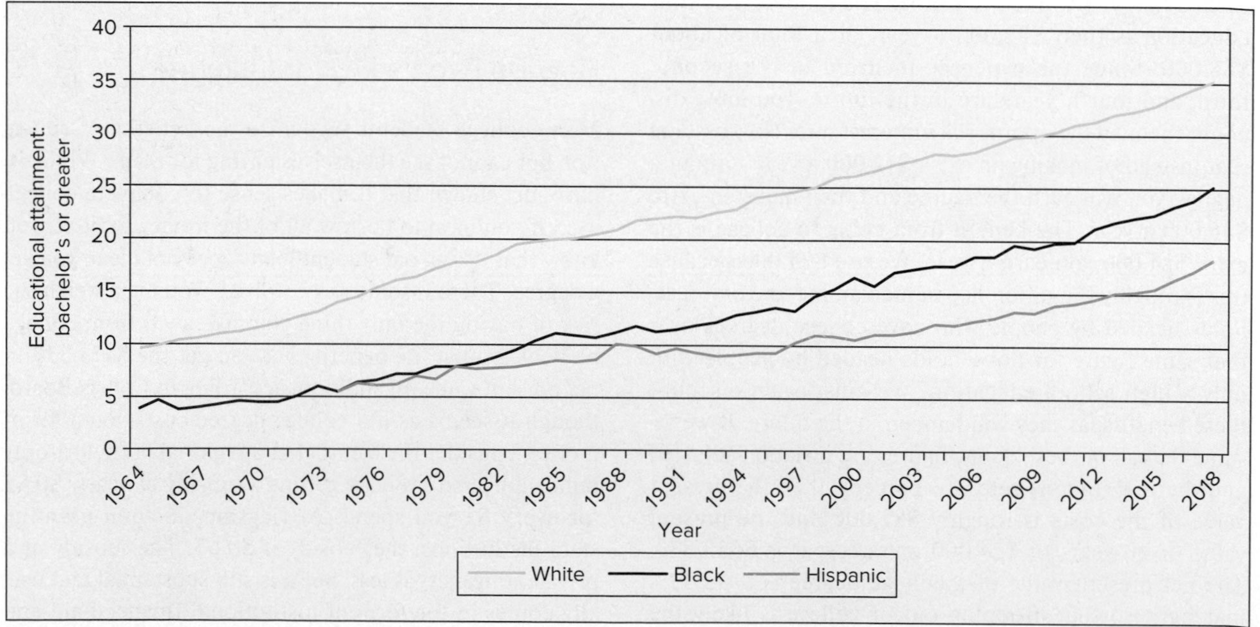

Summary

You now understand why a college education is an expensive thing to provide and why those costs have been rising faster than inflation over the years. You know that a part of that rapidly rising set of costs is associated with the cost of textbooks. You understand that the principle of present value is useful in seeing why borrowing money to pay for a college education is a wise, though potentially risky, investment in future income potential and that the source of funds for students has increasingly moved from grants to loans. Finally, you observed that though higher educational attainment is higher in the United States than it is in most countries, that advantage is evaporating as other countries' citizens are rapidly increasing their levels of educational attainment.

Key Terms

advance

royalty

Quiz Yourself

1. Which of the following has experienced the slowest increase?
   a. Overall prices
   b. College textbook prices
   c. College tuition
2. Subsidies to higher education
   a. exist for public universities only.
   b. exist for both public and private universities.
   c. that make higher education free to everyone would (from economists' perspective) be wise.
   d. can only be given to students (rather than universities).
3. What are the key reasons why college costs are higher than high school costs?
   a. Research expenses
   b. College faculty salaries are higher than K–12 faculty salaries
   c. Subsidies to education cause increased demand for it
   d. All of these
4. The textbook publishing industry has a great deal in common with the pharmaceutical industry in that there are __________ fixed costs and __________ marginal costs.
   a. high; high
   b. high; low
   c. low; high
   d. low; low
5. Authors are typically paid for their work
   a. based on a percentage of the sales at college bookstores.
   b. based on a percentage of the sales from publishers to bookstores.
   c. a fixed amount regardless of sales.
   d. on a per-page basis.
6. The economic tool that proves the value of an expensive college education is
   a. the production possibilities frontier.
   b. the yield curve.
   c. supply and demand.
   d. present value.
7. The cost of educating a college student is
   a. less than the cost of educating a high school student because college classes are generally large.
   b. equal to the cost of educating a high school student because, although college teachers make more money, their classes are generally larger.
   c. less than it used to be.
   d. much greater than the cost of educating a high school student because college professors make more money and teach fewer hours per week.
8. The United States has a ______ level of educational attainment than most countries when considering all age groups. It ranks _____ than that when you look at the 24- to 35-year-old group.
   a. higher; lower
   b. higher; higher
   c. lower; lower
   d. lower; higher

Short Answer Questions

1. Suppose there is a fixed level of external benefit (accruing to the general public) of students getting a college education. Suppose it exactly equals what community colleges are currently charging, and a subsidy is set so that community college becomes free. Show why it is likely that community colleges will raise tuition almost immediately.
2. Distinguish between what you have learned in this class that could be described as an external benefit and that which is likely only a private benefit.

Think about This

Your education, from kindergarten through college, benefited you and it benefited society. The proportion of a typical college education paid by the student has risen in recent years. How much of your college education do you pay? (Consider the state appropriation to your school if it is public, the federal and state financial aid that you get, and the value of the guarantee on any of your student loans.) Is this the right division of the burden?

Talk about This

How did cost figure into your choice of school? Did you have lots of options? If you could have gotten a "full ride," where would you have gone?

Behind the Numbers

Department of Education, National Center for Education Statistics: nces.ed.gov/programs/digest

- Enrollment
- Spending
- Funding sources

Department of Education, National Center for Education Statistics: nces.ed.gov/programs/coe/

- International comparisons of educational attainment

U.S. Census Bureau: www.census.gov/topics/education/educational-attainment.html

- Educational attainment by race/ethnicity

Bureau of Labor Statistics: www.bls.gov/cpi

- Textbook and tuition prices
- Overall prices

CHAPTER THIRTY-EIGHT

Poverty and Welfare

Learning Objectives

After reading this chapter you should be able to:

LO1 Describe how poverty is measured and summarize the problems associated with that measure.

LO2 Summarize the demographics of poverty in the United States.

LO3 List and describe the programs that exist for the poor.

LO4 Describe the cash and in-kind programs designed to assist the poor and explain why voters may prefer in-kind programs over cash assistance.

LO5 List the incentives and disincentives of welfare.

LO6 Summarize the welfare reform issues that we currently face.

Chapter Outline

Welfare and its reform have been political issues from the time when the first "relief" bills were passed by Congress in the 1930s. In the 1990s, President Bill Clinton vowed to "end welfare as we know it," and in 1996, a compromise was reached between his administration and the Republican majority in Congress. In 2019, the political left resurrected the idea of universal basic income, a type of welfare that would guarantee everyone a cash income.

Today, there exists a wide variety of programs that provide assistance to people in need, and we review them in this chapter. Some of these programs, such as TANF, SNAP, and WIC, read like an alphabet soup; others have catchy names, like Head Start and Medicaid; still others have more straightforward names, like the School Lunch and Breakfast Program. Each program is designed to help poor people in specific ways. Some disburse cash; others provide goods or services at little or no cost.

After defining what constitutes a state of "poverty," we describe the people who meet the criteria. We present and discuss the history of poverty, and we discuss why the measure of poverty we outlined might not be adequate to the task of ascertaining who needs assistance. We then describe the programs that are available to the poor. We divide the programs into those that provide cash and those that provide goods and services. We discuss why we make such a division. Last, we discuss, in general terms, the incentives and disincentives inevitably associated with welfare programs, and we show why it is so difficult to solve the problems of those who live in poverty.

Measuring Poverty

What does being "poor" really mean? Are you poor only if you are on the verge of starvation? This absolutist position would suggest that poverty in the United States is almost entirely gone. As we will see later in our discussion, one of the most significant health problems of America's poor is that they are obese rather than starving. On the other hand, there is the position that poverty is a relative concept. We note that someone who has the living standard of a median-income Somalian is in poverty in the United States but not in Somalia, and an American today with an average income has a living standard that 100 years from now will likely be considered unacceptably poor. To see this point, note that the poor of today live in larger homes than all but the very richest Americans did in 1900.

The Poverty Line

Surveys have established reasonably well that low-income families of four spend roughly one-third of their income on food. Defining the **poverty line** as the level of annual income sufficient to provide a family with a minimally adequate standard of living, we created the first poverty line by multiplying the cost of a minimally sufficient diet by three, the reciprocal of one-third. In successive years, the amount has been raised by the amount of increase in the consumer price index (CPI). For other family sizes, a similar methodology is used where the reciprocal of the fraction of income spent on food by low-income people of that family size is multiplied by the cost of the minimally sufficient diet. In 2017, these numbers were $12,488 for one person, $15,877 for two people, $19,515 for three people, and $25,094 for four people. The **poverty rate** is the percentage of people in households whose incomes are under the poverty line. In 2017, the poverty rate in the United States was 12.3 percent.

poverty line
The level of income sufficient to provide a family with a minimally adequate standard of living.

poverty rate
The percentage of people in households whose incomes are under the poverty line.

poverty gap
The total amount of money that would have to be transferred to households below the poverty line for them to get out of poverty.

Another important measure of poverty is the **poverty gap**, a representation of the total amount of money that would have to be transferred to households below the poverty line in order for them to get out of poverty. The poverty gap in the United States was $84 billion in 2017.

Who's Poor?

Table 38.1 shows the basic demographics of the U.S. population and that portion in poverty. Many people think that most poor people are African American. While many academics are quick to dispel that myth, they often perpetuate another with a counter-assertion that most poor people are white. Neither is true if you separate

Table 38.1 Who's poor.

Source: U.S. Census Bureau. Current Population Survey, www.census.gov/topics/income-poverty/poverty/data/tables.html

Demographic	General Population (in millions)	Percentage of the General Population	Percentage of Those in Poverty	Poverty Rate (%)	People in Poverty
White alone, not Hispanic	195.3	60.5%	42.8%	8.7	17.0
Hispanic	59.1	18.3	27.2	18.3	10.8
Black alone, not Hispanic	42.5	13.2	22.7	21.2	9.0
Male	158.1	49.0	43.7	11.0	17.4
Female	164.4	51.0	56.3	13.6	22.3
Under 18	73.4	22.7	32.3	17.5	12.8
18 to 64 years	198.1	61.4	55.9	11.2	22.2
65 and over	51.1	15.8	11.8	9.2	4.7
Female-headed household, no husband present	48.0	14.9	33.7	27.9	13.4
No high school diploma*	22.4	6.9	13.8	24.5	5.5
High school graduate (no college)*	62.7	19.4	20.0	12.7	7.9
Some college (no degree)*	57.8	17.9	12.8	8.8	5.1
Bachelor's degree or higher*	76.9	23.8	9.2	4.8	3.7

*There are different thresholds for different compositions of each group. These figures are for a single adult under 65, two adults, two adults and one child, and two adults and two children, respectively.

European Americans from Hispanic Americans. Table 38.1 shows disproportionate numbers of African Americans (who also do not identify as Hispanic) and Hispanics are in poverty and that they comprise a majority of the Americans living below the poverty line. It is obvious that there is a significant degree of racial and ethnic distinction in U.S. rates of poverty.

The data indicate that women are more likely to be in poverty than men; and, if we define "families" as not including single adults, then of families in poverty, half are in female-headed households while 39 percent are families of married couples. Given that female-headed households with children make up only 14.9 percent of the general population, poverty is clearly a women's issue.

It is also true that children under 18 make up 32.3 percent of those who are poor, though they comprise only 22.7 percent of the general population. This is a poverty rate among children of 17.5 percent. Whether this indicates that the poor have more children or that raising children can itself lead families into poverty can be debated. Clearly, the picture of poverty is this: Minorities, women, and children are poor in numbers vastly out of proportion to their numbers in the general population.

Another key indicator of poverty is education or, more properly, the lack of it. Those with a bachelor's degree experience poverty at one-fifth the rate of high school dropouts. Simply completing high school cuts the chance of being in poverty nearly in half, and simply attending college reduces the chance of being in poverty from 12.7 percent to 8.8 percent. Completing college reduces the rate even further. Only 1 in 21 households headed by a college graduate is in poverty.

Poverty through History

Figure 38.1 shows that although the number of people in poverty is modestly higher than it was in 1959, the poverty rate has fallen dramatically. As we will discuss later, the poverty rate shown fails to account for the many government benefits.

In considering the decline in the general trend in poverty, be aware of jumping to quick conclusions. The poverty rate has remained largely unchanged since the middle 1960s when the "war on poverty" actually began. From that time to the present, it has neither fallen below 11 percent nor, until the Great Recession, gone above 15.2 percent. The systemic reduction, as a matter of fact, occurred between 1959 and 1969, before the enactment of many antipoverty programs. Noting that the shaded bars in Figure 38.1 indicate recessions, we can see that the poverty rate has increased during recessions and decreased during periods of growth. Democratic presidents Kennedy and Johnson get much of the credit for the pre-1969 reduction in the poverty rate. However, this was more greatly attributed to economic opportunities as a result of a strong economy than anything these

FIGURE 38.1 Poverty since 1959.

Source: U.S. Census Bureau. Current Population Survey, www.census.gov/topics/income-poverty/poverty/data/tables.html

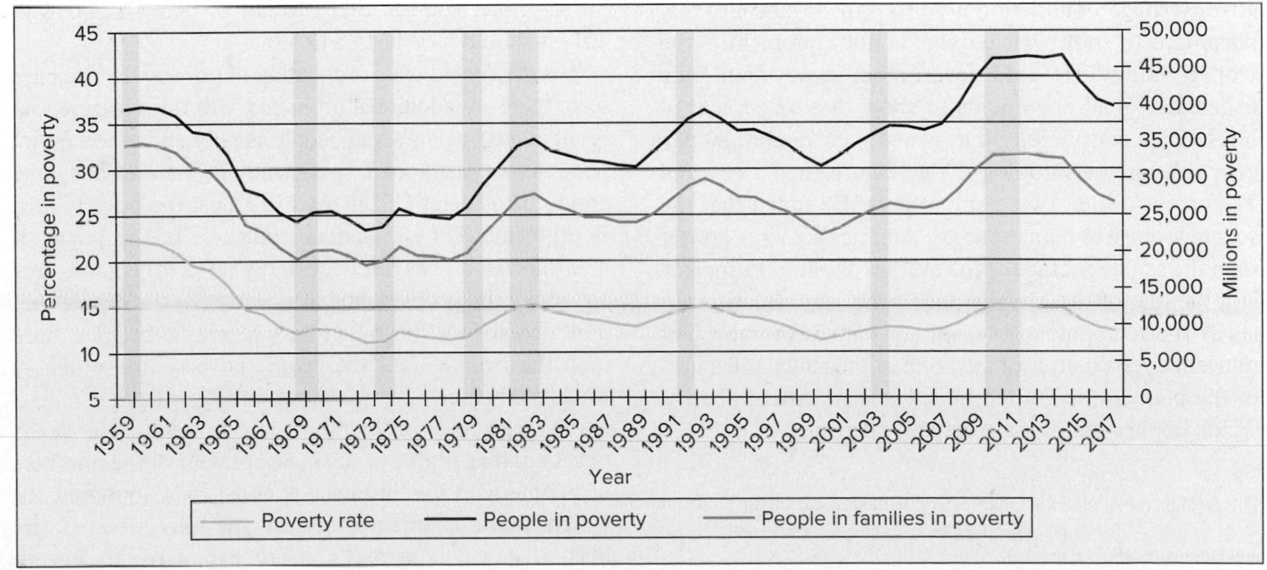

administrations did for the poor. The bulk of the pre-1969 decline took place prior to 1965 when antipoverty programs first began to become law. Since 1969, Democrats and Republicans have nearly identical records with respect to poverty. Generally speaking, the poverty rate is a reflection of the health of the overall economy.

Problems with Our Measure of Poverty

There is a host of reasons why using three times the cost of a minimally sufficient diet as a measure of poverty is inadequate to the task of measuring who is poor. First, it does not distinguish among families that are intact with one income earner and families that either are not intact or for other reasons have day-care costs. Because nearly 34 percent of families living in poverty are headed by single women with children under 18, this is potentially a significant problem. The one-third fraction used in the original poverty measure came from a survey conducted when there were fewer such female-headed households, so the poverty line could be understated by all or part of the cost of day care. The U.S. Census Bureau has two different surveys from which it estimates typical child-care costs, and those surveys give significantly different results. For instance, for a child under five, the median cost of care is $100 per week in one survey and $149 per week in the other. Regardless of which one is correct, ignoring these costs, even if there are many children in poverty who are watched by grandparents (30 percent), significantly understates poverty.

Although this indicates that poverty is understated, there are problems with the measure that indicate that poverty may be overstated. Robert Rector of the conservative Heritage Foundation used to provide statistics that purported to show that poverty is not a problem in the United States.[1] He used government surveys and published statistical documents to show that 42 percent of households considered poor owned their homes, 80 percent had air conditioning, 75 percent owned a car, and 31 percent owned two or more cars. He noted that the square footage of living space of America's poor is greater than the square footage of the average Western European, and the diet of the average poor American equals or exceeds the recommended daily allowances of important nutrients. As a matter of fact, one of the singular features of the poor in the United States is their rate of obesity, which implies that few are actually starving.

[1] The most recent version is available at www.heritage.org/research/reports/2015/09/poverty-and-the-social-welfare-state-in-the-united-states-and-other-nations.

Specifically on the point of wealth, 1.7 million poor families own homes worth between $150,000 and $300,000. There are hundreds of thousands of people in the United States who have little income but who are worth hundreds of thousands of dollars. Some are even millionaires. Admittedly, it is a small number of people like this who are rich but called poor. However, it is important to note that the poverty line measures only people's income relative to a fixed standard that ignores measures of wealth.

Another shortcoming of the formula that determines the poverty line is that it only includes cash income. Thus, programs that the poor take advantage of that are not cash-driven are incorrectly and absurdly omitted as if they have no value. For instance, the $250 of SNAP benefits that a family might receive each month is not counted, and if they found a subsidized rental apartment and free medical care, these benefits would not be counted either. Depending on the study, failing to include income that is in forms other than cash overstates poverty by between two and four percentage points.

As we saw in Chapter 6, the CPI that is used to update the poverty line each year has many shortcomings. Best estimates are that prior to 2008 it has overestimated the cost of living by a full percentage point and in subsequent years by eight-tenths of a percentage point. Because the increase in the poverty line is generated using this flawed measure, it is likely that the poverty line has long been overstated relative to its real value in the 1960s. Figure 38.2 indicates that although the lower line, the adjusted version, tracks the upper line throughout the 1960s, the spread is significant enough that if you take the 1959 poverty line as the base on which to build the adjusted poverty line, you see that instead of being $25,094 in 2017 it should have been $15,926.

Besides the possible overstating of poverty that we have seen, there are additional problems with this measure that result in mislabeling some people as poor and others as not poor. As we mentioned, specifically in the previous paragraph, the general CPI is used to adjust the poverty line. Because the CPI is a general indicator of the prices of many goods, it does not necessarily reflect the goods that are bought by people living in poverty. To the degree that poor people buy things that have increased in price more than the overall CPI, the "true" poverty line probably would fall between the two shown in Figure 38.2.

The way costs of living vary from area to area leads to yet another source of mismeasurement of the numbers of people who live in poverty, and it is a source about which there is uncertainty of the direction of the bias. Because it is much more expensive to live in

FIGURE 38.2 Poverty line with and without CPI adjustment.

Source: U.S. Census Bureau. Current Population Survey, www.census.gov/topics/income-poverty/poverty/data/tables.html

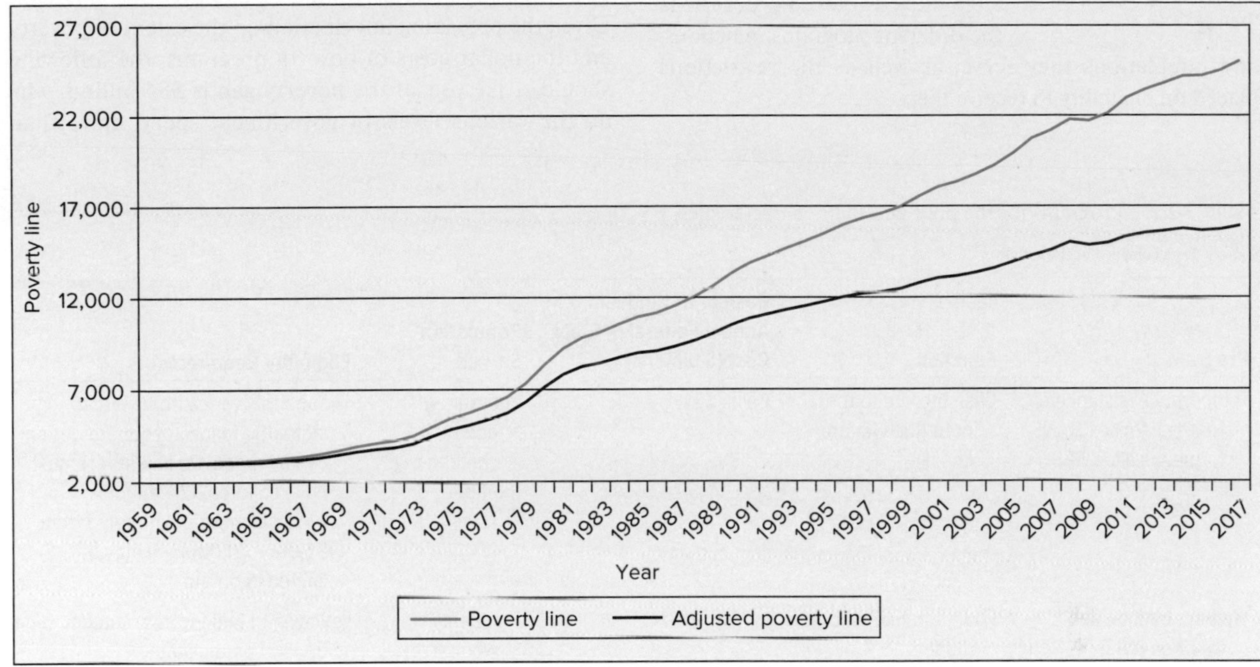

San Francisco, California, than in Appleton, Wisconsin, for example, families of four in San Francisco with incomes that are a single dollar over the poverty line figure of $25,094 are significantly worse off than families of four in Appleton with incomes one dollar under the poverty line. In this way, the poverty rate underestimates both urban poverty and poverty on the coasts. It overestimates the incidence of poverty in rural areas and small cities in the South and the Midwest.

There is a final reason to doubt official poverty numbers, and that is a missing $2 trillion. In Chapter 6, when we talked about national income accounting, we briefly explained the sources of the numbers that comprise GDP. It turns out that data used by the U.S. Census Bureau add up to substantially less, $2 trillion less, than the source numbers for personal income used in GDP calculations. While much of the missing $2 trillion is the in-kind transfers mentioned above, this certainly does not account for all of it. It is clearly true that most of that probably goes to the nonpoor. Some of it must also be in the hands of the poor, so there are clearly some who are labeled poor who are not.

Poverty in the United States versus Europe

As referred to in the opening, most countries have their own measures of poverty and they are not directly comparable. Timothy Smeeding, one of the foremost economists on the subject of poverty and income inequality, has attempted to create those comparable measures. He used the U.S. poverty line, adjusted it for different currency values, and looked at the percentage of people in various European countries who would fall below this line. Using this measure, he noted that U.S. poverty rates were higher than eight of the nine countries examined. When he focused strictly on income inequality, measured by the percentage of people living on incomes below 40 percent of a country's median disposable income, he found that the United States had the most unequal income of any of the countries compared. Generally speaking, therefore, poverty is a bigger problem in the United States than it is in Europe.

Programs for the Poor

In Kind versus In Cash

The programs available to the poor are many and complicated. They are better understood as varying from state to state rather than being one consistent program across the country. Furthermore, these programs are best understood as being divided between cash payments and provisions of goods and services in forms other

in-kind subsidies
Provisions of goods and services in forms other than cash.

than cash. Economists refer to the latter types as **in-kind subsidies.** Table 38.2 describes the different programs, functions, and populations they serve, as well as the restrictions placed on eligibility to receive them.

Why Spend $866 Billion on an $84 Billion Problem?

Given the preceding information on the extent of poverty and the dollar costs of poverty programs, the following should strike you: If the poverty gap is $84 billion, why do the various levels of government spend more than

Table 38.2 Programs for the poor and their characteristics, FY2017.

Sources: Data compiled by the author.

Program	Function	Cash or In-Kind and Annual Federal + State Cost ($ billions)	Population Served	Eligibility Requirements
Temporary Assistance to Needy Families (TANF); formerly called AFDC	Cash income to the poor (the welfare check)	Cash, $31.1	Poor parents and their children under 18	Though this varies from state to state, the following generalization can be made: Recipients (1) must have children; (2) cannot have much wealth (ranging from $1,000–10,000); (3) may be limited in duration
Women, Infants, and Children (WIC)	Food, formula, and diapers	In-kind, $5.7	Pregnant women and new mothers	Low wealth and income; cutoffs depend on the state
Food Stamps (now called SNAP)	Vouchers that can be spent only on food	In-kind, $68.2	All poor	Low wealth and income; cutoffs depend on the state; recipients can remain on the program for only 24 consecutive months
Medicaid		In-kind, $581.9	All poor	Low wealth and income; cutoffs depend on the state
Section 8 or Housing Authority Apartment	Reduced rent or low-cost housing	In-kind, $37.0	All poor	Low wealth and income; cutoffs depend on the state
Head Start	Day care; preschool	In-kind, $8.9	Poor with children under 5	First come, first served for anyone at or below the poverty line with up to 35 percent of enrollment between 100 percent and 130 percent of the poverty line
National School Lunch Program (NSLP)	Lunch and breakfast	In-kind, $17.9	Poor with school-age children	Anyone below 130 percent of the poverty line pays nothing, and anyone below 180 percent of the poverty pays a reduced price
Supplemental Security Income (SSI)	Cash assistance to "deserving poor"	Cash, $54.6	Disabled, widow(er)s, and orphans	Someone (a parent, guardian, or spouse) must be disabled or be deceased
Earned Income Tax Credit (EITC)	Negative tax; boost low-pay workers	Cash, $61.8	Working poor	Based on family size; phases in at incomes up to $14,250, then phases out for incomes between $24,350 and $51,500; family of four maximum is $5,716

10 times that on poverty programs? The answer is twofold: (1) There are people above the poverty line in need whom we choose to help, and (2) poverty programs must be terribly inefficient if it genuinely takes $866 billion to cure an $84 billion problem.

Table 38.2 shows that billions more are spent on goods and services than are spent in cash benefits. Including some minor programs not mentioned in Table 38.2, cash benefits total around $148 billion, whereas in-kind benefits total $719 billion. Clearly, the government spends far more money on programs that give it control over recipients' behavior.

From a societal point of view, our response to poverty is clear. We want the poor to have enough to eat, adequate medical services, adequate housing, and so on. Instead of providing them with enough money to pay for these things, the government provides them with what it thinks they need.

If there is a family whose members enjoy good health, it is conceivable they would rather have more money spent on food and less on medical care, but they cannot make that substitution. People who live in poverty are denied the ability to make basic decisions when they are given specific goods and services rather than money. In many studies of the poor, it is clear that they value cash more than the goods they are provided. Some SNAP recipients show exactly how little they value their benefits by selling them for 50 cents on the dollar.[2] Why haven't programs been designed so that people in need receive cash and are then encouraged to make their own decisions on how to spend it?

There are several reasons, but three come to mind. First, through elected officials, voters have made it clear that they do not trust the judgment of the people who receive government benefits concerning what goods they buy. Many believe that if the poor could make good decisions, they would not be poor.

Second, people are more concerned with the welfare of needy children than with the welfare of adults. If you look at the programs with this in mind, you will see that nearly all of them require the presence of a child for an adult to be eligible. If we want to guarantee services for children, it makes more sense to give the adult access to such services rather than cash. This minimizes the likelihood that the money will be diverted by adults away from the targeted children.

Third, some welfare benefits seem designed more to provide those who tender them with a feeling of magnanimity than to benefit the poor. If voters/taxpayers are interested in their own happiness rather than the happiness of the poor, they may want to see policies that provide the poor with goods and services. Such voters would, perhaps, want some kind of assurance that their money went to its intended purpose.

Is $866 Billion Even a Lot Compared to Other Countries?

Though the United States spends $866 billion on its antipoverty programs, the Smeeding analysis puts this in perspective by noting that European antipoverty programs are far more aggressive. He notes that after accounting for taxes and various welfare programs, the system in the United States reduces poverty (defined by him as the percentage of people living below 50 percent of median household disposable income) by only 26 percent, whereas the average European country's programs reduce their poverty by more than 60 percent. He also notes that where OECD countries devote 55 percent of their antipoverty spending on cash programs, the United States devotes only 17 percent to cash programs.

Incentives, Disincentives, Myths, and Truths

While no one has ever intended this to be the case, many of the programs designed to help the poor are blamed for ensuring that people who live in poverty and receive benefits have no incentive to become self-sufficient. The existence of welfare is accused of giving people a reason not to work. It is blamed for encouraging young women both to get pregnant and to carry the pregnancy to term. Welfare is indicted for encouraging recipients to have more children so that their WIC will be extended and their SNAP and TANF payments increased. The structure of TANF's predecessor, Aid to Families with Dependent Children (AFDC), was blamed for breaking up poor families by giving them the incentive to have the father leave. Together, these problems created the concern that welfare was becoming a way of life and that people were getting used to it.

From a theoretical perspective, each of the preceding arguments has merit, but the evidence from economic studies is not one-sided. First, there are several counterclaims. Birthrates among teenagers climbed steadily from

[2] Early studies of the impact of using SNAP cards instead of food stamp vouchers showed a decrease in fraud by 67 percent. More recently, fraud has increased, focused primarily in smaller retail outlets.

WELFARE'S BEST URBAN LEGEND

The world of welfare is replete with urban legends. My favorite goes something like this: "I was standing in line at the grocery store one day behind a nicely dressed woman who was buying beer, steak, shrimp, and a whole bunch of stuff I couldn't afford. She had them put the steak and shrimp on her SNAP card and used her cash to buy the beer. She packed up her groceries and went to her brand new SUV." In teaching this subject for years, I have heard this story in countless renditions from students who were either customers or grocery employees. The story is almost always the same. While the story may be about fraud, it is also quite likely about their misinterpreting the actions of a foster parent.

Most states give foster families WIC, SNAP, and Medicaid cards to pay for the food and medical expenses of the children in their care. That some of these families are wealthy enough to afford nice meals and nice vehicles does not diminish society's obligation to pay them for the service they are providing by caring for orphaned, discarded, or abused children or those children whose parents are in prison.

the 1960s through the early 1990s and leveled off when the states and then the federal government instituted welfare reforms designed to curb benefits. The truth is that the real dollar value of benefits per recipient is lower today than it was in the late 1960s. Thus, if poor teenagers were really considering the value of welfare in making decisions about having children, teen pregnancy rates would have fallen from the mid-1970s on as the real value of the benefits fell. It is more likely that the culture and teen sex drives had more to do with teen pregnancies than the prospect of receiving welfare checks.

Second, although it was and still is true that the more children you have, the more benefits you get, there is no systematic evidence that people on welfare had more children because they were on welfare. If welfare mothers were concerned only for themselves and the benefits they could get, it would make sense that they would have children so they would be eligible for more benefits. What had to have been evident to them, however, is that the increase in benefits does not cover any more than the increased cost of raising an additional child. Unless we want to claim that the poor do not care about their children, there is little likelihood that rational women would get pregnant and do the work of raising an additional child in order to keep a few extra dollars a month. They could make more money with less effort if they engaged in almost any other form of work.

Third, it is true that families on welfare are far more likely to have absent fathers, but it is hard to say whether the father's leaving was caused by the need to be welfare-eligible or the family became welfare-eligible because the father left. In order to accept the argument that welfare caused an epidemic of absent fathers, you must hold the cynical belief that a well-meaning father would abandon his children so they could receive benefits. Although this might have been the case prior to 1996, today, after welfare reform, the abandonment would have to be complete. A mother now has to name and state the last known location of absent fathers when they apply for benefits. Clearly, whether the need to apply for welfare leads to the breakup of families that would have stayed together is debatable. The reason that some welfare programs are contingent on a parent's absence stems from the conviction that if there are two able-bodied adults in a household, one of them should be working. Either the problem of absent fathers is a coincidence or it is the price society is paying for building welfare requirements around a view that families with both parents present should not be eligible for assistance (unless one is disabled) because at least one should be working.

Fourth, under AFDC, that is, prior to the welfare reforms of 1996, welfare dependency had been growing at an alarming rate. Some 26 percent of recipients had been receiving benefits from the program for 10 years or more at the same time that the percentage of families that had been on welfare for very short periods of time was falling. In addition, daughters of recipients were tending to become recipients themselves. These circumstances and others like them led Congress and the president to agree to change welfare programs to incorporate limits on the length of time people could receive benefits and to require that recipients become gainfully employed.

Welfare Reform

Is There a Solution?

To be successful, a social safety net must meet three goals:

1. The program that is designed cannot be so expensive that the taxpaying public will not sustain it.

2. The program must have an incentive built in that makes beneficiaries want to leave it.
3. The program must provide enough of a level of basic necessities that recipients have a socially acceptable standard of living.

The problem facing policy analysts in the United States has always been that these goals cannot be satisfied simultaneously.

Any program must have a phaseout level of income. If the phaseout is too quick, meaning that for every dollar you earn you lose significant welfare benefits, the disincentive to work will be too profound. The AFDC program reduced benefits by nearly a dollar for every dollar the recipient earned. This nearly 100 percent take-back rate meant that without a salary at least twice the minimum wage in a job, a single parent with two small children requiring day care would be far better off on welfare than working.

If the phaseout is too slow, then too many people will be getting welfare benefits and not enough will be paying taxes. Though this is possible, it violates the first goal, that of having a program that does not cost too much money. On the other hand, the phaseout can be slow and of low cost to taxpayers. The problem will then be that there will not be enough money for recipients to survive.

The implicit choice made by policy makers prior to the welfare reforms that were instituted in 1996 was to give up on providing incentives to leave the program. The increase in long-term dependency on the program can, at least in part, be blamed on this decision. The near 100 percent take-back rate on AFDC left people with no earned income better off than people making $10,000 a year. The result was that only those recipients who could invest in an education could ultimately afford to leave the program.

Welfare as We Now Know It

In the 1996 reforms, the problem of welfare dependency was tackled by simply putting a clock on eligibility. The institution of time limits was an acknowledgment of the concern that dependency was wrong and that monetary incentives for relinquishing benefits were too expensive. Instead of being offered incentives to leave the program, people are now told how long their benefits will be provided. States are given block grants of money (TANF) that they are supposed to use to aid their poor. Instead of distributing it as cash benefits, as they did under AFDC, they can now spend it on job training, child care, or tax breaks for businesses that are willing to hire welfare recipients. States frequently set time limits and establish work requirements for some programs. Supplemental Security Income (SSI) rules for disability have changed such that some people who were once eligible for full benefits are now eligible for only partial benefits.

A relatively old idea has resurfaced in the last few years: a universal basic income. Pushed by those on the political left, it would provide a guaranteed level of income to everyone. It would leave all choices (including whether or not to work and on what to use the money) to the individual. The idea has gained little traction among moderates and conservatives.

Is Poverty Necessarily Bad?

There are many economists who object to the implied premise of this entire chapter: namely, that poverty is a bad thing. Without a carrot—wealth, and a stick—poverty, these economists believe that people would have little incentive to "work hard and play by the rules."[3] If accepted as valid, this philosophy would suggest that there is a trade-off between rates of economic growth and rates of economic inequality. There is evidence from the 1980s through today that countries with low rates of economic inequality have low rates of economic growth, but there is much disagreement about whether the former causes the latter.

[3]This phrase was often used by President Clinton as a political mantra.

Summary

You now understand how poverty is measured, who is poor in the United States, and how the percentage of the population that is poor has changed through the last 60 years. You are able to describe some of the significant problems presented by the official poverty rate. You are familiar with the many programs that exist for the poor, note that most of the programs grant the recipients goods and services rather than money, and understand why the government does this. Last, you are aware of the incentives and disincentives in the welfare state, and you know some of the details of welfare reform that emerged in the late 1990s.

Key Terms

in-kind subsidies
poverty gap
poverty line
poverty rate

Quiz Yourself

1. Poverty is a(n) _____ concept in that a person with a particular level of income in the United States may be considered in poverty, while a person with that same income in Somalia may be in the upper quarter of income earners.
   a. relative
   b. absolute
   c. irrelevant
   d. fictitious
2. In a simple 300 million-person world of all four-person families, if the poverty line is $20,000 and half of the 10 million families (with 40 million poor people) earn $17,500 and the other half earn $15,000, then the poverty gap is
   a. $200 billion (= 10 million * $20,000).
   b. $400 billion (= 20 million * $20,000).
   c. $150 billion (= 20 million * $2,500 + 20 million * $5,000).
   d. $37.5 billion (= 5 million * $2,500 + 5 million * $5,000).
3. In a simple 300 million-person world of all four-person families, if the poverty line is $20,000 and half of the 10 million families (with 40 million poor people) earn $17,500 and the other half earn $15,000, then the poverty rate is
   a. 3.33% (10 million/300 million).
   b. 13.33% (40 million/300 million).
   c. 16.66% (50 million/300 million).
   d. 96.33% ([300 million − 10 million]/300 million).
4. Using a poverty line of $20,000, under the current system of calculating the poverty rate, which of the following people is not considered in poverty and probably ought to be?
   a. A rural family whose sole income is from a minimum wage ($18,000) position
   b. A rural family whose combined income is $24,000
   c. A New York City family whose combined income is $21,000
   d. A retired couple whose multimillion-dollar estate yields them no income
5. Using a poverty line of $20,000, under the current system of calculating the poverty rate, which of the following people is considered in poverty and probably ought not to be?
   a. A rural family whose sole income is from a minimum wage ($18,000) position
   b. A rural family whose combined income is $24,000
   c. A New York City family whose combined income is $21,000
   d. A retired couple whose multimillion dollar estate yields them no income
6. The distribution of aid to the poor between in-kind and in-cash is
   a. roughly equal.
   b. weighted heavily toward in-cash benefits.
   c. weighted slightly toward in-kind benefits.
   d. weighted heavily toward in-kind benefits.
7. The most obvious pattern in poverty rates is the degree to which they are higher during
   a. Democratic administrations.
   b. wars.
   c. Republican administrations.
   d. recessions.
8. The evidence is that welfare reform in 1996 resulted in __________ the number of people on welfare.
   a. a substantial increase in
   b. a slight increase in
   c. a substantial decrease in
   d. no impact on
9. Which of the following is the most expensive welfare program?
   a. Medicaid
   b. SNAP
   c. TANF
   d. WIC

10. Which of the following attributes of welfare programs serve as an incentive to get off the program?
    a. Medicaid disappears when income is above 133 percent of the poverty line.
    b. TANF payments increase when there are more children.
    c. In some states, there is a maximum number of months you can collect SNAP benefits.
    d. WIC provides food to pregnant women.

Short Answer Questions

1. Compare the data on who is in poverty to whatever stereotype you may have had prior to reading this chapter.
2. What do the data suggest with regard to poverty and the age profile of those in poverty relative to the age profile generally?
3. What measure of poverty would give you the lowest possible estimate of the amount of money you would need to solve the nation's poverty problem? Why would only spending that amount not likely be a good solution to the problem?
4. If you were to construct a poverty measure, what would you put into the calculations to deal with the issues listed in the chapter?

Think about This

The wealth of one person, Bill Gates, is about equal to the annual poverty gap in the United States in one year, $84 billion. The United States has a more significantly unequal division of income than any other industrialized country. What are the consequences of that unequal distribution?

Talk about This

What other "urban legends" exist about the poor and welfare? What research could be conducted to dispel these legends or prove them to be factual?

For More Insight See

Blank, Rebecca M., "Evaluating Welfare Reform in the United States," *Journal of Economic Literature* XL (December 2002).

Journal of Economic Perspectives 11, no. 2 (Spring 1997). See articles by Peter Gottschalk; George Johnson; Robert Topel; and Nicole Fortin and Thomas Lemieux, pp. 21–96.

Journal of Economic Perspectives 12, no. 1 (Winter 1998). See articles by Dale Jorgenson; and Robert Triest, pp. 79–114.

Smeeding, Timothy, "Poor People in Rich Nations: The United States in Comparative Perspective," *Journal of Economic Perspectives* 20, no. 1 (Winter 2006).

Wolff, Edward, "Recent Trends in the Size Distribution of Household Wealth," *Journal of Economic Perspectives* 12, no. 3 (Summer 1998).

Behind the Numbers

U.S. Census Bureau: www.census.gov/topics/income-poverty/income.html

- Income by sex
- Income by race

U.S. Census Bureau, Current Population Survey: www.census.gov/topics/income-poverty/poverty/data/tables.html

- Poverty rate
- Poverty gap

White House Office of Management and Budget (OMB): www.whitehouse.gov/omb/historical-tables

- Federal spending on programs for the poor, detailed functional tables

The Heritage Foundation; paper by Robert Rector: http://www.heritage.org/poverty-and-inequality/report/how-poor-are-americas-poor-examining-the-plague-poverty-america

- Statistics of those in poverty

CHAPTER THIRTY-NINE

Head Start

Learning Objectives

After reading this chapter you should be able to:

LO1 Describe the purpose and premise behind the Head Start program.

LO2 Analyze Head Start using present value concepts.

LO3 Summarize the evidence regarding the efficacy of the Head Start program in both the short term and long term.

LO4 Use the concept of opportunity cost to evaluate the Head Start program.

Chapter Outline

Established in 1965, the Head Start program serves 899,374 children under the age of five at an annual cost of more than $9.2 billion. It began on the seemingly sound premise that early intervention in the lives of children can pay dividends later in the form of improved educational outcomes, reduced crime rates, and other socially desirable outcomes. Thus, Head Start has enjoyed broad political support, despite a vigorous debate over whether it has engendered a long-run positive influence.

We explore the notion that early intervention in the lives of children is worth the investment of funding Head Start. We offer a cautionary note concerning the effectiveness of a short-term investment in early childhood education. We fully describe the program and show the increase in enrollment and funding that Head Start has enjoyed. In addition, we describe its mission, its faculty, and its children. We examine the evidence of the success of Head Start as well as the evidence of its shortcomings, and we offer a final thought on the opportunity cost of fully funding it.

Head Start as an Investment

The Early Intervention Premise

When social scientists looked at the problem of poverty in the 1960s, many hoped that, with enough money, poverty could be significantly reduced and perhaps permanently eliminated. Early evidence gave them great hope. The poverty rate fell from more than 20 percent in 1960 to less than 11 percent a decade later, but it never fell below that. Though $866 billion was spent on poverty programs in 2017, the official poverty rate continues to remain between 11 and 15 percent.

More troubling has been the degree to which people whose annual incomes are lower than the poverty line have settled into habits that keep them in poverty. At the inception of Head Start, people thought that early intervention in the lives of children could lessen or even eliminate some of the sources or causes of poverty. Theoretically, children given academic skills, life skills, and health care to promote a "head start" on life would be more likely to succeed.

The early intervention premise suggests two things about money spent on a quality early education. By interrupting a cycle of poverty, we save future taxpayers money. This can be analyzed using the Chapter 7 concept of present value. It also implies that people other than the child and the parent benefit when a child gets high-quality care. We examine this aspect as well.

Present Value Analysis

The founders of Head Start hoped that money invested early in the education of young children would pay for itself in the long run: Students who may not ordinarily be associated with those likely to succeed would graduate from school, live with good standards of hygiene, earn respectable incomes, and pay taxes. Ideally, using the economic concept of present value, we would be able to prove that, like any good investment, Head Start would pay for itself. As you know, present value is found by discounting future payments by projecting interest rates in a way that puts future and present dollar figures on an even basis. Because human nature is to want things now rather than later, dollars paid now are more valuable to people than dollars paid in the future. Therefore, if the present value of the dollars spent on early education is less than the present value of the stream of benefits, then any such early education program is a good investment.

Suppose it could be shown that having a child in Head Start reduced a child's likelihood of dropping out of school, getting pregnant, and committing crimes for which jail time was required. Suppose it could also be shown that Head Start increased the likelihood that the child would grow up to be a fully functional taxpayer.[1] If that were true, it still would not necessarily justify the investment. From a strictly economic perspective, the present value of the increased costs associated with Head Start would have to be exceeded by the present value of the benefits as measured by increased taxes, reduced welfare, and imprisonment costs.

External Benefits

When people other than the consumer or producer of a good get a benefit from it, economists refer to this as a **positive externality.** The argument is that when parents choose child care, people other than themselves, their child, or the day-care worker are affected. By choosing a high-quality option, other parts of society benefit because the presumption is that the child is more likely to be a productive citizen in the future. Whenever there are such external benefits, economists will generally conclude that some form of subsidy is warranted.

positive externality
The benefits that go to someone other than the consumer or producer of a good.

The Early Evidence

The efficacy of the premise underlying the desirability of early intervention was fortified by studies from the 1960s through the 1980s, showing how effective early childhood education could be. The most prominent of these studies followed several hundred young, poor children, half of whom were given an excellent preschool experience free for two years, and half of whom were given nothing. The half who went to preschool not only performed better on IQ tests when they entered school, but also performed better in school, were less likely to commit crimes as teens, and graduated at far higher rates than the group that did not get that early education. By nearly every measure, the children given the "head start" stayed ahead.

Advocates of Head Start maintained that for every dollar spent on early childhood education, five dollars would be returned in increased tax revenues and reduced welfare spending. While not reported in present value terms, recalculating it that way using reasonable interest rates suggests that such an investment would be a good one. Armed with that early evidence, Head Start began with great hope that in a generation or two, early childhood education would make significant inroads into poverty in the United States.

The Remaining Doubts

Even in the early years, some people questioned the premise that the investment in early childhood education could have the kind of return that was projected. These doubts were based mainly on the implausibility that a few years of preschool could enable children to overcome the effect of poverty and other social problems. Although most Head Start programs are offered for half days during the school year, even children in the all-day, all-year form of Head Start spend only 4,600 hours in the enriching environment. The rest of their childhood, 153,000 hours, may be spent in poverty-stricken homes, crime-ridden neighborhoods, and educationally deficient schools. Regardless of how good the 4,600 hours is, it is hard to imagine that its influences would be strong enough to enable children to prevail over all the other influences in their lives.

Critics also point to flaws in the original study that showed the great potential for early intervention. Children in the original study were placed in a classroom that was nearly ideal, and their teachers were better equipped, physically and educationally, than any national program could ever hope to be. Critics doubted whether the program could be duplicated and used for the rest of the country.

The Head Start Program

Ever since its beginning in 1965, Head Start has enjoyed significant growth in appropriations but has never had a

[1]Later in this chapter, you will see that there is an open debate over whether Head Start has had any of these effects.

budget sufficient to be called "fully funded." A fully funded program would have enough money, staff, and facilities to handle all children who are eligible for the program. In reality, there have been long waiting lists in some cities for Head Start services.

Head Start is much more than day care, and it is not merely a preschool. Under reforms enacted in the early 1990s, it has become a center of learning for the entire family. Teachers are charged not only with creating a wholesome environment for children but also with making sure parents know of the available social resources for economically troubled families. The teachers make sure that immunization and health records are up to date, and they help parents develop personally, professionally, and as caregivers.

The evidence shows that Head Start centers are performing these tasks very well. Professional accreditation agencies have found that centers are well within the standards for early childhood education, certifying the vast majority of centers as "good" or better.

By 2017, there were 899,374 children enrolled in Head Start, at an average cost per child of nearly $10,257. As can be seen from Figure 39.1, inflation-adjusted spending and enrollment stayed relatively flat from 1965 to 1990. Though enrollment began at nearly 750,000 and fell through the 1970s to a low of 333,000, it rebounded through the early 1980s to a half million, where it stayed until 1990. Similarly, inflation-adjusted spending on the program stayed between $750 million and $1 billion (1982 dollars) from its inception through 1990.

Beginning in 1990, President Bush (George Herbert Walker) and Congress attempted to change Head Start. They sought either to fund it fully or to open slots for many more students. By 1997, enrollment reached 800,000, with the stated goal of reaching 1 million children by 2000.

While enrollment fell short of that goal, it has continued to rise. Also in 1997, new standards came into place that required teachers to attain a higher degree of certification. The new standards were then used to justify increases in teachers' salaries. These reforms increased the cost of the program substantially. Though enrollments increased 67 percent, spending increases were even more dramatic. Inflation-adjusted spending increased by more than 204 percent from 1990 to 2001.

In the first decade of the 2000s, enrollment was averaging about 908,000. It sharply increased in 2011 to more than 960,000 but has since fallen to its lowest level since 2001, at a little more than 899,000.

The children who are enrolled in Head Start do not mirror those in the general population, and they do not mirror the population living below the poverty level. According to data collected by FACES (from 2014 to 2018) in Fall 2014, while 60 percent of the general population and half the people living in poverty were white, non-Hispanic, 28 percent of the children in Head Start were

FIGURE 39.1 Head Start spending and enrollment.

Source: U.S. Department of Health & Human Services. https://eclkc.ohs.acf.hhs.gov/about-us/article/head-start-program-facts

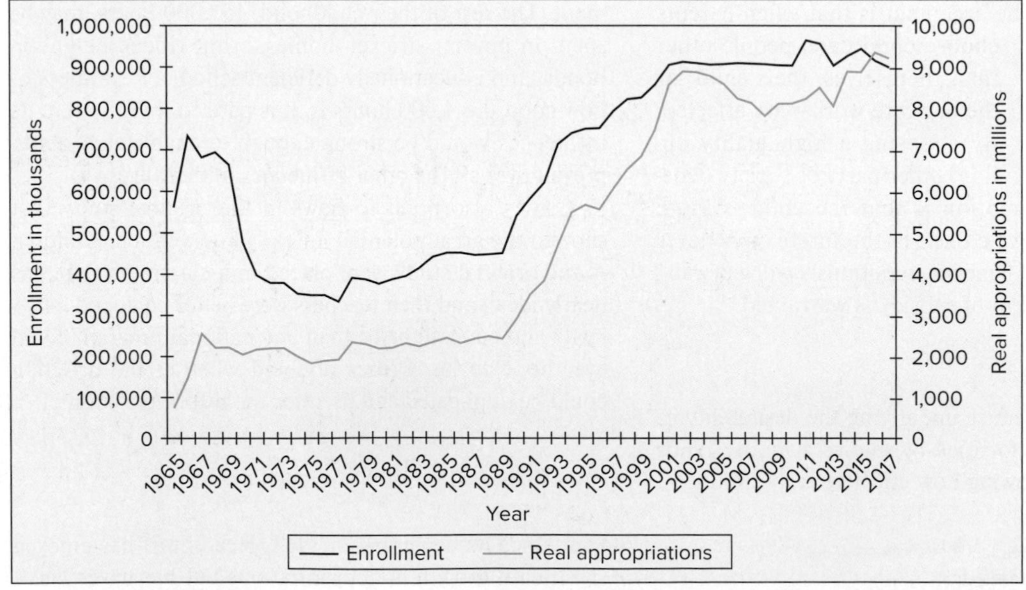

white. While only 14 percent of the overall population and 29 percent of the poverty population were black, non-Hispanic, 22 percent of the Head Start population was black. Similarly, Hispanics were overrepresented, in that they comprised only 17 percent of the general population and 33 percent of the poverty population but constituted 42 percent of the Head Start population.

In 2014, children with disabilities were significantly overrepresented in Head Start. Though 7 percent of children (ages 4 and under) were disadvantaged in this way, children with such disparities represented 14 percent of the children in Head Start.[2]

The families of Head Start children are overwhelmingly poor, and their levels of educational attainment are low. Thirty-one percent of Head Start families had household incomes below 50 percent of the federal poverty line, and 67 percent had household incomes below 100 percent of the federal poverty line. Nearly half of families reported an inability to afford basic needs such as shelter, clothing, food, and medical care within a 12-month period. Approximately 45 percent of Head Start families were headed by biological or adoptive mothers only, whereas only 3 percent were headed by biological or adoptive fathers only. According to the 2018 Program Information Report (PIR), the highest level of education obtained by the child's parent or guardian at enrollment was primarily a high school diploma or GED, at 45 percent. Another 23 percent did not complete high school nor earn a GED. With regard to government assistance, nearly 53 percent of families were receiving benefits from the Women, Infants, and Children (WIC) program; 50 percent were receiving benefits from the Supplemental Nutrition Assistance Program (SNAP); 9 percent were receiving cash benefits or other services from Temporary Assistance to Needy Families (TANF); and 7 percent were receiving Supplemental Security Income (SSI).

According to the PIR, 42 percent of single parents/guardians were not working, and in 14 percent of two-parent families, neither parent/guardian was working. In these cases, Head Start serves as an augmented preschool function only. In a little over one-quarter of two-parent families, both had jobs. Here, Head Start also provides a significant and free day-care service. For single-parent families, 58 percent of parents/guardians were working, whereas only 26 percent were both working in two-parent families. Again, whether the parents view the day-care function as more important than the preschool function, the child nevertheless gets good care and an education simultaneously. Moreover, parents are assisted in being better parents through the various family services that Head Start offers, including parenting education, asset building, substance abuse prevention and treatment, and mental health services.

In 2018, the Head Start staff was composed of 246,000 paid employees and more than 1 million volunteers. Of those volunteers, more than 70 percent were current or former Head Start parents. Regarding formal education of paid staff, nearly 70 percent of classroom teachers had at least an associate degree in early childhood education.

The Evidence

The basic premise of Head Start is that it is literally an educational "head start" and that the students who graduated from it ought to do better down the road than similarly situated[3] students who did not participate. For the first several decades of the program, there was virtually no evidence that test scores, dropout rates, graduation rates, or any other measure of educational achievement in later years was enhanced when students attended Head Start. Most of the studies showed a decreasing influence and found that most of the benefit of Head Start was gone by the third grade and that none was evident by the sixth grade. Those studies that did show intended benefits, such as one by Oden, Schweinhart, and Weikart, showed that children who participated in a Head Start program in the 1970s in Colorado and Florida were, 17 years later, less likely to drop out of high school and less likely to commit crime. The problem was that the positive results were never able to be replicated in other places.

As the General Accounting Office (GAO), the investigative wing of Congress, reported in 1997, there were no national studies that showed, in a compelling way, that anything long lasting was achieved in Head Start. A study by Janet Currie and Duncan Thomas put it quite well: "In summary, despite literally hundreds of studies, the jury is

[2]Head Start serves students to age 5.

[3]Not all studies of Head Start compare children's abilities adequately. For instance, if you put a child of educated, financially well-off parents in a dilapidated building with a lousy teacher, you will probably get better results than you will if you put a poor child of a single, uneducated teenage mother in a new building with a great teacher. The home environment is remarkably important. This means that unless you control statistically for home environment variables, you get study results that are not indicative of the effectiveness of the program. Good studies of Head Start must compare "equally situated" children. The standard statistical control mechanism is to analyze siblings where one was in the program and another was not in the program.

still out on the question of whether participation in Head Start has any lasting beneficial effects."

In its 1994 and 1998 reauthorizations of the law that created Head Start, Congress commissioned a national study on the long-term benefits of the program. By 1999, a highly regarded committee of scholars settled on a methodology and a set of goals for collecting the relevant data. That process resulted in a final report that went to Congress in 2010. The positive results reported in that study showed that for narrowly defined groups on narrowly defined measures there was indeed an impact. Moreover, scholars began to assert that despite the lack of evidence on long-term benefits, the program may be worth its costs if only for its short- and medium-term benefits.

Those benefits included that participants were less likely to repeat kindergarten or first grade and were less likely to be placed in special education during that time. There were also modest improvements in reading and verbal test scores. In addition, Head Start children were healthier (had lower obesity rates) because part of Head Start is parental education and because children in Head Start are fed nutritious meals while they are in the program. In the teacher–parent contacts, immunization records are reviewed and, when necessary, doctor and dentist referrals are made. Parents of Head Start children are more aware of the many services available to them and their children, an awareness that explains, in part, why they are enrolled in other forms of federal assistance.

Since that 2010 report, several newer studies have been produced that have shown more general and long-lasting results. A 2016 report of the Hamilton Project (an initiative of the left-leaning Brookings Institution) shows that participants had higher high school graduation rates and higher rates of continuing their education beyond high school. An interesting additional finding is that former participants, when they are parents themselves, are more likely to engage in (what they describe as) positive parenting (teaching colors, numbers, and shapes to their own young children while also avoiding spanking).

The Opportunity Cost of Fully Funding Head Start

If tax money had no opportunity cost, Head Start would not be controversial. In the tradition of the medical profession's Hippocratic oath, Head Start clearly does no harm. Whether it does any good and, if so, whether that good is enough to justify the costs are other questions. Head Start costs $10,257 per year per student, more than most day-care centers charge for a year of service, even though most day care is nine hours a day, all year, and Head Start is only four days a week during the school year. According to the Pew Research Center, day-care costs per four-year-old child range from $5,000 per year in the rural south to more than $12,000 per year in New York. As noted in Chapter 38, the U.S. Census Bureau has two different surveys from which it estimates typical child-care costs that place the median cost of care (for children under 5) at between $100 and $149 per week.

If the federal government wants to provide free day care for poor children, it can do it for less money than it spends on Head Start. If Head Start genuinely provides a measurable "head start," it should show up more clearly in efficacy studies. The question for economists is whether Head Start is the best use of money–and that question centers on the notion of opportunity cost. Would poor parents and their children be better off if the funds simply provided day care?

Make no mistake about it, the opportunity cost would exist whether or not Head Start was effective. The worst billion-dollar-per-year government program and the best billion-dollar-per-year program have the same opportunity cost: $1 billion of other programs or tax cuts.

What differentiates an effective program from an ineffective one is that when we fund a program that does not perform, we do not consider alternatives designed to meet the same goal that might perform better. The conventional wisdom among politicians is that Head Start is living up to its billing. They think that it is a good net present value investment. The lost opportunity to experiment with a better alternative program cannot be ignored.

Summary

You now understand that Head Start is a federally funded program that provides early childhood education to nearly a million children at a cost of $9.2 billion per year. You are able to use the concepts of investment and net present value to understand the premise of the program. You know that despite the efforts of economists and others to verify the worth of the program, the evidence that the program works is rather scant and is the subject of ongoing research. You can see that, as with any other expenditure, there is an opportunity cost to the program.

Key Term

positive externality

Quiz Yourself

1. From an economic perspective, the tool one would use to analyze the costs and benefits of Head Start would be
   a. present value.
   b. supply and demand.
   c. production possibilities.
   d. marginal net benefit.
2. If Head Start were a good long-run investment from a strictly economic perspective, for current children enrolled in the program it would
   a. make them happier.
   b. help their parents with subsidized day care/preschool.
   c. increase the likelihood of future success as adults.
   d. increase the likelihood that they knew the alphabet going into kindergarten.
3. Though the high-quality preschool experience is a private benefit for the children and their parents, the economic justification for Head Start is based on
   a. external costs.
   b. its low total cost.
   c. the increase in reading ability of participants going into kindergarten.
   d. the external benefits to society.
4. The early evidence on programs like Head Start made it clear that
   a. the rate of return to these programs was very low.
   b. the net present value of the external benefits was positive.
   c. the short-run benefits were not worth the costs.
   d. the long-run benefits were not worth the costs.
5. The typical Head Start teacher is
   a. an ill-trained minimum-wage worker.
   b. a professional credentialed worker making more than the typical day-care worker.
   c. a college graduate making $30,000 a year or more.
   d. a professional with a master's degree or higher.
6. Current evidence suggests that the long-term benefits of Head Start are
   a. sufficiently positive to make the net present value positive.
   b. sufficiently positive such that when added to the short- and intermediate-term benefits, the net present value is positive.
   c. spotty/inconsistent.
   d. curiously negative.
7. The intermediate-term external benefits of Head Start
   a. focus on reducing the likelihood of the children ending up in prison.
   b. focus on reducing the likelihood that the children will become pregnant as teenagers.
   c. are significant if you know that the children would qualify for subsidized free day care anyway.
   d. are significant in that they reduce the likelihood of the children needing expensive special education in elementary school.

Short Answer Questions

1. How would the present value analysis of Head Start change if interest rates rose/fell?
2. Suppose you identified an alternative to Head Start that could be tried (on the same population). Describe how would you determine whether the alternative worked better than Head Start.

Think about This

The notion of calculating the present value of external benefits and comparing that to the present value of extra costs in evaluating Head Start is a purely economic way of looking at the program. Is this the only way? Is it the right way? Whether or not society benefits from their participation, does society owe these underprivileged children such a program?

Talk about This

Suppose the evidence was that Head Start was completely ineffective from a present value perspective. What would you do with the money that is spent on the program? What programs are we forgoing?

For More Insight See

Bauer, Lauren, and Diana Schanzenbach, "The Long-Term Impact of the Head Start Program," http://www.hamiltonproject.org/assets/files/long_term_impact_of_head_start_program.pdf.

Congressional Budget Office, *Research Provides Little Information on Impact of Current Program,* April 1997.

Currie, Janet, *Early Childhood Intervention Programs: What Do We Know?* April 2000, http://www.brook.edu/dybdocroot/es/research/projects/cr/doc/curie20000401.pdf.

Currie, Janet, and Duncan Thomas, "Does Head Start Make a Difference?" *American Economic Review* 85, no. 3 (June 1995), pp. 341–364.

Garces, Eliana, Duncan Thomas, and Janet Currie, "Longer-Term Effects of Head Start," *American Economic Review* 92, no. 4 (Sept. 2002).

Head Start Impact Study: Final Report January 2010, www.acf.hhs.gov/sites/default/files/opre/hs_impact_study_final.pdf.

National Head Start Impact Research, U.S. Department of Health and Human Services. Head Start Impact Study, http://www.acf.hhs.gov/programs/opre/hs/impact_study/index.html.

Oden, Sherri, Lawrence Schweinhart, and David Weikart, *Into Adulthood* (Ypsilanti, MI: High/Scope Press, 2000).

Behind the Numbers

Department of Health and Human Services, Administration for Children and Families: Early Childhood Learning and Knowledge Center (ECLKC): Head Start: Head Start Program Facts: Enrollment History: https://eclkc.ohs.acf.hhs.gov/about-us/article/head-start-program-facts

- Enrollment
- Teachers
- Funding

Department of Health and Human Services, Office of Planning, Research and Evaluation (OPRE), Head Start Family and Child Experiences Survey (FACES): www.acf.hhs.gov/sites/default/files/opre/faces_fall_2014_child_family_data_tables_final_clean_toacf_122217_508.pdf

- Characteristics of enrollees

U.S. Census Bureau: www.census.gov/topics/income-poverty/income.html

- Characteristics of people in poverty

CHAPTER FORTY

Social Security

Learning Objectives

After reading this chapter you should be able to:

LO1 Describe Social Security's basic tax and benefit structure.

LO2 Detail the history of changes to the Social Security program since its inception.

LO3 Explain the economic rationale for Social Security.

LO4 Enumerate the effects of Social Security on work and savings.

LO5 Explain the origin and purpose behind the Social Security Trust Fund.

LO6 Summarize present estimates of the future financial health of the Social Security system and evaluate the options for ensuring its long-run solvency.

Chapter Outline

When most people think about Social Security, they envision retirement checks for the elderly. Social Security has a much broader scope, including benefits for eligible widows and orphans in addition to medical and disability insurance. In this chapter, we concentrate on retirement benefits.

We begin by reviewing the history of Social Security as a government pension program, and we include its tax, benefit, and structure. We then turn to why it is needed. We discuss the effects of Social Security on work and savings. Last, we discuss why insolvency for the Social Security Trust Fund is likely without reform and what reform might look like.

The Basics

The Beginning

In 1935, the Social Security Act was passed and signed into law by President Franklin Roosevelt. The stock market crash of 1929 and the Great Depression of the 1930s caused great upheavals in people's financial circumstances. Unemployment reached a high of 25 percent. People who had been wealthy investors before the crash were lucky if they had a job that would allow them to at least live from paycheck to paycheck after the crash. Many banks closed when, as a result of the stock market crash, their investments were insufficient to pay their depositors. In this circumstance, even people who saved diligently and invested prudently for their retirement found themselves without savings. Social Security guaranteed a safety net, come good times or bad, to generations who retired from the late 1930s on. At the time, it was not intended that Social Security be the only income on which a person lived. In 2018, 44 percent of unmarried recipients received more than 90 percent of their income from Social Security.

Today, Social Security provides guaranteed retirement benefits averaging about $1,461 a month to 47 million American people over the age of 62. Social Security is a **pay-as-you-go pension** system where current

pay-as-you-go pension A system where current workers' taxes are used to pay pensions to current retirees.

workers' taxes are used to pay pensions to current retirees. This is unlike a traditional **fully funded pension** system where, for every benefit dollar it is required to pay in the future, there is an offsetting amount currently invested that is sufficient to pay off that dollar. It is the pay-as-you-go aspect that allowed money to go to the elderly right away (the first checks went out in 1936), but, as we will see, it is also this aspect that currently puts Social Security in the most jeopardy.

fully funded pension
A system that has an amount currently invested that is sufficient to pay every benefit dollar it is required to pay in the future.

Taxes

Social Security taxes (technically called FICA, or Federal Insurance Contribution Act taxes) are **payroll taxes.** That is, the amount workers pay is based on what workers earn from their work. This is different from an income tax in that interest, dividends, and other forms of unearned income are not subject to this tax. In addition, not all payroll is taxed; taxes are paid only up to a limited amount of income called the **maximum taxable earnings.** In 2019, this amount was $132,900, which means that workers did not have to pay the old-age portion of the Social Security tax for income they earned beyond that point. Both the employer and employee pay an equal amount of this tax so that if you have to pay $1,000 in tax, so does your employer. The self-employed pay both parts of the tax.

payroll taxes
Taxes owed on what workers earn from their work.

maximum taxable earnings
The maximum of taxable earnings subject to the payroll tax.

Benefits

On the benefit side, eligible retirees get benefit checks that are based on what they made during their working years. The **average index of monthly earnings (AIME)** is the monthly average of the 35 highest earnings years (capped by the maximum taxable earnings for each respective year) adjusted for wage inflation. The AIME is put into a formula that generates the **primary insurance amount (PIA).**[1] Single people are paid the PIA and married couples get 1.5 times the highest of their PIAs or the sum of their individual PIAs, whichever is higher. For full benefits, workers cannot begin to collect until they reach the **retirement age,** though they can collect partial benefits at age 62.

average index of monthly earnings (AIME)
The monthly average of the 35 highest earnings years adjusted for wage inflation.

primary insurance amount (PIA)
The amount single retirees receive in a monthly check if they retire at their retirement age.

retirement age
The age at which retirees get full benefits.

Although the payroll tax structure is such that everyone with income under the maximum taxable earnings pays the same rate of tax, the benefit structure is such that, in net, Social Security redistributes income to the lower end of the income scale. To see this, consider the following example. Assume, inflation-adjusted, a person earns $5,000 per month for 35 years, so that person's AIME is $5,000. Inflation-adjusted, the employee and the employer each pay $382.50 (7.65% × $5,000) per month in taxes. In 2019, that person would get a monthly Social Security check of $2,137. If someone else were in a similar situation with one-fifth the income, that person and his or her employer would combine to pay one-fifth the tax, but the benefit would be $794 per month. Thus, this employee pays one-fifth the tax but receives one-third the benefit. The person at the lower end of the income scale has a benefit dollar-to-tax dollar ratio that is twice that of the upper-income person. This is by design, and, as such, the program serves to redistribute money down the income line.

Changes over Time

Since its inception, Social Security has added benefits. Payments to widows and orphans, called survivor benefits, have been part of Social Security from its inception. Disability insurance, for workers who are unable to work for long periods of time, was added in 1956, and basic, highly subsidized health coverage (called Medicare) was added in 1966.

Table 40.1 shows how the tax rate, the maximum taxable earnings, and the retirement age have changed since the program began. This table shows how Social Security's components have been altered to ensure its survivability. As you can see, tax rates have risen, in part not only to pay for the other benefits described previously but also to guarantee that retirement benefits would be there for each generation. The tax rate has risen from 1 percent to 7.65 percent, while the

[1] The formula for 2019 was 90 percent of the first $926 plus 32 percent of the next $4,657 plus 15 percent of the remainder up to a maximum benefit that is computed using the maximum taxable earnings for each of the work years. This formula is adjusted yearly for inflation. For more information, see www.socialsecurity.gov.

Table 40.1 History of Social Security's components at selected points in time.

Year	Maximum Taxable Earnings ($)	Old-Age and Disability Tax Rate (% of payroll)	Medicare Tax Rate (%)	Total Tax Rate That Both Employers and Employees Pay (%)	Retirement Age*		Benefits†
					Year of Birth	Age	
1937	$ 3,000	1.000%	0%	1.000%	1937	65	OA, S
1950	3,600	1.500	0	1.500	1950	66	OA, S
1955	4,200	2.000	0	2.000	1955	66 + 2 months	OA, S
1960	4,800	2.250	0	2.250	1960	67	OA, S, DI
1965	4,800	3.625	0	3.625	1965	67	OA, S, DI
1970	7,800	4.200	0.600	4.800	1970	67	OA, S, DI, HI
1975	14,100	4.950	0.900	5.850	1975	67	OA, S, DI, HI
1980	25,900	5.080	1.050	6.130	1980	67	OA, S, DI, HI
1985	39,600	5.700	1.300	7.000	1985	67	OA, S, DI, HI
1990	51,300	6.200	1.450	7.650	1990	67	OA, S, DI, HI
1995	61,200	6.200	1.450	7.650	1995	67	OA, S, DI, HI
2000	76,200	6.200	1.450	7.650	2000	67	OA, S, DI, HI
2019	132,900	6.200	1.450	7.650	2019	67	OA, S, DI, HI

*Until 1983 the retirement age was 65. In 1983, the law was changed to increase it depending on year of birth. 1938, => 65 + 2 months; 1939, => 65 + 4 months; 1940, => 65 + 6 months; 1941, => 65 + 8 months; 1942, => 65 + 10 months; 1943–1954, => 66; 1955, => 66 + 2 months; 1956, => 66 + 4 months; 1957, => 66 + 6 months; 1958, => 66 + 8 months; 1959, => 66 + 10 months; 1960 on, 67.

†OA = old age; S = survivor; DI = disability; HI = health insurance (Medicare)

maximum amount subject to tax has risen from $3,000 to $132,900. The retirement age has also risen. People born before 1938 can retire with full benefits at 65; those born after 1960 must wait until they are 67. A somewhat complicated transition formula determines the retirement age of those born between 1939 and 1959. In short, in contrast to the view that Social Security has been a monolithic and unalterable program, there have been many changes that have both broadened its scope and ensured its survivability.

Why Do We Need Social Security?

If you have worked through other issues chapters in this book, you know that economists believe that government intervention in private enterprise must be justified on at least one of the following three grounds:

1. The need to control **externalities**, that is, effects created by an unregulated market on people other than the buyer or seller, such as pollution, secondhand smoke, and drunk driving.
2. Concern about significant moral or ethical problems associated with the good being sold, for example, drugs, prostitution, and pornography.
3. Sellers or buyers are incapable of making rational decisions, because people either cannot be counted on to exercise wisdom or have inadequate information upon which to base a wise decision.

externalities Effects created by an unregulated market on people other than the buyer or seller.

It is a combination of the first and third reasons that makes some form of compulsory-saving/retirement-benefit program necessary in the eyes of economists.

Ideally, rational and wise people will save money for retirement based on their preferences for consuming now versus consuming later. They will realize that money spent now has an opportunity cost, namely, money that cannot be spent later. Investment markets allow people to save or borrow as they please. If all the assumptions about well-functioning markets are valid in the investment market, then there is no reason for government to force people to save. They will save the right amount for themselves.

In opposition to the rationale put forth by economists is the contention that people may not save the right amount for themselves. This is an argument that has little appeal among economists. Many economists maintain that if the government were not taxing workers for this purpose, workers could be saving the money independently, and saving or not saving would therefore be their choice.

On the other hand, two arguments against a completely free market approach have some appeal among economists. First, our humanity prevents us from letting others starve. If people do not save for themselves, someone else will be forced to support them. Their decision not to save affects others. These "others" could be children, relatives, friends, or government. Social Security prevents people from not saving the right amount, and it protects others from compensating.

Second, our rationality stems from our ability to learn from our mistakes. In most situations, and especially in most markets, we learn from our mistakes. For instance, if the first time you go grocery shopping for yourself you buy nothing but marshmallows and Red Bull, you will quickly learn that you need vegetables and fruits in your diet. However, if you fail to save enough for retirement, you cannot just decide to live the first 65 years of your life over again. Government often prevents us from this sort of mistake.

There are few guarantees that we will always do the right thing ourselves. There are other examples of this: (1) You cannot borrow money before age 18 without a cosignature; (2) you cannot drop out of school before you are 16; and (3) you cannot drink until you are 21. Society fears that you might suffer irreparable bankruptcy, poverty, or alcoholism, respectively; and it wants government to ensure that you will not make mistakes that cannot be undone. For these reasons, the question among economists is not whether some form of government-run retirement is needed but what form that system takes and how to fund it so that it is financially stable.

Social Security's Effect on the Economy

Effect on Work

Before Social Security was implemented, 51 percent of men over age 65 worked. Today, that number is 24 percent. While there is much dispute on the degree to which Social Security itself caused this to happen (in fact, this number has risen in recent years), Social Security has clearly made it easier for people to retire. This has good as well as bad aspects. Though the retired may be happier being retired, the economy is deprived of their labor and output. On the other hand, as more people retire, positions open throughout the labor market, and people move up to fill vacated positions. Paradoxically, this is a circumstance in which the economy is hurt even though everyone in it is happier. (Revisit Chapter 6 and the section "Real Gross Domestic Product and Why It Is Not Synonymous with Social Welfare" for more information.)

Effect on Saving

Most economists believe that if people had to save for their own retirement (i.e., there was no Social Security program), they would save more than they do now. Though these economists disagree on the magnitude of this effect, they have concluded that the existence of Social Security reduces the amount of money that is saved in the economy. This is primarily due to the **asset substitution effect.** If the government is taxing you on your earnings now and promising a pension payment later, the government is, in effect, saving for you. If the government is saving for you, you will likely save less for yourself.

Two counteracting effects to this are the *induced retirement effect* and the *bequest effect.* As mentioned, people are clearly retiring earlier than they did in the past. If Social Security did not exist, and people had no hope of ever retiring, they might not save anything. On the other hand, because Social Security makes retirement a possibility, people may save so as to retire earlier than they otherwise would have chosen. The **induced retirement effect** thus increases national savings because people need to save more if they are going to retire earlier than they would have without Social Security.

asset substitution effect
Government is saving for you; thus you will save less for yourself.

induced retirement effect
People need to save more if they are going to retire earlier than they would have without Social Security.

Another impact of Social Security is that it may increase national savings if the elderly are putting aside more money for bequests, that is, money that will go to younger family members when their elders die. It may be that Social Security provides a stable enough income for the elderly that they choose to save enough to pass on a larger inheritance than they would have if there had been no such program. The **bequest effect** thus increases national savings because people save more so as to give larger gifts to their descendants than they would have without Social Security.

bequest effect
People save more to give larger gifts to their descendants, thus increasing national savings.

Economists dispute the net effect of Social Security on savings. Martin Feldstein, in particular, was the first to estimate the effect of Social Security on savings. In 1974, he concluded that there was a dramatic reduction in savings. This was disputed by other economists, led by Alicia Munnell in 1977 and Dean Leimer and Selig Lesnoy in 1982, all of whom estimated that the net effect was zero. Not to be silenced, in 1996, Feldstein published revised estimates for 1992, when personal savings were actually $248 billion, indicating that it would have been $646 billion without Social Security. The result is that there is little agreement except for a middle ground that appears to indicate a small net negative impact of Social Security on savings.

Will the System Be There for Me?

Why Social Security Is in Trouble

There has always been a concern about whether Social Security could maintain the existing benefit structure. Tax rates have always risen faster than benefits have been added because the retired population has grown faster than the working population. In 1982, a significant concern was raised that the pay-as-you-go system could not handle the demographic bulge of the post–World War II baby boom. In the years following World War II, until around 1960, some 2.5 percent of all women gave birth each year. The advent of the birth control pill, the increased availability of abortion, and the social unrest of the 1960s and 1970s significantly altered America's birthrate. By 1976, only 1.5 percent of women gave birth each year.

As a result, the baby-boom generation now represents 24 percent of the current population. Because of this, the number of taxpaying workers per benefit-receiving retiree will continue to fall precipitously. In 1950, there were more than 16 workers paying taxes for every retiree who was collecting benefits. Today, the number is 2.8, and current projections say it will drop to 2.2 by 2030 and to 2.0 by 2095. Figure 40.1 presents an overview of this situation.

The Social Security Trust Fund

Social Security Trust Fund
A fund established in 1982 to hold government debt, which will be sold as necessary when tax revenues are less than benefits.

To combat the demographic problem, the **Social Security Trust Fund** was established in 1982 to collect more taxes than were needed to pay current benefits.

FIGURE 40.1 Workers per retiree history and projections.

Source: Social Security Administration. https://www.ssa.gov/OACT/TR/2018/

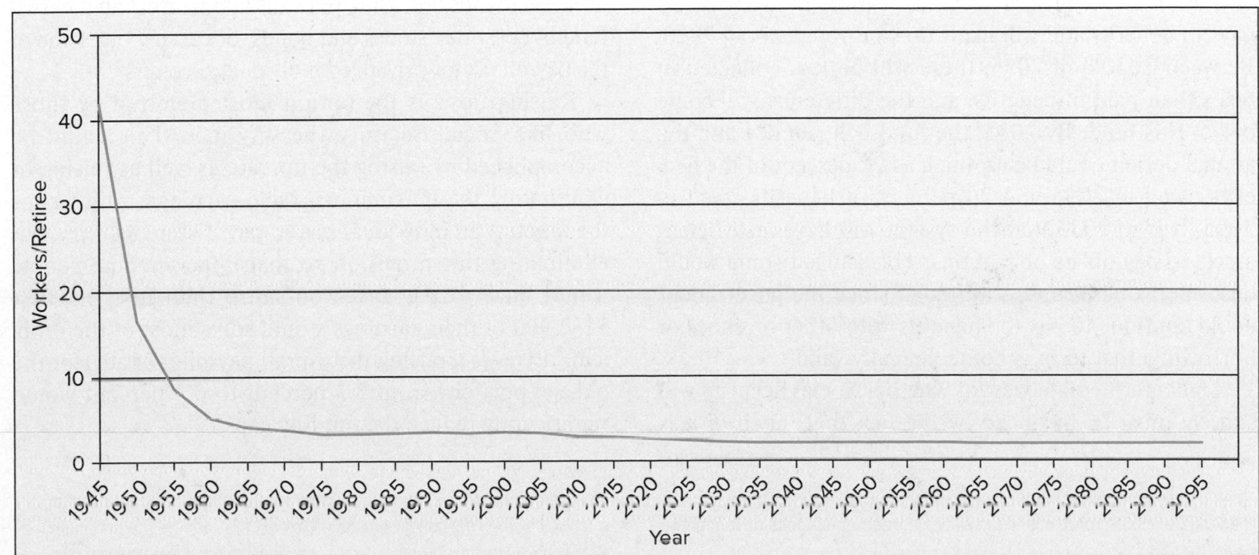

In later years, there would thus be enough money to pay benefits to baby-boom retirees. In 2018, there was approximately $2.8 trillion in U.S. government debt in this fund.[2]

Whether this actually constitutes a true trust fund is debatable. It is a collection of debt that will either be issued for the first time or be reissued to the public when there is less in Social Security tax revenues than benefits to pay. One way of looking at this issue is that the trust fund is money that was collected using the Social Security tax, rather than the income tax. This was begun in the 1980s and early 1990s to reduce what would otherwise have been a much larger deficit. If you look at it this way, the national debt that grew to $21.5 trillion by 2018 actually only grew to just $15.7 trillion (and just $13.4 trillion if you count Federal Reserve holdings of the national debt). As a result, should surpluses be available, we would be reducing the true national debt to allow ourselves the ability to borrow much more later. Either way, it is essentially the same. Reissuing debt and borrowing money are functionally identical.

The Social Security trustees periodically issue reports that attempt to project how long this trust fund will suffice. They issue three different predictions based on three different sets of assumptions. The "optimistic" report is based on assumptions that economic growth will be higher than we have seen in the recent past, life spans will be shorter than current health trends are likely to yield, and interest rates will be lower than they are likely to be. The "pessimistic" report is based on assumptions of slow growth, long lives, and high interest rates.

The "intermediate" report is the most widely quoted, and it indicates that the Social Security system generally (except for 2010 through 2011 when revenues were down as a result of the recession) collects more in taxes than it pays in benefits and will likely do so through about 2020. Between 2020 and 2035, there will be less collected in taxes than paid in benefits, and the difference will come out of this fund. By 2035, the fund will run dry and the annual deficit could be as much as 22 percent of the benefits owed in 2035 and 26 percent of benefits owed in 2095. It is in 2035 that the system will have insufficient assets to pay off its obligations. This is what some would describe as bankruptcy, although since the government could continue to pay the benefits with other revenues or borrowing, that term is not technically valid.

This intermediate view of whether Social Security will survive must be balanced by the fact that much of it is based on assumptions that may or may not materialize. For instance, if the optimistic view holds, and the economy grows a single percentage point per year more than predicted, the problem is mostly solved. Changes, for example, in immigration policies that allow more workers to enter, could help solve the remainder of the problem. In addition, if inflation and interest rates are slightly less than predicted, Social Security insolvency is far from certain. As a matter of fact, an increase in something as unrelated as the divorce rate would make the problem worse. Husbands and wives typically get less in benefits married than they do if they are divorced.

The long and the short of it is that economists cannot be sure that Social Security will be bankrupt. Significantly altering what many consider to be the nation's greatest social program on the basis of economic assumptions that may or may not come true strikes many as unwise. This is especially true, from the point of view of economist and Social Security expert Peter Diamond. He noted that even if the trust fund is exhausted, the taxes paid will be sufficient to cover 75 percent of benefits. On the other hand, the possible solutions that we next describe also require several years to be effective if the goal is to make the program 100 percent solvent into the future.

Options for Fixing Social Security

The options for saving Social Security are plentiful, and they range from radical to timid. They all include a mixture of the following elements: raising payroll taxes, raising the retirement age further, cutting benefits to upper-income recipients, changing the target from indexing benefits using wage inflation to indexing using price inflation, investing the trust fund in corporate stocks and bonds, or carving out some of the payroll tax for privatized individual accounts.

Raising taxes is the option most preferred by those who like Social Security the way it is. This could be accomplished by raising the tax rate as well as raising or eliminating the maximum taxable earnings, which caps the amount an individual has to pay. Estimates vary, but eliminating this provision so that upper-income people would have to pay taxes on more than just the first $132,900 of their earnings would solve most of the problem.[3] Likewise, raising the overall payroll tax rate (for the old-age portion) from 5.3 percent to 6.3 percent would significantly reduce the funding gap.

[2] As you may recall from Chapter 10, "Monetary Policy," or Chapter 12, "Federal Deficits, Surpluses, and the National Debt," the federal government owes itself $8 trillion.

[3] The degree to which it would help close the funding gap depends on whether you also changed the benefit structure to reflect this change. The maximum AIME is based on the maximum taxable earnings for each relevant year.

Another alternative would be to raise the retirement age. Typically those who like this option argue that Social Security's original retirement age was established based on life expectancy, which in 1935 was 65. If the retirement age is exactly life expectancy, then people who die at or before expectancy pay a lifetime of taxes and get no benefits. This ensures that there is enough money to pay for those who die after expectancy. Currently life expectancy is 79. For those who make it to 65, men can expect to live another 18 years, women 21 years. Though people are living much longer, the problem is that there is less Social Security retirement money to go around. Depending on how quickly a change is made, raising the retirement age to 70 would solve about one-third of the problem. If the retirement age were not raised to age 70 until 2075, as some suggest, it would be of no help in resolving the problem scheduled to occur in 2035.

One of the great successes of Social Security is that it has brought the poverty rate among the elderly down greatly. On the other hand, many retirees have enjoyed financial success without government help. Some have succeeded so well in this area that they are getting Social Security checks but have no need for them. The median net worth for a Social Security recipient is currently about four times that of a nonrecipient. One proposed solution to Social Security's problems is to subject its beneficiaries to a **means test.** Those with high incomes or great wealth would get less of their PIA than those who depend on the monthly check. Depending on how much a wealthy person's check is reduced, this could significantly help prevent the program's insolvency. Denying Social Security to anyone whose other income is greater than $50,000, for example, would eliminate the solvency issue altogether.

means test
Determination of the amount of one's government benefit on the basis of income or wealth.

Less radically, means testing could be introduced by using a hybrid form of indexing espoused by economists Pozen, Schieber, and Shoven. They suggest indexing benefits for upper-income retirees using price inflation rather than wage inflation. Because the former is usually one percentage point lower than the latter, this would have the effect of slowly reducing the benefits paid to upper-income retirees. On the other hand, this could create problems. If benefits to the wealthy are reduced too much, this could seriously discourage savings among the upper- and upper-middle-income earners. Also, political support for the program might be seriously jeopardized, as it would resemble a welfare program more than a universal retirement program.

Another way to save the system would be to invest the Social Security Trust Fund in corporate investments that yield higher rates of return. As mentioned previously, the trust fund buys government debt that "yields" between 2 and 3 percent. In this sense, the government (the Treasury) owes the government (the trust fund) money and has to pay itself interest. Proponents of this solution contend that if the government invested the money in corporate stocks and bonds, the higher rates of return would generate enough to pay retirees' benefits.

There are problems with this approach. First, government would be responsible for picking stocks and might not do very well. Second, the process of picking government investments might be unduly politicized. Given politicians' practice of giving in to special interests, it is not beyond the realm of possibilities that such investment would not be in the general interest. Third, though corporate securities do better in the long run than government bonds, they are also riskier.

The last option suggests that individuals be allowed to invest part of their taxes themselves. In the 2000 presidential election, candidate George W. Bush made this a cornerstone of his solution to the Social Security crisis. The precipitous declines in global stock markets that began in 2000 and did not rebound until 2003 seriously undercut the political support such an option was beginning to build. With his reelection in 2004, President Bush again pushed this option front and center. What he suggested was a system by which younger workers would have a portion of their taxes placed in an account under their control. Opponents of the president's plan focused on the fact that the guaranteed Social Security benefit would be significantly reduced while supporters countered that the proceeds of the accounts, if investments returned their normal historical rates, would more than make up the difference.

In late summer 2005, Hurricanes Katrina and Rita took over the headlines, and the subsequent political damage to President Bush ended his ability to sell a major change to Social Security.

During his 2008 presidential campaign, Barack Obama rejected all forms of privatization and instead suggested that the 6.2 percent old-age portion of the Social Security tax be reimposed on incomes over $250,000. President Obama never offered a solution during his eight years in office, and President Trump's campaign doubled down on this inaction by pledging not to make any of the adjustments that economists insist are necessary to maintain full retirement obligations. Since taking office, President Trump has not considered any significant changes to the program.

Summary

You now understand what Social Security is. You know its basic tax and benefit structure as well as the changes that have been made to the program since its inception. You recognize the economic rationale for having the system and the effects of the program on work and savings. You learned that, under present estimates, the system will be unable to fully meet its obligations by 2035, what the Social Security Trust Fund is, and what the options are for fixing the system so that it will not only be there for you but be good for you as well.

Key Terms

asset substitution effect
average index of monthly earnings (AIME)
bequest effect
externalities
fully funded pension
induced retirement effect
maximum taxable earnings
means test
pay-as-you-go pension
payroll taxes
primary insurance amount (PIA)
retirement age
Social Security Trust Fund

Quiz Yourself

1. Social Security's revenue emanates from taxes on
   a. all income.
   b. payrolls.
   c. capital.
   d. estates.
2. One of the reasons a government-run annuity system such as Social Security may be better for society than simply relying on private savings is that
   a. no one would save for themselves.
   b. people, being overly risk averse, will save too much.
   c. people, being risk neutral, will save too much.
   d. people, having imperfect foresight, will save too little.
3. The average index of monthly earnings is indexed
   a. for wage inflation.
   b. for consumer price inflation.
   c. for producer price inflation.
   d. via a combination of wage and price inflation.
4. Since its inception, the portion of earnings that has been subject to the Social Security tax has
   a. remained roughly intact.
   b. increased substantially.
   c. decreased slightly.
   d. decreased substantially.
5. In 2019, a worker who earned \$150,000 would have __________ in Social Security taxes taken out of his or her pay and __________ would also be paid by the employer.
   a. \$20,333.70; \$20,333.70 (both equal to \$132,900 × 0.153)
   b. \$10,414.80; \$10,414.80 (both equal to \$132,900 × 0.0765 + \$17,100 × 0.0145)
   c. \$10,166.85; \$10,166.85 (both equal to \$132,900 × 0.0765)
   d. \$11,475.00; \$11,475.00 (both equal to \$150,000 × 0.0765)
6. The asset substitution effect implies that Social Security will __________ from where it would have been without it.
   a. increase savings
   b. increase work
   c. decrease work
   d. decrease savings
7. The question of whether Social Security increases or decreases savings depends mostly on whether the __________ effect outweighs the __________ effect or vice versa.
   a. bequest; asset substitution
   b. bequest; induced retirement
   c. asset substitution; induced retirement
   d. interest; asset substitution

Short Answer Questions

1. Why would comparing the benefit and tax structure of Social Security to what might be achieved in a private investment alternative be valid, and why might it not be valid?
2. How would a change in immigration policy affect the projected solvency of the Social Security system?

3. How much would an individual receive in benefits if she had a constant (wage-inflation adjusted) monthly income of $6,000, and how would that compare to someone who had an income one-third that size?
4. What economic concept do you use to compare benefits received in the distant future with taxes paid in the past, present, and in the near future?

Think about This

How much risk is appropriate for a government-run annuity system? Is there an appropriate risk–return calculation to be made? Is Social Security risk free? What about political risk?

Talk about This

Defenders of the status quo in Social Security note the extremely low administrative costs of the system relative to those associated with private investment houses. Critics of the status quo note that the real rate of return to future recipients is so much less than the long-term historical average of stocks that paying the extra administrative costs would be worth it. Who's right? Given the methods of saving Social Security described in this chapter, which combination would you employ to save it?

For More Insight See

Aaron, Henry, "The Myths of Social Security Crisis: Behind the Privatization Push," *NTA Forum* 26 (Summer 1996).

Clark, Robert, "Social Security Financing: Facts, Fantasies, Foibles, and Follies," *American Economic Review* 94, no. 2 (May 2004).

Cogan, John F., and Olivia S. Mitchell, "Perspectives from the President's Commission on Social Security Reform," *Journal of Economic Perspectives* 17, no. 2 (Spring 2003).

Diamond, Peter, "Social Security," *American Economic Review* 94, no. 1 (March 2001).

Feldstein, Martin, "Social Security and Saving: New Time Series Evidence," *National Tax Journal* 49, no. 2 (June 1996), pp. 151–163.

Hyman, David, *Public Finance: A Contemporary Application of Theory to Policy,* 7th ed. (11th ed. Cengage, 2013).

Journal of Economic Perspectives 10, no. 3 (Summer 1996). See articles by Edward M. Gramlich; and Peter A. Diamond, pp. 85–88.

Leimer, Dean, and Selig Lesnoy, "Social Security and Private Saving: New Time Series Evidence," *Journal of Political Economy* 90, no. 3 (June 1982), pp. 606–642.

Pozen, Robert, Sylvester J. Schieber, and John Shoven, "Improving Social Security's Progressivity and Solvency with Hybrid Indexing," *American Economic Review* 94, no. 2 (May 2004).

Rosen, Harvey S., and Ted Gayer, *Public Finance* (New York, NY: McGraw-Hill/Irwin, 2010).

Steuerle, C. Eugene, and Jon M. Bakija, *Retooling Social Security for the 21st Century: Right and Wrong Approaches to Reform* (Washington, D.C.: Urban Institute, 1994).

Behind the Numbers

Social Security Administration: www.socialsecurity.gov

- Enrollment
- Tax structure
- Benefit structure

Social Security Administration, Trustees Report: www.ssa.gov/OACT/TR/2018/

- Trust fund projections
- Enrollment projections

CHAPTER FORTY-ONE

Personal Income Taxes

Learning Objectives

After reading this chapter you should be able to:

LO1 Explain the structure of federal income taxes.

LO2 Describe the concepts of horizontal and vertical equity and how they apply to the issue of taxation.

LO3 Summarize the trade-off that exists between simplicity and horizontal equity when people are making tax policy.

LO4 Describe how taxes can alter the incentives of people to work, save, and engage in other socially desirable outcomes.

LO5 Summarize the debates over taxes.

Chapter Outline

In 2018, income taxes accounted for $1,684 billion of the $3,330 billion that made up federal revenue. As Figure 41.1 suggests, the rest came from payroll (FICA), corporate, customs, excise, estate, and miscellaneous taxes. Personal income taxes nearly comprise the majority of the revenue government receives. These taxes also provoke many of the disagreements between Republicans and Democrats. Each party fights for policies it believes are best for the nation and that help its constituencies.

Usually, the political fights surrounding the personal income tax code are related to whether the rich pay their "fair share." To look at these controversies with any insight, we will need to understand the way taxes work and who pays them before we get into which party has the better claim on taxes.

We start with a discussion of how federal income taxes work in the United States. Following that, we discuss whether and how income taxes alter the willingness of people to work and save and how capital gains fit into this picture. We then introduce surprising news about who actually pays taxes. At the end, we present some of the interesting tax debates that typically separate Republicans and Democrats.

How Income Taxes Work

Federal income taxes[1] in the United States are collected through a series of estimates that are corrected on April 15 of the year after the tax year. When you get a new job, you are required to complete a W-4 form on which you provide information that will help your employer determine how much tax should be withheld from each of your paychecks. **Withholding** is the deduction from your paycheck in which you and the government estimate how much tax you are going to owe during a year so you can pay it a little at a time rather than all at once. On April 15, you use the amount you actually earned, as reported to you on a W-2 or a 1099 form, to compute what you actually owe. People who have had too much withheld get a tax refund. If they have too little withheld, they must pay the remaining balance by April 15.

withholding
Deduction from your paycheck to cover the estimated amount of taxes you are going to owe during a year.

[1] This chapter is exclusively about federal income taxes. Though state income taxes often start with the federal definitions, there are key differences.

FIGURE 41.1 Federal taxes and their sources in billions.

Source: Office of Management and Budget. https://www.whitehouse.gov/wp-content/uploads/2019/03/hist-fy2020.pdf.

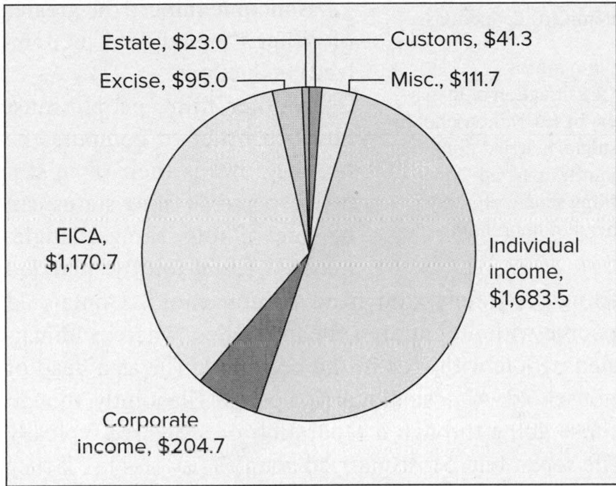

As you can see from Figure 41.2, the amount of tax you owe looks complicated. In reality, tax computations are simple for most people because, thanks to a 1986 law, most people can skip the most complicated step, itemizing deductions, and fill out as few as 10 lines on their tax forms. Still, for many others, tax forms, rules, and procedures are complicated and jargon-filled. To understand how taxes affect people, we must first learn about those forms, rules, procedures, and jargon.

The tax you owe is, of course, influenced by how much you earn. The **adjusted gross income (AGI)** is the total net income from all sources. To get that number, add together all of your income from the traditional sources (wages, salaries, tips, interest, and dividends). Then add any net profit from businesses and rental apartments, any profit you have from asset sales (called **capital gains**).

adjusted gross income (AGI)
Total net income from all sources.

capital gains
Any profit generated by selling an asset for more than was paid for it.

deductions
Amounts by which AGI is reduced; the greater of either the standard deduction or itemized deductions.

To determine how much of that adjusted gross income is taxable, you must first consider deductions.

Deductions (amounts by which AGI is reduced) are complicated by the fact that they are the greater of either a minimum

FIGURE 41.2 Federal income taxes, 2018.

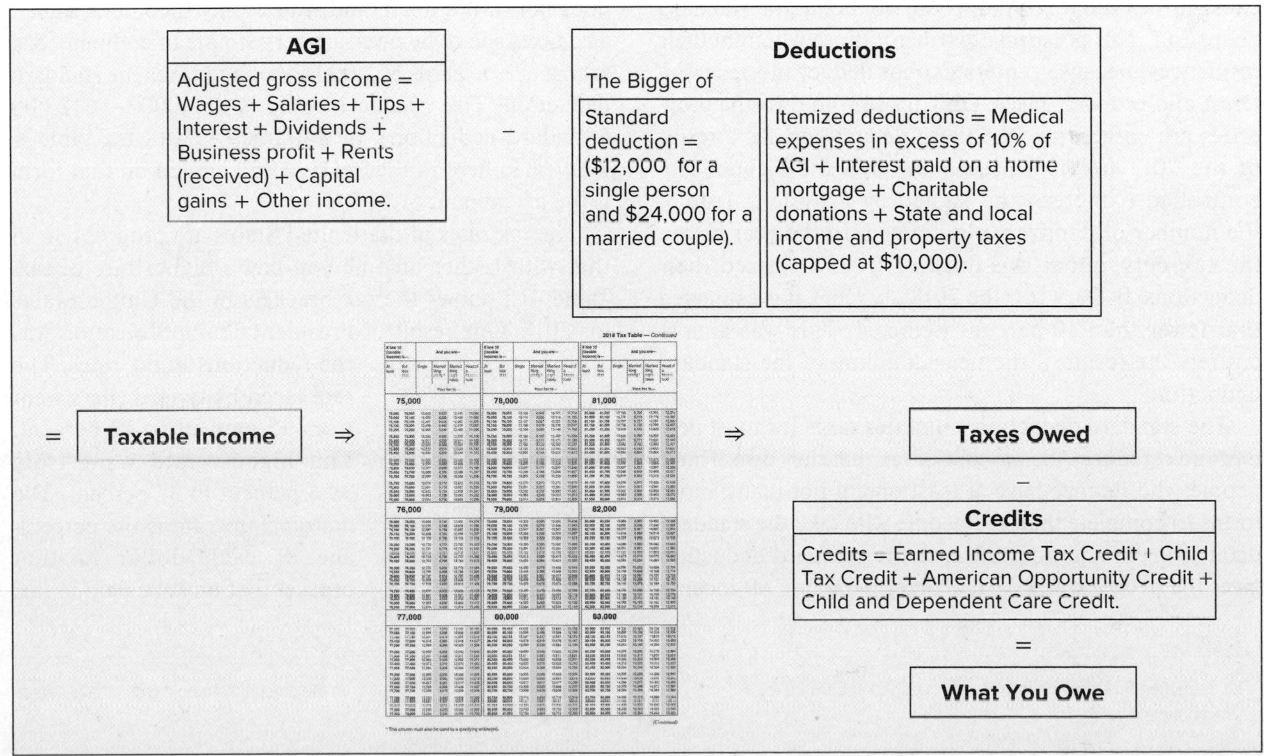

level or the sum of particular expenditures, the value of which is money that will not be taxed. The minimum level of deduction is called the **standard deduction,** and this is the amount that most people take. **Itemized deductions** are for particular expenses on which government does not want taxes paid. The reason most people can compute their taxes relatively easily is that they skip this complicated step. Rather than itemizing deductions, they accept the value of the standard deduction.

standard deduction
The minimum level of deduction.

itemized deductions
Deductions for particular expenses on which the government does not want taxes paid.

deductible
Approved types of expenses for income tax purposes.

When people itemize (that is, "list"), they add up those things that are **deductible** (approved types of expenses) and instead of reducing their taxable income by a fixed amount, they reduce it by the sum of those expenses. For instance, when people buy homes, they typically have mortgage payments. In the early years of paying a mortgage, the payment is almost entirely interest. That interest is deductible. Other deductible items that are listed include state and local income and property taxes,[2] charitable donations, and certain (usually very high) medical expenses.

Most people do not itemize their deductions because if they did, the total would not equal the standard deduction. This is especially true for those who rent their residences, because renters cannot deduct mortgage interest and property taxes. Only those who own the properties are entitled to take these deductions. As a result of the 2017 tax cuts passed through the Republican-controlled Congress and signed by President Trump, the number of itemizers plummeted. In the year before the tax cuts, about one-third of filers itemized their deductions. In 2019 (for the 2018 tax year), it is estimated that fewer than 10 percent itemized. This was almost entirely the result of the near doubling of the standard deduction.

The standard deduction simplifies taxes for most people, and it reduces the amount of tax that they owe. Those people who itemize have at least one, if not many, more forms to complete than the people who take the standard deduction. In addition, because the standard deduction gives the people who take it a larger reduction off income than they would otherwise get, it reduces their tax burden. **Taxable income** is therefore adjusted gross income minus (the greater of either the standard or itemized) deductions.

taxable income
Adjusted gross income minus (the greater of either the standard or itemized) deductions.

filing status
Classification of taxpayers based on household: single, married filing jointly, married filing separately, and head of household.

Another thing people must know in order to compute the tax they owe is their **filing status.** A person's filing status can be one of four things: single, married filing jointly, married filing separately, and head of household. Unmarried people without children file as singles, whereas unmarried people with kids in the household file as a head of household. Almost all married people file jointly, though those going through a separation or a divorce typically file separately. Most married couples pay less tax if they file jointly, though some couples file separately because they balk at sharing financial information with one another. In the 2018 tax year, for married couples the standard deduction was $24,000; for single people it was $12,000.

The tax tables show the amount most people owe in tax. To read tax tables, find the column that contains the filing status. Then read the row to find the amount of taxable income. As an example, take a single person who does not own a home and whose only income is salary. The taxes she or he owes are very simple to compute. Say such a person earns $52,000 a year and takes the standard deduction. The taxable income is $52,000 − $12,000 (standard deduction), or $40,000. A 2018 tax table is duplicated here in Figure 41.3, and circled on that form is the tax amount of $4,745.[3]

The tax rates in the United States are **progressive** in that with higher income you pay a higher rate of tax. Table 41.1 shows the tax brackets in the United States for 2018. One result of President Trump's election was the reductions in tax rates. The rate faced by typical filers went from 15 percent to 12 percent. The highest rate went from 39.6 percent to 37 percent. The **marginal tax rate** is the percentage of each dollar in that bracket that must be paid in tax.

progressive taxation
Those with higher income pay a higher rate of tax.

marginal tax rate
The percentage of each dollar in a bracket that must be paid in tax.

[2] The deduction for state and local taxes is capped at $10,000 for a married couple.

[3] That represented a $1,000 cut from the amount someone would have owed under the 2017 tax code.

FIGURE 41.3 Tax table for 2018.

Source: Department of the Treasury Internal Revenue Service. "2018 Tax Table." 1040 Tax and Earned Income Credit Tables. www.irs.gov/pub/irs-pdf/i1040tt.pdf.

2018 Tax Table

If line 10 (taxable income) is—		And you are—			
At least	But less than	Single	Married filing jointly *	Married filing separately	Head of a household
		Your tax is—			
39,000					
39,000	39,050	4,525	4,302	4,525	4,411
39,050	39,100	4,536	4,308	4,536	4,417
39,100	39,150	4,547	4,314	4,547	4,423
39,150	39,200	4,558	4,320	4,558	4,429
39,200	39,250	4,569	4,326	4,569	4,435
39,250	39,300	4,580	4,332	4,580	4,441
39,300	39,350	4,591	4,338	4,591	4,447
39,350	39,400	4,602	4,344	4,602	4,453
39,400	39,450	4,613	4,350	4,613	4,459
39,450	39,500	4,624	4,356	4,624	4,465
39,500	39,550	4,635	4,362	4,635	4,471
39,550	39,600	4,646	4,368	4,646	4,477
39,600	39,650	4,657	4,374	4,657	4,483
39,650	39,700	4,668	4,380	4,668	4,489
39,700	39,750	4,679	4,386	4,679	4,495
39,750	39,800	4,690	4,392	4,690	4,501
39,800	39,850	4,701	4,398	4,701	4,507
39,850	39,900	4,712	4,404	4,712	4,513
39,900	39,950	4,723	4,410	4,723	4,519
39,950	40,000	4,734	4,416	4,734	4,525
40,000					
40,000	40,050	4,745	4,422	4,745	4,531
40,050	40,100	4,756	4,428	4,756	4,537
40,100	40,150	4,767	4,434	4,767	4,543
40,150	40,200	4,778	4,440	4,778	4,549
40,200	40,250	4,789	4,446	4,789	4,555
40,250	40,300	4,800	4,452	4,800	4,561
40,300	40,350	4,811	4,458	4,811	4,567
40,350	40,400	4,822	4,464	4,822	4,573
40,400	40,450	4,833	4,470	4,833	4,579
40,450	40,500	4,844	4,476	4,844	4,585
40,500	40,550	4,855	4,482	4,855	4,591
40,550	40,600	4,866	4,488	4,866	4,597
40,600	40,650	4,877	4,494	4,877	4,603
40,650	40,700	4,888	4,500	4,888	4,609
40,700	40,750	4,899	4,506	4,899	4,615
40,750	40,800	4,910	4,512	4,910	4,621
40,800	40,850	4,921	4,518	4,921	4,627
40,850	40,900	4,932	4,524	4,932	4,633
40,900	40,950	4,943	4,530	4,943	4,639
40,950	41,000	4,954	4,536	9,954	4,645
41,000					
41,000	41,050	4,965	4,542	4,965	4,651
41,050	41,100	4,976	4,548	4,976	4,657
41,100	41,150	4,987	4,554	4,987	4,663
41,150	41,200	4,998	4,560	4,998	4,669
41,200	41,250	5,009	4,566	5,009	4,675
41,250	41,300	5,020	4,572	5,020	4,681
41,300	41,350	5,031	4,578	5,031	4,687
41,350	41,400	5,042	4,584	5,042	4,693
41,400	41,450	5,053	4,590	5,053	4,699
41,450	41,500	5,064	4,596	5,064	4,705
41,500	41,550	5,075	4,602	5,075	4,711
41,550	41,600	5,086	4,608	5,086	4,717
41,600	41,650	5,097	4,614	5,097	4,723
41,650	41,700	5,108	4,620	5,108	4,729
41,700	41,750	5,119	4,626	5,119	4,735
41,750	41,800	5,130	4,632	5,130	4,741
41,800	41,850	5,141	4,638	5,141	4,747
41,850	41,900	5,152	4,644	5,152	4,753
41,900	41,950	5,163	4,650	5,163	4,759
41,950	42,000	5,174	4,656	5,174	4,765

If line 10 (taxable income) is—		And you are—			
At least	But less than	Single	Married filing jointly *	Married filing separately	Head of a household
		Your tax is—			
42,000					
42,000	42,050	5,185	4,662	5,185	4,771
42,050	42,100	5,196	4,668	5,196	4,777
42,100	42,150	5,207	4,674	5,207	4,783
42,150	42,200	5,218	4,680	5,218	4,789
42,200	42,250	5,229	4,686	5,229	4,795
42,250	42,300	5,240	4,692	5,240	4,801
42,300	42,350	5,251	4,698	5,251	4,807
42,350	42,400	5,262	4,704	5,262	4,813
42,400	42,450	5,273	4,710	5,273	4,819
42,450	42,500	5,284	4,716	5,284	4,825
42,500	42,550	5,295	4,722	5,295	4,831
42,550	42,600	5,306	4,728	5,306	4,837
42,600	42,650	5,317	4,734	5,317	4,843
42,650	42,700	5,328	4,740	5,328	4,849
42,700	42,750	5,339	4,746	5,339	4,855
42,750	42,800	5,350	4,752	5,350	4,861
42,800	42,850	5,361	4,758	5,361	4,867
42,850	42,900	5,372	4,764	5,372	4,873
42,900	42,950	5,383	4,770	5,383	4,879
42,950	43,000	5,394	4,776	5,394	4,885
43,000					
43,000	43,050	5,405	4,782	5,405	4,891
43,050	43,100	5,416	4,788	5,416	4,897
43,100	43,150	5,427	4,794	5,427	4,903
43,150	43,200	5,438	4,800	5,438	4,909
43,200	43,250	5,449	4,806	5,449	4,915
43,250	43,300	5,460	4,812	5,460	4,921
43,300	43,350	5,471	4,818	5,471	4,927
43,350	43,400	5,482	4,824	5,482	4,933
43,400	43,450	5,493	4,830	5,493	4,939
43,450	43,500	5,504	4,836	5,504	4,945
43,500	43,550	5,515	4,842	5,515	4,951
43,550	43,600	5,526	4,848	5,526	4,957
43,600	43,650	5,537	4,854	5,537	4,963
43,650	43,700	5,548	4,860	5,548	4,969
43,700	43,750	5,559	4,866	5,559	4,975
43,750	43,800	5,570	4,872	5,570	4,981
43,800	43,850	5,581	4,878	5,581	4,987
43,850	43,900	5,592	4,884	5,592	4,993
43,900	43,950	5,603	4,890	5,603	4,999
43,950	44,000	5,614	4,896	5,614	5,005
44,000					
44,000	44,050	5,625	4,902	5,625	5,011
44,050	44,100	5,636	4,908	5,636	5,017
44,100	44,150	5,647	4,914	5,647	5,023
44,150	44,200	5,658	4,920	5,658	5,029
44,200	44,250	5,669	4,926	5,669	5,035
44,250	44,300	5,680	4,932	5,680	5,041
44,300	44,350	5,691	4,938	5,691	5,047
44,350	44,400	5,702	4,944	5,702	5,053
44,400	44,450	5,713	4,950	5,713	5,059
44,450	44,500	5,724	4,956	5,724	5,065
44,500	44,550	5,735	4,962	5,735	5,071
44,550	44,600	5,746	4,968	5,746	5,077
44,600	44,650	5,757	4,974	5,757	5,083
44,650	44,700	5,768	4,980	5,768	5,089
44,700	44,750	5,779	4,986	5,779	5,095
44,750	44,800	5,790	4,992	5,790	5,101
44,800	44,850	5,801	4,998	5,801	5,107
44,850	44,900	5,812	5,004	5,812	5,113
44,900	44,950	5,823	5,010	5,823	5,119
44,950	45,000	7,834	5,016	5,834	5,125

If line 10 (taxable income) is—		And you are—			
At least	But less than	Single	Married filing jointly *	Married filing separately	Head of a household
		Your tax is—			
45,000					
45,000	45,050	5,845	5,022	5,845	5,131
45,050	45,100	5,856	5,028	5,856	5,137
45,100	45,150	5,867	5,034	5,867	5,143
45,150	45,200	5,878	5,040	5,878	5,149
45,200	45,250	5,889	5,046	5,889	5,155
45,250	45,300	5,900	5,052	5,900	5,161
45,300	45,350	5,911	5,058	5,911	5,167
45,350	45,400	5,922	5,064	5,922	5,173
45,400	45,450	5,933	5,070	5,933	5,179
45,450	45,500	5,944	5,076	5,944	5,185
45,500	45,550	5,955	5,082	5,955	5,191
45,550	45,600	5,966	5,088	5,966	5,197
45,600	45,650	5,977	5,094	5,977	5,203
45,650	45,700	5,988	5,100	5,988	5,209
45,700	45,750	5,999	5,106	5,999	5,215
45,750	45,800	6,010	5,112	6,010	5,221
45,800	45,850	6,021	5,118	6,021	5,227
45,850	45,900	6,032	5,124	6,032	5,233
45,900	45,950	6,043	5,130	6,043	5,239
45,950	46,000	6,054	5,136	6,054	5,245
46,000					
46,000	46,050	6,065	5,142	6,065	5,251
46,050	46,100	6,076	5,148	6,076	5,257
46,100	46,150	6,087	5,154	6,087	5,263
46,150	46,200	6,098	5,160	6,098	5,269
46,200	46,250	6,109	5,166	6,109	5,275
46,250	46,300	6,120	5,172	6,120	5,281
46,300	46,350	6,131	5,178	6,131	5,287
46,350	46,400	6,142	5,184	6,142	5,293
46,400	46,450	6,153	5,190	6,153	5,299
46,450	46,500	6,164	5,196	6,164	5,305
46,500	46,550	6,175	5,202	6,175	5,311
46,550	46,600	6,186	5,208	6,186	5,317
46,600	46,650	6,197	5,214	6,197	5,323
46,650	46,700	6,208	5,220	6,208	5,329
46,700	46,750	6,219	5,226	6,219	5,335
46,750	46,800	6,230	5,232	6,230	5,341
46,800	46,850	6,241	5,238	6,241	5,347
46,850	46,900	6,252	5,244	6,252	5,353
46,900	46,950	6,263	5,250	6,263	5,359
46,950	47,000	6,274	5,256	6,274	5,365
47,000					
47,000	47,050	6,285	5,262	6,285	5,371
47,050	47,100	6,296	5,268	6,296	5,377
47,100	47,150	6,307	5,274	6,307	5,383
47,150	47,200	6,318	5,280	6,318	5,389
47,200	47,250	6,329	5,286	6,329	5,395
47,250	47,300	6,340	5,292	6,340	5,401
47,300	47,350	6,351	5,298	6,351	5,407
47,350	47,400	6,362	5,304	6,362	5,413
47,400	47,450	6,373	5,310	6,373	5,419
47,450	47,500	6,384	5,316	6,384	5,425
47,500	47,550	6,395	5,322	6,395	5,431
47,550	47,600	6,406	5,328	6,406	5,437
47,600	47,650	6,417	5,334	6,417	5,443
47,650	47,700	6,428	5,340	6,428	5,449
47,700	47,750	6,439	5,346	6,439	5,455
47,750	47,800	6,450	5,352	6,450	5,461
47,800	47,850	6,461	5,358	6,461	5,467
47,850	47,900	6,472	5,364	6,472	5,473
47,900	47,950	6,483	5,370	6,483	5,479
47,950	48,000	6,494	5,376	6,494	5,485

* This column must also be used by a qualifying widow(er).

Table 41.1 Marginal tax rate.

Status	10%	12%	22%	24%	32%	35%	37%
Single	$0–9,525	$9,525–38,700	$38,700–82,500	$82,500–157,500	$157,500–200,000	$200,000–500,000	$500,000–
Head of household	$0–13,600	$13,600–51,800	$ 51,800–82,500	$ 82,500–157,500	$157,500–200,000	$200,000–500,000	$500,000–
Married filing jointly	$0–19,050	$19,050–77,400	$77,400–165,000	$165,000–315,000	$315,000–400,000	$400,000–600,000	$600,000–
Married filing separately	$0–9,525	$9,525–38,700	$38,700–82,500	$82,500–157,500	$157,500–200,000	$200,000–500,000	$500,000–

This means that our single person making $52,000, with taxable income of $40,000, has a tax rate of zero on the first $12,000 of AGI, pays 10 percent on the next $9,525, pays 12 percent on the next $29,175, and pays 22 percent of the remainder.

tax credits
Amounts by which you reduce the tax owed.

Even after you have figured your tax, this is not what you actually owe. There are many **tax credits** that now go into the computation. We will focus on four important ones. The first, the earned income tax credit, is designed for the working poor. This can be a substantial increase in your take-home pay if you have children and do not make a lot of money. In 2018, for those with at least two children, the credit amounted to as much as $5,828. The second important credit is the Child Tax Credit. For those married couples who make less than $400,000, this credit amounts to $2,000 per child. This constituted a doubling of the 2017 Child Tax Credit and was done to offset the elimination of the previous mechanism ($4,000 per child in exemptions from taxable income) for assisting taxpayers who have children. The third major credit is the Child and Dependent Care tax credit. For the majority of families with child-care expenses, this credit allows for between 20 percent and 35 percent (again, depending on AGI) of those expenses to come off the tax bill. The last of the major credits is the American Opportunity Credit. This allows for up to $2,500 of college-related expenses to come off the tax bill.

There is an important distinction between tax credits and deductions. A tax deduction comes off taxable income, so the savings to taxpayers are whatever their marginal tax rate is times the amount of the deduction. For example, if a person is in the 12 percent tax bracket, a $1,000 deduction is worth $120. A $1,000 credit, on the other hand, is $1,000 off the tax bill. Tax credits are therefore better than deductions if the two are in equal amounts.

There is another aspect of the distinction between credits and deductions that is important. When the political parties are debating taxes, there is often a discussion of whether there should be a tax deduction or credit for something. Because credits are more costly to the government than deductions, we can imagine that the choice facing policy makers for the tax cut would be a $2,500 deduction or a $500 credit. For people in the 12 percent tax bracket, a $2,500 tax deduction is worth between nothing (because they still end up with insufficient deductions to get over the standard deduction) and 12 percent of $2,500, or $300. For people in the 24 percent bracket, a $2,500 deduction is worth up to $600. The net result of this is that credits are better than deductions when they are in equal amounts and that for tax reductions of equal cost to the government, credits are better than deductions for the poor. For the rich, the opposite is true: Tax deductions are preferred over tax credits.

For people with a variety of income sources and many deductions, the rules are very complicated. The vast majority of people are not in this predicament. You must own a farm or business, have a significant and actively changing investment portfolio, have significant medical expenses that you have to pay yourself, work in an environment where you get high pay but have to pay for lots of work expenses (like an employee in sales), or have some other strange source of income in order to have overly complicated income taxes.

A provision that was eliminated in the 2017 tax cuts was personal exemptions. It used to be that for every person in the household, there was a $4,000 exemption (which also was subject to AGI limits). The net effect of eliminating the personal exemption, the near doubling of the standard deduction, and the doubling of the Child Tax Credit was that effective tax rates dropped for families with children.

Issues in Income Taxation

Horizontal and Vertical Equity

One question that always arises with regard to income taxes is whether they are fair. The very definition of "fair" requires some thought. To be fair, it seems clear that equal people should be treated equally. This concept, called **horizontal equity**, is not in much dispute. People who earn the

horizontal equity
Equal people should be treated equally.

same income, from the same sources, with the same family structure, and are the same in every other dimension should pay the same taxes.

vertical equity
People across the income scale are treated fairly with regard to ability to pay.

Where the controversy lies with most people is the issue of **vertical equity.** That is, are people across the income scale treated fairly with regard to their ability to pay? As you saw with Table 41.1, people at the upper end of the income scale pay much more in tax and much higher percentages of tax than people at the lower end.

Equity versus Simplicity

There is a distinct trade-off between horizontal equity and simplicity. This is because it is difficult to clearly establish the question of "sameness" that is at the heart of the definition of horizontal equity. Most economists who study the issue of taxation want the tax code to be **neutral.** For instance, to ensure neutrality, income earned from work must be treated the same as income made from investments. The problem is that in order to accomplish neutrality, the tax code would have to be very complicated. Consider capital gains income.

neutral
When applied to a tax code, the implication that it does not favor particular forms of income or expenditure.

When assets are bought and later sold at a profit, there is capital gain. Under the principles of neutrality, capital gain should be taxed—the question is how much? This question arises because there are problems with capital gains that do not affect earnings from work. First, much of the increase in the value of an asset is simply the compensation for inflation. We tax all gains rather than just the inflation-adjusted gains because this is easier. Second, some assets are difficult to evaluate, so capital gains are taxed only on realization (when you actually have the profit in hand) rather than accrual (when the asset price increase happened). This undertaxes capital gains by letting the holder of them defer the tax.

Taxing on realization rather than accrual is simple, but it creates a different problem whose solution only creates another problem. Because there is no tax until an asset is sold, when a person dies while in possession of an asset, there are capital gains. Perhaps there is no paperwork to find out when it was bought, so there is no way of finding out exactly how big the capital gain is. To solve this, all capital gains, and therefore all taxes owed on those gains, are forgiven at death. This is called the *stepped-up basis.* It assumes that all assets were purchased on the day the person died. However, solving one problem creates yet another. There is an incentive for the elderly to hold assets with large capital gains rather than sell them, because doing so avoids the capital gains tax.

Thus, the problem is that there is a trade-off between simplicity and equity. In order to be simple, the tax code must violate equity, and in order to be fair, it must violate simplicity.

Incentives and the Tax Code

There is an active debate among politicians and economists about the effects of income taxes on the behavior of people. Two of the most interesting issues are how such taxes affect people's willingness to work and save. Republican politicians and conservative economists are convinced that the existence of income taxes causes people to work and save less. Democratic politicians and liberal economists are convinced that people do not work and save any less and may, in fact, work and save more.

This is because there is a fundamental disagreement between economists concerning the relative importance of what economists call the **substitution effect** and the **income effect.** Any time you change the price of something, in this case either the take-home wage rate or the after-tax interest rate, you create these two effects. The substitution effect moves people toward the good that is now cheaper or away from the good that is now more expensive. As an example, if there are only two goods, apples and oranges, and the price of apples increases, you would move toward oranges. This is not the end of the story, though. There is also an income effect. This can go either direction and depends on the Chapter 2 concepts of normal and inferior goods. If a good is inferior, the increase in price lowers your real spending power and you would move back toward that good. If a good is normal, the opposite occurs.

substitution effect
Purchase of less of a product than originally wanted when its price is high because a lower-priced product is available.

income effect
An increase in price lowers spending power; if the good is normal, this further lowers consumption; if it is inferior, it can increase consumption back toward where it was (or even further). This effect works in either direction.

Do Taxes Alter Work Decisions?

One of the most well-researched questions in economics is the effect of take-home pay on the number of hours worked. To the untrained observer this may not seem like a very difficult question, but it actually is. The substitution effect is the more obviously seen effect. Because taxes reduce take-home pay for every hour worked, the incentive to work, rather than stay home and relax, is lessened. Thus, you reduce your work effort.

The other side of the story, though, is the reduction in income. If you do the work that is necessary to generate a certain standard of living, then you will have to work more hours to have the income to sustain that standard of living. The empirical research suggests that if taxes do alter the work decision, it is only very slightly. Most estimates suggest that the substitution effect is exactly countered by the income effect. That is, an increase in taxes has no effect on work effort, though a 2013 estimate suggested that a 10 percent reduction in after-tax wage rates generates a 4 percent reduction in work hours. Either way, taxes do not substantially alter the incentive to work.

Do Taxes Alter Savings Decisions?

A similar result has been found on after-tax interest rates. Though there is disagreement in methodology that generates a disagreement in the conclusion, many economists believe that an increase in tax rates has little or no effect on saving behavior. This also suggests that the substitution effect and income effect completely counter each other. There are, though, estimates that suggest that the net is not zero. In particular, Michael Boskin (in a 1976 paper) estimated that a 2.5 percent decrease in the after-tax interest rates results in a 1 percent decrease in savings.

Taxes for Social Engineering

If taxes do not substantially alter the incentive of people to work or save, then you might think that policy makers would have given up on using taxes to get people to do other desirable things. However, this is not the case. President Clinton proposed and Congress enacted a plan to use tax credits to provide an incentive to go to college. Tax deductions and credits for a variety of desirable outcomes have been tried at a variety of different times. Typically, these tax breaks do not result in more of the desired outcome but simply subsidize the people who were already engaging in it.

President Bush was less fond of tax changes of this type, but President Obama jumped right in with billions of targeted tax deductions and credits in his 2009 Economic Recovery Act (i.e., his stimulus package). In that package, there were tax credits for first-time home buyers, for buyers of hybrid cars, and even for buyers of energy-efficient water heaters. The belief that the federal income tax code can be used to motivate socially desirable activities is deeply held in the halls of the capitol, yet there is little evidence that these tax credits have a significant impact.

Who Pays Income Taxes?

A vastly misunderstood concept of income taxation is who it is that pays. For years, Republicans and Democrats alike have perpetuated the myth that middle-class Americans pay this tax and the rich do not pay their fair share. A look at Table 41.2 should begin to dispel that myth. The first column indicates the percentile of tax returns; the second and third columns indicate the percentage of income earned and taxes paid by everyone at or below that percentile.

From this table you can draw several myth-breaking conclusions. First, the bottom half of taxpayers pays less than 2 percent of the income tax, while the top half pays the remaining 98 percent. Second, the top 10 percent of taxpayers accounts for 73 percent of federal income taxes paid, while the rest of taxpayers account for only 27 percent. Third, if it were true that the rich were not paying as much as the middle class, the second column would not always exceed the third. It does, and the rich pay far more tax than do the rest of us.

Table 41.2 Distribution of taxes, 2016.

Source: Internal Revenue Service. Statistics of Income: Individual Income Tax Returns. https://www.irs.gov/uac/soi-tax-stats-individual-income-tax-returns.

Percentile of Taxpayers, Bottom x% of Returns*	Cumulative Percentage of Adjusted Gross Income	Cumulative Percentage of Taxes Paid
10	0.00%	0.00%
20	0.47%	0.02%
30	1.92%	0.09%
40	4.25%	0.36%
50	7.51%	1.00%
60	11.76%	2.19%
70	17.63%	4.49%
80	25.24%	8.22%
90	36.52%	15.69%
100	51.42%	26.50%
	100.00%	100.00%

*Example: The bottom 40 percent of taxpayers earn 4.25 percent of adjusted gross income and pay 0.36 percent of all federal income taxes.

FIGURE 41.4 Income and tax distributions.

Source: Internal Revenue Service. "Statistics of Income: Individual Income Tax Returns." www.irs.gov/uac/SOI-Tax-Stats-Individual-Income-Tax-Returns.

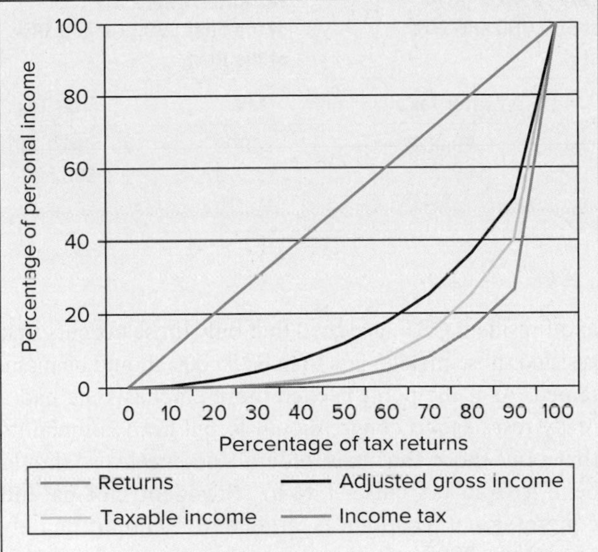

Figure 41.4 portrays the same information graphically. If all income and taxes were earned and paid equally, it would represent a straight line. The degree to which the income earned, shown as AGI, is bowed is the degree to which income earned is unequal. If taxes were paid mostly by the middle class, then the tax curve would be above the income curve. Since the opposite is true, it should be clear that there is significant effective progressivity in the tax code.

Tax Debates

One of the central themes of the political debates is whether tax cuts should be across the board or targeted. Republican presidential candidates offer across-the-board tax cuts, whereas Democratic presidential candidates offer tax cuts that are targeted to specific populations. The difference in philosophy is essentially two differences of opinion: whether most of the tax cuts should go to the people who pay most of the tax or whether the tax code should be used to encourage particular behaviors and help people with the least income.

On the first difference of opinion, it is clear that any across-the-board tax cut must go mostly to the rich since it is they who pay the vast majority of income taxes. Thus an across-the-board tax cut by definition favors the rich. Whether this is fair criticism is relative. If you look at where most of the dollars go in such a cut, it is indisputable that the rich get most of the money. On the other hand, this is because they pay the most. Giving a tax cut to the poor gives a tax cut to people who pay very little federal income tax.[4]

Because of the progressivity of the tax code, simply reducing the tax rate by a fixed percentage not only gives more of a tax break to upper-income taxpayers, but it also changes the income distribution in a way that favors upper-income Americans. To see how, consider Table 41.3. The second column indicates before-tax income, showing a circumstance where the upper-income person makes 10 times what the lower-income person makes. The third column indicates the tax that would be paid under the simple hypothetical tax code where 10 percent of the first $50,000 and 20 percent of the rest is paid in tax. The progressivity of the income tax is displayed here in that the upper-income household makes 10 times as much as the lower-income household but pays 15 times as much tax. The fourth column shows the after-tax income. Again, note that the effect of the progressive income tax is to reduce the ratio of spending power of the high-income to lower-income person from 10 to 1 to 9.44 to 1. The fifth and sixth columns show the effect of a 10 percent reduction in tax rates. The 10 percent tax rate becomes 9 percent and the 20 percent tax rate becomes 18 percent.

Republicans and Democrats will interpret Table 41.3 in two entirely different ways. Republicans will say that under both tax codes the upper-income people are paying 15 times the taxes that the lower-income people are paying. Moreover, they will claim that any tax cut that helps the poor will change the distribution of taxes to be even further slanted to upper-income people. Democrats will focus on the distribution of the after-tax income figure and note that an across-the-board tax cut increases the ratio of an upper-income person's after-tax income to a lower-income person's after-tax income from 9.44 to 9.51. As a result, though an across-the-board tax cut keeps the percentage of government funded by each group the same, it changes the after-tax income distribution in favor of the rich.

Another great debate centers on unraveling the 1986 tax reform law that eliminated most social engineering from the tax code. Prior to that year, thousands of provisions were included to induce people to do a variety of things. The law passed in 1986 eliminated almost all of them. Slowly, but steadily, the Clinton administration sought provisions to again urge people in particular

[4]Tax cuts to the poor typically result from increasing the earned income tax credit. This credit often exceeds the amount of tax owed by a substantial amount. Many low-income families pay "negative taxes," so a tax cut to them simply makes this more negative.

Table 41.3 Hypothetical example of the effect of a 10 percent cut in tax rates on income distribution.

		Tax Code where Tax = 10% of the First $50,000 and 20% of the Rest		Tax Code after a 10% Cut in Tax Rates where Tax = 9% of the First $50,000 and 18% of the Rest	
	Before Tax	Tax	After Tax	Tax	After Tax
Lower-income person	$10,000	$1,000	$9,000	$900	$9,100
Upper-income person	$100,000	$15,000	$85,000	$13,500	$86,500
Ratio	10	15	9.44	15	9.51

directions. For instance, they sought and got partial tax deductions and credits for higher education.

After his election in 2000, George W. Bush sought and got two substantial personal income tax cuts. The first, in 2001, cut marginal tax rates, phased in an increase in the Child Tax Credit, and phased out the estate (inheritance) tax. The second, in 2003, sped up the timetable on the 2001 tax cuts and reduced the tax rate on corporate dividends.

Taken together, the beneficiaries of these tax cuts were middle-income and higher-income families with children and the wealthy. Middle-income families with children saw dramatic declines in their effective rates as the Child Tax Credit jumped from $200 to $1,000 per child. The wealthy saw a sizable reduction in their taxes as well with the reduction in marginal income tax rates by 3 to 5 percentage points (depending on bracket), the reduction in the rate at which dividends are taxed, and the phasing out of the estate tax.

One of the central questions of the 2008 presidential campaign was whether the 2003 tax cuts should be allowed to expire in 2011. President Bush repeatedly attempted to convince a skeptical Democratic Congress to make the cuts permanent. Senator McCain vowed to make them permanent were he elected. Then candidate and President Obama argued that only those tax cuts that assisted those making less than $250,000 should be maintained. As if the point needed more emphasis, he had a ready response to congressional Republican complaints that only those that paid federal income taxes should benefit from tax cuts: "I won." President Obama and congressional Democrats argued for and ultimately passed the 2009 stimulus. In it were provisions cutting taxes for anyone who paid Social Security taxes. This included billions of dollars for millions of taxpayers whose federal income tax liability was zeroed out as part of the plan. The midterm elections of 2010 constituted a significant shift in the other direction as Republicans made historic gains in both the House and Senate. One consequence of those changes was that the Bush tax cuts were extended through 2012, setting up an obvious election issue for both parties. In a democracy such as that which exists in the United States, elections have consequences, and regardless of the politics of the time, taxes are always going to be a focal point for debate.

The tax package passed in 2017 reversed this trend by eliminating the miscellaneous tax deductions category (where people were able to deduct a variety of different expenses). It also capped the deductibility of state and local taxes at $10,000 for a married couple.

Summary

You now understand how federal income taxes work and are able to apply that knowledge and the concepts of horizontal and vertical equity to the U.S. tax code. You understand the trade-off that exists between simplicity and horizontal equity and understand that in theory taxes can alter the incentives of people to work and save but that little effect has actually been shown. You know that this has not stopped policy makers from using taxes to motivate socially desirable outcomes. Last, you understand the debates over taxes that began during the 1990s and continue today.

Key Terms

adjusted gross income (AGI)
capital gains
deductible
deductions
filing status
horizontal equity
income effect
itemized deductions
marginal tax rate
neutral
progressive taxation
standard deduction
substitution effect
taxable income
tax credits
vertical equity
withholding

Quiz Yourself

1. The tax brackets have higher tax rates for more taxable income. This makes the federal income tax
   a. proportional.
   b. regressive.
   c. progressive.
   d. integrative.
2. Because there are ___________________, adjusted gross income is always ___________ taxable income.
   a. deductions; less than
   b. deductions; greater than
   c. credits; greater than
   d. credits; less than
3. One of the challenges of creating an income tax system is that there is a trade-off between
   a. taxing wages and taxing salaries.
   b. progressivity and regressivity.
   c. simplicity and fairness.
4. If Congress wants to use $100 billion on tax cuts, the version that would help a family of four making $40,000 a year would
   a. lower marginal tax rates by one percentage point.
   b. increase the standard deduction by $2,000.
   c. increase the Child Tax Credit by $1,000.
   d. index the tax brackets for inflation.
5. If the tax system is progressive and someone is in the 25 percent tax bracket, this means that ______________ is owed in taxes.
   a. 25 percent of his or her salary
   b. 25 percent of his or her adjusted gross income
   c. 25 percent of his or her taxable income
   d. less than 25 percent of his or her taxable income
6. Taxes on interest income have the potential to create
   a. an incentive or disincentive to save.
   b. a disincentive to work.
   c. an incentive to invest.
   d. a disincentive to cheat on taxes.
7. Suppose politicians are debating whether to tax college professors less than high school teachers (at the same level of income). This would violate
   a. the Constitution.
   b. vertical equity.
   c. horizontal equity.

Short Answer Questions

1. Suppose someone were to say that they earned $100,000 per year, that they paid less than $10,000 in federal income taxes, but that their marginal tax rate was 25 percent. Could that be true?
2. Use the tax tables in the chapter to compute the taxes of someone taking the standard deduction, having a spouse, three children, and $70,000 in income.
3. Explain why someone who cared about the poor and energy savings would advocate for a tax credit rather than a tax deduction if $100 billion was going to be devoted to tax cuts to promote energy-saving changes to behavior.
4. Explain why an across-the-board tax cut would benefit those at the higher end of the income scale more than it would affect those at the bottom end.

Think about This

There were many changes that resulted from the 2017 law that cut taxes for many (and raised taxes for a few). One of those changes was the capping of deductions for state and local taxes at $10,000. That cap was not indexed for inflation, which means that in coming years, the cap will impact more and more families. Tax brackets are indexed for inflation. Should every provision in the tax code be indexed?

Talk about This

The Democrats tend to work toward tax code adjustments that help those at the lowest end of the income scale; Republicans do the opposite. As a college graduate you are likely to start at the low end and become part of the high end. Are your attitudes about a political party going to stay the same or change as your income circumstances change?

For More Insight See

Boskin, Michael J., "Taxation, Saving and the Rate of Interest," *Journal of Political Economy* 86, no. 2, pt. 2 (April 1978).

Citizens for Tax Justice, *The Hidden Entitlements* (Washington, D.C.: Robert S. McIntyre, 1996).

Hyman, David, *Public Finance: A Contemporary Appli-cation of Theory to Policy,* 6th ed. (Fort Worth, TX: Dryden Press, 1999), esp. Chapters 13 and 14.

Slemrod, Joel, "Do We Know How Progressive the Income Tax Should Be?" *National Tax Journal* 36, no. 3 (September 1983), pp. 361–369.

Slemrod, Joel, *Do Taxes Matter? The Impact of the Tax Reform Act of 1986* (Cambridge, MA: MIT Press, 1991).

Behind the Numbers

White House Office of Management and Budget (OMB): www.whitehouse.gov/omb/historical-tables

- Federal revenue sources

Internal Revenue Service: www.irs.gov

- Tax rates and brackets

Internal Revenue Service: www.irs.gov/statistics/soi-tax-stats-individual-income-tax-return-form-1040-statistics

- Income and tax distribution

CHAPTER FORTY-TWO

Energy Prices

Learning Objectives

After reading this chapter you should be able to:

LO1 Define a cartel.

LO2 Model how a cartel can make its members large sums of money.

LO3 Show why cartels are not typically stable and describe the conditions necessary for creating cartel stability.

LO4 Evaluate whether OPEC qualifies as a cartel.

LO5 Summarize the history of inflation-adjusted oil and gasoline prices.

LO6 Model the role of expectations to explain why events can cause gasoline prices to change quickly.

Chapter Outline

The world runs on petroleum products. Whether it is gasoline for automobiles, diesel fuel for trains and trucks, or home heating oil, modern society could not survive without oil. With proven oil reserves at 1,661 billion barrels, roughly 565 billion barrels more believed to be yet undiscovered, and oil consumption running at a little over 101 million barrels a day, it is likely that oil reserves will be gone in the second half of the 21st century.

In this chapter, we review the history of oil and gasoline prices and discuss the causes and effects of significant changes. We consider the Organization of Petroleum Exporting Countries (OPEC) and how it developed and collapsed, recovered, and re-collapsed as an effective oil cartel. We also talk about why gasoline prices were so unstable for so long but have since stabilized. We look at electricity prices and why the industry lends itself to monopoly, and why this has led to government price regulation. Last, we consider the future and try to get an idea of where the oil industry might be 50 to 100 years from now.

The Historical View

Oil and Gasoline Price History

Gasoline prices, which were never stable, skyrocketed in the 1970s. Although several events coincided during that decade to increase prices, many politicians declared that this period was the beginning of a general long-term "energy crisis." A brief look at Figure 42.1 suggests that the crisis was actually short run in nature. As a matter of fact, by 1998, the prices of crude oil and gasoline had fallen to a point at or near their 30-year lows. Crude oil prices doubled in the 1999–2000 time frame, doubled again in the 2003–2005 time frame, and doubled once again from 2007 to July 2008. Non-inflation-adjusted gasoline prices reached all-time highs of above $4 per gallon during the July 4th weekend of 2008 and began a six-month plummet that ended with them dropping in some areas of the United States to below $1.30 per gallon by Christmas 2008. Crude oil prices fell nearly 75 percent during that same span. Prices climbed steadily back once the Great Recession ended and spiked in early 2011 as turmoil in the Middle

FIGURE 42.1 Inflation-adjusted gasoline and domestic and imported crude oil prices, 2018 (2005 dollars).

Source: U.S. Energy Information Administration. www.eia.gov.

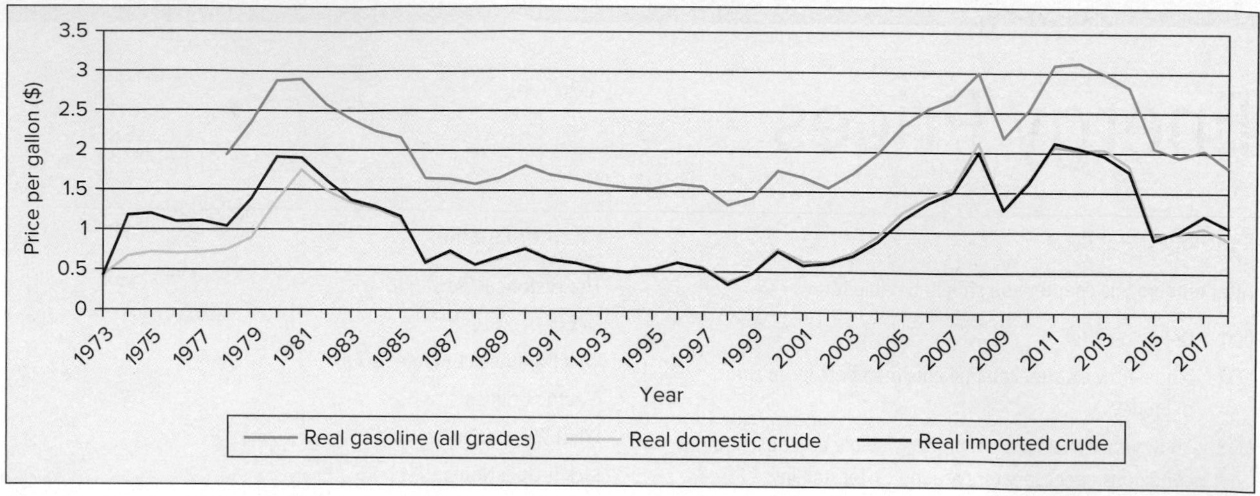

East created significant uncertainty about oil availability. Once hydraulic fracturing and directional drilling technologies took hold (in 2014), prices fell. In recent years (2015–2019), prices have largely stabilized.

The top curve in Figure 42.1 shows the path of gasoline prices (adjusted for CPI-measured inflation) since the general conversion to unleaded fuel in 1978. The middle curve tracks the price of domestically produced crude oil, and the bottom curve shows the price of imported crude. Though oil prices are usually quoted in barrels, the prices have been converted to gallons for use here, and the prices have been adjusted for inflation. For context, a barrel is 42 gallons, so a price of $61 per barrel is the same as $1.50 per gallon.

Geopolitical History

Some geopolitical history will provide insight into why oil prices changed. As you can see from Table 42.1, oil is not evenly distributed throughout the world. You can surmise from this that the politics of the Middle East, and the Persian Gulf in particular, have been important in determining oil supplies.

Table 42.1 Global reserves by region.

Source: U.S. Energy Information Administration. www.eia.gov

Group	Barrels in Reserve (in billions)	Percentage of World Reserves
Persian Gulf OPEC	794	48
Non-Persian Gulf OPEC	395	24
Rest of the world	472	28

The Arab–Israeli wars of 1967 and 1973 generated a great deal of animosity between Arab nations and the Western world. The United States in particular was castigated because it supported Israel. The United States provided both substantial intelligence and weapons that helped the Israelis to prevail in taking (in 1967) and then holding (in 1973) the West Bank of the Jordan River from Jordan, the Golan Heights from Syria, and the Gaza Strip and Sinai peninsula from Egypt.

After this, Arab nations, angered by U.S. aid to Israel, refused to sell oil to the United States and much of the rest of the Western world. Though this did not lead to the rationing of gasoline in the United States, it did in Great Britain. This embargo also resulted in marked increases in prices. Figure 42.1 indicates that these first jumps in oil prices occurred in 1973 and 1974.

The significant price increases in the late 1970s resulted from the economic power that OPEC wielded as an oil cartel. How cartels are created and how they can raise prices substantially will be thoroughly explained later in this chapter; but suffice it to say, in inflation-adjusted terms, crude oil and gasoline prices reached record highs during this time. Gasoline hit $1.40 a gallon, the 2018 equivalent of $3.89, and crude oil hit $40 per barrel, the 2018 equivalent of $111.

In the late 1970s, the Iranian Revolution occurred. This made Iran's neighbors such as Iraq, Kuwait, and Saudi Arabia very nervous. There is some dispute as to who the aggressor was, but these fears proved to be well founded, when in 1980 Iran and Iraq went to war. Although this war had many impacts more morally significant than its effect on the price of oil,[1] the impact on the price of oil changed the business of oil forever.

Because modern weapons are expensive, both Iran and Iraq were strapped for cash, and each country had only one realistic way of raising money, each began to sell as much oil as it could. While their official production figures do not show it, likely because they had to lie to fellow OPEC members, greater production allowed them to purchase more and better weapons.

As oil prices rose through the 1970s, Iran and Iraq began to pump more oil. Additionally, other nations engaged in efforts to find new sources of oil. New reserves were found in the North Sea, Mexico, and in many other countries, and these reserves began to be exploited. In 1982 and 1983, a major recession rocked the United States and Europe, depressing demand for oil. As a result of these factors, the price of oil collapsed. Ultimately, by 1986, the price per barrel fell to less than $10, and the average price per barrel at the end of the year was $12.51.

When the Iran–Iraq war ended in 1988, oil prices began to recover but reached only the $15 level—a little more than 30 cents per gallon. At the end of the war, Iraq owed Saudi Arabia and Kuwait $40 billion each, as it had borrowed feverishly to buy weaponry. At $15 per barrel, Iraq could not afford to both pay these debts and rebuild its war-torn country. Adding to the insult that Iraq felt, Kuwait and Saudi Arabia were not budging on OPEC production quotas, and Iraq felt that it had done Kuwait and Saudi Arabia a favor by fighting Iran in the first place. As we will see later when we discuss cartels, production quotas must be low to keep prices high.

On August 2, 1990, Iraq invaded Kuwait, and the United States was convinced it was poised to continue the attack into Saudi Arabia. The fear of another war in the Persian Gulf sent oil prices to nearly $30 per barrel very quickly, which caused the average price for the year to be $20 per barrel. With the American- and British-led victory in the Gulf, prices stabilized through 1998 at between $10 and $15 per barrel.

Beginning in late 1998, OPEC reasserted itself with a series of production cuts that led the price of crude oil to top $30 per barrel in the spring of 2000. Another politically inspired set of price swings occurred prior to and in the aftermath of the Iraq war in 2003. Gas prices spiked at over $2 per gallon in many U.S. cities in the month before the war. Once the conventional aspect of the war ended without major petroleum shortages, the price of gasoline came back to a more normal level ($1.25 to $1.50). Between 2003 and 2005, the Iraqi insurgency prevented a continuous flow of oil from that country and, coupled with increased worldwide demand for oil, prices spiked once again.

Historical highs were set in 2004 and 2005 in nominal terms, and for the first time in 25 years, the inflation-adjusted record price for oil began to be challenged. Inflation-adjusted gasoline prices briefly exceeded record levels in the weeks following Hurricane Katrina. Events in 2006, 2007, and 2008 propelled prices even higher. In 2006, the Bush administration was warning Iran against pursuing nuclear weapons. Oil markets reacted with significant concern that the administration was contemplating military action. At the same time, continued conflict in Nigeria and growing world demand from China and India were causing prices to increase. In 2007 and into 2008, investors looking for a place to make money started driving up world crude oil prices by speculating in oil futures. Their bet was that the growth of China and India coupled with the flattening of world oil production would create a severe oil shortage. (Note in Figure 42.2 that at 85–88 million barrels per day, world oil production was stagnant from 2005 through 2011.)

The Middle East in general and the Persian Gulf in particular have proven that they can rival the Balkans in the old adage that "they produce more history than they can consume locally." The price of oil is inextricably tied to the political, military, and religious tensions of the region, tensions that are historically significant but would likely be dismissed in the West were it not for the oil.

A Return to Irrelevancy

Though the Great Recession caused prices to temporarily plummet from $150 per barrel down to below $40 per barrel, the economic recovery of 2009–2014 helped OPEC restore its long-run price targets of $100 per barrel. What happened next was a repeat of the experience of the 1980s.

There is a cliché in economics that goes: "The cure for high prices is high prices." That economic truism results from the motivation to innovate. That innovation is intensely motivated by high prices. In the early 1980s, the high prices of the day directly motivated the search for and the provision of oil in places that it was previously

[1]Iraq first used poison gas on Iranian soldiers and its own citizens, Iranians recruited children to serve as soldiers, the Reagan administration sold the Iranians weapons while using the profits to fund the Nicaraguan contras, and the CIA gave intelligence support to Iraq.

FIGURE 42.2 Worldwide oil production, 1970–2018.

Source: U.S. Energy Information Administration. https://www.eia.gov

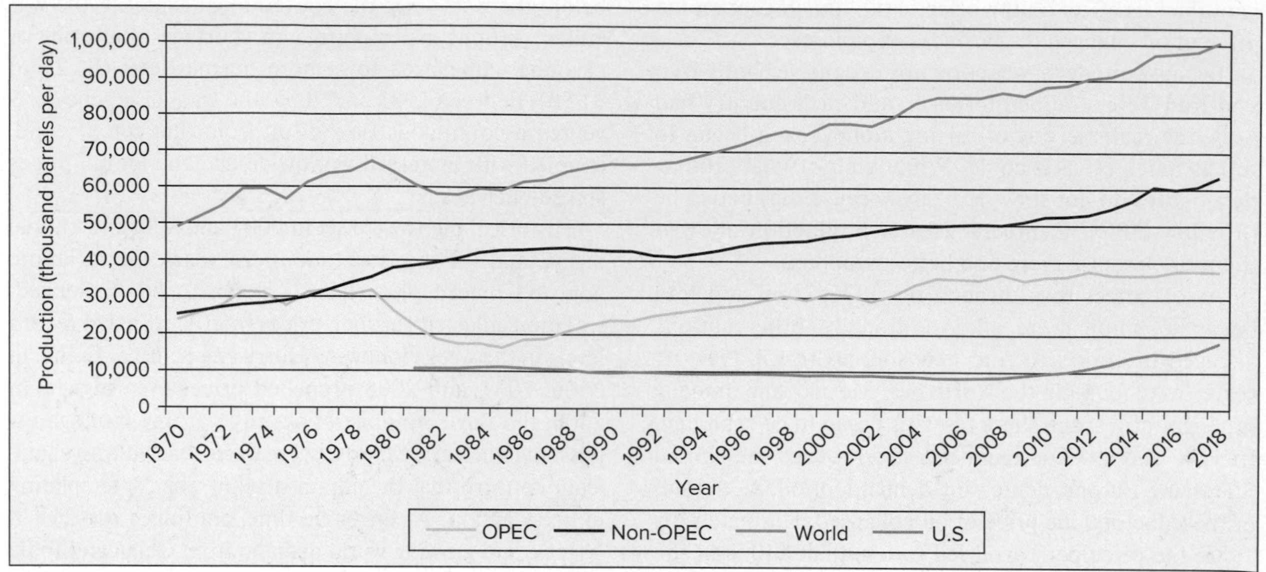

known to exist but thought to be to too difficult to extract: Alaska, the North Sea, and the Gulf of Mexico. Those new supplies eliminated the prerequisite monopoly power cartels need to create artificially high prices via the conspiratorial restriction of output. Fairly quickly, $40 per barrel oil dropped below $10 per barrel.

In 2014, three technologies came to full fruition: hyper-accurate seismologic imaging, hydraulic fracturing, and directional (usually horizontal) drilling. The first allowed oil companies to find mini-pockets of oil and precisely map their size and location. The second allowed those companies to, if necessary, break up the rock in

OIL BENEATH MY CHURCH PEW

By way of illustration on a small and personal scale, look at the *Google Earth* image of my place of employment: Indiana State University. A dormant and capped oil well on a campus parking lot inspired the (obviously not-by-coincidence former professor-of-petroleum-engineering-turned-) university president to have a company look for oil on campus. Using the new seismological technology, they were able to find several mini-pools of oil on or near campus. One was below my church, Central Presbyterian (that sits a block west of Hulman Center), and the other was below a recreation field near our first-year residence halls. It generates more than $180,000 per year in royalties for the university.

Though a small-scale example, this occurred all over the United States during this time frame. Thought to be dormant, oil fields were reopened, and U.S. production of oil tripled from its 2004 low. On an aggregated level, these technologies caused the United States to resume its place as the number one producer of petroleum in the world.

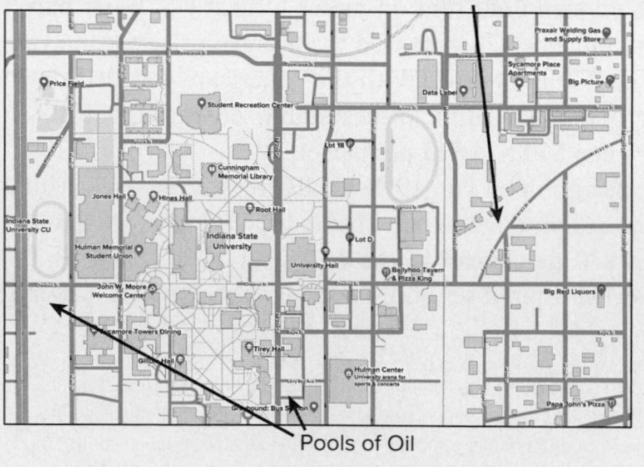

FIGURE 42.3 Oil prices and rig counts.

Sources: The American Oil & Gas Reporter. http://www.aogr.com/web-exclusives/us-rig-count/ and U.S. Department of Energy. https://www.eia.gov

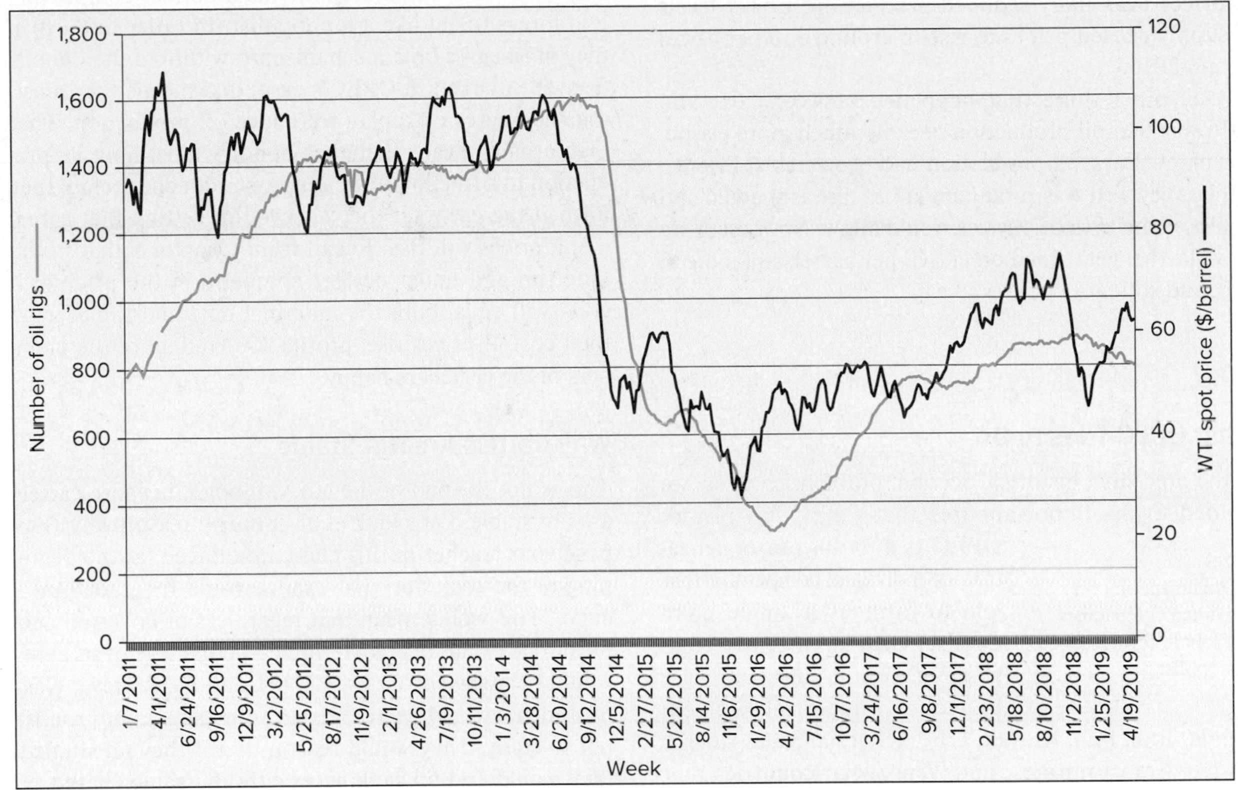

which the oil was located so as to allow it to be profitably pumped. The third allowed those companies to extract oil by drilling one vertical bore and then to turn their drill bits horizontally to access each mini-pocket one at a time. From new oil fields in North Dakota to re-opened ones in Texas and Oklahoma, U.S. oil production increased markedly. Drillers in the Permian Basin of West Texas and Eastern New Mexico have recently taken advantage of these technologies. As a result, U.S. production has more than doubled since 2006. U.S. oil production alone is responsible for 61 percent of the world increase in oil production since that year.

OPEC can no longer restrict output sufficiently to increase its profits. An unmercifully complicated economic diagram will be skipped in favor of this relatively straightforward assertion: In order for cartels to keep prices high, the production by entities outside the cartel must be limited. When production outside the cartel is large, any price-increasing reduction in production of the cartel can be quickly matched by price-decreasing extra production by the outsiders.

The opposite economic truism, "the cure for low prices is low prices," can also be seen in Figure 42.3, which maps 2014–2016 oil prices against data on oil rig counts. When the price of oil plummeted from $100 per barrel in 2014 to under $30 per barrel in 2015, many producers waited to see if the new lower prices would remain. When they did and after losses mounted, they stopped drilling. The number of active rigs in the United States dropped from 1600 to below 400.

Note that, during this time, there is a lagged relationship between rigs and price. If you "pull" the data on rigs to the left by about three months, it sits right upon the data for prices. What that means is there is a delayed reaction by drillers to changes in prices. The reason for the lag can be explained by the shutdown condition. Remember that just because a firm is losing money does not mean it will immediately stop producing. As long as the price is greater than average variable cost–which in this case is the cost of running the rig once you have located the oil–the firm will produce. It was only when the price dropped below the average variable cost or when the operators had to move the rig to another place that drilling slowed. The long-run drop in prices eventually reduced production. Lower levels of supply caused prices to rise to around $50 per barrel in mid-2016.

One other thing that happened between 2014 and 2016 was that oil production became much more elastic. For many years, oil production had been stable. Prior to 2014, every well was producing oil as fast as it could and as fast as the laws of physics would allow. Now, there are oil wells that get turned on at $40 per barrel, still more at $50, and still more at $65.

OPEC

What OPEC Tries to Do

In the preceding historical account of the price of oil, we alluded to the important role that OPEC has played. OPEC is a **cartel** (an organization of individual competitors that join to form as a single monopolist) that is currently composed of Algeria, Angola, Congo, Ecuador, Equatorial Guinea, Gabon, Iran, Iraq, Kuwait, Libya, Nigeria, Saudi Arabia, United Arab Emirates, and Venezuela: countries that export oil. Taken together, they have, as Table 42.1 shows, 72 percent of the proven oil reserves in the world. There was a time when this gave them enormous political power to wield. Through the 1990s, however, oil prices were such that the cartel seemed to be powerless, only to be revived in 1999 and 2000. How did all this happen?

cartel
An organization of individual competitors that join to form a single monopolist.

When groups of people, firms, or countries have little power as individuals but perceive their joint power as great, they hypothesize themselves as a joint force. If something exists or arises that binds them together and there are not too many of them to organize, there is a chance they can make it work. These ingredients were present when, in the late 1960s and early 1970s, Middle Eastern oil-exporting countries saw that together they could punish Israel's main supporters and make a profit at the same time.

This turned a loose organization, OPEC, into a powerful oil cartel. Cartels can exist in many different industries where a small number of competitors make up the vast majority of the suppliers of a commodity. The trouble is all cartels have a self-destructive tendency and OPEC was no different.

How Cartels Work

Cartels work because the individual perfect competitors join forces to act like a monopolist. In order to do this, they must agree on a mechanism to withhold their goods from the market. In OPEC's case, that means they must, together, agree on a plan to reduce oil production. That plan usually means that each country must limit its production to a fraction of what it was producing before they formed the cartel. If they succeed in getting that agreement, prices will rise. Recall from Chapter 5 that in the long run and under perfect competition the price of a good will equal both the marginal cost and the average total cost. If prices rise, profits rise, and all of the members of the cartel are happy.

Why Cartels Are Not Stable

This is not the end of the story, though, because cartels are not stable. Let's look at an intuitive reason why. Suppose your teacher in this class announced, at the beginning of the semester, that exams would be graded on a curve. This would mean that regardless of how well people did on exams, a predetermined percentage of students would be assigned As, Bs, Cs, Ds, and Fs. A clever class of students would band together to make a joint promise not to study. They would reason that if they all studied, they would end up ranking exactly the same (based on their aptitude for economics) as they would if they did not study at all.

Let's add here the outlandish assumption that students have no desire to study economics for fun and that they just want the grade for as little effort as possible. What would happen then? Would no students study? The scheme might work for the first quiz, but it would start falling apart as one or more students eventually sneaked off to study. They would see that it was in their interest to study because they could get better grades. Eventually, other students would notice that some were cheating. They would see their own grades drop in relation to those of their peers as the cheaters passed them by. Noncheaters would then start to cheat—that is to say, they would study. If, as we speculate, everyone ends up studying as they would without the prior agreement, then the agreement has become meaningless.

This is rather close to what happened with OPEC. Countries saw that they could make money by cheating. A country committed to cheating would see that cheating paid because at their agreed-upon production their marginal revenue (the new, high cartel price) was greater than the marginal cost, so the country could make a profit. That profit would greatly exceed the profit previously received at the cartel's imposed quota. As in our previous example, using grading on a curve where everyone schemed together, individual greed induced cheating on the collective, and this caused all gains to evaporate. Cheating by OPEC members led not only to the disappearance of the large profits but also to the evaporation of all economic profits.

Further hurting OPEC was the introduction of other, non-OPEC countries into the mix. A large importer, Great Britain, motivated by high prices to find its own sources, found oil in the North Sea. Moreover, it found enough to both solve its own problems and become an exporter. Mexico and other countries also found oil and began selling it in large quantities. Although OPEC tried to persuade these countries to join in a larger, more powerful cartel, none agreed. They reasoned that they could still sell at or slightly below the cartel price, and they could do so without any production quotas. Figure 42.2 highlights this fact by showing that, as a percentage of total world oil production, OPEC is no longer the biggest producer. Other nations are producing oil and taking market share from OPEC.

Back from the Dead

The 1990s saw oil prices fall dramatically and remain below historical averages until 1999, when prices took a sudden jump higher. How did OPEC, which seemed dead, come back to life? In fact, the potential profitability of OPEC never disappeared. It was only the behavior of the individual countries that dissipated potential profits. Throughout 1998 and 1999, OPEC began a series of production cuts that eventually totaled 4.3 million barrels per day. They thus drove up world prices. Unlike previous oil price spikes, they chose to let up before a major inflation episode struck the United States. OPEC was once again controlling world oil prices.

Why Did Prices Change So Fast?

It takes months for an empty tanker to leave the United States, arrive in the Persian Gulf, be loaded with crude oil, arrive back in the United States, be offloaded, and have the crude oil refined into gasoline. If that is true, how is it possible that the price of gasoline at a neighborhood gas station can change by 20 percent in a week? The answer takes us back to Chapter 2 and the determinants of supply and demand. Remember that the expectations of the future price of a good affect both the current supply curve and the current demand curve.

Remember, too, that if the price is expected to rise, there will be little to no delay in the demand curve moving to the right and the supply curve moving to the left. This is because consumers will want to stock up before any price increase fully takes effect, and producers will want to hang on to what they have in hopes of being able to sell it for more later. The impact of this is that prices will rise now in anticipation of price increases later.

To see how this works in the oil industry, recall the reaction in the United States to Iraq's invasion of Kuwait. Within days, gasoline prices went up by as much as 25 cents per gallon. How did this happen? Starting with the oil-importing companies and ending with the gas stations, each wanted to buy and store all the product it could before the prices increased. Normally, no one in gasoline production keeps significant quantities in storage. It costs money to store oil and other petroleum products.

The oil companies thus hurried to fill their tankers before the price increased too much. Refineries rushed to get tankers lined up to sell them their crude oil; distributors did the same thing, and so did gas stations. At every stage, the demand for product rose because firms wanted to put as much cheap input in storage as possible. They would then have more to sell when the prices rose.

Also true in such circumstances is that at every stage, firms do not want to sell out of their storage to provide someone down the line with product to store—that is, unless the buyer is willing to pay more. Prices rise and storage tanks fill. If there were an actual gasoline shortage, this would not be bad: It would be beneficial to have the extra oil in storage.

When prices are anticipated to fall, the opposite happens: Firms attempt to get rid of product. Because firms will want to get as much as possible for the gasoline that is in storage and will empty storage tanks only when it is clear that prices will in fact fall, prices decrease more slowly than they increase. Prices did fall after the Gulf War, and they fell by more than the 25 cents they had increased, but the decrease took much longer than the increase had taken.

The ultimate example of rapid price swings based on price expectations occurred the afternoon and evening of September 11, 2001. In response to concerns, both real and imagined, over the availability of gasoline, prices at some stations tripled. Some stations, particularly in the Midwest, were charging \$1.40 per gallon in the morning hours prior to the terrorist attacks and were charging more than \$4.00 per gallon later that day.

While some price increase could be explained by changes in wholesale prices (they increased between 5 and 10 cents per gallon that day), the bulk of the price jump occurred because of a rumor-fed fear that prices would dramatically rise if refineries were shut down or oil imports stopped. While consumer advocates and attorneys general were upset, consumers in particular were not blameless. Two-hour gas lines were not uncommon that afternoon and evening fueled by the same rumor-fed fear that if they did not fill up then, the price would be higher the next day. But by morning it became apparent that refineries were not in jeopardy, and prices fell to previous levels.

Is It All a Conspiracy?

There is a common view in the general public that gasoline prices are all a conspiracy and that deals are cut in back rooms to set the price of gasoline. If that were true, it would be against the law both federally and in every state in which it occurred. Absent an explicit conspiracy, what would explain the fact that prices increase not just rapidly (which is explained by the "expected price" phenomenon from Chapter 2) but at almost exactly the same time from gas station to gas station?

When a station gets its supply, the price it pays changes to reflect changing wholesale prices. Were that the end of the story, then prices would change only when stations got a new supply. The twist is that the cost of the gasoline in the ground is quite literally "sunk" and therefore ignored. Remember from Chapter 5 that fixed/sunk costs are ignored when setting the profit-maximizing price. It is only the cost of replacing that gasoline, its opportunity cost, that concerns the profit-maximizing gas station. Because that price changes daily, even if the gasoline in the underground tank is a week old, gas stations will adjust their price daily to reflect the cost of replacing it.

Why would the prices at neighboring gas stations change within minutes of one another, and why would it take only hours for price increases to be reflected across town? The answer to these questions revolves around the fact that the industry is governed by oligopoly. The neighboring stations must keep their prices at or below one another so when wholesale prices change there is economically explainable tendency for the resulting retail prices to be equal or, at least, close. In most communities, though there are many gas stations, there are but a few wholesale suppliers. The wholesale suppliers face rapidly changing national spot markets for gasoline and keep their prices aligned with their competitors (few as they may be) in order to maintain their gas station customer base. Because only a few wholesalers are selling to the same set of retailers at the same wholesale price, and because those retailers are pricing according to the replacement cost of the gasoline, it should not be surprising that gas prices seem to change at the same time across a community.

From $1 to $4 per Gallon in 10 Years?

We need to take a step back to understand something about the "price" of oil. As Table 42.2 shows, there is not one price. Every grade and type of crude oil has a price based on the ease with which you can refine it into saleable products like gasoline. As a result there can be a 25 percent difference in the crude oil price between the output of countries and even within countries. When oil prices are mentioned on the news, they typically choose a representative type. The most often-quoted oil prices are Brent Sea, Saudi Light, and West Texas Intermediate.

Still, by whatever measure, the price of oil skyrocketed between December 1998 and 2008. For data consistency purposes the U.S. Department of Energy produces a weighted average of imported oil prices that it calls the Refiner Acquisition Cost of Imported Oil.

Table 42.2 Crude oil prices, various types.*

Source: U.S. Energy Information Administration. www.eia.gov

	Price of Oil			
Variety of Oil	**Apr-07**	**Apr-11**	**Mar-16**	**May-19**
West Texas Intermediate	$63.98	$109.53	$37.55	$58.87
Brent Sea (U.K.)	$67.49	$123.26	$38.21	$68.38
Saudi Light	$62.65	$117.81	$35.29	$69.95

*The quoted prices for West Texas Intermediate and Brent Sea are spot prices, whereas the quoted prices for Saudi Light are landed costs.

FIGURE 42.4 Refiner acquisition cost, December 1998–January 2009.

Source: U.S. Energy Information Administration. https://www.eia.gov

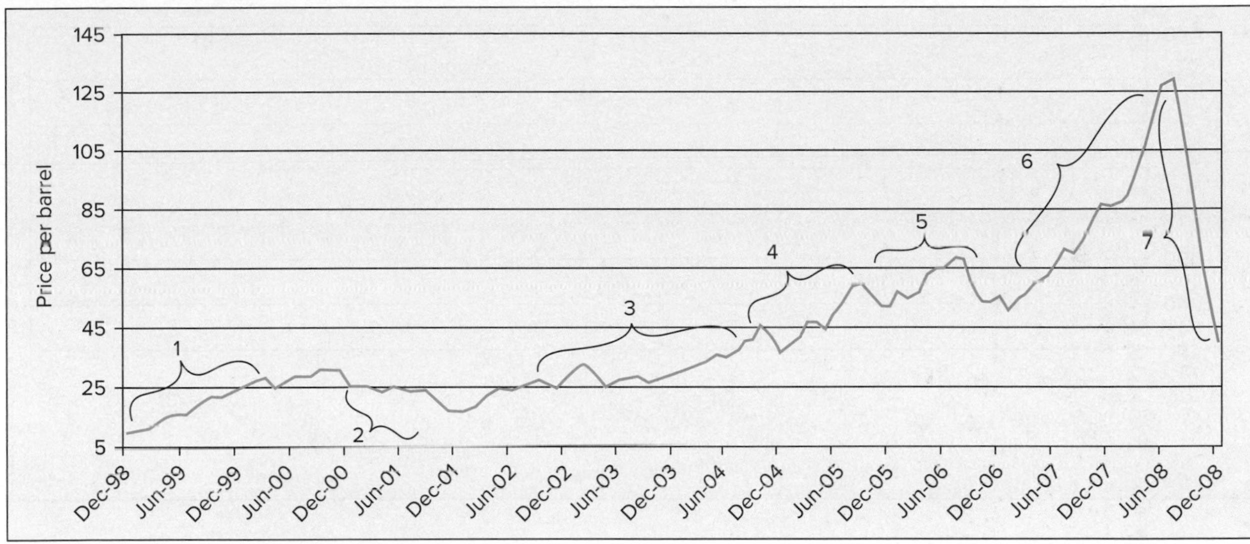

1—OPEC production cuts; low stocks of oil; bad weather.
2—Release of oil from the Strategic Petroleum Reserve; recession.
3—Political unrest in oil-producing Venezuela and Nigeria; war in Iraq.
4—Hurricanes damage platforms in the Gulf of Mexico.
5—Threatened conflict between the U.S. and Iran; Nigerian civil war heats up.
6—Global commodity speculation given increases in Chinese and Indian demand and stagnant production.
7—Global financial crisis and recession.

Figure 42.4 shows how that measure increased over the 10-year period from late 1998 to early 2009.

What caused this rapid increase in prices? The short answer is increased world demand coupled with problems in the world oil supply chain brought about by increased OPEC discipline, political unrest in oil-producing countries, and the U.S.-led war in Iraq. Gasoline prices, which tend to closely follow crude oil prices, were also impacted by limited U.S. refining capacity.

The main factors in increasing demand between 2002 and 2008 were the global economic expansion coming out of the 2001 recession; the significant increase in miles driven by the typical American; the substitution by Americans from more fuel-efficient cars to less fuel-efficient vans, pickups, and SUVs; and the long-term expansion of demand in India and China.

Americans have steadily migrated to less fuel-efficient vehicles. Whereas cars made up 70 percent of the U.S. fleet in the late 1990s, they now make up 44 percent. Though the fuel efficiency of cars has increased and the fuel efficiency of vans, pickups, and SUVs has increased, the impact of moving to the larger vehicle has totally eliminated the benefit of greater gas mileage. As you can see from Figure 42.5, this increase in demand, combined with a variety of supply issues, caused gasoline prices to spike.

Chinese demand for petroleum has increased markedly as well. Once a net exporter of fuels, China is now a leading importer. Over the last 19 years, while global petroleum demand has increased 29 percent, China's petroleum demand increased 171 percent. Over the next few years, China is expected to account for more than one-third of the increase in world oil demand.

Just as there is more than one variety of oil, there is also more than one variety of gasoline. Gasoline is not simply "regular," "plus," or "premium." For environmental reasons, gasoline is formulated for the particular climate and environmental conditions of local areas as well as state and local laws. Gasoline prices are also impacted by state and local taxes. These taxes average 29.52 cents per gallon, with Pennsylvania, California, and Washington topping the charts at 58.70, 55.70, and 49.40 cents, respectively, and Alaska, Texas, and South Carolina having the lowest taxes, at 14.34, 20, and 20.75 cents, respectively.

FIGURE 42.5 Gasoline prices, December 1998–January 2009.

Source: U.S. Energy Information Administration. https://www.eia.gov

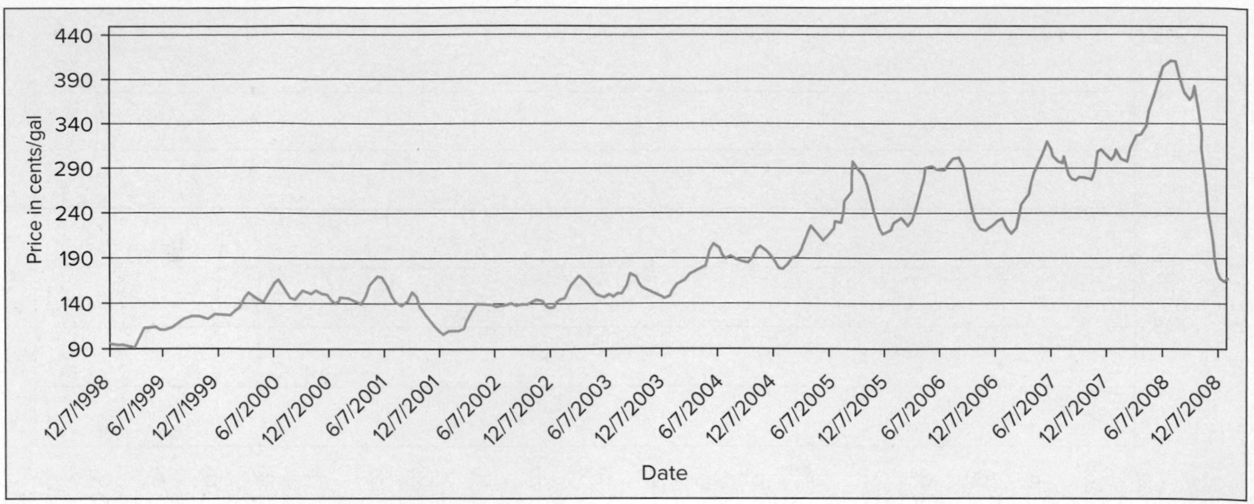

Though gasoline can be imported directly, more than 90 percent of gasoline is produced by a limited number of refineries in the United States from crude oil. Figure 42.6 shows the location and capacity of refineries in the United States. Of significant note is that the refineries along the Gulf Coast of the United States are susceptible to hurricanes. The four hurricanes that hit the area in the summer and fall of 2004, and five more in 2005, highlighted this particular bottleneck. In 2004, with the hurricanes coming in one after the other, ships carrying crude oil from Venezuela and Africa could not make it to port, thereby constraining U.S. supplies of gasoline. Hurricane Katrina decimated the Port of New Orleans and in the process dramatically affected gasoline prices in the late summer and early fall of 2005.

Who is to blame for all this? Mostly ourselves. The U.S. government has chosen to limit new exploration and the creation of more refining capacity, largely for environmental reasons. The BP spill in the Gulf of Mexico only underscored the doubt many Americans had regarding the potentially enormous consequences of drilling in environmentally sensitive locations. It also doesn't help that Americans generally are to blame for driving more miles and driving less fuel-efficient cars. The war in Iraq cut supplies coming from that country, with Iraqi oil production still not back to pre-invasion levels. Blaming the Chinese for increasing their appetite for driving is clearly hypocritical but they are, so we can blame them too. Finally, OPEC has become far more disciplined in its management of cartel prices. In the end, we are running on a global energy system where, if anything goes wrong, prices escalate rapidly, and between 1998 and 2008 many things went wrong.

Electric Utilities

Electricity Production

While it took more than a century for Edison to capitalize effectively on Benjamin Franklin's dreams for electricity with his lightbulb, it did not take that long for the United States to become dependent on it. Similarly, while the motivation for building the Hoover Dam may have been economic stimulation, flood control, and irrigation, the by-product of cheap electricity was credited with allowing millions to live and find work in southern California.

For the most part, electricity is produced by regulated utility companies. These companies incur substantial fixed costs that present nearly insurmountable barriers to entry. These fixed costs include the power plant itself as well as the transmission lines and transformers that get the electricity into homes so that consumers can use it.

Their variable inputs are sometimes nearly free, as is the case with hydroelectric, wind, and solar power; but more typically, oil, natural gas, coal, or nuclear fuel must be purchased. Where you live often determines how your electricity is produced. Nationally, burning coal to produce electricity through steam turbines accounts for 40 percent of electricity produced. Nuclear power accounts for 20 percent of electricity production, while

FIGURE 42.6 Refinery locations and capacity in the United States.

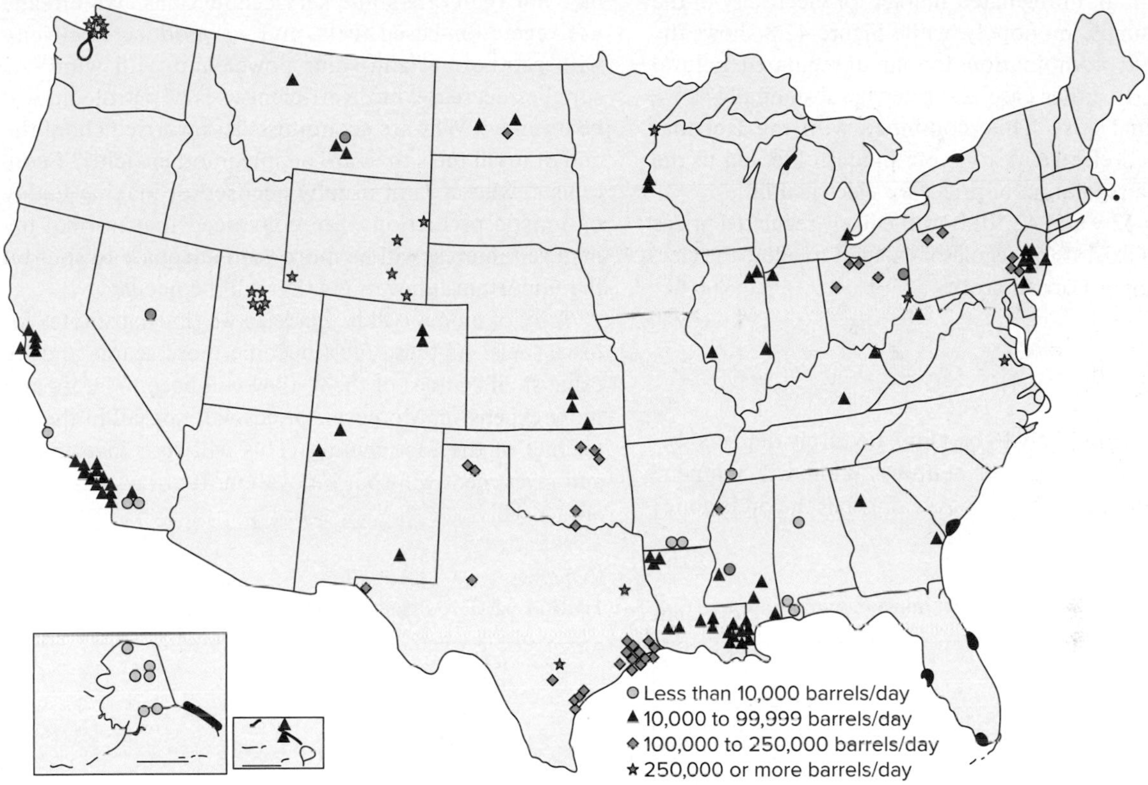

natural gas accounts for as much as one-third of electricity production during the summer months and as little as 20 percent during winter months. Hydroelectric power and other renewables account for the remainder.

The distribution of that reliance varies substantially across the country. The Pacific and Mountain West regions produce 15 to 20 times the amount of electricity through the turbines of their dams than does New England. Nuclear power provides almost 70 percent of the electricity usage in Connecticut, but nothing in Washington State and less than 10 percent in Maine. Not surprisingly, burning coal is a main source of electricity where coal is abundant.

Why Are Electric Utilities a Regulated Monopoly?

Because of the high fixed costs of production, the residential electricity market is characterized by monopoly because these costs tend to deter entry. Whether or not the proper model for this market is that of a natural monopoly or a simple monopoly depends on the type of electricity produced and the distance of transmission.

A **natural monopoly** exists when there are high fixed costs and diminishing marginal costs. In nuclear and hydroelectric power, the variable costs are low. In nuclear power, the rods themselves are cheap, relative to the amount of coal that would have to be purchased to produce the same electricity. On the other hand, the personnel that are required at a nuclear facility are highly trained and compensated, on top of which when things go wrong at a nuclear facility, they can go terribly wrong. In hydroelectric power, the variable input is free because the water that drives the turbines is accomplished with gravity. In both cases, the cost of the facility is enormous relative to the costs of the variable inputs. Even when coal, oil, or natural gas are burned to generate electricity, the market tends toward monopoly because of the high fixed costs of the transmission network.

natural monopoly Exists when there are high fixed costs and diminishing marginal costs.

Figure 42.7 shows what the price-output combination would be in an unregulated market for electricity in the case of a simple monopoly, while Figure 42.8 shows the price-output combination for an unregulated natural monopoly. In either case, the price is substantially above the marginal cost. This, combined with the fact that people need electricity to live a modern life, led to the widespread regulation of prices for electric utilities.

Figures 42.9 and 42.10 show the likely regulated prices that would exist if the regulators sought to allow the electric companies normal profits.

What Will the Future Hold?

Oil reserves are likely to be almost entirely depleted before the end of the 21st century. What will happen? Will we revert to the Stone Age once all the oil is gone? No. There are no perfect substitutes for oil and gas today, but there are some serviceable ones. We already use vegetation-based fuels, and we produce electricity with geothermal and solar power and with wind. As supplies decrease, more efficient uses of petroleum will be invented. Why are economists less worried about the end of fossil fuels than are people in other fields? Economists, who are not usually accused of making highly optimistic predictions, are convinced that normal human self-interest will be more than adequate to spur on the important innovations that will be needed.

A lot of money will be made as we find substitutes for fossil fuels. As these fuels become more scarce and we exhaust all sources of them, they will become more and more expensive. Moreover, prices will not fall in the latter half of the 21st century. This will spur investment, and investment will spur innovation. It always has and it always will.

FIGURE 42.7 An unregulated simple monopoly.

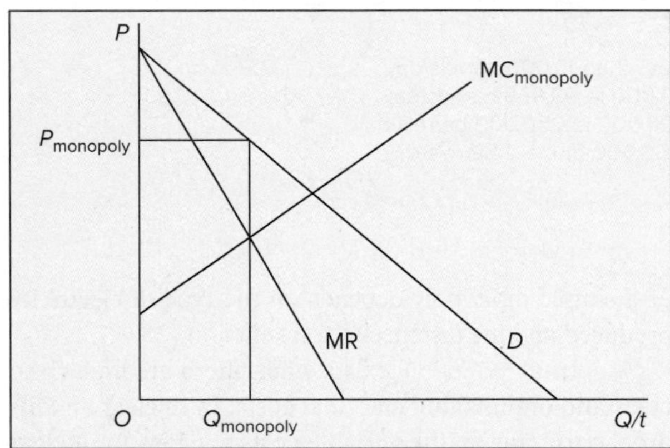

FIGURE 42.8 An unregulated natural monopoly.

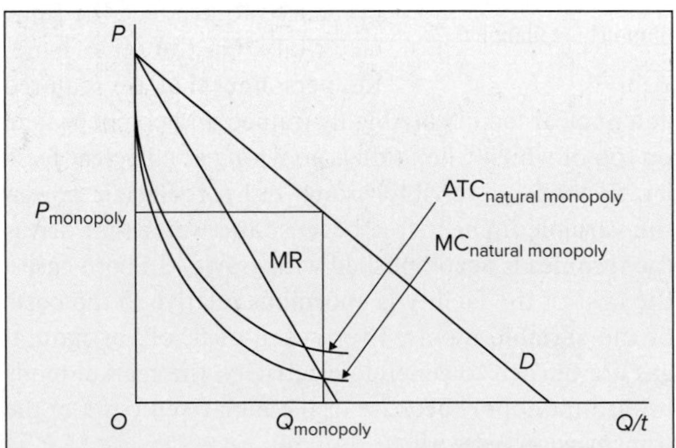

FIGURE 42.9 A regulated simple monopoly.

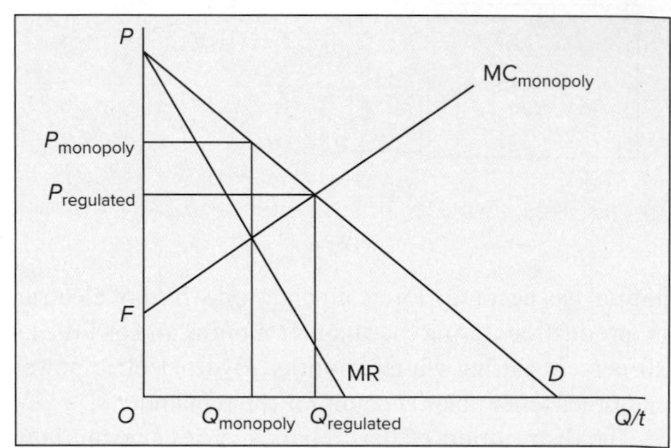

FIGURE 42.10 A regulated natural monopoly.

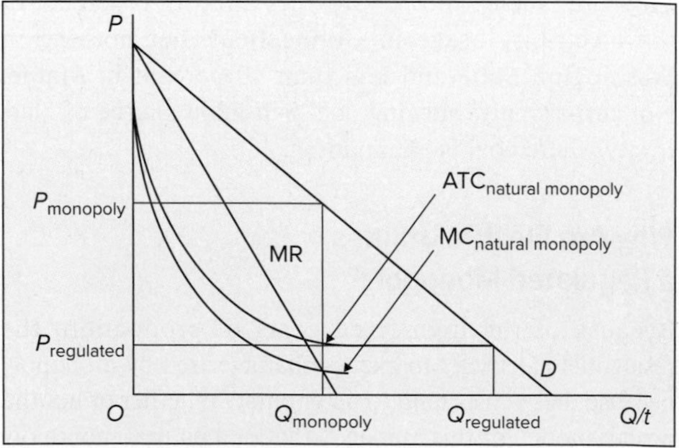

Consider this: If you were an oil company and you anticipated the end of your current form of business, you would spend as much money as it took to find a way to continue to sell fuels to your current customers. You would spend money on a variety of promising leads. You would try, for example, to use renewables to fuel existing cars, and, if that did not work, you would experiment with high-power, quick-charge batteries that you could sell, so cars could run on electricity.

Evidence of the power of the profit motive is all around us. It has been known for a half century that there was thick oil in relatively thin layers of rock in the Bakken formation, a deposit of oil shale that runs from North Dakota through eastern Montana and into southern Canada. It was simply too expensive to exploit using conventional vertical drilling, because if you drilled down and hit the oil, only a small portion would be recoverable. The oil was too thick to flow toward the well. In the last 10–15 years, horizontal drilling and hydraulic fracturing (dubbed "fracking") have unleashed three or more decades' worth of natural gas in Pennsylvania, and the same process is being exploited in North Dakota. The potential is that this oil could completely supply U.S. needs that have heretofore come only from imported oil. It is only because oil prices rose during the 2000s that anyone bothered to consider this possibility. At $100 per barrel, interesting drilling tactics are profitable that are not so profitable at $40 per barrel.

Nearly any problem can be solved with the proper incentive, and profit is one of the oldest and most effective incentives of all.

Kick It Up a Notch

Going back to the question of how cartels work, consider Figure 42.11. On the left panel is the market for oil. If the market were governed by perfect competition, then the price-quantity combination would be P_{comp}, Q_{comp}. This price would be carried over to the right panel, which would show the cost functions of a representative oil-producing country. Recall from Chapter 5 that the long-run equilibrium in such a market would mean that the price line would come tangent at the bottom of the average total cost (ATC) curve, where it would also intersect marginal cost (MC). Thus the representative oil-producing country would sell q_{comp}, because this is where marginal revenue (MR) intersects marginal cost (MC). At this level of production, it would make only normal profit, that is, the profit consistent with the return expected in other industries.

FIGURE 42.11 A model of a cartel.

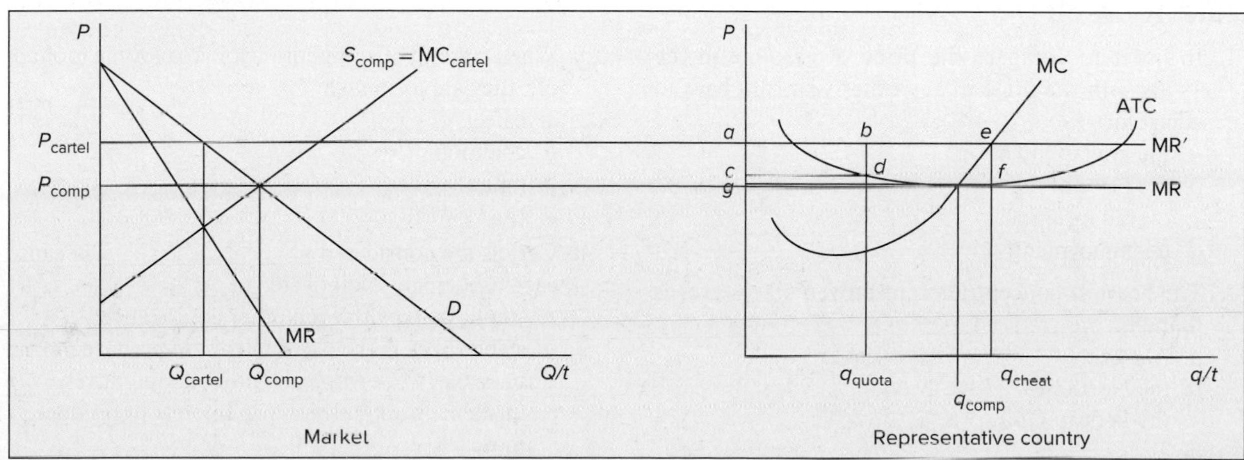

If it joined a cartel with other, similar countries, then the model for the market would be monopoly rather than perfect competition. If that were the case, then the cartel would jointly produce only Q_{cartel} and would charge P_{cartel} because that's where marginal revenue (MR) intersects marginal cost (MC) on the left panel of Figure 42.11. Because total production of all countries combined would be less than before, the representative country's production would also have to be less than it was previously. Some negotiations between the member countries would result in each one being allocated a quota, labeled q_{quota}. If the representative country produced q_{quota} and received P_{cartel} per barrel, it would make an economic profit, that is, profit above normal, in the amount of *abcd*.

Cartels are not stable because cheating pays. The right-hand panel of Figure 42.11 shows this; see that at q_{quota}, MR′ was greater than MC. Countries that cheated did so hoping that no one would notice. A country committed to cheating would see that cheating paid. Looking again at Figure 42.11, you see that at the new high cartel price, P_{cartel}, the country would maximize profit at q_{cheat}. This is where MR′ equals MC. That profit, *gaef*, would greatly exceed the profit previously received at the cartel's imposed quota. As in our previous example, using grading on a curve where everyone schemed together, individual greed induced cheating on the collective and this caused all gains to evaporate. Cheating by OPEC members led not only to the disappearance of the large profits (*gaef*), but also to the evaporation of all economic profits.

Summary

Now that you have completed this chapter, you know what a cartel is, that OPEC is a major oil-producing cartel, why cartels work to make their members large sums of money, and why they are not stable. You know that, inflation adjusted, the price of oil and the price of gasoline have been historically unstable and that this instability has been a consequence of geopolitics and the inherent instability of cartels. You understand why it is that events in the Middle East can alter prices at the pump within a few days. Finally, you understand why electricity prices are typically regulated.

Key Terms

cartel

natural monopoly

Quiz Yourself

1. In order to compare the price of gasoline in the 1970s with the price in any other year, you have to adjust for
   a. the availability of oil.
   b. the price of oil.
   c. overall inflation.
   d. unemployment.
2. The heaviest concentration of proven oil reserves is found in
   a. Alaska.
   b. the North Sea.
   c. the Persian Gulf.
   d. Texas.
3. When a group of competitors joins to form a monopoly, they are forming a
   a. cartel.
   b. coalition.
   c. union.
   d. trust.
4. Cartels are considered ________________ because each participant is motivated to ________________.
   a. stable; work with each other cooperatively
   b. stable; work in their own interest to produce more
   c. unstable; work with each other cooperatively
   d. unstable; work in their own interest to produce more

5. Gasoline prices in early 2019 were between $2.25 and $2.75 per gallon. They were
   a. the highest nominal prices and highest inflation-adjusted prices in American history.
   b. the highest nominal prices but were not the highest inflation-adjusted prices in American history.
   c. neither the highest nominal prices nor the highest inflation-adjusted prices in American history.
   d. the highest inflation-adjusted prices but were not the highest nominal prices in American history.
6. In the early 2000s, a world event could cause gas prices to rise and fall dramatically and immediately. In the late 2010s, that was no longer true. What changed during that time?
   a. Increased supply elasticity
   b. Increased demand elasticity
   c. Decreased supply elasticity
   d. Decreased demand elasticity
7. Cartels typically require that the firms agree to form a(n) ______. By that standard, OPEC should _____ be considered a cartel.
   a. monopoly; absolutely
   b. monopoly; not
   c. oligopoly; absolutely
   d. oligopoly; not

Short Answer Questions

1. There have been other cartels through history: most notably drug cartels in the 1980s in Colombia and during more recent times in Mexico. They never suffered from cheating. Why?
2. At the height of the 2008 financial crisis, in the time it took a completely full oil tanker to travel from Saudi Arabia to the United States, the price of oil fell nearly $50 per barrel. Use the expected price formulation to explain how that could happen.
3. What would be the principal obstacle preventing a cartel from emerging in the production of beef?
4. Why might the cartel model still make sense even when OPEC produces less than half of the world's oil?

Think about This

All energy consumption involves externalities that are recognized. Given that we have spent billions of dollars militarily defending access to oil, should we consider that an externality too? Aren't the consumers of energy indirectly compelling increased spending on the military?

Talk about This

Oil prices are highly sensitive to output changes. Hurricanes, terrorist acts, and other unexpected occurrences regularly cause the price of oil to increase by 10 percent within the course of a month, only to fall again when the trouble subsides. Should the federal government use its strategic petroleum reserve to counter these effects or should it use the reserve only in a true emergency?

For More Insight See

Adelman, Morris, *Genie Out of the Bottle: World Oil since 1970* (Cambridge, MA: MIT Press, 1995).

Behind the Numbers

Global energy resource data.

U.S. Energy Information Administration: www.eia.gov

- Gasoline prices
- Crude oil prices
- Global reserves by region
- Oil consumption

CHAPTER FORTY-THREE

If We Build It, Will They Come? And Other Sports Questions

Learning Objectives

After reading this chapter you should be able to:

LO1 Apply the concept of local substitution to issues of sports.

LO2 Summarize the evidence regarding whether sports franchises impact overall economic activity.

LO3 Analyze the profitability versus championships trade-off from a team owner's perspective.

LO4 Summarize the basics of sports labor economics history and its key vocabulary.

Chapter Outline

Sports offers an interesting venue in which to ask economic questions. For instance, if you are the mayor of a city whose citizens want a sports franchise, are you better off if you get one from another city or do you mount a campaign to garner an expansion franchise? If it will enhance the chances of getting a franchise, do you build a billion-dollar stadium and hope you get a team to put in it? Now suppose you are a mayor of a city that already has a franchise whose owner is threatening to leave. Do you build the franchise owner a stadium, even though the one the team is in is only 25 years old? The question that underlies all these decisions is whether a sports franchise is an important economic attraction for a city. Mayors make deals all the time to attract other kinds of major employers. Why not a sports franchise?

To change perspective, suppose now that you are an owner of a franchise. What would make you want to move your team to a different city or hold your own city hostage to build you a stadium? How do you decide whether to bid for high-priced talent? Can you compete in the financial arena if you do? Can you compete on the field, the pitch, the ice, or the court if you do not?

These are all questions that arise in all sports, and they are all economic in nature. We answer each by looking at them from two perspectives: the city's and the team owner's. Because no discussion of the economics of sports today would be complete without a discussion of labor, we include that, too. We try to determine how society went from sports as games to sports as business.

The Problem for Cities

Expansion versus Luring a Team

One of the emerging trends of the 1990s, like the 1950s, was the sudden increase in the desire among owners of sports franchises to move their teams from one city to another. Compared to other sports, baseball has been relatively stable. It has increased in numbers of teams, but existing teams have tended not to move. Other sports, however, have seen teams move all over the place. That being said, the most famous relocations occurred with the Dodgers and Giants relocating from New York to California during the 1950s. That made good economic sense for the sport at the time. The movement of the Rams and Raiders out of Los Angeles during the 1990s, on the other hand, made little economic sense for the National Football League.[1] In those franchise shifts, movement resulted from a city's offering enticements to owners. In each case, the franchise owner has made millions.

A city must decide on its strategy when it seeks to attract a team. While each sport has added new teams in the last 30 years, such expansion is not always the surest way for a particular city to get a team. In part, this is because there's no guarantee that a given sport will expand or will choose a particular city. Football and baseball added only two teams each between 1970 and 1990. Though the 1990s saw increased expansion in both sports, many cities have waited in line for an expansion franchise, only to be spurned. When cities lose patience, they may turn their attention to finding teams that are in financial trouble and offering their owners the lure of millions of dollars as well as profit guarantees.

Cities that have been disappointed in the expansion process and have subsequently sought out financially troubled teams. Some have succeeded in getting them, albeit at a high cost. After St. Louis lost the football Cardinals to Arizona, it sought, but was denied, an expansion team, while franchises were granted to Jacksonville and Charlotte instead. It turned, then, to luring an existing team. The Los Angeles Rams wanted a stadium built in Los Angeles containing revenue-producing luxury boxes, and the owner threatened to move if demands were not met. As part of its expansion bid, St. Louis was already in the process of building such a stadium. When Los Angeles refused to build one, the Rams moved to St. Louis. Before their Super Bowl year, the team attracted fewer fans than it had drawn in Los Angeles. Nevertheless, the owner made more money because corporations paid hundreds of thousands of dollars for luxury boxes.[2] Nashville experienced a similar situation when the Oilers moved from Houston. In each case, a city stood in line, was denied a team, and managed to buy its way in anyway.

In its pursuit of a team, a city has to decide whether it should build a stadium in hopes that a team and a franchise will come. This "if you build it, they will come" strategy is fraught with uncertain payoffs. St. Louis built it, and the Rams did come. St. Louis then failed to renovate it, and the Rams left. St. Petersburg built it, and no one came. In hopes that the Chicago White Sox would move, the Tampa–St. Petersburg area built a new stadium, but, at the last minute, the city of Chicago and the state of Illinois agreed to build the White Sox a new stadium. The White Sox are still in Chicago. Though the Tampa Bay area ultimately got an expansion franchise, the wait lasted 10 years, and the city may have to build another new stadium because the facility in which the team plays is considered one of the worst places to see a baseball game in the major leagues. Building in hopes of getting a franchise sometimes works and sometimes does not. In 2018, the NFL's San Diego Chargers did something completely different. They moved to Los Angeles and played in an undersized soccer stadium while a facility was constructed.

While these lessons regarding expansion apply to the American sports world of the NFL, NBA, MLB, and NHL, they don't apply to soccer. Quite literally, a city in England could get its local club team into the Premier League, England's top league, in just a few seasons. Unlike American sports, where the franchises are in the league as long as they wish to be and expansion is quite limited, in European soccer, the teams have to remain competitive in order to stay in their respective leagues. At the conclusion of each season, two to three soccer clubs are "relegated." That means they are dropped from the Premier League down to a lower league, and the three top lower league teams are promoted to the Premier League for the next season. A city desiring a place in the Premier League could, theoretically, purchase enough talent on the open market for soccer players to win enough games over enough seasons to go from being a local soccer club to playing Manchester United (the Yankees of the Premier League). This also leads to the odd result that in England in 2012–2013, there were six London-area teams in the Premier League and sizable cities with no teams.

The magical story of Leicester City being promoted after the 2013–2014 season, being forced to go on an incredible winning streak to avoid relegation in 2014–2015, and then winning the Premier League in 2015–2016 only serves to make the point that soccer really is different. It should be noted, however, that in Spain's LaLiga Barcelona and Real Madrid have finished one–two in every year but one from 2008–2009 to 2015–2016. In the Premier League, it is

[1]The only economic aspect of the decision not to have a team in the second largest city in the United States that makes sense is that the Rams and Raiders rarely sold out the Los Angeles Coliseum. This meant that not only were their games blacked out during that time, but also the network slated to cover the game could not cover any other game during that time. With no team in Los Angeles, there were no game blackouts and that meant more ad revenue to the networks, which could potentially mean a higher bid for broadcast rights.

[2]In 2016 the story was completely reversed. The new owner used the stadium contract with St. Louis to try to force improvements. That contract required that the stadium be in the top 25 percent of NFL stadiums and that if it wasn't, the city and state would make sufficient renovations so that it was. When the city and state refused, the Rams relocated back to Los Angeles.

only a little more equitable in outcomes. Since 2000–2001, the top five teams (Manchester City, Manchester United, Arsenal, Chelsea, and Liverpool) have accounted for all but five of the 57 top three finishes, and two of those occurrences were in 2015–2016.

Does a Team Enhance the Local Economy?

From a rational perspective, a city needs more reasons for having a franchise than just wanting to have one. To this end, the justification that most proponents give for getting a team is that doing so is an investment in the city's future. If that were true, the jobs gained, tax income generated, and prestige gained from having a team would genuinely be enough to pay for the costs of building the stadium. Because most mayors consider economic development a vital responsibility of their terms in office, you might think that enticing a team to move in would be the same as enticing any other major employer to relocate to a city. Does it not make sense for a mayor who seeks to draw a major employer to an area to also seek out a sports franchise that will employ many people?

While the reasoning sounds good, sports franchises simply do not generate very good jobs for people other than the athletes. Whether the jobs are created in the facility or are in surrounding restaurants, their pay scale is relatively low, and the jobs come with few benefits. Moreover, though each baseball team has 81 home dates, in basketball the number is 41, and in football it is a mere 8. You cannot build a local economy with only a few workdays a year.

It turns out that whether a sports franchise can be an economic cornerstone is a well-researched question. You may be surprised to know, though, that in nearly every study on the subject, economists have concluded that sports teams do next to nothing to improve economic activity in a city. The research has focused on whether cities that have lost franchises did any worse economically than they would have had they not lost the team. Research also questioned whether cities that were granted a franchise did any better than they would have without one. The conclusion that was consistently drawn was that a city's economic activity was almost totally unrelated to whether it had a franchise.

The reason that sports teams do not add much to a local economy is that money spent on tickets, parking, and memorabilia is mostly local. This is referred to as **local substitution**, and it means that local people are going to games instead of eating out or going to movies or other things they would have done locally with their money. In the larger picture, sports is just a branch of the entertainment industry. Having a team changes how entertainment dollars are spent, but it does not change the amount that is spent. To make a somewhat exaggerated point, the Queens Park Rangers were relegated from the Premier League in 2013. As such, their fans had five other London-area Premier League teams to see when they were relegated. There was no loss of economic activity, even soccer-related

local substitution
The effect of the substitution of one economic activity for another within a community, so the net effect is zero.

SPRING TRAINING AND THE NCAA

The competition for teams is confined to neither the big-time professional leagues, nor even professional team sports. Beginning in the 1990s, first in Florida and then years later in Arizona, cities began attempting to lure Major League Baseball teams and their spring training sites. The threats made by teams became far more real in the 2000s as many threatened to move to Arizona for their annual training during the months of February and March. In fact, while at one time there were fewer than 10 teams in Arizona during spring training, half the league now trains there. It can be argued that the cities in the competition to be spring training sites are more rational because (according to their own market research) more than half of attendees at spring training games come from outside the area. Some people choose their spring break vacation site based on where their favorite team locates. If this is the case, the local substitution effect can be said to be minor.

It is also worth noting that, although college teams do not threaten to move, the NCAA has. It was once located in Overland Park, Kansas (a Kansas City suburb), and that city benefited from garnering a disproportionate number of NCAA men's basketball tournaments. In 1999, the NCAA extracted many concessions from the city of Indianapolis and moved there. With it, they brought the ability to locate major tournaments in the city and state. The men's Final Four is in Indianapolis in every fifth year. In the other years, Indianapolis gets an opening weekend set of games, or a second weekend round, or the women's Final Four. Again, because the vast majority of the people in attendance are from out of town, the local substitution argument is negated, and because it is on a repeating basis, the city's reasoning is somewhat more defensible.

economic activity, in London as a result of their relegation. In this sense, arguing whether a city should attract a sports team is like arguing whether a city should fight to attract a Walmart Supercenter. Both produce about the same gross revenue and employ large numbers of people at low wages. The difference is that for a Walmart, much of the money leaves the local area in payment for the store's goods, and for a team, huge amounts of money go to a few rich stars.

Although some cities may not feel they have "arrived" or are "major league" until they have at least one baseball, basketball, hockey, or football team, they pay a very high price for that honor. Some cities grow in population to the point where a team is justified, but they have none. Austin, Texas, is now the largest Standard Metropolitan Statistical Area without any major league football, basketball, hockey, or baseball franchise. When people in Austin, Texas, look at the attention that a small city of less than 100,000 gets each year with the Packers in Green Bay, they may conclude that they will not be living in an important area until they have one. If image is everything, then it may be worth it to assess citizens millions in taxes to get a franchise. Otherwise such outlays of money are highly questionable.

Why Are Stadiums Publicly Funded?

That outlays for stadiums are questionable as a means of creating economic growth does not prevent the issue from arising. Public funding of stadiums can be explained in terms of **positive externalities** and bargaining power.

positive externalities The benefit that a person other than the buyer or seller receives as a result of a transaction.

The positive externalities are the benefits to the fans of having a team in the city that are in excess of what they get from going to the games. There are millions of sports fans who enjoy having a team in their city whether or not they ever go to a game or watch it on television. They enjoy following the team in the newspaper and talking about the team with their friends. Because they value that experience, voters, having decided that they want to keep a team, are willing to pay taxes to keep the team. This is similar to their willingness to pay taxes to support the arts when they do not attend concerts or museums.

Having seen why voters may be willing to pay taxes to keep a team, we need to look at why they end up having to pay to keep a team. Because teams have demonstrated a willingness to move, and cities have demonstrated a willingness to lure the teams of other cities, all of the bargaining power belongs to the team owner. One of the things that we assumed in Chapter 5 when we discussed perfect competition was that there were many buyers and many sellers and that none had any market power. Here, the market power is concentrated with the owner, who can move the team if voters do not pay for the stadium.

The Problem for Owners

To Move or to Stay

Owners are the big winners in sports when teams relocate. Owners understand that an individual team's worth is based on how much it can earn from memorabilia sales, luxury boxes, and, in the case of baseball, local TV revenue. They also know that it is to their advantage to have many interested cities for their teams and to do little to discourage talk of moving.

Unfortunately, owners are often at cross-purposes with their leagues since it may be in the best interests of the leagues to have stable teams. Each owner knows that the sport is harmed by movement. Each owner knows that he or she would make a great deal of money by moving the team. As a result, it is in the communal best interests of sports that teams do not move around too much. However, it is in every individual owner's best interests to consider moving, threaten to move, and sometimes actually move. This is why baseball and football have ownership rules that require agreement of two-thirds to three-quarters of the other owners for a team to move or be sold. Though the owners of the Minnesota Twins, Pittsburgh Pirates, and Chicago White Sox threatened to move their baseball teams, none have. In football, owners have seen the money that others have made in moving. To keep the option open for themselves, they have routinely approved other owners' moves.[3]

When teams relocate, it is because the owners want to make more money. Some relocations lead to the need for new team mascots; new mascots mean vast increases in sales of shirts, hats, and other memorabilia. The Browns reaped such benefits when they moved to Baltimore and became the Ravens. The Oilers also benefited when they moved to Nashville and became the Titans. Even teams that should have changed their mascots but did not reaped revenue from the sales of memorabilia. For instance, the Jazz moved from New Orleans to Utah, and the Lakers moved from Minneapolis to Los Angeles.

[3]An exception to this was the refusal of the NFL to let the Seahawks move from Seattle to Los Angeles. This location was too lucrative to just let someone have.

Each move meant sales to a whole new set of fans in the new city.

Football teams usually move to gain stadiums with luxury boxes. Such boxes provide a significant source of extra revenue for a team. Though television contracts for football are admittedly large, the NFL spreads the revenue equally among the teams. The teams therefore get the same amount, whether they are in New York or Green Bay. Because the league's contract with the players dictates salary costs for all the teams, owners are left with small margins of profitability and a motivation to look for alternative sources of revenue. Luxury boxes make the difference. Because luxury-box revenue is not shared between the teams the way ticket revenue is shared, potential revenue from such boxes has been enough of an incentive for the Rams to move from Los Angeles to St. Louis, the Oilers to move from Houston to Nashville, the Browns to move from Cleveland to Baltimore, and the New England Patriots to nearly move from the Boston area to Hartford, Connecticut. Oddly enough, in each case, luxury boxes improved team finances enough to warrant movement from a larger metropolitan area to a smaller one.

To Win or to Profit

Some teams are worth very little where they are and would be worth much more if they moved. The Kansas City Royals and Minnesota Twins are two baseball teams that cannot simultaneously field consistently competitive clubs and earn a profit. In baseball, team revenues are largely affected by local television deals. The Yankees' TV deal, for example, dwarfs that of the combined size of the Royals, Twins, Mariners, and a number of other "small-market" teams. The Royals were sold for $96 million in 1996 on the condition that the team would not leave Kansas City for at least 10 years. Had the owners been able to at least threaten to move to another city, chances are good that they would have sold for many times more than $96 million. A move to someplace like Charlotte, Orlando, or another large, growing city would generate a lucrative local TV deal. It may be, however, that the only owner with sensitivity toward his city and the team's fans was the late Ewing Kaufman, whose will required that anyone who bought the team be required to keep it in Kansas City for a decade. For a prospective owner, nothing can be better than to be able to buy a struggling team for under $100 million and to sell it 10 years later for a billion. This is probably a temptation that a living owner will not forgo. But for a resurgence in 2014 and 2015, the Kansas City Royals could easily have gone down in history with the Washington Senators, who moved and became the Texas Rangers, and the Seattle Pilots, who moved and became the Milwaukee Brewers.

This is not to say a small-market team cannot win. Some teams will win if they construct a superior farm system and are lucky enough to see their players mature at exactly the right time. This happened with the Royals in the late 1970s, and again in the mid-2010s with the Twins in the middle 1980s, with the Mariners in the middle 1990s, and with the Rays in 2008 through 2010. Unfortunately, if a team is that lucky, free agency will limit the time that the team can win and remain profitable.

The Cubs, Red Sox, Yankees, and Dodgers will always be ready to buy talent as soon as the players are eligible for free agency. As further evidence of this problem, a special committee appointed by the commissioner of baseball noted that, from 1994 to 1999, no team whose payroll was in the bottom half of major league baseball won a playoff game. Though the Rays bucked the trend for three years, their roster was raided prior to the 2011 season. Only two members of the 2015 Royals were on the roster by mid-2018. The Royals went from championship contenders to 106 losses because they rapidly unloaded talent. Small-market owners understand that to profit, they must sacrifice by losing players. That results in losing games.

This is also not to say that a team with money will always buy the right talent. Table 43.1 shows that a willingness to bid for free agents helps teams to get into the playoffs, but also that it is far from a slam dunk. Between 2010 and 2015, there were 56 teams making the playoffs. Twelve came from the bottom third of team salaries, 22 came from the middle third, and 22 came from the top third. In terms of World Series participants during that same period, of the 12 teams, five came from the top third, six from the middle third, and one from the bottom

Table 43.1 Salary ranks and playoff appearances.

Year	Number of Teams Qualifying for the Playoffs	Number of Playoff Teams with Team Salaries in the Top 10	Number of Playoff Teams with Team Salaries in the Bottom 10
2010	8	4	1
2011	8	2	2
2012	10	5	2
2013	10	3	3
2014	10	5	2
2015	10	3	2

third. During that time, not buying free agents clearly diminished a team's prospects of playing in October and November, but dumping a great deal of money on free agents was no guarantee of winning a ring.

This trend created a countervailing attempt to do precisely the opposite among some lower-revenue franchises. As will be discussed later in the chapter, the Royals, Astros, and Brewers (as well as the better-funded Cubs) chose to lose so as to accumulate draft choices for the purpose of winning (albeit for a short period) with inexpensive talent.

In early 2009, the NBA, as quietly as possible, borrowed $132 million to help its struggling franchises make payroll. Though their short-term troubles could be tied to the state of the economy in late 2008 and early 2009, it is a long-term challenge for all sports leagues when there is a marked imbalance in team revenues. Owners face the "win or make money, but you can't do both" challenge when they are at the bottom of the league in team revenues.

Similarly, in NASCAR, the top teams with the top names and millions in sponsorship money can field teams that win 90 percent of races. Since 2007, Joe Gibbs Racing, Hendrick Motorsports, Roush Racing, Stewart-Hass Racing, and Richard Childress Racing have accounted for all but 10 of the 169 Chase participants and all but one champion.

The ultimate example of this phenomenon occurred with the Premier League's Manchester City. Purchased in 2008 by a group from Abu Dhabi who invested millions in garnering worldwide talent, the team was sold in 2009 to Sheikh Mansour, an individual estimated to be worth $30 billion from a family estimated to be worth a trillion dollars. With massive investments, the team won Britain's FA Cup in 2011 and the 2012 Premier League for the first time in 44 years, all while losing nearly $200 million a year.

Don't Feel Sorry for Them Just Yet

While it may be tempting to feel sorry for the "poor" owners who lose money each and every year on their franchises, you can probably leave the Kleenex in your pocket. As Tables 43.2 and 43.3 indicate, even though baseball and football franchises may claim to lose money each year, the return on their investment is still substantial. How? Because history suggests that the team will sell for substantially more than the owner paid for it. Economist

Table 43.2 Purchase prices, current values, and rates of return on selected Major League Baseball franchises.

Source: *Forbes*. www.forbes.com.

Team	Purchase Price on Most Recent Sale (Year)	*Forbes* Magazine 2019 Estimate of Value (Millions)	Real Annual Rate of Return
New York Yankees	$10 million (1973)	$4,600	14%
St. Louis Cardinals	$150 million (1996)	$2,100	12%
Los Angeles Dodgers	$2 billion (2012)	$3,300	7%
Kansas City Royals	$96 million (2000)	$1,025	13%
Washington Nationals	$450 million (2006)	$1,750	11%

Table 43.3 Purchase prices, current values, and rates of return on selected National Football League franchises.

Source: *Forbes*. www.forbes.com.

Team	Purchase Price on Most Recent Sale (Year)	*Forbes* Magazine 2018 Estimate of Value (Millions)	Real Annual Rate of Return
Pittsburgh Steelers	$2,500 (1933)	$2,585	18%
Dallas Cowboys	$150 million (1989)	$5,000	13%
Oakland Raiders	$180,000 (1966)	$2,420	20%
Phoenix Cardinals	$50,000 (1932)	$2,150	13%
New Orleans Saints	$70 million (1985)	$2,075	11%

Rodney D. Fort specializes in sports economics, even writing a textbook devoted to it. Having collected financial data on NFL and MLB franchises over the years, he has come to the conclusion that it is the capital gain that makes these investments truly valuable.

You might expect there to be high real rates of return on owning powerhouse franchises like the Yankees, Cardinals, and Dodgers in baseball and the Cowboys and Steelers in football. On the other hand, even teams without much of a history of success earned substantial profits for their owners. For comparison, it should be noted that these real rates of return (of 7 to 20 percent) are better than typical alternatives. Specifically, real stock market returns average between 5 and 8 percent.

The Sports Labor Market

What Owners Will Pay

When we think about the market for talent in any sport, we must recognize that it is fundamentally no different from any other labor market. Firms will hire the marginal laborer as long as the contribution of the employee to revenue equals or exceeds the money that must be paid to that employee. This concept, called the **marginal revenue product of labor,** is important in any firm. In sports, the marginal revenue product of labor is the money that the team generates in revenue because a particular player is on the team. It would include any increase in revenue that results directly from their performance as well as all that revenue that results indirectly, say in the form of memorabilia sales, from the player being on the team. So, a star may make a team win, which causes it to draw more fans. But the star's presence may also cause sales of team logo jerseys to increase. In deciding whether to sign a player to a large contract, an owner must decide whether the player is worth the money. If the player generates at least as much in revenue to the team as the salary that the player commands, then the player is worth it.

marginal revenue product of labor
The additional revenue generated from hiring an additional worker.

What Players Will Accept

The issue for players is whether the pay they are offered to play for a team exceeds their next best offer. This next best offer is a player's **reservation wage.** It is the least that the player will sign for, because anything less makes an offer from some other team or some other job more desirable. Before the days of lucrative sports contracts, players quit their sports before they otherwise would have because outside offers were better. Depending on the institutional structure of the sport, a player's reservation wage can be very high because he[4] will have offers from other teams, or it can be very low because the player is able to offer his services to only one team. In the latter case, the reservation wage is the next best job, but outside of the sport.

reservation wage
The least amount that a player will accept because it is the next best offer.

The pay that a player will end up getting will thus be between the most it can be, the marginal revenue product of labor, and the least it can be, the reservation wage. This gap can be enormous.

The Vocabulary of Sports Economics

Franchise owners, of course, spend their time attempting to increase revenues and fighting increases in expenditures. We have dealt with the revenue side and the luxury-box solution, but the expenditure side is more complicated. The problem owners face is players who are **free agents.** It is increasingly difficult to compete in the major sports without an ability to buy talent. Total gate receipts for the average "small-market" major league baseball team is between $40 million and $75 million. The 1997 Florida Marlins lost millions winning the World Series, and the owner proceeded to sell all of the team's high-salaried players the following year. Though this practice occurs most often in baseball, it is done in other sports as well. In basketball, for example, once Michael Jordan left the Bulls, the owner of the team traded, sold, or decided not to renew contracts on Pippen, Rodman, and a host of others. As a result, the Bulls became the first team to win a championship in basketball and follow that with a season in which they were eligible for the **draft** lottery. The Cleveland Cavaliers went from the NBA finals to the draft lottery in 2019 after losing LaBron James to free agency.

free agent
A player who is able to offer services to the highest bidder.

draft
The process by which new talent is assigned to teams.

The draft is a mechanism designed to provide competitive balance. By allowing teams that finished poorly to draft first, the leagues infuse the poorer teams with the best of the young talent. One problem with such a draft is that it motivates teams to play badly to vie for the first pick. This was

[4] "He" is appropriate here as long as big money is associated only with men's professional team sports.

the accusation in the NBA when, in hopes of getting Ralph Sampson with the first pick in the 1983 draft, the Houston Rockets played very badly. While never proven conclusively, the concern was they were playing badly intentionally. In 1985, the NBA created a system whereby the teams that did not make the playoffs were entered into a lottery. In 1990, the system was changed so that the chance of winning was higher for the poorer performing teams.[5] None of the systems devised to prevent "tanking" (the purposeful losing so as to qualify for better draft positioning) have succeeded. If anything, tanking is more common now than ever. The Cubs, Royals, and Astros turned tanking-created draft choices to championships. The Philadelphia 76ers have tanked their way to relevance in the NBA. Before that, the 1997 San Antonio Spurs tanked their way to being able to draft future Hall of Famer Tim Duncan.

It is difficult, if not impossible, for a team to win without great talent; and unless it manages to find that talent through the draft, it must bid for the talent of players who are free agents. With the single exception of the 1998 NBA lockout, the ultimate winners in labor negotiations during the last several years have been the players. Athletes have successfully negotiated for greater access to free markets for their talent. Free agency has increased average salaries faster than revenues from TV or ticket sales so that today, a single player can earn more in a year (though only in nominal terms) than it cost to build Yankee Stadium in 1923.

Quite often, today's owners must decide whether to make money or to win games. It is unfortunate that for more than a few teams, in more than a few sports, these are conflicting goals. Owners within each of the major sports have complained about their inability to earn a profit or at least break even. Because only a few players are on the free agent market each year and because many teams consider themselves just a few wins short of either contending for the playoffs, or better, winning a championship, the price that players are able to command is quite high.

Sports franchise owners have attempted to institute **salary caps,** in order to protect themselves from themselves. That is, they want to protect themselves from being tempted to bid against one another. Other than baseball, each major professional team sport has some form of salary cap in place. The owners hope to lessen their costs at the expense of players by limiting the amount of money they can bid against each other for talent. Sometimes it is not in the best interests of the owners to have strict salary caps. During the 1980s, the NBA allowed teams to have one player's salary not count against the cap as long as any further signings were done at the minimum. This rule, called the Larry Bird exemption, was instituted so that teams could keep a great, marquee player.

salary cap
The maximum in total payroll that a team can pay its players.

Another avenue for allowing small-market teams to succeed is to implement a general sharing of revenues, or at least a sharing of the television revenues. Because football does **revenue sharing** well and baseball does not, you would expect a more fluid mix of winners and losers in football than in baseball. That is, in fact, what we saw in the 1990s. Two baseball teams dominated the decade, the Atlanta Braves and the New York Yankees, both of which had a "local" television market via cable that was, in fact, thoroughly national. Neither, of course, shared the revenue it got with the other baseball teams, and this gave them an absurd advantage in bidding for high-priced talent.

revenue sharing
The process by which some revenues are distributed to all teams rather than simply the teams that generate them.

In a simpler time, sports were games played by men who were happy to be paid at all. Owners were happy to oblige by hardly paying them. There were no women's professional leagues and no laws requiring high schools and colleges to fund women's athletics. Without a doubt there was grumbling among players about their pay, but not until 1977 did business considerations begin. In that year, baseball had an epiphany. An arbitrator declared two players free agents and the sport was forever changed. Within a few years, other sports also gained forms of free agency and players who had had virtually no right to the economic benefits of the free competitive market began to get rich.

Prior to 1977, all players in all team sports were bound to the team they played for the previous year. Having this so-called **reserve clause** in contracts meant that the only choice players had was to either play for what the owner offered or retire. Whereas star players in their later years had the sort of leverage that was afforded by the support of public opinion, lesser players did not. Even when Joe DiMaggio, considered by many the best right-handed hitter of all time, held

reserve clause
A contract clause that requires that players re-sign with the team to which they belonged the previous year.

[5] Specifically, of the 29 teams in the NBA, 13 do not make the playoffs and are in the lottery as a result. Like the lotto, each team's logo is printed on Ping-Pong balls. A team has one ball plus one for each team they were behind in the race to the playoffs. Thus the worst team in the league has 13 of the 91 balls in the hopper. As a result, their probability of getting the first pick is 14.3 out of 100.

out for a better contract by going home to San Francisco to open a restaurant, he ultimately came back to the Yankees for much less than he was worth. Going back to our discussion on the reservation wage, with the reserve clause in place, the reservation wage for players bound by it was very low.

From 1977 on, each sport has engaged in collective bargaining agreements that have given players more and more freedom of movement and contracts that are much more lucrative in terms of salaries and incentives. These agreements usually require teams to pay a minimum salary. Baseball's minimum salary was set at $300,000 in 2004 and adjusted for inflation thereafter. Hockey's minimum salary had been the lowest of the major sports and is now the highest, at $700,000. The NBA has a minimum salary chart that is based on years of service. For a rookie, the minimum salary for the 2018–2019 season was $582,180 while for a 10-year veteran it was $1,662,176. The interesting thing about the NBA system is that it works against veterans who wish to finish their careers as role players. If you refer to Chapter 33's discussion of the minimum wage, this is an example of how this type of minimum wage can actually hurt someone it was intended to help.

In each sport, players are bound to the team they played for the previous year for a period of time that ranges from four to six years, depending on the sport. These collective bargaining agreements have decidedly raised the reservation wage of players with the requisite experience to have earned free agency. For free agents, the reservation wage is the next best offer from another team. That is usually very close to their marginal revenue product.

Thus free agency and other aspects of collective bargaining agreements have raised average salaries in all sports far faster than inflation. Though there is dispute among economists as to how much credit for this change goes to free agency, average salaries have ballooned. They increased sevenfold in 25 years in baseball, sixfold in basketball in 20 years, and sixfold in football in 20 years. This increase may be attributed to an increase in the marginal revenue product of players, which has come about in part because the sports are more popular, they draw larger gates and television audiences, and sales of memorabilia have grown. For whatever reason, consider this: In the 1920s, Babe Ruth became the first player to earn more than the president. In 2019, the minimum major league salary exceeded the president's by more than $150,000.

Of course when you change a system, good and bad outcomes ensue. Along with higher pay and benefits for players arrived at through collective bargaining agreements, professional sports has endured **strikes** and **lockouts.** Each sport has lost at least part of a season to this sort of work stoppage. A strike, a refusal by the players to work, is usually voted for when the players want something in a new contract that is quite different from the status quo. A lockout, a refusal by the owners to let the players work, is usually instituted when the owners want to make extensive changes in existing contracts.

strike
An action by labor to deny employers the services of the employees.

lockout
An action by employers to deny employees access to their jobs.

Baseball owners have tried other avenues to get around the competitive nature of bidding on free agents. After 1986, baseball free agents found that owners were no longer willing to bid on their services. The change was so abrupt that it caught many off-guard. Subsequently, players began to suspect that it could only have resulted from the collusion of the owners not to bid on each other's players. In 1987, the first case went to an arbitrator. The owners offered the "How could we possibly collude?" defense, arguing that such an arrangement would have been impossible to enforce among themselves. It was not lost on millions of baseball fans or the arbitrator that, in a different era, a different set of owners had managed to collude to keep African Americans and Hispanics from the game until 1946. Various arbitrators found that baseball owners had in fact colluded and were ordered to pay $280 million in damages.

To illustrate how much, or how little, power each side has, consider the alternatives a player has. If a league has a structure that prevents owners in the league from bidding against one another, then players have little choice but to accept what the team offers—that is, unless the player has value in another league. For most athletes, this power only exists for two-sport stars. For soccer players, however, there are myriad other leagues in other countries willing to pay players. A player on a Premier League team doesn't just have options to move to another team; he has options to move to another league. The Spanish and German leagues, for instance, regularly sign players who have played in the Premier League.

What differentiates team sports like baseball, football, hockey, and basketball from individual sports like golf and tennis is that individual sports have no "owners" with whom to negotiate. Players can make as much as they want. They just have to win.

One problem with team sports is that it is under the control of a small number of self-serving owners. They pay the talented players. Unfortunately, anytime only a few bosses bid on talent, the bosses are usually satisfied, and the talent usually grumbles. In golf and tennis, there are no owners, so golfers and tennis players never grumble. They accept the direct relationship that exists between winning and income. While I am a fan of many sports, auto racing, and, in particular, National Association of Stock Car Auto Racing (NASCAR),[6] is interesting to me as an economist. It is something like golf and tennis in that individual achievement is vital. It is also something like team sports in that an individual driver must rely on a host of others doing their jobs. In auto racing, there are so many different owners and so many different drivers that something like perfect competition exists. Moreover, there is easy entrance and exit from the market because anybody with sufficient capital can start a new team and attempt to qualify for major events like the Daytona 500 or Indianapolis 500. Additionally, there are enough buyers and sellers of talent that the prices arrived at for talent seem fair to all concerned. The only issue that could upset this balance would be if NASCAR, Indy Racing League (IRL), or Formula 1 got so indifferent to driver safety that drivers were forced to band together to fix a problem. Thus, they would become adversaries instead of partners with the owners and sponsors. Unless something like this happens, racing will probably remain an example of how, under perfect competition, all parties get what they are worth and are worth what they get.

[6]NASCAR is the governing body of the most notable of several stock car racing circuits. Stock cars are called "stock" because they look vaguely like regular passenger cars that you can buy at your local dealer.

Summary

You now understand how economic principles can be applied to the issues of sports. In particular, you learned that, despite the obvious attempts of cities to acquire franchises through expansion and by luring others, there is no economic evidence to suggest that having a franchise enhances a city's economic stature. You know that owners are not only on the opposite side of this particular bargain, but they also face a problem of their own. They must negotiate with players; if they are doing so in a small market, they must often decide whether they wish to make money or win. Last, you are now familiar with the basics of sports labor economics history and the vocabulary that is central to it.

Key Terms

draft
free agent
local substitution
lockout
marginal revenue product of labor
positive externalities
reservation wage
reserve clause
revenue sharing
salary cap
strike

Quiz Yourself

1. The value of a sports franchise to a city's economy depends greatly on
   a. the sale of memorabilia to citizens.
   b. the degree to which non-ticket-based sales increase.
   c. the degree to which restaurant revenues rise.
   d. the degree to which noncitizens spend money in the city.
2. Most baseball franchises have ____________ over the years, while the sale price of the typical team has ____________.
   a. earned a profit; fallen
   b. lost money; fallen
   c. earned a profit; risen
   d. lost money; risen
3. The typical problem for generating parity in sports leagues is that
   a. there is no mechanism for bringing in new talent in a way that helps the bad teams.
   b. there is no means by which players on one team can move to another.
   c. without a salary cap and with unlimited free agency, big city, high-revenue teams have an advantage.
   d. no one wants it.

4. The economics of soccer are very different than the economics of other sports. This is the result of the fact that
   a. in soccer, there are leagues that compete with one another for players.
   b. soccer gives players more freedom.
   c. football, baseball, hockey, and basketball are perfectly competitive systems.
   d. there is more money in soccer than there is in football, baseball, hockey, and basketball combined.
5. Economists note that a reason exists for policy makers to subsidize sports stadiums, and it is that
   a. they bring in billions of dollars to their communities.
   b. they result in large increases in city payrolls.
   c. they result in enormous increases in taxes.
   d. the teams make people happy—even those who don't go to the games.
6. Which of these gives owners the greatest control?
   a. Free agency
   b. A reserve clause
   c. Arbitration
   d. A strike

Short Answer Questions

1. How did the reserve clause serve to allow owners to pay something close to the players' reservation wage rather than their marginal revenue product of labor?
2. Use the local substitution argument to consider what the economic value of your college's basketball team truly is.
3. If someone from the arts community were to argue for a subsidy to garner an arts festival, how would the local substitution argument apply and how might the external benefits argument apply?

Think about This

The U.S. women's national soccer team has a record of accomplishment. To put it generously, the men's team doesn't. Still, when the men qualify for the World Cup, they are paid many times what the women earn, even when the women win the women's World Cup. The reason is quite simple. The revenue sources (television contracts, tickets, etc.) associated with the men's 2022 World Cup in Qatar are expected to total $6 billion. For the 2019 women's version in France, the number was $131 million. Steph Curry, of the NBA, earned $37 million in 2019. The salary cap in the WNBA is $110,000. Why? The NBA television rights sell for more than $3 billion per year. For the WNBA, those rights are less than $50 million per year. Male athletes earn more than female athletes because the men generate significantly greater (worldwide) viewership. Is that enough of a reason for the disparity in compensation?

Talk about This

The Indianapolis Colts used an implied threat to move as a means by which to induce the state of Indiana and the city of Indianapolis to build them a new stadium. This is somewhat ironic since the same family used the fact that Indianapolis built them a stadium in the 1980s to leave Baltimore. To what degree are the combined threats by owners to leave their respective cities a conspiracy?

For More Insight See

Kahn, Lawrence M., "The Sports Business as a Labor Market Laboratory," *Journal of Economic Perspectives* 14, no. 3 (Summer 2000).

Sheehan, Richard, *Keeping Score: The Economics of Big-Time Sports* (South Bend, IN: Diamond Communications, 1996).

Siegfried, John, and Andrew Zimbalist, "The Economics of Sports Facilities and Their Communities," *Journal of Economic Perspectives* 14, no. 3 (Summer 2000).

CHAPTER FORTY-FOUR

The Stock Market and Crashes

Learning Objectives

After reading this chapter you should be able to:

- LO1 Describe how stock prices are determined and what stock markets do.
- LO2 Apply the concept of present value to the fundamental elements of stock prices and describe how prices can deviate from their fundamental value.
- LO3 Distinguish between types of corporate bankruptcy.
- LO4 Differentiate the impact of a typical bankruptcy from one where deception was a key component.

Chapter Outline

Even to many of the people who invest in it, the stock market is a mystery. Investors buy stocks, that is, shares of the value of a company. As stockholders, they have the right to vote in shareholders' meetings and a right to a prorated share of dividends. The questions of what makes the prices of stocks go up and down in general and why prices actually soar or plummet on any particular day have perplexed both stockholders and economists for many years.

Figures 44.1, 44.2, and 44.3 show the values of three important indexes of the stock market. In each, the level of each of these indices is in gold and the common logarithm (the log base 10) is in black. You can see that the level of each has grown over time though each saw major declines in 2000 and again in 2008. However, taking the long-run view, stocks have increased markedly during the last 37 years. You can also see that the plunge in late 2008 brought each index back to a level that was similar to its 2001 low. Graphs such as these are deceiving though, if you just look at the level, which is why the logarithmic scale is useful. For instance, when looking at historic swings from 25 or even 70 years ago, what is imperceptible on the level scale is quite noticeable on the logarithmic scale. You may recall that the Dow Jones and S&P 500 each grew rapidly in the 1920s and then plunged in the 1930s. It is impossible to see those decreases on the level scale but much easier to see it on the logarithmic scale.

What could cause stocks to increase by more than 50 percent in four months, as they did in 1982? What could cause a stock market to lose 20 percent of its value on a single day, as it did in October 1987? Assuming that the price of a share of stock does, in fact, represent the value of that share of the company in question, how can the value of anything change so fast?

The ultimate question of what actually determines stock market prices is the focus of this chapter. We explore what traditional economic theory suggests on the subject of how stock prices are determined. We discuss how a stock market can advance economic growth by helping to transfer financial capital into the hands of the people who can use it best. We show that if a stock market is "efficient," small investors–investors who invest relatively small amounts of money–do not need to take a lot of time thinking about their investments because it will not do them much good. We move to a discussion of the causes and effects of some of history's stock market crashes and what might be done to prevent them. We finish with a discussion of bankruptcy and the accounting scandals of 2001 and 2002.

FIGURE 44.1 The Dow Jones Industrial Average (DIJA), 1896–2018.

Source: finance.yahoo.com.

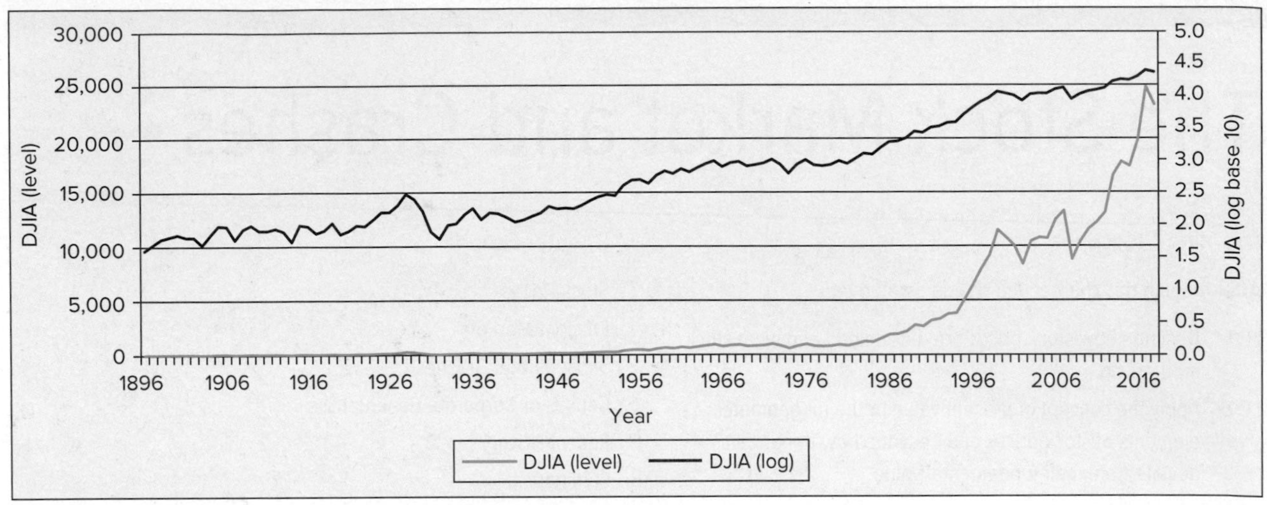

FIGURE 44.2 Standard & Poor's (S&P) 500, 1870–2018.

Source: finance.yahoo.com.

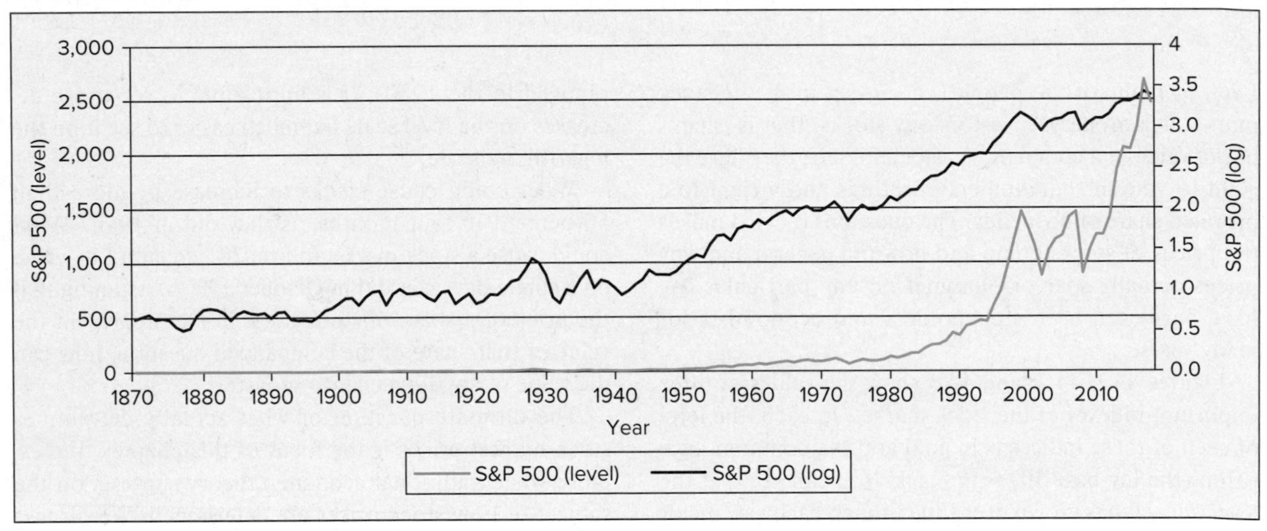

Stock Prices

How Stock Prices Are Determined

Traditional economic analysis has always suggested that the value of any asset is based on three things: the flow of returns that come from the asset, the amount that the asset is expected to sell for when it is sold, and the rate at which the future flow of those returns is "discounted." To compute the value of a stock, we add the payments that come in at different times. To meaningfully compare those payments, we use the concept of present value that we introduced in Chapter 7.

Although the math for computing present value is somewhat complicated, the concept is not hard to understand. If there are 1 million shares of a company and the company profits are exactly $1 million, then the earnings per share is exactly $1. How much would you pay for a share of stock that would yield earnings of $1/year

FIGURE 44.3 NASDAQ Composite Index, 1980–2018.

Source: finance.yahoo.com.

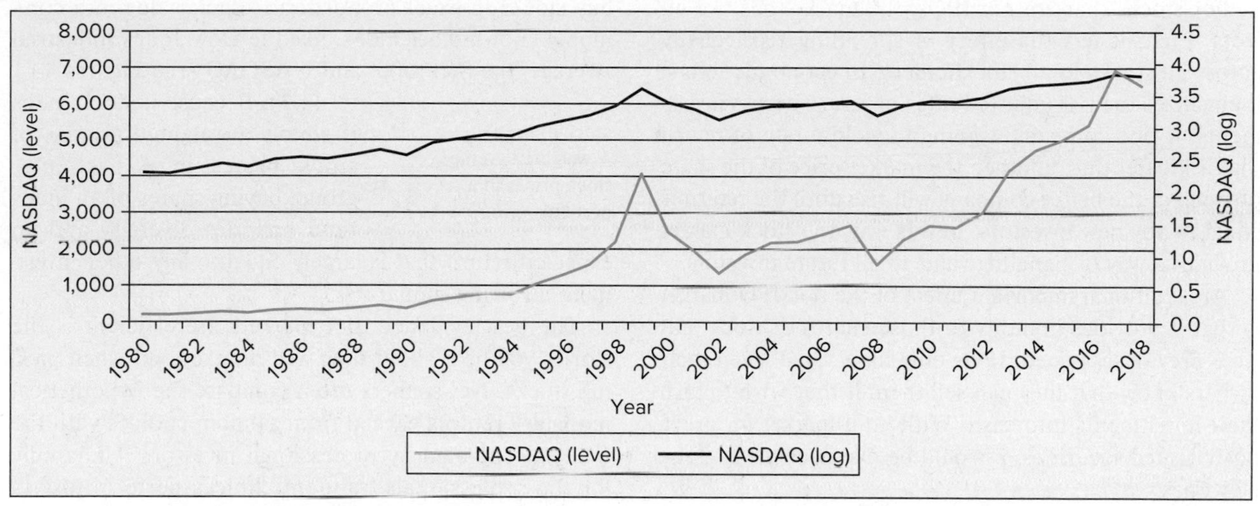

forever? What it is worth is the present value of that $1 each year. Recall that you learned in Chapter 7 that one of the components of present value is the interest rate. Sometimes we change the jargon a bit and refer to it as the discount rate, but it is the same concept: the amount by which future payments are discounted. In the previous example, if you are confident of being paid $1/year/share forever, the present value is the reciprocal of the interest rate. If the interest rate is 5 percent, then the present value is $20. If it is 10 percent, the present value is $10.

Because we rarely act as if companies will last forever, we usually judge the value of a stock to be the present value of its expected dividend payments plus the present value of its expected final sales price. Both of these present values are greatly determined by the interest rate.

The price of a share of stock can move as a result of a change in any of the three variables. A change in the profit expectations will change both dividend expectations and final sale price expectations. These in turn will change the price of the stock. A change in interest rates will also change the stock price. In the end, though, the ultimate long-term value of a stock is determined by its profit expectations and the interest rate. These are known as **fundamentals,** elements that determine a stock's price that make long-term economic sense.

fundamentals
Elements that determine stock prices that make long-term economic sense—profit expectations and interest rates.

What Stock Markets Do

Stock markets exist as an efficient way of getting available financial capital to whichever investors make the best use of that financial capital. Stock markets set share prices, thereby providing investors information about which companies are doing well and which are not. Stock markets allow firms that need influxes of money to get what they need, and they allow investors to invest money in places that provide good returns.

Though most of the shares traded on any particular day are stock issued many years before, an important function of a stock market is to support new companies with investors' funds. When a company sells stock for the first time in an attempt to raise money for expansion, this **initial public offering (IPO)** turns what is typically a small, privately held firm into one that now has stockholders, issues dividends, and has a board of directors.[1] It allows companies to grow far beyond what owners can borrow or otherwise raise themselves. Though such firms can incorporate and sell stock among a limited number of people,[2] an IPO opens up the possibility that

initial public offering (IPO)
A company's first sale of stock to the public in an attempt to raise money for expansion.

[1] Sometimes IPOs are not so small. When AT&T spun off its hardware division to focus on its wireless business, that IPO was very large.

[2] Such an entity is called an S-corporation

an unlimited number of people, or even other corporations, can become its investors.

For stocks that are not IPOs, the market has two effects. First, it has the effect of spreading risk equally across all stocks to all stockholders. In economic terms, it equalizes the risk-adjusted rates of return across investments. If one company is going to yield a rate of return that is greater than another, the market price of the share of stock of the better company will rise until the return is equal to any new investors. In this way, the stock market provides a way of signaling value to all future investors.

An additional important effect of the non-IPO market is that it provides liquidity to those shares of stock that were previously issued. IPOs only have value when their owners know that they can sell them if they wish to turn their investments into cash. Without a market for previously issued securities, it would be overly costly to issue new ones.

Efficient Markets

A market is labeled **efficient** by economists if all available information is accounted for in the market. For instance, if markets are efficient, the price of a share of stock will encapsulate everything that investors know about that stock. If investors are concerned that a product that a company sells is likely to generate cumbersome lawsuits, for example, the market price will fall by the value that the market places on the uncertainty it is feeling about the company and on the expected legal exposure.

efficient market
All information is taken into account by participants in a market.

What this "efficient market hypothesis" means for everyday investors is that they do not have to worry about outsmarting the market. The Wall Street gurus who spend every waking minute looking for new information on the market will place buy and sell orders. This will cause prices to move up and down in appropriate ways as new information on profits, risks, and interest rates are available. Because that information will be absorbed into the market long before most other investors find out about it, most other investors cannot take advantage of it. As unlikely as it may seem, new investors can simply invest in whatever they like, knowing that the chances are good that anything they pick will have the same chances of doing as well as anything else a professional outside Wall Street might pick.

While maintaining a diverse portfolio of investments is less risky than picking a specific stock, investors do not always have enough money to buy a variety of different stocks. Such investors can invest in index funds, which buy stocks in exact proportion to their value in a commonly known **stock index,** like the Dow Jones Industrial Average, the S&P 500, and NASDAQ (see Figures 44.1 to 44.3). Because a stock index is simply a weighted average of stock prices in a particular group, buying shares of an index fund provides diversity and an expected return that is largely equal to any other investment involving similar risk.

stock index
A weighted average of stock prices in a particular group.

The best evidence that markets are efficient is the stories you hear about how well monkeys do when picking stocks. Newspapers often compare the hypothetical monetary returns earned from random choices with the returns generated by professional investors. Unhappily for the professionals, random choices perform just as well as their selections.

Stock Market Crashes

The American stock market "crashed" twice in the 20th century, once in October 1929 and again in October 1987. In both cases, a loss of at least 25 percent of the stock market's total value was experienced in a matter of days. The real question that economists who believe that stock markets are rational have to answer is this: Is it possible that expectations of things that are fundamental can change for everyone simultaneously and by amounts necessary to change stock prices that much?

If the answer to that question is "no," that things that are fundamental cannot change that much or that fast, then the stock market is not much more socially useful than a casino. On the other hand, if you can explain everything that occurs in a stock market in terms of changes in fundamental economic variables, then, the stock market is socially useful.

Bubbles

It is crucial for us to know how a stock market, or how any market, crashes. If people invest their savings for retirement, college, or anything else, and their investments are going to be subject to wild swings, then it is important to know whether increases in stock prices happen because of increases in value or because of what economists call **bubbles.** A

bubble
The state of a market where the current price is far above its value determined by fundamentals.

bubble of any kind grows slowly and looks very nice while it exists, but, when bubbles break, they break fast and ugly. The metaphor of a bubble is often used to describe an asset market that grows beyond all economic reason.

The two fundamentals that go into the formula for the value of an asset are the flow of payments it produces and the interest rate. The price of a stock can change significantly if either of these changes a great deal. Economists are not overly concerned about this, and their lack of concern becomes justified when the stock prices of companies that are believed to generate losses in the short run and great profits in later years vary quite a bit with a change in interest rates. This variability does not bother economists much even if the stock price can change by a large percentage in a short time. The expected flow of payments, or profits, also is not likely to change quickly enough to change the price of the stock greatly or quickly.

The main source of crashes and the bursting bubbles is more likely to be abrupt changes in the sale price that is projected for the future. This is especially true if our expectations of future prices are based, at least in part, on current prices. For instance, because today's price is $90, you may think the price next year will be $100. If the price today were $80, you might expect that the future price might be $90, and so on.

The bubble bursts when a stock price falls and you think this indicates that it will be worth less next year. That makes you think that its value today is lessened. Now you start thinking that its value will be even less next year, and its current value becomes even less in your mind. This vicious cycle spirals the value of the stock down, and it can happen very fast. As we discussed earlier, nearly every stock in the world lost around 25 percent of its value within hours of the start of the October 1987 crash.

If stock market crashes had no impacts other than hurting some of the investors who hung on too long, there would be no issue of concern. The problem is that stock market crashes have real impacts on average families. When stocks are doing very well, people feel richer, and they are richer. They do not have to save as much because their previous savings are doing so well. As a result, they feel comfortable buying new homes, cars, major appliances, and furniture that they would not have purchased if in poor financial times.

Homes, cars, appliances, and furniture are all goods that have to be made by industry, and industry runs on its workers. When the demand for their labor is high, workers get more hours, better pay, and a host of other benefits. With better pay, workers are richer, and they buy more and more. This is an economically virtuous cycle in which good times create more good times. A good stock market causes a good economy, and a good economy fosters an even better stock market. Unfortunately, we cannot avoid the reality that what rises can also fall. When the stock market falls, people lose wealth, and they then buy fewer goods. Stock values fall even lower; consumption drops even further.

Japan's equivalent to the DJIA, the Nikkei Index, remained depressed during a time in which the American stock market values increased almost tenfold. The virtuous cycle that existed in the United States during the period from 1990 to 2019 and the vicious cycle that existed in Japan during the same period give testimony to two important conclusions: (1) A stock market's health influences the rest of the economy and (2) stock prices can rise and fall very quickly.

Example of a Crash: NASDAQ 2000

In 1999, the NASDAQ increased 84 percent from 2,208 points to 4,069 points on the back of a technology sector that seemed to grow without bound. By March 10, 2000, the NASDAQ was above 5,000 points. The NASDAQ did not finally bottom out until October of 2002 when it reached a low of 1,114 points. What could have happened that an entire market index would lose 78 percent of its value in 31 months (see Figure 44.4)?

There are a number of explanations. Some of them revolve around our notion of the bubble, while others are more fundamental. Many of the hottest companies in the already-hot technology sector were operating with staggering losses while being touted as leaders of the "new economy." As a matter of fact, for the early Internet technology companies, earning a profit was a sign of "stagnant thinking." New-economy thinking led firms to plow everything they made into improving name recognition and market share. To this end, the 1999 and 2000 Super Bowl broadcasts were filled with elaborate multimillion-dollar-per-minute ads for these companies.

Expectations for these companies were that losses now would be more than compensated for with massive profits later. If you do the math, which we will avoid here, you will see that anytime you have losses early and profits much later, the net present value of this investment can change quite rapidly with reasonably small changes in interest rates or profit expectations.

To see this, take a hypothetical Internet stock that is expected to lose $1 per share for 10 years and then make

FIGURE 44.4 NASDAQ Composite Index, 1999–2003.

Source: MSN Money. "NASDAQ Composite Index." Last updated July 22, 2019. https://www.msn.com/en-us/money/indexdetails/fi-a3oxnm.

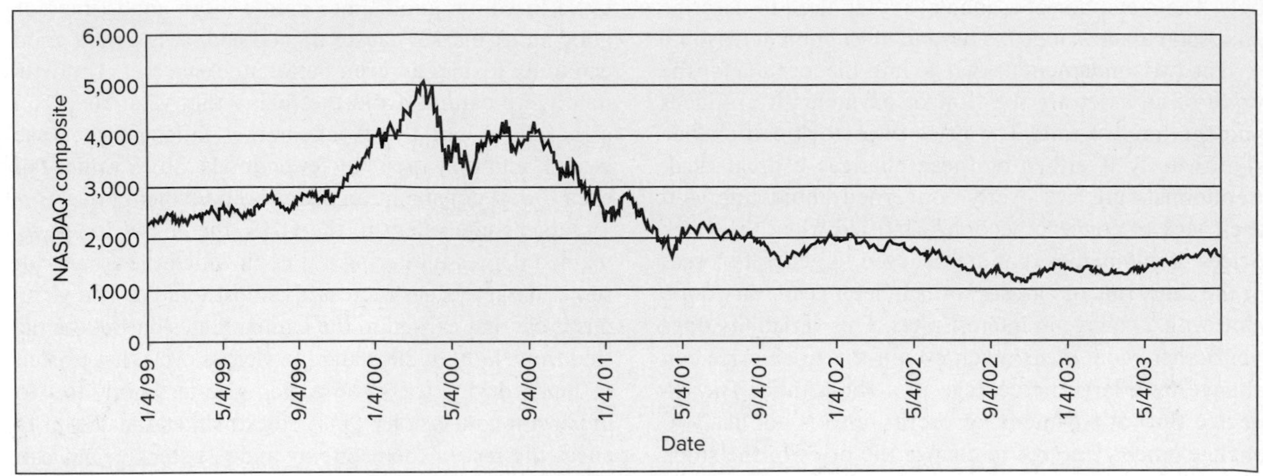

$5 per share thereafter. If the appropriate interest rate on a comparably risky investment is 10 percent, then, using the fundamentals, the stock would be worth $14.44. If you increase the interest rate to 11 percent, the stock's value would drop to $11.23. A 10 percent increase (1 percentage point) in the interest rate would translate to a 22 percent drop in the value of the stock. If the expected profit to the company had been spread evenly throughout the lifetime of a company of equal value, an increase in the interest rate of 1 percentage point would only decrease the value of the stock to $13.13. Thus, one explanation of the drop in the NASDAQ is that interest rates rose during the period.

A second explanation of the drop in the NASDAQ is diminished profit expectations. Again, because the profits were expected to come much later in the process, small changes had large effects. Continuing with our hypothetical Internet company, a drop in profit expectations to $4 per share, even keeping interest rates constant at 10 percent, would drop the value of the share of stock to $10.22. Thus, a 20 percent drop in profit expectations decreases the share price 29 percent.

The final explanation for the 1999 spike and the 2000–2001 tumble is the bubble explanation. Recall that a bubble is the metaphor for an asset whose value has stretched far beyond its fundamental value, based on the notion that expected increases in the asset price are self-fulfilling. There is little doubt that the buying frenzy among investors in 1999 and early 2000 was fed by the desire by many not to be left out of "the next Microsoft" or "the next Intel." Thus, if people buy without regard to the fundamentals, a bubble is created, and when fundamentals are reexamined, bubbles burst.

Causes of Corporate Bankruptcies

In the aftermath of the September 11, 2001, attacks on New York City's World Trade Center buildings and the recession of 2001, the Enron Corporation declared **bankruptcy.** Enron, which at the time was the U. S.' seventh largest corporation in terms of revenue, declared bankruptcy, owing more than $5 billion and lacking the ability to pay the interest on that debt. Companies or individuals declare bankruptcy when they lack the necessary funds to pay their **creditors.** Kmart and Global Crossing (a transcontinental Internet provider) also declared bankruptcy during the same period of time. However, the Enron bankruptcy made far more news. Why? Kmart served many more customers, and Global Crossing was more in debt ($12 billion), but Enron's demise was potentially far more damaging.

bankruptcy
A legal status entered into when a company or individual cannot pay its debt.

creditors
The people or institutions to which a company or individual owes money.

Bankruptcy

When a corporation cannot pay its creditors, it must either renegotiate the repayment schedule that it has with its creditors or declare bankruptcy. When a company declares bankruptcy, it has two choices: It

Chapter 11 bankruptcy A form of bankruptcy that protects a corporation from creditors so as to get its financial affairs back in order.

Chapter 13 bankruptcy A form of bankruptcy that allows a corporation to sell off all of its assets and pay its debts all in an effort to preserve as much value as possible for its stockholders.

can try to reorganize and go forward or it can simply give up. The former, called **Chapter 11 bankruptcy,** protects a company from its creditors so as to give the company time to get its financial affairs back on track. The latter, called **Chapter 13 bankruptcy,** lets the company sell off its assets in an orderly fashion so as to preserve as much value as possible for the last-in-line stockholders. Nearly every case of corporate bankruptcy you hear on the news is of the Chapter 11 variety.

When a company declares bankruptcy, a judge is appointed to oversee its financial affairs. Major financial decisions, such as the sale of assets, must first be approved by the judge.

Why Capitalism Needs Bankruptcy Laws

While on the surface it may seem strange that the ability to avoid debts would be viewed as a "good" thing, under capitalism bankruptcy laws actually aid economic efficiency. Without the ability to seek protection from creditors, even a temporary inability to pay debts would make it so that any creditor could foreclose on the business. This could reduce or even eliminate the business's ability to improve its financial condition. It would happen because, while it would be in the collective interest of the creditors for the company to get back on its feet, it would be in their individual interest to be the first in line to get their money repaid.

Suppose, for example, that a company owes money to three different banks. Suppose, too, that the company has insufficient funds to pay these creditors this year but that, given the chance, it can probably make enough money over the next few years to pay them what it owes. Further suppose that if the company sells its assets, it can pay what it owes to only two of the three banks. Without the protection of Chapter 11 bankruptcy, it would be in the interests of each of the banks individually to foreclose because each would not want to be the one bank that wasn't paid. In an apparent contradiction, it might easily also be in the banks' interests for the company to be allowed to continue without anyone foreclosing. Bankruptcy laws enable firms to continue under judicial supervision and afford all concerned the hope that they will pay off their debts.

The Kmart and Global Crossing Cases

When Kmart and Global Crossing filed for Chapter 11 bankruptcy in 2002 and 2018, economists found the reasons to be familiar and not all that troubling. Kmart, in the middle of a discount store sandwich with Walmart and Target, went bankrupt because it was not able to discount as deeply as Walmart, nor was it able to market to upscale consumers as effectively as Target. Global Crossing took a gigantic gamble borrowing billions to string fiber-optic cable under the oceans, connecting Europe, Asia, and North America with Internet-friendly broadband connections.

Bankruptcies like these do not trouble economists in the way they appear to disturb people in the press, bankers, and shareholders. Economists argue that when companies get outcompeted, it's right that they lose money. Furthermore, when they do it long enough, they should go out of business. They maintain that capitalism works only when the promise of profit is countered by the threat of bankruptcy. Incompetence and risky business decisions that turn out badly must have consequences, and in the cases of Kmart and Global Crossing, this is exactly what happened. Kmart suffered from management and marketing strategies that were not up to those of the competition. Global Crossing operated on the premise that intercontinental Internet bandwidth would be a hot commodity, and it used debt to finance its decision. AT&T, which is in the same market and raised its money with sales of stock and reinvested profits, also made little money in this market. It survived because its losses resulted only in disappointing earnings to stockholders. Global Crossing, on the other hand, could not generate enough profit to pay the interest on its $12 billion debt.

Both Kmart and Global Crossing declared bankruptcy even though they possessed more in assets than they owed creditors. Kmart had $16 billion in assets and $2 billion in debts, while Global Crossing had $22 billion in assets and $12 billion in debts. There were two problems, though: The assets were listed at book value rather than market value, and the assets were not such that they were producing revenue.

Two examples may illustrate the problem. When Kmart builds a store and outfits it, it may cost $10 million, but there is no one who will pay $10 million for it after it is built. Similarly, it may have cost Global Crossing $20 billion to lay fiber-optic cable from one end of the ocean to another, but that by no means suggests that anyone would be willing to buy it from Global Crossing for that amount of money.

To illustrate further the circumstance in which there are many assets and no revenue from those assets with which to pay creditors, suppose a company is worth $5 billion and borrows $10 billion to buy gold coins. It has an asset worth $10 billion but has no revenue to pay the interest on the debt. Now suppose the company takes those coins and drops them one by one in the ocean between New York and London. Our hypothetical company now has $15 billion in assets on its books, but the coins that are apparently worth $10 billion may actually be worth next to nothing. There is genuinely $10 billion worth of debt with no revenue in sight to pay for the interest that is accruing on it.

What Happened in the Enron Case

Usually, it is not that difficult to say what a business does. Walmart, for example, is a discount retailer; GM makes cars; and State Farm sells insurance. To get a handle on what happened in the Enron case, you have to understand Enron's actual business activities. What did Enron do to make money? It was an energy trading company. It bought electricity, oil, natural gas, gasoline, and other energy sources from producers, with the intent of reselling them to industrial companies and utilities. It made money by "buying low and selling high." It did this rather well for several years during the 1990s. Later, it started getting into sideline businesses such as the buying and selling of bandwidth for the Internet.

"Buying low and selling high" is always good business practice, but it is hard to sustain because economic profit always induces entry (i.e., new competition), especially when there are few barriers. Enron had few competitors in the early 1990s, but when other companies saw that profits were achievable, they began to enter. Without barriers to entry, Dynegy Inc., Reliant Energy, El Paso Energy, Duke Energy North American, and Calpine Corp. joined the competition, and they raided Enron for valued employees. Had this been the end of the story, there would not have been much of a story at all. It would have been the typical "company has idea, exploits it for as long as it can, and then settles for normal profits."

Enron's management wanted to continue generating extraordinary profits, and its executives were paid almost exclusively in stock and stock options. One of the classic problems in corporate capitalism is called the **principal–agent problem**, a problem that occurs when the owners of the company (the shareholders) are motivated by long-term profitability for the company, and the managers are motivated by monetary gain for themselves. When chief executive officers (CEOs) are paid high salaries, they may avoid potentially lucrative business avenues that might be accompanied by some level of risk. The problem is that the agent, in this case the CEO, is not making decisions consistent with the principals' (in this case the stockholders') wishes. The primary concern in this example of the principal–agent problem is that salaried CEOs will avoid risking their jobs and will err on the side of caution.

principal–agent problem The problem that occurs when the owner of an asset and the manager of that asset are different and have different preferences.

For years, it has been taken on faith that the best way for stockholders to get the CEO to do their bidding was to tie the CEO's compensation to stock performance. One version of this has the CEO paid only in stock. Thus, when stock prices are low the CEO is paid less than when the stock price is high.

An extreme version of this scheme is in place when management is paid in stock options. Stock options are authorizations that allow those who hold them to buy a specific number of shares of stock at the price stated on the option. They are enormously valuable when the stock price is above the option price but have no value when the underlying stock price is below the option price. Enron's compensation package for its managers was a combination of stocks and options.

Enron's management compensation was thus tied to stock performance, and in the eyes of Enron shareholders, this was good. Their perception was that management decisions that affected the company in good ways were rewarded, while those that affected the company in bad ways were punished. It unfortunately also put management in a position such that if it could deceive the *markets* into thinking that it was doing better than it actually was, then management could enrich itself. This is not new. This is the primary reason why accounting firms exist. They are supposed to guard against such deception by reviewing the corporate financial statements of the companies they audit so as to certify to the public that when a company says it earned $1 billion, it actually did.

Enron's deception took the form of high-debt, off-the-books gambles. Enron created several subsidiaries, named, for whatever reason, for "Star Wars" characters, and it saddled each with millions in debt. Each subsidiary had a high-risk, high-return niche market. None of this would be interesting except for the fact that the debt of these firms was secured by assets of the larger corporation. That in turn would not be interesting except that this debt was deceptively noted in Enron financial statements.

Enron would state that it was owed money by other companies; it would report this as an asset but would not mention that it was also a debt. Even more troubling, the smaller subsidiaries would borrow from banks to pay Enron the interest, thus raising Enron's reported profits. In the final analysis, Enron was overstating its profits by $1.2 billion and its assets by even more.

When the scheme collapsed in the fall of 2001, there were two fatally wounded companies: Enron and its accounting firm, Arthur Andersen. Andersen had certified Enron's books to be accurate when they demonstrably were not. It had participated in the creation of the subsidiaries and had gone along with the attempt to cover things up by issuing a reminder to employees working on the Enron account to shred "unneeded" documents. Though this "reminder" was technically a simple restatement of company policy, everyone at Andersen who worked on the Enron case knew that it meant to shred the evidence.

Why would an accounting firm participate in such fraud? It again boils down to the principal–agent problem. The lead accountant in any firm wants to please his or her clients. The clients pay the firms millions in fees per year for which the lead accountants are handsomely rewarded. The *principal,* the accounting firm, must trust the action of its *agent,* the lead accountant. Their interests are sometimes at odds because the accounting firm is worthless without a reputation for honesty. That reputation was effectively sold by the lead accountant, without Andersen's knowledge or consent. The importance of all this was that Andersen was destroyed by the actions of its lead accountant in the Enron case.

Why the Enron Case Matters More Than the Others

Cases like Kmart and Global Crossing really do not have much influence on the economy as a whole, but cases like the Enron debacle are potentially ominous signs of a systemic problem. Economically speaking, Kmart's loss was Walmart's and Target's gain. Global Crossing took a giant risk that didn't work for them. The risk associated with buying Global Crossing stock was pretty well understood, and if international bandwidth markets had taken off as quickly as investors had expected, they would have made a fortune. Because they did not, and because the firm was very much in debt, the stockholders were left with nearly worthless stock. Enron stockholders were simply lied to by Enron management. Investors must be able to trust what is on financial statements.

Investors take calculated risks. They assemble the information and make decisions based on that information. The area of uncertainty that investors expect is that of the return to be received from their investments. Some companies make a profit and others do not. They seek to avoid the uncertainty over the complete truthfulness of financial reports by insisting on independent audits. If accounting firms aid the company's deceptive tactics rather than uncover them, then investors are left with two areas of uncertainty: (1) Will the company make money? and (2) Will the financial statements tell the truth? The additional uncertainty about the accuracy of audits raises the required rate of return on stocks and results in inhibiting some profitable business avenues.

As a direct result of problems evidenced by Enron and Andersen, other companies began to reveal their own "overstatements" of profits. One by one, Xerox, WorldCom, and other corporate giants came out with earnings "corrections." As a result, investors continued to lose confidence through 2002, and stock values dropped an additional 20 percent from levels that were already 20 percent to 60 percent below the levels of March 2000. It was not until the early spring of 2003 that the markets began to recover from the effects of these scandals.

Recent History

As the economy grew out of the 2001 recession, stocks were slow to recover. By mid-2008, however, the DJIA and S&P 500 had reached or exceeded their March 2000 levels (though the NASDAQ stood at barely half its all-time high). What was behind this resurgence? Profits and persistently low long-term interest rates, fundamental determinants of stock market value, reasserted themselves during 2006 through early 2008.

In 2008, the bursting housing bubble spread to the financial sector. Companies, especially financial services companies, with significant exposure to housing finance were the first to drop. By Labor Day 2008, it was clear that the problems of the housing and financial services industry would not be confined to those industries.

Not all drops in the stock market result from bursting bubbles. When the automakers and their parts suppliers experienced a dramatic drop in sales and losses topped $10 billion per quarter at GM, few economists were calling it a bubble. These changes were part of the fundamental aspect of what stock markets do. When profit expectations fall because of poor sales, stock prices fall.

Bank and insurance stocks were hit by a very high level of uncertainty. The across-the-board drop in these stocks was due to investor concern about their ability to distinguish between healthy and vulnerable financial institutions. The concern was magnified by the fact that the rating agencies, Standard & Poor's and Moody's, failed to forecast the problems with housing generally and AIG in particular.

Beginning in late 2009, the economy began to recover (albeit at a painfully slow pace), the stock market made significant gains. These gains were driven by the two fundamentals: profit expectations and interest rates. Corporate profits increased much faster during this period than did any other economic measure. The reason was that employers of all varieties found that once they got past the recession's bottom and had made adjustments to their labor force, the remaining workers were quite productive. Sales increased while, for the most part, costs did not. The result was higher profits, and those higher profits created expectations of higher future profits. Combined with low interest rates, the result was a 314 percent rise in the DJIA from its March 2009 lows to its highest level in late 2018.

Summary

You now understand how stock prices are determined and what stock markets do. You recall the fundamental elements of stock prices and how prices can deviate from their fundamental value. You were able to see these concepts at work as you read about the stock market declines of 2000. You learned about the economic need for bankruptcy law and the consequences of the accounting scandals and bankruptcies of 2001 and 2002. Finally, you know that the drop in stock market prices during 2008 and 2009 resulted from fundamental changes to profitability of firms in both the financial and goods-producing sectors.

Key Terms

bankruptcy
bubble
Chapter 11 bankruptcy
Chapter 13 bankruptcy
creditors
efficient market
fundamentals
initial public offering (IPO)
principal–agent problem
stock index

Quiz Yourself

1. The fundamental value of a share of stock is based on the present value of expected future
   a. dividends.
   b. revenues.
   c. profits.
   d. costs.
2. A stock index is the
   a. weighted sum of stock prices.
   b. simple sum of stock prices.
   c. geometric average of stock prices.
   d. consensus view of professional economists.
3. If you invested in 20 different companies and chose those companies at random, you would be counting on the ____________ market hypothesis and its implication that you would do as well as you would with any other investment strategy.
   a. random
   b. complete
   c. stock
   d. efficient
4. Stock market crashes tend to result when stocks get ____________ their fundamental values.
   a. too far below
   b. too close to
   c. too far above
   d. confused with
5. A stock market exists
   a. only to service the sale of new issues, called IPOs.
   b. to provide liquidity to all stocks, including recent IPOs.
   c. to help policy makers make better choices.
   d. to provide income to retirees.

6. When a company wants to get protection from its creditors so that it can restore itself to a profit-making entity, it can declare Chapter ________ bankruptcy.
   a. 7
   b. 9
   c. 11
   d. 13
7. The principal–agent problem centers on the separation of
   a. supply and demand.
   b. investors and savers.
   c. owners and managers.
   d. interest and dividends.
8. The Enron bankruptcy was more troubling to the financial sector than the Global Crossing bankruptcy because Global Crossing
   a. took enormous risks, but Enron was deceptive in its accounting practices.
   b. was in a dying sector, but Enron was deceptive in its accounting practices.
   c. was poorly managed, but Enron took enormous risks.
   d. took enormous risks, but Enron was in a dying sector.

Short Answer Questions

1. Explain why the announcement of higher interest rate targets by the Federal Reserve (if they were at least somewhat of a surprise) would likely result in lower stock prices.
2. Explain why, if a company's profits are growing at rates greater than the current interest rates and have been expected to continue doing so for several more years, a stock price can greatly exceed what might otherwise seem reasonable for the sum of the assets of that company.
3. Explain why a stock market must exist for the resale of stock first issued many years ago for newly issued stock (an IPO) to garner significant interest among investors.
4. Explain how the "bubble" process, in which expectations get way out in front of reality on the upside, can be duplicated on the downside, causing a stock to fall below a reasonable level.

Think about This

Not all asset bubbles are related to stocks. In 2005, there was a concern about housing prices on the coasts exceeding all rational prices. One of history's bubbles involved tulip bulbs. The problem is that bubbles are easier to recognize in retrospect. Are there any assets you can think of that currently look like a bubble?

Talk about This

Stock markets are designed to allow corporations to raise initial capital. In providing liquidity to previously issued securities, they enhance that function. For these benefits, we devote some of our best and brightest financial minds. Is that a good use of resources?

For More Insight See

Journal of Economic Perspectives 4, no. 2 (Spring 1990). See articles by Joseph E. Stiglitz; Andrei Shleifer and Lawrence H. Summers; Peter M. Garber; Robert J. Schiller; Eugene N. White; and Robert P. Flood and Robert J. Hodrick.

Behind the Numbers

Yahoo finance: finance.yahoo.com

- DJIA, S&P 500, NASDAQ

CHAPTER FORTY-FIVE

Unions

Learning Objectives

After reading this chapter you should be able to:

LO1 Describe why labor unions exist and model how they alter the bargaining relationship between employers and employees.

LO2 Distinguish between a competitive labor market and one where there is market power only with the employer, only with the employee, and when both have power.

LO3 Differentiate between labor unions that seek to raise wages by reducing supply and those that seek to raise wages by using collective bargaining as a monopolist.

LO4 Summarize the history of unions in the United States.

Chapter Outline

The role of labor unions in the United States has been the subject of controversy for more than 100 years. As the economy developed from agriculture to industrial manufacturing, labor issues came to the forefront. Although the struggle to organize labor to demand better treatment began much earlier, it was not until the 1930s that legislation was enacted giving workers the right to bargain collectively and to join unions. Unions grew in influence and membership, with their representation in the workforce peaking at nearly 30 percent in 1975. That year saw the beginning of a long and rapid decline, and unions now represent only 10.5 percent of the total workforce and 6.4 percent of the private workforce.

On a theoretical level, we discuss here why unions are usually desirable in a manufacturing economy, and we show how they can serve the best interests of both laborers and the economy as a whole. We then survey the early struggles, pertinent laws, and successes and failures of unions. We use two measures of union power to illustrate the health of labor in the United States, and we conclude with some insights into the ways unions are making the transition to the 21st century.

Why Unions Exist

The Perfectly Competitive Labor Market

When the United States was almost entirely agrarian in nature, aside from those who were enslaved, indentured, or otherwise beholden to masters of one sort or another, people worked mainly for themselves. Obviously, if you work for yourself, and outside influences are not at work, your pay and working conditions cannot be unfair since your productivity determines your wealth. As the United States grew throughout the 19th century, however, it evolved into an economy where fewer and fewer people worked for themselves. With the Industrial Revolution, more and more people began to work for companies that manufactured goods. The supply and demand model of the economy supports us in concluding that any time one person buys something from another person, there are gains to both sides. This applies to labor as well.

Figure 45.1 indicates that if the good being sold is labor, and the price at which it is sold is the wage, then, like any market in perfect competition, there is an

FIGURE 45.1 A labor market under perfect competition.

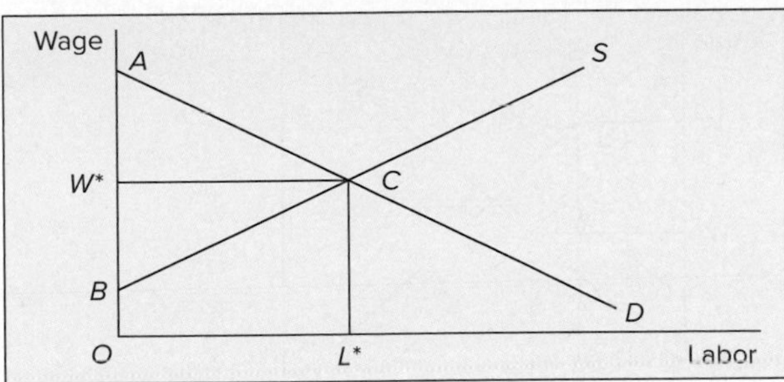

equilibrium wage and an equilibrium amount sold that make both parties better off than they were before the transaction took place. In Figure 45.1, at equilibrium the wage paid is W^* for L^* labor. The firm that hires the labor pays it OW^*CL^*, values it at (i.e., generates revenue from the sales of output from it of) $OACL^*$, and therefore gets the difference that is its consumer surplus (or profit) of W^*AC. The workers get paid OW^*CL^* when it costs them only $OBCL^*$ in opportunity cost to provide their efforts. As a result, they get producer surplus of BW^*C. There is no other wage-labor combination that provides as much surplus to the combination of both workers and firms as this one.

In a fairly subtle way, we assumed that there was perfect competition in the labor market. This means that there are many independent firms and many independent—that is, nonunion—workers, so neither buyers nor sellers of labor have any control over the wage. Perfect competition also requires that all parties involved have good information about their alternatives.

A Reaction to Monopsony

We can safely assume that the labor market can be accurately modeled by perfect competition when the city is very large and the job is not particularly specialized. For instance, there are many carpenters in large cities, and there are many contractors who hire them. On the other hand, competition can be a lot less than perfect. The most extreme example of this would be a so-called company town, where only one firm buys labor in a particular area. Though company towns tend to be rare today, towns like Redmond, Washington, with Microsoft, and State College, Pennsylvania, with Penn State University, are close. On the other hand, history is filled with companies that literally owned entire towns. Mining towns were especially likely to be company towns, with all the problems of paternalistic control and domination of workers with which they have been associated.

The case where the specialization is so narrow that there are at most only a few potential buyers of a skill is one that is somewhat different in cause but similar in effect. This is fairly common in high-skill specialties where there is only one employer in a large area. You may be actually sitting at a chair in such a location. While assistant, associate, and full professors in colleges earn pretty good salaries, adjunct professors at colleges and universities are paid very little. Faculty at mid-level universities often earn around $90,000 and teach four to six courses per year. Though there are research and service obligations to their jobs, their salaries translate to between $15,000 and $22,500 per course. Adjuncts are often paid less than $3,000 for a semester-long course. Many colleges are in towns where they are the only employer of people with masters and doctoral degrees (especially in the arts and humanities). For that reason, for highly educated people who are in the college town as a result of their spouse's work at the college, the school can offer to pay them very little and still get relatively high-quality instruction.

Regardless of the reason, if it is the case that there is only one employer in an area, that employer has power that is very similar to the monopoly power enjoyed by utilities. Recall that under monopoly there is only one seller of a good and that seller can charge very high prices. When the market has only one buyer, a **monopsony** exists. In a monopsony, the seller rather than the buyer is exploited.

monopsony
A market with only one buyer.

Figure 45.2 shows how monopsony alters the perfectly competitive markets depicted in Figure 45.1. Before analyzing the detail of the graph, though, we need to review a little labor vocabulary. As we mentioned briefly in the explanation of Figure 45.2, the demand curve for labor represents how much money an additional worker can generate for the firm as that worker increases production and therefore sales revenue. This is called the **marginal revenue product of labor**, and it is equal to the demand curve, because the firm will be willing to pay up to the amount of money it can make from its workers' efforts in order to garner all possible profit out of its labor force.

marginal revenue product of labor (MRP_L)
The additional revenue generated from hiring an additional worker.

In addition, because there is only one buyer of labor, the firm is not looking at an equilibrium wage that it must pay its employees. The firm decides how much labor it wants, and it pays the minimum required to get that labor. To get more workers, it not only has to pay the new workers more; it also has to pay all workers more. Thus if

FIGURE 45.2 A company town and a monopsony market for labor.

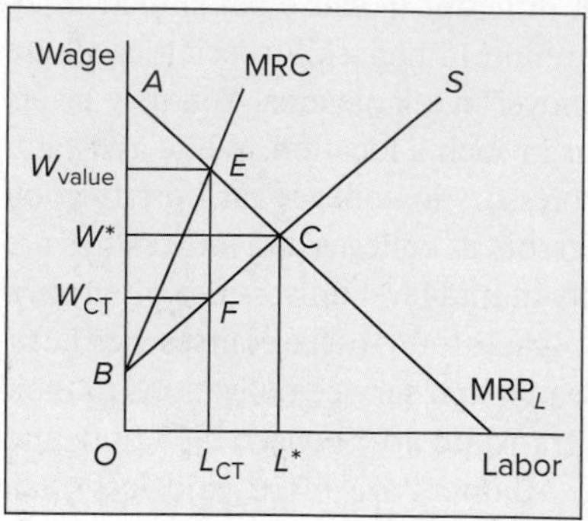

FIGURE 45.3 The impact of licensing.

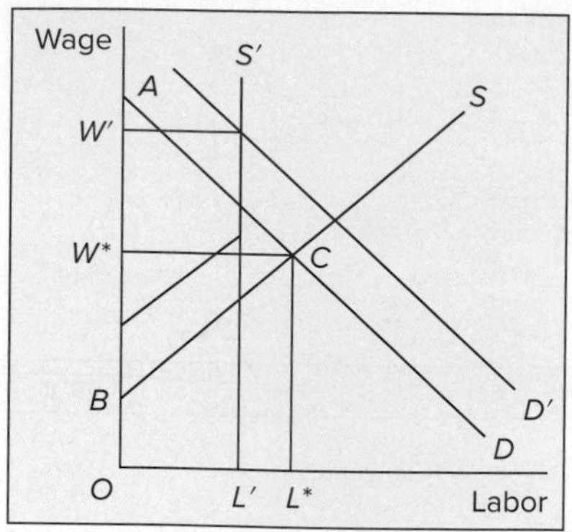

the firm wants to hire more workers, its costs do not rise along the supply curve; they rise faster. The cost of increasing hiring is therefore not the supply curve but the curve that is labeled the **marginal resource cost (MRC)** in Figure 45.2. This shows the increase in total labor costs to the firm of buying increasing amounts of labor.

marginal resource cost (MRC)
The increase in total labor costs to the firm of buying increasing amounts of labor.

To solidify this in your mind, consider Table 45.1. The first column represents the wage that is paid. The second is the quantity supplied. The third, the total cost to the employer, is the product of the first and second. The final column is the difference in the total cost from one worker to the next. Notice that it rises substantially faster than the first column.

The monopsonist firm maximizes profit when it hires at the point where the marginal revenue product of labor equals the MRC. In Figure 45.2, this is L_{CT} (i.e., in a company town) rather than L^* workers. To find what these workers are paid, we take L_{CT} up to the supply curve to get W_{CT}. If we want to know what these workers are worth, we go up to the demand curve to find that the amount of money they are making for the company is W_{value}. It should be clear that under monopsony workers do not earn what they are worth. Note that under perfect competition, at L^*, workers earn their marginal revenue product of labor; that is, they earn exactly what they are worth.

Table 45.1 Relationship between supply and marginal resource cost.

Wage	Quantity Supplied	Total Cost to the Employer	Marginal Resource Cost
5	1	5	
6	2	12	7
7	3	21	9
8	4	32	11
9	5	45	13

A Way to Restrict Competition and Improve Quality

Some unions and professional organizations enhance the pay of their members by restricting the supply of workers and increasing the value of their members. Thus Figure 45.3 alters Figure 45.1 by reflecting the reduction in potential workers as a changing of the shape of the supply curve. First, the supply curve moves to the left because there is a cost to the employee of learning how to become skilled in this area. The costs to the newly licensed employees are reflected in the general movement of the supply curve to the left. Because the number of openings for training in the field, here noted as L', is limited, the supply curve is perfectly inelastic at that point. Because there is an improvement in skills of the workers and the quality of their work, there is a movement of the demand curve to the right. This raises the wage to those who ultimately work in the field. Among others, the American Medical Association, the American Bar Association, the International Brotherhood of Electrical Workers, and the Plumbers and Steamfitters[1] all follow this pattern.

By restricting the ability of people to become workers in a particular field, these types of unions keep the supply of workers down. You cannot practice medicine or law without a license, and that license serves as a mechanism to restrict competition. While you can wire your own house or do your own plumbing, in many communities you cannot sell these services to others without a license.

[1]The United Association of Journeymen and Apprentices of the Plumbing and Pipe Fitting Industry of the United States and Canada.

The other side of Figure 45.3 is the increase in demand. Because of the training that union plumbers and electricians get, we can model their increased productivity and quality as an increase in the demand for their services. Thus, having a certification process also increases the pay of these workers, because an increase in the demand occurs for their services. As you can see, the net result is an increase in the price of these services and an uncertain effect on the numbers of these services that are provided.

If, on the other hand, the net effect of unionization of this form is that the labor sold is reduced, then unionization detracts from economic efficiency. Otherwise, unionization is neutral or good for it. Though there is considerable debate among labor economists, they tend to suggest that the net impact of licensing is generally negative.

A Reaction to Information Issues

Another reason that the actual market for labor may not be the perfectly competitive version is that workers may not have good information about other positions they might fill. Workers who explore other prospects tend to be viewed as disloyal by their bosses and co-workers. To avoid this perception as well as the effort of looking for a new job, people may not know what they are worth elsewhere. Though it was not stated above, one of the things that makes the perfectly competitive labor market perfect–workers earn what they are worth–is that workers who are paid less than market wages know it and will move on to other, better-paying jobs. If they do not know about the other jobs, they are not likely to move even when they are poorly paid or poorly treated.

There are a couple of ways that this tends to hurt workers. The first, as stated above, is that there is a tendency for employers and co-workers to distrust people seeking better jobs, especially when those better jobs are with competitors. Therefore, there is sociological "peer pressure" that prevents workers from finding out what they are worth. Second, employers are not above conspiring with one another to instill fear into workers. This occurs when there are a limited number of firms that collude in agreeing not to bid against one another for workers. When this works, each of the firms can threaten "disloyal" workers with statements like "you will never work in this town again."

A Union as a Monopolist

Unions exist to ensure that workers get at least what they are worth in a perfectly competitive market and possibly more. Laborers band together in unions so they can force employers to provide them with wages that are equal to their marginal revenue product of labor. They do this by countering the market power that firms have with market power of their own. Unions are most effective when they are the single seller to a firm's single buyer. Sometimes, unions such as the United Auto Workers, the United Mine Workers, and the Teamsters[2] provide labor to many different buyers of labor. In such cases, it is the union that possesses the sole market power.

FIGURE 45.4 A union's effect on wages in a perfectly competitive labor market.

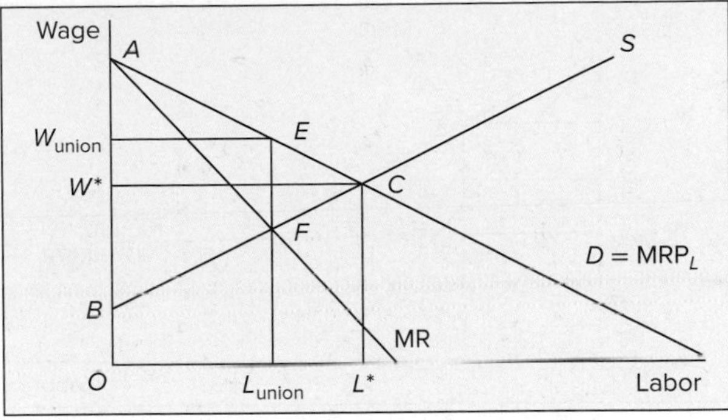

The formal model of unions is the same as the model of monopolies. In Figure 45.4, you see the impact of having a union control all labor. The marginal revenue to the union is set equal to the supply curve to find the amount of labor the union wishes to provide. This occurs at L_{union}. That means that wages are higher than before, as W_{union} exceeds W^*. If we look at unions as if they existed in a vacuum, it would appear they are bad for the economy. That is because the consumer surplus falls by less than producer surplus grows, so unions appear to hurt the economy.

Unions did not spontaneously arise, and they do not exist in a vacuum. In some cases, poor treatment, poor pay, or both poor pay and poor treatment encouraged workers to organize. For others, Figure 45.4 depicts what happens. When unions simply use their monopoly power to sell labor to different competitive firms, the existence of the union detracts from economic efficiency. We can see, though, that some workers lose opportunities to work, because L_{union} is less than L^*. We also see that the gain to those who keep their jobs is greater than the loss to those who lose theirs, because the producer surplus increases. Clearly, the firms that do the hiring are worse off as their consumer surplus is reduced. The net effect is that unions reduce the total amount of the surplus.

[2]The United Automobile, Aerospace, and Agricultural Implement Workers of America; the United Mine Workers of America; and the International Brotherhood of Teamsters, Chauffeurs, Warehousemen and Helpers of America, respectively.

FIGURE 45.5 The union fights the one-company town, or monopoly versus monopsony.

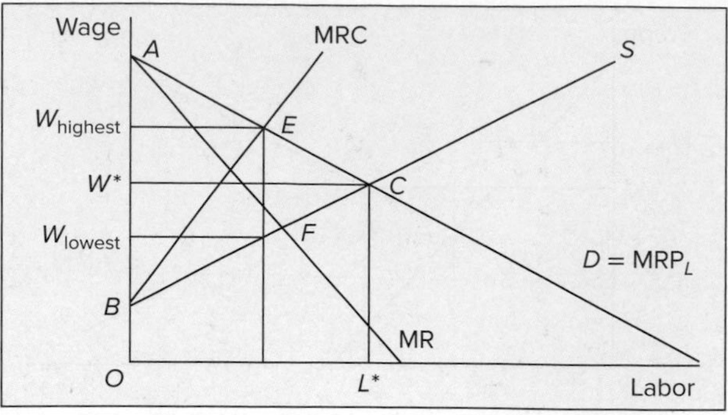

To compare those unions that exist as a reaction to monopsony power to the case without the union, we need to combine Figures 45.2 and 45.4. In Figure 45.5, we can model the labor versus management negotiation. In its monopolistic form, the union will want to set the wages at $W_{highest}$. This is what the union would demand if it were bargaining with many different employers. The "company" that rules the company town will want to pay what it would have paid if it were bargaining with many independent workers, W_{lowest}. There are some sophisticated economic models that are designed to predict the outcome of bargaining between unions and firms, but at this point we have difficulty making good predictions about where within the range the wages will ultimately settle.

Once a wage has been agreed on in this range, the number of workers the employer will hire depends on the supply and demand curves. To find out exactly how many will be hired, remember that since we are not going to be at equilibrium, it will be the lower of quantity demanded and quantity supplied at that wage. To find quantity demanded at that wage, take that wage to the demand curve. Similarly, to find quantity supplied, go over to the supply curve. As long as the bargaining process works out between what unions want and what firms are willing to pay, the economy is better with a union in a company town than it is without a union in a company town. The result of the bargain is that deadweight loss is reduced.

The History of Labor Unions

Labor organizations have existed in the United States since shoemakers banded together near the end of the American Revolutionary War. Labor's battle was largely unsuccessful until the beginning of the 20th century, though, because courts saw their actions as restraint of trade or conspiracy. Thus any union that organized and struck an employer for better conditions or better wages had these actions stopped by the courts.[3]

Before laws began to support laborers' attempts to form unions, and before unions had any rights under the law, there were court rulings that were decidedly anti-union. At one point, in a dispute between workers and a company that made railroad cars, sympathetic railroad workers refused to handle cars made by that particular company. The company retaliated by having U.S. mail cars attached to the "offending" company's cars. When railroad workers then uncoupled the mail cars from the company's cars in sympathy for the company's workers, they were jailed for conspiracy to tamper with the U.S. mail. From the end of the Civil War to 1914, the courts, Congress, and most presidents were beholden to large corporate interests, interests that saw that union members were fired, jailed, beaten, and killed. Seldom were they successful in getting pay increases.

All that began to change in 1914 when President Woodrow Wilson, a Democrat, was able to work with a Congress controlled by the Democrats. In that year, laws were enacted to grant labor rights. Although one of these laws, the Clayton Act, was overturned by the Supreme Court, its passage marked a clear dividing line between the political parties. Republicans sided with management and Democrats with organized labor.

Through the 1920s, Republicans controlled both the presidency and Congress and nearly no headway was allowed for labor unions. The Great Depression, which started in 1929, changed the economic and political landscape. As millions of workers lost their jobs, Democrats were voted into office; and, under the presidency of Franklin Roosevelt, Congress enacted the Norris–La Guardia Act, the National Industrial Recovery Act, and the Wagner Act, among others. These laws reestablished labor rights that had been granted under the Clayton Act, and they created new ones. Under these acts, workers were given the right to organize and bargain collectively. Additionally, they stipulated that exercising these rights could no longer be construed as conspiracy to restrain trade. The law now stated that whenever a majority of workers voted for union representation, the union was held to represent all workers, whether nonunion workers wanted to be represented or

[3]See Campbell R. McConnell, Stanley L. Brue, and David A. MacPherson, *Contemporary Labor Economics*, 11th ed. (New York: McGraw-Hill, 2017), Chapter 10.

not. In actuality, it was often the case that when a firm's workers were represented by a union, membership in that union was required as a condition of employment for all the employees.

These rights did not apply to everyone. Most notably, government employees were still forbidden from striking, but the new laws did give labor a great deal of muscle. As the economy surged out of the depression and into World War II, strikes were becoming commonplace. Strikes were considered serious enough that, during World War II, Congress temporarily gave the president power to seize control of industries in which strikes were considered to be jeopardizing the production of war material.

In the year following Japan's surrender in World War II, nearly 120 million workdays, 1.9 percent of all potential work time, were lost to strikes. In part, this was because a wide disparity existed between where wages were going before the war and where they were as a result of a wartime freeze. Since wages were frozen for much of the war, workers wanted to at least be paid what they would have been paid had the freeze not been in place. Management liked the low current wages and argued that the health insurance benefits that were put in place to balance the wage freeze were sufficient to compensate for the freeze.

As a result of depression-era laws, labor maintained nearly all of the bargaining power and was quite successful in achieving its aims. Organized labor was so successful that to keep its power in check, a Republican Congress passed the Taft–Hartley Act over President Harry Truman's veto.

The Taft–Hartley Act amended the Wagner Act in ways that created a greater balance of power in labor-management battles. It allowed states to determine whether they would allow workers who did not want union representation to work for a company for whom a majority wanted union representation. It also allowed the president to order a cooling-off period, temporarily ending any strike that threatened the economic health of the nation.

In 1962, President John Kennedy issued an executive order that gave federal employees the right to unionize and to bargain collectively in ways they had not been able to do under the Wagner Act. Though still unable to strike, they were granted grievance procedures. Other protections were instituted that led greater numbers of public employees to form and to join unions.

A look at Figure 45.6 shows that since the time of President Kennedy, there has been a general decline in the number of workers who belong to unions. Figure 45.7 shows the reduction in union strength in the form of declining work stoppages. Though union power peaked in the middle 1970s, the decline has been long and consistent. The exception has been the relative health of public employee unions. Figure 45.6 shows that the percentage of all workers who are unionized and the percentage of private-sector employees who are unionized have fallen dramatically since the 1980s. It further shows that the

FIGURE 45.6 Union membership as a percentage of the workforce.

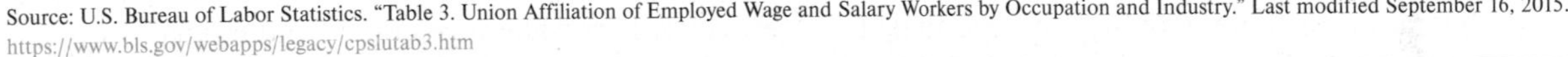
Source: U.S. Bureau of Labor Statistics. "Table 3. Union Affiliation of Employed Wage and Salary Workers by Occupation and Industry." Last modified September 16, 2015. https://www.bls.gov/webapps/legacy/cpslutab3.htm

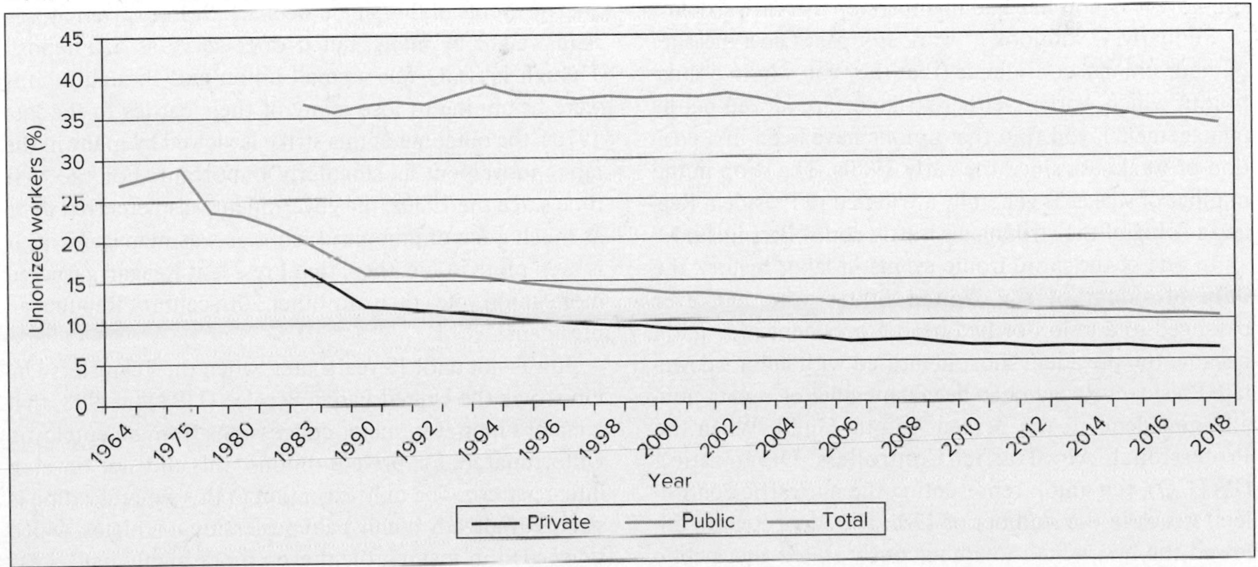

FIGURE 45.7 Lost time from strikes and lockouts.

Source: U.S. Bureau of Labor Statistics. https://www.bls.gov/web/wkstp/annual-listing.htm

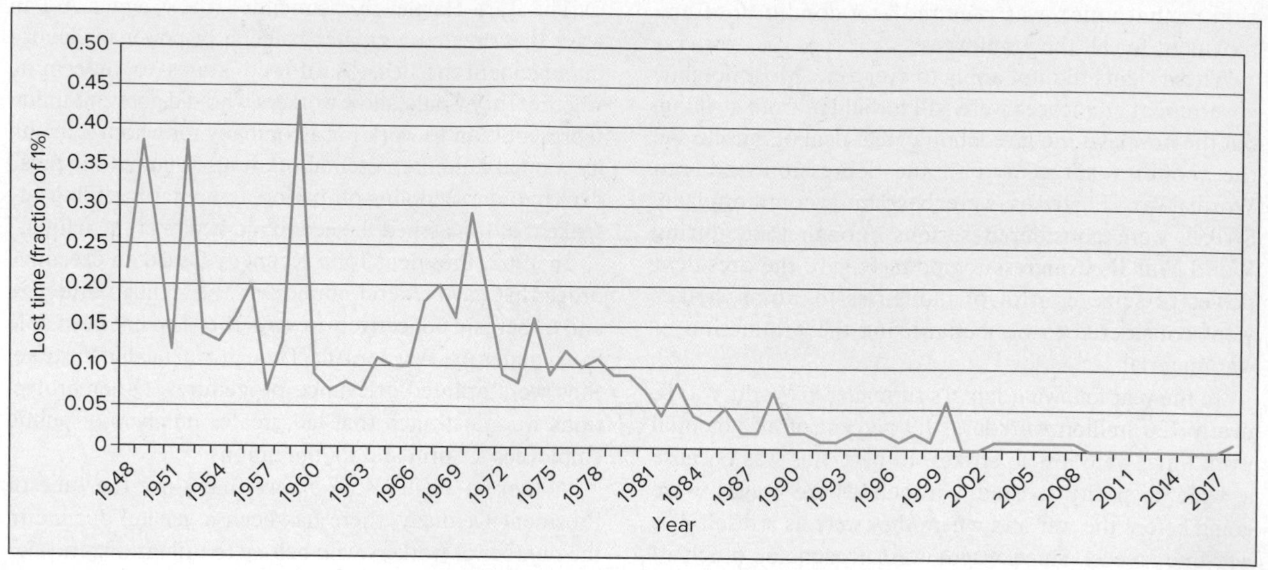

percentage of public employees who are unionized has stayed at a relatively constant 35 percent to 40 percent.

This difference between the health of public and private employees' unions is most clearly seen in just a few unions. The United Auto Workers lost nearly half of its 1.5 million members between 1978 and 1995. In 2018, their membership was only 395,000. The United Steelworkers of America once numbered 1.3 million; today membership is half that. On the other hand, the American Federation of State, County, and Municipal Employees Union has had membership increase sixfold.

Similarly, if you look at work stoppages as a measure of labor unions' confidence (that they can win in a situation in which workers either strike or are locked out by management), you find that unions have been in a position of weakness since the early 1980s. The drop in the number of strikes is generally attributed to President Reagan's firing of the striking air traffic controllers in 1981.

In one of the more ironic events in labor history, the only president of the United States who had ever belonged to a union or had been a president of a union became the president most identified with labor's downfall. President Reagan had been a member of, and eventually president of, the Screen Actors' Guild. When the Professional Air Traffic Controllers Organization (PATCO), the union representing the air traffic controllers, struck in the summer of 1981, President Reagan followed the law, which unambiguously stated that public employees who engaged in strikes were to be terminated. At the time, hardly anyone thought he would actually follow through and fire the controllers, and virtually everyone thought he would hire them back after the strike was settled. When they struck, he fired them. He then ordered his secretary of transportation not to negotiate with them, because they were fired and no longer held legal status as employees. Instead, he ordered every available air traffic controller in the military to fill in until new controllers could be recruited and trained.

The events of this single week in 1981 are given inordinate weight by many, but it does serve as a timepost. Though PATCO was a small union and though unions were beginning to lose many of their battles in the late 1970s, the outcome of this strike is viewed by many in the labor movement as singularly important. For the first time since the 1930s, the government was perceived to be as much a foe of unionized labor as was management. It is even more ironic, then, that President Reagan garnered more union votes than any other 20th-century Republican president.

It was not until 17 years later, when the Teamsters Union struck the United Parcel Service (UPS) in 1998, that a major union won major concessions from an employer. Unfortunately for private unions, this did not develop into a pattern. The only exception to this generalization is strikes by already highly paid professional athletes, which succeeded in making them even more highly paid. Less than one-tenth of 1 percent of all work time was lost to strikes over the late 1990s, a consequence that can be attributed to the realization on the part of labor that they would lose any confrontation.

The ultimate reasons that organized labor won the UPS strike are the same as the reasons that any union wins a strike. The workers were not easily replaceable and the company that employed them had competitors that were taking its market share. The labor market of the late 1990s was such that finding dependable workers was difficult. This contrasts with strikes such as the strike by Caterpillar's Peoria, Illinois, workers in the early 1990s. At that time, dependable workers willing to take jobs at $15 to $25 an hour were not difficult to find. In 1998, such workers were much more difficult to find. Thus, the Teamsters would demand higher wages. Another difference was that UPS saw its market share in the overnight delivery business disappear. The fear that customers would not return after the strike induced the company to settle. Conversely, Caterpillar had less of a concern that competitors would or could take market share for long because of Caterpillar's dominance in the heavy construction equipment industry.

In July 2005, the AFL-CIO (the largest federation of unions in the United States) had its most significant defections in decades as the Teamsters and other unions abandoned the umbrella organization. The dispute centered on whether the financial resources of the unions should be devoted to electing politicians sympathetic to union concerns or whether they should be devoted to increasing union membership by unionizing previously unorganized industries.

Where Unions Go from Here

Unions composed of men and women who work in the public sector will likely survive long into the future, as there are far fewer pressures on them than there are on unions in the private sector. For instance, if a car company decides it can no longer afford its union's pay demands, it can move its production facilities to a location where the workers are only too happy to take the jobs at whatever wage/salary the company is offering. On the other hand, if a city cannot afford its firefighters' wage demands, it must negotiate. It cannot move to a location where it can hire other firefighters and pay lower wages.

Unions in the private sector are likely to have continuing difficulty for three basic reasons. First, because employment growth has been most evident in service and retail industries where many employers hire only a few employees each, unions have found it much more difficult to organize these workers. Second, because manufacturing in areas like automobiles and steel is susceptible to international trade pressures to keep costs down, unions will have a hard time winning concessions even in industries in which they are still strong. Third, the impact of Walmart and other major retailers on consumer good manufacturers has been enormous. When firms are faced with a specific retailer that is responsible for nearly half their sales, and that retailer demands significant cost concessions, unions representing the employees of those manufacturing firms are faced with a tough choice. Either they give in to wage reductions or risk having their jobs relocated to foreign lower-cost venues. For these reasons, the picture for private-sector unions is rather bleak.

In general, the health of private-sector unions will depend greatly on whether we return to the days when only a few major employers hired most workers. The information age has seen many start-up companies lure workers away from larger companies. The wages of computer engineers, programmers, and the employees who actually make computers are pretty close to what these workers are worth. If, on the other hand, the computer industry begins to centralize around only a few major employers and start-ups become rare, unions may finally be able to convince these information technology workers to be organized. Unless that happens, public-sector unions may dominate the labor movement by the end of the 21st century.

Public-sector unions play an increasing role in our economy and in our politics. Public employees are attached to their employer for a much longer period of time than private-sector employees. This is largely the case because public-sector employees remain on defined-benefit pension plans that reward longevity with one employer. Those pensions pay off very well for those people who join the police force, or the firefighters, or the school system when they are young and stay with them until retirement. None of these professions pay well in terms of salaries, but they have benefit packages that well exceed what is typical for private-sector workers in that salary range. This is especially true when you count the near certainty of continued employment and the very low employee contribution rates for those benefits. The future for public-sector employees likely will continue or fall on the basis of these public-sector unions' ability to retain that benefits advantage. They understand this very well, which is why public-sector employee unions are some of the most prolific contributors to politicians who protect their interests.

That strength, in 2018, turned into a vulnerability. That year, the Supreme Court ruled that public-sector unions were inherently political even when they were only dealing with wages and benefits. The reasoning was that these wages and benefits are paid by taxes, and taxes are inherently political. That meant that workers were being unconstitutionally compelled to contribute to political positions they may not hold. In this case, the court ruled that membership could not be mandated. That may ultimately mean that public union membership will begin to decline.

Kick It Up a Notch

Referring back to Figure 45.2 and using the notions of consumer and producer surplus introduced in Chapter 3, we can see that monopsony is worse than perfect competition. Firms do better because they pay less, and workers do worse because they make less. The net to society is reduced by *EFC* because the consumer surplus to firms is $W_{CT}AEF$, while the producer surplus to workers shrinks to $BW_{CT}F$. That combined area is less than the optimal level by *EFC*. We can conclude from the preceding that if the problem that unions combat is monopsony, then unions can make things better by moving the market toward its original equilibrium.

In Figure 45.4, we see that the fall in consumer surplus is $W_{union}AE$, and the increase in producer surplus is $BW_{union}EF$. As a result, there is a net reduction, and unions appear to hurt the economy. Remember, unions do not exist in a vacuum and are typically a reaction to something operating against workers.

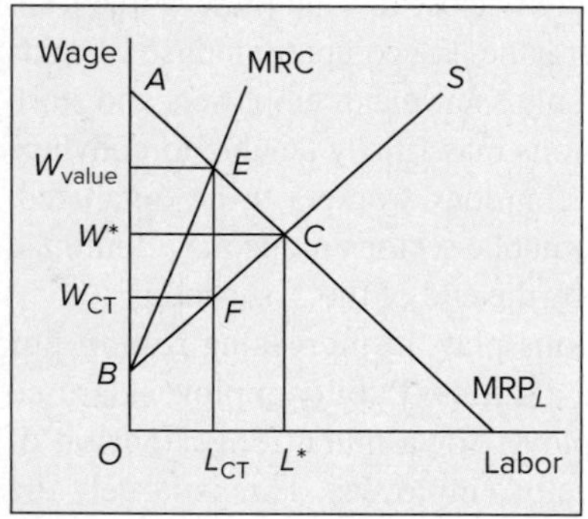

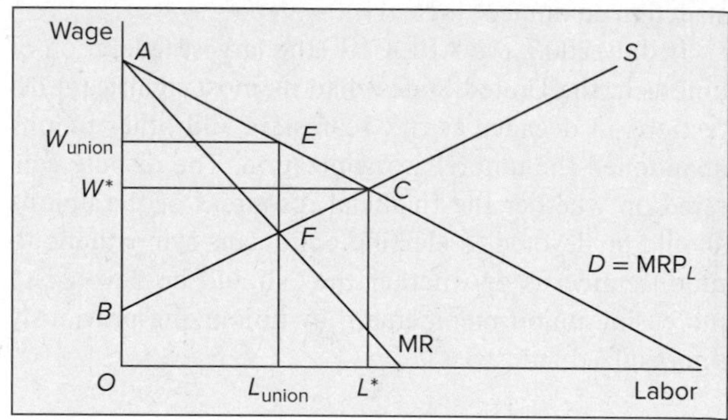

Summary

You now know why labor unions exist and how they alter the bargaining relationship between employers and employees. You understand how a competitive labor market differs from one where there is market power with only the employer, with only the employee, and when both have power. You see that labor unions differ in that some seek to raise wages by reducing supply, whereas others seek to raise wages by using collective bargaining as a monopolist. Last, you now understand how unions were first formed in the United States, and you are able to project where unionization is going in the United States.

Key Terms

marginal resource cost (MRC)

marginal revenue product of labor (MRP_L)

monopsony

Quiz Yourself

1. When there is only one employer in a city, the model that economists use is
   a. monopoly.
   b. monopsony.
   c. perfect competition.
   d. monopolistic competition.
2. When there are many employers in a city and one union, the model that economists use is
   a. monopoly.
   b. monopsony.
   c. perfect competition.
   d. monopolistic competition.
3. Under perfect competition, marginal resource cost ___________ supply; under monopsony, marginal resource cost ___________ supply.
   a. equals; equals
   b. equals; is greater than
   c. equals; is less than
   d. is greater than; is less than
4. A union that trains and restricts supply has an effect on the supply curve that moves it to the ___________ and, at a point, makes it ___________.
   a. left; vertical
   b. left; horizontal
   c. right; vertical
   d. right; horizontal
5. The United Auto Workers, the United Mine Workers, and the Teamsters try to raise wages by __________. The United Brotherhood of Electrical Workers and the Plumbers and Steamfitters try to raise wages by ___________.
   a. increasing the value of the members' work to employers; using monopoly power
   b. using monopoly power; doing to the same thing
   c. using monopoly power; increasing the value of the members' work to employers
   d. increasing the value of the members' work to employers; doing to the same thing
6. Labor unions have greater representation in ___________ employees.
   a. public
   b. service
   c. manufacturing
   d. retail
7. Since the early 1970s, work stoppages have
   a. plummeted.
   b. remained constant.
   c. increased slowly.
   d. increased rapidly.

Short Answer Questions

1. Explain why the marginal resource cost rises faster than the supply curve for labor.
2. Explain why, in a negotiation between a monopolistic union and a monopsonistic company in a town, there would not be a single outcome of wage and quantity like there is if only one of those two conditions hold.
3. Explain why there has been such a reduction in the number of work stoppages.
4. Use the context of the monopoly–monopsony tension to explain why public employees are so heavily unionized.

Think about This

The ability of unions to have their demands met has decreased markedly since the 1981 PATCO strike. Work stoppages have also decreased since that time. Are unions just not trying to make their influence known or do they not strike knowing they have little chance of winning?

Talk about This

The *Janus v. AFSCME* Supreme Court ruling will likely diminish the political power of public unions. From a First Amendment perspective, the ruling makes sense (you can't compel someone to belong to an organization with a political agenda different from your own), but from an economist's external-benefit perspective (nonmembers benefit from the work of union members in increasing wages), it doesn't. Should public employees be required to be members of their union?

For More Insight See

McConnell, Campbell R., Stanley L. Brue, and David A. MacPherson, *Contemporary Labor Economics,* 10th ed. (New York: Irwin/McGraw-Hill, 2013), esp. Chapters 10, 11, and 13.

Behind the Numbers

Bureau of Labor Statistics: www.bls.gov/cps/cpslutabs.htm
- Union membership

Bureau of Labor Statistics: www.bls.gov/wsp
- Work stoppages

CHAPTER FORTY-SIX

Walmart: Always Low Prices (and Low Wages)—Always

Learning Objectives

After reading this chapter you should be able to:

LO1 Describe the importance of Walmart in the U.S. economy.

LO2 Demonstrate that the grocery sector continues to have a variety of competitors with monopolistic competition being an adequate model to explain it.

LO3 Summarize the winners and losers that occur when Walmart enters a community.

Chapter Outline

Depending on whom you talk to, Walmart is either one of the great American success stories and the driving force behind a surge in productivity, or it is the emblem for low-wage, no-benefit, dead-end jobs, and the destroyer of small business. The reality is that it is all of that. Begun by Sam Walton as a small discount store in Bentonville, Arkansas, it has grown over several decades to become the largest nongovernmental employer in the United States, responsible for nearly 3 percent of U.S. GDP. With nearly every new store, there is a debate about whether a new Walmart is good or bad for the community. Several communities have banned large discount stores on the argument that what Walmart brings, low-priced merchandise and low-wage jobs, is not worth the cost in terms of other lost jobs and lost local character. In this chapter, we explore the pros and cons of "big-box stores" in general and Walmart in particular.

The Market Form

Most communities that have Walmart Supercenters have other large grocery chain–affiliated stores as well. Also in the mix are individually owned stores. Your prototypical community will have stores of all varieties. From warehouse stores like Sam's and Costco to the "supers" (Kmart, Walmart, and Target), to the national chains (Kroger), to the national holding companies (e.g., Ahold Delhaize USA is a holding company with regional stores like Stop & Shop and Giant and Cerberus Management is a private equity holding company that includes Albertsons and its subsidiaries, like Safeway), to the regional chains (Wegmans, Winn-Dixie, and Publix, etc.), the grocery business is large and diverse. The market form that best describes this set of conditions is monopolistic competition. Though very small towns may have only one grocery store (monopoly) and small cities may have just two or three (oligopoly), the vast majority of Americans live in a community in which three of the four types of stores are present.

Every grocery store has a monopoly of sorts based on its location but is faced with competition from other stores as consumers are willing to travel short distances past one store to go to another. Many people have a preference for stores that include or do not include some goods. While some are intimidated by a "super" store, others are attracted to them because they can do grocery shopping, have their pharmacy needs met, and pick up a power tool all in one location. Some consumers want the "hometown proud" feeling of a locally owned store because they want to be on a first-name basis with their meat cutter and appreciate the fact that the owner sponsors a local Little League team. Monopolistic competition fits this market quite well.

A look at Figure 46.1 and Table 46.1 clearly shows that the regional and top national grocery store companies and holding companies are widely dispersed throughout the United States with little likelihood that any one firm could gain a monopoly in any but the smallest of communities. Table 46.2 shows the percentage of total grocery sales by the top 10 firms. However you examine the data, the concern that Walmart is establishing a monopoly is not supported.

Table 46.1 National grocery chains, locations, and establishments.

Firm	Number of States	Number of Establishments
Albertsons*	35	2,300
Aldi	35	1,600
Kroger*	35	2,800
Target**	50	274
Trader Joes	41	488
Walmart Supercenters	50	3,568
Whole Foods Market*	42	479

*Includes stores operated under a banner of the parent company.
**There are 274 Target stores that are 170,000 square feet or larger, offering a full grocery selection. Target has 1500+ stores that have a limited grocery selection.

FIGURE 46.1 Store locations of the regional grocery store outlets in the United States.

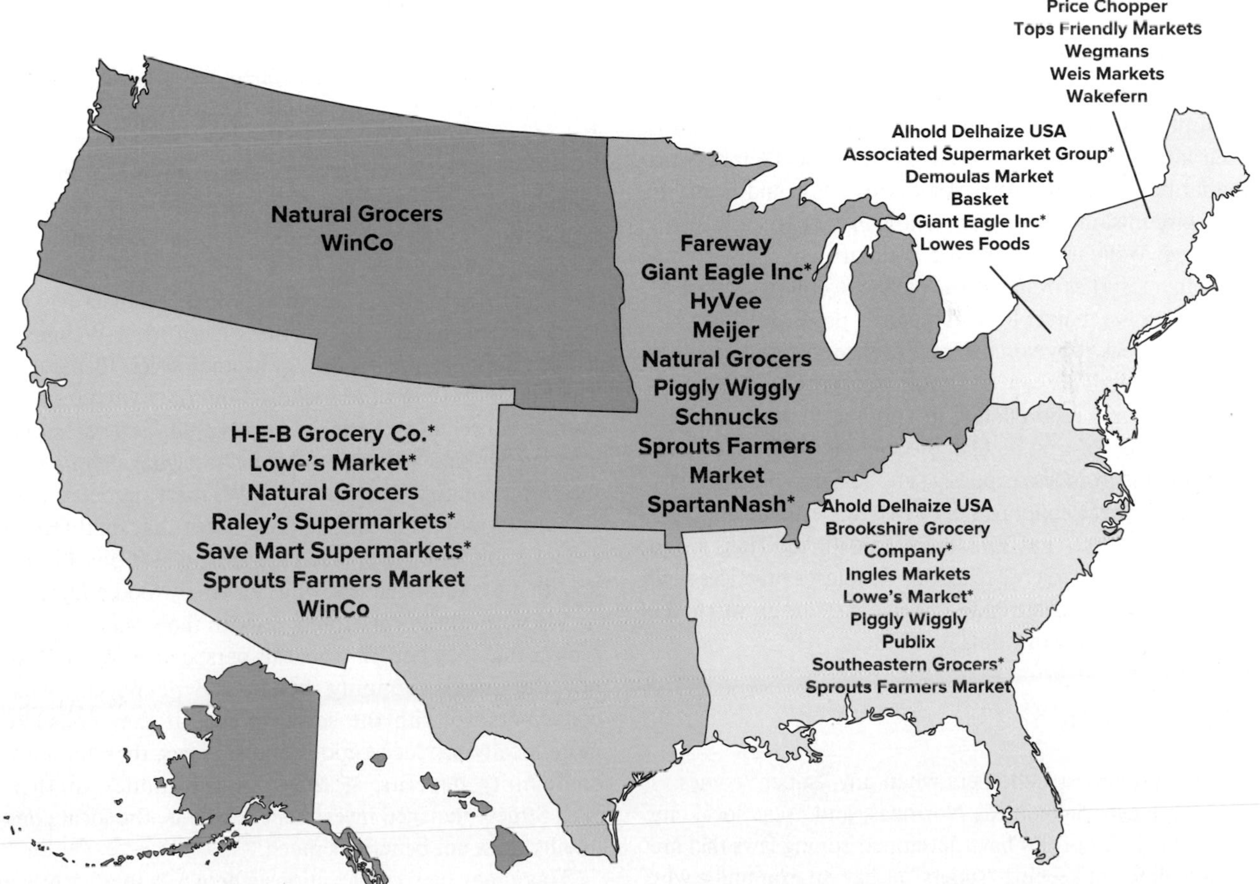

* Includes stores operated under a banner of the parent company.

Table 46.2 Top 10 grocery store chain sales in the United States.

Source: stores.org

Rank	Company	Annual Sales (billions)	% of Top 10 Sales ($771 b)
1	Walmart*	$375	48.62%
2	Kroger	$116	15.03%
3	Target	$72	9.32%
4	Albertsons	$60	7.75%
5	Royal Ahold Delhaize USA	$43	5.60%
6	Publix	$35	4.48%
7	H-E-B Grocery	$22	2.85%
8	Meijer	$17	2.22%
9	WakeFern/ShopRite	$16	2.11%
10	Whole Foods Market	$15	2.00%

*Albertsons and subsidiaries

A similar concern is the degree to which Walmart affects its suppliers. To many firms, large and small, Walmart is their largest buyer. Were Walmart to become their only potential buyer, the problem of monopsony would occur. In that circumstance, companies are forced to reduce the prices to Walmart for fear that Walmart will refuse to buy from them. Just as Walmart can "make" a company by vastly expanding the market for a company's products, it can just as easily break it by compelling the firm to produce goods more cheaply. This can, and often does, result in the company outsourcing production to another country, reducing wages and benefits at its U.S. production facilities, or making products from less expensive and less durable materials. The left-leaning Economic Policy Institute estimated in 2015 that between 2001 and 2013, there were 400,000 jobs lost in the United States solely because of Walmart's practices such as this. They further attribute 15 percent of the growth in the U.S. trade deficit with China to Walmart.

Who Is Affected?

There are many stakeholders when any "super" comes to town and, especially in the Northeast and West, local city and county authorities have developed zoning laws that are clearly aimed at keeping "supers" at bay. In examining why some object to the introduction of a Walmart Supercenter into a community, it helps to look at who wins and who loses. First, as a group, consumers unambiguously win because Walmarts tend to charge substantially less for identical items when comparisons are made between its prices and those of other big national or regional grocery stores like Kroger, Safeway, Food Lion, or Albertsons. Often, Walmart can sell its staple items (like milk and bread) for less than independent grocers pay their suppliers. Second, workers may win or lose depending on two things: (1) whether there is a net increase in jobs or whether the jobs gained at the Walmart are countered by lost jobs at competitors, and (2) what Walmart pays its employees. Third, taxpayers may win or lose depending on whether or not there is a net addition to sales in the community that results in a net increase in sales taxes. Finally, some of the owners of small businesses and other existing corporate retailers may be affected negatively, while others may benefit from such an endeavor. Let's examine some data.

Most Consumers Stand to Gain—Some Lose Options

We'll take each set of stakeholders in turn, starting with consumers. The gain to consumers from paying less for their groceries is substantial. The average Walmart Supercenter sells between $100 and $150 million worth of goods in a year. Estimates vary considerably, but a trade association of mass marketers once estimated that Walmart's prices were 15 percent to 22 percent lower than national averages. Competition has reduced that margin. That suggests that the logistical advantages that Walmart has enjoyed are slowly eroding as others learn from Walmart's tactics. Suppose the average consumer saves 10 percent. The gain to the consumers who voluntarily switch from an average store to a Walmart Supercenter is (per store) between $10 and $15 million annually. Aggregate that over the entire country. Ten percent of Walmart's grocery sales amount to more than $50 billion. Given that total federal spending on food assistance (SNAP and WIC) is $74 billion, that is a rather large savings for family food budgets.

Whatever these consumers do with the saved money, it is clear that they benefit from this perspective. Whether or not the local economy benefits depends on what consumers do with the saved money. If they consume more locally produced goods and services, then the local community benefits. If they put the money in their Wall Street-managed investment accounts, the local community does not benefit as much.

There may be some locations where a "super" drives a locally owned store out of business and doing so makes some consumers worse off because they now have their optimal grocery option removed from their set of choices. To ballpark that loss, suppose a family used to pay $1,000 more a year on groceries at a locally owned store than they would have at a Walmart and did so because they liked the personalized service available at that store. They have shown through their "revealed preferences" that this option is worth at least $1,000. For every 1,000 consumers affected, the loss would be $1,000,000. What seems likely is that consumers as an aggregate are better off, though some may be worse off.

Workers Probably Lose

It's hard to tell what the impact will be on workers because it is unclear whether there will be any net addition (or net loss) to the workforce. If there is a net addition, it may not be great enough to offset the loss associated with the fact that, despite recent increases in their own wages, Walmart's pay, including benefits, is usually lower than a unionized grocery store. A representative sample of recent Walmart openings shows that they employ approximately 300 people per store. However, there are problems with that number: First, about half of the jobs are part time, and second, the literature on displacements suggests that between 75 percent and 133 percent of such jobs will be displaced elsewhere in the community.[1] If we assume that a work year contains 2,080 hours, and, further, if we assume Walmart pays its employees $5 less per hour than its competitors, there will be a loss to the community of workers that is $3 million per store. To change this perception, in 2018, Walmart announced a companywide minimum wage of $11 per hour.

Sales Tax Revenues Won't Be Affected Much

The question of whether taxpayers will gain or lose depends on whether the net sales in the state increase. The literature on the degree to which new supercenters increase total sales in a community suggests that between 70 percent and 80 percent of their sales displace sales that would have taken place in that community anyway. The problem with saying that sales taxes would therefore increase is that (1) a sizable portion of the sales are for tax-exempt items like food and (2) very little of the taxable sales would go to people who would have spent their money outside the state.

The latter point is important because sales taxes in many states go directly to the state. Therefore, whether the sales are in the particular community or in one of the neighboring counties, the sales taxes collected are the same. So, though more sales taxes would be collected in the community, there would be little effect on total sales tax collections.

Some Businesses Will Get Hurt; Others Will Be Helped

The impact of Walmart and other "supers" on other stores in the area is not clear. IGA (an association of independent grocers) suggests that its members not try to "out-Walmart" Walmart. Its website stated that they "believe that a good grocery store isn't a sprawling, impersonal example of cookie-cutter commerce, but a community hub owned and operated by the very people who know the area best–the citizens." As a result, they support local charities, sponsor many local children's athletic teams, stock food products not often stocked at a "super," happily take special orders for meats not typically carried by the "supers," cut meat on-site rather than having it delivered already packaged, and their owners are on-site and part of their communities. At least some of Walmart's growth has been at the expense of these stores.

What is also important in the mix is that Walmarts tend to lead to the creation of complementary businesses. This "pull-factor" has been estimated to increase the creation of other retail business and other economic activity. A new Walmart is likely to "pull" retail sales from neighboring counties. That also leads to new fast-food and chain sit-down restaurants and other retailers. Walmart can be the instant critical mass for an undeveloped or depressed area to become economically vibrant.

Of course they "pull" from somewhere. A study of Walmart's impact on community tax bases shows that though there is a statistically significant increase in the tax base in a community when a Walmart comes to town, communities see their tax bases fall. From a regional perspective, the net, while positive, is much smaller because the decline in adjacent communities' tax bases wipes out two-thirds of the benefits to the community with the new Walmart.

Community Effects

Sociologists have entered the Walmart discussion by pointing out that the introduction of "supers" has the impact of displacing stores that are owned by people who are also community leaders. This suggests that there is a further external cost to Walmarts in that they damage a community's noneconomic fabric. They also argue that after controlling for a host of other variables, shortly after a Walmart enters a market, local rates of poverty rise.

[1] One nonacademic source suggests that Walmart gets so much more work out of an employee that the total number of workers falls when a Walmart comes to town.

Summary

The net result of any new Walmart is what you might expect. Consumers mostly win and workers mostly lose; some businesses win and others lose, with the net being somewhat positive depending on the particulars of the community. If the new store simply replaces sales that would have occurred in the town anyway and the gain in employment is offset completely by the closing of other businesses, then what consumers gain is approximately equal to what workers lose. If, as is more likely, there is some net addition to employment and complementary businesses grow alongside the Walmart, then it is a net addition to the community. The local business leaders will gain or lose depending on whether they try to go head-to-head with Walmart or they attempt to complement the Walmart by selling what Walmart does not, service.

Quiz Yourself

1. Walmart constitutes ___ of U.S. GDP.
   a. less than 1 percent
   b. about 3 percent
   c. 15 percent
   d. more than 25 percent
2. The impact of a new Walmart on a community's consumers is
   a. significantly positive for those that get lower prices.
   b. somewhat negative for those that prefer a personal touch (if stores offering it close).
   c. substantially negative in all aspects.
   d. a combination of *a* and *b*.
3. The impact of a new Walmart on a community's workers is
   a. only positive in that new jobs are created.
   b. only negative because better-paying jobs at competitors are lost.
   c. positive and negative because new jobs are created, but they often displace better-paying ones.
   d. only positive because Walmart pays better than their competitors.
4. We can measure how much someone values the personal touch of a small grocery store by using the amount extra they pay at that store even when there is a Walmart in town. Economists call that
   a. revealed demand.
   b. revealed preference.
   c. parsing the preference.
   d. noting the demand.
5. The impact of Walmart on its suppliers is
   a. unambiguously positive.
   b. unambiguously negative.
   c. positive and negative in that Walmart enlarges the market for their products but demands a much lower price than they typically receive.
   d. negligible.
6. The predominant market form for the grocery business in the majority of U.S. cities is one of
   a. monopoly.
   b. oligopoly.
   c. monopolistic competition.
   d. perfect competition.
7. Walmart's entry into the grocery business in the 1990s
   a. turned it into a monopoly.
   b. had no impact on the market form; it remained perfectly competitive.
   c. had no impact on the market form; it remained monopolistically competitive.
   d. had no impact on the market form; it remained an oligopoly.

Short Answer Questions

1. Theory suggests that Walmart might be able to come in, drive out competitors, and then raise prices. Data suggest that it doesn't happen. What would explain why Walmart doesn't do this?
2. Give an example of a "pull effect" that you have seen with a new large retail operation in your city or town, and explain whether this is simply an example of local substitution.
3. What are the strategies that grocery stores use to survive when a new Walmart locates in their area?
4. What is the gain to consumer surplus associated with a new large retailer, and why might that not be enough to overcome the losses associated with it?

Think about This

Walmart's entry into the grocery business in the 1990s had an important effect in lowering the price of groceries to poor people. Should this be taken into account when establishing the poverty line?

Talk about This

Major American companies that used to manufacture their goods in the United States are now manufacturing their goods in China because Walmart puts enormous pressure on the company to lower prices. This is because its practice is to tell a manufacturer what it will pay for a good. If the company wishes to sell its goods in a Walmart, it will lower prices. This is good for you in that you get goods at a lower cost. It is bad for the U.S. employees of the business because they lose their jobs. What is the net good/bad in your mind?

For More Insight See

Boyina, Manjula, "An Examination of Pull Factor Change in Non-Metro Counties in Kansas: A Study of the Economic Impact of Walmart Construction," *Kansas Policy Review* 26, no. 2 (Fall 2004).

Franklin, Andrew W., "The Impact of Walmart Supercenter Food Store Sales on Supermarket Concentration in U.S. Metropolitan Areas." Paper presented at the USDA conference, "The American Consumer and the Changing Structure of the Food System," Arlington, Virginia, May 3–5, 2000.

Hicks, Michael J., *The Local Economic Impact of Walmart* (New York: Cambria Press) (2007).

Stone, Kenneth E., Georgeanne Artz, and Albert Myles, *The Economic Impact of Walmart Supercenters on Existing Businesses in Mississippi:* www2.econ.iastate.edu/faculty/stone/mssupercenterstudy.pdf

CHAPTER FORTY-SEVEN

The Economic Impact of Casino and Sports Gambling

Learning Objectives

After reading this chapter you should be able to:

LO1 Describe the potential economic impact of casino gambling in the context of the local substitution problem.

LO2 Apply the concept of externalities to casino gambling.

LO3 Describe why the local substitution problem depends greatly on where the casino is located.

LO4 Distinguish between daily fantasy and other sports betting.

Chapter Outline

When state and local governments encounter financial difficulties, one of the first solutions brought to the table is the licensing revenue that would follow from allowing for the expansion of casino gambling. Whether it be the introduction of gambling to the state or its expansion to a new part of the state, the argument goes something like this: "If we open a new casino, gaming companies will hire people to build it, more people to run it, and they will all be paying more in taxes." This "everyone wins" scenario is plagued with the same logical flaw as the "if we build it, they will come" argument for publicly funding the construction of a new sports stadium. This is in addition to the negative externality that is created for casino communities.

The Perceived Impact of Casino Gambling

The perception that gambling has an enormous economic impact on a community is understandable. Millions of Americans set foot in a casino each year, leaving nearly $41 billion. The casinos themselves employ 362,000 people while paying more than $10 billion in taxes. That, in a nutshell, is why gambling became one of the "answers" to state budget crises that stemmed from the 2001 recession and were once again turned to by states looking to close budget gaps in 2009 through 2011.

Local Substitution

The problem with the argument that a casino is an economic boon to its host community is that the money that goes into the casino came out of the pockets of some other businesses and therefore does not increase total economic activity in the community. To explain why, I will use my hometown as an example.

Terre Haute, Indiana, is known for two things: It was the college town for Larry Bird, and it is the home of the U.S. penitentiary that housed and then executed Timothy McVeigh. It is also home to economic and population decline. Once considered a major city in the state, it currently struggles to be noticed by the state's leaders. In 2017, and again in 2019, local leaders proposed that the solution to Terre Haute's economic woes included a casino. The proposal required approval by the state legislature. It failed in 2017 but passed in 2019.

It is unambiguously true that such a facility would cost approximately $100 million to construct and that many of those construction jobs would be filled by citizens of the city. It is also true that once operational, a casino in Terre Haute would employ hundreds of workers at all levels of pay and responsibility. The problem is that money would, in large part, come from people who already spend their entertainment dollars in the city.

The confusion over whether casinos are an economic answer to a community's problems results from the fact that the thing right in front of you often masks the equally sized but more dispersed negative impacts. This is true even if there are not the negative social consequences associated with gambling.

When properly examined, the bulk of the money that is spent on gaming in a community is money that usually comes from inside the community. The only substantial impact comes when a casino is located in a relatively rural area with a major market unserved by an existing casino. Thus residents of Cincinnati used to drive to Indiana's neighboring Aurora to gamble when they otherwise would not have gone across the Ohio River to spend their entertainment dollars. Chicago, Illinois, is on the Illinois and Indiana border. Four cities on the Indiana side of the border, East Chicago, Gary, Michigan City, and Hammond, all have casinos, but these mostly serve the Chicago metropolitan area.

A casino in Terre Haute might draw Indianapolis residents, but it is not close enough to make it an obvious success. There are casinos just to the southeast and northeast of Indianapolis, so people could easily go there instead without traveling quite as far. In the end, the people most likely to patronize a Terre Haute casino are people who already spend their entertainment dollars in Terre Haute. We know that this is exactly what will happen because it is exactly what happened to the people of eastern Indiana in 2011 when ground was broken on a new casino in Cincinnati. The two casinos in eastern Indiana faced significant competition in late 2012 and suffered from the fact that their main customer base now has a newer casino much closer to home. In 2017, one of those weakened casinos sought to move some of their licenses to Terre Haute. Likewise, casinos were built in the Chicago area in 2011, and the result was declining casino revenue in Gary, Indiana. In 2019, the Indiana legislature agreed (pending a referendum in the county that includes Terre Haute) to allow one of the licenses in Gary to move to the city.

This Indiana example is playing out in many states. Whether it be gambling in Wisconsin, Missouri, or anywhere else, the names change, but the idea stays the same.

The "Modest" Upside of Casino Gambling

Senior Economist Thomas A. Garrett of the St. Louis Federal Reserve notes, "Although economic development is used by the casino industry and local governments to sell the idea of casino gambling to the citizenry, the degree to which the introduction and growth of commercial casinos in an area lead to increased economic development remains unclear." The evidence, as Dr. Garrett puts it, favors a "modest impact." In particular, the impact depends on where the casino is (rural or urban) and whether there is a large, unserved market nearby.

Were there no externalities associated with casino gambling, the Garrett data would suggest that it is no different from any other recreational activity. That it is unlikely to be a significant driver of local development would not preclude it from being part of the larger solution of economic growth. Again, looking at Indiana's experience shows that the impact of casino gambling is quite modest. From 1991 to 2001, the period of significant casino growth in the state of Indiana, the annual growth rate in personal income in counties with a casino was 5.3 percent, whereas in counties without a casino that annual growth rate was 5.2 percent.

Further, the notion that casinos are a boon to community tax collections is partly wrong and partly deceiving. Much of the revenue attributed to the casino would have been paid by other entertainment operators were there no casino. Concentrating the dollars paid into one source doesn't make them any greater. The real increase in tax revenue attributable to casinos exists because the effective tax rate on a gambled (and lost) dollar is substantially higher than the effective tax rate on a dollar spent at a restaurant or bowling alley. It is a tax increase that brings revenue to local governments, not an increase in economic activity. The allure of casinos (for politicians) is hard to deny. They offer the possibility of raising taxes without the negative political consequence.

The Economic Reasons for Opposing Casino Gambling

The economic reasons to oppose this modest economic growth opportunity are the same as the reasons to oppose or limit the sale of tobacco, alcohol, drugs, and prostitution. Gambling is quite clearly addictive. Addicts of all varieties will do anything to satisfy their desires. Gambling addicts will incur large amounts of credit card debt, mortgage their homes, and put their families in terrible financial condition before seeking help. This leads to another problem: Gambling is associated with costs borne by someone other than the gambler or the casino. In the presence of **externalities,** free markets produce more of the good or service (including gambling entertainment) than is consistent with economic efficiency.

externalities
Effects of a transaction that hurts or helps people who are not part of that transaction.

Psychologists who study gambling addicts contend that most problem gamblers became attracted to it because they won significant sums of money their first time. This creates an emotional high in the same centers of the brain that drug addiction affects and, like drug addicts, gamblers continually try to repeat that high. Of course, they can't win over the long run. Casinos make money, money that used to belong to gamblers. To a statistician, gambling has a negative "expected value." That means that the average person who brings in $100 to a casino will leave with less than $100. This is because the gambles themselves are never "fair." Whether it's craps, poker, blackjack, or any other game, the "house" has a **"vig,"** or percentage of the average gamble that is its take. The "vig" is what pays for the employees, the facility, and the profits to the casino company. This is why there are few gamblers who earn significant income gambling.

vig
The expected percentage of any gamble that a casino will keep.

This, of course, is no different from any other form of entertainment. You never leave a movie theater with more money than you went in carrying. Assuming the movie was good, you do not complain because you got to see it. The allure of gambling is that you will win. When your first experience with gambling is like mine (I fed $40 in quarters into a slot machine in 20 minutes and won nothing), casino gambling has no appeal. On the other hand, psychologists insist that when you win big, there is a "high." It is a high that could potentially lead to addiction. As a result, you can make an economic argument against casinos on the same grounds you argue that cocaine or methamphetamine should be illegal.

That addiction can also create other negative behaviors by the gambler, and those behaviors can affect innocent third parties. When gamblers borrow extensively to support their addiction to gambling, the result can be high rates of bankruptcy. Higher bankruptcy rates lead to higher interest rates for the rest of society because credit card companies cannot distinguish people using their credit cards to buy food, clothing, or pay hotel bills from those who use their cards to support a gambling addiction. In addition, the money that gamblers use to support their habit could have been put to better use on food, clothing, or other goods for their family. When gamblers divorce, leaving spouses and their children on public assistance, those consequences are an external cost of gambling. Left unregulated or untaxed, any such market that produces external costs will produce too much.

Sports Gambling and Daily Fantasy

In traditional sports gambling, you place a wager on which team is going to win. In most sports where there are more people who think that one team will beat another, a point spread is offered whereby the expected winner must win by more than the spread in order for the person betting on that team to win. Prior to a 2018 ruling by the Supreme Court that allowed sports betting anywhere it was approved by the state, there were very limited locations in the United States (Nevada, Oregon, Delaware, and Montana) in which it is legal to bet on the outcome of a game. As states approve sports betting, chances are high that this type of gambling will increase dramatically.

One relatively new entrant into the world of sports gambling is the business of "daily fantasy." It attempts to classify itself as a game of skill (legal everywhere) instead of as a game of chance (legal in only a few places). To understand how daily fantasy makes that argument, you must understand its history. Daily fantasy is a spinoff on fantasy sports, which itself is a spinoff of the very old rotisserie baseball. In the latter two, two or more people would create a league and draft players. The performance of those players over the course of a season would determine the winner of the league. Instead of a team scoring traditional runs, goals, or points, the individual players' statistics would be converted into points using an agreed-upon standard. In football, touchdowns, yards rushing or passing, defensive points allowed would be converted into league points. In baseball, runs batted in, runs scored, earned run average, etc., would be converted into league points for each game played. In some leagues, you would have an opponent each day or each week, and if you scored more points, you won, and if not, you lost. In other leagues, it was simply a running total of your league points against others' league points.

That was all fine for people who were content playing for nothing of real value. Gamblers want instant results. A season-long league doesn't suit their tastes. Instead, the daily fantasy business created one-day leagues. You draft before games start, and when the day is over you know the statistics, the league points, and the winners. Unlike traditional season-long fantasy leagues where a group of friends would gather around a table at one time and draft players, in daily fantasy, you log into a website and buy players using a credit card. The price on any particular player is a function of their expected performance. The price of a superstar is much higher than the price on a lesser-known player. It is this aspect on which backers of the assertion that daily fantasy is a game of skill make their case. A well-informed, statistically savvy analyst can choose cheaper players and beat the stars. They can get more points and a higher net payout if they buy the right players, not just the popularly chosen ones. Though there are more than 30 fantasy sports sites, between DraftKings and Fan Duel they controlled 95 percent of the market in 2016. The vig for each is similar, between 6 percent and 15 percent, and depends on the sport.

The legal distinctions that enabled daily fantasy to exist began to unravel in 2016 as several states began to outlaw participation by their residents. Some states created a distinction between legal residents physically in the state and those outside the state; others did not.

It is worth noting that sports gambling in the rest of the world is largely legal. Nine of 20 Premier League (soccer) teams sport gambling sites on their jerseys, and all 20 have some associate sponsor. BWIN.com sponsors LaLiga's Real Madrid but only after it had previously sponsored Barcelona.

While some may believe that there is or is not a legal distinction between casino gambling, traditional sports gambling, and daily fantasy, there is clearly no economic distinction and no distinction regarding the negative externalities associated with gambling. Whatever side you are on with regard to the balance between the individual's right to participate in these forms of entertainment and society's concern for the impact of gamblers' behavior on others, should probably be the same regardless of the type of gamble.

Summary

You now understand that it is easy to overstate the impact of a new casino on the economy of a community. The impact is "modest" because of the degree of local substitution. Casinos are not a perfect solution to a community's desire for better jobs, higher incomes, and greater tax revenues. You also know that gambling is addictive and that economists consider addictive goods worthy of regulation. Finally, you recognize that a casino produces external costs, and like any good where that happens, an unregulated, untaxed market will produce too much gambling. You understand that this is all likely to increase with the legalization of sports betting (both directly and through fantasy sports).

Key Terms

externalities

vig

Quiz Yourself

1. The argument that casinos have little economic impact on a community is based on the notion of
   a. supply.
   b. demand.
   c. opportunity cost.
   d. local substitution.
2. Economists generally believe that a new casino in a city that already has them would likely have a(n) ________ economic impact.
   a. enormously negative
   b. modestly negative
   c. enormously positive
   d. modestly positive

3. Which one of the following communities would likely see the greatest economic impact from a new casino?
   a. Plainfield, IN (just outside Indianapolis)
   b. Gary, IN (outside Chicago and already has one)
   c. Terre Haute, IN (Indianapolis is 70 miles away; no other population center is closer than 180 miles)
   d. Las Vegas, NV

4. The percentage that casinos make on the average bet is called the
   a. vig.
   b. rip.
   c. take.
   d. rob.

5. The argument that increasing the number of casinos in a state will increase overall tax revenue in the state is
   a. substantially correct, because they pay substantial taxes.
   b. overstated but still partially correct, because there is local substitution, but gambling profits are taxed more heavily than other profits.
   c. understated because they pay more taxes than is generally known.
   d. wrong because casino profits are not taxed.

6. The concern that gambling affects not only the gambler and casino but also others is called a __________ and suggests that there would be too __________ production in an unregulated or untaxed market.
   a. positive externality; much
   b. negative externality; much
   c. positive externality; little
   d. negative externality; little

Short Answer Questions

1. If you were in a political argument with someone taking the side of the casino industry and she pointed out that casinos pay significant taxes, how would you (being on the other side) respond?
2. Suppose you were in a political argument with someone who wanted to locate a casino in your city (supposing that it had none), because there was a large city across the river in another state (also without one), and he pointed out that you could lure all those people in that large city to spend their money in your city. Supposing that you were against it, how would you counter that particular point?
3. What externalities exist when there is a casino, and how might those externalities be dealt with in a way that would allow a casino while also mitigating the externalities?

Think about This

Casino companies, Walmart, and sports teams make the same case with regard to economic development, and they are mostly wrong for the same reasons: local substitution. Why do they still succeed in overstating their economic impact?

Talk about This

The effect of gambling addiction is similar to the effect of other addictions, though it is less apparent to others. Alcoholics, drug addicts, and so on are easier to spot. Part of the problem is that inveterate gamblers can be successful at their addiction (winning a televised poker championship) or unsuccessful (and losing everything), while no one becomes a successful meth addict. Is gambling a problem only for the losers? Should casinos allow people to lose only a particular amount of money?

For More Insight See

Evans, W. N., and J. Topoleski, "The Social and Economic Impact of Native American Casinos," NBER Working Paper No. 9198: http://papers.nber.org/papers/w9198

Garrett, Thomas A., *Casino Gambling in America and Its Economic Impacts,* Federal Reserve Bank of St. Louis: http://research.stlouisfed.org

Garrett, Thomas A., and Mark W. Nichols, *Do Casinos Export Bankruptcy?* Federal Reserve Bank of St. Louis: http://research.stlouisfed.org/wp/2005/2005-019.pdf

Behind the Numbers

American Gaming Associations: www.americangaming.org

- Taxes, wages, revenue, and visitations

CHAPTER FORTY-EIGHT

The Economics of Terrorism

Learning Objectives

After reading this chapter you should be able to:

LO1 Describe the economic impact of the September 11, 2001, terrorist attacks.

LO2 Apply the aggregate supply–aggregate demand model to show the impact of the attacks.

LO3 Describe how insurance works and why the increased uncertainty after the attacks affected insurance markets.

LO4 Explain the concept of the "rational" terrorist.

Chapter Outline

This chapter explores the impact of terrorism and its continuing threat on the U.S. and world economy, as well as why economists analyze a terrorist as they would look upon any "rational" economic actor. In doing so, we will review the economic impact of September 11, 2001. As we progress, you will learn how economists apply the notions of uncertainty, risk, and insurance when exploring the economic impact of terrorism and why self-protection against terrorism negatively affects those that do not protect themselves. Further, you will see that a rational terrorist will seek to maximize benefits to himself at a minimum of costs.

The Economic Impact of September 11th and of Terrorism in General

Osama Bin Laden's Al-Qaeda operatives claimed (in the immediate aftermath of the attacks) that the damage inflicted by their attacks on the United States totaled more than $1 trillion. While that figure was hard to justify at the time, true damage estimates are, nonetheless, difficult to construct. In order to properly estimate the damage, you must begin with the costs associated with the demolition and the ensuing cleanup of World Trade Center (WTC) and Pentagon debris. Then, you must to add the costs of rebuilding the affected portion of the Pentagon and replacing the WTC commercial and transportation facilities.[1] You must also include the lost earning potential of the more than 3,000 victims. You cannot stop there. The war on terrorism, and the ancillary increases approved in defense spending because of that war, has added $100 billion annually to the federal budget. Adding the cost of the war and occupation of Iraq[2] and Afghanistan and the subsequent overt and covert wars against ISIS to the mix sends the total much higher, and begins to make the $1 trillion claim of Bin Laden seem not so implausible.

There are other costs you must include as well: any and all other money you have to spend because of the attacks that you would not have had to spend had the attacks not occurred. When that is complete, you have to add the money that could have been earned that might not now be earned. Thus, when survivors seek counseling because of their trauma; when we all demand greater

[1] The Institute for Analysis of Global Security estimates these costs at between $10 billion and $13 billion.

[2] Setting aside whether the war in Iraq was really about terrorism, it is unlikely Iraq would have been invaded had there not been the terrorism argument in the background.

security at airports, large sporting events, and other potential targets; or, whenever we forgo an opportunity to travel because of the risk that we feel is present, these expenses must be included among all the other economic impacts of the attacks.

Starting at the top, the WTC and the adjacent buildings were insured for $4 billion. The damage to the Pentagon cost another $1 billion to repair. Next, the four planes were worth between $50 million and $100 million each. These are costs related to the direct damages that resulted from the attacks, but they are by no means the only costs or the only damages.

There was income lost as a result of these buildings being attacked. Those in the WTC and surrounding buildings who did not perish did not produce goods and services for several days as their employers sought new operation facilities. Many of the people and companies housed in the WTC towers were engaged in offering financial services, and they had purchased insurance against loss of income. Estimates of these losses suggest that upward of $10 billion was paid to these companies to compensate them for that lost income. Total insurance estimates of the cost of the New York attacks were between $25 billion and $30 billion. As a result, many of the victims of the attacks received some form of monetary compensation, either from employers or from organizations like the Red Cross.

In economic terms, accounting for the loss of those who died is somewhat more difficult, depending as it does on estimating the value in money that a victim would have been worth over his or her entire projected lifetime. Economists have little trouble developing a dollar figure, but it is clear that saying that the life of Mary the secretary was worth $750,000 and that of Sally the investment banker was worth $3.6 million raises controversy.

A first pass at estimating what was lost to the economy as a result of the deaths of 3,000 people is to establish the present value of their future earnings. These were highly trained and highly paid people. If you assume that the average person killed earned $75,000 in salary and benefits, was 40 years old, and had a life expectancy of 35 more years, then such a calculation would have each person worth approximately $1.7 million. With 3,000 deaths, that yields a little over $5 billion.

In addition to what we have presented so far, there is the lost production of those 100,000 or more New York residents who would have been producing goods and services in the weeks following the attacks but were not able to because their bosses were still attempting to find new office space, reestablish phone and computer connections, and regain electric power. This includes the inhabitants of the WTC itself as well as the people who worked in surrounding buildings that were evacuated because of the damage done to them.

Now consider the losses outside of New York and Washington that must be associated with the attacks. Airlines in particular were hard hit. The resulting drop in passenger flights led them to lay off more than 100,000 employees. Nationwide, in all sectors of the economy from mid-September through the end of 2001, new filings for unemployment insurance increased from just over 300,000 per week to nearly 650,000 per week. Although these numbers diminished to between 400,000 and 450,000 for most of 2002 and 2003, the employment outlook remained weak during this period. In 2016, the Institute for Analysis of Global Security placed the total cost of the attacks at $2 trillion.

All of the preceding examples are clearly costs to society, but in what will appear to be quite contradictory, GDP accounting will score some of these losses as economic positives. The money it cost to tear down the damaged buildings and begin rebuilding the WTC and Pentagon came from two main sources. The federal government put forward $40 billion for this effort, and insurance companies were responsible for another $25 billion. The resulting increase in government spending likely had a positive impact on GDP, and because the insurance companies footing the bill were mostly foreign rather than domestic—while the demolition and rebuilding efforts occurred in the United States—this, too, had the effect of boosting GDP.

Increases in military spending, government spending on internal security, and spending on airport security have led and will also continue to lead to increases in GDP. Of course, none of this is likely to make us better off than we were on September 10, 2001. We only hope that by spending this extra money we will be as secure today as we thought we were on September 10th. Spending more to accomplish the same thing boosts reported GDP but does not make us better off.

Modeling the Economic Impact of the Attacks

If you have studied Chapter 9, "Fiscal Policy," you are familiar with what economists call aggregate demand shocks (unexpected events that cause aggregate demand to change). Clearly, the attacks of September 11th qualified as "shocks" under any definition. Retail sales during the

FIGURE 48.1 The post-9/11 aggregate demand shock.

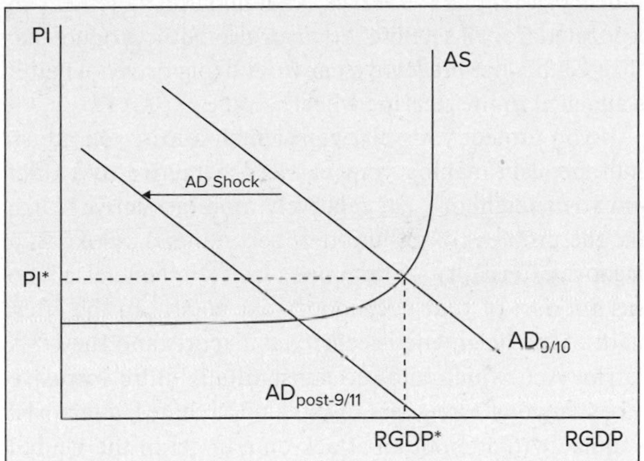

FIGURE 48.2 The post-9/11 aggregate supply shock.

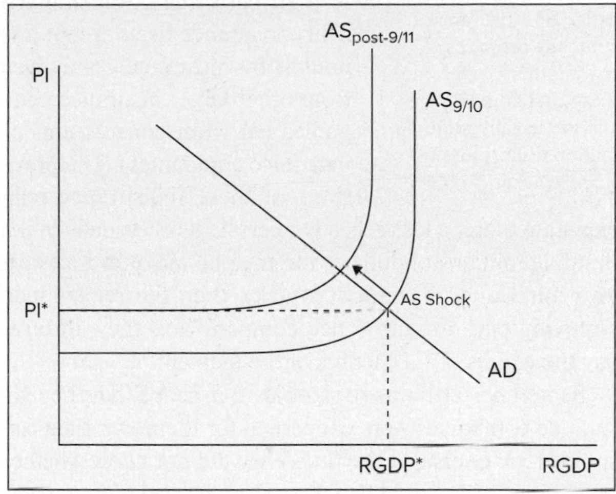

week of September 11th were dramatically lower than they otherwise would have been. This, and a variety of other indices of consumer confidence, all took very serious hits in the fall of 2001. Complicating things further, business confidence, which is typically measured by looking at businesses' hiring, layoff, and investment plans, was also adversely affected by the aftermath of the attacks. These effects in combination created the clearest example of an aggregate demand shock in decades. Figure 48.1 shows the impact of these shocks on the aggregate demand–aggregate supply model. Lower aggregate demand reduces equilibrium RGDP and overall prices.

As we will see in the section on insurance, premiums paid by businesses in high-risk areas rose substantially as well. That would lead to an aggregate supply shock. Though this effect was likely less than the relative importance of the aggregate demand shock, it is important to note, and Figure 48.2 depicts that aspect.

Insurance Aspects of Terrorism

When dealing with a world of uncertainty, rational people seek insurance because they view themselves as better off if they can pay something upfront to minimize the financial consequences of a foreseeable, but not necessarily predictable, problem. We insure our cars and our homes because, although the likelihood of a financially catastrophic incident is low, the consequences of a problem could be so severe that we are better off avoiding it by paying an insurance company to take the risk for us. The insurance company is only too happy to sell us the insurance because they get more money than they expect to have to pay, and the uncertainty in their payouts is relatively low because they are spread among so many people. They have actuaries who tell them how many homes are likely to be damaged in fires or how many automobiles they are likely to have to repair or replace.

Terrorism insurance in a place where terrorist acts are somewhat predictable (like Israel) is likely to be very expensive but also likely to be available because insurance companies can anticipate the number of buses and restaurants that will be destroyed. These many small-scale attacks are insurable because no single one of them jeopardizes the long-term survival of the insurance company. September 11th changed much of that thinking. It was the worst insurance outcome in American history, easily surpassing the previous record set by Hurricane Andrew.[3]

In the post–September 11th world, insurance companies have become leery of insuring major commercial landmarks. A major attack of a nuclear, biological, or chemical nature, or even another airliner hijacking directed at a major population center is enough to cause insurance companies to fear for their own survival. For a while, insurance carriers refused to offer insurance on major new construction projects, did not renew policies on major commercial landmarks, and insisted that acts of terrorism be excluded from the policies' payout provisions.

This is not without precedent. After Hurricanes Andrew and Hugo in the late 1980s and early 1990s, insurance companies began pulling out of the Gulf Coast region of the United States for fear that they could not survive another hurricane. They stayed because they were able to buy

[3]The monetary damage from Hurricane Katrina and Superstorm Sandy each subsequently surpassed this record.

reinsurance
The form of insurance where one insurance company promises to pay another (larger one) if the first company has a large (usually multiple million dollar) loss from a single event.

reinsurance and pass the cost on to their customers. Reinsurance is like insurance itself except it is bought by insurance companies from other larger insurance companies (or from consortiums of insurance companies). The provisions of these reinsurance policies state that if a loss exceeds a certain level (usually in the multiple millions of dollars) for any one major event (such as a hurricane or terrorist attack), then the reinsurance company pays the insurance company and they, in turn, pay the claims of the victims of the incident.[4]

September 11th was so significant in scope that the reinsurance companies were concerned for their own financial survival. Of course, at the time, they did not know whether September 11th would be followed by several more attacks or not. The anthrax scare of late 2001 and early 2002 only added to the uncertainty. Insurance works well when the level of uncertainty to the party doing the insuring is somewhat low. Reinsurance works well when the uncertainty to the insurance company is large but is manageable to a reinsurance company. Nothing works when no one has any level of confidence in the risks involved.

The solution was re-reinsurance, where the U.S. federal government became the insurer of last resort. No one buys terrorism insurance from the government; there are no re-reinsurance agents selling to homeowners or businesses. The government will sell reinsurance to insurance companies and re-reinsurance to reinsurance companies. Few pieces of legislation initiated by the George W. Bush administration passed with as much support as the bill authorizing the government's involvement in the reinsurance market. This was partly because much of the financial community and labor unions were on the same side of the issue.

Buy Insurance or Self-Protect or Both

When faced with any uncertainty, a rational economic actor can do one or both of the following: protect him/herself or buy insurance against the loss. We have already extensively discussed the latter, so let's talk a bit about self-protection. Suppose you live in a community in which automobile theft is rampant. You can buy a car with an electronic alarm, an ignition that will start only with a special key (such that the car cannot be "hot-wired"), or a tracking system like "Lo-Jack" that allows a stolen car to be located from a satellite. You can also buy a product like "The Club" that prevents a car from being driven when it is attached to the steering wheel.

If you protect yourself against such a loss, you are simultaneously making your car less attractive to a thief and your neighbor's car relatively more attractive. This, like the problem of pollution or secondhand smoke, is a negative externality. Your actions hurt someone else who was not part of your decision to take action. In the aftermath of the heightened security at airports and the USA Patriot Act, which allowed substantially more intrusive surveillance of foreigners in the United States, a terrorist is unlikely to attempt an attack on a target in the United States, let alone a U.S. airport, and far more likely to target Americans or American interests in other, less secure locations. That puts Americans in those locations in more danger than they would have been had these security measures not taken place in the United States.

Terrorism from the Perspective of the Terrorist

Economists who study terrorism examine terrorists in the same manner as economists who study crime examine criminals who engage in crimes of profit: as rational people behaving in their own self-interest. You can quarrel with this interpretation if you like, and many people have a hard time calling a suicide bomber "rational" in this sense, but terrorists are in it for something. That "something" is usually political. Irish Republican Army (IRA) terrorists wanted Northern Ireland returned to Irish control or at least wanted the English out of Ireland. Palestinian terrorists want some, most, or all of what is now Israel as a Palestinian state. Sudanese, Filipino, and antiabortion terrorists have political goals. ISIS sought a global Islamic State. Whether you are a terrorist or a freedom fighter often depends on which side of the power structure you support.

This "rational terrorist model," like the "rational criminal model," suggests that terrorists have a goal, devote resources to achieve that goal, weigh benefits and costs, and determine the best way of reaching the goal is to take all such actions where the marginal benefit equals or exceeds the marginal cost. Because the goals are political, the actions must have a political impact, which means they must garner media attention. They garner the most media attention when attacks are gruesome, affect innocent people, and occur where the media exist. They are the least costly to the terrorist when the targets are relatively unguarded and easy to attack. That

[4]Hurricane Katrina challenged the ability of insurance companies to buy reinsurance for hurricanes because the fear was that global warming had so changed the probability of major hurricane damage occurring in an area that State Farm and others refused to write new policies in states susceptible to hurricanes. After leaving the market in 2009, State Farm reentered the market in 2012. However, to the degree that climate change increases the severity of future hurricanes, reinsurance will become increasingly important.

means that from the perspective of Al-Qaeda, the September 11th attacks were nearly perfect. The lax security at U.S. airports; the high-profile nature of the World Trade Center, the Pentagon, and the Capitol Building or White House (whichever building Flight 93 was destined to attack) in the media meccas of New York and Washington, D.C.; and the obvious innocence of the people on the planes and in the buildings made them the perfect targets for terrorism.

The worldwide reaction, the wars in Afghanistan and Iraq, and the public's willingness to give up some degree of its freedoms and privacy combined to make the costs of terrorism to the terrorist substantially greater. The substantial increase in the counterterrorism budget of the CIA and the FBI and the new powers granted to these organizations make a terrorist act in the United States far more expensive to execute. The lack of any coordinated (by Al-Qaeda/ISIS) attack in the United States between September 11th and the writing of this edition suggests that terrorists may have weighed the costs and benefits and taken the stance that attacks on U.S. interests in the United States are not worth it. On the other hand, terrorists have clearly not surrendered. Attacks around the globe, embassy bombings, assassinations of U.S. diplomats, and attacks on places where Americans congregate overseas suggest terrorists are targeting easier locations using smaller groups or individuals. Economists refer to this, and any other occurrence where one alternative gets more expensive so that the other is chosen, as the *substitution effect*.

The Madrid train bombing in 2004 and the London subway bombings in 2005 illustrate this substitution effect very well. Because terrorists apparently thought it was easier to get into Spain and the United Kingdom than it was to get into the United States, they chose targets that were "less expensive." Though in the United States, the 2013 Boston bombing also fits this pattern.

Unprecedented expenditures on increased security generally have motivated terrorists to find the softest, most high-profile targets. The attacks in 2016 in France and Belgium were examples of this. Clearly the United States is not immune from attack, but so far, at least, it has been limited to lone wolf attacks. The incidents such as the ones in Boston, San Bernardino, Orlando, Pittsburgh, Charlottesville, and Las Vegas are likely to be what we face.

Summary

You understand that economists' estimates of the damage inflicted by Al-Qaeda on September 11, 2001, encompass a wide variety of issues, from the loss of the buildings, to the loss of economic output, to the economic consequences of the loss of lives. You recognize that insurance issues become more complicated as the level of uncertainty rises but that reinsurance helps to resolve those issues. Finally, you know that economists view terrorists as rational economic actors attempting to get the biggest result for the least expense in the same way that any other goal-oriented person would. As a result, we can predict that as we tighten security in one area in response to an attack, they will seek other targets. In particular, lone wolf attacks become the norm rather than coordinated, high-profile attacks.

Key Term

reinsurance

Quiz Yourself

1. Many economists generally
   a. accept the notion that a human life is worth the value of the chemicals that can be extracted from it.
   b. argue that a human life is worth the sum of the person's future income.
   c. argue that the loss to society resulting from "wrongful death" is the present value of the person's income.
   d. reject the notion that any dollar value can be used to estimate the value of a human life.
2. The destruction of the World Trade Center and damage to the Pentagon and the accompanying work to rebuild and repair led to ___________ to the insurance companies and ___________ in GDP.
   a. gains; gains
   b. losses; losses
   c. losses; gains
   d. gains; losses

3. Economists call the reduction in consumer confidence that resulted from the September 11th attacks an ___________ shock which leads to the ___________.
   a. aggregate demand; aggregate demand curve shifting left
   b. aggregate demand; aggregate demand curve shifting right
   c. aggregate supply; aggregate supply curve shifting left
   d. aggregate supply; aggregate supply curve shifting right
4. Economists call the increase in insurance costs that resulted from the September 11th attacks an ___________ shock, which leads to the ___________.
   a. aggregate demand; aggregate demand curve shifting left
   b. aggregate demand; aggregate demand curve shifting right
   c. aggregate supply; aggregate supply curve shifting left
   d. aggregate supply; aggregate supply curve shifting right
5. The chief effect of reinsurance is that
   a. insurance premiums are higher.
   b. insurance companies are prevented from engaging in fraud.
   c. insurance companies can offer insurance without fear of a major event causing them to go out of business.
   d. consumers are protected against easily anticipated occurrences.
6. The government's role in terrorism insurance is that of
   a. a primary provider.
   b. a reinsurance provider of last resort/re-reinsurer.
   c. innocent bystander.
   d. disinterested observer.
7. The negative externality associated with self-protection from terrorism suggests that
   a. terrorists cause more damage than they think they will.
   b. people engage in less self-protection than they should.
   c. people engage in the right amount of self-protection.
   d. a person who self-protects makes someone else relatively more vulnerable.
8. Under many economic models of terrorism, the terrorist is assumed to act
   a. without regard for incentives, costs, or benefits.
   b. in a predictable way, since they maximize costs subject to minimizing benefits.
   c. in a predictable way, since they maximize benefits subject to minimizing costs.
   d. with no predictable nature.
9. Substitution, in the context of the "rational terrorist model," suggests that heightened security at airports will
   a. end terrorism.
   b. cause terrorists to target airports even more as they attempt to show their strength.
   c. cause terrorists to seek alternative targets.
   d. inspire even more terrorism around the globe because it will show them they have succeeded.

Short Answer Questions

1. Talk to anyone born prior to 1935, and they know exactly where they were when they heard Pearl Harbor had been attacked; they can also tell you how life was different before and after that day. Talk to anyone born prior to 1995, and they can tell you a similar story regarding September 11, 2001. Have that latter conversation and focus on their experiences with either air travel or large-event attendance (such as an NFL game). Describe the opportunity cost of all the extra security effort we expend now relative to what existed before those attacks.
2. The key to providing a secure facility/event is imagining how terrorists think. With that in mind, if you wanted to get away with a terrorist act, describe the single "best" (easiest, biggest) target in your community (or on your campus). Describe how you would secure that target from such an attack.

Think about This

One of the things that counterterrorist intelligence agents must do is put themselves in the position of the terrorist. Take 10 minutes and think about your hometown. What action could terrorists take that would have the maximum impact for the least cost to themselves? Would that action necessarily be suicidal?

Talk about This

Do you agree with the contention that terrorist actions can be viewed as "coldly rational"? Would you characterize the actions of terrorists who kill themselves in conducting their operations as rational?

For More Insight See

Brauer, Jurgen, "On the Economics of Terrorism," *Phi Kappa Phi Forum* 82, no. 2 (Spring 2002).

INDEX

Page numbers followed by n indicate material found in footnotes.

A

D

E

F

G

H

J

K

L

M

N

O

Q

R

S

T

U

V

W

X

Y